GW01046795

THRUSHES

HELM IDENTIFICATION GUIDES

THRUSHES

Peter Clement and Ren Hathway

With additional illustrations by Clive Byers and Jan Wilczur

CHRISTOPHER HELM

A & C Black • London

To Angela

The plates in this book by Ren Hathway are
dedicated to the memory of
Alison Gregory
the closest of friends and the greatest inspiration

© 2000 Peter Clement, Ren Hathway, Clive Byers, and Jan Wilczur

Christopher Helm (Publishers) Ltd., a subsidiary of A & C Black
(Publishers) Ltd., 35 Bedford Row, London WC1R 4JH

0-7136-3940-7

A CIP catalogue record for this book is available from the
British Library

All rights reserved. No part of this publication may be
reproduced or used in any form or by any means — photographic,
electronic or mechanical, including photocopying, recording,
taping or information storage and retrieval systems — without
permission of the publishers.

Typeset and designed by D & N Publishing, Baydon, Wiltshire, UK

Printed in Spain by Artes Gráficas Toledo S.A.U.
D.L. TO: 1560-2000

CONTENTS

INTRODUCTION

Thrushes are one of the few families which are so well known that they need almost no introduction. They are one of the most widely distributed of passerine groups, and through their attractive (though not necessarily the brightest) plumages, their lilting and musical songs and, in the case of several species, their close association with most of us living in towns, villages and the edges of large cities, we have come to know some of them rather well. Whether it is as a garden or town park bird, a denizen of deep and dark forests, a seasonal visitor or coastal migrant, most people regularly (knowingly or unwittingly) come into contact with at least one or two members of the tribe. Whilst some, perhaps most, species are easily seen and have become tame and approachable through long periods of association with man and his environment, others have remained shy, secretive and extremely elusive. Within their dense forest and seemingly impenetrable habitat some of these birds easily match the poorest known species of pittas, rails, crakes or some of the most skulking warblers.

Although we know comparatively little of their exact origins, thrushes belong to an Old World family which most probably originated in central or southern Asia, where many species, particularly the older and more primitive species of *Zoothera* thrushes, are still found. Within the last 10 million years or so, they have spread throughout the continents and, with the exception of New Zealand (whose only species were introduced from Europe) and Antarctica, and are found on all major landmasses. They are only entirely absent from the polar regions and the hottest of deserts (although some are regularly found on passage or in winter in some of the most barren parts of the Sahara). Some of the remotest islands in the world's major oceans have been colonised, although it is possible that the arrival of the birds now resident there happened before these areas became the remote islands we know today.

One of the many attractive qualities of thrushes is that they can be found in the Old World from the Tamyr to Kamchatka and south through the great landmasses of Asia and Africa to the Cape, Sri Lanka and much of Indonesia, and in the New World from Alaska to Tierra del Fuego. They are also, for the most part, attractive, active and easily seen birds. Their songs, which are an added appeal in themselves, are musically accomplished and usually given from open perches, which makes the singer easily detected. Moreover, most of the *Catharus* and *Turdus* thrushes and several species of *Myadestes* are highly developed singers and contain some of the most musically adept of any of the songbirds. This degree of visibility, the allure of their songs, and their frequent association with man (several on practically every continent are familiar as garden birds in at least part of their range) have resulted in their songs being a common source of poetic inspiration and spiritual uplift.

Most thrushes – 'true thrushes' as we will refer to them for the purposes of this book – are, or have recently evolved from, birds of forests. Many species still live deep within the darkest of thick forest cover, whilst others have moved out to occupy a wide range of more open habitats, usually with the provision that there is some tree cover within the habitat. For one Central American species – Sooty Thrush *Turdus nigrescens*, which lives in large areas of virtually open, treeless areas of the páramo (high-altitude areas of open damp valley grassland with mosses and bunch-grasses together with patches of dwarf bamboo and densely growing shrubs) – this may literally mean that its sole contact with its original habitat is a single windblown tree in the vast extent of its upland wilderness. In between these extremes there is a range of tree-dominated habitats where thrushes may be found, including open woodlands and plantations (of the temperate regions), parks (including those in the middle of large capital cities), orchards and gardens, and acacia and savanna woodlands of the tropics. This range of habitat occupancy is best shown by some species which in parts of their range (i.e. Europe and part of North America) are frequently found in contact with man and are regular garden birds but which elsewhere (e.g. Siberia, northern Canada) are the shyest of forest dwellers. There is a frequently told story of a group of Russian biology students from Tomsk who were in England some years ago to study conservation methods. No sooner had they boarded their bus for the journey from the airport to the centre of London than they were wide-eyed with amazement at the number of 'Black Thrushes' inhabiting the local suburban gardens. They were further amazed by the tameness of Blackbirds and Song Thrushes, both of which are extremely shy and retiring birds in their homeland area of Siberian taiga forest.

Most of those species which inhabit open country and the edges of woodland and forests are often found foraging or feeding in any open area of ground that provides a supply of invertebrates. The typical foraging behaviour of these birds – busily turning over piles of leaves and decaying vegetation whilst eagerly searching with a beady eye for anything that moves – is a joy to watch. Some of these leaf-turners are particularly adept at flinging discarded vegetation some way from their area of digging. In some English beechwoods in autumn it is possible to see deep scrapes and holes in the layers of leaf-litter made by these birds intent on finding a meal, and it would be easy to assume that such digging had been done by a rabbit or badger. Not only do they depend on a range of invertebrate prey to survive, which is critical when nestlings are being fed, but they can adapt from being insect-eaters to fruit- and berry-eaters when these are ripe. As such they often come into conflict with those who have grown the fruits for human consumption, but in only a few areas are they considered a pest.

The flycatcher-thrushes *Neocossyphus*, arguably true thrushes in the widest sense, are almost exclusively invertebrate-dependent (as far as is known) and have evolved foraging habits which come close to (or mimic) those of the 'true' flycatchers. Such foraging methods include hovering and collecting insect prey in flight, and picking food items from the most spindly of leaves and twigs whilst almost motionless in hovering flight. The rock-thrushes *Monticola* have adapted to a more sedate form of foraging, a watch-and-wait strategy, very energy-efficient and, for some of the more open-country species, similar to that employed by shrikes. The birds sit on a tall or prominent perch such as a rock or trees (or in many cases the top of a roadside pole carrying power cables), and survey the ground immediately below for suitable prey to become active. Once a potential meal comes into view the bird pounces, collects it and returns to its former perch to dissect and eat its victim.

The feeding methods of the whistling-thrushes *Myophonus* differ yet again. These birds occur mostly in areas of swift-flowing streams in the well-forested hills of southern Asia, being mostly all dark or blackish-blue and showing cobalt-blue patches and silvery spots at the tips of certain feathers. Most forage at the edges of the streams and spend their time hunting for small fish, crustaceans and aquatic insects. One or two species feed by sitting on a large rock in the middle of the stream and waiting for small fish (alive or dead) to rise to the surface, at which point they quickly dash in and grab the intended prey before it slips away.

For those species which spend their entire lives within the depths of forests (most *Zoothera* and some *Turdus* thrushes, and several of those in monotypic genera) we have only a sketchy idea of their lives. We generally know some of their behaviour, actions and foraging methods, but less about their courtship and breeding. For some species, however, data are extremely limited and several (e.g. Fawn-breasted Thrush *Zoothera machiki*, New Britain Thrush *Z. talaseae* and Guadalcanal Thrush *Z. turipavae*) have been seen by ornithologists on only a handful of occasions. For these species we can only guess at their lifestyles. Some (e.g. Moluccan Thrush *Z. dumasi*, Red-backed Thrush *Z. erythronota*, Ashy Thrush *Z. cinerea* and race *neilgherriensis* of White's/Scaly Thrush *Z. dauma*) are particularly mystifying since they appear, intriguingly, to have little or no song, which raises more questions than answers. For instance, male defence of a territory may not be necessary in the traditional sense because pairs appear to be distributed at such low densities that territories are known by the individuals or pairs concerned without the need to advertise or defend them. This presupposes that individuals communicate with each other through short, brief contact calls or they rarely ever spend any length of time out of each other's sight. Are they perhaps so advanced that they communicate by sounds inaudible to the human ear? If so, why would they need to? Moreover, if they have no song or do not spend long periods singing, advertising or defending territories, it follows that they must have more time for foraging or other activities. However, since the area in which they live is probably the optimum of the available habitat, it is equally likely that foraging is not an onerous business or unduly time-consuming. Thus we are left with the impression that much of the daily routine of these birds, outside the breeding season (which appears to be fairly short), is taken up by doing not very much. The low densities of these birds, and their apparent inability either to adapt to anything outside of pristine forest habitat or to communicate with each other or competitors, represent an intriguing problem which can only be unravelled by much more detailed fieldwork.

The purpose of this book is to provide the interested reader with a detailed account of each of the true thrushes. In line with other handbooks in this series we have concentrated most effort on the identification of these birds, together with details of where they can be found and their main field characteristics, such as their song or behaviour. We have been equally concerned with documenting as accurately as possible the current status and population of each species, particular emphasis being given to those in decline or at risk of extinction, together with any information on measures taken, proposed or required to prevent or reverse the downward trend. Overall, our aim has been to give equal attention to all species of the thrushes in their most characteristic and attractive aspects, so we have tried to capture the spirit and allure of these birds by describing not only what they look like and what they do but also the wild places in which they live. Whilst the identification and location of these birds has been the principal aim of the book, we have also given some emphasis to the ecological aspects where possible, but we are aware of the limitations that a work such as this can provide on this aspect. It is not principally intended for use as a field guide but as a reference to provide a greater level of detail than given in most other guides. Regrettably, the scope and space of the present work does not allow for a more technical account of thrush biology, but a number of key references are given in the bibliography which will provide a broader background for those interested in this aspect.

Using this book will allow the reader to identify both the familiar and the unfamiliar species of thrushes they are likely to see or seek out; and it will give background depth and insight into the species for anyone wishing to know more or seeking clarification. We include our own and others' information from the field and from museums, supplemented by an extensive search of the available literature. However, with such a vast abundance of information in papers published in an ever-increasing number of journals, and in a range of languages, some information may well have been overlooked. We would be extremely grateful to hear of any omissions or errors that may have been made, together with any work (in progress or in future) which looks at the ecology of these birds and particularly those species of which we know so little.

This is only the second monograph to be written on the thrushes, and the first for a hundred years. In the 100 years since Henry Seebohm and R. Bowdler Sharpe produced their two-volume *A Monograph of the Turdidae* between 1898 and 1902 much has happened. Not only have great advances been made in our understanding of the species, the genera (and to a somewhat lesser degree, the relationships between them) but also 12 new species have been described in that time. The vast compendium of information provided by Seebohm and subsequently Sharpe was, at the time, a great step forward in our knowledge of these species. The two volumes of their work (which are widely credited to and colloquially known as Seebohm's, despite being largely completed by Bowdler Sharpe following the untimely death of Seebohm in 1895), together with the exquisitely detailed illustrations by the gifted Dutch artist J. G. Keulemans, set a benchmark in enhancing our understanding and appreciation of the birds in the family. More importantly this work has been a source of immense inspiration to all of those involved with the present book. It is our modest hope and intention that this work will stand a similar test of time and will, hopefully, become a worthy successor to those great ornithological luminaries. It will, in addition to providing a unique source of information on the thrushes of the world, identify the gaps in our knowledge of these alluring species which we hope those who follow on will be able to fill.

ACKNOWLEDGEMENTS

It would be wrong to pretend that a work like this is just the product of one or two people, especially when the amount of detail given to a family of birds such as the thrushes, which span the entire temperate and tropical zones of the planet, is considered. We are particularly grateful to all of the following who have helped in some way in providing advice, comments and information and made this book more accurate, authoritative and attractive in the process: Per Alström, Dr Hans Altmann, David Anthony, Hem Sagar Baral, Peter Barthel (*Limicola*), Leo Batten, Tommy Bird, Patric Blomquist, Axel Bräunlich, Mark Brazil, Andy Brown, James Cadbury, Geoff Carey, Clive Byers, Dave Capper (BirdLife International), Peter Colston, Gail & Barry Cooper, Dave Cooper, Maria Luisa da Silva, Reginald David, Allan Drewitt, Bob Edgar, Jonathon Ekstrom, Dave Fisher, Peter Flint, Ben Fraser, Simon Gillings, Martin Goodey, Graeme Green, Simon Harrap, Andreas Helbig, Jon Hornbuckle, Tim & Carol Inskipp, Stuart Jack, Krys Kazmierczak, Aleem Khan, Guy Kirwan, Jaan Lepson, Tim Loseby, Teus Luijendijk, Tony Marr, Nick Mason, Dr Jochen Martens, Rod Martins, Carole McCormick (BirdLife International), Jon McCracken, Giuseppe Micali, Dominic Mitchell, Marie Morin, Frank Murphy, Eddie Myers, Professor Ian Newton, Hope Oatman, Urban Olsson, David Pearson, Dave & Carol Powell, Doug Pratt, Colin Richardson, Peter Roberts, Allan Sander, Rick Simpson, Dr D. W. Snow, Geert Spanoghe, Mike Spicer, Andy Stoddart, Andy Swash, Bryan Sykes, Richard Thewlis, Bryan Thomas, Richard Thomas, Cyril Walker, Jan Wendeby, Nick Williams, Dale Zimmerman and Dan Zetterström.

We would particularly like to thank those who were kind enough to lend their time, effort and information on more remote areas or certain species – Des Allen (Japan), Mark Andrews (Cameroon), Dr John Ash (Ethiopia, Somalia), Jonathan Baillie (Olivaceous Thrush *T. o. xanthorhynchus*), Bas van Balen (Indonesia), Brinley Best (Ecuador), K. David Bishop (Indonesia), David Boertmann (Greenland), Mark Brazil (Japan), Ian Burfield (Ring Ouzel), Geoff Carey (Hong Kong, China), Mark Catterall (Red-backed Thrush), Mike Chong (Malaysia), Gordon Clarke (Somalia), Pete Davidson (Red-backed Thrush), Ed Dickinson (Philippines), Chris Doughty (Australia), Will Duckworth (Laos), Guy Dutson (New Guinea, Solomon Islands), Chris Eastwood (New Guinea), Walter G. Ellison (*Catharus* thrushes), Woei-horng Fang (Taiwan), Jeff Foster (Hawaiian Islands), Kimball Garrett (Varied Thrush), Dave Gibbs (Indonesia, Solomon Islands), Phil Gregory (New Guinea, Australia), Steve Howell (Mexico), Tim & Carol Inskipp (India, Nepal), Toru Ishizuka (Japanese and Izu Islands Thrushes), Allan Keith (Dominican Republic), Frank Lambert (Indonesia), Peter Kennerley (Hong Kong, China, Japan), Nedra Klein (La Selle Thrush), Greg Lasley (Mexico), Steve Latta (La Selle Thrush), Paul Leader (Hong Kong), Jeremy Lindsell (Uganda), Charles Lyon (Hawaiian *Myadestes*), Dr Konstantin Mikhailov (Russia), Andy Mitchell (Cuba), Peter Morris (Madagascar), Klaus Malling Olsen (Denmark), the late Henri Ouellet (Bicknell's Thrush), Mark Pearman (South America), Gunnlaugur Petursson (Iceland), Rob Pople (Ecuador), Anand Prasad (India), Chris Rimmer (Dominican Republic), Francisco Rivas (Dominican Republic), Don Roberson (California), Craig Robson (South-East Asia), Phil Round (Thailand), Gehan de Silva (Sri Lanka), Tom Snetsinger (Hawaiian *Myadestes*), Soren Sorensen (Faroes), Alfred Twinomusuni (Oberlaender's Ground-Thrush), Kathy Wakelee (Hawaiian *Myadestes*), Barry Walker (Peru, Bolivia), George Wallace (Cuba), Kate Wallace (Dominican Republic), Deepal Warakagoda (Sri Lanka), Kanchana Weerakoon (Sri Lanka), David Wells (Malaysia), Rob Williams (South America) and Robin Woods (Austral Thrush).

We are extremely indebted (as always) to the staff at the Natural History Museum, Tring, for access to the national collection, in particular thanks are due to Mark Adams, Peter Colston, Robert Prys-Jones, Cyril Walker and Michael Walters; in addition a huge vote of thanks goes to Effie Warr, the Librarian at Tring who dealt with all queries and cries for help (no matter how often or obscure the document) with great calm, patience and fortitude. The staff of several other museums and collections around the world deserve equal thanks for their help in providing information or letting us have specimens on loan – David Allan of the Durban Natural Science Museum, Durban, South Africa; J. Phillip Angle, James Dean and Pamela Rasmussen, National Museum of Natural History, Smithsonian Institution, Washington DC; Dr Ernst Bauernfeind of the Naturhistorisches Museum, Vienna, Austria; Walter E. Boles of the Australian Museum, Sydney; Jaime J. Cabrera of the National Museum, Manila, Philippines; Tamar Cassidy of the Transvaal Museum, Pretoria, South Africa; René Dekker of the National Museum of Natural History, Leiden, Netherlands; Terri Elder of Nelson Provincial Museum, Nelson, New Zealand; Dr Renate van den Elzen of the Museum Koenig, Bonn, Germany; Dr Per Ericson of the Swedish Museum of Natural History, Stockholm; Kimball Garrett of the Los Angeles County Natural History Museum, Los Angeles, California; Gene Hess of the Delaware Museum of Natural History, Delaware; Emanuel Levine, Mary Lecroy and Paul Sweet of the American Museum of Natural History, New York; Dr Michel Louette of the Koninklijk Museum voor Midden-Afrika, Tervuren, Brussels, Belgium; A. Msimanga of the National Museum, Bulawayo, Zimbabwe; Steve Ottery of the Isles of Scilly Museum, England; Eric Pasquet of the Muséum National d'Histoire Naturelle, Paris; Fred Sibley and Paul Whitehead of the Peabody Museum of Natural History, New Haven, Connecticut; Dr Pavel Tomkovich of the Zoological Museum of Moscow; Philip Unitt of the San Diego Natural History Museum, California; David Willard of the Field Museum of Natural History, Chicago; Takeshi Wada of the Osaka Museum of Natural History, Osaka, Japan; Anna Wong of the Sabah Museum, Kota Kinabalu, Sabah, Malaysia.

Special thanks are also due to Gerda Flumm, Miou Helps, Tanya & Steve Rooke and Mike Wilson for their help and expertise in the translation of several important papers and documents. PC would also like to thank both Nigel Collar and Adrian Gardiner or their extensive help and comments on the first draft of the entire text, and Dr Andreas Helbig for his help with information on the DNA work being undertaken on various species.

In addition we would like to pay tribute to the many people who have helped with the production of the plates and artwork in so many ways. For their help with illustrations thanks go to Clive Byers, Ashley Fisher, Alma Hathway, James Siddle, Kris Webb and Jan Wilczur. RH offers particular thanks to Colin Bradshaw for having faith right from the start, teaching the basics and for the first break as an artist (illustrating a paper on *Catharus* thrush identification), also Stuart Jack, James Siddle, Mashuq Ahmad and Nigel Wheatley for much intelligent (and some not so intelligent) discussion on the finer points of bird identification. For their help, advice and criticism thanks are also due to Bob Flood, Pete Fraser, Bob Hibbet, Jeremy Hickman, Dominic Mitchell, John and Irene Miller, Dave and Carol Powell, Ann and Roger Symonds, Will Wagstaff and Royston Wilkins; for their warmth and hospitality Frank Murphy, Hope Oatman and Jackie Bogardus in the United States; also Paul and Teri Roberts, Sarah and Carl Russell in the U.K.

PC would like to express a huge debt of thanks to Angela for her kind understanding, love and patience during the long years that the book was in production. RH would also like to thank his family for years of support, most particularly Alma Hathway and Suzie Hewitt on Tresco; also to all the good close friends in providing support at times of low ebb and without whom there would never have been the confidence to see it all through. Heartfelt appreciation especially to the following – Mush Ahmad, Debbie Hewitt, Beth Hilton, Stuart Jack, Jojo Johnston, John and Chris Ryan, Katharine Sawyer, James Siddle, Viv Stratton, Kris Webb (Spider), Nigel Wheatley, Chas Wood and Jo Wrigley, and to Ellen and Neil Gregory; and last, but not least, to Alison.

LAYOUT AND SCOPE OF THE BOOK

Species numbers

Each of the species included in the book is given a unique reference number which identifies it on the plates and in the texts, and is applicable solely to this work and has no other purpose or significance. Under English name is any alternative name (in parentheses) where known or in common usage; this is not an exhaustive list and doubtless there are many local or dialectal names missing (e.g. the local or native names of some of the Caribbean and Indonesian species). Following the English name is the scientific name, then the plate number. The original scientific binomial is also given followed by the type locality (i.e. where the first recorded specimen was collected, photographed or described).

The plates

With one exception, all the main plumages of each of the 162 (including two of the three extinct) species have been depicted on the plates, together with those of the most recognisable races or geographically distinct forms. The single exception is the Amaui *Myadestes woahensis* from Hawaii, which was seen only by the naturalist who discovered it in 1825. The specimens taken at the time of its discovery were lost (two were recently thought to have been rediscovered), no description other than a few brief notes exists and, unsurprisingly, no painting or illustration was made. Recent opinion on the species, however, has suggested that it may possibly have been a race of a similar species (now endangered) on another Hawaiian island.

The plates have been painted from specimens both living and in museums and, where possible, verified by the use of field data, photographs or, in some cases, particularly where no other source exists, illustrations in other published guides. In the latter case the exquisitely detailed plates by Keulemans in Seebohm and Sharpe's monograph have been one of the greatest points of reference. Keulemans had the advantage of being able to illustrate most of the birds from fresh specimens which were sent by collectors to the British Museum for identification and inclusion in the national collection. At that time many of the species had not been previously illustrated (or only poorly) and the species concept and sequence order was, at best, rudimentary. Perhaps more importantly it was in the latter part of the era when society as a whole was still coming to terms with the Darwinian view that many of the species were, in fact, related to each other. The monograph had a total of 130 plates illustrating what were then thought to be a similar number of species (or slightly fewer), but many of the birds illustrated have since been reclassified as subspecies and only 76 of those currently considered to be full species are illustrated. Moreover, the Seebohm/Sharpe monograph restricted itself to the thrushes in *Geocichla* (now *Zoothera*), *Turdus* (which also included some of the present *Catharus* thrushes), *Merula* and *Mimocichla* (the latter two now subsumed within *Turdus*), and did not extend to any of the other genera or species included in this work.

In this present book most of the adult individuals on the plates are illustrated in new (i.e. newly moulted) or fresh plumage, except where stated otherwise; this is to show them at their best or at the most developed stage of the plumage. In the majority of cases both sexes are illustrated, but in a few, where females are identical to males, only one is depicted. In those cases where worn plumage differs extensively from freshly moulted individuals, this is also shown on the same plate. In some species, particularly the *Monticola* thrushes, the fresh plumage partially or entirely obscures the breeding plumage and both are illustrated. For the majority of species, however, the differences between fresh (autumn and winter; non-breeding) and worn (summer; breeding) plumage are largely indistinguishable in the field (but very clear on birds in the hand). Worn plumage usually only remains so for short periods during the summer or breeding season, and is probably best detected in the hand or from very close views in the field (usually only in fairly extreme cases), when the somewhat ragged edges to individual (mostly flight and tail) feathers are evident.

In most cases immature and/or juvenile plumages are also shown, but have been largely restricted to those species where the juvenile and first-year plumages are either particularly distinctive or differ from that of the adult(s). In general the juvenile plumage (i.e. that assumed on leaving the nest for the duration of about two or three months prior to the first moult) consists mostly of a duller version of that of the respective adult, with spotted or mottled underparts (and, sometimes, streaked parts of the head and back). For a few species the juvenile and immature plumages are still unknown or undescribed; others, regrettably, have been poorly described and therefore incorrectly shown in several existing field guides.

A few flight illustrations have been included, mostly of the *Zoothera* thrushes to show the distinctive underwing pattern. These have been kept to a minimum (others appear in the body of the text) to show the most striking features of birds in flight, such as wing-bars or tail patterns, which may be detectable on a good view in the field. Where the species is recognisable in flight or has distinctive flight characteristics (e.g. communal roosting or flocking together in flight), a black and white illustration is given in the text.

All the plates have been arranged so that they follow the same order as the text, except in a few instances where we have shown similar and potentially confusing species alongside each other. In one or two cases geographically related groups of species are shown together, or follow on for ease of reference and for comparison with similar-looking species. In other instances, this has not always been possible owing to the number of similar species, but the summary caption to the plate and the identification section of the main text indicate which species most closely resemble the bird under discussion, and which should be considered when the observer is confronted with an unfamiliar species. Each of the individuals illustrated is to scale within each plate, but the scale differs between plates.

The captions on the facing pages to the plates provide a brief summary of the range and habitat for each species together with the distinctive features of the age and sex of the bird illustrated.

The maps

The maps show the seasonal or (for entirely sedentary birds) annual distribution of each species. The ranges shown are a condensed view of the area occupied, with more detailed information on the species status is found in the text on distribution. The breeding areas are shown in yellow and the wintering areas in blue, with the range for entirely resident or sedentary species is shown in dark green. For some areas where the species only occupies a small area arrows have been used to indicate this and for some of the migration routes we have hatched this in blue to show that birds may be expected to occur within this area at certain times of their annual cycle of movements for which more information will be found in the text on movements.

Species accounts

Identification

The introductory and often brief opening section contains essential information on the species's size (given in centimetres and inches), with minimum and maximum body lengths (males are usually slightly larger than females), and usually the most obvious features of its shape, stance or plumage, to enable the bird to be identified. Where relevant to identification, reference is also made to the number of races and the major differences from the nominate (i.e. first named or discovered) race. In several cases, particularly island endemics, the account begins with a reference to the restricted range of the species to highlight the point that outside of this area it is extremely unlikely, if ever, to be encountered.

Confusion species Most species have similarities with others whether closely or more distantly related, and one of the purposes of the book is to ensure that individual birds are correctly identified and that an uncommon or rare ones are not mistaken for a more likely or common one. For each species this subsection gives details of other species with which it is most likely to be confused (including species not covered in this book), with the emphasis placed on those aspects of structure or plumage which will help the observer in correct identification. For some distinctive or obvious species this may not be relevant or necessary, with a few species or subspecies being the only thrushes in various parts of the world and having no similar counterparts. In one or two species (particularly those in parts of South America) the main differences are in the calls or the song, and the use of vocalisations is essential in comparing the different species; this may also be mentioned here but details of these differences are given in the section dealing with voice.

Description

This section gives detailed information on the plumage or range of plumages of the adults and immature birds and, where recognisable in the field (or in some cases in the hand), the first- or second-summer plumages are included. The section starts with reference to whether the sexes of the adults are alike, similar (but sometimes separable) or different; in cases where the adults are identical no separate description is given for the adult female. Unless stated otherwise, the nominate race is described here. In some species (e.g. Swainson's Thrush) the nominate race has a very limited distribution and is generally less well known than another race, in which case the nominate will be mentioned under the section on geographical variation. The final part usually deals with the plumage of immature birds, usually that acquired shortly before leaving the nest (juvenile plumage) and that which succeeds it following the moult (first-year plumage), which may have to serve the individual for almost a full year. Juvenile birds may still have down on the head or upperparts, feathers in pin and usually short or not fully grown tails, and their first plumage only lasts a short time (probably no more than 3–4 months). Immatures (first-year plumages or older) are much more like the adults in size and plumage features. In the Palearctic the first-year plumage is frequently referred to (when it is possible to distinguish it at all) as first-winter and first-summer plumages, based on the time of year that the bird is encountered. In practice, the differences between first-year and adult plumage is very slight and mainly in the presence of new feathers which are clearly definable as adult, i.e. they lack any trace of immature

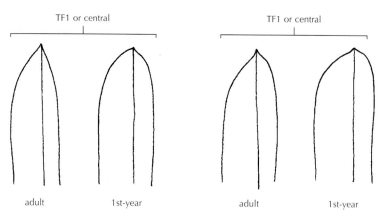

TF1 or central   TF1 or central

adult   1st-year   adult   1st-year

Tail feathers of adult thrush showing differences in shape between adult (right) and first-year bird.

characters. In the hand these are easier to see and for most thrush species ageing is usually confirmed by the shape of the tail feathers. In first-year birds the tips of the tail feathers are tapered and more pointed, whilst those of adults are more clearly rounded.

In North America the equivalent descriptions of these plumages (beyond juvenile, which is only applicable for approximately the first three months of the bird's life and is called *juvenal* are referred to as (i) hatching year (HY) – a bird in the year of its birth until 31 December in its first full plumage following juvenile moult, (ii) after hatching year or second year (AHY or SY) – a bird in at least its second calendar year (although, since most passerines moult from their first-winter/HY plumage to one virtually inseparable from the adult, this does not apply very widely; but for some thrushes there is a distinct phase when the remains of the first-winter/HY plumage are still detectable in its first-summer/AHY/SY plumage), and (iii) adult/ASY – a bird which has achieved full plumage (for some this will be in the autumn of its second calendar year or at least in its third year.

Descriptions normally follow the same format, enabling the reader to find the relevant parts of the plumage in all of the birds described. This order usually starts with the head, particularly the forehead, crown and nape (also the face and chin and throat where these are the same colour), followed by the rest of the upperparts and then the tail. The wings are described separately, beginning with the wing-coverts, alula and primary coverts, then the flight feathers (primaries, secondaries and tertials, although when both 'flight feathers' and tertials are described, the term 'flight feathers' applies just to the primaries and secondaries). The face is then described, unless it has already been covered with the rest of the head, together with details of the supercilium and/or other facial markings, which may include a submoustachial and/or malar stripe (very few thrushes show definite or well-marked moustachial stripes). The underparts are described from the chin and throat to the breast, belly, flanks and undertail-coverts; for those species in which the underparts are uniform these parts are not given separately. It concludes with details of the bare (or soft) parts; bill, legs and feet; where relevant, eye-ring and postocular spot colours are normally also given here.

Every effort has been made to be consistent in the description of plumage colours but the range of shades, mainly in blacks, greys and particularly browns, shown by the majority of thrushes is not always easy to convey. Moreover, the addition of some colour tones such as olive, tawny or buff is designed to make the colours more widely understood. However, without a baseline definition these are just as likely to be misunderstood since what is brown, grey-brown or dark brown to one eye may be judged differently by another. In addition, there is high degree of variation that can be given to basic colours through changes in natural light and shading and its effect on subtle plumage tones. Ridgway (1912) compiled what is now regarded as the standard work on the names of colours and was widely used for many of the early species descriptions in the ornithological literature. This work has recently been updated and revised by Smithe (1975), but we have eschewed use of or reference to these works since neither is widely available or practical without direct reference to individuals in the hand; the former work is now out of print and expensive to obtain secondhand.

In the description of plumage coloration several 'rules' must be kept in mind. Firstly, light, as already acknowledged, plays a large part in the way that the colours are appreciated by the human eye. This is particularly true when identifying forest birds in shade or beneath deep cover; strong overhead light will increase the level of contrast and make dark colours paler and pale colours lighter or greyer; similarly, shaded or obscured light will inevitably make dark colours darker so that any heavy colour with an element of reddish may appear brown, brown may appear black, and so on; in good even light birds in the foliage of a well-leaved tree can appear both lighter and with a greenish tinge. Similarly it should be remembered that birds in vegetation rely on certain plumage features, e.g. bars or spots, to break up the plumage as a way of camouflaging their presence, and as such may be difficult to detect. In the description of colours it should also be borne in mind that basic colours are modified by compound qualifiers that precede them; thus grey-brown is browner than brownish-grey; in any compound description the main colour is modified by the preceding adjectival qualifier.

Foxing One of the chief problems encountered when using museum specimen skins as the basis for descriptions of thrushes is that of foxing. This is basically a colour-change process that occurs, apparently naturally, following the death of the individual, and is more prevalent in some species than others. In the main this is the change from light brown to a darker or deeper and rufous (i.e. foxy), tone, particularly in those species which are in life plain brown or olive-brown. For instance, virtually all of the *Catharus* thrushes in life are brown to grey-brown on the head and upperparts; some are redder-brown and others are tinged greyish; however, most specimen skins are distinctly browner than olive. In addition, fading of the colour tones in museum specimens is also a factor to bear in mind; in one species, Spotted Nightingale-Thrush, the colour changes are particularly pronounced, with the underparts mostly bright or deep primrose-yellow (spotted with black) in life whereas in all preserved specimens the underparts lose all traces of yellow and become white. Colour changes such as this are not restricted to the *Catharus* thrushes, however, as several olive-tinged *Turdus* thrushes are also known for the amount of foxing and fading they undergo. Future students of thrush plumages and morphology would be well advised to use, where possible, as much material from life as they can, since descriptions based purely on specimens may be deficient in certain colour characters present in life.

Leucism and albinism It also seems appropriate to mention here that thrushes, and in particular (but not exclusively) certain well known species (e.g. Blackbird and American Robin), exhibit a fair degree of leucism or, more rarely, total albinism. Leucism is manifest by individuals showing a degree of white, off-white or pale buff in the plumage, from almost total coverage to individual parts, including the primaries and/or secondaries or one, some or all of the tail feathers. There appears to be no absolute rule as to how leucistic birds appear, except that as far as is known from existing records the phenomenon is confined to *Turdus* species only. The offspring of leucistic birds can show similar markings, totally different ones or none at all. From what is known it appears that both leucism and albinism are due entirely to poor or unstable geneflow and that some species and individuals are more prone to exhibit certain characteristics than others. We have made no attempt to document the variation of leucistic birds recorded except for one species. The exceptional case that departs from this rule concerns the 'schizochromistic' morph on the limited number of individuals recorded showing the characteristics) of Varied Thrush. Individuals showing this condition (which includes the sole U.K. and western Palearctic record) lack the normal orange or reddish colour in the plumage and replace it with white or pale-greyish white (see plate 13). As far as we are aware, there are no known cases of melanism or partial melanism in thrushes.

Geographical variation

In the classification of species we have adhered to the biological species concept (BSC) which recognises racial or subspecific status to closely allied forms (these can, in the main, be distinguished either in the field or in the hand). All races or subspecies are detailed in this section, giving the visual features that differentiate them from the nominate. In some cases there are variations or plumage 'morphs', which are also described here. Some races may differ only weakly, slightly or subtly in colour tone or size from others, and hence are probably only identifiable in the hand. It should be remembered that some subspecies vary considerably, perhaps more than is generally understood, since the boundaries of each may be poorly marked or incompletely known; moreover, since there is in most cases a clinal change between pure individuals or pairs of respective neighbouring subspecies, many will be intermediate.

At least two of the North American *Catharus* and several of the South American *Turdus* thrushes have a number of subspecies adopted (and further ones proposed) on grounds of fine differences. Where races or subspecies have been proposed which show only slim differences from others (e.g. in subtle shading of the plumage or solely by measurements in millimetres alone, and either way determined only by a comparison of museum specimens), we accept them as currently valid and present details supporting their differences. However, we consider that further research may invalidate their status, and take the view that subspecies proposed on the basis of minor or subtle differences involving small sample sizes should be treated with great caution, since in many cases these will reflect only individual variation.

We also provide references and descriptions of races where there are marked differences which may lead to them being adopted as full species in their own right. In cases where the present taxonomic assessment of species/subspecies is confused or controversial we have included a brief summary of the problem or a justification for the inclusion or exclusion of a particular taxon. This is to inform the reader of the need for further research or review and to present the source material for those seeking further details.

BSC versus PSC Our reasons for adhering strongly to the Biological Species Concept (BSC) as opposed to the Phylogenetic Species Concept (PSC) are more than adequately set out by Snow (1997), who advocated strongly in favour of the retention of the BSC using the *Turdus merula* (Blackbird) complex as an example. This is a single species complex which ranges from the Azores and Canary Islands east through Europe and western Asia, showing varying plumages, sizes and proportions, e.g. differing wing shapes depending on whether they are resident, migratory or confined to remote islands. Although there are ecological differences between the various forms within the complex they are clearly a species assemblage which has been derived from an ancestral stock which most probably inhabited the western Palearctic – the area where the species has its greatest concentration and widest continuous distribution. Beyond this there are other distinct allopatric forms further east in the Himalayas, China and the Indian subcontinent, but for any one of them we have no indication (on present knowledge) whether any or all might prove to be reproductively isolated, i.e. behave as a separate species. Snow argued that:

> At the two extremes of size (based on male wing-length) are *T. m. maximus* of the Himalayas (144–167 mm) and *T. m. azorensis* from the Azores (117–127 mm). *T. m. maximus* should perhaps be treated as specifically distinct from the western Palearctic forms under either of the species concepts; not only is it huge, but it differs quite markedly in plumage, and by its song and calls; *T. m. syriacus*, of Turkey and the Levant, may form a link with the European populations, being intermediate in size, but further studies of these central and southwest Asian populations would be needed to establish how isolated they are from one another and whether the variation is clinal. At the bottom end of the size range, *T. m. cabrerae* of Madeira and the Canary Islands (122–129 mm) is about as small as *azorensis* and differs in having darker female plumage, a less rounded wing and a slightly longer tail. In Europe and North Africa, there is clinal variation between the very large eastern continental populations and the very small Atlantic island populations, which the BSC recognises by a number of subspecific names...
>
> If there is some difficulty under the BSC in deciding whether the eastern Palearctic and Oriental groups of Blackbird-like forms should be treated as conspecific with *merula*, the problem for the PSC would involve the whole range from the Atlantic islands to China. The Azores population would certainly be a phylogenetic species; the Madeiran and Canary Islands populations would demand detailed study. They are certainly isolated from one another and further research, including molecular analysis, would very likely bring to light diagnosable differences not only between Madeira and Canary Island birds but perhaps also between populations of different Canary Islands...
>
> Himalayan *maximus* and Chinese *mandarinus* would certainly be given species status, while the *simillimus* group of peninsular India and Sri Lanka would probably be treated as three species, as they comprise three rather distinct allopatric groups. Central Asian *intermedius* might well be treated as a species, as would the main bulk of the western Palearctic mainland populations within which variation is clinal. This clinal variation would not be given formal taxonomic recognition. In fact, a major re-examination of the whole complex would be necessary before any final decision could be made on the division, into a number of phylogenetic species, of what is now treated as polytypic *Turdus merula*.

Thus it seems clear that there would be no advantages in the adoption of a PSC-based approach to the classification of thrushes since one of the main tenets of the PSC approach, that it is a much easier or simplistic approach (and is based on discernible or diagnosable differences between taxa), proves to be undeliverable: even with one of the commonest and widespread thrush species in the world, a thorough and more detailed analysis is needed before any coherent decisions can be made. Without doubt the same could be said equally of large groups or complex species such as American Robin, African and Olive Thrush, White-throated and White-necked Thrushes. The (admittedly conservative) BSC approach is justifiable when so much still remains unknown about the relationships of individuals and groups within the family. Moreover, whilst no single species concept will satisfy the multiple purposes of what is understood and accepted as an integral 'species', adherence to the BSC will maintain some taxonomic stability and provide a basis for continuing communication at least for the foreseeable future.

Voice

Thrushes in the main are highly vocal birds, and we have given details of the most frequently used calls and songs, together with song periods and, where known, preferred song-perches and positions. For most of the forest-living thrushes, calls are principally given to maintain contact, either the 'here am I where are you' type, or a lower, more intimate call between paired birds at close range. Calls given in agitation or alarm range from notes registering simple disturbance to outright and frequently protracted panic depending on the cause, but they are usually sufficient to fend off the disturbance or to bring it to the attention of others. Whilst we have attempted to be comprehensive in our coverage of calls, there may be some species which utter notes in both calls and song which are not given here. This may be because the species is poorly known, the notes are dialectal or particular to a given race or only given for a short period in the year (e.g. when young are in the nest or shortly after they have fledged).

The nest calls of parents to young or the squeaky (and not especially distinctive) calls of nestlings are not included here as we feel these are more relevant to a specific work on the breeding biology of thrushes. As the primary purpose of this work is identification, we have given calls by young birds which are, in general, at least three months old (possibly younger in some of the *Catharus* or *Myadestes* thrushes), since prior to that age fledglings, still dependent on parental care and feeding, maintain a begging squeal first perfected whilst in the nest.

Thrushes are justly famous throughout the world for their songs (indeed for some species their vocal qualities have been the reason for their decline), and are among the finest avian singers; as such, they are capable of a wide range of variation and modulation within their tonal structures. We have striven for accuracy in attempting to describe the complex nature of these songs, which can barely be done more than perfunctory justice, through the medium of imitative transcription and onomatopoeia, to convey the huge range of modulated tones and pitch given by these masterclass songsters. Sonagrams are not used in this book as the differences between species with very similar calls or songs will convey very little to most fieldworkers and even to experienced birdwatchers who are unfamiliar with the range of notes given by these birds (although, of course, we recognise that, increasingly, there are a number of fieldworkers who are becoming adept at using these for identification).

As an aid to providing observers with as complete coverage as possible and as a celebration of their musical qualities, a CD is being prepared separately which contains the songs of almost all the species in the book. Regrettably, however, despite the inclusion of a wealth of recordings from various ornithologists and sound-recordists around the world, this is not comprehensive. This is due principally either to the inaccessibility of certain species when they are singing or to the absence of known songs in certain species: wider recognition of the latter problem will, it is hoped, encourage future work to focus on improving our understanding.

Status and distribution

This section starts with a brief account of the status of the species throughout most of its range. It is acknowledged that there are wide degrees of variation in density or abundance between areas within a range; for some species this may be due to seasonal shifts in the population or because individuals are less easy to see or detect at certain times of the year (e.g. when birds are moulting they are much less visible). No attempt, except in certain cases, has been made to show areas of greatest density or abundance, since for many species the information does not exist. However, where certain population figures are known (or estimated), we have given them to show relative areas of abundance or scarcity. For some species the highest density is at, or certainly close to, the centre of the range, but for a number of species areas of optimum breeding habitat are at, or close to, the edge of the range (e.g. Redwings, Eyebrowed and Dusky Thrushes all breed in higher numbers at the northern edge of their breeding range along the tundra zone than further south).

Following the details of status the known breeding or wintering distribution is given. Setting the distributional limits of species is inherently difficult in that this tends to overstate the area shown as occupied at the edges and in less well known parts of the range. In a wider context it is also acknowledged that there are limits to the accuracy of showing the distribution of any species in this fashion, except for perhaps those that are extremely well known and/or occupy very small areas (e.g. mountain ranges or small islands). The range of any species is dependent on a number of factors, not least the status or relative abundance of each species and the amount of preferred habitat. Moreover, the ranges shown may be the maximum recognised for the species and one not attained or occupied every year, or perhaps only when the population is cyclically high.

Whilst there is a wealth of information on the distribution of species largely based on where the appropriate habitat indicates they should occur, there is very little information on why some species are particularly scarce or seemingly absent from large tracts of apparently suitable habitat. In general very little is known of the ecology of many of the forest thrushes, particularly those in large areas of tropical forest; the deep-forest *Zoothera* thrushes are, for example, among the least known birds.

Movements

This section gives detailed information on movements outside the breeding and wintering seasons, principally to and from the breeding areas and the timing of these movements, or where the species undertakes random or nomadic wanderings. It also outlines the sedentary or resident nature of species and summarises (where known) information on the occurrences of birds outside their normal (i.e. native) areas, from the unusual but regular visitor to the extreme vagrant. Several of the *Catharus* and *Turdus* thrushes, together with notable examples of the *Monticola* and two *Zoothera* thrushes, are long-distance migrants covering up to 6000 miles (10,000 km), whilst others make movements of only limited duration and distance. Some of the higher-ground species make largely altitudinal movements to escape the worst of severe winter weather at high elevations. Most of the *Zoothera* thrushes are highly sedentary and make little or no movements (that we know of), so that occurrences only

Fieldfares and Redwings gathering before migration.

marginally outside their normal range are all the more noteworthy and included here. Some African species make short-distance movements ahead of the seasonal rains (especially to the breeding areas), but these are poorly known and would benefit from further investigation.

Habitat

Information given in this section refers to the preferred habitat or that in which the species is most frequently found. Whilst we have attempted to include all the habitats occupied it is possible that we may have omitted one or two local habitat types. All thrushes are chiefly forest dwellers, or have in the recent past emerged from being forest-dwelling birds and adapted to more open types of habitat (e.g. plantations, scrub and upland heaths), usually provided that there are adequate amounts of cover for them to take refuge when danger threatens. Very few live in areas completely devoid of some kind of tree or tree-scrub cover. Those least tied to forests are perhaps the majority of the *Monticola* thrushes, which have largely adapted to more arid areas of dry open country with a slight to well-developed cover of scrub. Even these have not entirely abandoned their reliance on tree/scrub cover, perhaps with the exception of some individual Rock-Thrushes which occasionally overwinter in the Ahaggar range of southern Algeria and the massifs of Air province, northern Niger. Some of the South American *Turdus* species, together with one or two races of Island Thrush, may occur temporarily in very sparse areas but this is usually only for brief foraging trips, and they retreat to tree cover when threatened by predators or severe weather; in some cases these may be the only trees for a considerable distance. As noted elsewhere, several species have become attached to man and live within villages, towns and cities, especially where it is beneficial for food or protection to do so. In some cases this may only be true for part of the population and we have attempted to be as accurate in documenting this as possible. We have omitted certain urban habitats which are used by only small numbers of the population of the relevant species.

Within this section we include the altitude range of those species which live at some elevation, but for many species this is not uniform throughout their range and exceptions will most likely occur depending on the parts of the range and times of the year. It should also be borne in mind, particularly for the more wide-ranging and migratory species, that thrushes are as likely to occur in unusual habitats as any other migrant temporarily forced off-course. As an example of this both White's and Siberian Thrushes, the two longest-distance migrants of the *Zoothera* family, and which normally prefer the depths of forests, have occurred on remote (and almost treeless) islands off the coast of north-west Europe at times when they should have been in South-East Asia.

Behaviour

This section begins with the sociability of species in question, mainly whether birds are likely to be encountered alone, in pairs or (at certain times of the year) in loose or mixed-species flocks. Most thrushes are territorial birds, particularly when breeding, and even winter feeding areas are fairly rigorously defended by some species. As would be expected, most thrushes usually occur in pairs throughout the course of the year, but often only single birds will be seen by the casual observer. Apart from a few of the more common or widespread species the only time of the year that pairs are likely to be seen together is during the brief courtship period and the longer time devoted to feeding young. At the opposite extreme there are those, mostly northern breeding species (and all *Turdus* thrushes), which occur in loose association or small groups, mostly at plentiful sources of food or communal roosts.

(*Left*) Male Blackbirds fighting for territorial domination.

Aggression posturing of males defending territory or feeding areas.

Within this section we have omitted comments on individual species's habits, particularly comfort activities such as head-scratching and bill-cleaning, together with resting, roosting, sunbathing and dust-bathing, as they are an everyday part of the life of the bird. These are dealt with more specifically in the extended section on thrush behaviour (*see* page 43). Reference is made to the flight of the individual where it is particularly distinctive or has a characteristic action. The flight of almost all the thrushes is fast, direct and slightly undulating over longer distances. However, slight variations give a different emphasis to the mode of flight, with both Mistle Thrush and Fieldfare having long bounding undulations, whilst the smaller Redwing can look more like the smaller Starling *Sturnus vulgaris* when moving in flocks. Forest-dwelling thrushes are particularly adept at a rapid flight through seemingly impenetrable areas of dense stands of trees together with hanging vines, lianas and creepers, but generally keep low and dive into the deepest of cover when danger threatens. We have not dwelt here on the specifics or mechanics of thrush flight except in those circumstances where it is particularly relevant for the identification of the individual species. In a couple of instances we include data from research undertaken on speed and rates of progress made by migrating birds as detected by satellite tracking and ringing, to show how far and how fast birds of this size can cross large areas.

Foraging and food How birds feed is often a critical feature in identifying their family, whether it is on the ground, in a tree or (including several thrushes) in flight. In the *Behaviour* section foraging and feeding methods are described, although for many thrushes there will be little actual difference between the patterns of activity. Most thrushes are probably best described as omnivorous; they are

Adult male Rock Thrush carrying food.

perhaps best adapted as insectivores but readily take to a wide variety of berries, fruits and seeds at certain times of the year. Within this seemingly wide range of food they are largely opportunistic and will take whatever is most readily available. Few species are entirely dependent on only a limited number of invertebrates for survival, although for some forest species large numbers of ants or termites may comprise a sizeable proportion of their daily needs. Most food items are given as general descriptions (e.g. ants, beetles, etc.) as for the majority of species detailed analyses of diet are lacking. Moreover, in a book mainly devoted to the identification of these birds, space is limited to the general nature of their food items. We attempt to give details of all known food items but when dealing with a family of birds that has a wide choice of food, the range of items taken by the less familiar species is much greater than we are aware.

Breeding

In this section we have given a brief summary of the breeding data relevant to the identification of individual species. This mainly includes dates of the start and duration of the breeding season, nesting materials, position of nest; and number and colour of eggs. Where known we have also included data on number of days between egg-laying and hatching (incubation) and the fledging period of nestlings, and finally any information on multiple broods. Regrettably, space does not allow for more

Male Blue Rock-Thrush in Display flight.

details. Regrettably, space does not allow for more details of the features of (and differences between) nestlings and downy fledglings (illustrated below). Data on these together with details of adult courtship, display and pair-bonding are subjects which require some depth to convey all the subtleties and differences, in particular the display actions shown by all the thrushes – one of the more active, visible and excitable groups of birds in their territorial and sexual displays. We have made reference to parts of the display for species where males make characteristic display-flights as part of their courtship, notably the *Monticola* thrushes. For many of the *Zoothera* thrushes this activity is either unknown or displays are not part of their sexual courtship. For a number of *Turdus* thrushes, which have an extremely active and prolonged courtship and display period, an immense amount of information exists. For the western Palearctic species reference will be found in Cramp *et al.* (1988); or as a detailed essay on the daily progress of a close-knit group of Blackbirds studied over a period of several years in southern England, the interested reader will find *A Study of Blackbirds* (Snow 1958) a delight. There is also a monograph on *The Fieldfare* (Norman 1994), one of the commonest and most successful thrushes, which has expanded its breeding range in Europe during the course of the 20th Century.

Adult female Blackbird on nest.

Nestling thrushes at 3–4 days.

Nestling thrushes at c. 10–12 days with downy feathers and wings in pin.

Fledgling Turdus *thrush at c. 20 days.*

Adult Song Thrush feeding brood of young.

Adult Song Thrush feeding brood of young.

Moult

As in most passerines all thrushes have two moult periods during the year. The moult that follows the breeding season is a complete or full moult involving replacement of all feathers for adult birds, whilst for birds born within the year it is only a partial moult as some of the wing and tail feathers are retained for a full year until they are replaced at the complete moult stage as adults. Some species have a partial moult at the end of the winter or non-breeding period, during which some of the body feathers and wing-coverts are replaced. Birds in newly moulted feathers are known as fresh-plumage birds whilst the older and more abraded plumage of the summer or breeding season is usually referred to as worn plumage.

In North America the complete moult of adults is known as the prebasic moult (leading to the basic plumage) and that which occurs before the breeding season is known as the prealternate moult (leading to the summer or alternate plumage); the only thrushes that display significantly different winter and summer plumages are three of the rock-thrushes *Monticola* of Africa and Asia. In these species the fresh or summer plumage is obscured for most of the winter by broad dull brown or sandy tips which wear off before spring and the onset of the breeding season to reveal the brilliance of the summer plumage. Very little work has been done on the moult patterns of thrushes in the tropical zones but it is extremely likely that their moult patterns are similar to those of the temperate regions.

The complete (or prebasic) moult usually takes places from July to September but can begin up to one month earlier and terminate up to six weeks later depending on the breeding season and the success or individual birds. For all thrushes the moult takes place in the breeding area or very close to it, and is usually complete (or substantially so) before those that migrate begin to depart for their wintering areas. Body feathers are replaced by the emergence of new feathers which displace existing ones, resulting in a gradual transition from old to new feathers. The flight feathers are replaced individually or in groups of two and three, beginning with the inner primaries and continuing out to the tips of the wing, and the same feathers are moulted equally on both wings at the same time. The tertials are usually moulted together at about the same time as the primary moult begins and usually before the secondaries are replaced. The secondaries are also replaced individually, and this begins a short while after the start of the replacement of the primaries, but these feathers are replaced from the outers inwardly. The tail feathers are also replaced from the innermost or central feathers

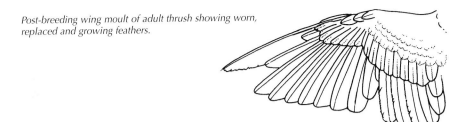
Post-breeding wing moult of adult thrush showing worn, replaced and growing feathers.

outwards, but this may not always proceed at an equal rate on both sides of the tail. The moult is usually completed with the replacement of the outermost (smallest) primary and the outermost tail feathers. Individual birds in moult are usually fairly obvious by the scruffy or dishevelled state of their plumage, most often by the varying stages of growth in the tail feathers and at closer range (or more especially in the hand) by the contrast in the shape and newness of the old and new feathers.

Moult in first-year birds follows a similar pattern but begins slightly later and is only a partial replacement of the body feathers and a varying numbers of the lesser, median and greater coverts; the number of coverts replaced varies within and between species. For instance it has been found that early broods and the more southerly populations of some species often replace more greater coverts than subsequent broods or more northerly breeding birds, and that variation can occur from year to year. For those that moult some of the greater coverts it is usually the inner greater coverts that are replaced, while none of the other wing or flight feathers is moulted. In some species this is evidently on certain individuals (depending on time of year) since many retained greater coverts (from juvenile plumage) have pale or buffish tips and are generally longer or more oval-shaped than the uniform, shorter and more rounded replaced feathers.

The spring, pre-breeding or prealternate moult of (both adult and first-year) thrushes is much less obvious and concerns only a smaller number of feathers. Depending on the species it may concern the replacement of some of the head, face and body feathers but the wing and tail feathers are usually retained until the complete post-breeding moult. In some individuals this may mean that old and new wing-coverts are retained for a whole year or that by the time of the complete moult most of the old (or oldest) coverts will have been lost or abraded through natural wear. Again depending on the species, moult of feathers at this time of year can begin as early as January and continue into early April, but for several species of *Turdus* thrush (and very probably several others) it may be a gradual process that continues throughout the winter. For most thrushes the spring marks the time when the breeding plumage is revealed though the abrasion of broad pale tips to some of the body feathers, but for others which have no obscuring pale tips it is a time when the plumage acquired six months previously begins to show the first signs of wear.

This is, of course, a fairly generalised summary of how the periods of moult affect the various species covered by this book. It is not intended to be a detailed account of how the annual replacement of certain feathers is undertaken; rather, it is an aid to understanding how birds may appear in the field. Also included are some references to the essential information on the appearance and ageing of moulting birds in the hand, but more extensive summaries can be found on the wider subject of bird moult in Humphrey & Parkes (1959, 1963), Palmer (1972) and Payne (1972). For detailed information on moult in North American passerines a good summary is available in Pyle *et al.* (1997), and for Europe see Svensson (1992).

Measurements

Apart from the total length, given in the Identification section in centimetres and inches, all linear measurements given here are in millimetres. Measurements are given chiefly as a guide for comparing similar-sized birds in the field or for use, mainly by ringers/banders, on birds in the hand. Some species have slight differences in leg or wing length, which, with practice, may be recognisable in the field, especially when considered in relation to the stance of the bird in question.

Wing length is measured from the carpal joint (bend of the wing) to the tip of the longest primary on the flattened wing chord (in the folded position). Bill length (except where stated) is the length

Measurements of overall length of bird.

Measurements of flattened wing chord.

Tarsus measurements.

Measurements of bill length and depth.

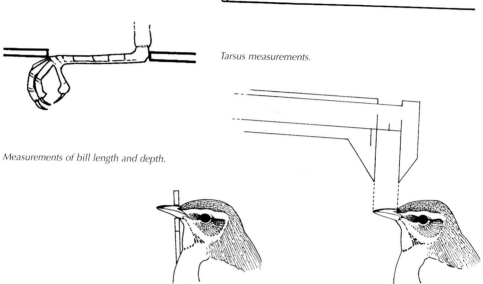

of the culmen from the base of the feathers (the exposed part of the culmen) to the tip of the upper mandible (see diagram). Tarsus length is the distance between the 'knee' joint at the upper end of the tarsus to the 'ankle' joint of the middle toe. For some species, mostly those in the Palearctic or Holarctic, this is from live birds captured for ringing (Svensson 1992, Pyle *et al.* 1997), but for most of the other species measurements from live birds are not readily available and museum specimens have been used.

It should be borne in mind when comparing museum data with live birds that (a) some species or specimens may not have been measured using the flattened wing chord, and (b) up to a 3% reduction occurs in dead or prepared specimens owing to the natural processes of skin shrinkage. For those sources of information other than our own, the method of measurement has not always been cited. In addition, some measurements, particularly where only one or two individuals have been sampled, may include those taken from worn birds or from juveniles which may be slightly smaller or shorter than adults in fresh plumage (although most immatures will have fully grown feathers within a few weeks of leaving the nest), or from adults in primary moult which can also give shorter measurements. Some caution is also needed in comparing bill data, since not all authors use the same method as ourselves (alternatives are tip of bill to nostrils or the base of the skull) and without the method of measuring being clear, comparisons may be inappropriate. Unless otherwise stated, all measurements refer in the first instance to the nominate subspecies and are given in the order of wing, bill and tarsus. These are followed by those measurements for the named subspecies, concluding with the weight (given in grams).

We have avoided the use of tail measurements in this book since there are, in the main, no species which are dependent on tail length for identification. More importantly, we feel that the tail offers the greatest scope for error amongst those who are not fully experienced with morphometric techniques. Moreover, for measurements of the tail to be of practical use, only a fully grown adult should be used, as it is not always possible to ascertain whether the tail is still growing. In theory the length of the tail should be from the base of the central tail feathers to the tip of the longest feather. In practice the undertail-coverts provide a good cover for the base of the tail and the right point is not always easily located, especially on some thrushes.

All measurements given are either taken from existing (and acknowledged) literature sources or are our own either from living birds or from museum specimens, chiefly those from the British

Museum collection at Tring, the U.S. National Museum of Natural History (Smithsonian Institution) and the American Museum of Natural History in New York.

The data on weight are entirely from published reference material and from ringing/banding reports from observatories, ringing groups, etc. These weights are intended purely as a guide to the average adult weight, bearing in mind that weights of individuals change over the course of the year in response to natural conditions (weather, migration and, in the case of females, egg development).

References

At the end of each species account there is a list of references which are relevant to the details included in the particular account, including plumage details, behaviour or, for many species (especially for which there is very little information), calls or song; in some cases records of birds in new (or previously unknown) areas of occurrence are deemed sufficiently worthy to cite the source for others' future reference. Most of the references at the end of each account are of papers in ornithological journals, since references to guides or handbooks could appear under almost any species. For some species we have made use of regional handbooks to provide the most recently available information.

A complete list of all references used in this book is given at the end. This is not a comprehensive bibliography but aims to be up-to-date, with details of each of the species. The references are mainly from papers and books that we have used for identification, range, movements and breeding. We hope that the references cited will provide future students and interested readers with a thorough background in all aspects of the biology of the birds in this book.

CLASSIFICATION OF THE THRUSHES

In common with several other species, family groups and world family orders, the first authors to set out an ordered structure to the thrushes were Seebohm (1881) and Seebohm and Sharpe (1898–1902). These two, together with several later authors who reviewed arrangements of species, were concerned with the correct position of these birds in relation to their nearest relatives (i.e. those of perceived descent) or to those with which they shared similar features. The early years of the 20th Century saw a number of changes in the order and, not surprisingly, differences of opinion arose between authorities on the characters that defined or separated species as being worthy of inclusion within certain families. The consensus order arrived at by Hartert (1910) included the thrushes (and the chats) as a subfamily of the Muscicapidae – a large grouping which also included the babblers, mockingbirds, wrens, dippers, Old World flycatchers and accentors. This large assemblage reflected the facts that he found it impossible to draw a distinction between the families, that the 'muscicapids merge gradually into the so-called turdids', and that those species which could not satisfactorily be classified in either of these families 'may be considered a timalid' (babbler).

The order produced by Hartert remained largely unchanged over the following 40 years and formed the basis of the classification by Mayr & Amadon (1951). At the 11th International Ornithological Congress in Basle in 1954 this order was adopted by the committee set up to arrive at an agreed standard list of the bird families of the world. The committee found that 'for the reasons stated by Hartert' the Turdidae, Sylviidae (Old World warblers) and Muscicapidae should be combined in a single family, the Muscicapidae. This order of passerines, referred to as the 'Basle sequence', was subsequently adopted (with minor amendments and additions) by the editor and authors continuing Peters' *Checklist of the Birds of the World*; in the case of the Turdinae these were in fact written by S. Dillon Ripley in 1964. Within the family groups Ripley listed individual species according to the understanding of how each species related to the next. This order was widely adopted until the development of comparisons based on mitochondrial DNA analysis. It is also perhaps worth noting the fact that Vaurie (1959), in his widely respected work on *The Birds of Palearctic Fauna*, regarded the conclusions of the Basle sequence as not particularly satisfactory and adopted the earlier sequence proposed by Wetmore (1930), subsequently revised in 1960. With regard to their classification of thrushes, however, Vaurie and Wetmore differed little from that of Ripley, with the sole exception of treating Siberian Thrush *Zoothera sibirica* as a member of *Turdus*.

The thrushes are a group of closely related families with Old World origins and close affinities to several others of similar ancestry. In particular they share vocal characteristics with the babblers; this link is probably closest through *Geomalia*, here treated as turdine but often considered timaliine. No comprehensive DNA study exists on the phylogeny of thrushes, which is surprising given the pace at which some other families have been the subject of analysis; our knowledge would clearly benefit from an in-depth study of the whole family. The relationship with the chats is now less clear than previously thought since Sibley & Ahlquist (1990) and Pasquet *et al.* (in prep.) have shown that the chats are more closely genetically related to the Muscicapinae (i.e. Old World flycatchers) than they are to *Turdus*, although all muscicapid flycatchers and thrushes are definitely monophyletic. However, since the relationships between the muscicapid flycatchers, small chats and thrushes are still unclear, we continue to unite them all in the one family Muscicapidae. The sister group of this family is the Sturnidae–Mimidae group (starlings and thrashers) which also includes the Cinclidae (dippers). This is supported by DNA hybridisation (Sibley & Ahlquist 1990, Sheldon & Gill 1996) as well as by some phenotypic evidence (Martínez del Rio 1992). The DNA evidence places the thrushes after the dippers in Cinclidae on the basis that whilst dippers are not directly related or descended from thrushes they were an earlier branch of the muscicapid family tree which diverged before the splitting off of the turdine/muscicapid stock. In their work on the biochemical relationships of certain turdine groups Pasquet *et al.* (in prep.) confirm that the Turdinae should be restricted to the 'true' thrushes. After the thrushes Sibley & Ahlquist (1990) and Sibley & Monroe (1990) place the Old World flycatchers in the Muscicapinae, including the chats, but also the large generic groups of *Bradornis*, *Rhinomyias*, *Cyornis* and *Muscicapa*.

Thrushes are medium-sized, slim-bodied songbirds with slender bills; rounded heads; 10 primaries; booted or scutellated tarsi, usually long and strong as an adaptation to terrestrial foraging; toes well developed with the hind toe opposing the three forward-pointing ones to enable a firm perching grip; rictal bristles present at the base of the bill; mainly square-ended tail but also sometimes rounded and with 12 (exceptionally 14) feathers; and wings either short and fairly rounded at tips or long and pointed. The tongue has a blade-like reedy tip and the syrinx is tracheo-bronchial. The eggs usually have a pale base colour and are extensively spotted; the young are mostly spotted in their first juvenile plumage. Moult is, in most adults, restricted to a single complete replacement in the autumn; thrushes lack a spring moult but some areas of the plumage change by abrasion, the tips of feathers wearing away. Food is taken mainly on the ground but also from trees and vegetation, and consists mostly of invertebrates and fruit.

The casual observer comparing the morphological characters of the thrushes will see fairly clearly that there are links to and comparisons with the babblers, robins and chats and, in the New World, with the mockingbirds (*Mimus*, mimic thrushes) in which several of the Caribbean species of thrush were originally placed. In the latter case links to the mockingbirds may be more apparent than real since they are now considered to be more closely related to the starlings and mynas (Sturnini), and any similarities are due more to evolutionary convergence than to recent common ancestry. In addition several species of babbler (another Old World family with its origins probably in southern Asia) show close morphological similarities with the thrushes. In particular the five species of quail-thrush *Cinclosoma* from Australia and New Guinea resemble thrushes in shape and many actions, and are similarly ground-loving insect foragers, but have short and rather weak-looking wings and slightly longer, more graduated tails with rounded tips. Similarities with the thrushes is purely one of evolutionary convergence (it is presumably ecologically beneficial to share similar characteristics) and, as far as we know at present, not to any closer genetic linkage. Moreover the situation is further confused in that several groups of otherwise unrelated birds share the colloquial name 'thrush' as part of their common or English name. Particularly relevant here are the *Amalocichla* shrike-thrushes (Australia and New Guinea) and the antthrushes (Formicariidae) of South America, but apart from size and a superficial resemblance in structure (which allows them to show similar behavioural traits or actions, especially in foraging techniques), neither of these shares a direct relationship with the thrushes. In addition the Australian robins *Petroica* are actually flycatchers. In the New World, the Icteridae, which comprises the cowbirds, grackles, oropendolas and orioles, also contains 17 species to which the name blackbird has been applied. For example, the widespread Red-winged Blackbird *Agelaius phoeniceus* of North and Central America is one of several closely related species which bear this name, but this is purely a convenient descriptive term referring to the birds' plumage and, since icterids are of New World origin, such 'blackbirds' bear no relationship at all to true thrushes.

Taxonomy and relationships

The taxonomy and species sequence in this book follows that of Sibley & Monroe (1990) on the basis that their classification 'is the first to be based on a single objective criterion, namely the degree of similarity between the DNA of species representing the major groups of living birds.' It is, however, worth pointing out that the order in Sibley & Monroe (1990) differs only very slightly from that set out in Ripley (1952, 1964). Where we have differed from this order the justification for doing so is given, mainly on the basis of more recent information on the species (not necessarily DNA analysis), or where there is doubt or insufficient proof to adopt decisions, particularly in the review of subspecies. As an instance of the latter there have been a number of papers since Sibley & Monroe's classification which have shed new light on the relationships of certain species/subspecies. Moreover, it is not clearly stated by either Sibley & Ahlquist (1990) or Sibley & Monroe (1990) where, or for which species, DNA material has been examined. In some instances of rare, threatened or restricted-range species it is extremely unlikely that blood samples and DNA profiles have been examined. Moreover, in acknowledging the classification of Sibley & Monroe (1990) as the one that we have largely followed, a few words on the previous classifications are necessary to set this in context.

In their evaluation through the evidence of DNA, Sibley & Ahlquist (1990) found that the Muscicapidae consisted of two subfamilies, the Turdinae (the 'true' thrushes) and the Muscicapinae, which they further subdivided into two distinct groups or tribes, the Muscicapini, including the Old World flycatchers, and the Saxicolini, including the chats, robins or chat-like thrushes. In particular they found that the true or typical thrushes in the Turdinae (*Monticola*, *Zoothera*, *Turdus* and *Catharus*) are closely related and that whilst *Myadestes* has slightly more distant affinities it is closer to *Catharus* than to any other family.

In Ripley's broad 1964 assessment of the family no distinctions were drawn between the true thrushes and the chats, since they were regarded as members of a single family and examples could be found where one merged into the other (thus agreeing with the earlier view of Hartert 1910). From the DNA evidence Sibley and Monroe (1990) incorporated all remaining chats and chat-like thrushes in the Saxicolini. The two notable exceptions are *Zeledonia* (Wren-thrush of Central America) and *Drymodes* (Australian scrub-robins) which have been removed to the Parulini tribe of the Emberizinae and Corvoidea respectively. The principal change made by Sibley & Monroe (1990) to Ripley (1964) was to draw a clearer distinction of the Turdinae as a subfamily of the Muscicapidae on the basis of molecular evidence. Under their arrangement the Turdinae comprise the following genera.

Genus	no. of species
Neocossyphus	4
Monticola	13
Myophonus	7
Geomalia	1
Zoothera	36 (+1 extinct)
Cataponera	1
Nesocichla	1
Cichlherminia	1
Sialia	3

Myadestes	12 (+1–3 extinct)
Cichlopsis	1
Entomodestes	2
Catharus	12
Platycichla	2
Psophocichla	1
Turdus	65 (+1 extinct)
Chlamydochaera	1
Brachypteryx	5
Heinrichia	1
Alethe	6

This treatment reflects the following changes. First, the subfamily includes the genus *Neocossyphus* as an early offshoot of the thrushes although previously classed variably as belonging elsewhere within the Muscicapidae due to the predominantly flycatcher-like behaviour when foraging. Within *Neocossyphus*, Sibley & Monroe (1990) included the two members previously comprising the genus *Stizorhina*, although several earlier authors, notably Bannerman (1953), had also pondered on the exact relationship of the two *Stizorhina* flycatcher-thrushes to that of the extremely similar *Neocossyphus* ant-thrushes. Analysis of the DNA of all four species (Pasquet *et al.* in prep.) confirms that they are all closely related but the two flycatcher-thrushes are not as closely related as the two ant-thrushes and the latter are of more recent descent.

Second, the Hawaiian genus *Phaeornis* is now subsumed within an expanded *Myadestes*, following the work of Pratt (1982), who found songs and behaviour to be extremely similar. Biochemical studies by Fleischer and McIntosh (in prep.) support the inclusion of the Hawaiian thrushes within *Myadestes* but have not yet resolved the relationships of the various species. It is now widely believed that an ancestral member of the genus, possibly similar to the present Townsend's Solitaire *M. townsendi*, the only truly migratory member of the family, colonised the Hawaiian archipelago from mainland North America in the last 10,000 years and became widespread throughout whilst adapting differently to the environments of each of the islands. Several authors, principally Stejneger (1887), have commented on the similarity of Kamao *M. myadestinus* to Townsend's Solitaire, the only real or appreciable difference being in the proportions of the wings, tail and legs (a possible adaptation to a non-migratory lifestyle). We have included all former *Phaeornis* species within *Myadestes* and have (pending further investigation) retained all of the other nine species within the genus.

The genus *Pseudocossyphus* formerly consisted of three species, all endemic to Madagascar. Traditionally it was considered closely related to *Monticola* but smaller than all except *M. rufocinereus* (the main differences relating solely to wing structure). Ripley (1952) put them within *Cossypha* (chats) because they show some affinities with several of the muscicapid chats, but Goodwin (1956) argued in favour of retaining *Pseudocossyphus*. More recently detailed work by Farkas (1971, 1973, 1974) has shown that the differences are within the limits of variation embraced by *Monticola* and that they have many structural and behavioural traits in common. Langrand (1990) retained *Pseudocossyphus* without giving reasons but, apparently unaware of the work of Farkas, proposed that a taxonomic review was required. We follow Dowsett & Dowsett-Lemaire (1993), Urban *et al.* (1997) and Morris & Hawkins (1998) in subsuming all three species within *Monticola*.

Finally, the *Amalocichla* were included within the Turdinae by Ripley on the grounds that the two New Guinea species involved are thrush-like in behaviour and (at least the larger of the two) morphologically similar to some *Zoothera* species. Sibley & Monroe (1990) lacked DNA material from *Amalocichla* but regarded the inclusion of the genus with the thrushes as tentative at best, and cited Olson (1987) who considered that they were more closely related to the Acanthizidae (thornbills) of Australia. We agree with this and as such they are not considered within the scope of this work.

In summary, this book deals with the 'true thrushes' and whilst it is recognised that, owing to their systematic closeness to the thrushes, it should also perhaps include the bluebirds *Sialia*, the single species of Fruithunter *Chlamydochaera*, the six shortwings *Brachypteryx* and *Heinrichia* and the six alethes *Alethe*, these are included within the accompanying volume to this work on *Robins and Chats*, simply for the purposes of space and of identification, as they are more similar in appearance to the similar-sized chats.

Whilst we recognise that the inclusion (or exclusion) of some of those within the Turdinae as classified by either Ripley (1964) or Sibley & Monroe (1990) in this book will not meet with the approval of all taxonomists, it is a satisfactory grouping from which advancing knowledge will be able to clarify the relationships between these birds. The rapid advances that have been made in recent years in mt-DNA profiling will become more widely applied as the ability to 'read' species's (or individual birds') profiles develops. However, although an outstanding achievement, it is not a method that can always easily be applied to species of which we know very little. Moreover, some of those 'species' on which we need much more information are among the most elusive animals alive on the planet, and as such require considerable research effort. In the near future it is likely that sampling of mt-DNA will be able to determine the same data from a feather sample. It is likely, given our advancing knowledge, that in a decade or so from now our view of species relationships will have improved substantially.

The genera of thrushes

Neocossyphus

Four species, all endemic to Africa. Medium or medium-small thrushes with relatively short (and in two species broad-based) bill and long tail, rounded wings (with short primary projection) and plumage predominantly russet-red to rufous; mainly arboreal but occasionally forage lower or on the ground; juveniles are similar in colour to the adults and largely unspotted. The two ant-thrush species are mainly ground-dwelling, the two flycatcher-thrushes mainly arboreal (mid- to upper canopy) and, apart from plumage coloration, the two pairs appear to have little in common. The two flycatcher-thrushes have previously been considered more closely related to the true muscicapid flycatchers in their own genus *Stizorhina*. However, although seemingly unalike in behaviour, structure, voice and breeding, the similarities of plumage are particularly strong in that Rufous and Red-tailed Ant-thrush are almost uniformly rufous with dull greyish heads; Finsch's Flycatcher-Thrush and White-tailed Ant-thrush extend this similarity with extremely similar areas of white in the tail. Moreover, not only do they occur in the same areas of Africa, the respective 'species-pairs' have, on occasion, been noted foraging within the same mixed-species group at ant or termite swarms. Several theories have been advanced as to how and when these species evolved or diverged from each other (White 1962, Dowsett & Dowsett-Lemaire 1993). It may have occurred in the fairly recent past, but whilst plumage characters continued to be shared it resulted in a notable divergence in feeding behaviour and bill structure.

The affinities of *Neocossyphus* as a whole were, until recently, somewhat uncertain and largely unresolved. Several authorities considered the genus not to belong the thrushes at all – the species in question show some anatomical differences (particularly the un-thrushlike syrinx) from the rest of the family (Ames 1975, Jensen 1989). Olson (1989) suggested the creation of a larger subfamily unit Myadestinae, within the larger Muscicapidae, to incorporate *Neocossyphus* (and *Stizorhina*) together with *Myadestes*, *Modulatrix* and *Pinarornis*, since they all have chat-like affinities and a modified turdine syrinx. Keith *et al.* (1992) acknowledged such ideas but retained all four species within the Turdidae as a loose assemblage grouped between *Alethe* and *Modulatrix*. *Alethe* is now considered by Sibley & Monroe (1990) to be closer to the true thrushes whilst *Modulatrix* and *Pinarornis* continue to remain puzzling. Dowsett & Dowsett-Lemaire (1993) divided the species pairs within the group and resurrected *Stizorhina* for *fraseri* and *finschii* on the basis of the structural and behavioural differences. In defence of this they considered that they did not share a common origin and that the similarities could equally be the result of convergence. Furthermore, they agreed with White (1962) in that there was no morphological justification for treating *finschii* as anything more than sub-specifically distinct from *fraseri*. In support of this they quoted the observation of hybrids between the two in eastern Nigeria (where the two taxa are closest), and the fact that the songs of the two are similar, differing only in speed of delivery and pitch. The recent work by Pasquet *et al.* (in prep.), through the analysis of the DNA of the four species within the group, has confirmed the affinities of the *Neocossyphus–Stizorhina* grouping. First, all are closely related and that all are properly included within *Neocossyphus* and, more importantly, there is cladistic evidence to show a relationship with *Myadestes*. Perhaps more surprisingly, their work reveals that the Old World flycatchers are not (as previously believed) naturally related to *Neocossyphus* and are an assemblage of species with convergent ecological and evolutionary patterns.

Monticola

Thirteen species distributed throughout the Afrotropical, Palearctic and Oriental regions. Medium-sized thrushes but including four species closer to redstarts *Phoenicurus* in size, the genus as a whole seeming to connect the thrushes to the chats. *Monticola* thrushes are characterised by slender bills which broaden at the base (in the smaller species), small and inconspicuous rictal bristles (well-developed frontal bristles in the three Madagascan species), long wings and short tails, and in all but one species (Little Rock-Thrush) the sexes differ. In several species the males are mainly blue or cobalt-blue on the head and upperparts with chestnut (varying from orange to deep rust-chestnut) on the underparts; African species have (again with the exception of Little Rock-Thrush) very similar distribution of blue and chestnut areas. Females of all species are predominantly brown or barred darker or paler, with some, particularly the African species, sharing the orange underparts of the males. The bills are black or dark horn-brown. Songs of most species show affinities with several of the chats in containing scratchy notes or phrases and some more musical notes, but several, including two of the Madagascar species, have extremely fine songs with well-developed flutelike melodic phrases.

They are all principally birds of rocky and montane terrain but several of the African and Oriental species are more closely associated with woodlands or forests, particularly Miombo Rock-Thrush, which is almost entirely confined to miombo woodland in the hill country of southern-central Africa. Six species are migratory, although one, Sentinel Rock-Thrush, is mainly an altitude migrant. The Rock-Thrush and Blue Rock-Thrush are both long-distance migrants, with birds at the eastern limits of the breeding range covering some of the longest distances travelled by passerines to winter within Africa, mostly south of the Sahara. The relative position of the *Monticola* thrushes within the entire family of thrushes is unclear but they may be distantly related to wheatears *Oenanthe* and redstarts, in the similarity of red or orange in the plumage of males, in the red in the tail of Rock-Thrush, and in the similar behavioural habits and tail-quivering of Rock- and Little Rock-Thrush. Considered on size, structure, general thrush-like behaviour together with some clear chat-like affinities they are systematically best placed at the start of the true thrushes.

Changes to previous taxonomic classification: *M. pretoriae* (Transvaal Rock-Thrush) is here considered to be a clinal variation of the nominate form of *M. brevipes* (Short-toed Rock-Thrush); see Farkas (1962, 1966) and Clancey (1968). Morris & Hawkins (1998) separate Amber Mountain Rock-Thrush *M. erythronotus* from Forest Rock-Thrush *M. sharpei* on morphology but we feel that a comprehensive mt-DNA analysis is required in order to substantiate this claim.

Myophonus

Seven species virtually all restricted to southern Asia (from the Dzungarian Ala Tau, the Tien Shan range and central China south to Sri Lanka and Indonesia), the sole exception being that resident in the mountains of Taiwan. Seebohm (1881) considered that the *Myophonus* whistling-thrushes should be excluded from the Turdidae on account of their longer first primary, which in his opinion indicated closer affinity with the babblers. However, Delacour (1942) showed clearly that they are related to the Turdinae on structure, behaviour and habitat occupation, the only doubt resting on the fact that in juvenile plumage the young are only indistinctly spotted. This treatment was supported and adopted by Ripley (1952) who considered *Myophonus* as a primitive off-shoot of the true thrushes, and by Sibley & Monroe (1990).

Medium to large thrushes with strong hooked-tip bills and long legs, the plumage being essentially dark blue approaching navy as a ground colour, with a panel of bright violet- or cobalt-blue on the lesser coverts (not always easy to see in the field). In four whistling-thrushes the blue body plumage is overlain with a varying amount of metallic blue (from violet to cobalt) to silvery-white tips on the upper and underparts, the silvery-white tips being most obvious on the median coverts of the nominate race of Blue Whistling-Thrush. Recent work has found that the bright violet-blue areas are highly developed in their reflection of ultraviolet light, unique in a passerine, and which has implications for colour signalling in birds (Andersson 1996, 1999). In addition, almost all of the species in the genus have a silvery-whitish blue to dull violet chevron on the forehead to over the eyes, but in one species (Sunda Whistling-Thrush) this is fairly dull and in another (Sri Lanka Whistling-Thrush) entirely absent. The females are, for the most part, very similar or slightly duller but in two species the females are clearly browner but retain the metallic blue patch across the lesser coverts. All are principally birds of fast-running streams or rivers in mountain forests but they sometimes wander to forests well away from water, and in winter some move to lower levels where rivers may be slower-flowing.

There has been some confusion over the spelling of the generic name, which has included *Myophoneus*, *Myiophoneus* and *Myiophonus*; this was discussed by both Delacour (1942) and Deignan (1965), the latter concluding that *Myophonus* is correct and that the previous names are erroneous applications. Although Sibley & Monroe (1990) agreed with Deignan they perpetuated the use of the incorrect *Myiophonus*.

Geomalia

A monotypic genus endemic to Sulawesi, of uncertain affinity and widely considered not to be a thrush and to have closer affinities to the babblers. However, it also shows some, perhaps distant, affinities with the *Zoothera* thrushes with which it has been classed, but its true position has yet to be fully established. Ripley (1952, 1964) placed it within the Turdinae, although Stresemann (1931), who originally described the species, and White & Bruce (1986) concluded that it was more closely related to the babblers. Coates & Bishop (1997) adopt the view of White & Bruce and maintain it within the babblers while acknowledging that its true position is unclear. Sibley & Monroe (1990) cited the discussion by White and Bruce but, without explanation, maintained it within the thrushes. It is characterised by a thrush-like bill, short rounded wings and a long graduated tail; the plumage is dark brown to slate grey-brown above and deep rufous or orange below. The voice is apparently undeveloped and apart from a thin repeated whistle it is not known to sing. *Geomalia* is ground-dwelling, usually beneath thick vegetation, extremely shy and generally very little known. Until more specific data, principally evidence from DNA profiling, is available, we see no reason to remove this from the Turdinae, though we recognise that there are good grounds, principally on morphology and behaviour, for placing it closer to the babblers.

Zoothera

Thirty-six species distributed throughout the world mainly in Africa and Asia, with two species in Australasia and singles in North and Middle America. They are usually referred to as ground-thrushes, considered an older, more primitive family than *Turdus*, and show several behavioural traits (e.g.

slowly bobbing the entire body or just the tail) not exhibited by any other thrushes. The song of many species is unremarkable, usually simple in structure and frequently merely a single note or phrase repeated with little or no variation. Some, however (e.g. Siberian and Oberlaender's Ground-Thrush), have a richer, more melodious voice and recall some of the musical phrases given by *Turdus* thrushes. *Zoothera* thrushes are similar in structure to many *Turdus* thrushes, but the genus includes both larger and smaller species. The bill is usually stout and broad-based, and often no longer than the breadth of the head, but five Asian species have longer bills whilst conversely three African species have quite short ones; in all species the rictal bristles are well developed. The wing is generally shorter and more rounded than similar-sized *Turdus* thrushes, and the tail square-tipped, generally shorter (except in one or two species) and composed of 12 feathers except in certain species which have 14. The legs and feet are sturdy and lack scutellated divisions, and are usually pale or flesh-coloured. The sexes either alike or different. The range of plumage is also variable as in *Turdus* thrushes but several species have dark crescents or tips to both the upper- and underparts. All *Zoothera* thrushes are distinguished by the broad, contrasting underwing markings consisting of white bases to the secondaries and inner primaries, black (or blackish) tips to the under greater-coverts and axillaries, and white bases to the coverts, creating a geometric pattern. Several species have vertical black or blackish patches through the eye and across the cheeks, a pattern also shown by several immatures in the genus (where it is absent in the adults). All species are mainly ground feeders in dense montane or tropical forests and several are extremely poorly known either in terms of their behaviour, breeding or voice. Several in the *Z. dauma* group are very poorly known and some current subspecies (e.g. *neilgherriensis* and *imbricata*) may prove to be good species in their own right (see below).

The African species have in the recent past been considered closer to *Turdus* (White 1962, Hall & Moreau 1970) than the present grouping within *Zoothera*. Doubts about the true affinity of the African species have been expressed largely on the basis of strong vocal differences (for those species where songs are known) compared to the more primitive modulated whistles of several Asian species (Dowsett & Dowsett-Lemaire 1993). In our opinion, however, the African species exhibit many similar characters to other *Zoothera* thrushes, not least the distinctive underwing pattern together with other morphological characters; moreover, not all Asian species have songs based on single-note variation (in fact the race *aurea* of White's/Scaly Thrush has quite a musical song). There are also good reasons to support the idea that the African and Asiatic members of *Zoothera* are more closely related than is apparent. Spot-winged and Spotted Ground-Thrushes share close morphological characters, as do Orange-headed and Orange Thrush, and Crossley's and Abyssinian Ground-Thrushes, suggesting a linkage or common ancestor. In all three instances it is tempting to speculate on how recent this ancestry could be, since they are now more distantly separated by at least 65 million years following the parting of the two continents. A more detailed review of the genus is overdue (as is the reappraisal of several of the species within it i.e. the *Z. dauma* grouping). Until such a detailed review of the genus is available we are content to unite the African species within the genus.

Both Ripley (1962) and Sibley & Monroe (1990) included Varied Thrush and Aztec Thrush within *Zoothera* although AOU (1998) maintain *Ixoreus* for the former and *Ridgwayia* for the latter. These were retained because of their distinctive plumages and because the links to *Zoothera* thrushes in the Old World are not particularly clear (and may never have existed). However, both show plumage features, mainly the distinctive geometric or 'geocichline' underwing pattern of *Zoothera* thrushes and neither exhibits particularly marked changes in morphology that separates them (except in terms of their isolated distribution from their nearest congeners) from the remaining members of *Zoothera*. We agree with the more conservative approach and maintain them within *Zoothera*, pending further research.

The status of several Indonesian and South-East Asian species remains obscure. In particular both Red-backed Thrush *Z. erythronota* and Chestnut-backed Thrush *Z. dohertyi* are shy and little-known residents of primary forests on small Indonesian islands and differ from each other only slightly in the plumage of the head and face. Ripley (1962) listed both of them under *Z. erythronota* and included the race *mendeni*, known only from a single specimen collected in 1938. However Eck (1976) and White & Bruce (1986) considered that there was no reason to treat *dohertyi* as conspecific with *erythronota*; whilst we are content to agree with this approach the position of each is not entirely clear. There are other, as yet unnamed, races of *Z. erythronota* on Taliabu, Buton and Kabaena islands which may, on the limited evidence available, be similar to *mendeni*.

Kivu Ground-Thrush *Z. tanganjicae* was considered conspecific with nominate *Z. piaggiae* by Ripley (1962), Dowsett & Dowsett-Lemaire (1993) and Urban *et al.* (1997), with Sibley & Monroe (1990) supporting the earlier view of Prigogine (1977) that the two are separate species. Clement (1999a) concluded that the differences in plumage (principally the head to nape colour and the wing to tail ratio) and the altitudinal separation were no more than differences elsewhere in the species (e.g. between the races *rowei* and *piaggiae*). Information on this species group is insufficient to support further substantial changes and further work is required, since the African *Zoothera* have not always been treated consistently with others in the genus.

Kibale Ground-Thrush *Z. kibalensis*, known from only two male specimens collected in 1966, was described as a full species by Prigogine (1978), but Dowsett & Dowsett-Lemaire (1993) considered the taxon to be only subspecifically distinct as the claimed plumage differences were considered to be no greater than that which exists between *Z. c. graueri* and nominate *Z. c. camaronensis*. Several authors have questioned the validity of *kibalensis* on the slender evidence and lack of further records from a relatively well worked area of Central Africa, suggesting that the specimens were hybrids and that *kibalensis* is invalid. We refer to *kibalensis* within the account for *Z. cameronensis* but acknowledge that its continued recognition is unlikely.

The White's Thrush *Z. dauma* complex is an extremely difficult group. Ripley (1962) classed all 'scaly' thrushes as belonging within the *Z. dauma* species group and included *major, horsfieldi, machiki, heinei* and *lunulata*. These have subsequently been shown – mainly by Ford (1983), Ishihara (1986) and White & Bruce (1986) – to be species in their own right and were treated as such by Sibley & Monroe (1990). The basis for these splits is mostly morphological, behavioural and (especially in the Australian species) the degrees of sympatry where the ranges overlap. It seems possible that both *neilgherriensis* and *imbricata* (currently treated as within *Z. dauma*) will be given full species status in the near future, both of them clearly being relict outposts, highly sedentary in small isolated niches of deep forest habitat with no contact with each other and possibly only very limited contact with congeneric members of the group in the case of the former and none at all in the latter. Furthermore it seems, from the limited information available on voice, and hence display and territory defence mechanisms, that mate attraction and/or interbreeding with a stranded migrant representative of *dauma* would be unlikely since both have only rudimentary songs at best or, in the case of *neilgherriensis*, possibly none at all. Further work on these birds is required, chiefly the response to *dauma* and *aurea* songs and, if achievable, the response to each other's songs. However, it may be that they have songs which are either given for very short periods in the early or pre-dawn period or possibly for the greater part inaudible to the human ear.

San Cristobal Thrush *Z. margaretae* was treated by Ripley (1962) as a single species comprising nominate (from San Cristobal) and *turipavae* (from Guadalcanal) and this treatment was followed by Sibley & Monroe (1990). However, the work of Gibbs (1996) on this little known and rarely seen species has revealed that the two differ more widely morphologically than previously recognised and that *turipavae* is specifically distinct; we follow Gibbs in treating these as separate species.

Cataponera

A monotypic genus endemic to Sulawesi. A medium-sized thrush with fairly short rounded wings, long bill and strong sturdy legs. The plumage is olive or dark olive-brown on the crown with a prominent black supercilium extending to the sides of the nape; the underparts are slightly paler or with a cinnamon or reddish tinge to the undertail-coverts. An unobtrusive species living at mid- to low levels in trees or on the ground beneath dense foliage in evergreen montane forests. It is extremely secretive, rarely seen and little known. In shape, structure and behaviour it appears closely related to *Turdus* thrushes, but it also displays some habits and behaviour of the babblers, especially the laughingthrushes *Garrulax* and may, on further examination, prove to be more appropriate to that genus.

Nesocichla

A monotypic genus confined to five of the islands in the Tristan da Cunha archipelago in the South Atlantic. Similar to *Turdus* species in shape and structure but characterised by small, rounded wings, large bill and fairly long and strong-looking legs and feet. The plumage is mostly brown or reddish- or rufous-brown, mottled or streaked orange-buff on the underparts. It is mainly a ground-dweller and occurs in a variety of habitats mostly above 300 m. It is considered to be a primitive relative of *Turdus* thrushes and most probably of New World origin: the passerine landbirds of Tristan are (based on the winds) thought to have colonised from South America (Rand 1955). It may prove on DNA analysis to lie within the range of *Turdus*, but morphologically it also has some similarities with the following genus – *Cichlherminia*.

Cichlherminia

A monotypic genus confined to several islands in the Caribbean. A large and stoutly built thrush with fairly long and rounded wings (third to fifth primaries equal longest, first primary about a third the length of the longest, and second intermediate in length), short tail and large, stout bill with arched culmen. The frontal bristles are numerous and strong. The legs are strong or stout but never longer than twice the culmen length. The upperparts are variably warm or dark russet-brown, the wings olive-brown, and the underparts heavily patterned with white or yellowish centres forming large central spots (with pointed tips) and brown fringes. This is a forest-dwelling species found at all levels from the ground to the upper canopy. It is considered to be a primitive relative of *Turdus* thrushes, but also shows some surprising similarities in plumage to Tristan da Cunha's monotypic *Nesocichla*.

Myadestes

Thirteen species, distributed throughout the Hawaiian archipelago (where six species are endemic of which one and possibly now three are extinct), Middle America, several of the Caribbean islands (where two species are island endemics) to northern South America. These thrushes are small with a slim shape, fairly long and slightly rounded tail, short legs and a short broad-based bill; sexes similar and juveniles conspicuously spotted especially on the underparts, which show a scalloped pattern with buff, yellowish or whitish centres emarginated evenly or finely with black, creating a distinctive pattern of spots. The wings are rounded with the third to fifth primaries longest, and occasionally also the sixth; the first primary is short and the second intermediate in length, with the secondaries also fairly long. The central pair of tail feathers are longest and all the outers slightly shorter and tapered towards the tip. The bill is short, flat and relatively weak, with partly covered oval nostrils and fairly long or well-developed frontal bristles. The tarsus is short and rarely is longer than the middle toe and claw. The plumage is generally unremarkable, with a range of grey to green and brown (rufous in one species) predominating; some species have white eye-rings; the adults usually show a band of buff or white at the base of the secondaries or extending to the inner primaries, white tips to the tail and pale outer webs to the outer tail feathers.

The song of most species is a variety of whistling phrases but two species – Cuban and Rufous-throated (both island endemics) – are truly exceptional in their use of modulated whistles, buzzing tones, bell-like notes and flute-like trills. Most are arboreal, being found from mid-height to canopy level in forest trees, and are usually sedentary or make limited altitudinal movements with the sole exception of Townsend's Solitaire, a long-distance migrant which moves north to central Alaska to breed. Nests are usually a cup of moss placed low in a tree or on the ground. The Hawaiian species were formerly separated into *Phaeornis* owing to their island endemism (and were thought to have evolved separately) but their plumage, vocal and behavioural similarities with *Myadestes* (Pratt 1982) are now widely accepted. However, on behaviour and vocal grounds they could also be considered close to several *Catharus* thrushes, particularly the sedentary montane species of Middle America.

Ripley (1964) included Black-faced Solitaire *Myadestes melanops* and Varied Solitaire *M. coloratus* within the Andean Solitaire *M. ralloides* grouping, but we follow Ridgely (1976), AOU (1983) and Hilty & Brown (1986) in considering both to be worthy of full species status on the basis of distinctive morphological and range differences.

Cichlopsis

A monotypic genus, widely but sparsely distributed throughout various areas of northern South America, indicating a relict distribution. It is poorly known, being similar to *Myadestes* with which it was formerly classed but subsequently considered to be sufficiently distinct to warrant its own genus. It is characterised by a long tail, a fairly short rounded wing (wing-point between primaries 3 and 5) and a stout two-tone bill (similar to but longer than any *Myadestes*), with a deeper upper mandible and well-developed culmen ridge and similarly well developed frontal and rictal bristles at the base of the bill. The tarsus is rather short and about the same length as the middle toe. The plumage is uniform rufous-brown with a paler throat-patch, lacking the prominent wing-bar and white outer tail feathers of *Entomodestes*. The stance is more horizontal than in *Myadestes* and *Entomodestes*; it also differs from *Myadestes* in voice and nest location.

Entomodestes

Two species of limited distribution, restricted to the Andes of northern South America. Morphologically similar to *Myadestes* solitaires in shape and structure but larger and with longer tails. Analysis of mt-DNA by Pasquet *et al.* (in prep.) confirms that they are more closely related to *Turdus*. They are characterised by a long and graduated tail with the outer feathers tapering to a point from about mid-length. The bill is prominent and broad-based, the nostrils large and isolated from the feathers at base of forehead. The tarsus is prominently divided into scutellated sections. The wings are rather rounded with short primary projection and all primaries are broad and of equal width for the entire length. The plumage is largely black or black with rich rufous upperparts and white face-patch, both species having broad white wing-bars and outertail-feathers which are seen to good effect in their dashing flight.

Catharus

Thirteen species mostly confined to the Americas except Grey-cheeked Thrush, which crosses into the Old World and breeds in extreme north-east Siberia. Most of those in Middle America are sedentary or move altitudinally, but six species are highly migratory with extremes moving from northern Canada and Alaska to central South America. The sexes are similar and juveniles spotted in their first plumage. They are characterised by their generally small size, northern or migratory species having fairly long and pointed wings with a short first primary and third and fourth primaries longest. In sedentary species the wing is shorter with rounded primaries, fourth and fifth being longest. The tail consists of 12 feathers and is slightly rounded. The bill is relatively short and broad at the base with an arched culmen, the nostrils not covered by well-developed frontal bristles which are either reduced, slender or absent. The tarsus is long and usually about twice the length of the culmen; in tropical breeding species the tarsus and toes are quite stout. The plumage of most species is between grey-brown through olive-brown to warmer rufous-brown on the crown and upperparts (in some species the crown is contrastingly darker than the rest of the upperparts): the underparts are either plain off-white or greyish to yellow with variably restricted or poorly defined spots, smudges or light streaks on throat and breast except in Wood Thrush, which is boldly spotted with black. Some of the Central and South American species have bright orange or reddish-orange bills set against otherwise dull olive plumages. Several species, e.g. Hermit Thrush and Veery, together with several of the sedentary species from Central America (Slaty-backed and Ruddy-capped Nightingale-Thrushes), have remarkable songs and are widely acknowledged as being among the finest songsters in the New World. Most of the montane species (of Central and northern South America) are extremely shy and infrequently seen, in general inhabiting the lower levels of dense vegetation where they are more often heard than seen. The northern migratory species tend to be more arboreal, although all species are principally ground-feeding birds. Wood Thrush, the largest *Catharus*, has previously been placed in its own genus *Hylocichla*, but is now widely regarded as being more closely related to the members of *Catharus* breeding in temperate North America and wintering in the Neotropics, based on structure (particularly on the length of the outermost primary), behaviour and song together with other morphological characters.

Platycichla

Two species restricted to South America. They are similar to (and poorly separated from) the *Turdus* thrushes in size, shape and structure. They are medium-sized thrushes with a rounded wing, short bill, medium tarsus (bill and legs shorter than most *Turdus*) and rounded tail, with outer feathers shorter than the central pair, some of which are almost pointed at the tips. The first primary is short and the third to fifth primaries longest or equal; the secondaries are also long. The bill has an arched culmen, with frontal and rictal bristles also pronounced and strong: the tarsus is equal to or shorter than the length of middle toe and claw. The plumage is uniform grey or brown. Goodwin (1957) argued in favour of maintaining *Platycichla* as distinct from *Turdus* on the basis of these slim morphological differences. Ridgely & Tudor (1989) recommended that it should be incorporated within *Turdus* but maintained it themselves. We support this retention pending further investigation.

Psophocichla

A monotypic genus, confined to Africa south of the Sahara. Widely treated as within *Geocichla* = *Zoothera* (Chapin 1953–1954, Irwin 1984) and *Turdus* (Ripley 1964, Hall & Moreau 1970). It shows some similarities with *Zoothera* thrushes on the face pattern, particularly the Spotted Ground-Thrush *Z. guttata* of East and South Africa, but clearly differs by the lack of typical underwing pattern which leaves it closer to many *Turdus* species. Irwin (1984) discussed the position of *Psophocichla* and concluded that it is probably sufficiently isolated and distinct to merit the maintenance of the monotypic genus. Relationships with *Zoothera* are not particularly clear and it may possibly be as close to Spot-winged Thrush *Z. spiloptera* of Sri Lanka as to *Z. guttata*. The wing is also more like *Turdus* in shape, longer and more pointed, but the tail is short: the bill is large, broad and deep at the base. The legs are long and contribute to a very upright stance. Similar in plumage to members of both *Turdus* and *Zoothera* with grey upperparts, striped face pattern and prominent spots on otherwise white underparts recalling both Mistle Thrush *T. viscivorus* and Spotted Ground-Thrush. However, it seems clear that the relationship with *Turdus* is equally (if not more) distant and that resemblance to both Mistle Thrush (with which Hall & Moreau thought it formed a superspecies) and Song Thrush *T. philomelos* is entirely superficial and due to convergence. Until the position of the genus is clarified through DNA study we are content to agree with Irwin (1984), Sibley & Monroe (1990), Dowsett & Forbes-Watson (1993) and Urban *et al.* (1997) that *Psophocichla* is valid.

Turdus

Sixty-five species of world-wide distribution. Medium to large thrushes with rounded heads, medium or long, pointed wings, fairly prominent bill (stout in some species) and usually with long tail and legs. They are characterised by having the first primary extremely small and the third to fifth the longest (in some the sixth may equal the longest). The bill has a straight or slightly arched culmen, with some having a moderate angle to the gonys (usually only visible in the hand); the nostrils are round or oval and partly feathered posteriorly and usually show well developed rictal and frontal bristles. The tail has 12 square-tipped feathers which are always much longer than the closed wing-tip (usually extending to the tips of the uppertail-coverts). The legs are stout or strong and the tarsus of moderate length. Sexes are either different or identical and juvenile plumage is always spotted. The plumage of adults is frequently uniform, with black, brown or chestnut-brown predominating, but some species also have reddish or bright orange-rufous on the underparts, whilst others have greyish tones on the upperparts. Several species are also spotted or streaked on the underparts. Two species confined to the Caribbean (one of which is extinct), formerly classed as *Mimocichla* (the mimic thrushes – because thought to represent a possible connection with the mockingbirds) are predominantly blue or bluish-grey.

16 species are migratory, including some of the longest-distance passerine migrants with several high northern latitude species moving south to winter within temperate and tropical zones. Many forest-dwelling species of Africa and the Neotropics are either extremely sedentary and rarely occur outside their preferred habitat or may make short-distance movements following the rainy seasons. The voice in practically all *Turdus* thrushes is particularly well developed and these birds are well known for their rich lilting melodic songs, which contain characteristic phrases common to many species, but which once learned are easily told apart. Like the *Zoothera* thrushes they are mainly ground-feeders, but many of the truly forest species have become almost totally arboreal and forage in trees well above ground level. Nests are often elaborate structures of woven plant material in a deep substantial cup-shape structure frequently lined with mud and placed well above the ground, usually in a tree, but for some species any similar structure that offers a suitable opportunity may be utilised. The eggs are predominantly pale green to pale or turquoise-blue but occasionally whiter, with most being finely spotted or speckled with brown to reddish-brown and in some overlain with larger, irregular patches of lilac, mauve or grey. Within the classification of the Turdinae the *Turdus* thrushes are traditionally placed last, as the most developed of all the thrushes.

There are several differences between Ripley's treatment of the *Turdus* thrushes and that of Sibley & Monroe (1990), the main being a small number of splits which has increased the species count from 62 to 66. Neither Ripley (1962) nor Hall & Moreau (1970) recognised *Psophocichla* and considered the characters shown by the sole member of the genus to be within the range of *Turdus*. Of the other African species, apart from a slight re-ordering, Sibley & Monroe (1990) followed Hall & Moreau (1970), who divided Ripley's arrangement of the subspecies in the two Northern Olive Thrush *T. abyssinicus* and Southern Olive Thrush *T. olivaceus* into a new grouping of Olive *T. olivaceus* and African Thrush *T. pelios*. This had the effect of (i) uniting under *T. olivaceus* the previously separated Taita Thrush *T. helleri*, Somali Blackbird *T. ludoviciae* and Yemen Thrush *T. menachensis*, and (ii) separating African Thrush *T. pelios* from Central and West Africa and dividing it into five further subspecies.

Keith and Urban (1992) later reviewed this treatment in line with that used both by Sibley & Monroe (1990) and subsequently adopted by Urban *et al.* (1997). This identified the limits of the four members of the superspecies comprising *T. olivaceus* (Olive), *T. pelios* (African), *T. libonyanus* (Kurrichane) and *T. tephronotus* (Bare-eyed Thrushes). It also united all remaining races (of the previous *abyssinicus/olivaceus* grouping) south of Somalia under Olive Thrush and also included *helleri*, *ludoviciae* and *menachensis* within the complex on the basis of vocal and certain morphological evidence. Whilst Keith & Urban (1992) appreciated that these three were isolated from other races (and hence were probably in the process of diverging into full species) it was considered that the principal differences of plumage were not sufficient to determine full separation since they still have the orange underwing-coverts, a factor linking all others in the *olivaceus* complex. At best it was considered that they were dull-coloured members of the complex, and *menachensis* although geographically more distant, is probably best regarded as an allospecies within the group.

This arrangement has not found universal acceptance, however, and Collar & Stuart (1985), Collar *et al.* (1994) and Zimmerman *et al.* (1996) have persisted with the previous treatment of *T. helleri* as a full species on the basis of clear morphological differences and its isolation from any other member of the *olivaceus* species grouping. Collar *et al.* (1994) and van Perlo (1995) have also treated the similarly isolated *ludoviciae* in northern Somalia as a full species, while in the Yemen, Collar *et al.* (1994) along with the two most recent works dealing with the birds the Arabian avifauna, Hollom *et al.* (1988) and Porter *et al.* (1996), regard *menachensis* as a full species, Yemen Thrush.

As Hall & Moreau (1970) stated, and which remains equally true 30 years later, there is wide disagreement between the treatment proposed by different authorities. A more consistent standard of agreement will, in all probability, only be established by biochemical comparisons. Whilst we have no wish to confuse or complicate this matter further we have sought to align our view with that of previous authors, notably Keith & Urban (1992), which has, perhaps regrettably, meant retention of *helleri*, *ludoviciae* and *menachensis* at the subspecific level, since we feel that a convincing case has not been made for them to be split into species. At the same time we have adopted a stronger morphological approach to those races which seem distinctly closer to African Thrush than previously considered. The races *nigrilorum*, *poensis*, *centralis* and *chiguancoides* continue to be controversial and we are of the opinion that the morphology of these races is closer to that of the predominantly West African distribution of African Thrush than the present arrangement of Olive Thrush.

The Asian and Palearctic grouping of the *Turdus* thrushes by Sibley & Monroe (1990) follows closely that of Ripley (1964) and both extend this grouping to include the (Malaysian–Indonesian–Pacific) distribution of Island Thrush *T. poliocephalus*. This is an acceptable arrangement since this species, divided into one of the largest number of subspecies – currently 50 – is morphologically close to the Blackbird *T. merula* complex (Europe–East Asian distribution) and shares many similar characteristics of voice, behaviour and reproduction. A very similar pattern of distribution is shared by the 90+ species of white-eyes *Zosterops*. These are a group of Old World passerines widely distributed throughout Africa, southern Asia to China, Japan and Indonesia. More interestingly, they also extend their range through many of the Indonesian islands to New Guinea and east to Fiji and Samoa, which mirrors that of Island Thrush (except that white-eyes occur on slightly more islands) including the southerly extent of the range to Norfolk and Lord Howe Islands (where two species are now thought to be extinct, as are the races of Island Thrush which also formerly occurred there). The difference between treatment as full species as opposed to subspecies is that all the species of *Zosterops* are considered the result of several successive invasions of the island groups from the mainland (Lack 1971). Island Thrush on the other hand has attained its present distribution by a single invasion from one point of origin, expanding and diversifying into a wide number of island races.

Clearly, proof of this may lie in the examination of mt-DNA patterns of each of the *T. poliocephalus* races but we would be surprised if it revealed anything other than a close lineage, probably from *T. merula* stock and probably of fairly recent origin. The species as a whole remains poorly known and requires considerable investigation of its biological composition to determine its affinities and origins: the distribution of races involves a baffling mosaic in which strongly differentiated forms interpose between similar ones and virtually identical forms are stranded at great distances from each other. Under modern-day species concepts it would be easy to consider many races worthy of full species status (a process already initiated by some authorities considering certain taxa in several better studied areas). Some authors have linked *T. o. ludoviciae* to this group (as the sole non-island resident) on the basis of its overall slaty plumage, but its linkage to the *T. olivaceus* group is well established through voice and plumage, most notably the orange-buff underwing-coverts not shown by any of the *T. poliocephalus* group.

Both Vaurie (1959) and Ripley (1964) regarded Grey-backed Thrush *T. hortulorum* as a single species but Sibley & Monroe (1990) separated nominate *hortulorum* and *dissimilis* (Black-breasted Thrush) as full species on the basis of the wide separation in their respective breeding ranges with no known intermediate zones, so that, together with Tickell's Thrush, they form a superspecies. We follow this arrangement and accord full species status to both *T. hortulorum* and *T. dissimilis*.

The South American grouping of *Turdus* thrushes by Sibley & Monroe (1990) followed Ripley (1964) closely. However, Black Thrush *T. infuscatus* was split from Glossy-black Thrush *T. serranus* on the basis of the wide gap in the distribution between Honduras to Colombia. The two slaty-thrushes, Andean *T. nigriceps* and Eastern *T. subalaris*, previously considered as only subspecifically separated, are now regarded as full species on the basis of their isolated ranges. The species limits in the three very similar thrushes, Pale-vented *T. obsoletus*, Cocoa *T. fumigatus* and Hauxwell's *T. hauxwelli*, are complex and poorly understood. Hellmayr (1934) considered *fumigatus* and *hauxwelli* to be conspecific but Gyldenstolpe (1945) showed that in parts of Brazil they were sympatric and best regarded as separate species. Ripley (1964) accepted this and separated both, with *obsoletus* as a race of *fumigatus*, but Meyer de Schauensee (1966, 1970) separated *obsoletus* while continuing to treat *hauxwelli* as a race of *fumigatus*, subsequently (1970) revising this to include *hauxwelli* within the *obsoletus* complex. Snow (1985) looked at museum specimens from the contact zones of *fumigatus* and *hauxwelli* where he found considerable individual variation, and concluded that all populations (including *obsoletus*) should be treated as conspecific pending further investigation. Ridgely & Tudor (1989) found this unsatisfactory on the basis that the evidence for such a treatment was not yet available but that all three were closely allied and should be considered as allospecies.

The specific status of all three is further confused by the position of *orinocensis*, originally considered to be a race of *T. fumigatus* on the basis of its morphological characters (Hellmayr 1934, Ripley 1964). It has also more recently been considered a race of *obsoletus* on the basis of its altitude preference (Meyer de Schauensee & Phelps 1978). Ridgely & Tudor (1989) argued that despite Snow's work on the individuals of the contact zones little new information on the level of differences between the three taxa had been established and a more specific field study was required which included behaviour, courtship, breeding behaviour and altitudinal preferences together with DNA analysis of the entire complex. Whilst the need for such a detailed study is still urgently required we follow the treatment of Ridgely & Tudor, which allows species status to *obsoletus*, *fumigatus* and *hauxwelli* whilst retaining *orinocensis* as a race of *T. fumigatus*.

The relationship of the component subspecies within the White-necked Thrush *T. albicollis* grouping has been considered unsatisfactory on the basis of behaviour, vocal and altitudinal differences. We follow AOU (1983) and Ridgely & Tudor (1989) in distinguishing birds of Middle America and the Andes of northern South America as White-throated Thrush *T. assimilis* from the more lowland forest birds within the *albicollis* grouping. The position of the little known race *daguae* of north-west Colombia and central Ecuador is possibly less well defined than others within the species group but on the basis of voice and behaviour it is considered part of *T. assimilis*, although it has been proposed as worthy of full species status.

Finally, the two similar species of western Mexico, Rufous-backed Thrush *T. rufopalliatus* and Grayson's Thrush *T. graysoni*, considered as a single species under Ripley (1964), are here treated as full species following Phillips (1981) and given limited support by Howell & Webb (1995), who also considered that the status of the two required further study.

USE OF ENGLISH NAMES

English names used in this book largely follow those in Sibley & Monroe (1990), which in turn adhere closely to those of Voous (1977) and Vaurie (1959) for Holarctic species, Keith *et al.* (1992), Dowsett & Forbes-Watson (1993) and Urban *et al.* (1997) for African species, and Ridgely & Tudor (1989) for the Neotropics. However, in certain cases we have preferred the use or retention of other names for the reasons set out below. The pursuit of a uniform standard of names may be an ideal but in ornithological practice it seems as far away now as ever. Whilst we have no wish to lessen the importance of such an aim, we feel that it is equally essential that there is regional and local agreement on the use of names, otherwise they are likely to become redundant. Any attempt to impose or create names locally or regionally by distant authors would be unwise and, as has frequently been the case, unnecessary.

In the following two cases some comment is required on the current usage of English names. The use of White's or Scaly Thrush for *Zoothera dauma* is particularly difficult since both names apparently have equal usage in the western and eastern parts of the range. Over most of Europe the bird is known as White's Thrush in honour of Gilbert White (the eminent 18th-century English naturalist), but over most of Asia Scaly Thrush appears to be assuming priority. Although known to science since 1790 White neither saw nor named the bird but it was first named in his honour by Eyton in 1836. The name has remained in common usage ever since, and it seems especially fitting to commemorate a distinguished naturalist through such an exquisite and enigmatic species. Moreover, the alternative name is a perfunctorily descriptive epithet which has none of the attraction and lacks a sense of ornithological history and integrity, which is largely out of step with the tradition of honouring respected naturalists. As Mearns & Mearns (1988) have indicated, species have been named after certain people completely unconnected with ornithology and for no other reason than they were the financial patrons of expeditions to distant parts of the world (frequently for reasons other than natural history). It has recently been proposed (Beaman 1994) that Scaly Thrush should be the name used in Asia, notwithstanding that none of the recent field guides to Japan, nor even Cheng (1987), uses this name, and that the name in Russia (and the former U.S.S.R.) is 'Spotted' or 'Golden' Thrush. However, we appreciate that White's may not, in future, have a significance to increasing numbers of locally based ornithologists and, in this one instance, we give equal status to Scaly Thrush as the name in use. In doing so we realise that this will not receive universal approval but on the basis of common usage and as a reference point which acknowledges local or regional requirements it is a pragmatic way of achieving a name that can be recognised and used by all.

The second point at issue is the usage of 'thrush' or 'robin' for the Central and South American species of *Turdus*. Prior to the lists of Meyer de Schauensee (1966, 1970) all were referred to as robins, but strictly speaking this is incorrect and inconsistent with the 'true robins' of Europe and Australia. AOU (1983, 1998) changed some of the robins into thrushes but remained inconsistent in its approach. Ridgely & Tudor (1989) and Howell & Webb (1995) used the family name for each of the species with the exception of American Robin which is probably too familiar and widely known ever to be successfully changed to its more correct title.

Other differences from Sibley & Monroe (1990) on the use of English names are (12) **Rock-Thrush** (the prefix Rufous-tailed or Mountain is unnecessary); (18) **Sri Lanka Whistling-Thrush** (now in line with the change to the national name); (54) **Bassian Thrush** and (55) **Russet-tailed Thrush** (split following Ford [1983] and named following Simpson & Day [1989]); (61) **Bonin Islands Thrush** (the reduction to Bonin Thrush seems unnecessary); (105) **Tickell's Thrush** (the change to Indian Grey Thrush is unnecessary; Tickell's is the name most widely used and commemorates the ornithologist who discovered the species in 1833); (111) **Blackbird** (a qualifying epithet seems unnecessary, since the New World blackbirds Icteridae are unlikely to be confused with those in Europe or Asia; only the elevation of certain Asiatic races to full species might require the adoption of the prefix Common or Eurasian, and we agree with Beaman [1994] that the former is preferable to the latter); (114) **Kessler's Thrush** (the change to White-backed Thrush is unnecessary as the existing name is sufficient to distinguish the species); (119) **Izu Islands Thrush** (the reduction to Izu Thrush is unnecessary; the bird is known throughout Japan as Izu Islands Thrush from the transcribed name of Seven Islands Thrush); (125) **Chinese Song Thrush** (the similarity to Song Thrush is plain and infers a close affinity with the more widespread species from Europe; previously known as Eastern or Verreaux's Song Thrush, Chinese is now considered preferable); (145) **Mountain Thrush** (the prefix 'American' seems unnecessary since there is no other Mountain Thrush; moreover it is not widespread throughout the Americas).

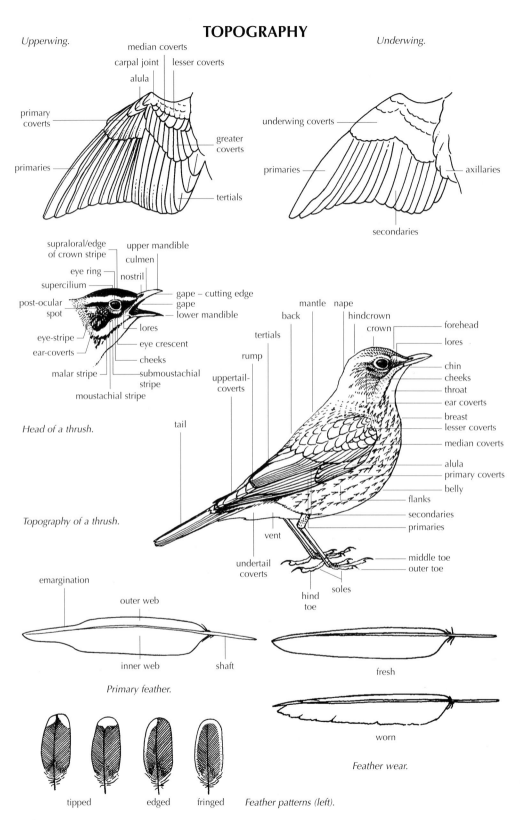

TOPOGRAPHY

Upperwing.

median coverts
carpal joint — lesser coverts
alula

primary coverts

primaries

greater coverts

tertials

Underwing.

underwing coverts

primaries

axillaries

secondaries

supraloral/edge of crown stripe — upper mandible
culmen
eye ring
nostril
supercilium
post-ocular spot
gape – cutting edge
gape
lower mandible
eye-stripe — lores
ear-coverts — eye crescent
cheeks
malar stripe — submoustachial stripe
moustachial stripe

Head of a thrush.

Topography of a thrush.

tail

tertials

rump

uppertail-coverts

back — mantle — nape — hindcrown — crown
forehead
lores
chin
cheeks
throat
ear coverts
breast
lesser coverts
median coverts
alula
primary coverts
belly
flanks
secondaries
primaries
middle toe
outer toe

vent
undertail coverts
hind toe
soles

emargination
outer web
inner web — shaft

Primary feather.

fresh

worn

Feather wear.

tipped — edged — fringed — *Feather patterns (left).*

VOICE AND VOCALISATIONS

As would be expected in a group of birds that chiefly inhabits forests thrushes are very vocal, since contact between pairs or family groups is important. The calls of most thrushes are single or double notes uttered largely to maintain contact between pairs of adults and dependant young or for the purpose of alerting others to the presence of danger. Call notes are used in the daily activities of most passerines primarily as a method of contact or location, including between parents and young. They also perform other functions, mostly concerning food but also in the maintenance of the pair-bond and in alerting conspecifics and other species to the presence of a predator; indeed, thrushes are frequently the first to raise the alarm. Moreover, they are used as threats in territorial disputes or aggression between rival males of the same or similar species. It has been estimated that Blackbirds can communicate up to seven different pieces of information through calls, aside from song and subsong, whilst others (mostly European species) can relay up to 21 items (Simms 1990); little is known of the voice patterns of the remoter or deep-forest species, but further work may reveal that their abilities to communicate are equally sophisticated. However, work on parrots suggests that the species with the widest vocabularies are those that are sociable for part of the year and territorial for the rest of it, whilst those which are either solitary or sociable all year have less complex repertoires. This may prove true of thrushes also.

Redwing in song.

Songs, especially in thrushes, are more complex arrangements of notes and phraseology, often in more than one key. They are sexually related, controlled by hormones and given to express the presence of a male on territory advertising for a female, to maintain the pair-bond and/or to defend a territory. Several species incorporate some of their call notes, or variations, into their songs, whilst others have entirely different notes. One of the most accomplished singers in the subfamily is Lawrence's Thrush, which has no song phrases of its own but individual males can give perfect imitations of the songs of as many as 50 other forest species; collectively at least 170 species are known to be imitated by this thrush.

Songs given by birds on territory serve to identify the singer and his (most singing thrushes are males) status and intentions. Anyone who has heard the dawn chorus in a temperate forest in Europe, Siberia or North America can testify to the far-carrying songs of certain *Turdus* or *Catharus* species for up to half a mile (or more for certain notes), most songs being given from high perches in trees. *Monticola* thrushes also sing from a prominent position on a rock- or cliff-face so as to enable the widest broadcast of the song. Some species are year-round songsters with periods of greatest activity at the start of or during the breeding season, with less active periods at other times of the year. Other species restrict their song to the courtship period and cease at or immediately before the eggs hatch.

The extremely fine and musical songs in the thrushes are due to the arrangement of the syringeal muscles (the syrinx) in the throat and also the highly developed neuro-physiological processes in the brain to coordinate muscle power and tonal production. In some species, the notes given in the songs overlap to produce the effect of a double or multiple note (i.e. one note beginning before the preceding note ends). In the Wood Thrush sonagrams have shown that there is a part of the song when four separate notes, which have no harmonic relation to each other, may be given simultaneously. This suggests that in some species, including Cuban and Rufous-throated Solitaires (since they have a particularly complex note structure containing modulated whistles and buzzes), there is a more highly developed acoustic or vibratory mechanism operating in addition to the syrinx. Even in species such as the Blackbird, the song contains some complex phrasing, and captive birds have been quick to learn changes in pitch and can be induced to sing in different keys.

Virtually all thrushes, with the exception of several *Zoothera* species, have extremely well developed vocal powers; indeed some of the better known songsters are renowned for their musical accomplishments. Whilst none of the thrushes is as widely celebrated for its musical inspiration as the closely related Nightingale *Luscinia megarhynchos* or to a slightly lesser extent the Robin *Erithacus rubecula*, both the Song Thrush and Blackbird have inspired poets (particularly Tennyson and Browning) in Europe and the American Robin features heavily in the chorus line of a well-known and enduring song in the U.S.A. At least three of the *Catharus* (Swainson's, Hermit and Wood) thrushes breeding in North America are considered to be the finest singers on the continent, whilst two of the Caribbean *Myadestes* (Cuban and Rufous-throated) solitaires are accorded the same esteem in their regions.

BEHAVIOUR

Foraging

The general foraging behaviour of most thrush genera can be summed up in a few words. *Neocossyphus* are either almost entirely arboreal and spend long periods watching from high branches and waiting for passing prey, or conversely spend long periods on the ground foraging for ants or taking advantage of the invertebrates flushed by columns or swarms of army ants. *Monticola* are alert but patient and sedate birds, usually seen unhurriedly surveying the ground below a high perch from which they make sudden dashes when a meal appears. *Myophonus* spend long periods foraging on the edges of streams. *Zoothera* thrushes are best characterised as being elusive, diffident, forest-dwelling, ground-loving birds with largely cryptic plumage (exceptions being Siberian and Varied Thrushes). *Myadestes, Cichlopsis* and *Catharus* are solely New World thrushes and best thought of as largely plain coloured (the exception to this being Wood Thrush), small to medium-small size and generally shy or retiring woodland birds, many of which occur at high altitudes or northern latitudes. Finally, the large family of *Turdus* thrushes defy simple description and are best thought of as widespread, generally easily seen, attractive, ground- and tree-loving birds with a nervous or excitable nature.

Blue Whistling-Thrush picking food from surface of fast-flowing stream.

Pied Thrush in typical foraging pose, waiting and watching for movement.

All thrushes generally show similarities in many of their actions. Those that spend long periods on the ground have a fairly unhurried action, largely dictated by their style of watch-and-wait foraging for ground-living or wood-boring invertebrates and their larvae. Walking, hopping and running are all common forms of movement used to cover foraging areas. Some species have a particularly distinctive stance, varying from horizontal with head held low (listening close to the surface of the ground as in Song Thrush) or head and neck held high to survey the immediate vicinity (as in

Fieldfare). Many species, particularly among *Turdus* thrushes, employ a range of foraging techniques similar to those used most frequently by the Blackbird. Many of the far-flung and high-altitude races of Island Thrush reveal their affinities to this (perhaps not so distant) relative by their simple actions, behavioural traits and contact and alarm calls, all of which are redolent of the bird more familiar to most European birdwatchers as an urban-dwelling species. Variations on these actions are used by several of the other families when feeding on the ground. More unusually, several *Zoothera* ground-thrushes (particularly in the *dauma* group) have developed a seemingly nervous, bobbing or slowly rising and falling motion whilst walking slowly over the ground in search of prey. The derivation of this action, which recalls a similar feeding action in Jack Snipe *Lymnocryptes minimus*, is unclear but presumably beneficial to the foraging bird.

A considerable part of the lives of all birds is taken up in acquiring sufficient food for individual fitness and successful reproduction. For many thrushes finding food is a relatively simple exercise requiring only minimal effort and a sufficient area to supply their needs. The floors of different types of forests and woodlands offer a significant supply of prey, since for many species the areas in which they obtain most of their sustenance is comparatively small. Many of the seed-eating passerines require a much larger area, as food availability is dependent on the seasonal cycle of the plant species. Whilst a supply of prey items is critical to its survival, thrushes are particularly cosmopolitan in their diet with no species known to be entirely dependent on a single species of invertebrate or fruit. Moreover, few areas of the world have so few invertebrate species that large territories are required to ensure a sufficient supply.

Most of the species that are resident in, or migrate to, the northern temperate latitudes are principally insectivores, and the young are entirely dependent on a sufficiency of insects and their larvae, but outside the breeding season the food choice becomes wider with the seasonal abundance of ripening fruit. Some *Monticola* thrushes are more restricted to animal diets and there is no evidence of them taking fruits or seeds, but in two species (Blue-capped and Cape Rock-Thrushes) there is evidence of their feeding on nectar. For those species living in the tropics the diet is more evenly balanced over time, since different species of forest tree provide a succession of fruiting seasons throughout the year.

Several *Monticola, Myophonus* and *Turdus* thrushes are known to take small lizards and amphibians, in the former case as a regular part of their diet (given their more arid habitats) whilst in the latter case this is possibly more down to opportunism (although reports of urban Blackbirds and Song Thrushes taking tadpoles from garden ponds appear to be increasing). The *Myophonus* thrushes, being more closely attached to the margins of water, take a variety of aquatic insects together with crabs, molluscs and other crustaceans, and two of the larger species (Sunda and Blue Whistling-Thrushes) are also known to take nestlings and small mammals. As they are clearly opportunistic feeders, possibly all thrushes will take whatever suitable food is available to them. In perhaps what is the most extreme instance of this they will take the young of other birds, exemplified by adult Tristan Thrushes which actively seek out and take nestlings and young of several other island endemic passerines and, perhaps exceptionally, have been known to attack and kill adult White-bellied Storm-Petrels *Fregatta grallaria*.

Within forest habitats foraging is simply a matter of locating and collecting the item of food (search and pursue) with many species, particularly the *Zoothera* thrushes, found in damp or moist areas where both adult and larval invertebrates are likely to be most numerous and easily taken. In more open habitats, many observers will be familiar with thrushes diligently waiting and surveying the surface of the ground for movement. Several species, particularly tropical forest dwellers which are otherwise extremely solitary or territorial, often gather at a fruiting tree to share in the abundance of easy pickings without showing any aggression towards either their own species or other thrushes. Some species, particularly those in South America, are principally arboreal and have an equal dependency on fruit as much as they have on invertebrate prey. Most thrushes (particularly *Turdus* and several *Myophonus*) at certain times of the year, e.g. autumn (in the northern hemisphere), take to eating buds, berries and fruit from a range of trees, saplings, bushes and shrubs.

Their slim shape, light frame and quick actions all assist in the detection of food, and the manoeuvrability of the individual helps to feed itself and to collect a supply for dependent nestlings. The bill is shaped for quick seizure of small, soft-bodied prey, but in the larger terrestrial species it can also be used to probe into or sift through soft earth or decaying vegetation. They have an amazing ability to hear the underground movements of invertebrates and many can detect worms, beetles and other creatures below the surface of the ground and dig down to find them with astonishing accuracy. Some forest species adopt a similar strategy when sifting through the accumulated piles of leaf-litter or lightly probing in decaying vegetation in search of invertebrate prey. Such species, however, actively dig into the deep piles of litter and, using the bill to flick dead leaves aside, pursue their goal down through several inches of accumulated detritus; some species also scratch with both feet or move leaves or larger objects out of the way by jumping backwards. In a few cases 'tools' are used in feeding: Song Thrush, African Thrush, Malabar and Blue Whistling-Thrushes (and possibly other African *Turdus* species) use stone anvils in breaking open snail-shells to get at the soft inner body. Why this use of anvils (which can include other hard surfaces strong enough to achieve the desired result) is limited to just a few species is a matter of conjecture. Blackbirds, which are known to rob Song

Fieldfare picking berries from tree.

Song Thrush breaking snail shells at an anvil.

Thrushes which have broken open a shell, are apparently unable to adopt the method for themselves. Of all the thrushes only these four species are known to use a tool to assist in the process of food gathering; in birds as a whole this is rare and largely restricted to a few passerine species.

The *Myadestes* solitaires of Central and North America spend long periods foraging at various levels in forest trees and vines and can often take to the air in flycatcher-like sallies after insects. Two of the African *Neocossyphus* species closely resemble large flycatchers and also pursue insects from forest trees making short, rapid airborne sallies after passing insects. Further similarities are shown in their abilities to hover briefly on the outside of the most fragile branches and collect insect prey. Whilst their size and structure is adapted for this method of feeding it is interesting to speculate as to whether it the result of hybridisation or an evolutionary adaptation that has largely become redundant for thrushes. Curiously, the other two species in *Neocossyphus* are almost entirely ground-feeders, and although they also take other small invertebrates are almost restricted to several species of forest ants (hence their name ant-thrushes). Work now being undertaken on the DNA profiles of these four species should reveal more about their origins and current affinities.

Relationships with man

Thrushes, particularly those in the large and widespread genus *Turdus*, are well known largely because of the frequency with which we come into contact with several species during the course of our daily lives. In many cities and suburbs around the world, and in more rural areas, thrushes are familiar to us either as garden, parkland or local woodland birds. They are large enough to be noticed and attractive in their appearance, exhibiting a shy but curious manner, and are often quick to take food that is put out. They are neither too small to be overlooked nor too numerous to be considered a nuisance. They have recognisable calls and most (certainly those with which people are familiar) have a pleasing and melodious song associated with the various seasons of the year. Moreover, although not always widely appreciated, they are persistent survivors in the face of various types of human activity. Countless birds come to grief through collisions with traffic, whilst smaller numbers are injured or killed by hitting pylons, telegraph wires, buildings and windows; domestic cats, as co-inhabitants of the human environment, are estimated to kill at least a million birds (which clearly includes a high percentage of thrushes) in the U.K. alone each year. Habitat destruction and modification takes a further toll as gardeners, town planners and developers unwittingly rip out hedges and shrubs which provide roosting and nesting sites, so that the density of sustainable territories becomes markedly reduced.

Sociability

One main characteristic of the *Turdus* thrushes breeding in temperate latitudes is their sociability or group-dependence, compared to those in the more tropical latitudes and other thrush genera. Several *Turdus* thrushes are particularly sociable and spend much of the non-breeding period in flocks. In Europe and western Asia, migrant and wintering flocks of Redwings and Fieldfares are a common sight from the end of September to April and, for many people, mark the onset of the winter. Similarly, most of the high-altitude Himalayan, central Chinese and eastern Siberian species winter at lower levels in small (and often mixed) groups. In North America, migrating flocks of American Robins (which in some areas can exceed a thousand individuals) mark the beginning of the fall and the return of the spring especially to places where the species is mainly a summer visitor. Few other thrushes occur in such impressive numbers, but several species occur in small parties (mostly comprising family groups) at the end of the breeding season. Birds from the tropical forests are seemingly less dependent on social gatherings and mostly only gather together at common sources of food (e.g. fruiting trees).

Preening and comfort actions

Necessary maintenance or comfort activities include bathing and preening, which generally take place in less exposed areas than when foraging (since they require a greater amount of attention on the part of the individual and less time spent watching for predators). Comfort activities such as sunbathing, dust-bathing and 'anting' are more related to the removal of parasites than the condition of the feathers. In passerines (as in most birds) there are a considerable number of external parasites that infest the feathers or the skin surface of the bird and these are probably best detected when exposed to sun or dust, which stimulates movement of the parasites. Sun-bathing also assists the synthesis of vitamin D from the preen gland at the base of the tail. In Europe on sunny days Blackbirds and, to a lesser extent, Song Thrushes and Fieldfares can be seen on patches of ground spreading their wings open and fanning the tail to catch the maximum effect of the sun's heat whilst often holding the head to one side with eyes closed, almost in a trance-like state. Blue Rock-Thrushes are also known to spend periods sun-bathing in much the same position as *Turdus* thrushes but also whilst more upright and with the bill pointing at the sky.

Blackbird sunbathing.

Anting, although only recorded in a few (mostly *Turdus* and *Zoothera*) thrushes, chiefly in those species which are best known (principally Blackbird and Fieldfare in Europe, and American Robin in the U.S.A.), is probably a more widespread activity than currently known. This may involve the direct application of the bird picking up individual non-stinging ants (mostly of the Formicinae and Dolichoderinae subfamilies) by the bill and applying formic acid and other fluids to the feathers. Another method, more commonly used by thrushes (although Blackbirds appear to use both in equal amounts), is simply to permit the ants to wander all over the body (especially between the feather bases) and leave a trail of formic acid whose insecticidal properties help with the eradication of ticks, fleas, flat-flies and feather lice.

All birds preen, ensuring that the plumage is maintained to its best condition, primarily for the purposes of insulation and flight but also for use in display and camouflage. After foraging, feeding and roosting, preening and feather maintenance are usually the most time-consuming activities. Preening involves either a slight, rapid adjustment of feathers to remove dirt or ectoparasites or a more prolonged comfort activity usually following bathing, and includes the repair or maintenance of feathers and feather structure, spreading the preen oil (taken from the base of the tail) over the plumage. Thrushes use any available sources of water in which to bathe, including small puddles along forest paths and the margins of small streams, rivers or ponds. In more extreme cases some tropical forest species use water trapped in leaves or bromeliad cups, whilst any of the more urban species frequently utilise garden ponds, leaking taps or birdbaths put out by helpful gardeners.

Redwing bathing.

Bathing is a vigorous activity, often undertaken following a nervous inspection of the intended site to ensure that there are no predators lurking. First the breast and belly are dipped into the water followed by the head, with water being splashed over the upperparts by flapping the wings to shower the whole bird (and a good deal else). This is repeated several times with noisy flaps of the wings as the bird becomes more invigorated and refreshed by the activity. Having completed this part the bird then moves to a nearby branch to begin the next stage of preening with the head and bill, having first wiped the bill several times across the side of the branch. This is accompanied by several almost violent shakes of the body and whirring of the wings to get rid of excess water. During this process the bird frequently rubs its bill or the sides of the head over and across the rump and uppertail-coverts as it collects oil from the preen gland and spreads it over the rest of the body. Most thrushes bathe alone but some species, particularly those which are more communal, bathe together and up to 40 Fieldfares have been recorded bathing on the edge of a lake. More exceptionally, some Ring Ouzels breeding at higher altitudes have been known to 'bathe' on snow-covered ground. During the moulting period some species bathe twice a day but once is more normal. There is little information on the bathing habits of the lesser-known species, and for some desert-fringe species (e.g. the rock-thrushes) it can only be assumed that they have some access to damp areas within their territories.

Roosting

Roosting and roost sites are important for territory-holding birds and need to be a safe haven for the hours of total inactivity. For many thrushes, particularly the sedentary species which inhabit forests or well-wooded areas, this is a matter of selecting the most suitable area of available habitat. Most *Monticola* thrushes are invariably solitary and roost high up in the crevices of a rockface, or in the uppermost branches of a tree; in northern India and central China the eaves the roof cavities of houses are used by Blue Rock-Thrush. Wintering Ring Ouzels in North Africa also roost amongst rocks and boulders. Most thrushes, especially those which inhabit the damp floor of extensive forests and spend virtually their whole lives alone or in pairs, roost alone and are particular in their choice of roost site and the company (if any) they keep. Like most passerines, thrushes roost by fluffing out the body plumage and tucking the head and bill under the closed wing. They remain motionless in this position for long periods, particularly those sedentary species which winter in the northern latitudes.

Several thrushes, principally the more familiar *Turdus* species (e.g. Blackbird, Fieldfare, Redwing and American Robin), have communal roosts. Some of the lesser known species may also share this habit as Great Thrush of northern South America is known to gather in roosts of up to 40 outside the breeding season. Communal roosting has benefits for the individuals involved but since thrushes are territorial birds, the pre-roosting gathering and dawn dispersal is frequently accompanied by ritualised posturing, aggression and alarm calling to determine the respective position of individuals within the roost. Some roosts are used throughout the year; by breeding males in the summer months and by juvenile birds from about July onwards, but very few roost communally during the moult period.

Some Blackbird roosts are traditional and known to have been in use for several decades; at roosts which have been well studied in southern England numbers have occasionally exceeded 2,000 individuals in the non-breeding season. Similarly, some winter roosts of Redwings and Fieldfares have exceeded 20,000 birds, with Fieldfares slightly outnumbering Redwings (Simms 1978). Such roosts are uncommon in most of lowland England where there is an abundance of cover, and more often number between several hundred and a thousand individuals, but are more frequent in the towns and cities of northern and central Europe. Norman (1994) recorded an exceptional 25,000 Fieldfares at a Warwickshire roost in March 1977 and another in excess of 200,000 (shared with Blackbirds) in the département of Nord, France in January 1975. Roosts of this size clearly indicate that birds move some distance to attend these roosts. Batten (1977) studied the movements of Blackbirds attending a large thrush roost in the suburbs of north-west London (perhaps the largest known in Britain) and of over 6,500 birds ringed most were recovered within 5 km and only about 1 in 50 moved more than 25 km, although it was also clear from subsequent recoveries in Sweden and France that the roost contained a few birds of continental origin. A Redwing roost in Northumberland attracted birds from as far away as 19 km and another in Warwickshire included birds from up to 13 km distance (Simms 1978).

Communal roosts appear to have the main benefit of providing a high degree of protection from predators. Within Blackbird roosts, however, each bird maintains a discreet distance of at least 60 cm from its nearest neighbour, indicating that comfort and the shared body warmth present in roosts of Starlings and other communally roosting birds appear to be less important. In the London roost Batten (1977) found that the thickest bushes and most sheltered parts of the trees or bushes were used for roosting and, although there was no appreciable change in the temperature or humidity within the roost there was an average reduction of about 73% in the wind speed and hence wind-chill factor. Since wind-chill factor is critical in terms of heat loss from an individual, the position of birds within the roost is critical. On nights with a high wind chill, birds in the most favoured locations suffered only about 60% of the weight loss of birds in more exposed positions, so that the hourly loss of weight for some individuals was calculated to be about 0.54g whilst for others it could be as high as 0.7g. It was also found that putting birds artificially closer to each other resulted in the birds becoming more disturbed, leading to less time asleep and consequently a greater loss in weight.

Few other thrush species appear to roost in such densities or at traditional sites. Mistle Thrushes may roost together in small numbers which may only be in family or related groups of up to 20 or more (exceptionally 50) individuals (Simms 1978). Mistle Thrush roosts have been recorded in trees and shrubs as well as in creepers and clumps of mistletoe but as in the Blackbird, a distance of approximately 60 cm is kept between individuals in the roost. Song Thrushes appear to be more solitary in their roosting habits, with most probably going no further than a convenient shrub or tree, although they are frequently recorded roosting in small numbers with other thrushes. Simms (1978) also recorded roosting Song Thrushes in heather, low scrub, coastal sand-dunes and amongst sacks of peat.

Winter roost sites in Europe are mainly in woodlands and these are frequently conifer woods, well-wooded hedges and areas of scrub with brambles, although reedbeds have also been used. Fieldfares appear to be alone in roosting occasionally on the ground in winter, although there are also records of migrant Ring Ouzels doing so in southern Scotland; Simms (1978) recorded instances of Fieldfares roosting on heather moors in the Pennines of England as well as on ploughed fields, stubble, grasslands and marshes, presumably where trees were absent. On the evidence of Blackbirds, breeding pairs will roost within the territory and display alarm and aggression to other Blackbirds or thrushes. By the end of August, communal roosts are in operation although they do not reach a peak until the mid-winter, depending on the severity of the weather, since prolonged freezing in temperate latitudes will initiate movements of the birds. The period of communal roosting also varies with the species, with most of those frequently found in communal roosts in northern Europe forming roosts between September and the following spring, with declining numbers from February onwards. However, for the Mistle Thrush, which is one of the earlier breeding species (but possibly no more so than many Blackbirds from the southern parts of the range), territories are established early in the year and communal roosting is abandoned during December. Also Blackbirds which winter in southern Europe but breed in the north continue to roost communally whilst the local birds are establishing territories.

48

THE HISTORICAL RECORD

The fossil record of thrushes from the Pleistocene (between 12,000 and 1.8 million years ago) is, as it is for most of the passerines, extremely scant and there is very little that relates specifically to any of the main thrush genera. This is largely because passerines with such fine, fragile bones are unable to withstand fossilisation and hence leave very little trace of their existence. Most of what is known comes from work undertaken on fossils in the western Palearctic, especially Europe; at least some information on the early *Turdus* thrushes exists but virtually nothing is known of the origins, development and distribution of the other species. The earliest record appears to come from the middle Pleistocene of Europe and refers to a species of *Turdus*, possibly an early or prototype Blackbird or Ring Ouzel (C. Walker pers. comm.). There are, however, numerous reports of *Turdus* species having been found in 'Pleistocene' deposits, particularly cave excavations, but, regrettably many of these have not been checked and could refer to any period from the lower Pleistocene onwards.

The family as a whole has its greatest number of representatives in the temperate and tropical regions of the Old World where it most probably originated. Olson (1971) postulated from fossil remains in Bavaria that the ancestors of the suboscine passerines arose in the Old World tropics early in the Tertiary period (60+ million years ago) and spread widely throughout the world. These early forms were later largely replaced by the more advanced oscines (species with a highly developed syrinx – the songbirds) throughout their entire range, except in South America which had become isolated during the Tertiary period. The isolation of birds in South America allowed widespread development and spread of the suboscines (collectively, the remaining suborders of the passeriformes, with poorly developed syrinx) over the period when the more advanced oscines were replacing their earlier relatives in the Old World. This has had the consequence of a diverse and widespread group of over 1,000 specialised suboscines surviving in South America to the present day. However, invasions into the New World of the oscine passerines most probably occurred very early since a number of New World genera (including *Turdus*) are now particularly well established throughout the Americas and the Caribbean. The table below shows the distribution of all thrushes between the temperate and tropical regions of the Old and New Worlds.

	Temperate region	Tropical region
OLD WORLD	47	49
NEW WORLD	14	52

Turdus thrushes were certainly present in northern Europe about 500,000 years ago; with several species (e.g. Blackbirds, Song Thrushes and Redwings) all having left some traces of their existence in the interglacial period between the most recent ice ages. *Turdus* thrushes probably originated in Asia, where 12 species are still widely distributed, with six species having moved west to colonise Europe and a further nine resident in eastern and southern Asia. The colonisation of the New World, probably by several invasions, has been dramatic, with 15 species now resident or breeding in Central America (including Mexico) and a further 18 in South America.

It is interesting that so many *Turdus* species developed at such a distance from their perceived area of origin, particularly as only one species of *Turdus* – American Robin – occurs in the whole of North America, making it unlikely that any of the colonists arrived by way of a Bering Sea 'bridge'. Alternatively, if they did arrive by this route, it appears that the temperate forests of the north (similar in type and character to those of eastern Asia) were unable to sustain them. The present spread and diversity of the thrushes in tropical South America clearly suggests that these species are best adapted to the dense humid forests with some having further developed a preference for the montane habitats along the Andean chain.

Within the whole of Africa there are only six *Turdus* species, but of these, three – African, Olive and Kurrichane – are very similar and together with Bare-eyed Thrush show all the signs of relatively recent descent from a common ancestor. All of the former three species are particularly well dispersed in a number of subspecies south of the Sahara, each demonstrating a dependence on various types of forest.

The Olive Thrush also provides the best example of convergent evolution in Old and New World thrushes, since the Rufous-bellied Thrush from eastern Brazil to Argentina is so similar that it would probably be considered conspecific if the two species shared the same continent. As Moreau (1966) remarked, 'it might be considered evidence of recent colonisation across the south Atlantic, but especially in view of the limited repertory of colour and pattern within the genus *Turdus* it seems better to regard the resemblance between these two thrushes as due to convergence'. This is also supported by the fact that several other South American *Turdus* thrushes, notably Chestnut-bellied and to a certain extent Austral Thrush share this plumage characteristic of bright orange or rufous on belly and flanks. Moreover, it appears that various shades of red occur on the underparts of several unrelated *Turdus* species from the pale tawny colour in Eyebrowed *T. obscurus* and the southern race confinis of American Robin *T. migratorius* through to the deep rufous-red of Izu Islands Thrush *T. celaenops*, several races of Island Thrush *T. poliocephalus*, and La Selle Thrush *T. swalesi*, plus all other North American races of American Robin.

Immediately east and west of the African continent there are two island endemic species of *Turdus*, Olivaceous Thrush and Comoro Thrush. The former occurs on São Tomé and Príncipe in the Gulf of Guinea, the latter on three of the four islands in the Comoros group in the Indian Ocean. Whilst neither shows any particular morphological affinity or resemblance to any of the other African species they share similarities with each other (principally barring on the underparts, a feature found in very few *Turdus* thrushes) despite being separated by over 2500 miles and the continent of Africa. It is easy to speculate that they may have derived from a common ancestor, possibly from mainland Africa, whose stock has since died out. However, this raises the question as to why a common mainland ancestor left no linkage through an extant species, since the African continent on the whole is not inhospitable to the family; there is a parallel between these two thrushes and the two species of *Zoonavena* swifts, although the Comoroan species also appear on Madagascar. It is also interesting that the only thrushes on Madagascar are three small *Monticola* species.

In the Oriental region there are only two resident or breeding *Turdus* species in South-East Asia, and both of these (Blackbird and Island Thrush) occur largely at the extreme margins of the region, although a few other members of the genus spend the winter there. The reasons for this lack of *Turdus* thrushes are not particularly clear but may relate to climate habitat choice (*Turdus* are generally more temperate birds), competition with other species or simply predation. However, the single species within *Cataponera* from Sulawesi is morphologically similar to the *Turdus* thrushes.

Further historical questions arise about the widely varying forms that make up the Island Thrush *Turdus poliocephalus* group. This species is distributed on approximately 56 islands from northern Sumatra and Borneo east through New Guinea to Fiji and several other island groups in the southwest Pacific and north to Taiwan. Until recently the range also extended south to Lord Howe Island about 400 miles (650 km) off the coast of Australia. Within this range are a number of variations of plumage from all black or dark brown types to those with white, creamy or pale orange head to breast and others with varying degrees of rufous or chestnut on the underparts. Moreover, the distribution pattern appears random with no apparent clinal change in plumage, with dissimilar birds on neighbouring islands and similar types more distant from one another. This apparently random spread may be unravelled by the use of mitochondrial DNA profiling to compare affinities within the group. Another equally intriguing aspect is that during its colonisation of far-flung islands it must have encountered larger islands such as Australia or even the Asian mainland but on continents it presumably encountered species already in the niches it would have filled, and therefore failed to become established; whereas on islands those niches were vacant. It may be that there are affinities to Izu Islands Thrush which inhabits a small group of islands south of Japan, but this remains to be determined. What is clear is that based on size, structure and perhaps more importantly vocal characteristics, the group is connected to and possibly closely related to the Blackbird of Europe and Asia.

FUTURE RESEARCH AND CONSERVATION OF SCARCE THRUSHES

Thrushes as a subfamily are numerous and widely dispersed throughout almost all regions of the world; they are only naturally absent from New Zealand and the polar regions. They are a common sight in areas with large human populations but equally so in emptier rural areas. However, their high degree of familiarity may be deceptive, since in the most isolated and remote parts of the planet there are some species, particularly in the genera *Zoothera* and *Turdus*, of which we know very little. At least 29 of the 162 species of thrush can be classed as poorly known, largely on the basis of small populations and often a distribution remote from centres of human habitation, but in some cases they are just plain numerically rare. Most of them are shy or elusive, and our knowledge of them or their ecological niche is particularly sparse. The causes of their low population levels are neither well researched nor widely understood. In most cases the circumstance appears to be entirely natural and not connected to habitat loss or destruction (which is a recent feature) although this will, very probably, limit any future expansion.

Table 1. Species/subspecies with small populations/restricted ranges

	Island endemic
Sri Lanka Whistling-Thrush *Myophonus blighi*	X
Slaty-backed Thrush *Z. schistacea*	X
Moluccan Thrush *Z. d. dumasi*	X
Z. d. joiceyi	X
Red-backed Thrush *Z. e. erythronota*	X
Z. e. mendeni	X
Chestnut-backed Thrush *Z. dohertyi*	X
Ashy Thrush *Z. cinerea*	X
Orange-sided Thrush *Z. peronii*	X
Everett's Thrush *Z. everetti*	X
Crossley's Ground-Thrush *Z. crossleyi*	–
Oberlaender's Ground-Thrush *Z. oberlaenderi*	–
Black-eared Ground-Thrush *Z. c. camaronensis*	–
Z. c. graueri	–
Grey Ground-Thrush *Z. p. princei*	–
Z. p. batesi	–
Sunda Thrush *Z. andromedae*	X
White's Thrush *Z. dauma neilgherriensis*	–
Z. d. imbricata	X
Amami Thrush *Z. major*	X
Horsfield's Thrush *Z. horsfieldi*	X
Fawn-breasted Thrush *Z. machiki*	X

(continued overleaf)

Table 1 (continued)

	Island endemic
New Britain Thrush *Z. t. talaseae*	x
Z. t. atrigena	x
San Cristobal Thrush *Z. margaretae*	x
Guadalcanal Thrush *Z. turipavae*	x
Geomalia *Geomalia heinrichi*	x
Sulawesi Thrush *Cataponera turdoides*	x
Olivaceous Thrush *Turdus olivaceofuscus xanthorhynchus*	x
Olive Thrush *T. olivaceus helleri*	–
T. o. ludoviciae	–
Island Thrush *T. poliocephalus mareensis*	x
T. p. xanthopus	x
Plumbeous-backed Thrush *Turdus reevei*	–
Marañón Thrush *T. maranonicus*	–
Unicoloured Thrush *T. haplochrous*	–
La Selle Thrush *T. swalesi*	x

There are a number of factors common to all of them. Almost without exception, they are tropical species with their origins in pristine forests, and both the forests and the species they support may once have had much larger ranges. Nearly two-thirds (21) of the 29 species are island endemics and of the remaining five African species four are endemic to ecological islands of montane forests.

The problems and vulnerability of island endemics are well known. Small populations and ranges expose species to rapid decline in the face of habitat change and, in particular, to the effects of alien species (including diseases). High levels of predation from introduced rats and cats are often to blame for island extinctions – but even within their island distribution and despite an apparent abundance of suitable habitat some thrushes appear to be widely dispersed at very low densities. The race *joiceyi* of Moluccan Thrush occurs on the Indonesian island of Seram, which is still relatively heavily forested, but although it was first described to science in 1921 it has only subsequently been recorded there on very few occasions. For the African species it is undoubtedly true that most of the montane forests where they occur are relicts from a previously more extensive and continuous area (Moreau 1966). From a modern-day perspective the thrushes in Table 1 appear to display an inability to adapt or change to wider or secondary types of forest habitats.

It is probably fair to say that for most such species there have been fewer than a hundred sightings (or specimens collected) since they were first described, mainly during the latter years of the 19th Century. The majority are *Zoothera* thrushes, the archetypal forest or ground-thrush with camouflaged plumage, but also *Turdus* thrushes, and both the monotypic *Geomalia* and *Cataponera* fit this category. Although several species of *Catharus* nightingale-thrushes are extremely difficult to see, they show neither such limited habitat choice nor such restricted ranges as are shown by the species under discussion here. The four Hawaiian *Myadestes* have also been excluded from this discussion since they do not appear to have been restricted in their natural ranges. Their decline to small (if still extant) populations is the result of recent human interference, i.e. a combination of habitat destruction and modification, the introduction of predators and the spread of diseases to which they lacked immunity.

The genus *Zoothera* is one of the oldest of the thrushes and probably the most primitive since it shows little evidence of being adaptable to other, more recent habitats. It comprises 36 species, of which approximately half (18) are extremely rare; 15 species are island endemics, have limited distribution and are poorly known. Three of these (New Britain, San Cristobal and Guadalcanal Thrushes) are known from only very few sightings, while three others (Moluccan, Ashy and Amami

Thrushes) are in decline and are considered endangered, and one (Bonin Islands Thrush) is extinct. Of the remainder only two (White's and Siberian Thrushes, both long-distance migrants) have a large distribution. *Turdus* by contrast is the largest genus of thrushes and collectively shows more adaptability and a much wider habitat preference or niche occupation. Over most of the range of *Turdus* it is a relatively successful genus; there are however, in addition to the five species included here, one or two others which may be restricted by a specific habitat choice (they may be vulnerable to threats to their remaining areas of habitat) but are not included here on the basis of more extensive original distributions. The ones listed here have apparently naturally limited ranges and all display the same restrictions and inability to adapt to wider habitats. The same applies to the monotypic *Geomalia* and *Cataponera*; so little is known of the first of these that uncertainties persist about its true affinities and confirmation is still required that it is in fact a thrush rather than a babbler; the single member of *Cataponera* is equally elusive, and whilst it appears to be related to the *Turdus* thrushes it also shows several babbler-like (or at least laughingthrush-like) features which set it apart.

For most of these species (particularly the African *Zoothera*) it is unlikely that more than 2,000 pairs exist, and for many it is highly likely that there are far fewer than this. The population of Amami Thrush is currently thought to be approximately 75 pairs (Khan in prep.) whilst that of the Taita Hills race *helleri* of Olive Thrush is probably also less than 100 pairs (Collar *et al.* 1994). With the exception of La Selle Thrush (an island endemic suffering from increased habitat destruction) and Amami Thrush, none of the species in this list is apparently in immediate danger of declining to beyond recoverable limits, but continued habitat depletion will severely increase that risk. More importantly, as several occur in extremely remote areas and are only infrequently seen, any one of them could become extinct within a matter of years without the fact becoming immediately apparent.

The rarity of these species is unlikely to be attributable to a single cause, but more information is still required on the factors which limit their numbers and distribution. Assemblages of species (in this sense all tropical forest species) typically contain a diverse collection of wide-ranging and specialist foragers of both rare and common species. A proportion of the species in an assemblage will be lower in overall numbers than other members of the assemblage. The higher the number of species in the assemblage the greater the likelihood that more species will naturally occur in low numbers, since they occupy a specialised niche (and within seemingly extensive habitats their specialised niche is fully occupied) or their preferred habitat is very restricted in area.

There is, at any rate, an underlying assumption that the more abundant and widespread species have broader habitat choices, can utilise a greater range of resources, and have broader environmental tolerances than those with ecologically or geographically restricted habitats. Some of the work on the causes of rarity has looked at habitat choice or niche occupation as a key to the limiting factors for certain species, but the mechanisms by which rare or specialist habitat species relate to the overall species diversity of the assemblage are less well understood, and to explain why such a considerable proportion of all tropical thrushes are rare requires more work on species dynamics.

Limits to populations

Part of the problem of identifying factors that limit population growth in any species lies in the determination of how, and how much, each factor affects the balance of all species populations. All birds are regulated by the resources available to them within the area occupied; these are mainly food, water, shelter, nesting sites and a mate. In restricted species a constraint on any one of these will have a more critical effect and its impact on the species will be greater, and within a shorter timescale, than it will on more widespread species. For restricted populations of scarce sedentary species the trend depends entirely on the ratio of births to deaths since there is no recruitment into the population from elsewhere.

A factor that may be decisive in the success of species is mobility. For many species their distribution is limited by their inability to find and colonise new areas of suitable habitat, even within relatively short distances. Coupled to this is the additional ability to establish themselves in a new area having reached it. This raises the question of whether rare species have poorer or more limited colonisation abilities than common species. Many that are presently rare – and this includes several thrushes in Table 1 – have declined because of habitat (and hence range) reduction in recent times. The previous expanse or extent of their habitat may have meant that it was never a necessity for them to have dispersal abilities to more than a neighbouring part of the same forest. Where large areas of forest have been felled, such birds display no ability to move to or recolonise areas of suitable habitat, especially those (should they exist) at some distance. As a general rule, species with effective dispersal abilities have mainly stable or increasing ranges, whilst those with poor dispersal abilities are decreasing.

There is, however, good reason for some species not to have well-developed dispersal abilities if the probability of encountering new and unoccupied territory is very low. From the distribution pattern of the species under consideration here, it would appear that as most have limited ranges, their powers of mobility or abilities to colonise new areas are also limited. It could be expected that three of the four African *Zoothera* species may have better powers of mobility since they occur across parts of Africa which are separated by huge distances of lowland habitats generally inhospitable to them.

It is also possible that these species retreated to the montane forests during the last 10,000 years when there may have been other intermediate areas of suitable habitat available. This can be compared to the distances of mobility of other (admittedly *Turdus*) thrushes in the region. The species which inhabit Marsabit forest in northern Kenya do so having reached it directly from the other parts of their ranges; in the case of the *abyssinicus* subspecies of the Olive Thrush, it is a distance of at least 80 miles (130 km) from the nearest population, since Marsabit is not, and apparently has never been, connected to any other forests (Moreau 1966). Moreau also pointed out that a distance of 200 miles (320 km) across the Red Sea was not a barrier to the ancestors of Yemen Thrush, which must have reached its present distribution from within the African continent. The key difference appears to be that those species which show good mobility or well-marked colonising abilities, as in the species of African *Turdus*, are birds of the canopy or forest edge and not, as is the case with most of the restricted-range species, birds of the interior of deep forests.

On this basis it can be assumed that whilst the species under discussion here occur at low densities, the annual increment to their populations is equal to the losses and, apparently, remains constant irrespective of their overall density. It can also be assumed that these species will persist at low density within a restricted habitat indefinitely, providing there is no adverse change in the factors or conditions that maintain the balance in the population. What is unclear is the proximity of these species' populations to their minimum viable or sustainable limits. More particularly, is the limitation or restriction due entirely to naturally causes, e.g. predation, parasitism or competitive exclusion or, as has been suggested, is it more closely linked to evolutionary mechanisms? If they are so specialised and unable to tolerate change or adapt to the pressures on their environment, does this mean that they have always been (and will in the future be) restricted in numbers and ranges or are they relict or redundant species approaching the end point of a line of evolutionary divergence?

The causes of limitation or range restriction and the apparent inability or incapacity of certain thrushes to survive in a wider range of habitats requires further research in order to understand the status of each. Such research would undoubtedly repay dividends in the knowledge gained not only for the conservation of these birds but also for other species with a similarly rigid and conservative habitat preference or niche.

In summary, although little is known of the details, it can be assumed that some, if not all, of these tropical forest thrushes are regulated by a density-dependent mechanism – their numbers are kept within limits by habitat availability, competition for food, predation levels and possibly parasites. A considerable amount of information remains to be discovered about the movements or interactions of individuals or pairs, spatial distribution (and its influences on populations) together with foraging and dispersal patterns by the use of radio-tracking, but until such time they will remain attractive, intriguing but highly elusive exotic species.

THREATS/EXTINCTION

In such a large and widely dispersed family of birds it is intriguing but perhaps unsurprising, given current pressures on wildlife globally, that three species might have become extinct in recent times and that several more are increasingly at risk of following them into oblivion. More worryingly, perhaps, is the number of species (and subspecies) where we have little or no idea of their current population status or, in one or two cases, whether they still exist at all. Perhaps those most at risk are the Hawaiian solitaires, the Kamao and Olomao. The most recent estimates put the total population of each species at 20 individuals or fewer, but sightings are so infrequent (apart from their sheer rarity, much of their habitat is inaccessible) that they could already have slipped into extinction, and indeed this is now accepted to have happened (Reynolds & Snetsinger 2000). The most recent sighting of a Kamao was in 1996, while there have been no accepted sightings of the Olomao since 1980 (although a 1988 report is widely considered valid). Reasons for the decline of these birds are not clear and may involve a combination of factors: habitat fragmentation, increased losses to introduced predators and the rapid spread of avian malaria and avian pox are likely all to have have taken their toll. A third species, the Puaiohi, also from Hawaii, could until recently have been ranked with the above two since it was also thought to have a population of under 20 individuals in 1983, but in 1996 several were caught and taken into a captive-breeding project. In 1999 the first young were hatched in captivity, and were subsequently released back into the wild on Hawaii. The species remains, however, critically endangered.

These three Hawaiian species are perhaps the thrushes which face the greatest threat, but they are not alone and, with the exception of the Palearctic, every continent contains a number of thrushes whose population is perilously low and facing an uncertain future. There are several reasons for their declines but these can be best summarised under two main themes, habitat destruction and restricted range.

If we assume the worst scenario, the 20th Century witnessed the demise of three species – Kamao, Olomao and Grand Cayman Thrush – and possibly as many as six subspecies: Forest Thrush (*C. l. sanctaeluciae*), Cuban Solitaire (*M. e. retrusus*), Island Thrush (*T. p. poliocephalus*, *T. p. mareensis*, and *T. p. vinctinctus*), and Black-headed Thrush (*T. o. caucae*). The immediate future of six other species (all listed in Table 1) – Ashy Thrush, Amami Thrush, Olive Thrush (race *helleri*), Puaiohi, Unicoloured Thrush and La Selle Thrush (together with two other subspecies of Island Thrush) – appears particularly bleak. Another eight species (most of which have restricted ranges) – Sri Lanka Whistling-Thrush, Red-backed Thrush, Chestnut-backed Thrush, Oberlaender's Ground-Thrush, Forest Thrush, Cuban Solitaire, Grey-sided Thrush and Chinese Song-Thrush – are also considered to be declining and could well be seriously at risk within a matter of years. Without intervention they face an inevitable fate. Only by the setting aside of completely inviolate sanctuary areas (of sufficient size and habitat) will the impacts of habitat loss now be reversible. Such reserves are particularly important for restricted-range species. But in addition to the creation of reserved areas, protection must mean that measures will be taken against those whose actions, wittingly or otherwise, affect the future well-being of protected species. The purpose of any areas set aside as reserves for wildlife is (and in certain areas continues to be) severely undermined by the lack of any enforcement to ensure that the status of protected species is fully and widely realised as meaning exactly that.

Common and widespread species also face problems of their own. The hunting and taking of some species (notably Song Thrush in Europe) for food has, at present, an unknown effect on the population but is clearly an additional burden on a population otherwise beset by declines caused by pesticide poisoning and habitat erosion. Elsewhere the removal of individuals from the wild as cage-birds for their songs may also be compromising their viability at a time when they are already under stress from habitat loss. In North America the increase and spread of the brood-parasite Brown-headed Cowbird is having a widespread effect on the breeding population of the Wood Thrush and is showing signs of similarly affecting some populations of Swainson's Thrush and could, in future, if left unchecked, result in huge depletions in the distribution and abundance of both species.

We must be optimistic, but also throw our weight behind international conservation organisations, particularly the work of Birdlife International, as they struggle with the problems that beset the world's wildlife. There could be no better legacy to those who come to review the situation of thrushes at the close of the 21st Century that not one of the species here regarded as facing an uncertain future will have by then passed beyond the line of extinction.

PLATES 1–60

PLATE 1 *NEOCOSSYPHUS* THRUSHES

1 Rufous Flycatcher-Thrush *Neocossyphus fraseri*   Text page 179

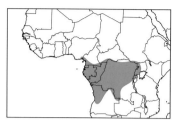

West and Central Africa: Bioko and SE Nigeria east to Uganda and NW Tanzania and south to C Angola. Lowland forests, secondary woods, edges of abandoned cultivation.

a Adult: short bill, cinnamon-brown upperparts, greyer face, pale orange-buff bases to flight feathers (wing-bar in flight); dull orange below.
b Adult tail: gingery- or rusty-buff edges to dark tail.
c Juvenile: like adult but darker above and duller below; may be streaked or mottled on breast.

2 Finsch's Flycatcher-Thrush *Neocossyphus finschii*   Text page 180

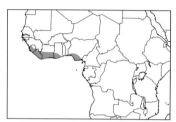

West Africa: Sierra Leone east to Nigeria. Dense primary and secondary lowland woods, swamp forests.
a Adult: short bill, cinnamon-brown upperparts, greyer head and face, and dull orange below.
b Adult tail: white outer wedge to black tail.

3 Red-tailed Ant-Thrush *Neocossyphus rufus*   Text page 181

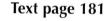

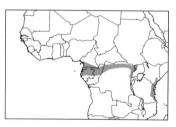

West Africa: S Cameroon to Kenya south to C Tanzania. Moist forests, secondary woods; prefers drier riverine and coastal forest in the east.
a Adult: mostly rust-brown with darker olive head, and bright rufous-orange underparts.
b Adult tail: as upperparts but with paler outer feathers.
c Juvenile: like adult but duller and finely streaked orange-buff above, olive below.

4 White-tailed Ant-Thrush *Neocossyphus poensis*   Text page 182

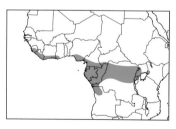

West and Central Africa: Sierra Leone to Kenya and N Angola. Primary and secondary forests, forest edges and clearings, also forest patches.
a Adult: dark brown upperparts, chin and throat paler; dull rufous-orange underparts.
b Adult tail: black with white wedge to tips of outer feathers.
c Juvenile: like adult but face flecked paler and dark olive tips to breast.

PLATE 2 MADAGASCAR ROCK-THRUSHES

5 Forest Rock-Thrush *Monticola sharpei* Text page 184

N and E Madagascar. Dense montane rainforests, including relict forests and secondary woodlands.

a Adult male: blue-grey head to upper breast and mantle; central tail feathers and tips to all outers dark brown; bases to outer tail feathers and underparts deep orange.

b Adult female: brown head and upperparts, tail like male; broadly streaked with white on chin to upper breast.

c Juvenile: heavily spotted on head, wing-coverts and underparts, bill yellowish; tail like adults.

d Adult male *erythronotus*: bluish head and face only (does not extend to upper breast), chestnut-brown upperparts.

e Adult female *erythronotus*: warm brown upperparts, white chin and throat not as extensively streaked as nominate female; warmer buff-brown below.

6 Benson's Rock-Thrush *Monticola bensoni* Text page 185

S-C Madagascar. Low trees, sparse scrub in rugged or rocky terrain often near cliffs, also rocky gorges; in non-breeding season in dry riverbeds, canyons and hillsides with scattered boulders.

a Adult male: head to upper breast and upperparts dull grey-blue; uppertail and sides of tail rufous; underparts orange.

b Adult female: head and upperparts grey-brown; tail like male but appears all dark and has dark tips to all feathers; broad white stripe on centre of chin and throat, underparts spotted pale brownish.

7 Littoral Rock-Thrush *Monticola imerinus* Text page 187

S and SW Madagascar. Lowland semi-open savanna, grassy steppes and sandy scrub with euphorbias.

a Adult male: pale grey head to breast and mantle, dark brown tail and orange underparts.

b Adult female: grey-brown head and upperparts except for light orange uppertail-coverts; chin and throat streaked with white.

c Juvenile: like adult female but finely spotted above and scalloped on breast.

5c

5b

5a

5e

5d

7c

7a

7b

6b

6a

gppw

PLATE 3 ROCK-THRUSHES (1)

8 Cape Rock-Thrush *Monticola rupestris*   **Text page 188**

S Botswana and South Africa to extreme SW Mozambique. Foothills, cliffs, gorges and rocky or boulder-strewn hillsides in mountains and loose scree-slopes.

a Adult male: blue-grey head, rufous-brown upperparts; rump to sides of tail and underparts rufous or rufous-orange.

b Adult female: lacks blue-grey head, is browner with darker streaks; pale, poorly defined submoustachial, dull rufous-orange underparts.

c Juvenile: like adult female but more heavily spotted on head and upperparts and barred underparts.

10 Short-toed Rock-Thrush *Monticola brevipes*   **Text page 190**

SW Angola, Namibia and N South Africa. Rocky outcrops in open hills, also wooded kopjes, stony slopes in mountains, escarpments.

a Adult male: white to pale bluish head to crown; grey or bluish-grey upperparts, chin and throat and black face; rump and sides of tail to rest of underparts bright orange.

b Head of adult male *pretoriae*: forehead to nape whitish, grey above; lacks bluish tinge.

c Adult female: head and upperparts dark brown, rump and tail as male, chin and throat pale buff streaked or fringed darker.

d Juvenile: like adult female but heavily spotted on head and upperparts and scalloped with pale yellowish and dark fringes or bars below.

13 Little Rock-Thrush *Monticola rufocinereus*   **Text page 198**

East Africa and SW Arabia: Eritrea and N Somalia south to E Uganda and N Tanzania, also SW Saudi Arabia and W Yemen. Forests and wooded areas in rocky ravines, cliffs or gorges with scrub and thornbush.

a Adult male: ash-grey head and upperparts to centre of breast; rump to sides of tail and rest of underparts orange.

b Adult female: as male but slightly paler and may have pale or whitish chin.

c Juvenile: heavily spotted above and below; rump and tail as adult.

PLATE 4 ROCK-THRUSHES (2)

9 Sentinel Rock-Thrush *Monticola explorator* Text page 189

S and E South Africa east to SE Transvaal. Open hillsides and plateaus with short grass and rocky outcrops, boulderfields or bare slopes.
a Adult male: blue-grey head to breast, darker blue upperparts; rump to sides of tail orange and underparts rufous-orange.
b Adult female: brown upperparts but rump and sides of tail like male but duller; chin to breast mottled whitish.
c First-year male: like adult male but duller and plumage obscured by buffish tips.
d Juvenile: as adult female but duller, finely spotted paler above, with pale edges to wing-coverts and tertials; dark tips to throat and breast.

12 Rock Thrush *Monticola saxatilis* Text page 194

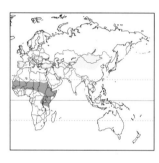

Palearctic, wintering in Africa mostly south of the Sahara. Dry, stony or rock-strewn areas including steppes, heaths, scree-slopes, hills, crags, mountain slopes, gullies, ravines, wadis, dry riverbeds, boulderfields and valleys.
a Adult male: pale blue head to upper mantle, white patch on back and rufous-orange on uppertail-coverts and sides of tail; underparts rich orange.
b Adult female: upperparts grey-brown with pale buffish tips; rump to sides of tail deep rufous-orange; underparts heavily barred or scalloped pale buffish-orange with dark fringes.
c Juvenile: very like adult female but generally more barred above (especially rump) with broad pale wing-bars on tips to coverts; paler below with broader fringes.
d First-summer male: like adult male but plumage may have paler tips to face, scapulars and wing-coverts, underparts more broadly fringed paler.

9d

9c

9a

9b

12d

12c

12b

12a

JPPW

PLATE 5 ROCK-THRUSHES (3)

11 Miombo Rock-Thrush *Monticola angolensis*   **Text page 192**

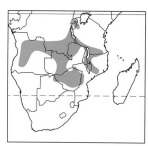

SE Zaire to N and S Tanzania to W Zambia, Zimbabwe, N Mozambique, NE Botswana and central and northern Angola. Locally in open miombo woodland in upland areas.

a Adult male: pale blue-grey upperparts with black tips and streaks; rump to sides of tail bright, underparts orange.

b Adult female: paler than male and upperparts more heavily tipped or streaked with black, broad malar stripe and orange on breast variably tipped with black.

c Juvenile: grey upperparts boldly spotted with pale yellowish and blackish fringes above and broad grey tips to white underparts.

14 Blue-capped Rock-Thrush *Monticola cinclorhynchus* **Text page 199**

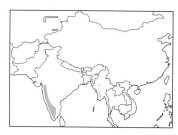

E Afghanistan, N Pakistan to Kashmir east through Himalayas to Arunachal Pradesh and Assam; winters W Peninsular India, parts of Assam and SW Burma. Forests and open moist deciduous woods.

a Adult male: deep blue crown and nape, chin to sides of neck; black ear-coverts and most of upperparts except for white patch in wing; blue-black tail, orange rump and underparts.

b Adult female: grey-brown head and upperparts (uppertail-coverts sometimes darker and barred gingery-brown); white below with heavy dark bars or scalloping.

c Juvenile: like adult female but more heavily spotted below and more broadly fringed black above.

15 White-throated Rock-Thrush *Monticola gularis*   **Text page 201**

E Siberia to Amurland, Mongolia, Manchuria, NE China and N Korea; winters in S China and SE Asia to E Burma: forests and open woodlands on hills and valleys.

a Adult male: like Blue-capped but has smaller patch of white in wing, lacks blue on chin to sides of neck and has white stripe on centre of chin and throat (usually only visible in head-on view).

b Adult female: brown to olive-brown upperparts, mottled with dark bars and pale edges or tips to mantle and scapulars; underparts boldly scalloped.

c First-year male: like non-breeding male; plumage obscured with greyish to golden-buff tips on upperparts and paler tips to orange underparts.

11b

11c

11a

14c

14b

14a

15b

15c

15a

JPPW

PLATE 6 ROCK-THRUSHES (4)

16 Chestnut-bellied Rock-Thrush *Monticola rufiventris* Text page 203

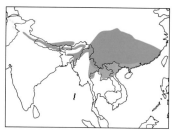

Himalayas of N Pakistan to SE Tibet, NE India, and mountains of N Burma, NW Thailand and S China. Winters at lower altitude to Bangladesh, N Laos and N Vietnam: open forests or scattered trees, mostly firs also oaks, rhododendrons on steep hillsides.

a Adult male: deep blue crown and upperparts (latter mottled black); black face with blue-black chin and throat; underparts chestnut.

b Adult female: olive or olive-brown upperparts narrowly barred darker; broad pale or whitish-buff patch at rear of ear-coverts and heavily mottled underparts.

c Adult male (winter): as spring and summer but darker and with pale tips to mantle, scapulars, with wing-bar on greater coverts.

d Juvenile male in transition: as first-year bird but with more prominent pale tips to head, face and underparts.

17 Blue Rock-Thrush *Monticola solitarius* Text page 205

Palearctic and Oriental; SE Europe to Japan, Indian subcontinent, China, SE Asia and Philippines; winters within breeding range and in N Africa and Arabia. Rocky hills, quarries, outcrops, scree-slopes, boulderfields and limestone valleys, gorges, steep cliffs (both coastal and montane), plus castles, churches and ruins; *madoci* in vicinity of mines and caves.

a Adult male: uniform deep blue (slightly darker or blacker centres to wing and tail); in sunlight becomes metallic blue.

b Adult female: grey to bluish-grey above with paler fringes and tips; pale buffish face, narrowly barred below.

c Juvenile: like adult female, but darker and less visibly barred above; chin to breast more heavily spotted or mottled.

d Adult male *philippensis*: violet-blue head to breast and upperparts, orange-rufous underparts.

e Adult male *madoci*: smaller than nominate with shorter tail; generally not as deep blue.

PLATE 7 WHISTLING-THRUSHES (1)

18 Sri Lanka Whistling-Thrush *Myophonus blighi* **Text page 210**

Central Sri Lanka. Damp forests and ravines with rivers or streams.
a Adult male: small size, shy and unobtrusive; all black with metallic blue flash on wing (usually hidden by scapulars); all-dark bill; often best detected by call.
b Adult female: dark brown, paler below with metallic blue flash in wing (usually hidden by scapulars).

22 Malabar Whistling-Thrush *Myophonus horsfieldi* **Text page 214**

WC India: forests with fast-moving streams and torrents.
a Adult: mostly black with metallic blue on forehead and wings, rump, flanks and tail.
b Juvenile: mostly sooty-black except for wing-coverts; becomes progressively blue during first year.

23 Blue Whistling-Thrush *Myophonus caeruleus* **Text page 215**

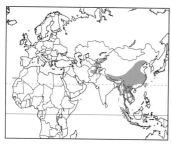

Central Asia to C China, Himalayas, N India, SE Asia, Malay Peninsula, Sumatra and Java. Montane and hill forests with streams and rivers, caves: *crassirostris* occurs in mangroves.
a Adult: bluish-black (appears all black in shade), deeper blue on wings and tail, spotted or streaked with fine silver tips; all-dark bill.
b Juvenile: sooty-black indistinctly spotted with bluish wings and tail.
c Adult *temminckii* head/bill: heavily spotted with pale silver-blue tips on forehead to crown; eye brown; orange-yellow bill.
d Adult *crassirostris* head/bill: eye dark brown; heavy yellow bill.
e Adult *dicrorhynchus* head/bill: dull blue-black with reduced spotting; eye brown; bill mostly yellow with dark culmen.

18b

18a

23c

23d

23a

23b

23e

22a

22b

PLATE 8 WHISTLING-THRUSHES (2)

20 Sunda Whistling-Thrush *Myophonus glaucinus*   **Text page 212**

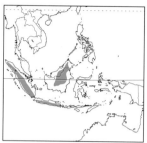

Sumatra, Borneo, Java, Bali. Forests with streams in foothills and mountains, also caves and crevices in rocky outcrops.

a Adult male: deep bluish-black or tinged purplish-blue with bright blue (but rarely visible) lesser coverts; lacks metallic spotting on body.

b Adult female: as male but duller or darker and lesser coverts slightly darker blue.

c Juvenile: dark brown with fine pale streaks above and broadly spotted or streaked on breast to flanks.

d Adult male *borneensis*: blue-black with bluish sheen on throat and breast; wings, rump and tail browner than nominate; lesser coverts bright violet-blue without bluish sheen on edges to flight feathers.

e Adult female *borneensis*: almost entirely uniform dark brown with (usually hidden) purplish-blue lesser coverts.

f Adult male *castaneus*: forehead a band of metallic blue; crown to upper mantle, chin to breast and upper belly black with dark purplish-blue sheen; rest of upperparts chestnut-brown becoming bright cinnamon on edges to flight feathers; patch of bright blue on lesser coverts.

g Adult female *castaneus*: as male but face brown tinged greyish; crown to nape and upper mantle dark brown with purplish sheen.

21 Malayan Whistling-Thrush *Myophonus robinsoni*   **Text page 213**

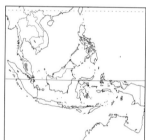

Peninsular Malaysia. Evergreen forests with fast-flowing rivers and streams, ravines and gullies.

Adult male: entirely black or blackish-blue except for deep purplish-blue forehead to sides of crown and bright metallic blue lesser covert patch and metallic purplish-blue tips to breast and upper belly; bill mostly bright yellow with dark culmen.

20a

20b

20c

20d

20e

20f

20g

21

PLATE 9 WHISTLING-THRUSHES (3), GEOMALIA AND SULAWESI THRUSH

19 Shiny Whistling-Thrush *Myophonus melanurus*   Text page 211

Sumatra. Hill and montane forests with rivers and streams.
a Adult male: mostly black but blue forehead to sides of nape; blue flash in wings (often obscured by scapulars) and tips to body feathers; black bill.
b Adult female: duller or browner than male with blue forehead to eyes but reduced amount of bluish tips on body.

24 Taiwan Whistling-Thrush *Myophonus insularis*   Text page 218

Taiwan. Montane forest with ravines and fast-flowing rivers.
a Adult in shade: blackish-blue except for blue forehead to eyes, wings, tail and tips to underparts; all-black bill.
b Adult in sun: becomes entirely metallic blue except for flight feathers and undertail-coverts; eye ruby-red.

25 Geomalia *Geomalia heinrichi*   Text page 219

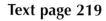

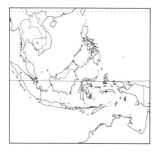

Sulawesi. Undergrowth of rainforests.
Adult: long brown tail, dark brown above and warmer or rufous below; mostly ground-loving, very shy and rarely seen.

62 Sulawesi Thrush *Cataponera turdoides*   Text page 273

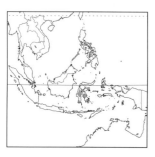

Sulawesi. Evergreen montane forests.
a Adult: olive-brown with warmer brown in wings and paler underparts, broad yellow eye-ring and black lores to sides of nape.
b Juvenile: lacks black lores to nape but eye-ring prominent and spotted above and below.
c Adult *abditiva*: as nominate but more prominently warmer rufous-brown in wings and undertail-coverts; underparts deeper olive-brown; black on lores less extensive.

24a

24b

19a

19b

62a

62b

62c

25

CliveByers

PLATE 10 PIED AND SIBERIAN THRUSHES

31 Pied Thrush *Zoothera wardii*   **Text page 226**

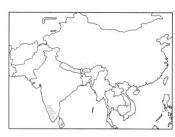

Himalayas of N India, Nepal and Assam; in winter mostly S India and Sri Lanka. Broadleaved woods and forests.

a Adult male: very distinctive; black above and mostly white below with long white supercilium and tips to wing-coverts and tertials; rump and uppertail-coverts also tipped white; flanks tipped black.

b Adult female: as male but black replaced by brown; supercilium and tips to wing-coverts buffish-white; underparts scaly with brown crescents.

c First-year: very like adult female but darker olive-brown and underparts darker mottled with pale centres.

36 Siberian Thrush *Zoothera sibirica*   **Text page 233**

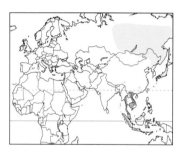

Siberia to Ussuriland, Amurland, Sakhalin, Japan and NE China; winters mostly SE Asia. Extensive conifer forests and alder-thickets in lowland taiga and river valleys; in winter to montane forests.

a Adult male: very distinctive; slate-grey tinged blue with long white supercilium; white tips to tail and undertail-coverts; yellow legs.

b Adult female: brown or olive-brown with paler buff face pattern, supercilium buffish (less clean than male); underparts scaly; legs pale buffish-brown.

c First-year male: greyer or more bluish-grey than adult and supercilium usually less extensive; paler below with pale spots; may show pale tips to wing-coverts.

d First-year female: like adult female but more extensive pale tips to wing-coverts; supercilium usually less defined, underparts more heavily spotted with pale centres.

e Adult male *davisoni*: darker than nominate with less white tips to tail and undertail-coverts, white only on centre of belly to vent.

f Juvenile: like female but darker, face and underparts more mottled; pale buffish tips to wing-coverts.

31c

31b

31a

36b

36a

36d

36c

36e

36f

PLATE 11 INDONESIAN *ZOOTHERA* THRUSHES

27 Moluccan Thrush *Zoothera dumasi* Text page 221

Seram and Buru, Indonesia. Dense moss-forests.

a Adult: large bill, upperparts rich russet; darker brown on wings and face to belly; pale eye-ring; broad white tips to wing-coverts; belly whitish.

b Juvenile: more spotted and mottled than adult with pale central shaft-streaks on scapulars and broad dark malar stripes.

c Adult male *joiceyi*: more extensively darker brown above (only crown and nape russet); single wing-bar on tips of median coverts.

28 Chestnut-capped Thrush *Zoothera interpres* Text page 222

S Thailand, Malaysia, Indonesia to Philippines. Submontane forests, forested hills and lowland primary forests.

a Adult: chestnut on crown to nape; deep blue-grey upperparts, broad white tips to wing-coverts; black face to breast.

b Adult *leucolaema* (Enggano): upperparts (including tail) browner than nominate; face to sides of breast black, chin and throat white.

c Juvenile: like small version of adult but heavily streaked above with pale orange-buff; white in wing tinged orange and heavily spotted below.

29 Red-backed Thrush *Zoothera erythronota* Text page 223

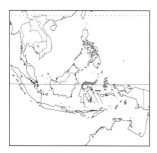

Sulawesi. Primary and secondary evergreen forests.

a Adult: very distinctive; russet crown to back; black wings with two broad wing-bars; white patches on face; black chin to breast and bars on rest of underparts.

b Juvenile: like adult but has pale buffish central shaft-streaks.

c Adult (unnamed Taliabu race): black face with white patch on ear-coverts, no wing-bar; wings and underparts blackish.

30 Chestnut-backed Thrush *Zoothera dohertyi* Text page 225

Lombok to Timor, Lesser Sunda Islands. Undergrowth of montane primary forests, mist-forest and woodlands.

a Adult: black crown to nape; mantle to rump chestnut (brighter on uppertail-coverts); wings black with broad white wing-bars; black and white face; chin to breast black, spotted on flanks.

b Juvenile: as adult but duller brown and head to breast and flanks spotted or barred darker; wing-bars buffish.

PLATE 12 ASIAN AND INDONESIAN *ZOOTHERA* THRUSHES

32 Ashy Thrush *Zoothera cinerea* **Text page 227**

Luzon and Mindoro, Philippines. Primary and secondary forests of foothills and mountains.
Adult: extremely shy and rarely seen; grey crown and upperparts with broad white wing-bars; black and white patches on face and heavily spotted underparts.

33 Orange-sided Thrush *Zoothera peronii* **Text page 228**

Timor, Lesser Sundas. Lowland deciduous forests, woodlands with scrub or thickets.
Adult: orange-brown upperparts, more rufous on rump and base of tail; black and white face; chin to upper breast plus belly to undertail white; breast and flanks deep orange.

34 Orange-headed Thrush *Zoothera citrina* **Text page 229**

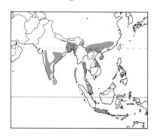

N Pakistan to Sri Lanka, SE Asia and S China, Andamans and Nicobars, Peninsular Malaysia, Sumatra and Java. Damp forests and woodlands, preferring well-wooded forests with bushy undergrowth.
a Adult male: entire head and underparts deep orange; slate-grey wings and upperparts; white median coverts and undertail-coverts.
b Adult female: as adult male but upperparts browner or tinged olive; wings warm brown.
c Juvenile: dull brown except for more rufous on head and face and grey wings with pale buff streaks on mantle and scapulars.
d Adult *cyanotus*: as nominate or slightly paler but with distinctive black and white face pattern.
e Adult *albogularis*: deeper or rufous-orange on nape to breast and white lores to chin; lacks white in wing.

35 Everett's Thrush *Zoothera everetti* **Text page 232**

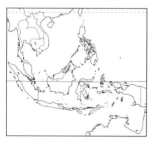

N Borneo. Undergrowth and damp areas of lower levels of submontane deciduous forests.
a Adult: very shy and retiring; deep brown upperparts, pale face, dark malar and warm orange underparts.
b First-year: like adult but with fine shaft-streaks above, paler but more heavily scaled or scalloped below.

PLATE 13 VARIED AND AZTEC THRUSHES

37 Varied Thrush *Zoothera naevia*   **Text page 236**

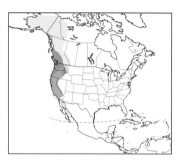

Alaska to SW Alberta, N Idaho and NW California; winters mostly within the breeding range, east to Montana and S Baja California. Dense conifer forests.

a Adult male: very distinctive; (bluish) slate-grey upperparts contrasting with bright orange supercilium, wing-bars and chin to breast; black breast-band.

b Adult female: like adult male but browner and generally lacks grey; orange also slightly paler and breast-band paler or incomplete.

c Juvenile: like adult but upperparts brown to grey-brown and finely streaked pale orange-buff; lacks breast-band and underparts tipped darker.

d First-year male: very like adult but dark tips to upperparts; pale tips to tertials; wing-bars duller and paler tips to breast-band.

e Adult 'grey morph': very rare but entire plumage lacks any orange and is replaced by white; breast-band grey.

38 Aztec Thrush *Zoothera pinicola*   **Text page 239**

Mexico from Sonora to Guerrero and Oaxaca. Forests and ravines of pine or pine-oak.

a Adult male: very striking but frequently shy: mostly brown with fine pale streaks and whitish or pale grey uppertail-coverts; pale brown to whitish patches in wing; pale tips to dark tail.

b Adult female: like male but head to breast and upperparts browner and prominently streaked paler.

c Juvenile: very distinctive with extensive pale yellow or golden-yellow spots and streaks on upper- and underparts; white patch in wing with broad pale grey tips.

PLATE 14 AFRICAN GROUND-THRUSHES (1)

39 Abyssinian Ground-Thrush *Zoothera piaggiae*   **Text page 240**

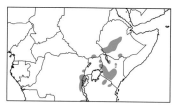

Sudan and Ethiopia south to N Tanzania, Uganda and Zaire. Undergrowth of evergreen montane forests.
a Adult: olive-brown cheeks, crown and upperparts; rufous-brown forehead and underparts; two broad white wing-bars and broad white eye-ring.
b Juvenile: mostly dull brown heavily streaked with pale shafts and spotted on underparts; whitish wing-bars.
c Adult *hadii*: very like nominate, slightly darker above.
d Adult *tanganjicae*: more extensively rufous or russet on head to nape and rump to base of tail.

41 Orange Ground-Thrush *Zoothera gurneyi*   **Text page 244**

Discontinuous from C Kenya south to E South Africa, also in S Zaire and C Angola. Undergrowth of evergreen montane forests.
a Adult: olive-brown upperparts and orange on lores to flanks; belly white with two white wing-bars; smudge through eye.
b Juvenile: mostly brown with fine pale buff streaks above and dark spots below, buffish-white wing-bars and smudge through eye.
c Adult *otomitra*: upperparts paler with heavier smudge through eye and pale ear-coverts.

42 Oberlaender's Ground-Thrush *Zoothera oberlaenderi*
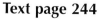
Text page 246

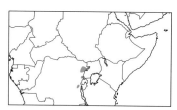

E Zaire to SW Uganda. Undergrowth of tall forests.
Adult: rufous-chestnut head to nape and underparts (belly white) and brighter rufous on rump and base of tail; white eye-ring broken by narrow smudge through eye.

39a

39b

39c

39d

42

41a

41c

41b

CliveByers

PLATE 15 AFRICAN GROUND-THRUSHES (2)

40 Crossley's Ground-Thrush *Zoothera crossleyi* **Text page 242**

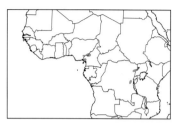

Isolated populations in SE Nigeria and S Cameroon; S Congo; NE Zaire. Middle levels and undergrowth of mature montane primary forest.
a Adult: distinctive face pattern of blackish cheeks and ear-coverts and halved white eye-ring; mantle olive-brown; rufous sides of neck to flanks; two broad white wing-bars; pale tips to outer tail feathers.
b Adult *pilettei*: upperparts more heavily brown to olive-brown and smaller pale tips to tail.

43 Black-eared Ground-Thrush *Zoothera cameronensis* **Text page 247**

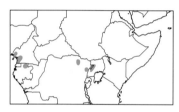

Isolated populations in S Cameroon; NE Gabon; NE Zaire and W Uganda. Dense undergrowth of lowland and temperate forest.
a Adult male: small; black bars on face; rust-orange above with two white wing-bars; pale face and deep orange below.
b Adult female: paler than male and less rust-brown above; duller white tips to wing-coverts.
c Juvenile: face like adult with pale streaks on upperparts and spots on buffish-orange underparts; wing-bars also buffish-white.
d Adult *graueri*: greyer above than nominate, duller rufous-orange below, sometimes with sparse streaks on breast; face washed pale orange and bold black streaks.
e Adult *kibalensis*: very like nominate; face pattern distinct on pale buffish base; more rufous above and bright orange below.

44 Grey Ground-Thrush *Zoothera princei* **Text page 249**

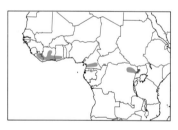

Discontinuously from Sierra Leone to W Uganda. Dense undergrowth of lowland evergreen forests.
a Adult: upperparts grey-brown tinged olive; two white wing-bars and pale tips to outer tail feathers; two dark bars on face and sparsely streaked on throat.
b Adult *batesi*: very like nominate but more olive-brown hind-crown to back; lower throat has few (if any) indistinct dark streaks; breast tinged warmer orange.

PLATE 16 ASIAN AND AFRICAN SPOTTED THRUSHES

45 Spotted Ground-Thrush *Zoothera guttata* **Text page 250**

Discontinuous in E and S Africa; Sudan; S Tanzania and N Mozambique; S Zaire; Malawi; E Cape Province, South Africa. Understorey of coastal and lowland evergreen forests.
a Adult: olive-brown upperparts, two white wing-bars; prominent face pattern and heavily spotted underparts.
b Adult *fischeri*: very like nominate but more olive upperparts, spots more widely distributed on underparts, and (on average) paler base to bill.

46 Spot-winged Thrush *Zoothera spiloptera* **Text page 252**

Sri Lanka. Undergrowth and bamboo clumps in dense forests.
a Adult: olive-brown upperparts, pale or whitish face with two broad blackish stripes, double white wing-bars and spotted underparts; black bill.
b Juvenile: Mostly brown above with pale streaks, brown below with darks spots or bars; dark stripes on face.

96 Groundscraper Thrush *Psophocichla litsitsirupa* **Text page 325**

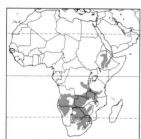

Eritrea to C Ethiopia; E Zaire and W Tanzania to Angola, Namibia, Botswana and South Africa. Open woodland (acacia, miombo and savanna); also moorland and dry heath with grass and junipers.
a Adult: a very upright, short-tailed thrush; grey-brown above, no wing-bars; prominent bars on face, heavily spotted below.
b Juvenile/first-year: like adult but heavily streaked pale orange-buff and tips to wing-coverts; underparts also buffish.
c Adult *simensis*: upperparts more heavily brown and underparts more heavily buff to buffish-brown.
d Adult *stierlingi*: paler above and whiter below than nominate.

96a

96c

96d

96b

46a

46b

45a

45b

PLATE 17 WHITE'S AND AMAMI THRUSHES

50 White's Thrush *Zoothera dauma*   **Text page 257**

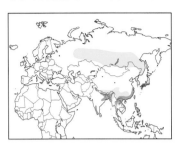

Siberia; Urals to Ussuriland, Amurland, N Mongolia, N Manchuria, N Korea and N Japan; Himalayas from N Pakistan to S China and parts of SE Asia; SW India; Sri Lanka; winters from N India and most of SE Asia, S China and S Japan. Mature oak and fir forests.

a Adult *dauma*: bold pattern of olive and yellow subterminally with black crescents on upperparts and whitish face, underparts with bold black tips; bold black and white underwing and white tips to outer tail feathers in flight.

b Adult *aurea*: slightly larger and paler than nominate.

c Juvenile *dauma*: like adult but shows more extensive pale yellowish areas above with olive tips and pale central shaft-streaks; underparts more spotted than scalloped.

d First-winter *dauma*: very like adult and only reliably told by some retained juvenile wing-coverts.

e Adult *neilgherriensis*: very like nominate but upperparts slightly darker, and rump to tail warmer.

f Adult *imbricata*: slightly smaller than nominate and darker above, visibly light peachy to warm buff below.

51 Amami Thrush *Zoothera major*   **Text page 262**

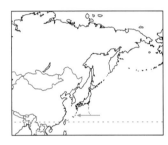

Amami Oshima, Ryukyu Islands. Wet or moist primary forest.

Adult: very like White's but slightly larger with pale yellow central shafts and broad blackish-brown crescents; rump and uppertail-coverts paler, less broadly tipped blackish (except for longest upper-tail-coverts); underparts buffier with yellow on bases to belly and flanks, underwing duller or greyish.

50b

50b

50d

50c

50a

50f

50e

51

50f

CliveByers

PLATE 18 INDONESIAN AND AUSTRALIAN *ZOOTHERA* THRUSHES

52 Horsfield's Thrush *Zoothera horsfieldi* **Text page 263**

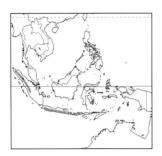

N Sumatra, Java, Bali, Lombok and Sumbawa. Undergrowth of montane deciduous, rhododendron and open Casuarina forests.
Adult: very like White's Thrush but slightly smaller, upperparts deeper olive-russet and less mottled with pale subterminal shaft-streaks (most restricted to forehead, crown and sides of nape).

53 Fawn-breasted Thrush *Zoothera machiki* **Text page 263**

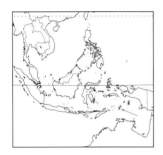

Tanimbar, Lesser Sunda Islands. Lowland and gallery forests, including degraded and secondary forests and scrub.
Adult: uniform (unbarred or scaled) upperparts with warm russet-brown rump and uppertail-coverts; pale buffish face to breast and bars on sides of breast to flanks.

54 Bassian Thrush *Zoothera lunulata* **Text page 264**

E Australia and Tasmania. Heavy forests and lowland coastal rainforests or eucalyptus woodlands.
a Adult: olive-brown upperparts, no pale yellow subterminal tips and broad blackish crescents at tips; rump and uppertail-coverts more heavily olive and barred black; breast also olive, rest of underparts white scalloped black.
b Adult *macrorhyncha*: very like nominate but with browner tail and longer, heavier bill.

55 Russet-tailed Thrush *Zoothera heinei* **Text page 266**

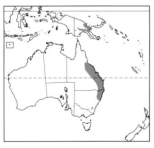

New Guinea; Solomon Islands; E Australia. Rainforests and dense wet eucalypt woods of lowland valleys, also primary forests and adjacent thickets.
a Adult: like Bassian Thrush (separated altitudinally); rump and uppertail-coverts narrowly barred (appearing absent in some) and tinged warmer rufous; central tail feathers warm or russet-brown.
b Juvenile: like adult with less pronounced black crescents.
c Adult *papuensis*: smaller and more golden-buff subterminally with extensive dark bars and scallops.

55a

55c

55b

54a

54b

52

53

CliveByers

PLATE 19 ASIAN AND PACIFIC ISLAND THRUSHES

26 Slaty-backed Thrush *Zoothera schistacea* **Text page 220**

Tanimbar, Lesser Sunda Islands. Dense lowland primary and secondary forests. (See map below.)
a Adult male: deep grey upperparts, broad white wing-bars; black chin to breast and heavy black spots on rest of white underparts.
b Adult female: less black on crown and generally fewer spots on rest of underparts.

47 Sunda Thrush *Zoothera andromedae* **Text page 253**

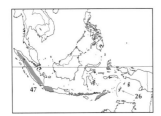

Sumatra to Timor; also the Philippines. Undergrowth of wet or moist hill and montane forests.
a Adult: Large head and bill, dark grey face and grey upperparts scaled with black tips and prominent black scallops to pale greyish underparts.
b Juvenile: like adult but browner and more heavily scalloped below; white tips to crown and nape and pale buffish streaks on mantle and scapulars.

56 New Britain Thrush *Zoothera talaseae* **Text page 267**

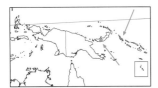

New Britain, Papua New Guinea; Bougainville, Solomon Islands. Montane mist-forests.
Adult: blackish-slate on head and upperparts, two broad white wing-bars; white underparts with distinctive scalloped flanks.

57 San Cristobal Thrush *Zoothera margaretae* **Text page 268**

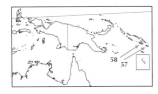

Makira, Solomon Islands. Undergrowth of montane primary forests.
Adult: olive-brown upperparts (with slightly darker fringes), white tips to coverts (indistinct on medians) and heavily scalloped below.

58 Guadalcanal Thrush *Zoothera turipavae* **Text page 269**

Guadalcanal, Solomon Islands. Montane forests. (See map above.)
a Adult (below): dusky olive-brown above and heavily scalloped below with greyish flanks; small dark bill.
b First-year: similar to adult but with orange-buff tips to wing-coverts.

61 Bonin Islands Thrush *Zoothera terrestris* **Text page 272**

Ogasawara Islands, Japan. Extinct.
Adult: mostly brown head and upperparts, broadly streaked darker, rufous-brown rump to base of tail; flanks tinged rufous-brown.

58a

PLATE 20 ASIAN THRUSHES

48 Plain-backed Thrush *Zoothera mollissima*   **Text page 254**

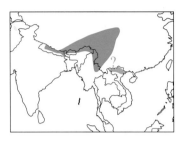

Himalayas from N Pakistan to SE Tibet, Assam, N Burma; S China from W Szechwan and NW Yunnan; winters to lower levels and N Vietnam. Alpine meadows, boulderfields with juniper and rhododendron.

a Adult male: plain olive-brown upperparts; mottled face and dark rear edge to ear-coverts and boldly scaled underparts.

b Juvenile/first-year: like adult but duller and with pale buffish shaft-streaks on upperparts.

49 Long-tailed Thrush *Zoothera dixoni*   **Text page 256**

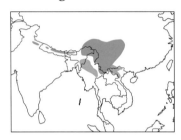

Himalayas from N India to SE Tibet and Burma, east to Szechwan and NW Yunnan; winters at lower levels and N Vietnam. Dense fir, oak and rhododendron forests, also dwarf juniper forest.

a Adult: like Plain-backed but with longer tail, pale tips to wing-coverts and bolder scallops below.

b Juvenile/first-year: like adult but with pale buff central shaft-streaks to upperparts.

59 Long-billed Thrush *Zoothera monticola*   **Text page 270**

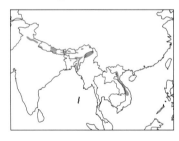

Himalayas from N India to Arunachal Pradesh, N and E Bangladesh, NW Burma; also N Vietnam. Undergrowth of dense fir forests.

a Adult: large bill, dark olive-brown upperparts, brown wings and heavily streaked underparts.

b Juvenile/first-year: like adult but has narrow pale orange-buff shaft-streaks and broad pale tips to wing-coverts; spotted below.

60 Dark-sided Thrush *Zoothera marginata*   **Text page 271**

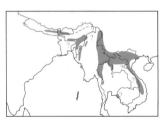

Himalayas of E Nepal to Bhutan; Assam to Arunachal Pradesh; N and E Burma, N Thailand, N Laos and N Vietnam. Dense undergrowth in deciduous, broadleaved and fir forests.

a Adult male: like Long-billed but browner or more rufous above with well-defined face pattern and scalloped underparts.

b Juvenile: like adult but has fine buffish streaks above and bars below.

PLATE 21 HAWAIIAN THRUSHES AND TOWNSEND'S SOLITAIRE

65 Kamao *Myadestes myadestinus*   **Text page 276**

Kauai, Hawaiian Islands. Dense wet montane forests. Probably extinct.
a Adult: plain brown above, greyish mottled whitish breast, whiter on belly; bill short and broad-based.
b Juvenile: heavily spotted above with pale tips to wing-coverts; heavily scalloped underparts.

67 Olomao *Myadestes lanaiensis*   **Text page 278**

Molokai, Hawaiian islands. Montane rainforest. Probably extinct.
Adult: grey-brown head and olive-brown upperparts, pale buffish-orange patch at base of secondaries; buffish below.

68 Omao *Myadestes obscurus*   **Text page 279**

Hawaii. Dense wet montane forests. (See map below.)
a Adult: small size, short stout bill; grey-brown head and olive-brown upperparts.
b Juvenile: heavily spotted above; pale tips to wing-coverts; breast to belly scalloped with pale centres and dark-brown fringes.

69 Puaiohi *Myadestes palmeri*   **Text page 281**

Kauai, Hawaiian Islands. Wet montane forest with steep-sided ridges and valleys.
a Adult: short-tailed; drab olive-brown with grey face and white eye-ring; pale grey breast.
b Juvenile: brown above, spotted pale buff; pale tips to wing-coverts; eye-ring often incomplete; broadly scalloped below.

70 Townsend's Solitaire *Myadestes townsendi*   **Text page 282**

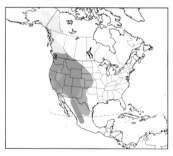

SE Alaska to S Dakota to New Mexico and C Mexico; winters S British Columbia to Texas and California. Conifer forests and wooded ravines above treeline.
a Adult: slender with upright stance, long tail; mostly grey-brown; prominent eye-ring, buffish patch on closed wing and white outer tail feathers.
b Juvenile: heavily spotted above with pale tips to greater coverts; pale buff below with dark bars or scalloped pattern.
c Adult in flight: pale wing-bar and white outer tail feathers.

65a

65b

67

68a

69a

69b

68b

70b

70a

70c

CliveByers

PLATE 22 SOLITAIRES (1)

71 Brown-backed Solitaire *Myadestes occidentalis* **Text page 284**

Mexico to Honduras. Cloud-forest.
a Adult: head grey with broad white eye-ring and dark submoustachial, rufous edges to wings; white tips to outer tail feathers.
b Juvenile: heavily scalloped above; underparts yellowish-buff with closely scalloped pattern.

72 Cuban Solitaire *Myadestes elisabeth* **Text page 286**

Cuba. Dense humid forests with limestone outcrops, rocks and cliffs. (See map below.)
a Adult: olive-brown above, white eye-ring, white in outer tail.
b Juvenile: extensively spotted and flecked with buff and dark fringes on upperparts; dusky tips to underparts.

73 Rufous-throated Solitaire *Myadestes genibarbis* **Text page 287**

Jamaica to St Vincent. Montane rainforests and lowland evergreen forests.
a Adult: upperparts slate-grey, white outer tail feathers: distinctive face pattern and deep rufous throat.
b Juvenile: upperparts spotted with orange-buff centres; underparts barred blackish.
c Adult *sibilans*: much darker grey above with broad deep orange submoustachial.

74 Black-faced Solitaire *Myadestes melanops* **Text page 288**

Costa Rica to W Panama. Humid or cool forests, tree-clad slopes and ravines, second-growth woods.
a Adult: slate-grey with jet-black face and silvery-white underwing-coverts; broad-based orange bill.
b Juvenile: mostly dark or sooty-grey with pale buff spots and streaks above; underparts mottled with pale buff centres and dark brown tips.

77 Slate-coloured Solitaire *Myadestes unicolor* **Text page 291**

Discontinuous; S Mexico to Nicaragua. Cloud-forest, humid, evergreen and pine-oak woodlands and bushy slopes.
a Adult: uniform dark slate-grey with blacker wings and tail, white tips to outer feathers.
b Juvenile: like adult but slightly darker, and large pale buff spots with blackish edges and fringes above and whitish-buff centres to underparts.

PLATE 23 SOLITAIRES (2)

75 Varied Solitaire *Myadestes coloratus* Text page 289

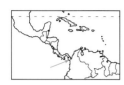

E Panama to NW Colombia. Damp forests, forest edges; foothills and mountains.
a Adult: face black; head, face and underparts grey with rust-brown upperparts and black wings and tail; bill yellow.
b Juvenile: Heavily spotted with pale tawny-buff above and paler or whitish-buff below.

76 Andean Solitaire *Myadestes ralloides* Text page 290

Andes from Colombia to Peru and N Bolivia. Humid and cloud-forests, secondary woodlands.
a Adult: rufous-brown above and lead-grey below; in flight has pale or silvery wing-bar and tips to tail.
b Juvenile: like adult, mottled with pale buff tips above and dark bars to grey underparts.

78 Rufous-brown Solitaire *Cichlopsis leucogenys* Text page 292

Disjunct in south-east Venezuela, Guyana, Surinam; SW Colombia, NW Ecuador; C Peru and E Brazil. Dense rainforests.
a Adult: mostly rufous-brown with warmer brown wings and tail; undertail-coverts warm buff.
b Juvenile: like adult but with pale buff streaks to head and upperparts and tips to wing-coverts.
c Adult *peruvianus*: chin and throat bright rufous-orange; rest of underparts slightly duller.

79 White-eared Solitaire *Entomodestes leucotis* Text page 293

Andes in C and S Peru to N Bolivia. Montane forests. (See map below.)
a Adult: very striking, mainly jet-black below with rufous or deep chestnut upperparts and a large white face-patch; in flight shows broad white wing-bar.
b Juvenile/first-year: like adult but upperparts slightly duller with paler tips.

80 Black Solitaire *Entomodestes coracinus* Text page 294

Andes of W Colombia to NW Ecuador. Cloud-forests.
Adult: jet-black with white face, bend of wing and edges to tail.

75b

76b

76a

75a

78b

78a

78c

79b

79a

80

PLATE 24 NIGHTINGALE-THRUSHES (1)

81 Black-billed Nightingale-Thrush *Catharus gracilirostris*
Text page 295

Costa Rica to W Panama. High-altitude forests, secondary forests and woods, clearings above treeline, patches of elfin forest and thick páramo vegetation.
a Adult: small size, all-dark bill, slate-grey crown and pale grey throat; pale tawny-brown breast-band.
b Juvenile: head duller than adult; breast dark reddish-brown streaked whitish, belly barred with brown.

82 Orange-billed Nightingale-Thrush *Catharus aurantiirostris*
Text page 296

Mexico to Colombia and N Venezuela. Understorey of rain- and cloud-forests, secondary woods, plantations, dry thorn scrub, bamboo and brush.
a Adult: bright orange bill, rufous-brown upperparts, pale greyish face and paler grey breast and flanks.
b Juvenile: pale central shaft-streaks on crown to scapulars; median coverts with pale yellowish tips.
c Adult *costaricensis*: darker olive head and upperparts than nominate; tail dark rufous-brown.
d Adult *melpomene*: russet olive-brown upperparts, deepest on forehead to nape; greater coverts edged rich olive-brown.
e Adult *phaeopleurus*: face to crown grey, upperparts olive-brown but rump to base of tail warmer brown, lower throat to breast pale grey.
f Adult *aenopennis*: upperparts paler but with warm rufous edges to wing and tail; face pale olive-brown.

84 Russet Nightingale-Thrush *Catharus occidentalis*   Text page 300

Mexico. Understorey of humid cloud-, pine–oak and fir forests.
a Adult: rich or russet upperparts, pale grey underparts with buff spots on breast; flesh-coloured lower mandible to dark bill.
b Juvenile: darker brown upperparts than adult and pale orange-buff spots on forehead to upper rump; pale buff tips to median coverts and edges to greaters.

81a

81b

82b

82a

82c

82d

82f

82e

84a

84b

PLATE 25 NIGHTINGALE-THRUSHES (2)

83 Slaty-backed Nightingale-Thrush *Catharus fuscatur* **Text page 298**

Discontinuous from S Costa Rica to N Venezuela and N Bolivia. Undergrowth of humid, mossy montane forests.
a Adult: slate-grey upperparts, head blacker with prominent pale whitish eye and bright orange bill.
b Juvenile male: brown on head and upperparts; throat to breast pale buffish-brown; belly greyish.

85 Ruddy-capped Nightingale-Thrush *Catharus frantzii*
Text page 301

Mexico to Panama. Thick undergrowth and floor of pine–oak and conifer cloud-forests, woodlands and ravines.
a Adult: russet or russet-olive above with rufous forehead to nape, face whitish-grey; underparts paler.
b Juvenile: dark olive-brown with paler centres; breast and flanks dull olive barred darker.
c Adult *alticola*: forehead to crown and nape deep ruddy-brown becoming deep olive-brown.

86 Black-headed Nightingale-Thrush *Catharus mexicanus*
Text page 302

Mexico to W Panama. Undergrowth of cloud-, humid and lowland forests.
a Adult: olive-brown upperparts with sooty head and face and bright orange eye-ring, bill and legs.
b Juvenile: head dark olive-brown, upperparts with light orange-buff streaks; pale subterminal tips to median and greater coverts.
c Adult *fumosus*: similar to nominate but face is greyer, chin to breast also grey.

87 Spotted Nightingale-Thrush *Catharus dryas* **Text page 304**

Discontinuous from S Mexico to extreme NW Argentina. Edges and undergrowth of humid evergreen cloud-forests.
a Adult: black head, olive-grey above and pale yellow underparts spotted with grey; bill and legs orange.
b Juvenile: dark olive-brown above with pale buff streaks; head streaked with brown; dark olive below finely mottled with pale yellowish-buff centres.
c Adult *maculatus*: upperparts darker olive and underparts deeper yellow with bolder spots.

85a

85c

85b

86a

86b

86c

87c

87a

87b

83a

83b

PLATE 26 NORTH AMERICAN *CATHARUS* THRUSHES (1)

88 Veery *Catharus fuscescens*   Text page 305

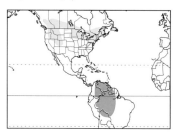

S Canada and U.S.A.; winters Colombia to Brazil. Forests and wooded mountains, preferring mixed woods of oak and pine with good undergrowth.

a Adult: reddish or rufous-brown upperparts, breast yellowish-cream lightly spotted, indistinct eye-ring and greyish flanks.

b First-year *fuliginosus*: as nominate but slightly warmer brown upperparts, stronger arrowhead spots on upper breast and pale tips to greater coverts.

c Adult *salicicolus*: less rufous than nominate and more olive-brown above; breast has well-defined brown spots.

d Juvenile *fuscescens*: upperparts heavily spotted with pale buff tips, breast mottled with pale brown becoming bars on flanks.

92 Hermit Thrush *Catharus guttatus*   Text page 315

Alaska, Canada and U.S.A.; winters in W and S U.S.A. and N Mexico. Coniferous, deciduous or mixed forests.

a Adult *guttatus*: upperparts grey-brown or tinged olive becoming warm brown on rump and chestnut on tail; edges to wings also warm brown; underparts mostly white heavily spotted black.

b Juvenile *guttatus*: shows olive-brown wings and warm brown rump and tail; heavily spotted with pale buffish on upperparts (streaks on scapulars) and mottled or barred darker below.

c Adult *faxoni*: upperparts darker or browner grading to warmer brown edges to flight feathers and rump and tail; heavily spotted with black below.

d Adult *auduboni*: largest race; upperparts pale greyish-olive, tail duller than nominate and flanks slightly paler grey; underparts white with blackish spots.

PLATE 27 NORTH AMERICAN *CATHARUS* THRUSHES (2)

89 Grey-cheeked Thrush *Catharus minimus* **Text page 308**

Extreme NE Siberia and N Canada; winters from Colombia to Brazil and N Peru. Dense forests, scrub and thickets.
a Adult: grey-brown tinged olive upperparts; indistinct eye-ring and pale greyish face; blackish spots on pale cream breast.
b Juvenile: upperparts heavily tipped pale buff; pale buff tips to greater coverts and greyish bars below.
c First-winter *aliciae*: as nominate but slightly colder olive above and duller below; pale buff tips to greater coverts; flanks washed brownish-olive.

90 Bicknell's Thrush *Catharus bicknelli* **Text page 310**

SE Canada to NE U.S.A.; winters Hispaniola. Forests of balsam and red spruce.
Adult: very like Grey-cheeked (not always separable in field) but upperparts more olive-brown, tail warmer brown, edges to wings warmer olive, face finely streaked paler; base of bill extensively yellow.

91 Swainson's Thrush *Catharus ustulatus* **Text page 312**

Alaska, Canada, W and NE U.S.A.; winters S Mexico to Brazil and N Argentina. Spruce and deciduous forests, alder thickets.
a Adult: olive-brown upperparts tinged grey; distinctive pale lores and broad eye-ring; small blackish spots on breast.
b Juvenile: olive-brown above, heavily spotted pale buff; pale buffish tips to greater coverts; barred dark olive below.
c Adult *swainsoni*: upperparts paler than nominate; rump browner and breast creamy-buff heavily spotted.
d First-year *oedicus*: as nominate but paler above; some pale buff tips to greater coverts; whiter below with smaller spots.

93 Wood Thrush *Catharus mustelina* **Text page 319**

SE Canada and E U.S.A.; winters from C Mexico to Panama. Breeds in dense broadleaved woods; winters in humid forests.
a Adult: larger than other N American *Catharus* thrushes; reddish-brown crown to nape; brown above, boldly spotted below.
b Juvenile: duller than adult, spotted and streaked with pale buff on upperparts; pale buff tips to wing-coverts.

PLATE 28 AFRICAN *TURDUS* THRUSHES (1)

97 African Thrush *Turdus pelios* **Text page 326**

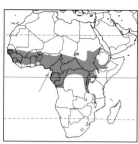

W and C Africa, Senegal to Ethiopia south to Gabon and Zaire. Dry, humid or moist forests, riverine forests and open woodlands, clearings and forest edges including villages.

a Adult: pale grey-brown above and breast pale grey; chin and throat streaked grey-brown, flanks washed orange, belly and undertail-coverts white or whitish. Yellow bill.

b Juvenile: as adult with pale orange streaks on crown and mantle; pale buffish-orange tips to wing-coverts: heavily spotted with brown on breast and flanks.

c Adult *centralis*: slightly darker above; chin and throat heavily streaked; breast grey to orange-grey; flanks peach-orange.

d Adult *chiguancoides*: similar to *saturatus* but slightly paler above; breast off-white or greyish, belly and flanks fawn-buff.

e Adult *saturatus*: breast grey to greyish-buff becoming whitish on upper belly; flanks usually orange.

f Adult *nigrilorum*: browner or grey-brown above; heavily streaked chin to sides of lower throat; breast and flanks pale grey-brown, centre of belly to undertail white.

g Juvenile *nigrilorum*: as nominate juvenile but darker above and may be more heavily spotted below.

h Adult *poensis*: as *nigrilorum* but heavily tinged olive above; more extensive dingy grey on breast, upper belly and flanks.

97a

97b

97d

97c

97e

97f

97g

97h

JPPW

PLATE 29 AFRICAN *TURDUS* THRUSHES (2)

101 Olive Thrush *Turdus olivaceus*   Text page 333

E and S Africa, discontinuously south from Eritrea and Ethiopia south to S Zaire, C Angola, C Namibia and South Africa. Montane and lowland evergreen forests. See also Plate 30.

a Adult: dark olive-brown above; chin and throat white streaked blackish, breast buff, grey- or light olive-brown becoming orange on belly.

b Juvenile: upperparts more olive than adult, streaked with pale orange with pale orange-buff wing-bars; underparts pale orange heavily spotted blackish-brown.

c Adult *stormsi*: upperparts dark brownish-olive (some greyish-olive); breast deep orange tinged light brownish-olive, rufous-cinnamon on belly and flanks.

d Adult *baraka*: brownish-grey above; breast to belly deep tawny, lower breast and flanks more often tinged heavily with chestnut.

e Adult *abyssinicus*: less olive than nominate and slightly paler brown with a greyish cast on upperparts; yellow to orange eye-ring; sides of throat streaked dark brown, greyish-olive on lower throat and breast, bright orange on lower breast, belly, flanks.

f Adult *milanjensis*: upperparts slightly darker than nominate; chin and throat buffish-white striped blackish; upper breast olive-buff to olive-brown tinged orange; centre of breast and upper belly deep orange; undertail olive-brown with white shafts.

g Adult *smithi*: like nominate but slightly paler above; pale yellow eye-ring; chin and throat less heavily streaked; breast to flanks grey or greyish-buff tinged orange, centre of lower breast to vent light orange.

h Adult male *bocagei*: upperparts tinged grey; stripes on throat narrower than other races; breast ashy-brown tinged orange on sides of breast and flanks; centre of lower breast and belly white.

i Adult male *nyikae*: like *smithi* with heavier streaks on off-white to buffish chin and throat; lower throat and breast dull orange-buff tinged grey to dingy olive-brown; pale orange on sides of belly, rusty on flanks; belly to undertail white.

j Adult male *oldeani*: like *nyikae* with darker olive upperparts; greyish underparts, belly dull olive tinged orange, flanks grey-brown; eye-ring orange.

101b

101a

101c

101d

101f

101g

101e

101i

101j

101h

JPPW

PLATE 30 AFRICAN *TURDUS* THRUSHES (3)

98 Bare-eyed Thrush *Turdus tephronotus*　　　Text page 329

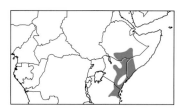

S Ethiopia to NE Tanzania. Dry or semi-arid country, light wood-lands, grasslands with woods and thickets.
a Adult: upperparts grey; prominent patch of bare yellow skin around eye; breast grey, deep orange on lower breast to flanks.
b Juvenile: as adult but with pale tips to wing-coverts and heavily spotted with dark brown below.

99 Kurrichane Thrush *Turdus libonyanus*　　　Text page 330

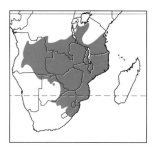

Burundi and NW Tanzania to Angola, Transvaal and Natal. Woodlands from light bush and miombo to secondary growth, forest clearings.
a Adult: upperparts grey tinged olive; large bright orange-yellow bill and orange eye-ring, broad white submoustachials bordered with bold black malar stripes; bright orange flanks; rest of underparts white.
b Adult *verreauxi*: paler grey above than nominate, eye-ring and bill slightly deeper orange; legs and feet bright yellow.
c Juvenile: as adult but with pale buff streaks on upperparts and tips to wing-coverts, spotted on underparts.

101 Olive Thrush *Turdus olivaceus*　　　Text page 333

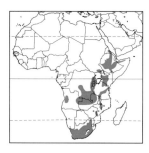

East Africa discontinuously south to C Angola, C Namibia and South Africa. Montane and lowland evergreen forests. See also Plate 29.
a Adult *roehli*: like *helleri* but dark olive-brown above and greyer on breast; dull orange centre of breast and flanks.
b Adult *helleri*: blackish-grey above; flight and tail feathers blackish; thin yellow eye-ring; flanks rufous-orange.
c Adult *ludoviciae*: head to nape and upper breast blackish; thin pale yellow eye-ring; rest of upperparts dark lead-grey; underparts also grey; bill, legs and eye-ring yellow.
d Juvenile *ludoviciae*: heavily spotted and streaked above; wing-coverts have whitish spots at tips; underparts dull grey-brown, mottled with whitish-buff and brown tips.

101a

101b

101c

101d

99a

99b

99c

98a

98b

JPPW

PLATE 31 ENDEMIC ISLAND THRUSHES

63 Tristan Thrush *Nesocichla eremita*   Text page 274

Tristan da Cunha. Sheltered valleys or gullies to plantations, orchards, thickets, moorlands and scattered trees.

a Adult *eremita*: brown above with pale orange-buff tips to wing-coverts, heavily blotched or streaked darker brown below.

b Adult *procax*: as nominate but slightly larger and more rufous-brown above, face mottled pale brown, broad pale orange at tips of median coverts; more and stronger orange on underwing.

c Juvenile *procax*: heavily and broadly streaked pale orange-buff above; broad pale orange-buff tips to tertials and wing-coverts; heavily mottled below.

100 Olivaceous Thrush· *Turdus olivaceofuscus*   Text page 332

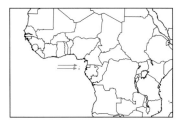

São Tomé and Príncipe. Lowland moist forest, woods and edges.

a Adult: olive-brown head and upperparts and barred or scalloped underparts.

b Juvenile: as adult but with fine pale buff flecks or streaks above and heavy dark brown spots below.

103 Comoro Thrush *Turdus bewsheri*   Text page 338

Comoro Islands. Evergreen primary forests and forest edges.

a Adult *bewsheri*: deep brown tinged olive above; chin and throat white becoming scaly on breast and belly.

b Adult *comorensis*: as nominate but slightly darker brown above; sides of chin and throat streaked brown; underparts unscaled with pale or dull brown on breast and flanks; centre of belly white.

c Adult *moheliensis*: like *comorensis* but browner spots and streaks on cheeks and ear-coverts; chin and throat spotted brown extending to warm brown breast with slightly browner tips.

103b

103c

103a

63c

63b

63a

100a

100b

PLATE 32 ARABIAN AND ASIAN THRUSHES

102 Yemen Thrush *Turdus menachensis* Text page 337

SW Arabia. Steep, rocky hillsides, slopes and wadis with vegetation, including acacia or juniper scrub.

a Adult: olive-brown above, paler below with greyish tinge to plumage; chin and throat heavily streaked brown.

b First-year: as adult or slightly darker; pale buff tips to wing-coverts and dark bill.

108 White-collared Blackbird *Turdus albocinctus* Text page 345

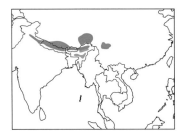

Himalayas from S Kashmir to SE Tibet, Bhutan, Assam and east to Szechwan; winters within breeding range and south to Manipur. Open conifer and mixed forests, forest edges and margins, also in dwarf rhododendron.

a Adult male: almost entirely black except for broad white collar and yellow bill.

b Adult female: browner than adult male with collar less distinct and pale buff to greyish-white. Some females darker with less distinct collar.

c Juvenile: lacks collar; dark upperparts heavily streaked with pale or rusty-buff; underparts heavily mottled with dark tips.

110 Grey-winged Blackbird *Turdus boulboul* 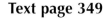 Text page 349

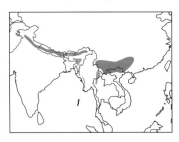

Himalayas from N Pakistan (not Kashmir) east to Bhutan, Arunachal Pradesh, Yunnan and SW Szechwan; outposts in Kwangsi and N Laos; winters at lower levels and south into Assam and Burma. Damp broadleaved forests with undergrowth, tall conifer forests, clearings.

a Adult male: almost entirely black except for broad pale greyish wing-panel; yellow bill.

b Adult female: olive-brown, slightly paler below with pale buffish-brown wing-panel.

c First-year male: like adult male but blackish-grey body and whitish chin and tips to underparts.

d Juvenile male: dark brown above streaked whitish-buff; heavily barred/mottled below; wings like adult; sexes separable early age.

108b

108a

108c

110d

110a

110b

110c

102a

102b

PLATE 33 RING OUZEL AND BLACKBIRD

109 Ring Ouzel *Turdus torquatus*   Text page 346

Scandinavia and Europe to Caucasus; winters S Europe, N Africa and Middle East. Wild rock-strewn uplands with stunted trees, heather moorlands with outcrops, crags or boulders.

a Adult male: jet-black with white crescent on breast and edges to wing-coverts, grey-edged flight feathers and underparts.

b Adult female: as male but brownish-black above and crescent on breast frequently obscured by dark tips; pale tips on body usually more extensive to undertail.

c Adult male *alpestris*: as nominate male but with broader, more extensive pale edges above and below.

d First-winter female: like adult female but breast-band may be entirely obscured by dark tips; broad greyish edges to wing-coverts and fringes to body feathers.

e Juvenile: blackish-brown above with pale buff streaks to head, mantle and scapulars, pale centre of chin and throat; no breast-band.

111 Blackbird *Turdus merula*   Text page 351

Canary Islands, Palearctic, Indian subcontinent and Oriental region (introduced Australia and New Zealand). Deciduous forests and woods, old hedgerows, orchards, gardens, parks, squares. See also Plate 34.

a Adult male: glossy black; orange-yellow bill and eye-ring, dark legs.

b Adult female: dark brown, slightly paler below, palest on chin and throat; sometimes warm brown on breast; bill mostly dull brown.

c Juvenile: mostly dark brown, heavily streaked with pale orange-buff; broad pale tips to wing-coverts; mottled pale buff and brown below.

d First-summer male: like adult male but dull eye-ring, all-dark bill, flight feathers and (some) wing-coverts browner-black.

PLATE 34 ASIAN BLACKBIRDS

111 Blackbird *Turdus merula*   Text page 351

Canary Islands, Palearctic, Indian subcontinent and Oriental region (introduced Australia and New Zealand). Deciduous forests and woods, old hedgerows, orchards, gardens, parks, squares. See also Plate 33.

a Adult *kinnisii*: entirely bluish slate-grey with orange-yellow bill and broad eye-ring; legs pale yellow.

b Adult male *nigropileus*: blackish-brown with black cap and slightly darker wings; orange-yellow bill and eye-ring; legs pale yellow.

c Adult female *nigropileus*: grey-brown often with paler area on chin and belly; cap usually slightly darker than body.

d Adult *spencei*: very like *nigropileus* but slightly darker brown on body and division of darker cap less distinct; broad grey edges to wings.

e Adult male *simillimus*: like *spencei* but more blackish-brown above, brown below; legs and feet orange-yellow.

f Adult female *simillimus*: like male but paler or greyer-brown.

g Adult female *aterrimus*: grey-brown above, buffish-brown below.

h Adult male *mandarinus*: black above and brownish-black below; larger than nominate.

i Adult female *mandarinus*: as male or sootier-brown; may be paler or browner on breast.

j Adult male *maximus*: largest race; all sooty-black, no eye-ring and usually dull yellow bill; legs as nominate.

111a

111c

111b

111d

111e

111f

111g

111i

111h

111j

PLATE 35 CHESTNUT THRUSH AND FIELDFARE

113 Chestnut Thrush *Turdus rubrocanus*   Text page 366

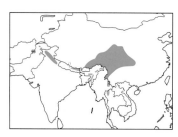

Himalayas of E Pakistan to SE Tibet, Arunachal Pradesh and C and SE China; in winter also to NW Burma and NW Thailand. Conifer and mixed forests.

a Adult male: head ash-grey (slightly paler on collar); chestnut body, black wings and tail.

b Adult female: as male but duller body, head also darker.

c Juvenile: head and face dark, pale buff streaks to scapulars, pale chin and throat, heavily spotted underparts.

d Adult male *gouldi*: head and face dark slate, chestnut on body brighter than on nominate.

e Adult female *gouldi*: as male but head and face grey, duller chestnut on body and wings and tail browner.

122 Fieldfare *Turdus pilaris*   Text page 387

Palearctic; Scotland to C Siberia; winters mostly in Europe and Caspian to Kazakhstan. Woods and mixed and deciduous forests, wintering in more open areas.

a Adult: grey head, dark chestnut back and wings; rusty-buff sides of breast and broad dark tips to most underparts; in flight shows large white patch on underwing.

b Juvenile: like adult but greyer above with narrow pale buff central shafts and dark tips; heavy black streaks and spots below.

122a

122b

113d

113e

113c

113a

113b

PLATE 36 PALE AND KESSLER'S THRUSHES

114 Kessler's Thrush *Turdus kessleri*   Text page 367

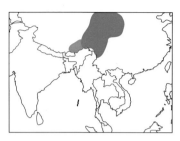

W and C China to Tibet; winters in breeding range and SE Tibet. Montane dwarf juniper and conifer forests, low rhododendron and willow scrub.

a Adult male: large; black head, wings and tail; pale buff mantle and sides of breast; chestnut back, scapulars, belly and flanks.

b Adult female: grey-brown head to breast; wings and tail darker; pale greyish-buff on mantle and sides of breast; light orange on rump, belly and flanks.

c Juvenile: similar to adult female but with pale buff streaks on head, prominent on scapulars.

117 Pale Thrush *Turdus pallidus*   Text page 372

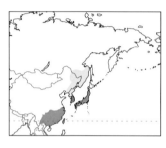

E Siberia, Amurland and Ussuriland to N Manchuria; winters in C and S Japan to Taiwan, S Korea and S China. Dense mixed and deciduous montane and submontane forests.

a Adult male: head and face grey; upperparts pale brown to light chestnut; flight feathers grey-brown; white tips to outer tail.

b Adult female: like adult male but duller or more olive and with streaks on whitish chin and throat.

c First-year male: like adult female but head and face olive-grey flecked paler; prominent pale submoustachial and dark malar, pale tips to greater coverts.

d Juvenile: mostly brown to olive-brown above heavily streaked buffish-orange; mottled below with dark brown spots.

PLATE 37 TICKELL'S AND JAPANESE THRUSHES

105 Tickell's Thrush *Turdus unicolor* **Text page 341**

Himalayas from N Pakistan to Sikkim and Bhutan; winters at lower levels from Pakistan to Bangladesh. Open broadleaved or mixed forest.

a Adult male: almost entirely ash-grey, slightly paler below and white undertail-coverts; orange-yellow bill, eye-ring and legs.

b Adult female: like male but browner with prominent pale submoustachial and dark malar.

c First-year male: like adult female or slightly greyer with pale buff tips to wing-coverts.

d Juvenile: like female but browner with pale buff streaks to upperparts and tips to wing-coverts; underparts heavily spotted black with orange on flanks.

107 Japanese Thrush *Turdus cardis* **Text page 344**

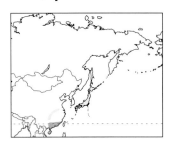

Breeds Japan and C China; winters S China from Yunnan to Hainan and Vietnam. Dense, dark forests on hills and mountains.

a Adult male: all-black upperparts to breast, black spots on white belly and flanks; yellow bill.

b Adult female: olive-brown grey-tinged upperparts and heavily streaked underparts, sides of breast tinged rust-orange.

c Juvenile: brown to olive-brown above heavily streaked with pale buff and dark tips; underparts mottled with brown spots.

d First-summer male: distinctive black head to breast; slate-grey above and boldly spotted below.

e First-year male (variation): resembles female, lacking black on chin to breast, but has all-grey head and upperparts tinged with olive, pale buff-brown tips to greater coverts.

PLATE 38 ASIAN *TURDUS* THRUSHES (1)

104 Grey-backed Thrush *Turdus hortulorum*   Text page 339

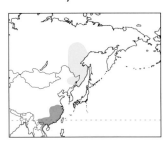

E Siberia to N China; winters SE China to N Vietnam. Oakwoods and mixed woods, also wintering in open woods, bamboo clumps, scrub.
a Adult male: grey upperparts to breast; bright orange sides to breast and flanks.
b Adult female: olive-brown head and upperparts (may be tinged grey), dark malar; bold spots on orange breast and flanks.
c Juvenile: as adult female but heavily streaked pale buff above and more extensively spotted brown below.

115 Grey-sided Thrush *Turdus feae*   Text page 368

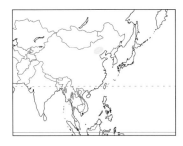

N China; winters NE India to E Burma and NW Thailand. Dense, damp broadleaf woods and forests on hills and mountains.
a Adult male: bright olive-brown above with white supercilium and cheeks; white chin and grey lower breast and flanks.
b First-year female: like adult male but sometimes brownish or tinged grey below.

116 Eyebrowed Thrush *Turdus obscurus*   Text page 369

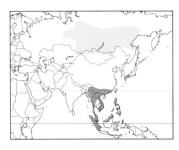

W Siberia to Kamchatka; winters S China, SE Asia to Philippines. Dense forests, extensive taiga and mixed forests.
a Adult male: grey head and face with white supercilium and cheeks; olive-brown above, orange breast and flanks.
b Adult female: like adult male but lacks grey on head, supercilium usually less distinct; paler or duller below.
c First-year male: like adult male but greyish-brown head and face, pale buff tips to greater coverts; often pale orange below.
d Juvenile: brown above, heavily streaked with pale orange-buff; dull orange with dark spots below.

PLATE 39 ASIAN *TURDUS* THRUSHES (2)

106 Black-breasted Thrush *Turdus dissimilis* **Text page 342**

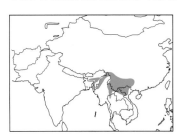

NE India, N Burma and S China to N Vietnam. Damp evergreen woods and forests, wintering at lower levels in scrub jungle.
a Adult male: black head to breast; slate-grey upperparts and bright orange belly and flanks.
b Adult female: dark olive-brown head and upperparts, whitish submoustachial and dark malar leading to spots on breast.
c Juvenile: heavily flecked or streaked pale buff above with well-defined pale buff tips to wing-coverts; spotted below.

118 Brown-headed Thrush *Turdus chrysolaus* **Text page 374**

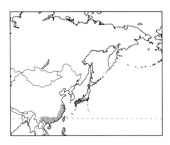

Kurile Islands, C Sakhalin and C Japan; winters S Japan to SE China and Taiwan. Dense forest and scrub, wintering in lowland cultivated areas, fields and scattered woodlands.
a Adult male: russet-brown above with blackish face to centre of breast, deep orange below with white belly to undertail-coverts.
b Adult female: as male but slightly paler above and duller below with brown face and streaks on throat.
c Juvenile: like female but heavily streaked pale buff above and brown spots below.

119 Izu Islands Thrush *Turdus celaenops* **Text page 375**

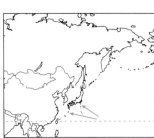

Japan. Deciduous and mixed woods of fir or laurel forests, open secondary woods, orchards and large gardens.
a Adult male: black head to breast, russet-brown above and deep orange below with whitish belly.
b Adult female: as male but head duller with whitish chin and throat.
c Juvenile: mostly russet-brown above with large pale buff streaks and spotted with brown below; pale submoustachial.

PLATE 40 DARK-THROATED THRUSH

120 Dark-throated Thrush *Turdus ruficollis*   Text page 377

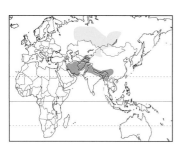

W and C Siberia, W Mongolia and NW China; winters Iran to Kazakhstan to S China and N Burma. Conifer and deciduous forests, undergrowth of dense taiga forest, wintering in grassy areas, forest edges and rhododendron thickets.

a Adult male *atrogularis*: grey upperparts, black face and breast, white belly and flanks and pale yellow base to bill.

b Adult female *atrogularis*: slightly duller or more olive upperparts, dark face and whitish tips to chin and black on breast, some dark streaks on flanks.

c First-year male *atrogularis*: like adult male but pale tips to wing-coverts, whitish sides to throat and pale tips to black on throat and breast; bill duller and less extensively yellow.

d First-year female *atrogularis*: like same-age male but duller or more olive-tinged above, black streaks below extending to flanks.

e *atrogularis* **tail pattern**: all dark and shows no orange or red.

f Adult male *ruficollis*: deep red or reddish-chestnut on face (including supercilium) to breast, outer tail also rufous-red; belly and flanks off-white; upperparts as *atrogularis* or slightly paler grey.

g Adult female *ruficollis*: as male but red on face and tail less extensive; may be streaked blackish on throat and breast; chin whitish.

h First-year male *ruficollis*: like adult male but red on face and breast paler, less extensive and usually mottled with pale or whitish tips.

i *ruficollis* **tail pattern**: dark brown central pair and outerwebs to several inner feathers but most outers are rufous-red.

j First-year *ruficollis x atrogularis*: chin to breast mottled warm brown to purple-black; malar also black infused with red.

k Adult *ruficollis x atrogularis*: chin to breast purple-black; tail variable from normal to deeper rufous or chestnut and may have darker webs to outer feathers.

l Juvenile *atrogularis*: mostly grey above, heavily streaked pale buff on head and upperparts, prominently on mantle and scapulars; breast may have buffish wash heavily mottled with blackish spots.

120c

120b

120a

120d

120e

120g

120f

120h

120i

120j

120k

120l

PLATE 41 DUSKY THRUSH

121 Dusky Thrush *Turdus naumanni* Text page 381

C and E Siberia south to N Mongolia; winters Ussuriland, N Korea, China, SE Tibet and NE India. Open forests, woods and dwarf willows, wintering in open forests, cultivated areas and parks. See also Plate 42.

a Adult male *naumanni*: brown or grey-brown upperparts, bright rufous edges to scapulars, warm brown rump to base of tail; edges to flight feathers warm brown to rufous, underparts mostly rufous.

b Adult female *naumanni*: as male but lacks rufous on scapulars and edges to flight feathers, tail less rufous; paler on chin and throat with broad dark malar, rufous on underparts variable.

c First-winter *naumanni*: like adult male above but underparts more like female and rufous variable.

d Juvenile: heavily streaked with pale buff and dark brown tips above; wings and rump to tail like adult; black spotting below.

e Adult male *naumanni* variation: some males in breeding season (probably first-years) have head and face more as adult female.

f Adult male *eunomus*: black on head and upperparts broken by broad white supercilium, chin and throat; rich brown fringes to scapulars and wing-panel; tail mostly dark brown edged chestnut; underparts heavily black fringed broadly white.

g Adult female *eunomus*: as male but upperparts much browner and lacks heavy contrast, also reduced extent of warm brown edges, and wing-panel broken into broad brown edges to feathers; underparts similar but usually less bold.

h *naumanni* × *eunomus* intergrade: variable but upperparts like *naumanni* and black on underparts infused with reddish.

i First-winter male *eunomus*: as adult female but wings like adult male.

j Adult male *eunomus* **head, worn plumage**: much paler or grey-brown.

k Adult male *naumanni* × *eunomus* **intergrade**: head and upperparts as *eunomus* but underparts show reddish patches of *naumanni*.

121b

121c

121a

121d

121e

121g

121h

121f

121j

121i

121k

PLATE 42 DARK-THROATED AND DUSKY THRUSH VARIATIONS AND INTERGRADES

120 Dark-throated Thrush *Turdus ruficollis* **Text page 377**

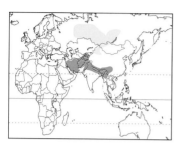

W and C Siberia, W Mongolia and NW China; winters Iran to Kazakhstan to S China and N Burma. Conifer and deciduous forests, undergrowth of dense taiga forest, wintering in grassy areas, forest edges and rhododendron thickets.

a Adult male *ruficollis* × *atrogularis*: normal upperparts but has red in tail and black on breast also infused with reddish-brown.

b First-winter female *ruficollis*: as same-age female *atrogularis* but with rusty-brown streaks on breast and reddish in tail.

c First-winter female *atrogularis*: as same-age male *atrogularis* but usually with whiter throat and lighter streaks below; no red in tail.

d First-winter female *ruficollis*: can be as extensively red on throat and breast as adults.

121 Dusky Thrush *Turdus naumanni* **Text page 381**

C and E Siberia south to N Mongolia; winters Ussuriland, N Korea, China, SE Tibet and NE India. Open forests, woods and dwarf willows, wintering in open forests, cultivated areas and parks. See also Plate 41.

a First-winter male *naumanni*: showing variable extent of pale throat and rufous on underparts.

b First-winter female *naumanni*: as same-age *T. ruficollis* but more extensive spots on breast, few narrow streaks; breast and flanks with rufous or orange centres or streaks; rump to tail as adult.

c First-winter male *naumanni* × *eunomus*: head and upperparts as *eunomus* but browner above, underparts with reddish-brown centres.

d First-winter male *eunomus*: as adult male but upperparts greyer and rich brown wing-panel incomplete; black below more broken.

e Adult *naumanni* × *eunomus*: as adult *naumanni* above but darker, with rich brown wing-panel, extensively reddish-brown below.

f First-winter female *naumanni*: variably brown to rufous-brown above, lightly spotted black on breast and reduced orange or rufous below.

120a

120b

120c

120d

121b

121a

121c

121d

121e

121f

PLATE 43 EUROPEAN AND ASIAN THRUSHES

123 Redwing *Turdus iliacus*

Text page 389

Palearctic, Iceland to E Siberia; winters Europe to S Caspian. Birch or mixed conifer woods, wintering in woods, copses and open fields.
a Adult: grey-brown above, long white supercilium, heavily streaked underparts with rust-red flanks.
b Juvenile: like adult but with broad pale buff streaks on crown to mantle and scapulars and underparts heavily spotted black.
c Adult *coburni*: as nominate except heavy brown tinge above and broader streaks below.
d Juvenile *coburni*: as nominate but browner; dusky olive on breast.
e Adult underwing: rust-red to deep rufous.

124 Song Thrush *Turdus philomelos*

Text page 392

W Palearctic to C Siberia; winters S Europe, N Africa and Middle East (introduced SE Australia and New Zealand). Woods, copses, thickets, hedgerows, parks and gardens.
a Adult: warm brown above with paler flecked face and indistinct tips to wing-coverts; black spots below.
b Juvenile: as adult or slightly paler with pale buff streaks and orange-buff tips to wing-coverts.
c Adult underwing: deep yellowish-buff.

125 Chinese Song Thrush *Turdus mupinensis*

Text page 396

C and S China. Montane broadleaved and mixed forest and wood-land.
a Adult: like Song Thrush (no overlap) but with well-defined face pattern, pale tips to wing-coverts and larger spots below.
b Juvenile: as adult but heavily streaked pale buff above; washed buffish below.

126 Mistle Thrush *Turdus viscivorus*

Text page 397

W Palearctic to C Siberia, C Asia and W Himalayas; winters in south of breeding range and in N Africa to N Pakistan. Woods, open forests, fields, orchards, parks and gardens.
a Adult: large size, pale grey-brown above, boldly spotted below with white corners to tail.
b Juvenile: as adult but with pale buff spots and streaks above, broad pale tips to wing-coverts and less heavily spotted below.

PLATE 44 ISLAND THRUSH (1)

112 Island Thrush *Turdus poliocephalus*   Text page 357

Indonesia to SW Pacific. Montane temperate, pine and cloud-forest, also above the timberline in sparse or dense scrub, tree heather, ferns, grassland and boulderfields.

a Adult *niveiceps* (Taiwan): white head; rest of upperparts jet-black, centre of breast black becoming cinnamon or orange-chestnut on belly and flanks.

b Adult female *niveiceps*: mostly brown above, head and face with varying amounts of white; usually white supercilium behind eye.

c Juvenile *niveiceps*: as adult female but paler buffish head and streaks and tips to wing-coverts; dull orange-buff with black tips below.

d Adult male *deningeri* (Seram): head creamy-white or tinged buff; rest of plumage brownish-black.

e Adult *poliocephalus* (Norfolk Island; probably extinct): head to upper breast pale grey to light buffish; rest of plumage black with white streaks on undertail.

f Adult *ruficeps* (Fiji): head to upper breast light golden-brown to rufous-buff; rest of plumage black or glossy black.

g Adult *tempesti* (Fiji): pale grey head to breast, slightly darker on crown; rest of plumage black or brownish-black.

h Adult *albifrons* (Vanuatu): head to breast white or creamy-white; rest of plumage black with white tips to vent and undertail-coverts.

i Adult *pritzbueri* (Vanuatu; probably extinct): like *albifrons*, head to breast creamy- or greyish-white; rest of plumage black or blackish-brown.

112c

112a

112d

112b

112e

112f

112g

112h

112i

PLATE 45 ISLAND THRUSH (2)

112 Island Thrush *Turdus poliocephalus*　　　Text page 357

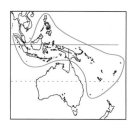

Indonesia to SW Pacific. Montane temperate, pine and cloud-forest, also above the timberline in sparse or dense scrub, tree heather, ferns, grassland and boulderfields.

a Adult *vitiensis* (Vanua Levu, Fiji): dark grey crown and upperparts, paler face to breast, dark grey belly to undertail-coverts, tinged rufous on belly; legs and feet bright yellow.

b Adult *xanthopus* (New Caledonia): dark brown tinged warmer brown above, cinnamon-brown below.

c Adult *vinitinctus* (Lord Howe Island; Extinct): head grey-brown, rest of upperparts russet-brown tinged olive, vinous- or cinnamon-brown below.

d Adult *malindangensis* (NW Mindanao, Philippines): dark grey-brown above, paler grey chin to upper belly, flanks brownish.

e Adult *erythropleurus* (Christmas Island, Indian Ocean): head and upperparts olive-brown, throat and breast pale grey, lower breast to flanks orange.

f Adult *javanicus* (central Java): mostly dark brown, slightly paler or buff-brown on face to belly.

g Adult *carbonarius* (central New Guinea): almost entirely blackish except for slightly browner-black head to breast.

h Adult *nigrorum* (Negros, Philippines): head and upperparts dark grey-brown, paler or lighter grey below.

i Adult *thomassoni* (N Luzon, Philippines): glossy black except for brownish-black head, nape and breast.

j Adult *versteegi* (W New Guinea): blackish-brown except for slightly paler head to nape and breast.

PLATE 46 ISLAND THRUSH (3)

112 Island Thrush *Turdus poliocephalus* Text page 357

Indonesia to SW Pacific. Montane temperate, pine and cloud-forest, also above the timberline in sparse or dense scrub, tree heather, ferns, grassland and boulderfields.

a Adult *whiteheadi* (E Java): grey-brown head to breast and upperparts; belly and flanks rusty-rufous; undertail-coverts streaked.

b Adult *indrapurae* (C Sumatra): head brown, becoming darker brown on upperparts and breast; belly and flanks rufous.

c Adult *hygroscopus* (C Sulawesi): head and face to breast pale brown, rest of upperparts dark brown; belly and flanks rich rufous-orange.

d Adult *seebohmi* (N Borneo): dark sooty-brown head, breast and upperparts, rufous belly and flanks.

e Adult *fumidus* (W Java): head and upperparts brown, slightly paler on breast and rufous-orange on belly and flanks.

f Adult *celebensis* (SW Sulawesi): head and face to breast dusky olive-brown, upperparts dark grey-brown; belly and flanks deep orange.

g Adult *katanglad* (Mindanao, Philippines): head and upperparts brown, chin to breast pale buffish-brown, upper flanks and belly rufous.

h Adult *schlegelii* (W Timor): head and face to breast grey-brown, upperparts dark grey-brown tinged olive; rest of underparts rust-orange.

i Adult *mindorensis* (Mindoro, Philippines): head to breast pale grey-brown, rest of upperparts sooty-brown; sides of lower breast brown, flanks rufous.

j Adult *layardi* (Fiji): olive-brown head and upperparts, chin to breast pale grey, brown on breast, rufous-orange on belly and flanks.

112a

112b

112c

112d

112e

112f

112g

112h

112i

112j

PLATE 47 ISLAND THRUSH (4)

112 Island Thrush *Turdus poliocephalus* Text page 357

Indonesia to SW Pacific. Montane temperate, pine and cloud-forest, also above the timberline in sparse or dense scrub, tree heather, ferns, grassland and boulderfields.

a Adult male *efatensis* (Vanuatu): sooty-blackish, browner on nape, chin, sides of neck to breast; vent and edges to undertail whitish.

b Adult female *efatensis*: as male but dark brown with rich rufous-buff on belly and flanks.

c Adult *placens* (Vanuatu): head and upperparts dull brown; chin to breast grey-brown; belly and flanks warm rufous-buff to chestnut in females; white tips to undertail.

d Adult *whitneyi* (Vanuatu): entirely sooty-black, slightly paler or browner on chin to breast.

e Adult *becki* (Vanuatu): brownish-black tinged grey below; white tips to undertail-coverts.

f Adult *bougainvillei* (Solomon Islands): blackish-brown or tinged grey on head to breast.

g Adult *mareensis* (New Caledonia; Extinct): black with blackish-brown underparts and white tips to undertail.

h Adult *vanikorensis* (Vanuatu): sooty blackish-brown, perhaps tinged slightly greyer below, and white tips to undertail.

i Adult *hades* (Fiji): entirely glossy black except for bright yellow bill, legs and eye-ring.

j Adult *malekulae* (Vanuatu): blackish-brown or tinged grey-brown below, white tips to undertail-coverts.

k First-year *kulambangrae* (Solomon Islands): entirely blackish-brown (as adult), but with rufous-buff tips to wing-coverts and underparts.

PLATE 48 AMERICAN ROBIN

161 American Robin *Turdus migratorius*   **Text page 440**

N America to Mexico; winters mostly in south of range. Forests and woods from bottomlands to timberline, also tundra, meadows, alder thickets, wooded farms, hedges, fields, lawns, gardens.

a Adult male: blackish head with broad broken eye-ring, dark grey upperparts, white tips to blackish tail, streaked chin and throat and deep orange-rufous underparts.

b Adult female: like male (some inseparable) but paler, head less dark, tinged browner above, duller orange below with pale tips.

c Juvenile: mostly brown above with extensive pale spots (with dark tips) or streaks, and dull orange with blackish spots below.

d First-winter male: more like adult but with incomplete sooty-brown head, greyish-white tips to wing-coverts, and underparts more like female with whitish tips.

e Adult male *achrusterus*: black on head tipped pale grey; upperparts slightly browner or dusky-brown; white tips to tail indistinct; underparts paler, on average, and tawnier-rufous.

f Adult female *achrusterus*: as male or slightly browner on head and broadly tipped pale grey; underparts slightly sandier, usually with paler tips.

g Adult male *nigrideus*: darker on head and upperparts; tail as nominate; slightly deeper rufous below; chin and throat more heavily streaked and undertail-coverts grey.

h Adult male *confinis*: palest race; uniform pale grey-brown head and upperparts; few or no white spots to tip of tail (but white edge to tip of outermost feather); short whitish supercilium; underparts buffish to yellow (especially in female).

161a

161b

161c

161d

161e

161f

161g

161h

PLATE 49 CENTRAL AND SOUTH AMERICAN THRUSHES

140 Chestnut-bellied Thrush *Turdus fulviventris*   Text page 415

Andes of E Colombia and W Venezuela, also S Colombia to N Peru. Cloud-forest and secondary woodland.

a Adult: head black, upperparts slate-grey tinged brown; breast grey and bright orange on rest of underparts.

b Juvenile: duller than adult with dark streaks on head, pale orange-buff streaks on scapulars and tips to wing-coverts; spotted below.

141 Rufous-bellied Thrush *Turdus rufiventris*   Text page 416

N Brazil to N Argentina. Lowland humid woodlands, groves, plantations, forest clearings, patches of scrubby bushes.

a Adult male: olive-brown head and upperparts, streaked throat and tawny-buff upper breast becoming rufous-orange on belly.

b First-year: as adult but with pale orange-buff tips to wing-coverts and diffuse brown spots on duller breast and belly.

156 White-throated Thrush *Turdus assimilis*   Text page 434

Mexico to N Ecuador. Moist lowland and foothill forests and lower-elevation cloud-forests.

a Adult *assimilis* (see also Plate 50): dark brown tinged olive above; chin and throat boldly streaked dark brown; bright yellow eye-ring; white crescent on upper breast; pale buffish to olive-grey below with buff-brown on lower breast and flanks.

b Juvenile: as adult but eye-ring brown, pale buff streaks on head, orange-buff tips to wing-coverts; warm buff-brown below with dark brown tips.

162 Rufous-collared Thrush *Turdus rufitorques*   Text page 443

S Mexico to El Salvador. Cloud-forest and pine–oak woods and woodland with brush or scrub, pastures and edges of cultivation.

a Adult male: very distinctive; mostly black with broad rufous-orange collar extending to chin and breast.

b Adult female: mostly brown or greyish-brown, pale indistinct orange-buff collar, lightly streaked on throat.

c Juvenile: dark upperparts heavily streaked pale buffish-orange above and spotted dark brown below.

162a

162b

141b

162c

141a

140a

156b

156a

140b

PLATE 50 WHITE-THROATED AND WHITE-NECKED THRUSHES

156 White-throated Thrush *Turdus assimilis*   Text page 434

Mexico to N Ecuador. Moist lowland and foothill forests and lower-elevation cloud-forests.

a Adult *assimilis* (see also Plate 49): dark brown tinged olive above; chin and throat boldly streaked dark brown; white crescent on upper breast; pale buffish to olive-grey below with buff-brown on lower breast and flanks.

b Adult *daguae*: upperparts deep brownish-olive tinged rust-brown; breast to belly and flanks sepia-brown, narrow eye-ring and dark bill.

c Adult *lecauchen*: upperparts dark olive-grey, bill and eye-ring bright yellow, streaks on throat blackish-brown; breast to flanks grey or olive-grey tinged peachy-buff.

d Adult *oblitus*: like lecauchen but more heavily tinged olive-brown above; breast, upper belly and flanks buffish-brown; legs and feet yellow.

e Adult *rubicundus*: variable olive to heavily rufous-brown above; breast and flanks dull olive or olive-grey, latter sometimes faintly tinged orange-buff.

157 White-necked Thrush *Turdus albicollis*   Text page 436

South America; Colombia to Brazil and NE Argentina. Undergrowth of rain-forest, mature second-growth areas and montane forest.

a Adult: head and face dark brown becoming brownish-olive above; heavily streaked chin and throat, white crescent on upper breast; breast greyish becoming orange-rufous on flanks.

b Juvenile: as adult but duller, heavily streaked with pale orange-buff and tips to wing-coverts; throat pale with dark malar and mottled with dark brown spots.

c Adult *spodiolaemus*: as nominate but more rufous-olive above; black streaks on throat broader or heavier.

d Adult *crotopezus*: like *spodiolaemus* but darker on mantle to rump; longest uppertail-coverts grey-brown; breast to upper belly dingy grey tinged buffish, flanks tawny or tinged olive; bill mostly dark.

157b

157a

157d

157c

156b

156d

156a

156c

156e

PLATE 51 SOUTH AMERICAN THRUSHES (1)

143 Pale-breasted Thrush *Turdus leucomelas*   Text page 418

Colombia to Brazil, S Peru and NE Argentina. Humid forest edges and clearings.
a Adult: grey head and rust-brown upperparts; greyish-buff breast to flanks and white centre of belly and vent; bill olive-yellow.
b Juvenile: as adult but flecked or streaked pale yellowish-buff above; pale buff tips to wing-coverts and spotted below.

146 Black-billed Thrush *Turdus ignobilis*   Text page 422

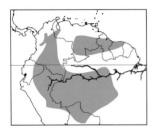

Colombia to Surinam and Ecuador. Forest edges to wooded areas, grassy plains, parks, pastures and gardens.
a Adult: almost entirely olive-brown with white throat (streaked dark brown) and belly to undertail-coverts; black bill.
b Juvenile: as adult but flecked or streaked with pale buff above and spotted below.
c Adult *debilis*: as nominate or slightly darker but throat whiter; breast and flanks paler grey; centre of belly to undertail creamy-white.

152 Yellow-eyed Thrush *Turdus nudigenis*   Text page 430

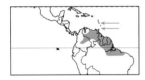

Lesser Antilles to Venezuela and NE Brazil. Gallery forest and rainforest edges, lightly wooded areas, clearings, bamboo clumps.
a Adult: generally plain olive-brown, paler olive on breast; distinctive broad yellowish-orange eye-ring.
b Juvenile: as adult but with pale buff flecks or streaks above and tips to wing-coverts, spotted below; eye-ring narrower.

153 Ecuadorian Thrush *Turdus maculirostris*   Text page 431

W Ecuador to NW Peru. Deciduous and semi-deciduous forest edges, open areas with grass and scattered trees.
Adult: very like (out-of-range) Yellow-eyed Thrush but upperparts less brown and has narrow eye-ring.

154 Unicoloured Thrush *Turdus haplochrous*   Text page 432

N Bolivia. Lowland woodland and seasonally flooded riverine forest.
Adult: olive-brown upperparts, breast to belly brownish and indistinct streaks on throat.

PLATE 52 SOUTH AMERICAN THRUSHES (2)

144 Creamy-bellied Thrush *Turdus amaurochalinus*   Text page 419

Brazil to C Argentina. Lowland forest edges, clearings and small woods, edges of cultivation, parks and large gardens.
a Adult: olive-brown above with bright yellow bill (breeding), black lores, streaked throat, buffish breast, creamy-white belly.
b Adult: grey-breasted form.
c Juvenile: browner than adult with fine pale streaks and tips to wing-coverts; buffish below heavily mottled dark brown.

147 Lawrence's Thrush *Turdus lawrencii*   Text page 423

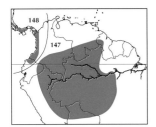

S Venezuela to N Bolivia and C Brazil. Wooded swamps, along streams, seasonally flooded dense rainforests.
a Adult male: almost uniform olive-brown, slightly paler below, white belly to undertail; prominent eye-ring and yellow bill.
b Adult female: slightly paler below with narrow eye-ring and duller bill.

148 Pale-vented Thrush *Turdus obsoletus*   Text page 424

Costa Rica to Colombia. Humid and wet forests, gallery forests and tall secondary forests. (See map above.)
a Adult: dark brown with rufous tinge above and white lower belly to undertail; in flight shows bright orange underwing-coverts.
b Juvenile: duller above than adult with pale buff streaks and tips to wing-coverts; mottled brown on breast; belly and flanks paler.

149 Cocoa Thrush *Turdus fumigatus*   Text page 426

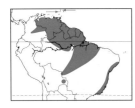

Lesser Antilles to C and E Brazil. Dense tropical forest, secondary woodlands, gallery forests, forest edges and clearings, open woodlands, plantations. See also Plate 53.
a Adult: almost entirely warm rufous- or cinnamon-brown; throat whitish streaked with brown, bill dark.
b Juvenile: darker than adult with orange-buff streaks above and tips to wing-coverts; breast mottled yellowish- or orange-buff and brown.

150 Hauxwell's Thrush *Turdus hauxwelli*   Text page 427

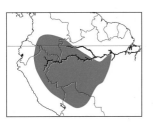

Colombia to Peru and C Brazil. Dense humid lowland primary and secondary forest.
Adult: head and upperparts dark brown; throat white streaked dark brown; breast warm earth-brown; belly white.

148b

148a

144b

144a

144c

150

147b

147a

149b

149a

Clive Byers

PLATE 53 CARIBBEAN THRUSHES (1)

128 Grand Cayman Thrush *Turdus ravidus*   Text page 401

Formerly Grand Cayman Island. Dense lowland forests. Extinct.
a Adult: almost entirely deep ash-grey with white undertail-coverts; bill, legs and eye-ring coral-red.
b Tail pattern: dark grey tail with broad white tips to outer four feathers.

129 Red-legged Thrush *Turdus plumbeus*   Text page 401

Bahamas to Dominica. Edges of rainforest and coastal woodland, mangrove, scrub, pinewoods and coffee plantations.
a Adult *rubripes*: slate-grey upperparts, paler below with black tail and white tips to outer feathers; white chin and submoustachial; orange-buff flanks.
b Juvenile *rubripes*: as adult but mottled with darker tips to head and pale buffish-orange tips to wing-coverts; spotted below.
c Tail pattern *ardosiaceus*: broad white tips to outer tail feathers.
d Adult *plumbeus*: short white submoustachial and chin divided by extensive area of black throat to breast; bill black to dusky red.
e Adult *ardosiaceus*: slightly paler grey above and below and streaked black and white chin. Bill, eye-ring, legs and feet coral-red.

149 Cocoa Thrush *Turdus fumigatus*   Text page 426

Lesser Antilles to C and E Brazil. Dense tropical forest, open, secondary and gallery woodland, edges, clearings and plantations. See also Plate 52.
a Adult *personus*: dark face and mostly brown upperparts, paler buff-brown below with indistinct streaked throat; grey-brown bill.
b Adult *aquilonalis*: paler brown and less rufous above with warm brown edges to wing-coverts; chin and throat white heavily streaked brown; underparts paler or more orange-brown.

129a

129b

129c

129d

129e

128b

128a

149b

149a

PLATE 54 CENTRAL AMERICAN THRUSHES (1)

151 Clay-coloured Thrush *Turdus grayi*   **Text page 428**

Extreme SE Texas and N Mexico to N Colombia. Moist to damp lowland forest, woods and edges of cultivation, coffee and banana plantations.

a Adult: dull or clay-brown with darker upperparts, pale throat diffusely streaked darker, rest of underparts pale orange-buff; dull greenish-yellow bill.

b Juvenile: as adult with fine pale buff streaks to most upperparts and median coverts; fine pale buff tips to median and greater coverts. Underparts mottled dull brown, belly yellowish-orange barred with diffuse dull-brown tips.

c Adult *casius*: as nominate but browner-olive above and deep clay or buff-brown on breast, flanks and underwing-coverts; paler or orange-buff on belly to undertail.

d Adult *incomptus*: duller than nominate and similar to *casius*; flanks brownish washed grey.

158 Rufous-backed Thrush *Turdus rufopalliatus*   **Text page 438**

Mexico. Deciduous and mixed forests to woodland edge, dense shrubbery and scrub; also plantations.

a Adult: cinnamon or deep rufous on upper- and underparts; grey head and dark grey wings and tail; chin and throat white with black streaks.

b Juvenile: as adult but duller above, with buff flecks and shaft-streaks on crown and nape, buffish streaks and dark fringes on mantle to scapulars, broad orange central streaks on median coverts, and browner greater coverts with pale tips.

159 Grayson's Thrush *Turdus graysoni*   **Text page 439**

Tres Marias Islands, W Mexico. Dry or semi-arid forests, also plantations.

Adult: like Rufous-backed Thrush, but duller above; head and face tinged olive, mantle and back pale cinnamon tinged olive; grey or grey-brown scapulars and rump; breast greyish-buff becoming warmer on flanks and off-white on centre of belly.

151a

151c

151d

151b

159

158a

158b

PLATE 55 CARIBBEAN THRUSHES (2)

64 Forest Thrush *Cichlherminia lherminieri*   Text page 275

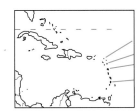

Guadeloupe to Montserrat, West Indies. Primary and secondary evergreen rainforest and undergrowth.
a Adult: head and upperparts warm brown; broad pale eye-ring and pale eye; oval-shaped chevrons and brown fringes to feathers below.
b Juvenile: as adult but darker with indistinct pale streaks above and smaller, more contrasting spotted pattern below.
c Adult *dominicensis*: darker brown on head and upperparts; breast with fewer blackish-brown tips forming smaller chevrons on breast, larger spots with whitish centres on flanks.

127 White-chinned Thrush *Turdus aurantius*   Text page 400

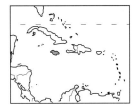

Jamaica. Wooded hills and mountains, citrus and banana groves.
a Adult male: dark grey head and upperparts, paler grey-brown below with distinctive white patch on inner wing-coverts.
b First-year: as adult but duller, with diffuse dark tips below.

155 White-eyed Thrush *Turdus jamaicensis*   Text page 433

Jamaica. Wooded hills, mountains, gullies and ravines, sometimes coffee plantations.
Adult: brown head, whitish eye; slate-grey upperparts and dull buff underparts with white upper breast.

160 La Selle Thrush *Turdus swalesi*   Text page 439

Hispaniola. Understorey of subtropical rain- and cloud-forests.
a Adult: head, upperparts and upper breast blackish; rufous lower breast and flanks, whitish streaks on chin.
b Adult *dodae*: as nominate but mantle heavily tinged olive.

160a

160b

127b

127a

155

64a

64c

64b

PLATE 56 SOUTH AMERICAN THRUSHES (3)

135 Andean Slaty-Thrush *Turdus nigriceps*   **Text page 410**

Ecuador and NW Peru to NW Argentina. Humid montane forests.
a Adult male: slate-grey upperparts with slightly darker head, narrow pale eye-ring, heavily streaked chin and throat and paler ash-grey underparts.
b Adult female: warm brown upperparts, face flecked paler and eye-ring narrow; breast variably brown to warm brown, paler on belly to undertail.

136 Eastern Slaty-Thrush *Turdus subalaris*   **Text page 411**

S Brazil to extreme NE Argentina. Humid and dense riverine forest, woodland canopy, plantations.
Adult: like Andean but upperparts more uniform, tinged bluish; white crescent on upper breast, pale ash-grey breast to flanks.

137 Plumbeous-backed Thrush *Turdus reevei*   **Text page 412**

W Ecuador to NW Peru. Forests and secondary woodlands, edges and clearings.
a Adult male: blue-grey head and upperparts, pale eye; throat with dark streaks, breast white to greyish-buff, flanks peach-buff.
b Adult female: as male but slightly browner on head and face.
c Juvenile: heavily streaked above with pale orange-buff and dark tips and scaled tips to underparts.

139 Marañón Thrush *Turdus maranonicus*   **Text page 414**

S Ecuador to NW Peru. Dry deciduous woodlands, also forest edge, mimosa scrub and irrigated agricultural areas and mango groves.
a Adult: earth-brown upperparts (including face) with slightly darker tips forming indistinct scaly pattern; underparts white with extensive dark brown crescents on breast and flanks.
b Adult: front view.
c Juvenile/first-year: as adult but with fine streaks above and fewer dark tips; pale orange-buff tips to wing-coverts and broad dark bars below.

PLATE 57 CENTRAL AMERICAN THRUSHES (2)

131 Sooty Thrush *Turdus nigrescens*　　　　　Text page 404

Costa Rica to W Panama. High-altitude volcanic lavafields, páramo, bushy areas of scrub, bogs and pastures.

a Adult male: entirely sooty-black with whitish eye and orange-yellow bill and legs.

b Adult female: as male but deep chocolate-brown on head and body.

c Juvenile: sooty-brown above with pale yellowish streaks; median and greater coverts have yellowish-orange spots at tips; underparts spotted blackish-brown on yellowish ground colour; pale eye.

133 Black Thrush *Turdus infuscatus*　　　　　Text page 407

Mexico to Honduras. Humid evergreen and pine-oak cloud-forests and forest edges.

a Adult male: all black with bright yellow bill, eye-ring and legs.

b Adult female: almost entirely brown with warmer brown underparts and streaked throat.

c Juvenile: similar to adult female with pale orange-buff streaks to head and upperparts and pale orange tips to wing-coverts; underparts spotted dark brown or blackish.

d First-summer male: similar to adult with grey-brown head and upperparts except for some black feathers on mantle and back, underparts greyish with black tips on belly.

145 Mountain Thrush *Turdus plebejus*　　　　　Text page 420

Mexico to W Panama. Tall evergreen cloud-forests, open woodlands and forest edges.

a Adult: almost entirely uniform dark or dull olive-brown except for faint streaks on chin and throat and paler centre of belly; bill black.

b Juvenile: as adult but with pale buff streaks to upperparts and pale tips to median and greater coverts; underparts have dark brown spots.

c Adult *differens*: slightly more olive or olive-brown on upperparts; underparts more heavily tinged light olive-brown.

133c

133a

133b

145b

133d

145c

145a

131c

131a

131b

Clive Byers

PLATE 58 SOUTH AMERICAN THRUSHES (4)

130 Chiguanco Thrush *Turdus chiguanco* Text page 403

Andes of C Ecuador to WC Argentina and C Chile. Open dry country, short grass areas with scattered bushes or cacti.

a Adult: almost entirely grey-brown tinged olive, slightly paler below with streaks on throat; bill bright yellow.

b Juvenile: like adult but pale buff steaks to crown and mantle and tips to wing-coverts; heavy mottling on face and underparts.

c Adult male *anthracinus*: almost entirely sooty-black; bill and legs orange-yellow.

d Juvenile *anthracinus*: like nominate juvenile but generally darker above and duller below.

132 Great Thrush *Turdus fuscater* Text page 406

N Colombia and N Venezuela to SE Peru and NW Bolivia. Humid cloud-forest and Polylepis patches, edges and clearings, hedges, isolated scrub.

a Adult: large; appears long-tailed; head and upperparts brown, slightly paler or more olive below; yellow bill and eye-ring.

b First-year: like adult but slightly paler with orange-buff streaks and dark tips, mottled with pale buff streaks and dark tips below.

c Adult *cacozelus*: as nominate but paler olive-brown above and buffish-olive on breast and flanks.

d Adult *ockendeni*: sooty-black or deep blackish-brown above, underparts uniform dark brown; bill and legs yellowish-orange.

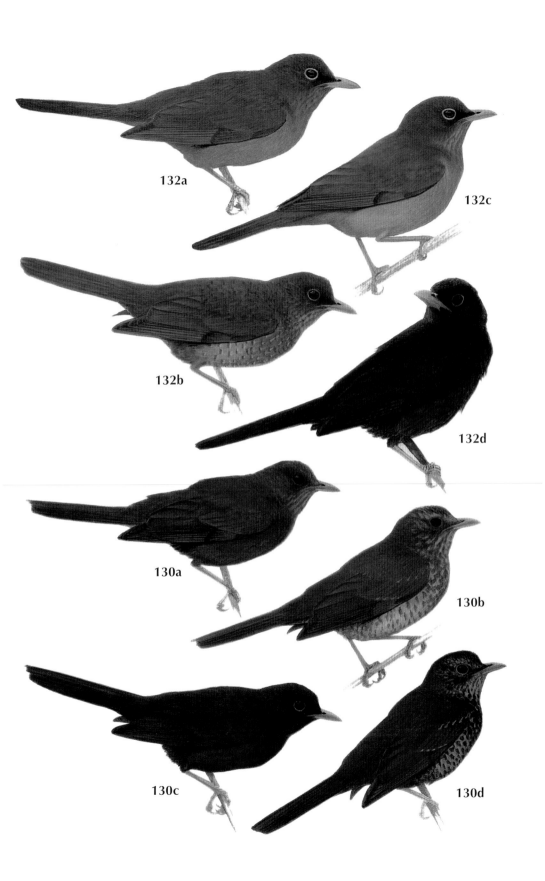

132a

132c

132b

132d

130a

130b

130c

130d

PLATE 59 *PLATYCICHLA* THRUSHES AND GLOSSY-BLACK THRUSH

94 Yellow-legged Thrush *Platycichla flavipes* Text page 322

Discontinuous; N, E and SE South America, Trinidad and Tobago. Humid rain- and cloud-forests, deciduous and secondary woods, coffee plantations, large gardens with tall trees.

a Adult male: black head to breast, wings and tail; slate-grey elsewhere and with bright yellow legs, bill and eye-ring.

b Adult female: warm brown head and upperparts, paler or more gingery on chin and throat and orange-buff flanks.

c Adult female *polionota*: as nominate but slightly darker or colder above; duller below, belly paler or whitish.

d Adult male *xanthoscelus*: entirely glossy black.

e Adult female *xanthoscelus*: as nominate female but duller below.

95 Pale-eyed Thrush *Platycichla leucops* Text page 324

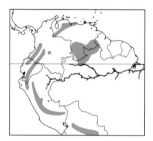

Discontinuous from Colombia and S Venezuela to E Peru and Brazil. Humid montane and cloud-forests, wooded ravines, tall dense secondary woodlands.

a Adult male: entirely glossy black with pale bluish-white eye.

b Adult female: entirely dark olive-brown, paler below; eye pale grey to grey-brown.

c Juvenile: as adult female but with orange-buff streaks on head to scapulars and tips to wing-coverts and blackish spots below.

134 Glossy-black Thrush *Turdus serranus* Text page 408

N Colombia and N Venezuela to Peru and NW Argentina. Humid, montane cloud-forests and secondary forests and woods.

a Adult male: entirely glossy black except for bright yellow bill, eye-ring and legs.

b Adult female: dull olive-brown tinged rust-orange below with pale yellowish eye-ring and legs.

PLATE 60 SOUTH AMERICAN THRUSHES (5)

138 Black-hooded Thrush *Turdus olivater*   Text page 413

Discontinuous; Colombia to Brazil. Cloud-forest, forest edges, clearings, open woodland, coffee plantations, open country with scattered trees.

a Adult male: head to breast black, rest of upperparts deep olive-brown; underparts pale sandy- to buffish-brown; bill and eye-ring yellow.

b Adult female: lacks black head and breast, slightly paler above and below; chin and throat indistinctly streaked.

c Adult male *caucae*: head and face black; throat dingy whitish streaked black; breast and upper flanks greyish-olive becoming pale on belly to undertail-coverts.

d Adult male *roraimae*: black on head merges with upperparts (darker olive-brown than nominate); chin and throat streaked blackish extending across lower throat; breast to flanks and belly light orange.

e Juvenile male: like male but duller and black less extensive; pale orange tips to wing-coverts and fine buff streaks on scapulars; black spots on throat and breast.

142 Austral Thrush *Turdus falcklandii*   Text page 417

Chile, S Argentina and Falkland Islands. Forests and woodlands including secondary woods, and dense tussock-grass near boulder beaches and rocky outcrops.

a Adult *falcklandii*: blackish head and warm brownish-olive upperparts; streaked chin and throat; rich buff-brown to ochre-brown below.

b Juvenile *falcklandii*: like adult but heavily streaked with pale orange-buff and blackish tips to upperparts and dark brown spots on pale buffish underparts.

c Adult *magellanicus*: paler or more greyish-olive upperparts; blackish forehead and crown often obscured by olive-brown fringes; chin and throat paler and more heavily streaked blackish, rest of underparts also paler.

d Juvenile *magellanicus*: dark head; brown upperparts heavily streaked yellowish-buff with pale buff tips to wing-coverts; dark brown spots below.

138b

138a

138c

138d

142c

138e

142d

142b

142a

1 RUFOUS FLYCATCHER-THRUSH *Neocossyphus fraseri*   **Plate 1**
(Rufous Thrush, Rufous Flycatcher, Fraser's Rusty Flycatcher)
Muscicapa Fraseri **Strickland, 1844,** *Proc. Zool. Soc. London*: 101 – Fernando Po.

IDENTIFICATION 20 cm (8″). A medium-sized rufous to dark rufous thrush, which resembles a large or lethargic flycatcher, of west-central Africa; at close range has a short (and relatively broad-based) bill and short legs, a rounded head, plump body and fairly long, thin tail. Almost uniform in appearance with deep rufous or cinnamon-brown upperparts, slightly brighter on the rump and outer tail feathers, darker on the head; shows a broad pale rust-orange wing-bar (more prominent in flight) and slightly paler rust-orange underparts. Feeds in trees in a manner frequently suggestive of a flycatcher but also of a cuckooshrike, dashing about from mid-tree height to upper canopy between periods of inactivity. **Confusion species** Most likely to be confused with Finsch's Flycatcher-Thrush (2), which is slightly darker above and below and with white tips to the outer tail feathers and no wing-bar. From White-tailed Ant-Thrush (4), which is usually more closely associated with the ground and ant swarms, by slightly paler upperparts and lack of any white in tail. From similar Red-tailed Ant-Thrush (3) by upright stance, shorter broad-based bill, more flycatcher-like shape and behaviour in trees (and not in undergrowth), short legs and broad wing-bar in flight (more prominent on underwing). In parts of the range Rufous Flycatcher-Thrush and both Red-tailed and White-tailed Ant-Thrushes may all attend the same ant swarms, but Rufous Flycatcher-Thrush usually remains in vegetation and rarely spends any time on the ground.

Taxonomic note This bird was originally classified as a flycatcher Muscicapidae in the genus *Stizorhina*, but is now regarded as more closely allied to the thrushes in *Neocossyphus*. The exclusion of 'flycatcher' from the species's name by Britton (1980) is acknowledged and seems morphologically justified, as the species appears more thrush-like than a flycatcher; but for the present we agree with Keith *et al.* (1992) that the connection should be maintained. Since 'Rufous Thrush' is the name most frequently used, this is likely to be preferred in time. Dowsett and Dowsett-Lemaire (1993) consider *finschii* a race of *fraseri* on the basis of observed hybrids between the two taxa in eastern Nigeria.

DESCRIPTION Sexes alike. **Adult** Forehead to crown and nape brown or tinged grey-brown; mantle, back and scapulars deep rufous or cinnamon-brown, tinged olive; lower back (in some also faintly on upper back), rump and uppertail-coverts bright rufous-brown. Tail brown or warm brown but outer two tail feathers, and outerweb and tip of next innermost, paler gingery- or rusty-buff (which shows on undersides of closed tail). Lesser coverts as scapulars, median coverts dark brown with pale or rust-orange tips, greater coverts similar but with narrow and indistinct pale edges; alula and primary coverts brown to dark brown but outerwebs of primary coverts olive-brown; flight feathers brown to dark brown, outerwebs of primaries cinnamon-brown or tinged orange-brown and with a short or indistinct buffish panel on closed wing at base of inner primaries, secondaries edged rust-brown or slightly paler at bases and also with indistinct panel on closed wing; tertials brown or tinged olive-brown. Underwing-coverts light or pale orange with darker bases to axillaries but paler bases to primaries and secondaries, creating a broad wing-bar (which contrasts with dark underside of flight feathers) in flight. Face brown or grey-brown flecked paler orange-buff on cheeks and ear-coverts, also sometimes greyish flecked with pale orange-buff on sides of chin and throat; centre of throat finely barred darker, lower chin and throat similar but becoming more heavily tawny or dull rust-orange on breast and rest of underparts, sometimes paler orange on centre of belly, vent and undertail-coverts. Bill broad-based, short and fairly stubby, dark brown or black. Legs and feet variably light brown to brownish-pink but feet may be greyish. **Immature** Juvenile is very similar to adult but darker or duller brown on upperparts and paler or buffish-orange, washed duller or greyish, on head, breast, belly and flanks; chin and throat pale or whitish-grey, flecked or mottled slightly darker on lower throat and upper breast.

GEOGRAPHICAL VARIATION Three races; variation poorly defined. Both *N. f. rubicunda* and *N. f. vulpina* are virtually identical in the field to nominate birds but *vulpina* has slightly brighter central tail feathers, and both differ marginally in the extent of pale orange at the base of the undersides of the flight feathers, and may also show some variation in the tones of the underparts; *rubicunda* may, on average, be slightly darker or deeper rust-orange, whilst *vulpina* is paler or brighter orange. Both races may also show slightly heavier or warmer rust-brown on the mantle, back and scapulars.

VOICE Usual contact note, most often given when taking flight, is a short thin *seet*; also has a pleasant, slow and rising whistle *weeee-weeee-weeooouuu* or a shorter, sharper *sweet-sweet-sweet* (recalling similar notes of Nuthatch *Sitta europaea* in Europe) and occasionally given with some harsher or dry *swit-swit-swit-swit* notes when in territorial pursuit of intruder; alarm call varies in intensity depending on state of anxiety from soft or feeble *sweeet* to a louder, more repetitive scolding *tswit-tswit-tswit* when mobbing an intruder near the nest or young. Song is composed of similar notes to the call but is usually short, rather subdued, thrush-like and given only during courtship display; commonly begins with a loud trill.

STATUS AND DISTRIBUTION Common or locally common.

N. f. fraseri Bioko (Fernando Po).

N. f. rubicunda Mt Cameroon and most of southern Cameroon but generally avoids the western parts of the country; also the Calabar area of extreme south-east Nigeria to Gabon, Congo and south-western Zaire (Kasai), south through northwest Angola to the Cuanza River in west-central Angola.

N. f. vulpina Extreme southern Sudan (Aloma Plateau and Bengengai, where uncommon), central, northern and north-eastern Zaire south to extreme north-west Zambia; western and southern Uganda (Budongo, Bugoma, Bwamba to Mbarara, Malabigambo and Teto forests east to Mpigi, Kampala, Entebbe, Kifu and Mabira forest) and south to Rwanda and Bukoba, north-west Tanzania.

MOVEMENTS Sedentary, but recorded twice in the Oban Hills (Cross River National Park) in extreme south-eastern Nigeria, where it may be a rare resident.

HABITAT Lowland forests, secondary woodlands, old plantations or trees at edges of abandoned cultivation; in West Africa also secondary forest adjacent to oil palms. Occurs up to 1400 m (4620′) in Uganda; in southern Sudan it is an uncommon resident of gallery forest.

BEHAVIOUR Occurs alone, in pairs or, in the non-breeding season, frequently in mixed-species flocks. Usually at mid-height to canopy levels of trees in forests and woodlands; may occur at lower levels or down to the ground to feed at ant swarms, and, particularly during the rainy season, often in or near clearings and in trees overhanging streams. Forages through the foliage of branches or flits nimbly from branch to branch like a cuckoo-shrike Campephagidae. May make occasional passes or sorties after nearby flying insects, e.g. on out-of-reach foliage; generally does not fly-catch from a perch. Has a habit of quickly or rapidly flirting the outer tail feathers. Vociferous in defence of territory or young but freezes and remains silent and motionless in response to some avian predators, e.g. African Goshawk *Accipiter tachiro*. Food mostly invertebrates, particularly caterpillars, but also ants, termites, beetles, cicadas, millipedes and occasionally small snails and small fruits.

BREEDING Season: probably all year round but especially during the rains – January to October (Congo and Zaire), August to December (Cameroon). Nest: a large and generally untidy loose collection of material in a shallow cup made mostly of moss, fine roots and dry or decaying leaves; usually in open cavities, e.g. base of large hole on side of tree, broken branches, stumps or old woodpecker or barbet hole; has been known to utilise the old nest of African Thrush (95); building and incubation entirely by female. Eggs: 1–2; little known but reportedly pale blue with reddish-brown or dark reddish-purple markings. Fledging period: 14 days.

MOULT No information.

MEASUREMENTS (n=42) Wing 90–105; tarsus 18.5–23.5; bill (culmen) 10–12.5, (to gape) 14.5–16.5; *vulpina* (n=11) wing 92–108; *rubicunda* (n=5) wing 92–96. Weight, male (n=35) 30–44 g, female (n=21) 27–39 g (Keith *et al.* 1992).

REFERENCES Britton (1980), Keith *et al.* (1992).

---

2 FINSCH'S FLYCATCHER-THRUSH *Neocossyphus finschii* Plate 1
(Finsch's Rusty Flycatcher, Finsch's Rufous Ant-Thrush)
Cassinia finschii Sharpe, 1870, *Ibis* 2(6): 53, pl. 2, fig. 2 – Fantee.

IDENTIFICATION 18.5–20 cm (7¼–8″). Very similar to Rufous Flycatcher-Thrush (1) (with which it has no overlap) in shape, stance and behaviour – an all dark brown thrush with warmer or cinnamon-brown underparts, short bill, short legs and white tips to the outer tail feathers. Relatively little known but frequents the thickest, densest parts of primary and secondary forests; more likely to br seen fly-catching than Rufous Flycatcher-Thrush and generally less frequently in low vegetation or on the ground than either Red-tailed (3) or White-tailed (4) Ant-Thrushes, but note that this species and White-tailed Ant-Thrush frequently occur together at ant swarms. **Confusion species** Most similar to allopatric Rufous Flycatcher-Thrush which has paler upperparts, a prominent wing-bar and no white tips to outer tail feathers. Overlaps for much of its range with White-tailed Ant-Thrush but best separated by voice, shorter bill and legs, lack of prominent wing-bar, paler chin and throat and more arboreal behaviour including sideways flicking of the tail and active fly-catching. Red-tailed Ant-Thrush is more terrestrial, horizontal in stance and longer-legged, with brighter or more orange patch on rump and outer tail feathers but no white at tips of tail.

Taxonomic note Originally classified as a flycatcher Muscicapidae in the genus *Stizorhina*, but now regarded as more closely allied to the thrushes in *Neocossyphus*. See also the taxonomic note under Rufous Flycatcher-Thrush regarding hybrids with that species in eastern Nigeria.

DESCRIPTION Sexes alike. **Adult** Forehead to crown and nape grey-brown or greyish olive-brown, mantle, back and scapulars dark olive-brown; lower back, rump and uppertail-coverts rich chestnut or rufous-brown. Tail dark brown but central pair of feathers tinged rust-brown, outer tail feathers extensively white on distal half of inner-web and base of outerweb; next innermost has large area of white at tip (on both webs). Lesser coverts as scapulars, medians slightly darker or browner and faintly tipped dull orange-buff, greaters similar but narrowly and indistinctly edged and tipped pale orange; alula brown edged slightly paler or light orange; primary coverts brown or lightly tinged olive-brown and may show a fine pale orange edge; flight feathers brown, narrowly edged russet on outerwebs or primaries and outer secondaries, inner secondaries and all tertials edged olive; bases of secondaries also broadly dull deep orange; ill-defined rust-orange wing-bar at base of inner primaries. Underwing-coverts pale tawny-orange or rusty-buff on axillaries with pale orange or orange-buff base to flight feathers. Lores grey or tinged greyish-olive and finely spotted or flecked with pale orange-buff on cheeks and ear-coverts; thin or narrow blue or pale blue eye-ring, usually only visible on lower half of the eye. Chin and throat pale buff becoming pale tawny or dull orange on lower throat; breast to sides of neck dull orange over olive or olive-brown bases; lower breast, belly and flanks to undertail-coverts rich or bright orange to rufous-chestnut on sides of breast and flanks. Bill black or blackish-brown on base of lower mandible. Legs and feet variable from pale to dusky to flesh or reddish-flesh, and pale or grey-brown. **Immature** Unknown.

GEOGRAPHICAL VARIATION None. Monotypic.

VOICE Very similar to that of Rufous Thrush but generally slower and lower-pitched. Call a rapidly repeated four-note *tswe-tswe-tswe-tswe* or a slightly longer, more drawn-out *tsw-tswee... tsweeeee*, also a long, plaintive whistled *wee... weeeee-eee*. Alarm call, usually uttered on approach of predator, a buzzing *word-word-word*. Song period in Liberia May to October (Gatter 1997). Responds to taped play-back of its call (whereas Rufous Flycatcher-Thrush does not).

STATUS AND DISTRIBUTION Locally common to rare. Coastal lowlands of southern Sierra Leone, Liberia (up to 800 m/2640' in Wologizi Mountains, and up to 900 m/2970' on Mt Nimba),

southern Ivory Coast (south of Sipilou-Gagnoa-Abengourou), southern Ghana (where uncommon), extreme southern Benin and southern Nigeria (south of Ibadan, Ife and Mamu forests but also reported from Kagoro). May also be a rare resident in southern Togo, but only one record.

MOVEMENTS Sedentary.

HABITAT Undergrowth and low-level vegetation of primary and secondary lowland forests, swamp forest and thick or dense woods to about 1500 m (4950'). Usually occurs in the thickest, densest parts of the forest.

BEHAVIOUR Usually alone or in pairs. Highly territorial, but may join mixed-species foraging flocks at ant swarms in non-breeding season. Occurs in deep forest in understorey and lower canopies of trees and thick vegetation, often near streams or damp areas. Much less dependent on ant swarms than Red-tailed or White-tailed Ant-Thrushes; also sits motionless for long periods on a horizontal branch or creeper. More frequently hawks like a true flycatcher, including sallying from perches to take passing insects, fast sweeping flights, and hovering to take insects from under leaves or foliage. Food mostly small insects, ants, termites, beetles, grasshoppers and flies.

BREEDING Very little known; a bird was collecting nest material from base of epiphytes in southern Nigeria in March; birds in breeding condition were recorded in Liberia from June to December, with an independent young in September.

MOULT Most of the 17 individuals examined in the hand in Liberia between June and October were moulting (Gatter 1997).

MEASUREMENTS (n=24) Wing, male 93–105, female 97–102; tarsus 20–24; bill (culmen) 10.5–13, (to gape) 16–21. Weight 33–41 g (Keith *et al.* 1992).

REFERENCES Gatter (1997), Keith *et al.* (1992).

3 RED-TAILED ANT-THRUSH *Neocossyphus rufus* Plate 1

Pseudocossyphus rufus Fischer & Reichenow, 1884, *J. Orn.* 32: 58 – Pangani.

IDENTIFICATION 22.5–25 cm (8¼–9¾"). A plain reddish-brown thrush of Central and East Africa. Almost uniform in coloration, but slightly darker or tinged olive on the upperparts, particularly the head and neck, with the rump and outer tail feathers rich or brighter rust-brown, the underparts dull rust-brown. Generally shy or secretive but presence often given away by its fairly frequently uttered sibilant call note. Less common or frequently met with in the west of its range. **Confusion species** Unlikely to be confused with any other thrush except the very similar Rufous Flycatcher-Thrush (1) which is smaller, more arboreal, lacks the rufous tail, has a different underwing pattern and is more upright with a shorter bill. White-tailed Ant-thrush (4) is duller brown above and on the breast and has a blackish centre to the tail with prominent white spots at the tips of the outer three feathers. Note that Red-tailed Ant-Thrush, White-

tailed Ant-Thrush and Rufous Flycatcher-Thrush may all occur together at the same ant swarm in parts of the range.

In East Africa both Northern *Phyllastrephus strepitans* and Terrestrial *P. terrestris suahelicus* Brownbuls are similar but smaller and slenderer, the former having rufous-brown on the rump and uppertail-coverts, the latter a whitish belly, and both with white on the chin and throat. Fischer's Greenbul *P. fischeri* also has a rufous-brown tinge to the uppertail-coverts and tail but is generally more heavily olive above with a pale or cream-white eye.

DESCRIPTION Sexes alike but male is brighter than female. **Adult** Forehead to crown, face and nape grey tinged olive-brown, becoming browner on mantle, back and inner scapulars; outer scapulars richer brown or rufous with orange-rufous edges; rump and uppertail-coverts rich or deep rust-brown. Tail long and brown to rufous-brown with outer 2–3 feathers paler orange. Lesser coverts orange-rufous, median and greater coverts orange, tinged olive and edged or fringed rufous; alula olive tinged or washed with warm rufous-brown; flight feathers dark brown (appearing blackish in flight) broadly edged rufous-brown or orange rufous-brown with outerwebs of primaries browner; tertials olive-brown. Underwing-coverts pale orange-rufous or yellowish-orange. Feathers of chin and throat greyish with dull orange tips, becoming brownish or rust-brown on upper breast; rest of underparts orange to rust-orange or tinged with cinnamon on flanks and undertail-coverts. Eye brown or dark brown. Bill black or blackish-grey. Legs and feet variable from pale brown to purplish-grey, pale lilac-flesh or flesh-coloured. **Immature** Juvenile similar to adult but duller or more olive-brown above and flecked paler with fine pale orange-buff central shafts and paler or tawny-brown tinged with olive on under-parts.

GEOGRAPHICAL VARIATION Two races; variation clinal and not well marked. Birds of the race gabunensis have darker grey heads and chin and throat and the breast is also darker and more infused with olive or olive-brown.

VOICE Most frequent call is a descending or wavering sibilant peeeeyew or tit-teeeeyew, occasionally extended into tsip-wi-wheeeeer or seeyew-peeeyew and repeated fairly frequently; at ant swarms gives a high-pitched trilling chrrrr-chrrrr or prrr... prrrr, also used on take-off and in flight. Alarm or distress note of birds near the nest or young is a thin or high-pitched tseem and a sharp, rasping treet. Song consists of the call notes, somewhat more drawn-out and followed by a long descending, rattling trill, accelerating and descending in pitch.

STATUS AND DISTRIBUTION Fairly common (rufus) or uncommon (gabunensis).

N. r. gabunensis Southern Cameroon to the Ogooue River, central Gabon, east through northern Congo and northern Zaire (Uele, Kisangani and Kivu) to Budongo, Bwamba and Maramagambo forests, western Uganda. Has also been recorded in south-west Central African Republic (Carroll 1988, Quantrill 1995).

N. r. rufus Coastal forests of eastern Kenya north to the lower Tana River to about Bura and in the

south to the Shimba hills, Zanzibar and in Tanzania south along the coastal lowlands to about Mikindani but also the East Usambara Mountains, Nguru and Pugu hills and the foothills of the Uluguru Mountains.

MOVEMENTS Mostly sedentary but has occurred once in Boni Forest, southern Somalia, in August 1970 (Ash & Miskell 1983, 1998).

HABITAT Moist forests, secondary woodlands and bushed thickets up to c.1400 m (4620′); in Uganda gabunensis occurs between 700 and 1400 m (2300–4620′); in Kenya occurs in slightly drier riverine and coastal forest.

BEHAVIOUR Generally shy and secretive, though may become more approachable at ant swarms where it is a dominant species; usually more heard than seen and detected by its frequently given (especially at dawn) sibilant call note. Forages on the ground among leaf-litter beneath trees, may (particularly in East Africa) venture out into more open areas of tracks in the early morning when undisturbed. Regularly attends ant swarms and may join mixed-species foraging flocks in the forest canopy. Food is mainly insects, particularly small ants, beetles, grasshoppers, caterpillars, spiders, millipedes and occasionally small snails.

BREEDING Season: possibly year round, nestling in Cameroon in November; Gabon in December and January; northern Congo in April and May (with female in breeding condition in September); Kenya in April; Zanzibar in September. Nest (only three known): a shallow cup-shape structure or platform of plant stems, fibres, rootlets and dry leaves on a platform of dry leaves and other roots; placed up to 4–10 m (13–33′) from the ground in a hole of a tree or in the crown of a broken or rotting tree-stump. Eggs: 2, dull white but heavily (almost entirely covered) speckled or spotted with brown or reddish-brown (Brown 1970). Incubation by female only.

MOULT No information.

MEASUREMENTS (n=31) Wing, male 112–127, female 107–117; tarsus 27.5–31; bill (culmen) 13–15, (to gape) 17.5–21; gabunensis (n=10) wing 107–112; tarsus 26–29; bill (culmen) 12.5–16, (to gape) 19–23.5. Weight (n=12) 53–80 g (Keith et al. 1992).

REFERENCES Ash & Miskell (1983, 1998), Britton (1980), Brown (1970), Carroll (1988), Keith et al. (1992), Quantrill (1995), Zimmerman et al. (1996).

4 WHITE-TAILED ANT-THRUSH *Neocossyphus poensis*   Plate 1

Cossypha poensis Stickland, 1844, *Proc. Zool. Soc. London*: 100 – Clarence, Fernando Po.

IDENTIFICATION 20–22 cm (8–8¾″). A slim, dark, fairly long-tailed forest thrush usually seen foraging low down or on the ground; widely distributed from the coastal forests of West Africa east to western Kenya. Sooty-brown on the head and upperparts; tail darker or blacker-brown with

prominent white tips to outer three feathers; shows broad rufous-chestnut wing-bar and dark wing-tips in flight; underparts pale or dull rufous-orange. **Confusion species** Only likely problem is Finsch's Flycatcher-Thrush (2), which is more arboreal (and hence conspicuous), has different voice and feeding behaviour, perches in more upright posture, flicks open its white tail feathers, has smaller bill, shorter legs and slightly duller underparts, and lacks the broad wing-bar in flight. Red-tailed Ant-thrush (3) overlaps in parts of Central Africa, but is more uniform reddish-brown tinged olive on head and upperparts, and has deeper rust-brown underparts and dark reddish-brown tail with paler reddish outer feathers and no white spots at tip. Note that White-tailed and Red-tailed Ant-Thrush plus either Rufous (1) or Finsch's Flycatcher-Thrush may attend the same ant swarms. Also initially similar to Grey-chested Illadopsis *Kakamega poliothorax*, which is smaller, grey not rufous below, and lacks white tips to outer tail feathers. Brown-chested Alethe *Alethe poliocephalus* has whitish supercilium, shorter tail, brown breast and whitish remaining underparts.

DESCRIPTION Sexes alike. **Adult** Entire upperparts dark or sooty-brown faintly washed olive on mantle, back and scapulars. Tail slightly darker brown but outermost feather paler brown on narrow outerweb and extensively white at tip half of innerweb, tips of next inner two with reduced amounts of white (least on innermost). All coverts as scapulars or with slightly paler brown fringes when worn; flight feathers also brown but with rufous-chestnut on outerwebs to bases of primaries, forming indistinct panel on inner primaries and bases of secondaries, innerwebs bright orange or orange-rufous forming a broad wing-bar in flight; edges of innermost secondaries and tertials tinged olive. Underwing-coverts pale orange extending to base of inner primaries and secondaries. Lores to over eye, cheeks and ear-coverts and sides of nape grey or flecked darker, becoming grey-brown on sides of neck. Chin and throat pale or whitish-grey, becoming dull grey or olive-brown across upper breast; lower breast to centre of belly pale rufous; sides of belly and flanks more heavily cinnamon or dull rufous-orange; vent and undertail-coverts orange. Bill short and either black with brown on lower mandible (male) or entirely blackish-brown (female). Legs and feet pale whitish-flesh to pink or pale flesh-brown. **Immature** Juvenile little known but thought to be similar to adult except for paler flecks on cheeks and ear-coverts and dull dark olive tips to lower throat and breast (Bannerman 1936).

GEOGRAPHICAL VARIATION Three races; variation clinal and not well marked. Birds of race *pallidigularis* are very slightly paler brown or more heavily tinged olive on upperparts and wings, the olive wash extends across the pale orange breast, the belly is paler orange, flanks and undertail-coverts heavily rufous-orange. *Praepectoralis* is slightly larger than the nominate race and also slightly warmer or browner, tinged olive on the upperparts; the face is duller, the throat grey-brown. The breast is more heavily or extensively washed olive over deep orange. Has slightly less white at the tips of the outer tail feathers; the white is restricted to the innerweb and extreme tip of the outerweb and extends to 23 mm compared to c. 36 mm in nominate.

Taxonomic note Birds in Kenya and Uganda have a noticeable amount of individual variation in the brown tones of the head and upperparts and as such we follow Zimmerman *et al.* (1996) in considering *kakamegoes* and *nigridorsalis* as synonymous with *praepectoralis*.

VOICE Call a single short ascending whistle, *weeeuu*, *wheeu* or *weeeeeeeeeeeeet* or *wurrrrrrreeeeeeeet*, frequently repeated; also reported to give a sharp or abrupt *tizz* followed by a rapid ticking when about to fly; alarm notes a sharp *sip-sip* and a low, sharp or ticking *prrrt-prrrt* when disturbed or excited, frequently given when attending ant swarms; in defence of territory or pursuing intruder gives loud *heer her-hih*. Song a rich and typically thrush-like *wurreeeet t'ree ueeeeeeeet*, rarely heard; sings from undergrowth and up to 15 m (50') in a tree; also known to give a subdued version when attending ant swarms.

STATUS AND DISTRIBUTION Locally common, otherwise uncommon to rare.

N. p. poensis Forests of Sierra Leone, Liberia (including Wologizi Mountains, and Mt Nimba) and the coastal forests of Ivory Coast (north to Comoe and Sipilou), Ghana (where very rare: 2 records), Togo (extremely rare: 1 record) and southern Nigeria; more widely in Cameroon, Gabon, Bioko (Fernando Po) and the Congo (possibly including the Mayombe forest). May also occur in extreme southwest Central African Republic (Carroll 1988).

N. p. pallidigularis Northern Angola.

N. p. praepectoralis Northern and eastern Zaire (Equateur district south to about Kinshasa and east to Kivu province), western Uganda (Budongo, Bugoma, Bwamba to Maramagambo, Impenetrable and Malabigambo forests), northern Rwanda and western Kenya (Kakamega, South Nandi and North Nandi forests).

MOVEMENTS Sedentary.

HABITAT The undergrowth and mid-levels of trees and creepers of primary and secondary forests, including forest edges and clearings; also forest patches in savanna from sea-level to c.1500 m (4950') in most of the range but between about 700 and 1500 m (2300–4950') in Uganda and between 1700 and 1900 m (5600–6270') in western Kenya, exceptionally at 2520 m (8310') in Rwanda (Dowsett-Lemaire 1990).

BEHAVIOUR Shy, secretive and frequently overlooked; usually alone except when feeding young, but up to four may occur together (Gatter 1997); rarely occurs in mixed bird parties. Has a characteristic habit of raising and lowering tail, either wagged fairly rapidly or occasionally slowly; flicks tail sideways when alarmed or agitated, when white tips easily seen. Forages on or near the ground in thick or tangled undergrowth; may emerge into the open on paths or forest trails and known to bathe in roadside puddles after rains at dusk and dawn; most frequently seen when following ant swarms. Flight generally slow and fluttering. Food includes insects, principally small black ants and termites, also larvae, beetles, grasshoppers, millipedes and spiders; also, perhaps exceptionally, some seeds and small hard-stoned fruits.

BREEDING Unknown but birds in Zaire in June and November were considered to be in breeding condition and young were seen in April–May and October; birds in breeding condition noted in Liberia April–July and a fledgling in mid-September; young birds in Cameroon in September, November and December; fledglings in Nigeria in June; birds in breeding condition in Cameroon in September and Angola in February.

MOULT Birds in Liberia were in the process of moulting wing feathers in late July and August–October, advanced stages of moult in November–

February, fresh plumage in February–March, and worn plumage in May–June.

MEASUREMENTS (n=20) Wing, male 102–112, female 97–109; tarsus 27.5–30; bill (culmen) 12.5–14.5, (to gape) 19–23. Race *praepectoralis* (n=3) wing 98–112; tarsus 25–30.5; bill (culmen) 13.5–14.5, (to gape) 20–21. Weight (n=62) 43–60 g (Keith *et al.* 1992).

REFERENCES Britton (1980), Carroll (1988), Dowsett-Lemaire (1990), Gatter (1997), Keith *et al.* (1992), Zimmerman *et al.* (1996).

5 FOREST ROCK-THRUSH *Monticola sharpei* Plate 2

Cossypha sharpei Gray, 1871, *An. Mag. Nat. Hist.* (4)8: 429 – Madagascar [forests east of Ambatondrazaka (Lake Alaotra), *fide* Grandidier (1879) *Hist. phys. nat. pol. Madagascar, Ois.* 1: 370].

IDENTIFICATION 16 cm (6¼"). Endemic to Madagascar. A small chat-sized rock-thrush recalling both redstarts *Phoenicurus* in the rich orange plumage of the rump, tail and underparts; the tail pattern recalls that of wheatears. Male has blue-greyish head to mantle and back and extends to upper breast. Female is mostly brown or pale greyish-brown with broadly streaked throat and breast and barred belly and flanks. **Confusion species** Similar to Littoral Rock-Thrush (7) but male is distinguished by smaller bill and deeper or more bluish upperparts extending to the chin and breast, and the rich orange, not grey, tail. Female differs from female Littoral by smaller bill and much darker or browner head and upperparts with rich or deep russet outer tail feathers and prominent streaks on barred underparts. Very similar to Benson's Rock-Thrush (6) but male Forest has deeper bluish-grey head to breast (except race *erythronotus* where blue restricted to head) and upperparts (duller or greyer in Benson's) and has brighter orange underparts; female greyer above and below and lacks well pronounced streaks on chin to breast except for broad pale centre to chin and throat. Not known to occur in same habitat or overlap with Benson's.

DESCRIPTION Sexes differ. **Adult male** Centre and upper forehead to nape and sides of neck blue-grey becoming slightly darker on mantle, back, scapulars, lesser and median coverts; lower forehead to eyes grey-blue, lores black; may show paler area over eyes. Rump warm gingery- or rufous-brown, uppertail-coverts slightly brighter orange. Central tail feathers and tips to all and distal edges to outermost feathers blackish-brown; remaining outer feathers bright or deep russet-orange, undertail pattern orange with dark brown tip. Greater coverts dark brown or tinged dark bluish, rest of coverts and flight feathers blackish-brown. Chin and throat to upper breast greyish-blue as on forehead or marginally paler than that on rest of head, some feathers on sides of lower breast darker bluish-black; rest of underparts and

underwing-coverts bright or deep orange, thighs brownish. Bill black. Legs and feet brown to blackish-brown. In worn plumage head and upperparts, especially back and scapulars, become tinged brownish. **Adult female** Forehead to nape and sides of crown pale brown tinged slightly warm brown; mantle, back, scapulars, lesser and greater coverts warm or russet-brown becoming bright rufous-brown on rump and uppertail-coverts. Tail warm rufous-brown basally, darker towards tip; some females, however, show warm brown bases to outer tail feathers and darker central and tips to all outer feathers, similar to male. Wings brown but finely edged warmer brown on flight feathers and more broadly edged on tertials. Underwing-coverts light or pale orange-buff. Face brown or pale brown with pale or whitish-buff moustachial and browner or darker submoustachial and malar stripes; centre of chin and upper throat white or whitish, becoming tawny-brown on sides of lower throat, often spotted or mottled with pale creamy-buff. Breast brown, heavily and broadly striped pale whitish or creamy-buff and brown extending to upper belly and upper flanks; belly pale buffish-brown barred darker, flanks similar but slightly darker; undertail-coverts similar or slightly warmer or gingery-brown. **Immature** Juvenile brown on head to mantle, back and wings heavily marked with fairly large pale orange-buff spots edged dark brown at tips of feathers; rump dull orange-brown but barred or tipped darker brown. Wings and tail as adult female but greater coverts more finely spotted with pale orange-buff at tips. Face heavily mottled with pale buff and brown. Chin and throat mottled pale buff with browner edges and/or tips extending more heavily on breast, upper belly and upper flanks; belly pale or yellowish-buff mottled or finely spotted darker, undertail-coverts tinged warm or ginger. Bill yellow to yellowish-orange with a dark culmen. First-year males show blue on head to back before pale juvenile spots have disappeared. Adult plumage is assumed by gradual reduction in amount of spots in plumage.

GEOGRAPHICAL VARIATION Three races; variation clinal but well marked in *erythronotus*. Male of race *erythronotus* differs from nominate male by slightly larger size and larger bill, more bluish tone which only extends over the head to nape, face and throat (not extending onto breast). Mantle, back, scapulars and wing-coverts rich chestnut-brown; rump and uppertail-coverts bright orange-brown. Tail bright orange with dark brown central feathers and distal tips to all outers. Rest of underparts to undertail deep orange, deepest (almost chestnut on some) on the breast. Female similar to nominate female but has warmer brown upperparts especially on back, bright gingery or rufous-brown uppertail-coverts and all undertail feathers; wings dark brown, fringed chestnut. Underparts similar to nominate female but less white on sides of lower throat. Breast and flanks warm buffish-brown, broadly streaked sandy-buff; centre of belly to undertail-coverts like nominate but paler buffish or yellowish. Male of race *interioris* slightly larger than nominate male and, on average, has darker, more extensive tips to tail.

VOICE Not well known and generally silent. Call a high-pitched *hweet* and low *krrrrr*; alarm call is a quiet *tseet-tak-tak* or *tak-tak-tak*. Song is a series of melodious, thrush-like whistling phrases including *teedew teedew* or *teeooo teeooo teeooo* broken by long pauses (Morris & Hawkins 1998). The race *erythronotus* sings most frequently at dusk but also on occasions during the day.

STATUS AND DISTRIBUTION Common or fairly common but frequently overlooked; considered Near-Threatened (Collar *et al.* 1994).

M. s. erythronotus Restricted to northern Madagascar: the Massif de Tsaratanana (Montagne d'Ambre or Amber Mountain) at 1000–1300 m (3300–4290') east to about Ambohitsitondroina–Ambanizana (western Masoala Peninsula).

M. s. sharpei Sambava to Tolagnaro, usually above 800 m (2640'), eastern Madagascar.

M. s. interioris High Plateau near Antananarivo

(Ambohitantely, Manjakatompo and Fianarantsoa), eastern-central Madagascar.

Taxonomic note Morris & Hawkins (1998) and Sinclair & Langrand (1998) considered *erythronotus* a full species, the Amber Mountain Rock-Thrush; the latter authors also include Benson's Rock-Thrush as race of Forest Rock-Thrush.

MOVEMENTS Sedentary.

HABITAT Dense, humid, mid-level and montane rainforests of eastern Madagascar, including relict forests and occasionally secondary woodlands between 800 and 2050 m (2640–6765'), including forests of *Ilex* and small forests in river valleys, where it occurs low down in thick vegetation and on the ground, also at forest edges. The race *erythronotus* is confined to the rainforests of Montagne d'Ambre.

BEHAVIOUR Secretive and usually quiet but often approachable and not especially shy; usually alone or in pairs. Forages low down in thick vegetation or on the ground, but also rises up to mid-level in secondary forests and scrub. Hops and flies low over the ground but also spends long periods motionless on low branches and often makes long dashes to seize prey on the ground. Food is mostly insects but also some fruit and berries.

BREEDING Very poorly known. Season: September or October to February. Nest: a cup-shaped structure of plant stems, twigs and roots, usually placed in a bush or hole in a tree or a crevice in a rock-face up to 2 m (7') from the ground.

MOULT No information.

MEASUREMENTS Wing, male (n=18) 74.5–83.5, female (n=12) 66–75.5; tarsus 23.5–26; bill (culmen) 10.5–15, (to gape) 16–20; *interioris* (n=5) wing 77.5–80.5; *erythronotus* wing, male (n=12) 78–85, female (n=6) 74.5–81.5; tarsus 24–27; bill (to feathers) 13.5–15.5, (to gape) 18–21.5. Weight apparently unrecorded.

REFERENCES Dee (1986), Langrand (1990), Morris & Hawkins (1998), Rand (1936), Sinclair & Langrand (1998).

---

6 BENSON'S ROCK-THRUSH *Monticola bensoni*   Plate 2

Monticola bensoni Farkas, 1971, *Ostrich* suppl. 9: 83–90 – Ankarefu, Antinosy Cy, Madagascar [corrected to 23°21'S 44°48'E in the Onilahy drainage, southern Madagascar – Collar and Tattersall (1987)].

IDENTIFICATION 16 cm (6½"). Endemic to southern Madagascar, where very localised and seemingly attached to patches of vegetation near or adjacent to cliffs and boulder canyons. Only recently described and has been considered a race of Forest Rock-Thrush (5) but now separated on ecological requirements, behaviour and plumage. Male has head and upperparts dull grey-blue extending to upper breast; uppertail and sides of tail rufous, but centre and tip of tail dark; rest of underparts dull orange. Female grey-brown with mottled underparts and pale stripe down centre of throat. An African Red Data Book species, where considered Insufficiently Known and

Vulnerable (Collar and Stuart 1985, Collar *et al.* 1994, Langrand & Goodman 1996), but probably now better classified as at Lower Risk on the basis of more recent evidence of a larger distribution than previously thought (Collar 1999); no decline or immediate threat has been detected. Confusion species Very similar to Forest Rock-Thrush but the ranges and habitats do not overlap. Male Benson's has the head and upperparts duller grey, chin to upper breast pale grey, rump and uppertail-coverts more extensively dull reddish-orange; dark brown fringes of outer tail feathers restricted to distal tips on Benson's whilst on entire edge of Forest. The blue-

grey on breast of nominate race of Forest is slightly more extensive (restricted to upper breast on Benson's). Benson's has dark grey wings, which are darker or more rufous in Forest; bill of Benson's much finer or flattened along the culmen. Female Benson's is similar to female Forest but distinctly greyer-brown on head and upperparts; has white central stripe with dark grey not brown sides of chin and throat; usually shows a fairly distinctive pale eye-ring; underparts pale with fine greyish streaks. **DESCRIPTION** Sexes differ. **Adult male** Head and upperparts grey-blue, lower back slightly greyer, rump and uppertail-coverts bright reddish-orange. Central pair of tail feathers dark brown; all outers orange or dull rufous-orange, edged slightly darker (only on distal half of outermost feather) and tipped dark or blackish-brown. Median and greater coverts dark grey to grey-brown with fine pale grey fringes, flight feathers dark grey-brown with paler grey outerwebs and pale brown to warm buffish-brown edges to inner primaries and secondaries forming pale panel on closed wing, tertials similar but with paler grey edges to outerwebs; underwing, coverts and axillaries reddish-orange as on flanks. Lores and ear-coverts slightly darker greyish-blue than rest of head. Chin, throat and upper breast pale greyish-blue as head; centre of breast to undertail-coverts orange or dull reddish-orange. Bill dark brown to blackish. Legs and feet dull black, but may appear paler. **Adult female** Head and upperparts grey-brown, slightly more earth-brown on forehead and usually with fairly conspicuous eye-ring; uppertail-coverts bright or rufous-orange. Tail with central pair of feathers dark brown, all outers bright orange but with darker brown outerwebs (closed tail usually appears dark) and dark tips to all feathers. Wings as upperparts or slightly darker on innerwebs. Chin and throat brown as head but with distinctive white chin and narrow central streak down centre of throat, bordered by grey-brown malar; breast to belly and undertail-coverts spotted or streaked pale brown with whitish edges and pale grey centres. **Immature** Juvenile male has grey head spotted or speckled with fine light grey spots and paler grey band across belly. Immature female almost entirely pale grey, except for rufous-brown tail, and spotted or speckled with paler grey.
GEOGRAPHICAL VARIATION None. Monotypic.
VOICE Call a long, high-pitched *veed*; alarm is a deep *tock* or *tack*, frequently repeated as *tak-tak-tak*; also a thin *queek* distress call. Song described as quiet, melodious, sweet whistled trilling phrases, resonant and interspersed with some rasping or guttural notes; may also mimic other species, particularly Madagascar Paradise Flycatcher *Terpsiphone mutata*, Crested Drongo *Dicrurus forficatus* and Madagascar Wagtail *Motacilla flaviventris*. Sings from prominent rock or tree or from dense shrubbery at foot of cliff, etc., at all times of day from before dawn through heat of day, though mostly in early morning.
STATUS AND DISTRIBUTION Locally common. South-central Madagascar mainly between the Mangoky and Onilahy rivers; the northern bound-

ary extends east from about Bejangoa to Andringitra and includes the main areas of the Isoky-Vohimena Forest, the Isalo Massif, east to the Andringitra Massif, south to about Ankarefo and west to Ankazoabo. Exact limits not defined and range may be larger than currently known; has also been seen in Zombitse Forest Reserve, near Sakaraha, mostly in non-breeding season; may also extend north to the Makay Massif and the Bemaraha Plateau (Farkas 1971) and west to the Mikoboka and Analavelona ranges and east to the isolated domes near Ambalavao and Fianarantsoa (Langrand & Goodman 1996).
MOVEMENTS Poorly known; see Distribution. In austral winter the few records available imply dispersion to lower levels and slightly different habitat from breeding; has occurred south to Zombitse and north to the Mangoky River region and south to Sakaraha.
HABITAT Breeds at 400–2580 m (1320–8500') in low trees or sparse scrub in rugged or rocky terrain often adjacent to cliffs, particularly isolated and extensive steep cliff-faces which rise out of rolling plains and hillsides, also rocky gorges with bushes and short trees or patches of ground-layer vegetation. Also appears to favour burnt areas with regenerating vegetation. Outside the breeding season has been found in dry riverbeds, canyons and hillsides with scattered boulders; occasionally in patches of mature forest.
BEHAVIOUR Usually alone or in pairs, though several pairs may occupy an extensive cliff-face (e.g. 6 males or pairs within 2 km of one locality). Keeps low to the ground or cover of rocks, boulders and cliff-faces; may forage in vegetation islands, bushy patches and adjacent small trees and bushes; birds at one non-breeding locality were found perching on roadside telephone wires. In the grasslands of Zombitse-Vohibasia National Park has been seen foraging in village gardens; not shy and seemingly adapts well to human presence. During the heat of the day, may spend long periods sheltering in the foliage of trees or bushes. Males give active display-flights in the breeding season from high rocky peaks and crags. Forages in a redstart-like manner; on the ground moves with quick hops; also regularly pursues (for several metres) and catches insects in flight. Flight is mostly low, fast and direct. Food most probably solely insects, including flies taken in flight.
BREEDING Poorly known. Season: late October to about January; either double-brooded or a late-summer breeding bird. Nest: a thin or flat cup-shaped platform made almost entirely of thin strips of plant material, especially roots and plant stems, usually placed in a crevice or cavity in a cliff or rockface, exceptionally in a hole in the roof of a house or on a ledge or among rocks.
MOULT No information.
MEASUREMENTS Wing 79–86; tarsus 25.5–28; bill (culmen) 15–16, (to skull) 19–20.5. Weight 24–28.5 g (Langrand & Goodman 1996).
REFERENCES Collar (1999), Collar & Stuart (1985), Collar & Tattersall (1987), Collar *et al.* (1994), Dee (1986), Farkas (1971), Langrand (1990), Langrand & Goodman (1996).

7 LITTORAL ROCK-THRUSH *Monticola imerinus* **Plate 2**

Cossypha imerina **Hartlaub, 1860, *J. Orn.* 8: 97 – St. Augustine Bay, south-east Madagascar.**

IDENTIFICATION 16 cm (6½"). Endemic to Madagascar where it inhabits the coastal scrub and dune country of the subdesert area in the south and south-west. Male has grey head to upper breast and upperparts with dark brown tail, bright orange underparts. Female is pale grey to greybrown with warmer orange or rufous rump and uppertail-coverts and dull buffish or greyish-buff underparts which are slightly or subtly scaled darker. Both sexes are longer-billed than the other two rock-thrushes of Madagascar. **Confusion species** Similar to Forest Rock-Thrush (5) but much greyer and lacks the distinctive rich orange and brown tail pattern of the male or the streaked and barred pattern of the underparts of the female. Both sexes of Littoral have longer and strongerlooking bills and are greyer above; males are also pale grey from chin to breast, while females have only the centre of chin and throat white and lack the prominent stripes onto the breast. Unlikely to be found in same habitat as Forest and no overlap in ranges. Benson's Rock-Thrush (6) is also similar but much bluer-grey but with paler grey upperparts; further separated on habitat. Female Benson's differs by brown (not grey or grey-brown) upperparts and dingy or pale grey underparts.
DESCRIPTION Sexes differ. **Adult male** Entire head and face to nape, mantle, back and scapulars to lesser and median coverts pale grey or tinged bluish-grey, rump and uppertail-coverts slightly paler or duller and tipped brownish-grey. Tail dark brown with all outer (except outermost) feathers finely edged pale bluish-grey (in hand may show fine orange innerwebs to some inner tail feathers but not central pair). Greater coverts dark brown broadly edged and tipped pale bluish-grey in fresh plumage, becoming less grey when worn; alula dark greyish-black; primary coverts and flight feathers dark or blackish-brown, finely edged pale greyish-buff in fresh plumage; tertials similar but more broadly edged greyish. Lores to eye darker grey-blue than on forehead and face. Chin and throat to breast pale grey or bluish-grey; lower breast, belly and flanks to underwing-coverts bright orange, slightly paler on axillaries; vent to undertail-coverts creamy or tinged with orange, thighs grey flecked with orange. Bill long and slender, black, upper mandible finely hooked at tip. Legs and feet black. **Adult female** Forehead to crown, mantle, back and scapulars pale grey or light grey-brown, some birds having some fine dark streaks on crown. Rump pale brown becoming warm or light orange on longest uppertail-coverts. Tail dark or blackish-brown edged with warm brown. Wings, including coverts and alula, brown finely edged pale bluish-grey, primary coverts quite broadly edged pale bluish-grey; in worn plumage edges to flight feathers pale buff-brown; underwing-coverts pale or tinged peachy-buff. Face pale or buffish-brown finely mottled with whitish spots on sides of chin and throat; centre of chin and throat have narrow stripe of white or whitish edged pale grey-brown and forming short streaks on sides of lower throat; breast and sides of neck off-white with indistinct grey-brown scaling, becoming pale yellowish-buff on the belly; flanks greyer, undertail-coverts light creamy-buff or tinged orange. **Immature** Juvenile similar to adult female but heavily mottled or spotted on upperparts with variably sized white or whitish spots on forehead, crown and nape (small) to mantle and back (larger), and barred darker at tips of feathers. Median and greater coverts grey or greybrown tipped whitish-buff. Chin and throat pale buff, young female developing broad pale central stripe on centre of chin and throat at an early age, becoming scaled or scalloped with pale or yellowish-buff and fine dark brown edges on breast, belly and flanks. Juvenile male shows individual orange feathers on lower breast and belly as it progresses towards adult plumage; vent and undertail-coverts light or whitish orange-buff.
GEOGRAPHICAL VARIATION None. Monotypic.
VOICE Call is several short harsh or scratchy notes including a soft *kirr-tak-tak-tak* alarm note. Song consists of short scratchy phrases including *cheearr tu-tu-tu* and longer phrases of clear whistles and scratchy notes frequently repeated, usually given from low, open perch (Morris & Hawkins 1998).
STATUS AND DISTRIBUTION Common or very common. The coastal belt of south and south-west Madagascar from the Mangoky River and Manombo (uncommon or scarce north of Toliara) south to about Cap Sainte-Marie and east to Lac Anony; may extend to the extreme south-east corner at Taolanaro (Fort-Dauphin).
MOVEMENTS Sedentary.
HABITAT Mostly lowland semi-open savanna, grassy steppes or sandy scrub, including dunes and edges of beaches, with low to medium vegetation and interspersed with euphorbias (particularly *Euphorbia stenoclada*) rarely at any elevation – max. c.200 m (660') at Cap Sainte-Marie.
BEHAVIOUR Similar to that of Forest Rock-Thrush; not shy but otherwise secretive or generally inconspicuous and alone or in pairs. Forages on the ground in the open where it hops over vegetation; when disturbed, has characteristic habit of flying up to a high vantage point and watching intruder in upright stance with neck and head held prominently forward and bill tilted up at an angle; otherwise may spend long periods motionless on low perch in bushes and undergrowth. Food mostly insects, berries and some fruit.
BREEDING Very poorly known. Season: October to February. Nest: a cup-shaped structure of twigs, plant stems and roots lined with similar or softer

plant material. Eggs: 2, greenish-blue.
MOULT No information.
MEASUREMENTS Wing, male (n=7) 79–86, female (n=5) 76.5–81; tarsus, male 26.5–28.5, female 25.5+; bill (to gape) 18.5–21.5, (to feathers) 14–17.5. Weight apparently unrecorded.
REFERENCES Dee (1986), Morris & Hawkins (1998).

8 CAPE ROCK-THRUSH *Monticola rupestris* Plate 3

Turdus rupestris Vieillot, 1818, *Nouv. Dict. Hist. Nat.* (nouv. ed.) 20: 281 – near Cape Town [= Table Mountain, Sclater, 1930, *Syst. Av. Aethiop.*: 449].

IDENTIFICATION 21–22 cm (8¼–8¾"). An endemic rock-thrush of South Africa, slightly larger than many others of the region and deeper or more richly coloured. Deep blue-grey head to chin and throat; mantle, back and scapulars rich or warm rufous-brown with some darker centres and paler tips; rump, uppertail-coverts and sides of tail rufous, wings and tail dark or blackish-brown; breast to undertail-coverts rich rufous or deep orange. Female lacks the blue-grey head, which is replaced by brown finely flecked or streaked darker, and has a whitish (becoming orange-buff) centre of chin and upper throat. **Confusion species** Very similar to other rock-thrushes in the region. Male Sentinel Rock-Thrush (9) has a paler grey head which extends onto the mantle and breast, and the rest of the upperparts are blue-grey; females have dark brown upperparts, pale faces and mottled brown and white underparts. Cape usually found at lower altitudes than Sentinel and more closely confined to rocky or montane habitats. Male Short-toed Rock-Thrush (10) has blue-grey upperparts and a pale or whitish forehead and crown; female smaller than female Cape with more uniform upperparts and paler underparts with a large pale chin and throat. Male Miombo Rock-Thrush (11) is also smaller and has light grey head, face and most upperparts tipped or spotted black.
DESCRIPTION Sexes differ. **Adult male** Entire head slate blue-grey to throat, sides of neck and nape; lores to eye blackish. Mantle, back and scapulars russet-brown with broad blackish central shaft-streaks, tipped paler or orange, some tips to scapulars and lesser coverts sometimes pale buff or greyish. Rump and uppertail-coverts rufous-brown or chestnut. Tail dark or blackish-brown on central feathers, all outers broadly edged rufous-brown or chestnut. Median coverts as scapulars, greater coverts black or blackish finely edged pale rufous or cinnamon (becoming pale or whitish-buff when worn), alula and primary coverts black, flight feathers black finely edged pale orange-buff or light orange, tertials similar and edged warm buff or tipped paler when worn, light orange when fresh. Breast to undertail-coverts and underwing-coverts rufous-orange to buffish-brown, often tipped paler on centre of breast and belly. Bill black. Legs and feet dark blackish-brown or black. **Adult female** Head and face pale brown or greyish-brown on forehead to crown, cheeks and ear-coverts; tips to cheeks and ear-coverts flecked darker or blackish; nape to mantle, back and scapulars brown or grey-

ish-brown streaked blackish; rump and uppertail-coverts deep rufous-orange. Tail dark or blackish-brown on central pair and progressively rufous or rufous-orange with some brown towards tips of all outers except outermost, which are slightly paler orange. Wings as male but more broadly edged pale buff or pale buff-brown on edges to secondaries and tertials. Pale or whitish ill-defined moustachial and sides of throat finely streaked or flecked dark brown and pale orange-brown, centre of throat whitish or pale buff to buffish-orange forming a broad stripe; breast to upper flanks and belly rufous-orange, becoming paler on lower belly and vent. Undertail-coverts pale buff, lightly washed orange. **Immature** Juvenile similar to adult female but generally darker rufous-brown above and heavily spotted or scaled with pale buff edges and tips to head, face, nape, mantle, back and scapulars; wings are blackish but edged dusky-rufous or paler buff on inner secondaries and tertials; chin and throat as female but rest of underparts dark rufous, mottled with darker or blackish subterminal bars on breast and with pale orange-buff tips and lighter buff tips on belly and flanks, the latter with fine dark or blackish barring.
GEOGRAPHICAL VARIATION None. Monotypic.
VOICE Call a thin whistle varying in pitch and tone; alarm note is a guttural *burrr* or a thin whistle (given when predators are near). Usually calls with head and bill tilted upwards and tail fanned out. Song, given by both male and female, is a variable series of mellow whistles, *weetleooo pee pee chitrrr, whittoo chu whee chu chrruu-chrruuu*, etc., broken with short 1–2 second pauses and usually terminating in rising buzzing trill; also includes brief imitations of other birds (Maclean 1988). Sings mostly in the evening or early morning.
STATUS AND DISTRIBUTION Common or locally common. Breeding resident in south-west, southern and more widely in eastern Cape Province, South Africa, south of the Orange River and north into southern and eastern Orange Free State, the Drakensberg range in Lesotho, Natal and Swaziland, also throughout most of the high areas of the Transvaal (north to the Soutpansberg) and the Lebombo Mountains of eastern Swaziland and extreme south-west Mozambique; also in extreme south-east Botswana (Kanye to Mafeking area).
MOVEMENTS Largely sedentary but may be an altitude migrant in parts of the range, e.g. Lesotho, where more frequently recorded at lower altitudes in winter months.

188

HABITAT Throughout most of its range it occurs in foothills, cliffs, gorges and rocky or boulder-strewn hillsides in mountains and loose scree slopes often with scattered vegetation, grassy areas, bushes or stunted trees, isolated or abandoned buildings, quarries etc.; occurs down to sea-level in south-west Cape Province. In parts of its range, e.g. De Aar, Northern Cape, it enters large gardens in non-breeding season.

BEHAVIOUR Rarely found away from preferred habitat where usually solitary or in pairs. Wary and often sits motionless on rocky crag or ledge for considerable periods of time. Spends long periods of time on the ground or rockface where it forages by hopping; also forages on flowering aloes. Occasionally perches on a rock or tree used as a lookout point. Often flicks wings when landing but not habitually; in some parts of its range it has become tame and approachable around human settlements and perches freely on buildings. Feeds

mostly on invertebrates including spiders, milli-pedes and land molluscs but has been known to take small frogs, also nectar, particularly flowering aloes, and some fruit.

BREEDING Season: September to February. Nest: an untidy cup-shaped structure made mostly of grasses, twigs, roots and some dry soil, and lined with fine grasses, dry aloe leaves and small roots, usually placed in a thin crevice, on a ledge or crack in a rock, occasionally in (or under) an aloe tree or hole in a building. Eggs: 2–3, exceptionally 4, pale blue spotted finely with brown or rust-brown spots. Nestlings fed by both parents. Is an occasional brood host to the Red-chested Cuckoo *Cuculus solitarius*.

MOULT No information.

MEASUREMENTS Wing, male 105–119, female 106–115; tarsus 28–31; bill (culmen) 21–25. Weight 60–64 g (Maclean 1988).

REFERENCES Maclean (1988).

9 SENTINEL ROCK-THRUSH *Monticola explorator* Plate 4

Turdus explorator **Vieillot, 1818,** *Nouv. Dict. Hist. Nat.* **(nouv. ed.): 260 – mountains of the Cape of Good Hope.**

IDENTIFICATION 16.5–18 cm (6½–7″). An attractive and richly coloured rock-loving thrush endemic to rocky terrain in south and east South Africa. Smaller than the Cape Rock-Thrush (8) with which it is often found, and has a softer or violet-blue head and breast to nape and sides of neck; mantle and back bluish-grey with wings and central tail feathers dark or blackish-grey; rump and uppertail-coverts to outer tail feathers bright orange; rest of underparts rich or deep orange. Female lacks any blue-grey and is mostly brown above with a streaked or mottled paler face to breast, grey upperparts and pale or dull orange underparts. **Confusion species** Male is similar to male Cape Rock-Thrush, but slightly smaller with blue-grey head and breast extending to the mantle and back; female differs by much paler face, mottled throat and breast and paler or duller underparts. Usually occurs at higher altitude than Cape Rock Thrush and more frequently occurs in montane grasslands. Male Short-toed Rock-Thrush (10) is also similar but has paler or whiter forehead and crown and bright or deep orange breast; female Short-toed has a pale or whitish unmottled chin and throat and pale orange on the breast and upper belly.

DESCRIPTION Sexes differ. **Adult male** Entire head and face (except for blackish lores to eye) to breast, sides of neck and lower nape soft or violet blue-grey. Mantle, back and scapulars (to lesser coverts) darker bluish-grey with centres of feathers darker, rump and uppertail-coverts deep orange. Central tail feathers dark or blackish-brown with all outer feathers deep or bright orange with varying amount of dark brown or blackish on tip of outerweb. Median coverts as scapulars or slightly bluer, greater

coverts dark or blackish-grey finely fringed paler or greyish, alula and primary coverts black; flight feathers also black but with fine pale grey edges and tips to secondaries (which become pale buff in worn plumage); tertials the same or more broadly tipped pale grey. Underwing-coverts orange becoming rich or deep orange on rest of underparts. Bill black. Legs and feet dark or blackish-brown. **Adult female** Forehead to crown and nape brown or tinged grey and flecked paler; mantle, back and scapulars brown or grey-brown with some paler tips on mantle and back in worn plumage; rump and uppertail-coverts pale or dull orange. Tail as male but central feathers brownish-black and all outers dull orange. Wing as male but lacks bluish tinge and edges to coverts and flight feathers finely buff; may show some bluish-grey tips to lesser coverts; under-wing-coverts tawny-buff. Face mostly mottled dull brown with pale buff or greyish-buff spots that become pale buff streaks on sides of chin, cheeks and sides of neck; ear-coverts brownish streaked finely with pale buffish. Chin and throat to breast mottled pale buff and pale or tawny-brown with occasional darker tips; sides of breast usually tinged warm buff or buffish-orange. Lower breast to upper belly dull or dingy orangey-buff often tinged brown; flanks and belly dull or pale orange with paler tips to flanks. Undertail-coverts deeper or warmer orange, longer undertail-coverts whitish. **Immature** Juvenile very similar to adult female but duller brown and more heavily spotted with pale buffish tips on upperparts; rump and uppertail-coverts pale or dull tawny-buff; black tips form scaly pattern on throat, breast and flanks. First-year birds similar to adults but plumage obscured in fresh plumage by pale or buffish tips.

GEOGRAPHICAL VARIATION Birds from Swaziland have been separated into *tenebriformis* on the basis of darker grey upperparts, more intense blue throat and breast, and darker underparts, but this appears at best to be clinal and not consistent throughout; division into two races is not supported here.

VOICE Call a thin or high-pitched whistle very similar to that of Cape Rock Thrush; alarm call a soft descending *tre-e-e-e-ee-ee-ee-e*. Song a lively melodious warbling series of fairly short phrases, *worr, chilli-chilli, worr, treeo, treeo, worr...* interspersed or varied with *chi-chi* or *troo-tree* and other similar chattering phrases; females also sing but give only a shorter *chu-chu-chu-chree-chree-chree...* version of the male's song (Maclean 1988, Newman 1983). Song given from prominent perches close to the nest site.

STATUS AND DISTRIBUTION Common or locally common. Endemic to south and east South Africa from the southern Cape Province east through the southern Karoo to north-east Cape Province, the Drakensberg range in Lesotho, southern and eastern Orange Free State, inland Natal and south-east Transvaal (north to about Lydenburg). More widely distributed at lower altitude in non-breeding season.

MOVEMENTS An altitude migrant although many birds at lower levels are resident. Ranges from sea-level to high plateaulands slightly above 3000 m (9900'), but most birds occur above 1200 m (3950') and in Lesotho absent below 2000 m (6600'). Birds breeding at the highest levels move to lower levels in winter, usually down to c.600 m (2000'). Birds from Lesotho move north-east in non-breeding season to winter in the Lebombo Mountains (Mt Meponduine) in extreme southern Mozambique. Has occurred as a vagrant to the eastern Cape, Zululand and north and central Transvaal.

HABITAT Open hillsides and plateaulands generally above 1200 m (3960') with short-grass pastures and rocky outcrops, boulderfields or bare slopes; also fond of recently burnt grassland areas and felled plantations, and occasionally near human settlements.

BEHAVIOUR An erect, alert rock-thrush with a generally upright posture and bill held slightly upward, hence the name Sentinel, when the male stands guard on favoured perches near the nest site. Usually alone, in pairs or small loose groups; in prime habitat pairs nest within 500 m (1500') of each other. Active, hopping rapidly over stones and loose scree, perching prominently on roadside wires, posts, rocks, boulders and termite mounds. In parts of its range, usually at the higher levels, occasionally visits and perches on buildings. Often in company or loosely associated with Cape Rock Thrush in areas of overlap. Frequently flicks wings after alighting. Forages on the ground amongst rocks and grassy tufts and feeds mostly on small insects, e.g. ants and termites, but also beetles and moths and their larvae; also takes seeds and some fruit.

BREEDING Season: September to December, possibly extending to February in Lesotho. Nest: a large cup-shaped structure of dry grass stems, twigs, roots, moss and lichens lined with finer grasses and rootlets and built solely by the female, usually well hidden under a stone or boulder, in a crevice or on a ledge, also under large grass tufts on hillsides. Eggs: 2–3, rarely 4, plain greenish or sky-blue, sometimes finely speckled or spotted reddish-brown. Incubation period 13–14 days by female only. Fledging period 16 days, nestlings fed by both parents.

MOULT No information.

MEASUREMENTS (n=22) Wing, male 100–108, female 95–104; tarsus 32–35; bill (culmen) 19–22.5 (Urban *et al.* 1997, Maclean 1993). Weight apparently unrecorded.

REFERENCES Maclean (1988), Newman (1983), Urban *et al.* (1997).

10 SHORT-TOED ROCK-THRUSH *Monticola brevipes*   Plate 3

Petrocincla brevipes Waterhouse, 1938, in Alexander, *Exped. Int. Africa* 2: 263 – 'Tans Mountain, Damaraland, near Walvis Bay.

IDENTIFICATION 18 cm (7"). A small rock-thrush of the dry western and interior areas of south-west Angola, Namibia and South Africa; often appears long-billed or large-headed and short-tailed. Males of the nominate race have a variable amount of white or whitish-blue on the forehead and crown to nape; the mantle, back and scapulars are blue-grey, rump and uppertail-coverts deep or bright orange, central tail feathers brown or blackish-brown, as are the innerwebs of the outer tail (outer edges orange). Face to chin and throat blue or blue-grey, lores black, rest of underparts bright or deep orange. Females have uniform dark brown upperparts except for the orange on the rump to outer tail, the large area of pale or whitish on the chin and throat, and pale orange on the breast and belly.

Confusion species Male is similar to that of both Cape (8) and Sentinel (9) Rock-Thrush (range overlaps only with Cape) but is smaller than Cape and has white on forehead to crown (or sides of crown), except in the race *pretoriae*; main differences from Cape are paler blue of head and face and blue-grey on mantle and back, and from Sentinel pale forehead or crown and lack of blue extending to the throat. Female is also similar to female Cape and Sentinel but the large unmottled area of whitish on the chin and throat, slightly paler, more uniform upperparts, and the pale orange on the breast and belly are the best distinguishing characters. Miombo Rock-Thrush (11) male is also similar but is out of range of Short-toed, has slightly paler blue on head and upperparts, and is spotted or mottled with black on upperparts; female has heavily streaked or barred upperparts, lacks the orange rump and outer edges of the tail, and has broad dark malar stripes, pale chin and throat, and whitish belly to undertail-coverts.

DESCRIPTION Sexes differ. **Adult male** Forehead and crown to nape variable from white (in worn plumage) to pale whitish-blue, becoming darker blue across crown (in some, mostly in fresh plumage, the blue extends from forehead to nape but sides of crown are white forming a supercilium). Mantle, back and scapulars blue-grey, rump and uppertail-coverts bright or deep orange. Tail has central feathers dark or blackish-brown as are inner-webs to most outer feathers, with broad orange or orange-rufous outerwebs to all outer feathers, broadest on outermost pair. Median coverts dark grey or blackish fringed with pale grey or bluish-grey, greaters similar but finely edged pale bluish-grey or whitish, alula black, primary coverts also black but finely edged paler; flight feathers black with fine bluish-grey outerwebs (but edged duller or browner when worn), tips to secondaries narrowly whitish, tertials similar but more broadly edged bluish-grey and tipped buff. Underwing as under-parts. Lores black, occasionally extending to ear-coverts; cheeks and lower ear-coverts pale grey or bluish-grey extending to chin and slightly darker on throat and sides of nape. Breast and remaining underparts deep or bright orange or orange-rufous. Bill black. Legs and feet black. **Adult female** Fore-head to crown and nape dark brown or tinged grey, slightly darker on mantle, back and scapulars; rump to tail as male but central tail feathers (and inner-webs to most outers) browner. Wings as male but brownish-black and coverts, secondaries and ter-tials finely edged pale buffish-brown in fresh plumage. Lores to eye dark or blackish-brown, becoming brown on cheeks and ear-coverts flecked or finely streaked paler or whitish. Chin and throat pale buff or whitish and edged or fringed with brown forming streaks on sides of throat and neck and across lower throat. Breast to upper flanks and upper belly warm orange or orange-rufous, becom-ing paler or washed orange on lower belly to vent and undertail-coverts. **Immature** Juvenile exten-sively spotted or scalloped on head to back and chin to breast with pale yellowish centres and dark fringes which gradually wear to buff tips on upper-parts and black bars on breast, flanks and upper belly; black flight feathers also narrowly edged yel-lowish-buff and tipped more broadly, with a yel-lowish-buff wing-bar across the tips of the greater coverts. Rump and tail as adult but rump usually barred with dark tips. Tail as adult. First-winter male is identifiable by bluish-grey upperparts spotted with pale buff tips (of juvenile plumage) to head and nape; underparts (except for sides of breast) buffish-orange barred with dark brown crescents at tips; first-year female darker or duller brown on upper-parts with pale buff spotting and paler buff on underparts, lightly washed orange with small or fine dark bars or crescents at tips.

GEOGRAPHICAL VARIATION Two races; varia-tion clinal and mainly concerns head colour of male and upperparts of female. Male of race *pre-toriae* has forehead to crown and nape paler grey (remains grey when worn); the grey on face to throat and on mantle, back and scapulars lacks the bluish tinge and is mousier; the orange underparts are slightly deeper or heavier and the edges to the flight feathers are buffish not bluish-white. Female is generally darker or browner especially on the head and face, and shows less grey on the upper-parts; the dusky speckling on the underparts is also heavier or more pronounced.

VOICE Most frequent call is a thin *tseeep*. Song, not well recorded, mostly a series of whistled phrases jumbled together and recalling those of the other rock-thrushes of the region; also includes some mimicry of other species with which it comes into contact.

STATUS AND DISTRIBUTION Common or locally common.

M. b. brevipes Resident in south-west Angola (Iona Post to Mossamedes escarpment), discontin-uously south through Namibia to the northern Cape Province and the northern Karoo east to about 23°E (Urban *et al.* 1997).

M. b. pretoriae South-east Botswana (to about Molepole), western Transvaal and south-western Orange Free State, also isolated populations between 29° and 30°E in north-eastern Orange Free State and at Siteki. Reportedly also in the Lebombo Mountains in Swaziland (Clancey 1968, Urban *et al.* 1997, Maclean 1993) but Harrison *et al.* (1998) found no evidence of this in surveys for the South African Breeding Birds Atlas.

Intergrades between the two races occur in cen-tral and northern Cape Province; Farkas (1966, 1979) and White (1967) considered *pretoriae* a valid species.

MOVEMENTS An altitude migrant, dispersing widely at lower levels in winter; there are records of individuals outside the range in eastern Botswana and the northern Transvaal.

HABITAT Rocky outcrops in open hilly country, also wooded kopjes, stony slopes in mountains, escarpments and sides of river valleys usually with some scattered shrubs or small stunted trees, in some parts of the range found around human set-tlements, villages and edge of towns, especially during the non-breeding season.

BEHAVIOUR Usually alone or in pairs perching on the ground or in trees, or roadside wires; gen-erally shy or wary but in parts of its range has become tame and often seen perching on build-ings. Forages mostly on the ground in a chat-like manner, usually in the open but also under trees and bushes, feeding mostly on insects but also small scorpions and some seeds.

BREEDING Season: August or September to Janu-ary (Botswana and Transvaal), November to March (Namibia). Nest: a loose or bulky cup of dry grass, roots and similar plant material, lined with fine grasses; usually well hidden in a tree or bush under a rock or among the roots of a tree on a rockface or side of a steep crevice or valley, occasionally on a ledge. Eggs: 2–3, sky-blue to greenish-blue.

MOULT No information.

MEASUREMENTS Wing, male 100–108, female 96–102; tarsus 23.5–27; bill (culmen) 20–27; *pretoriae* wing, male 100–105 (Urban *et al.* 1997, Maclean 1988). Weight apparently unrecorded.

REFERENCES Clancey (1968), Farkas (1966, 1979), Harrison *et al.* (1998), Maclean (1988, 1993), White (1967).

11 MIOMBO ROCK-THRUSH *Monticola angolensis* Plate 5
(Angola Thrush)

Monticola angolensis Sousa, 1888, *J. Sci. Math. Phys. Nat. Lisboa* 12: 225, 233 – Caconda, Benguella, Angola.

IDENTIFICATION 18 cm (7"). A small to medium-sized rock-thrush confined to miombo woodland in rock-covered hills or plateau areas of southern and southern-central Africa. The male has a pale grey-blue head, face and most of the upperparts (except for the orange rump to outer tail) with black mottling on the central nape, mantle, back and scapulars; the blue-grey of the head extends to the throat; the breast to belly and flanks is deep orange or rufous and the vent to undertail-coverts is white or washed with orange. Females are generally drab and pale brown with a heavy dark malar stripe, fine dark bars and streaks on the upperparts, lacking the orange on the rump and tail; the tail is pale brown (finely barred darker) and the underparts are pale orange or buffish-orange, barred darker on the breast and whitish on the belly. **Confusion species** Once seen well neither adult is likely to be confused with any other rock-thrush, as the dark spotting on the upperparts of the male is distinctive and the general brown tones of the female, together with the lack of colour on the rump and tail, differ considerably from the other rock-thrushes of the region; separated on range and habitat from the similar Cape (8), Sentinel (9) and Short-toed (10) Rock-Thrushes.

DESCRIPTION Sexes differ. **Adult male** Head and face pale blue-grey with dark or blackish lores, blue-grey extending across upperparts to mantle, back and scapulars where some (highly variable between individuals) feathers are tipped with black forming a mottled pattern on nape, mantle, back and scapulars; cheeks and ear-coverts may also be dark grey or greyish-black. Rump and uppertail-coverts bright or deep orange, sometimes also barred narrowly with black. Central tail feathers black or blackish-brown, all outers having dark or brownish innerwebs but broadly edged bright or deep orange on outerwebs with narrow dark bar at tip. Median and greater coverts blackish on innerwebs but broadly edged pale grey-blue on outers and tipped with black, alula black finely edged pale buff, primary coverts and flight feathers black or blackish-brown finely edged pale bluish (may be edged pale buff on inner primary coverts) or more broadly on inner secondaries and tertials, this fading to pale buff or whitish when worn; tertials similar or darker on innerwebs, outerwebs pale bluish-grey, spotted or barred black. Underwing-coverts heavy or deep rufous-orange. Breast to upper flanks deep orange or rufous (heaviest or deepest on centre of breast), becoming paler or whiter on belly to vent and undertail-coverts, sometimes undertail-coverts washed pale orange. Bill slender and tapering, black. Legs and feet black. **Adult female** Head and face finely mottled or flecked brown and pale buff, mostly pale buff with browner tips to feathers, darker brown tips to lores and paler or whitest on submoustachial region. Mantle, back and scapulars variable from pale buffish-brown to greyish-brown closely mottled, vermiculated or barred darker with brown, and tips to feathers also brown; rump and uppertail-coverts similar but with brown or warm buff-brown and narrow black bars. Tail has brown to dark brown centres and pale edges, but edges and all outers have broad orange or chestnut innerwebs and are spotted or barred blackish. Median and greater coverts as scapulars or becoming greyish-brown, alula dark brown, primary coverts dark brown finely fringed with pale buffish-brown, spotted or streaked darker. Flight feathers dark brown broadly edged pale buffish-brown or light grey-brown (may be barred or spotted darker), tips of primaries mostly unbarred; tertials pale brown to pale grey-brown fringed subterminally with black and edged with light orange to pale buff. Underwing-coverts light orange. Broad pale buff submoustachial and dark brown malar stripe bordering pale buff centre to chin and throat; breast and flanks dull orange (variably paler or lighter orange) and may be finely or broadly tipped dark brown or blackish, sometimes flanks paler or buffish; belly to vent and undertail-coverts whitish or light cream or washed lightly with pale orange. Thighs orange. **Immature** Juvenile heavily spotted above and below with broad pale beige or light buff centres to head, face, nape, mantle, back and scapulars with broad dark brown to blackish fringes, with feathers on mantle and back more elongated and coming to a point at tip. Median coverts tipped the same or with pale orange centres; greater coverts buffish-orange with fine dark or blackish bars at tip; flight feathers dark brown, secondaries finely fringed blackish, primaries finely fringed pale buff. Face to breast, belly and flanks as upperparts but mottled paler buff on centre of feathers or at tips and fringed dark olive to dark brown, paler or whiter on belly and undertail-coverts.

First-year bird is very similar to adult female but has mantle, back and scapulars (and tips of wing-coverts) more heavily mottled and spotted with buff, grey and black. Tail dark brown spotted blackish on outerwebs of central pair, all outer feathers orange with blackish subterminal fringe and pale brown outer fringe. Underparts paler than adult, throat finely spotted and breast to belly and flanks buffish barred or mottled dark brown with orange feathers showing through as age progresses; undertail-coverts usually cream and unbarred.

GEOGRAPHICAL VARIATION Two races; variation not well marked. Male of race *hylophila* has the breast and flanks paler and less contrasting less than in nominate, the belly and undertail-coverts white. Variation appears to be clinal as the populations at extreme ends of the range are highly distinct but there is a wide area of intermediacy between the two; females inseparable. The race '*niassae*' is now considered to fall within the range of variation shown by nominate *angolensis*.

VOICE Call a rising two-note fluty whistle with the second higher than the first; also a chattering alarm call. Song a variable series of high-pitched and sweet or melodic phrases, *pe-pe-per-pee-pew, per-per, pee-pew pweetweet*, successive phrases sometimes differing slightly in tone, *tlee tee too too it* or *heooo heo hehe... wheooouu'u'u'u seeti seeti... heeiou'u tch site-situ...*, and often containing mimicry of other birds in the vicinity. Males sing from well below the canopy and neither call nor song is very loud.

STATUS AND DISTRIBUTION Uncommon to locally common.

M. a. angolensis South-eastern Zaire from northern Lake Tanganyika from about Katenga, also around Lake Kivu in south-west Rwanda, north-east Burundi and adjacent areas of Tanzania (Kibondo). Also southern Tanzania south of about 9°S from Kigoma to Lake Rukwa, east to Nandembo and Nachingwea, south into Malawi (except the west); also southern Zaire to northern and western-central (but not western) Zambia south to extreme north-east Botswana (first bred November 1995) and in the west through eastern-central Angola to the central plateau.

M. a. hylophila Western Malawi, south to southern Zambia and most of Zimbabwe except the extreme north-east and the south; also adjacent areas of northern Mozambique (Manica and Tete districts) and eastern Sofala district between the Inyamadzi and Buzi rivers (Clancey 1971, Urban *et al.* 1997).

MOVEMENTS Largely resident but some evidence that birds in southern Tanzania wander in the period March to September when it becomes locally numerous and has wandered into Botswana; also only recorded along the western shore of Lake Malawi in June to October; scarce migrant or visitor to western Zambia and parts (Inyangna and Chimanimani Mountains) of the eastern highlands of Zimbabwe. Single extralimital record from Dodoma, central Tanzania (Britton 1980).

HABITAT Not a bird of open rocky areas (though may occasionally be found along the edges), as it is more or less confined to open *Brachystegia* (miombo) woodland, usually in upland or hilly areas, across the entire range; also found in *Baikiaea* woodland and mountain acacia *Brachystegia glaucescens* and along edges of *Eucalyptus* plantations. Occurs mostly between 600 and 2000 m (1980–6600'). Pattern of distribution is highly localised, and absent from many areas of apparently suitable habitat; may be dependant on availability of trees with suitable nestholes.

BEHAVIOUR Usually alone, in pairs or in small associated groups; shy, unobtrusive and easily overlooked, although in defence of territory or recently fledged young it becomes quite bold. Spends long periods in open miombo woodland, flitting from branch to branch, but forages mostly on the ground in leaf-litter and rotting vegetation and under logs; also hawks or drops shrike-like onto insect prey from low perch in trees or bushes. When disturbed flies up into a tree and sits motionless before quietly making its escape. Family parties, especially of recently fledged birds, may make use of telegraph wires crossing open country as vantage points. Feeds mostly on insects, particularly ants and termites, but also crickets, worms, moths and their larvae, spiders and centipedes, also occasionally small legless lizards.

BREEDING Season: August to December but mostly September to November. Nest: a large and untidy or bulky structure supporting a small cup made of dry coarse grasses, plant stems, roots and vine fibres and twigs, lined with fine grass; some nests lack the supporting structure and are quite sparse in construction and eggs can even be laid on a scraped hollow in rotten wood, usually placed in a hole or fork in a tree, on a stump or along a branch up to 3 m (c.10') from the ground. Nests and territories appear to be occupied and defended over several years. Eggs: 3–4, pale or turquoise-blue, unmarked or erratically spotted with reddish-brown. Incubation by both male and female. Incubation period 13–15 days. Fledging period 18–21 days, young fed by both parents. Two broods; three (in three months) are not unknown (Maclean 1988, Ginn *et al.* 1989, Urban *et al.* 1997).

MOULT No information.

MEASUREMENTS Wing, male 91–104, female 92–101; tarsus 23–28.5; bill (culmen) 19.5–22.5. Weight 44 g (Maclean 1988).

REFERENCES Clancey (1971), Ginn *et al.* (1989), Maclean (1988), White (1967).

12 (COMMON) ROCK THRUSH *Monticola saxatilis* Plate 4

(Rufous-tailed Rock-Thrush)

Turdus saxatilis Linnaeus 1766, *Syst. Nat.* (ed. 12): 294 – Switzerland.

IDENTIFICATION 17–19 cm (6¾–7½"). The most widespread of the rock-thrushes. A distinctive, chat-like, dumpy but often upright, short-tailed and long-winged shape (has long primary projection typical of long-distance migrant). Male in summer has pale blue head and slate-grey upperparts except for large white patch on the back, deep reddish-orange underparts and base and edges to the brown tail. Female is pale brown to brown, mottled paler or buffish on the upperparts and barred underparts with deep rust-orange base and edges to the tail. Winter male more like female, with greyish-blue head and upperparts heavily spotted or mottled and barred darker; underparts similarly barred pale buff, light orange and blackish except for the undertail-coverts, flight feathers and tail, which are as summer plumage. **Confusion species** Most likely problem is with Blue Rock-Thrush (17), particularly male of eastern race *philippensis* which, however, lacks the white back and has an all-dark tail and bright blue head and upperparts extending to the breast; female and immature Blue Rock-Thrush (of all races) have uniform upperparts and are generally darker or browner with a longer tail. Female and immature Rock-Thrush are paler, browner and more heavily mottled on the upperparts. Unlikely to be confused with female or immature rock-thrushes elsewhere in range owing to lack of heavy barred upperparts and presence of rusty or rufous base of tail. Little Rock-Thrush (13) is smaller and with a longer tail; the grey on the head of the male extends to the centre of the breast and has no white on the back; female is similar to the male and lacks the barring or scaled pattern of female Rock-Thrush.

DESCRIPTION Sexes differ. **Adult ('summer') male** (late February to late July or early August) Entire head to upper mantle, chin, throat and sides of neck pale blue except for slightly darker or greyer-blue lores; mantle and scapulars grey or slaty-blue but may be variably tipped paler blue; back white and some feathers on lower mantle and inner scapulars may also be tipped white (in heavily worn plumage extent of white may be larger); rump and uppertail-coverts dark grey-blue but longest uppertail-coverts rufous-orange. Tail brown to dark brown but bases to all feathers and edges to outers broadly rich rufous-orange. Median coverts black, finely tipped paler or whitish-buff, greaters black or browner-black and in fresh plumage sometimes tipped white (greatly reduced or absent in breeding birds); alula and primary coverts black or blackish-brown, the latter finely edged or tipped whitish; flight feathers and tertials blackish-brown, the latter sometimes showing slightly paler tips (pale tips of flight feathers usually worn down by mid- to late spring and most April birds have black wings, though some may retain some or all pale tips until well

into the breeding season). Axillaries and underwing-coverts as underparts, which are deep rufous-orange, deepest or heaviest on breast and upper belly and slightly paler or whitish on vent; birds in spring (February–April) may show pale or buffish-orange tips anywhere on underparts. Bill, legs and feet black or blackish-brown. **Adult 'winter' male** (late August to early February) Head and face pale grey or greyish-brown but bases to crown and nape bluish to blue-grey, finely barred subterminally with grey-brown or blackish and tipped pale yellowish-buff on forehead to nape; face finely tipped pale or yellowish-buff and streaked the same on ear-coverts. Lores dark greyish-blue with pale buff tips. Mantle, back and rump slightly heavier greyish-slate or grey-brown (may also show some bluish bases) with dark brown or blackish subterminal bars and pale buff tips; bases to feathers of lower mantle, back and rump white with pale grey tips (show as an obscure whitish patch); rump and uppertail-coverts dark grey but longest uppertail-coverts rufous or cinnamon, all with paler or whitish tips. Tail as in breeding plumage. Wings as in breeding plumage but median coverts have whitish to pale sandy-buff tips and unmoulted inners may have pale or whitish central shaft, greater coverts have broad pale sandy to greyish-buff edges (may be tinged bluish) and paler or whiter tips; alula and primary coverts dark brown with narrow whitish-buff tips; flight feathers dark brown with thin buff or pale sandy-buff edges and tips (to all feathers in fresh plumage); tertials similar but more broadly tipped pale buff to pale sandy-buff. Chin and throat white but sides duller or greyish-buff and tipped finely with brown, feathers on sides of lower throat sometimes with blue-grey bases; breast, belly and flanks barred pale buffish-orange to orange at base of each feather; broad dark brown subterminal band and pale or whitish-buff tip variable in extent on each feather, creating a barred pattern, heavier on breast and more widely spaced on belly and flanks; vent and undertail-coverts dull rufous-orange with paler orange edges and tips and few dark spots at tips. Late December/January birds have fewer pale tips to upperparts and barred underparts but some still show traces of non-breeding plumage on crown, throat, breast and belly in late May and early June. Early spring adults have chin and throat pale blue like rest of head, face with fine pale tips; underparts as in summer but with paler tips, undertail-coverts slightly paler orange. **Adult 'summer' female** Similar to non-breeding adult male but much browner with no blue or blue-grey at bases of feathers. Forehead and crown to scapulars and rump pale brown to greyish-brown but with fine black subterminal spots and pale buff tips or light orange-buff on crown, nape and sides of neck;

mantle and back have indistinct dark central shafts and dark brown subterminal bars and buffish or creamy-buff bases and broad pale or sandy-buff tips; rump and uppertail-coverts dark rust or rufous-orange barred darker and slightly duller than on male, longest tail-coverts tipped paler. Tail dark brown with rufous-orange at base and bright rufous-red edges to all outerwebs. Lesser and median coverts brown or dark brown finely tipped pale, sandy or yellowish-buff (pale tips sometimes absent by early winter), greater coverts brown to dark brown with fine pale or sandy-buff tips; alula and primary coverts dark or blackish-brown, the latter finely fringed or edged pale buff; flight feathers dark or blackish-brown, browner on tertials which have broad sandy- or greyish-buff tips; underwing-coverts pale rufous-orange. Lores to eye grey-brown forming thin indistinct line; thin pale or cream eye-ring; cheeks and ear-coverts finely mottled brown with pale or sandy-buff tips. Centre of chin and throat whitish, sides dark brown mottled paler with pale or yellowish-buff tips; remaining underparts creamy-buff or light orange-buff on breast (occasionally to sides of neck), flanks all subterminally barred darker, heaviest with dark brown edges and subterminal tips on breast, narrowest on centre of belly and vent and with pale or yellowish-buff tips; vent and undertail-coverts usually unbarred pale or buffish-orange. Bill dark or blackish-horn with paler base to lower mandible. **Adult 'winter' female** Very similar to breeding plumage but with more extensive pale tips and subterminal dark or blackish spots and bars on forehead to upperparts, with broad pale buff to sandy-buff tips extending to sides of rump. Median and greater coverts have broad pale fringes or tips, as do alula and primary coverts; flight feathers and tertials dark brown broadly tipped creamy-buff to light sandy-buff. Face more prominently mottled fine pale grey-brown and light yellowish to cream, centre of chin and throat white and sides mottled with fine brownish spots; breast to upper belly and upper flanks as sides of throat but more yellowish-orange with darker brown subterminal bars and pale buff tips; rest of flanks pale orange-buff with dark brown subterminal bars and pale yellowish tips. **Immature** Juvenile very similar to non-breeding adult female (many are inseparable even in hand) but possibly slightly paler brown and with pale buff tips to upperparts which may show as clear spots with slightly darker fringes on late summer birds. Wing-coverts, flight feathers and tertials have broad pale buff to pale orange-buff tips. Underparts more clearly scalloped with pale buff centres and brown fringes but by late August or early September these are replaced with broad white tips, dark centres and orange bases to feathers. **First-winter male** Probably not always separable from adult male in field, but (increasingly through winter) shows bluish tinge to crown, mantle, scapulars and sides of throat; chin and throat whitish with some blue feathers becoming more extensively bluish towards

spring; also some white begins to show on back. **First-winter female** As adult female (and not always separable with certainty in field) but generally more heavily barred above and below and possibly with more contrasting pale tips; head and upperparts spotted with pale buff and dark or blackish-brown fringes to feathers, creating heavily mottled or scaled pattern; lower mantle and back more broadly tipped and appear more heavily barred; upper rump grey-brown with fine blackish subterminal bars and pale tips, becoming rufous-orange on lower rump and uppertail-coverts with dark or blackish subterminal bar and pale buff tip; tail and flight feathers brown with broad pale orange edges to outers. Wing-coverts as adult but greater coverts and tertials have broad pale buff fringes and pale buff spots at tips; underwing-coverts as adult but paler orange. Underparts also duller and lack any warm or orange-buff tones on breast and flanks and more closely or heavily but often diffusely barred or scaled with brown and buff tips; chin and throat more extensively pale or yellowish-buff, undertail-coverts warm or bright rufous. **First-summer male** Very similar to adult male but less bright overall, retaining juvenile flight and tail feathers as well as some outer greater coverts and hence showing browner (worn) wings; head and face pale blue with pale greyish tips to some feathers; tips to mantle and scapulars often with faint dark subterminal bars and worn whitish tips; greater coverts may have vestigial or retained whitish tips, and orange underparts may have pale or whitish tips and faint dark bars on flanks. **First-summer female** Very similar to adult female and often cannot be aged with confidence. First-winter birds are possibly told (depending on time of year) by amount of wear on retained flight and tail feathers, particularly the pale tips to the wing-coverts and tertials.

Twice recorded hybridising with Blue Rock-Thrush, both times in Italy (Cramp et al. 1988).

GEOGRAPHICAL VARIATION No races currently recognised but birds from Central Asia ('turkestanicus') and eastern Turkey ('coloratus') have been proposed as separable (Stepanyan 1964), the former by a paler grey head and face and the latter by deeper or more saturated colours, particularly the underparts, which average deeper or more rust-red. However, these differences do not appear consistent as there is considerable variation in colours and sizes between individuals throughout the range. Birds in the east average slightly smaller, show a more attenuated bill and have a slightly longer second primary (equal to the third) (Vaurie 1955).

VOICE A variety of contact notes given: a soft diu or ju, a plaintive and mournful piping huep-huep-huep or hewet-hewet-hewet recalling the similar tone of Bullfinch Pyrrhula pyrrhula, and a chak or tchak; alarm notes are a soft uit-uit by female in mild alarm near nest, a rattling kschrrr or scur-r-r-r similar to that of Woodchat Shrike Lanius senator, and a more emphatic or scolding tchack or schak-schak in greater anxiety, often running into a longer phrase in continued mobbing of a predator, *uit-schak-schak-schak*.

Song a soft flowing series of melodious fluted phrases and some mimicry of other species within the vicinity (e.g. Chaffinch *Fringilla coelebs*), similar to that of Blue Rock-Thrush (17) but softer and may begin with several isolated or unconnected phrases. Very chat-like in overall tone with several scratchy notes amongst the more melodious whistling phrases, recalling song of Northern Wheatear *Oenanthe oenanthe*. Also has soft continuous subsong of twittering, gurgling, rattling notes. Song usually given from top of tree, bush, rock or stony scree-slope or cliff-face; also has rising, then looping and descending display-flight when song given. Both sexes sing, but most active song (and display-flight) given by male; sings mostly from April to July or early August, but appears to utter subsong throughout the year although probably less frequently in wintering area; young birds are able to sing at c.3 months.

STATUS AND DISTRIBUTION Uncommon or locally common; has declined considerably in central Europe this century. Breeds from central-northern Portugal and much of Spain discontinuously east through southern France, Switzerland and west-central Austria, Corsica, Sardinia, Italy (except the north), northern Sicily; still present in a few small outposts in Czech Republic but numbers declined during 20th century; Slovakia east to the Carpathians and Moldova and south through Romania to the Balkan states, northern and central Greece to the Taiyetos Oros (Peloponnese), the larger Ionian Islands, Crete and the Aegean islands of Thasos, Samothraki and Samos.

Breeds throughout most of Turkey, but nowhere common and especially sparse in the west, west-central and south-east (except the extreme south-east), and east through Iran (mostly the mountainous areas of the Elburz and Zagros and absent from most of the Dasht-e-lut desert) through Afghanistan and occasionally in the area of Quetta, northern Baluchistan, Pakistan; a few (up to about 12) pairs breed on the isolated outpost of Mt Hermon, northern Israel, above 1650 m (5450'); may also breed in the Sharra highlands of western Jordan (Andrews *et al.* 1999). In North Africa breeds in the High and Middle Atlas of Morocco and in northern Algeria (Aures and possibly elsewhere in the coastal ranges).

In southern Russia breeds in parts of the southern Crimea and the Caucasus; and continuously (from north-east Iran) through southern Turkmenia and most of Tadzhikistan, then east through the Tien Shan, the Karatau and Kirgiz Alatau, eastern Kazakhstan north to about the latitude of Semipalatinsk and at several isolated hill ranges in central and southern Kazakhstan; the Tarbagatai, the central Altai range (possibly locally in north-east Altai), north through the Sayan range (where it may be extremely local) to about Krasnoyarsk and the upper Yenisei; east through the southern slopes of the Tannu Ola range, Mongolia and in northern China from central and northern Sinkiang (mostly north of the Takla Makan desert) east to the Ala

Shan in Kansu, Inner Mongolia and the southern Khinghan range in southern Manchuria (where generally rare or scarce).

In winter to Africa mostly south of the Sahara, except for outposts in southern Algeria and possibly elsewhere along the coasts of Algeria and Libya; may also winter in small numbers along the Iranian coast of Arabian Gulf, southern Oman and Yemen. Winters in small numbers from Senegal and Gambia (probably also southern Mauretania) south to north-east Sierra Leone and Mt Nimba, Guinea/Liberia/Ivory Coast, erratically east through southern Mali, northern Ivory Coast, Ghana (where generally scarce or uncommon), Togo (3 records), northern Nigeria (and at Igbetti in the south) and northern Cameroon (north of 8°N). Passage migrant and may also winter, infrequently, in the Ahaggar range of southern Algeria and the massifs of Air province, northern Niger. More numerous east of south-central Chad and northeast Central African Republic, southern Sudan, Eritrea (occasional or irregular in northern Somalia) and Ethiopia (possibly also Djibouti) south to north-east Zaire, northern and central Uganda, Kenya and central Tanzania, south to about Tabora and east to Dar es Salaam and Zanzibar. In Africa a vagrant to southern Somalia, Rwanda and northern Zambia.

MOVEMENTS Migratory; a migrant to northern breeding range from wintering area in sub-Saharan Africa north of the tropical forests.

Present in wintering area from October to March and early April; departs wintering areas in Kenya and northern Tanzania in March and April and from Sierra Leone and Nigeria in early April; passage west of Nigeria mostly February to March. Passage through coasts of North Africa (where much more numerous than in autumn) from March to early May, with most birds passing late March and early April; a sparse but regular migrant through the oases of central and southern Libya from March to May; in Middle East and Arabia passage from February to late April or mid-May, though most noticeable (more numerous in spring) on northerly passage through Israel from mid-March to early June (with peak late March to late April).

Arrives (males usually a few days before females) at breeding areas in southern Europe from February onwards but more northerly European sites not occupied until mid-April; in Greece and Cyprus (slightly more numerous in spring than autumn) main passage is late March and April (occasionally earlier: mid- to late February or later into May); arrives in Kazakhstan and the Central Asian foothills in early May and the high-altitude sites in Turkey, the Caucasus and further east not until mid- or late May. Evidence of passage further east lacking and less common in spring than on return migration, but known to move through the higher areas of eastern Iran, and from the hills of Sind to Baluchistan, northern Pakistan, Kashmir and western Punjab, north-west India.

Southern departures from breeding range in Europe and much of Asia follows post-juvenile dispersal in early to late August when early migrants (mostly first-winter birds) have reached Morocco east to Egypt (except Libya, where virtually unknown on autumn passage) and Israel. Direction of passage mostly east of south as records in western Sahara relatively scarce, though passage and arrival in Nigeria (where uncommon in winter) from late September; crosses Sahara in broad front from the end of September to late November. Rare on passage through north-west India and northern Pakistan in August and September, with most records in early September, occasional birds to late October and exceptionally November in Sind.

Passage through Cyprus (where generally a scarce migrant), Israel and Egypt fairly light, with most from the last few days of August to the end of September or early October (exceptionally to end of November in Israel); in Jordan extremely rare autumn migrant with only two records, both in early October.

Passage through Arabia and along the Red Sea from late August to late November (most September–October). In Gulf States a scarce migrant from August to November with scattered records (much less common than in spring) in Bahrain, Kuwait, Saudi Arabia and Oman in December and January. Arrives in Ethiopia and Somalia from late August and early September but peak arrival not until early October; passage through northern Somalia about the same time but more usually from late September; arrives in Uganda and central Kenya from mid-October and southern Kenya and northern Tanzania from late October to mid-November, further west in central Sudan and southern Chad in mid-October, and in Nigeria about a month later. Present on Mt Nimba from mid-December to mid-March but also earlier records in September and October. Thus birds breeding in north-east China and wintering in East or Central Africa travel at least 8100 km (5500 miles) between areas. Some evidence of site-fidelity on wintering grounds, with one individual returning to the same area in northern Tanzania for three successive winters.

In late spring overshooting migrants have reached Scotland, Norway and Sweden and elsewhere in northern and central Europe. A scarce passage migrant to Cyprus and a vagrant to British Isles (17 up to 1996), Denmark (6), Norway, Sweden, Estonia, Netherlands (3), Belgium, Germany, Canary Isles, Seychelles, Sikkim, Kiangsu, eastern China and Honshu, Japan (May 1982).

HABITAT A variety of dry, stony or rock-strewn areas from Mediterranean steppe to heaths, scree-slopes, hills, crags, mountain slopes, gullies, ravines, wadis, dry riverbeds, boulderfields and valleys, usually with some low or stunted vegetation including shrubs, juniper or willow scrub usually above 600 m (2000'), with most at 1500–2700 m (4950–8910') but reaching 3000 m (10,000') in places, e.g. Afghanistan; also old castles, ruins, roofs of buildings, edges of cultivation, especially vineyards and, on migration, edges of cultivation, hayfields, woodlands, hill-tops, fences, parks, gardens (including large towns and cities) and coastal headlands; has been recorded at 5000 m (16,500') in the Karakoram range. In winter in more lowland habitat of grasslands with scattered acacia, rocky outcrops and savanna, but occurs up to 3000 m (10,000') in East Africa; also stony gullies with scattered woodland, hillsides, canyons, open moorland with scattered trees or rocks and bare or burnt ground; in Kenya frequently winters in coastal scrub on sandy beaches and dunes.

BEHAVIOUR Alone or in pairs, although several pairs may occupy the same stretch of habitat; occurs in small groups or loose associations on migration. Often perches upright and recalls wheatear *Oenanthe* but has long pointed wings and short tail, which is often wagged, flicked or flirted; on the ground walks, runs and hops in long bounds, perches readily on rocks, trees and telephone wires. Flight is usually low, slightly undulating or dipping and fast, but male has rising butterfly-like and floating display-flight and a rapid plummeting escape flight from predators. Forages mostly on the ground and by hunting in shrike fashion from a prominent perch, pouncing on prey on ground mostly amongst rocks; also takes some insects in flight by short fly-catching sallies. Food is mostly insects, particularly beetles, wasps, damselflies, small dragonflies, grasshoppers, ants, spiders and their larvae; also small lizards, earthworms, snails and small frogs; takes a small amount of fruit including cherry, rowan, grapes, currants, elderberries, and (mostly in wintering area) mulberries, many direct from tree.

BREEDING Season: late April to July. Nest: a neat cup of grass, roots and moss lined with finer dry grasses and moss; may also include some fur or small feathers; usually placed in a ledge or crevice in a rock or scree-slope, rockface, cliff, wall, ruin or crag, under rocks or boulders, on rare occasions in a tree hole. Eggs: 3–4, exceptionally 5–6, pale blue or with faint reddish-brown speckles or spots at larger end. Incubation period 14–15 days by female only. Fledging period 14–16 days; young fed by both parents but mostly the female. Two broods but possibly only one in northern and extreme southern (e.g. Israel) parts of the range.

MOULT Complete post-breeding moult of adults begins mid-July or occasionally early August and completed from early August to early September. Partial pre-breeding moult of head and body, occasionally including some lesser and median coverts (more rarely the greater coverts or tertials) from mid-November to December and completed from late January to early March. Partial post-fledging juvenile moult of head, body, lesser and median coverts from (c.6 weeks of age) late June to mid-August and fully completed by early September. Pre-breeding moult of first-winter birds at about the same time as that for adults, from November to February or March.

MEASUREMENTS Wing, male (Europe and Africa) 119–131, (Tien Shan, India and Mongolia) 115–126, female 112–126; tarsus 26.5–30; bill (from skull) 23–27. Weight, male (summer) 40–65 g, female (summer) 45–65 g (Cramp *et al.* 1988, Urban *et al.* 1997).

REFERENCES Andrews *et al.* (1999), Stepanyan (1964), Tucker & Heath (1994), Vaurie (1955).

13 LITTLE ROCK-THRUSH *Monticola rufocinereus* Plate 3

Saxicola rufocinerea **Rüppell, 1837,** *Neue Wirbelt., Vögel*: **76, pl. 27 – Simen Province, northern Abyssinia.**

IDENTIFICATION 15–16 cm (6–6¼"). A diminutive but stout or stocky rock-thrush of south-west Arabia and parts of East Africa. Adults are mostly grey on the head to breast and mantle and back, but the rump to base of tail and remaining underparts are orange, the tail pattern recalling that of a Bluethroat *Luscinia svecica* with a dark inverted 'T' and red in the outer feathers, whilst some of its habits – e.g. tail-quivering – recall those of a redstart. **Confusion species** Most likely to be confused with eastern races of Redstart *Phoenicurus phoenicurus* which, however, have white or whitish forehead, black lores, face, chin and throat to breast, pale panel in the wing, shorter bill and a much longer tail with red only in the tail and extending to the outer feathers. Little Rock-Thrush is shorter-tailed and has a longer slender bill. All other rock-thrushes are much larger and Red-tailed Wheatear *Oenanthe xanthoprymna*, which is unlikely to occur within range, is paler above with white underparts. The race of Black Redstart *P. ochruros phoenicuroides* which winters in extreme northeast Africa is much blacker on the upperparts and chin to breast, and remaining underparts are deep orange; females and first-year birds are almost uniformly dull grey-brown with reddish-orange uppertail-coverts and outer tail feathers.

DESCRIPTION Sexes almost alike. **Adult male** Forehead to crown deep ash-grey; nape, mantle, back, scapulars and wing-coverts duller or olive-grey (or may appear tinged brownish). Rump deep orange to orange-rufous on uppertail-coverts. Tail mostly deep orange-rufous except for dark brown central feathers and tips to all outers and distal edges of outermost pair, forming distinctive inverted dark T; undertail shows only dark terminal band. Flight feathers dark or blackish-brown finely edged pale brown on secondaries and more broadly on tertials, becoming pale buff in worn plumage; alula black or blackish; underwing-coverts light or pale orange. Base of bill and lower forehead to over eyes pale bluish-grey, extending as a short supercilium; lores black, cheeks and ear-coverts to chin, throat and breast grey or dull bluish-grey, forming bib or breast-band; sides of lower breast and rest of underparts rich orange, thighs greyish-brown. Bill (slender and finely hooked at tip), legs and feet black, soles of feet greyish. **Adult female** As male except for slightly paler or duller (on average) olive-brown tinge on upperparts and chin to breast; lower breast often finely barred. Chin and throat also whitish or pale whitish-grey. In worn plumage has pale or whitish tips to upper lores, sides of crown and nape, cheeks and sides of throat. **Immature** Juvenile heavily spotted or mottled above and below with large pale buff-edged blackish spots; spots on crown and nape smaller and closer together. Rump and uppertail-coverts orange. Tail as adult but

duller. Tips of median and greater coverts pale orange-buff, edges to secondaries pale buff or buffish-brown; tips of tertials pale buffish to light orange. Chin and throat pale buffish, finely barred at tips; breast, belly and flanks also barred darker.

GEOGRAPHICAL VARIATION Two races; variation not well marked. Female of race *sclateri* is darker grey on the chin, throat and neck (and more similar to the male) than the nominate. Both sexes of this race are stated to have more dark brown on the outer tail feathers, but this feature is very variable and some African individuals can have as much as some Arabian birds.

VOICE Mostly silent but has a soft *trrt* or *tyyt* alarm note. Song a pleasant series of variably pitched scratchy and flute-like melodic notes, *tryyh-rrr-tvirirp-tschak-tschak* or *tsurr-sureet, skeee, tsee-ee-tsurrrrr* or *steeee skurrree skirrrrrr*, fading towards the end and recalling the general tone of Blue Rock-Thrush (17). In non-breeding season often gives a very soft warbling subsong, usually only audible from a few feet. Song usually given from high perch in bush, tree or rock-face.

STATUS AND DISTRIBUTION Uncommon or locally common.

M. r. rufocinereus Eritrea south to western and central Ethiopia east to northern Somalia (where locally common) and south to the highlands of western and central Kenya and the borders of northern and eastern Uganda (Kidepo Valley National Park, Mt Kakamari, Mt Moroto and Sebei). A scarce and uncommon wanderer in non-breeding season (November to March) to the Imatong and Didinga mountains of southern Sudan (but no recent records) and to Longido, the western scarp above Lake Natron, and the Kerio Valley, southern Kenya, also to Lobo Lodge, northern Serengeti National Park in northern Tanzania (Zimmerman *et al.* 1996, Urban *et al.* 1997).

M. r. sclateri Asir mountains of south-west Saudi Arabia, north to about Kawkaban south to western Yemen.

MOVEMENTS Largely resident but see Distribution. Makes seasonal appearances in parts of its range where it is not known to breed, e.g. southern Sudan between November and March, but may be poorly recorded from adjacent areas; occurs at slightly lower altitudes – down to 600 m (1980') – in Yemen in winter; thus movements to, and occurrence in, areas at the edge of the range poorly known.

HABITAT Upland or semi-montane forests and wooded areas in rocky ravines, forest clearings and grass-covered rocky escarpments, cliffs or gorges with scrub, edges of cultivation (particularly orchards); in parts of range around buildings and in isolated areas of thornbush, edges of wadis, and thickets in savanna or open bush including acacias, junipers and euphorbias; between 1400 and 2500 m (4620–8250') in Africa and between 800 and 3000 m (2640–9900') in Arabia (Brooks *et al.* 1987).

BEHAVIOUR Alone or in pairs; several pairs may nest in fairly close proximity. Often tame and confiding; many actions similar to both Redstart and Black Redstart; spends long periods sitting and watching from vantage point before darting after an insect on or near the ground, eating it on the ground and returning to same or similar perch; may also pursue flying insects in flycatcher-fashion; perches upright with tail pointing vertically downwards on rocks and low branches, also shivers or quivers tail nervously whilst perched. On the ground runs and hops in manner of small thrush. In parts of its range more active at dusk and dawn. Food mostly insects including grasshoppers and beetles which it takes in flight or searches for on the ground; also caterpillars and some fruit, particularly *Rosa abyssinica* and *Olea chrysophylla* (Urban *et al.* 1997).

BREEDING Poorly known. Season: February to May and June, also September and October (Urban & Brown 1971) and December (Betts 1966). Nest: mostly of tree bark, moss and animal or human hair, placed in fork of bush or shrub or cleft of large tree, rocky crevices up to c.1.3 m (c.4') from the ground; also recorded on beam in hut. Eggs: 3, plain bluish-green or turquoise-blue, may have some small or fine reddish-brown spots at larger end. Both male and female feed the young. Probably two broods.

MOULT No information.

MEASUREMENTS Wing, male 77–90, female 80–85; bill (culmen) male (n=36) 13–16, female (n=32) 13.5–16, (to skull) male 19–20.5, female 18–21; tarsus, male 24–27, female 22.5–26. Weight (Kenya birds) 20–27 g (Urban *et al.* 1997).

REFERENCES Betts (1966), Brooks *et al.* (1987), Smith (1957), Urban & Brown (1971), Urban *et al.* (1997), Zimmerman *et al.* (1996).

14 BLUE-CAPPED ROCK-THRUSH *Monticola cinclorhynchus* Plate 5
(Blue-headed Rock-Thrush)

Petrocincla cinclorhyncha Vigors, 1832, *Proc. Zool. Soc. London*: 172 – Himalayan mountains [restricted to Simla by Baker (1921) *J. Bombay Nat. Hist. Soc.* 27: 719].

IDENTIFICATION 17–18 cm (6¾–7"). A medium-sized rock-thrush (smaller than others of the region) of the Himalayas (summer) and southern India (winter). Males are very distinctive with deep cobalt-blue on the crown to nape and chin and throat; the face to mantle, back, scapulars and wings are black with a broad white wing-patch on the secondaries; the rump, uppertail-coverts and remaining underparts are bright orange. Females are olive-brown or tinged grey on the head and barred or scalloped whitish or yellowish-buff, with dark brown underparts and no white wing-patch.

Confusion species Most like the widely separated (but closely related) White-throated Rock-Thrush (15), which lacks blue on the face and has white on the central throat. Female from female White-throated by lack of barred upperparts. Both sexes of Blue Rock-Thrush (17) are more uniformly dark; males are deep grey-blue with no orange or white in the wing, females darker brown with paler spotting, not bars or scallops, on the underparts. Male Rock Thrush (12) has paler blue head and upper mantle and white back to upper rump; female is paler brown with pale yellowish-buff spotting or streaks on upperparts, lighter bars on underparts, and brown tail with rufous base. The larger Chestnut-bellied Rock-Thrush (16) has a bright cobalt-blue crown to nape and rump to tail, with mantle and back tipped deep blue (not uniform black), no white wing-patch and much deeper rust-red underparts. Female more broadly barred and less scalloped on underparts, with distinctive face pat-

tern formed by a pale yellowish-buff stripe from lores to eye and patch at lower edge of ear-coverts.

Taxonomic note Previously considered conspecific with White-throated Rock-Thrush (15).

DESCRIPTION Sexes differ. **Adult 'summer' male** Forehead to crown, nape and centre of upper mantle bright cobalt-blue, overlying black bases to feathers, blue often appearing as streaked. Edges of scapulars deep bluish-black. Lores (occasionally across base of bill) to over eye, cheeks, ear-coverts, sides of nape to sides of neck, mantle, back and scapulars jet black. Rump and uppertail-coverts bright or rufous-orange. Tail fairly short and black but edges to bases of all feathers bright or metallic blue. Lesser coverts bright metallic blue (black when worn), showing as broad blue panel on closed wing; median coverts black with small bright blue edges or centre of tip; greater coverts black or blackish-blue with outers broadly edged or entirely pale or cobalt-blue; alula black and primary coverts also black but fairly broadly edged light blue; flight feathers black or blackish, all (except outer two primaries) narrowly edged pale blue; base of secondaries (and lowest tertial) white, showing as broad wing-bar in flight; rest of tertials black narrowly edged bluish, but often appearing entirely black. Underwing-coverts bright or deep rufous-orange. Chin and throat (to sides of throat) deep cobalt-blue, breast to vent and undertail-coverts bright or deep orange, heaviest or deepest on breast. Bill black, base of lower mandible yellowish outside breeding season. Legs and feet variable from olive-brown, greyish or bluish-slate to pale silvery-grey but may also be greenish, soles usually dull or dirty yellow. **Adult 'winter' male** Forehead to nape darker or blackish with broad dark subterminal tips and fine pale buff tips obscuring most of deep blue crown to nape; only supercilium from above lores to rear of ear-coverts is deep blue. Face dull black continuing on sides of neck to mantle, back and scapulars, all heavily scalloped with broad pale buff or light orange-buff tips. Chin and throat paler or duller blue and obscured by thin or fine pale orange-buff tips; edges and tips to inner secondaries and ter-tials also browner, rest of tertials sometimes also broadly pale buff. Some birds show very pale or whitish-blue centre or sides to chin and throat. **Adult female** Forehead and most upperparts pale grey-brown tinged olive on mantle, back and scapulars; rump similar but with large pale buff spots and dark brown fringes forming bars; upper-tail-coverts the same, slightly warmer, more gin-gery-brown or barred darker. Tail short, grey-brown. Median and greater coverts brown nar-rowly edged paler or light buff-brown on edges to greaters; alula pale brown, primary coverts similar to greaters; flight feathers brown or pale brown finely edged buff-brown, broadly on edges to inner secondaries and tertials. Underwing-coverts pale or very light orange-buff with darker or browner tips to greater underwing-coverts. Lores brown or dark brown with broad yellowish-buff stripe along upper lores; pale or indistinct buffish or creamy-buff eye-ring; ear-coverts faintly or narrowly spot-ted or streaked light buff, sides of nape slightly olive-brown. Chin and throat white or whitish-buff becoming pale buff-brown or lighter buff at sides and edged finely with dark brown forming a scal-loped pattern, larger and more prominent on sides of neck, breast, belly and flanks, with pale buff centres mixed with yellowish-buff and broadly fringed dark brown; lower flanks and undertail-coverts tinged warm yellowish-buff. Upper mandible black, lower brownish-horn. Legs and feet variable from slate to brown or pale greyish-brown. Some females have extensive pale buff barring and dark brown tips on rump and warm brown or tawny-buff and dark brown barring on uppertail-coverts; some also have sides of nape and neck heavily flecked or streaked white or whitish-buff. **Immature** Juvenile similar to adult female but upperparts entirely spotted or streaked with pale buff or light orange-buff with dark brown fringes, forming a heavily spotted pattern on head, nape, mantle, scapulars and back (largest spots on crown, scapulars and back); rump similar but spots smaller and more broken by darker or browner centres (juvenile male has uppertail-coverts bright orange barred darker). Tips to median and greater coverts pale buff or light yellowish-buff as are tips to tertials. Tail brown tipped rufous. Face heavily flecked pale buff and brown. Underparts as adult female but heavily and more uniformly scalloped pale or whitish-buff with dark brown tips. Imma-ture male shows metallic blue on lesser coverts at early age (July onwards) whilst rest of plumage is still juvenile; attains deep or rufous orange on rump and uppertail-coverts and on breast to belly by August, although some birds still show reduced black tips to belly into first-winter plumage in Sep-tember and October; white patch in wing notice-able from mid- to late August. Subadult male similar to adult winter plumage but usually with narrower pale brown edges and tips to feathers. Subadult female has pale buff tips to greater coverts (retained into following spring) and slightly duller pale brown tips to the tertials.

GEOGRAPHICAL VARIATION None. Monotypic.

VOICE Call a sharp *peri-peri* slightly rising in tone, and outside of the display or breeding season a rarely given grating call; the alarm is a loud *goink-goink, tri-goink* or *tri-goink-goink*, the first note whistled and the second and third lower in pitch, often given repeatedly. Song resembles that of a Stonechat *Saxicola torquata* in quality but more thrush-like in tone, a clear and repeated *rit-prileee-prileer* or a more extended *tew-li-di, tew-li-di, tew-li-di, tew* or occasionally with harsher notes such as *tra-trree-trreea-tra* and a *seer-twik-twik* given monotonously with varying emphasis. Song usually delivered from top of tree, usually pine but also in descending display-flight on outstretched wings; most song given in early morning and evenings from mid-March to mid-June but also not unknown at intervals throughout the day.

STATUS AND DISTRIBUTION Common. Breeds from the Hariab Valley and the Safed Koh in eastern Afghanistan east through the Himalayas from north-ern Pakistan to Kashmir (possibly also Gilgit), Nepal, Sikkim, Bhutan and western Arunachal Pradesh and south or south-west into the hills of Nagaland and the Cachar, Khasi and Garo hills of Assam. In winter mostly western peninsular India from the Western Ghats (south of the Tapti River) south to Kerala and western Tamil Nadu; eastern birds also winter in parts of Assam (Cachar Hills) and probably a sparse winter visitor to Arakan Yoma, south-west Burma. In some years some birds may linger north of the main wintering range in Madhya Pradesh (apparently reg-ular in Bandhavgarh National Park), Uttar Pradesh and around Mt Abu, Rajasthan, India.

MOVEMENTS Migratory; a summer breeding visi-tor to the Himalayas and hills of north-east India from about mid-April, occasionally late March; most northerly birds on passage during April and these and high-altitude birds probably not settled on territory until early May. Southward departure begins in September (possibly late August) and passage across most of peninsular India recorded west to about Karachi and east through Bang-ladesh to about Manipur to middle and late Octo-ber, late birds still in high-mountain passes of Nepal into early October. A scarce or rare passage migrant (may be commoner than the few records suggest) to Andhra Pradesh and Orissa. Perhaps a scarce or rare winter visitor to central Pakistan but the few February records are judged to refer to birds on early return passage (Roberts 1992).

HABITAT Forests and open moist deciduous woods of the foothills and lower mountain slopes between 1200 and 2200 m (3950–7250') throughout most of the Himalayas, but slightly higher to about 3000 m (10,000') in Kashmir and Sikkim and occasionally as low as 900 m (2970') in northern Pakistan or about 1000 m (3300') in Sikkim and Bhutan; in winter to between 610 and 2380 m (2000–7850'). Also occurs in mixed fir and bamboo forests, boulder-covered grassy slopes with stunted trees, and edges of plantations, especially coffee and cardamom. In winter in similar habitat but also occurs at lower altitudes in more open areas on the lower foothills and edges of the plains; also in mango groves.

BEHAVIOUR Usually alone or in pairs and somewhat shy; during the breeding season becomes secretive or elusive and quick to take flight at the first sign of disturbance; may join mixed-species foraging flocks in winter. Perches erect or upright in trees; when alarmed sits almost bolt upright and wags tail slowly up and down. Flight usually swift and direct with rapid wing-beats, but also flies silently through forest. Forages mostly from high vantage point, flying down to capture insect prey before returning to original position; also in trees from mid- to lower canopy, but not unusual on the ground searching leaf-litter. Also makes occasional aerial sallies after flying insects. Food is mostly insects and their larvae, snails, worms and some seeds, berries and nectar from plants such as *Erythrina* and *Salmalias*; also occasionally small lizards, skinks and frogs.

BREEDING Season: May (possibly late April) to July. Nest: a neat cup of grass, twigs, roots, bark strips and moss, lined with pine needles, finer grasses, roots and lichens or a few animal hairs, usually placed on the ground under a rock or in a rocky crevice, under a grass tuft, amongst the large roots of a tree, in a hole in a bank or occasionally on a tree-stump about 3 m (10') from the ground. Eggs: 3–4, exceptionally 5, white to pale yellowish-cream or deep buff heavily speckled with fine reddish spots. Nest building and incubation by the female, but feeding and care of young by both sexes. Probably two broods (recently fledged young in northern Pakistan at end of August).

MOULT Post-juvenile moult of all body feathers and some wing feathers from July to September or early October. Postnuptial moult of adults complete by late August or September.

MEASUREMENTS Wing, male 99–108.5, female 96–108; bill (from skull) 21.5–26; tarsus 24–27. Weight 29–41 g (Ali & Ripley 1983, Roberts 1992).

REFERENCES Ali & Ripley (1983), Roberts (1992).

15 WHITE-THROATED ROCK-THRUSH *Monticola gularis*   Plate 5
Oroecetes gularis Swinhoe, 1862, *Proc. Zool. Soc. London*: 318 – Tianjin, China.

IDENTIFICATION 18–19 cm (7–7½"). The eastern counterpart of allopatric Blue-capped Rock-Thrush (14), with which it used to be considered conspecific. Crown to nape bright cobalt-blue, face to sides of neck, mantle and upper back black tipped buff or buffish-brown, rump to tail rich or rufous-chestnut; wings black with white patch on base of secondaries and tail dark grey with bluish or greyish-blue base; underparts rich or rufous-orange with white mesial stripe on throat to upper breast (difficult to see unless bird facing observer). Females pale brown heavily scaled or scalloped on the underparts, with a poorly defined narrow white or pale buffish central stripe on the lower throat and upper breast; the upperparts are barred darker on the lower back to tail. **Confusion species** No overlap in range with the slightly smaller Blue-capped Rock-Thrush; cobalt-blue chin and throat and no white instantly separates male; female is more similar but White-throated is more heavily and visibly barred on the upperparts and the cheeks and ear-coverts are more heavily mottled. Chestnut-bellied Rock-Thrush (16) is much larger with no white in the wing; male has deeper blue upperparts, bluish-black chin and throat and deep rust-chestnut breast to undertail-coverts; female is extensively barred above and below and has a well-defined face pattern and pale or yellowish-buff area above the lores. Eastern race *philippensis* of Blue Rock-Thrush (17) is also initially similar but has much bluer, almost violet-blue head, face, upperparts and breast and deep orange under-parts; female much darker than female White-throated and lacks any scalloping or barring.

DESCRIPTION Sexes differ. **Adult male** Lower forehead and upper lores black; upper forehead to nape bright cobalt-blue with black bases to feathers and often appears streaked. Cheeks, ear-coverts, sides of nape and neck to mantle, back and scapulars black, in worn plumage pale buffish-brown. Lower back, rump and uppertail-coverts deep or rich rufous-chestnut. Tail grey-brown but edges and bases to all but central pair pale greyish-blue, some birds also showing bluish wash to central pair; upper back occasionally with pale blue tips, lower back occasionally with black tips. Lesser coverts have bright metallic cobalt-blue panel on closed wing; median coverts black; greaters blackish or finely edged blackish-blue; alula blackish-brown, primary coverts same or finely edged pale blue; flight feathers blackish-brown finely edged blue-grey on outerwebs with broad white patch at base of inner secondaries, which shows as a short whitish patch in flight. Underwing-coverts pale orange. Lores to lower cheeks, sides of chin, throat, breast and upper flanks rich rufous or rust-orange; centre of chin and throat to centre of upper breast white (usually shows in the field only when facing observer from lower throat or centre of upper breast); belly to undertail-coverts orange, palest on undertail-coverts. Bill black to dark brownish-horn. Legs and feet flesh-pink to grey or tinged brownish. In fresh plumage (autumn and winter) similar to summer dress, but obscured by brown or brownish-black tips to forehead, crown and nape and broad pale, golden-buff or light orange-buff tips and edges to mantle, back and scapulars, becoming broad pale or whitish-buff tips to median and greater coverts and tertials. Underparts duller than in summer and obscured by pale buffish tips to sides of chin, throat and breast. **Adult female** Forehead to crown and nape brown or medium olive-brown tinged with grey, extending in some to centre of upper mantle; rest of upperparts barred with olive-brown bases, broad black subterminal bars and single creamy-buff spots at tips or yellowish-buff tips on lower back and warmer or light orange-buff bars and tips to rump and uppertail-coverts. Tail brown; may show slight reddish-brown tinge to central feathers with fine paler tips to all feathers. Wings brown but median and greater coverts have black subterminal bars and broad pale buff tips, median coverts usually blacker than greaters and tips to greaters broader or more obvious; tertials similar to greater coverts; in fresh plumage edges to flight feathers and tertials narrowly warm or light cinnamon-brown. Underwing-coverts pale yellowish-cream. Upper lores form narrow blackish line to eye, with narrow pale buff eye-ring; lower lores pale or whitish and finely mottled with orange-buff and dark brown tips; cheeks and ear-coverts brown, finely spotted whitish-buff. Chin and throat white or whitish in centre and broadly scalloped pale buff-brown with black tips at sides, extending to breast and becoming larger or heavier scalloping with darker tips; belly and undertail-coverts pale or yellowish-buff. Bill dark purplish-brown with paler or pinkish base to lower mandible. **Immature** Juvenile very similar to adult female but underparts more heavily barred blackish-brown and yellowish-buff. Sexes separable at early age, male having uppertail-coverts grey with rufous-orange tips, blackish flight feathers with pale buff patch at base of secondaries, and rust-orange underwing-coverts; female more heavily spotted with yellowish-buff and brown bars on upperparts, uppertail-coverts barred darker and lack any orange, flight feathers brownish but outerwebs of secondaries pale rufous, and underwing-coverts yellow or yellowish-orange. First-winter male similar to adult in winter but generally has pale yellowish or golden-buff edges, and tips to feathers of upperparts thinner. First-summer males show paler, retained, greater coverts, alula and primary coverts which contrast against the newer black median coverts, mantle and tertials.

GEOGRAPHICAL VARIATION None. Monotypic.

VOICE Generally silent but may give occasional *tsip* or *tseep* flight call or a soft *queck-quack* note, often interspersed with sharp *tack-tack* notes, like two stones knocked together. Song generally very sombre and melancholy, exceptional for a rock-thrush and includes several whistled phrases that could have been given by a human; resembles that of Blue Rock-Thrush (17) but slower, a series of long low flute-like whistling notes rising slightly, also one or two more complex ringing phrases interrupted by a short, repeated *chat-at-at*. Usually sings from a high perch in tops of trees; similar song given whilst in active flight through the tops of trees. Song period relatively short, from May to end of June or sporadically to middle of July.

STATUS AND DISTRIBUTION Uncommon, widespread and generally dispersed. Breeds in eastern Siberia in the Amur river basin north to about 55°N along the Zeya river and west to about 115°E along the Argun river in the south-east Transbaikal region (may also breed further west along the Shilka River south of Chita), south into extreme eastern Mongolia, northern Inner Mongolia east through Heilungkiang including the Khabarovsk region of the Amur and south to northern Hopeh, north-east China and extreme northern North Korea. Cheng (1987) included the Zhongtiao Shan of southern Shansi Province within the breeding range.

In winter in southern China from Fukien and Kwangtung west to southern Yunnan, sporadically to western, central and eastern Burma (Mt Victoria and the Shan States), Thailand (except central but generally uncommon), Laos, where scarce or local (Duckworth *et al.* 1999) and most of Cambodia to southern Vietnam (except west Tonkin and north Annam; probably a scarce visitor to central Annam); a scarce visitor to Peninsular Malaysia and Singapore.

MOVEMENTS Migratory; breeds in northern China north to the Amur River basin and winters in southern China, south to northern Burma and eastern and peninsular Thailand and southern Laos; spring passage though eastern China and North Korea mid- to late May with first birds singing on territory in Manchuria in last week of May and arrivals in breeding area of middle Amur by middle of May; more northerly parts of range not reached until the first days of June. Return movements mostly in mid- to late September and October through eastern and southern China (west to eastern Mongolia) and North Korea; widespread on passage but nowhere common, most birds in wintering area from November to March. A vagrant to Taiwan (May 1996), Hong Kong (7+ records including an overwintering bird from end of November 1990 to April 1991), Singapore (3 winter records) and once in South Korea (May 1930) and several in Japan (exact number unknown).

HABITAT Mostly forests and open woodlands on hillsides, mountains and river valleys with cliffs and crags, showing preference for firs (including those in small clearings in evergreen forests), mainly cedars and spruces, but also found in birch woods, larches, maples and ash groves; on high ground found in scattered groves of trees along ridges but also in more densely wooded areas. In the north of its range also occurs on the edge of the taiga in swampy areas overgrown with blueberry, marsh rosemary and birch scrub. On migration occurs on hills and in coastal scrub and bushes; in winter mainly evergreen and deciduous forests from the lowlands to about 1220 m (4000′).

BEHAVIOUR Usually alone or in pairs with male much more visible than the seemingly more retiring female. Often perches on a high or prominent lookout with only the top of the head visible; may also sit motionless for long periods on low branch. Forages in trees at middle to low levels and in undergrowth in forests as well as birch scrub and rock-strewn open forests with low trees. Feeds mostly on insects (including wasps) and their larvae, but diet largely unknown and possibly little different from other rock-thrushes.

BREEDING Season: June and July. Nest: a simple cup-shaped structure of dry grasses, rootlets and some moss, usually placed on the ground under a shrub or amongst tree roots; breeding territory occupies a large area. Eggs 3–5, exceptionally 6,

white with small rust-brown speckles and spots, usually at the thicker end. Nestlings fed by both parents. Two broods.

MOULT Complete post-breeding moult of adults from mid- to late July to early September. Post-juvenile moult at same time begins late July and completed by late August to early September.

MEASUREMENTS Wing, male 95–102, female 92–99; tarsus 22.5–25.0; bill (culmen) 15.5–18.0. Weight 34–40 g (La Touche 1925–1930).

REFERENCES Cheng (1987), Dementiev & Gladkov (1954), Duckworth *et al.* (1999), La Touche (1925–1930).

16 CHESTNUT-BELLIED ROCK-THRUSH *Monticola rufiventris* Plate 6

Petrocincla rufiventris Jardine & Selby, 1833, *Illustr. Orn.* 3: 129 – Himalayan district [restricted to Simla by Ripley (1961) *Synopsis Birds India Pakistan*: 523].

IDENTIFICATION 23–25 cm (9–9¾"). The largest of the rock-thrushes. Male has deep blue upperparts with blackish bases on mantle and back and brighter aquamarine-blue on the rump and uppertail-coverts; the face and sides of neck are black, with deep rust-orange or maroon underparts. Female is much duller and generally browner, barred darker on the upperparts but with a fairly distinctive face pattern of pale eyering and large pale buff patch at lower rear edge of the ear-coverts; the underparts are heavily mottled or spotted with dark brown and pale or yellowish-buff. **Confusion species** Male is most likely to be confused with the slightly smaller and slenderer eastern race *philippensis* of Blue Rock-Thrush (17) which lacks the black face and sides of neck and has duller, more uniform blue upperparts with the blue extending to the breast. Female from all races of Blue by the face pattern and more boldly mottled underparts. All other rock-thrushes eliminated on size, face pattern (females) and lack of white in wing (males). Female is initially similar to female Siberian Thrush (36) but is generally more upright and has a distinctive face pattern (some female Siberian show a similar pattern but generally whitish supercilium only extends to behind ear-coverts and fades); Siberian also shows barring on upperparts, dark malar stripes, pale or whitish lower belly to undertail-coverts, and diagnostic '*Zoothera*' underwing pattern. Confusion with Long-tailed (49) and White's (50) Thrushes is eliminated on size and underpart coloration.

DESCRIPTION Sexes differ. **Adult male** Forehead to crown, nape and centre of upper mantle deep cobalt- or aquamarine-blue; sides of upper mantle to back and scapulars deeper blue overlying black bases to feathers, becoming paler metallic aquamarine on rump and uppertail-coverts. Tail deep blue-black with black shafts and outer edges to all feathers. Lesser coverts bright metallic blue; median coverts bluish-black and greaters black or outers edged bluish-black; alula blue-black on

outerwebs and black on innerwebs; primary coverts deep bluish with darker or blackish tips; flight feathers black with light bluish (in fresh plumage) outer edges to all (except outer two) primaries (becomes bluish-black when worn) edged broadly on secondaries; tertials mostly deep bluish-black. Lores, cheeks, ear-coverts and sides of neck black. Chin and throat to centre of upper breast dull or blackish-blue with some paler or brighter metallic tips to lower throat; breast to undertail-coverts and underwing-coverts deep rust or chestnut. Bill black; may have greyish base to lower mandible. Legs and feet black or purplish-black, soles grey or yellowish-grey. In fresh plumage (autumn and winter) has pale or greyish-buff tips or fringes to throat and upper breast, mantle, scapulars and centre of back; narrow pale tips to black wing-coverts and tertials; sides of lower breast also sometimes blackish-blue. **Adult female** Forehead to nape, mantle, back, scapulars and uppertail-coverts grey or greyish olive-brown (may show some blue on forehead and forecrown), flecked or scaled darker with dark or blackish-brown subterminal bars on mantle and back, becoming dark bars with paler grey-brown centres and tips on lower back to uppertail-coverts. Tail brown edged grey-brown (may also show a bluish wash) on bases of all outers. Wing brown or dark brown, greater coverts edged greyish-olive; alula dark brown, primary coverts as greaters; inner secondaries edged greyish-olive becoming broader on outerwebs of tertials. Upper lores to eye flecked pale yellowish-buff above broad dark brown stripe; pale buff eye-ring; cheeks and ear-coverts dark brown narrowly flecked pale or whitish-buff; broad pale or whitish-buff submoustachial stripe from base of bill to below ear-coverts; sides of neck tipped or spotted whitish or creamy-buff, showing as patch behind ear-coverts. Chin and throat dark brown with broad whitish central stripe and thinner streaks on sides of lower throat; breast, belly and flanks mottled or spotted with dark brown centres, grey-brown edges and pale or whitish-buff tips; vent and undertail-coverts similar but more heavily barred. Bill dark horn-brown. Legs and feet dark brown to dark purple. **Immature** Juvenile similar to adult female but much darker or blackish-brown with large pale beige or buffish triangular-shaped spots on forehead (where small) to back (largest on mantle and back) becoming light orange-buff bars and blackish-brown tips on rump and uppertail-coverts. Edges to scapulars have pale buff central shaft-streaks and large spots with dark brown edges at tips. Greater coverts brown with darker brown edges and pale buff tips; tips to tertials also pale brown. Underparts heavily spotted with large pale buff centres to dark-edged feathers, darkest on breast; chin and throat also mottled with darker tips or very pale buff with few dark tips. Spots mostly triangular in shape, becoming more barred on belly and undertail-coverts. First-winter male shows rust or maroon-chestnut on underparts, bluish wings and spots on scapulars, and bluish tail by end of June and early July whilst rest of plumage as juvenile; first-year birds similar to adults but recognisable by retained (variable in number) greater coverts.

GEOGRAPHICAL VARIATION None. Monotypic.

VOICE A sharp querulous *quach* contact note; a high shrill *sit sit*, *tick* or *stick* notes often included in the jay-like rasping or croaking *churrr*, *chhrrr* or *chaaaaa* when disturbed; warning note between adults at the nest is a plaintive *pwee pwee*. Song a pleasant series of short warbling phrases, similar in tone to Blue-capped Rock-Thrush (14), an ascending (though may begin with a descending) note or whistle and repeated *seee-twiddle-dee-it* variably interpreted as *jero–terry–three*, *fir-tar-ree* occasionally varied or interspersed with *tewleedee-tweet-tew* or *til-tertew* or similar notes. Subsong, usually given much later in the year, recalls the bubbling and warbling notes of Common Starling *Sturnus vulgaris* but more broken with wheezing and grating notes. Song usually given from the top of a tall tree from late February (Thailand) to about the middle or end of July.

STATUS AND DISTRIBUTION Fairly or locally common. Breeds in northern Pakistan from the Murree hills and possibly Swat east through the Himalayas of Kashmir and northern India and Nepal and south-east Tibet (where scarce) to Sikkim, Bhutan and Arunachal Pradesh, and to northern Bengal, Assam, Nagaland, Manipur, Mizoram and the hills of western, northern and eastern Burma (where distribution poorly known), north-west Thailand (Doi Inthanon), northern Laos (above 1500 m/4950'), possibly also Tonkin, and to southern China from Yunnan and southern Szechwan east to southern Hupeh and western Fukien.

In winter to lower altitudes within the breeding range but also reaches the Chittagong region and the higher parts of south-east Bangladesh, other areas of high ground in north-west Thailand (Thanon Thong Chai and Khun Tan ranges, where uncommon), northern Laos and north Tonkin, Vietnam.

MOVEMENTS Partial or altitude migrant, moving to lower levels within or immediately adjacent to the breeding range, but occurs sporadically or erratically on the plains of northern India and Bangladesh. Most movement away from the breeding areas is from October to March. A rare visitor to the Islamabad region and a vagrant to Hong Kong (4 records).

HABITAT Open forests or stands of scattered trees, mostly of firs especially spruce, juniper or fir, also oaks, rhododendrons and deodar on steep hillsides, rocky slopes, cliffs, gorges or wooded ravines between 1000 and 3400 m (3300–11,220'), exceptionally to 4460 m (14,700') at Gosainkund, Nepal. In eastern Himalayas appears to avoid dense deciduous forests but throughout much of the range in southern China occurs in fir and pine forests. In winter occurs usually below 2380 m (7850'), but rarely below c.1200 m (3960') except in severe weather.

BEHAVIOUR Usually alone or in pairs; inconspicuous when breeding but otherwise not usually shy, although keeps mainly to the inner part of foliage on larger branches; male is, however, more likely to be seen on top of tree or a prominent branch; usually perches very upright and habitually sways its tail slowly back and forth. Forages both within trees and on the ground (including sides of streams), where it hops; flight is strong and quite fast; often chases insects on the wing like a large flycatcher or drongo *Dicrurus*, and has a distinctive display-flight, sailing out from a tree top or similar perch in a wide horizontal arc on flat wings and tail spread before returning to original perch. Food mostly insects, particularly beetles, grasshoppers, cicadas, butterflies and moths and their larvae, plus worms, small lizards and frogs; some berries also taken.

BREEDING Season: April to July. Nest: a large pad or cup of dry grass, moss, leaves, twigs and pine needles or other locally available plant material on a small platform of small twigs and lined with rootlets and fine grasses, usually placed in holes or crevices in cliffs or on a ledge, occasionally in a tree hole or amongst the roots of a tree or on a bank. Eggs: 3–4, pale cream-yellow and washed with pink and finely spotted or speckled with deep pink, pale or reddish-brown or brick-red usually at the larger end. Nest built by both sexes but incubation by female only. One brood.

MOULT Little known; adults are still in post-breeding moult with the tail feathers partially replaced by mid- to late November.

MEASUREMENTS Wing, male 117–130, female 111–124; tarsus 25.5–30; bill (from skull) 24–28. Weight, male 50–61 g, female 48–56 g (Ali & Ripley 1983, Roberts 1992).

REFERENCES Ali & Ripley (1983), Fleming *et al.* (1979), Roberts (1992).

17 BLUE ROCK-THRUSH *Monticola solitarius*

Plate 6

Turdus solitarius Linnaeus, 1758, Syst. Nat. (ed. 10): 170 – Oriente [= Italy, ex. Willoughby, *vide* Hartert (1910) *Vög. pal. Fauna*: 674].

IDENTIFICATION 20.5–23 cm (8–9"). Males are almost uniform deep bluish with blacker wings and tail and have long, slender bills and an upright stance when perched; in winter slightly browner. Seen at their best in good sunlight, metallic blue plumage is obvious. Females are variable with brown crown and upperparts and a heavily mottled buffish face, chin and throat becoming barred browner on the rest of the underparts, some birds resembling males with bluish tinges to the upperparts and wing-coverts. Juveniles similar to females but more heavily spotted buff on the upperparts. Most races similar but eastern race *philippensis* very distinctive with slightly paler bright blue upperparts (except for blackish wings and tail) and throat to breast and deep orange or rufous-orange breast to flanks and undertail-coverts. **Confusion species** Males are unlikely to be mistaken for any other thrush except for Blue Whistling-Thrush (23), which is larger, bulkier and longer-tailed with metallic bluish spots to the body and lesser coverts and white tips to the median coverts. Eastern race Blue Rock-Thrushes resemble Blue-capped (14), White-throated (15) and Chestnut-bellied (16) Rock-Thrushes, all of which are deeper or blackish-blue on the mantle, back and wings, and brighter or paler blue on the crown and rump; all three also have black faces; Blue-headed has a white patch in the wing and White-throated has a white centre to the orange-sided throat and rest of underparts. Female is similar to female Rock Thrush (12) but has longer tail and longer, slenderer bill, and lacks the paler or more finely barred underparts, warm buff flanks and rufous base to the tail. Female Blue-capped is slightly smaller and paler with gingery-brown rump and uppertail-coverts, less heavily barred and more scalloped underparts, yellowish-buff undertail-coverts; female White-throated is similar to Blue-capped but has pale throat, browner breast and heavy mottling on the upperparts. Differs from female Chestnut-bellied by slimmer shape, less heavily or boldly barred underparts and no distinct pale throat-patch.

DESCRIPTION Sexes differ. **Adult 'summer' male** Entire head and body (except for blackish lores to eye and possibly across ear-coverts) deep azure-blue, slightly glossy in tone (shows brighter or more metallic blue in strong sunlight). Tail black but edges to base of central pair and outer edges of all outers slate-blue. Lesser and median coverts blackish-centred and broadly edged slate-blue; greater coverts, alula and primary coverts black edged slate-blue on outerwebs (except alula) and finely edged whitish towards tip; flight feathers black, outerwebs to base of primaries and (more extensively) secondaries edged slate-blue; tertials similar to secondaries but more broadly edged; slate-blue edges to all wing-coverts and flight

feathers usually worn down or absent after May (some as early as April on edges to flight feathers), when tips to secondaries and primaries may also begin to show fine buff (i.e. worn) tips; underwing-coverts dark grey with slate grey-blue tips. Bill fairly long and slender, black. Legs and feet dark brown to greyish-black or black. In late summer may appear darker or greyer with blackish bases to forehead, crown, mantle and back; slate greyish-blue generally duller or browner. **Adult 'winter' male** Fresh-plumaged birds from about September–December onwards have the forehead to nape tipped grey or finely sandy-buff at tip, and slate-blue bases to feathers largely concealed; mantle, back and scapulars have dull dark grey subterminal bar and pale or sandy-buff tips which may extend faintly to rump and uppertail-coverts, which are otherwise dull slate-blue; also has slate-blue edges to secondaries, primaries and tertials and more extensively on edges of base of tail. Lores dull or dark bluish, cheeks, ear-coverts to chin and throat finely mottled or flecked with brown tips; rest of underparts slate-grey, may also be (variable in extent) barred blackish with dull sandy-buff or off-whitish tips. Wings as in summer but with pale buff edges or tips to coverts and flight feathers. Tail has pale slate-grey fringes. **Adult 'summer' female** Forehead and crown to mantle, scapulars, rump and uppertail-coverts dark grey-brown with dark greyish-blue bases to feathers and darker subterminal bars and pale buff tips. Tail dark brown to brownish-grey; can show a faint slate-blue tinge on edges to bases of feathers. Lesser coverts grey-brown to slate-blue; median coverts dark or blackish-brown and finely tipped off-white or pale buff; greater coverts blackish-brown, variably edged lighter brown or tinged slate-blue with very fine whitish edges; alula and primary coverts black or blackish-brown finely tipped pale buff; flight feathers blackish-brown, narrowly edged paler brown; tertials similar but finely fringed buffish-brown. Underwing-coverts grey or blackish-brown broadly fringed darker or tinged bluish and streaked buff. Paler or browner edges to feathers usually reduced or absent from about May. Lores to cheeks, ear-coverts and sides of neck mottled buff-brown with darker bases; may show greyish in front of eye, narrow dull buffish eye-ring, mottling on ear-coverts more streaked, and rear ear-coverts as nape. Chin and throat as face but often more heavily mottled or completely pale buff with darker fringes; breast brown to dark brown mottled with dark subterminal bars and pale buffish tips; belly and flanks to undertail-coverts variable from same as breast and clearly barred with broad pale buff or buffish-brown bars to greyish or dark grey-brown on sides of breast and flanks with barring restricted to centre of belly; undertail-coverts more broadly barred warm buff and dark brown or blackish. Bill as male or slightly greyer-black. Legs and feet dark brown. Some variation in plumage of upperparts possibly age- or wear-related, as some females more like adult male with tinges of glossy dark blue on head and body and on fringes to wing-coverts, but with broad brown edges to under-parts, and chin, throat and undertail-coverts buffish as in most females. **Adult 'winter' female** As summer plumage but with more extensive grey-brown tips overlying slate-bluish bases; may show some blue on mantle and scapulars to rump and uppertail-coverts, but also dark subterminal bars and pale or whitish tips. Some birds have thin or narrow bluish edges to greater coverts. Face as in summer but more heavily streaked. Chin and throat to breast extensively mottled pale buff with darker fringes and darker or browner bases, feath-ers on breast showing as distinct pale spots; rest of underparts bluish, heavily barred pale or buffish and blackish or dark brown but some birds may be greyer. Wings and tail as in summer but with pale buff tips. **Immature** Juvenile very similar to adult female (and possibly not separable with certainty in field) but paler, lacks any bluish tinge and has pale buff, yellowish or off-whitish spots to most of upperparts with fine dark brown or blackish tips, heaviest spotting on forehead to nape and upper mantle. Tail brown, narrowly edged pale greyish-blue at bases but edges mostly abraded by March of first year; some first-year birds may show whitish tips. Median and greater coverts dark brown with narrow pale grey-blue edges becom-ing whitish towards tips; in autumn unmoulted greater coverts have dull brown edges and contrast with fresh inners; alula dark brown; primary coverts, tertials and flight feathers brown to dark brown with pale or whitish tips to primary coverts and narrow buff fringes, becoming broader buff tips to tertials. Face dull dark brown finely (but often densely) flecked or spotted with dull or pale buffish-brown, each feather having a darker or blackish border. Chin and throat dark brown, heavily flecked or finely spotted paler or buffish with dark grey or greyish-buff bars at tips of feath-ers; rest of underparts similar or more heavily mot-tled with narrow bars at tips to pale or buffish-brown centres. **First-summer male** Similar to adult male but more greyish-brown and barred with broad brown feather edges and tips to upperparts; retains juvenile greater and primary coverts, ter-tials, flight and tail feathers to end of first summer and consequently wings and tail looks much browner with no pale or greyish-blue edges; greater coverts usually have broad whitish tips to outers and primary coverts also show pale buff edges and tips; tail feathers narrower and with more pointed tips than adult. **First-summer female** Similar to adult female with variable amounts of pale blue on bases to body feathers; retains same juvenile feathers as in first-summer male (and has same pale or whitish tips to greater and primary coverts), and usually a distinct contrast between new scapulars and old tertials; but differences not always marked, so ageing not always possible.

Twice recorded hybridising with Rock Thrush in Italy (Cramp *et al.* 1988).

GEOGRAPHICAL VARIATION Five races; varia-tion largely clinal and poorly defined except in one race, *philippensis*. Birds of the race *longirostris* are, on average, slightly smaller than nominate birds and the males are also slightly paler, brighter or more greyish-blue on the forehead, cheeks, chin and throat in fresh plumage but not always separa-ble with certainty when worn. Females and juve-niles are paler or greyer above and slightly paler below than nominate females, the throat is more uniform, the breast has paler spots and the sandy-buff belly and flanks are less heavily (more nar-rowly) barred (as in nominate females, some, perhaps older individuals may show a blue or bluish tinge to the upper- and underparts).

Race *pandoo* is slightly larger and darker blue than nominate with male more leaden-blue except for the dusky-blackish wings (in fresh plumage the blue feathers are largely obscured by dark brown, with pale buffish tips on head and face and black-ish subterminal bars and greyish tips to body), tail also blackish but washed blue. Female also darker or colder brown and generally shorter-winged; upperparts dull greyish-blue (or, in some, more heavily tinged blue) with head, nape and mantle slightly browner, face to throat and breast greyer than nominate and spotted finely with dull white; rest of underparts bluish finely barred blackish and off-white; in winter most body feathers subtermi-nally blackish and tipped white.

Some individuals of both *longirostris* and *pan-doo* are so similar, also to nominate males, as to be inseparable in the field. Birds from Bengal, Assam, Sikkim and Burma are, on average, darker or bluer and more strongly contrasting dark and pale on the body plumage.

Race *madoci* is smallest and has a noticeably rounded wing-tip; male is more wholly blue and slightly darker on the throat than *pandoo*, female dull brown and more heavily suffused with blue especially on upperparts; face, chin and throat suf-fused with buff or buffish-brown. Bill, legs and feet black.

Most distinct are males of the race *philippensis*, which have head, upperparts (except for blackish wings and tail) and chin to breast violet-blue or bluish-slate, paler or brighter blue on throat, sides of neck and sides of breast; lower breast, belly, flanks, underwing-coverts to undertail-coverts orange-rufous to maroon, some showing bluish tips to flanks and thighs. In fresh (i.e. non-breeding) plumage, head and upperparts barred with black and brownish-grey tips, and red on underparts sim-ilarly obscured by dark bars and pale tips. Female is darkest of any race with grey-brown upperparts, finely mottled blackish and white bars; lower nape often paler, creating pale collar; lower back and uppertail-coverts tinged bluish-grey to bluish-black; underparts pale buff or greyish-buff and barred or scalloped blackish, most prominently on belly and flanks, and sometimes also washed pale rufous. Bill black in male and brownish in female. Both sexes have a slightly but noticeably shorter tail than other races. Immature male has upperparts, head and upper breast darker brown with pale buff tips to crown, nape, mantle and scapulars and from the throat to the upper breast, and has dark brown subterminal bars and pale buff tips to belly and flanks. First-winter birds similar to same-age nominate birds with dark underparts but usually show more heavily speckled or spangled head, face and most of underparts; first-summer male is duller blue than adult.

Distribution note 1: Birds in Japan and adjacent islands (previously separated as *magna*) have proportionately larger bills and tarsi and the chestnut on the belly is, on average, much darker than that of the birds in the rest of the range.

Distribution note 2: Intermediates between *pandoo* and *philippensis* occur in Sikkim, Bengal and southern China (north to the Yangtze and southern Hupeh and east to Fukien and Kwangtung, and occur in winter in Assam, Meghalaya and northern Thailand); they show a variety of mixed orange-rufous and blue patches on the belly, flanks and/or undertail-coverts.

VOICE Mostly silent outside of breeding season but has a sharp high-pitched whistled *uit-uit* or *veeet-veeet*, occasionally given as a rapid *vivivi...*; a varied vocabulary of alarm or distress calls, most commonly a deep *tak-tak* or a more Blackbird-like *tchuk* or repeated *tchuk-tchuk*; appears to alternate this with a high *tsee*, *pee*, *peet* or *peep*, which may occasionally be given as *tsii*, *tzick* or *tschik* or even as a soft croaking note; the harsh *tak* or *chak* is occasionally given as an extended rapid *chakerack-ack* or *schrrrackerr* or a more Blackbird-like *chack chack chack eritchouitchouitchouit tchoo tchoo* and a harsh churring or rattling *trrr* which may be run into *trr ti chak chak*. During courtship both sexes give *ssrrrt* and longer *ruissssrrrt* notes; during nestling period male also gives a musical chuckling contact-note in flight when approaching the nest.

Song a fluty series of rather high-pitched or piping Blackbird-like notes, *chu sree*, *chur tee tee* or *wuchee-trr-trrt*, usually of 3–5 phrases (some of which may be rather scratchy in tone) before repeating, often after a lengthy pause; song given in autumn more melodious and descending. Song may be given from perch on rock, cliff, building or dead tree, etc., or whilst in long, slow, descending glide (which may also begin with a short upward spiral) with wings half-closed or in parachute fashion, ending with a level or slightly upward glide to a perch. Subsong usually a series of low, rambling, warbled notes often containing some scratchy or harsh notes; has been likened to the chattering notes given by Common Starling *Sturnus vulgaris*; song given during or just before mating may also be a variation of the subsong; most song (in European part of range) January to June, also sings in late winter or prior to spring departure. Females also sing, but much less often than males and perhaps only in defence of territory (both winter and summer); similar to that of male but shorter and with some harsher notes, but may conclude with a rising *tudelit*.

STATUS AND DISTRIBUTION Common or locally common.

M. s. solitarius Southern Europe from Portugal and northern Spain (where range disjunct) more continuously from central and southern Spain east through the Balearics, coastal southern France and the southern Alps, where more extensive, coastal lowlands of Italy (except the north-east), Corsica, Sardinia, Sicily; also in southern Switzerland; continuously south along the Adriatic coast (from about Trieste) of Yugoslavia and Croatia to Albania, Greece, Crete (except the northern-central areas) and most of the Ionian and Aegean islands, north to southern Bulgaria and east through most of northern Turkey (where scarce) north to the southern Caucasus and south to Cyprus (breeding mostly along the Kyrenia range), Lebanon, western Syria, northern and central Israel (south to the Judean hills) and the highlands of western Jordan (south to about Petra). In North Africa from Morocco and the Saharan Atlas of Algeria (and possibly also some of the north coast ranges) to northern Tunisia; may also breed occasionally in northern Egypt. Has also bred in Senegal (Rouchouse 1985) in 1983 and 1984 and possibly subsequently, the small, apparently sedentary population there being augmented in the northern winter.

Winters within much of the breeding range usually at lower altitudes, but birds (particularly females) from Switzerland, northern Greece, central and eastern Turkey and the southern Caucasus completely desert the breeding area; an unknown proportion of birds move south to winter in parts of central and southern Algeria notably the Ahaggar and Tibesti massifs, coastal Libya (Tripoli and Cyrenaica), through most of Israel, western highlands of Jordan and the Sinai area of northern Egypt, Eritrea, northern Somalia and southern Saudi Arabia (possibly east to the western Gulf), also in parts of the Sahara Desert in central Sudan and southern to eastern-central Chad. In the west small numbers winter in Air province, northern Niger, around Nouakchott and possibly elsewhere in western Mauretania and south along the coast of Senegal; occasional inland and recorded in Gambia (3 records mid-November to early March) but perhaps overlooked, also the Loma and Tingi Mountains of north-east Sierra Leone and regular in small numbers (singles) on Mt Nimba in southern Guinea/northern Liberia/western Ivory Coast from October to April. May also be regular in small numbers in western Mali. Extremely scarce or a vagrant to Ghana, northern Nigeria (6 records, all late October–March), northern Cameroon (3+ records) and northern Central African Republic.

M. s. longirostris Central and southern Turkey (but largely absent from the central Taurus and south-east) perhaps with an area of *solitarius–longirostris* intergradation in north-east Iraq (south to about Baghdad); Iran (principally the north-west and the Zagros and Elburz ranges) to Turkmenia, southern Tadzhikistan, Afghanistan, northern Pakistan (southern Baluchistan to North-West Frontier Province) and Baltistan (Kashmir), intergrading with *pandoo* in eastern Afghanistan and along the north-western border with Pakistan.

In winter to much of Arabia south to Oman (where local or uncommon) and north-east Africa from Sudan (possibly also north-east or eastern Egypt), Eritrea, Ethiopia and northern Somalia north to eastern Israel (scarce), southern Iraq and intermittently east to southern Afghanistan, western and central Pakistan (where it reaches the Makran coast) and north-west India.

M. s. pandoo Pamirs of southern Tadzhikistan and north-east into the western Tien Shan range where it straddles the border with south-west Sinkiang, China; south to about Chitral in extreme northern Pakistan and Ladakh, Kashmir east through the Himalayas of northern India, southern and south-east Tibet (but not the Tibetan plateau), central Nepal, Sikkim, Bhutan, northern Bengal, Assam and Arunachal Pradesh (where generally scarce) in southern China from Yunnan (where it intergrades with *philippensis*) and western Szechwan east to Kwangtung and north to the Yangtze.

In winter to most of lowland or peninsular central Pakistan, India, Nepal (below 1400 m/4600'), Sri Lanka (where variably scarce or annual in small numbers), Andaman and Nicobar Islands, and east through Bangladesh to northern Burma and most of Thailand, Laos, Vietnam, southern China (including Hong Kong where singles are occasional in summer) and Hainan, south to Malaya, Borneo, Brunei and Sumatra. Winter birds in Assam and Meghalaya with variable amounts of rufous or rufous-chestnut on the lower belly and vent may be intergrades with or referable to *philippensis*.

M. s. philippensis Eastern Russia from southern Amurland, south through Korea to north-east China south to southern Shansi, Honan (possibly also Hupeh) and Shantung; also in Japan from southern and western Hokkaido and Honshu south through the Nansei Shoto including the Daito, Izu, Ogasawara and Iwo Islands to the Batanes Islands (northern Philippines). Has bred Taiwan but not in 20th century.

In winter overlaps with the winter range of *pandoo* in southern China south of the Yangtze south to Taiwan, Hong Kong, Hainan, also southern Korea (and offshore islands) in the west to south-east Yunnan, Tenasserim, western Burma, north-west, north-east, central, south-east and southern Thailand and Peninsular Malaysia (where overlaps with resident *madoci*) to Laos, Cambodia and Vietnam, and from Malaysia and north Borneo (and Sarawak) east to the Philippines (where widely distributed throughout), Sulawesi (Talaud, Sangihe, Siau, northern Sulawesi and Manadotua), Moluccas (Taliabu, Sula, Buru, Bacan, Seram, Ambelau, Ambon, Tayandu, Tapat, Halmahera, Ternate and Tidore) and the Palau archipelago.

M. s. madoci Peninsular Malaysia, including Talibon and Langkawi islands and southern peninsular Thailand north to at least Krabi and on some of the inshore islands in the Gulf of Thailand; a vagrant to Singapore.

MOVEMENTS Migrant; partial and altitude migrant. Birds from breeding areas in southern Europe and north-west Africa mostly resident or partially migratory; high-altitude birds, e.g. those in the High Atlas of Morocco, move to lower levels.

Departure from breeding areas begins in August, possibly slightly later in eastern Turkey and the Caucasus (October records not unusual in Armenia), with passage through North Africa, the Middle East, Arabia and across the Sahara in September and early October (occasionally late August), though passage through Israel is considered to be slight and non-breeding birds there are more nomadic; main passage period through Egypt is mid-September to mid-October or slightly later, when first arrivals noted in Sudan, Chad, Eritrea and northern Somalia; most southerly wintering birds, e.g. those in Senegal (see also above) and elsewhere in West Africa, not usually present until mid-November. Return passage is generally earlier than that of Rock-Thrush, with early birds back in southern breeding areas from late February to mid-March; passage through Egypt, Israel and Jordan in February and slightly later (March and early April), in central Israel to late April and early May; territories in central and northern Turkey and the Caucasus not usually reoccupied until mid- to late April or May.

Race *longirostris* is a spring migrant to Turkmenia in April and occasionally mid- to late March, and a scarce migrant in mid-February and March through eastern Israel; this race (or nominate *solitarius*) is a scarce passage migrant and uncommon winter visitor to the United Arab Emirates, eastern Saudi Arabia (scarce migrant to Central Province), Bahrain and Oman from September–April exceptionally (early May in UAE and July in Bahrain); in autumn moves to lower altitudes in Afghanistan and Pakistan (from some of the valleys of North-West Frontier Province south to northern Baluchistan, Salt Range south through the hills and plains west of the Indus to Cape Monze and around Karachi) from mid-September and October to mid-April. A rare but probably overlooked vagrant to Socotra (single record, female December 1996).

Race *pandoo* is a common summer migrant to most of the Himalayas, north to the Pamirs from April to September or early October; movements to wintering areas in September and early October in the north and later in October further south; average arrival dates in Thailand and Burma are about the last ten days of September, exceptionally early September in northern Thailand (late August in Hong Kong) with return passage in early April; vagrant to Malaya, Taiwan (October 1932) and the Tokara Islands, Japan (May 1988).

Race *philippensis* is an uncommon and local summer visitor to Hokkaido from mid-April to the end of September; a winter visitor to Hong Kong from late September (exceptionally early August) to late April or early May and a scarce or locally common winter visitor to South-East Asia from mid-September or October to April or early May. In north Borneo and Sarawak a winter visitor in small numbers from November to January but in

Brunei occurs from mid-October to mid-April. In the Philippines and the Moluccas it is a regular winter visitor from October to March (except for the Batanes Islands where it is resident) with extreme dates of 21 September (arrival) and 19 May (departure). A vagrant to Manokwari (Irian Jaya), January 1994, Port Moresby (Papua New Guinea), January 1986, and a bird showing the characters of this race occurred in Nepal in December 1973. Has also occurred in Australia: first-year male at Noose Heads National Park, south-east Queensland, late October to early December 1997.

Birds of the nominate race are vagrants to Belgium, Germany, Sweden and Britain (4 records) but some records in Europe have been considered escapes. In North America one on Unalaska Island, Aleutians, in spring 1996 was assumed to be an escape but a single in Goldpan Provincial Park, British Columbia, 6 June 1997 will be the first for the continent if accepted.

HABITAT Usually found in rocky limestone hills, quarries and outcrops, mountain plateaus, scree-slopes, boulderfields and karst valleys, gorges, steep cliff-faces (both coastal and montane), often with low or stunted tree or vegetation growth; also castles, churches, monuments and ruins including city walls, and in parts of the range it also occurs in towns and cities, perching on roofs, gutters and ledges, even (e.g. in India) entering houses and outbuildings; in the Malay Peninsula *madoci* is frequently seen in the vicinity of mines and caves in or near lowland forests, and breeds on offshore rocky islets, e.g. Ko Phi Phi, near Krabi, Peninsular Thailand; occurs from sea-level (to about 300 m below in the northern Judean desert) to about 3300 m (10,900′) in Central Asia (exceptionally to about 4000 m/13,200′ in Ladakh and to 4880 m/16,100′ in Dolpo and Mt Everest region), slightly lower, to about 1800 m (5950′) in China and 1500 m (4950′) in Pakistan. In winter in similar habitat at generally lower altitudes and often occurs on dry or arid rocky outcrops, desert wadis, large gardens, orchards and edges of cultivation. In India *longirostris* often in untypical open or stony country, including rocky stream- or riverbeds and in the vicinity of brick kilns; in Japan and the Moluccas *philippensis* is exclusively coastal, occurring in a variety of shoreline and coastal freshwater habitats.

BEHAVIOUR Usually alone or in pairs but several pairs may have overlapping territories in areas of high density; may occur in loose aggregations of 3–4 on migration when may even occur with Rock-Thrush. Generally shy or unobtrusive when breeding but may be more approachable in winter and in areas where accustomed to people. Spends long periods sitting erect on prominent perch, surveying the ground below for insects on which it pounces; on the ground walks or hops, on occasion walks with wings drooping and tail semi-erect; usually flicks tail as part of normal action. In flight very similar to Rock-Thrush but with longer tail; usually flies low over the ground but also may make escape-flight from intruders through mine-shafts, tunnels, etc.; wing-beats shallow and very elastic, except for more rapid escape-flight; on landing often bobs down, flicks wings and flirts tail or flicks it upwards. Forages in areas of soft earth but also makes shrike-like sorties after prey; also (particularly *philippensis*) makes fly-catching sallies after flying insects, and takes some fruit. Food mostly insects including grasshoppers, locusts, beetles, flies, ants, some butterflies or moths and their larvae; also centipedes, spiders, molluscs, worms, snails, lizards, small snakes, mice and occasionally frogs and toads; fruit includes olives, figs, vines, hawthorns and seeds and berries of ivy, lantana.

BREEDING Season: January to May (*madoci*), late March or early April to late June or early July. Nest: a large or bulky cup-shaped construction of dry grass, rootlets, plant stems, soft or fibrous bark, moss, lined with finer material and grasses, feathers or down and occasionally animal hairs; usually placed in hole, crevice or between boulders in a cliff or between rocks, under an overhang, wall of an old building or in a drainage pipe, exceptionally in a hole in a tree; site often used in successive years. Eggs: 3–5, exceptionally 6, pale blue or glossy bluish-green, either unmarked or finely spotted or speckled with reddish to brown spots or mottling usually at the larger end. Incubation period 12–15 days. Fledging period about 16–18 days. Nest built mostly by female but young fed and cared for by both parents. Two broods, but northerly breeding birds may only have one.

MOULT Post-juvenile moult in late June (in southern breeding birds) but most in July and August, occasionally September and early October, replaces entire head and body feathers, lesser and median coverts and some (inner) greater coverts; rest of the wing and tail feathers are retained until second autumn. Post-breeding moult of adults more prolonged from late (occasionally early) July to October; no spring moult but breeding plumage is assumed by wear or abrasion of feather edges. Record of male *longirostris* half-way through moult in late May (Cramp *et al.* 1988).

MEASUREMENTS (n=43) Wing, male 121–133, female 116–128; tarsus 28–31; bill (to skull) 26–32.5; *longirostris* (n=35) wing, male 114–127, female 113–125; bill (to skull) male 26.5–30, female 26.5–30; *pandoo* (n=30) wing, male 111–136, female 111–126; tarsus male 25–32, female 25–30; bill (to skull) male 24.5–30, female 25.5–28.5; *philippensis* (n=38) wing, male 113–128, female 112–124; *madoci* (n=5) wing, male 112–114, female 107–110. Weight (n=31) 50–70 g; *longirostris* (n=13) 43–53 g; *pandoo* male (April–June) 37–52 g, female (May–June) 45–54.5 g; *philippensis* male 39–56 g, female 46–60 g (La Touche 1925–1930, Ali & Ripley 1983, Urban *et al.* 1997).

REFERENCES Ali & Ripley (1983), Chasen (1940), Gregory *et al.* (1996), de Greling (1992), Harrison (1954), Hicks & Finch (1987), La Touche (1925–1930). Rouchouse (1985), Tucker & Heath (1994), Urban *et al.* (1997).

18 SRI LANKA WHISTLING-THRUSH *Myophonus blighi*   **Plate 7**
(Arrenga, Ceylon Whistling-Thrush, Bligh's Whistling-Thrush)

Arrenga blighi Holdsworth, 1872, *Proc. Zool. Soc. London*: 444, pl. 19 – banks of Lemastota-Oya, 4200 feet, Haputale, Uva, Ceylon.

IDENTIFICATION 20–21.5 cm (8–8½"). Endemic to the hills and mountains of central Sri Lanka, where very scarce. The smallest of the whistling-thrushes, extremely shy and frequently difficult to see. Male has black head and face, blue-black body and edges of otherwise black wings, but in field, without good light or prolonged view, usually appears entirely black; bright blue lesser covert patch is rarely seen in field as mostly covered by scapulars. Wing very short and rounded; when closed, tips of primaries reach to tips of uppertail-coverts. Female even more retiring than male; brown or rich chestnut-brown with an equally inconspicuous bright metallic blue lesser covert patch. **Confusion species** Most likely problem is local race *kinnisii* of Blackbird (111), which occurs in similar areas but is slate- or bluish-grey with a brownish tinge below, but best distinguished by longer tail and orange eye-ring, bill, legs and feet.

DESCRIPTION Sexes differ slightly. **Adult male** Entire head black, rest of body (upper- and under-parts) deep or inky blue-black except for black or sooty-black rump, uppertail-coverts, tail and flight feathers. Lesser coverts bright metallic or cobalt-blue, median and greater coverts black with blue-black edges to greaters; alula, primary coverts and flight feathers black with blue-black edges to primary coverts and inner primaries and secondaries; underwing-coverts, lower belly, vent and undertail-coverts also sooty-black. Bill entirely black with fine hooked tip to upper mandible. Eye dark brown. Legs and feet dark brown or blackish. **Adult female** Entire head and underparts earth-brown or rich chestnut-brown; mantle and scapulars with deep purplish-blue sheen; bright purplish-blue patch on lesser coverts at bend of wing. Rump and uppertail-coverts cinnamon-brown; flight and tail feathers dark brown. Base of forehead and face slightly paler or warmer brown than crown. Chin and throat pale brown, becoming slightly darker or deeper on rest of underparts. In fresh plumage edges to flight and tail feathers warm or rich brown. **Immature** Juvenile similar to adult female but with thin or fine pale orange-buff central shaft-streaks to forehead, crown, nape, face, chin, throat and breast. Underparts slightly paler or warmer rust-brown than adult. Lacks any purple sheen. Wings and tail brown with rich or rufous-brown edges. First-year male shows deep bluish bases to head, breast and belly, and bright blue lesser coverts within first six months.

GEOGRAPHICAL VARIATION None. Monotypic.

VOICE Call a thin or shrill, sibilant, high-pitched whistled, *seer eer*, reminiscent of a creaking metal gate, given in flight or whilst on the ground; may be either restricted to the first sylla-ble or repeated several times in quick succession; can be heard above the noise of rushing water (Warakagoda 1997). Calls given frequently in defence of the territory and at (or whilst leaving) the roost. Song, rarely heard, a drawn-out plaintive whistling note; displaying males utter a short undulating high-pitched whistle which may be preceded by a series of shrill, sibilant warbling notes. Males in defence of the territory utter a scolding song, composed of high-pitched notes slightly more musical in tone than the normal call.

STATUS AND DISTRIBUTION Scarce. Endemic to the hills of Central and Uva provinces, Sri Lanka; probably confined to the Peak Wilderness Sanctuary, the montane forests above Hakgala, Horton Plains National Park and recently recorded in the Matale area of the Knuckles Range (Dumbara Hills). Has declined in recent years possibly as a result of habitat destruction in favour of commercial plantations (Hoffmann 1984); now classed as Endangered by Collar *et al.* (1994).

MOVEMENTS Sedentary.

HABITAT Undergrowth of damp heavy forest and fern-clad wooded ravines and gorges, often with rivers and streams and usually above 900 m (2970'), mostly between 1200 and 1800 m (3960–5940') and exceptionally to c.2200 m (7260'). Seldom far from wooded streams or ponds.

BEHAVIOUR Shy, retiring and generally unobtrusive; female even less likely to be seen than male but both probably frequently overlooked owing to their unobtrusive behaviour. Can go long periods undetected in or under a bush, only revealing its presence by calling. Usually seen alone but members of pair rarely far apart; pairs occupy a territory throughout the year, the male actively defending it with vigorous chases and calls. Roosts communally in trees close to boundary with another territory. Very active and restless in search of food; most active at dusk and dawn. Forages low down in and under vegetation and on the ground in damp hollows and on the edges of ponds and streams. Hops and runs rapidly on the ground and frequently spreads the tail; flight is fast and generally low. Feeds mainly on insects, snails, small frogs, lizards, geckos and possibly seasonally ripe fruit.

BREEDING Season: January to May, occasionally to July. Nest: a large, neat cup-shaped structure of green moss, plant stems and decaying leaves, lined with fern rootlets, usually placed on a ledge or among rocky crevices on the side of a river or torrent, occasionally in the fork of a tree or on a fern-covered tree-stump up to 3 m (10') from the ground. Eggs: 1–2, pale greenish-white with a few faint reddish-brown spots or blotches at the larger end. Incubation by female only but both adults feed nestlings.

MOULT No information.

MEASUREMENTS Wing, male 103–113, female 97–110; bill (to gape) 26–30.5, (to feathers) 17.5–20, depth of bill 5–7; tarsus 32–37 (Ali & Ripley 1983, Delacour 1942). Weight apparently unrecorded.

REFERENCES Ali & Ripley (1983), Collar *et al.* (1994), Delacour (1942), Henry (1971), Hoffmann (1984), Warakagoda (1997).

19 SHINY WHISTLING-THRUSH *Myophonus melanurus*   Plate 9
(Sumatran Whistling-Thrush)

Arrenga melanurus **Salvadori, 1879, *Ann. Mus. Civ. Genova* 14: 227 – Mount Singalan, West Sumatra.**

IDENTIFICATION Male 24–29 cm (9½–11½"); female 22–25 cm (8¾–10"). Endemic to the mountain forests of Sumatra. Small to medium-sized whistling-thrush; wings long and pointed with long or well spaced primary projection. Mostly jet-black or deep blackish-blue with bright metallic tips to most of the body and wings, small panel of metallic blue on lesser coverts (may be obscured); lores to eye black, centre of forehead to over eyes bright blue, often extending as a supercilium. Bill, legs and feet black. Female slightly duller than male. **Confusion species** Only possible problem is the larger, generally deeper blue Blue Whistling-Thrush (23) which (in Sumatran race *dicrorhynchus*) has a bright yellow bill (with dark culmen), darker or blacker underparts and reduced (or completely lack) pale blue spots on forehead to over the eyes.

DESCRIPTION Sexes alike. **Adult** Jet-black but centre of forehead to over eyes, face, crown, nape (including sides of nape) and neck, mantle, back and scapulars tipped deep metallic violet-blue, sometimes extending to tips of chin, throat and breast; rump and uppertail-coverts unspotted browner-black than body. Lesser coverts bright deep metallic blue and (when not covered by scapulars or breast feathers) show as bright blue patch at bend of wing; median and greater coverts blackish-brown with bright blue edges and tips to greaters; alula and primary coverts blackish, latter edged deep blue, flight feathers blackish-brown narrowly edged bluish on primaries and broadly edged deep blue on secondaries and tertials. Tail mostly blackish-brown but middle of central pair and edges to bases of all outers deep blue. Lores to eye black. Lower belly to vent and undertail-coverts also blackish-brown. Bill black; hooked tip to upper mandible. Eye hazel-brown. Legs and feet black. **Adult female** Similar to male, including violet-blue forehead and supercilium; but duller brown flight feathers, dull bluish lesser coverts and browner tail and underparts. **Immature** First-year bird entirely sooty-black with blackish-brown tinge to rump, uppertail-coverts, tail and flight feathers. Underparts also more brownish-black than above. Forehead to over eye finely tipped buffish or whitish; fine pale buffish shaft-streaks to breast and flanks. Sides of crown to sides of nape and neck to mantle and edges of scapulars and inner lesser coverts tipped deep metallic blue. Bill mostly black with yellowish base to lower mandible.

GEOGRAPHICAL VARIATION None. Monotypic.

VOICE Call a high-pitched ringing screech.

STATUS AND DISTRIBUTION Common or fairly common. Endemic to Sumatra.

MOVEMENTS Sedentary.

HABITAT Hill and montane forests with rivers and streams on the slopes of the higher mountains above 800 m (2640').

BEHAVIOUR Usually alone or in pairs; generally shy and inconspicuous, but in parts of its range quickly acclimatises to man and becomes tame and inquisitive. Forages in trees at mid-level but also spends long periods low down or on the ground of mossy forests, usually near water. Feeds principally on vegetable matter, some fruit and seeds, and a variety of insects and their larvae.

BREEDING Very little known. Nest: a large cup-shaped structure of living moss and other plant fibres placed against the trunk or in the fork of a tree or along a thick branch; adults feeding young recorded in May.

MOULT No information.

MEASUREMENTS Wing, male 114–132, female 114–127; tarsus, male 37–43, female 33.5–39; bill (n=11) (to gape) 25–31, (to feathers) 11–20.5, depth of bill 5.5–8 (Delacour 1942). Weight apparently unrecorded.

REFERENCES Delacour (1942), MacKinnon & Phillips (1993).

20 SUNDA WHISTLING-THRUSH *Myophonus glaucinus* **Plate 8**

Pitta glaucina Temminck, 1823, *Pl. Col.*, livr. 33, pl. 194 – Java.

IDENTIFICATION 24–26.5 cm (9½–10½"). A large, sturdy-looking thrush with a large head, long wings and broad wing-base; nominate race is slightly smaller than those on Borneo and Sumatra. Like other whistling-thrushes these birds are deep bluish-black to purplish-blue with a bright blue, but equally rarely seen, lesser covert patch; lack any metallic spotting; *castaneus* from Sumatra differs by having the mantle to tail, wings and belly ruddy or chestnut-brown. All three races are island endemics. **Confusion species** Blue Whistling-Thrush (23) is larger, has a bright yellow bill and is spangled or spotted with metallic blue on the head and nape to mantle.

DESCRIPTION Sexes almost alike. **Adult male** Forehead to crown and face to sides of nape and neck bluish-black with forehead to over eyes more clearly or visibly deep blue; mantle (occasionally from hindcrown), back, rump and uppertail-coverts to scapulars, sides of throat and breast deep purplish-blue, with bright blue lesser coverts. Tips of median and greater coverts and edges of primary coverts and flight feathers deep bluish-black; rest of flight feathers and tail black, but edges to outer tail feathers violet or diffusely violet only on outerwebs. Some individuals show pale or whitish bases on back, lower breast, belly and flanks, and some have belly to undertail-coverts blacker or blackish-brown. Bill black with hooked tip to upper mandible. Eye dark hazel-brown. Legs and feet black. **Adult female** Similar to male but duller or darker and lesser coverts sometimes darker blue. **Immature** First-year bird extremely dark brown with some pale centres to crown. Central shafts on lores, ear-coverts, nape, sides of neck, chin and throat pale buffish-white, more broadly forming spots or streaks on breast, belly and flanks.

GEOGRAPHICAL VARIATION Three races; variation relatively well marked. Adult male *borneensis* is similar to nominate but larger and darker, and the deep purplish-blue is less prominent on the upperparts and almost invisible on forehead to nape. Overall mostly purplish-blue-black with a more prominent bluish sheen to throat and breast. Wings, lower back, rump, uppertail-coverts and tail browner than nominate, the lesser coverts bright violet-blue but without any bluish sheen on edge of flight feathers. Belly and flanks to undertail-coverts and thighs more dark brown than black; can show white bases to feathers of the back and breast to belly and flanks. Bill larger than in nominate, jet-black. Eye variable from dark blue to dark brown. Legs and feet jet-black, soles of feet yellow. Adult female is almost entirely dark brown with (rarely seen) purplish-blue patch at base of lesser coverts.

Adult male *castaneus* is also larger than nominate and has the lower forehead to lores and eye black; upper forehead to over the eyes has a frontal band of deep metallic blue, slightly brighter and higher on forehead than in nominate; crown to nape, sides of neck and upper mantle black with a deep or dark purplish-blue sheen. Mantle, back, rump, uppertail-coverts, scapulars to median and greater coverts deep ruddy or chestnut-brown, becoming bright cinnamon on the edges of the flight feathers and tertials. Lesser coverts to bend of wing has a patch of bright blue. Innerwebs of flight feathers brown. Tail bright cinnamon-brown becoming slightly darker towards tip. Chin and throat black, sides of throat to breast, upper belly and upper flanks black with a dark purplish-blue sheen; lower flanks and belly brown becoming warm or chestnut on vent to undertail-coverts; can also show some white at bases to back, breast, belly and flanks. Thighs brown. Adult female *castaneus* has forehead and lores to eye rich or deep brown; face brown tinged greyish, crown to nape and upper mantle dark brown with a purplish-sheen; crown and nape can also be blackish. Rest of upperparts, including lesser coverts to bend of wing as adult male but cinnamon on belly duller. Underparts warm brown or cinnamon-tinged or washed greyish; chin and throat (and thighs) earth-brown. Juveniles resemble adult female with bluish sheen on upper nape; sides of neck and chin to breast and upper belly have paler centres to feathers which gradually darken with age to black.

Taxonomic note Some differences in opinion between authorities exist over the treatment of these races. Chasen (1935) considered that each merited full species status but Delacour (1947) recognised only *glaucinus* and most subsequent authors, principally Ripley (1964) and more recently Sibley & Monroe (1990), have followed this treatment. Van Marle & Voous (1988) suggested that *castaneus* is a distinct species and should be treated separately. However, in view of the similarities in size and structure, but the considerable differences in plumage and habitat occupation (nominate *glaucinus* and *castaneus* are primarily montane birds, whilst *borneensis* also occurs into the lowlands), a detailed study of the vocalisations and an examination of their DNA profiles is clearly urgently required before adopting any further lumping or splitting.

VOICE Has a variety of loud ringing notes, *ooweet-oweet-tee-teet*, often followed by a softer *truuu-truuu*; alarm note is a harsh or raucous *cheet* or *tee-ee-eet... tee-ee-eet* and also a three- or four-note squirrel-like chattering chortle. Song is a loud series of clear, melodious whistles similar to those given by Orange-headed Thrush (34) or Hill Blue-Flycatcher *Cyornis banyumas*, with short pauses and ending with some *chet-chet* notes; usually given from tree or crag.

STATUS AND DISTRIBUTION Locally common.

M. g. borneensis Lowland forests, foothills and mountains of Borneo.

M. g. castaneus Hills and mountains of Sumatra.

M. g. glaucinus Mountains of Java and Bali.

MOVEMENTS Sedentary.

HABITAT Forests with streams in the foothills and mountains, also around caves and crevices in rocky outcrops; nominate birds on Java occur from about 800 to 2400 m (2600–7920') on Java and slightly lower in parts of Bali, *castaneus* occurs from 400 to 1500 m (1300–4950') on Sumatra, and *borneensis* occurs locally in the lowland forests to about 2400 m (8000') on Borneo, occasionally to about 2700 m (9000') on Mt Kinabalu.

BEHAVIOUR Similar to that of Blue Whistling-Thrush but less heavily tied to water and may be more widely found in forests. Typically fans tail like other whistling-thrushes. Forages along streams and watercourses and is frequently most active in the open in early morning and evening, but at other times of day is elusive and remains hidden within low vegetation. Feeds on insects and their larvae, principally aquatic insects, snails and molluscs, also frogs, crickets, beetles, slugs, termites, centipedes, worms and woodlice; also takes some fruit and has been known to take small mammals.

BREEDING Season (West Java) September to April or early May. Nest: large cup-shaped structure of fern leaves, moss, roots usually placed in a cave or hole in cliff or rocks over or near a stream, waterfall or river. Eggs: 2, variably pale pinkish, greenish-white or cream-coloured, finely speckled and/or capped with deep pink or reddish.

MOULT No information.

MEASUREMENTS Wing, male 132–150, female 132–142; *castaneus* male 132–147, female 132–139; *borneensis* wing, male 141–155, female 137–153; bill (n=11) (to gape) 26.5–34, (to feathers) 19.5–23; *castaneus* (n=2) (to gape) 30–33.5, (to feathers) 21; *borneensis* (n=9) (to gape) 36.5–45, (to feathers) 18.5–24; depth of bill (all races) 7.5–10.5; tarsus, male 35.5–41, female 34–37; *borneensis* 39.5–43.5; *castaneus* 39.5–45 (Chasen 1935, Delacour 1942). Weight apparently unrecorded.

REFERENCES Chasen (1935), Delacour (1947), van Marle & Voous (1988), Ripley (1964), Sibley & Monroe (1990).

21 MALAYAN WHISTLING-THRUSH *Myophonus robinsoni* Plate 8

Myiophoneus robinsoni Ogilvie-Grant, 1905, *Bull. Brit. Orn. Club* 15: 69 – Mengkuang hebah peak, Pahang state.

IDENTIFICATION 25–26 cm (10"). A sooty, blackish-blue whistling-thrush endemic to the highlands of the main range, Peninsular Malaysia. Has deep purplish-blue forehead to sides of crown, bright metallic blue lesser covert patch and metallic purplish-blue tips to breast and upper belly; bill is bright yellow with a dark culmen. Female similar but duller or browner. **Confusion species** Overlaps with race *dicrorhynchus* of Blue Whistling-Thrush (23) which is slightly larger and has silvery-white tips to the median coverts and metallic blue spotting or spangling on the upperparts (greatly reduced in size compared to nominate birds) and on the breast, upper belly and flanks. Malayan is smaller with a slenderer bill and rounded wings and is somewhat browner than Blue particularly on the underparts.

DESCRIPTION Sexes almost alike. **Adult male** Entirely sooty-black or blackish-blue except for deep purplish-blue forehead to over eye and navy or purplish-blue tinge to face, crown, nape, tips of mantle, upper back and scapulars. Lesser coverts to bend of wing and bases of median coverts have a patch of bright metallic blue. Tips of median and edges and tips of greater coverts, outerwebs of primaries (except outermost two) and secondaries also deep metallic blue but those on median coverts often inconspicuous or absent. Innerwebs to flight feathers and all tertials blackish or brownish-black; underwing-coverts blackish-brown. Tail blackish with deep bluish or purplish-blue sheen to edges of central feathers. Chin, throat, breast and belly to upper flanks sooty-black with metallic purplish-blue tips to sides of throat and across breast to upper belly; flanks tinged purplish-blue; rest of underparts black or sooty brownish-black with white bases to feathers often showing. Bill mostly yellow with dark brown culmen or base to upper mandible. Legs and feet black or blackish-brown. **Adult female** Similar to male but slightly browner-black and not as extensively tipped or washed purplish-blue (individual feathers have smaller areas of bluish); underparts also browner with smaller metallic purplish-blue tips to breast and upper flanks. **Immature** Poorly known and undescribed. Probably very similar to adult in first year with dull sooty-black plumage or may show a dull bluish tinge to upperparts.

GEOGRAPHICAL VARIATION None. Monotypic.

VOICE Contact note is a thin, high-pitched *tseee* frequently repeated when alarmed or disturbed. Song very similar to that of Blue Whistling-Thrush but much softer.

STATUS AND DISTRIBUTION Uncommon. Peninsular Malaysia, endemic to the hills of Selangor and Pahang (and possibly elsewhere in mountains over 900 m/3000') south to the Genting Highlands. Most frequently (but not consistently) seen on Fraser's Hill; considered Near-Threatened (Collar *et al.* 1994).

MOVEMENTS Sedentary.

HABITAT Broadleaved evergreen forested hills and secondary forest edge, between 755 and about 1510 m (2500–5000') with streams and fast-flowing rivers, also in ravines and wooded gullies.

BEHAVIOUR Not well known but many habits and actions as those of Blue Whistling-Thrush (including spreading the tail when feeding on the ground). Generally less confined to running water and often forages in woodlands or at edges of roads through woodlands, particularly in the early morning. Predominantly crepuscular, shy and difficult to observe; usually alone or in pairs. Has bounding gait from rock to rock, frequently pausing with erect posture and head cocked up at an angle. Occasionally perches in trees above narrow streams or over roads. When disturbed flies off rapidly for a short distance before dropping back quickly to the ground. Food largely unrecorded but probably very similar to the range of invertebrate prey, and possibly also some carrion and fruit, as taken by others members of the genus.

BREEDING Season: March and September, possibly also the intervening months. Nest: a cup-shaped structure of plant fibres, mostly of tree-ferns, bryophytes and dead leaves, usually placed in an epiphytic fern or on a branch, creeper or vine. Eggs: 1–2, pale bluish-grey and finely specked with pale pinkish-brown.

MOULT No information.

MEASUREMENTS Wing, male 141–151, female 130–134; tarsus 38.5–46; bill (n=6) (to gape) 35–36, (to feathers) 21–23, depth 8.5–9 (Delacour 1942, Medway & Wells 1976). Weight apparently unrecorded.

REFERENCES Delacour (1942), Glenister (1971), Medway & Wells (1976).

22 MALABAR WHISTLING-THRUSH *Myophonus horsfieldi*   Plate 7

Myophonus Horsfieldii Vigors, 1831, *Proc. Zool. Soc. London*: 35 – Himalayan mountains [restricted to Malabar by Baker (1923) *Hand-list of Indian birds*: 93].

IDENTIFICATION 25–30 cm (10–11¾"). The whistling-thrush of the hills of western and southern India. Unspotted sooty-black or blackish-blue on the head and upperparts except for the shallow V of bright cobalt-blue on the forehead to over the eyes and the patch on the lesser coverts; underparts blackish but tipped metallic blue on the breast, belly and flanks. Rarely found away from forested streams or torrents. **Confusion species** No other whistling-thrush in range; cobalt-blue forehead, yellow bill and lack of spots separate it from the similar but larger Blue Whistling-Thrush (23). Closer to the range of Sri Lanka Whistling-Thrush (18) but larger with bright cobalt-blue forehead. The sympatric races of European Blackbird (111) are distinctly paler, particularly *nigropileus* of the Western Ghats, and readily distinguished by the bright or deep yellow bill, eye-ring, legs and feet.

DESCRIPTION Sexes almost alike. **Adult male** Entirely blackish or blackish-blue with a prominent metallic blue sheen; centre of forehead to over the eyes has a broad V of cobalt-blue. Mantle, back, scapulars increasingly to rump and uppertail-coverts deep or royal-blue sheen. Lesser coverts to bend of wing have a patch of bright cobalt-blue (may be hidden or obscured by body feathers); edges and tips to median and greater coverts, alula, primary coverts, outerwebs of flight feathers and tertials deep blue. Tail blackish but all feathers heavily blue-black on outerwebs (least on outermost). Chin and throat to sides of neck black, rest of underparts black but feathers on breast, belly and flanks broadly tipped metallic blue; vent blackish-brown as are thighs and undertail-coverts, both of which have deep blue sheen. Bill hooked at tip, black. Eye dark brown. Legs and feet black, soles dirty whitish. **Adult female** Blue tips to underparts not as broad. **Immature** Almost entirely sooty-brown or blackish, wings (except lesser and median coverts) and tail as adult.

GEOGRAPHICAL VARIATION None. Monotypic.

VOICE Call is a series of short, harsh notes; alarm a shrill and very high-pitched or piercing *kree-ee* reminiscent of a Hill Myna *Gracula religiosa* given usually whilst in or about to take flight. Calls very early in the morning, often well before dawn. Song a loud and rich rambling series of whistled notes travelling up and down the scale, very human-like in tone and quality. Song period mostly from February to September but also occasionally in December and January.

Nestlings are frequently taken from the wild and reared as cage-birds for their beautiful song, and can be taught to whistle a complete tune. In some areas this practice has greatly reduced the population of this bird.

STATUS AND DISTRIBUTION Fairly common. Western India and parts of central and central-eastern India, from the northernmost Western Ghats in western Gujarat (Mt Abu) and southern Rajasthan south to western Karnataka and western Kerala and extending east from southern Gujarat through central Madhya Pradesh along the Satpura range to extreme north-west Orissa; east in the south from the Western Ghats to the Nilgiri Hills and the Shevaroy Hills in Tamil Nadu.

MOVEMENTS Partial or short-distance altitude migrant; in monsoon moves to lower-altitude foothills and adjacent areas of the plains but usually remains near streams and rivers. A scarce or rare visitor to Andhra Pradesh and southern Orissa.

HABITAT Forests or tangled vegetation with tall trees and fast-moving rocky streams or torrents; also shady moss-covered ravines and cardamom plantations up to about 2200 m (7260'); rarely seen away from water but occasionally on adjacent forest paths, trails or gardens.

BEHAVIOUR Usually alone or in pairs; bold and seemingly fearless, quickly adapting to human settlement and frequently entering outhouses and gardens. Forages on the ground or in shallow water, and hops from rock to rock in stream- or riverbeds, occasionally taking food from the surface of the water. Frequently perches in trees, also in caves or rock slopes. Flies low and fairly fast; on landing (and occasionally when just perched) raises its tail high over its back, then lowers it slowly whilst simultaneously spreading it. Feeds mostly on aquatic insects and their larvae, also worms, small frogs, snails and crabs; the latter are battered open on a stone regularly used for the purpose; also some fruit, particularly figs and berries.

BREEDING Season: chiefly May to September but in the south of the range can begin as early as February or March. Nest: a large or bulky cup-shaped structure of moss, roots and grass lined with fine rootlets and moss, occasionally held together or reinforced with mud; usually placed on a ledge or crevice in a rock beside or behind a waterfall and soaked with continual spray; in part of the range nests in entrances to tunnels and drainage pipes; exceptionally has nested in the rafters of a house

or church and even up to 12 m (c.40′) in a tree. The same site and nest is frequently used in subsequent years or with new materials added on top of the old. Eggs: 2–3, occasionally 4, pale clay or pale greenish to greyish-stone, sparsely spotted with pale reddish spots and lavender blotches. Incubation period 16–17 days. Nest building, incubation and feeding of young by both adults. Two broods.

MOULT Post-juvenile moult of body feathers and lesser, median and inner greater coverts and tertials. Complete postnuptial moult of adults begins with wing and tail feathers from September to November.

MEASUREMENTS Wing, male 139–170, female 142.5–154; tarsus 38–47; bill (n=69) (to gape) male 32–35.5, female 29.5–35.5, (culmen) 20–26, depth of bill 7.5–10. Weight 101–130 g (Delacour 1942, Ali & Ripley 1983).

REFERENCES Ali & Ripley (1983), Delacour (1942).

23 BLUE WHISTLING-THRUSH *Myophonus caeruleus* Plate 7
(Himalayan Whistling-Thrush, Violet Whistling-Thrush)

Gracula (caerulea) **Scopoli, 1786,** *Del. Flor. Fauna Insubr.***, fasc. 2: 88; ex Sonnerat 'merle bleu de la Chine', 1782, Voy. Ind. Orient.: 188, pl. 108 – China [restricted to Canton by Stresemann (1924)** *Abh. Ber. Mus. Dresden* **16(2): 28].**

IDENTIFICATION 31–35 cm (12¼–13¾″). A large dark blue to dark violet-blue thrush, often found near streams and rivers in forest in mountainous areas of southern Central Asia, the Himalayas, China, Burma, South-East Asia, Malaysia and parts of Sumatra. Distinctively marked with shining or metallic blue tips to many of the head and body feathers and with a large (but not always well seen) patch of metallic blue on the lesser coverts and white or silvery-white tips to the median coverts; wings and tail otherwise deep blue-black. Large yellow bill with a dark culmen and hooked tip, except for nominate race which has an all-black bill. **Confusion species** Overlaps with very similar Malayan Whistling-Thrush (21) in Peninsular Malaya, Sunda Whistling-Thrush (20) in Sumatra and Java, and Shiny Whistling-Thrush (19) also on Sumatra. Malayan is slightly smaller and duller or generally browner on the underparts; has metallic blue spots or spangled tips to the breast and upper belly and lacks any bluish spotting on the upperparts and has no white or silvery-white tips to the median coverts. Sunda Whistling-Thrush has no metallic spotting and an all-black bill, Shiny Whistling-Thrush is smaller, has a black bill and is generally not as deep or blackish-blue on the head and upperparts or on the belly to undertail, but has deep violet-blue chevron on forehead to over eyes. Both Grandala *Grandala coelicolor* and male Blue Rock-Thrush (17) are smaller and have all-dark bills. All crows are much blacker and lack the deep blue-black body plumage.

DESCRIPTION Sexes almost alike. **Adult male** Entirely bluish-black or dark indigo-blue spotted with lighter metallic or violet-blue tips to forehead and sides of crown above eye forming a solid patch, otherwise erratically spaced over the crown, nape, mantle, back, scapulars and rump to uppertail-coverts, the latter often less distinctly spotted; can show white central shaft-streaks on lower back. Some individuals show varied patterns of metallic blue spotting more heavily or densely grouped over the eye and sides of nape, centre of mantle and on underparts. Tail broad and rounded at tip, entirely deep indigo or blue-black except for black feather-shafts and outer edges to all feathers. Lesser coverts extensively metallic or purplish-blue forming solid patch at bend of wing. Median coverts dark bluish-black tipped metallic blue; in some birds, however, tips (especially outers) are spotted silvery-white. Greater coverts, alula, primary coverts and flight feathers deep blue-black on outerwebs, all innerwebs and tips sooty-black; outer primaries entirely black; tertials dark bluish-black but innerwebs sooty-black; underwing-coverts also deep blue-black with metallic blue tips. Lores to eye black; cheeks, ear-coverts and sides of neck blue-black heavily tipped or streaked metallic blue extending to chin, throat, breast and belly; larger spots on flanks with white bases to feathers and short (but variable in length) central shaft-streaks which may extend to lower breast; vent and undertail-coverts bluish-black or blackish, less heavily spotted or tipped metallic blue; undertail-coverts unspotted. Thighs

215

sooty-black. Bill hooked at tip, black (smaller or thinner than most of the other races). Eye variable from dull dark yellow to light orange to dark brown. Legs and feet black, soles yellowish. **Adult female** As the male but slightly duller or sootier above with less metallic blue tips and tinged browner on underparts. **Immature** First-year bird mostly sooty-blackish with deep violet-bluish tinge to head, face, nape, mantle, wings, tail and flight feathers; median coverts may show a few pale violet-blue specks or spots. Back to rump and upper-tail-coverts sooty-black. Chin, throat, sides of neck sooty or dark brownish-black with thin or fine whitish central shaft-streaks and spots on cheeks, ear-coverts, over eye, chin, throat, sides of neck to breast and belly. Bill black.

GEOGRAPHICAL VARIATION Seven races; variation largely clinal and not well defined.

Race *temminckii* is very similar to the nominate with deep blue-black on most of body and most prominent on wings and tail. Centre of forehead to over the eyes is heavily spotted with metallic blue tips forming a narrow patch and streaks erratically across crown, back, scapulars, rump and upper-tail-coverts (and silvery-blue shaft-streaks on nape and mantle), continuing onto rump and uppertail-coverts (both of which have fine white shaft-streaks). Prominent patch of purplish-blue on lesser coverts to bend of wing; tips of median coverts, especially outers, silvery-white but generally duller in females. Lores to eye, chin and throat black but ear-coverts, sides of neck, chin and throat heavily spotted or streaked metallic blue, with larger blue-green spots on breast and belly; belly may also show fine whitish shaft-streaks. Vent sooty-black. Underwing-coverts sooty-black tinged deep blue. In worn plumage metallic blue tips wear to thin paler streaks on upperparts and sides of face and neck. Eye usually much browner than nominate *caeruleus*. Bill slightly larger than nominate and hooked at tip, orange to orange-yellow with dark brown to blackish base, culmen and/or tip. Legs and feet black, soles yellowish-grey. Female similar to male but slightly smaller and generally duller, the tips of the median coverts dull whitish. First-year *temminckii* has sooty- or brownish-black body except for bluish tinge to crown, nape, mantle, scapulars and heavily on wings and tail. Upper mandible mostly dark or brownish, lower dull yellowish. Metallic blue tips appear in first-winter plumage on forehead, crown and mantle.

Race *turcestanicus* is similar to *temminckii* but slightly duller overall, with brownish flight feathers, belly, flanks to vent and undertail-coverts, and longer wings and tail.

Race *eugenei* is similar to both *temminckii* and *caeruleus* but lacks the white or silvery-white tips to the median coverts and has a larger or heavier bright yellow bill with some black on the culmen and at the base.

Race *crassirostris* is virtually identical to the nominate but slightly smaller with a smaller, stouter bill; the upperparts, breast and belly are spangled metallic blue and the face (except lores

and cheeks) have more and finer metallic blue streaks extending to the sides of neck, nape and throat; the median coverts are tipped white or whitish-blue; and on average there is more basal white feathering on the lower back, lower breast, belly and flanks. The underwing often shows a white patch at the base of the primaries. Eye dark brown. Bill yellow. Immature similar to nominate but with pale central shaft-streaks on underparts and white bases showing through; bill mostly black but with yellow edges and gape.

Race *dicrorhynchus* is the dullest, slightly larger, with a larger bill than the nominate. Adults are dark blue-black with the metallic spotting greatly reduced or vestigial. Centre of forehead, nape and sides of neck are faintly spotted, very faint on mantle and back. Scapulars also tipped metallic blue but much reduced; large patch of dull purplish-blue on lesser coverts to bend of wing; tips to median coverts silvery-white. Face and crown sooty-black, the chin and throat with small metallic bluish spots becoming larger (but no more prominent) on breast and more widely spaced on belly; flanks, lower belly to undertail-coverts brownish or sooty-black; lower back, lower breast, belly and flanks with large white bases. Eyes brown. Bill large and yellow with a dark or blackish culmen. Juvenile all sooty-brown with a faint bluish tinge to crown, mantle (with indistinct pale central shafts), wings (especially flight feathers) and tail; belly to undertail-coverts browner than on breast or upperparts, flanks similar with indistinct whitish central shafts. Bill black.

Race *flavirostris* is like *dicrorhynchus* but with a visibly shorter tail; overall much blacker-blue or purplish and appearing black at a distance; metallic blue tips are smaller and appear as crescents on tips of forehead, sides of crown, nape and, well spaced, mantle and upper back to scapulars, chin, throat, breast and belly (larger on breast and belly). Wings and tail faintly blue-black but appear mostly black, with thin or faint white tips or crescents to median coverts. Back to rump and uppertail-coverts and lower belly to undertail-coverts and wings sooty-black. Bill large, stout, yellow with a black culmen. Legs and feet black. Immature dull blackish with bluish tinge to wings and tail.

Taxonomic note Eck (1974) and van Marle & Voous (1988) have proposed that *flavirostris* is a separate species: Large Whistling-Thrush.

VOICE Call a piercing sharp whistle (*caeruleus*) or strident, ringing and far-carrying *tzeet-tze-tze-tzeet* (*eugenei*); alarm note is a loud, shrill *kreee* or *scree*, occasionally continued into *scree-chit-chit-chit*. Song a thin, slightly undulating whistling warble of several musical notes, e.g. *tew-tew* or *tih-tih*, often preceded by a loud, ringing *tzeet-tzeet* and including several harsh or grating Jay-like notes and ending with a rising *tzeeet-tzuit-tzuit-zuit-zuit*; may follow a lilting pattern. That of *eugenei* is loud and reminiscent of Black-collared Starling *Sturnus nigricollis*. Song usually given on the wing or when perched on a rock, crag or tree; also has a softer or more subdued subsong rather creaky or jumbled and continues more or less continuously for up to 3 minutes. Often sings in state of agitation whilst pursuing intruder from breeding territory. Song often given before dawn; mostly from end of February (exceptionally from late January) to end of June and again from mid-August to end of September; subsong more usually heard in September and October.

STATUS AND DISTRIBUTION Common, but often thinly or patchily spread; *dicrorhynchus* is only locally common.

M. c. turcestanicus Southern Kirgizstan and Tadzhikstan to the Tien Shan, north to the Dzungarian Ala Tau; in the south to the western Pamirs (apparently absent in the eastern range) and northern Afghanistan.

M. c. temminckii Afghanistan (except the area occupied by *turcestanicus*) to north-east Iran and east through the mountain ranges of northern Pakistan from Baluchistan (where rare) and continuously from the valleys of Indus Kohistan to Chitral, Baltistan and Kashmir to the Himalayas of Himachal Pradesh, northern India and east through Nepal, Sikkim, Bhutan, Assam, northern Bengal, south-east Tibet and Arunachal Pradesh, north-east India to about 96°E (where it intergrades with *eugenei*), south into southern and south-west Burma, Nagaland, and Manipur to the Chittagong Hills and Meghalaya Plateau of Bangladesh. In winter at lower levels to the foothills below the breeding range; in Pakistan occurs south to the Salt Range, including Lahore and occasionally Jhang; in northern India in the northern Punjab and in the east into north-west Thailand (where generally rare or very scarce).

M. c. eugenei Mishmi Hills of north-east Assam and most of Burma (northern, southern and eastern, plus Tenasserim – excluding the range of *temminckii*), southern China from southern Szechwan (meets *caeruleus* in the Omei Shan region but degree of integration, if any, unknown) to Yunnan and western Kweichow south to western, northwest and north-east Thailand, Cambodia, Laos and Vietnam (though generally rare in the south). Mostly sedentary but moves short distances southward in winter, apparently wandering as far as south-east Thailand (Delacour 1948) but records could also refer to *crassirostris*.

M. c. caeruleus Central and eastern-central China from south-east Kansu and eastern Szechwan (mostly east of the range of *eugenei*), east to Shansi, Hopeh, Kiangsi and Chekiang and in the south to Kweichow, Kwangtung (including Hong Kong), Fukien and northern Kiangsi. In winter along the Yangtze Valley and south into eastern Burma, northwest and north-east Thailand, Laos and Tonkin, northern Vietnam; status uncertain (possibly a vagrant) in Cochinchina, southern Vietnam.

M. c. crassirostris South-east and Peninsular Thailand to the islands in the Gulf of Siam, south to Tarutao and Langkawi islands, Perlis and Kedah, north-west Peninsular Malaysia.

M. c. dicrorhynchus Malay Peninsula from extreme southern Thailand (Pattani province) south to the hills of Selangor and northern Pahang (to about 1800 m/5950'), also the hills of western Sumatra (up to 1000 m/3000'); has also been recorded from Mulu Caves area, Sarawak (M. Chong pers. comm.).

M. c. flavirostris Mountains of Java up to 1060 m (3500').

MOVEMENTS Partial or altitude migrant, some birds winter at lower altitudes, though many birds remain fairly high in the Himalayas, and descends to the foothills and plains adjacent to the breeding range, though usually in the area of forest with streams. Outside of the breeding season may remain in or close to breeding site and some birds endure periods of frost and snow at high levels whilst other are found in woods or forests some way from nearest water.

HABITAT Broadleaved, evergreen and mixed deciduous forests with streams or rivers, including torrential rivers, also in dry karst valleys and ravines, open hillsides, limestone outcrops and gorges with caves, wooded cliffs and gullies along river valleys, occasionally at high elevations in sparse bush, thornscrub or stunted trees near streams but generally reluctant to breed above the treeline; *crassirostris* also occurs along forest edges and in mangroves. Breeds at sea-level throughout most of China (including Hong Kong where often found in urban habitat (gardens and parks among skyscrapers) but elsewhere mostly between 1000 and 3650 m (3300–12,050') in the Himalayas but lower limit variable from 2700 m (8900') in the Baluchistan to about 1200 m (3960') in the western Himalayas and 1500 m (4950') in Nepal; has also been recorded at 4800 m (15,850') in Khumbu, Nepal, in May and to 5180 m (17,100') (Biswas 1961). In winter occurs in similar habitat at lower levels.

BEHAVIOUR Usually alone (especially in winter) or in pairs, but established pairs usually remain together throughout the year. On the ground actively hops or jumps from stone to stone, including those in rushing torrents; also walks and runs with large bounding strides, climbs hillsides and cliff-screes with long hops often with wings partially open, running with short steps and frequently fanning or spreading the tail half open when perched. Forages in riverbeds and takes floating items of food from surface of rivers, also on paths, cliffs or forest floor, turning over leaves with its bill in typical *Turdus* thrush fashion, many other habits redolent of European Blackbird (111). Often crepuscular and active until well after dark and spends long periods of the day inactive sitting on a low branch in dense undergrowth. Flight swift and powerful on large wings; frequently raises tail high over back and lowers it slowly, often fanning it open whilst doing so; may repeat this several times especially on landing. Is particularly aggressive to birds of prey and owls on the breeding territory and has a fairly elaborate aggression display involving puffing out the breast and adopting aggressive postures. Feeds mainly on worms, snails, slugs, small crabs, frogs, other aquatic crustaceans and molluscs, water beetles, grasshoppers, insects and their larvae, particularly of cockchafers; snailshells opened by hammering them against a large stone; also known to take small birds, especially nestlings and other small creatures; takes ripe berries especially of dogrose and mulberry, and other vegetable matter.

BREEDING Season: January to May in Selangor, February to April in southern Burma and Malaysia; October to June (*flavirostris*); end of April to August elsewhere; breeding territory and nest frequently used for several years in succession. Nest: a large or bulky cup-shaped structure mainly of green moss, lined with finer roots, grass stems, fern fronds and some mud, occasionally also some horsehair, usually placed on a ledge, mossy bank or in a hollow or crevice of a boulder, rock walls or cliff, under an overhang behind a waterfall, in or under a dead tree-stump, in a cave, below a bridge, or in the rafters of a forest bungalow or outhouse. In Hong Kong an urban bird, frequently nesting on buildings; more rarely known to nest in a tree up to 12.5 (c.40') from the ground. Nests re-used in subsequent years, often accumulating into a sizeable structure. Eggs: 3–4, occasionally 5–6, variably pale creamy or whitish-buff (or tinged pink) to pale green or bluish or olive-grey or pale buffish-brown with fine or light pinkish or faint reddish smudges or speckles, the reddish speckles or spots sometimes covering the entire egg. Nest built and nestlings fed by both sexes. Usually two broods, but perhaps only one at highest altitudes.

MOULT Post-juvenile moult from late July to October; post-breeding moult of adults from mid- or early July to late August or early September.

MEASUREMENTS Wing 158–182; tarsus 47–54; bill 29–32, depth of bill 8–9; *turcestanicus* wing, male 179–200, female 168–184; tarsus 45–52; bill 37–38, depth of bill 9; *temminckii* wing, male 167–192, female 155–184; tarsus 48–55; bill (from skull) 33–36, depth of bill 9–10; *eugenei* wing, male 165–181 (exceptionally to 188), female 154.5–178; tarsus 48–54.5; bill 34–37, depth of bill 9–10.5; *crassirostris* wing 153–182; tarsus 45.5–55; bill 32–36, depth of bill 10.5–12; *dicrorhynchus* wing, male 155–187, female 158–169; tarsus 50–55; bill 35–44, depth of bill 12–13; *flavirostris* wing 168–182; tarsus 48–56; bill 44–46, depth of bill 14–15. Weight, male (summer) 136–194 g, (winter) 191.5–231 g; female (summer) 156.5–211 g, (winter) 153–160 g (Delacour 1942, Ali & Ripley 1983, Medway & Wells 1976).

REFERENCES Ali & Ripley (1983), Biswas (1961), Delacour (1942), Eck (1974), Inskipp & Inskipp (1991), van Marle & Voous (1988), Medway & Wells (1976), Smythies (1986).

24 TAIWAN WHISTLING-THRUSH *Myophonus insularis* Plate 9
(Formosan Whistling-Thrush)
Myiophoneus insularis **Gould, 1862,** *Proc. Zool. Soc. London*: 280 – Formosa.

IDENTIFICATION 28–30 cm (11–11¾"). Endemic to Taiwan. A medium-sized whistling-thrush with a robust appearance; plumage is entirely deep inky or blackish-blue with a paler metallic blue chevron on the forehead and lesser coverts (latter not always visible); lores and flight feathers black. In good light becomes much brighter metallic blue with a ruby-red eye (duller in shade). **Confusion species** Very similar to allopatric Malabar Whistling-Thrush (22), with which sometimes considered conspecific, but slightly larger with a smaller amount or more crescent-like area of deeper or darker metallic blue across the forehead to over the eyes. On Taiwan unlikely to be confused with any other species.

DESCRIPTION Sexes alike. **Adult** Almost entirely blackish-blue or deep violet-blue with deep metallic blue across the upper forehead and over the eyes. Crown to rump and uppertail-coverts navy-blue over black. Tail black but with deep blue sheen to all except outermost feathers and tips and shafts of central feathers. Lesser coverts with small panel of bright metallic blue (not always visible); medians and greaters as the upperparts but tips to both (and edges to greaters) metallic blue, alula and primary coverts navy-blue with deeper blue edges to alula, primary coverts and outerwebs of secondaries and primaries, innerwebs and tertials blackish; underwing-coverts as body but greaters have white bases. Lores black (may extend in some across lower forehead); cheeks and ear-coverts black or blackish-blue. Underparts black but deep or navy-blue sheen to chin, throat and upper breast with broad bright metallic blue tips to breast, belly and upper flanks; lower belly to lower flanks, vent, thighs and undertail-coverts brownish-black. Bill fairly short but stout and thick, black. Eye bright red to deep reddish-brown. Legs and feet black. **Immature** Juvenile similar to adult but dull blackish with bluish tinge to wing-coverts, especially extensive on lesser coverts; also yellowish gape and base to lower mandible. First-year bird more similar to adult but head and face dull blackish, body and wings blue-black becoming more like adult with age.

GEOGRAPHICAL VARIATION None. Monotypic.

VOICE Call a loud sharp screaming whistle, *screee*, given with extra urgency or shrillness in alarm. Song a pleasant mixture of shrill rising and falling whistling and melodious phrases, a gently rising *tooo-tu-toot-duu* and *wooot-oot-duu* and including a few scratchy or guttural notes, followed by a series of high-pitched, slightly off-key piping notes and some melodious piping phrases or short trills. May begin quietly and increase in volume, or with the thin high-pitched piping note; overall pace is slow, unhurried and ponderous.

STATUS AND DISTRIBUTION Endemic to Taiwan where it is fairly common.

MOVEMENTS Sedentary.

HABITAT From sea-level (particularly along the island's north coast) to about 2400 m (7920') but principally in montane forests with mixed evergreen trees and bamboo and damp, dark, wooded ravines with fast-flowing streams and torrents usually between 400–2100 m (1320–6900') or occasionally slightly higher; also caves and crevices.

BEHAVIOUR Usually alone except in breeding season. Many habits and actions very similar to those of Blue (23) and Malabar (22) Whistling-Thrushes; spends long periods on the ground where it runs, hops and bounds from rock to rock in forest streams and riverbeds. Often sits motionless on a crag or boulder slowly opening and closing its tail whilst also gently raising it. Often fairly shy and most active at dusk and dawn. Flight is fast, swift and direct, usually low and close to the ground. Forages mainly in damp ground and on the banks of streams and rivers but also rocks in the middle of fast-flowing torrents. Food is mainly freshwater shrimps, aquatic insects (particularly Coleoptera) and their larvae; but lizards, frogs, grasshoppers, mantises and earthworms also taken.

BREEDING Season: April to July but mainly in late May and June. Nest: a fairly large but shallow cup-shaped structure of dead twigs, *Carex* stems, roots and moss, lined with finer roots; usually placed in a hole in rocks and trees up to 12 m (40') from the ground or among the roots of a tree, in crevices or between rocks. Eggs: 2–4, yellowish-pink to pale pinkish-buff sparsely or erratically speckled or spotted with small reddish-brown blotches or slightly larger greyish-lavender blotches. Incubation period 12–14 days. Nestlings fed by both parents.

MOULT No information.

MEASUREMENTS (n=9) Wing (unsexed) 152.5–164, male to 166, female 145–162; tarsus 43–49.5; bill (to gape) 29.5–36.5, (to feathers) 20.5–26, depth 8–10. Weight apparently unrecorded.

REFERENCES Hachisuka & Udagawa (1950–1951), Meyer de Schauensee (1984).

25 GEOMALIA *Geomalia heinrichi*   Plate 9
(Sulawesi Mountain Thrush)

Geomalia heinrichi **Stresemann, 1931, *Orn. Monatsb.* 39: 11 – Mount Latimojong, 2800, Celebes [Sulawesi].**

IDENTIFICATION 28–29 cm (11–11½"). The sole representative of the genus *Geomalia*. An extremely shy and rarely seen ground-loving bird of the damp forest floors above 1700 m in the mountains of central and northern-central Sulawesi. Has a brown head, diffuse dark malar stripe, dull orange underparts and dark brown back, wings and tail, the tail being graduated towards the tip. Short rounded wings and long tail are distinctive field marks. **Confusion species** Unproblematic when seen well, but might be mistaken for a babbler (see below), particularly a laughing-thrush, but no babblers on Sulawesi.

Taxonomic note The exact taxonomic position and affinities of this bird has given rise to considerable disagreement among several authorities. Although bearing several characteristics of a thrush it also shows some, perhaps slightly more, affinities to the babblers, particularly the laughing-thrushes *Garrulax*. Stresemann (1931a,b), who first described the species, thought it a babbler and placed it in a monotypic genus *Geomalia* since there was no obvious close relative in the babblers Timaliidae, a view supported by White & Bruce (1986). However, Ripley (1952) considered that the bird showed characteristics associated with the ground-thrushes and placed it within *Zoothera*; this was partly revised by Ripley (1964), who accepted its generic distinctiveness and placed *Geomalia* immediately before *Zoothera*, a treatment followed by Sibley & Monroe (1990). Without further research we see no reason to dissent here but note that Coates & Bishop (1997) followed White & Bruce (1986) who, however, suggested that the position of this species and the totally unrelated Malia *Malia grata* require further study to determine their exact affinities.

DESCRIPTION Sexes alike. **Adult** Forehead to crown and hindcrown deep or dark brown, slightly paler on nape and hindneck. Mantle, back, wing-coverts and scapulars to rump and uppertail-coverts dark or rich dark brown. Wings very short and wing-tips rounded; flight feathers slightly lighter brown than coverts and scapulars except for rich rust- or chestnut-brown edges to bases of primaries. Tail long and graduated towards tip (recalls some laughing-thrushes *Garrulax*) and deep umber-brown, outer two feathers slightly shorter and paler brown than central feathers; undersides pale reddish-brown. Face brown but streaked or flecked with paler or lighter brown. Sides of neck warmer or orange-brown; broad brown malar stripe from base of bill. Underparts deep or rich orange-brown, rufous on breast very slightly paler or spotted with brown on throat; flanks browner and centre of belly to undertail-coverts paler or orange-brown. On underwing, coverts black, base of under secondaries pale orange. Bill dark or blackish-horn, atypical in shape for a thrush: upper mandible has hooked tip and lower tapers towards tip. Eye brown. Legs and feet pale yellow or yellowish-olive. **Immature** Poorly known and undescribed; thought to be very similar to adult but has dark or blackish-brown mottling on breast and upper belly.

GEOGRAPHICAL VARIATION Two races; variation poorly marked. Race *matinangensis* is very similar to nominate birds but slightly darker on crown, neck and most of upperparts, which are generally browner; the underparts are also darker. White & Bruce (1986) considered these differences too trivial to warrant formal recognition as subspecies.

VOICE Call an intermittent, thin, high-pitched and insistent whistle for up to a second in length and repeated at intervals (Coates & Bishop 1997). Song unknown but may be a longer repetition of the call notes.

STATUS AND DISTRIBUTION Uncommon to rare; considered Near-Threatened (Collar *et al.* 1994).

G. h. heinrichi Latimojong mountains, south-central Sulawesi.

G. h. matinangensis Ile-Ile and (possibly elsewhere) the Tentolomatinan range, northern Sulawesi, and Mt Rorekatimbu, Lore Lindu National Park, central Sulawesi; Mt Tanke Salokko, Mekongga mountains, south-eastern Sulawesi.

MOVEMENTS Sedentary.

HABITAT Highland and montane forests, between 1700 and 3500 m (5600–11,550'), including rainforests, where it lives in, or under, thick undergrowth.

BEHAVIOUR Extremely shy and secretive, frequently overlooked; usually alone; even during the breeding season rarely seen in pairs. Inhabits the forest floor where it walks, or hops with wings held low and horizontal with the back, over vegetation, often flicking or twitching its tail in an agitated fashion. Has very short rounded wings and flies weakly generally over very short distances. Forages on the ground amongst rotting and decaying vegetation for beetles and their larvae, probably also takes other insects.

BREEDING Unknown.

MOULT No information.

MEASUREMENTS (n=4) Wing, male 121–128, female 117–130 (but variable, with some 110–113); tarsus (n=1) 43.5; bill (n=1) (culmen) 22, (to gape) 34; *matinangensis* wing, male 116–122 (White & Bruce 1986). Weight apparently unrecorded.

REFERENCES Coates & Bishop (1997), Collar *et al.* (1994), Ripley (1952, 1964), Sibley & Monroe (1990), Stresemann (1931a,b), White & Bruce (1986).

---

26 SLATY-BACKED THRUSH *Zoothera schistacea* Plate 19
(Slaty-backed Ground-Thrush)
Geocichla schistacea Meyer, 1884, *Zeitschr. ges. Orn.* 1: 211, pl. 8 – Tanimbar.

IDENTIFICATION 16–17 cm (6¼–6¾"). A little-known endemic of the Tanimbar Islands, Lesser Sundas, Indonesia. Like many other *Zoothera* it is generally shy or secretive and easily overlooked; inhabits lowland forests and found from the ground and understorey into the subcanopy. Possibly best found when singing during the wet season. A fairly small, attractive and distinctively marked thrush with deep grey upperparts and edges to the wings, two white wing-bars, broad white supercilium and ear-coverts, black chin to breast and white on remaining underparts broken by prominent black spots on lower breast to mid-belly. Legs and feet noticeably pale or flesh-coloured. **Confusion species** Unlikely to be confused with any other species when seen well. In flight shows white tips to outer tail feathers and two wing-bars (most prominently on tips to greater coverts).

DESCRIPTION Sexes almost alike. **Adult male** Forehead to crown black, becoming grey (with blackish centres to feathers) on hindcrown and nape. Mantle, back and scapulars to rump and uppertail-coverts deep grey. Tail blackish-brown tinged grey on central pair and bases to all outer feathers, with a wedge of white (1.5 cm; ½") on innerweb at tip of outer feathers and smaller spot at tip of next innermost. Lesser coverts black tipped grey, medians and greaters black broadly tipped white, forming double wing-bar; alula and primary coverts black; flight feathers blackish-brown, bases of inner primaries finely edged grey, secondaries narrowly edged greyish on inners becoming dark grey on edges to tertials; innerwebs of tertials grey-brown. Underwing-coverts silvery-white with black bases to greater coverts and silvery-white bases to flight feathers. Broad white supercilium from base of bill to over ear-coverts; lores to cheeks black, ear-coverts white. Chin, throat, sides of neck and entire breast jet-black; rest of underparts white (usually unspotted just below black on breast) or creamy-white, spotted with black on mid-belly, heaviest or most boldly spotted at sides and on flanks; flanks otherwise washed grey. Bill black. Iris dull blackish-brown or coffee brown. Legs and feet pale flesh to yellowish. **Adult female** Less extensively black on crown; black spots on underparts possibly less extensive. **Immature** Undescribed.

GEOGRAPHICAL VARIATION None. Monotypic.

VOICE Call a thin, high-pitched *tseee* or *tzee*; alarm is a similar harsh rasping *zheeeeee* or *zheeet*. Song a rich or melodious series, repeated at intervals, of up to eight sweet and clear whistled notes, the first longest, more drawn-out and upwardly slurred than the rest, which move alternately up and down the scale, finishing with a long upslurred high-pitched whistle (Coates & Bishop 1997); also a frequently repeated musical rising and falling series of short whistled phrases, *duuuu-weet... tu... yooo*, and a slower, more musical series of mellow notes. Sings from the ground and the middle and subcanopy of tall trees, but rarely visible.

STATUS AND DISTRIBUTION Common (Collar & Andrew 1988) or locally common. Tanimbar Islands (Yamdena, Larat), Lesser Sunda Islands, Indonesia. Fears over status perhaps unwarranted (see Habitat); Near-Threatened (Collar *et al.* 1994).

MOVEMENTS Sedentary.

HABITAT Lowland primary and secondary forests, preferring dense evergreen forest along watercourses; may be threatened by the loss of habitat due to destruction from commercial logging (Collar & Andrew 1988), but recently found in degraded forest on the edge of cultivation (Bishop & Brickle 1998).

BEHAVIOUR Little known; usually alone or in pairs, occasionally in small (perhaps family) groups; considered to be more active and visible during the wet season (Bishop & Brickle 1998). Forages on the forest floor and in low-level under-growth, but generally not as terrestrial as other thrush species of the region and often (especially when flushed from the ground) found high in the mid-storey or subcanopy of tall trees.

BREEDING Unknown.

MOULT No information.

MEASUREMENTS (n=4) Wing, male 96–99; tarsus 27; bill (n=2) (culmen) 18–19, (to gape) 26.5. Weight apparently unrecorded.

REFERENCES Bishop & Brickle (1998), Coates & Bishop (1997), Collar & Andrew (1988).

27 MOLUCCAN THRUSH *Zoothera dumasi*　　　Plate 11
(Moluccan Ground-Thrush)

Geocichla dumasi Rothschild, 1898, *Bull. Brit. Orn.* Club 8: 30 – Mount Mada, 3,000', Buru.

IDENTIFICATION 17 cm (6¾"). An attractive, small to medium-sized thrush with a heavy-looking bill; the wings also appear short and rounded. In common with several other *Zoothera* thrushes from the Indonesian/Wallacean region it is a shy, little-known and secretive inhabitant of the forest floor. The race *joiceyi* on Seram is very poorly known and has been seen on very few occasions since its discovery in the 1920s. Rich russet-olive upperparts but slightly darker tail, wings with two white bars at tips of coverts (only on tips of medians on Seram birds), white eye-ring above dark or blackish cheeks; chin and throat to breast black (more extensive on Seram birds), rest of underparts creamy-white with some black spots on sides of belly and flanks. Confusion species Unlikely to be confused with any other species; the only other thrush on Seram is Island Thrush (112) race *deningeri*, which is distinct with a white head and throat, yellow bill and legs.

DESCRIPTION Sexes alike. Adult Upperparts rich russet-brown tinged olive and slightly darker (overlying darker grey bases) on forehead to hindcrown; brightest or richest russet on centre of mantle to uppertail-coverts. Tail brown but central feathers chestnut tinged olive-brown as are the edges of all outers. Lesser coverts as scapulars; median and greater coverts blackish-brown broadly tipped white, forming double wing-bar; inner greaters broadly edged rufous-brown; alula and primary coverts dark brown with paler brown edges to primary coverts; all flight feathers brown finely edged warm or light russet-brown, more broadly edged on inner secondaries; tertials also russet brown, slightly darker or olive-brown on innerwebs; bases to all innerwebs of flight feathers white except outermost three primaries. Underwing has lesser coverts to bend of wing whitish with dark brown tips, median and greater coverts brown or dark brown with white bases to undersides of flight feathers. Lores (may also extend across lower forehead) black or blackish flecked with brown; pale or whitish eye-ring. Cheeks and ear-coverts black but rear of ear-coverts grey-brown; chin and throat to centre of breast and upper belly black; sides of breast to upper flanks brown or olive-brown; belly and rest of flanks white to creamy-white, with black or dark olive spots or bars on centre of belly or flanks; vent and thighs to undertail-coverts buffish-white. Bill fairly large and deep, black. Legs and feet yellowish or yellowish-flesh to pale greyish. Immature Juvenile similar to adult but much duller or browner with pale buffish streaks to crown, back and scapulars and small whitish-orange tips to median and greater coverts. Chin and throat whitish but sides of throat to breast mottled or spotted with blackish and dull whitish-buff, belly pale buffish-white with a few dark olive bars at tips, flanks brownish or light chestnut. Bill blackish. Legs and feet brown.

GEOGRAPHICAL VARIATION Two races; variation well marked. Race *joiceyi* has head to nape as nominate but mantle, scapulars and rest of upperparts tinged olive, becoming slightly darker or blackish-olive on lower back and rump; wings and tail darker brown, lacking any warmth; median and greater coverts black, medians tipped (possibly only on outers) with white spots; flight feathers also black or blackish-olive, the latter with narrow pale brown outerwebs, underwing-coverts black; face and underparts more extensively black to centre of upper belly and flanks (sides of breast may show some white tips), centre of belly white, undertail-coverts dull black spotted white at tips.

VOICE Generally silent but utters a thin *tseep* contact note or *tsree-tsree* flight call. Responds to imitations of its call (Coates & Bishop 1997).

STATUS AND DISTRIBUTION Numerically not uncommon or locally common on Buru but extremely shy; *joiceyi* extremely rare and little known.

Z. d. dumasi Mountains of Buru, Moluccas, Indonesia. Hartert (1924) reported this species on Wa Fehat, Gama M'Rapat and Mount Tagalago.

Z. d. joiceyi Highlands of Seram, Moluccas, Indonesia.

MOVEMENTS Sedentary.

HABITAT Dense lower montane moss-forests between 725–1515 m (2400–5000') on Buru and up to 1280 m (4220') on Seram. There have been very few sightings of *joiceyi* since it was first described in 1921, most recently (three together) in August 1987 (Bowler & Taylor 1993) and about seven in the north-east of the island in 1996 (Isherwood *et al.* 1997).

BEHAVIOUR Usually alone or in pairs. Extremely shy and skulks in deep forest undergrowth, foraging on the ground where it hops over the vegetation; often gives brief flick of the wings, especially when nervous. Easily disturbed and flies with rapid noisy wing-beats low through the forest understorey.

BREEDING Very poorly known; eggs on Buru recorded in early February and young birds in early April.
MOULT No information.
MEASUREMENTS (n=3) Wing, male 89–94, female 85–88; tarsus 31–32; bill (culmen) 17, (to gape) 23–26; *joiceyi* (n=1) wing 93; tarsus 35.5. Weight apparently unrecorded.
REFERENCES Bowler & Taylor (1989, 1993), Isherwood *et al.* (1997).

28 CHESTNUT-CAPPED THRUSH *Zoothera interpres*   Plate 11
(Chestnut-capped Ground-Thrush, Kuhl's Ground-Thrush)

Turdus interpres "Kuhl" = Temminck, 1826, *Pl. Col.*, livr. 78, pl. 458 – Java and Sumatra.

IDENTIFICATION 15–18.5 cm (6–7¼"). A fairly small or compact thrush with a discontinuous distribution from southern Thailand to the Lesser Sundas, Indonesia. Like several other *Zoothera* thrushes of the region it is shy and very retiring, and remains generally little known; but shows unmistakable combination of chestnut head (often looks dark or brown in the poor light of forest floor), grey upperparts with two broad white wingbars, white lores to eye, black chin to breast and white rest of underparts spotted black on upper belly and flanks. **Confusion species** Unlikely to be confused with any other species.

DESCRIPTION Sexes alike. **Adult** Forehead to crown and nape deep chestnut, brightest on nape. Mantle, back and scapulars to rump and uppertail-coverts dark or slate-grey. Tail grey-brown but central pair of feathers and edges to bases of all outers greyer-brown, tips of outer pair broadly, and next pair narrowly, tipped white. Inner lesser coverts as scapulars, outer lessers and median coverts pure white; greater coverts black with white tips to inner four (on outerweb); rest of coverts and flight feathers black but primaries, inner secondaries and tertials edged slaty or olive-grey, more broadly on tertials; underwing has white leading edge to coverts, axillaries and bases to median coverts slate- or blackish-grey with white bases, greaters black with white tips, bases to flight feathers also white. Lores whitish, some birds showing thin blackish line above lores to eye; cheeks and ear-coverts black but tips to upper and rear edge of ear-coverts white. Chin to sides of neck and breast black; rest of underparts white with some black fan-shaped tips forming bars on sides of belly and flanks; may also show olive spots or tips to lower flanks (where generally reduced in size). Bill dark brown or black. Legs and feet pale pink or yellowish-flesh. **Immature** Juvenile similar to adult but upperparts dull chestnut or rufous-brown with pale shaft-streaks and flecks on forehead, crown, nape and upper mantle; also has prominent gingery-buff and brown streaks or speckling on scapulars; lower back and rump greyish; whitish

or gingery-brown median coverts (outers may be edged blackish), gingery-brown greater coverts, tips white; tips to tertials gingery-brown. Face buffish-white with broad dark or blackish lines below eye and another on rear of ear-coverts. Chin and throat pale buff or whitish, breast blotchy black and buff or orange-brown with black tips, becoming white on underparts with black spots on belly. Legs and feet pale yellow.

GEOGRAPHICAL VARIATION Two races; variation well marked. Race *leucolaema* has crown to nape chestnut-brown (slightly paler than in nominate); mantle, back and scapulars to rump and uppertail-coverts russet-brown tinged olive; wings similar to nominate but lesser coverts olive-grey and medians and greaters black with broad white tips; primary coverts blackish-olive, flight feathers dark brown but broadly edged pale olive at bases of primaries; rest of primaries dark olive; outerwebs of tertials olive but innerwebs dark brown. Tail short and brown or deep olive-brown. Lores to eye blackish, as is most of (olive-washed) face. Chin to centre of upper breast white but sides of throat and rest of breast black; belly to undertail-coverts white or tinged buffish, flanks olive-brown or washed buff. Bill as nominate but longer, blackish. Legs and feet pale or yellowish, fleshy-pink to straw-yellow. Juvenile male has head and upperparts blackish-brown with narrow pale brown shaft-streaks; may show some russet-brown tips on back and scapulars; median coverts blackish with dull whitish to orange-buff fan-shaped spots, greaters tipped brown; lores to ear-coverts black, underparts white with heavy buff-brown wash spotted black on breast.

VOICE Mostly silent outside of the breeding season but has a sharp or ringing *turrr-turrrrr* alarm or distress call; female has a harsh *tac* note and a thin, soft but high-pitched and descending *tsi-i-i-i*, frequently used when feeding young and also given by young birds, though usually flatter in tone (Chong in prep.); young also have a short buzzy note. Song a slow series of rising, flute-like or liquid whistling phrases, e.g. *tooeetyu* or *towyeetoo*, interspersed with *soweetoee* and chirrups, *see-it-tu-tu-tyuu*; may also contain rough or grating notes and some high whistled notes, generally recalling the sweet musical song of White-rumped Shama *Copsychus malabaricus* but higher-pitched. Some singers give only short, hesitant and frequently repeated songs whilst others have an apparently more varied and continuous repertoire. Sings from low perches and mid-level of trees but also uses roofs of village houses (Coates & Bishop 1997). Song period (Java) April to July.

STATUS AND DISTRIBUTION Generally rare or scarce resident but easily overlooked; locally common on small offshore islands; the race *leucolaema* is common on Enggano (MacKinnon & Phillipps 1993). The species may occur more widely in forests of several other islands of Indonesia and the Philippines. In recent years very heavily exploited for the cage-bird trade in Indonesia, raising fears of its extinction on some islands in the Lesser Sundas.

Z. i. interpres Discontinuously south from southern peninsular Thailand (from about 10°N), Malaysia, Borneo, Java (where also occurs on small offshore forested islands e.g. Krakatau, Deli and Tinjil), Lombok, Sumbawa and Flores, and may also be a rare resident on several islands in the Sulu Archipelago in the south-west and on Basilan in the central southern Philippines. May also occur on Bali (requires confirmation). Possibly more widespread on mainland Sumatra than the existing records suggest (see Movements) as one adult and two juveniles for sale in Kota Agung bird market had apparently originated from within the southern part of the national park (Robson 1999).

Z. i. leucolaema Enggano Island, western Sumatra.

Taxonomic note Junge (1938) considered *leucolaema* merited species status.

MOVEMENTS Largely resident but has occurred (twice) on Mt Kerinci, Sumatra, with another near Tamping, Bukit Barisan Selatan National Park in August 1998.

HABITAT Lowland primary, deciduous and evergreen forests, forested hills and submontane forests, usually at 200–1000 m (660–3300'); also in partly degraded forests, woods and isolated woodland patches on the edges of cultivation. Recently recorded at 1400 m (4620') on Mt Gede, Cibodas, West Java (S. van Balen pers. comm.).

BEHAVIOUR Away from one or two islands where it is locally common and found around villages, e.g. Flores (singing from the roofs of houses), it is generally extremely shy and easily overlooked, spending most of its time alone or in pairs, in trees at mid-height but frequently low down or on the ground, skulking under vegetation or in thick or dense forests with heavy ground cover. Even in areas where it is known to be present it is extremely difficult to see well, its presence frequently only betrayed when it utters its soft call-note. On the ground hops or bounds before stopping, frequently remaining motionless for a short period before commencing foraging in leaf-litter. Occasionally seen in fruiting trees where it may associate with Chestnut-backed Thrush (30). Food little known except insects, larvae, snails and some earthworms; also known to take some fruit and seeds.

BREEDING Very little known; nest and juveniles only recently described (Smythies 1981, Round & Treesucon 1997). Season little known; April (Borneo, Java) or May to about late July or August; young birds being fed by adults in February on Flores (Verhoeye & Holmes 1998) suggests some earlier breeding or regional variation. Nest: a cup-shaped structure of moss and bamboo leaves lined with fine strips of plant material, usually placed up to 4 m (15') from the ground in a small tree or bamboo clump. Eggs: 2–3, pale greenish-white or pale greyish with lavender-grey mottling and heavily blotched reddish-brown. Fledglings fed by both parents (Round & Treesucon 1997).

MOULT No information.

MEASUREMENTS Wing, male 99–108, female 94–101; tarsus 22–29; bill (culmen) 13–16; *leucolaema* wing, male 97–108.5, female 97–102; tarsus 26.5–32.5; bill (culmen) 15–19.5. Weight apparently unrecorded.

REFERENCES Chong (in prep.), Coates & Bishop (1997), Junge (1938), MacKinnon & Phillipps (1993), Robson (1999), Round & Treesucon (1997), Verhoeye & Holmes (1998).

29 RED-BACKED THRUSH *Zoothera erythronota* Plate 11
(Red-backed Ground-Thrush, Rusty-backed Thrush)

Geocichla erythronota Sclater, 1859, *Ibis* 1: 113 – Macassar (Ujung Padang, S. Sulawesi).

IDENTIFICATION 19–21 cm (7½–8¼"). An attractive, small to medium-sized thrush found on five islands in Indonesia. Locally common or scarce. Has chestnut or russet-brown upperparts except for black wings and tail, two broad white wing-bars across tips of wing-coverts and at tip of outer tail feathers. The face is mostly white with a broad black stripe from below the eye. Chin to centre of breast black, broad white pectoral band from sides to centre of breast; rest of underparts are white, spotted erratically with black. Birds on Peleng and Taliabu have most of the face and underparts blackish. Two races (nominate and *mendeni*) fully described but there are as yet unnamed races recently discovered on Taliabu, Buton and Kabaena, Indonesia. Birds on Peleng and Taliabu have most of the face and underparts blackish whilst those on Kabaena have the upperparts mostly black with the rump chestnut-orange. **Confusion species** No problem species within range but very similar to the Chestnut-backed Thrush (30) of

Lombok to Timor, which has a black bill and black forehead to crown and nape and is heavily spotted on the underparts.

DESCRIPTION Sexes almost alike. **Adult male** Forehead and crown russet or chestnut-brown (but some may show blackish streaks on forehead, crown and upper nape), becoming paler or chestnut on lower nape, mantle, back, upper scapulars to rump and uppertail-coverts (rump and uppertail-coverts may also be reddish-chestnut); lower scapulars black or blackish-brown. Tail black with large white spots at tips of innerweb of outermost feather and tips of next inner two margined with white. Lesser coverts black, median coverts white (but inner medians may be entirely black), greater coverts black with broad white tips; rest of coverts and flight feathers black but has pale or white edges to bases of outer primaries; bases of inner primaries and secondaries white, forming white wing-bar in flight. On underwing, coverts whitish on lessers, axillaries dark or blackish-brown with white bases, median and bases of greaters blackish with white bases, tips of greaters and bases to outer primaries blackish-brown, bases to inner primaries and all secondaries white. Upper lores to over eye, base of bill, cheeks and ear-coverts white narrowly bordered black on supercilium and rear of ear-coverts; eye-ring also white but broken on lower edge and across cheeks by broad stripe of black; small, almost invisible patch of grey skin behind eye. Chin and sides of throat to centre of breast black above a broad white band from sides to centre of breast and bordered below by a narrower dark or blackish band; sides of lower breast, belly and flanks to undertail-coverts white, but broadly barred black on upper belly and flanks; flanks can also be warm buff-brown, and bars on lower flanks are grey. Bill pale bluish-green with paler or creamy tip. Legs and feet pinkish-flesh or pinkish-brown. **Adult female** Like male but paler on crown and mantle and barring on flanks less clearly marked (may be diffused with grey). **Immature** Forehead and crown brown with paler orange-buff spots at tips; scapulars dark olive-brown with thin light orange-buff central shaft-streaks. Lesser coverts have fine orange-buff central shafts and pale orange-buff tips. Chin to centre of throat whitish-buff; sides of throat (malars) to sides of neck and upper breast black, rest of underparts off-whitish or yellowish-buff and indistinctly barred with blackish tips to feathers. First-year bird similar to adult but has more extensive whitish submoustachial and ear-covert patch tinged buff.

GEOGRAPHICAL VARIATION Two (possibly three) races; variation well marked. The single specimen of the race *mendeni* has the entire upperparts, including wings and tail, brighter or cinnamon-brown; the face is black except for a narrow white patch above the eye and another on the ear-coverts; the underparts are entirely black. Underwing pattern typical of *Zoothera* thrushes. Bill slate-blue. Legs and feet flesh-pink. Another possible race has recently (1991) been discovered on Taliabu, Sula Islands, Indonesia (Davidson & Stones 1993, Davidson et al. 1995) but to date there are no specimens and all records are of a few brief sightings of extremely shy individuals. This population is seemingly closer to *mendeni* than

nominate but has uniform bright or rich chestnut upperparts from forehead to rump; wings and tail blackish lacking any white tips to coverts. Face black except for an oval patch of white behind eye; underparts blackish with a slightly metallic sheen except for chestnut undertail-coverts. Bill blue-grey. More recently (1999) two other unnamed races have also been discovered, the first on Buton Island (SE Sulawesi) is similar to nominate *erythronota* but black on the crown is more extensive and chestnut largely restricted to the nape; the rump is tinged more rusty-orange and shows less white on the ear-coverts and also lacks the white moustachial stripe. Legs pale purple on leading edge with pale blue at rear, claws pinkish. Birds on Kabaena (SE Sulawesi) have the upperparts almost entirely black except for some chestnut tips to the nape and chestnut-orange on the rump (M. Catterall pers. comm.). Further information on the population of all three races is needed before these individuals are assigned a name.

VOICE Call a thin, very high-pitched, upslurred note. Song virtually unknown and unrecorded, but reported to be a liquid and typically thrush-like series of notes (Holmes & Phillips 1996).

STATUS AND DISTRIBUTION The nominate race is locally common to uncommon or scarce; birds on Taliabu are extremely scarce and apparently at risk from habitat destruction; *mendeni* is known from a single specimen collected in August 1938. Considered Near-Threatened (Collar et al. 1994).

Z. e. erythronota Sulawesi (possibly restricted to north and north-central Sulawesi north of Lore Lindu National Park, or overlooked), Indonesia.

Z. e. mendeni Peleng Island (part of Banggai Islands), Sulawesi, Indonesia.

Three (unnamed) races occur on Taliabu, Sula Islands, Indonesia (Davidson et al. 1995) and Buton and Kabaena, Sulawesi (M. Catterall pers. comm.).

MOVEMENTS Sedentary.

HABITAT The nominate race occurs in primary evergreen forests up to about 1000 m (3300') and the single specimen of *mendeni* was taken at 300 m (1000'). The birds on Taliabu were seen in secondary forest at about 50 m (165') altitude in selectively logged and degraded forests with bamboo stands; birds on Buton were mostly in forest or along forest edge and always in the understorey; on Kabaena at least five birds were recorded in patches of degraded forest or scrub with scattered trees, apparently not shy and frequently came into the open on forest roads.

BEHAVIOUR Usually alone or in pairs, occasionally loose (possibly family) parties. Extremely secretive, retiring and easily overlooked (mostly seen by mist-netting) though recent sightings on Kabaena were not shy and frequently appeared in the open; forages unobtrusively low down in heavily shaded areas beneath trees, shrubs or more usually on the ground, where it behaves in typical thrush fashion, hopping or bounding over the ground or occasionally perching on low branches; also makes fast dashes after others invading its territory and also in escape flight from predators. Food mostly beetles but also other insects, their larvae and worms, snails, molluscs, etc.

BREEDING Almost unknown. A nest in April was in the fork of a low tree-stump (C. Byers pers. comm.).

MOULT No information.
MEASUREMENTS Wing (n=11) 106–118; tarsus 25.5–32.5; bill 14.5–17.5; *mendeni* wing 114. Weight apparently unrecorded.

REFERENCES Coates & Bishop (1997), Collar *et al.* (1994), Davidson & Stones (1993), Davidson *et al.* (1995), Holmes & Phillipps (1996), Stones *et al.* (1997).

30 CHESTNUT-BACKED THRUSH *Zoothera dohertyi* Plate 11
(Chestnut-backed Ground-Thrush)
Geocichla dohertyi **Hartert, 1896, *Novit. Zool.* 3: 555, pl. 11, fig. 3 – Lombok.**

IDENTIFICATION 16–18 cm (6¼–7″). A brightly coloured, attractive medium-sized thrush of the forests of several of islands in the Lesser Sundas, Indonesia. Distinctive contrast of black head to throat and breast, white face broken by a broad black stripe through eye and across cheeks, and rich reddish-chestnut upperparts; black wings and tail with broad white band across median coverts and tips of greaters. Rest of underparts white spotted with black. **Confusion species** Similar in overall plumage to nominate race of Red-backed Thrush (29) on Sulawesi, but widely separated geographically and has black bill and crown and spots (not bars) on flanks. Orange-sided Thrush (33) from East Timor is also similar but lacks the black crown and chin to throat and breast but has brown forehead to nape and unbarred or spotted deep orange or orange-rufous underparts.

Taxonomic note Previously considered a race of Red-backed Thrush but Eck (1976) discussed the reasons for treating it as a separate species.
DESCRIPTION Sexes alike. **Adult** Forehead to upper nape black. Lower nape to mantle, back and scapulars deep reddish-chestnut becoming brighter chestnut on rump and uppertail-coverts. Edges and tips of outer scapulars black or with deep reddish-chestnut centres. Tail black or blackish-brown with large white spots at tip of innerweb of outermost feather. Lesser coverts black, median coverts white and greater coverts black with white tips to most except for inner 2–3; rest of coverts and flight feathers black but with prominent white bases to primaries (forming small white panel) and edges to most outer primaries on closed wing. Lesser underwing-coverts to bend of wing white, bases of greater coverts and outer primaries black or blackish; bases of inner primaries and all secondaries white. Lores to eye and base of bill white; may show short, dark or blackish malar stripe; broad black longitudinal stripe through eye (interrupts supercilium) across cheeks; ear-coverts white extending up behind or over eye. Chin black but can also be whitish (perhaps through age or wear); throat, sides of nape and neck, throat and breast also entirely black. Sides of lower breast bright or rufous-chestnut; rest of underparts white but heavily blotched or spotted with black or variable amounts of bright chestnut on sides of lower breast and upper flanks. Bill black with pale base to lower mandible. Legs and feet whitish or flesh-white. **Immature** First-year bird (June) similar to adult but has browner forehead to crown and nape with pale buffish central shafts (more prominent and against darker brown bases in some). Scapulars also darker or duller brown, with pale cen-

tral shafts. White median and greater coverts with fine buffish-brown tips; inner medians can also be light buffish-brown. Face generally pale buff with broad dark or blackish streak from eye to sides of neck and darker malar stripe. Underparts pale buff but breast and upper flanks heavily mottled with blackish tips and pale brown bases or warm brown centres; lower flanks pale orange or gingery-buff.
GEOGRAPHICAL VARIATION None. Monotypic.
VOICE Call a harsh or scratchy contact note, a thin whistle and a thin or very high-pitched squeaking whistle; often difficult to locate calling bird. Song a series of typical thrush-like phrases of mellow, sweet, clear whistles, *weeeeoooowee-tid-deeeedidiyeee – eee*, together with more complex musical warbling notes broken by short pauses similar to that of Chestnut-capped Thrush but generally slower (Butchart *et al.* 1994, Coates & Bishop 1997). Sings from concealed perch in trees at mid-canopy level.
STATUS AND DISTRIBUTION Variably common, locally common or rare; however, in recent years exploited heavily for cage-bird trade owing to its beautiful song, and may be extinct on Lombok and close to extinction on Sumbawa. Resident on the Lesser Sunda islands of Lombok, Sumbawa, Flores, Sumba and on Mt Mutis, West Timor.
MOVEMENTS Sedentary.
HABITAT Ground strata and lower levels of montane primary forests, mist-forest and woodlands at 400–1700 m (1320–5610′); on Sumbawa and Flores most frequently met with in closed-canopy semi-evergreen rainforest at 750–950 m (2475–3135′). On Timor occurs higher, at 1050–2300 m (3465–7600′).
BEHAVIOUR Usually solitary but may be sociable, in groups of up to 5 at common source of food, where it is known to associate with Chestnut-capped Thrush (28). Habits similar to those of many other *Zoothera* thrushes of the region but not always as shy, secretive or retiring and may become approachable; its presence may be detected by its persistent high-pitched call. Forages on the ground as well as in trees.
BREEDING Unknown. Birds collected on Sumbawa were considered to be in breeding condition in May, with juveniles there and on Flores at the end of August and early September (Butchart *et al.* 1994).
MOULT No information.
MEASUREMENTS Wing (n=9) male 99–107, female 99–105; Timor birds wing 105–115; tarsus 27–30.5; bill 14–17 (White & Bruce 1986). Weight apparently unrecorded.
REFERENCES Butchart *et al.* (1994), Coates & Bishop (1997), Eck (1976).

31 PIED THRUSH *Zoothera wardii*   Plate 10
(Pied Ground-Thrush, Pied Blackbird, Ward's Thrush)

***Turdus Wardii* Blyth, 1842, *J. Asiat. Soc. Bengal* 11: 882 – Mysore below Seegore Pass.**

IDENTIFICATION 22–22.5 cm (8¾–9″). A very striking thrush of the Himalayas which winters in Sri Lanka. The male is a strikingly black and white thrush with a long, broad, white supercilium, black breast and white belly (barred blackish) to undertail; in flight the underwing pattern is typical of the genus and the white spots at the tail-tip are obvious. The female is similar but browner and well spotted or tipped white or pale buff, but shows the male, a slightly narrower, duller supercilium than the male. **Confusion species** Within range unlikely to be confused; presence of long white supercilium and spots on upperparts diagnostic. Male Siberian Thrush (36), which winters to further east, is initially similar but lacks the white spots, edges and tips to the otherwise black upperparts, and has duller or blackish underparts and a dark or blackish (not yellow) bill. Females differ by similar features but Pied are browner and have dark bars or scallops on the flanks while Siberian are browner above with pale or yellowish centres plus dark centres to the undertail-coverts.

DESCRIPTION Sexes differ. **Adult male** Head and upperparts black, slightly glossy except for long broad white supercilium from base of bill to sides of nape; rump and uppertail-coverts broadly tipped white or whitish. Tail black but outermost feather (and tips to outer 2–3, which have large white spots) mostly white with black outerwebs. Inner lesser coverts white bordered by some or all black outers; median coverts and tips to all greaters white; primary coverts black with broad white patch on innerwebs; secondaries and tertials also tipped white and finely edged white on outerwebs to primaries 3–6; underwing-coverts white on leading edge to bend of wing, black or blackish on greater coverts and white or silvery-white inner primaries and bases of secondaries. Lores to chin and throat black, rest of underparts white with erratic black spots on sides of belly and flanks, occasionally in broad row on flanks. Bill yellow but base of upper mandible dusky or black; in non-breeding season tip also becomes dark. Legs and feet yellow, yellowish-olive or yellowish-brown. Some birds, possibly first-years, have brownish or olive-brown nape and tips to lower back and rump and browner wings. **Adult female** Forehead to scapulars and lower back medium olive-brown or slightly darker or duller; rump and uppertail-coverts similar but greyer and tips of longest coverts white or whitish. Tail brown (except for central and outermost feathers) tipped broadly with white, outermost feathers white with brown outerweb. Dark olive with white or whitish-buff tips to outer lesser coverts, median coverts brown with broad white tips, greaters mostly brown with white triangular tips; alula dark brown with olive-brown outerweb; primary coverts dark

brown with olive-brown outerweb; flight feathers dark brown finely edged pale brown on outer three, inner secondaries more broadly edged warm brown, tertials olive-brown, darker on innerwebs and tipped white. Long broad whitish or whitish-buff supercilium from base of bill to sides of nape (usually narrower than that on male); lores dark brown or blackish, cheeks and ear-coverts brown; broad pale or whitish-buff sub-moustachial and narrow dark brown malar. Chin white or whitish-buff; throat with large white spots or ovals with dark or brown edges on brown or olive-brown ground, becoming whiter on lower breast with broad dark brown bars forming a heavily barred or scaled pattern; lower belly and undertail-coverts white. Upper mandible dusky-brown to orange-yellow, lower lighter or yellower. Legs and feet brownish-yellow. **Immature** Juvenile similar to adult female but with face to throat more buffish, streaked finely with brown tips and buff or pale buff shaft-streaks to forehead, crown, nape, mantle and scapulars. Orange-buff tips to lesser, median and greater coverts. Sides of lower throat and breast dark brown becoming more heavily mottled or scalloped with blackish tips on underparts except for centre of belly; undertail-coverts may show brown or dark brown edges. Subadult males often show darker or rich brown on face and upperparts and white or whitish-buff tips to chin, throat and breast, and have incomplete or flecked darker supercilium; tips of uppertail-coverts also usually whiter than in same-age females.

GEOGRAPHICAL VARIATION None. Monotypic.

VOICE Generally silent but occasionally utters a sharp chirping or spitting *ptz-ptz-ptz-ptz* alarm note. Song a short and relatively unmusical bul-bul-like warbling consisting of two-note *pie-dee* phrases occasionally ending with an upwardly inflected *zik*, repeated at intervals; usually given briefly at dawn in early spring from tree-top.

STATUS AND DISTRIBUTION Uncommon; considered Near-Threatened (Collar *et al.* 1994). Breeds in the Himalayas from Kulu Valley, Himachal Pradesh, northern India east through northern Uttar Pradesh to Nepal (where rare or very sparsely distributed), also south-east Assam in the Barail range, north Cachar; may also breed (*fide* Baker 1932, Ali & Ripley 1983) more widely in Sikkim and Bhutan to Arunachal Pradesh. Winters in Sri Lanka, mostly in the central and southern hills; may also winter in small numbers in the Yercaud and Kolli Hills region of Tamil Nadu, southern India (Karthikeyan 1994).

MOVEMENTS Migratory; entire breeding population moves south or south-west to winter in Sri Lanka; passage in autumn from September to October and recorded in the foothills of the Himalayan breeding range east to Bhutan and

Assam; in the south occurs annually in the Eastern Ghats, Mysore and the southern hill ranges of Kerala and Tamil Nadu; considerable numbers depart from Point Calimere in Tamil Nadu in autumn; arrives in Sri Lanka from early October to November. Northern route in spring appears to be different and more direct, as very few southern India records in spring but some recorded (exceptionally from late February) in Eastern Ghats; departs from Sri Lanka (occasionally recorded from southern India) in March and April (sometimes present to mid- or late May); first arrivals in breeding area from late March.

HABITAT Broadleaved woods and forests including well-wooded ravines and hillsides between 1500 and 2400 m (4950–7920′), also patches of thick dense woods in open country and edges of cultivation and gardens in parts of its range; often in areas of damp ground or near streams. In winter in similar habitat but also less well-wooded areas including scrubland, gardens and parks with suitable areas of good cover usually between 750 and 1500 m (2475–4950′); several birds frequently winter in the town park in Nuwara Eliya, central Sri Lanka.

BEHAVIOUR Generally shy and wary, especially in the breeding season, but males often more visible during rivalry battles over courtship or territory in May, and somewhat more approachable in winter; usually solitary or in pairs, but may form loose flocks on migration and in winter. On the ground hops, walks and bounds in search of food, usually under or close to tree cover; forages on the ground where it turns over dead leaves and rotting vegetation, and in bushes and trees. Feeds mostly on insects but also takes some berries and fruit, particularly mulberries, guavas and wild figs.

BREEDING Season: May to July. Nest: a large deep cup-shape of green moss, grass and some leaves with an inner lining of roots, mud and grass stems, usually placed in a fork of a branch or against the trunk of a small tree or tall shrub up to 5 m (16.5′) from the ground. Eggs: 3–4, white or tinged pale sea- or bluish-green and lightly speckled or spotted with pale reddish either over the entire surface or at the larger end. Nest building, incubation and care of nestlings undertaken by both parents. One brood.

MOULT No information.

MEASUREMENTS Wing, male 110–120, female 110–120; tarsus 26–29; bill (from skull) 25–28. Weight (n=6 autumn males) 52–72 g (Ali & Ripley 1983, Whistler & Kinnear 1932).

REFERENCES Ali & Ripley (1983), Baker (1932), Karthikeyan (1994), Whistler & Kinnear (1932).

---

32 ASHY THRUSH *Zoothera cinerea*   Plate 12
(Ashy Ground-Thrush)

Geocichla cinerea Bourns & Worcester, 1894, *Occas. Pap. Minnesota Acad. Nat. Sci.* 1: 23 – Mindoro.

IDENTIFICATION 20 cm (8″). An extremely shy and little known (but probably greatly overlooked) endemic of the forested foothills of the northern Philippines. Small and short-tailed; has a very distinctive grey plumage with two broad wing-bars, blackish wing-coverts and flight feathers finely edged slate-grey. Face pale but has two blackish stripes from the eye across the cheeks and rear of the ear-coverts; underparts white but heavily spotted with black on the throat and breast; in flight shows typical *Zoothera* underwing pattern. **Confusion species** Within its limited native range unlikely to be confused with any other species once seen well.

DESCRIPTION Sexes alike. **Adult** Entire upperparts slate-grey, slightly darker on crown and tips to mantle, back and scapulars. Tail dark brown with slate-grey wash to central feathers. Lesser coverts black, median coverts white, greater coverts black tipped white (usually not as broad as on medians), alula dark grey, primary coverts dark or blackish-grey finely edged white on tips to outerwebs; flight feathers dark or blackish-grey, secondaries edged blackish and primaries and tertials broadly edged slate-grey but base of inner primaries with diffuse pale patch. On underwing, coverts grey or blackish-grey, carpal area whitish flecked with grey, broad white band across bases of secondaries, flight feathers pale grey. Lores and base of bill whitish finely flecked grey, cheeks whitish with broad black stripe from below eye, ear-coverts also whitish-grey becoming blackish stripe at rear, in some lower edge of ear-coverts also blackish. Sides of neck as upperparts. Chin and throat whitish becoming heavily or densely spotted with black on sides, lower throat and centre of upper breast (often shows as black gorget); remainder of breast white with sparse black spotting, belly and flanks whitish with pale yellowish-buff wash or grey on flanks and less closely marked with smaller blackish spots, these becoming diffuse on lower flanks; lower belly, vent and undertail-coverts whitish. **Immature** Unknown.

GEOGRAPHICAL VARIATION None. Monotypic.

VOICE Unknown but may have a rich, typically thrush-like warbling song similar to Orange-headed Thrush (34).

STATUS AND DISTRIBUTION Uncommon to scarce. The Sierra Madre and Cordillera Central of northern and central Luzon south to about Laguna de Bay and Taal Lake, and the northern half of Mindoro, Philippines. Exact range poorly or only fragmentarily understood but is threatened by destruction of lowland forests, both legal and illegal (83% of forest cover has been destroyed since the 1930s on Luzon and by 1988 only 8.5% of forest cover remained on Mindoro), and from snaring by trappers; hence considered Vulnerable by Collar *et al.* (1999).

MOVEMENTS Very poorly known; up to 130 ringed in 7 years at Dalton Pass, Luzon, indicates some post-breeding dispersal (Dickinson *et al.* 1991).

HABITAT Primary and secondary forests of the foothills and mountain slopes between 400 and 1050 m (1320–3465′) on Luzon, and between 90–360 m (300–1190′) on Mindoro; formerly also in lowland forests. Found in forest with jagged limestone outcrops in Quezon National Park, in mossy forest and forest with a fairly open rattan-dominated understorey at Mt Makiling (near Manila), and in remnant ridgetop forest patches at another Luzon site.

BEHAVIOUR Very poorly known but is extremely shy and elusive, spending most of its life low down in thick vegetation or on the ground where it forages for insects and their larvae. Often ventures into the open on tracks and trails at dawn; once discovered, birds on territory may become confiding. Food items little known but includes figs and invertebrates; otherwise probably differs very little from food choice of other similar forest-dwelling thrushes in South-East Asia.

BREEDING Largely unknown; probably from February to June; juveniles recorded in May and early October (Dickinson *et al.* 1991, Collar *et al.* 1999).

MOULT No information.

MEASUREMENTS (n=3) Wing 109–112; tarsus 25.5; bill (culmen) 18. Weight apparently unrecorded.

REFERENCES Collar *et al.* (1994, 1999), Dickinson *et al.* (1991).

33 ORANGE-SIDED THRUSH *Zoothera peronii*   Plate 12
(Orange-banded Thrush, Orange-banded Ground-Thrush)

Turdus peronii **Vieillot, 1818, *Nouv. Dict. Hist. Nat.* (nouv. ed.) 20: 276 – New Holland [in error; corrected to Kupang, by Mayr (1944) *Bull. Amer. Mus. Nat. Hist.* 83: 155].**

IDENTIFICATION 19.5–21.5 cm (7¾–8½″). A medium-sized and brightly coloured thrush with a restricted range in Wallacea where fairly common and relatively easy to see; sings throughout the year. Has a whitish face and brown crown to nape becoming mostly chestnut-brown on the upperparts; wings dark brown with two broad white wing-bars at tips to coverts; breast to flanks is deep orange to orange-rufous becoming white on lower breast to undertail-coverts. **Confusion species** Unlikely to be confused with any other thrush in the region; most similar to Chestnut-backed Thrush (30) of West Timor which has a black head, whitish face and black chin to breast and heavily spotted underparts.

DESCRIPTION Sexes alike. **Adult** Forehead to hindcrown brown or deep chestnut-brown becoming paler or orange-brown on nape. Mantle, back and scapulars chestnut, deeper or rufous on rump and uppertail-coverts. Tail brown or tawny-brown on central feathers, outers having tawny-brown edges with large white wedge at tip of innerweb of outermost feather, occasionally with smaller white spot at tip of next innermost feather. Lesser coverts dark brown finely tipped white, medians white, inners sometimes with dark brown bases; greaters dark or chestnut-brown, inners with pale or gingery-brown edges and white crescents at tips; alula brown, primary coverts dark brown edged pale or whitish on outer edge; flight feathers dark brown, primaries edged finely with white becoming brown on outerwebs; secondaries and inner primaries white at base of innerwebs. On underwing, lesser coverts to bend of wing white; median and greater coverts to outer primaries greyish-brown with white tips. Lores pale or whitish-buff but sometimes finely flecked or spotted black; cheeks also white or whitish. Hind cheeks to ear-coverts broadly black extending to sides of neck (some have dark mark above eye); centre of ear-coverts white or whitish-buff, rear edge of ear-coverts black forming dark border. Submoustachial whitish or finely spotted with blackish and bordered by thin dark malar (often broken into series of continuous blackish spots). Chin and throat to centre of upper breast white, breast to flanks bright or deep orange or orange-rufous. Centre of belly (centre of lower breast in some) to vent and undertail-coverts white. Bill brownish-black, whitish at base of lower mandible. Legs lavender-grey; feet brown or brownish. In fresh plumage edges to secondaries and tips to tertials bright orange or gingery-brown, more broadly on tertials but upper tertial uniform with scapulars. **Immature** Juvenile unknown. First-summer bird brighter on mantle and scapulars with paler or buffish central shafts and fine or light orange-buff tips to tertials.

GEOGRAPHICAL VARIATION Two races; variation clinal. Race *audacis* has forehead, crown, mantle, back and scapulars darker or more heavily tinged cinnamon, extending to the central tail feathers and edges to bases of all outers; the underparts are deeper orange-rufous on the breast and flanks. Bill black or brownish-black in females, with greyish base to lower mandible. Legs and feet pale flesh.

VOICE Song (from recording made in West Timor) a series of three loud, ringing, upslurred clear whistles followed by a series of shorter staccato notes, variable in tone and sometimes including several short harsh *ksk* or chattering notes. Song may also include some more typical drawn-out thrush-like whistling notes mixed with shorter, harsher notes. Sings throughout year but more during or just before breeding (Coates & Bishop 1997).

STATUS AND DISTRIBUTION Locally common; formerly considered at risk (Collar & Andrew 1988) but now Near-Threatened (Collar *et al.* 1994).

Z. p. peronii West Timor (principally the forest reserves of Baun, Bipolo, Camplong and Kapan) and Roti.

Z. p. audacis East Timor to Wetar, Romang, Damar and Babar.

MOVEMENTS Sedentary.

HABITAT Lowland forests, woodlands with scrub or thickets up to c.1200 m (3960′) (White & Bruce

1986, Noske 1995). Nominate birds occur in small, remnant patches of deciduous forests up to 600 m (1980′).

BEHAVIOUR Alone or in pairs or exceptionally up to five together when feeding in fruiting trees. Largely terrestrial but not as shy as other *Zoothera* thrushes of the region and often seen foraging at mid-level and in the tops of trees in relatively open forest.

BREEDING Unknown.

MOULT No information.

MEASUREMENTS (n=15) Wing 100–112; tarsus 28.5–32.5; bill 16–20; *audacis* (n=5) wing 98–107. Weight apparently unrecorded.

REFERENCES Coates & Bishop (1997), Collar & Andrew (1988), Noske (1995), White & Bruce (1986).

34 ORANGE-HEADED THRUSH *Zoothera citrina* Plate 12
(Orange-headed Ground-Thrush)

Turdus citrinus Latham, 1790, *Index orn.* 1: 350 – India [restricted to Cachar by Baker (1921) *J. Bombay Nat. Hist. Soc.* 27: 718].

IDENTIFICATION 20–23 cm (8–9″). Extremely distinctive with several well-marked races ranging from the Indian subcontinent through much of South-East Asia to Java. Nominate birds have rich or deep orange head and underparts, except for the white undertail-coverts; the rest of the upperparts are leaden bluish-grey with a broad white wing-bar on the median coverts and pale or whitish tips to the dark grey tail; females are generally more olive or olive-grey on the upperparts. Some distinctive racial variation, with several races having well-marked face patterns of dark bars on whiter or pale orange lores, cheeks and ear-coverts, and on the submoustachial and chin and throat. Shy and easily overlooked in forest undergrowth but less reclusive than many other *Zoothera* species. **Confusion species** The orange and grey plumage and striking face pattern (where present in certain races) make confusion with other species unlikely.

DESCRIPTION Sexes differ. **Adult male** Entire head and face to nape, sides of neck and upper mantle deep or rufous-orange, some birds slightly paler orange on upper mantle; rest of mantle, back and scapulars to rump and uppertail-coverts deep bluish-grey with paler fringes forming a scaly pattern. Tail dark or blackish-brown but central feathers and outerwebs of all others fringed bluish-grey, tips of innerwebs to outermost feathers paler or whitish-brown. Lesser coverts grey-brown with paler grey tips, median coverts grey broadly tipped white, greater coverts dark grey with blackish central shafts and paler grey edges, and in fresh plumage paler grey tips to outers; alula dark grey, primary coverts the same or blackish broadly edged grey; flight feathers blackish-brown with broad pale bluish-grey edges to outerwebs; secondaries more broadly edged grey and tertials grey

with black central shafts. Underwing has coverts and axillaries bluish-grey with white bases, medians bluish-grey or lead-grey, tips of greaters and bases of secondaries and inner primaries white or whitish. Chin and throat to belly and flanks similar to head and face but slightly paler orange (some may show pale or whitish-orange chin and throat); vent, thighs and undertail-coverts white. Bill slaty-black with dark steely-horn lower mandible. Legs and feet pinkish-flesh or yellowish at rear with brownish front, feet similar or flesh-pink with yellowish soles. **Adult female** Forehead to crown or nape as male but darker, browner and tinged burnt-orange. Mantle, back and scapulars heavily tinged olive or greenish-olive; rump and uppertail-coverts grey but tips of longest uppertail-coverts olive-grey. Some females, however, are identical to males; colour of upperparts appears to be age-related, older birds resembling males. Wings as male except for pale olive-grey lesser coverts and olive tones of upperparts extending to edges of flight feathers; rest of flight feathers pale greyish-olive especially on secondaries and tertials. Tail tinged lightly olive-grey on central feathers and edges to all outers. Chin and throat whitish or pale orange and underparts generally paler or duller (except for breast which is often deepest orange). Bill brownish-horn, flesh-pink at base of lower mandible. Legs and feet light brown. **Immature** Juvenile has forehead to nape and upper mantle dull rufous or rust-brown with large pale yellowish-buff central shafts. Mantle and scapulars dull dark grey or bluish-grey (male) or browner in female, with pale buff central shafts; lower back, rump and uppertail-coverts also have pale grey central shafts. Median and greater coverts dark grey or grey-brown with fan-shaped light orange-buff tips; flight feathers bluish-grey (male) or tinged grey-brown (female). Face orange flecked or mottled duller or browner with narrow dark brown line from below eye to sides of neck and dark border to rear of ear-coverts. Chin and throat pale orange-buff with blackish gorget; breast and belly to flanks orange or light yellowish-orange heavily washed or spotted dark olive or olive-grey; upper breast may be darker or have a dark band. Juvenile female has edges to scapulars, rump and uppertail-coverts olive, as are edges to flight feathers and tertials. First-winter (August) bird more like the respective adult but retains juvenile plumage and pale flecks on head and upper mantle (also on uppertail-coverts on some) and has pale orange-buff medians and tips to greater coverts. Face has dark brown smudge below eye and dark brown rear edge to ear-coverts. Chin and throat very pale orange with dark brown malar; upper breast has band or gorget of dark olive-brown becoming mottled with dark brown over orange-brown on centre and lower breast to upper flanks.

GEOGRAPHICAL VARIATION Twelve races; variation largely clinal but well marked in some races.

Race *gibsonhilli* differs very little from nominate but is, on average, slightly brighter or deeper orange on head and upperparts; also has a slightly longer, heavier bill.

Race *innotata* very similar to nominate but brighter or deeper orange and lacks white tips to median coverts; female duller on head and underparts with grey of mantle and back tinged olive or olive-brown. May intergrade with nominate in parts of range; intergrades may have paler or whiter tips to median coverts.

Race *cyanotus* has lores to eye, base of bill and submoustachial stripes white, a broad dark brown vertical 'tear-drop' from upper eyelid through eye and over cheeks to sides of neck, forepart of ear-coverts white (extending to sides of throat) and rear ear-coverts broadly bordered dark brown (rear edge with thin whitish tips); forehead and crown to nape more olive than nominate birds. Thin or narrow pale orange (or tinged brownish) malar stripe and extensive area of white on chin, throat and centre of upper breast. Outer median coverts entirely white, greater coverts with pale grey tips. Bill as nominate female; legs and feet pale flesh tinged brown or brownish-yellow. Female similar to male and has mantle, back and scapulars more heavily tinged olive or olive-green than nominate.

Race *aurimacula* similar to *cyanotus* but not so well defined; lores, cheeks, ear-coverts and sides of neck whitish but flecked or tinged pale orange or brownish on edges of whitish-orange submoustachial stripe; malar stripe dark brown. Same dark brown stripe below eye (but often poorly defined) to sides of neck and border to rear of ear-coverts. Chin and throat pale or yellowish-white and may show some brownish spots on sides of throat; breast and flanks orange (usually restricted to breast in female) becoming pale orange on belly and lower flanks; centre of belly to vent and undertail-coverts white. Bill grey-brown, paler at base of lower mandible. Legs and feet flesh.

Race *courtoisi* very similar to both *cyanotus* and *aurimacula* but has face paler or more extensively whitish-buff from lores to ear-coverts (than *cyanotus*) and two dark brown bars from eye and at rear of ear-coverts; chin and throat pale chestnut-buff with dark brown malar (becoming dark brown spots on sides of throat); as in other races female slightly duller and has olive tinge to upperparts. Also differs from *aurimacula* in having a longer wing.

Race *melli* almost identical to *courtoisi* but smaller with a shorter wing.

Race *rubecula* (sexes identical) much darker or deep chestnut-orange on head and face to lower nape and entire underparts, except for white undertail-coverts (but some individuals may show paler or lighter orange on chin and upper throat). Bill black. Legs and feet variable from flesh-pink to yellowish or dark grey.

Race *orientis* identical to *rubecula* and separated solely on longer wing.

Both sexes of race *aurata* have deep or rich chestnut-orange on head, sides of neck and breast. Chin and throat pale orange (extending to cheeks and ear-coverts in female), undertail-coverts pale yellow or yellowish-buff. Male has dark lower eye-ring which continues as dark patch on cheeks; centre of belly to vent and undertail-coverts white. Juvenile and first-year birds much darker or browner on head and face with broad pale rufous or orange-buff spots and shaft-streaks to crown, nape and mantle; mottled blackish and orange on breast with broad dark stripe from below eye to sides of throat and on rear edge to ear-coverts.

Race *albogularis* lacks white tips to median coverts; deep or rufous-orange on head to nape and sides of neck; deep orange, tinged with chestnut, on breast, belly and flanks; white on chin and throat and on vent to undertail-coverts. Face whitish or pale orange with trace of face-bars in *cyanotus* with shadow of dark, poorly defined or smudged line from below eye to sides of throat, and dark orange-brown border to rear of ear-coverts, centre of ear-coverts may be whitish or pale orange; submoustachial whitish or very finely flecked pale orange and bordered with narrow brownish malar stripe (less defined on female). Female very similar but has greyish-blue upperparts washed or suffused green, heaviest on mantle.

Race *andamensis* is very similar to *albogularis* and lacks white tips to median coverts but deeper, darker (or slightly tinged olive) orange to orange-chestnut on head, face and underparts (especially flanks), except for chin and throat which is sometimes whitish on chin and finely spotted light orange; centre of belly to vent and undertail-coverts white. In hand or at close range some birds show faint trace of face-bars in *cyanotus*. Bill dark brown or black, pinkish-flesh at base of lower mandible. Legs and feet flesh-white. Females have greyish-blue upperparts suffused or washed olive-green, and show faint traces of broad vertical stripes down cheeks and ear-coverts.

VOICE Call a soft *chuk*, *tjuk* or *tchuk* and a loud screeching *teer-teer-teer* or *kreeee...* like a pencil scraping on slate; in flight a thin *tsee* or *dzeee* very like several other *Turdus* and *Zoothera* thrushes; also a loud harsh dry rattle; alarm note also very similar to that of Blackbird (111) but otherwise appears to be generally silent, especially in winter. Song a loud clear series of variably sweet lilting phrases or musical notes, recalling quality of Blackbird and structure of Song Thrush (124) (usually higher-pitched) owing to repetition of some phrases: *teeer-teerr teerrr* (*rubecula, orientis*) or *wheeper-pree-preeteelee, wheeeoo-peeerper... wheechee-leet... wheeeechee-leet, pir-whoo-peerrte-rate...* Also includes imitations of other bird songs and calls in the general vicinity, e.g. bulbuls, babblers, Common Tailorbird *Orthotomus sutorius* and Common Hawk-Cuckoo *Cuculus varius.* Song usually given whilst sitting motionless, wings held down by sides of body, from low (occasionally as high as 15 m/50') in a leafy tree or from dense cover. Sings mostly early morning and late afternoon; in Nepal from early April to late August; passage migrants in Hong Kong sing in April and May.

STATUS AND DISTRIBUTION Locally common or uncommon. Very popular as cage-bird on Java and numbers have severely declined in recent years owing to trapping for aviculture.

Z. c. citrina Margalla foothills, northern Pakistan, and east along the Himalayas of northern India from about Chamba, Himachal Pradesh, to Nepal, Sikkim, Bhutan and Arunachal Pradesh, south through Assam to Manipur and the Chittagong Hills of eastern Bangladesh, possibly also western and northern Burma (becoming progressively commoner in east of range). In winter in lower foothills from eastern Punjab, eastern Rajasthan and Madhya Pradesh (where scarce) and Orissa east to Bihar, Bengal, Bangladesh and the lowlands of Assam; irregular or erratic south to about Madras and an annual winter visitor, possibly in small numbers, to Sri Lanka.

Z. c. cyanotus Peninsular India from south-east Gujarat east through Madhya Pradesh to Bihar and Orissa (though absent from some apparently suitable areas) and parts of Andhra Pradesh, west through Maharashtra to Tamil Nadu, Karnataka and Kerala.

Z. c. innotata Exact range imperfectly known and may be more extensive than shown on map; throughout most of South-East Asia from southern Burma and western, southern and south-east Yunnan, southern China, north-west Thailand (possibly also northern, central and southern Laos where perhaps mainly a passage migrant) and Cambodia to southern Annam, Vietnam. In winter south to Peninsular Burma, north-east, eastern and southern Thailand to Peninsular Malaysia.

Z. c. melli Southern Kweichow, Kwangsi to northern Kwangtung and western Fukien; part of the population may be migratory moving south in non-breeding season; regularly winters in Hong Kong.

Z. c. courtoisi Breeds Anhwei, eastern-central China; wintering range unknown.

Z. c. aurimacula Hainan, E Tonkin and central Annam (south to about Cat Bin), Vietnam; possibly also northern Laos.

Z. c. andamensis Andaman Islands.

Z. c. albogularis Nicobar Islands (Great Nicobar, Camorta, Nancowry, Trinkat, Katchall, Bompoka and Car Nicobar).

Z. c. gibsonhilli Southern Tenasserim, Burma to Trang province, southern Thailand. In winter further south at lower levels along Peninsular Thailand and on several islands in the Gulf of Thailand, discontinuously south to about Selangor, Peninsular Malaysia; also annual in small numbers (1–2) in winter to Singapore.

Z. c. aurata AT 1000–1630 m (3300–5400') on Mt Kinabalu and Mt Trus Madi, northern Borneo.

Z. c. rubecula Western Java.

Z. c. orientis Eastern Java and Bali; intergrades with *rubecula* in west of range.

Taxonomic note Mees (1996) questioned the validity of *orientis* and considered that all birds on Java were referable to *rubecula.*

MOVEMENTS Migrant, partial migrant or resident; nominate *citrina* departs from breeding areas in September and early October, although most records for Peninsular Malaysia are 25 November to mid-April; return movements north in April and May to August. Most southerly wintering birds reach Tamil Nadu in October. Recorded primarily as an autumn or winter migrant at Fraser's Hill, Peninsular Malaysia, from August onwards, but mainly late November and December, with only very small numbers in April and May (Wells 1992). Two *aurata* were recorded at 1800 m (5940') on Mt Kinabalu in May 1998; these were considered to be displaced by extensive fires at lower levels (Robson 1998). Baker (1924) recorded nominate birds as not very rare in the Bihar plains, Bengal, in December and January. Although largely resident in most of its central Indian range, numbers of *cyanotus* increase from April to August in Bandhavgarh National Park, north-east Madhya Pradesh.

The nominate race is a rare, but annual and increasing, visitor to Sri Lanka (mostly October–December) but regular in winter to the lowlands of northern-central Pakistan; three in Islamabad in mid-February 1997 were the first in winter. Breeding *innotata* are fairly common in the breeding areas of north-west Thailand from May to end of October but absent from mid-November to April; otherwise a scarce migrant to most of Laos (where however it may also breed) and Singapore and a vagrant to Taiwan (Kaohsiung city), November 1998.

HABITAT Damp broadleaved evergreen forests and woodlands, including lowland and hill forests, preferring well-wooded areas with established but not too dense undergrowth of bushes and ferns, also bamboo forests, secondary woodlands and groves of trees on the edges of cultivation or plantations, often in damp areas, near streams or in shady ravines; *cyanotus* also occurs in large well-wooded gardens and orchards. Occurs from 250 m (825') up to 1830 m (6040') in the Himalayas and up to about 1500 m (5000') in Malaysia and on Java.

BEHAVIOUR Usually alone or in pairs, very shy, secretive and not easily seen but comparatively more easily seen than many *Zoothera* species and may congregate in small flocks in non-breeding season at common source of food. Forages low down or on the ground in, or under, thick vegetation and forest undergrowth; often crepuscular and most active in late evening or dusk, when may venture out into the open on paths or tracks; also feeds in fruiting trees and berry bushes; in parts of range regularly in mid- to subcanopy level. Hops or walks slowly and flicks leaf-litter and decaying vegetation aside with bill, also probes into damp earth mounds or mossy crevices. Flight is swift but silent; when disturbed flies to low branch and sits motionless in full view until intruder has passed. Feeds on the ground mostly on insects and larvae, particularly ants, termites, flies, spiders and small beetles, also worms, snails, slugs, leeches, berries and fruit; in Malay Peninsula fruiting figs provide major source of food in non-breeding season.

BREEDING Season: early April, May or June to August or September; *rubecula* October to May and possibly throughout the year. Nest: a large but shallow cup-shape of moss, twigs, bracken, grass, bark strips and rootlets combined with mud and lined with leaves, stems, fir needles, bamboo strips, moss and fern roots; usually in a fork of a small (especially mango) tree or (frequently coffee)

bush up to 4.5 m (15') from the ground. Eggs: 3–4, rarely 5, variable from pale cream-buff or pale greyish-blue to pale greenish-white and speckled and blotched with pale lilac and spotted or flecked with reddish-brown, often forming a cap at the larger end. Nest building and incubation by both sexes; known to be a brood-host to the Pied-crested Cuckoo *Clamator jacobinus*. Incubation period 13–14 days. Fledging period 12 days.

MOULT Post-juvenile moult complete by end of September or early October.

MEASUREMENTS Wing, male 111–126, female 105–123; tarsus 27.5–33; bill 19–25; *cyanotus* wing, male 105–119, female 102–116; bill 20.5–24.5; *innotata* wing 110–122; *courtoisi* wing 125; *melli* wing 115–121; *andamensis* wing 100–110; bill 17–19.5; *albogularis* wing 100–106; *aurimacula* wing 110–114.5; *rubecula* wing 102–109.5; tarsus 33–34; bill 26–28; *orientis* wing 111–114. Weight 56–67.5 g (Nepal, October), 48–60 g (Tamil Nadu, October); *cyanotus* 47–60 g (Whistler & Kinnear 1932, Ali & Ripley 1983).

REFERENCES Ali & Ripley (1983), Baker (1924), Fleming *et al.* (1979), Mees (1996), Roberts (1992), Robson *et al.* (1998), Wells (1992), Whistler & Kinnear (1932).

35 EVERETT'S THRUSH *Zoothera everetti*   Plate 12
(Everett's Ground-Thrush)
Geocichla everetti Sharpe, 1892, *Ibis* (6)4: 323 – Mount Dulit, north-west Borneo.

IDENTIFICATION 19 cm (7½"). A rare and little known thrush of the undergrowth and lower branches of montane forest in northern Borneo. Most likely to be seen on narrow trails in forests below Mt Kinabalu but disappears at first sign of intruder. Head and upperparts brown to olive-brown, tail slightly warmer or more russet-tinged, wings short and rounded. Face whitish or washed browner with a fairly broad dark malar and large dark bill, but best told by orange underparts. Ground-loving and usually in damp areas but easily overlooked and until recently seen by very few observers. **Confusion species** Within its very small and restricted range unlikely to be confused with any other species.

DESCRIPTION Sexes almost alike. **Adult male** Entire upperparts from forehead to scapulars and uppertail-coverts deep olive-brown. Tail brown but most feathers edged warmer or more russet olive-brown. Wing short and rounded, all coverts as scapulars; alula (longest feather projects beyond primary coverts) brown, primary coverts darker brown edged olive-brown; flight feathers dark brown edged pale brown on inner primaries and warmer or olive-brown on secondaries and tertials. Underwing has lesser coverts to bend of wing and axillaries white, medians and greaters dark brown, bases of inner primaries and secondaries white. Lores pale whitish-olive or finely tipped brown, extending as pale spot behind eye; cheeks whitish or buffish-white, ear-coverts similar or

greyer and flecked brown; broad submoustachial pale orange-buff and poorly defined against broad dark brown or blackish malar stripe. Chin and throat pale orange-buff, breast deep or dark orange and extending to flanks but sometimes feathers at sides of breast tipped brown; centre of belly white or whitish with orange tips to some feathers; thighs pale greyish-brown; vent and undertail-coverts white or washed pale orange. Bill fairly long, blackish. Legs and feet brown. **Adult female** Very similar to male but slightly browner on upperparts. **Immature** Juvenile unknown. First-year bird very similar to adult but has buffish central shaft-streaks, finely on head, nape and upper mantle and more broadly on edges to scapulars; tips to median and greater coverts orange-buff. Underparts light orange heavily spotted or mottled with black tips.

GEOGRAPHICAL VARIATION None. Monotypic.

VOICE Unknown.

STATUS AND DISTRIBUTION Rare; considered Near-Threatened (Collar *et al.* 1994). Confined to Sabah and Sarawak, northern Borneo, where found on Mts Kinabalu, Murud, Mulu, Dulit, Trus Madi and the Kelabit uplands.

MOVEMENTS Sedentary.

HABITAT Undergrowth and lower levels of trees and vegetation in submontane deciduous forests at 1210–2300 m (4000–7590').

BEHAVIOUR Extremely secretive and retiring; very difficult to observe, disappearing into thick

vegetation at the first sign of an intruder. Forages on the ground, usually in moist patches and near the edges of streams, taking mostly invertebrates: slugs, small worms, leeches and molluscs.
BREEDING Recorded breeding on Mt Kinabalu in May, nest low down in undergrowth vegetation.

MOULT No information.
MEASUREMENTS (n=5) Wing, male 108–112, female 108; tarsus 32.5–36.5; bill (culmen) 17–21.5, (to gape) 28–32. Weight apparently unrecorded.
REFERENCES Smythies (1981).

36 SIBERIAN THRUSH *Zoothera sibirica*   Plate 10
(Siberian Ground-Thrush)

Turdus sibirica Pallas, 1776, *Reise versch. Prov. Russ. Reichs* 3: 694 – Dauria, Siberia.

IDENTIFICATION 20.5–23 cm (8–9"). Male is dark slate or blackish grey-blue with tapering white supercilium, white centre of belly, broad white tips to dark undertail-coverts, bluish lower back and rump and blackish tail with whitish tips at corners; has distinctive contrasting *Zoothera* underwing pattern of white on lesser coverts and bases of flight feathers broken by black central band across the median and greater coverts. Female is olive-brown above with a buffish or creamy supercilium and long submoustachial and dark brown malar, tail with pale whitish or creamy-buff tips at corners, pale orange-buff tips to median and greater coverts, mottled underparts with paler centres and brownish fringes; underwing-coverts as the male but pattern brown and buffish. Immature similar to female but first-year male separable on body colour; may have indistinct or reduced white supercilium and mottled underparts. **Confusion species** Only possible problem species for male would be male Pied Thrush (31) viewed briefly; latter has extensive white tips to median and greater coverts and white tips to flight feathers, and is much whiter below but barred black on flanks. Female Siberian possibly confusable with several other brown thrushes but told by face pattern, plain brown upperparts, mottled underparts and distinctive underwing pattern. Most likely problem is the very similar female Pied Thrush, which is a browner version of the male with broad white tips to median and greater coverts, flight feathers and longest uppertail-coverts; the belly and flanks are much more heavily barred or scaled with black or dark brown. Female Chestnut-bellied Rock-Thrush (16) is separated by lack of supercilium and presence of broad pale submoustachial and patch at rear of ear-coverts and sides of neck, shorter and slightly thicker bill, large dark eye with pale or buffish eye-ring, and generally heavier mottled underpart pattern.
DESCRIPTION Sexes differ. **Adult male** Entire upperparts from forehead and crown to scapulars, rump and uppertail-coverts dark slate or blackish-grey tinged dark bluish; mantle, back, scapulars and rump may show narrow black tips. Tail black but central pair and edges to bases of all outers tinged grey, outermost with large white spot on innerweb at tip, and tips to next inner 2–3 also white or whitish but less than on outermost. Lesser coverts as scapulars, median coverts dark or blackish-grey narrowly edged paler or dark grey, greaters similar but with blacker innerwebs and bluish-grey outerweb and tips; alula and primary coverts black, the latter finely edged bluish-grey; flight feathers dark brown or black, primaries narrowly edged bluish-grey in fresh plumage, secondaries with broad diffuse dark bluish-grey edges, tertials similar with outerweb dark bluish-grey. Underwing distinctive: axillaries and lesser coverts to bend of wing white, tips to axillaries dark grey; median and greater coverts broadly grey or greyish-black but tips of greater coverts and bases to flight feathers broadly white, in flight showing as two broad white bands broken by a broad darker middle band. Lores, cheeks and ear-coverts black or blackish-grey but long white supercilium begins narrowly on mid-lores, broadening over eye and sometimes extending onto sides of nape. Chin and throat to sides of neck and breast as upperparts or slightly paler grey; may be tinged brownish in fresh plumage. Sides of lower breast, belly and flanks grey or paler, bluish-grey with narrow darker or blackish fringes, some feathers sometimes showing narrow whitish central shafts; central belly, vent and central undertail-coverts white; lower flanks and edges to undertail-coverts dark blackish-blue basally with broad white tips forming broad bars; white on belly and undertail-coverts on some may be tinged or washed greyish. Bill black. Legs and feet yellow or orange-yellow when breeding, becoming duller or brownish-yellow or purplish-

Tail pattern of Siberian Thrush.

horn with yellowish rear of tarsus and soles to feet in winter. **Adult female** Entire upperparts from forehead to scapulars, rump and uppertail-coverts olive-brown tinged warmer or rufous-brown, sometimes showing greyer-olive tinge on mantle to rump and uppertail-coverts. Tail has central feathers olive-brown and all outers slightly warmer or richer brown with white or creamy-white spots at tip of outermost feather and smaller spots at tips of next inners. Lesser coverts as scapulars or tinged grey; median and greater coverts olive-brown tipped (usually as a crescent, sometimes with slight central extension up shaft) rufous-buff and usually larger or more prominent on outer medians, tips to greaters slightly paler and usually more prominent on inners (but tips may be absent or small and buff or greyish-buff); alula and primary coverts dark olive-brown finely edged (but not at tips of primary coverts) paler or lighter olive-buff; flight feathers dark brown on innerwebs and broadly edged warm or rufous-brown on outerwebs, tips of tertials may also be slightly paler. Underwing pattern as male but lesser coverts and bases to flight feathers can be duller or buffish and central wing-bar of axillaries, median and bases to greater coverts dull olive-brown. Broad pale buff or creamy-buff (appears whitish) supercilium begins broadly on lores and extends to beyond ear-coverts, but often flecked, mottled or interrupted with olive-brown and often continues behind ear-coverts; very thin or narrow whitish eye-ring often indistinct or only visible on upper half of eye; lower lores, cheeks and ear-coverts olive-brown but flecked or mottled paler with light or yellowish-buff becoming flecks on ear-coverts; lower cheeks often paler or spotted with dark olive-brown; short dark or olive-brown submoustachial either continuous or interrupted from base of bill. Chin and throat pale buff or whitish but lower and sides of throat and neck spotted with dark olive-brown, breast and centre of upper belly similar or very lightly tinged with yellowish-orange, each feather tipped dark olive-brown forming bars; flanks and sides of belly with larger or paler centres to feathers, forming diffuse pale spots and edged and tipped (more broadly than edge) olive-brown, lower flanks with pale buffish-brown centres and diffuse olive-brown fringes; lower centre of belly and vent white or off-white; undertail-coverts creamy or white with some dark olive-brown bases and tips forming crescents. Bill dark brown or brownish-horn with pale yellowish base to lower mandible. Legs and feet pale or yellowish-brown or yellow. **Immature** Juvenile has head and upperparts, including wings, dark olive-brown but tips to lesser and median coverts have fine pale buffish-brown central shafts (broadening at tip), greater coverts brown with olive-brown edges and tips with pale buff or off-white spot at centre of tip; flight feathers brown edged olive-brown; wing-coverts and flight feathers become greyer in first-year male. Underparts pale buff on chin and throat tipped or barred darker brown becoming (in male) dull grey-brown or olive-brown on breast with large pale whitish-buff spots (with dark or blackish edges) slightly paler or light or grey to greyish-white on

belly streaked whitish on lower belly to undertail-coverts; flanks dark greyish or (in female) buff or buffish-brown tinged rufous and barred dark with a brown tip forming a barred or scaled pattern. **First-winter male** More clearly resembles adult but has dark brown tinge to forehead, crown and upper mantle; tail as adult but darker blue-grey, especially on central pair, and white spot on innerweb of outermost feather less defined; wings have fresh blackish median coverts (occasionally with some retained juvenile feathers) with white spots at centre of tip; retained juvenile greater coverts (usually outer feathers) are olive-brown and may show an off-white to buffish spot at tip, whilst newer feathers are as those on mantle and scapulars, lacking pale tip; rest of mantle, back, scapulars to rump as adult; flight feathers, primary coverts and tertials brownish-black (contrasting slightly with upperparts) and retained from juvenile plumage; outerwebs to flight feathers olive-brown. Underwing pattern as adult. Face variable and dependent on state of wear; in autumn/early winter, face pattern more like that of female and often indistinct; pale cream-buff or buffish-white supercilium can be long, short or uneven behind the eye or finely mottled with olive-brown, with pale buff eye-ring (absent in adult). Lores, cheeks and ear-coverts brownish-black and variably mottled or streaked buff or finely spotted buff on lower cheeks, and bordered below by thin but distinct dark or blackish malar; rear edge of ear-coverts may also be finely tipped pale buff. Chin and throat variably pale buff spotted dark brown at sides and more heavily across lower throat; lower throat and upper breast dark olive-brown, progressively dark grey on sides of breast; flanks and sides of belly variably interspersed with whitish-buff spots or tips (from juvenile plumage) on breast and sides of belly, and white or pale grey bases or central shafts on flanks; centre of lower belly and vent white; undertail-coverts white, broadly edged or fringed grey-brown or broadly tipped darker, forming a bold barred pattern. Bill blackish-brown with yellowish base to lower mandible. Legs and feet greyish-brown becoming yellow towards first summer. **First-summer male** Similar to adult but duller and browner-black, representing a transitional stage from first-winter plumage but lacking the juvenile spots or pale tips to upper- and underparts. Breeds in first summer. **First-winter female** Similar to adult female and probably not always separable with certainty, as some juvenile wing-coverts are retained as in same-age male; both adult and first-year have small pale triangular tips to greater coverts, but some retained inner greater coverts in first-year bird show generally larger and more obvious pale buffish tips contrasting with olive-brown primary coverts; also some first-year birds show fine black edges to tips of retained coverts (absent in adults). Apart from this there is little difference in overall tones of upperparts between the ages. At close range or in hand the shape of the tail feathers – pointed at tips – may be diagnostic, but not in all cases.

GEOGRAPHICAL VARIATION Two races; variation not well marked. Race *davisoni* very similar to nominate but, on average, slightly larger with slightly longer wings and tail. Both sexes slightly darker, blacker in male and darker olive in female, on forehead to crown, cheeks, ear-coverts and chin; white on innerwebs of tail feathers also reduced or almost absent, and shows smaller or reduced area of white on centre of lower belly and vent (may be completely absent); white on under-tail-coverts also less extensive.

VOICE Call a soft or virtually inaudible whistle, also a slightly stronger, more typically thrush-like *peep*, *seep* or *tseee* given when disturbed or from nocturnal migrants; winter contact note a soft whistled *chit* or *tsip*; alarm call a soft *tsss* or *chrsss* whilst that given by birds on territory recalls the dry rattling notes of Mistle Thrush (126). Song an extremely hesitant, halting or languid delivery punctuated by long pauses; typically gives a series of 2–3 whistled phrases, usually rich and clear, also varying in pitch with some notes deeper than others, often given as *tvee-tring* or *tvee-tryu*, *tvee-kvee* or *tvee-kwi-tring*. In Japan and Yenisei region also has a two-note phrase *yui'i-tss...* *yu'i-tss* or *tsss...sss...ss* occasionally included in the song, with a wavering quality to the final part of the phrase. Song occasionally interspersed with *choon* or *chveen* or a longer version of *hooweet-sirrr*, *heooweet-sirrr* and repeated at intervals. Song of *davisoni* less musical and more of a languid whis-tle: *feep-tss* or *tweet-tss* or *kleep-tss*, with phrases repeated after long pauses. Sings from a concealed perch typically from low to mid-height in an alder or spruce, occasionally higher atop a conifer or shrub; mainly in the early dawn and in parts of the range at dusk; may also sing for short periods throughout the day at the start of the breeding season. Song period mid-May to late July.

STATUS AND DISTRIBUTION Uncommon or rare, locally common to abundant summer breed-ing visitor along the Yenisei.

Z. s. sibirica Breeds in eastern Russia from about 85°E in Siberia (may be extending range west to about Mariinsk and possibly further west to about Omsk) to the Sea of Okhotsk, in the north to about 69°N along the upper Yenisei and to about 65–66°N on the upper Lena and east to the upper Kolyma, in the south to about 55°N in Ussuriland and Amurland, and slightly further south in the western (and occasionally also in the eastern) Sayan range and around Lake Baikal (where it may be irregular or infrequent) and south to about 45°N in the Sikhote-Alin north of Vladivostok; also to Khubsugul Lake in northern Mongolia, northern Inner Mongolia and Heilungkiang, north-east China, but exact limits imperfectly known; large parts of suitable habitat within the range appar-ently unoccupied.

In winter from Manipur Hills of extreme north-east India (where largely uncommon or rare) dis-continuously east through South-East Asia from south-east Burma, western and east-central Thai-land, also southern Peninsular Malaysia to Suma-tra and West Java; also Laos (where uncommon and mostly a passage migrant), Cambodia and most of northern Vietnam to Central Annam

(where possibly also a passage migrant). Rare or uncommon in winter in Hong Kong (perhaps also elsewhere in southern China) in October–April, and in Borneo, Sumatra (although up to 40 a day in some winters, e.g. 1991 and 1993/1994) and Bali. Has also occurred on Narcondam, Andaman Islands (once), and Nias Island (once).

Z. s. davisoni Breeds on Sakhalin (where uncommon to rare) and the southern Kuril Islands, mainly Kunashir and Shikotan (where scarce); in Japan on Hokkaido and northern and central Hon-shu; summering birds have also occurred on Sado, Shikoku, Kyushu and Tsushima.

In winter apparently mixes with nominate birds throughout much of South-East Asia but specifi-cally recorded in Tenasserim, eastern Burma, Peninsular Malaysia and Tonkin, Vietnam.

MOVEMENTS Migratory. Northern breeding birds (both races) move south from the breeding range in early September to mid-October (following post-breeding dispersal movements in August) across Siberia, China, Mongolia and in reduced numbers in Korea, where generally uncommon. Arrives in wintering areas from north-east India east to Malaysia from mid-October onwards, with some late arrivals in early December; migrants at Fraser's Hill, Peninsular Malaysia, appear late November to early December.

Departs from wintering areas in late March to late April, with main passage through northern Thailand in mid-April, but passage through China, Korea and eastern Siberia continues to late May and some birds in Mongolia in early June may still be on northward migration; certainly some birds arrive in northern breeding areas, e.g. along the Yenisei, only in mid-June. Males arrive back on breeding territory up to a week ahead of females. In central Japan birds arrive from late April to early May; return pas-sage of *davisoni* through Sakhalin is in late May and first half of June. May be a non-breeding summer visitor in small numbers to Korea.

A rare autumn migrant and winter visitor to Tai-wan, first recorded May 1987 and in 1991, 1994, 1995, 1996, 1997, 1998 and 1999, mostly in November–December; a rare passage migrant or winter vagrant to most of Europe, mostly involving single first-winter birds, but flocks have occurred twice in Poland (17–18 on 23 January 1976 and on 20 March 1978) and once in Hungary (25 together on 15 February 1947). Elsewhere the totals are Britain (7 to 1999), Ireland (1), France (5), Belgium (2), Netherlands (2), Norway (6), Sweden (1), Poland (10), Germany (11), Austria (2), Hungary (2), Bulgaria, Switzerland (1), Italy (3) and Malta (1). The single record in Israel was not accepted by Shirihai (1996). There is a specimen of *davisoni* from Mahableshwar, Western Ghats, India, dated April 1969 (Abdulali & Unnithan 1991).

Most movements are nocturnal but some local movements occur in daylight; usually moves in small flocks of up to 60, often in small mixed flocks with Eyebrowed Thrush (116).

HABITAT Breeds mainly in the extensive conifer-ous taiga of lowland Siberia; usually avoids pure broadleaved or deciduous forests; favours dense undergrowth of alder trees and bushes, alder–willow thickets and firs in stands of spruces, poplars, larches or birches, usually in moist areas like river valleys; in some areas also in low hills. Along the Yenisei most abundant in low riverine scrub away from spruce–birch forest but is also common in higher areas of alder scrub in spruce–birch forest. In Ussuriland breeds mostly along small rivers in mixed or conifer forests and those with alder–fir undergrowth. In Sakhalin breeds in the dense undergrowth of both lowland and montane conifer forests (but usually avoids river valleys) including dwarf bamboo in spruce–fir forests and stunted birch, mountain alder and dwarf cedars in spruce–birch groves; in north of range occurs in thick dark deciduous vegetation and alpine birch up to about 2400 m (7920'). In winter inhabits broadleaved and conifer forests on hills and mountains up to 1800 m (5950') in north-east India, and up to 2565 m (8460') in northern Thailand and similar elevations in south-east China.

BEHAVIOUR Usually alone or in pairs in breeding season. Very secretive or wary and often overlooked. Forages low down or on the ground, frequently turning over leaves and decaying vegetation under bushes and trees. In north of range often equally active (including singing) by night as by day. Readily takes flight when disturbed, often

flying off silently through dense forest to high perch in tree-top. Feeds mostly on worms and insects and their larvae, occasionally fruit such as cherries, currants and berries (including those of lantana) in winter.

BREEDING Season: end of May or early June to mid-August. Nest: a large, often untidy cup-shaped structure of grasses, plant stems and moss bound together with mud and lined with finer grasses, plant fibres and leaves, usually placed in undergrowth or fork of tree or branch of large shrub or crown of small spruce up to 4.5 m (14–15') from the ground. Eggs: 4–5, similar to those of Fieldfare (122), generally green or with a bluish base colour and finely speckled or spotted reddish or rufous. Incubation period 11–12 days, by both sexes.

MOULT Post-breeding moult of adults from mid- to late August; most are completed in early September. Post-juvenile moult is about the same time, from mid-July to late August or early September.

MEASUREMENTS Wing, male 114–127, female 113–124; tarsus 27.5–31; bill (to skull) male 21–24.5, female 22–25.5; *davisoni* wing, male 119–130, female 120–127. Weight 60–72 g (La Touche 1925–1930, Ali & Ripley 1983, Cramp *et al.* 1988).

REFERENCES Abdulali & Unnithan (1991), Ali & Ripley (1983), Cramp *et al.* (1988), La Touche (1925–1930).

37 VARIED THRUSH *Zoothera naevia* Plate 13

Turdus naevius **Gmelin, 1789, *Syst. Nat.* 1(2): 817, based on the Spotted Thrush Latham, 1783, *Gen. Syn.* 2(1): 27 – Nootka Sound, Vancouver Island, British Columbia.**

IDENTIFICATION 24–25.5 cm (9½–10"). A brightly coloured orange and brown or grey-brown thrush of north-west North America. Adult male in breeding plumage has greyish-blue upperparts from nape to tail, wings blackish with two broad orange tips to the wing-coverts and orange-brown edges to the flight feathers, blackish face with long pale orange supercilium behind eye to sides of nape; underparts orange broken by broad black breast-band. Female similar but slightly smaller and much browner above and paler or duller below. **Confusion species** Head and face pattern distinctive, and broad wing-bars separate both adults and immatures from any other thrush with orange underparts.

Taxonomic note Frequently placed in the genus *Ixoreus* (e.g. by the American Ornithologists' Union, on the basis that it is distinct from *Zoothera*) or in the older classification of *Geocichla* (along with most of the *Zoothera* species, especially the non-African species), and by some authorities within *Turdus*.

DESCRIPTION Sexes similar but separable in field. **Adult male** Forehead blackish becoming slate-grey on crown and hindcrown; nape to mantle, back and rump to uppertail-coverts variably

blue-grey to dark grey tinged brown, often showing blackish sides to neck and centres to feathers on mantle and back; base of longest uppertail-coverts darker grey than tips. Tail dark grey or blue-grey basally on central feathers with small white tips to each feather, broadest on outer feathers. Coverts bluish or blackish-grey but tips to median and greater coverts broadly orange or tawny-buff, alula and primary coverts dark grey or tinged blue-grey, flight feathers and tertials brownish-grey but inner primaries orange basally and edges of flight feathers pale orange extending to edges of tertials; tips of tertials often white or whitish on innerweb. Underwing has axillaries white tipped pale slate-grey, median coverts slate-grey extending to white-tipped greaters. Lores to eye black or blackish-grey extending to cheeks and ear-coverts. Bright orange supercilium extends from above eye to sides of nape. Chin and throat, including sides of throat and breast, bright orange; broad black band across centre of breast, rest of underparts pale orange or orange with paler tips, becoming paler orange-buff to whitish on belly and flanks, often with greyish crescent-shaped tips; undertail-coverts orange but longest feathers dark brown with whitish tips. Bill quite long, dark

Underwing pattern of adult Varied Thrush.

or blackish-horn on upper mandible, pale yellow-ish-horn on lower. Eye black. Legs and feet flesh-pink. Outside breeding season, upperparts lose blue-grey tinge and become dark grey to grey-brown from crown to uppertail-coverts. **Adult female** Similar to non-breeding male but slightly smaller and duller, tinged with olive on head and face to upperparts and tail; breast-band either lacking or very faint greyish or brownish; orange on underparts usually much duller with brown tips to white or whitish flanks and belly to vent, under-tail-coverts white or off-white with dull orange-brown tips to longest feathers. Supercilium often thinner and paler and usually shorter. **Grey and white variant** Upperparts slightly paler or lighter grey but supercilium, tips to wing-coverts, edges to flight feathers (including tips to tertials) and entire underparts (except for breast-band, which is greyer) white or pale greyish-white. Extremely rare; only one museum specimen known (Califor-nia State University), but the sole British record was of a bird in this plumage. **Immature** Juvenile similar in overall colour tone to female but has short or thin pale orange or orange-buff supercil-ium, brown ear-coverts often flecked paler, upper-parts brown or olive-brown with faint whitish shaft-streaks, median and greater coverts broadly tipped dull orange-brown; chin and throat pale or whitish-orange and lower throat, breast and sides of neck pale or tawny-brown mottled with darker brown tips forming a scaly pattern, lower and sides of breast to flanks dull orange-brown often smudged or scaly with rest of underparts becom-ing whitish; undertail-coverts white. **First-winter male** Similar to adult. Mantle and back grey or bluish-grey, with darker or browner edges to feath-ers (though some July immature males are olive-brown), slightly darker on scapulars, wings brown to dark greyish-brown (appear blackish) with tips of median and greater coverts broadly deep orange to orange-buff, outer feathers sometimes darker, having been retained from juvenile plumage (number of retained feathers varies) and fresh or replaced feathers with bluish edges; greaters similar, primary coverts may be narrow on outer feathers; bases and distal edges to primaries and tips to some secondaries and tertials also orange to pale orange. Tail as adult or greyish-brown with bluish wash at base, tips more pointed, and may have pale tip restricted to outer feather only. Chin and throat pale yellowish or washed light orange and may show a slight or nar-row dark malar at sides; black breast-band flecked or tinged grey or comprise feathers with yellowish to yellowish-orange centres and dark tips or cres-cents (usually more extensive at sides); sides of lower breast and belly variably pale to dull deep orange-buff, becoming tipped buff or olive-brown on flanks and centre of belly; vent and undertail-coverts white but tipped with dull olive-grey. **First-winter female** Very like female but generally duller with upperparts brown or grey-brown and retained juvenile coverts worn with brownish edges and contrasting with newer, paler edges to inner coverts; tail also browner with tapered (not rounded tips); underparts paler and breast-band (if present) much less distinct or greyer than in male. In extreme cases some individuals cannot be safely aged or sexed.

GEOGRAPHICAL VARIATION Two races; varia-tion largely clinal and based on the intensity of the female underparts. Validity of race *meruloides* often questioned. The upper body, wings and tail are paler or greyer except for the crown, which may be brown, while the underparts are paler or duller and have less white on the vent and sides of the undertail-coverts. Some males of this race are also lighter grey on mantle and back. Both sexes have a shorter, more rounded wing.

Other races have been proposed, notably *car-lottae* from Queen Charlotte Island, north-west British Columbia (Phillips 1986), where females are, on average, tinged tawny or reddish-brown above including the edges to the flight feathers, crown slightly paler than in nominate, underparts deep orange and tail with paler or buffish-brown edges. Phillips (1986) also described *godfreii* (from central British Columbia south to eastern Wash-ington and western Montana) as intermediate between nominate *naevia* and *meruloides* with medium-brown reddish-tinged upperparts and paler medium-orange underparts.

VOICE Call a weak but typically thrush-like *chuk*, *took* or *tschoook*; also a thin melancholy whistling *woooeeee*, most frequently given in winter. Song a variety of eerie, melancholy, sustained and vibrant notes, pure in tone and varying rapidly and unpre-dictably from high to low in pitch, with a sharp and buzzing (drill-like) resounding trill and on other occasions broken by a short pause. Each note begins slowly and swells to a rich full tone, some notes often prolonged and echoing, final notes finishing with a flourish which gradually dies away. Eerie quality enhanced by the depths of the fir forests; usually given from tops of trees, from March onwards.

STATUS AND DISTRIBUTION Common or locally common but numbers in wintering areas variable between years; in south of wintering range uncom-mon or rare in some winters.

Z. n. naevia Breeds on Kodiak Island and in sev-eral areas of the Alaska Peninsula; possibly also this race on the Seward Peninsula (where locally abun-dant); more continuously from south-east Alaska (Yakutat Bay) south through coastal (and islands of) British Columbia, east to the Cascade Ranges south through Washington and Oregon to north-west

California (Del Norte and Humboldt counties). In winter from extreme southern Alaska south through the breeding range to south-west California; casual or infrequent records inland in California.

Z. n. meruloides Breeds mainly east of nominate race, from north-central Alaska through the Yukon, north-west Mackenzie and interior British Columbia to south-west Alberta, eastern Washington, north-east Oregon, northern Idaho and north-west Montana. In winter occurs from southern British Columbia (possibly or occasionally to coastal south-eastern Alaska) to southern California (including San Mateo and Santa Cruz counties) and northern Baja California, east to Montana and north-central Idaho.

MOVEMENTS Migratory, though some birds may be only altitudinal migrants. Birds of nominate race move south to winter within the breeding range or slightly beyond in south-west California (where generally casual or irregular from October to early March, rarely into May, June and July). Both nominate and *meruloides* have been collected in San Diego county, south-west California. Departs from breeding areas in central Alaska in late August and September with only a few late birds lingering into early October. Some birds move only a very short way from mountains to adjacent valleys, whilst others cover considerable distances from their breeding areas (possibly accounting for occurrences out of normal range). Birds of eastern race *meruloides* appear to move further than nominate, with birds wintering further to the south (and possibly east). Return movements begin late March but birds are not back in breeding territories on Seward Peninsula until last third of April or early May. On migration has frequently been found with moving flocks of American Robins (161) and has occurred in similar flocks far east of usual migration routes, though apparently only rarely found with this species in California.

Regularly wanders east to Alberta and a rare but annual vagrant to Saskatchewan, Manitoba, Quebec, New Brunswick (including one wintering bird) and Nova Scotia; also an autumn vagrant to many of central and east coast states of U.S.A., from Wisconsin to Massachusetts, New York and New Jersey south to South Carolina (October 1993), Kansas, Kentucky, Tennessee and New Mexico between early November and mid-April, with most in December and January. Race *meruloides* has occurred north to Point Barrow and Prudhoe Bay, northern Alaska, mostly as overshooting migrants in late spring but also in summer (July) and in September; one (race unknown) occurred north to Cornwallis Island (Queen Elizabeth Islands) in July 1994, also in Arizona (January and February 1956, March 1958) and on Guadelupe Island (off western Baja California, Mexico). Outside of North America has occurred as a vagrant to Wrangel Island (June 1983) and England (November 1982).

HABITAT Breeds in dense conifer forests from sea-level to the summit of the Cascade Range, principally in old forests of tall firs, cedars, spruces and hemlocks together with a mixture of alders, poplars and maples and in glades and edges where there is an undergrowth of dogwood and wild currant. One of the few species to be found in the dense dark forests; often occurs in areas of streams, along the shores of lakes and in the humid coastal belt of forests that range along the western seaboard of north-west U.S.A., British Columbia and southern Alaska. In winter in similar habitat but often in oak woodlands and mixed oak and conifer forests; also partial to shady canyons.

BEHAVIOUR A shy retiring bird preferring the dark shaded areas of forest or fir woods than any open areas; also appears to have an affinity for damp areas and frequently sings on the wettest days. Often aggressive in defence of territory and in parts of range shows little fear of man. In flight like most thrushes has fairly bold, undulating wingstrokes, recalling American Robin (with which it may occasionally associate) but not as large or bulky in shape; flight through forest often fast and twisting. Forages and feeds low down in trees and undergrowth, and also on the ground where it searches amongst fallen leaves and rotting debris; in winter often feeds in more open areas. Appears to feed mostly on invertebrates with centipedes, small bugs, ants, snails, worms and small beetles occasionally supplemented by bees, wasps, flies, grasshoppers and crickets; also takes wild (occasionally cultivated) fruit including snowberries, honeysuckle, acorns, juniper berries, blueberries, blackberries, cranberries, mistletoe, raspberries, sumac, buckthorn, wheat and various weed seeds.

BREEDING Season: late April to mid- or late July. Nest: a bulky structure of soft moss, fir twigs, dead leaves, rotten wood, dry grass and plant stems lined with mud and soft or fine grasses; exceptionally placed near ground, but usually about 4.5 m (14–15') up, and in Alaska not infrequently as high as 7.5 m (25'), in small to medium-sized firs, alders or willow thickets, usually placed on a horizontal branch or against the trunk; some are built in forks in branches. Eggs: 3, exceptionally 5, pale blue with a sprinkling of fine brown to dark brown spots. Incubation solely by the female, 12–14 days; fledging period 13–14 days.

MOULT Adults undergo complete moult after breeding, from late June onwards, largely complete by the end of August or early September. Juveniles undergo a partial moult at about the same time, during which the head and body feathers, together with the median coverts and some of outer greater coverts and tertials, are replaced.

MEASUREMENTS Wing, male (n=100) 121–136, female (n=100) 118–133; tarsus 29.5–33; bill (culmen) 18–23 (Pyle *et al.* 1997). Weight apparently unrecorded.

REFERENCES Godfrey (1979), Pyle *et al.* (1987).

38 AZTEC THRUSH *Zoothera pinicola*

Plate 13

Turdus pinicola Sclater, 1859, *Proc. Zool. Soc. London*: 334 – southern Mexico, pine-forests of the tableland above Jalapa, Veracruz.

IDENTIFICATION 21.5–24 cm (8½–9½″). A scarce, very striking dark brown and white thrush endemic to the mountain forests of central Mexico. Male has a distinctive dark brown hood and is heavily flecked or mottled paler on much of the head and body; wings black with pale whitish or whitish-grey edges to greater-coverts and flight feathers; tail black but uppertail-coverts and tips of tail white. Underparts white. Female basically similar but lacks the dark hood and has head and breast more prominently streaked; also shows a broader supercilium and more white in the wing. Immature particularly striking with a much heavier pattern of pale buff spots and streaks above and golden-buff scaling or scalloping below. Unique and unmistakable. **Confusion species** None.

Taxonomic note Often classified (e.g. by the American Ornithologists' Union) in its own genus *Ridgwayia*; previously included in *Geocichla*.

DESCRIPTION Sexes differ. **Adult male** Forehead to crown, nape and upper mantle, chin and throat to breast dark sepia or blackish-brown (browner in sunlight), flecked (mostly on cheeks, ear-coverts, crown and nape) or streaked paler whitish and brown. May show narrow or indistinct pale brown supercilium. Back, scapulars to rump and uppertail-coverts unstreaked dark or blackish-brown, longest uppertail-coverts white. Tail black or blackish-brown, browner on outermost feathers and all feathers broadly tipped whitish-grey (more extensive on innerwebs than outers) and outerwebs of outermost feathers narrowly edged white. Median and greater coverts as scapulars, greaters broadly edged white, buffish-white on inners, becoming brown or blackish-brown on innerwebs; alula dark grey or blackish, primary coverts black tipped silvery-grey with blackish central shafts; flight feathers black with broad white midway patch on primaries (upper edge of patch often grey), also some white edges to tips of outer 2–4 primaries; inner primaries and all secondaries broadly silvery-grey or greyish-white at tips; inner secondaries blackish-brown tipped browner, tertials similar but broadly tipped pale grey. Underwing shows typical *Zoothera* pattern of white lesser and median coverts, blackish-grey greaters and pale or whitish bases to flight feathers. Chin and throat may be slightly paler brown than rest of head; breast usually sharply demarcated from rest of underparts, which are white or tinged buff with dark patch on lower flanks; some may show dark brown spots on flanks. Bill dark brown or blackish-brown. Legs and feet pale whitish-pink or flesh-pink. **Adult female** Similar to male but lacks hooded appearance and is generally paler brown and more prominently streaked with larger or broader pale buffish-brown centres or tips to head, face (except blackish lores), chin to breast and nape to scapulars and back. Has slightly paler

(more conspicuous) greyish-buff supercilium than male, and edges to flight feathers pale grey not whitish, pale tips to inner secondaries smaller and duller. Chin and throat dull buffish streaked with grey-brown; pale central shafts. Usually shows longer patch of white on outer greater coverts and at base of outermost primary. **Immature** Juvenile mostly blackish but heavily spotted, streaked or mottled golden-buff (variably whitish to rufous-buff) on head, back and scapulars, with broad streaks on edges to scapulars and greater coverts and tips to median coverts (juvenile female has streaks on upperparts broader and whiter); flight feathers as in adult but white tips duller and innerwebs to secondaries and tertials pale buff-brown. Lower back to rump cinnamon or reddish-brown edged darker or blackish-brown; uppertail-coverts have pale buff tips. Tail black with small white tips to all feathers. Supercilium broadly buffish-white; lores and area around eye usually black in juvenile male, more streaked in young female. Underparts heavily scaled or scalloped with pale whitish or golden-buff; centres to all feathers broadly edged black or blackish-brown; lower breast more finely edged, with paler, whitish centres to belly, vent and undertail-coverts; flanks blackish. Bill blackish with pale pinkish-brown base to lower mandible. Legs and feet brownish-pink becoming brighter pink with age.

GEOGRAPHICAL VARIATION None. Monotypic.

VOICE Call a thin, slightly quavering, whining *wheeerr*, *whieeer* or an upslurred rasping or buzzing *zrrip* or *prrip* or *prreep*, the latter almost disyllabic and sometimes given with a rolling or questioning tone; a more abrupt but metallic *whein* or *wheen* and a thin or nasal *sweee-uh* or upslurred *seeep* may be used as an alarm or disturbance note. Song not well known but apparently relatively unmusical, being a slightly louder repetition of the call note interspersed with clicking or twittering notes, sharp clucks and pauses (Hardy & Parker 1992, Howell & Webb 1995).

STATUS AND DISTRIBUTION Uncommon or locally common. Mostly resident. An endemic thrush of the high mountains of Mexico on the Pacific and interior slopes of south-east Sonora (Sierra Obscura) and south-west Chihuahua south through northern and eastern Sinaloa and Durango to Jalisco and east to Puebla, west-central Veracruz and northern Oaxaca; also in isolated outposts of Guerrero and southern Oaxaca. May also be a local resident in southern Coahuila to eastern San Luis Potosi and southern Hidalgo.

MOVEMENTS Largely resident but may move to lower levels in winter; localised movements or scarce resident in north-east Mexico; has occurred in northern Sinaloa, southern Jalisco and northern Michoacán. Since August 1977 has occurred (increasingly and probably now annually) as a vagrant to western Texas (4 records in Big Bend National Park; Chisos Mountains in January, May, July, August and October) and in spring and summer (recorded January, February, May, June, July, August and September) in south-east Arizona (18 records from the Huachuca, Chiricahua and Santa Rita Mountains) (Zimmerman 1991).

HABITAT Mostly forested ravines of pine or pine-oak or occasionally humid forests of the subtropical and montane zones at 1800–3500 m (5940–11,550′). Usually occurs in damp hollows or the moist floors or valley bottoms of ravines and canyons.

BEHAVIOUR Usually in pairs or small groups, occasionally up to 30 together, or mixes freely with other thrushes, particularly foraging flocks of American Robins (161) or Silky-Flycatchers *Ptilogonys cinereus*; often shy and difficult to see as it forages low down in bushes or thick vegetation or on the ground in dense cover; also sits motionless for long periods, and is best detected by call or song. Feeds mostly on berries and insects; vagrants in south-west U.S.A. have been recorded feeding on the fleshy fruits of Texas madrone *Arbutus texana*, grapes *Vitis arizonica*, manzanita *Arctostaphylos pungens* and hackberries *Celtis reticulata*, together with cultivated species such as *Pyracantha coccinea* (Zimmerman 1991).

BREEDING Very poorly known. Season: May to June in the south; later, possibly into early August, in the north. Nest: a deep cup of grass and other fibrous material usually covered or decorated with green moss in trees at mid- to upper levels of canopy cover. Eggs: 2, pale blue, unspotted.

MOULT Juvenile plumage is replaced by first-winter plumage by early to mid-September. Moult period of adults is unknown but like other thrushes a complete moult probably follows the breeding season.

MEASUREMENTS Wing, male 127–135.5, female 124–135; tarsus (n=11) 25–27; bill (culmen) 18–21. Weight (3 females) 67–78 g (Zimmerman 1991).

REFERENCES Hardy & Parker (1992), Howell & Webb (1995), Zimmerman (1991).

39 ABYSSINIAN GROUND-THRUSH *Zoothera piaggiae*   Plate 14

Turdus piaggiae Bouvier, 1877, *Bull. Soc. Zool. France* 2: 456 – Uganda [restricted to Lake Tana, northern Abyssinia, *vide* Chapin (1953) *Bull. Amer. Mus. Nat. Hist.* 75A: 579].

IDENTIFICATION 19–20 cm (7½–8″). An attractive but very shy or secretive ground-thrush, replacing the very similar Orange Ground-Thrush (41) in the highland forests of East Africa. Deep rufous-orange on the head and face with a prominent white eye-ring, becoming slightly more orange on the breast and flanks; upperparts olive-brown, brighter or warmer orange-brown on the rump and tail with two prominent bright white wing-bars at tips to wing-coverts. **Confusion species** In south-central Kenya (Mt Kenya and Aberdares) sympatric with similar but slightly larger Orange Ground-Thrush, but higher-altitude Abyssinian identified by unbroken white eye-ring, rich brown head, slightly warmer brown upperparts, smaller bill and lack of any grey or pale areas on crown or dark bars across cheeks and ear-coverts. In south-west Uganda, eastern Zaire, Rwanda and northern Burundi Oberlaender's Ground-Thrush (42) is very similar to race *tanganjicae* of Abyssinian; Oberlaender's has the entire head and face more rufous-orange, except for the diffuse or ill-defined black mark through the eye (interrupting the eye-ring), contrasting with the deeper or darker rust of the orange-rufous mantle, back and scapulars. The songs of both *tanganjicae* and Oberlaender's differ in structure.

Taxonomic note 1: The race *tanganjicae* has been proposed as a valid species – Kivu Ground-Thrush (Prigogine 1977) – but we follow Dowsett & Dowsett-Lemaire (1993) in treating it as conspecific. The differences between the two, principally the head-to-nape colour-tones and the wing-to-tail ratio are considered to be no greater than those which exists elsewhere, e.g. between races *rowei* and *piaggiae*; the claimed altitudinal separation is also based on limited evidence and requires confirmation that the two breeding populations are indeed completely allopatric (see Distribution and Habitat). The race *williamsi* (Macdonald 1948) is here considered a synonym of the nominate race.

Taxonomic note 2: Has previously been classified as belonging to the *Turdus* thrushes (see White 1962) but we follow Ripley (1964) in including this and the 'orange' thrushes of the region with *Zoothera*.

DESCRIPTION Sexes alike. **Adult** Forehead to fore-crown deep rufous-orange or rich chestnut-brown; crown, nape and ear-coverts browner becoming rich brown tinged olive on mantle, back and scapulars and more heavily or brighter olive-brown on rump, uppertail-coverts and base of tail; rest of tail rich or russet-brown on central feathers, darker towards tip and paler brown on outer feathers with white tips (on innerwebs). Lesser coverts as scapulars or with orange tips, median coverts black with broad white tips, greaters black on innerwebs and edged with olive or olive-brown on outers and tipped bright white; alula and primary coverts dark or blackish-brown; flight feathers brown or dark brown, outer primaries edged pale or orange buff-brown at base becoming olive-brown on secondaries and outer tertials; inner tertials dark or blackish-brown. Underwing has axillaries white with brown tips, median and greaters to bend of wing grey or grey-brown tipped white; bases of secondaries and all, except outermost two, primaries white. Lores to cheeks dusky- or cinnamon-brown, broad white eye-ring, small patch of bare skin often visible immediately behind eye; chin and throat to breast and sides of neck rich or deep rufous-orange, becoming orange on lower sides of breast and tinged olive-brown on flanks; centre of lower belly pale orange or white, vent to undertail-coverts white; thighs pale brown. Bill black or blackish-horn. Legs and feet pale flesh, flesh-pink or whitish to pale brown with white soles. **Immature** Juvenile similar to adult but generally paler and duller on head and upperparts, with fine pale orange-buff central shaft-streaks to crown, nape and more broadly or prominently on mantle, back and scapulars. Tips and edges to median and greater coverts pale or orange-buff. Lores, lower face and sides of neck orange-brown, finely mottled or spotted brown; may show dark mark through eye and over cheeks, rest of eye-ring pale buffish-white; dull orange-brown submoustachial and dark malar. Chin and throat dull buff becoming heavily mottled with black tips; breast, belly and flanks have pale orange bases and black tips interspersed with some deeper orange feathers on belly and flanks towards first-winter plumage. Winter birds (November onwards) may have finely streaked shafts on upperparts while orange on underparts may have remains of a few dark bars and tips to breast and upper belly.

GEOGRAPHICAL VARIATION Five races; variation not well defined. All races are extremely similar to nominate *piaggiae* in the field and differ principally in the extent or intensity of olive in the rufous or russet upperparts and the orange on the breast and flanks. Races *kilimensis* and *rowei* are tinged heavily browner-olive on mantle and back, more visibly olive in *rowei* than any other race; *kilimensis* is deeper orange to chestnut on breast and flanks whereas *rowei* is paler or lighter orange; immature *kilimensis* has darker mottling on underparts extending from chin and throat across breast and flanks. Race *hadii* is like nominate but more olive with very little russet tones on upperparts (except crown), mantle and tail generally darker and innerwebs to flight feathers blacker. Race *tanganjicae* ('Kivu Ground-Thrush') has forehead to crown and nape deep russet or chestnut extending onto upper mantle; rest of mantle, back and scapulars russet or deep orange-brown, heavily tinged olive and becoming rufous-orange or bright russet on rump and uppertail coverts; greater coverts black or blackish heavily tinged olive and boldly tipped white. Chin and throat as top of head, but lores to ear-coverts slightly darker or dusky. Adult female virtually identical to male but deep orange-rufous on head and face duller and that on chin and throat slightly lighter or paler; may show greyish wash on lower throat. Immature has median and greater coverts black or blackish, overlain with olive on greaters, tips dull off-white or whitish-orange. Chin and centre of throat paler or whiter than adult.

VOICE Mostly silent but gives a thin, high-pitched *seep* when disturbed; also a more typically thrush-like, throaty *chuc* or *tuc*, often running into a repeated *tuc tuc tuc*; has a sharp, rising *cry cry* alarm note. Song rich and typically thrush-like in tonal quality and in its repetition of a wide variety of phrases, mostly whistles on the same level interspersed with both softer and harsher notes and some trills: *wurrr teeeu weeeu... wur-weeeeu-tiWEE, wichu-tsik trrrrrrweeeeeu, seeesurrrWEE, tiuweee chikuchik wurweeeotuweeee...* May also end abruptly with a short soft *chuck* or *pseet*. Some regional variation in song occurs, as birds in Rwanda have longer, more rambling and rather different-structured song. Some repeated phrases recall those in song of Orange Ground-Thrush, which is generally flutier and mellower; does not respond to taped songs of either Orange or Oberlaender's. Sings vigorously throughout the breeding season, but at either end of the season may only perform in early dawn; song period late July to March. Sings mostly from concealed perch in forest understorey or subcanopy. Song of *tanganjicae* similar to that of nominate, with repeated phrases, but each phrase held slightly longer and usually with an upslurred second note; speed of delivery slightly slower, fairly similar to song of Oberlaender's in overall tone, but repeated double-note phrases distinctive.

STATUS AND DISTRIBUTION Locally common (but easily overlooked) to rare; when treated as a full species race *tanganjicae* considered Near-Threatened (Collar *et al.* 1994).

Z. p. hadii South-east Sudan (Imatong and Dongotona Mountains).

Z. p. piaggiae Discontinuously in Ethiopia in the western highlands north to about 10°N – with an April 1998 record in the Simien Mountains near Jinbar waterfall, Sankaber, some 360 km (225 miles) north of previous known limits (Demey 1999) – and southern and south-east highlands, Boma Hills, extreme south-east Sudan, northern and western Kenya (west of the Rift Valley, particularly Mt Nyiru and Mt Elgon to the Mau Escarpment) to Mt Moroto, eastern Uganda, and in the Rwenzoris of south-west Uganda and (usually above 1900 m/6270') in eastern Zaire south to the Kahuzi and Itombwe Mountains. (In parts of eastern Zaire and south-west Uganda nominate *piaggiae* and race *tanganjicae* are usually separated altitudinally, with *piaggiae* occurring at higher altitudes.)

Z. p. tanganjicae Hills and lower montane forests (usually below 2000 m/6600' but see also Movements) of Kigezi, Mt Muhavura and the Bwindi (Impenetrable) Forest, south-west Uganda, and eastern Kivu province, Zaire (principally Virunga Volcanoes, Nyungwe forest, Kahuzi Range, Itombwe Mountains, and Mt Kabobo), western Rwanda and north-west Burundi.

Z. p. kilimensis Discontinuously east of the Rift in central and southern Kenya from Mt Marsabit, Mt Kulal, Mt Nyiru, Karissia Hills, Mt Uraguess, Mt Kenya, Aberdares and Mt Kilimanjaro, northern Tanzania.

Z. p. rowei Extreme southern Kenya on Nguruman Hills and in the Loliondo and Magaidu forests, Arusha district, northern Tanzania (very little known and only recently recorded again in Loliondo area since its discovery in 1931) (Salempo 1994).

MOVEMENTS Mostly sedentary but race *tanganjicae* in Bwindi Forest, south-west Uganda, breeds down to about 1600 m (5280') and moves to about 2500 m (8250') or higher when not breeding (A. Twinomusuni pers. comm.).

HABITAT Undergrowth of evergreen highland forests usually in high rainfall areas at 1800–3300 m (5940–10,890'), mostly above 2300 m (7600') but also exceptionally lower to 1310–1560 (4320–5150') on Mt Marsabit; occurs in bamboo forest up to 3200 m (10560') on Mt Kenya, and may occur in pine plantations in Ethiopia and Kenya; *tanganjicae* occurs in ground and lower vegetation of lower montane forests 1530–2040 m (5050–6730'), possibly higher as the original type specimen – originally described as race *williamsi* of Abyssinian Ground-Thrush – was collected at 2900 m (9570') and the bird collected from the Virunga Volcanoes was taken at 2325 m (7670').

BEHAVIOUR Extremely shy (*tanganjicae* is rare and little known) and usually alone but two or three may occur in loose proximity in parts of the range (e.g. *piaggiae* in Ethiopia). Forages on the ground, where it hops, walks or runs, usually under trees or dense vegetation, occasionally up to 6–7 m (c.20') from the ground in fruiting bushes or trees, often in damp or moss- and lichen-covered areas near forest streams, but may venture into more open parts of the forest or in clearings or edges of paths; also flies to drink at waterholes in dry season, quickly retreating into cover at first sign of intruder. Feeds mostly on worms, millipedes, snails and insects and their larvae, for it searches the leaf-litter and ground vegetation; may also follow ant swarms and known to take fruit, mostly figs, berries and some seeds.

BREEDING Season: mostly at the onset of, or during, the rainy season – February to June (Ethiopia, Kenya, Sudan and Rwanda) or to July (Uganda) and again in September–December. Nest: a cup of moss (may occasionally also use other plant material) lined with small fern stems, fibres and roots, placed up to 5 m (16–17') from the ground, but usually much lower, in the fork of a branch or small tree, well hidden or concealed. Eggs: 2, pale bluish-green or more heavily greenish-blue, occasionally with lilac or purple-grey blotches and fine red, reddish-brown or chestnut spots. Young fed by both parents and remain with parents for up to 3 months following fledging.

MOULT Adults have complete post-breeding moult; body moult noted February–March, July–August and November–December.

MEASUREMENTS Wing, male 95–109.5, female 94–109; tarsus 31.5–36; bill (culmen) 19.5–24; *hadii* wing, male 98–100, female 95–99; bill 23; *kilimensis* wing 95–106; tarsus 32.5–37; *rowei* wing, male 97–102, female 98–99; *tanganjicae* wing 104–107. Weight, male 42–58 g, female 43–65 g.

REFERENCES Demey (1999), Dowsett & Dowsett-Lemaire (1993), Macdonald (1948), Prigogine (1977), Salempo (1994), Urban *et al.* (1997).

40 CROSSLEY'S GROUND-THRUSH *Zoothera crossleyi*   Plate 15

Turdus crossleyi Sharpe, 1871, *Proc. Zool. Soc. London*: 607, pl. 47 – Cameroon Mountain.

IDENTIFICATION 21.5–22 cm (8½"). A rare resident of three widely scattered areas in Central and West Africa. Mostly deep chestnut or russet-brown on the head (except for the prominent dark brown or blackish cheeks and ear-coverts), neck to breast and flanks; mantle to tail and wings generally browner or with russet or rufous tinge to the rump; shows two broad white wing-bars and fairly broad, broken white eye-ring. On the ground it has a very upright stance. **Confusion species** One of several very similar-looking thrushes from the deep forests of Central and West Africa. Differs from allopatric Orange Ground-Thrush (41) by deeper or darker chestnut-brown forehead and upperparts and orange or rufous-orange on the nape; the rump and uppertail-coverts are also more rufous than in Orange Ground-Thrush, although some males of latter can show warm or richer brown tones to the lower rump and uppertail-coverts and sides to tail-base. Chin and throat on Orange are more uniform with the breast than that on Crossley's which shows blackish bases to this area. Lesser, median and greater underwing-coverts are olive-brown on Orange but greyer or grey-brown on Crossley's. Oberlaender's Ground-Thrush (42) is slightly smaller and has richer chestnut extending across the mantle and back; it is also entirely rufous on the head and face, lacking any dark or blackish on the cheeks and ear-coverts (which are uniform, although some individuals may show a dark smudge through the eye). Black-eared Ground-Thrush (43) has a similar distribution but is easily told from Crossley's by paler face and broad dark streaks through the eye and on rear ear-coverts. Abyssinian Ground-Thrush (39) has a prominent complete white eye-ring and generally shows uniform ear-coverts and less white and more orange on belly and flanks. Grey Ground-Thrush (44) lacks any rich chestnut or orange-brown tones in the plumage.

DESCRIPTION Sexes alike. **Adult** Forehead and crown deep chestnut or russet becoming more rufous or rufous-chestnut on nape and sides of neck. Mantle, back and scapulars russet or brownish-chestnut and tinged olive on scapulars, becoming brighter or more rufous (and lacking any olive) on rump and uppertail-coverts. Tail brown or russet-brown with pale buff tips to outer two feathers (more extensive on outermost). Lesser coverts as scapulars, median coverts black or blackish-brown broadly tipped white, greater coverts similar but generally less broadly tipped white especially on outers (where white tips often absent); alula and primary coverts dark or blackish-brown; flight feathers brown or dark brown but broadly edged paler or russet-brown on primaries and olive-brown on secondaries; tertials russet-brown on innerwebs and olive-brown on outerwebs. Underwing has axillaries dark olive-brown, white tips to bend of wing; median, greater and primary coverts brown; white to silvery-white bases to all flight feathers (except outermost two primaries). Base of bill and lores to eye black, base of lower forehead and upper lores pale orange-buff forming short line above lores. Eye-ring white but broken on upper and lower eyelid; cheeks and short submoustachial black or blackish; ear-coverts also dark or blackish but heavily flecked or streaked orange-brown; rear of ear-coverts entirely orange-brown or rufous extending to sides of nape. Chin and throat orange or pale orange overlying visible black or blackish bases; lower throat and breast deep or rufous-orange and only slightly paler or lighter orange on belly and flanks; centre of lower belly to vent and undertail-coverts white. Bill substantial but comparatively short and deep at base, dark brown or black. Legs and feet pinkish or fleshy-white. **Immature** Juvenile similar to adult on upperparts but with buffish or light orange-buffish central shaft-streaks on crown, nape and mantle, often forming a paler collar; usually shows black patch on cheeks and rufous ear-coverts. Chin and throat black becoming buff, spotted or mottled black, on breast; flanks rufous and spotted darker. Bill mostly greyish but buffish-grey on base of lower mandible.

GEOGRAPHICAL VARIATION Two races; variation not well defined. Race *pilettei* very similar to nominate but has crown, nape and most of upperparts more heavily olive-brown and lacks the chestnut of nominate; tail also mostly brown with small white tips to outermost feathers. Chin slightly paler or whiter. Bill slightly smaller. Immature very like nominate but face paler or rufous-buff, chin and throat buff with only a poorly defined submoustachial, breast pale rufous-buff spotted and mottled with dark brown; undertail-coverts white; tips of outer greater coverts white becoming orange or rufous-orange on tips of inners.

VOICE Song a rich and mellow series of phrases of up to 10 notes; usually begins with two low notes then rises slowly up the scale and ends with thin high-pitched slurred *hor-her-heewo-chichiwo-tsitsi*, repeated at intervals with some variation between notes (Urban *et al.* 1997). Singing performed up to a month before and throughout breeding season; sings from concealed perch on the ground or up to 25 m (82') in canopy of primary forest.

STATUS AND DISTRIBUTION Uncommon to scarce or rare; considered Near-Threatened (Collar *et al.* 1994).

Z. c. crossleyi Obudu Plateau, Gotel Mountains and the Mambilla Plateau, south-east Nigeria, and Rumpi Hills, Mt Cameroon, Mt Kupe, Mt Manenguba, Sakbayeme and Nsimanden, southern Cameroon; also an isolated population near Mayombe, southern Congo.

Z. c. pilettei North-east Zaire: western parts of the Semliki valley from about Beni south to the Itombwe highlands near Kamituga (White 1967).

MOVEMENTS Very poorly known but one bird trapped at 650 m (2145') on Mt Cameroon in December was retrapped a month later at 200 m (660'), indicating a degree of altitude migration (Urban *et al.* 1997).

HABITAT Mid-levels and undergrowth, especially in ravines and other damp areas, of mature primary forests on mountains and plateaus between 1200 and 2300 m (4000–7590') in Cameroon, 500–600 m (1650–1980') in the Congo and between 960–1850 m (3168–6100') in Zaire.

BEHAVIOUR Very shy and secretive, often remaining motionless when disturbed; seen by very few ornithologists; usually alone or in pairs. Spends most of its life low down or on the ground amongst dense vegetation, occasionally rising a few feet from the forest floor to perch on a rock or low branch. Has an upright stance. Food little known but stomachs of collected birds contained insects and seeds.

BREEDING Unknown, but birds noted in breeding condition in Nigeria and Cameroon from April to June and in Zaire from August to November, indicating breeding season from end of the dry season and start of the rains.

MOULT No information.

MEASUREMENTS Wing, male 105–114, female 106–116; tarsus, male 31–37, female 32–37.5; bill, male (culmen) 17.5–20, (to gape) 23–25, female (culmen) 18.5–21, (to gape) 20–25; *pilettei* wing 107–115.5; tarsus 34–38.5; bill, male 20–23, female 20–22. Weight 63–82 g (Serle 1954, Urban *et al.* 1997).

REFERENCES Elgood *et al.* (1994), Serle (1950, 1954), White (1967).

41 ORANGE GROUND-THRUSH *Zoothera gurneyi*   Plate 14

Turdus gurneyi Hartlaub, 1864, *Ibis* 6: 350, pl. 9 – near Pietermaritzburg, Natal.

IDENTIFICATION 21–23 cm (8¼–9″). A small to medium-sized thrush of montane forests in parts of East and southern Africa where it is a shy and elusive bird, its presence often only given away by its pleasant song. The rounded crown and most of the upperparts are olive-brown, the forehead and upper lores are orange, with a white half eye-ring and dark smudge below the eye; two broad wing-bars; chin and throat to breast and flanks deep orange, often tinged brownish on flanks; centre of belly to vent and undertail-coverts white. Sexes alike but female usually slightly paler below. **Confusion species** Two problems are Abyssinian Ground-Thrush (39) in East Africa (with which it overlaps in central Kenya) and Olive Thrush (101) further south in Africa. Abyssinian is slightly smaller, lacks black facial markings, and has russet or rufous-brown forehead to crown, brighter olive-brown upperparts and wings, rufous-orange chin to breast, a well defined unbroken eye-ring and slightly smaller bill. Olive Thrush is much darker above, lacks wing-bars and face markings, and has paler or duller breast (depending on race), a yellow bill and orange underwing. Differs from allopatric Crossley's Ground-Thrush (40) on song and by more extensive dark face pattern, less olive on crown and upperparts, less rufous rump and uppertail-coverts, more uniform chin, throat and breast and olive-brown (not grey-brown) lesser, median and greater underwing-coverts.

DESCRIPTION Sexes almost alike. **Adult** Upperparts from forecrown to rump and uppertail-coverts olive-brown, washed grey (especially northern birds) on mantle, back and scapulars and sometimes appearing more heavily russet-brown on forehead and crown and on rump and upper-tail-coverts; tail the same but base russet-brown, outer feathers narrowly tipped white (often invisible in field). Scapulars as upperparts, median and greater coverts black or blackish-brown broadly tipped white, alula and primary coverts brown to dark brown; flight feathers also dark or blackish-brown but broadly edged pale or warm reddish-buff on outerwebs of primaries, creating a slight contrast on closed wing; tertials warm or russet-brown. Underwing has axillaries and lesser coverts to bend of the wing white, medians and bases to greater coverts dull or olive-brown tipped white, broad white band across bases of all secondaries and all (except outer two) primaries. Lores dusky-brown but upper lores to eye orange or rufous-orange; narrow and incomplete dull white eye-ring broken above and below by diffuse blackish smudge across cheeks (may also show small area of grey bare skin behind eye); ear-coverts orange-brown tinged olive, becoming pale greyish and finely streaked blackish, rear of ear-coverts indistinctly brown or blackish. Chin and throat to sides of neck, breast and flanks orange to russet-orange, usually warmest or brownest on throat and breast (but sometimes with olive-brown flecks or small spots at sides) and paler on lower breast and

flanks, except for lower flanks which are pale olive-brown. Short blackish malar. Centre of belly to vent and undertail-coverts white, thighs off-white or washed pale buff-brown. Bill entirely dark brownish-horn or black. Legs and feet pale flesh-pink. **Adult female** As male but generally less bright or so extensively orange on underparts. **Immature** First-year bird similar to adult but heavily mottled or broadly streaked with buff central shafts to upperparts including rump, streaks diminishing gradually from back, rump and tail towards head and neck; broad white wing-bars on tips of median and greater coverts but tinged or edged with pale orange; face has faint trace of blackish streak below eye; underparts paler or duller rufous-orange and variably mottled or barred with blackish tips, undertail-coverts buffish-white.

GEOGRAPHICAL VARIATION Five races; variation clinal and not well defined. The races *chyulu* and *usambarae* (previously separated by Clancey 1955) are here considered to be synonymous with *raineyi*. Race *otomitra* has upper forehead to crown and upperparts more heavily tinged grey and less olive; cheeks and ear-coverts often more blackish below eye, becoming paler or yellowish-olive and flecked or finely streaked with light yellowish-buff or greyish towards rear of ear-coverts; flanks washed olive. Race *raineyi* very similar to *otomitra* (some birds poorly separable) but with slightly darker grey crown and ear-coverts (with small pale yellowish-buff spots) becoming paler grey-brown on rest of upperparts, flanks also usually lacking olive tinge. Mt Kenya race *chuka* similar to nominate and *raineyi* but slightly larger with darker olive-brown upperparts, with grey or greyish on head and nape, slightly longer bill which in hand may show a hooked tip (present on some *raineyi*). Race *disruptans* slightly smaller than nominate with entire upperparts olive to olive-brown except for slightly heavier russet or cinnamon tinge on rump and uppertail-coverts, and orange upper lores and cheeks; wings and base of tail more heavily tinged reddish-brown, spots on tips of median and greater coverts slightly smaller; ear-coverts olive or olive-brown below eye and flecked paler or with light orange on rear of ear-coverts.

VOICE Call a thin *tsip* or *tseep*, a slightly longer chuckling *cureek* and a whistling or hissing trill; at dusk birds going to roost give a *ti-tue-tue-too-wee-to* (Urban *et al.* 1997). Song a fairly long series of varied, mellow, melodious, fluty phrases of 7–10 notes, often sustained for several minutes and beginning with *chee-choo-chee, cheelerooo trrooo...* or *wuree tew-tew* and rising slightly before falling away at the end; also a series of repeated slurred whistles on one note before rising to another and continuing with that note *reee-eee tureeee-tew, reee-eee tureee-tew... erreeee tew-tew rrriiiiii, errreeee-tew-tew-rriiii*, often interspersed with high-pitched but soft or almost inaudible whispered notes; also gives a more quavering or ringing *quee* *qui-urrrr tur-turileeee weet-weet*. In tone very similar to the song of Brown Robin *Cercotrichas/Erythropygia signata* which (in South Africa) inhabits the same forests but starts on a higher note and sings slightly faster. Sings from deep within forests and extensive woodlands, perching mainly at medium height in thick canopy but also in low cover; usually most vocal early morning and evening. Song period (southern Africa) from end of April to November or early December.

STATUS AND DISTRIBUTION Uncommon, locally common or scarce.

Z. g. otomitra Mt Kilimanjaro, Pare Mountains, East Usambara Mountains, Mt Oldeani, Mt Meru and Arusha National Park, North Pare Mountains, Nguru Hills, Uluguru Mountains, Njombe Highlands, Rubeho and Udzungwa Mountains, Mt Rungwe and the Ufipa Plateau, and in coastal forests at Kiono (Urban *et al.* 1997), all in northern, north-east and south-west Tanzania, Upemba National Park in south-east Zaire, Nyika Plateau in northern Malawi, and with an isolated population on Mt Moco, central Angola.

Z. g. chuka Southern Aberdares and Irangi, Chuka and Meru forests on the eastern and south-east slopes of Mt Kenya mostly between 1830–2300 m (6040–7590'), central-southern Kenya.

Z. g. raineyi Taita and Chyulu Hills usually between 1370–2140 m (4520–7060'), southern Kenya.

Z. g. disruptans Milanje Plateau of southern Malawi and the Vumba and Inyanga (Eastern) Highlands of eastern Zimbabwe south to the Chimanimani Mountains and the Lucite River; and in Mozambique north to the watershed of the Pungue River with an isolated population on Mt Gorongosa (central Mozambique). In the south to adjacent areas of northern and eastern Transvaal (south to the Soutpansberg). Intergrades with both *gurneyi* and *otomitra*.

Z. g. gurneyi Eastern Cape, area east of Buffalo River and west and north of Umtata in the Kambi Forest, north-east into Natal, South Africa; in November 1997 found in Mgwayitza Forest, north-west Swaziland.

MOVEMENTS Partial or altitude migrant. Many birds are resident in the lower to middle levels of montane forests but some, presumably those from higher altitudes, move to lower levels, usually between May and July, still remaining above 350 m (1150') in Zimbabwe, Transkei and the coastal districts of Natal; in south-east Kenya recorded down to 260–280 m (860–925') (Zimmerman *et al.* 1996); in Tanzania occurs down to 600 m (1980') in the East Usambaras; recorded in the Pugu Hills (south-west of Dar es Salaam) in May 1988 (Baker & Baker 1992).

HABITAT Nominate and *disruptans* breed in montane *Podocarpus* evergreen forest, where it inhabits undergrowth of ferns and mosses on slopes in damp areas, particularly along streams of the mistbelt. Usually breeds between 750 and 2500 m (2500–8250') but at 1800–2400 m (5940–7920') on Mt Moco, Angola, 1250–1750 m (4125–5775') in the Upemba highlands and down to 1200 m

(3960') in southern Malawi; *raineyi* ranges from 1370 to c.2300 m (4520–7590') while *otomitra* occurs from 1600 to 2500 m (5280–8250') throughout most of its range but exceptionally to c.3500 m (11,550') in bamboo forest on Mt Meru and down to c.900 m (2970') at Amani and in the Ngurus, at 900–1200 m (2970–3950'), exceptionally to 1830 m (6000'), in the East Usambaras, and 1050–1900 m (3465–6270') in the Udzungwa Mountains (Britton 1980, Zimmerman *et al.* 1996, Urban *et al.* 1997).

BEHAVIOUR Generally a shy or seldom-seen denizen of dense montane forests where it inhabits the darker areas of moist hollows, usually alone or in pairs. Considered to be crepuscular and often its presence is only betrayed by its song; usually more approachable in the early breeding season when singing birds defend territories. Flight usually swift and agile through the trees but rarely flies far. Spends long periods inactive in thick or tangled vegetation; forages on the ground, avidly searching the leaf-litter and moist soil by flicking aside fallen leaves and debris; may occasionally follow ant swarms. Feeds mostly on earthworms (especially when raising nestlings), also insects and their larvae, beetles, crickets, slugs and land molluscs, with small amounts of various seasonal wild fruits, e.g. berries (more in the north than south) taken from trees or on the ground.

BREEDING Season: January–May (Kenya), August–December (Tanzania), October–January (Malawi), September–December or January (Zimbabwe, Mozambique and South Africa). Nest: a deep cup-shaped structure made mostly of moss, twigs, dead leaves, root fibres and ferns, lined with fern roots, plant fibres and green moss, usually placed in the fork or along the branch of a small tree or sapling or in a bush or creeper against a tree-trunk, on a stump or in the crown of a tree fern, and up to 4 m (13') from the ground. Eggs: 2–3, turquoise-blue, either unmarked or with small reddish-brown spots or larger pale grey or mauve blotches. Incubation period 15 days. Fledging period 18–20 days, but young remain with parents for several successive months.

MOULT Very poorly known; adults moult primaries (but not secondaries, tail or body feathers) towards the end of the breeding period (January) in South Africa; others, possibly first-year birds, renew primaries, secondaries and tail feathers in April–May (Earlé & Oatley 1983).

MEASUREMENTS Wing, male 105–114, female 102–112; tarsus 32–38; *disruptans* wing, male 100–109.5, female 101–110; *otomitra* wing, male 105–116, female 105–113.5; *raineyi* wing 106–113.5; *chuka* wing, male 116–126, female 117–122; bill (culmen) male 21.5–25, female 20–25. Weight, male 44.5–64.5 g, female 48.5–76 g (Maclean 1988, Urban *et al.* 1997); in breeding pairs females are consistently heavier than males (Earlé & Oatley 1983).

REFERENCES Baker & Baker (1992), Britton (1980), Clancey (1955), Earlé & Oatley (1983), Maclean (1988), Newman (1983), Urban *et al.* (1997).

42 OBERLAENDER'S GROUND-THRUSH

Plate 14

Zoothera oberlaenderi

(Forest Ground-Thrush)

***Geocichla gurneyi oberlaenderi* Sassi, 1914, *Anz. Akad. Wiss. Wien, Math-Naturwiss.* 51: 310 – between Beni and Mawambi, north-eastern Congo.**

IDENTIFICATION 20 cm (8"). A small rich russet-brown *Zoothera* with an extremely restricted distribution, occurring in only a few forest localities in Central Africa where it remains little known. Has the entire head, face and nape rich or dark rufous-chestnut except for a dark smudge mark through the eye and a prominent broken white eye-ring. Upperparts similarly rich chestnut, becoming browner on wings and tail; broad white wing-bar on median coverts and smaller one on tips of greaters. Underparts progressively paler orange on upper belly and lower flanks. **Confusion species** Very similar to race *tanganjicae* of Abyssinian Ground-Thrush (39), to which it is closely related but slightly smaller in overall proportions and with different songs. Oberlaender's has entire head and face more rufous-orange, except for the diffuse black mark through the eye (interrupting the eye-ring) contrasting with the deeper rust of the orange-rufous mantle, back and scapulars. Black-eared Ground-Thrush (43) has prominent face-bars through the eye, across the cheeks and on the rear ear-coverts, and is usually duller both above and below. Orange Ground-Thrush (41), occurring well to the south and east of Oberlaender's, is similar to Black-eared but has browner upperparts and weaker face pattern. Crossley's Ground-Thrush (40) is slightly larger with contrasting dark or blackish cheeks and ear-coverts and browner mantle, back and rump.

Taxonomic note Previously considered a race of Orange Ground-Thrush and Abyssinian Ground-Thrush.

DESCRIPTION Sexes alike. **Adult** Forehead to nape, cheeks and ear-coverts deep or dark rufous-chestnut, slightly lighter on nape and sides of neck; broad white half eye-ring broken above and below by black smudge continuing onto cheeks; small patch of dark grey bare skin behind eye. Mantle, back and scapulars deep rufous or rusty orange-brown with pale olive-orange fringes to edges of scapulars and becoming brighter and more rufous on rump and uppertail-coverts. Tail bright or warm brown with rufous-brown on central feathers and bases to edges of all outer feathers. Wings much as in Abyssinian Ground-Thrush of race *tanganjicae*, with bold white spots on median coverts, greater coverts black overlain with olive and narrowly tipped white; flight feathers dark brown broadly edged pale rufous to orange-brown on primaries, more olive on secondaries and broadly on outerwebs of tertials. Underwing has whitish axillaries extending to bend of wing, becoming grey-brown on coverts and broad white band across base of secondaries and most primaries. Chin and throat to breast deep rufous-orange, paler on lower breast, flanks and belly; centre of belly, vent and undertail-coverts white. Bill black with paler base to lower mandible. Legs and feet pinkish-flesh to whitish. **Immature** Juvenile similar to adult but crown darker and nape mostly rufous; also crown to mantle has pale buff central shaft-streaks. Face dull rufous with dark patches from eye to cheeks and another on ear-coverts; narrow black submoustachial. Underparts as adult or slightly paler orange on breast and flanks, heavily mottled or spotted with dark or blackish-brown on breast and upper belly; rest of underparts white. Bill dark horn-brown. Legs and feet creamy (Urban *et al.* 1997).

GEOGRAPHICAL VARIATION None. Monotypic.

VOICE Not well known. Song a loud caroling series of typical mellow thrush phrases running up and down scale, fluty or ringing in tone, at medium to slow or unhurried pace (A. Twinonmujuni pers. comm.), often beginning with a three-note piping *tewee pip-pip-pip...* before running into main series of phrases, some of which sound slightly off-key and as if whistled by a human; usually no repetition of phrases but gives some similar notes in quick succession. Similar in quality to song of race *tanganjicae* of Abyssinian Ground-Thrush; also recalls tone and timbre of Blackbird (111) and Mistle Thrush (126) in Europe. Sings in trees at mid-height (7–10 m/21–33'). Song period usually fairly short, immediately before breeding season. Not known to respond to taped play-back of other species' songs.

STATUS AND DISTRIBUTION Very scarce; in mid-1980s it was classified as threatened and feared to be under some threat due to the depletion and degradation of its forest habitats (Collar & Stuart 1985); now considered Near-Threatened (Collar *et al.* 1994). Discontinuous in north-east Zaire from the Ituri Forest, Bondo-Mabe, Kamituga area, southern Kivu and Semliki Valley (which forms the border with Uganda) to the Bwamba and Bwindi (Impenetrable) forests, south-west Uganda.

MOVEMENTS Sedentary.

HABITAT Forests, mostly those containing tall stands of ironwood *Cyanometra alexandri*, at 700–1300 m (2310–4230') in the Ituri Forest, 1080–1420 m (3565–4686') in Kivu and to c.1616 m (5330') in the Bwindi Forest. Habitat destruction is a potential threat, and it may no longer occur in Bwamba Forest (which is now largely degraded or destroyed); forest clearance is also taking place around Kamituga (southern Kivu) (Collar & Stuart 1985, Collar & Andrew 1988).

BEHAVIOUR Alone or in pairs; lives on the forest floor in stands of tall trees, particularly ironwoods; found in more open areas, appearing to avoid dense forest and tangled undergrowth. Forages on the ground and feeds on insects and their larvae, also slugs.

BREEDING Virtually unknown; only one nest has ever been found (May–June 1998 in Bwindi Forest, Uganda, but later destroyed by squirrels); no eggs have ever been found; breeding season is most probably from the end of the dry season into the start of the rainy season. The nest in 1998 was built of dry grasses, vegetation strips and plant fibres (A. Twinomujuni pers. comm.). Fledglings

have been seen in the Itombwe Mountains, eastern Zaire, in March and September.

MOULT No information.

MEASUREMENTS Wing, male 95–103, female 95–102; tarsus 27–30; bill (culmen) male 19–22, female 18–21. Weight 41–48 g (Prigogine 1985, Urban *et al.* 1997).

REFERENCES Collar & Andrew (1988), Collar & Stuart (1985), Keith (1968), Keith & Garrett (1994), Urban *et al.* (1997).

43 BLACK-EARED GROUND-THRUSH   Plate 15
Zoothera cameronensis
Geocichla cameronensis Sharpe, 1905, *Ibis* (8)5: 472 – Efulen, Cameroon.

IDENTIFICATION 16.5–18 cm (6½–7″). A rare or extremely scarce ground-thrush of which very little is known, with a restricted range in West and Central Africa. Away from well-watched study sites most records are of trapped birds; appears to be mostly silent and the song is entirely unknown. Small with a short tail, short rounded wings and a heavy-looking bill; distinctive face pattern of broad dark lateral bands; russet-brown head, face and upperparts; orange to rust-orange below with two broad white wing-bars (which can show well in flight). **Confusion species** Similar to Crossley's Ground-Thrush (40) but differs on smaller size, shorter bill and face pattern: all dark brown or blackish cheeks and ear-coverts in Crossley's. Oberlaender's Ground-Thrush (42) also lacks the prominent face pattern and has the head and face (and rest of upperparts) more uniform deep or rich chestnut-brown with a broad broken white eye-ring; underparts also brighter or plainer orange, not tinged chestnut. Birds of race *graueri*, which are generally duller in tone than the nominate, are similar to Grey Ground-Thrush (44), especially race *batesi* with which it appears to overlap in north-east Zaire and western Uganda; *graueri* is generally dull greyish-brown on the forehead to nape, lacks any rich or russet-brown tones on the upperparts (except the tail), has a pale orange face (broken by two broad black bars) and dull orange breast to upper belly and flanks.

Taxonomic note 1: The race *graueri* was originally described as a race of Grey Ground-Thrush (44) under the name *Geocichla princei graueri*. Prigogine (1965) showed that the subspecies was more closely allied to Black-eared Ground-Thrush and thus it became *Z. c. graueri*. However, some authorities consider that this and several other African thrushes are more appropriate to *Turdus*, in which case it would need to be renamed *T. c. prigoginei* (Hall 1966) since *graueri* is preoccupied within the Olive Thrush complex by *T. olivaceus graueri*.

Taxonomic note 2: The race *kibalensis* (Kibale or Prigogine's Ground-Thrush) from Kibale Forest, western Uganda, was described (Prigogine 1978) from two specimens taken in 1966 originally

attributed to the race *batesi* of Grey Ground-Thrush (Friedmann & Williams 1968). Payne (1980) and Urban *et al.* (1997) questioned the species status of *kibalensis* and thought it might represent a hybrid of Black-eared and Grey Ground-Thrushes. Dowsett and Dowsett-Lemaire (1993) considered the specimens referable to Black-eared or else as possibly 'subspecifically distinct'. It is surprising that no further records have come to light in an area relatively well surveyed, unless it was a population on the edge of extinction; *Z. kibalensis* was classed as Indeterminate (Collar & Stuart 1985) and may be threatened by loss of mature forest in Kibale. However, we agree that the differences of plumage and size are no greater than those between *graueri* and nominate birds. Clement (1999a) discussed *kibalensis* as a race of Black-eared and the similarities of *Z. c. graueri* and *Z. p. batesi* (Grey Ground-Thrush) and concluded that until more information is forthcoming the affinities of both *graueri* and *batesi* are best regarded as indeterminate.

DESCRIPTION Sexes alike but separable. **Adult male** Forehead to crown and upper nape brown or dark brown; sides of lower forehead and lores pale peachy-orange; nape orange-brown becoming more orange on sides of neck. Mantle and back rich or deep rust-brown extending to inner scapulars and tertials; rump and uppertail-coverts heavier or deeper rust-brown. Tail brown but edges to bases (especially central pair) deeper or more rufous-brown. Lesser coverts as scapulars; median coverts black with large white spot at tips, greaters black or blackish-brown with large white spots at tips of outers (slightly duller in females), inners lack white spots and have broad rich or rufous-brown edges and lighter olive-brown tips; alula brown or dark brown and primary coverts dark or blackish-brown; flight feathers brown to dark brown but edges to outer 3–4 primaries pale rufous becoming deeper or richer brown on edges to secondaries. Lesser underwing coverts to bend of wing dark grey tipped white, axillaries to median and greater coverts white tipped black in male and browner in female, bases to secondaries and inner primaries white forming a broad white underwing-bar in flight. Lores to submoustachials, chin and throat pale peachy-orange; thin dark brown malar stripe; eye-ring buffish, broken above and below by black continuing across cheeks (to lower fore ear-coverts) and ear-coverts pale orange or orange-buff with broad black border and lower edge to rear of ear-coverts, forming two dark stripes across face. Lower throat, sides of neck and breast bright or deep orange or tinged rust-orange, slightly paler or whiter on centre of lower belly and olive or olive-brown on lower flanks; undertail-coverts off-white or faintly tipped orange. Bill large and heavy, black; may be paler at base of lower mandible. Legs and feet pale or whitish-pink, possibly white in some. **Adult female** Separable from male by uniformly paler rust-brown on head and upperparts and pale rufous on lower rump to sides of base of tail. Spots at tips of coverts less distinctly white, contrasting less against browner-black greater coverts. Face also much paler or buffish. **Immature** Juvenile and first-year bird similar to adult but have pale yellowish or orange-buff central shaft-streaks on forehead, crown, nape, upper mantle and scapulars; the white tips to median and greater coverts (present in nestling feathers) are finely edged with orange-buff; tips to inner medians and inner greaters entirely orange-buff. Orange on lower throat, breast and flanks flecked and mottled with brown; undertail-coverts pale or orange-rufous.

GEOGRAPHICAL VARIATION Three races; variation not well marked.

Race *graueri* is slightly darker or greyer (especially on forehead to nape) and less reddish on upperparts (except tail) than nominate, may show less white on tips of greater coverts (especially in females) and is duller rufous-orange on breast, upper belly and flanks, usually lacking any olive on flanks; centre of belly, vent and undertail-coverts white, or undertail-coverts may be buffish-white. In hand (or at close range) should show sparse streaks on breast, but on museum specimens these are very fine or almost absent. Face is like nominate but may have bolder black streaks through eye, on cheeks and at rear of ear-coverts on otherwise pale whitish face washed pale orange. Immature similar to nominate but forehead and crown dark brown tinged grey and with pale central shafts; mantle and back have rufous-buff central shaft-streaks; underparts pale rufous mottled with dark brown spots on breast; belly white but flanks rufous.

Race *kibalensis* slightly larger than the other two and has a well-defined face pattern on a pale buffish-brown ground colour; bare skin behind eye dark grey; crown and upperparts more rufous and nape slightly paler; throat, breast and flanks bright orange and centre of belly to undertail-coverts white; base of bill comparatively flat or depressed and base of lower mandible grey.

VOICE Mostly silent; has a thin or high-pitched *seep* in flight and this may be used as a contact note. Birds in the hand have given a more buzzing *srreeep* variation of this call on being released. Song unknown.

STATUS AND DISTRIBUTION Rare or very scarce.

Z. c. cameronensis Southern Cameroon, discontinuously from Korup National Park and the western Bakossi Mountains, Mt Cameroon, and the coastal forests at Efulen, Kribi, Ndian, Campo and Grand Batange, also in north-east Gabon. Hall & Moreau (1970) showed two specimens from southern Nigeria; these are now considered to have been in error.

Z. c. graueri Ituri Forest in north-east Zaire, and Budongo and Bugoma forests, western Uganda.

Z. c. kibalensis Kibale Forest, south-west Uganda; known only from 2 adult males collected at 1525 m (5032′) in December 1966.

MOVEMENTS Sedentary.

HABITAT Dense undergrowth of lowland and temperate forest, up to 1700 m (5610′) in Zaire. In Uganda known to occur in low herbaceous ground vegetation in pristine (i.e. unlogged) mature forests of ironwood and mahogany.

BEHAVIOUR Relatively unknown; extremely scarce and very secretive; possibly (and easily) overlooked but rarely seen even by those conducting surveys and most recent records are of birds trapped. Recent records from well-watched study sites suggest that birds on territory may become approachable by habituation. Spends long periods foraging on the ground amongst low-growing plants and turning over the leaf-litter. Flight usually low (within 2 m/6′ of the ground) and fairly fast. Food insects including beetles, ants and cockroaches, also small snails.

BREEDING Unknown; nest and eggs undescribed. Probably nests at the end of the dry season and in the long rains; females in Zaire and Uganda in breeding condition in May and June, fledglings in May, females on eggs in September and October (J. Lindsell pers. comm.); in Gabon males in breeding condition in December to January and immature in June (Urban *et al.* 1997).

MOULT No information.

MEASUREMENTS Wing, male 94–102, female 96–100; tarsus, male 27–29, female 26–28; bill, male 18–20, female 15.5–19; *graueri* male 103–106, female 96–102; tarsus 27.5–30.5; bill, male 18.5–20, female 17.5–18.5; *kibalensis* male 109 and 112; tarsus 30.5 and 33; bill 21. Weight 42–47 g; *graueri* 45–52 g (Prigogine 1978, Urban *et al.* 1997).

REFERENCES Clement (1999a), Collar & Stuart (1985), Dowsett & Dowsett-Lemaire (1993), Friedmann & Williams (1968), Hall (1966), Hall & Moreau (1970), Payne (1980), Prigogine (1965, 1978, 1985), Urban *et al.* (1997).

44 GREY GROUND-THRUSH *Zoothera princei* **Plate 15**

Chamaetylas princei Sharpe, 1873, *Proc. Zool. Soc. London*: 625 – Denkera (interior of Fantee).

IDENTIFICATION Male 21–22 cm; female 19–19.5 (7½–8½″). A little known and rarely seen *Zoothera* from the forests of West and Central Africa. Identified by the unspotted underparts and blackish patches on an otherwise off-white face, grey-brown crown to back becoming rich brown on the rest of the upperparts, and a double wing-bar of white spots; the breast is dull greyish-olive overlying paler orange ground colour (in some the breast is pale orange) with fairly long thin dark streaks on the upper breast. The bill is short but appears heavy and slightly arched; the wings have a short primary projection. Central African birds are slightly darker above and less heavily streaked on the breast. **Confusion species** Most closely resembles Black-eared Ground-Thrush (43) with which it shares the same facial markings, but Black-eared has richer or more russet-brown upperparts and orange below. Birds of the race *batesi* from Cameroon, Zaire and western Uganda are extremely similar and possibly identical to (and therefore synonymous with) the race *graueri* of Black-eared (see note below) but separable by its tawny-orange throat to lower breast and flanks and peachy-buff facial ground colour; *graueri* also has streaks on the throat and centre of the upper breast, and an all-dark bill. Spotted Ground-Thrush (45) is initially similar but paler brown above and heavily spotted below. Orange Ground-Thrush (41) has similar upper body but differs on face pattern and underpart coloration.

Taxonomic note Clement (1999a) discussed the similarities of the races *Z. p. batesi* and *Z. c. graueri* (Black-eared Ground-Thrush) and concluded that until more information is forthcoming their relationship is best regarded as indeterminate.

DESCRIPTION Sexes alike. **Adult** Forehead to nape and mantle grey-brown tinged with olive, becoming browner on lower back and scapulars; rump and uppertail-coverts rich or rufous-brown. Tail brown or deep brown but edges to base of tail also rich or rufous-brown, with white tips to outermost feathers (unlikely to be seen in field). Lesser coverts as scapulars, median coverts dark or blackish-brown broadly tipped white, greaters similar but less broadly tipped white and outers have pale or pale brown edges becoming slightly darker on inner greaters; alula pale or milk chocolate-brown, primary coverts dark brown; flight feathers dark brown broadly edged pale, light or tawny-brown becoming slightly darker on inner secondaries; tertials brown or olive-brown on outerwebs, slightly darker on innerwebs. Underwing has axillaries and lesser coverts to bend of the wing white, tips of axillaries and median and greater underwing-coverts dark grey or grey-brown; bases to secondaries and primaries (except outer two) white. Lores to eye and submoustachial pale buff or dull whitish; eye-ring dull grey or pinkish, with small

patch of bare skin behind eye greyish-flesh; upper and lower eyelid to cheeks a broad dark brown or blackish streak, hind ear-coverts pale buffish flecked finely with greyish tips, and rear edge to ear-coverts broadly black and may extend narrowly along lower edge of ear-coverts. Narrow but prominent dark brown malar stripe from base of lower mandible. Chin and throat pale or whitish-buff becoming dull greyish-olive on sides of neck to breast, and with a few narrow, sparsely distributed blackish-brown streaks on centre of upper breast; lower breast unstreaked pale or dull olive overlying pale orange ground colour (breast and flanks sometimes tinged pale orange to light tawny); belly and undertail-coverts whiter or whitish tinged with greyish or pale orange. Bill short and black; base to lower mandible pale pinkish-horn or whitish (male) or darker, more uniform (female). Legs and feet dull pinkish-flesh or -grey, dusky-brown on forward edge. **Immature** Similar to adult including face pattern, but browner and finely streaked with pale buff shaft-streaks on crown to lower back and scapulars, and dull orange-buff shafts and paler orange-buff or rust-orange tips to median and greater coverts; tips to greater coverts sometimes as white as in adult. Lores and chin pale buff, lower throat and upper breast dark or rufous-brownish spotted with dark brown becoming dull orange or orange-rufous on rest of underparts.

GEOGRAPHICAL VARIATION Two races; variation not well marked. Race *batesi* very similar to nominate in the field but, on average, more olive-brown on hindcrown to mantle, scapulars and upper back; rump, uppertail-coverts and tail are as nominate. Lower throat is, on average, duller or brownish-buff overlying pale orange becoming light greyish-brown overlying pale orange (or washed with olive) on breast, which has very few indistinct dark streaks (may be absent in most individuals); flanks are greyish tinged brown, becoming paler on centre of belly; undertail-coverts dingy or off-white (possibly paler in female). Bill as nominate. Legs and feet whitish-horn. Immature very similar to nominate but slightly paler brown on head, belly buffish-white.

VOICE Contact note between pairs is a long, high-pitched, rolling trill *tsssrrr* (Urban *et al.* 1997). Song unknown.

STATUS AND DISTRIBUTION Rare to extremely rare (Central Africa); locally common (West Africa).

Z. p. princei Discontinuously in a few forest localities in extreme eastern Sierra Leone (Gola Forest), Liberia (Wologizi Mountains east to Mt Nimba and the Douobe River and south to Sapo National Park), Ivory Coast (Tai National Park, Yapo Forest north to Lamto and Comoe National Park) and possibly also southern Ghana (two 19th-century records only).

Z. p. batesi Discontinuously in southern Cameroon (Korup National Park by one record, Mt Kupe, Efulen, Etembo, Bipindi, Kribi, Bitye and inland to Sangmelima and Yokadouma) to Lobaye prefecture, extreme south-west Central African Republic (Carroll 1988) and in north-east Gabon; Ituri Forest in north-east Zaire; western Uganda in Bugoma, Budongo and Bwamba forests (Dranzoa 1995) but probably no more than six records, virtually all of birds collected (Clement 1999a).

Serle (1957) documented a brief sighting in eastern Nigeria (Umuagwu) in August 1953 but was unable to confirm the record; as no further sightings have been made it is treated as unconfirmed by Elgood *et al.* (1994).

MOVEMENTS Mostly sedentary, but occurrences outside the known range either relate to new (i.e. previously unknown) localities or to seasonal movements which are at present very poorly known or understood in this extremely scarce and secretive bird.

HABITAT Thick or dense undergrowth and ground vegetation of lowland mixed evergreen forests, especially *Cyanometra*, up to 550 m (1815′) on Mt Nimba, Liberia, and to 610 m (2010′) in Cameroon.

BEHAVIOUR Extremely shy and secretive, a rare (and rarely seen) resident of tropical forests; easily disturbed, running rapidly through vegetation or taking flight at the first sign of an intruder. Usually occurs in pairs. Forages on the ground where it keeps to thick cover and searches through leaf-lit-

ter and decaying vegetation and digs into moss, soft earth and rotting wood; has been recorded as part of mixed-species flocks feeding at ant swarms. Feeds on insects, large grasshoppers, beetles, millipedes, larvae, spiders, worms and small snails; also known to take small frogs.

BREEDING Season: June–August (Liberia, Nigeria and Zaire), October–April (Gabon). Nest: a large or bulky cup of twigs, dead leaves and plant fibres lined fine roots, usually placed in the fork of a branch or trunk of small tree or on top of a bunch of dead leaves. Eggs: 1–3, turquoise-blue to bright green with lilac blotches and fine reddish-brown spots or speckles. Incubation by female only, but male brings food to nest; young fledge at c.12 days (Brosset & Erard 1986, Urban *et al.* 1997).

MOULT Birds examined in the hand in Liberia were in wing moult in December and January; adult in fresh plumage in April.

MEASUREMENTS (n=13) Wing, male 107–117, female 106–112; tarsus, male 31–35, female 32–35; bill, male (culmen) 16–17.5, (to skull) 19–24, female (culmen) 14–17, (to skull) 19–21; *batesi* (n=9) wing, male 102–112, female 101–111; tarsus 28–33; bill, male (culmen) 16–17, (to skull) 20–23, female (culmen) 14–17 (to skull) 17–22. Weight (n=16) 59–83 g (Urban *et al.* 1997).

REFERENCES Allport *et al.* (1989), Brosset & Erard (1986), Carroll (1988), Clement (1999a), Dranzoa (1995), Gatter (1997), Progogine (1978, 1985), Serle (1957), Urban *et al.* (1997).

45 SPOTTED GROUND-THRUSH *Zoothera guttata* Plate 16

Turdus guttatus Vigors, 1831, *Proc. Zool. Soc. London*: 92 – Algoa Bay, Africa [= Durban, Natal, Smith (1839) *Ill. Zool. South Africa, Aves* 2(8), pl. 39].

Taxonomic note Previously known as *Turdus fischeri*.

IDENTIFICATION 22–23 cm (8¾–9″). A large thrush with a discontinuous range in the coastal forests of East Africa, Malawi and eastern Cape Province of South Africa with indications of populations elsewhere in Africa from single specimens. Although neither shy nor particularly uncommon, it is an elusive, easily overlooked ground-dwelling bird of shaded forests (drier habitat on migration), very distinctive with olive-brown upperparts, two broad wing-bars, well marked face pattern and heavily spotted underparts. **Confusion species** Groundscraper Thrush (96) has a similar face pattern but has grey upperparts, no wing-bars and more upright gait and does not enter deep forest. Spotted Morning Warbler *Cichladusa guttata* from East Africa is smaller, lacks any face pattern or wing-bars and has a rounded rufous tail.

DESCRIPTION Sexes alike. **Adult** Forehead to crown and nape olive-brown becoming slightly paler or more olive on mantle, back, scapulars, rump and uppertail-coverts (in fresh plumage and good light may show faint rufous tinge). Tail simi-

lar or slightly warmer olive-brown at base and on central pair; most outers browner with broad white wedge and central shaft to innerweb of outermost feather (most noticeable in flight) and small spots (declining in size inwardly) at tips of next two inners (not always present). Lesser coverts as scapulars but tips may be paler or warm buffish-brown, median coverts white, greater coverts dark or blackish-brown edged olive-brown and broadly tipped white, forming two wing-bars, that on greaters extending across wing; alula and primary coverts dark brown, latter edged olive-brown; flight feathers and tertials dark brown edged paler or light olive-brown on inner primaries and scapulars. Underwing has coverts blackish-brown tipped white, axillaries white with olive-brown tips, broad white bases to all secondaries and all, except outermost two, primaries, showing as broad wing-bar in flight. Lores off-white merging with broad white eye-ring (broken by black line above and below eye extending across cheeks), small patch of bare skin behind eye variable from

off-white to pinkish- or purplish-blue, ear-coverts pale creamy except broad black streak on rear edge (upper part may be as brown as crown); sides of neck pale yellowish-buff finely spotted darker. Sides of chin and throat white or off-white broken by long thin blackish submoustachial stripe, centre of chin and throat white finely spotted with black; rest of underparts white, except for creamy or creamy-buff tinge to sides of breast and upper flanks, heavily spotted with black on breast and flanks; spots on breast may form rows whilst those on upper belly and rear flanks slightly smaller and may form bars; centre of belly and rest of underparts pure white. Bill dark or blackish-horn, with pale yellowish or pink base to lower mandible. Legs and feet bright pink or pale flesh. In fresh plumage slight rufous tinge to crown and upperparts, and buff to brownish-buff tips to median and greater coverts and edges and tips of tertials. **Immature** Juvenile similar to adult but generally slightly darker and spotted with pale buff on crown and pale buff and rust-orange on lower nape and mantle; sides of crown and cheeks rust-brown; wing-coverts have rufous or orange-buff central shaft and rust-orange tips; underparts buffier with denser, smaller blackish spots. First-year bird slightly more rufous on upperparts; probably inseparable from July. Note that presence or absence of buff or brownish-buff tips to greater coverts and tertials is not always indicative of age. **GEOGRAPHICAL VARIATION** Five races; variation weak. Race *fischeri* slightly smaller than nominate and paler or more olive and, on average, less rufous on upperparts; spots on breast and flanks smaller and sparser. On average also shows a greater area of pale pinkish or pinkish-grey at base of lower mandible and grey-brown towards tip. Race *belcheri* very like nominate but has belly and flanks whiter and lacks any buff; spots more heavily black. The single specimen of race *lippensi* has upperparts olive-grey. The single specimen (a first-year female) of *maxis* is darker or browner above than other races with the greater covert tips individually spotted with buff, declining inwardly in size; spots on breast and flanks more heavily pronounced and undertail-coverts orange-buff; wings also shorter than other races.
VOICE Generally silent but may give a soft or very high-pitched (almost inaudible), thin *tsee-tsee* or *tree-troo*, or a slightly louder but very short *psssss*, occasionally becoming a louder or more penetrating note. Foraging pairs often utter a similar note or a more sibilant *spspspppppp*. Wintering birds in Kenya give a series of *tswee* notes (Bennun 1987), possibly as a contact call. Song a pleasant and melodious series of up to 6 short, whistled phrases interspersed with brief pauses, *swee-toot-toodle, pree-pree-swee, swee-toot-toodle* (Maclean 1988), with some fluty notes *tru-whu-whee-er* included. Non-breeding birds (*fischeri*) in eastern Kenya give a slightly different version, possibly subsong, consisting of a series of dry, rather unmusical, almost unbroken notes *tcheew tu tu wee-u tuwi* or a more rolling *teerrlu toorrli teerrlu*. Sings from secluded perch in tall tree, usually within the lower canopy but occasionally at some height, in the depths of the forest; most song given early dawn and at dusk.
STATUS AND DISTRIBUTION Fairly common to uncommon (easily overlooked). Due to its wide and disjunct range consisting of small or indeterminate populations, habitat destruction and poor breeding success it is considered Endangered by Collar *et al.* (1994).
Z. g. maxis Lotti Forest, Imatong Mountains, southern Sudan, where known from a single specimen (first-year female) taken at 1250 m (4125') in October 1979 (Nikolaus 1982).
Z. g. fischeri Breeding area poorly known but recent evidence (Holsten *et al.* 1991) indicates southern Tanzania (Rondo Plateau and the Litipo Forest) and probably also northern Mozambique (Collar *et al.* 1994). In non-breeding season moves north to the coastal forests of south-east Kenya north to about Lamu (but principally Arabuko-Sokoke Forest region including Gede ruins and the Shimba Hills), and north-east Tanzania south to Pangani and the Pugu Hills.
Z. g. lippensi Upemba National Park, Zaire, where known from a single specimen taken at 1750 m (5775') in October 1973 (Benson & Benson 1975, Prigogine & Louette 1984).
Z. g. belcheri Malawi, where a small resident population of about 30–40 pairs is restricted to four submontane forests at 1200–1500 m (3960–4950') on Mt Chiradzulu, Mt Soche, Mt Thyolo and Mt Mulanje east of the Rift Valley (Collar & Stuart 1985).
Z. g. guttata Discontinuously through eastern Cape Province, Transkei from East London to KwaZulu-Natal, South Africa, with small populations in isolated forests at Dlinza, Entumeni and Ngoye forests and in the Oribi Gorge, southern Natal; in the non-breeding season to north-east of Durban to about Lake St Lucia but may also extend into southern Mozambique (Collar & Stuart 1985, Collar *et al.* 1994). Clancey (1993) suggested that birds in the north of this range, in northern KwaZulu-Natal, were more closely related to *belcheri*, but an analysis of specimens from across the range of *guttata* in South Africa by Harebottle *et al.* (1997) found no evidence to support this idea.
MOVEMENTS Partial migrant. Movements of nominate *guttata* not well understood but birds from breeding areas in the eastern Cape area move north into Natal and Zululand from April to September; some remain in Zululand during the winter months. Similarly most records of *fischeri* for the coastal forests of south-east Kenya are from late March to late November (Britton 1980), i.e. coinciding with the rainy season, mostly May to October, exceptionally (once) to mid-December; a passage migrant through the Pugu Hills (southwest of Dar es Salaam) in May. Migrates at night with many found dead from collisions with buildings and towers (Ginn *et al.* 1989, Maclean 1988).
HABITAT Breeds in coastal and lowland evergreen forests, preferring areas of thick canopy cover, shaded undergrowth and extensive patches of open leaf-litter or ground vegetation often with thicker, denser areas of undergrowth and vine

creepers at mid-height; usually found at mid- to low levels in humid forests, mostly in damp hollows or depressions and in scrub and rank vegetation along rivers and streams in forests. In Zululand in winter occurs in coastal forest on dunes, and in south-east Kenya drier *Brachystegia* forests. On migration occurs in moist bush, scrubland and wooded thickets.

BEHAVIOUR A retiring and inconspicuous, overlooked, but not necessarily always shy bird. Usually alone or in pairs; occasionally in loose, possibly family, groups. In south-east Kenya wintering birds, often in pairs, are known to establish small territories and return to the same area in subsequent years (Bennun 1987). Spends most of its time foraging low down in vegetation or in leaf-litter on the forest floor in shade beneath tall shrubs and bushes. Feeds in typical thrush manner by actively searching through deep leaf-litter and digging into rotting vegetation. Most activity is early morning and late evening but possibly intermittent throughout the day. Spends long periods on the ground standing motionless and well camouflaged, but if disturbed flies off at speed with a rapid, twisting escape flight before landing on a low branch. Food is mostly insects taken on the ground, particularly ants, termites and millipedes, also land molluscs and other invertebrates and their larvae, and seasonally available wild fruit and berries, particularly those of the snake lily *Scadoxus membranaceus*.

BREEDING Season: October to January; possibly later for *maxis*. Nest: a large cup-shaped structure of grass, leaves, roots, twigs, moss and mud, lined with fine grasses and small rootlets; placed up to 10 m (33') (usually much lower, 3 m/10') from the ground in a fork, against the trunk of a small tree or bush, on a horizontal branch or amongst thick bundles of creepers. Eggs: 2–3, pale greenish-blue heavily spotted and blotched with dark reddish and greenish-brown.

MOULT Post-breeding moult of adults completed in March–April; wing moult (of *fischeri*) complete by July, and presumably undergoes moult in non-breeding areas, though apparently variable, as some birds are in fresh flight feathers by early May whilst others still moulting inner secondaries.

MEASUREMENTS Wing, male 114–125, female 110–120; tarsus, male 30–33.5, female 31–34; bill (culmen) 23–26; *fischeri* wing, male 108–118, female 112–116; tarsus 28–32; bill 21–24; *belcheri* wing 112–119; *lippensi* wing 112; tarsus 30; bill 24; *maxis* wing 108; tarsus 31; bill (culmen) 24. Weight 45–65 g (Keith & Twomey 1968, Maclean 1988); *guttata* 72–78 g (Prigogine 1985, Urban *et al.* 1997).

REFERENCES Bennun (1987), Britton (1980), Clancey (1993), Collar & Stuart (1985), Collar *et al.* (1994), Ginn *et al.* (1989), Harebottle *et al.* (1997), Holsten *et al.* (1991), Keith & Twomey (1968), Maclean (1988), Nikolaus (1982), Prigogine & Louette (1984), Urban *et al.* (1997).

46 SPOT-WINGED THRUSH *Zoothera spiloptera*   Plate 16
(Spotted-winged Thrush, Spotted-winged Ground-Thrush)
Oreocincla spiloptera Blyth, 1847, *J. Asiat. Soc. Bengal* 16: 142 – Ceylon.

IDENTIFICATION 21–23 cm (8¼–9″). A shy endemic of the forested hills of Sri Lanka and most easily found when singing males are on territory. Distinguished by the olive-brown upperparts, two broad white wing-bars, black-spotted underparts, and whitish face with two dark stripes below the eye and at the rear ear-coverts. Juveniles quickly attain the face pattern of the adult. **Confusion species** Somewhat similar female Pied Thrush (31) is distinguished by its long whitish supercilium, white tips to the outer tail feathers, bars (not spots) on the flanks, and lack of facial pattern.

DESCRIPTION Sexes alike. Face generally duller or greyer in female. **Adult** Forehead to crown, nape, mantle and scapulars olive-brown becoming browner across lower back, rump and uppertail-coverts. Tail warm brown or tinged olive at base and edges of all outers. Lesser coverts as scapulars but outer 1–2 may show pale or whitish tips, median coverts dark or blackish-brown tipped white (some inners may lack white tip), greaters the same but also edged olive-brown; white tips to both median and greaters form two broad wing-bars; alula brown, primary coverts dark brown; flight feathers brown but all primaries broadly edged paler or light brown, secondaries edged

darker or more olive-brown, tertials almost uniform warm brown. Lores to eye pale or whitish; broad whitish submoustachial; finely barred darker or blackish and broken (or disjointed) malar stripe; broad vertical dark brown stripe from below eye to sides of throat; eye-ring whitish; ear-coverts whitish with blackish rear edge and white tips to rear of border on sides of neck. Chin and throat white or whitish as are rest of underparts but sides of lower throat, breast, belly and flanks heavily spotted with widely spaced black fan-shaped spots (those on belly and flanks usually smaller than on breast); sides of breast and flanks may also be washed with grey or latter with olive-brown; vent to undertail-coverts unspotted white. Bill blackish-horn, slightly paler at base of lower mandible. Legs and feet dark bluish-grey or greyish-flesh. **Immature** Juvenile has forehead to crown and nape brown, becoming warmer or rich brown on mantle, back and scapulars with darker or earth-brown central streaks and rufous-brown on rump and uppertail-coverts; wings and tail as adult but median and some inner greater coverts tipped light orange-buff. Face much buffier or orange-buff, cheek-patch and rear of ear-coverts blacker. Underparts light or pale orange-buff mottled or spotted darker with brown or dark brown tips. Bill brown with yellowish base.

GEOGRAPHICAL VARIATION None. Monotypic.

VOICE Contact note is a very soft, almost inaudible grasshopper-like *tzseee*, and alarm is a weak or feeble single chirping note. Song a rich, varied and sweet-toned series of short whistled phrases, including several resembling those given by humans. Usually delivered from a secluded perch in the lower branches of a tree or dense thicket, mostly in the early morning and just before dusk. Singing males on territory frequently imitate the songs of others (K. Weerakoon pers. comm.).

STATUS AND DISTRIBUTION Uncommon or locally common; easily overlooked especially when not singing. Considered Near-threatened by Collar *et al.* (1994) and Vulnerable by Hoffmann (1998) on the limited geographic range and the threats to forests from logging. Endemic to Sri Lanka, mostly the foothills of the wet zone of the central and south up to about 1800 m (c.6000'), with scattered populations in the dry zone.

MOVEMENTS Sedentary.

HABITAT Undergrowth and bamboo clumps in dense rainforests (including selectively logged forests) up to 2200 m (7260'), but mostly between 450 and 1500 m (1485–4950'), and in scattered drier woodland; also occurs along forest edges in cardamom jungles, cacao plantations and secondary scrub (Jones *et al.* 1998).

BEHAVIOUR Usually solitary and generally shy and inconspicuous, keeping well hidden in thick vegetation, but is also inquisitive and can be enticed into view by a whistled imitation of its song. May occasionally venture into the open at dusk along forest tracks. Spends most of its time foraging low down or on the ground where it vigorously searches through decaying vegetation and piles of leaf-litter; also forages in shrubs and bushes for invertebrates and berries. When disturbed or alarmed runs rapidly through the undergrowth. Food is poorly known but mostly insects, including spiders, moths, grasshoppers and their larvae, also earthworms together with fallen fruit e.g. wild breadfruit *Artocarpus nobilis*, and some berries.

BREEDING Season: February to December but mainly March to early May, and August to December or January in the north. Nest: a large loose cup of green moss, dead leaves and small twigs, lined with small fern fronds, moss, rootlets and fine hair or other fibres and generally recognisable by large scraps of material hanging loosely below the nest; usually placed up to 3 m (10') in the fork of a sapling or small forest undergrowth tree or in the crown of a tree-fern, occasionally on tops of tea bushes or on a ledge of a moss-covered rock, occasionally on the ground amongst the roots of a large tree. Eggs: 2–3, pale buff or pale bluish-green and densely covered with flecks, spots or blotches of lilac and reddish-brown. Incubation possibly by both parents; care of young by both birds. At least two broods.

MOULT No information.

MEASUREMENTS Wing (n=22), male 92–104, female 93–96; tarsus 29–34; bill (culmen) 17–20.5, (to skull) 22–23. Weight 70 g.

REFERENCES Hoffmann (1998), Jones *et al.* (1998).

---

47 SUNDA THRUSH *Zoothera andromedae*   Plate 19
(Andromeda Thrush, Sunda Ground-Thrush)

Myiothera andromedae Temminck, 1826, *Pl. Col.* livr. 66, pl. 392 – Java and Sumatra.

IDENTIFICATION 23.5–25 cm (9¼–10″). A shy and retiring thrush of lowland forests of Sumatra, the Lesser Sundas and montane forests on Java and several islands in the Philippines. Forages for long periods on the ground in leaf-litter and only rarely ventures into the open. Grey above, darker on wings and tail, with dark scales; the dark face is streaked whitish, the breast pale grey and flanks boldly marked with black chevrons. Has a large bill and appears large-headed. **Confusion species** Lack of a chestnut cap and white wing-bars separates Sunda from the smaller Chestnut-capped Thrush (28); male Siberian Thrush (36) is much darker grey above and below and has a long white supercilium; Horsfield's Thrush (52) on Lombok and Java is brown or golden-brown, scaled darker on both upper- and underparts.

DESCRIPTION Sexes alike. Female may be slightly browner-grey on the upperparts. **Adult** Entire upperparts from forehead and crown to uppertail-coverts slate-grey but tips to scapulars, lower mantle, back and upper rump slightly darker or blackish creating a partially scaled appearance. Tail dark brown but central pair tinged grey-brown and outer feathers brown. Lesser coverts as scapulars, median and greater coverts blackish but fringed dark slate grey-brown, greater coverts also broadly edged dark slate-grey; alula, primary coverts and flight feathers dark brown; longest alula projects beyond primary coverts. Underwing has lesser coverts to bend of wing white; axillaries, median and greater coverts dark or blackish-brown with white bases to axillaries; bases to secondaries and all (except outermost) primaries form a broad band of white. Lores pale or whitish-grey, pale or whitish eye-ring; cheeks and ear-coverts blackish-brown flecked or finely mottled whitish; broad pale grey submoustachial flecked finely darker and bordered below by long broad blackish malar stripe. Chin and throat off-white becoming grey on sides of throat and tipped slightly darker; breast and sides of neck also grey becoming whiter

on centre of lower breast; sides of lower breast, centre of upper belly and flanks distinctly patterned with diamond-shaped white centres broadly edged black and coming to a point at tip of each feather; thighs brown and edged grey; centre of lower belly and undertail-coverts white. Bill long and often hooked at tip, black or greyish with some yellow at gape. Legs and feet variable from ashy-pink to greyish-purple or light horn-brown, soles dirty white. In worn plumage edges to primaries and secondaries slightly paler or buffish-brown. **Immature** First-year bird darker brown with fine pale buff central shafts to crown, nape, mantle, back and scapulars, also pale orange-buff shafts on median coverts and pale orange-buff tips to both median and greater coverts. Edges and tips to tertials sometimes also finely orange-buff. Face more heavily mottled or spotted black and white. Chin white; breast, belly and flanks heavily scaled or mottled with whitish (or pale golden-buff on breast) centres and dark brown or blacker edges, forming chevrons. Bill as adult or with dark horn lower mandible.
GEOGRAPHICAL VARIATION None. Monotypic.
VOICE Undescribed, but birds noted singing in June.
STATUS AND DISTRIBUTION Local, uncommon or rare; probably easily overlooked. Discontinuous from (and imperfectly known in parts of its range) Sumatra (including Enggano Island), West Java (where only known from Gunung Gede-Pangrango), Bali, Lombok, Sumbawa, Flores (5 records of sightings or trapped since 1897), Timor, Wetar, Romang, Moa and, in the Philippines, on Luzon (Dalton Pass, Ipo Dam, Pangil and in Kalinga-Apayao province), Mindoro (Mt Hal-

con), Negros (Balinsasayao, Negros Oriental province) and Mindanao (Mt Apo, Mt Malindang, Mt Katanglad, Mt Hilong-Hilong and Mt Mayo).
MOVEMENTS Sedentary.
HABITAT On smaller islands such as Lombok, Sumbawa and Flores it is a bird of hill forests at 450–920 (1485–3035'), 1200–1300 m (3960–4290') on Bali, and 1200–1600 m (3960–5280') or slightly lower on Enggano. Birds on Java and in the Philippines occur in montane mossy forest above 1000 m (3300'); on Mt Malindang it occurs between 1360 and 2260 m (4500–7450').
BEHAVIOUR Usually alone or in pairs. Very shy and generally unapproachable, spending most of its time low down in dense forest undergrowth or on the ground; sometimes ventures out into the open on forest trails or paths but always cautious and quick to take flight at the first sign of disturbance. Usually flies low and fast into adjacent areas of cover. Forages on the ground amongst leaf-litter and decaying vegetation. Food includes insects and their larvae, spiders, snails, worms and small fruits.
BREEDING Very poorly known. Season: (West Java) September–April. Nest: small but firm cup of moss, fine roots, leaf stems, lichens mixed with mud and plant fibres usually placed low down in tree. Eggs: 2–3, buff or pale greenish and densely marked with fine rusty- or reddish-brown spots or speckles.
MOULT No information.
MEASUREMENTS Wing (n=12) 119–132; tarsus 30–33; bill (culmen) 22–26. Weight 108 g (Rand & Rabor 1960).
REFERENCES Dickinson *et al.* (1991), Rand & Rabor (1960).

48 PLAIN-BACKED THRUSH *Zoothera mollissima*   Plate 20
(Plain-backed Mountain Thrush)
Turdus mollissimus Blyth, 1842, J. Asiat. Soc. Bengal 11: 188 – Darjeeling.

IDENTIFICATION 25–27 cm (10–10½"). A large brown thrush of the Himalayas and mountains of southern China, where it breeds in rocky areas above the treeline. Has plain olive-brown upperparts with a rufous tinge (nominate race) to the wings and central tail feathers; outer tail feathers have white tips. In flight shows pale wing-bar and an underwing pattern similar to that of White's/Scaly Thrush (50). Underparts are pale or yellowish on the breast with dark brown scales or crescents. **Confusion species** Similar to a number of other thrushes of the region, principally Long-tailed Thrush (49), which has two fairly broad pale or white wing-bars, heavy or deeper crescents on the underparts, better definition to the face pattern (blackish ear-coverts) and a slightly longer tail and more noticeably pointed wings. White's/Scaly Thrush is much more heavily mottled above with broad dark tips forming scales to both the upper- and underparts; also has pale wing-bars and pale tips to the tail. Mistle Thrush (126) is also very similar but has spotted (not scaled or scalloped)

underparts, lacks the wing-bar and has a prominent contrasting underwing pattern in flight, slightly paler upperparts and slightly more white edging the longer tail.
DESCRIPTION Sexes alike. **Adult** Entire upperparts olive-brown from forehead to rump and uppertail-coverts, slightly darker on forehead to nape and tinged with warm or rufous-brown on mantle, back and scapulars, and slightly paler olive on rump and uppertail-coverts. Tail brown with large pale or whitish spots on innerwebs of outer feathers, outerwebs pale brown; central feathers tinged warm or rufous olive. Lesser coverts as scapulars; median and greater coverts brown edged and tipped olive-brown; alula and primary coverts brown with outerwebs paler or sandier-brown, tips darker or browner; flight feathers brown to dark brown with fine outer edge of pale or sandy-brown on primaries and broadly at base of secondaries, forming an indistinct panel on closed wing; bases to secondaries and innermost primaries pale or whitish, forming wing-bar in flight; edges to secondaries

254

duller or more olive-brown; tertials olive-brown on outerwebs and dark brown on inners. Underwing has lesser coverts white; median and greaters broadly dark or blackish-brown tipped white to bend of wing; bases of secondaries to inner primaries white. Lores pale buff or flecked darker or blackish, becoming more strongly blackish, with pale or yellowish-buff flecks, spots or tips, on cheeks and ear-coverts; pale or dull yellowish-buff submoustachial bordered below by long dark or blackish malar stripe; pale or buffish-white eye-ring; dark or blackish edge to ear-coverts on some. Chin and throat pale yellowish-buff or off-whitish tinged yellow with broad black tips or crescents to sides of lower throat, breast and sides of neck and extending heavily across whitish belly and flanks; vent white; thighs white but flecked olive. Undertail-coverts olive or olive-brown but broadly white around central shaft and at tip. Some birds are more heavily tinged or washed with yellow or yellowish-buff on breast and belly, and others have olive-brown bars or crescents on lower belly and lower flanks. Bill dark horn, base of lower mandible yellow. Legs and feet yellowish-flesh or yellowish-brown to flesh-brown. **Immature** Juvenile similar to adult but crown, nape, mantle, back and scapulars heavily streaked pale buff on central shafts. Sandy-buff tips to median coverts and some inner greaters. Face heavily mottled blackish and pale or yellowish-buff. Breast to flanks heavily or densely mottled with yellowish-buff bases and dark brown or blackish tips or fringes. Belly and lower flanks white with narrower tips or bars, and undertail-coverts olive-brown with pale or whitish central shafts. Bill black but edges to upper and lower mandible yellowish-flesh. Legs and feet yellowish-flesh.

GEOGRAPHICAL VARIATION Three races; variation clinal but poorly defined. Birds from the western end of the range (whiteheadi) are slightly paler above while those from the eastern end (griseiceps) are slightly darker, especially on the crown, which is browner and contrasts slightly with the rest of the upperparts. Whiteheadi is, on average, slightly smaller and lacks the warm or rufous tinge on the upperparts and has the forehead and crown uniform with the rest of the upperparts, but in fresh plumage is probably inseparable in the field.

VOICE Has a sharp or grating rattling alarm and a single thin chuck contact note but is otherwise generally silent, especially outside the breeding season, and reluctant to call even when alarmed. Song similar to that of White's/Scaly Thrush (50) (nominate race) but slightly faster and more varied with rich, musical or melodious whistling phrases such as plee-too or plee-chuu followed by ti-ti-ti or ch-up-ple-ooop, mostly continuous and not repeated (though some of the more rising, ringing phrases are), interspersed with pauses of up to 10 seconds between phrases. Sings from secluded perch within the upper canopy of tall trees or tops of rocky peaks or crags, usually at dawn and dusk, but also during the day especially in poor weather.

STATUS AND DISTRIBUTION Fairly common, but uncommon in southern China and rare in Pakistan.

Z. m. whiteheadi Rare or local in (and a summer migrant to) northern Pakistan, in the higher valleys of the Jamgarh and Mussian peaks and the Neelum to Kunhar watershed; resident and more numerous or frequent in Kashmir discontinuously east through the western Himalayas of northern India to about Kumaon and western Nepal (where it intergrades with nominate mollissima). In winter to lower levels within the range; the wintering range of breeding birds in northern Pakistan is unknown but is probably the western Himalayas.

Z. m. mollissima Central Nepal (east of whiteheadi) east to Sikkim, Bhutan, Arunachal Pradesh and southern and south-east Tibet, northern Bengal, Assam and northern Burma. In winter to Khasi Hills, southern Assam, Cachar, Manipur, northeast Burma and southern China in central and south-west Szechwan, north-west Yunnan.

Z. m. griseiceps Southern China from central and western Szechwan from the Min River south to the Likiang range and the Mekong–Salween divide, north-west Yunnan; in winter extends to northern Tonkin, Vietnam (where generally scarce).

MOVEMENTS All three races are altitude migrants, wintering from October to late March or April at lower levels between 1300 and 3600 m (4300–11,880') south of the breeding range, from north-east India and southern Assam to north-east Burma, north-west Yunnan and northern Vietnam (mollissima), or at lower levels of the breeding range (whiteheadi) between 900 and 2600 m (2970–8580') in forests (principally oak and fir); griseiceps breeds between 2400 and 4250 m (7920–14,025') but moves lower in winter within the breeding range while part of the population moves south-east to northern Tonkin. Whiteheadi is a rare winter visitor to Simla and annual at Banhavgarh National Park, north-east Madhya Pradesh, the only known wintering area in central India (Tyabji 1994).

HABITAT In breeding season occurs between 2400 and 4500 m (9900–14,850') on alpine rocks and boulderfields with juniper and dwarf rhododendron, and often in damp shady spots with moss-covered vegetation, usually around or above the treeline, also alpine meadows and pasture with rocks and scattered bushes, scrubby or rocky slopes and grassy hillsides. In winter in similar habitat but at lower elevation, usually at 1600–2895 m (5280–9550') In South-East Asia also open country with or without rocks or boulders, damp hillsides and edges of cultivation, stream valleys and paths through scrub or light forest. On migration may occur in fir clumps or woods and in undergrowth with berry bushes.

BEHAVIOUR Alone or in pairs in summer but may form loose or scattered flocks in winter. Generally easily overlooked but very shy and unapproachable, flying off rapidly at the least sign of disturbance or human intrusion; flight low and swift and swoops up to a low perch; in winter may fly to high perch in trees and remain motionless, depending on camouflage to avoid detection. Forages mostly on the ground in undergrowth or beneath tall trees, particularly in damp or shady places, also edges of fields and more open areas of vegetation away from trees. Feeds by both turning over leaves and decaying vegetation and probing in soft earth; food is mostly insects, small molluscs, leeches and snails, but also takes some fruit, berries and seeds.

BREEDING Season: late April to July. Nest: a large, deep, cup-shaped structure of dried grass, moss, black fern roots and fine plant stems; usually placed on the ground under bushes or dwarf rhododendrons, on rare occasions low in the fork of a bush or on a rocky ledge. Baker (1924) recorded *whiteheadi* as nesting on cliff ledges above the treeline. Eggs: 4, whitish, heavily spot-ted reddish or reddish-brown usually at the larger end, or with large underlying pale purple blotches. Nestlings and young fed by both parents.

MOULT Summer adults are still in worn plumage in mid- to late July, so they presumably commence post-breeding moult in late July or August.

MEASUREMENTS Wing, male 130–148 (to 161 in south-east Tibet), female 134–144; bill (to skull) 26–31; *griseiceps* wing 139–161; bill 28–30; *whiteheadi* wing, male 140–150, female 134–143; tarsus 30–31; bill 22–26. Weight 89–112 g (Ali & Ripley 1983, Vaurie 1955a).

REFERENCES Ali & Ripley (1983), Baker (1924), Tyabji (1994), Vaurie (1955a).

49 LONG-TAILED THRUSH *Zoothera dixoni*   Plate 20
(Long-tailed Mountain Thrush)

Geocichla dixoni Seebohm, 1881, *Cat. Birds Brit. Mus.* 5: 161 – Himalayas, Nepal and Darjeeling.

IDENTIFICATION 27–28 cm (10½–11″). A shy or scarce thrush of the high Himalayan forests of the treeline in summer and dense mid-level forests in winter. Crown and upperparts olive-brown with two buff or buffish-white wing-bars; tail also olive-brown with paler outer feathers and white wedge on innerweb and tip. Face well marked with blackish rear edge to ear-coverts; chin and throat pale yellowish-buff spotted or barred at sides, becoming more heavily barred or scalloped on breast and flanks. Not very vocal. **Confusion species** Extremely similar to Plain-backed Thrush (48) and best distinguished by presence of wing-bars on closed wing, lack of warm or rufous tones, better defined face pattern with blackish ear-coverts, and generally heavier bars or scales to the breast, belly and flanks; also weaker-billed and rather longer-tailed. Differs from Mistle Thrush (126) by more heavily olive upperparts, heavily scaled or scalloped (not spotted) underparts, wing-bars at tips of coverts, and pale wing-bar in flight and a prominent contrasting underwing pattern.
DESCRIPTION Sexes almost alike. **Adult male** Entire upperparts olive-brown, slightly darker or browner on forehead (with pale shaft-streaks) to nape. Tail brown, central pair tinged olive-brown and outer feathers darker brown with innerweb (of outer feather) broadly whitish-buff, whitest at tip, tip of next innermost also showing some white. Lesser coverts as scapulars, medians dark brown broadly tipped whitish or sandy-buff, greaters brown to dark brown and less broadly tipped whitish or sandy-buff; alula brown or edged sandy-brown, primary coverts similar but broadly and heavily tinged tawny or sandy buff-brown except tips; flight feathers brown broadly edged sandy-buff on primaries, becoming slightly paler brown at bases (shows as broad wing-bar in flight) and duller or browner on edges to secondaries and outerwebs of tertials, with brown innerwebs and finely pale buff tips of tertials. Underwing has lesser and median coverts to bend of wing white, tips of medians and bases of greaters dark or blackish-brown, tips to greaters white and bases of secondaries pale orange-buff. Lores, cheeks and ear-coverts light yellowish or creamy-buff finely tipped or flecked olive-brown and more heavily olive-brown on fore ear-coverts; broad blackish tips form dark rear border with narrow or fine pale yellowish or creamy-buff tips. Eye-ring green. Chin and throat pale yellowish or creamy-buff, becoming barred with blackish-brown on sides and across lower throat; breast more yellowish and heavily tipped or barred dark brown or blackish; sides of breast and flanks washed heavily olive-brown and tipped dark or blackish-brown, forming distinct scaled or barred pattern; centre of belly whitish and less heavily or broadly barred dark or blackish-brown, thighs olive-brown, vent white and undertail-coverts creamy-yellowish tinged or washed olive-brown at sides. Bill dark brown. Legs and feet dull yellow to light brown. **Adult female** Slightly smaller with brown bill and dull brownish-yellow legs and feet. **Immature** Juvenile very similar to adult but has very fine pale or yellowish-buff central shafts to forehead, crown, nape, mantle and scapulars, some feathers on mantle, back and scapulars tipped dark or blackish-brown, broad pale central shafts on inner scapulars; outerweb of outermost tail feathers more extensively whitish or pale buff; tips to median and greater coverts sandy-buff with thin, short central shafts towards tips, tertials having pale or sandy-buff tips to outerwebs. Underparts more heavily or densely barred and, apart from flanks, have generally smaller tips or bars; base colour of chin, throat and breast (and flanks in some) yellowish or pale yellow; undertail-coverts pale yellowish with reddish-brown fringes. Bill dark horn-brown. Legs and feet flesh-yellow to light brown.
GEOGRAPHICAL VARIATION None. Monotypic.
VOICE Call poorly known. Song a series of fairly

slow, slurred phrases mostly of a dry or hoarse *wu-ut-cheet-sher*, *wut-chet-shuur* interspersed with similar phrases and musical twitters, together with *too-ee* or just *ee-ee* phrases; may begin song with an upward *w'i-it* or include a similar note in the main song; final note of phrase usually given in slurred and stuttering manner. Sings from top or upper branches of fir trees but not always visible; mostly early in the morning, and briefly in the evening.

STATUS AND DISTRIBUTION Locally common or uncommon (easily overlooked). Northern India, the Himalayas from about the Sutlej River, Himachal Pradesh, possibly also the northern Punjab, east through Nepal, Sikkim, Bhutan, Arunachal Pradesh, south-east Tibet and central and western Szechwan from the Min River to north-western Yunnan; in the south from northern Bengal through Assam to northern Burma (possibly also western Burma; recorded early April 1995 on Mt Victoria). In winter to lower levels in southern Assam, Nagaland, Manipur and the northern Cachar Hills, northern and central Burma; also Kwangsi, south-ern China and northern Tonkin, northern Vietnam.

MOVEMENTS An altitude migrant moving to lower levels, generally 1220–2700 m (4120–8910') in winter. Four birds in western Burma in April 1995 were most probably migrants (Robson *et al.* 1998). A rare or scarce winter visitor to north-west Thailand (Round 1983); vagrant to Laos (Nam Ha, March 1997) (Duckworth *et al.* 1999).

HABITAT Dense forests of fir, oak and rhododendron above or along the treeline, also dwarf juniper forest and high-altitude scrub usually between 2100 and 4250 m (6930–14,025'). In winter thick or dense forests at lower levels, and often near streams; also more open country, hillsides and edges of cultivation (where it may come into contact with Plain-backed Thrush).

BEHAVIOUR Usually alone or in pairs but may form loose associations in winter. Many actions similar to that of Plain-backed Thrush; generally secretive, especially in summer, when it is a shy or retiring bird of the thickly vegetated forest floor or alpine scrub. Occasionally feeds in semi-open areas along paths, tracks or roadsides with cover nearby. When disturbed flies up into bushes or branches of trees and remains motionless until intruder has passed. Forages entirely on the ground where it searches for insects and their larvae, also snails and occasionally some berries.

BREEDING Season: May to July. Nest: a fairly large cup-shaped structure mostly of moss on a platform or base of twigs and lined with fine dry grasses; usually placed in a tree (mostly firs, oaks or willows) up to 3 m (10') from the ground. Eggs: 3, dull greenish, marked throughout or at the large end with reddish-brown speckles, spots or blotches.

MOULT No information.

MEASUREMENTS Wing 131–147; tarsus 34.5–40; bill (from skull) 24–30, mostly 26–28. Weight (n=4) 71.5–103 g (Ali & Ripley 1983, Vaurie 1955a).

REFERENCES Ali & Ripley (1983), Duckworth *et al.* (1999), Robson *et al.* (1998), Round (1983), Vaurie (1955a).

50 WHITE'S or SCALY THRUSH* *Zoothera dauma*   Plate 17

(White's Ground-Thrush, Speckled Mountain Thrush, Golden Mountain Thrush, Small-billed Mountain-Thrush [*dauma*], Tiger Thrush [*heinei/lunulata*]) * See note on page 39 regarding use of English names.

Turdus Dauma Latham, 1790, Index orn. 1: 362 – India [restricted to Kashmir by Baker (1921) J. Bombay Nat. Hist. Soc. 27: 720].

IDENTIFICATION 24–30 cm (10½–12") (*imbricata* 23–24 cm/9–9½"; *neilgherriensis* 25–27 cm/9¾–10½"; *aurea* 29–30.5 cm/11½–12"). A large, very striking thrush, with long wings and tail and a relatively small head; upperparts yellowish-olive heavily mottled with black crescent-shaped tips, underparts whitish with stronger black crescents. In flight shows prominent broad black and white bands across the underwing and dark centre to tail with prominent white tips. **Confusion species** Has a passing resemblance, especially in flight across open country, to Mistle Thrush (126), which has prominent white underwing-coverts and lacks the distinctive black and white pattern, with plain upperparts, less white in the tail, and spotted underparts. Young Mistle have more spotted upperparts (fading on the rump and uppertail-coverts) but lack the black crescents. Both Plain-backed (48) and Long-tailed (49) Thrushes have plain upperparts. Otherwise similar only to the other members of the species group (see Taxonomic note), particularly Amami (51), Hors-field's (52), Bassian (54) and Russet-tailed (55) Thrushes, but is isolated geographically from the last three and only occurs as a migrant in the area occupied by Amami.

Taxonomic note Ripley (1964) and previous authors considered that the entire White's Thrush complex comprised *Z. dauma* (50), *major* (51),

Underwing pattern of White's Thrush.

horsfieldi (52), machiki (53), lunulata (54), heinei (55), talaseae (56) and margaretae (57), and until recently this assemblage was treated as a single, widely distributed, species, *Z. dauma*. All except three of these (*machiki, talaseae* and *margaretae*) differ little in plumage but more substantially in size and song. Since then, various authors including Cheng (1976), Mees (1977), Ripley & Hadden (1982), Ford (1983) and White & Bruce (1986) have reviewed this approach. From their recommendations the present treatment of the entire complex has evolved, as summarised and adopted by Sibley & Monroe (1990). Whilst this is an acceptable modern approach – and consistent with similar divisions being proposed or made on other similarly related taxa – it may not be the most satisfactory arrangement. This is particularly true with regard to the birds on Java (to Bali and Lombok) and Taiwan, which have been classed as *horsfieldi* (in the case of Taiwan most probably in error); likewise the relationships of birds in southern India and Sri Lanka to those in Siberia and the Himalayas, and of those in New Guinea and adjacent islands to those in south-east Australia and Tasmania, need further work. It is also likely that some taxa presently considered as only subspecifically distinct will, in time, be treated as full species since, although they clearly share a relatively recent common ancestor, they are in the process of diverging from each other, and our understanding of species limits and composition is also changing. Further research using DNA sequences or profiles of all species/races in the complex will undoubtedly result in a better arrangement.

DESCRIPTION Sexes alike. Female has dark horn-brown bill. **Adult** Forehead to crown and nape dark olive with bases pale golden-yellow, light yellowish-buff central shafts and broad dark brown tips or fringes forming bars or scales. Sides of nape and neck more heavily edged blackish creating paler spotted pattern. Mantle, back and scapulars similarly olive at base becoming pale gold or golden-buffish broadly tipped blackish-brown, forming heavily scaled pattern (some dark tips not always forming bars); scapulars often have light yellowish-buff central shafts and subterminal spots. Rump and uppertail-coverts also olive but bases slightly paler or yellowish-olive and dark tips on rump slightly less heavily defined, uppertail-coverts variably tipped in extent (some of longest may have dark central shafts towards tip). Tail (12 feathers, occasionally 14 in east of range) brownish-olive on central two pairs, becoming dark brown on outers, broadly edged with white at tips of outer two feathers. Lesser coverts as scapulars but outers blackish tipped yellowish-buff and inners with pale or yellowish-buff shafts and tips; median coverts dark or blackish-brown broadly tipped pale cream, greaters similar or slightly paler and edged lighter or yellowish-brown, inner greaters more broadly tipped yellowish or yellowish-buff; alula brown and primary coverts brown or dark brown at base, broadly edged distally pale or whitish-yellow and broadly tipped blackish; flight feathers dark brown, primaries yellowish-brown to yellowish-olive on

Tail pattern of White's Thrush showing extent of white at tips of outer feathers.

outerweb, broadly edged golden-yellow, and on bases of inner primaries, secondaries similar but sometimes with duller brown edges, tips to inner primaries and secondaries dull whitish-buff to olive-yellow; tertials dull yellowish-olive but inner-web brown or dark brown. Underwing has lesser coverts to bend of wing white; base of medians white and broadly tipped black or blackish-brown; greaters blackish-brown and broadly tipped white, merging with broad white or silvery-white bases to secondaries and inner primaries, forming a very distinctive underwing-pattern in flight. Lores to eye whitish or pale greyish-buff with indistinct blackish tips, thin or narrow whitish or yellowish eye-ring, cheeks and ear-coverts yellowish and finely mottled with brown or olive-blackish flecks, rear edge of ear-coverts sometimes showing a broad dark border; broad but poorly defined whitish or whitish-buff submoustachial finely flecked darker and bordered below by thin dark malar. Chin and throat white or creamy-whitish with fine flecks becoming larger, dark brown crescents on centre of lower throat and upper breast; sides of lower throat yellowish, extending to sides of upper breast and barred with dark brown or blackish crescents; feathers of central breast pale yellow basally with dark brown tips, forming a heavily scaled pattern (amount of yellow at feather bases on underparts variable; some birds show olive at bases on sides of breast); belly and flanks white (may show yellow subterminally) and all boldly tipped with dark brown or black crescents on flanks, slightly smaller bars on lower flanks and centre of belly; undertail-coverts white occasionally with small blackish crescents; thighs white, finely barred greyish-brown. Bill dusky-blackish or brownish-black (has a small hook at tip), with dull yellow or yellowish-brown base of lower mandible. Legs and feet variably dusky or brownish olive-flesh to straw or deep yellow, soles paler or yellowish. In hand some individuals in fresh-plumage have fine pale yellowish filoplumes projecting beyond feathers on nape; tail has narrow pale yellowish or white tips, except outermost two feathers which are pale brown, whitish-brown towards tip, and next innermost has white tip (extent of white at tips of outermost two varies from 0 to c.20 mm); in worn plumage becomes slightly duller or greyish-olive on upperparts, tips of median and greater coverts whiter and edges to flight feathers duller and tinged greyish or olive; central tail feathers greyer or less olive; underparts whiter with less yellowish or buff in bases to feathers. **Immature** Juvenile very similar to adult but upperparts brownish-olive and more heavily mottled yellowish, becoming yellowish to orange-buff subterminally and broadly spotted or barred dark or blackish-brown on forehead, crown, mantle, scapulars and back; broad pale cream or orange-buff central shafts to mantle and scapulars and broadly subterminally yellowish to orange-buff on edges of scapulars and spotted black at tips; rump and uppertail-coverts paler or browner and more like adult with some yellowish-buff subterminally and indistinct dark spots becoming browner bars on uppertail-coverts. Tips to central tail feathers pale yellowish-buff. Median coverts blackish-brown with yellowish central shafts and broad spots at tips, greater coverts and flight feathers as adult. Face similar to adult but more finely mottled creamy-buff with darker tips; has thin pale cream eye-ring and short, poorly defined supercilium finely spotted darker. Underparts very heavily mottled on sides of neck and breast with whitish or creamy-buff on chin, becoming yellowish-orange and broadly spotted blackish-brown and more erratically spaced on lower breast; spots become bars on flanks and sides of belly; lower belly to undertail-coverts white with some dark bars or yellowish-brown spots. **First-year bird** Similar to adult and not always separable on plumage, but retains juvenile feathers on alula (usually longest feathers), greater coverts (unmoulted outers contrast with variable number of fresh, paler olive-brown inners, which are also slightly longer than unmoulted feathers), primary coverts, tertials, flight feathers and tail. Although no difference in pattern from adult, may show paler face and less broad or well-defined bars and slight contrast between shape and colour of retained outer coverts, which are shorter and more rounded or worn than the new (inner) median and primary coverts; flight feathers and tail more worn in first-year bird in late winter and spring compared to adult. In hand can be aged by shape of tip of central tail feathers – slight point at shaft tip (more clearly rounded at tip in adults) and olive in colour; first-year bird has graduated shape to point at tip which may have very fine buffish spot but usually absent in spring birds. Bill similar to adult female.

GEOGRAPHICAL VARIATION Four races (others have been proposed); variation clinal, most pronounced in *imbricata*.

Race *aurea* is slightly larger on average and probably not always separable (especially in worn plumage) in the field from nominate *dauma*, and only confirmed by wing measurements. In fresh plumage paler on face with much finer spots or flecks on cheeks, ear-coverts and submoustachial; chin and throat more extensively white. Bases to feathers of forehead to crown, nape, mantle, back and inner scapulars yellowish to golden yellowish-buff. Tail has 14 feathers (some western birds may

only have 12). Bill as nominate (including presence of small hook at tip) but more substantial, base to lower mandible whitish-flesh (may extend to cutting edges of upper); more likely to show dark tip. Legs and feet pale flesh or browner on toes.

Race *neilgherriensis* is darker on head and upperparts and lacks broad pale yellow or golden subterminal spots (some show diffuse yellowish-buff); bases of feathers more olive-brown with indistinct subterminal area of rich or warm-buff (or olive-buff on forehead to crown and nape) and dark or blackish-brown bars at tips (prominently on forehead, crown and nape); rump and uppertail-coverts slightly warmer or russet-brown and less heavily barred blackish-brown (blackish bars at tips sometimes absent). Tail also brown but central feathers slightly warm in tone, becoming darker on outers except outermost which has fairly broad whitish innerweb to tip. Wings as nominate but edges to inner primaries and secondaries more warmer brown and less golden in tone except for edges to outer primaries; tertials olive-brown becoming slightly warmer towards paler edges and tips. Underparts whiter, heavily scaled blackish-brown. Legs and feet as nominate but possibly more usually flesh-coloured.

Race *imbricata* similar to but smaller (24 cm/9") than nominate and colder or slightly darker olive than *neilgherriensis* on upperparts; also lacks warm or brown tones and has blackish-brown tips extending across rump and uppertail-coverts. Wings very similar to both nominate and *neilgherriensis* but may show darker or duller tips to greater coverts contrasting with paler tips to medians. Underparts much more heavily warm peachy to light rufous-buff (except for whitish-buff centre of chin to belly), with dark or blackish tips forming, on average, slightly narrower black bars than on *dauma* or *neilgherriensis*; undertail-coverts usually plain. Tail noticeably short, outer feathers paler brown with innerwebs of outermost two narrowly buffish-white (contrasts slightly with rest of feathers). Bill black, base of lower mandible horn-grey. Legs and feet variable from flesh-colour to brownish-flesh or bluish-brown.

VOICE Generally silent, apparently often reluctant to utter even alarm or distress calls but known to give soft (often inaudible beyond a few feet) Bullfinch-like whistle as contact between pair; also a typically thrush-like, drawn-out, high-pitched *seeh, seep, zieh* or *tzeep*, and a shorter, softer *tsi*; alarm call a dry *chuck chuck*; adults scolding an intruder at nest give a muffled churring or a *rrrarra* or *krrra*; alarm call of *imbricata* is a series of high-pitched notes.

Song variable between races. Race *dauma* gives a slow series of short phrases recalling Mistle Thrush in quality but broken or less connected, each phrase repeated two or more times and separated by equally long pauses: *pur-loo-tree-lay... dur-lee-dur-lee... drr-drr-chew-you-we-eeee*, or a more languid *chirrup cheweee chueu wiow we erp chirrol chup cheweee wiop*, occasionally interspersed with soft squeaks, twitters or chuckles and happily sustained for hours.

Race *aurea* has a slow, melancholic, seemingly endless (hours-long) series of thin whistles broken by pauses of similar duration, a thin and slightly rising or falling whistled *huuwiieee... weeeeooooooooo* or occasionally a more clearly two-note *pee-yuuuuu...* with the second syllable lower and much more drawn-out, the notes carrying considerable distances – up to a kilometre – and creating an eerie quality in the depths of dank dark forests. Two (or more) birds may sing at the same time, but at some distance apart, adding to the haunting quality of an echoing effect; when duetting, one bird is sometimes thought to give high notes and the other low notes e.g. '*wheeeee...whooooo...whooooo...weeeee...*'. In Ussuriland and Japan also known to sing with a prolonged even-pitched whistle occasionally, as in *dauma*, followed by a jumbled series of soft squeaking, twittering or warbling notes.

Song of *imbricata* only recently recorded (July 1997; information from D. Warakagoda pers. comm.) is a series of clear plain whistled notes repeated 6–8 times. Each whistle starts level in pitch and then smoothly descends, and is of about one second duration. The song is not loud but clearly audible at some distance and usually only given (probably from the roosting site) shortly before first light; it is repeated c.4–5 times and stops at first light. May indulge in duet with a second bird some distance away. A second song type consists of a series of short, soft, thin, reedy whistled notes for up to 30 seconds followed by a short pause before repeating, given with very little emphasis or carrying power, and thus easily overlooked. Song period appears to be February to April and immediately before and after the main breeding period from mid-July to early October.

Song of *neilgherriensis* appears to be undocumented. Some authors have likened it to that of nominate with a series of slow, short phrases, but no faunal work dealing with southern India provides any direct information. Baker (1924) had a contact who lived near a breeding pair but who 'never heard it sing once.' If *neilgherriensis* does in fact sing it may be of such quality and/or given for so short a period that it has remained undetected.

Song usually given from within foliage of upper canopy of tree, rarely on exposed perch at treetop; in Siberia and Japan *aurea* sings mostly at night and only rarely during the day, *dauma* sings at dawn but may also sing at other times, especially in poor weather, also occasionally in the evening. Turns head from side to side whilst singing and varies volume of song, thus difficult to locate singer. Song period (*dauma*) early April to mid-June, (*aurea*) mid- to late April (may sing intermittently as early as mid-March in Japan) to early July, with unmated birds singing in some areas into August.

STATUS AND DISTRIBUTION Fairly common (*dauma*); uncommon (*aurea, neilgherriensis*); rare (*imbricata*).

Z. d. dauma Breeds between 2320 and 3600 m (7650–11,880') – though generally sparse above 3000 m (9900') – in the Himalayas from northern Pakistan (Indus Kohistan and Murree, where slightly lower to 2100 m/6930') and Kashmir east through northern India and Nepal to Sikkim, northern Bengal, Assam, Bhutan, Arunachal Pradesh and south-east Tibet, also south to the hills of Garo, Khasi and Cachar to Manipur and Burma where it has been recorded from Mt Victoria and the Arakan Hills, north through the Upper Chindwin and north-east Burma and discontinuously south through the Southern Shan States to Tenasserim; in southern China extends to central and western Szechwan and northern Yunnan, also in parts of northern Thailand and isolated parts (e.g. Khao Luang and Khao Nok Ram) of Nakhon Si Thammarat and Trang provinces, Peninsular Thailand, Laos and Vietnam.

In winter occurs south into the foothills (up to about 1800 m/5940') of extreme north-east Pakistan and much of north-east lowland India south to southern Madhya Pradesh, eastern Maharashtra, Orissa and southern Bengal, southern Nepal, most of eastern Bangladesh (south to about Chittagong) and possibly also Mizoram, but nowhere common.

Distribution note 1: Breeding birds in South-East Asia, from eastern Burma to southern Vietnam and further east to include Taiwan and Iriomote in the Ryukyu Islands, have previously been separated into the race *affinis*, but whilst it is recognised that birds in this area require further investigation they are here considered inseparable from nominate birds.

Z. d. aurea Limits poorly known but ranges discontinuously in western Siberia in the southern Urals, reaching Perm in the extreme west; recorded breeding (or in summer) up to about 2600 m (8580') throughout most of Siberia from about 62°N along the Yenisey–Yeloguy confluence, south to about Krasnoyarsk and east along the Podkamennaya Tunguska and the upper Angara River to Lake Baikal, western Ussuriland (and may extend south through the Yablonovy range into extreme northern Mongolia), southern Ussuriland and Amurland, the southern coastal area of the Sea of Okhotsk and the Sikhote-Alin south into north-west and eastern Mongolia, mostly in the areas around Ubsunur (Uvs Nuur) and Kubsugul (Hövsgöl Nuur) Lakes, and north-east Inner Mongolia and north-west and northern Manchuria south into Korea, and in Japan from Hokkaido to Honshu. Reported to breed in the Tien Shan of western Sinkiang by Meyer de Schauensee (1984) but not confirmed by Cheng (1987).

In winter to Honshu, Shikoku and Kyushu and surrounding islands (Japan) and in southern China from the Yangtze valley west to Yunnan and east to Kwangtung, Fukien and Taiwan (where uncommon but recorded in almost every month except June and July), Hung-t'ou Hsu (Lanyu Is.), south to the Philippines (Luzon, Mindoro, Palawan, Catanduanes and Batan; old records from Fuga and Marinduque), southern Annam, Vietnam, central and southern Laos and north-west and north-east Thailand (rare) and irregularly to northern and eastern Burma.

Distribution note 2: Breeding birds in Ussuriland, Amurland, Manchuria, Korea and Japan (from Hokkaido to Honshu), previously separated as race *toratugumi*, are here considered synonymous with *aurea*. Similarly birds taken on Taiwan and previously separated as *hancii* and *affinis* are here considered synonymous with *aurea*; whilst it is acknowledged that, from the few data available, summering/breeding birds on Taiwan may represent either a distinct race or a smaller population of *aurea* (wing 133–145), we feel more work is needed to establish their exact relationships.

Z. d. neilgherriensis Resident in hills of southwestern peninsular India from northern coastal Karnataka (possibly also Goa) south to Kerala and western Tamil Nadu (Nelliampathi, Brahmagiri, Biligirirangans, Nilgiri and Palni hills) at c.600–2100 m (2000–6930').

Z. d. imbricata Resident in the hills of Sri Lanka between 450 and 2200 m (1485–7260'), but mostly above 900 m (2970').

MOVEMENTS Depending on race either resident (*neilgherriensis, imbricata* and some *dauma*), partial or totally migratory (some *dauma* and *aurea*), or an altitude migrant (some *dauma*).

Northern breeding birds are entirely migratory with entire population of *aurea* and some *dauma* (though most of the latter are largely sedentary or move east along the lower foothills) moving between south and south-east to wintering grounds in South-East Asia from north-east India (though *aurea* is a rare winter vagrant to Arunachal Pradesh and Assam) east to southern China, southern Japan, Taiwan and the Philippines. Longest-distance movements are from western Siberia (west of the Yenisei) south-east through Sinkiang and north-west Mongolia to Yunnan east to Kwangtung and Fukien. Most departures (following a period of post-breeding dispersal in August) are from late August or early September to late October or even early November. Most birds have left the central and southern Siberian breeding areas by mid-September. Passage through northern China and Korea from mid-September and northern Tibet later that month, arriving in most areas of southern China in October; a scarce winter visitor (average of 15) to Hong Kong from November to April; arrivals in northern India and Bangladesh from early November. Wintering birds in the Philippines from November (mostly Luzon) to March, exceptionally to early May.

Wintering birds depart northward from March onwards in northern India and southern China, but some birds are still present until late April. Passage through northern China and Mongolia from mid-April to late May. In southern Russia (Lake Baikal region) and further west (Novosibirsk region) earliest arrivals are in early May but most passage is mid-May to early June, although records from mid-April in extreme south are not unusual. Far eastern Siberia and Japanese birds move about the same time, departing from northern and central Japan in September and early October with stragglers remaining into the first week of November, but a comparatively short-distance migrant there, with some birds wintering in southern Japan. Returning birds back in central Honshu from late March but arrivals in Kuril Islands and Ussuriland not until mid-April, with passage through May.

Accidental visitor to Bangladesh (1 record), Peninsular Malaysia and Sumatra (3 records: October 1989, February 1994, July 1994), Panay, Philippines (December 1997) (but Panay only first studied ornithologically in 1990s, so vagrancy there possibly an unreasonable assumption); vagrant to most countries in the western Palearctic including Greenland (October 1954), Iceland (October 1939, October 1982 and November 1982) and the Faeroes (November 1938, autumn 1974) and west to the British Isles (50 to 1999), France (11) and Spain (3 including 2 on the Balearics); Belgium (17), Netherlands (11), Germany (c.27), Denmark (2), Norway (6), Sweden (October 1985), Poland (6), Finland (September 1961, October 1988), Austria (3), Italy (20), Sicily (October 1974), Corsica, Sardinia, Yugoslavia, Greece (autumn 1954, February 1965) and Romania (September 1981). Most records are in the period October to January but also September, February, April and May.

HABITAT Mature forests of oak and fir, mostly thick or dense spruce or *Pinus sibirica* forests of the taiga zone, montane or submontane forests with heavy or tangled undergrowth including ferns, rhododendron and bamboo clumps; has a preference for dense spruce but also mixed fir and broadleaf deciduous woods such as larch, birch and aspen, also sal (*Shorea robusta*) forests; also occurs at forest edges, ravines, clearings and frequently in moist areas, on moss-covered slopes and boulders or near streams; in winter and on passage in similarly well vegetated areas but often in more open areas of tree clumps, open hillsides, along streambeds or, in Korea or parts of Thailand, large parks and gardens including cities, e.g. Seoul.

BEHAVIOUR Usually alone or in pairs; generally shy and retiring, preferring the depths of well-wooded areas in which it remains hidden or camouflaged in the dappled light. Sedentary birds (i.e. *neilgherriensis* and *imbricata*) occupy territories all year round. Forages low down, mostly on the ground in damp or moist areas where it moves slowly, silently and deliberately, walking or running often along forest paths; has peculiar shivering or nervously bobbing or jerking gait recalling similar motion of Jack Snipe *Lymnocryptes minimus*, apparently used as a method of bring worms to the surface; also has a habit of slowly or rapidly raising and lowering tail and fanning tail open on downward stroke; in some areas occasionally becomes tame and approachable; turns over leaves and decaying vegetation in typical thrush manner and digs or probes in soft earth. Flight rapid and usually low and silent on long wings, recalling both Mistle Thrush and some of the Asiatic cuckoos by its short upward glide before landing on perch. Feeds mainly on insects, their larvae, grasshoppers, beetles and earthworms, slugs, leeches and snails; also berries and occasionally some fruit.

BREEDING Season: end April to June (*dauma*) or late July (*aurea*); March to June (*neilgherriensis*); March to May and July to October (*imbricata*). Nest: a broad cup-shaped structure of dry grasses, leaves or pine needles and roots mixed with large quantities of moss and lined with finer vegetation and bracken fronds, usually placed in the fork of a tree or branches in bushes up to 6 m (20') or perhaps exceptionally to 10.5 m (35') from the ground; occasionally on the ground, in a bank or among stones, boulders or moss-covered branches and undergrowth. Eggs: 3–4, variable in colour from pale yellowish-green to greenish-blue and light clay, and heavily spotted or freckled with pale reddish-brown; those of *neilgherriensis* are somewhat darker or browner and less well marked, clutch usually only 2 or occasionally 3. Nest-building and incubation by female alone but both adults tend the nestlings. Most races have single brood except for *imbricata*.

MOULT Adults have complete post-breeding moult from end of July to end of August or start of September. Post-juvenile moult, involving all head and body feathers, lesser coverts and inner medians and inner greater coverts, occurs in late summer from mid-July to early or (rarely) mid-August. Has partial moult of body feathers in March–April.

MEASUREMENTS Wing, male 137–150, female 135–150; tarsus 27–36; bill (to skull), male 22–31, female 21–29; *aurea* wing, male 155–176, female 149–172; tarsus 33–38; bill (from skull) 27–31; *neilgherriensis* wing 124–136; tarsus 28–32; bill (culmen) 27–29; *imbricata* wing 116–127; tarsus 27–30; bill (culmen) 26–27.5. Weight *dauma/ aurea* male 92–195 g, female 93–174 g; *imbricata* 89.5 g (Ali & Ripley 1983).

REFERENCES Ali & Ripley (1983), Baker (1924), Cheng (1987), Ford (1983), Mees (1977), Meyer de Schauensee (1984), Ripley (1964), Ripley & Hadden (1982), Sibley & Monroe (1990), White & Bruce (1986).

51 AMAMI THRUSH *Zoothera major* Plate 17

Geocichla major Ogawa, 1905, *Annot. Zool. Japan* 5: 178 – Amami-O-Shima.

IDENTIFICATION 29–30.5 cm (11½–12″). A slightly larger and longer-tailed relation of White's Thrush (50) of which it was, until recently, considered a race (see Ishihara 1986 and taxonomic note on White's Thrush). One of the rarest thrushes; restricted to the forests of central Amami Oshima, Ryukyu Islands. Appearance very like White's Thrush but song very different. **Confusion species** Unlikely to be confused with any other thrush except race *aurea* of White's which is a migrant and winter visitor to the region. See below for differences, most of which are easily determined on birds in the hand together with the number of tail feathers.

DESCRIPTION Sexes alike. **Adult** Almost identical to White's Thrush (particularly race *aurea*) but marginally larger and longer-tailed, with only 12 (not 14) rectrices. Has broad pale yellow central shafts and well defined subterminal bands and blackish-brown tips on upperparts whilst rump and uppertail-coverts are paler and not as broadly tipped blackish as White's, except for longest uppertail-coverts which are broadly tipped. Bases of primaries on upperwing show only limited pale buff compared to those on White's (which extend to bases of outer secondaries). Pale area of underwing smaller and duller or greyish compared to White's. The underparts often more buffish or creamy-white with more yellow on bases to feathers of belly and flanks, and possibly a little duller than whiter underparts of White's. Face more heavily mottled with blackish on cheeks and ear-coverts. Bill, legs and feet as White's. **Immature** Juvenile undescribed but probably similar to same-age White's.

GEOGRAPHICAL VARIATION None. Monotypic.

VOICE Calls similar, if not identical, to those of White's Thrush. Song differs from race *aurea* of White's by being much more *Turdus* thrush-like in tone and quality – a series of slow, varied, whistling or flute-like notes both rising and falling, e.g. *piri piri kyo kyo...* or *chirrup-chewee, chueu, wiow-we-ep, chewee-wiop* (Khan & Takashi in prep.), but retaining the repetitive quality of the song of some White's. Song period is mostly March to early May, and on some days in the autumn most song is given in the early morning, frequently before dawn and up to an hour after sunrise.

STATUS AND DISTRIBUTION Extremely rare, occurring at very low densities. Large areas of mature forests have been cleared on Amami Oshima in recent years and replaced by young unsuitable forest plantations, so that the species is considered vulnerable and in danger from habitat destruction (Collar & Andrew 1988). Recent data suggests that the population since 1990 is now stable at about 75 individuals (Khan & Takashi in prep.), but still regarded as Critically Endangered (Collar *et al.* 1994). Restricted to the forests of Kinsakubaru to Kamiya and Yuidake, Yuandake, Asado Anengachi, Akatochi Yama, Aminoko and Sekko, central district of Amami Oshima in the Ryukyu islands, Japan.

MOVEMENTS Sedentary.

HABITAT Prefers undisturbed wet or moist primary forest between 100 and 400 m (330–1320') (Brazil 1991) with annual rainfall in excess of 4000 mm, but has also occurred in secondary forest over 60 years old.

BEHAVIOUR Extremely shy and retiring; most of its behaviour, food and breeding biology is virtually unknown, but probably similar to that of White's Thrush.

MOULT No information.

MEASUREMENTS Wing 164–173 (4 birds); tarsus 41.5–44.5; bill (culmen) 31–33; Weight (1 bird) 172 g.

REFERENCES Brazil (1991), Collar & Andrew (1988), Collar *et al.* (1994), Ishihara (1986), Khan & Takashi (in prep.).

52 HORSFIELD'S THRUSH *Zoothera horsfieldi* Plate 18

Oreocincla horsfieldi Bonaparte, 1857, *Rev. Mag. Zool.* [Paris]: 205 – Java.

IDENTIFICATION 26.5–28 cm (10½–11″). An extremely scarce or rare (but probably greatly overlooked) resident of montane forests of northern Sumatra east to Lombok; very little known. Previously treated as a race of White's Thrush (50) but now considered sufficiently isolated to warrant distinct recognition (see taxonomic note on White's Thrush). Very similar to White's but generally somewhat darker or richer olive on the upperparts and less mottled with reduced amount of yellowish subterminally on the mantle, back and scapulars. **Confusion species** Unlikely to be confused with any other species apart from White's Thrush, which does not occur in Indonesia.

DESCRIPTION Sexes alike. **Adult** Extremely similar to White's Thrush but slightly smaller and has forehead, crown and upperparts much deeper or olive-russet with only a few pale yellowish-buff subterminal shaft-streaks (most of which are restricted to forehead, crown and sides of nape), latter and sides of neck also heavily tipped blackish-brown and sides of breast infused olive or olive-brown. Dark barring on rump on average lighter than in White's. Tail as in White's but with 14 feathers, outer two paler brown with small white tips on innerwebs (less than 15 mm or occasionally absent). Face similar to White's but generally darker and more infused with olive on lores and upper ear-coverts; submoustachial, cheeks and lower ear-coverts whitish but finely mottled or barred olive or olive-brown on submoustachial and with prominent broad dark brown malar. Bill as in White's. Legs and feet pale flesh-brown to duller dirty brown. **Immature** Juvenile similar to adult but has black bars and crescents on underparts less clearly defined.

GEOGRAPHICAL VARIATION None. Monotypic.

VOICE Very little known; a short thin *tzeet* and a soft monotonous whistle. Song a long, thin but loud whistle given at regular intervals; similar to that given by race *aurea* of White's Thrush. Appears to sing at times in concert with others, different pitches of song producing a choral effect (S. van Balen pers. comm.).

STATUS AND DISTRIBUTION Rare or uncommon resident, more frequent in East Java. Northern Sumatra south to Mt Kerinci and east through the highlands of Java, Bali and on the Rinjani volcano, Lombok; also recently seen on Sumbawa (Coates & Bishop 1997). Previously (and mistakenly) considered to occur as a rare breeding visitor to Taiwan; there are no recent breeding records of any White's Thrushes (*Z. dauma* group) on Taiwan, where the race *aurea* is known to be an uncommon or rare winter visitor (Fang in litt.).

Distribution note Included in volume 2 of *The Birds of the Malay Peninsula* (Robinson 1928) under *Oreocincla aurea horsfieldi* on the basis of three specimens from Peninsular Thailand, despite being called Javan Mountain Thrush. These specimens are referable to *affinis* which is now considered to be synonymous with the nominate race of White's Thrush.

MOVEMENTS Presumed to be an altitude migrant, reportedly commoner at lower levels in the winter months.

HABITAT The undergrowth and low vegetation of montane deciduous, rhododendron and open *Casuarina* forests between 920 and 2800 m (3030–9240′), although occurs down to c.1200 m (3960′) on Bali.

BEHAVIOUR An uncommon, rarely seen and probably greatly overlooked bird of dense mountain forests where it forages quietly on the ground; however on occasion it has been found to be tame or approachable. May occasionally venture out onto the edges of trails or paths. Food mostly snails, molluscs, invertebrates and worms but also berries and other small fruits.

BREEDING Poorly known. Season: (West Java) January to late February or March to November. Nest: compact cup-shaped structure of moss, twigs, grass and roots usually placed near the ground in a bush or along a moss-covered branch up to 2 m. Eggs: 1–2, pinkish-buff to greenish or yellowish-white, lightly blotched lavender-grey or spotted with pale brown (Hellebrekers & Hoogerwerf 1967). Probably two broods.

MOULT No information.

MEASUREMENTS Wing 133.5–145; tarsus 35–37; bill (culmen) 26–28, (from gape) 31–37 (Robinson & Kloss 1918). Weight apparently unrecorded.

REFERENCES Hellebrekers & Hoogerwerf (1967), Robinson & Kloss (1918).

53 FAWN-BREASTED THRUSH *Zoothera machiki* Plate 18

Geocichla machiki Forbes, 1883, *Proc. Zool. Soc. London*: 589, pl. 52 – Timor-Laut, Tanimbar Is.

IDENTIFICATION 21–22 cm (8½″). A scarce or rare resident of Tanimbar Island, eastern Wallacea, Indonesia. Until recently known from only 2–3 specimens collected in 1883 and at the turn of the century, not seen again until the mid-1980s (Collar and Andrew 1988) and again in November 1992 (Lewis 1993); more recently seen 3–4 times (Bishop & Brickle 1998, D. Gibbs pers. comm.); occasionally relatively easily observed. Requires further research into breeding behaviour and relationships with other *Zoothera* thrushes. Previously treated as a race of White's Thrush (50) but differs slightly in plumage, size and choice of habitat, and now regarded as a very poorly known species (see taxonomic note under White's Thrush). **Confusion species** No serious problem in range; the plain upperparts and warm rust-coloured rump differ considerably from the slate-grey Slaty-backed Thrush (26), the only other sympatric thrush.

DESCRIPTION (from three specimens) Sexes alike. **Adult** Forehead and crown brown or washed greyish, nape slightly paler. Mantle, upper back and scapulars olive-brown; may show orange-buff central shafts and blackish-brown tips to outer scapulars and slightly darker or browner tips to mantle, back and inner scapulars; lower back, rump and uppertail-coverts warm or russet-brown. Tail brown or warm brown, slightly duller than rump and uppertail-coverts, outermost feathers paler brown with whitish spot (at least 20 mm) on innerweb at tip. Median coverts blackish-brown broadly tipped whitish, greater coverts dark brown edged paler or olive brown and less broadly tipped whitish especially on inner greaters; alula brown or pale brown edged paler brown or light orange on outerweb, primary coverts blackish-brown and narrowly edged paler orange-buff on base of outerweb; flight feathers dark brown but broadly edged buffish-brown on outer primaries, and bases to inner primaries form a paler panel against rest of flight feathers, edges to secondaries paler earth-brown; tertials as secondaries but tipped whitish-buff. Underwing shows typical *Zoothera* pattern of white on lesser coverts and bases to axillaries and median coverts; greater coverts black or blackish-brown, tips white, bases of secondaries and inner primaries white. Lores to cheeks and lower ear-coverts pale buff, very finely flecked or spotted olive-brown, upper ear-coverts brown or olive-brown flecked paler, with thin olive malar stripe.

Chin and throat white becoming off-white, light beige on lower throat and sides of neck with fine ill-defined olive tips. Lower breast to upper belly light tan to yellowish-brown finely edged olive-brown becoming more heavily edged browner on lower breast and upper belly; flanks and lower belly white more heavily barred blackish-brown on flanks; undertail-coverts whitish with long central olive-brown stripe on centre of undertail-coverts. Bill sooty-grey above with yellow lower mandible. Legs and feet pale flesh. **Immature** Juvenile unknown, probably very similar to adult but with pale shaft-streaks on crown, nape and mantle and dark edges to rest of upperparts and mottled or blotched dark brown on breast and flanks.

GEOGRAPHICAL VARIATION None. Monotypic.

VOICE Call a thin but sharp *tsip* or *tsit*. Song a simple series of whistled or piping notes.

STATUS AND DISTRIBUTION Rare or scarce; considered Near-Threatened (Collar *et al.* 1994). Tanimbar (Timor-laut) Islands (Yamdena and Larat), Lesser Sunda Islands, Indonesia.

MOVEMENTS Sedentary.

HABITAT Lowland monsoon and gallery forests, degraded and secondary forest, scrub and forest edge.

BEHAVIOUR Usually alone in undergrowth or dense scrub but not shy; frequently seen in the early morning foraging in the open on the forest floor, along streams and watercourses, trails and roads; recently found to favour recently burnt areas (Lewis 1993). On the ground hops or runs in typical fashion.

BREEDING Unknown.

MOULT No information.

MEASUREMENTS (n=1) Wing 112; tarsus 30.5; bill (culmen) 20.5, (to gape) 26. Weight apparently unrecorded.

REFERENCES Bishop & Brickle (1998), Lewis (1993), White & Bruce (1986).

54 BASSIAN THRUSH *Zoothera lunulata* Plate 18
(White's Thrush, Olive-tailed Thrush, Speckled Thrush, Mountain Thrush, King Thrush, Tiger Thrush, Large-billed Ground-Thrush)

Turdus lunulata Latham, 1810, *Index Orn. suppl.*: xlii – Nova Hollandia [restricted to Sydney by Mathews (1920) *Birds Australia* suppl. 1, check-list: 147].

IDENTIFICATION 22–26 cm (8¾–10¼"). One of two *Zoothera* thrushes that occur on mainland Australia; formerly treated as a race of White's Thrush (50) but now recognised as a separate species. This and the following species – Russet-tailed Thrush (55) – coexist (but largely separated altitudinally) in the forests of north-east New South Wales and southern Queensland. **Confusion species** Very similar to White's (which is absent from Australia) and Russet-tailed Thrushes, but generally separable by heavier or more prominent scaling or barring on the tips to the upperparts, and olive, not rufous or russet, on the rump to base of the tail; some birds, particularly those in overlap

areas, may not always be separable with certainty in the field. Also differs vocally and probably (though not well understood) in habitat selection. Overlaps with Russet-tailed for c.350 km in eastern Queensland but occurs at higher levels.

Taxonomic note Ford (1983) discussed the *Zoothera dauma* complex in Australia and, as followed here, proposed the specific recognition of this and the following species.

DESCRIPTION Sexes alike. **Adult** Forehead, crown and nape to sides of neck like White's Thrush but slightly darker olive or olive-tan with small (often absent) pale yellowish-buff tips or subterminal spots and fine blackish bars at tips. Mantle, back and scapulars to rump and uppertail-coverts olive-brown or olive-tan, some birds appearing darker or tinged bronze; lacks pale buff or yellowish-buff subterminal spots (but at close range sometimes shows faint pale buff or yellowish-tan edges to outer scapulars or very fine central shafts on mantle and back); rump generally more olive; centres of uppertail-coverts sometimes paler, all heavily or broadly fringed blackish creating prominent scaly pattern. Tail (12 feathers) dark brown tinged olive, four central feathers sometimes slightly paler olive-brown, buffish tips to all feathers most prominent (up to c.20 mm but usually less on males than females) or whitest on outer pair. Median and greater coverts brown or olive-brown with pale buff tips on some, usually most prominent on outer medians and faint or narrow on greaters (edges to some greaters may be browner as are some outerwebs of primaries and outer secondaries). Broad white eye-ring, ill-defined blackish smudge below eye and pale buff forward ear-coverts, finely edged olive and becoming darker with fine blackish tips on rear ear-coverts; narrow but prominent dark malar stripe. Underparts whitish but washed light yellowish-buff on breast, some feathers on sides of lower breast and flanks also yellowish-buff subterminally, sides of breast also olive, all prominently tipped or barred blackish-brown on flanks and sides of belly, but more widely or erratically spaced on belly, which lacks any olive or yellowish. Upper mandible brownish-black to dark grey, lower brown or pale pinkish-brown. Legs and feet pale flesh-pink, greyish-fleshy or fleshy-white. **Immature** Juvenile similar to adult but has smaller blackish crescents on upperparts and pale tips to tail; underparts also mottled buffish with blackish spots instead of well defined crescents on centre of breast and belly. First-year bird retains juvenile feathers in wing and tail as in same-age White's Thrush.

GEOGRAPHICAL VARIATION Three races; variation clinal. Races *cuneata* and *macrorhyncha* have long heavy bills, and the upper mandible of *macrorhyncha* has a hooked tip; both are similar in plumage to nominate *lunulata* but *macrorhyncha* has a longer, browner tail with a warmer or brighter tinge to all feathers except the outermost, which is pale brown (paler on the innerweb) with a dull whitish tip. Some *macrorhyncha* may show a warmer or slightly browner tinge to the rump and uppertail-coverts; the underparts are slightly paler or whiter with a yellowish-buff tinge to the breast and some olive at sides of breast, heavily or densely scaled dark or blackish. *Cuneata* is, on average, slightly darker olive-brown, the upperparts with a russet tinge, and with a brown tail except for the central feathers, which are tinged olive, and an extensive area of white (up to 35 mm) on the innerweb of the outermost feathers. Has a slightly whiter chin and throat, becoming yellowish on lower throat and flecked or tipped brown, variable from yellowish-buff to pale cinnamon-buff broadly tipped dark brown forming bars or scales on breast, upper belly and flanks; ground colour to centre of belly and flanks whiter. The wing is also longer than in nominate. Bill black. Legs and feet yellowish-brown.

VOICE Mostly silent but gives a thin *seep* contact note in flight or when taking flight; also a sharp or insect-like *chi-lit* and occasional churring notes, possibly as an alarm or aggression call. Song a weak or subdued but tuneful Blackbird-like warbling and trills, carrying only a short distance; also a more drawn-out fluted two-note whistle connected with an upward inflection and occasionally developed into a melodious warble; and a series of very soft piping *hiss* notes given during the day. Song period unpredictable but recorded mostly in the southern winter and spring. Sings mostly at dusk, through the night and again in the early dawn for short periods but may also sing during the day in poor or dull weather.

STATUS AND DISTRIBUTION Fairly common.

Z. l. cuneata Atherton Tablelands, Herberton district, north-central Queensland, Australia.

Z. l. lunulata Extreme south-east Queensland, eastern and southern New South Wales to southeast South Australia in the Mt Lofty Ranges and Kangaroo Island; also on King and Flinders Islands.

Z. l. macrorhyncha Tasmania.

Taxonomic note some authorities (e.g. Ford 1983) consider *cuneata* and *macrorhyncha* to be synonymous.

MOVEMENTS Mostly sedentary but wanders locally when not breeding and occur in wetter areas of river valleys. In exceptionally dry years may become nomadic in search of suitable habitat. In April and May 1991 considerable numbers were forced into a number of new locations by a combination of drought and forest fires.

HABITAT Dense heavy forests, from c.700 m (2310') (sometimes as low as to c.550 m/1800') to c.1050 m (3465') (Holmes 1984) in humid tropical coastal rainforests and eucalyptus woodlands with wet sclerophyll scrub or underbrush; in places breeds in pine plantations. In non-breeding season may occur in more open drier areas including secondary forests and large secluded gardens.

BEHAVIOUR Usually alone or in pairs; very shy and secretive, preferring to forage quietly in undisturbed areas on the ground under thick vegetation, where it flicks through fallen leaves and decaying vegetation in search of invertebrates or worms; on occasion may emerge into the open in grassy clearings or forest edges; may be crepuscular. When disturbed crouches low and still or bounds or rapidly flies into cover, but may also remain motionless in tree or thick shrub, evading detection by its camouflaged plumage. Flies quickly and directly through forests, but over longer distances across more open areas the flight is more gently undulating or bounding on powerful wing-beats. Food, taken mostly from the ground, is insects, earthworms and molluscs supplemented by fruit from trees and bushes.

BREEDING Season: late June or July to December. Nest: large, rounded and substantial bowl-shaped structure of bark strips, fine twigs and stems, grasses and leaves, lined with moss and fine dry grass and roots and may be covered with bunches of moss; usually placed in the fork of a tree or branch, in a tree crevice, occasionally behind loose areas of bark, on a tree-stump or in the crown of a tree-fern up to 15 m (50') from the ground. Eggs: 2–3, pale green or bluish-green but also sometimes dull bluish-grey, greyish-green, buffish-stone or off-white, finely freckled, spotted or blotched light reddish-brown. Two broods. The same nest may be used in several subsequent breeding seasons.

MOULT No information.
MEASUREMENTS Wing, male 134–142, female 129–138; tarsus 31–35; bill 25–28; *cuneata* wing, male 138–148, female 135–140; bill (culmen) 28–32. Weight 90–120 g (Schodde & Mason 1999).
REFERENCES Ford (1983), Holmes (1984), Schodde & Mason (1999).

55 RUSSET-TAILED THRUSH *Zoothera heinei*   Plate 18

Oreocincla Heinei Cabanis, 1851, *Mus. Hein.* 1: 6 – Japan [in error; corrected to north Australia, Queensland, in J. Orn. 20: 237].

IDENTIFICATION 25.5–27.5 cm (10–10¾"); females smaller than males. An Australo-Papuan species in the White's Thrush complex, formerly treated as a race of White's (50) but now considered a separate species although very similar to the slightly larger Bassian Thrush (54), the only other *Zoothera* thrush in Australia. Mainly olive-coloured with fairly broad dark or blackish edges and tips, forming a predominantly scalloped pattern on the upperparts; dark fringes or tips narrower on the rump and uppertail-coverts and warm brown, extending to the base of the tail. Underparts also heavily barred with broad blackish bars at tips of individual feathers. **Confusion species** Only likely to be mistaken for Bassian Thrush (White's does not occur in Australia), which is generally more olive above, especially on the rump, and has heavier dark bars or scales on the upperparts, particularly on the rump, and white (not buff) tips to the tail. Also differs in song and habitat preference; where the two species occur together Russet-tailed is found at lower altitudes.
DESCRIPTION Sexes alike. **Adult** Entire upperparts olive or tinged russet with much finer blackish bars and edges to feathers, at close range (in hand, scapulars, mantle and lower back can show very thin or narrow pale central shafts); rump and uppertail-coverts very narrowly barred (appearing absent in some in field) and visibly tinged warmer rufous, and central tail feathers russet-brown on central two pairs becoming darker on outer feathers, outermost feather pale brown with extensive white (at least 20 mm) on innerweb, tips of outer two feathers white (white may extend thinly onto other outer feathers). Wings as White's but more rounded and tinged rufous; has cream or dull buffish tips to median and greater coverts, innerwebs to flight feathers and tertials browner, outerwebs to tertials olive or lighter olive. Broad whitish submoustachial fairly heavily spotted or flecked olive as are cheeks, ear-coverts and broad dark malar. Underparts very similar to Bassian, whitish but washed pale yellowish-buff on breast, with some feathers on sides of lower breast and flanks also tawny or yellowish-buff; sides of breast white (sometimes tinged olive), tipped or barred blackish-brown on flanks and sides of belly, generally with smaller bars or tips than on Bassian. Bill light

horn-brown or greyish-horn. Legs and feet variably light greyish-pink to light or straw-yellow. **Immature** Juvenile very similar to same-age White's and also resembles adult, but has less pronounced black crescents on upper- and underparts.
GEOGRAPHICAL VARIATION Four races; variation clinal and not well marked except for *papuensis* which is slightly smaller (21.5–23 cm/8½–9") and slightly darker than nominate.
     Race *papuensis* has forehead to crown and nape golden-buff subterminally and extensively barred dark or blackish-brown; mantle, back and scapulars also golden-brown or slightly darker and tinged olive; rump and uppertail-coverts warm or gingery in tone and (generally) with less or narrow black barring; tail dark brown with paler brown outer feathers and extensive (up to 5 cm/2") white on distal half of innerweb. Median and greater coverts blackish with creamy-white spot at tip of each feather forming a double wing-bar; flight feathers dark brown edged pale warm or golden-brown on primaries and outer secondaries; outerweb of tertials also warm brown, tipped creamy-buff. Chin and throat pale golden-buffish (including submoustachial) with fairly long dark malar and less extensive barring on lower throat. Bill black; lower mandible may be horn or dark brown except for a small whitish area at base. Legs and feet pale pinkish-flesh.
     Race *eichhorni* is very similar to but slightly smaller than *papuensis* and lacks any warm or gingery-ochre tinge to rump and uppertail-coverts; crown slightly paler; mantle, back and scapulars have darker olive bases and slightly narrower black edges or tips; underparts may have reduced barring; lower mandible, legs and feet light horn.
     Race *choiseuli* resembles *eichhorni* but with a longer wing and a more rufescent rump.
     Taxonomic note Ripley (1964) treated all taxa in the *heinei* group as part of the White's/Scaly Thrush complex in *Z. dauma*. Ford (1983) discussed the *Z. dauma* complex in Australia and reviewed the relationship of other forms in the group, concluding that *heinei* and *lunulata* were full species inhabiting Australia, with *papuensis*, *eichhorni* and *choiseuli* morphologically closer to *heinei* and, as such, races of that species. He also considered *papuensis* most probably worthy of

specific recognition but stopped short of doing so until such time as more is known of its calls and behaviour. Several other authors have classified all three subspecies under Bassian Thrush but we find Ford's evidence more persuasive. In addition, we have proposed elsewhere in this book that no further changes be adopted concerning the *dauma* complex until a comprehensive biochemical review is made.

VOICE Little known; mostly silent, but has a thin high-pitched whistling or hissing *tsee-ip* contact or distress call and a stronger, more pleasant whistling *wheeer doo* or *theea thooa* double-note; gives a chattering alarm call similar to that of Blackbird (111). Song unknown.

STATUS AND DISTRIBUTION Fairly common except for *papuensis* which is rare or little known. The race *choiseuli* is known from a single specimen taken in 1924.

Z. h. papuensis Widely scattered throughout New Guinea from the upper Utakwa River, Irian Jaya, in the west and more continuously from the Snow Mountains east to the Adelbert Mountains, Huon Peninsula, Eastern Highlands and some of the south-east ranges.

Z. h. eichhorni Eloaua and Mussau, St Matthias Islands, New Ireland province, Papua New Guinea.

Z. h. choiseuli Choiseul Island, Solomon Islands.

Z. h. heinei Eastern Queensland, north to about Ingham and south to about Gloucester, New South Wales, Australia. Range in New South Wales may be expanding; recorded south to Mosman, August 1992 (Morris & Burton 1993).

MOVEMENTS Sedentary.

HABITAT Rainforests and dense wet eucalyptus woods of lowland valleys between 300 and 750 m (990–2475′) (Holmes 1984). Occasionally to about 900 m (2970′); *papuensis* occurs in primary

hill forests between 490 and 1700 m (1615–5600′) but mostly occurs at c.1200 m (3960′); *eichhorni* occurs mainly in primary and secondary lowland rainforests and adjacent regrowth and thickets.

BEHAVIOUR Similar to that of White's Thrush; usually alone or in pairs (although family parties occur together in late breeding season) and generally shy and unapproachable; may be seen feeding on tracks or at the edge of forests, particularly in the early morning; *papuensis* is considered to be extremely secretive and generally little known – walks on the ground and has been seen to adopt a curious slow bobbing motion when foraging (P. Colston pers. comm.). Most sightings (especially outside Australia) are of birds flushed at close range from ground cover; may fly off at about 2–3 m (6–9′) above the ground level or rely on camouflage to avoid detection. Forages on the ground for invertebrates, including worms and molluscs; occasionally fruit.

BREEDING Season: August–January. Nest: similar to Bassian Thrush – a large cup or bowl of bark strips, dead leaves and dry grasses, lined with fine roots and covered with moss, usually placed up to 15 m (50′) in the fork of a tree or on an old stump and hidden by vegetation. Eggs: 2–3, pale green or greenish-blue with fine pale reddish or reddish-brown speckles.

MOULT No information.

MEASUREMENTS (n=12) Wing, male 122–130, female 122–128; tarsus 28–31; bill 30.5–34.5; *papuensis* (n=7) wing 108.5–119; tarsus 26–30; bill 23.5–29; *eichhorni* wing, male 103–112, female 107; tarsus 30–32; bill 25–27.5; *choiseuli* (n=1) wing 109; tarsus 26; bill 27. Weight 85–115 g (Ripley & Hadden 1982, Schodde & Mason 1999).

REFERENCES Ford (1983), Holmes (1984), Morris & Burton (1993), Ripley and Hadden (1982), Schodde & Mason (1999).

56 NEW BRITAIN THRUSH *Zoothera talaseae*   Plate 19
(Northern Melanesian Ground-Thrush, Black-backed Ground-Thrush, White-bellied Ground-Thrush, San Cristobal Ground-Thrush)

Turdus talaseae **Rothschild and Hartert, 1926,** *Bull. Brit. Orn. Club* **46: 53 – Talasea, New Britain.**

IDENTIFICATION 20–23 cm (8–9″). An almost unknown ground-living resident with a limited range in the highland forests of New Britain and Bougainville Islands. Until recently known only from eight museum specimens collected in 1925, 1971 and 1980. From specimens it is a slate-grey or black and white thrush with two white wingbars and a scaled or scalloped pattern on the sides of the underparts. **Confusion species** The distinctive plumage makes it unlikely to be confused with any other species; within its range the only other thrush in range is Island Thrush (112).

Taxonomic note Previously considered as a distinctive race of White's Thrush (50) (see Ripley & Hadden 1982).

DESCRIPTION Sexes alike. **Adult** Entire upperparts

deep or blackish-slate grey and continuous from lores across cheeks and ear-coverts (but cheeks often flecked while extending onto ear-coverts), slightly darker or blacker on head and lighter on rump and uppertail-coverts; mantle and back have black fringes, present but narrower on rump. Tail also blackish-slate with large white tips (at least 20 mm) to outer feathers. Median coverts white, greater coverts grey or dark slate-grey boldly tipped white; flight feathers slate-grey or slightly darker, narrowly edged grey-brown on outerwebs and slightly paler at bases of inner primaries and outer secondaries. Underwing has axillaries white with black tips, lesser coverts and bases to median coverts white and extending to bend of wing, tips of inner medians and all greaters black or blackish-grey towards bend of wing, bases to flight feathers white, becoming indistinct or diffuse on primaries. Chin and throat to sides of neck white as are rest of underparts, but sides of breast and flanks heavily edged black or blackish slate-grey forming large scales or semicircles extending towards centre of belly. Bill black but lower mandible and cutting edges to upper mandible paler or greyer. Legs and feet light horn-brown, dark grey or blackish. **Immature** Juvenile unknown but probably similar to adult with fine pale central shafts on head and upperparts and pale buff spots at tips of median and greater coverts.

GEOGRAPHICAL VARIATION Two races; variation not well marked. Race *atrigena* similar to nominate but darker or duller black on upperparts, including cheeks (no white flecking) and sides of head, and generally lacks darker edges on mantle and back. White tips to median and greater coverts also much smaller and more crescent-like than in nominate. Bill black. Legs and feet black (male) and brownish-black (female).

VOICE The only known note (from *atrigena*) is a thin or high-pitched peevish whistle, very similar to others in the White's Thrush complex. The song is unknown.

STATUS AND DISTRIBUTION Extremely rare and very little known; few records, but recent sightings on New Britain in late 1990s (D. Gibbs & G. Dutson pers. comm.). Previously known from only four specimens collected in 1925 and 1971 (Diamond 1971); *atrigena* is known only from four specimens

collected in June 1980 (Hadden 1981, Ripley & Hadden 1982). Listed as Near-threatened (Collar *et al.* 1994), but without specific information difficult to determine its true status. Probably never more numerous than the few records suggest; it may exist at very low density levels.

Z. t. talaseae Mount Otu, New Britain, and Umboi Islands, Bismarck Archipelago, Papua New Guinea.

Z. t. atrigena Crown Prince Range, Bougainville Island, Papua New Guinea.

MOVEMENTS Sedentary.

HABITAT Montane forests; on New Britain occurs at 580–1430 m (1910–4720'), on Umboi down to at least 1300 m; *atrigena* occurs in mist-forest at c.1500 m (4950').

BEHAVIOUR Generally shy, secretive and little known; has been seen very few times by ornithologists. Forages low down in undergrowth or on the ground. Feeds on insects and their larvae.

BREEDING Nest: constructed entirely of moss interwoven with fine rootlets. Eggs: 2, similar to those of Blackbird, but smaller and with fine rufous spots at broader end (Sharpe in *Ibis* 1926: 53–55).

MOULT No information.

MEASUREMENTS Wing 103–109; bill 21–25; tarsus 27.5–30; *atrigena* wing 96–100; tarsus 33–38; bill 20–27.5 (Hadden 1981, Ripley & Hadden 1982). Weight apparently unrecorded.

REFERENCES Coates (1990), Hadden (1981), Ripley & Hadden (1982).

57 SAN CRISTOBAL THRUSH *Zoothera margaretae* Plate 19

Turdus margaretae Mayr, 1935, *Amer. Mus. Novit.* 820: 4 – San Cristobal, 1900', Solomon Islands.

IDENTIFICATION 20–23 cm (8–9"). A shy or secretive endemic of Makira in the Solomon Islands and best detected by its call. A medium-sized thrush, dark olive-brown above with white spots at the tips of the wing-coverts, larger or more obvious on the greater coverts, short and fairly rounded wing, and a distinctive scaled pattern below; flushed birds fly off with a whirring sound. **Confusion species** Could only be mistaken for the similar but allopatric Guadalcanal Thrush (58) (previously considered a race of San Cristobal Thrush), which is more heavily marked on the underparts and lacks the pale or whitish tips to the median and greater coverts and tips to the tertials. **DESCRIPTION** Sexes alike. **Adult** Entire upperparts uniformly olive-brown but slightly darker or duller on head; rump and uppertail-coverts warmer or tinged rufous-brown. Tail uniformly brown. Median and greater coverts blackish-brown with white at tips of medians restricted to edges; large white spots at tips of greaters; primary coverts uniform brown to dark brown; flight feathers dark brown with warmer brown edges to outerwebs, tertials similar but with small whitish

subterminal spots at tips. Underwing has lesser coverts to bend of wing whitish, median and greater underwing-coverts blackish or dark grey, and broad white wing-bar at base of mid-primaries to inner secondaries. Upper lores and sides of crown pale or whitish, lower lores, cheeks and ear-coverts white with blackish tips becoming brown with whitish flecks. Chin and throat white or whitish with a poor or ill-defined whitish submoustachial bordered by dark olive or brownish tips; breast whitish in centre becoming olive-grey at sides, whitish subterminally with broad brown or blackish-brown fringes extending to flanks, but with larger white ovals and dark edges or fringes; sides of belly with narrower or thinner fringes, centre of belly to vent and undertail-coverts white or buffish-white. Bill black. Legs and feet pinkish-white. In fresh plumage may show darker tips or terminal band to feathers on back. **Immature** Very similar to adult but more scaly on upperparts with russet subterminal and dark or blackish bars at tips of mantle and back. Forehead to nape with pale spots or centres and olive-brown edges and tips. Underparts with less defined margins to breast feathers and sometimes brownish wash to centres.

GEOGRAPHICAL VARIATION None. Monotypic.

VOICE Call a thin, high-pitched, drawn-out, sometimes slowly descending *tseep* whistle, fairly typical of the genus; also may give a soft *chook*. Song a simple tuneless series of clicking and grating notes and short high-pitched whistles (Gibbs 1996). Sings and calls from deep within thickets; generally does not respond to taped calls or songs.

STATUS AND DISTRIBUTION Generally a little known and poorly documented species with very few sight records. Locally common within the preferred altitude range; considered elusive but not uncommon above 650 m (2145') (J. Hornbuckle pers. comm.). Endemic to Makira (San Cristobal), Solomon Islands. Considered Near-Threatened (Collar *et al.* 1994).

MOVEMENTS Sedentary.

HABITAT Ground vegetation and undergrowth of montane primary forests at 200–700 m (660–2310'), occasionally in secondary growth and overgrown gardens (Buckingham *et al.* 1995).

BEHAVIOUR Extremely shy and secretive, skulking in thick vegetation; in flight wings make a distinctive whirring sound; most sightings are of birds flushed from footpaths in the early dawn (the local name `babainitara' means `the bird that lives by the road') (Buckingham *et al.* 1995).

MOULT No information.

MEASUREMENTS (n=4) Wing, male 95–99, female 91–95; tarsus 34–37; bill (culmen) 24–26. Weight 60–71 g.

REFERENCES Buckingham *et al.* (1995), Collar *et al.* (1992), Gibbs (1996), Mayr (1935, 1936).

---

58 GUADALCANAL THRUSH *Zoothera turipavae* Plate 19
Zoothera margaretae turipavae Cain & Galbraith, 1955, *Bull. Brit. Orn. Club* 75: 92 – Turipava, 4100', mountains of Guadalcanal.

IDENTIFICATION 19.5–20 cm (7¾–8"). One of the least known thrushes in the world, restricted to Guadalcanal in the Solomon Islands. Head and upperparts dark or sooty-brown, no wing-bars and heavily patterned underparts of white or yellowish ovals broadly fringed with brown or blackish-brown. Slightly smaller in size but similar to other *Zoothera* thrushes in shape, but has relatively short bill and tail and long legs. **Confusion species** Similar to San Cristobal Thrush (57) but slightly smaller, darker above without pale tips to the coverts and tertials, more heavily patterned below with distinct pale or whitish ovals broadly edged darker, flanks greyer and tips to undertail-coverts buffish not white.

Taxonomic note Previously considered a race of San Cristobal Thrush (57).

DESCRIPTION Sexes probably alike. **Adult** Entire upperparts dusky-olive or earth-brown becoming slightly warmer or browner-olive on rump, upper-tail-coverts and centre of tail, rest of tail dark brown edged chestnut at base. Wings dark brown but edges to alula and secondaries rufous or chestnut forming a small, inconspicuous panel; underwing has typical *Zoothera* pattern. Face as top of head and upperparts or slightly browner, finely flecked buff and slightly darker behind eye; buffish eye-ring. Chin and throat pale greyish-white but sides of chin and lower throat flecked or indistinctly streaked olive-brown; breast, upper belly and flanks with large pale off-white or yellowish-buff (especially towards tip) oval centres to feathers, bordered with dark or blackish-brown, most heavily on breast and sides of belly; flanks greyish, centre of belly white with broad black fringes or tips but centre of lower belly white, undertail-coverts cinnamon or gingery-brown with whitish bases. Bill black with base to lower mandible greyish. Legs and feet greyish-fuscous to blackish but claws white or ivory. **Immature** First-winter bird has pale central shafts to most upperparts, wings slightly browner with bright orange-buff tips to median and greater coverts.

GEOGRAPHICAL VARIATION None. Monotypic.

VOICE Call a very thin, high-pitched *tsssss-ssss* similar to that of San Cristobal Thrush, occasionally drawn out into a short hiss. Song very distinct from San Cristobal Thrush, a long, loud, melodious series of upward or rising but slurred whistles, short trills and repeated modulated whistles, occasionally including the call note (Gibbs 1996). Sings mostly at dawn from low song-posts (up to 1 m from the ground) but also occasionally later in the day. Responds to playback of taped songs.

STATUS AND DISTRIBUTION Uncertain. Endemic to the mountain forests of Guadalcanal, Solomon Islands, but only known from very few records. Only one specimen (probably a first-year bird, taken in August 1953: Cain & Galbraith 1955) exists. The next record was of a singing bird on 11 March 1994 (Gibbs 1996) above Turipava, close to the type locality on Mt Mbutohaina in the central mountains of Guadalcanal (D. Gibbs pers. comm.), and one was at the same locality in 1997 (G. Dutson pers. comm.); no others have been seen or heard but much high ground on Guadalcanal remains largely unexplored.

MOVEMENTS Sedentary.

HABITAT Mist-forest above 1000 m (3300').

BEHAVIOUR Little known; secretive but not always shy. The single bird observed in the field in March 1994 kept on or close to the ground and was elusive but seemingly unafraid, singing apparently unconcerned by the presence of the observer just a few feet away (D. Gibbs pers. comm.).

MOULT No information.

MEASUREMENTS (n=1) Wing 90.5; bill 24.5; tarsus 36.5; Weight 53.5 g.

REFERENCES Cain & Galbraith (1955), Galbraith & Galbraith (1962), Gibbs (1996).

59 LONG-BILLED THRUSH *Zoothera monticola* **Plate 20**

(Large Brown Thrush, Greater Long-billed Thrush, Large Long-billed Thrush)

Zoothera monticola Vigors, 1832, *Proc. Zool. Soc. London*: 172 – Himalayas
[restricted to Simla-Almora area, *vide* Ticehurst & Whistler (1924) Ibis (11)6: 472].

IDENTIFICATION 27–29 cm (10½–11½"). Generally a stoutly built thrush of the Himalayas to Burma (also northern Vietnam) with a short tail and curved bill, dark brown above and spotted below with whitish mid-breast, belly and underwing, and olive-brown sides of breast and flanks. Very scarce but shy and undoubtedly easily overlooked. **Confusion species** Long bill, dark upperparts and short tail distinguish it from most other similar species of the region; main problem is likely to be Dark-sided Thrush (60) which is slightly smaller and browner, notably on the wings, with a shorter bill, better defined face pattern, scaled (not spotted) underparts, and buffish underwing.

DESCRIPTION Sexes alike. Female slightly smaller than male. **Adult** Entire upperparts from forehead to rump and uppertail-coverts dark brown, each feather fringed slightly darker, creating a suffused scalloped effect at close range; forehead to crown slightly paler or tinged rufous-brown. Tail short and brown with slightly paler brown outer feathers. All coverts and flight feathers brown to dark brown but tips to median and greater coverts may be slightly paler with broad paler edges to primaries. Underwing has axillaries dark brown with white bases, lesser coverts to bend of wing white; lower median coverts dark brown and greater coverts broadly blackish-brown tipped white; bases of secondaries and inner primaries white. Face brown, finely mottled paler brown on lores and whitish on cheeks with whitish streaks on ear-coverts. Broad blackish-brown malars to sides of upper breast. Centre of chin and throat white, finely spotted or speckled olive-brown; centre of breast whitish, heavily marked with large dark or blackish-brown spots, streaks or blotches; sides of breast to flanks olive-brown or tinged greyish-brown and diffusely spotted or blotched darker. Centre of belly off-whitish spotted with dark brown or grey-brown; lower flanks grey-brown. Undertail-coverts dark brown with white central shaft-streaks and broad white tips. Bill long and upper mandible noticeably decurved at tip, dark brown or black. Legs and feet light brown. In worn plumage some adults show faded or pale greyish-buff edges to median and greater coverts. **Immature** Juvenile similar to adult but browner with slightly shorter bill and light buff central shafts on forehead, crown, nape, mantle, back and scapulars, also on median and greater coverts and tertials; tips to median and greater coverts pale or dull orange-buff. Face heavily mottled with dark brown and pale orange-buff spots or tips. Underparts mottled with light yellowish or orange-brown bases and dark or blackish-brown bars at tips; flanks grey-brown with broad pale

buff central shaft-streaks. The pale orange-buff tips to median and greater coverts are retained into first-year plumage, as are some pale central shaft-streaks on crown and nape.

GEOGRAPHICAL VARIATION Two races; variation clinal and not well marked. Race *atrata* has head tinged brownish but rest of upperparts much darker or blacker-brown, with bases to feathers very deep or dark grey; the wings are also browner; underparts whitish as in nominate but more extensively tipped with black.

VOICE Generally silent but has a loud *zaaaaaaaa* alarm note. Song a loud but rather sad, mournful or melancholy series of up to three slow, plaintive whistles, *te-e-uw* or *sew-a-tew-tew*, with the middle note higher than the other two. Variations on this theme occur, e.g. *weech-a-wee-wuu*, with the soft-toned whistles initiated or intermingled with harsher or more rasping notes, *rrraee ti tuu* or *trrray tya tyee*. Sings for short periods (up to c.10 minutes only), mostly in the early morning and again at dusk (Martens & Eck 1995), usually from the tops of tall trees.

STATUS AND DISTRIBUTION Scarce to rare but very secretive; considered Near-Threatened (Collar *et al.* 1994).

Z. m. monticola Himalayas of northern India from (about Kulu) Garwhal, Himachal Pradesh east through Nepal to Sikkim, Bhutan, northern Bengal, Assam and Arunachal Pradesh and south to Nagaland, Manipur and Meghalaya, and to north-west Burma (Mizo, the northern Chin Hills and Myitkyina).

Z. m. atrata Western Tonkin south to Central Annam, Vietnam.

MOVEMENTS An altitude migrant wintering at lower levels within the breeding range. In Nepal winters at 915–2500 m (3020–8250') but has been recorded down to 250–300 m as a rare visitor to Chitwan National Park (825–990'); in Sikkim and much of Assam winters at 1500–2000 m (4950–6600') but in parts of Sikkim and Bhutan stays as high as 2900 m (9570'). Timing of these movements little known but passage birds in Nepal in April. A vagrant to the Chittagong Hills of eastern Bangladesh.

HABITAT Thick tangled undergrowth of dense fir forests including bamboo clumps or rhododendrons, often in damp areas of moss or moss-covered rocks or near streams, seeming to require open patches of moist or muddy earth or banks, at 2285–3350 m (7540–11,055') in the Himalayas, but mostly below 2700 m (8900'); but at 900–1900 m (2970–6270') in north-east India; little is known of the birds in Vietnam, which occur at around 1500 m (5000').

BEHAVIOUR Usually alone. Extremely shy and retiring, spending long periods on the ground in dense dark forest undergrowth; probably crepuscular, spending long periods inactive. Forages in swampy ground at the edges of streams and bogs, in streambeds and around boulders, or on damp forest floors, turning over dead or decaying vegetation and stones with its large bill. Flight rapid and usually makes for cleared areas, e.g. along streams, but prefers to escape notice by hopping quietly out of view into dense vegetation. Food mostly insects or their larvae; also some snails, worms and molluscs; has been known to take some fruit.

BREEDING Season: May to July. Nest: a bulky cup-shaped structure of earth, dry leaves and damp green moss with an inner lining of fine roots, small twigs, plant fibres and lichens, usually in the fork of a tree (mostly a rhododendron) or along a horizontal branch of a moss- or lichen-covered tree, up to 5 m (16.5'), exceptionally 7 m (23') from the ground. Eggs: 3–4, variably pale greyish-green, pale olive-green, pale cream to warm buffish-cream, with small reddish or reddish-brown spots or blotches.

MOULT No information.

MEASUREMENTS Wing, male 132–150, female 130–143; tarsus 33–36; bill (from skull) 41–46; *atrata* wing 129–134. Weight (n=2) 122–131 g (Ali & Ripley 1983).

REFERENCES Ali & Ripley (1983), Martens & Eck (1995).

60 DARK-SIDED THRUSH *Zoothera marginata*   **Plate 20**
(Lesser Brown Thrush, Lesser Long-billed Thrush)
Zoothera marginata **Blyth, 1847, *J. Asiat. Soc. Bengal* 16: 141 – Arakan.**

IDENTIFICATION 23–25.5 cm (9–10"). A stout, large-billed, rather short-tailed montane thrush ranging from the eastern Himalayas through southwest China to Vietnam. Upperparts dark olive with a rufous panel on the closed wing and a well-marked face pattern with contrasting dark and pale ear-coverts and broad malars bordering a pale throat; underparts heavily scaled on the breast and sides of belly, often appearing mottled or smudged in the field. **Confusion species** Most problematic is the largely sympatric Long-billed Thrush (59). Dark-sided is slightly smaller and browner, with a shorter bill, better defined face pattern, buffish (not whitish) underwing, and paler breast with dark scales (not spots). From both Plain-backed (48) and Long-tailed (49) Thrushes by long, hook-tipped bill, short tail and lack of wing-bars; face pattern and well marked underparts with heavy scallops are also good field characters. White's Thrush (50) is slightly larger with a shorter bill and longer tail, and is more heavily mottled or speckled with broad blackish-brown bars forming scales both above and below; in flight has distinctive underwing pattern and white tips to outer tail feathers.

DESCRIPTION Sexes alike but male has blacker head and breast markings. **Adult** Forehead to nape, sides of neck and upper mantle dark brown, rest of upperparts deep or dark rufous-brown tinged olive. Tail almost entirely dark rufous-brown except for slightly paler outer feathers (outermost has white outerwebs). Wings, including all coverts, deep or dark olive-brown with tips of greater coverts and outerwebs to primaries warm rufous-brown except for buffish-white bases; centres to median and greater coverts and innerwebs to flight feathers dark brown. Underwing has axillaries brown with buffish-white bases, lesser coverts white; medians dark brown and greaters buffish-white with dark olive-brown bases; secondaries and inner primaries have buffish-white bases. Lores, cheeks and ear-coverts finely mottled or flecked off-white and brown, more heavily flecked brown below eye and paler on ear-coverts; eye-ring purplish; rear of ear-coverts broadly marked very dark brown (female) or black (male) with fine white tips. Sometimes shows indistinct off-white submoustachial with fine flecks or spots of brown (female) or blackish-brown (male) and (often indistinct) dark brown or blackish malar which may extend to below cheeks. Chin and throat pale buffish-white, spotted with brown (female) or blackish-brown (male) on sides of lower throat and sides of neck; centre of upper breast as lower throat, sides of breast dark brown (female) or blackish-brown (male) with pale or light buffish centres which usually only show towards centre of breast; sides of breast olive-brown and may appear mottled or smudged; lower breast, flanks and sides of belly distinctly and heavily scalloped with pale whitish or yellowish-cream centres and broad olive-brown fringes; flanks often more uniform olive-brown, thighs olive-brown. Vent and undertail-coverts olive-brown basally, broadly tipped dull whitish or yellowish and edged olive-brown at sides. Bill long and curved or hooked at tip, upper mandible brown or blackish-brown, lower paler. Legs and feet vary from dirty flesh-brown to grey-brown or dark bluish-brown. **Immature** First-year bird slightly browner on upperparts and has thin or fine dull orange-buff central shafts to crown, mantle, back and scapulars; tips to median and greater coverts retained into first year of adult plumage; pale orange-buff tips to tertials. Underparts mottled rufous-buff with dark brown on tips to breast, heavier on sides of lower throat, lighter on belly and flanks.

GEOGRAPHICAL VARIATION None. Monotypic.

VOICE Generally silent but contact note is a soft deep guttural *chuck* or *tjuk*; the alarm note is high-pitched repeated *pit-pit-pit*. Song poorly known (and may only be given for very short periods) but has a short (less than a second), unobtrusive and thin downwardly inflected monotone whistle similar to that of race *aurea* of White's Thrush.

STATUS AND DISTRIBUTION Uncommon or scarce. Poorly known; described by Ali & Ripley (1983) and King *et al.* (1975) as a scarce or uncommon resident or altitude migrant from the Himalayas of western Nepal east through Sikkim, Bhutan, northern Bengal, Assam and Arunachal Pradesh to western and southern Yunnan, south-west China and south to Nagaland, Meghalaya, Manipur and Mizoram, also northern Burma, western, north-west, north-east and south-east Thailand east to northern and central Laos and western and eastern Tonkin to south Annam, central Vietnam.

However, recent examination of the records in northern India and Nepal (Grimmett *et al.* 1998) suggests the range is smaller and more fragmented than previously thought. In northern India and Nepal T. P. Inskipp (pers. comm.) found very few (c.10) records outside of the more continuous area from Meghalaya to Manipur and Nagaland and none at all in Assam and Arunachal Pradesh. Smythies (1986) gave no records from northern Burma and considered it a rare bird outside the area from the Chindwin river, the Chin Hills and the Arakan Yoma, western Burma; Cheng (1987) recorded it as a rare resident in southern Yunnan.
MOVEMENTS An altitude migrant moving to lower levels generally within the breeding range but down to about 1900 m (6270') in Sikkim; in Laos to about 600 m (1980'); in Thailand regularly down to c.300 m (1000') or even lower, on occasions to the limit of evergreen forest; there are also records of wintering birds in Nepal from 274 m (900') (Biswas 1961, Inskipp & Inskipp 1985); a winter vagrant (4 records) to the hills of north-east and south-east Bangladesh.

HABITAT Thick or rank undergrowth in dense deciduous, broadleaved evergreen and fir forests between 750 and 2570 m (2475–8500'), usually near streams or in damp areas. In winter also occurs in thick vegetation, e.g. sedge and reedbeds in damp hollows and along the banks of slow streams and rivers.
BEHAVIOUR Usually alone; very shy and secretive, spending long periods on the ground or in low vegetation; crepuscular in some areas. Usually flies up into tree when disturbed but often sits motionless in thick vegetation when intruders in vicinity. Forages over wet earth, especially moist streambeds and damp patches of rotting vegetation, using its long bill and frequently digging a hole (up to 30 cm/1' in diameter) in search of food, its body disappearing below ground level. Food is mostly insects, worms and molluscs.
BREEDING Season: May–August. Nest: a large cup-shape of green moss, rootlets, twigs, plant fibres and stems, lined with fine grass, fern roots or bamboo shoots, usually placed low down in a fork of a tree or on a stump up to 5 m (16.5') from the ground and concealed behind vegetation; occasionally on the ground. Eggs: 3–4, off-white to pale grey or greyish-green with a covering of reddish-brown spots or blotches, very like those of Long-billed Thrush. Incubation apparently by both sexes.
MOULT No information.
MEASUREMENTS Wing, male 122–130, female 124–129; tarsus 27.5–30; bill, male (to skull) 33–34, female 24.5–30, (to skull) 32–33. Weight 74 g (Ali & Ripley 1983).
REFERENCES Ali & Ripley (1983), Biswas (1961), Cheng (1987), Grimmett *et al.* (1998), King *et al.* (1975), Smythies (1986).

61 BONIN ISLANDS THRUSH *Zoothera terrestris*   Plate 19
(Bonin Thrush, Kittlitz's Thrush)

Turdus terrestris **Kittlitz, 1831, *Mem. Acad. Imp. Sci. St. Petersbourg* 1: 245, pl. 17 – Bonin Island.**

Extinct. Described by Kittlitz in 1831 from four individuals he collected in 1828, the species was never seen again despite searches by later naturalists and collectors in 1889 and the 1920s. Nothing is known of its behaviour or breeding biology; it occurred in woodlands in the coastal lowlands of Chichi-jima in the Ogasawara Islands south of Honshu, and may also have occurred on Haha-jima (Brazil 1991). Reasons for its demise are not clear but most probably related to the introduction of domestic animals to the islands. Adult birds were almost entirely rich brown, becoming rufous-brown or chestnut on the rump, uppertail-coverts and base of tail; the mantle, back and scapulars were heavily streaked black, formed by the inner-webs of the feathers; the hindcrown and nape may also have been lightly streaked. Wings were dark brown but the tips to median and greater coverts broadly light olive-brown, greater coverts black-ish, broadly tipped and narrowly edged light olive-brown, primary coverts black and broadly edged light olive-brown, with the same colour on the edge of base of the primaries and edges to secondaries, and broadly on the outerwebs of the tertials. Lores dark brown and cheeks and ear-coverts slightly duller or darker than the brown of the upperparts; narrow pale or dull yellow eye-ring. Chin and throat to centre of upper breast white or whitish but prominently streaked with long dark brown lines onto the sides and centre of the breast; sides of breast and flanks may also have been tinged rufous-brown, centre of belly to undertail-coverts white; females may have been more extensively white below. Bill dark or blackish-horn. Legs and feet pinkish-flesh.

The four specimens are now in the national museum collections in St Petersburg, Leyden, Frankfurt and Vienna.

62 SULAWESI THRUSH *Cataponera turdoides* Plate 9
(Mountain Thrush, Cataponera Thrush)
Cataponera turdoides Hartert, 1896, *Novit. Zool.* 3: 70 – Bonthain Peak, Celebes.

IDENTIFICATION 20–25 cm (8–9½"). A scarce endemic of Sulawesi; rarely seen and remains generally little known, with no photographs of birds in the wild. Medium-sized with fairly short rounded wings; orange-yellow dagger-like bill and sturdy legs; olive-brown cap to crown with a fairly prominent, broad black supercilium from the lores to the sides of the nape; small triangle of bare or yellow skin behind the eye; slightly paler below; northern birds (*abditiva*) have cinnamon- or rust-tinged undertail-coverts. **Confusion species** Highly distinctive, but Island Thrush (112) race *celebensis*, present in same area but in different habitat and at higher elevation, lacks the black supercilium and has darker upperparts, head and breast, rufous flanks and white central belly.

DESCRIPTION Sexes alike. **Adult** Forehead to hindneck dark olive-brown forming a cap bordered by broad black supercilium from lores and below base of bill to sides of nape (often ends broadly on nape); mantle to scapulars, rump and uppertail-coverts slightly lighter olive-brown or tinged warmer brown on mantle, back and scapulars. Tail warm brown edged slightly rust-brown on bases to all outer feathers. Wing-coverts (including alula and primary coverts) warm brown, flight feathers blackish-brown edged paler or warm olive brown, warmest on edges of scapulars and tertials; underwing-coverts greyish-olive to olive-brown with orange edges. Lores to below base of bill blackish, cheeks and ear-coverts light olive-buff or paler buff, becoming olive to olive-brown on sides of neck; eye-ring and small (but obvious) post-ocular patch behind eye deep orange-yellow. Chin and throat light olive becoming paler olive tinged grey on breast, upper belly, thighs and flanks; undertail-coverts olive-brown. Some birds have underparts paler or greyish-buff. Bill prominent, deep orange-yellow. Legs and feet yellow or bright orange. **Immature** Juvenile rich brown densely spotted with creamy-buff on underparts and streaked on upperparts. Bill very dark. First-year bird similar to adult but slightly darker brown with pale buff central shaft-streaks on crown, nape and upper mantle; underparts slightly paler or buffier, chin, throat and breast mottled with pale buff centres and dark brown tips forming bars; ear-coverts have pale buff central shaft-streaks.

GEOGRAPHIC VARIATION Four races; variation clinal and not well marked. Two races – *tenebrosa* and *heinrichi* – are known from very few specimens, *tenebrosa* being greyer-olive above and less olive below, with both webs of flight feathers dark rust-brown, while *heinrichi* has a supercilium that only reaches just beyond eye (not to nape) and lacks black lower lores to below base of bill.

Race *abditiva* similar to nominate but slightly darker or more olive-brown on upperparts and deeper rufous or chestnut-brown on wings (mostly wing-coverts and both webs of flight feathers), undertail-coverts and tail. Underwing-coverts light orange-brown and undersides of flight feathers pale orange-cinnamon. Lacks black at sides of base of bill. Chin and throat to breast deep olive becoming tinged bright cinnamon or light orange on belly and vent; lower flanks deep olive-brown. Juvenile like adult but streaked paler above and has light cinnamon or orange-reddish vent to undertail-coverts.

VOICE Virtually unknown; a thin and typically *Turdus*-like *tsiip*, a series of thin squeaks used as contact notes, and a chattering alarm call (Coates & Bishop 1997). Song a series of short, rich fluty, almost sad-sounding phrases: *toowip tu-wee, tu tee-tu-tee, tuee wip-wip-wip-wip-wip*, recalling that of Song Thrush (124). Sometimes the phrases are more complex in phrases where it includes mimicry of Yellow-vented Whistler *Pachycephala sulfuriventer*, which has a typical whipping whistler song, and songs or calls of Rusty-breasted Cuckoo *Cacomantis sepulcralis* and Sulawesi Babbler *Trichastoma celebense*. Also, most frequently in the morning, it has a quieter series of short whistled phrases of about 6–8 notes, repeated up to 10 times and followed by a more subdued song recalling a Blackbird (111) in tone but with the repetitive pattern of Song Thrush (E. Myers, P. Morris pers. comms.). Song delivered from an exposed perch 3–6 m (10–20′) from the ground in open forest, mostly at or before dawn and around dusk even during bad weather, also in late afternoon.

STATUS/DISTRIBUTION Uncommon to very scarce; little known.

C. t. abditiva Northern Central Sulawesi (including Lore Lindu National Park).

C. t. tenebrosa Southern Central Sulawesi (including Latimojong Mountains).

C. t. turdoides Southern Sulawesi (Lompobattang Massif).

C. t. heinrichi South-east Sulawesi (Mekonga Mountains).

MOVEMENTS Sedentary.

HABITAT Mostly evergreen montane forests with dense ground vegetation, usually between 1100 and 2400 m (3630–7920′).

BEHAVIOUR Extremely shy, secretive and easily overlooked. Occurs mostly alone or in pairs when breeding but also found in mixed foraging flocks with Malia *Malia grata*. Generally unobtrusive and arboreal in habits and appears to favour mid-canopy of trees where it forages in mossy fronds, epiphytes and tree-ferns, but also occurs low down in trees or dense vegetation or, more rarely, on the ground beneath dense foliage; hops along horizontal branches. Many habits and actions recall those of laughing-thrushes *Garrulax*, but shape and structure more typical of *Turdus* thrushes. Feeds mostly on small forest fruits taken from within trees and on insects.

273

BREEDING Unknown.
MOULT No information.
MEASUREMENTS (n=4) Wing, male 109–120, female 105–109; tarsus 33; bill (culmen) 21.5; *abditiva* (n=3) wing 122–132. Weight apparently unrecorded.
REFERENCES Coates & Bishop (1997), White & Bruce (1986).

63 TRISTAN THRUSH *Nesocichla eremita*   Plate 31
('Starchy')

Nesocichla eremita **Gould, 1855, *Proc. Zool. Soc. London*: 165 – Tristan da Cunha.**

IDENTIFICATION 22–23 cm (8½–9″). The only thrush in the Tristan da Cunha group, mostly brown with heavily streaked or blotched underparts, becoming reddish or more rufous-brown in the outer island races; has small rounded wings and robust legs and feet. Within its limited island range unlikely to be confused with any other species. **Confusion species** None.

DESCRIPTION Sexes alike. **Adult** Entire upperparts brown, closely blotched darker or blacker on forehead to crown, centre of mantle and back, with slightly paler or browner fringes on nape; fine warm brown streaks on forehead and crown and pale brown fringes to mantle, back and scapulars. Rump and uppertail-coverts olive-brown, except for longest uppertail-coverts which have dark brown centres and paler or olive-brown tips. Tail brown or edged olive-brown. Wings olive-brown with pale orange tips and edges to greater-coverts, edges and tips of primary coverts also pale orange; edges and tips of secondaries pale orange-buff (paler when worn); edges to outer primaries pale orange-buff. Underwing pale orange. Face gingery-brown streaked or blotched darker or blacker. Chin pale buff becoming mottled or streaked browner on throat, merging with warm brown sides of neck. Breast dark brown with pale orange-buff edges forming a heavily mottled or streaked pattern extending to belly and flanks; vent to thighs and undertail-coverts pale or light orange-buff. Bill large and powerful, black or blackish-horn with pale tip. Legs and feet dusky or blackish-brown. **Immature** Juvenile similar to adult but darker above with pale buff or orange-buff spots on forehead to nape and pale orange bases and shaft-streaks to mantle, back and scapulars. Rump and uppertail-coverts also have pale orange-buff central shaft-streaks. Breast blackish tipped pale buffish; belly pale buff with blackish spots. Bill blackish with pale horn tip. Legs and feet brown.

GEOGRAPHICAL VARIATION Three races; variation clinal and not well marked. Race *procax* is slightly larger and darker or more rufous-brown, with more extensively pale orange at bend of wing, tips of median coverts and edges to primary coverts and flight feathers, and more heavily orange on underwing. Face flecked or mottled pale brown on ear-coverts. Bill very dark brown. Legs and feet light horn. Race *gordoni* intermediate in extent of pale orange on tips of wing-coverts and edges of flight feathers; may also show whitish tips to tertials; cheeks, ear-coverts and supercilium paler and spotted or flecked light or warm brown; can show slight pale buffish-brown submoustachial and darker brown malar stripe. Underparts have liver-brown spots (streaks in nominate).

VOICE Call a thin or soft *seeep* whistle and a rasping *chirp* which may be contact notes, given with soft or heavy emphasis between pairs. Song a rich or fluty series of phrases preceded by *chissik, chissik* and a harsher *trrkk* before a repeated *swee swee swee* or *pseeooooee pseeooooeee*; also has a soft subsong which is almost inaudible beyond a few yards, consisting of melodic warbles and trills lasting for up to several minutes; usually given low within the canopy of a tree or from a secluded perch in the upper levels of a *Phylica arborea* bush.

STATUS AND DISTRIBUTION Usually fairly numerous, tame, inquisitive and easily seen, but birds on Tristan da Cunha are much more secretive than those on the neighbouring islands. In the 1960s and early 1970s considered vulnerable to predation from feral cats and in 1972–1974 the population was estimated to be between 40–60 pairs, a decline from 'a few hundred pairs' 20 years previously; feral cats have now been eradicated from Tristan but birds may still fall victim to black rats *Rattus rattus*. By the late 1990s the population on Tristan was thought to be endangered with less than six sightings between May 1998 and May 1999 (BirdLife in prep.) possibly due to the continuing presence of rats. On Inaccessible recent surveys indicate an increase from 100–150 pairs in 1972–1974 to c.850 pairs in 1993; the population on Nightingale (including Middle and Stoltenhoff) was estimated at between 330–560 pairs in 1972–1974. The species, currently listed as Near-Threatened (Collar *et al.* 1994), is now considered to be at risk from the potential introduction of grazing animals, cats and rats to the other islands (BirdLife in prep.).

N. e. eremita Tristan da Cunha.
N. e. gordoni Inaccessible Island, Tristan da Cunha group.
N. e. procax Nightingale, Middle and Stoltenhoff Islands, Tristan da Cunha group. Fraser *et al.* (1994) recorded the introduction (illegally) of an unknown number of this race onto Tristan da Cunha.

MOVEMENTS Sedentary.

HABITAT A wide variety of well-vegetated areas, from sheltered valleys or gullies (gulches) to plantations, orchards, thickets, wet heath, moorlands and scattered trees, also bracken in valleys and grassy clearings in undergrowth, *Phylica* scrub, tree-fern tangles and dense tussock-grass areas (especially race *procax*), ferns and rocky and boulder-strewn slopes. Birds on Nightingale and Inaccessible regularly forage along beaches and in and among penguin colonies, and on Inaccessible they regularly enter Great Shearwater *Puffinus gravis* and other seabird breeding burrows; nominate birds are found mostly above 300 m (c.1000'), only descending to lower levels in severe winters.

BEHAVIOUR Usually alone or in pairs, occasionally in small loose groups. Hops and runs on the ground in typical thrush-like gait; frequently flicks or flirts the wings open when calling. Forages on the ground beneath trees, in grassy clearings and *Phylica* thickets, turning over leaves and moss. Food caterpillars, insects (mainly Coleoptera, beetles, weevils), ticks, snails, earthworms, seeds and berries, especially those of *Nertera depressa* and *Empetrum rubrum*; also scavenges carrion from dead birds and dead fish, and eats the contents of seabirds' eggs (which it cracks open with its strong bill and consumes with its strong brush-tipped tongue), and kills and eats nestlings of Tristan *Neospiza acunhae* and Wilkins's Buntings *N. wilkinsi* and Inaccessible Island Rail *Atlantisia*

rogersi; known to attack and kill fully adult White-bellied Storm Petrels *Fregatta grallaria* (Ryan & Moloney 1991).

BREEDING Season: September to late January or early February. Nest: a large, neat, cup-shaped construction mostly of grasses or coarse tussock-grass and other dead vegetation, lined with moss, usually placed on the ground or up to 0.3 m (1') from it and well hidden in or under tussocks, a rock or on a ledge on a cliff, occasionally on an exposed site, e.g. rock-face or in shacks. Eggs 2–3, usually 3 in *procax* and 4 *gordoni*, pale green and speckled with reddish-brown. Fledging period c.20 days; chicks fed by both parents.

MOULT Post-nuptial moult of adult from late November or early December to early March is a complete moult, beginning with the flight feathers followed by the body and tail feathers. Juveniles undergo an incomplete moult into adult plumage.

MEASUREMENTS Wing 99–111; tarsus 35.5–38; bill 21.5–23; *procax* wing 112–119; tarsus 38–39; bill 23–24; *gordoni* wing, male 109–121, female 104–115; tarsus 37–42; bill 21–26.5. Weight 78–124 g (Elliott 1957, Fraser *et al.* 1994).

REFERENCES BirdLife International (in prep.), Elliott (1957), Fraser *et al.* (1994), King (1981), Ryan & Moloney (1991).

64 FOREST THRUSH *Cichlherminia lherminieri* Plate 55
Turdus L'Herminieri Lafresnaye, 1844, *Rev. Zool.* [Paris] 7: 167 – Guadeloupe.

IDENTIFICATION 24–27 cm (9½–10½"). A large, stocky thrush with a stout bill and long legs, endemic to four islands in the Lesser Antilles. Generally dark brown above with a variable pattern of pale bases to the underparts with brown to blackish-brown tips forming a pattern of large chevrons; large yellow bare patch around the eye, yellow bill and legs. **Confusion species** No obvious problems in the range, but Pearly-eyed Thrasher *Margarops fuscatus* has a very similar pattern below, although it also has white on tail, more white on belly, a pale eye and a slightly longer, thinner, yellowish-brown bill.

DESCRIPTION Sexes alike. **Adult** Entire upperparts and face warm or russet-brown, slightly darker on forehead and crown and paler on nape; rich brown uppertail-coverts and base of tail becoming darker brown towards tip. Olive-brown edges to secondaries and tertials, innerwebs to flight feathers warm brown; underwing-coverts white with brown edges to outerwebs, undersides of flight feathers pale orange. Lores dark brown; cheeks and ear-coverts brown, finely flecked with pale buffish central shaft-streaks, broad deep yellow eye-ring and small patch behind eye. Chin and throat dull yellowish-white, finely streaked warm sandy-buff to gingery-brown, becoming more heavily gingery on edges to lower throat and upper breast; breast white with heavy sandy-buff or gingery suffusion, lower breast, belly and flanks

with a very distinctive pattern of large white chevrons (pointed at lower end) sharply emarginated with dark brown fringes; feathers of lower belly and vent centrally white or yellowish with brownish fringes, thighs brownish, undertail-coverts white with tips of longest feathers brown. Bill bright or deep yellow. Legs and feet yellow.

Immature Juvenile very similar to adult but head and face slightly paler brown with fine pale buffish central shaft-streaks on crown, nape and mantle, and pale or rusty buffish-brown shaft-streaks on scapulars; cheeks and ear-coverts finely mottled pale buffish-brown. Underparts more mottled or spotted, with less defined brown edges to feathers of lower breast and belly and whitish or orange-buff in centres.

GEOGRAPHICAL VARIATION Four races; variation clinal and moderately well marked.

Race *dominicensis* slightly smaller (23 cm/9") and much darker above, with blackish-brown forehead to lores, crown and nape becoming dark brown washed olive on entire upperparts, slightly more olive on edges to wings. Tail similarly dark brown or washed olive-brown. Face dark mahogany-brown with paler orange or buffish-tawny flecks. Chin and throat mottled darker brown than face with rich buff to tawny-orange on breast and rich olive-brown streaks, breast with few (if any) light or yellowish-buff centres and blackish-brown tips, becoming browner on lower breast with whitish centres and diffuse black spots; belly and flanks with same pattern as nominate, tips of lower flanks and sides of belly forming arrow-like marks; centre of belly to undertail-coverts white except for longest which are edged olive-brown.

Race *lawrencii* has upperparts reddish-brown, intermediate in colour between nominate and *dominicensis*, with white centres to feathers on breast and belly longer and more pointed and edges darker brown, centres to central breast pale tawny or buffish-brown; throat feathers edged rufous, not pale brown.

Race *sanctaeluciae* similar to nominate but slightly smaller, upperparts, on average, slightly paler, and wings and tail slightly longer; spots on breast buffish and much larger than in nominate; belly also more extensively white.

VOICE Call a loud abrupt *chuck-chuck* often extending into a rapid harsh or scolding chatter. Song a loud, far-carrying but melodious, fluty, whistling cadence; may include harsher notes or extended phrases such as *tiwiiieee*, and a loud whistling or squealing puppy-like yelping note (Bond 1979, Hardy & Parker 1992). Song usually given from a concealed perch.

STATUS AND DISTRIBUTION Nowhere common; previously (to about 1980) also on St Lucia but now considered to have been extirpated by the Yellow-eyed Thrush (152). May also suffer from food competition and brood parasitism by the Shiny Cowbird *Molothrus bonariensis*, hunting by humans, loss of habitat and predation from introduced rats, mongooses and native snakes, especially the venomous fer-de-lance *Bothrops*

lanceolatus (Diamond 1973). Considered Near-Threatened (Collar *et al.* 1994).

C. l. lherminieri Guadeloupe, West Indies.
C. l. dominicensis Dominica, West Indies.
C. l. sanctaeluciae St. Lucia, West Indies but not seen since about 1980 (D. Anthony pers. comm).
C. l. lawrencii Montserrat, West Indies.

MOVEMENTS Sedentary.

HABITAT Forests, mostly primary and secondary evergreen rainforests and undergrowth in semi-arid forests, particularly favouring open forests with little undergrowth. Found at all levels from forest floor to the canopy of tall trees; *dominicensis* is found in open glades in dense woods.

BEHAVIOUR Shy and generally little known; occurs mostly alone or in pairs. On the ground runs rapidly into cover when disturbed. Feeds in typical thrush manner, scratching for insects amongst the dry leaf-litter and decomposing vegetation with its strong legs and feet; also takes some berries and fruit.

BREEDING Season: April–July (possibly longer). Nest: a bulky cup-shaped structure of moss, dried leaves, some plant material, vines and twigs, placed low down in a bush, tree fern or tree. Eggs: 2–3, greenish-blue and unspotted.

MOULT No information.

MEASUREMENTS Wing, male 133.5–144, female 132.5; tarsus, male 42–44.5, female 40; bill (culmen) 24.5–26.5; *dominicensis* wing, male 120.5–125, female 118–119; *lawrencii* wing 136.5; *sanctaeluciae* wing, male 134.5, female 132.5–144 (Ridgway 1907). Weight apparently unrecorded.

REFERENCES Diamond (1973), Hardy & Parker (1992), King (1981), Ridgway (1907).

65 KAMAO *Myadestes myadestinus* Plate 21
(Large Kaua'i Thrush)

Phaeornis myadestina Stejneger, 1887, *Proc. U.S. Natn. Mus.* 10: 90 – Kauai, Hawaiian Islands.

IDENTIFICATION 18–20 cm (7–8"). A medium to small solitaire, endemic to Kauai in the Hawaiian Islands, probably now extinct. Most easily recognised by the short, stout, broad-based bill but plumage is rather unremarkable, with brown forehead, crown and most upperparts, face slightly paler and greyish, breast and flanks mottled paler or whitish, and belly to undertail whiter. **Confusion species** Most similar bird is the smaller, closely related Puaiohi (69), also endemic to Kauai, but separated by the whiter underparts, browner head and face, the short, broad-based black bill and the dark not pinkish legs and feet. Kamao gives a full wing-quiver whilst Puaiohi only gives a quick flick of the wing. Kamao and Puaiohi are no longer likely to occur in the same habitat. Lone juveniles are unlikely to be separable with confidence, but size and leg colour should be distinctive. Kamao might also be confused with the more vociferous Japanese Bush Warbler *Cettia*

diphone, which is smaller and slimmer, with a longer tail, thinner bill and prominent pale supercilium; it was introduced into the Hawaiian Islands in 1930 and is now present in parts of the former range of Kamao.

DESCRIPTION Sexes alike. **Adult** Forehead to crown, nape and upper mantle drab brown or faintly tipped grey or greyish-olive in worn plumage; rest of mantle, back, scapulars, rump and uppertail-coverts olive to olive-brown. Tail brown, central feathers and bases to all outers paler or olive-brown, outer two buffish-brown and outermost with small white spot at tip. Median coverts as scapulars or edged warmer olive-brown, greaters brown edged pale buff-brown or olive-brown on inner greaters; alula dark brown; primary coverts also dark brown but finely edged olive-brown on outerwebs; flight feathers brown narrowly edged light warm brown on inner primaries and more broadly sandy-brown on secondaries, forming panel on closed wing; tertials dark brown edged and tipped pale olive-brown, with small panel of pale orange-brown or rufous at bases to inner primaries and secondaries; underwing-coverts silvery-white lightly tinged buff on bases to flight feathers. Lores to cheeks and ear-coverts olive or olive-brown with fine pale buff spots or streaks; may show pale or ill-defined malar stripe. Chin and throat to sides of neck, breast and upper belly pale pearl-grey lightly mottled or dappled with whitish centres, becoming paler or whiter on lower belly, lower flanks and undertail-coverts; flanks may show some olive-brown. Bill short and stout, broad at base, black. Legs and feet black or blackish-brown. **Immature** Juvenile similar to adult but heavily spotted with pale buff centres to forehead, crown and nape, with more prominent spots with blackish-brown fringes on mantle and scapulars to centre of back, rump and uppertail-coverts. Lesser and median coverts have whitish-buff tips and greaters have buff-brown subterminal spots and blackish tips; secondaries and tertials may also show buff-brown spots at tips. Face flecked paler with faint dull beige or whitish-buff submoustachial and thin dark malar. Chin and throat pale yellowish-buff finely mottled darker; breast, belly and flanks heavily scalloped with pale yellowish-buff and dark fringes, less heavily on vent with plain yellowish-cream undertail-coverts.

Specimens are in BM Tring and the Smithsonian Institute, Washington (see also Wakelee & Fancy 1999).

GEOGRAPHICAL VARIATION None. Monotypic.
VOICE Call a shrill, high-pitched 'police-whistle', a cat-like rasping alarm note similar to, but higher-pitched, than that of Omao (68), and a short hissing note. Song a series of musical phrases in a complex structure containing flute-like whistles, trills and musical warbles recalling the song of a *Turdus* thrush, but given with less emphasis. Sings from both fairly low and high perches, particularly dead branches at the tops of trees; quivers its wings whilst turning its head from side to side; also sings in flight, rising up into the air before dropping back suddenly into a low bush or shrub. Most song given in the early morning and late afternoon.
STATUS AND DISTRIBUTION Like many native bird species on the Hawaiian Islands (including three of the four *Myadestes*) this thrush was formerly (end of 19th century) extremely common to abundant, and still fairly common in parts of the range in mid-1930s; from mid-1940s declined drastically (but seen regularly into mid-1970s) and population estimated at approximately 200 individuals in 1968–1973, but by 1981 fewer than 20 individuals were thought to remain in the same area (Scott *et al.* 1986). Since the early 1980s records have become scarcer; the last documented sighting was in 1992 but there was an apparently reliable record in January 1996 (T. Snetsinger pers. comm.). The species was classed as Critical by Collar *et al.* (1994) when only a few individuals remained, and it was thought unlikely to survive long into the 21st century. A more recent review of all the rare breeding birds in Hawaii suggests that it is indeed already most probably extinct (Reynolds & Snetsinger 2000). Reasons for the decline are uncertain but the spread of avian malaria by mosquitoes seems likely to have been a factor. Endemic to Kauai, Hawaiian Islands.
MOVEMENTS Sedentary.
HABITAT Dense montane forests and forest edges, in the latter years of the 1980s confined to the wet montane forest area of Alakai Swamp (above 6000 mm rainfall per year), though also occasionally (unconfirmed) reported from the Pihea Ridge trail above Kalalau Valley. Formerly occurred more widely from sea-level to montane forests with deep steep-sided ravines or ridges in mesic and wet forests.
BEHAVIOUR Tame and easily approached even whilst in full song. Perches in an upright or erect stance and quivers its wings and tail in a nervous manner but also spends long periods motionless. Forages in trees and bushes; food mostly fruit especially olapa, lapalapa, ohia ha, kanawao, ohelo, painiu, pukiawe, kawau, kolea, mamaki, lobelias and pilo, and berries of thimbleberry together with the fleshy flower bracts of the ieie vine; may also take invertebrates, especially caterpillars but also spiders, weevils, damselflies and beetles and their larvae (Wakelee & Fancy 1999).
BREEDING Unknown.
MOULT No information.
MEASUREMENTS Wing (n=8) male 103–107, female 100–103; tarsus 33–34; bill (culmen) 12.5–14, depth 5–7, width (at base) 9–10. Weight apparently unrecorded.
REFERENCES Collar *et al.* (1994), Munro (1960), Pratt *et al.* (1987), Reynolds & Snetsinger (2000), Scott *et al.* (1986), Wakelee & Fancy (1999).

66 AMAUI *Myadestes woahensis*   Not illustrated
(Oahu Thrush)

Phaeornis woahensis Wilson & Evans, 1899, *Aves Hawaiiensis*, introd.: xiii. (Oahu). Amended to *Turdus woahensis* Bloxam in Wilson & Evans, 1899, following Olson (1996).

Extinct. Very little is known of this bird, which lived in the forests of north-east Oahu, where it was discovered in 1825. It was later reported as being about 7½" (19 cm) long with the upperparts olive-brown, the extremities of each feather much lighter in colour; the belly was pale ash-grey, tail and wings brown and the bill had bristles at the base; it had a melodious song and was fairly common. Several individuals were collected but subsequently lost, and the bird was not described for science until 1899. It became extinct between its discovery and the visit of the next naturalist to survey the island.

Olson (1996) recently located two specimens on which the original description is almost certainly based, and regards them as representing, at best, a subspecies of Olomao (67). The AOU (1998) consequently treated the validity of the species as uncertain. However, it may be best to regard the identity of the recently found specimens as speculative in view of the long gap since the loss of the originals.

REFERENCES AOU (1998), Olson (1996).

67 OLOMAO *Myadestes lanaiensis*   Plate 21
(Lanai Thrush)
Phaeornis lanaiensis Wilson, 1891, *Ann. Mag. Nat. Hist.* (6)7: 460 – Lanai.

IDENTIFICATION 16–18 cm (6¼–7"). A critically endangered or possibly extinct endemic of Molokai in the central Hawaiian Islands, where there have been no confirmed sightings in the past 20 years. Head and face grey-brown becoming olive-brown on the rest of the upperparts, with a fairly prominent pale buffish-orange patch at the base of the secondaries; chin and throat pale grey, rest of the underparts creamy-white or tinged buff. **Confusion species** Very similar to the Omao (68), which is greyer on the forehead to crown, richer brown above and much duller or greyer below; the ranges of the two species have never overlapped. Japanese Bush Warbler *Cettia diphone* is similar but smaller with a longer tail, pale supercilium and pale bill. **DESCRIPTION** Sexes almost alike. **Adult male** Forehead to crown and nape grey-brown becoming olive-brown on rest of upperparts; centre of upper mantle tinged grey. Tail brown or olive-brown on central pair and bases to all outer feathers except outermost, outers pale brown with outerweb whitish tinged pale buff-brown. Median and greater coverts brown edged olive-brown; alula dark brown; primary coverts dark brown finely edged olive-brown; flight feathers brown finely edged olive-brown on primaries and along secondaries, tertials slightly paler brown or tinged more uniformly olive-brown, with a small, square pale orange-buff patch at base of secondaries; underwing-coverts silvery-white extending to bases of secondaries. Face grey or greyish-olive, finely flecked or spotted whiter. Chin and throat to breast pale grey, paler or duller on breast and creamy-white on belly and vent, and tinged buff on undertail-coverts. Bill black. Legs and feet black or blackish-brown with yellow soles. **Adult female** Similar to male but slightly darker or browner on head and less tinged grey on upperparts. Underparts whiter with only throat to centre of breast pale grey. **Immature** Juvenile heavily flecked and spotted on upperparts with pale buff centres and dark olive-brown edges and tips on head and face; has large triangular spots with blackish edges on rest of upperparts; rump and uppertail-coverts more broadly barred or mottled with pale buff and dark olive-brown tips. Tail as adult but with whitish outer feathers. Pale buff subterminal spot and dark brown edges and tips to median and greater coverts; rest of wings as adult but with pale brown edges; primary coverts dark brown with olive edges; tips to tertials and scapulars also narrowly pale buff. Chin and throat whitish becoming heavily mottled off-white to pale yellowish-buff, with dark brown fringes forming oval-shaped scalloped pattern on breast, belly and flanks. Pale centres and spots on upperparts progressively wear off to reveal more adult-like plumage but crown appears to retain streaking longest (still present on some birds in July). Pale buff spots at tips to wing-coverts and tertials also wear down to narrow whitish tips.

GEOGRAPHICAL VARIATION Two races; variation clinal. Race *rutha* poorly differentiated from nominate but slightly larger, with slightly darker olive-brown upperparts; throat and breast greyer and belly to undertail-coverts whiter; bill averaged slightly longer and broader.

VOICE A variety of call notes, most given from cover, including a sharp cat-like rasping note, and a shrill 'police-whistle' call similar to the Omao's. Song a series of melodious thrush-like notes loosely and haltingly run together, similar to that of Omao, given repeatedly through the day and sometimes into the night. Sings ventriloquially from both high exposed perches and low down, frequently from a concealed perch. Birds on Lanai were considered not to sing (Munro 1960).

STATUS AND DISTRIBUTION Originally on Molokai, Lanai and Maui in the Hawaiian Islands. The population of this bird declined drastically during the 20th century and (if it survives) is now reduced to a few sparsely distributed individuals. Previously widespread, it has declined due to habitat loss compounded by the introduction of cattle, goats and deer, along with direct predators such as rats, cats and montgooses; in recent times, the spread of avian malaria by mosquitoes has undoubtedly exacerbated the problem. The chances of reversing the present situation appear to be negligible and the species is unlikely to survive long into the present century, as Molokai is not thought to be sufficiently high or large to provide a viable disease-free refuge (Wakelee & Fancy 1999); classed as Critically Endangered by Collar *et al.* (1994), but may already be extinct.

M. l. rutha Endemic to Molokai, central Hawaiian Islands, where probably fewer than 20 individuals persist scattered through impenetrable forests in two or three areas on the Olokui Plateau (previously also the Ohialele Plateau). Formerly common in the late 1800s throughout forests at all elevations, and widespread but less numerous in the early 1900s; a survey in 1936 had only one record and it was presumed extinct soon afterwards; it was rediscovered in 1964 and a population estimate of 19 individuals was made in 1979–1980 (Wakelee & Fancy 1999). The most recent confirmed record was in 1980 with another, considered to be valid, in 1988 (T. Snetsinger pers. comm.).

M. l. lanaiensis Formerly on Lanai where common until about 1923 (extirpated by 1933), and historically (race unknown) on Maui where described as abundant in the 1860s but never seen again. Increasing human population, and depletion and destruction of forests were thought to be responsible for its demise.

MOVEMENTS Sedentary.

HABITAT Montane rainforest, where it occurs in low trees with epiphytes, tree-ferns and undergrowth at all elevations, but most recently mainly above 1000 m (3300′).

BEHAVIOUR Shy and retiring, solitary. Keeps mainly to cover in low trees and undergrowth and is usually only detected by calls. Has several habits common to all the Hawaiian thrushes, e.g. upright or erect stance when perched and quivering of wings and trembling body when excited or alarmed. Usually only flies short distances but may fly-catch and take insects and fruit whilst in flight. Forages low down and feeds mostly on berries, fleshy fruits (similar to those taken by Omao and Kamao), flowers, insects and small snails.

BREEDING Virtually unknown; only three nests ever found. Nests reportedly in thickest undergrowth or dense clumps of vines and ferns (Munro 1960) but Perkins (1903) described three nests 25–30 m (80–90′) up in trees and made no mention of undergrowth. Nest: bulky and loosely constructed, mostly of dried leaves, ferns, mosses, twigs and fine rootlets very similar to that of Omao.

MOULT No information.

MEASUREMENTS Wing (n=33) 87–96.5; tarsus (n=33) 32–36.5; bill (to feathers) (n=29) 13–15; width (at base) 7.5–9; depth (at base) 5–5.5 (Wakelee & Fancy 1999). Weight apparently unrecorded.

REFERENCES Collar *et al.* (1994), King (1981), Munro (1960), Perkins (1903), Wakelee & Fancy (1999).

68 OMAO *Myadestes obscurus* Plate 21
(Hawaiian Thrush)

Muscicapa obscura Gmelin, 1789, *Syst. Nat.* 1(2): 945, based on the 'Dusky Flycatcher' Latham, *Gen. Synop. Birds* 2(1): 344 – in insulis Sandwich = Hawaii.

IDENTIFICATION 18.5–19.5 cm (7¼–7¾"). A small, inconspicuous thrush with a short, stout bill, restricted to the native forests and high-level scrub on Hawaii. Forehead, crown and face grey-brown, underparts grey, upperparts dull olive-brown with slightly warmer brown wings, tail slightly darker with paler outer feathers. Has a distinctive loud song and is far more often heard than seen. Rapidly declined since mid-20th century, doubtless owing to habitat destruction and the spread of avian malaria; but appears to be surviving, and may have developed some disease resistance; now mainly found in any numbers in the higher, less disturbed parts of its island range. **Confusion species** Identification unproblematic; does/did not occur with any other Hawaiian *Myadestes*. Northern Mockingbird *Mimus polyglottos* is much larger and has white in the wings and edges to the longer tail. There are, as yet, no records of Japanese Bush-Warbler *Cettia diphone* on Hawaii but confusion with this smaller, vociferous species may occur if it becomes established there.

DESCRIPTION Sexes alike (separable on wing measurements). **Adult** Forehead to nape grey-brown, perhaps paler or greyer on forehead to crown. Mantle, back and scapulars to rump and uppertail-coverts olive-brown, tinged warmer brown on upper mantle and scapulars. Tail dark olive-brown but outer feathers paler or lighter brown. Median and greater coverts and alula as scapulars but centres to greaters darker brown; alula and primary coverts dark brown edged slightly paler; flight feathers dark brown but edged narrowly brown on primaries becoming more broadly warmer brown on edges to secondaries; outerwebs of tertials olive-brown, innerwebs dark brown; underwing-coverts pale or silvery-white. Lores dark ash-grey; cheeks and ear-coverts brown or greyish-brown and sometimes flecked white. Underparts mostly plain or dull grey, greyest on breast, paler on belly and flanks to vent and thighs; lower flanks olive-brown; undertail-coverts white. Bill short and stout, black. Legs and feet brown to greyish-black. **Immature** Juvenile similar to adult but heavily spotted or streaked, with broad pale buff central shaft-streaks on crown and large pale buff spots on mantle, back and edges to scapulars; lower back and rump barred or mottled with pale buffish subterminally and brownish bar at tip. Ill-defined whitish-buff tips to lesser coverts; median and greater coverts similar but with large pale whitish-buff subterminal spot and fine dark bar at tip; edges and tips to secondaries and tertials also finely pale buff. Face dull olive-brown and finely streaked paler. Chin and throat pale grey, breast to belly scalloped with pale whitish- or yellowish-buff centres and blackish-brown fringes (dark edges sometimes narrowest on centre of breast and belly); vent and undertail-coverts whitish. First-year bird retains some or all pale buff tips to median and greater coverts and tips to tertials into following spring (March). Has been known to breed in first-year plumage (Wakelee 1996).

GEOGRAPHICAL VARIATION None. Monotypic.

VOICE A variety of calls, but frequently gives a sharp rasping note recalling inquisitive mewing of Grey Catbird *Dumetella carolinensis* and alarm call of Townsend's Solitaire (70); given repeatedly when disturbed; also a froglike croak and a high-pitched 'police-whistle' trill given between pair members (similar to that of the Kamao), and a rising series of buzzing or twangy notes often ending with a chirp. Song mostly composed of jerky up-and-down phrases of liquid chirps *wichiiweeeooo* interspersed with short slurred whistles, very loud, distinctive and pleasant; when displaying, has an upward song-flight terminating in a rapid descent into the forest. Also has a longer but softer subsong given in October to February. Usually sings from a regular high perch, often on the top branch of a (usually dead) tree, mainly early in the morning including in the pre-dawn darkness as well as at intervals during the day and until after sunset, but subsong usually given from perches hidden in vegetation. Song given by both sexes throughout the year but males sing more during non-breeding period; most song usually given between January and May and least during August and September (Berger 1972, Wakelee & Fancy 1999).

STATUS AND DISTRIBUTION Resident and highly sedentary, current population estimated at 170,000 individuals from surveys in 1976–1979 (Scott *et al.* 1986), but the area now occupied is less than 30% of its former range (Wakelee & Fancy 1999). Thought to have suffered from increased rates of predation, destruction of forests and spread of avian diseases, principally avian pox and malaria, contributing to its rapid decline in the 20th century. Endemic to the main island of Hawaii where it remains fairly common to locally abundant in the rainforests of Hamakua-Puna and Kau districts; a small isolated population still exists on Mauna Loa but it disappeared from Kona and Kohala mountains where it was common a century ago. A recent attempt has been made to translocate birds to the leeward side of Hualalai Volcano.

MOVEMENTS Largely sedentary but may make short-distance movements to feed on caterpillar hatches.

HABITAT Thick dense mesic and wet forests, mostly of native ohia *Metrosideros polymorpha* forest and mixed ohia and koa *Acacia koa* forest usually above 1500 m (4950′) but down to c.700 m (2310′) – and formerly to c.300 m (1000′) – in the Puna district; also subalpine and alpine ohia scrub between 600 and 2515 m (2000–8300′), exceptionally to 3500 m (11,550′), on lava flows with patches of stunted vegetation above the treeline on Mauna Loa; favours tree-ferns and moss-covered tree-trunks and branches.

BEHAVIOUR Usually alone or in pairs, but often in small flocks in the non-breeding season and in small numbers at fruiting trees; fairly shy and retiring, spending long periods sitting almost motionless with wings drooped, but also active in foraging for insects. Like all Hawaiian thrushes it has an upright stance when perched and quivers its wings in a seemingly agitated state when excited or alarmed or whilst singing. Hops on the ground but not known to walk or run. Rarely flies far in a single flight but may fly-catch and take fruit in mid-air; the wings make an audible whirring sound; forages all day, even during heavy rain. Feeds low down in vegetation, chiefly on fruit and berries, including olapa, ohelo, kopiko, kawau, lapalapa, maile, mamaki, akia, guava, olopua, akala, naio, holly berries and pilo fruits, plus apple blossom and koa flowers and invertebrates, including worms, spiders, bees, wasps and other insects and their larvae.

BREEDING First nest was not found until 1968. Season: throughout the year, nest-building beginning in January but main period April–August; most young fledge May to August but recently fledged young also seen in October. Nest: a fairly bulky cup-shaped structure of dead leaves, fronds, moss (usually of several species) and bark fibres, lined with grass, fine fern rootlets, pine needles and koa flowers; usually placed in trees or tree-ferns, including cavities in trees or along branches up to 12 m (40′) from the ground but most well below this level; birds on Mauna Loa thought to nest on ground. Built solely by female. Eggs: 1–2, pale greyish-white, heavily freckled or spotted with reddish-brown or lavender. Incubation period 15–17 days. Nestlings fed by both parents; fledging period 17–21 days. Two broods if first brood started in early spring.

MOULT Complete moult of adults from July to December; partial moult of first-year birds at same time but retaining secondaries, primaries, primary coverts and tail feathers to at least August; some first-years may not complete moult until February.

MEASUREMENTS (n=7) Wing, male 99–103, female 94–96.5; tarsus 34–35; bill 13.5–15. Weight 49–53 g (see also Wakelee & Fancy 1999).

REFERENCES Berger (1972), Fancy *et al.* (1994), Munro (1960), Pratt *et al.* (1987), Ralph & Fancy (1994), van Riper & Scott (1979), Scott *et al.* (1986), Wakelee (1996), Wakelee & Fancy (1999).

69 PUAIOHI *Myadestes palmeri*   **Plate 21**
(Small Kauai Thrush)
Phaeornis palmeri **Rothschild, 1893,** *Avifauna Laysan*: **67 – Halemanu, Kauai.**

IDENTIFICATION 16.5–18 cm (6½–7″). A critically endangered small thrush endemic to Kauai in the Hawaiian Islands. Overall rather drab with short tail, long pinkish legs and fairly prominent bill; upperparts dull olive-brown but face slightly greyer with a white eye-ring and short malar stripe; chin to breast pale grey, belly to undertail whitish.
Confusion species Very similar to the larger Kamao (65), another Kauai endemic (possibly already extinct) which is slightly browner above and paler or faintly mottled on the breast, with a short, stout bill and a longer tail. Puaiohi has a paler, greyer face with a white eye-ring, longer, thinner bill and pinkish-flesh legs (black on Kamao); also told by its quick wing-flick whilst Kamao and other Hawaiian *Myadestes* have a full wing-quiver. Three introduced species may pose problems. Juvenile White-rumped Shama *Copsychus malabaricus* shows similar pattern to immature Puaiohi and has pink legs, but told by prominent white rump. Hwamei *Garrulax canorus* also similar but larger with richer or rust-brown plumage, yellow bill and legs, no white in tail and pale bluish eye-ring. Japanese Bush-Warbler *Cettia diphone* is smaller and generally grey-brown with a distinct whitish supercilium.
DESCRIPTION Sexes alike. **Adult** Smaller than other Hawaiian thrushes with fairly long bill and short tail. Forehead to nape grey tinged olive-brown, rest of upperparts olive-brown tinged greyish (head and upperparts can appear uniform grey-brown). Wing-coverts as upperparts; rest of flight feathers olive-brown edged narrowly or finely paler brown; underwing-coverts silvery-white. Tail brown but central pair warmer as rest of upperparts, and outer feathers pale buff-brown on outerweb of outermost and whitish on distal half of innerweb. Face pale grey, mottled, flecked or finely spotted whitish, some birds showing small whitish spot above eye or incomplete white eye-ring; whitish submoustachial and bordered below by narrow dark malar (not always visible in field); chin to breast and sides of upper flanks grey becoming olive-brown on lower flanks; belly to undertail-coverts whitish. Bill black, fairly slender and somewhat longer than the similar, but larger Kamao. Legs and feet flesh-pink to pinkish-tan.
Immature Juvenile very similar to adult but forehead to crown and upperparts brown, finely spotted or scalloped with pale whitish- or yellowish-buff; lesser, median and greater coverts have pale or yellowish-buff subterminal spots and darker tips. Edges to tertials more olive-brown and tips pale buff. Whitish eye-ring present within first month but often incomplete. Chin white, throat to breast olive-grey but lower breast and rest of underparts prominently marked with large spots or scales formed by pale yellowish or off-white feathers with broad dark brown fringes; narrower dark edges on centre of lower breast and belly;

undertail-coverts off-white. **First-year bird** Upperparts become more uniform olive-brown although some birds retain yellowish subterminal spots and dark tips to wing-coverts into following year; flight and tail feathers also retained from juvenile plumage. Face mostly pale grey-brown with dark malar. Underparts mostly pale grey-brown, becoming more olive on flanks with some remnant scalloping on throat, breast (sometimes with a necklace effect or in faded version of fresh plumage) and flanks and dark crescents or chevrons on belly for several months into second calendar year. Bill dark greyish-horn. Legs and feet as adult.
GEOGRAPHICAL VARIATION None. Monotypic.
VOICE Call a fairly loud, rasping, toneless hiss, usually given from cover and frequently repeated; alarm note is a harsher hiss; also gives a low throaty growl. Song a simple wheezing reedy but ventriloquial *puaiohiiii*, high-pitched and rising, like the squeak of an unoiled wheel, broken by long pauses; similar to but shorter, louder and more reedy than that of Kamao (63) and of Apapane (Honeycreeper) *Himatione sanguinea*. Has a whispering version as subsong. Also gives a distinctive rapid fluttering whinnying, transcribed as *whehehehehehehe*. Both sexes give subsong and whinnying note. Sings all year but mostly before and during the breeding season, peaking in April and May; whinnying given as contact call between adult and juveniles mostly during April to October. Sings mostly in the early morning and late afternoon and evening, also during light rain (and after storms); most song given from tops of trees and middle to upper canopy, but also (only rarely seen) in display-flight.
STATUS AND DISTRIBUTION Endemic to Kauai, (now restricted to the Alakai Swamp region and some of the drainage streams), Hawaiian Islands. Formerly much more widespread in suitable habitat above 1000 m (3300′) but never thought to be common, and extirpated from much of its lower-elevation habitat by early 1900s; not seen in the 20th century until two found in the south of the Alakai swamp region in 1941. A survey of the Alakai swamp in July 1960 found 17 individuals and further surveys there between 1968–1973 found two other isolated populations, neither of which appear to have survived the hurricanes that struck Kauai in 1982 and 1992. An estimate for the years 1976–1983 put the total at only 20–54 birds (Scott *et al.* 1986) in some 20 km² of the Alakai swamp region. However, since 1992 it has been seen more regularly, with 18 records in early 1994 alone, when, however, it was still classed as Critically Endangered (Collar *et al.* 1994); thus the population was estimated to have been around 300–500 individuals in the early 1990s (T. Snetsinger pers. comm.). More recent estimates have put the population at around 150 individuals and by summer 1999 the population was judged

to be between 150 and 300 individuals (with an extensive survey planned for 2000) (Reynolds & Snetsinger 2000). The reasons for its decline are not certain, but are probably chiefly loss of habitat and the introduction of predators and the spread of avian malaria by mosquitoes. The species is now the subject of a conservation management programme and has bred successfully in captivity from eggs collected from the wild in 1996; the hatched young were released in early 1999 into managed areas of the Alakai swamp (Snetsinger *et al.* 1999).

MOVEMENTS Sedentary.

HABITAT Mesic wet montane forest with steep-sided ridges and stream valleys with koa *Acacia koa* and ohia *Metrosideros polymorpha* forest together with other native fruiting trees such as ohia ha, olapa, lapalapa and broussasia above 1050 m (3465′); most surviving birds are found in wet montane forest in the Alakai swamp region with rainfall in excess of 6000 mm per year. Requires steep ravines and cliff walls for nest sites and prefers those with *Sadeleria squarossa*.

BEHAVIOUR Extremely shy, very secretive and found in seemingly impenetrable habitat; solitary or sometimes in pairs, keeping to the undergrowth in dense forest often near streams. Generally more terrestrial than other Hawaiian *Myadestes*, regularly hopping on ground and along branches; flight usually fast, direct and low, with loud whirring sound. Has bill-clapping, wing-whirring and wing-spreading display in response to threat; wing-whirring frequently used on arrival and departure from nest. When perched adopts a typical upright stance on long legs. Occasionally catches insects in flight but more usually takes them from leaf clusters whilst hovering. Forages low down in vegetation, along moss-covered branches and tree-trunks, sometimes on the ground, taking fleshy fruits of native plants such as olapa, kanawao, ohelo and ohia ha, berries of lapalapa, and some seeds; also insects and their larvae, including beetles (particularly ones found on koa trees), damselflies, weevils and caterpillars, plus spiders and snails.

BREEDING First nest found in 1981. Season: April to September but main period April to June. Nest: a cup-shaped structure of woven fibres of bryophytes, ferns and fine grasses with an outer covering of mosses, leaves, liverworts, sedges and ferns; has typical *Myadestes* feature of a long trailing mass of material below the nest; constructed entirely by female and placed in a cavity on a steep-sided cliff wall or earth bank above a stream, the entrance usually well concealed by tall vegetation, e.g. ferns; occasionally uses ledge on cliff wall away from stream; rarely holes in trees. Successful nests frequently reused. Eggs: 2, very similar to those of Omao, pale greyish to white and spotted with lavender and reddish-brown. Incubation period 14 days. Nestlings fed by both parents and occasionally by birds from previous broods (including those up to one year old). Fledging period 17 days. Has several broods per year; up to five nesting attempts have been documented (Snetsinger *et al.* 1999).

MOULT Complete post-breeding moult of adults falls between July and December with a peak for most birds in October–November following breeding; body moult usually initiated before start of wing and tail moult. First-year birds have partial moult at about same time but variable between July and February, depending on time of hatching.

MEASUREMENTS Wing (n=9) 85–92, (2 immatures) 84–89; tarsus 35–37; bill (culmen) 15–17. Weight 37–43 g (Snetsinger *et al.* 1999).

REFERENCES Berger (1972), Collar *et al.* (1994), Kepler & Kepler (1983), King (1981), Pratt *et al.* (1987), Scott *et al.* (1986), Snetsinger *et al.* (1999).

70 TOWNSEND'S SOLITAIRE *Myadestes townsendi*   Plate 21

Ptiliogonys Townsendi Audubon, 1838, Birds Amer. (folio) 4, pl. 419, fig. 2 – Columbia River [= near Astoria, Oregon, *vide* Amer. Orn. Union (1910) Check-list North Amer. Birds (ed. 3): 359].

IDENTIFICATION 20–22 cm (8–8¾″). A small-billed, slim-shaped grey-brown solitaire of much of the U.S.A. and western Canada with an upright stance, a long tail with a slightly notched tip and a pale wing-bar in flight. Much slimmer and longer-tailed than most 'true' thrushes, with a small broad bill, pale eye-ring and orange panel at base of secondaries when perched. **Confusion species** Distinguished from female and immature Western *Sialia mexicana* and Mountain Bluebirds *S. currucoides* by longer shape, lack of orange on the breast or any blue in the wings and tail. Most likely to be confused with bigger, larger-billed Northern Mockingbird *Mimus polyglottos* but is duller grey, lacks double wing-bar and contrastingly pale underparts. In Mexico initially similar Brown-backed Solitaire (71) has warm or olive-brown upperparts and lacks any grey in the plumage. Out of range Slate-coloured Solitaire (77) is slightly smaller with uniform grey wings and body with blacker tail, broader white eye-ring and no orange panel in closed wing.

DESCRIPTION Sexes alike. **Adult** Entire upperparts plain or mouse-grey but crown very slightly darker, some birds also having pale tips on forehead; broad white eye-ring; mantle, back and scapulars tinged with pale brown in fresh plumage; tail black with dark grey central feathers, white outerwebs to outer feathers and tips of all other outers, with slight notch at tip at rest. Median coverts almost uniform with upperparts but greaters darker brown edged pale grey (especially at bases) or buffish and tipped whitish in fresh plumage (often absent in breeding birds), alula and primary coverts blackish-brown, flight feathers the same but with a long pale orange-buff panel at base of secondaries and pale orange-buff square at base of inner primaries (separated from first by blackish-brown outerwebs), tertials blackish edged white. In flight shows a pale tawny-buff wing-bar at base of inner primaries and buffish-orange at base of secondaries. Underwing has axillaries white becoming pale buff-brown on wing-coverts broadly edged dark brown with broad pale orange or buffish-orange band across base of secondaries and inner primaries. Lores dark grey but may be obscured by paler tips. Cheeks and ear-coverts grey to pale grey streaked finely with pale brown. Chin and throat whitish becoming grey on rest of underparts slightly paler or whitish-grey on vent and undertail-coverts. Bill short, laterally flattened at base where it becomes broad, black. Legs and feet short, dark grey to black. **Immature** Juvenile has entire head to nape, mantle, back and scapulars heavily spotted with pale whitish-buff centres and blackish crescent-like tips, densely spotted on forehead to nape and face, larger spots more widely spaced on mantle and scapulars; large pale whitish-buff tips to greater coverts and tertials and fairly broad pale orange edges to inner secondaries; rest of wings and tail as adult but central feathers blackish-brown; chin and throat similar to face and head but spots whitish with grey edges; breast to flanks and belly larger whitish or pale buff spots with dark bars at tips, forming barred or scalloped pattern. Eye-ring as in adult. Bill, legs and feet as adult.

GEOGRAPHICAL VARIATION Two races; variation poorly or weakly defined and very difficult to detect in the field. Race *calophonus* very similar to nominate; slightly darker or browner in fresh plumage on upperparts, especially crown and rump, with richer or deeper buff patches at base of flight feathers and edges to inner secondaries.

VOICE Call a thin, high-pitched, ringing whistle – variations on *tink*, *eeek*, *tew*, *whee*, *waa*, *clink* or *cre-eek*, often repeated monotonously; low *chirk* contact call between adults; *kree* also used as alarm. Song a loud, rapid, rising and falling warble of complex melodious notes including ringing or bubbling phrases and fluty whistles; may begin and end softly with loud middle portion; has been compared to the quality of the song of Black-headed Grosbeak *Pheucticus melanocephalus* and the tempo of a Warbling Vireo *Vireo gilvus* or the notes given by Purple Finch *Carpodacus purpureus*. Usually delivered from the top of a tree or bush but also occasionally in song-flight, the bird hovering at the peak of its flight before diving back to its perch. Sings throughout the year but has periods of inactivity in late summer and generally much less vocal during winter, when song generally softer, though has been known to sing in a snowstorm.

STATUS AND DISTRIBUTION Uncommon or fairly common.

M. t. townsendi Breeds in North America from east-central and south-eastern Alaska (Porcupine River and the upper Yukon River), south through the Yukon (except extreme north) to the central-western Mackenzie Mountains, and Nahanni National Park in south-west North-west Territories to central British Columbia, southern Vancouver Island and south-west Alberta, with an outpost in the Cypress Hills of Alberta and south-west Saskatchewan. In U.S.A. from Washington south and south-west through the Cascades and Sierra Nevada to southern California (Mt Pinos, San Bernardino Mountains, San Gabriel, San Jacinto, White, Inyo and Panamint Mountains), the Sheep Range in south-east Arizona and possibly in the Kingston Mountains of south-east California; in the east to south-east Wyoming (possibly also north-west Nebraska), the Sangre de Cristo range from central Colorado south to central New Mexico (where it also occurs in the White, Black and Mongollon Mountains), the White Mountains of eastern-central Arizona and possibly elsewhere in the state to the San Francisco Mountains and the Kaibab Plateau of north-east Arizona; the most easterly breeding birds inhabit the Black Hills of south-west South Dakota, south-east Montana and north-east Wyoming (Bowen 1997).

May be absent as a breeding bird from large areas of apparently suitable habitat within the range given above; Bowen (1997) considered it absent from most of northern, western and south-western British Columbia between 53°N and 59°N; status in south-east Alaska is uncertain.

In winter generally at lower altitudes from southern British Columbia and southern Vancouver Island east to southern Alberta (exceptionally north to southern Alaska) south through most of the breeding range to central and southern California (Peninsular Range), northern Baja California and northern Chihuahua south and east to Durango, northern Zacatecas and west-central Nuevo León, Mexico; in the east to southern Montana, south-west North Dakota south to eastern Nebraska, eastern Kansas and western Missouri, north-western Oklahoma to western and north-west Texas.

M. t. calophonus Resident in Mexico from extreme eastern Sonora and western Chihuahua south through the western Sierra Madre Occidental to Zacatecas and possibly northern Jalisco.

MOVEMENTS The nominate race is an altitude and partial migrant to lower levels up to about 3180 m (10,000') in the south of the breeding range (though rare locally in the interior and at the coast), from south-east Alaska (Juneau) and southern British Columbia east through Saskatchewan (where it has overwintered on several occasions), Manitoba (scarce or uncommon) to southern Quebec (6 records but has also overwintered), south to southern California, north-east Arizona, central New Mexico, central Texas and northern Mexico in northern Baja California and much of north-east Mexico. Disperses from breeding areas from mid-July to mid-August; autumn migration begins in August but most birds move in September and early October and are present on winter territories from October to April. Spring migration chiefly mid-March to at least mid-April and (perhaps exceptionally) to mid- or late May in southern California, but some birds are still present on winter territories up to 10 May.

In autumn and early winter a casual, irregular or erratic vagrant to Manitoba, Ontario, Quebec, New Brunswick, New Hampshire, New York (2 records), Nova Scotia, Newfoundland and Rhode Island south through most of the central and eastern U.S.A., though variably rare in some states, e.g. first Indiana state record was November 1995; no records from any of the Gulf States east of Arkansas and Atlantic coast states north to New Jersey; also recorded Guadelupe Island (off Baja California).

HABITAT Conifer forests, particularly relatively open stands (including edge of burnt or logged areas) of pine, firs, juniper, spruce and hemlock usually with little or no vegetation cover and near fast-moving streams; also stunted spruces and dwarf willows on high mountain slopes, cliffs and well-wooded ravines up to and above the timberline between 350 and 3630 m (1155–12000′); in Mexico in drier or semi-arid pine-oak forests. On migration and winter at lower levels in open woodlands, oak and pinyon-juniper woods, also in wooded foothills, canyons, ravines, chaparral and semi-desert scrub; may also occur on the edge of suburban areas.

BEHAVIOUR Usually conspicuous; alone or in pairs though loose aggregations of up to 10 come together at common sources of food, e.g. junipers, on migration or in winter are not unknown; also gathers in larger groups prior to and during migration or at stopover sites. Most usually seen perched or sitting upright on fairly open or exposed perch (often on dead branch or snag) at top of tall tree or post, and resembles a large flycatcher in shape, making a rapid dive onto ground-based prey and sallies as high as 30 m into the air (often above the tree canopy) to catch insects in flight, usually returning to point of departure; may also hover when picking berries from tree. In flight again resembles a flycatcher or bluebird, with fairly long tail and dashing flight, but also remains motionless for long periods. Forages on the ground and in (usually berry-bearing) trees; occasionally secretive and skulks in low vegetation thickets, only flying when disturbed. In winter both sexes vigorously defend small territories of feeding trees, usually junipers, indulging in violent struggles in their defence. Feeds mostly on insects, e.g. moths, beetles and their larvae, ants, flies, bees and wasps, most of which it catches in flight; also (especially in winter) takes a variety of berries, mostly juniper (often exclusively) either from the tree or on the ground, but also red cedar, mistletoe, mountain ash, buckthorn, hawthorn, hackberry and rosehips, plus cherries, ivy berries and pine seeds.

BREEDING Season: May (but pair formation in April) to July or early August. Nest: a cup-shaped structure of strips of bark, plant stems and dry grasses, also small twigs, pine needles and roots, covered with blackish moss and lined internally with fine grasses and sedges; built entirely by female; usually on or near the ground (e.g. on a roadside bank), low down in bush or shrub, often in a small hollow at the base of a tree or under an over-hanging bank of a stream, or less usually under rocks. Eggs: 3–4, exceptionally 5, variably dull white, bluish-white, greyish, greyish-blue, beige or pale pink, evenly spotted with brown, purple, reddish-brown, yellowish-brown or occasionally larger lavender-grey blotches. Incubation period 11–14 days. Fledging period 10–12 days. Two broods.

MOULT Adults have single complete postnuptial moult from mid-July to mid- or end of September; midsummer birds often in heavily worn plumage which is lightly tinged with brown and the whitish tips to the greater coverts and edges to the tertials are often totally abraded; no spring moult. Postnuptial moult of juveniles begins in July and complete by end of September; all or only outer greater coverts, alula, primary coverts and flight feathers including the tertials and all tail feathers are retained. Shape of the tail feathers may be indicative of age in the hand, but overlap occurs and some intermediate birds will be impossible to age.

MEASUREMENTS (n=43) Wing, male 108.5–123, female 105.5–118; tarsus, male 19–24, female 20–22.5; bill (culmen) 11–13; *calophonus* (n=4) wing, male 109–115, female 110.5–112. Weight 30–35 g.

REFERENCES Bent (1949), Bowen (1997), Godfrey (1979).

71 BROWN-BACKED SOLITAIRE *Myadestes occidentalis*   Plate 22

Myadestes [obscurus] occidentalis Stejneger, 1882, *Proc. U.S. Natn. Mus.* 4: 371–374 – Tonila, Jalisco.

IDENTIFICATION 20.5–21.5 cm (8–8½″). A grey and olive-brown solitaire from the highland forests and clearings of Mexico to Honduras. Head grey with broad white eye-ring and submoustachial, olive-brown upperparts with rufous edges to wing-coverts and flight feathers, with pale buffish wing-bar in flight; dark tail with white outer feathers; underparts paler grey. **Confusion species** Townsend's Solitaire (70) is similar but has slightly paler all-grey head, upper- and underparts, and small orange-buff patch at base of primaries, no white submoustachial. Slate-coloured Solitaire (77) is slightly smaller and uniformly grey (slightly darker in tone) with bold white eye-ring and pale pinkish legs and feet. From any of the *Catharus* nightingale-thrushes by upright stance, broad white eye-ring, grey underparts and white outer tail feathers.

Taxonomic note Formerly known as *Myadestes obscurus*.

DESCRIPTION Sexes alike. **Adult** Forehead to crown whitish-grey (may merge with upper lores in some), crown to nape and upper mantle darker or slate-grey (may be faintly washed olive), broad white crescents around eye forming almost complete eye-ring; mantle and upper back brownish-olive tinged rust-brown on mantle and scapulars and greyish-olive on lower back, rump and uppertail-coverts. Tail blackish-grey but central feathers greyish-olive and outers edged pale brown or greyish-buff towards tip and tipped white, next inner pair with tip off-white or pale greyish-white, several remaining feathers finely tipped white (probably only visible at close range in field). Lesser to greater coverts brown edged rust-brown on outerwebs; alula and primary coverts blackish-brown, latter edged rust-brown as on coverts, flight feathers dark brown broadly edged rust-brown on secondaries and tertials, base of secondaries and inner primaries with a panel of pale rust-orange forming short wing-bar in flight; innerwebs of tertials dark brown; underwing has coverts pale buffish-brown or warm buffish and tipped dark brown, with whitish-buff bases to secondaries and inner primaries. Lores to eye black with narrow off-white line across upper lores to eye, cheeks and ear-coverts grey finely streaked or flecked whitish-buff, broad off-white submoustachial from base of bill to below cheeks and thin blackish malar at sides of pale grey or whitish chin and throat, sides of lower throat pale grey becoming greyer on breast to flanks, centre of lower breast to belly pale grey or whitish or faintly washed olive, undertail as belly or slightly paler. Bill blackish or dark horn. Legs and feet pale greyish-brown to pinkish-flesh. **Immature** Juvenile has entire head to mantle, back, scapulars and rump heavily spotted or scalloped with pale or yellowish-buff centres and fine black fringes to feathers, slightly darker or smaller on head to nape; wings and tail as adult but edges to wing-coverts and flight feathers brighter brown and tips to greater finely spotted white. Face darker or greyer with dull whitish eye-ring; whitish-buff submoustachial and thin dark malar; chin and throat whitish-buff with some faint darker tips, breast and flanks yellowish or yellowish-buff with thin dark fringes forming a heavily scalloped effect, belly and lower flanks greyer and thinly edged darker, vent and undertail-coverts whiter. **First-year bird** Gradually assumes adult plumage on body but tips to median and greater coverts and feathers on head and face to chin and throat retain juvenile spots well into first year of life.

GEOGRAPHICAL VARIATION Three races; variation slight and poorly marked. Race *insularis* very similar to nominate but with slightly heavier rusty tinge and more extensively greyish on mantle and upper back; edges to secondaries may be paler or buffish and forehead, crown and submoustachial

also tinged light olive; pale buff or white on submoustachial, chin and throat also slightly more extensive; flanks slightly tinged olive. Legs and feet brown. Race *oberholseri* poorly separated from nominate but, on average, has brownish-olive more heavily tinged grey and underparts slightly darker or purer grey; legs reddish-brown.

Other races have been proposed, e.g. *deignani*, based on the variation in plumage colour but the degree of variation shown by existing races suggests that the creation of further races will only add confusion to an already unsatisfactory position.

VOICE Call a metallic, slightly querulous, upwardly rising whistle, *wheeu* or *yeeh*, pairs often indulging in duet-calling; alarm call is a nasal rasping *shiehh*. Song a series of squeaky jangling metallic notes, beginning hesitantly (first notes may be repeated several times between long pauses without running into full song) before becoming a rapid burst rising to a jumbled crescendo; highly ventriloquial and given from a secluded perch although sometimes in flight, repeated at frequent intervals and given throughout the year, but mostly from February to May and less often in June and July; a characteristic sound of the highland forests within the range.

STATUS AND DISTRIBUTION Common or fairly common.

M. o. occidentalis Eastern and central Mexico from southern Tamaulipas, Nuevo León and San Luis Potosi south to Guanajuato, northern Distrito Federal and northern Oaxaca; western Mexico from south-east Sonora through south-west Chihuahua to Durango, Nayarit and Guanajuato, also central Guerrero to southern Oaxaca.

M. o. insularis Tres Marias Islands, Mexico.

M. o. oberholseri Southern Mexico from Chiapas south to Guatemala, El Salvador on the volcanoes of Santa Ana, San Salvador and Los Esesmiles, and western Honduras (east to the Comayagua Valley). See Movements regarding possible occurrence in Belize.

MOVEMENTS Largely resident or sedentary but some birds move to lower levels in western Mexico in winter. Has apparently wandered to Belize, but Howell & Webb (1995) questioned whether the record might refer to an escaped cage-bird.

HABITAT Forests; mostly cloud-forests in the humid upper tropical zone of open semi-arid evergreen and deciduous woodlands, usually between 600 and 3500 m (1980–11,550'), also pine-oak woods and forests; frequently in clearings or along tracks; also favours streams or damp ravines.

BEHAVIOUR Usually alone or in pairs but will associate loosely with feeding flocks of other species such as bluebirds *Sialia* and, in parts of the range, Slate-coloured Solitaire. Habits very like those of Townsend's Solitaire but keeps mostly to low or mid-level vegetation in forests and clearings.

BREEDING Season: February to July. Nest: mostly of local grasses, covered with green moss and lined with finer grasses and some feathers; usually on the ground or in a burrow, sometimes on a sloping bank or at the foot of a tree and partially or entirely hidden beneath a fern or similar plant.

Eggs: 2–3, greenish-white with small reddish-brown spots mostly at the larger end. Incubation period 17 days.

MOULT Post-breeding period from August to September.

MEASUREMENTS Wing, male 98–107.5, female 97–108; tarsus 19–23; bill (culmen) 11–13; *oberholseri* wing, male 97–106, female 96–103.5; *insularis* wing, male 96.5–100, female 95–97. Weight apparently unrecorded.

REFERENCES Dickey & van Rossem (1938), Howell & Webb (1995).

72 CUBAN SOLITAIRE *Myadestes elisabeth*   Plate 22
(Ruiseñor)

Muscicapa elisabeth Lembeye, 1850, *Aves Isla de Cuba*: 39, pl. 5, fig. 2 – Cuba.

IDENTIFICATION 19–20.5 cm (7½–8"). Endemic to Cuba. Like other solitaires this is a plain, slender, long-tailed bird which more resembles a flycatcher than a thrush. Posture and actions also recall a flycatcher with upright stance and tail held vertical. Mostly plain olive-brown above, whiter below, with a white eye-ring, buffish-orange patch in the wing and white in the outer tail. Inconspicuous and more frequently heard (see Voice) than seen as it perches in the upper branches of tall trees. **Confusion species** La Sagra's Flycatcher *Myiarchus sagrae* lacks the pale submoustachial stripe, has a cinnamon-brown tail and usually holds itself horizontally, the tail in line with the upperparts.

DESCRIPTION Sexes alike. **Adult** Upperparts mostly olive-brown or slightly browner on crown, nape and mantle. Median coverts brown edged warmer brown, greater coverts dark brown, finely edged olive-brown; alula, primary coverts and flight feathers dark brown forming a dark patch on wing, the latter finely edged pale buffish-brown more broadly on secondaries; bases of secondaries have a small patch of warm buffish-brown; tertials as secondaries but broadly edged pale olive-buff on outerwebs; underwing has coverts whitish edged pale orange except for browner outer greaters, bases to flight feathers silvery-whitish on inner secondaries, becoming pale orange on bases to outers. Tail brown, central pair edged olive, outer feathers whitish on outerwebs and broadly on tips of inners; tips of penultimate outer feathers also white (occasionally a small spot on inner third). Lores dark olive becoming paler on cheeks, ear-coverts finely streaked tawny-buff; conspicuous white eye-ring and fairly broad whitish or pale buff moustachial, bordered by fairly short narrow dusky-brown submoustachial stripe. Entire underparts whitish, creamy-white on chin and throat; breast and flanks washed greyish-olive becoming more heavily olive on lower flanks; belly to undertail-coverts white. Bill small, blackish or dark horn on distal half of lower mandible and paler at base. Legs and feet brownish or yellowish-brown.

Immature Juvenile similar to adult but more olive and extensively spotted and flecked buff on head and face and with larger buffish spots and indistinct dusky edges or fringes to mantle, back and scapulars; tips to median and greater coverts pale orange. Underparts greyish-buff with occasional dusky tips mostly on breast and flanks.

GEOGRAPHICAL VARIATION Two races; variation poorly defined. Race *retrusus* (now extinct) was slightly greyer and less olive on upperparts, no tawny or buffish tinge to pale ear-coverts, pale buff supercilium across upper lores to eye, paler eye-ring and slightly smaller bill; underparts almost pure white with pale grey on breast.

VOICE Call a short whistle. Song a series of sustained flute-like harsh or discordant (almost machine-like) *zheeee* or *zhe-ee-ee-e* phrases, repeated deliberately at varying pitch, and interspersed with higher, sometimes wavering melodious whistles, short scratchy notes, brief warbles and trills resembling the sound of running a wet finger around the rim of a glass (Gundlach 1893, Garrido & Kirkconnell in prep.); far-carrying but ventriloquial, delivered from within the tree canopy. Sings throughout the year but less so at certain times, e.g. March (Raffaele *et al.* 1998). Considered the best singer in Cuba (the local name 'Ruiseñor' means Nightingale), and one of the most distinctive and remarkable songsters of the West Indies (Bond 1979).

STATUS AND DISTRIBUTION Endemic to Cuba where locally common but possibly threatened due to habitat destruction through the expansion of cacao, coffee and tobacco plantations. Considered Near-Threatened (Collar *et al.* 1994).

    M. e. elisabeth Sierra Maestra, Sierra del Magüey, Sierra de Moa, Toa and Baracoa Mountains of eastern Cuba (Holguin, Santiago de Cuba and Guantánamo provinces) and Sierra de los Organos, Sierra del Rosario and the Sierra de la Güira in western Cuba (Pinar del Rio province).

    M. e. retrusus Ciénaga de Lanier, Isle of Pines, Cuba; now considered extinct, not seen since about 1970.

MOVEMENTS Sedentary.

HABITAT Dense humid, deciduous and pine forests, usually on limestone with outcrops, jumbles or rocks and cliffs; the race *retrusus* formerly inhabited dense woods bordering the Ciénaga de Lanier (Bond 1979).

BEHAVIOUR Forages in trees (usually at canopy level) and catches insects whilst hovering. Feeds mostly on insects, berries, small fruits (including ripe palm nuts) and seeds. May occasionally descend to lower levels of trees more rarely to the ground.

BREEDING Season: February to July. Nest: a cup-shaped structure of palms fibres, roots, hair, moss and lichens, the entrance usually concealed by a

286

bromeliad and situated on the side of a bank or steep slope; also in tree cavities and crevices in cliffs or rock-faces up to 6 m (19.5') from the ground. Eggs 3, similar to those of other solitaires, pale greenish-brown and spotted with reddish-brown (Bond 1979, Pratt 1982).

MOULT No information.

MEASUREMENTS (n=35) Wing 75–96; tarsus 19–25; bill 10–12.5 (to nostril) 7.5–9.5; *retrusus* (n=1) wing 88.5; bill 12. Weight 21.5–33 g (G. Wallace unpub. data).

REFERENCES Bond (1979), Garrido & Kirkconnell (in prep.), Gundlach (1893), Phillips (1986), Pratt 1982), Raffaele *et al.* (1998).

73 RUFOUS-THROATED SOLITAIRE *Myadestes genibarbis* Plate 22
(Martinique Solitaire, Siffleur Montagne, Mountain Whistler, Soufriere Bird)

Myidestes [sic] genibarbis Swainson, 1838, *Nat. Libr. Flycatchers*: 134, pl. 13 – Africa or India [= Martinique, *vide* Sclater (1871) *Proc. Zool. Soc. London*: 270].

IDENTIFICATION 19–20.5 cm (7½–8"). An attractive slim small thrush of the forests of the Caribbean islands; like all solitaires it has an upright stance with the tail pointing almost vertically down. Upperparts, wings and tail slate-grey with white outer tail feathers (darker above with olive on rump and uppertail-coverts in St Vincent), white cheek crescents and broad white sides to the bill, pale grey below but with deep rufous throat to upper breast and undertail-coverts. Probably best detected by its remarkable, almost ethereal song. **Confusion species** None likely; the only solitaire in its range.

DESCRIPTION Sexes almost alike. **Adult male** Upperparts dark slate-grey, slightly darker on forehead to crown and nape, some feathers on lower back and rump sometimes tinged olive-brown. Median coverts, edges to inner greaters and tertials grey; alula, flight feathers and outer greaters blackish-brown with fine grey edges to primaries, more broadly grey towards tips of secondaries; bases to secondaries pale grey (may show on closed wing); underwing-coverts mostly grey, becoming darker grey on greater underwing-coverts, bases to primaries and secondaries white. Tail blackish-brown but central pair slate-grey and outer feathers white with next innermost mostly white. Lores to eye blackish, cheeks and ear-coverts dark grey or blackish finely flecked whitish with a small white crescent just below eye; sides of neck as upperparts. Fairly broad but short white submoustachial from base of bill bordered below by thin blackish malar. Chin white but throat to centre of upper breast bright or rich rufous-chestnut; rest of breast to belly slate-grey, paler on sides of lower belly; flanks similar but tinged rufous and vent to undertail-coverts rich rufous-brown. Bill black. Legs and feet yellow or yellowish-orange. **Adult female** As male but tends to show more white on chin and tips to throat. **Immature** Juvenile similar to adult but head to nape, mantle and back spotted with fulvous or orange-buff centres or shafts; tips to median and greater coverts rich orange-brown or cinnamon; crescent on lower cheeks pinkish; underparts similar to adult but with blackish bars at tips of breast and upper belly.

GEOGRAPHICAL VARIATION Six races; variation moderately well defined.

Race *sanctaeluciae* is, on average, slightly darker on upperparts with more white on inner-webs of outer tail feathers; chin and throat whitish, more extensively orange on centre of lower belly.

Race *dominicanus* has rufous on throat darker and less extensive, with a longer white submoustachial and broad streaks on ear-coverts; lower breast pale grey becoming whitish-grey on belly.

Race *montanus* similar to *dominicanus* but slightly smaller with a shorter tail; rufous on throat slightly paler or brighter, becoming tawnier on belly, lower belly whiter; may only show faint (if any) whitish streaks on ear-coverts.

Race *solitarius* slightly larger than nominate with longer tail, whole of chin and throat rich rufous or rufous-chestnut (may show some small white tips) and submoustachial whitish becoming rufous or rufous-chestnut, malar black; cheeks and ear-coverts seem to lack fine whitish streaks; belly pale greyish lightly tinged rufous.

Race *sibilans* much darker on upperparts with coal-black forehead; crown and nape to sides of neck, mantle and wing-coverts dark grey tinged olive on lower back, rump and uppertail-coverts. Tail also black but central feathers greyish-black tinged olive-brown, outer feathers (extensively on outer two, restricted on third) whitish but with dusky outerwebs. Wings black but with prominent square patch of white on inner primaries on closed wing, tertials edged pale grey; underwing-coverts dark grey with broad white wing-bar at base of secondaries. Cheeks and ear-coverts dark grey with small white crescent below eye and fine whitish flecks on ear-coverts; thin white submoustachial becomes deep orange below cheeks, sometimes flecked grey bordered by thin blackish malar stripe extending to sides of neck; chin white, throat and upper breast orange-rufous, sides and lower breast to flanks grey, belly pale grey, lower belly, vent and undertail-coverts pale orange-rufous; thighs slate-grey. Bill black. Legs and feet yellowish to pale yellowish-brown.

VOICE Call a single drawn-out whistle, *teut* or *toot*, similar in tone to a police-whistle. Two or more birds (pairs?) may call to each other in turn, with each bird uttering a clear plaintive whistle. Song an eerie and highly ventriloquial series of semi-discordant whistles and trills; similar to

Cuban Solitaire but usually shorter and with higher-pitched and clearer whistles; consists mainly of 3–4 notes, the second either higher or lower than the first (or may repeat the phrase on the same pitch) but increasing in volume; may conclude or intersperse it with flute-like whistles and ringing or bell-like trills (Bond 1979, Evans 1993). Some notes sound similar to human whistles (and are extremely easy to imitate; birds are said to incorporate new phrases whistled by humans), whilst the flute-like notes recall Hermit Thrush (92). Sings in a very upright posture with the tail drooped (Peters 1926).

STATUS AND DISTRIBUTION Fairly common. Has decreased in Haiti due to habitat destruction.

M. g. solitarius Jamaica.
M. g. montanus Hispaniola.
M. g. dominicanus Dominica.
M. g. genibarbis Martinique, Lesser Antilles.
M. g. sanctaeluciae St Lucia, Lesser Antilles.
M. g. sibilans St Vincent, Lesser Antilles.

MOVEMENTS An altitude migrant; birds on Jamaica and Hispaniola descend to lower elevations in winter (November–March/April).

HABITAT Montane rainforests, also humid lowland evergreen forests usually at 240–650 m (800–2200') on Martinique and 660–880 m (2200–2900') on St Vincent; on Martinique found amongst tree-ferns and bamboo in steep ravines.

BEHAVIOUR Fairly common but easily overlooked and more frequently heard than seen, often sitting motionless and silent in the depths of vegetation and only usually detected by its prolonged whistling call. Forages in trees, tree-ferns and bushes in or on the edge of forests, usually fruit trees and in damp areas. Feeds on small berries, fruit and insects.

BREEDING Season: March to August. Nest: a bulky cup-shaped structure usually placed in a bush, or on the ground beneath a vine-covered tree-trunk, stump or boulder, in a crevice in the fork of a tree, crown of a tree-fern or heart of a bromeliad (up to 15 m/50' from the ground), or on the side of a steep, mossy bank over a stream. Eggs 2, white or pale bluish-white, finely spotted with reddish-brown.

MOULT No information.

MEASUREMENTS (n=15) Wing (nominate and *dominicanus*), male 87–96, female 84.5–94.5; tarsus 20.5–23.5; bill (culmen) 10–13; *sanctaeluciae* (n=5) wing, male 85–92, female 82–92.5; *sibilans* (n=12) wing, male 83–92, female 87–91; tarsus 20.5–25.5; *montanus* (n=8) wing 84–93; *solitarius* (n=10) wing, male 89–96.5, female 88.5–95.5. Weight apparently unrecorded.

REFERENCES Bond (1979), Evans (1993), Hardy & Parker (1992), Peters (1926).

74 BLACK-FACED SOLITAIRE *Myadestes melanops* Plate 22

Myiadestes melanops Salvin, 1865, *Proc. Zool. Soc. London* (1864): 580, pl. 36 – Tucurrique, Costa Rica.

IDENTIFICATION 16–18.5 cm (6¼–7¼"). A shy, forest-dwelling solitaire of Central America. Like other solitaires a slim or slender upright bird which often sits motionless and silent for long periods and hence is often overlooked. Generally slate-grey with a jet-black face and bright or silvery-white underwing-coverts which show well in flight; bill broad at base and orange; legs also orange. Beautiful song has an ethereal quality so birds much prized and persecuted (in Costa Rica) as a songbird. **Confusion species** When seen well, size, shape and stance should eliminate most other species. Varied Solitaire (75) is similar but has rust-brown upperparts. Slaty-backed Nightingale-Thrush (83) is more thrush-like in shape and generally blacker except for the whitish belly, and has a whitish eye with an orange eye-ring and longer orange legs. Black-headed Nightingale-Thrush (86) has a black head but brownish-olive upperparts and white on the chin, throat and belly to undertail-coverts. Sooty Thrush (131) is much larger, more horizontal (and thrush-like) in shape, generally blackish-brown with a pale eye and yellow bill.

Taxonomic note Considered by some authorities (e.g. Ripley 1964) to be a race of Andean Solitaire (76). 2. Black-faced, Varied (75) and Andean Solitaires form a superspecies (Sibley & Monroe 1990).

DESCRIPTION Sexes almost alike. **Adult male** Forehead to lores, cheeks, chin and upper throat black, eye-ring area; rest of upperparts slate-grey or bluish-grey but may show buffish tips to upper forehead and sides of crown when worn. Wing blackish-brown, tips to median and edges and tips to greater coverts and tertials slate blue-grey; flight feathers blackish-brown but bases to inner primaries and secondaries pale grey or light slate, except for small square black patch at base of inner secondaries; edges to outer secondaries also finely greyish; underwing has coverts pale grey, silvery-white at tips, bases to secondaries and primaries silvery-white, very prominent in flight. Tail blackish or blackish-brown with outer feathers whitish, especially towards tip. Entire underparts from lower throat pale bluish-grey, slightly paler on belly and flanks. Bill short and broad at base, orange. Legs and feet bright orange or yellowish-orange. **Adult female** Very similar to male and not always distinguishable in field but slightly duller, especially on upperparts, and back tinged olive. **Immature** Juvenile mostly sooty-grey with pale buff spots and streaks on crown and nape; larger spots with darker or sooty-black fringes on mantle, back and scapulars to uppertail-coverts. Median and greater coverts pale buff-brown or blackish subterminally with pale tips to medians often lost before those on greaters. Face brown flecked pale buff; underparts mottled heavily with pale buff centres to feathers and dark brown edges and tips, whitish or buffish on belly. Wings and tail as adult; attains black face before immature plumage on body entirely lost. Bill dark on upper mandible. Legs and feet pale orange.

GEOGRAPHICAL VARIATION None. Monotypic.

VOICE Call a thin rising nasal *ghank* or throaty *rrau* and a more liquid *quirt*; the alarm note is an excited buzzing *shweee* or *shoo-wee-ee*. Song a beautiful series of high thin clear whistles interspersed with more melodic, flute-like, liquid notes, with rising and falling phrases creating an ethereal quality; given in a fairly leisurely fashion with frequent long pauses between phrases: *eeo-lay* or *teedleedlee... tleedleee... lee-dah... lee-doo*, with variations; may also give 2–3 note phrases on their own. Usually delivered from undergrowth, most frequently in late afternoon and evening, but also from secluded perch high in the forest canopy; females also sing but not as well or for as long as males. Song period March to about mid-May; some may sing or give a subsong between October and March.

STATUS AND DISTRIBUTION Common in protected areas and on the Caribbean slope but numbers have declined, through persecution for the cage-bird trade elsewhere. Breeding resident on both Central and Talamanca Cordilleras in Costa Rica south to the highlands of Chiriquí and Veraguas, western Panama.

MOVEMENTS Some post-breeding dispersal to lower elevations from November to February, regularly down to 450 m (1500′) and occasionally as low as 100 m (330′). Wandered to the north coast of Panama (Almirante, Bocas del Toro) in October 1963 but this record considered by Wetmore *et al.* (1984) possibly to refer to an escaped cage-bird;

also recorded on some offshore islands (e.g. Cebaco), where it may be regular.

HABITAT Cool humid and wet mountain and foothill forests of the upper tropical and subtropical zones, usually between 900 and 2750 m (3000–9000′) in Costa Rica, 750–2940 m (2500–9700′) in Panama. Inhabits tree-clad slopes, ravines and gullies, occasionally at forest edges and in secondary-growth woods or thickets, also thick or dense bushes in areas of cultivation.

BEHAVIOUR A shy, normally solitary, rather lethargic (hence infrequently seen) bird of dense undergrowth, including bamboo, in montane humid forests; often sits motionless allowing close approach before disappearing with a dashing flight showing the white in the wings; sometimes forages or sings higher in the canopy; most feeding takes place low down in the vegetation, sometimes on the ground, and birds will take berries or seeds by hovering. Food is mostly berries but also insects.

BREEDING Season: April–June. Nest: a scanty cup-shaped structure of thin dark roots and plant fibres, stems and liverworts, with an outer covering of green moss and liverworts and an inner lining of finer material; usually in a niche in a mossy bank, or in a crevice or hole in a tree-trunk up to 3.5 m (10′) from the ground, occasionally in a moss-covered crevice in a tree or along an epiphyte-laden branch. Eggs 2–3, white or pale pinkish, finely spotted reddish or rufous-brown, particularly at the larger end. Fledging period 15–16 days.

MOULT No information.

MEASUREMENTS (n=20) Wing, male 84–91.5, female 82–91; tarsus, male 20–23, female 18.5–23; bill (culmen) 10.5–13. Weight (2 males) 30–32 g (Wetmore *et al.* 1984, Slud 1964).

REFERENCES Slud (1964), Wetmore *et al.* (1984).

75 VARIED SOLITAIRE *Myadestes coloratus* Plate 23

Myadestes coloratus Nelson, 1912, *Smithsonian Misc. Coll.* 60(3): 23 – Mount Pirri, neat head of Rio Limon, eastern Panama.

IDENTIFICATION 16–18 cm (6½–7″). A poorly known and rarely seen solitaire with a small range in eastern Panama and extreme north-west Colombia. Has slate-grey head and underparts, black face and chin, and deep tawny upperparts including the wings and tail. A fine singer recalling Black-faced Solitaire (74) but generally quieter or softer in tone with more structured phrases. **Confusion species** Unlikely to be problematic when seen well; Black-faced Solitaire is initially similar on head, bill colour and underparts, but has entirely slate-grey (not brown) upperparts. Slaty-backed Nightingale-Thrush (83) occurs in the same area but is much blacker on the upperparts, with a pale eye and whitish belly. **Taxonomic note** Often considered (e.g. by Ripley 1964) a race of Andean Solitaire (76).

DESCRIPTION Sexes alike (but separable at close range and in the hand). **Adult male** Forehead to lower crown, lores to eye and chin to cheek black becoming grey on ear-coverts. Crown to nape slate-grey becoming tawny-brown tinged rust on mantle and scapulars to uppertail-coverts (deepest rust-brown on edges to scapulars, rump and uppertail-coverts), upper mantle more visibly tawny-brown. Median and greater coverts deep tawny-brown, slightly paler on edges to greaters; innerwebs of greaters blackish; alula, primary coverts and flight feathers blackish but secondaries finely edged and tertials broadly edged rich tawny-brown; underwing has dark grey coverts becoming silvery-white at bases of secondaries and inner primaries, very obvious in flight. Tail has central feathers grey or blackish, edged warm brown, but outer

feathers paler or brownish with whitish tips to innerwebs of outermost two. Lower throat to belly grey or slate-grey except for whiter lower breast, belly and vent. Bill, legs and feet orange. **Adult female** Similar to male but has crown and upper nape tinged olive-brown and lower flanks to vent olive-brown or tawny-brown. **Immature** Juvenile has entire head and face dark slate-grey but heavily obscured with pale brown tips, forming spots or streaks; mantle, back and scapulars to rump similar but more extensively brown with rich buff central shaft-streaks and broad terminal spots and dark slate tips. Median coverts rich buff with fine slate bars at tips; greater coverts dark slate-brown with rich buff-brown edges to outerwebs; alula and primary coverts mostly blackish-brown; secondaries blackish-brown on innerwebs and rich brown on outerwebs forming small panel on closed wing. In hand underwing shows broad white patch across bases of secondaries. Tail black but outer two feathers pale grey-brown with white tips to innerwebs. Underparts mostly slate-grey with large pale buff spots and slightly paler central shafts. May and June birds more closely resemble adults with blackish lower forehead, lores and chin to base of bill, but retain some juvenile spots on crown, mantle, back and underparts; becomes greyer as spots wear off.
GEOGRAPHICAL VARIATION None. Monotypic.
VOICE Outside the breeding season may give single harsh notes (from the song) as single calls, harsher in tone than in Black-faced Solitaire. Song a series of rich liquid phrases rising and falling, similar to Black-faced Solitaire and in tone recalling a swinging rusty gate. Includes some softer

notes (usually at the start): *see-see, see-at-you... seeeeleeeuu... see-see, see-at-you*; often sounds melancholy but may be interspersed with harsher disyllabic notes (M. Pearman pers. comm.).
STATUS AND DISTRIBUTION Common within limited range but very poorly known. Breeds in the Cerro Tacarcuna, Cerro Pirre, Altos de Nique and Cerro Quia of the Darién highlands of eastern Panama and extreme north-west Chocó, Colombia.
MOVEMENTS Sedentary.
HABITAT Moist forests and forest edges in foothills and mountains of the upper tropical and subtropical zones above 800 m (2640') to about 2200 m (6600').
BEHAVIOUR Generally little known and extremely shy, most records being of birds singing or caught in mist-nets; remains hidden in dense cover of the undergrowth but may occasionally be seen in the open in the lower levels and branches of trees or bushes.
BREEDING Largely unknown and unrecorded; possibly from about March or April (or perhaps earlier) to at least May–June (juveniles). Possibly two broods, as suggested by evidence from museum specimens: recently fledged nestlings (heavily spotted and with very short tails) taken in May and June at the same time as more fully developed immatures taken.
MOULT Few data, but full-grown immature in moult in early August.
MEASUREMENTS Wing, male 84–93, female 84.5–88.5; tarsus 20.5–23; bill (culmen) male 13.5–15.5, female 13–15 (Wetmore et al. 1984). Weight apparently unrecorded.
REFERENCES Wetmore et al. (1984).

---

76 ANDEAN SOLITAIRE *Myadestes ralloides*   Plate 23
Muscipeta ralloides d'Orbigny, 1840, *Voy. Amer. Merid.* 4, pt. 3, Ois.: 322 – Chulumani, Prov. Yungas, east side of the Cordillera, Bolivia.

IDENTIFICATION 16.5–18 cm (6½–7"). A slim, short-billed solitaire of the northern Andes (south to Bolivia) and coastal mountains of Colombia and Venezuela. Appears mostly dull brown or grey in secluded forests, but at close range warm rufous-brown above and lead-grey below, with a silvery wing-bar and edges to the tail in flight. Generally unobtrusive, spending long periods sitting upright and trogon-like on a horizontal branch; more easily detected when singing, but ventriloquial and thus still elusive. **Confusion species** Similar to allopatric Varied Solitaire (75) but lacks all-black face and (except for race *plumbeiceps*) has brown to olive-brown on crown and nape, darker bill, silvery-grey wing-bar and pale edges to tail.
DESCRIPTION Sexes alike. **Adult** Forehead and face to sides of crown deep slate-grey, crown to nape grey tinged heavily olive to olive-brown, mantle, back and scapulars rufous-brown or tinged olive becoming browner on lower rump and uppertail-coverts. Tail blackish-brown except for deep brown central feathers, all outer feathers

tipped white and outermost two pale grey on outerwebs and inners mostly off-white. Lesser coverts as scapulars or tinged slightly browner; medians the same but with darker bases, greater coverts blackish-brown edged bright olive-brown; alula and primary coverts blackish-brown finely edged olive-brown; flight feathers dark greyish-black finely edged pale olive-brown, with a small pale buffish-brown panel at base of inner secondaries on closed wing; tertials as flight feathers but more broadly edged warm brown on outerwebs. Underwing has coverts grey with silvery-white bases to secondaries and inner primaries, showing as wing-bar in flight. Lores to eye blackish or dark slate-grey. Chin and throat to sides of breast and flanks deep slate-grey (chin can sometimes be pale grey), belly whitish-grey and extending to undertail-coverts which are tipped with darker grey; flanks tinged cinnamon brown. Bill rather short and broad at base, upper mandible dark slate or brownish-horn, lower similar or pale orange-yellow (more extensive in some) at base.

Legs (fairly short) and feet burnt sienna to horn-brown. **Immature** Juvenile similar to adult in general plumage but entire head and face has small pale buffish-brown subterminal spots with darker tips, larger spots on mantle, edges of scapulars and tips to median and greater coverts; underparts dark slate-grey heavily obscured by pale buffish-brown shaft-streaks and pale buff tips. First-year bird retains juvenile plumage on tips to median and greater coverts.

GEOGRAPHICAL VARIATION Four races; variation not well defined. Race *plumbeiceps* very similar to nominate but deeper or richer rufous-brown on upperparts (including edges to flight feathers), with entire crown to nape slate-grey (except for birds in western Ecuador, which have hind-crown/upper nape tinged brownish) and underparts slightly darker grey, lower mandible entirely yellow. Race *venezuelensis* has paler brown upperparts, flanks more heavily tinged olive, legs and feet dull yellow, upper mandible blackish-brown, lower dull yellow. Central Colombian race *candelae* has crown and upperparts dark tawny, breast darker grey.

VOICE Call a throaty *rraou*. Song a slow, leisurely series of deliberate clear flute-like whistles occasionally interspersed with harsher or more guttural notes broken by frequent pauses: *lee-day... leedle-lee... lulee... ur-lur... turdelee... see-see... eee-oh-lay... teul-teul...*, with some notes more sustained than others and some singers giving only a shorter series of phrases; the last notes are either rising or lower than the others. Song usually repeated after a slightly longer gap than the pauses between phrases; some regional dialect apparent with northern birds apparently having a greater proportion of drier or harsh notes than others. The song is quite loud and far-reaching but extremely ventriloquial, singing birds frequently remaining undetected. Usually given from the lower canopy of a tall forest tree, mainly at dusk and dawn. Females also sing but quality inferior to male. Sings all year but less frequently outside the breeding season.

STATUS AND DISTRIBUTION Common or fairly common.

M. r. ralloides Northern Peru, south of the Marañón River, through the Andes of Amazonas, San Martín and eastern La Libertad east and south to central Cochabamba and more recently to Chuquisaca, Bolivia.

M. r. plumbeiceps Andes of central and western Colombia south through the Andes to western Ecuador.

M. r. candelae Upper Magdalena Valley, Colombia.

M. r. venezuelensis Northern and western Venezuela from the Perijá Mountains and the coastal ranges of Carabobo and Distrito Federal west to the Andes of Lara and Trujillo; also recently (April 1995) discovered in the Sierra San Luis, Falcón (Boesman 1997); south through the East Andes in Colombia and eastern Ecuador to extreme northern Peru, north of the Marañón River.

MOVEMENTS Sedentary.

HABITAT In dense areas of humid and cloud-forests and also in some second-growth woodlands and, at higher altitudes, dwarf vegetation; usually between 1200 and 2900 m (3960–9570') but also down to c.800 m (2640') on the Pacific slope of the Andes, and rarely to 4500 m (14850') in Venezuela.

BEHAVIOUR A shy or retiring, usually solitary bird which spends considerable periods inactive and is therefore inconspicuous and, unless singing, easily overlooked amongst the dense canopy of mid-level trees. Forages along branches and amidst the vegetation of medium to tall trees, but also fly-catches and gleans insects from the outside of more distant leaves; rarely occurs on the ground, but often nests there and frequently attends ant swarms. Food mostly insects but also berries and other small fruits.

BREEDING Season: March to November, with eggs noted in March, April and July, but presumably also later as juveniles noted in southern Peru in December. Nest: a small cup of moss usually on the ground on a bank or old stump or log, usually concealed with creepers. Eggs: 2, dull white finely speckled with reddish-brown at larger end.

MOULT No information.

MEASUREMENTS (n=12) Wing, male 84–89, female 83–87; tarsus 19.5–21; bill (to skull) 11.5–15, depth 3.5–4. Weight 25.5–30 g (J. Hornbuckle pers. comm., Rahbek *et al.* 1993).

REFERENCES Boesman (1997), Rahbek *et al.* (1993).

77 SLATE-COLOURED SOLITAIRE *Myadestes unicolor*   Plate 22

Myiadestes unicolor Sclater, 1857, *Proc. Zool. Soc. London*: 299 – Cordova, Veracruz, Mexico.

IDENTIFICATION 19–20.5 cm (7½–8"). A dark grey solitaire of the highlands of central Mexico to central Nicaragua. As in other solitaires has a short bill and upright stance with tail pointing vertically downward. Almost uniform dark slate-grey with blacker wings and tail, broad white eye-ring and white tips to outer tail feathers. An excellent song-bird much persecuted in eastern Mexico by bird-catchers. **Confusion species** Brown-backed Solitaire (71) is brown or rufous-brown on the mantle, back, scapulars and wings and has a short whitish submoustachial stripe.

DESCRIPTION Sexes alike. **Adult** Upperparts slate-grey, slightly paler on forehead and tinged with olive on mantle, scapulars and back to rump and uppertail-coverts. Median and greater coverts blackish-brown, greaters edged and tipped slightly paler; alula and primary coverts blackish and flight feathers dark grey-brown, latter edged slate-grey; bases to secondaries have a small square patch of light orange (may show only at close range); tertials broadly edged grey or greyish-olive but inner-webs browner; underwing has coverts whitish tinged buffish-grey, darker on outer coverts, bases to flight feathers silvery-white or light buffish on inner secondaries. Tail blackish-brown but central feathers grey-brown, outer two paler brown tinged grey, becoming whitish at tip. Lores to eye black; broad white crescents above and below eye, almost circling it, cheeks and ear-coverts to sides of neck grey, thin ill-defined whitish submoustachial (often flecked darker) bordered by narrow dark malar. Underparts dull grey, slightly paler on chin and throat and on belly to flanks; sides of lower breast and flanks may also be tinged olive. Bill dark grey or blackish-horn. Legs and feet flesh or pinkish to light brown. In worn plumage wings become browner with sandy-buff edges to outer-webs. **Immature** Juvenile similar to adult but slightly darker with fine pale buff spots on crown and nape and larger spots with darker edges and fringes on mantle, scapulars and uppertail-coverts. Median and greater coverts have pale orange tips. Underparts have pale whitish-buff centres to feathers mottled darker with brownish or dark brown bases at tips, heaviest on breast.

GEOGRAPHICAL VARIATION Three races; variation not well defined and separation is mainly on size (decreases from north to south but only by a few mm) and variation in the tone of grey. Race *pallens* is, on average, slightly paler on chin and throat and greyish-white on centre of belly; edges to flight feathers (especially at base) may be paler or pale buff, especially on females. Race *veraepacis* slightly paler or purer grey above with buffish-grey edges to flight feathers (in fresh plumage), and is darker grey on breast, paler on belly; has almost complete whitish eye-ring and pale buffish-grey spot on lower lores; outer tail feathers purer grey and tinged brownish-grey.

VOICE Most frequent call is a hard dry nasal *rrank* or *rran* and a more buzzing *zzrink*, possibly used as an alarm. A fine singer of beautiful, ethereal and haunting quality; often begins slowly or hesitantly with a few poor or uncertain notes before giving a varied series of clear or quavering fluted piccolo-like whistles that rapidly rise and fall and end with a long loose trill.

STATUS AND DISTRIBUTION Fairly common (Mexico and Honduras) or uncommon. Population in eastern Mexico has been drastically reduced (if not totally extirpated) by the activities of bird-catchers.

M. u. unicolor Southern Mexico in south-east San Luis Potosi, Hidalgo, Puebla, northern and south-eastern Oaxaca, Veracruz and western and central Chiapas.

M. u. veraepacis Disjunct in the highlands of Guatemala, northern Honduras and Los Esesmiles, El Salvador; also a rare resident or altitude migrant in the Cockscomb and Maya Mountains, Belize.

M. u. pallens Northern-central Nicaragua.

MOVEMENTS Not well understood but some birds winter at lower altitudes (February and March in El Salvador); has been recorded almost at sea-level in southern Veracruz (Los Tuxtlas) and Belize, where recorded as common in August (Howell *et al*. 1992).

HABITAT Cloud-forests, humid evergreen and pine–oak woodlands and bushed slopes of the upper tropical and subtropical zones between 1000 and 2700 m (3300–9000') in Mexico and El Salvador, slightly lower into the lower tropical zone at 300–1850 m (990–6100') in central Chiapas, Guatemala and Honduras (Gómez de Silva 1999).

BEHAVIOUR Generally shy and unobtrusive, keeping to the undergrowth of deep woods and densely shaded ravines. Forages low down but also at higher levels in berry-bearing shrubs and trees.

BREEDING Season: poorly known; at least March. Nest: completely of green moss and lined with fine roots, well concealed in a niche or crevice in a bank, or under an overhang or the large fronds of a fern. Eggs unknown but probably very similar to those of other *Myadestes* solitaires.

MOULT No information.

MEASUREMENTS Wing, male 90–103.5, female 93–97.5; tarsus 20–21.5; bill (culmen) 10.5–12; *pallens* male 89.5–98, female 88–95; *veraepacis* male 92–103, female 93–98.5. Weight apparently unrecorded.

REFERENCES Gómez de Silva (1999), Howell *et al*. (1992).

78 RUFOUS-BROWN SOLITAIRE *Cichlopsis leucogenys*   Plate 23
Cichlopsis leucogenys Cabanis, 1851, *Mus. Hein.* 1 (1850): 54 – Brazil.

IDENTIFICATION 20.5–21 cm (8–8¼"). A medium-sized, slender, mostly reddish-brown solitaire which, apart from its short legs, could be mistaken for one of several similar *Turdus* thrushes. Best distinguished by short bill (usually clearly divided in colour of upper and lower mandibles), broad dark malars, and tawny-orange centre of chin and throat, becoming warm or tawny-brown on breast and pale greyish on belly. Birds of races *peruvianus* and *chubbi* have more extensive bright orange on the throat and upper lores and supercilium (that on *chubbi* darker or browner). Immatures are undescribed. Song inferior to that of other solitaires, usually consists of scratchy trills and twittering notes.
Confusion species Generally similar to many female thrushes of the region, particularly Yellow-legged (94) and Pale-eyed (95), but best told

by more upright shape and stance and, in good view, small or shorter two-tone bill, unstreaked tawny-orange (or darker) throat, and combination of pale grey belly and bright orange-buff under-tail-coverts.

DESCRIPTION Sexes alike. **Adult** Forehead to crown, nape and entire upperparts rich russet or rufous-brown extending to wing-coverts, tertials and edges of flight feathers; flight feathers darker brown; underwing-coverts silvery-white faintly washed orange. Tail fairly long, deep cinnamon-brown, outer feathers paler or only tipped cinnamon. Face brown but mottled slightly paler on lores; thin fine pale flecks on ear-coverts. Chin and throat bright orange or tawny-orange bordered by broad brown malars, becoming warm tawny- or olive-brown on lower throat and breast and dull grey on sides of lower breast, flanks and belly; slightly tinged buffish-brown on flanks; vent and undertail-coverts light buffish-brown or tinged orange-buff. Upper mandible blackish, lower bright yellowish-orange. Legs and feet dull green-ish or yellowish-brown. **Immature** Unknown.

GEOGRAPHICAL VARIATION Four races; variation slight and not well marked. Race *gularis* very similar to nominate but may show more rufous-brown across breast ,and belly may be tinged dull ochre-brownish; undertail-coverts pale orange-buff. Race *peruvianus* has centre of chin and throat and upper lores brighter rufous-orange, sides of chin and throat darker brown extending to cheeks and ear-coverts; breast duller olive-brown and belly to flanks dark grey washed olive-brown, undertail-coverts bright yellowish-buff or tinged rufous. Eye dark hazel. Legs and feet greenish-brown, claws yellowish-horn. Race *chubbi* slightly larger and darker on upperparts with thin yellow eye-ring, deep rich brown on head, nape, mantle and back, becoming rufous-brown on rump and uppertail-coverts; face to upper lores, chin and throat deep chestnut-brown becoming rich chestnut on lower throat; upper breast olive-brown becoming grey on lower breast to upper flanks; thighs and lower flanks warm brown becoming bright orange-buff on undertail-coverts; under-wing-coverts bright orange-buff. Legs and feet brownish-black to dark grey.

VOICE Call a thin sharp penetrating whistle, *tsr-reeee*, and a louder *sueeet* alarm call. Song a series of rambling unmelodious sharp whistled phrases interspersed with some harsher or twittering notes: *tleeowit-tsiii-trrrrr-tr-tr-teeoo*, etc., recalling Eastern Slaty-Thrush (136). Song usually rapidly delivered from concealed perch in low to medium-height canopy; frequently raises or flutters its wings whilst singing.

STATUS AND DISTRIBUTION Local or uncommon in some areas, with some forest loss in its limited elevational range. Resident. Considered Near-Threatened (Collar *et al.* 1994).

C. l. leucogenys Brazil, in south-eastern Bahia and Espírito Santo.

C. l. gularis The tepuis of the Gran Sabana, south-east Venezuela, and adjacent Guyana and discontinuously east into Surinam.

C. l. chubbi North-west Ecuador, western slope of the western Andes in Esmeraldas and Pichincha.

C. l. peruvianus Central Peru on eastern slope of the Andes (Cerros del Sira, Huanuco and Rio Perene, Junín).

MOVEMENTS Sedentary but has been recorded once in western Colombia (Yatacue, upper Anchicaya valley, western Valle de Cauca) in August 1977.

HABITAT Dense primary rainforests in the lower montane and lower subtropical ranges at 750–850 m (2475–2800') in Brazil and at 550–1300 m (1815–4290') elsewhere.

BEHAVIOUR A shy inconspicuous bird usually alone and occurring at lower levels of the interior of forests, perching horizontally in low trees, shrubs and other vegetation, unlike other, more upright-perching *Myadestes* solitaires. Forages and feeds in underbrush and forest floor leaf-litter.

BREEDING Virtually unknown; only one nest found, positioned well above the ground in the fork of a tree.

MOULT No information.

MEASUREMENTS *chubbi* (n=2) wing, male 107, female 108; bill (culmen) 20; tarsus 26.5–7; *gularis* wing, male 102; tarsus 21.5. Weight 61 g.

REFERENCES Chapman (1924), Hilty & Brown (1986), Meyer de Schauensee & Phelps (1978), Sick (1993).

---

79 WHITE-EARED SOLITAIRE *Entomodestes leucotis*   **Plate 23**
Ptilogenys leucotis Tschudi, 1844, *Arch. Naturg.* 10: 270 – Peru.

IDENTIFICATION 23–24 cm (9–9½"). A very striking solitaire of the eastern slope of the Andes from central Peru to northern Bolivia, but far more often heard than seen. Mainly jet-black below and on the wings, with rufous or deep chestnut upperparts and a large white face-patch; in flight shows broad white wing-bar at base of flight feathers and prominent white outer tail feathers (contrasting with black inners). **Confusion species** If seen well fairly unproblematic; the only other solitaire with a similar white

face-patch – Black (80) – is allopatric and all-black above.

DESCRIPTION Sexes almost alike. **Adult** Forehead to hindcrown jet- or glossy black; nape to scapulars, rump and uppertail-coverts deep chestnut or rufous-brown, tail black but outer two feathers blackish-brown at base with distal half white on both webs, showing well on undertail of perched bird. Median and greater coverts as scapulars; alula, primary-coverts and flight feathers black but with white patch at base of inner

primaries, and outer edges may be thinly buffish-brown; tertials rufous but blackish on innerwebs. May show some white at bend of closed wing from long axillaries. In flight shows broad white wing-bar at base of primaries. Underwing has coverts whitish and snowy-white axillaries and bases to secondaries. Broad creamy or snowy-white patch from base of bill extends across cheeks and ear-coverts. Underparts mostly jet or glossy black but (especially female) may also show some rufous or chestnut on flanks. Bill small or short but pointed, upper mandible black, lower yellow to yellowish-orange. Eye variable from crimson to chocolate-brown. Legs and feet black. **Adult female** As male but has duskier-brown crown and hindcrown, black of underparts sometimes infused with rufous or deep chestnut on flanks. Iris brown. Legs and feet vary from brown to pale dusky-yellow. **Immature** Juvenile has pale central shaft-streaks to median and greater coverts and shorter pale central shaft-streaks on crown, nape and mantle. First-year bird similar to adult but slightly duller brown above. In hand or at close range in the field, tips of tail feathers pointed. Bill brown. Legs and feet yellow or yellowish-grey to pale grey-brown.
GEOGRAPHICAL VARIATION None. Monotypic.
VOICE Generally silent and song rarely heard.

Gives a series of single weak *chick* or *chuck* notes, which may be part of the song or single call notes. Song a far-reaching peculiar sustained ringing *wreeeeeeeeenhh*, nasal and metallic, almost like a harmonica or tuning-fork. Ventriloquial and usually given from a concealed perch within the canopy of medium to tall trees.
STATUS AND DISTRIBUTION Fairly common. Breeds along the eastern slope of the Andes in central and southern Peru (north to Amazonas) to northern Bolivia (La Paz and Cochabamba).
MOVEMENTS Sedentary.
HABITAT Usually in medium to tall trees in montane forest and forest edge or clearings between 1500 and 2800 m (4950–9240').
BEHAVIOUR Usually alone or in pairs, but known to form loose congregations in fruiting trees and joins mixed-species feeding flocks when not breeding. Generally shy or nervous and very difficult to see, except in escape flight. Forages in trees and feeds on insects, seeds, berries and fruit.
BREEDING Unknown.
MOULT No information.
MEASUREMENTS (n=5) Wing 113–119; tarsus 24–26; bill (to skull) 17–18.5. Weight, male 55–78 g, female 63 g (J. Hornbuckle pers. comm.).
REFERENCES Fjeldså & Krabbe (1990), Ridgely & Tudor (1989).

80 BLACK SOLITAIRE *Entomodestes coracinus* Plate 23

Myiadestes coracinus Berlepsch, 1897, *Orn. Monatsb.* 5: 175 – near San Pablo, Prov. Tuquerres, south-western Colombia.

IDENTIFICATION 23 cm (9"). A striking but inconspicuous and rarely seen (but more frequently heard) inhabitant of mossy forest within a limited range in the northern Andes. Similar to White-eared Solitaire (79) but all black apart from a red eye, black and orange bill, and white face, underwing-coverts (showing as carpal tufts), inner-webs to flight feathers and outertail-feathers (the latter seen to good effect in dashing flight). **Confusion species** Unmistakable overall, and could only be mistaken for the allopatric White-eared Solitaire, which is rufous above.
DESCRIPTION Sexes alike. **Adult** Entirely jet-black and slightly glossy except for white from base of bill to cheeks and lower ear-coverts, inner-webs to flight feathers, underwing-coverts and distal halves of outer two tail feathers. Tail quite long, otherwise sooty-black. Underwing has coverts silvery-white and long, producing small tuft on side of breast, and base of secondaries also silvery-white, producing broad wing-bar in flight. Eye red. Upper mandible black, lower orange. Legs and feet blackish-brown. **Immature** Juvenile very similar to adult but with paler shaft-streaks and spots to tips of scapulars and coverts; flight feathers browner and underparts mottled darker with whitish tips to breast, belly and flanks.
GEOGRAPHICAL VARIATION None. Monotypic.

VOICE Call a thin weak high-pitched *tszeeeeeeeeee*, slightly buzzing in tone. Song poorly known; said to be similar to White-eared Solitaire.
STATUS AND DISTRIBUTION Uncommon or locally common within a restricted range. Ranges south through the western Andes in west-central Colombia (north to Cerro Tatama, in southern Chocó) to north-west Ecuador (Esmeraldas and Pichincha).
MOVEMENTS Poorly known; possibly an altitude migrant as absent for long periods of the year in parts of the range when the mossy forests dry out, e.g. only recorded in upper Anchicaya Valley, Colombia in May–June and October–November.
HABITAT Wet, mossy (cloud) forests between 400 and 1900 m (1320–6270'), but most usually between 600 and 1600 m (1980–5280'), where it often occurs in clearings and along edges; also enters some second-growth woodlands.
BEHAVIOUR Generally shy, unobtrusive and extremely wary, most often seen only in departing dashing flight. Usually occurs alone or in pairs at most levels (except on the ground and in the open canopy) of forests, but also known to congregate in small, loose flocks at fruiting trees.
BREEDING Season: July. Nest: a cup of moss, lined with fine brown rootlets, placed in and

anchored to stems of thick vegetation, including bromeliads and aroids or creepers; also on trunks of trees or tree-ferns. Eggs: 2, light glossy green, speckled randomly with fine brown spots (Beltran 1992).

MOULT No information.

MEASUREMENTS (n=2) Wing, male 111.5, female 108; tarsus 25; bill (culmen) male 13.5, female 11.5, width (at base) 6–7, depth (at base) 5.5. Weight apparently unrecorded.

REFERENCES Beltrán (1992), Hilty & Brown (1986), Ridgely & Tudor (1989).

81 BLACK-BILLED NIGHTINGALE-THRUSH Plate 24
Catharus gracilirostris

Catharus gracilirostris Salvin, 1865, *Proc. Zool. Soc. London* (1864): 580 – Costa Rica (Volcan de Cartago).

IDENTIFICATION 13.5–16 cm (5¼–6¼"). The smallest of the nightingale-thrushes from Central America, identified by its size, all-dark bill, olive-brown upperparts, slate-grey crown and pale grey chin and throat above a tawny-olive breast-band.
Confusion species Ruddy-capped (85) is similar but has a bright orange lower mandible, a rich ruddy-brown crown, russet tone to upperparts and paler underparts with a brownish-olive wash to sides of breast. Orange-billed (82) is larger with darker head and back and a bright orange bill and eye-ring.
DESCRIPTION Sexes alike. **Adult** Forehead to sides of crown or hindcrown slate grey-brown gradually becoming rich or warm olive-brown on entire upperparts (except for sides of neck which are lighter olive-brown), also median and edges to greater coverts, scapulars, secondaries (may be more gingery-brown), primary coverts and tertials; alula and innerwebs to primary coverts and flight feathers duller brown than rest of upperparts; edges to tail feathers as rest of upperparts but centres duller brown. Underwing-coverts dark grey-brown. Face mostly slate-grey as on forehead, but cheeks slightly paler. Chin and throat greyish-white diffusely streaked greyish, breast with a band of olive-tawny or pale brown (less defined on some); belly and flanks pale grey slightly paler or whiter on lower belly, vent and undertail-coverts. In worn plumage loses warm brown tones of upperparts. Bill black. Eye brown or dark brown. Legs and feet brownish-horn. **Immature** Juvenile similar to adult but has entire head duller and infused with grey-brown on crown and nape and dark grey tinged olive on forehead, face, chin and throat; wing-coverts have pale edges; breast has dark reddish-brown mixed with grey smudges or whitish central shaft-streaks, belly whiter with brown tips to feathers forming bars, lower flanks brown.
GEOGRAPHICAL VARIATION Two races; variation slight and poorly defined. Race *accentor* is extremely similar to nominate but has upperparts slightly more heavily tinged reddish-brown, blacker legs and feet, paler breast-band and slightly stouter bill; several authorities have questioned the validity of this race.
VOICE Call a high-pitched descending *pseeeeew*, a thin penetrating *sic* or *seeet* and a short harsh chat-

tering wren-like buzzy *chrrr* often running into a trill. Song very like that of Russet-capped Nightingale-Thrush (84) but thinner, somewhat buzzier and less musical; up to 3 clear fluted whistles, followed by a tinkling, jumbled trill that rises and falls, often sounding out of tune; repeated after a short pause, successive phrases often differing slightly (Stiles & Skutch 1989, Hardy & Parker 1992).
STATUS AND DISTRIBUTION Common to abundant.
  C. g. gracilirostris Cordillera Central and Cordillera de Talamanca, Costa Rica.
  C. g. accentor Mountains of Chiriquí, western Panama.
MOVEMENTS Sedentary.
HABITAT Damp or moist cold high-altitude forests of the upper subtropical, montane and temperate zones between 1800 and at least 3500 m (5940–11,550'); also in secondary forests, woods by pastures and clearings above the treeline, and patches of elfin forest and thick vegetation with tall shrubs in the páramo zone.
BEHAVIOUR Alone or in pairs, often fairly tame or approachable; forages on the ground, in shrubs and low down in trees, occasionally venturing into the canopy; hops or dashes on the ground or along branches, stopping suddenly and remaining motionless before dashing after an insect; also forages in moss or lichens growing on trees and branches; turns fallen leaves in typical thrush-fashion; flicks wings and raises tail before lowering it slowly. Feeds mostly on insects, larvae, worms and invertebrates as well as a wide range of berries.
BREEDING Season: March to June. Nest: a bulky cup of roots and green moss, lined with fine grasses and small rootlets, usually placed up to 5 m (16') in dense shrubbery or low trees. Eggs: 2, greenish-blue, spotted or speckled reddish-brown or deep chestnut.
MOULT No information.
MEASUREMENTS (n=14) Wing, male 73–78.5, female 70–76; tarsus 30.5–33.5; bill (culmen) 12–14.5; *accentor* (n=8) wing, male 71.5–78.5, female 66–74 (Wetmore *et al.* 1984). Weight apparently unrecorded.
REFERENCES Hardy & Parker (1992), Stiles & Skutch (1989), Wetmore *et al.* (1984).

Catharus aurantiirostris

Turdus aurantiirostris Hartlaub, 1850, *Rev. Zool.* [Paris] (2)1: 158– Venezuela [restricted to Caracas by Hartlaub (1851) *Contrib. Orn.*: 80, pl. 72].

IDENTIFICATION 15.5–17 cm (6–6¾"). A widely distributed thrush of Central and South America, with bright orange bill, orange eye-ring and orange or yellow-orange legs and feet. Upperparts rufous- or olive-brown (three races with grey head), slightly more rufous on the rump and uppertail-coverts, face pale greyish, breast and flanks variably pale or heavier grey, belly whitish. Often very difficult to see as it spends most of its life low down or on the ground amidst thick tangled vegetation; most often detected by its almost constantly repeated song. **Confusion species** Most likely to be confused with Russet (84) and Ruddy-capped (85) Nightingale-thrushes; the former has a dark bill and buff, not grey, breast, while the latter has a dark upper mandible, and both have the forehead to nape usually much brighter brown than on the mantle and back; Ruddy-capped is much darker brown above and lacks any olive tones; both species lack an orange eye-ring and have pale legs. Black-headed Nightingale-thrush (86) has an orange bill, eye-ring and legs but is much more olive above with a much blacker head. The songs of Russet, Ruddy-capped and Black-headed are generally much more musical and melodious than Orange-billed; Russet's is tinnier in quality, Ruddy-capped and Black-headed's are more flute-like and contain whistles, trills and buzzy phrases; Ruddy-capped also includes some warbling phrases. Black-billed Nightingale-thrush (81) is smaller with an all-dark bill, and occurs at higher altitude.

DESCRIPTION Sexes alike. **Adult** Entire upperparts from forehead and including wing-coverts rufous-brown or tinged olive; edges of primary coverts, secondaries and tertials slightly paler or brighter rust-brown, innerwebs to flight feathers dark brown; rump as upperparts or brighter/deeper rust-brown; underwing has coverts grey with silvery-white bases of secondaries and inner primaries. Tail as uppertail-coverts or more rufous. Underwing-coverts greyish-white. Lores to cheeks and ear-coverts off-white to grey becoming washed olive-brown on rear of ear-coverts; bright orange eye-ring. Chin and throat whitish washed grey, breast and flanks similar but heavier grey, lower flanks tinged olive-grey; belly to vent and undertail-coverts whitish or tinged pale yellowish on lower belly. Bill bright orange to coral-red. Legs and feet variably orange or orange-brown, front of legs sometimes dull flesh-pink or tinged brownish. **Immature** Juvenile similar to adult but with very dark brown upperparts and diffuse pale central shaft-streaks to crown, nape, mantle, back and scapulars, becoming spots towards tips; median coverts have pale yellowish or orange-buff tips (present on some greaters); warm brown edges to secondaries and tertials and warm rufous edges to

tail feathers. Edges to primary-coverts and outer primaries pale orange or gingery. Face sooty-brown mottled with fine yellowish streaks, chin and throat white or off-white, breast dull grey-brown with pale yellow-buff centres forming pale spots or with brown bars at tips, belly and flanks yellowish-white with grey-brown or dull grey tips forming faint bars. Bill blackish to brownish-orange (may show dark culmen ridge).

GEOGRAPHICAL VARIATION Fourteen races; variation not well defined except in three races, and most concerns the extent or intensity of olive on the otherwise brown to rufous-brown upperparts; three races from south-west Costa Rica to western Colombia differ significantly in having the head and face grey.

Race *birchalli* darker or tinged more rufous on head to nape and upperparts, slightly warmer or richer brown on rump and uppertail-coverts. Cheeks and ear-coverts tinged grey-brown, underparts but slightly heavier grey on flanks.

Race *costaricensis* slightly smaller and darker or duller olive on upperparts but forehead to crown particularly darker and rump warm or rufous-brown tinged olive; tail dark rufous-brown; edges to primary coverts and secondaries quite bright gingery-brown.

Race *barbaritoi* similar to *griseiceps* (see below) but has head and upperparts olive-brown without rufous tinge.

Race *inornatus* has similarly olive-brown (or greyish-tinged) upperparts to *phaeopleurus* (see below) but duller, lacking any rufous tones, and lores, chin, throat and underparts whiter and more like nominate except for grey sides to breast and flanks.

Race *insignis* has upperparts more like nominate but duller and darker or greyer except for dark brown wings and warmer brown tail; underparts similar to *costaricensis* with slight streaks on dull whitish throat.

Race *melpomene* is slightly more russet olive-brown on entire upperparts than nominate, and slightly darker or reddest on forehead to nape and warmer or rufous-brown on rump and uppertail-coverts; central tail feathers and edges to all outers rich olive-brown. Greater coverts also edged rich olive-brown but innerwebs brown, and primary coverts brown broadly edged olive-brown, flight feathers also brown but outer primaries and secondaries edged warm brown; inner secondaries and tertials darker. Underwing-coverts duller than in nominate, greyish olive-brown. Cheeks and ear-coverts brown, slightly duller than rest of head. Chin to breast whitish-grey, but paler grey or washed olive on sides of breast, rest of breast grey, flanks pale grey and tinged with olive-brown. Bill bright orange usually with darker culmen and tip.

Race *bangsi* is extremely similar to (and sometimes doubtfully separable from) *melpomene* but well marked birds are heavily warm rufous tinged olive-brown on upperparts, edges to greater and primary coverts and flight feathers, and edges to base of tail; underparts as *melpomene* but vent darker or greyer.

Race *clarus* has entire upperparts warm olive-brown, slightly darker on forehead to nape and more rufous on edges to scapulars, tips of greater coverts, flight feathers, rump and uppertail-coverts, central tail feathers and edges to all outers. Underwing-coverts silvery-grey. Lores pale greyish-olive becoming brown on upper lores to over eye and cheeks, grey on ear-coverts; sides of neck olive-brown. Chin and throat white becoming pale grey on sides; lower throat to upper breast white washed grey; rest of breast grey extending to lower breast and flanks; belly to vent and undertail-coverts white. Legs and feet yellow.

Race *aenopennis* very like *clarus* but on average has upperparts slightly paler olive with warm rufous on edges to scapulars, coverts, flight feathers and rump to edges of tail feathers. Face like upperparts but paler olive-brown tinged grey on lores, cheeks and ear-coverts. Chin and throat white or faintly streaked darker, becoming streaked with greyish-buff at sides of throat; breast greyish or washed buff, slightly heavier buff at sides and on flanks; belly to undertail-coverts white.

The following three races from south-west Costa Rica to western Colombia have the face to crown and nape grey.

Race *russatus* has grey forehead to nape merging into upper mantle; rest of mantle and back light olive becoming warm cinnamon-brown on median and greater coverts; edges to primary coverts, outer primaries and secondaries rusty or rufous-orange, slightly darker on edges to tertials; innerwebs to flight feathers brown. Tail rufous on edges to darker centres. Grey of underparts also slightly darker than on nominate. Legs and feet yellowish-brown to pale orange.

Race *griseiceps* has forehead to nape and most of face grey, slightly paler on latter, becoming olive tinged brown (but less heavily than in *phaeopleurus*) on entire upperparts including wing-coverts and edges to outer tail feathers; edges to primary coverts and flight feathers bright gingery-buff, duller on inner secondaries and olive-brown on tertials; underwing-coverts pale grey. Chin and throat white spotted diffusely with grey, becoming pale grey on breast, upper belly and flanks; whitish on centre of belly to vent and undertail-coverts or with dark tips to some undertail-coverts. Bill bright orange-yellow but culmen often dark. Eye-ring orange. Legs and feet yellowish-orange.

Race *phaeopleurus* has lores, face and forehead to crown and hindcrown grey, becoming olive-grey on nape, rest of upperparts olive-brown but rump to base of tail slightly warmer or more rufous, edges to central tail feathers grey-brown; edges to primary coverts, outer secondaries and primaries warmer brown, inner secondaries and tertials olive-brown, innerwebs to flight feathers

pale brown. Face as crown but slightly paler; chin and throat white diffusely spotted greyer, sides of lower throat to breast pale grey, slightly heavier on lower breast and flanks, centre of belly to undertail-coverts white. Bill orange-red; females usually show dark culmen. Legs and feet yellow.

VOICE Call a scratchy or squeaky *mew* or *miaow* recalling Grey Catbird *Dumetella carolinensis*; also a dry or nasal *waaa-a-a-a*, often prolonged into a chatter and recalling similar notes given by Veery (88); also a *chirp* or a repeated euphonia-like *chirr chrit*, either low- or high-pitched and soft or loud, and a more scolding or alarmed *chirr-rr*. Song varies throughout the range but generally poor and unmusical for this family, recalling a bunting Emberizidae in overall tone and delivery; consists mostly of a variety of squeaks, chirps, warbles, twangy notes and trills grouped into rapid short jumbled phrases, best transcribed by Eisenmann (1950) as *ts-teyt, teweet, tisteet, witsteeyt, steeweea, tiststeet, tsipeeareet, tseea*, but mostly too thin and high-pitched to be considered melodious; typically repeats several phrases, e.g. *chirp, tsip, wee-ee, tsirrip-tsip* several times before changing; may also include some of the call or alarm notes within the song, such as *che-what ch-r-r-r*. Usually sings from cover of thick low vegetation or on the ground, and although bird sings for prolonged periods from same perch it remains motionless and difficult to detect. Sings all year but most actively in the breeding season, followed by a comparatively quiet period; sings throughout the day but generally much more at dawn and dusk.

STATUS AND DISTRIBUTION Common or fairly common.

C. a. melpomene Mexico in north-east Puebla, west-central Veracruz, Oaxaca and Chiapas (possibly occurs further north to southern Guerrero).

C. a. clarus Mexico from southern Nuevo León and south-west Tamaulipas and south through eastern San Luis Potosi to Guanajuato, Hidalgo, Mexico also south-east Sinaloa, western and central Durango, Nayarit, Jalisco, Colima, Michoacán, Guerrero and western Puebla. In winter spreads to the coastal lowlands north to central Sinaloa and south to central and southern Oaxaca.

C. a. aenopennis Mexico from north-east Sinaloa to south-west Chihuahua. In winter extends north to extreme southern Sonora and south to Colima and north-central Michoacán.

C. a. bangsi Southern Mexico, central Chiapas to El Salvador, Honduras and Guatemala.

C. a. costaricensis Northern-central Nicaragua and northern Costa Rica from the Central Cordillera to the upper Reventazon valley to Turrialba volcano, north, possibly continuously, to Cordillera de Tilarán; also an isolated population in the hills of the Nicoya Peninsula.

C. a. russatus Mountains of south-west Costa Rica in the General Terraba–Coto Brus region of the southern Pacific slope and the Cordillera de Talamanca, Chiriquí Mountains of western Panama.

C. a. griseiceps Mountains of western Panama, from eastern Chiriquí to Veraguas and possibly Cocle.

C. a. sierrae Colombia, in the Santa Marta Mountains.

C. a. phaeopleurus Colombia, in the middle and upper Cauca valley and upper Dagua and Patia valleys south to the upper Guaitara valley, western Nariño.

C. a. aurantiirostris Eastern Colombia, in the Perijá Mountains and the eastern slope of the eastern Andes in Norte de Santander; in Venezuela the coastal mountains in Distrito Federal, Miranda west to Carabobo south to northern Guarico; the Serra San Luis in Falcón; Lara, and the Andes of western Táchira.

C. a. inornatus Colombia, on the western slope of the eastern Andes in Sogamoso valley, Santander.

C. a. insignis Colombia, on the eastern slope of the eastern Andes in southern Boyacá and the upper Magdalena valley.

C. a. birchalli North-east Venezuela in Sucre and northern Monagas, and on Aripo, Trinidad.

C. a. barbaritoi Venezuela in the Perijá mountains and the upper Rio Negro.

Taxonomic note 1: Monroe (1968) considered *costaricensis* and *bangsi* indistinguishable from *melpomene*.

Taxonomic note 2: The grey-headed races *russatus*, *griseiceps* and *phaeopleurus* were formerly treated as specifically distinct as Grey-headed Nightingale-thrush *C. griseiceps*.

MOVEMENTS Largely sedentary but occurs in some numbers as a non-breeding visitor from October to April to the Pacific slope in southern Sonora south to Michoacán and the adjacent lowlands including Colima, where it reaches sea-level. These may be birds from the northern parts of the range in Sonora and central Chihuahua, which are less numerous (if not entirely absent) from November to March, but these movements are still poorly understood (see Phillips 1986). *Griseiceps* has also been recorded in winter on islands (e.g. Cebaco, Afuera) off the coast of Veraguas, Panama (Eisenmann 1950). Vagrant to Laguna Atascosa, Texas, April 1996 (first U.S. record) (Papish *et al.* 1996).

HABITAT Thick understorey vegetation in high-altitude rain- and cloud-forests, humid areas of pine-oak forests, drier thorn scrub, bamboo thickets, brush tangles, edges, clearings and tangled thickets, plantations (mostly coffee) and second-growth woods, including patches at field margins usually between 400 and 2500 m (1320–8250') in Mexico and Central America and between 600 and 2900 m (1980–9570') in Colombia and Venezuela; also, in some parts of the range, large unkempt gardens including those in fairly large towns such as Boquete, Chiriquí, Panama.

BEHAVIOUR Generally shy and retiring and keeps low in dense dark areas of thick undergrowth, but occasionally ventures into the open on a path or cleared area. Spends most of the time low down or on the ground where it hops or runs; ascends to medium heights (c.15 m/50') in trees, shrubs and bushes in search of berries. Rarely flies far but on landing cocks or flicks tail, lowering it slowly, and if nervous or uncertain often repeats the action, accompanied by a brief flick of the wings. Usually alone or in pairs and wary but, depending on vegetation, appears to be seen more frequently in Mexico and Panama than elsewhere, and often seen at ant swarms. Feeds mostly on small insects and spiders, worms and other invertebrates; also on berries and seeds.

BREEDING Season: March to June (Mexico) or to August in Costa Rica, possibly later (September or October) in Colombia. Nest: a large or thickly walled cup of coarse, dry material studded with green moss and lined with fine grass stems, dry acacia leaves, roots and other fibres, occasionally small flowerheads; usually placed just above the ground or up to 3 m (10') from it in a thick bush, thicket, small tree, hedge, or even in maize or coffee bush. Eggs: 2 or rarely 3, variable from pale blue to pale grey (in *costaricensis* pea-green) and speckled or blotched with brown and pale lilac-blue spots. Incubation by the female alone, period 13–15 days. Fledging period 13–17 days. Juveniles in April, August and October, Colombia; two, possibly three broods.

MOULT No information.

MEASUREMENTS (n=14) Wing, male 76.5–86, female 74.5–80; tarsus 28.5–34; bill (culmen) 13.5–16; *inornatus* wing 76; *insignis* wing 77–79; *melpomene* (n=14) wing, male 76–86, female 75–81; *clarus* (n=10) male, wing 83.5–88, female 78.5–83; *costaricensis* (n=12) wing, male 75.5–83, female 69.5–76.5; tarsus 28.5–30; *russatus* (n=16) wing, male 77–83, female 72.5–78; *griseiceps* (n=19) wing, male 72.5–84, female 73.5–81 (Wetmore *et al.* 1984). Weight apparently unrecorded.

REFERENCES Behrstock & Eubanks (1997), Eisenmann (1950), Fjeldså & Krabbe (1990), Hilty & Brown (1986), Howell & Webb (1995), Monroe (1968), Papish *et al.* (1997), Phillips (1986), Ridgely & Tudor (1989), Skutch (1960), Wetmore *et al.* (1984).

83 SLATY-BACKED NIGHTINGALE-THRUSH   Plate 25
Catharus fuscater
M(yioturdus) fuscater Lafresnaye, 1845, *Rev. Zool.* [Paris] 8: 341 – Bogota.

IDENTIFICATION 17.5–19.5 cm (6¾–7¾"). A shy and retiring slate-coloured thrush of wet mossy montane forests in parts of Central America and the Andes of South America. Generally slate-grey above, head often blacker with a flat crown, prominent whitish eye and bright orange bill; underparts paler or light grey often tinged buff-brown and centre of belly whitish. Gives a variety of pure bell-like whistles and spiralling trills. **Confusion species** Spotted Nightingale-thrush (87) overlaps in southern Mexico to Honduras but rarely co-occurs; has an all-black body, dark eye and dark olive (not slate-grey) upperparts, and is spotted with black on yellow underparts. Male Pale-eyed Thrush (95) is larger and entirely black (whitish eye lacks the eye-ring) with yellow bill and legs.

DESCRIPTION Sexes alike. Female averages deeper in colour, upper mandible usually darker. **Adult** Forehead to crown and nape blackish and darker than rest of blackish-grey upperparts; slightly paler grey on nape to rump and scapulars; wings (except slightly browner wing-coverts, alula and primary coverts) and tail blackish-brown; underwing-coverts grey or pale grey. Lores to over eye and cheeks black becoming dusky-brown on ear-coverts; thin orange or reddish-orange eye-ring. Chin and throat dull, off-white or white washed grey, becoming heavier grey or buffish on breast; centre of breast and belly to vent whitish with a yellowish wash in fresh plumage; flanks grey or greyish-buff becoming greyish buff-brown on undertail-coverts. Bill reddish-orange to vermilion or with dark culmen. Eye milky-white. Legs and feet yellow to bright orange-red. **Immature** Juvenile much browner on head and upperparts (including wings and tail), has slightly paler edges to primary coverts and outermost primaries; underwing-coverts brownish-grey. Chin whitish, throat pale buffish-brown, duller on flanks; centre of belly paler tinged grey, vent whitish, undertail-coverts dull brown. Eye dark.

GEOGRAPHICAL VARIATION Seven races; variation largely clinal and not well marked.

Race *hellmayri* similar to nominate but slightly blacker on upperparts except for slightly browner wings and tail. Chin and throat pale whitish-grey, breast to flanks grey, heaviest or darkest on lower flanks, centre of belly to undertail-coverts white in fresh plumage but dull whitish or washed greyish when worn; thighs grey-brown. Some birds are tinged brown on chin to flanks and undertail-coverts may be brownish-buff.

Race *mirabilis* also similar to nominate but in fresh plumage underparts washed slightly paler yellow with buffish-grey throat and upper breast; white on lower breast and belly duller.

Race *mentalis* slightly darker and tinged olive on upperparts from lower nape to rump, with only head blackish, wings and tail also blackish-brown; underwing-coverts grey to dark grey. Chin and throat pale buffish-brown, becoming browner on upper breast; lower breast darker or greyer extending to flanks; centre of belly pale yellow; undertail-coverts brown.

Race *caniceps* similar to *mentalis* with slight contrast between blackish-brown head to cheeks/ear-coverts and greyish-olive lower nape to scapulars/back; wings and tail blackish-brown; underwing-coverts grey. Chin and throat white becoming infused with buff or greyish-buff on sides and across upper breast; centre of lower breast, belly and vent whitish to pale yellow; flanks greyish; undertail-coverts pale greyish-buff. Eye slate.

Race *opertaneus* similar to nominate but brownish above, with a distinctly brownish-grey breast, more brownish flanks and darker underwing-coverts.

Race *sanctaemartae* by far the darkest race with forehead, crown and face to chin blackish and throat to flanks smoky-grey.

VOICE Call a catlike *meeaaaaaah* or *meeow* and a more buzzing *wheeety* or *whewty weer*; also a high-pitched whistling *poeeeee* and a low, grating *khroum-khroumn* alarm notes. Song very like that of Black-faced Solitaire (74) or Spotted Nightingale-thrush but less hurried and more ethereal and hauntingly flute-like, usually consisting of 2–3 alternating notes, *peee leee, peee-o-lay* or *toh-toh-tee, tee-toh* or interspersed with more complex notes such as *tlee-to-tleedelee, too-luuu-tee* or *to-wee-tlee*, repeated slowly at intervals. Usually given from low undergrowth, occasionally higher, and somewhat ventriloquial (singing birds are extremely difficult to see).

STATUS/DISTRIBUTION Common (Costa Rica); elsewhere uncommon or locally common.

C. f. hellmayri Costa Rica (Caribbean slopes of Guanacaste, Cordilleras de Tilarán and de Talamanca north to Cerro Santa María (Cordillera de Guanacaste) and Pacific slope, mainly Cordillera de Tilarán and the Dota Mountains) and western Panama (Chiriquí and Veraguas).

C. f. mirabilis Mt Pirre area of eastern Darién, Panama; possibly also this race or *hellmayri* on Cerro Jefe, eastern Panama province.

C. f. fuscater Mt Tacarcuna in eastern Panama; Perijá Mountains and the eastern Andes in Colombia south to Santander and western and north-east Ecuador (Pichincha south to El Oro and Loja); possibly also to south-east Ecuador – recently trapped at 1900 m at Quebrada Avioneta where it may be a scarce resident along the east Andean slope (Rasmussen *et al.* 1996); also the Andes of western Venezuela (from Trujillo to Táchira and western Barinas).

C. f. sanctaemartae Santa Marta Mountains, northern Colombia.

C. f. opertaneus Northern end of the western Andes, Rio Herredura, Frontino, Antioquia, Colombia.

C. f. caniceps Northern and central Peru (Piura and northern Cajamarca west to the Rio Zana valley and south to Junín).

C. f. mentalis South-east Peru (Puno) to northern Bolivia.

MOVEMENTS Sedentary.

HABITAT Dense undergrowth of humid, moist or mossy montane forests of the upper subtropical and lower montane zones, between 600 and 3250 m (1980–10,725′), often near streams.

BEHAVIOUR Very shy or retiring and often extremely hard to see; usually on or near the ground in the thickest part of the forest undergrowth, though occasionally climbs higher into fruiting trees. In some areas more active at dawn and ventures out into forest edges, clearings or along forest trails. Very active on the ground, where it hops in long bounds and stops, alert, and flicks wings constantly and nervously; also flicks wings on alighting. Forages on or near the ground, often in leaf-litter, mostly on small bugs and other insects and their larvae, also spiders and small fruits and berries; in parts of its range it regularly attends swarms of army ants.

BREEDING Season: December to July. Nest: a substantial cup-shaped structure mostly of rootlets, leaves and moss, lined with small fibres, fine grasses and placed low down, but can be up to 3 m (10') from the ground in an undergrowth bush or small tree. Eggs: 2, April–August (Costa Rica), December and January, pale greenish white to pale blue, thickly spotted and blotched with rufous or chestnut-brown. Juveniles March to July.

MOULT No information.

MEASUREMENTS (n=19) Wing, male 85.5–90.5, female 82–86.5; tarsus 33.5–35; bill (to skull) 17–19.5; *mirabilis* (n=10) wing, male 83.5–88, female 80–83; *hellmayri* (n=14) wing, male 81.5–94, female 78–89; tarsus 31–37.5; bill (culmen) 14.5–16.5. Weight 33.5–36 g (Wetmore *et al.* 1984, Rahbek *et al.* 1993).

REFERENCES Rahbek *et al.* (1993), Rasmussen *et al.* (1996), Wetmore *et al.* (1984).

84 RUSSET NIGHTINGALE-THRUSH *Catharus occidentalis* Plate 24

Catharus occidentalis Sclater, 1859, *Proc. Zool. Soc. London*: 323 – Totontepec, Oaxaca.

IDENTIFICATION 15.5–18 cm (6–7"). A shy russet thrush with a pale greyish breast and flanks, endemic to the mountains of Mexico. The race *olivascens* is much more olive-tinged on the upperparts but may show a russet tinge to the crown. **Confusion species** Very similar (also in song) to Ruddy-capped Nightingale-thrush (85) but latter slightly greyer below with an orange-yellow lower mandible without a dark tip, and in flight lacks a pale buff wing-bar; prefers much denser, wetter habitat. Orange-billed Nightingale-thrush (82) has a bright orange bill and eye-ring and brighter legs; only russet is on the rump and uppertail-coverts. Veery (88), a migrant through the region (mostly from Veracruz to Yucatán Peninsula and Belize), has darker, more contrasting flight feathers, a buff breast with small dark spots extending to the upper belly, and bright pink legs.

   Taxonomic note Previously considered conspecific with Ruddy-capped Nightingale-Thrush (Phillips 1969).

DESCRIPTION Sexes alike. **Adult** Forehead to crown and nape russet or rich russet-brown, becoming faintly tinged with olive on rest of upperparts to base of central tail feathers and edges to all outers; innerwebs to rest of tail brown; wings russet but brighter on edges to greater and primary coverts and outer primaries and secondaries; slightly darker on edges to tertials; median coverts as scapulars; innerwebs to flight feathers brown; underwing has grey-brown coverts with whitish bases to some feathers and pale buff bases to flight feathers forming a broad wing-bar. Face paler greyish or washed brown, tinged olive-buff and flecked paler on cheeks and ear-coverts. Chin and throat white finely spotted or flecked darker olive-buff, sides of throat and neck also greyish, breast same or greyish-olive, occasionally with slightly paler or yellowish bases. Belly whitish or washed grey, flanks light greyish-olive or with a brownish wash; undertail-coverts white or pale yellowish. Upper mandible dark horn or blackish, lower pale or flesh-pink with dark tip. Legs and feet pale flesh-pink. **Immature** Juvenile darker warm russet-brown above than adult with heavy pale orange-buff spotting or flecking on forehead to nape, mantle, back and upper rump; spotting on scapulars more widely spaced, tips to median coverts and edges to greaters pale orange-buff. Chin and throat dull whitish or yellowish becoming heavily spotted or mottled yellow and dull brown on lower throat, breast and flanks; belly more whitish with dull olive-brown shaft-streaks and tips; undertail-coverts dull yellowish-brown.

GEOGRAPHICAL VARIATION Three races; variation clinal and not well marked. Race *fulvescens* very similar to nominate but slightly larger with more rufous or russet on forehead to crown, rufous-olive upperparts and rich rufous tail and edges of wings. Face warm olive-brown; chin and throat finely streaked with olive-buff on lower and sides of throat and neck; breast grey infused or streaked olive-buff; flanks grey but centre of lower breast and belly white, slightly mottled darker. Race *olivascens* has upperparts and face less brown and more olive, extending to wings and tail; crown warmer brown on some birds; breast whitish-buff with large, ill-defined greyish spots.

VOICE Call a low-pitched, quiet, slightly gruff *chuk* or *chruh* and a nasal mewing *reear*, similar to that given by Orange-billed Nightingale-thrush. Song a varied series of thin fluted spiralling and falling phrases, *she-vee-ee-i-lu* or *chee ti-ve*, usually ending on a thin or high note; may also include a harsher *shweee* at the end; usually repeated in fairly rapid succession.

STATUS AND DISTRIBUTION Common or fairly common.

   C. o. olivascens Northern Mexico in south-eastern Sonora and western Chihuahua south to northern Sinaloa and north-west Durango. Recorded in winter in south-eastern Sinaloa.

   C. o. fulvescens Mexico, discontinuously in the mountains of southern Sinaloa and southern Durango; southern Coahuila and Nuevo León (area around Monterrey) and extreme south-west Tamaulipas; Jalisco and Guanajuato to México, Guerrero and western Puebla.

C. o. occidentalis Central Mexico in eastern San Luis Potosi; Veracruz, Puebla and Oaxaca east to Mt Zempoaltepec and the Río Molino areas.

MOVEMENTS Largely resident but some birds may move south from the northern parts of the range in winter; these movements are not fully understood.

HABITAT Open understorey vegetation of humid cloud-forests, but also in drier pine-oak and fir forests in the subtropical and lower temperate zones, between 1500 and 3500 m (4950–11550').

BEHAVIOUR Fairly active in undergrowth and on the ground, behaviour very similar to most other *Catharus* thrushes in the region, but generally somewhat more confiding than those breeding in North America; unless singing may seem scarce or elusive. Forages on the ground usually under fairly dense vegetation but may appear in the open in the early dawn on forest tracks; also feeds in fruiting trees at higher levels. Food mostly insects and some fruit.

BREEDING Very little known. Season: April to early July. Nest: mostly of plant material, grass and covered with moss, usually placed at low to mid-levels in bushes or trees in thickets, occasionally on the ground. Eggs 2–3, unspotted pale blue.

MOULT No information.

MEASUREMENTS (n=10) Wing, male 80.5–90.5, female 75–84.5; tarsus 30–33.5; bill (culmen) 13-15.5; *fulvescens* (n=22) wing, male 85.5–96.5, female 79.5–88.5; *olivascens* (n=4) wing, male 87–96.5, female 85–89. Weight apparently unrecorded.

REFERENCES Howell & Webb (1995), Phillips (1969, 1986).

85 RUDDY-CAPPED NIGHTINGALE-THRUSH   Plate 25
Catharus frantzii
Catharus frantzii Cabanis, 1861, *J. Orn.* 8 (1860): 323 – Volcán del Irazu.

IDENTIFICATION 15–18 cm (6–7"). An infrequently seen but common resident of the highlands of central and southern Mexico to western Panama. Upperparts russet or russet-olive with a brighter rufous forehead to crown and nape, face to throat whitish-grey and underparts paler or duller grey, with a distinctive dark upper and bright orange lower mandible. **Confusion species** Very like both Orange-billed (82) and Russet Nightingale-thrushes (84); differs from former (especially birds which show a rich brown crown) by lack of bright orange bill and eye-ring and yellowish-orange legs and feet; underwing of both very similar but coverts darker grey on Ruddy-capped and silvery-white on flight feathers slightly more extensive. Russet has dark tip to lower mandible and paler grey underparts, which may be washed buff on the lower throat and mottled on the breast; in the hand both Orange-billed and Russet show a pale buff wing-bar at base of flight feathers on underwing, lacking in Ruddy-capped. Differs from both on voice (slightly in case of Russet), habitat preference and colour of eggs. Lack of spots on underparts distinguishes it from migrant North American *Catharus* thrushes.

Taxonomic note Previously considered conspecific with Russet Nightingale-thrush (Phillips 1969) but now known to occur sympatrically with Russet and Orange-billed in parts of its range (notably Mexico and Costa Rica), breeding generally above the level of Orange-billed and below that of Russet, although there is some overlap at the extremes of these ranges and nests of both Ruddy-capped and Russet have been found within a matter of metres of each other.

DESCRIPTION Sexes almost alike. **Adult male** Forehead to crown and nape rich russet or deep ruddy-brown, brightest on crown; mantle, back and scapulars olive-brown washed russet including edges to wing-coverts and flight feathers; uppertail-coverts, central tail feathers and edges to all outers deep rufous-brown. Underwing has coverts grey-brown with silvery-white undersides to the flight feathers. Face greyish or tinged olive extending around eye and to ear-coverts. Central chin and throat whitish, becoming streaked greyish olive-buff on sides; breast, flanks and belly pale grey and tinged olive on breast; lower belly to undertail-coverts whitish. Upper mandible black, lower orange-yellow. Legs and feet flesh to greyish or brownish-flesh. **Adult female** Differs in extent of grey or greyish-buff on breast; some birds whiter on belly. **Immature** Juvenile similar to adult but forehead to nape dull or dark olive-brown with slightly paler centres to forehead, crown, nape, mantle and scapulars; wings also have slightly paler edges, Face generally darker or sootier than adult, breast dull olive with darker tips extending to flanks; feathers of whitish throat and flanks also tipped olive or olive-brown, forming bars on throat, lower breast, belly and flanks. Bill as adult but with dark tip to lower mandible. Legs and feet pale flesh.

GEOGRAPHICAL VARIATION Five races; poorly or only weakly defined. Most differences concern the intensity/saturation of the brown or olive-brown colour of the crown and upperparts, and the extent of pale grey or white on the underparts.

Race *alticola* has forehead to crown and nape deep ruddy-brown becoming deep olive-brown on rest of upperparts, including edges to wing-coverts and flight feathers except for edges to outer primaries, which are slightly paler or brighter olive-brown; tail dark rufous-brown. Underparts and underwing-coverts may be slightly darker grey, especially on throat and breast in fresh plumage.

Race *confusus* similar to nominate but tinged reddish-brown on upperparts with brownish wash to breast, remaining underparts slightly whiter.

Race *omiltimensis* similar to nominate but paler or duller on upperparts with olive or olive-rust brown contrasting against brighter crown; underparts mostly whitish or pale grey on breast.

Race *wetmorei* similar to nominate but crown duller, back paler (more like *omiltimensis*) and breast paler or browner.

Several other races have been proposed (Phillips 1986) but there seems to be a high degree of individual variation and some evidence of clinal variation between the populations; the level of variation, mostly concerning the intensity of the colour of the forehead and crown and the upperparts, together with the depth of white or grey on the underparts, does not appear to warrant further splitting.

VOICE Contact note is a sharp rising whistle, *whooeeet*, or a quavering *whierrr* or *wheeer*; alarm note is a hoarse *rrerrk* or *worrk*, also a harsh *correeee*. Song is a beautiful, ethereal and varied series of musical phrases similar in tone to Russet Nightingale-Thrush but richer and more musical with flute-like trills, whistles and warbles, *shee-vee-li-ee-ree* or *shee-vee-shee-oo* broken by short pauses; has been likened to the quality of the *eeoolay* notes given by Hermit Thrush (92) (Howell & Webb 1995, Stiles & Skutch 1989). Song period usually coincident with the onset of the rainy season and varies throughout the range; *alticola* sings from late May to late July, *frantzii* from mid-March to early June; song usually given in early morning and again in evening; also known to sing in poor or misty weather; usually performs from a low, concealed perch.

STATUS AND DISTRIBUTION Resident. Common or fairly common.

C. f. alticola Southern Mexico from central and southern Chiapas east and south-east to Guatemala, Los Esesmiles and Volcán de Santa Ana in El Salvador, Honduras and northern Nicaragua.

C. f. confusus Eastern Mexico from south-eastern San Luis Potosí to central Veracruz and northern Oaxaca.

C. f. omiltimensis Southern Mexico from Jalisco and central Michoacán to eastern Morelos; central-southern Guerrero and central-southern Oaxaca.

C. f. frantzii Mountains of Costa Rica to western Chiriquí, Panama.

C. f. wetmorei Southern Costa Rica to Volcín de Chiriquí, western Panama (mainly above 2000 m/

6600' but down to about 1600 m/5280' at Cerro Punta: Wetmore 1984).

MOVEMENTS Largely resident but some may make casual or altitude movements to lower levels in winter; these movements are poorly understood, since most birds appear to remain within the breeding area throughout the year. See note under Geographical Variation; it is possible that some 'out of range' records simply involved extreme variants of the local race.

HABITAT Thick tangled undergrowth and ground vegetation in moist, humid or semi-humid pine-oak and conifer cloud-forests, forest edges and clearings, woodlands and ravines, occasionally in bamboo thickets, vines and creepers of the subtropical and lower temperate zones between 1350 and 3500 m (4455–11,550').

BEHAVIOUR A shy, wary and usually solitary bird, best detected by its song but occasionally seen in the open at forest edges or in clearings, on trails, etc., but never far from cover. Hops or bounds thrush-like when on the ground. Habitually lowers its head to a horizontal position and opens its wings slightly when about to fly; also sometimes hold its wings below the level of the tail when on the ground. Forages on ground and frequently follows ant swarms, but also feeds in bushes, thickets and scrubby undergrowth, mostly taking insects and berries.

BREEDING Season: February to July. Nest: a bulky cup of green moss, liverworts, plant stems and fibres, vines and dry grass, lined with rootlets, dry leaves and occasionally horsehair; usually placed near a stream and up to 4 m (13') from the ground in a tangled thicket, fern-clump, cypress tree, moss-covered branch or similar vegetation. Eggs: 2, pale blue varying from greyish to greenish-blue, heavily marked or spotted with brown to cinnamon or reddish-brown, mostly at the larger end. Incubation solely by the female, period 15–16 days. Fledging period 14–16 days; young fed by both adults. Single-brooded.

MOULT No information.

MEASUREMENTS (n=21) Wing, male 79.5–89, female 78–87.5; tarsus 33–36; bill (culmen) 13.5–16.5; *alticola* (n=14) wing 82.5–89.5; *omiltimensis* wing 86.5; *wetmorei* (n=20) wing, male 85–90.5, female 78.5–84.5; bill (culmen) 17.5–19.5. Weight 28 g (Wetmore *et al.* 1984, Phillips 1986).

REFERENCES Phillips (1969, 1986), Rowley & Orr (1964), Skutch (1960), Wetmore *et al.* (1984).

86 BLACK-HEADED NIGHTINGALE-THRUSH   Plate 25
Catharus mexicanus

Mal(acocychla) mexicana Bonaparte, 1856, *Compt. Rend. Acad. Sci. Paris* 43: 998 – Jalapa, Veracruz, Mexico.

IDENTIFICATION 14.5–16.5 cm (5¾–6¼"). An olive or olive-brown nightingale-thrush from the mid-level forests of Central America. Has a sooty-black head and greyish face with bright orange eye-ring, bill and legs, and greyish underparts with an olive

or brownish wash on the breast and whitish throat and undertail. **Confusion species** Similar to several other nightingale-thrushes but only Spotted (87) has black head; much more olive above than Orange-billed (82), Russet (84) or Ruddy-capped

(85); Slaty-backed (83) is more uniformly slate-grey on the upperparts and has a pale eye.

DESCRIPTION Sexes almost alike. **Adult male** Forehead to crown and nape black or sooty-black, sometimes tinged grey-brown on the forehead; lores to cheeks and ear-coverts dark grey; thin bright orange eye-ring. Mantle to uppertail-coverts and scapulars dark olive or olive-brown extending to edges and tips of greater coverts, edges of primary coverts, flight feathers and tertials; innerwebs of greater and primary coverts, alula and flight feathers dull brown. Tail also dull brown with olive-brown edges to central feathers. Chin and throat whitish, centre of lower throat silvery-white, edges dull olive or greyish-olive becoming a dull olive wash across breast; belly and flanks white or greyish-white, belly sometimes washed yellowish; lower flanks dull olive; undertail-coverts whitish-buff. Bill bright orange with dark base to culmen. Legs and feet straw yellow to bright orange. **Adult female** Similar to male but black on head often obscured by olive-brown on forehead to crown and tips of hindcrown, blackest on nape and sides of upper neck; some show tinges of warm olive-brown on rump and uppertail-coverts; base of tail dark rufous. Underparts more heavily olive. Bill as male with culmen more extensively dusky-brown. **Immature** Similar to adult but head sooty- or dark olive-brown, and crown and nape to mantle and scapulars tinged olive with narrow light orange-buff central shaft-streaks; tips to median and greater coverts with pale orange subterminal spots and darker or blackish tips with pale fringes. Greyish chin and throat off-white; breast, flanks and belly mottled with sooty-olive and pale yellowish-buff centres with dark olive fringes; lower belly to undertail-coverts paler or whitish-buff.

GEOGRAPHICAL VARIATION Three races; variation not well marked. Race *cantator* is slightly smaller and much greyer on face to chin and throat with olive wash on grey breast and flanks, paler on centre of belly, and vent to undertail-coverts whitish. Upperparts show some brown on forehead obscuring black on crown and nape; rest of upperparts slightly more heavily tinged brown over olive, especially on rump to base of tail and central tail feathers. Race *fumosus* smallest, extremely like nominate but face very slightly greyer, chin and throat to breast also grey and without olive on underparts; flanks pale to medium grey; centre of belly to undertail-coverts whitish.

VOICE Call a sharp, ascending *seeet* or *dzeeet*, a plaintive mewing *rreahr* or *meeahh*, and a rising *chowr*; alarm note is a short dry nasal chattering or buzzing *chrrr* or *gerrr*. Song consists of up to 6–8 thin, high-pitched, flute-like whistles, usually including a sharp and distinctive *sreek*, clear whistles, trills and buzzing notes, some phrases repeated several times in typical thrush manner; overall recalls Orange-billed but more melodi-

ous. Sings at any time of day but mostly at dawn, infrequently outside the breeding season, usually from a low 3 m (10') concealed perch in a bush or low tree.

STATUS AND DISTRIBUTION Common to abundant resident.

C. m. mexicanus Mexico from southern Tamaulipas through Veracruz and Hidalgo to Oaxaca and western Chiapas.

C. m. cantator Mexico in the highlands of eastern Chiapas, Guatemala and Honduras, intergrading with *fumosus* across large areas of northern Nicaragua.

C. m. fumosus Nicaragua (north-central highlands sporadically or locally to the Caribbean lowlands) and Costa Rica to the Caribbean slope of the mountains in Bocas del Toro, Chiriquí and Veraguas, western Panama.

MOVEMENTS In winter locally to almost sea-level in parts of the range (Mexico); occasionally found to higher levels above the known breeding range – 1000 m (3300') along the Caribbean slope and to 1500 m (5000') on the Pacific slope of Costa Rica.

HABITAT Inhabits the lower storey and undergrowth of cloud-forest, humid and lowland forests of the tropical and subtropical zones, also drier forests in the higher areas of the range along the Pacific slope of Costa Rica and second-growth woodlands at 300–800 m (1000–2600') along the Caribbean slope of Costa Rica and slightly higher, 700–1300 (2300–4300'), on the Pacific slope to western Panama, and at 750–1800 m (2475–5940') in Mexico.

BEHAVIOUR A shy and generally elusive, solitary species which keeps low or on the ground in moist or humid forests. On the ground it bounds in a series of springing hops before coming to an abrupt halt and standing almost erect before progressing again. Flies low and usually for only short distances, disappearing into thick cover. Forages on the ground and along low branches by probing into or pecking through leaves and leaf-litter. Feeds mostly on insects and their larvae, also beetles and a substantial amount of fruit.

BREEDING Season: March to July. Nest: a large cup of green moss and rootlets with a finer lining of leaves and an external covering of moss; usually up to 3 m (10') along a branch or in a fork in thick undergrowth, vegetation or shrub. Eggs: 2, pinkish-white, finely speckled reddish-brown, usually at the larger end.

MOULT No information.

MEASUREMENTS (n=16) Wing, male 83–95.5, female 82.5–90; tarsus 28–33; bill (culmen) 13.5–15.5; *cantator* (n=8) wing 84.5–92; *fumosus* (n=20) wing, male 81–90, female 78.5–87. Weight 30–34 g (Griscom 1930, Wetmore *et al.* 1984).

REFERENCES Griscom (1930), Howell & Webb (1995), Wetmore *et al.* (1984).

87 SPOTTED NIGHTINGALE-THRUSH *Catharus dryas* Plate 25

Malacocichla dryas Gould, 1855, *Proc. Zool. Soc. London* (1854): 285, pl. 75 – Guatemala.

IDENTIFICATION 16.5–19 cm (6½–7½″). A shy and retiring bird of the undergrowth of montane forests of the highlands of southern Central America and the Andes to extreme north-west Argentina. Very distinctive with a black head, grey or olive-grey upperparts and slightly darker wings and tail and pale to bright yellow underparts spotted grey or black, with grey sides of the breast and flanks; bill, legs and feet orange. **Confusion species** The underparts are diagnostic. Slaty-backed Nightingale-Thrush (83) is similar but almost uniform slate-grey, with a blackish head or face, greyish unspotted underparts (paler in nominate birds) mottled with pale yellow, paler yellow on the belly.

DESCRIPTION Sexes almost alike. **Adult male** Forehead to crown and nape, lores, cheeks, ear-coverts and sides of chin and throat sooty-black, thin bright orange-yellow eye-ring. Rest of upperparts olive-green to olive-grey or mouse-grey but innerwebs to greater coverts, primary coverts, flight feathers and tertials dark brown; longest uppertail-coverts tinged olive-grey, central tail feathers olive or olive-brown, all outer tail feathers dark brown. Underwing-coverts whitish with grey tips, silvery-grey bases to flight feathers. Chin and throat pale yellow, very faintly or finely spotted grey or blackish-grey, breast slightly heavier buffish-white to apricot-yellow; rest of underparts pale yellow finely spotted dark grey or black on breast and belly, sides of breast and flanks grey or lead-grey, vent and undertail-coverts white. Bill orange or reddish-orange. Legs and feet reddish-orange. **Adult female** Very similar to adult male but mantle, back and scapulars more heavily tinged brown, bill with culmen ridge partly blackish. **Immature** Generally dull or dark olive-brown, slightly darker on head with fine pale buff central shaft-streaks on crown, nape, mantle and scapulars; lores, forehead, cheeks and ear-coverts black streaked brown; underparts dark olive except for pale or whiter chin and finely mottled or streaked pale yellowish-buff centres to breast and flanks with darker or browner olive edges and tips; belly less heavily mottled.

GEOGRAPHICAL VARIATION Five races; variation clinal and not well marked. Birds from western end of range of *ovandensis* in eastern Oaxaca have been separated as *harrisoni* (Phillips & Rook 1965) on redder bill and eye-ring, yellow on nape forming a narrow collar, and upperparts, on average, more olive, but these birds are generally regarded as within level of variation in *ovandensis*, as the species as a whole shows a wide range of variation, particularly in the olive tones of the upperparts, yellow of the underparts and colour of the bill, eye-ring and legs.

Race *maculatus* has upperparts (but not head or face) darker olive or olive-brown and underparts

deeper or apricot-yellow, the dark grey spots much more boldly or heavily pronounced, some spots on lower breast sometimes appearing to form complete band.

Race *ovandensis* olive or greyish-olive on lower nape to scapulars, rump and uppertail-coverts, with wings and tail slightly greyer; underparts (except for sides of breast and flanks) lemon-yellow spotted with dark grey.

Race *ecuadoreanus* has head and face black or blackish-grey and rest of upperparts grey-brown; underparts apricot-yellow spotted blackish-grey, sides of lower breast and flanks grey, vent whitish; eye-ring, bill and legs bright red.

Race *blakei* very similar to *maculatus* but has throat washed pale or buffish-brown.

VOICE Call a dry, nasal or bleating *rrehr, rreh'hu* or more extended *reh'chew*. Song a series of rich fluted phrases similar to those of Slate-coloured (77) and Black-faced (74) Solitaires or Wood Thrush (93) in quality: a liquid or more wavering *tru-lee* or *chee-lolee, trolowee* or *clee-oo-leew clee-oo-low* or *whee-i-lee wee-i-lou* repeated several times and interspersed with some whistled notes or phrases; also clacks bill loudly (Howell & Webb 1995, Hilty & Brown 1986, Stiles & Skutch 1989). Singing birds are often hard to find as they sing in flight through the forest undergrowth.

STATUS AND DISTRIBUTION Locally common to uncommon.

C. d. ovandensis Highlands of eastern Oaxaca (Sierra Madre de Chiapas) and Chiapas, Mexico.

C. d. dryas Guatemala on the Pacific slope and in Sierra de las Minas, and in Honduras on Volcán de Puca east to the Tegucigalpa region, also western Ecuador. The presence of nominate birds in western Ecuador (see Peters 1964) is probably best regarded as provisional given the presence there of *ecuadoreanus*.

C. d. maculatus Eastern Colombia at the head of the Magdalena Valley, Huila, and the eastern slope of the Andes from Boyacá to Macarena Mountains, southern Meta; also Venezuela from north-west Zulia, southern Táchira and south-west Lara and the eastern slope of the eastern Andes to eastern Ecuador (but rare in the south: only one record – August 1992 – in Zamora-Chinchipe province) south through the eastern Andes of north-central Peru.

C. d. ecuadoreanus Andes of Pichincha to El Oro and Loja, western Ecuador.

C. d. blakei Tarija, southern Bolivia, to Jujuy and Salta, north-west Argentina.

MOVEMENTS Sedentary.

HABITAT Humid evergreen cloud forests of the upper tropical and subtropical zones between 1200 and 3000 m (3950–9900′) in Central America and 700 to 2300 m (2310–7590′) in South

America, where it inhabits the low edges and undergrowth, particularly near ravines and streams. **BEHAVIOUR** Usually alone, in pairs or small mixed groups occasionally with Ruddy-capped Nightingale-thrush (85). Shy and extremely unobtrusive, preferring the cover of dense undergrowth, more often seen than heard and easily overlooked; but occasionally responds to whistled imitations of its call. Hops on the ground and forages in the undergrowth, turning leaves in typical thrush-fashion; also occurs, alone or in pairs, at army ant swarms. **BREEDING** Poorly known. Season: September,

February to April. Eggs: bluish-white speckled or spotted with rusty-brown and grey.
MOULT No information.
MEASUREMENTS Wing, male 92–102, female 91–93; tarsus 34.5–35.5; bill (culmen) 15–16; *ovandensis* wing, male 103–108, female 100–102.5; *maculatus* wing 87–95; tarsus 34.5–35.5. Weight 34–36 g.
REFERENCES Hilty & Brown (1986), Howell & Webb (1995), Phillips (1986), Phillips & Rook (1965), Rasmussen *et al.* (1996), Stiles & Skutch (1989).

88 VEERY *Catharus fuscescens*   Plate 26
(Willow Thrush, Wilson's Thrush)
Turdus fuscescens Stephens, 1817, in Shaw, *Gen. Zool.* 10(1): 182 – Pennsylvania.

IDENTIFICATION 17–19.5 cm (6½–7¾"). A small, stocky thrush of the damp woods and thickets of southern Canada and northern U.S.A., wintering in the tropical forests from Colombia to Brazil. Has a relatively small, rounded head and short stocky bill. Fairly shy or retiring, its presence often only given away by its rolling flute-like song. Adults are alike but there is some regional variation between the races from uniform warm brown to cinnamon or reddish-brown on the upperparts, face paler or flecked brown, chin white with brown malar stripe, dark spots on lower throat and breast, pale pearl-grey spots or smudges to rest of underparts. **Confusion species** Adult Grey-cheeked (89) and Swainson's Thrushes (91) have heavier, larger and better defined spots on the lower throat and breast, and both are darker on the upperparts, but western race *salicicolus* of Veery is very similar and best separated on face pattern (partial eye-ring and grey cheeks), grey flanks, and quantity, colour and intensity of breast-spots (note Swainson's has a pale buff eye-ring and upper lores). Hermit Thrush (92) has a thin white eye-ring and is generally duller brown above with a russet tail, some races e.g. *guttatus* and *faxoni* with a rufous tinge to the flight feathers and others (western) with extensive blackish spotting on a whitish breast. Wood Thrush (93) is also similar but much larger with very prominent spotting below and chestnut-brown head to mantle and back.
DESCRIPTION Sexes alike; female only separable in hand on wing measurements within corresponding age groups (see Suthers 1993). **Adult** Forehead to crown, nape, mantle, back and scapulars warm reddish- or rufous-brown becoming more olive on rump and uppertail-coverts. Tail dark brown but edged warm or tawny-brown on outer tail feathers. Wings as scapulars but median and greater coverts have slightly paler warm buff-brown edges and tips, alula blackish-brown, primary coverts dark brown edged slightly paler or olive-brown, tips dark brown; flight feathers dark brown with fine, warm olive-brown edges particularly to outer primaries. Tertials as coverts broadly edged warm olive-brown on outerwebs. Under-

wing-coverts whitish-buff. Face mottled finely with grey and pale brown, streaked finely with warm brown over eye and on cheeks and rear of ear-coverts; lores grey or greyish-white, indistinct or faint off-white partial or incomplete eye-ring (usually absent on upper fore part of eye), pale buff or greyish submoustachial bordered by poorly defined dark brown malar stripe. Chin whitish, becoming yellowish-cream on throat and sides of neck and lightly spotted dusky-brown, spots often triangular in shape, becoming indistinct and poorly defined across breast; lower breast, belly and flanks pale grey with diffuse brown spots on lower breast and centre of upper belly; lower flanks washed pale brown, lower belly to vent and undertail-coverts white. Bill dark brownish-horn with pale yellowish or flesh-pink base of lower (and cutting edges of upper) mandible. Eye dark brown. Legs and feet deep flesh-pink. **Immature** Juvenile has head and upperparts similar to adult but darker brown tinged rufous, heavily spotted with pale brown to creamy-buff tips, spots on crown and mantle more rounded than on scapulars, spots on rump and uppertail-coverts less distinct and tawnier-brown; dull blackish malar stripe; underparts whitish with warm or orange-buff tinge to throat, breast, flanks and undertail-coverts; breast more heavily spotted black, becoming thinner bars on belly and flanks; median and greater coverts tipped pale tawny- or golden-buff, tertials similar. First-winter birds similar to adult but distinguished by pale buff tips to greater coverts and pale orange-buff tips to tertials (although these are often lost by late winter/early spring). Tips of tail feathers more sharply pointed than adult.
GEOGRAPHICAL VARIATION Three races; variation largely clinal and poorly defined; moreover, individual variation can be enough to confound identification even in the hand. Race *salicicolus* slightly more olive-brown on upperparts and only faintly tinged rufous compared to nominate (recalling olive-brown nominate race *ustulatus* of Swainson's but best separated by lack of pale upper lores and lack of broad pale eye-ring, grey

face and grey flanks); generally has buffish breast and well-defined brown spots which are darker, slightly broader or more rounded and not as triangular as in nominate. Race *fuliginosus* (poorly defined; many birds intermediate and indeterminate) slightly larger than nominate, and slightly deeper or warm reddish-brown above than either nominate or *salicicolus*, with sharply defined reddish-brown arrowhead-shaped spots (larger than on nominate) extensively across breast.

VOICE Most frequent call is an abrupt fluted *veer whee-uu* or *kwee-eh* which may be part of the song, also a slow or slurred *hee-oo* or *weee-oo*; alarm note is an abrupt low *wuck*, almost quacking in tone, often repeated in a harsh or scolding rasp. Regarded as one of the sweetest singers among North American thrushes, with an ethereal, slightly resonating quality to its descending, rolling or ringing vibrant 3–5 notes *wree-u, wree-u, wree-u, wree-u* or *ree-ree-er, vee-ur, veer, veer, veer*, often with the last note prolonged into a *veeooo* or a slurred *rayeeoh*. Song very similar to parts of Hermit Thrush song, but consists of quickly repeated descending phrases whereas Hermit has a rising then falling opening phrase of spiralling notes repeated after a lengthy pause.

Song occasionally heard in wintering area but does not usually begin singing until on breeding territory – often the first sign of the bird in spring – from early May to the end of July; has favoured song perches at variable heights which are used in successive years; sings throughout the day but most frequently at (including shortly before and after) dawn and dusk.

STATUS AND DISTRIBUTION Common, but has declined throughout much of its North American breeding range since the mid-1960s.

C. f. fuscescens Eastern Canada from southern Ontario to southern Quebec, New Brunswick and Nova Scotia south through New England to northern New Jersey, Pennsylvania and north-east Ohio and south through the Appalachians of western Maryland (includes parts of Washington D.C.), West Virginia, Kentucky, North Carolina, eastern Tennessee and extreme north-west Georgia. In winter to northern South America but full extent of range imperfectly known, from Colombia to Venezuela and Guyana to south-central Brazil (see below).

C. f. fuliginosus Eastern Canada in south-west Newfoundland, Anticosti and Madeleine Island, possibly also extreme south-central Quebec. In winter only recorded in Brazil, where range probably as for the other two races but exact area unknown.

C. f. salicicolus Western Canada from central-southern British Columbia (extending to the coast in some areas, with singing birds on territory in Hyder, extreme south-east Alaska, in June 1990 and May–June 1991) east through south-central Alberta, southern Saskatchewan, southern Manitoba and western and southern Ontario (intergrades with *fuscescens* in southern Ontario); south in U.S.A. to northern and eastern Washington, west-central and extreme north-east Montana, northern, central-southern and eastern North Dakota, northern and central Minnesota, Michigan

and central Wisconsin, Illinois, central and eastern Iowa, extreme northern Indiana and extreme north-west Ohio; also north-east Oregon, Idaho, north-central Nevada and extreme northern Utah east to southern Wyoming and south through the Rockies to central Colorado, western Wyoming (with an isolated area in the Black Hills area of western South Dakota and eastern Wyoming), also north-east Arizona and an isolated outpost (may not breed annually) in central Arizona. In winter to Colombia, Venezuela and Mato Grosso in central Brazil (see below).

Taxonomic note At least two other races have been proposed: *levyi* from Alberta to northern Michigan and Wisconsin, and *pulichorum* from the higher areas of west Maryland to northern Georgia (see Phillips 1991 and Pyle *et al.* 1997). The differences cited are principally in the tone of the upperparts, the ground colour of the breast and distinctiveness of the breast spots. However, all of these are extremely fine and difficult to determine (colour of the upperparts changes with light intensity) in the field and possibly in the hand (without comparative material), and intergrades must confuse the situation further.

Distributional note 1: Races *fuscescens* and *salicicolus* occur together in northern South America from eastern Colombia through Venezuela, Guyana and western Amazonian Brazil south to northern Bolivia and north-west Mato Grosso, but are nowhere common and their exact ranges are poorly known; also occur (possibly infrequently) in the east to São Paulo state, south-east Brazil.

Distributional note 2: There is one winter record (race uncertain) from Louisiana, December 1983 (Zink & Dittman 1992).

MOVEMENTS Migratory. Moves south in autumn through the coastal and eastern U.S.A. west to a line south from eastern Nebraska to eastern Texas; small numbers pass through eastern Mexico (especially Yucatán, where uncommon to rare), but most may well move out over the Atlantic as recorded along the eastern seaboard of Massachusetts, Maryland and Virginia. Passage usually begins in mid- to late August and continues into September; most breeding areas are deserted from late August onwards. Peak date of autumn passage through Minnesota is 31 August (Winker *et al.* 1992). Late migrants linger in northern parts of the breeding range into early October, and as late as mid-October in New York state and the third week of October in New Hampshire. Recorded on passage through Colombia in October and in the northern Bahamas (where rare but possibly overlooked) from mid-September to mid- or late October; also rare or uncommon on passage eastern Mexico (Veracruz), Honduras (mostly on coast and islands), Jamaica, Cuba (12 September–14 October), Costa Rica and Panama (most records last week of September to early November) and rare on Curaçao, Netherlands Antilles (2 records). From the few records available from mid-October to early April birds move south through western Amazonia to winter in the cerrado region of southern Brazil and eastern Bolivia; return movements are to the east of the autumn route though central Amazonia (Stotz *et al.* 1992).

Direction of return movements between north-north-west to north-north-east but unknown in spring in Colombia and apparently much fewer then pass through Panama. First returning migrants in southern states throughout April and early May; has been recorded north to Washington D.C. and New York state in early to mid-April; in northern U.S.A. and Canada arrives in mid-May (average peak of spring migration in Minnesota 15–16 May) although late migrants still on passage over the Caribbean and through the southern states in the last week of May and exceptionally into the first week of June. Less common or rarer in spring in Cuba (April and early May), Jamaica and along the east and north coasts of Panama to Nicaragua and Belize. Migrant *fuliginosus* occur in spring along the Atlantic coast from Virginia to Massachusetts.

Ringing recoveries suggest that males migrate before females in spring but in autumn adults and immatures migrate at the same time. Long-distance tracking of migrants by NASA revealed that the maximum flight distance of night-flying individuals was 285 km at an average ground speed of 25 km per hour; flights lasted from 3.5 to 8.5 hours at varying altitudes of between 200 and 1000 m (660–3300′); some, however, were above 2000 m (6600′) and all lasted until about half an hour before dawn (Cochran *et al.* 1967, Cochran 1972). Average flight distance in both spring and autumn 2040 km with limit of c.2850 km (Odum *et al.* 1961).

Rare visitor to Vancouver Island, and a vagrant to California (11 records to 1998, 8 from mid-October to early November, 3 from mid-May to mid-June), Bermuda (frequent, mostly in October, twice in spring), Virgin Islands, Guatemala, Peru (1 record), Chile (1 record), British Isles (3), Sweden; also two 19th-century records from Germany.

HABITAT Breeds in forests and wooded mountain slopes of the temperate lowlands of North America, with a preference for mixed woods of oak and pine with a well-developed undergrowth, but also found in hemlocks and damp or moist woods or willows, poplars, aspens and alders along side-rivers and streams. In the north of the range occurs in broadleaved woods with a good undergrowth layer, but less frequently in conifer woods than other thrushes of the region although occurs in firs and tamarack swamps in the Great Plains region; in the Rockies reaches above 2500 m (8250′) in hillside woods, thickets and scrub and areas of dry brush. On passage occurs in similar habitat but also coastal scrub, woodlands and mangroves; in winter inhabits the edge of rainforest and secondary growth in Venezuela and Brazil.

BEHAVIOUR Generally fairly shy, secretive and solitary, preferring to feed on the forest floor or in thickets when on breeding territory, but elsewhere can become tame and approachable and then feeds in the open, hopping then stopping to turn over leaves; most actions are quick, purposeful but dignified, interspersed with pauses when the bird is motionless; many actions recall those of similar-sized Hermit Thrush but lacks latter's pronounced tail movements; flight through the forest is quick and usually straight or slightly bounding, but rarely flies far when on territory, preferring to dive into cover. Feeds chiefly on the ground on a wide variety of invertebrates but also forages in the mid- to lower canopy of trees and takes a range of wild fruit; invertebrates are mainly bugs (especially leafhoppers), beetles, ants, flies, wasps, moths and their larvae, grasshoppers, spiders and sometimes snails and earthworms; wild fruit includes blackberries, blueberries, cherries, dogwood, elderberries, wild grapes, juneberries and strawberries.

BREEDING Season: mid-May to late July or early August. Nest: a large, loose structure usually of dead or decaying leaves together with weed stalks, dry grasses and bark strips, placed low down in a tree or bush or often on the ground including in or amongst mossy hummocks; in wet areas often builds a flat platform of dead leaves as a base; exceptionally up to 7.5 m (c.25′) from the ground in firs, maples, alders or birch. Eggs: 3–4, exceptionally 5, pale or greenish-blue, usually unspotted or rarely finely spotted with brown. Incubation period 10–12 days. Fledging period 10–11 days. Possibly two broods. In parts of the range a brood-host to the parasitic Brown-headed Cowbird *Molothrus ater*; up to 87% of nests in Alberta and Manitoba known to be parasitised (Friedmann *et al.* 1977).

MOULT Adults undergo complete post-breeding moult from mid-July to late August; post-juvenile moult of immatures affects the head, body, lesser and median coverts, also some of the greater coverts and tertials about the same time, but usually complete by mid-August, exceptionally early September.

MEASUREMENTS Wing, male (n=100) 91–106, female (n=100) 89–103; tarsus, male 27–32.5, female 27.5–32; bill (culmen) 12.5–15.5, (to skull) male 17–18.5, female 16–18.5; *fuliginosus* wing, male 94–104, female 94–100; *salicicolus* wing, male 95.5–103.5, female 89–101. Weight 26–39 g (Pyle *et al.* 1997).

REFERENCES Cochran (1972), Cochran *et al.* (1967), Friedmann *et al.* (1977), Moskoff (1995), Odum *et al.* (1961), Pyle *et al.* (1997), Stotz *et al.* (1992), Suthers (1993), Winker *et al.* (1992), Zink & Dittmann (1992).

89 GREY-CHEEKED THRUSH *Catharus minimus* **Plate 27**

Turdus minimus Lafresnaye, 1848, *Rev. Zool.* [Paris] 11: 5 – Bogotá, Colombia.

IDENTIFICATION 16.5–19.5 cm (6½–7¾") (see note below on sizes of *aliciae*). One of a group of *Catharus* thrushes that breed in the vast forests of Alaska to the Labrador coast of eastern Canada and winter in Central and South America. Generally olive-grey tinged duller or grey-brown on upperparts; cheeks and ear-coverts similar but flecked paler or greyer, with a thin, indistinct pale eye-ring; underparts whitish with poorly defined malar stripes and dark spots on pale yellowish-washed breast, flanks washed grey-brown, belly to undertail-coverts white but washed grey. **Confusion species** Most likely to be confused with Bicknell's (90), Swainson's (91) and Hermit (92) Thrushes; for differences from Bicknell's see that species. Best told from Swainson's by greyish cheeks to ear-coverts, generally greyer tinge to olive upperparts, lack of pale lores and of broad buffish eye-ring (but Grey-cheeked can show narrow greyish-buff eye-ring, usually on rear of eye), spots on breast generally lighter or smaller; from Hermit by lack of any warm or russet tones in wings or tail, the larger, paler race *auduboni* of Hermit being paler but with more extensive black triangular spots on breast, flanks and upper belly. Veery (88) and Wood Thrush (93) are also initially similar but the former has more rust-brown upperparts, pale buff sides to throat and breast, and smaller indistinct dark spots on breast (note that western and central Canadian race *salicicolus* is also very olive-toned and best separated by face pattern, grey flanks and colour and intensity of the spots on the breast: dark and well-defined in Grey-cheeked and brownish to greyish and poorly defined on Veery); Wood Thrush is larger and less confusable, with darker brown upperparts and reddish-brown tinge to crown and mantle, a large white eye-ring and large bold black spots on the underparts.

DESCRIPTION Sexes alike. **Adult** Forehead and crown to mantle, back, scapulars, rump and uppertail-coverts greyish-olive tinged brown or grey-brown on mantle and back (in some, particularly in Newfoundland, mantle and back sometimes tinged lighter olive and rump and uppertail-coverts tinged brown). Tail greyish-olive, but bases and innerwebs of all feathers warmer or olive-brown. Median and greater coverts olive-brown or slightly darker with paler brown edges, alula (very small) dark brown, primary coverts pale brown, flight feathers dark brown finely edged paler brown (and more broadly on secondaries), tertials similar to flight feathers but more broadly edged pale or olive-brown in fresh plumage. Underwing has coverts olive or olive-grey but tips to lesser coverts tipped whitish or pale buff and base of secondaries also broadly whitish-buff forming a broad bar across underwing. In spring and early summer, wear causes plumage to become greyer and lose some olive tinge. Lores pale buffish-grey or greyish, cheeks and ear-coverts olive but tipped or flecked grey creating a paler area; thin, poorly defined pale buffish or grey eye-

ring (often only visible at rear of eye), rear of ear-coverts flecked darker or olive-brown. Chin and throat off-white or pale buffish-cream bordered by dark brown malars (comprising a series of small arrow-marked spots), breast and sides of neck white or washed pale yellow or cream and closely spotted on centre of breast with small triangular dark brown spots, duller or indistinct at sides, on buff or buffish-brown ground colour; flanks and sides of belly greyish-olive or shaded greyish, usually paler or greyer on belly, vent to undertail-coverts whitish. Bill dark horn with base of lower mandible (not usually extending beyond nostril) pale pinkish, occasionally pinkish-grey or, in breeding males, orange-yellow. Legs and feet flesh-pink or pinkish tinged light greyish-brown or blackish. **Immature** Juvenile has forehead and most upperparts greyish-olive tinged brownish or more olive than in adult with whitish shaft-streaks to crown, mantle, back and scapulars becoming buffish or buffish-brown on rump and uppertail-coverts. Median and greater coverts tipped buff to form wing-bar; face pale buff finely spotted black and can show a distinct pale eye-ring; breast white tinged pale buff at sides, and throat and breast spotted black, becoming black bars on flanks and belly. First-winter plumage as adult but cheeks streaked or flecked slightly paler or greyer, centre of breast washed pale or olive-yellow, sides of breast pale buff, spots on lower breast, upper belly and upper flanks often smudged or merging into rows, retained greater coverts from juvenile plumage sometimes with whitish-buff tips (can be absent through wear), and edges to primary coverts (but not tips, which are dark) bright olive-brown, as are edges to flight feathers, with browner olive at bases; tips of inner tertials also whitish. In the hand, tail feathers more tapered than in older birds. Bill as adult but base to lower mandible pale flesh, yellow gape.

GEOGRAPHICAL VARIATION Two races; variation clinal and weakly defined. Most differences between races not appreciable in the field and based mainly on size, particularly length of wing, and on subtle changes in colour tones of upperparts. Race *aliciae* averages slightly larger (17–19.5 cm; 6¾–7¾") and slightly colder olive or brownish-olive above, particularly crown, and generally duller below; flanks washed brownish-olive; pale base to lower mandible also, on average, bright yellow (in breeding season) and slightly more extensive (extending beyond nostril).

VOICE Most frequent call is a downward slurred *wee-ah, wee-oh, pe-uu, vee-ah* or *vee-er*, (any one phrase which can also be given abruptly or sharply on its own) higher-pitched and more nasal than that of Veery; also a range of short *what* or *chuck*, a light *pheeu* and a harsh scolding note; on migration has a thin, flycatcher-like *wheesp* or *pweep* contact note; night-flying migrants give a variable *pe-i-i-i-r, cheerrr* or *whe-errr*, initially similar to that given diurnally on territory, but stressing the highest-frequency part of the call in the mid-section and with a more abrupt end than that of night-flying migrant Bicknell's (Evans 1994). Song a series of high-pitched notes starting slowly with a *wee-oh* or *chook-chook*, repeated several times, followed by a staccato *chee-chee* and concluding with a light but descending *wee-oh wee-oh* or *wheee-er*, also a *we-tichi-whee, witchee-u*. Sings from the top of a tall tree, but also from lower bushes and in short songflight; usually given at dawn and dusk but also through the night. Song period very short and mostly from arrival on breeding territory (although heard infrequently on spring migration in South America) to early or mid-July; females also give weak songs whilst incubating eggs or brooding the young.

STATUS AND DISTRIBUTION Common to locally common.

C. m. minimus Breeds Newfoundland and southern Labrador south to St Pierre and Miquelon Islands. In winter to north-east Colombia and possibly north-west Venezuela.

C. m. aliciae Breeds in north-east Siberia from the central and lower Kolyma River (possibly very scarce in latter locality) east to the Chukchi (Chukot) Peninsula, most of Alaska (except the coastal north-east), where generally scarce or local especially on the south-east mainland (but common to abundant on the Seward Peninsula), northern Canada from the Yukon and northern Mackenzie south-east to about Eskimo Point, southern Keewatin and from north-west British Columbia through southern Mackenzie (possibly also the Caribou Mountains of northern Alberta) to north-west Saskatchewan, northern Manitoba and extreme northern Ontario; also most of western, central and eastern Quebec and central and northern Labrador. In winter to extreme eastern Panama (Darién), Colombia, Venezuela (scarce or rare – 4 records – in Amazonas), Guyana and north-west Brazil south to eastern Ecuador and northern Peru.

MOVEMENTS Migratory. All birds move between south and south-south-east to wintering areas mainly through the eastern states of central and southern Canada (west to western Alberta) and the eastern U.S.A., mostly via the Mississippi flyway and east of the Mississippi to Bermuda (where a scarce or casual migrant). Post-breeding dispersal begins mid- to late July. Usually departs from northern breeding areas in the last third of August and early September, and most have left central Alaska by 10 September; further south departures appear to be mostly in September and peak passage through eastern U.S.A. is late September and early October; exceptionally late birds recorded as far north as New York state as late as mid- to late November. Presumably crosses the Caribbean in a single flight as it is vagrant or accidental only on most islands but is a fairly common migrant through east-central Mexico (from southern Veracruz to the Yucatán Peninsula, possibly south to northern coast of Honduras) from late September to November, and rare (or probably greatly overlooked) in Guatemala, Honduras, Nicaragua and Panama, uncommon in Costa Rica. Casual or scarce in winter in lowland Costa Rica and generally uncommon as a wintering bird from early October to early May in Colombia; the main wintering range is from Venezuela east to Guyana and south to the western Amazon basin of north-west Brazil west to eastern Ecuador and north-east Peru (east of the Andes). The exact wintering area in central Amazonian Brazil remains largely unknown; it is a migrant in small numbers through Manaus from mid-October to early December, and from the beginning of March to mid-April (Stotz *et al.* 1992). Present in Venezuela from September to May but many elsewhere in the wintering range arrive later and leave earlier.

Return route opposite that in autumn, with most passage over the Caribbean and through eastern Central America north to north-east Mexico, although much less frequent in Panama, no spring records at all in Costa Rica, and only 4 (to 1991) in Bermuda. Early arrivals in southern U.S.A. at the end of the second third of April, southern Canada in early May, but those breeding at the northern edge of the range take up to another month to arrive on territory, with late migrants still on northerly migration in the first week of June as far south as Louisiana (Ouellet 1993). Arrives in north-east Siberia from first days of June through to the middle of the month (Portenko 1989).

A rare or scarce migrant to western U.S.A., notably Shemya (Aleutians), California (19 records to 1997, most between 12 September and 31 October with 2 late May and early June), Texas, eastern Wyoming, Montana, Arizona (1 record – September 1932), western Kansas, Cuba, Martinique (Windward Islands) and Curacao (Netherlands Antilles). Vagrant to Clipperton Atoll (Pacific Ocean), Surinam, Greenland (2), Iceland (2), British Isles (43 records and almost annual in appearance), Norway, France, Germany and Italy.

A nocturnal migrant moving usually singly but in peak periods of migration may travel in larger numbers, all heading in the same direction; has been noted on migration in east coast of U.S.A. in small flocks. Distances of up to 200 km (130 miles) a day have been covered on its spring migration (Bent 1949).

HABITAT Breeds in dense stands of conifers, usually tamarack and black spruce, also in mixed deciduous and fir forests with shrubby thickets, stunted spruce, dwarf willows and alders in damp or moist areas up to 1000 m (3300') and along the broad tundra edge beyond the treeline. In the east of its range breeds in more open forests. In winter occurs in the lower levels of forests in the tropical and subtropical zones, especially forest edges and more open areas, also some secondary woods with dense undergrowth, old or abandoned plantations and damp thickets. In Venezuela occurs up to 3000 m (9900') north of the Orinoco but to the south only found at about half this level (Meyer de Schauensee *et al.* 1987). On migration occurs almost anywhere suitable, from woods, copses, thickets and hill-tops to headlands and areas of low coastal scrub, roadside thickets, parks and large gardens; at such times often in company with other migrants including Swainson's Thrushes. On migration and in parts of the wintering range appears to become extremely elusive and very difficult to detect, preferring to remain on the ground or concealed in fairly dense vegetation.

BEHAVIOUR Generally shy and retiring, preferring the cover of undergrowth or thick vegetation, in both summer and winter quarters. Usually solitary or in pairs; spends much time on the ground walking and hopping about in typical thrush-like pose, taking few steps then stopping to wait and search the ground for prey. Apart from when singing rarely seen above mid-height in trees. Forages in low branches and vegetation and on the ground amongst the leaf-litter and rotting vegetation. Food mostly insects including beetles, weevils, ants, some wasps and bees, grasshoppers, moths, sowbugs and caterpillars (the latter particularly during autumn migration), also spiders; takes seeds and fruit such as blackberry, cherry, dogwood, elderberry and, also during the autumn, *Aralia racemosa* (Bent 1949).

BREEDING Season: early June to late July or early August. Nest: mostly of fine grasses, leaves, sedges and thin strips of bark, occasionally some moss, held together with a little mud to form a compact, firm structure, lined with fine grasses and flower heads; usually placed low down in bushes, willows or alders up to 6.5 m (20′) from the ground or on the ground. Eggs: 3–4, rarely 5–6, pale or dull greenish-blue, variably spotted, speckled or blotched with pale or darker brown; in some the spots are almost invisibly small. Incubation period (*aliciae*) 12–14 days. Fledging period 11–13 days.

MOULT Similar to most thrushes that breed in northern latitudes. Both adults and first-year birds undergo a moult which in adults is a complete renewal of all feathers between mid- (or early) July and end of August, whilst first-year birds retain greater coverts, some tertials, and all flight and tail feathers; the moult in both adults and first-year birds is completed in August or early September before the autumn departure.

MEASUREMENTS Wing, male (n=100) 96–109, female (n=100) 93–106 (Pyle *et al.* 1997); *minimus* wing, male (n=18) 101–111, female (n=13) 98–107 (Cramp *et al.* 1988); tarsus, male 28–32.5, female 27.5–31; bill (culmen) 11.5–14.5, female (to skull) 11.5–15; *aliciae* wing, male 94.5–108, female 95–103.5; tarsus 29–32; bill (culmen) 12.5–14.5. Weight (both races) male (May–June) 26–34 g, female 27–36 g; male (October) 30–50 g, female 30–45 g (Cramp *et al.* 1988); vagrants at Fair Isle (October 1953) 24 g, (October 1958) 27 g (Williamson 1954, Davis 1959).

REFERENCES Bent (1949), Davis (1959), Evans (1994), McLaren (1995), Meyer de Schauensee & Phelps (1978), Ouellet (1993), Phillips (1986), Portenko (1989), Stotz *et al.* (1992), Williamson (1954).

90 BICKNELL'S THRUSH *Catharus bicknelli*   Plate 27

Hylocichla aliciae bicknelli Ridgway, 1882, *Proc. U.S. Natn. Mus.* **4**: 377 – near the summit of Slide Mountain, Ulster County, New York.

IDENTIFICATION 17–19 cm (6¾–7½″). Extremely similar to Grey-cheeked Thrush (89) and away from the breeding area, particularly when alone on migration, probably not always separable with certainty. Described as a race of Grey-cheeked in 1939 but recently (1995) accepted as a full species. Differences are extremely subtle in size and plumage and more distinct in the songs, with no overlap in breeding or wintering ranges and no known intermediates; slightly different breeding habitats and marked differences in mt-DNA (Ouellet 1993). Slightly warmer olive brown and less grey above, with uppertail-coverts and tail slightly warmer brown or chestnut than the more uniform olive-brown of Grey-cheeked (note, however, that some Grey-cheeked can show slightly warmer tones to the upperparts and brighter tails which can appear to have a warm brown tinge and in itself may not be a reliable separation feature: see McLaren 1995); throat buffier, rest of underparts duller; bill has larger area (half to two-thirds) of colour on base of lower mandible, and orange-yellow (half or less on Grey-cheeked) and straw or pinkish-yellow). Very restricted breeding population and range, and may be declining, threatened or endangered (Rimmer 1996). **Confusion species** Apart from Grey-cheeked Thrush (see Description below), differs from other similar species as those for Grey-cheeked but may also require fine or detailed examination of lone migrants to eliminate western race of Veery (88). May show some similarities to Hermit Thrush (92) in warmth of tail but Hermit has rump, uppertail-coverts and base of tail brighter or rich chestnut even in the palest races (e.g. *auduboni*), and overall presents more of a contrast than the upperparts of Bicknell's.

DESCRIPTION Sexes alike. **Adult** Forehead to crown and upperparts olive-brown lacking any tinge of grey; on average warmer in tone and closer to the brown tones of some (eastern) Swainson's Thrushes (91); uppertail-coverts and tail slightly warmer brown or tinged chestnut. Edges to flight feathers in fresh plumage generally bright or warm olive in tone. Face similar to Grey-cheeked but less grey and cheeks and ear-coverts warmer or more olive-toned and have fine pale buff shafts. Throat buffish, becoming pale buffish-cream on breast, rest of underparts duller with greyish wash except for whiter vent to undertail-coverts. Bill dark horn with orange-yellow basal half to two-thirds of lower mandible. Legs and feet light purplish-flesh or tinged brown on tarsus and with feet darker brown. **Immature** Juvenile buffish-brown above with variable amounts of pale buff central shafts on nape, mantle and scapulars; greater coverts have pale buff spots at tips forming short wing-bar. Underparts heavily spotted or speckled with pale buff centres and dark bars at tips of breast and upper belly and flanks. First-winter birds more similar to adults but retain wing and tail feathers of juvenile plumage together with some greater coverts, tertials and primary coverts; thus may show fine pale buffish to buffish-white tips to greater coverts. Underparts and bill as adult.

In the hand there are differences which cannot be appreciated in the field. Bicknell's is, on average, smaller (though there is a shade of overlap) with wing 81.7–98.8 mm compared to 93.5–111 mm in Grey-cheeked; feet darker brown than Grey-cheeked, which has light flesh-brown legs tinged dark brown, toes even darker; soles of Bicknell's vary from pale flesh to pale or dull yellow but are brighter in Grey-cheeked and contrast more with upper surfaces of toes.

GEOGRAPHICAL VARIATION None. Monotypic.

VOICE Call a single *wee-ooo, pee-oo* or *psee-uuu* (similar to notes in the song) or a sharper *shrip*, abbreviated to a *chirp* note given on occasion or repeated after a short interval; also utters Veery-like chattering notes when defending territory from rival males; also has a snarling note in aggressive display; night-flying migrants have a call that differs from that of Grey-cheeked, a short and descending *cree-e-e* (Evans 1994). Contact and territorial calls also given in wintering area. Song is similar to but more even in pitch than that of Grey-cheeked, beginning with two or three low *chuck* notes followed by a high-pitched phrase, with a pause about midway and rising slightly towards the end, *chook-chook, wee-oo, wee-oo, wee-o-ti-t-ter-ee*, closing (after a short pause) with a thinner, slightly higher-pitched *shre-e-e-e*; on average the high and low frequencies are recognisably different from that of race *minimus* of Grey-cheeked. However, occasionally begins by repeating the first phrase and not concluding with the rest of song, and also utters the final part of the song without the prelude (Bent 1949, Ouellet 1993). Song period fairly short from end of May to end of June, but some individuals may sing into early July.

STATUS AND DISTRIBUTION Locally common within limited range but difficult to locate when not singing. Entire breeding population estimated to be between 7500 and 15,000 pairs (Rimmer 1996). Breeds in Canada in southern Quebec to about Sept-Iles, the Gaspé Peninsula, Magdalen Island (where it may now have disappeared), through northern New Brunswick to the Cape Breton Highlands and south-western Nova Scotia (though disappeared from parts of northern Nova Scotia since the mid-1950s); and in the U.S.A. discontinuously south through the higher ranges of the Catskill and Adirondack Mountains in New York state; Green Mountains, Vermont, and White Mountains, New Hampshire, and mountains of northern Maine. Possibly also (or only erratically) in north-east Massachusetts (Mt Greylock), where

it last nested regularly in 1973 (Atwood *et al.* 1996). In winter to Hispaniola and (probably in smaller numbers or a scarce visitor to) Puerto Rico and St Croix (Virgin Islands).

MOVEMENTS Migratory, but very rarely recorded on migration; has been recorded, sparsely, in both migration seasons in most of the east coast states from Quebec to Florida and the Bahamas (Wallace 1939, Ouellet 1993). May occur, perhaps exceptionally or as an early migrant, in the last few days of April in New York and Nova Scotia (McLaren 1995) but more usually in early May, and arrives on breeding territory in Vermont and New Hampshire (and doubtless elsewhere in New England) in the last week of May (passage or arrivals from 17 May) and early June (Rimmer *et al.* 1996). Departs from New England breeding sites at end of September or early October. A vagrant to Bermuda (November 1957, December 1995 to February 1996) and Cuba (October 1965, October 1968).

Some evidence of winter site-fidelity from work on birds in Dominican Republic, with up to 7 individuals recaptured in subsequent years within 50 m of their original points of capture; of these 3 were caught in the same net in successive years (Rimmer *et al.* 1999).

HABITAT Breeds primarily in stunted balsam firs and red spruce, on rugged, misty or cloudy mountain slopes, hill-tops or tree-line areas, usually above 900 m (2970') but between 175 and 1160 m (575–3830') on the Gaspé Peninsula; in recent years has been more frequently recorded in small areas of second-growth forest largely as a result of human destruction of prime forests. In winter found in moist, broadleaved forests from sea-level to about 2200 m (6600'), but most occur in montane forests; however, also reported from the National Botanical Garden in Santo Domingo, Dominican Republic.

BEHAVIOUR Actions and foraging behaviour are very similar to that of Grey-cheeked; considered by many to be shy or elusive but others (Wallace 1939, Bent 1949) have found it wary but approachable. Most activity in the breeding season appears to be in the early morning and evening, with fairly long periods of silence and inaction in the daytime. Wintering birds in Dominican Republic appear to make short-distance movements from broadleaf to pine forests to roost, with some evidence that birds roost communally in the canopy of pine forests. Forages on the ground and low in vegetation in the interior of forests, but also along forest edges. Feeds predominantly on insects during the breeding season, particularly on ants, blackflies, moths and their larvae; in late summer and autumn takes quantities of fruit and berries, including blueberry, barberry, snowberry, deadly nightshade, spicebush, wild grape, woodbine and poison ivy.

BREEDING Season: June to late July. Nest: a cup constructed mostly of moss and twigs together with plant stems, dry leaves, bark strips, rotting wood or animal hair lined with black rootlets and grasses, occasionally externally covered in green moss or lichens. Usually placed in a concealed location against the trunk or along the branches 1–4 m (3–13′) from the ground in a fir (or occasionally birch). Eggs: 3–4, white, with variable amounts of small or fine brown spots. Incubation period 13–14 days. Nestlings fed by both parents but mostly by the female (Wallace in Bent 1949). Fledging period 11–12 days.

MOULT Juvenile plumage is replaced by partial moult during early August (in late-fledging birds this may not be complete until early September), the wing (including some of the greater coverts and tertials) and tail feathers being retained into first summer. Adults have completed a post-breeding moult by the end of August or early September.

May have a restricted or very partial moult or replacement of some wing or tail feathers in spring. **MEASUREMENTS** Wing, male (n=84) 87–98, female (n=30) 80–96 (Pyle *et al.* 1997); wing, male (10) 88–98, female (n=7) 85–93 (Cramp *et al.* 1988); wing, male 85–98.5, female 82–95; tarsus, male 27.5–30.5, female 27.5–30; bill (culmen) male 11–16.5, female 12–14 (Ridgway 1907, Ouellet 1993). Weight 24.5–30 g (Rimmer *et al.* 1999).
REFERENCES Atwood *et al.* (1996), Bent (1949), Evans (1994), McLaren (1995), Ouellet (1993), Ridgway (1907), Rimmer (1996), Rimmer *et al.* (1996, 1999), Wallace (1939).

91 SWAINSON'S THRUSH *Catharus ustulatus* Plate 27
(Olive-backed Thrush)

T*urdus ustulatus* Nuttall, 1840, *Man. Orn. U.S. and Canada* (ed. 2): vi, 400, 830 – forests of the Oregon [= Fort Vancouver, Washington].

IDENTIFICATION 16.5–19.5 cm (6½–7½″). An olive-brown *Catharus* thrush with a wide breeding range in northern and western North America; short-billed and fairly short-tailed appearance, usually showing prominent buffish spectacles (pale lores and eye-ring); west coast breeding birds (nominate *ustulatus*) are warm brown above while eastern birds are olive-brown above. Has olive-brown or reddish-brown (not grey) cheeks and ear-coverts; throat and breast creamy-yellow or buff, heavily spotted black. **Confusion species** Northern and eastern breeding birds are very similar to Grey-cheeked Thrush (89) but Swainson's is generally darker above with a distinct pale loral stripe to the eye and a complete pale eye-ring, although some Grey-cheeked (particularly first-winter birds) also have well defined but narrower eye-rings. Western birds are more likely to be confused with Veery (88) but have distinctive face pattern, heavy spotting on the breast, and buffish-brown not grey on the flanks (for separation of autumn Swainson's and Veery in western U.S.A. see Roberson 1980). Hermit Thrush (92) is also similar and has a conspicuous eye-ring but is slightly smaller and (depending on race) has variably toned upperparts from brown to olive or grey-brown; all, however, have warm brown wings and the same or contrasting reddish-brown tails, with nervous wing-flicking and tail-pumping actions. Wood Thrush (93) is larger and has a different, more full-bellied shape and is eliminated on reddish-brown tinge to the crown and mantle and large bold spots on the underparts. Vagrant Swainson's in Europe are similar to the larger, paler brown Song Thrush (124), which has more extensively spotting on the underparts.
DESCRIPTION Sexes alike. **Adult** (*C. u. swainsoni*) Forehead to crown and nape deep olive-brown, becoming tinged with olive-grey on mantle, back and scapulars; rump and uppertail-coverts usually browner than mantle and back. Tail dark olive with blackish innerwebs. Median and greater

coverts dark olive or blackish edged finely with brownish-olive; alula and primary coverts blackish-brown tinged olive, flight feathers greyish-black, finely edged olive on outer primaries and secondaries on closed wing; tertials dark olive. Underwing-coverts mostly off-white with grey-brown tips to medians and bases of greaters. Lores, brown or slightly darker with very fine pale tips, upper lores to eye with a line of pale buff joining pale or warm buff eye-ring, forming 'spectacles'; cheeks and ear-coverts olive-brown and indistinctly flecked or mottled with buff extending to sides of nape. Chin and throat pale buff becoming deeper or creamy-buff on breast; malar stripe of sooty wedge-shaped spots, upper breast also marked with slightly larger wedge-shaped blackish-brown spots that become more rounded or oval on central and lower breast. Sides of lower breast, flanks and thighs buffish- or light olive-brown smudged with slightly darker brown; vent to undertail-coverts white. Bill blackish-horn with base of lower mandible pale yellowish to yellowish-pink and variably to flesh-pink or tinged pale lilac. Legs and feet flesh-pink or tinged variably purple, grey, brownish-grey; rear of legs and soles slightly paler. In spring and summer plumage becomes worn and upperparts including wings and tail paler or slightly greyer. **Immature** Juvenile has upperparts mainly olive-brown with wings and tail darker; pale buff shaft-streaks on forehead to mantle and scapulars; rump and uppertail-coverts less heavily streaked. Median and greater coverts have small whitish-buff spots (occasionally extending as streaks along shaft), greater coverts finely edged olive-grey. Chin and throat to breast mostly buffish, breast and sides of breast to flanks spotted blackish or with dark olive-brown bars, belly whitish, undertail-coverts pale grey. Face also mostly buffish with fine blackish flecks, broad pale buff eye-ring and blackish malar stripes. First-winter bird similar to adult but with some median and most greater coverts retained from juvenile plumage, and can show pale buff or whitish tips (sometimes absent or restricted to shaft); tertials also retained and much more worn than in adults. Tips of tail feathers usually more pointed and sometimes pale buff.

GEOGRAPHICAL VARIATION Four races (others have been proposed); variation clinal but moderately well marked. Differences are mainly in tone of upperparts, from olive or olive-grey in east to browner or warmer brown in west (including worn plumage), but away from breeding areas not always easily (especially in field) identifiable to race. In fresh (i.e. autumn) plumage, eastern adults more richly coloured or brownish than in spring, when plumage worn and tinged greyer. There is widespread lack of conformity of treatment, but whilst we recognise the more clearly marked races it is our view that the situation as it currently exists in the literature is unnecessarily confusing. Apart from the main east–west divide (i.e. olive-backed to russet-backed birds) there is little real need for an array of racial recognition to suit a taxonomic ideal based on very subtle degrees of colour change probably invisible to most field observers without a set of specimens for comparison. In our view a conservative approach is required to prevent recognition of further subdivisions and we therefore maintain the arrangement set out by Ripley (1964). However, we agree with previous authors that there needs to be an entire overview of the races of this (and possibly other *Catharus*) thrushes based on non-morphological characteristics and until such work has been completed there should be no adoption of further races without a comprehensive review and justification. See also Phillips (1991) and Pyle *et al.* (1997) for further racial separation.

Nominate race *ustulatus* is visibly separable from *swainsoni* (described above) as the upperparts are deeper or warmer brown, uppertail-coverts and base of are almost rufous-brown, breast washed brownish-buff and spots smaller; in fresh plumage the whitish undertail-coverts are tinged buff. In spring, upperparts slightly duller or less rufous

Race *almae* very similar to *swainsoni* but significantly paler or greyer and less olive on head and upperparts, especially in worn plumage; underparts are, on average, paler or whiter, spots darker (palest birds from north of range have previously been separated as *incanus*).

Race *oedicus* similar to nominate *ustulatus* but slightly paler or greyer-brown (especially in worn plumage), less rich or lacking rufous on upperparts (except for uppertail-coverts), paler on underparts with less heavy spots; the bill also averages slightly smaller.

Some western birds, including both *almae* and *oedicus*, can show reduced or less distinct spectacles and the buffy loral stripe and eye-ring is more like that of Veery.

VOICE Call a soft mellow *pwink, pwit, whit, whiut* like a drop of water in a bucket, or a *whiuh* or *hwee*, also a sharper, more buzzing *rrehrr*. Migrants frequently give the *whit* call note and

night-flying migrants give a single, mellow or plaintive and far-carrying whistled *queep*, making it possible to detect the flight route of individuals. Song fine and beautiful (considered by some to be second only to that of Hermit Thrush): a series of up to 15 sweet musical phrases rising or spiralling upwards in pitch *whao-whayo-whiyo-wheya-wheeya* or ending on a thin sharp note, *whip-poor-will-a-will-e-zee-zee-zee*, occasionally interspersing *wit* or *a-will* into the phrases. Sings mostly in the early dawn and evening, fairly commonly well into the night; sometimes in the afternoon; occasionally in concert with up to 20 others in the same area of forest. Occasionally sings before the start of, and during, spring migration, including weak song in Brazil and Colombia in late March and April and more strongly from late March to early May in Central America and the southern U.S.A.; but song period otherwise extends to late July or early August.

STATUS AND DISTRIBUTION Widespread and locally common but habitat destruction on its wintering grounds is considered to have contributed to the decline in the overall population in the 1980s (Roberson and Tenney 1993). Cowbird brood-parasitism is also suspected of having a negative influence on numbers.

C. u. ustulatus Breeds in the Alaska Peninsula (intermittently or sporadically north to the southern Seward Peninsula) and coastal south-east Alaska south through coastal British Columbia to western Washington (west of the Cascades), western Oregon to central Nevada and southern and western California west of the Cascades and the Sierra Nevada ranges; also probably this race in an isolated outpost in eastern Arizona (San Francisco peaks), although Phillips *et al.* (1964) considered the breeding birds of eastern Arizona to belong to the more northerly *swainsoni*. In winter from the coastal slopes (rare or local in interior) of central and southern Mexico, from Tres Marias Islands, north-west Nayarit and southern Tamaulipas (small numbers may also winter on the Yucatán Peninsula) south to Honduras, Costa Rica and the mountains of Bocas del Toro, western Panama.

C. u. almae (including *incanus*) Eastern and south-east Alaska (apart from coastal areas) east through the Yukon, western Mackenzie and northern British Columbia to west-central Alberta south along the Rockies to north-west Utah, Colorado and northern New Mexico; probably also this race in northern Nebraska, eastern Wyoming and eastern Montana. Winters from Colombia (possibly occasionally in Panama – January to March specimens from Veraguas to Darién) to northern Peru.

C. u. oedicus Breeds from northern Washington south along the eastern slope of the Cascades through central and south-west Oregon to south-central California (Santa Barbara and San Diego counties, also once on Santa Catalina Island). In winter from Tres Marias Islands and Nayarit, west-central Mexico, south to east-central Guatemala and north-west Costa Rica. A bird collected in March 1953 in Chiriquí, Panama, was assigned to this race by Wetmore *et al.* (1984).

C. u. swainsoni Canada from central British Columbia and central and north-east Alberta east through central and northern Saskatchewan, also a separate population in southern and south-west Saskatchewan east through Manitoba, Ontario, Quebec to southern Labrador to Newfoundland, Anticosti Island, New Brunswick and Nova Scotia and south in the U.S.A. from northern New England, Catskills and Adirondacks in New York sporadically (and probably declining) south through the Appalachians from the Allegheny hills of western Pennsylvania to west Maryland and southern Virginia; west around the great lakes to northern Michigan, Wisconsin and northern Minnesota. In winter sporadically in Honduras, central and eastern Panama (Veraguas to Darién), more continuously southwards from Colombia, Venezuela, southern Guyana and western Brazil to Ecuador, northern and north-eastern Peru, central Bolivia, and northern Argentina (Tucumán).

MOVEMENTS Migratory. Autumn departure from breeding areas in late August, September and early October, but disperses from breeding areas a month or more earlier, e.g. most breeding birds in central California have left the breeding area by late July but are present elsewhere within the region in August and September. Passage through much of the U.S.A. is in September to mid-October. Migration takes place on a broad front; preferred direction is due south but birds from Nova Scotia and northern New England move west of south. In parts of its range it becomes erratically numerous, e.g. Point Pelee, Ontario, but elsewhere in the central and southern states and the northern plateau of Mexico it is scarce or much rarer numerically than in spring. In southern California it is a fairly common coastal migrant (rare in the interior) to late October or exceptionally early November. Passage through Mexico (except Yucatán Peninsula where uncommon or scarce) and most of Central America in September and October (average arrival date in Honduras first week of October) whilst further south passage and arrival dates are correspondingly later in October and November. Birds may show winter site-fidelity; one ringed in Jujuy, northern Argentina, in January 1964 was retrapped in the same place four years later (Sick 1993).

Common to abundant migrant throughout Costa Rica and Panama (commonest in October but rare in winter and uncommon in spring) and passage and winter visitor to Colombia and western Brazil from early to mid-October to late April. *C.u. swainsoni* is a scarce or rare migrant to Bermuda and through much of the Caribbean (mostly to the southern Bahamas, Cuba, Jamaica, Swan Island, Isla de Providencia and Cayman Islands) between mid-September and end of November (although there is a December record from Bermuda), and an uncommon passage migrant to the Netherlands Antilles; has occurred in El Salvador as a rare winter visitor and a spring migrant in varying numbers.

Return movements are the reverse of those in autumn and passage through most of U.S.A., although in comparatively small numbers in the south-western states in April except for southern and interior California where common and widespread (occasionally abundant) from mid-April (from late March in Cuba) to late May; a common spring migrant in south-east Arizona but rare elsewhere. Arrives in breeding areas late April and early May (often not common until mid-May), with passage through Central America completed by the first few days of May, although some birds still on passage through northern Mexico and southern U.S.A. to the most northerly parts of the range in the first week of June; average arrival date in New York state is mid-May (earliest 24 April), but then common to abundant to early June. Has occurred as an overshooting migrant to central and northern Alaska. A rare vagrant in spring to Bermuda and on Meighen Island, North-west Territories, northern Canada and at least twice at Prudhoe Bay, western Alaska. Eastern (olive-backed) race birds are rare autumn vagrants to California.

Elsewhere a vagrant to Iceland (3 records), Britain (21 to 1996), Ireland, Norway, Finland, Belgium, Germany, Austria and Italy (March 1878); there is also an old (October 1893) record from Kharkov, Ukraine.

HABITAT When breeding, mainly the understorey of lowland Norway and white spruce forests, up to 2725 m (9000′), including dwarf or stunted spruce on hillsides; also hemlock and deciduous forests (usually mature tall forests) containing a proportion of spruce, balsam and dense alder thickets; also secondary stands of mixed forest. Often in well shaded damp areas, near streams or boggy hollows with willows, aspens or poplars. On migration occurs in similar habitat, but more often in the tops of trees, including smaller deciduous woods and thickets, orchards, parks, gardens, coastal and roadside thickets, desert oases and clumps of bushes. In winter occurs in humid or moist deciduous or semi-evergreen forests and fruiting trees (used as shade trees in and around coffee plantations) usually below 2000 m (6600′); in Honduras and possibly elsewhere race *ustulatus* is not found below 600 m (1980′); similarly *swainsoni* occurs in the lower montane forests of the Andes in northern South America.

BEHAVIOUR Generally shy or retiring and solitary, usually in lower to middle tree levels – it is the most arboreal of the *Catharus* thrushes – but also spends long periods on the ground where it keeps to fairly thick cover, walking and hopping and forages in leaf-litter. It also feeds at mid- to canopy level in trees and bushes; flight fairly fast or dashing and may slowly raise and lower tail for several seconds after landing; also flicks and twitches the tail stiffly when nervous or alarmed. In winter almost entirely arboreal, feeding primarily in fruiting trees; also takes berries from trees and bushes whilst hovering. Usually alone or in pairs in breeding and winter but forms loose flocks on migration when also found associating with migrant Grey-cheeked Thrush and Veery. Feeds (sometimes by short fly-catching sallies) mostly on insects, particularly ants (on passage and in winter attends army ant swarms), beetles, weevils, bees, wasps, flies craneflies, crickets, mosquitoes, bugs and caterpillars; also small earthworms plus fruit, particularly blackberries, raspberries, dogwood, spicebush, grape, wild cherries, elderberries and some seeds.

BREEDING Season: late May to early July. Nest: a neat cup-shaped construction of mosses, fine sedges, leaves and fine grass stems and plant fibres, bracken, lichens, moss and thin strips of bark (and occasionally decorated with loose strips of yellow birch bark) lined with similar but finer material of dead leaves, lichens and rootlets; usually placed between 0.75 and 10 m (30') from the ground (but most are within 2–3 m/6–9') on a low horizontal branch in thickets of spruce or balsam fir, tamarack, cedar or willow, usually up to several metres out from the trunk; sometimes on a tree stump. Eggs: 3–4, exceptionally 5, whitish-blue, evenly marked with small spots or speckles of pale, reddish- or even yellowish-brown. Incubation period 12–13 days, by female alone. Fledging period 10–12 days; both adults feed the young. Suffers heavy brood-parasitism from Brownheaded Cowbird *Molothrus ater*.

MOULT Post-juvenile moult begins in mid-August and is completed by the end of September; it involves the replacement of the body feathers and the lesser wing-coverts, also occasionally some median and greater coverts and tertials, but not all the greater coverts or rest of wing and tail feathers; wing-coverts, flight and tail feathers are retained

into first summer. Adults undergo complete postbreeding moult in July to early September and are then indistinguishable from first-year birds (except for the latters' retained and often pale-tipped wing-coverts). However, Cherry (1985) found that some birds depart from the breeding area before starting or during the early stages of the moult. The proportion of the population doing this is unknown but some individuals had moved at least 250 km from the breeding area whilst others had travelled no further than 30 km.

MEASUREMENTS Wing, male (n=100) 91–104, female (n=100) 87–100 (Pyle *et al.* 1997); *swainsoni* wing, male (n=17) 94–107, female (n=21) 93–102 (Cramp *et al.* 1988)*; *ustulatus* wing, male (n=30) 92–102, female (n=30) 90.5–99; *almae* wing, male 96–102, female 93.5–100; *oedicus* wing, male 92–100, female 89–96.5; all races except *swainsoni* tarsus, male 27–31, female 25.5–28.5; bill (to skull) male 16–18.5, female 15–17; *swainsoni* bill (culmen) 11.5–15; tarsus 26–31. Weight 25.5–39 g (Rahbek *et al.* 1993).

*Several museum specimens in the BMNH and AMNH collections have wing-lengths (flattened chord) down to 91 mm (PC).

REFERENCES Cherry (1985), Ornat *et al.* (1989), Phillips (1991), Phillips *et al.* (1964), Pyle *et al.* (1997), Rahbek *et al.* (1993), Roberson (1980), Roberson & Tenney (1993), Sick (1993), Wetmore *et al.* (1984).

92 HERMIT THRUSH *Catharus guttatus* Plate 26

Muscicapa guttata Pallas, 1811, *Zoogr. Rosso-Asiat.* 1: 465 – Kodiak Island, Alaska.

IDENTIFICATION 16–18 cm (6¼–7"). A small, compact thrush with a slender bill and relatively long tail; common and widespread throughout much of North America, wintering much farther north than other *Catharus* thrushes (south to southern Mexico and Guatemala). Very nimble and unobtrusive in its actions as it moves silently on the ground or through the branches; a rich, fluty, melodious singer. Adults are slightly variable between a complex number of races in the colour of the upperparts: olive-brown, warm brown or greyish-brown on the head to back contrasting with brown (*auduboni*) or rich chestnut-brown (*faxoni*) on the wings, rump and tail; underparts whitish with greyish flanks and variably spotted dark brown or black according to race. Frequently flicks wings and cocks or pumps tail, a distinctive feature for poorly seen birds. **Confusion species** Contrasting rich brown or rufous rump and tail against a duller or plainer brown head, mantle and back is virtually diagnostic from all other North American thrushes; no other species shares the colour of the tail although some Bicknell's Thrushes (90) may approach it in warmth but on Bicknell's this colour is restricted to the tail and it contrasts less with the rest of upperparts. Bicknell's

usually lacks a prominent eye-ring or it may only be partly present, and has a prominent orange-yellow base to the lower mandible (and cutting edges of upper). Veery (88) has uniform warm brown or cinnamon upperparts; the palest races of Hermit have contrasting upperparts and rump and tail. Russet (84), Orange-billed (82) and Ruddy-capped Nightingale-Thrush (85) have uniform warm brown or dark chestnut-brown upperparts but lack the rufous tones of the tail and are plain or uniform buff below. In Europe, Song Thrush (124) is much larger, has uniform mid- to warm brown upperparts and is much more heavily spotted below.

DESCRIPTION Sexes alike. **Adult** Forehead to nape, mantle, back and scapulars grey-brown or tinged olive becoming warmer brown on lower back; rump and uppertail-coverts warm brown becoming rust-brown on tips of uppertail-coverts, tail rust-brown at base grading to chestnut on outerwebs at tip, innerwebs darker or browner. Median coverts dark brown with paler or lighter brown edges and tips, greater coverts similar but edged warm brown; alula and primary coverts dark brown, latter edged warm brown, flight feathers warm or rufous-brown on edges and outerwebs of base of flight feathers, tips of primaries and all

Underwing pattern of Hermit Thrush.

tertials brown; underwing-coverts whitish to pale grey with dark tips to greaters, broad pale band across base of secondaries and inner primaries contrasting with dark tips to flight feathers (shows also on upperwing). Lores pale buff mottled darkish grey, often showing (but absent on western birds) a pale line across upper lores (appearing as short or indistinct supercilium) to thin but prominent (occasionally indistinct or absent) whitish eye-ring; cheeks and ear-coverts brown or grey-brown streaked broadly with pale whitish- or yellowish-buff. Can show short ill-defined brown or darker-spotted malar stripe; chin and upper throat white, lower throat and breast whitish to buff heavily spotted blackish, sides of lower throat greyish or smudged darker on sides of breast, belly and vent whitish-grey, undertail-coverts white. Bill dark horn with dull yellowish- or flesh-pink base to lower mandible. Eye dark brown. Legs and feet flesh-pink. **Immature** Juvenile very similar to adult but crown, nape, mantle, back and scapulars finely streaked or tipped buff, median and greater coverts having wedge-shaped buff spots at tips. Underparts dull white tinged buff on breast, blackish spots on lower throat (may also show dark malar) and centre of breast becoming barred with dusky-brown or blackish tips on lower breast, belly and flanks, the latter washed greyish. First-winter bird very similar to adult but distinguished by small pale buff tips to median and greater coverts and more finely on tips of tertials (often abraded by end of October), whereas pale tips to greater coverts may be retained into first summer. Birds from northern breeding races have paler tips to greater coverts than darker-backed birds from west of range.

GEOGRAPHICAL VARIATION Eight races; variation clinal but fairly well marked from west to east from pale greyish-olive to rich brown on crown to mantle and back; nominate *guttatus* is approximately midway along this cline (see also note below).

Grey or grey-brown upperparts
Races *auduboni, slevini* and *sequoiensis* have forehead and crown to mantle, back and scapulars pale greyish-olive or lightly tinged greyish olive-brown, tail slightly duller than nominate and flanks also slightly paler grey. In addition

auduboni, the largest race, has an almost white ground colour to underparts, except for grey on flanks, and is fairly heavily marked with black triangular or arrowhead spots on lower throat and breast, becoming more rounded and dark brown on belly and flanks; undertail-coverts pale buff; also shows a slightly heavier malar stripe; *slevini* and *sequoiensis* are probably inseparable in the field but *slevini*, is, on average, slightly smaller and more lightly spotted on a whiter breast, whilst *sequoiensis* has a slightly brighter or more rufous rump and heavier spots on breast. Race *polionotus* has upperparts pale grey-brown tinged olive on head to mantle, back and scapulars, and white undertail-coverts; overall like nominate *ustulatus* of Swainson's Thrush (91) but rump dull rufous rump and tail rusty or chestnut.

Brown or dark-backed race
Race *nanus* very similar to nominate and probably not safely separable in the field but generally smaller with warmer or slightly darker rufous-brown on mantle and back, slightly deeper rufous or russet-brown uppertail-coverts and chestnut tail, the spots on breast and belly larger and blacker, flanks darker grey, often washed brown. Legs and feet pale or lavender-grey becoming tinged bluish at rear.

Warm or rich brown upperparts
The eastern race *faxoni* is slightly more complex, with two morphs recognised differing in tone of upperparts. Some birds have a dull or dark brown head becoming warm brown on nape to mantle and scapulars, whilst others are distinctly greyer-brown, both however having broad rust- or rufous-brown edges to median, greater and primary coverts (not always easy to see in the field and sometimes absent altogether), also the tertials and edges to flight feathers (more extensive than in nominate) with a reddish-brown rump and tail; tips of primaries and outer secondaries dark brown. Underparts largely white, cream or yellowish-buff on the lower throat (finely streaked darker) to breast and flanks, spotted or smudged dark brown on sides of throat and breast, becoming paler brown on sides of lower breast and merging into buffish, tawny-brown or brownish-grey on flanks; centre of belly, vent and undertail-coverts white. In the hand base of bill broader or appears more swollen at base. Race *crymophilus* very similar to *faxoni* but darker above; considered by some (e.g. Phillips 1991) to be based on foxed specimens and thus synonymous with *faxoni*.

Taxonomic note As in other *Catharus* thrushes (chiefly Swainson's) there is considerable variation in opinion over the number of subspecies of Hermit Thrush. Up to 13 other races have been proposed (see Aldrich 1968, Phillips 1991), some of which subdivide and replace those with more extensive ranges (e.g. *nanus*) listed here. All recently proposed races concern small or relatively discrete populations which show slight differences from those elsewhere in the range. Almost all characters cited in support of these splits are extremely marginal and concern slightly paler or darker upperparts, strength of definition of the underpart spotting, bill shape and wing length. Very few of these differences, apart from the more obvious extremes of upperpart colour tones, are apparent in the field and most are only detectable in series of museum specimens. The identification in the field (in some cases in the hand) of some of these proposed races outside of the breeding areas is generally impractical. Although some subdivisions are probably legitimate – the species as a whole exhibits a considerable degree of geographic variation – a detailed overview of their ranges (possibly involving new or fresh specimens) is required to determine exact characters, racial limits, and areas of overlap and intergradation. The current problems of plumage colour are extremely confused (and confusing to all but museum specialists) and may be no more than clinal (see also this section under Swainson's Thrush). Phillips (1991) went some way towards a complete review of the species but used old and very probably 'foxed' specimens and may have been misled into making arbitrary divisions of clines. Until such time that a thorough review of this species (and possibly other *Catharus* thrushes) is completed, acceptance of further races or the fragmentation of existing 'good' races appears unnecessary and speculative; see also Pyle *et al.* (1997) and Lane & Jaramillo (2000).

VOICE Most frequent call is a variety of *tuck*, *wuck*, *chuck*, *chup*, *choop*, *quit*, *quoit* or *wit* notes, also a harsh *pay* and a ringing *cheeeee* or *seeee*; in autumn gives a soft catlike *meow* and a *churr* like an Eastern Bluebird *Sialia sialis*; alarm note is a scolding *tuk-tuk-tuk*. Mostly silent on migration but occasionally gives a soft *prrrt* (Speirs 1985), *quoit* or *chuck*. Song similar to (and easily confused with) that of Wood Thrush, a rich, beautiful and spiralling upward *oh, sferal, sferal* followed by a mixture of phrases at different pitches such as *oh, holy, holy* or *HEUUU vardle vardle* followed by *HEEE veery veery* and *HERR vardle vardle*, or *high-up, high-up, look-up, look-up*, the last two phrases sometimes being a repeated variation on *purity* or *sweetly*, in a rich cadence with the first note longest and lowest in pitch, the remainder clear and sweet, fading at end of phrase and ending with a down-slurred flourish. Studies of sonagrams reveal that certain high notes within the song are inaudible to the human ear. Considered as one of the finest singers amongst the American thrushes (and by some as the finest songbird in all North America), best heard in the solemn stillness of a dark dense forest in the quiet of sunrise or sunset. Sings from atop a dead or living tree but may also give song from lower levels. Sings most often in the early morning and late evening but in some areas sings throughout the day, and in areas of high density males often indulge in concert singing. Usually only sings when on territory but occasionally gives a thin whispering subsong on fine days in March and April (Bent 1949) and possibly earlier; recorded in wintering birds in Mexico. In northern breeding areas song period continues to end of July or mid-August.

STATUS AND DISTRIBUTION Common and widespread; in south-west U.S.A. an uncommon or locally common summer resident.

C. g. guttatus Breeds in southern Alaska, from the Alaska Peninsula (rarely or intermittently north to the coastal forests of Norton Sound and southern Seward Peninsula) west to about Shumagin Island, also Kodiak Island and islands along the coast to Cross Sound east to southern Yukon and central British Columbia, western Canada. In winter from southern Vancouver Island and north-west Washington south along the west coast of the U.S.A. east to central Oregon and central Colorado south to western Texas, Baja California, southern Sonora, southern Coahuila, Tamaulipas and possibly south-west San Luis Potosi and northeast Veracruz, northern Mexico (Phillips 1991) to eastern Texas.

C. g. nanus Breeds along the coastal areas of south-east Alaska and western British Columbia including Queen Charlotte and Vancouver Islands. In winter from south-west British Columbia south through the western U.S.A. to southern Nevada and south-west New Mexico and southern Baja California. Has also been collected in Veracruz in January 1975 (Winker *et al.* 1992).

C. g. slevini Breeds in the Cascade range of Washington and Oregon south through central northern California and the coast range of northern and central California (to Monterey County; possibly also this race in Santa Ynex Mountains of Santa Barbara County). In winter from extreme southern Arizona (possibly also extreme southern Nevada) south to Sonora and Sinaloa (possibly also to Michoacán and Hidalgo), northern Mexico and south in Baja California to the Sierra de la Laguna.

C. g. sequoiensis Breeds in the Sierra Nevada range of central and eastern California to western Nevada south to the mountains of southern California, San Bernardino Mountains, Mt Pinos (and probably San Jacinto Mountains). In winter from south-east Arizona, central and western Texas, south to Sonora and southern Tamaulipas, northern Mexico. Has occurred east to North Dakota, Kansas, Oklahoma, north-east Texas and Louisiana (but see comments under Geographic Variation).

C. g. polionotus Breeds in the Blue Mountains of eastern Washington, eastern Oregon, Nevada, south-west Utah (Pine Valley Mountains) and central eastern California (White and Inyo Mountains, south through the Panamint Mountains and Clark Mountains). In winter from south-east Arizona and most of Mexico (except south and east Veracruz, eastern Oaxaca and the Yucatán Peninsula); possibly also to central southern Guatemala (where uncommon or scarce) but requires confirmation.

C. g. auduboni Breeds along the Rocky Mountains from south-east British Columbia south to western Montana, Idaho, Wyoming, eastern Nevada through Utah to western and central Colorado (possibly also in south-east), central and south-east Arizona, New Mexico and extreme western Texas (Guadalupe Mountains). In winter throughout most of northern and central Mexico (except south and east Veracruz, eastern Oaxaca and the Yucatán Peninsula) but also southern Baja California, central Chiapas, southern Guatemala and extreme north-west El Salvador (Howell & Webb 1995, Phillips 1986, Unitt & Estrella 1996).

C. g. faxoni Breeds in central Yukon and the Mackenzie Range to north-east British Columbia, Alberta east through northern Ontario (southern outpost of the range in the Cypress Hills of south-west Saskatchewan) to Quebec (though largely absent from the southern shore of Hudson Bay, south-west Manitoba and southern Ontario; small outpost along part of the northern shore of Lake Erie) and southern Labrador, New Brunswick and Nova Scotia south into U.S.A. from north-east Minnesota, northern Wisconsin and northern Michigan to New York (including Long Island) and New England south from northern Pennsylvania and extreme north-west New Jersey to south-east West Virginia and western Virginia; small outposts in central Ohio. May also occur irregularly or sparingly south into eastern Tennessee and north-west North Carolina.   In winter through most of southern and eastern U.S.A. from southern central California and southern Arizona and northern central New Mexico north and east to central Massachusetts (and in recent mild winters to northern Vermont, southern New Hampshire and southern Maine [Rockland]), Rhode Island, southern Connecticut, southern New York and New Jersey, central Pennsylvania (also regularly on islands in western Lake Erie) and southern Ohio, possibly also southern Indiana and southern Illinois south through south-east Missouri to south and east Oklahoma, central Texas and east along the Gulf coast to southern Florida and Bermuda, more rarely the Bahamas.

C. g. crymophilus Breeds throughout Newfoundland. Winter range largely unknown but maybe within that of *faxoni*; recorded on migration in New York, Virginia and Georgia.

Distribution note Howell & Webb (1992) documented sightings and tape-recorded territorial singing birds at c.2700 m (8900′) in an area of the Sierra San Pedro Martir, northern Baja California, in June 1991, and cited previous observations from this area in June 1984 and July 1985. These records may refer to a range extension of one of the races breeding in central or southern California or of non-breeding/summering birds of one of the more northerly breeding races which winter in this area of northern Mexico. Has also bred (subspecies unknown) in north-east Kansas and in the Black Hills of south-west South Dakota.

MOVEMENTS Migratory (mostly nocturnal) with most races entirely deserting the breeding range except for *nanus* and possibly *faxoni*, which winter within the southern part of their breeding ranges; moves south to winter within the southern states of the U.S.A. and Mexico south to southern Guatemala. Autumn departures from northern parts of the range in late September; birds from Alaska and the Yukon arrive in southern Canada and Washington state from early October, and onward passage south continues through October into early November. Birds from central and east-

ern Canada and north-east U.S.A. move south or south-south-west from mid-September to late October and arrive in wintering areas in the southern U.S.A. and northern Mexico from the middle of September, but main passage (and arrivals in central and southern Mexico) appears to be in October and early November. Passage of migrants through Chicago and the great lakes area is from mid-August to mid-November with peak in mid-October. Average arrival date in southern California mid-October; in Tamaulipas, north-east Mexico, late October. Guatemala wintering records are from early November to mid-April.

Migration usually completed in stages with periods of 2–4 days, on average, stopover or off-passage, when birds may be seen at any available resting or feeding place along the route, including parks in major cities (e.g. Central Park, New York). Stopover period linked to climatic features or fitness of individuals. Direction of migration usually along natural features, e.g. hills or river corridors, but ringing in north-east U.S.A. in autumn indicates higher percentage of adults move along the coast than immatures (Ralph 1981).

Winters further north than any other *Catharus* thrush, with birds of the races *guttatus* and *nanus* wintering in western U.S.A. north to Washington and southern British Columbia, whilst in the east *faxoni* winters north to coastal Massachusetts, Rhode Island, southern Connecticut and southern New York state, and is now regular in small numbers in Bermuda and the northern Bahamas from early October to mid-April Thus any *Catharus* thrush seen in the U.S.A. in winter is most probably a Hermit.

Return movements in spring are the reverse of the routes taken in autumn but numbers vary from year to year, birds being common to abundant in some years whilst almost absent in others. Hermits are usually the first of the *Catharus* thrushes to arrive back on breeding territory. They arrive in the southern breeding areas in early April and the central and northern states from later that month. In central Canada and even southern Alaska first arrivals are in mid-April but more usually recorded from early May in latter area. Birds still on passage mid-May with migrants on the move in central and northern Mexico, Arizona and southern Texas in early and mid-May.

Accidental north through central Alaska to Point Barrow, Southampton and Seymour Islands (Northwest Territories, Canada), and James Bay, northern Ontario; generally rare north of known wintering range in northern U.S.A. and eastern Canada; a vagrant to western Greenland (2 in May, 1 in June, 2 in October), Jamaica, Cuba (1 in December), Guadalupe Island (Mexico), Iceland (8 in September–December), British Isles (6, including 2 in spring), Sweden (1 in April), Germany (4), Luxembourg (1), Switzerland and Italy (November 1901).

HABITAT Breeds in coniferous, deciduous or mixed forests (usually in open forest or woodland and along forest edge of spruce or hemlock and other northern hardwoods, e.g. maple, beech or birch, also black spruce, from sea-level to the tree-line, and in drier canyons with mature stands of trees often with a considerable undergrowth layer (or near cliffs or rock-faces in Alaska). Along the western seaboard breeds in the Pacific rainforest zone and on the Alaska Peninsula in the arctic-alpine zone. In California prefers moist forests of redwoods and broadleaved woods on (generally north-facing) slopes in areas of extensive bogs and swamps, but further north generally breeds in dry pine, scrub oak and fir woods, particularly in jack pine *Pinus banksiana* and Engelmann spruce *Picea engelmanni*. In winter occurs in much the same kind of habitat as in summer but also tropical deciduous forest and woodlands, chaparral woods and thickets, generally more widespread down to sea-level and common in a variety of woods, including montane and submontane mixed oak-pinewoods, often near streams in valleys, from foothills and canyons to parks and shrubberies of large gardens even on the edges of towns and cities; usually most numerous in areas of berry-bearing bushes and shrubs, descending in altitude as montane berry-bearing trees become bare; avoids open fields and meadows. Unitt and Estrella (1996) noted habitat and elevation differences between *slevini* and *guttatus/auduboni* in winter in southern Baja California. The former occurred in lowland tropical deciduous woodland below 1300 m (4300′) whilst the latter two were in oak-pine woodland with a heavily vegetated understorey above 1600 m (5280′).

BEHAVIOUR Usually a quiet, shy, retiring and solitary bird, inhabiting the forest floor or very close to it, flitting rather nervously with nimble actions through the lower levels of trees and bushes. On the ground hops and has an upright gait, tail also often held cocked up at an angle; quick to take alarm, silently dive into thick cover and sit on a low branch; also raises the crown feathers when alarmed. Often found in more open forests and woods than other North American thrushes, feeding quite frequently along woodland edges. Invariably flicks wings and/or tail in nervous motion or quickly raises tail and then lowers it slowly, most often on landing. Forages in fairly typical thrush fashion by moving quickly over the ground stopping suddenly and surveying the immediate area, also turning over dead leaves and decaying vegetation on the forest floor. Feeds in short bursts of activity alternated with periods of almost total inertia when sits motionless on a prominent perch. Occasionally fly-catches either from the ground or darts out warbler-fashion from

a high bush or tree. Food is mostly invertebrates and their larvae supplemented by a range of fruit especially in autumn and winter, when becomes almost dependent on berry crop; invertebrates consist chiefly of ants, beetles, bees, wasps, bugs, caterpillars, flies, grasshoppers and spiders, plus a few snails and small worms; fruit is mostly berries including blueberry, pokeberry, holly, mistletoe, elderberry, blackberry, dogwood, greenbrier and various creepers, plus wild cherry, red cedar, grape and poison ivy (Bent 1949).

BREEDING Season: May to August. Nest: a large but compact structure of small twigs, strips of wood or bark, dry grasses, leaves, ferns and moss lined with pine needles, plant stems, willow catkins, roots or fine grasses, sometimes up to 3 m (10′) from the ground in a tree but usually on the ground in a dip under a low-growing tree or bush which effectively hides the nest; in some areas in tussocks of wet bogs surrounded by larches and other firs, in others on drier ground surrounded by bearberry or sandwort; built by female only. Eggs: 3–4, occasionally up to 6, pale greenish-blue or pale blue, occasionally finely marked with small brown spots. Incubation period 11–13 days solely by the female, but male feeds incubating female. Fledging period 10–15 days. Two, exceptionally three broods in a season.

MOULT Adults undergo complete post-breeding moult in August and September. Post-juvenile moult to first-winter plumage is a partial moult of head and body feathers and lesser and median coverts, most inner greater coverts and occasionally tertials, before departure to wintering grounds, from early August to late September or October; exceptionally, it is delayed or arrested until arrival in winter quarters.

MEASUREMENTS Wing, male (n=100) 81–110, female (n=100) 78–103; tarsus 27.5–33; bill (culmen) 12–13.5; *faxoni* wing, male 89.5–100, female 82–94; bill (to skull), male 17–19, female 16.5–18.5; *sequoiensis* wing, male 90–98, female 86–94; *auduboni* wing, male 97–106, female 94–106; *nanus* wing, male 84–95, female 82–87.5; *polionotus* wing 98.5–106 (exceptionally to 110.5). Weight, male 27–37 g, female 27–32 g, autumn immatures 26–36 g; *slevinii* 18–21 g (Pyle *et al.* 1997).

REFERENCES Bent (1949), Howell & Webb (1992), Lane & Jaramillo (2000), Phillips (1991), Phillips *et al.* (1964), Pyle *et al.* (1997), Ralph (1981), Speirs (1985), Unitt & Estrella (1996), Winker *et al.* (1992).

93 WOOD THRUSH *Catharus mustelina* Plate 27

Turdus mustelinus Gmelin, 1789, *Syst. Nat.* 1(2): 817, ex Latham, 'Tawny Thrush' – in Noveboraco [New York].

IDENTIFICATION 19.5–21.5 cm (7¾–8½″). A large, stocky, very distinctive thrush of much of eastern North America; has a larger head and bill than any other similar *Catharus* thrush of the

region. Reddish-brown on forehead to mantle, becoming duller, more brownish-olive on wings, rump and tail; bold white eye-ring and streaked face, underparts white but heavily spotted black.

The beautiful ethereal song contains clear fluty bell-like notes descending in scale and ending in a high trilling. In the past 30 years has disappeared from much of the breeding range owing to the destruction of forests in both its summer and winter ranges; this, together with a high degree of brood-parasitism by cowbirds, is causing a continuing decline. **Confusion species** Unproblematic when seen well, the combination of reddish-brown on the head and large black spots extending to the flanks and vent below being diagnostic. Recalls Brown Thrasher *Toxostoma rufum* in pattern but has dark eye, short bill and tail, spots not streaks below, and no double white wing-bar (in adults). **Taxonomic note** Previously placed in the monotypic genus *Hylocichla* on the basis of plumage and behavioural (mainly posture) differences from *Catharus* thrushes. We follow Avise *et al.* (1980) and Winker and Rappole (1988) in finding insufficient grounds to retain it a separate genus.

DESCRIPTION Sexes alike. **Adult** Forehead dark brown or uniform with russet-, reddish- or cinnamon-brown on crown to nape and mantle, becoming browner on lower mantle and back to wings and tail, but centres to median and greater coverts and innerwebs to tertials darker brown or blackish, edges to scapulars and outerwebs of tertials warmer brown, edges to outer primaries bright cinnamon-brown. Lores blackish with a thin line of white across upper lores; distinctive white eyering; cheeks and ear-coverts brown mottled or streaked white. Chin and throat to cheeks white finely spotted black, often showing a prominent malar stripe; rest of underparts whitish or with a buffish wash on breast, and with large round black spots on breast, belly and flanks; vent, thighs and undertail-coverts white. Bill quite substantial with blunt tip, blackish-horn with a (pale) yellow, yellowish-brown or pale flesh base to lower mandible. Eye dark brown or black. Legs and feet bright or pale flesh-pink. **Immature** Juvenile similar to adult but has darker olive-brown upperparts with warm tinge to crown and mantle and pale buff spots on tips to crown, nape and mantle; wings darker but tips to median and greater coverts often pale buff forming two distinct wing-bars. Underparts as adult but spots sooty-brown, less circular and more pointed or triangular, those on lower breast and flanks often smudged. First-winter bird more closely resembles adult except for retained outer greater coverts which are paler brown with indistinct pale orange to cinnamon-brown tips, contrasting with newer (replaced) darker inner coverts; primary coverts may also be narrow and slightly abraded, brownish with narrow pale edges. Pyle *et al.* (1997) stated that first-summer and adult birds can also show buff tips to greater coverts, but these are usually less numerous and not as distinct as in first-winter birds.

GEOGRAPHICAL VARIATION None. Monotypic.

VOICE Most frequent call is a liquid *pip pip pip* or *kuk kuk kuk* or a sharp harsh *pit pit pit* which becomes a *quirt quirt quirt quirt* or *quick-quick-quick*; may also give a plaintive *whew* when alarmed or in human presence, also a rattling *trurr* and a thin, high-pitched squeaky whistle *tsee tsee*; occasionally gives a hoarse descending *heer* recalling the similar but more abrupt *veer* note of Veery. In wintering areas usually best detected by sharp contact notes. Alarm call very infectious and quickly picked up and repeated by other individuals in area, usually taking flight away from the intruder. An accomplished singer with a beautiful and ethereal song consisting of a series of 3–4 clear fluty phrases broken by long pauses, given as either *cheer-uu-lee... cheer-uu-lee-ah... ch cheero cheero lee* or *EEEohlay... Ayolee... ahleelee... AAleahlolah... ilolilee*, usually initiated with a low *kuk kuk* and interspersed with call notes and terminating with a soft guttural trill (Bent 1949); song given at dusk may close with a repeated series of soft *pit pit* notes. Sings from mid- to canopy level in trees (mostly in proclamation of territory) but usually from a concealed perch, also from branches lower down in trees, bushes and bare branches, and even occasionally from the ground; most song given in early morning (including before dawn) and again at dusk, also often after summer rains. Comparison of songs from two well separated parts of the range found only minor and subtle differences (Whitney 1989). Song period, mostly late April to end of July but occasionally heard in subdued song in winter quarters in March, also sometimes sings into August, exceptionally to October.

STATUS AND DISTRIBUTION Common but breeding range has declined over the last 20 years and is probably still declining owing to loss and fragmentation of habitat and poor breeding success. Breeds in extreme south-east Canada and eastern U.S.A. from south-east Ontario and south-west Quebec east to New Brunswick and south-west Nova Scotia, where the range is slowly expanding; south in the U.S.A. along the eastern seaboard from New Brunswick, south-west Maine, New Hampshire and Vermont south to northern Florida and west to Minnesota, central (along the Missouri River) and south-eastern South Dakota, eastern Nebraska, eastern Kansas, eastern Oklahoma and eastern Texas; absent from coastal south-east Texas and southern Louisiana. May breed infrequently or erratically in northern Nova Scotia, southern Manitoba, eastern North Dakota and parts of the former range in west-central Kansas and Oklahoma (Roth *et al.* 1996).

In winter occasional to rare in southern Texas and northern Florida; more exceptionally, recorded in winter in North Carolina. In Mexico from southern Tamaulipas and south-east San Luis Potosí but more regularly or commonly along the Gulf coast slope from southern Veracruz south to the Pacific slope of eastern Oaxaca, most of the Yucatán Peninsula (especially Quintana Roo), Belize, Guatemala and Honduras south to Costa Rica and western Panama; casual or sparingly in eastern Panama but most numerous in Bocas del Toro and Chiriquí.

MOVEMENTS Migratory. Entirely deserts the breeding range and moves south or south-south-west to winter from southern Texas and occasionally

Florida through eastern Mexico south to Panama; sporadic or at much lower density in winter than in summer. Primarily a trans-Gulf migrant, rare in south-east Texas and north-east Mexico.

Disperses from breeding area usually to forest edges and second-growth areas in late July and August but remains well into the autumn in vicinity of breeding grounds with only small-scale movements in early September; most southward movement noticeable later in month and in October, and virtually all have left by November; occasional November (throughout month) records as far north as New Hampshire, New York, New Jersey and Pennsylvania. A frequent but generally uncommon vagrant and winter visitor to Bermuda from end of September to end of April; rare migrant through Cuba (14 September to 21 November) and small numbers may remain until February. Crosses Gulf of Mexico in broad front (small numbers follow the coastal route from southern Texas into northern Mexico) with departures from most of the eastern Texas coast east to western Florida in southerly or south-easterly direction, with arrival points from southern Veracruz to the western or northern Yucatán Peninsula (a crossing of 950–1300 km/ 593–812 miles). Arrives in wintering range in central Mexico from late August to October but most in October and early November; earliest date in Honduras in mid-October and in Panama at about the same time. Individuals often winter site-fidelity. Wintering birds in Mexico appear to defend small (c.150 m²) territories (Rappole et al. 1989).

Return movements (reverse of autumn direction) take place in April with many birds moving north out of the wintering range from western Panama to central Mexico in late March, but not unknown in central and northern parts of the breeding range (Virginia) in mid- to late March and two old specimen records in Louisiana in February; most arrivals in southern states are in early April with northern birds, e.g. Michigan and Wisconsin, back on territory from mid-April; in north-east U.S.A. most arrive in early May (rare in April); late birds still on passage in late May.

Rare overshooting visitor to Saskatchewan; vagrant to western U.S.A. (Idaho, Colorado and California – where there were 16 records to 1998, 8 in August–November and 6 in spring including 3 singing birds in June, and 2 in December, 1 remaining until March; also to western Mexico (Sinaloa, Distrito Federal, Guerrero and Tres Marias Islands, Nayarit), also Bermuda, Bahamas, Puerto Rico, Jamaica, Hispaniola, Cayman Islands, Curacao (Netherlands Antilles) (October 1951), El Salvador, Colombia (December 1975), Guyana, Falkland Islands (Port Stanley, February 1970), Iceland (October 1967), Azores (19th Century) and British Isles (October 1987).

HABITAT Breeding habitat is mostly thickly wooded areas of broadleaved trees (mostly northern hardwoods – beech, maple, hemlock, gums, dogwood, hornbeam and oaks) with areas of shrubby and decaying vegetation, including rhododendrons and blueberry, up to c.600 m (2000'), with plenty of shade and moist or wet hollows or close to swamps or streams; in some areas, however, also found in woods on drier hillsides. Within last 100 years has taken to nesting in town parks and large suburban gardens where suitable habitat exists. In winter occurs in the undergrowth or thickets of damp or moist lowland tropical forests and plantations such as bananas. In Costa Rica it winters in the humid forests of the upper tropical and lower subtropical zones but appears to avoid the dry forest area.

Habitat destruction and fragmentation of large tracts of forest in both summer and winter ranges have contributed greatly to the decline of the Wood Thrush over the latter years of the 20th century. Birds breeding in smaller areas of forest suffer increased effects of predation and nest parasitism, the latter particularly by Brown-headed Cowbird *Molothrus ater*, resulting in a poorer breeding success than those nesting in more extensively forested areas. In the wintering range the continuing depletion of tropical forests forces birds in suboptimal habitat where they are forced to wander and appear to suffer higher mortality (Roth et al. 1996).

BEHAVIOUR A generally shy, solitary and retiring bird of the forest floor, undergrowth and lower branches of trees where its presence often remains undetected until it calls or sings; in parts of the range has become a common bird of towns and edges of cities where it loses its shyness and often feeds in shrubbery and flowerbeds or on lawns. Usually alone but in winter may consort loosely with several other individuals and occasionally join mixed-species flocks. On the ground hops and walks in short agile steps in much the same manner as other smaller *Catharus* thrushes, but also runs fairly fast over short distances; nervous and always wary of intruders, frequently flicking wings and quick to take flight at the slightest provocation; flight direct or slightly undulating and more like a larger thrush, but lighter and usually faster with rapid twists as it dives into cover. When alarmed both adults and young raise the feathers on the crown and seem to be crested; can also fluff out the body feathers, creating a pot-bellied appearance (Lane & Jaramillo 2000). Feeds in trees and bushes, but mostly on the ground, investigating and turning over leaves with its bill; in winter quarters attends army ant swarms. Takes adult and larval invertebrates including ants, moths, spiders, millipedes, beetles, flies, bugs, snails, earthworms and cankerworms, also small salamanders; wild fruit food consists mostly of berries including gallberry, mulberry, pokeberry, grape, dogwood, blackberry, elderberry, spicebush, black gum, black cherry and honeysuckle, plus small amounts of cultivated fruit (Bent 1949).

BREEDING Season: May to mid-August. Nest: a large structure with a deep cup mostly of dry grasses or similar plant material such as weed stalks and leaves, similar to American Robin (161) in size and shape, usually with a middle layer of mud and lined with small brown rootlets; occasionally contains pieces of light-coloured paper, rags or pieces of long grass. Usually placed in a shaded area on or in the fork of a branch, occasionally against the trunk, between 0.6 and 22 m (2–72'; average 4 m/13') from the ground in a tree, bush, shrub or vine, exceptionally on the ground. Built by female only. The same nesting site is used in successive years. Eggs: 3–4, rarely 5; second or subsequent clutches usually only 2–3, variable in colour from pale green to pale blue or greenish-blue, recalling American Robin (161) but smaller and more pointed at one end. Incubation 11–14 days, solely by the female. Fledging period 12–13 days; young forage for themselves from 20–23 days, independent at c.30 days. Two broods when first early and successful.

Brood-parasitism by Brown-headed Cowbird, especially in mid-western U.S.A., considered to have a severe impact on breeding success especially for those breeding in small woods. Incidence of parasitism most prevalent in mid-western states and least in the eastern parts of the range (Hoover & Brittingham 1993).

MOULT Adults undergo complete post-breeding moult during July and August, exceptionally to mid-September, and can appear very short-tailed at the end of July. Juveniles have partial post-juvenile moult from c.6 weeks of age, late July to mid-September, when the feathers on the head and body, together with the lesser coverts and some of the median coverts and tertials, are renewed.

MEASUREMENTS Wing, male (n=100) 100–116, female (n=100) 96–112; tarsus 28.5–33; bill (culmen) male 16–19, female 16–18, (to skull) male 19–22, female 18.5–20.5. Weight, male April–September 44–54 g, female 43–54 g; male October 48–71 g, female 53–72 g (Cramp et al. 1988, Pyle et al. 1997).

REFERENCES Avise et al. (1980), Bent (1949), Hoover & Brittingham (1993), Lane & Jaramillo (2000), Pyle et al. (1997), Rappole et al. (1989), Roth et al. (1996), Slud (1964), Whitney (1989), Winker & Rappole (1988).

94 YELLOW-LEGGED THRUSH *Platycichla flavipes* Plate 59

Turdus flavipes Vieillot, 1818, *Nouv. Dict. Hist. Nat.* (nouv. ed.) 20: 277 – Brazil [= Rio de Janeiro *vide* Hellmayr (1934): 425].

IDENTIFICATION 22–23 cm (8½–9"). A distinctive black and grey (or all-black) thrush of the mountains of northern South America. Females are duller and much browner with streaky throats, pale bellies and undertail-coverts, but both sexes have dark eyes, yellow to orange eye-rings and bright yellow legs and feet (also bill when breeding). **Confusion species** Male unlikely to be confused with any other species once seen well. Glossy-black Thrush (134) is the only real confusion possibility but the all-black race of Yellow-legged only occurs on Tobago and is easily separated elsewhere by the grey upper- and underparts of mainland birds. Male of the closely related Pale-eyed Thrush (95) is all black with a pale bluish-white eye and no eye-ring. Female more likely to be confused with those of several other species, particularly Pale-eyed Thrush, and is best distinguished by the thin yellow eye-ring, paler underparts, prominent streaking on chin and throat, and (normally) yellow bill (some Yellow-legged females may have all-dark bills). Female Black-hooded Thrush (138) is also very similar with an all-yellow bill, but slightly larger with a slightly paler, more uniform tawny-brown belly and flanks, no white on lower belly and vent to undertail-coverts, and often a faintly darker head and breast-band as in the male. Both sexes of Cocoa Thrush (149) lack any olive tinge in the plumage, are much more rufous above and below, and the wings and tail are reddish-brown. Pale-vented Thrush (148) is extremely similar but allopatric, lacks an eye-ring and has an all-dark bill and white or whiter undertail-coverts. Clay-coloured Thrush (151) is paler and more uniformly buffish-brown, lacks an eye-ring, has a reddish-

brown eye, paler and more diffusely streaked throat and a greenish- or yellowish-olive bill. Black-billed Thrush (146) also lacks the yellow eye-ring and is generally darker brown with a whiter, brown-streaked chin and throat, cleaner and more extensively white belly, and all-dark bill.

DESCRIPTION Sexes differ. **Adult male** Entire head and nape to sides of neck, chin, throat and breast to upper belly jet-black. Mantle to uppertail-coverts and upper scapulars slate-grey with slightly darker tips to mantle and back, creating a faint scaly effect. Lower scapulars, all wing-coverts, alula and primary coverts black, flight feathers blackish-brown on innerwebs and tips of primaries. Underwing-coverts dark grey or blackish towards axillaries. Outer tail feathers shorter than central pair, black. Some variation in amount of black on underparts, confined to the breast in some whilst in others extending more to centre of upper belly; rest of belly and flanks (and sides of lower breast in some) dull grey, slightly paler or whiter on undertail-coverts, sometimes showing white tips creating a scaly or crescent-like pattern, thighs blackish-grey. Eye dark with thin, bright yellow or orange-yellow eye-ring. Bill, legs and feet bright yellow but in non-breeding season bill becomes darker or dusky-yellow. **Adult female** Forehead and crown to scapulars warm or rufous olive-brown, slightly deeper or warmer on edges of scapulars and wing-coverts, rump and uppertail-coverts slightly greyer; all wing-coverts and alula gingery-brown, flight feathers dark brown but secondaries and outer primaries edged paler or light warm brown, tertials dark brown fringed slightly paler. Underwing has bright pale orange coverts, silvery-brown flight feathers. Tail dark gingery-brown tinged olive.

322

Lores to eye pale gingery-buff becoming darker on face, cheeks and ear-coverts finely flecked pale-buff. Chin and throat pale whitish- or yellowish-buff and with a weak pale yellowish submoustachial and lower throat, diffusely streaked darker buff or brownish. Breast to upper belly and flanks warm brownish-buff becoming whiter on centre of belly to vent and greyer or browner on lower flanks; undertail-coverts yellowish-brown with buffish-white central shafts and dull grey or brownish tips. Bill mostly dark horn with thin yellowish culmen and tip. Eye dark with thin yellow eye-ring. Legs and feet yellow or yellowish-brown. **Immature** Juvenile has dark brown upperparts (slate-brown in juvenile male with black wings and tail) and pale orange spotting to crown, mantle, back and scapulars. Chin whitish becoming yellowish-buff on throat and yellowish on breast, spotted finely with brown on chin and throat, becoming dark brown bars and tips on breast and flanks. First-winter bird has yellowish-orange tips to median and greater coverts and first-summer birds still retain thin white tips to greater coverts, forming a thin wing-bar.

GEOGRAPHICAL VARIATION Five races; variation clinal but well marked in some races.

Race *venezuelensis* extremely similar to nominate (some birds indistinguishable) but, on average, is duller grey on mantle, back and belly; some whitish on chin; bill and eye-ring pale orange-yellow; female more olive on upperparts with grey edges to rump and uppertail-coverts, slightly paler on throat, greyish-white on belly, and white on undertail-coverts.

Female of race *polionota* similar to that of *venezuelensis* but slightly darker on upperparts and much paler or duller on upper- and underparts and less warm in overall tone, centre of belly whiter, undertail-coverts whitish to dull grey; male very similar to that of *venezuelensis* and nominate.

Male of race *melanopleura* variable: some resemble nominate, others are black or mostly black with dark grey on back to rump and uppertail-coverts, black on face to belly merging with grey on lower belly, flanks and vent (the blackest or highest density of black individuals of this race are found in north-east Venezuela). Female *melanopleura* similar to nominate or slightly duller brown below.

Male of race *xanthoscelus* entirely black and glossed slightly bluish in tone, but some, perhaps in worn plumage, show irregular patches of grey bases to feathers on mantle to back and rump, and on flanks and belly; female very similar, if not identical, to *melanopleura*.

VOICE Call an abrupt *tsrip* or whistled *sreeet* alarm note and a typical thrush-like *chuck* or *cluck*. Song a series of rambling, loud, liquid and clear thrush phrases, *tsreep, tsreh-tsreh-tsreh, tsrip-tsip-tsip*, or *swet to-weeea*, given repeatedly (or more squeaky in tone) at medium pace and interspersed with variable quality of mimicry (often poor) of other bird songs, those on Tobago including imitations of manakins and spinetails, those in Brazil covering a wider variety including alarm calls from seedeaters and kingbirds to Swallow-tailed Kite *Elanoides forficatus*, parrots and even a Budgerigar *Melopsittacus undulatus* (ffrench 1973, Hilty & Brown 1986, Ridgely & Tudor 1989). Sings from highest treetops usually within the canopy; song period (*xanthoscelus*) April to July. Frequently persecuted by bird fanciers for its fine song.

STATUS AND DISTRIBUTION Fairly common or locally common.

P. f. venezuelensis Santa Marta Mountains and the east slope of the East Andes in Norte de Santander, Colombia, to northern and western Venezuela south to the Gran Sabana and Alto Paragua.

P. f. melanopleura Sierras of north-east Venezuela in Anzoategui, Sucre and Monagas, Margarita Island and Trinidad. (Occasional all black birds occurring on Trinidad are considered to be native individual variations and not migrant *xanthoscelus* from neighbouring Tobago.)

P. f. xanthoscelus Tobago.

P. f. polionota Cerro Roraima of southern Venezuela (Bolívar) to western Guyana and extreme northern Brazil (Roraima).

P. f. flavipes South-east Brazil from southern Bahia to Rio Grande do Sul south to eastern Paraguay (Alto Paraná to Ñeembucu) and Misiones; possibly still in northern Argentina, where the only records are 2 specimens taken in October and November 1894, 12 males collected at two localities in northern Misiones in October 1953 and September–October 1954, and sight records by W. H. Partridge in Iguazú National Park in September 1959 (Hayes *et al.* 1994, M. Pearman pers. comm.).

MOVEMENTS Poorly known. May be a partial migrant to lower altitudes when not breeding, as it is absent from mountainous parts of the south of the range; may only have been a non-breeding austral migrant or visitor to Misiones between September and November (Hayes *et al.* 1994).

HABITAT Occurs between 500 and 2000 m (1650–6600′) but down to just over 300 m (1000′) on Tobago; in humid rain- and cloud-forests, also deciduous and secondary woodlands, coffee plantations and large gardens with tall trees. In parts of its range found in the same areas of forest as Eastern Slaty (136), Rufous-bellied (141) and White-necked (157) Thrushes.

BEHAVIOUR Usually alone or in pairs; generally shy and rarely seen well, males being more often detected by their singing. Forages in bushes and trees from mid-height to tree-tops, often congregating in fruiting trees. Feeds on small fruits and insects.

MOULT No information.

MEASUREMENTS Wing, male (n=16) 108–119, female (n=12) 105–111; tarsus 22.5–26; bill (culmen) 13–18; *venezuelensis* wing, male 108–118 (exceptionally to 106), female 107–110; *melanopleura* wing, male 105–118, female 105–113; *polionota* wing, male 113–123, female 116; *xanthoscelus* wing, male 112–121, female 106–116. Weight 59–72 g (ffrench 1973, Sick 1993); *melanopleura* (both sexes) 52–67 g.

REFERENCES ffrench (1973), Hayes *et al.* (1994), Hilty & Brown (1986), Ridgely & Tudor (1986), Sick (1993).

95 PALE-EYED THRUSH *Platycichla leucops* **Plate 59**

Turdus leucops Taczanowski, 1877, *Proc. Zool. Soc. London*: 331 – Ropaybamba, Peru.

IDENTIFICATION 20–22 cm (8–8¾"). An all-black thrush with a prominent pale eye, yellow bill, legs and feet of the mountains of Venezuela and much of the northern and central Andes. Females are much browner, lack the pale eye and are very similar to several other female thrushes of the region. **Confusion species** Male is almost unmistakable, being the only South American black thrush with whitish eyes. Female is very similar to female Yellow-legged (94) but lacks the yellow eye-ring and streaking on chin and throat, with warm or ginger undertail-coverts (yellowish with grey or brown tips in Yellow-legged). Female Glossy-black Thrush (134) is slightly larger, has a narrow yellowish eye-ring and entirely uniform brown underparts. Female Black-hooded Thrush (138) is also slightly larger, has a thin yellowish eye-ring, is paler buff-brown on the entire underparts and has dull yellow bill and legs. Both of the initially similar Black-billed (146) and Pale-vented (148) Thrushes have extensive areas of white on the belly, vent and undertail-coverts. Cocoa Thrush (149) is much more richly brown above and below, and has a white, darker-streaked chin and throat. Clay-coloured Thrush (151) has paler underparts, especially on chin and undertail-coverts, lacks any greyish on the belly and has a greenish- or yellowish-olive bill.
DESCRIPTION Sexes differ. **Adult male** Entirely glossy black in the field but at close range or in the hand shows metallic greenish-blue tinge to upper- and underparts and wings, sometimes when worn showing grey patches or bases to feathers of underparts. Bill bright yellow. Eye pale bluish-white with pale orange-yellow eye-ring. Legs and feet yellow or orange-yellow. **Adult female** Entire upperparts dark olive-brown, slightly paler or tinged or streaked paler with yellowish-buff on edges to primaries and on cheeks and ear-coverts. Chin and throat off-white or buff becoming streaked or spotted with brown on mid- to lower throat, often showing thin yellowish submoustachial and dark brown malar to sides of throat; breast to belly warm buff-brown, centre of belly greyish washed buff-brown and becoming warmer or ginger in tone on flanks and white on vent and undertail-coverts, latter often with pale brown fringes. Underwing-coverts variably pale to deep orange or cinnamon. Bill yellow or yellowish when breeding, brown at other times. Eye brown to grey-brown. Legs and feet dusky yellowish-brown to brown. **Juvenile** Dark brown; wings and tail blackish-brown. Heavily mottled and barred yellowish to orange buff on underparts with dark brown or blackish tips to the feathers forming bars or crescents. Pale tips to crown, nape and mantle

becoming pale buff central shaft-streaks to scapulars and pale orange-buff tips to median and greater coverts.
GEOGRAPHICAL VARIATION None. Monotypic.
VOICE Song a broken series of varying musical or squeaky phrases delivered in typical thrush style, *wheero-weet, chup-e, ez-t, e-ta, ti't, eez, cheur-ez-weet...*, often loudest in or with stress on opening phrase and interspersed with some higher-pitched notes and interrupted with brief or long pauses; some phrases are good imitations of other species and include mimicry of Swainson's Thrush (91) (Hilty & Brown 1986, Ridgely & Tudor 1989). Sings from tops of trees within the canopy; song period (Peru) at least October to November.
STATUS AND DISTRIBUTION Uncommon or possibly locally common (but overlooked). Coastal mountains of northern Venezuela, Miranda and Lara to the Andes of Táchira; in Colombia on the east slope of the East Andes in Meta and the West Andes in Valle, the upper Magdalena Valley in Huila and recently (August–September 1997) in Cauca province; south through the Andes (on both western – south to Pichincha and El Oro – and eastern slopes) in Ecuador, eastern Peru to northwest Bolivia (south to western Santa Cruz). Also the tepuis of Bolívar and Amazonas, southern Venezuela and adjacent areas of high ground (including the Merumé Mountains) in Guyana and Roraima, northern Brazil.
MOVEMENTS Mostly sedentary but has been recorded at lower altitudes in adjacent lowlands.
HABITAT Humid and damp montane and cloud forests of the subtropical zone; also well-wooded ravines, tall, dense secondary woodlands between 1000 and 2000 m (3300–6600'), exceptionally down to 900 m (2970') on Pacific slope in Valle, Colombia.
BEHAVIOUR Very retiring, wary and infrequently seen; usually singly or in pairs, but known to occur in small numbers at fruiting trees. Forages in trees from mid-height to tree-tops, though rarely in open canopy. Feeds on fruit, mainly berries.
BREEDING Virtually unknown. Season: probably April to June (based on a pair in Colombia carrying food and recently fledged young, both in June). Nest: mostly of moss with some plant and vegetable fibres, placed up to 3 m (c.10') in a tree (Hilty & Brown 1986).
MOULT No information.
MEASUREMENTS Wing (n=15) male 110–118, female 108–115; tarsus 23.5–27; bill 15–18. Weight apparently unrecorded.
REFERENCES Hilty & Brown (1986), Meyer de Schauensee & Phelps (1978), Ridgely & Tudor (1989).

96 GROUNDSCRAPER THRUSH *Psophocichla litsitsirupa* Plate 16
Merula litsipsirupa Smith, 1836, *Rep. Exped. Centr. Africa*: 45 – between the Orange River and the Tropic.

IDENTIFICATION 21.5–22 cm (8½–8¾"). A common and mostly resident thrush of open country and edges of acacia woodland in most of East and South Africa. Often appears larger and more robust than it is and the short tail and relatively broad wings add to this impression. A medium-sized thrush with a broadly striped face with pale lores and heavily spotted underparts; top of head to mantle, rump and scapulars grey-brown, flight feathers and tail slightly darker with a contrasting orange panel at the base of the flight feathers in flight. Recalls Mistle Thrush (126) but with a shorter tail. **Confusion species** Throughout most of East Africa unlikely to be confused with any other thrush except Spotted Ground-Thrush (45), which is a similar but shyer bird of dense coastal forests with two broad white wing-bars and a less strongly marked face. In the north of the range Song Thrush (124) occurs as an erratic visitor but is smaller, has a longer tail and shorter bill, is more horizontal in stance, lacks a strong face pattern and is browner above. Spotted Morning Warbler *Cichladusa guttata* is similar but smaller, has a bright reddish-brown tail (rounded at the tip) and a white chin and throat.

Taxonomic note The systematic position of this species, as the sole representative of a monotypic genus, has been discussed by a number of authors, mainly Milstein (1968), Hall & Moreau (1970) and Irwin (1984). Although showing affinities with several *Turdus* species, especially Song and Mistle Thrushes, Groundscraper appears to be a true ground-thrush possibly linked to *Zoothera* (on plumage and behavioural characters) but, despite its resemblance to Spotted Ground-Thrush, it lacks a contrasting underwing pattern. In addition, unlike any *Zoothera* thrush and very few *Turdus*, perched birds frequently give an elaborate wing-flick, revealing the bright orange panel at the base of the flight feathers. Whilst some *Turdus* thrushes have quick, nervous wing-flicks, none appears to have developed it as much as in this species. These differences, although slight and within the range of plumage and behavioural variation shown in *Turdus* as a whole, are considered sufficient to warrant placement in its own genus.

DESCRIPTION Sexes almost alike, female generally less heavily spotted below. **Adult** Forehead and crown to mantle, back and rump and scapulars grey or pale greyish-brown, often streaked darker brown; at close range forehead to mantle streaked finely darker. Wing-coverts dark brown finely edged pale buffish-brown, alula and primary coverts blackish-brown; flight feathers dark brown but bases orange-buff forming a contrasting panel on open wing in flight; edges to secondaries and tertials pale greyish-buff or buffish-brown. Underwing-coverts and axillaries pale orange-buff. Tail similar to flight feathers with paler buffish edges

and buffish-white tips to outer feathers. Lores to eye and area immediately behind eye whitish; fairly broad white or pale cream eye-ring (often not visible in front of eye), cheeks and ear-coverts pale cream or whitish, finely flecked darker, with blackish stripe above and below eye to centre of cheeks and ear-coverts; rear edge of ear-coverts also blackish, forming a distinct face pattern. Very thin line of blackish moustachial, broad white sub-moustachial and thin blackish-brown malar stripe. Chin and throat white, as are most underparts but sometimes with tinge of orange-buff on lower throat and breast, and greyish wash to breast and flanks; lower edge of malar merges into heavily spotted underparts on white ground extending to lower belly and flanks; thighs and undertail-coverts white. Bill fairly long, brown or brownish-horn, base of lower mandible and cutting edges to upper yellowish. Legs and feet dull straw-brown or pale yellowish-flesh. **Immature** First-winter birds are similar to adults but slightly browner on upperparts with yellowish-buff central shafts and dusky subterminal spots on head, nape, mantle and back, and with light buff fan-shaped tips to median and greater coverts, inner secondaries also showing orange-buff tips, and broad pale buff tips to outer tail feathers; underparts more heavily suffused pale orange-buff with smaller spots. First-year female generally less heavily spotted on underparts.

GEOGRAPHICAL VARIATION Four races; variation clinal and not well marked; some authorities, e.g. Irwin & Benson (1966) and Britton *et al.* (1980), treat *stierlingi* as synonymous with the nominate race. Race *simensis* has upperparts tinged more visibly brown and ground colour of underparts buff, heaviest on sides of breast, black spots bolder and more distinct, underwing-coverts deep buff. Race *stierlingi* very similar to both nominate *litsitsirupa* and *simensis* but has upperparts (in fresh plumage) paler grey and ground colour of underparts whiter or pale grey; bill averages slightly shorter than nominate. Race *pauciguttatus* is paler grey above, slightly longer in wing and bill, and whiter with fewer spots below.

VOICE Call an onomatopoeic *lit-sit-sirupa* or *tsi-tsi-tsi-rufa*, hence the scientific name, also a *tlee-tlo-tlee-tleek*; in flight frequently utters a dry or coarse note recalling similar call of Starling *Sturnus vulgaris*; also has a sharp *chee-chee* alarm call. Song is a brisk, ringing or whistling *sweet sweet, wip wip trrooee-tli-tli-trrooee, troo-troo, tzz tzz, tweet-tweet-chichiruchee-tru-chitrroo...*, also given as *pray-do pray-do now-then now-then*, and a more repetitive *pit-it-it-chi-chi-chee*, the phrases repeated but varying in tone (Benson 1946, Newman 1983, Ginn *et al.*, 1989) and often including mimicry of other species such as Didric Cuckoo *Chrysococcyx caprius* and Greater Blue-eared

325

Starling *Lamprotornis chalybaeus*. Sings late into the evening and after dusk, also in early dawn; often sings before or during rain and in the middle of storms.

STATUS AND DISTRIBUTION Locally common to scarce.

P. l. simensis Highlands of Eritrea and the western and central highlands of Ethiopia, south to about Yavello, Mega and Arero.

P. l. stierlingi Southern Zaire, north to about Baraka, Dogoda, Kabinda and Kabalo, and the western shore of Lake Tanganyika, central and eastern Angola, north-western, south-west and northern Zambia, Malawi (west of the Rift valley) to western and southern Tanzania (north to about the Ufipa Plateau and the Udzungwa Mountains).

P. l. pauciguttatus Namibia (north-central) and southern Angola to north-west Botswana and western Zimbabwe.

P. l. litsitsirupa Extreme north-east Cape Province east through Orange Free State and the Transvaal to Natal, Swaziland and southern Mozambique south of the Limpopo (but generally scarce); also east to central and eastern Botswana and north to southern and central Zimbabwe.

MOVEMENTS Largely resident or sedentary but in parts of the extensive range makes some seasonal movements, mainly during the non-breeding season, but poorly understood; occurs in south-west Tanzania August to November and absent from parts of the breeding range in Zimbabwe June to August; in South Africa becomes more numerous in Kruger National Park during December to February and there are extralimital records in the Orange Free State and northern Cape Province.

HABITAT Mostly open or light miombo woodland including acacia and savanna woodland or larger areas of moorland and dry heath with grass, also areas of junipers up to about 1900 m (6270') or 2200 m (7000'+) in Eritrea; in the south of its range found in dry brush of acacia and mopane woodlands, also thorn-scrub and bush to the edges of cultivation and open areas with relatively few trees, cleared areas, *Eucalyptus* plantations and shortly grazed grass swards, occasionally in parks and large gardens in towns.

BEHAVIOUR Has a very characteristic alert and erect or upright gait, either when settled on the ground or perched (as it frequently does) on roadside wires – an impression enhanced by the fairly short tail. Also has an odd habit of flicking one wing out at a time. Often quite tame and approachable; usually in pairs or small loose groups, and when on the ground hops and runs swiftly, stopping occasionally to look around; often perches on a rock. Has a quick dipping flight (recalling Mistle Thrush) with rapid wing-beats, and when alarmed takes flight to the top of a tall tree. Forages on lawns or short grass swards in clearings and edges of cultivation and roadsides; like many other thrushes flicks over dead and fallen leaves in search of food, and is also reported to scratch at the surface of the ground in the manner of a chicken. Feeds mostly on invertebrates including land molluscs, worms, beetles, grasshoppers, moths and their larvae, but has been known to take small lizards and skinks; also takes seasonally available berries such as mulberry and mistletoe.

BREEDING Season: March to July or August in the north and July or August to January in the south; may extend to March in Namibia and Botswana. Nest: a bulky cup of twigs, mud or dung, grass and roots together with pieces of paper, rags and string lined with plant tendrils, flower petals, feathers, plant down, cotton wool or whatever is available; usually placed up to 7 m (23') from the ground in a fork or along a branch of a tree; in South Africa often near the nest of Fork-tailed Drongo *Dicrurus adsimilis* (Maclean 1988). Eggs: 2–3, occasionally 4, pale turquoise, creamy- or greenish-blue and slightly glossy, spotted or blotched reddish-brown or pale to lilac-blue. Incubation period 14–15 days; by both parents. Fledging period 18 days; young fed by both parents and by up to two other adult helpers.

MOULT Adults in Botswana and Zambia begin postnuptial moult in late October and early November, usually completed in January; replacement of flight feathers usually in January. Juveniles moult into first-year plumage from early November.

MEASUREMENTS (n=43) Wing, male 121–140, female 120–130; tarsus, male 27–35, female 30–34; bill (culmen) 21–26; *pauciguttatus* wing (n=3) 123–132; *simensis* wing 122–142; bill 18.5–22; *stierlingi* wing 121–136; bill (culmen) 18–22. Weight (n=39) 67–84 g (Urban *et al.* 1997).

REFERENCES Benson (1946), Ginn *et al.* (1989), Hall & Moreau (1970), Irwin (1984), Irwin & Benson (1966), Maclean (1988), Milstein (1968), Newman (1983), Traylor (1965), Urban *et al.* (1997), White (1960).

97 AFRICAN THRUSH *Turdus pelios*   Plate 28

Turdus pelios Bonaparte, 1851, *Consp. Av.* (1850) 1: 273 – ex Asia centrali [= Fazoglu (Fazughli) Sudan].

IDENTIFICATION 20.5–23 cm (8–9"). The common thrush of much of West and Central Africa. Similar in plumage to both Kurrichane Thrush (99) and Olive Thrush (101) with which it forms a superspecies. In parts of its range behaviour recalls Song Thrush in Europe, feeding on the ground on lawns and large gardens; elsewhere a shy forest dweller. Slight differences in plumage between races but nominate birds are pale grey-brown above with darker grey-brown wings and tail; chin and throat variably streaked pale or grey-brown, breast to upper belly pale grey or washed orange, flanks variably pale buff to light orange, belly and undertail-coverts whitish. **Confusion species** From Kurrichane by grey-brown upperparts and lack of pale supercilium, white throat or belly, although race *centralis* has white on the throat; Kurrichane also has an orange eye-ring and heavy dark malar stripes, rich yellowish-buff on the flanks and underwing-coverts (grey-brown in nominate African but a deeper buff in Kurrichane race *verreauxi*). From Olive by its longer, slimmer shape, longer legs, slightly longer yellow (not orange) bill and generally paler, greyer plumage (rarely found in same habitat), Olive being much darker olive to olive-brown above, with breast pale buff to olive-grey, belly deep tawny to orange-buff, and usually with a more prominent yellow-orange eye-ring.

Taxonomic note: See Olive Thrush for discussion on racial divisions between African and Olive Thrushes.

DESCRIPTION Sexes alike. **Adult** Forehead to crown, nape, mantle, back and scapulars pale grey-brown washed olive, some showing darker centres to mantle and back; rump as back or slightly paler, uppertail-coverts also similar or browner. Tail as upperparts but with darker centres to central feathers. Median and greater coverts uniform with rest of upperparts or very slightly browner or finely tipped paler; alula and primary coverts dark brown, flight feathers also dark brown finely edged paler, tertials brown with outerwebs of outer feathers slightly paler. Underwing has coverts as flanks or slightly heavier orange, flight feathers also very pale orange at base. Lores dark brown, cheeks and ear-coverts as upperparts or slightly paler buff, mottled or finely flecked pale buff or buffish-orange; sides of throat variably streaked brown or grey-brown on pale buff, sometimes with heavier malar stripe. Centre of chin and throat white or pale buffish with short brown streaks. Breast pale grey, greyish-buff or dusky buffish-brown, sides of lower breast and flanks pale tawny-orange. Centre of lower breast and belly to undertail-coverts white; thighs pale buffish or greyish-white (some individuals have much whiter underparts than others and the orange is restricted in some to upper areas of flanks). Bill orange or yellowish-orange, sometimes with dark brown culmen. Eye light brown with a poorly developed yellowish or light orange eye-ring. Legs and feet pale brown, brownish- or greenish-yellow to dirty flesh-brown. **Immature** Juvenile very similar to adult, sometimes slightly paler above, but with pale orange central shaft-streaks on crown and mantle; heavily spotted or blotched dark brown on breast and upper flanks and has pale buffish-orange or light tawny tips to median and inner greater coverts. Face finely flecked or spotted light orange and brown; chin also white spotted pale brown or grey-brown; flanks washed greyish. Bill yellow.

GEOGRAPHICAL VARIATION Six races; variation clinal and not well marked. Most differences concern the tone of the upperparts, in particular the intensity of brown and degree of olive, but also the intensity of grey on the breast and the colour of the flanks and belly.

Race *centralis* is slightly darker than nominate above and more heavily streaked with brown on sides of whitish chin and throat; breast variable from plain or dingy grey to orange-grey or brownish, becoming peachy buffish-orange on sides of belly and flanks, and light or bright orange on underwing-coverts. Legs and feet variable from pale grey, dirty yellowish and yellowish-brown to dull brownish-green.

Race *saturatus* similar to two previous races but slightly darker above with less heavy streaks on sides of chin and throat, breast grey or greyish-buff becoming paler, whitish or dingy white on upper belly and underwing-coverts, flanks orange; some individuals (previously separated as *adamauae*) are variable and are dull buff to off-white and show no orange. Legs and feet dirty-yellowish flesh, brownish-yellow or grey-brown.

Race *chiguancoides* similar to *saturatus* with olive underparts tinged paler or ashy-brown but, on average, has slightly heavier streaks on sides of chin and throat; upperparts more olive and breast greyish, pale grey or greyish buff-brown; belly and flanks have orange replaced by off-white or dull whitish-buff (in worn plumage may show tinge of rich or fawn-buff on sides of lower breast and flanks); underwing-coverts pale tawny-orange or orange-rufous; vent and undertail-coverts white with grey-brown bases to some outer feathers. Bill yellow-orange to dull yellowish-brown; legs and feet pale brown, brownish-grey, grey to pinkish-yellow.

Two other races, *nigrilorum* and *poensis*, have restricted ranges in West Africa and are very similar to each other. Race *nigrilorum* is slightly browner or more greyish-brown above and has well-streaked chin and throat to sides of lower throat; breast and flanks pale greyish-brown, centre of lower breast and belly to undertail-coverts white, latter often with broad ashy-brown edges and tips; underwing-coverts pale tawny- or light orange but may be deeper or browner. Race *poensis* very similar with upperparts more heavily tinged olive and breast to upper belly and flanks more extensively dingy grey or greyish-brown.

Taxonomic note The races *nigrilorum*, *poensis*, *centralis* and *chiguancoides* have previously been classed as races of Olive Thrush (101), most recently by White (1970) and Mackworth-Praed & Grant (1973); Urban *et al.* (1997) included races *baraka*, *graueri* and *stormsi* (here classed as races of Olive Thrush) within African Thrush; *chiguancoides*, *saturatus* and *nigrilorum* have also been classed (e.g. Bannerman 1936) as races of Kurrichane Thrush.

VOICE Most frequently given notes are a thin clear whistle and a hoarser *chuk* or *churp*, either singly or doubly, usually uttered on or before taking flight. Alarm call is a repeated or harsh *chuk-ukukukukuk*, rising slightly in tone. Song a long melodious series of clear phrases and slurred whistles broken by some hesitant guttural notes, most phrases repeated at least twice and occasionally as many as five times: *tureep tureep tureep weeu-weeu-weeu-cureep-churEEP*, or variations such as *trierieu trierieu ureetew-ureetew... slurreeep slur-reeep swrp-swrp-swrp, weet-tweeyu tweeyu...* (Zimmerman *et al.* 1996). Reported to mimic other species (Urban *et al.* 1997). Song given from before dawn and throughout the day from mid-February or March to early October (West Africa, Uganda) from the branches of small trees or shrubs; may sing all year in parts of its range but most frequently during the wet season and least in the dry.

STATUS AND DISTRIBUTION Seasonally or locally common, very common in Uganda; *poensis* uncommon or scarce.

T. p. pelios Central and northern Zaire (mostly north of the Congo River) north to western and central-southern Sudan (south of about 14°N to a line from Tambura to Shambe and the Baro River) and east to Eritrea and central and eastern Ethiopia. Possibly also this race (or *centralis*) west to the Central African Republic, southern Chad and eastern Cameroon.

T. p. centralis Southern and south-east Sudan (south of *pelios*), western and southern Ethiopia to western Kenya (Mt Elgon east to the Kerio valley, Kabarnet, Baringo and Elmenteita to Lake Nakuru and more locally to the Laikipia Plateau), Uganda, Rwanda, Burundi, eastern Zaire (where intergrades with *pelios*) and north-west Tanzania. Probably also this race (or nominate *pelios*) north and west to the Central African Republic, southern Chad and eastern Cameroon.

T. p. chiguancoides Senegal (south of about 14°N) and the Gambia east to southern Mali, south through central Guinea to Sierra Leone, northern (montane) and coastal Liberia, Ivory Coast (commonest in Guinea zone; absent in south), northern Ghana, central and southern Burkina Faso and extreme south-west Niger; intergrades with *saturatus* in western Ghana.

T. p. saturatus Western Ghana (intergrades with *chiguancoides* in the west) east to Nigeria (less common north of the Guinea zone) and north to about Filingue in extreme south-west Niger, Cameroon including the Cameroon highlands (but not the higher altitudes of Mt Cameroon and Adamawa plateau or the drier parts of the east and extreme north) south to Gabon and east through Congo to north-west Zaire (north of the Congo River) where it intergrades with nominate *pelios*. Birds in eastern Cameroon may also be nominate *pelios* or *centralis*.

T. p. nigrilorum Mt Cameroon above 750 m (2500'), rarely down to 515 m (1700'). Intermediates with *saturatus* occur on the lower slopes (generally below 600 m) of Mt Cameroon (Serle 1962) and the Bamenda highlands.

T. p. poensis Southern and eastern highlands of Bioko (Fernando Po).

MOVEMENTS Mostly resident but clearly undertakes some seasonal and probably short-distance movements, as only recorded in some parts of the range during the rains, e.g. a wet-season visitor to the northern/Sahelian parts of the range; race *chiguancoides* is a wet-season visitor to the middle and upper reaches of the Gambia River and north-central Mali, coastal Liberia, Ghana and Chad, and increases in numbers in northern Nigeria in the wet

season (March to October) and south to around Ibadan in the dry season (January to March).

HABITAT A mixture of dry, moist, humid and damp forests, also riverine forests and open woodlands, clearings and forest edges including villages, usually between 700 and 2000 m (2300–6600'), *nigrilorum* occurring in montane forest to 2880 m (9500'), but in parts of West Africa *saturatus* occurs between sea-level and 455 m (1500'), exceptionally to 695 m (2300'), in dense coastal scrub, rocky outcrops, edges of cultivated areas (especially yam farms and banana plantations), thickets, savanna, golf-courses and (in parts of the range) gardens in town and city suburbs.

BEHAVIOUR Usually alone or in pairs; generally rather shy and retiring, preferring the cover and shade of overgrowing vegetation but several – up to a dozen or slightly more – may gather at fruiting trees. Forages low down in vegetation or on the ground where it flicks over dead leaf-litter and vegetation, but feeds in the open when undisturbed; frequently feeds in typical fashion in the open on lawns and in large gardens where it recalls the actions and feeding behaviour of a Song Thrush in similar habitat in Europe; also reported to crack snail shells on a stone anvil (Mackworth-Praed & Grant 1973, Walsh & Walsh 1983). Forages mostly in the early morning but also again in early afternoon and at dusk; feeds mainly on fruit (reported to favour that of the nim tree *Azadarichta indica* in West Africa, including figs and papayas, berries and seeds (red peppers), but also worms and some insects and their larvae, ants, beetles, millipedes, snails, earthworms and occasionally small fish.

BREEDING Season: nests recorded in all months (Uganda) but most breeding activity occurs in the wet season (March–September/October in West Africa) and April–July in Ethiopia, November–March elsewhere. Nest: a bulky cup of rotted or coarse grasses, plant fibres, moss and mud lined with fine dry grasses, leaves, plant fibres and roots, usually placed (often conspicuously) up to 12–13 m (c.40') but mostly below 10 m (33') from the ground along a horizontal branch or in the fork of a tree or a clump of vines (usually in fruit trees), bush or banana palm; may utilise previous nest or that of another species, e.g. Laughing Dove *Streptopelia senegalensis*. Eggs: 2–3, occasionally 4, pale blue, bluish-green or more rarely cream and slightly glossy, with variable fine reddish-brown or brown spots or speckling and larger blotches of lavender or pale purple (in some no blue ground colour is visible and egg appears to be entirely rufous). Incubation by female only but nestlings fed by both parents. Two broods.

MOULT Race *saturatus* is in worn plumage in eastern Nigeria in August and completing moult in September and October (Serle 1957). In mountains of northern Liberia *chiguancoides* recorded in wing moult from January to May.

MEASUREMENTS Wing, male 105–121, female 103–118; tarsus, male 25–32, female 27–29; bill (culmen) male 17–22, female 16–20, exceptionally 24.5; *centralis* wing 105–122; *chiguancoides* wing, male 112–125, female 104–115; *saturatus* wing, male 107–122, female 106–120; *nigrilorum* wing, male 109–120, female 104–118; tarsus, male 33–35, female 33–34. Weight, male 46–70, female 51–72 g (Maclean 1988, Mackworth-Praed & Grant 1960, 1973, Serle 1962, Urban *et al.* 1997).

REFERENCES Bannerman (1936), Mackworth-Praed & Grant (1960, 1973), Maclean (1988), Serle (1957, 1962), Urban *et al.* (1997), Walsh & Walsh (1983), Zimmerman *et al.* (1996).

98 BARE-EYED THRUSH *Turdus tephronotus*　　　Plate 30

Turdus tephronotus Cabanis, 1878, *J. Orn.* 26: 205, 218, pl. 3, fig. 2 – Tiva River and Ndi, Taita, Kenya.

IDENTIFICATION 20–21.5 cm (8–8½"). A grey to grey-brown thrush with distinctive eye-markings and a patchy distribution in north-east Africa. The head and upperparts are grey with darker grey-brown wings and tail. Has an area of bare pale yellow skin around the eye, with blackish streaks on the throat and a greyish breast becoming deep orange or orange-rufous on the lower breast, belly and flanks. **Confusion species** Most likely to be confused with the very similar African (97), Kurrichane (99) and Olive (101) Thrushes, Kurrichane being closest. All three lack the diagnostic pale yellow around the eyes. African has orange flanks and a white belly. Olive is darker on the head and olive above, with a narrow yellow-orange eye-ring, brownish throat with less distinct streaks, grey-brown olive-tinged breast, and (on *abyssinicus*, the race in most of the range of Bare-eyed) more white on centre of belly. Kurrichane has greyish olive-brown upperparts, narrow orange eye-ring, dark malar stripes and whitish submoustachials, greyish-buff breast, orange on lower breast and flanks, and white centre of belly to undertail-coverts.

DESCRIPTION Sexes almost alike, female slightly paler below. **Adult** Forehead and crown to mantle, back, scapulars and rump deep grey, slightly paler on head and nape, some feathers on mantle and scapulars having darker bases showing; uppertail-coverts darker grey. Tail dark grey with slightly paler grey edges to outer feathers. Median coverts dark grey finely edged paler, greaters similar but with darker centres, alula, primary coverts and flight feathers dark grey or grey-brown finely edged paler or light ashy-grey, tertials similar but broadly edged pale ashy-grey. Axillaries and underwing-coverts deep or bright orange. Lores dark grey, with broad area of pale yellow skin around eye tapering into ear-coverts; cheeks and ear-coverts otherwise ashy-grey. Sides of chin and throat whitish streaked blackish, centre of lower throat to breast dull grey (forming band across breast) becoming tinged orange on centre of breast, lower breast to belly and flanks deep orange or orange-rufous, lower belly and vent white (may show pale brown tips), undertail-coverts as flanks or slightly paler. Bill bright orange-yellow to orange-brown. Legs and feet orange-yellow. **Immature** First-year bird similar to adult but greyer below and mottled with dark spots on breast and upper belly.

GEOGRAPHICAL VARIATION Monotypic, but some clinal variation with northern birds some-times slightly darker grey on upperparts and breast, streaks on the throat more pronounced, and orange on the belly deeper; proposed as race *australoabyssinicus* (Benson 1942).

VOICE Call a soft mellow or whinnying *tu*, *tew* or *que* repeated several times when on the ground; also a rattling *chirrrrrr* and more sibilant *tsick* or *chusick* alarm note repeated several times in quick succession. The song is typically thrush-like in quality, a short series of quavering trills followed by more musical or higher-pitched notes: *quir-rrrrrrrr turr chyik*, *thro-throo-thrit* or *squirrrrr-gyurrr tyip-tyip tew-tew-tew* or *kewerr-kewrr slleep-ee-ee*; also a *huu-huu-tsri-tsritsritsritsrisri* (Mackworth-Praed & Grant 1960, Zimmerman *et al.* 1996). Sings from the tops of trees.

STATUS AND DISTRIBUTION Uncommon or locally common. Breeds from southern Ethiopia and southern Somalia (west of about 46°N) south through eastern and east-central Kenya to Wajir, the Ndotos, Horr valley south to Kajiado, Namanga, the Tsavo and Taita region (but possibly very thinly distributed or absent from the central areas) to north-east and east-central Tanzania (east of Mt Kilimanjaro) and south-west to Dodoma.

MOVEMENTS Little known but considered to wander throughout the range in the non-breeding season; there are records from Dar-es-Salaam and more recently from Selous Game Reserve in south-central Tanzania, a considerable distance south of the previous known range (Britton 1980).

HABITAT Occurs mainly from sea-level to 1600 m (5300') in fairly dry or semi-arid country in light or open woodlands, thornbush, rocky scrub, grass-lands with woods or thickets, orchards, edges of cultivation and occasionally large gardens. Occurs in coastal scrub-forest in the Mombasa area (and possibly elsewhere along the coast) of Kenya.

BEHAVIOUR Little known; usually alone or in parties of up to 3, fairly shy and unobtrusive but may become confiding near buildings. Has a characteristic habit of frequently quivering or nervously vibrating the tail when perched. When disturbed flies rapidly but silently into thick cover. Forages mostly on the ground close to or under thick clumps of bushes or other vegetation, and feeds mostly on insects and their larvae, in particular beetles and caterpillars, occasionally wild fruit.

BREEDING Season: March–June and November–December. Nest: a cup of grasses, twigs, roots and dead leaves, lined with finer grasses and roots, usually placed some way (up to 3.5 m/10') from the ground in a tree or bush. Eggs: 2–3, pale bluish-green and marked at the upper end with spots or blotches of dark rufous, grey and violet (Mackworth-Praed & Grant 1960).

MOULT Almost unknown. Adults in complete post-breeding moult in July.

MEASUREMENTS (n=31) Wing, male 100–115, female 105–114; tarsus 27.5–31.5; bill (culmen) 21–27.5. Weight (n=12) 45–55 g (Urban *et al.* 1997).

REFERENCES Benson (1942), Britton (1980), Mackworth-Praed & Grant (1960), Urban *et al.* (1997), Zimmerman *et al.* (1996).

99 KURRICHANE THRUSH *Turdus libonyanus* Plate 30

Merula libonyanus Smith, 1836, *Rep. Exped. Centr. Africa*: 45 – near Kurrichane, western Transvaal.

IDENTIFICATION 21–23 cm (8¼–9″). A large, relatively long-tailed thrush of southern Africa, similar in plumage to two other African thrushes – Olive (101) and African (97), with which it forms a superspecies. Forehead and crown greyish-brown, rest of upperparts including wings and tail pale or ashgrey tinged olive, rump slightly greyer than mantle, with a large bright orange-yellow bill and narrow orange eye-ring, white submoustachials bordered with distinct or interrupted black malar stripes to sides of lower throat, breast pale grey or greyish-buff, flanks and sides of belly pale to bright orange, centre of belly to undertail-coverts white. **Confusion species** Most likely problem is Olive Thrush, which is darker above and, according to race, usually heavier or more brightly marked below, from dull to deep or bright orange on the belly and brown on breast, lacking any white on the face or the strong malar stripes. Olive is more a forest thrush, Kurrichane more an open (mixed or light) woodland bird, but the two may be in close contact in thickets or forest clearings. African is also very similar but is slightly browner above and paler below, sides of throat streaked pale buff-brown, breast pale grey to greyish-tawny, flanks pale orange with white centre of breast to undertail-coverts. Songs of all three differ. Bare-eyed Thrush (98) is also similar but greyer above, with a large orange-yellow area around the eye and orange on the underparts extending across most of the belly.

DESCRIPTION Sexes almost alike. **Adult male** Forehead and crown greyish-brown (with slightly darker centres) becoming slightly paler greyish tinged olive on nape to mantle, back and scapulars; rump and uppertail-coverts slightly paler. Tail as upperparts but outer feathers slightly paler brown. Wings slightly darker grey-brown than upperparts, alula blackish-brown, primary coverts grey-brown, edges to outer primaries and secondaries pale orange-buff; edges to tertials greyish-buff. Pale grey or tinged buffish-brown supercilium, lores as cheeks or streaked slightly darker, eye-ring narrow and bright orange, extending as small post-ocular spot (in non-breeding season this area becomes paler or yellow). Cheeks and ear-coverts as forehead and crown but flecked or streaked paler, submoustachials white or yellowish-white extending broadly to sides of lower throat and bordered on sides of throat by long black malar stripes from sides of chin (on some –

perhaps exceptionally or in older birds – the black spots form broken gorget across lower throat). Centre of chin and throat white or pale yellowish-white, breast pale grey or greyish-buff. Sides of lower breast yellowish or light orange becoming orange or orange-rufous on flanks and sides of belly to underwing-coverts (where often deeper orange), centre of lower belly to vent and undertail-coverts creamy- or whitish-yellow. Bill fairly large and prominent, bright orange-yellow (paler in non-breeding season), culmen and tip often dusky or brownish. Eye brown. Legs and feet variable: light grey, grey-brown, pale brown, pale pinkish-flesh, yellowish-brown and light orange-brown. **Adult female** As male but slightly smaller, browner and duller grey-brown on lower throat and upper breast. **Immature** First-year bird similar to adult but streaked on crown and spotted rusty-buff on tips of mantle and scapulars, wing-coverts with orange-buff tips and underparts paler, with less well-defined malar stripe and blackish-brown spots on breast to belly and flanks, lower mandible with yellow base. Bill dark horn,

GEOGRAPHICAL VARIATION Five races; variation clinal and very slight.

Race *tropicalis* differs very little from nominate but, on average, has upperparts slightly paler or greyer and tinged olive-brown, with orange-buff edges to lower scapulars and tips to greater coverts, greyish-buff breast becoming orange (paler than nominate but darker than *verreauxi*) on lower breast and flanks (tinged paler or buffish when worn), and rich orange- or yellowish-buff underwing-coverts; centre of belly to undertail-coverts white.

Race *verreauxi* is also paler grey on upperparts and central tail feathers, but innerwebs of flight feathers buff or buffish-brown and show well in flight; ear-coverts streaked grey-brown and whitish, upper breast greyish-buff becoming yellowish-orange or orange-buff on breast and flanks, underwing-coverts orange, eye-ring and bill slightly deeper orange than nominate and legs and feet bright yellow.

Race *chobiensis* (considered by some authorities, e.g. Mackworth-Praed & Grant [1963], Urban *et al.* [1997], to be an intermediate, synonymous with *verreauxi*) has slightly paler or greyer upperparts, breast also slightly paler than nominate but flanks as nominate.

Race *peripheris* only marginally differs from (and may be synonymous with) *verreauxi* by paleness (on average) of underparts, but some individuals deeper orange and upper breast dark grey-brown; upperparts, including wings and tail, darker or browner than nominate.

VOICE Call a loud sharp whistling *peet-peeoo*; also a *tsee-tse-oo* or *pss-chew, pss-chewi* or *tse-tseeoo* often repeated, a high-pitched *witteet, witteet*, and a soft *tsit* often uttered just prior to taking flight; alarm note is a thin sharp tit-like *tsit* or *pit-pit – pitchoo*. Song a mellow series of phrases comprising trills and whistles, usually given in short phrases of 4–10 notes beginning with or containing *sweet-wit-wit-weet* and *sweety-weet-weet* and *wip-weedle, weedle, weety-wip-weet*, often including mimicry of other birds' notes (Maclean 1988); or a pleasant *rrreeeee treeeeee qurileeeee* or higher *tsurrreeeeee* (*tropicalis*) (Zimmerman *et al.* 1996). Usually sings from tall trees; frequently sings after rain, often before dawn and again in the evening, and occasionally on moonlit nights. Main song period spring to early summer.

STATUS AND DISTRIBUTION Common or locally common resident throughout most of its range, but scarce or uncommon in the north-west.

T. l. tropicalis South-east Burundi and north-west Tanzania (where uncommon or discontinuous to about Mwanza and the Minziro Forest Reserve to central, southern (where more numerous) and north-east Tanzania (north to about Amani and the East Usambara foothills, south through Zambia (except the west), Zimbabwe (except the south-west) and most of Mozambique (north of the Limpopo River) to northern Transvaal, South Africa.

T. l. verreauxi Southern Zaire from the Kasai River and Moba on Lake Tanganyika south to west-central and south-east Angola (Malange, Cuanza Sul, Lunda to western Huila and Moxico).

T. l. chobiensis Northern Botswana (Okavango delta east to about Francistown) and adjacent areas of north-east Namibia and the Caprivi Strip and western Zambia.

T. l. libonyanus Eastern and south-east Botswana (mostly east of a line from Francistown south to Gaborone) and the Transvaal to Swaziland and Natal, South Africa.

T. l. peripheris Central and southern Natal (south to about Transkei), South Africa, north to about Maputo, southern Mozambique.

MOVEMENTS Mostly resident or sedentary, but some birds move short distances, and there are a few records from the northern Cape Province, Orange Free State (5 records) and Lesotho (1 record).

HABITAT A variety of woodland habitats from acacia savanna and light bush (miombo) to small woods, *Brachystegia*, mopane and second-growth areas and clearings in evergreen forests, edges of cultivated areas in orchard-bush, parks and large gardens in towns and suburbs, particularly those with tall trees; also mangroves.

Occurs from sea-level to about 1900 m (6270') but mainly at 900–1500 m (2970–4950') in Malawi. Mostly a bird of lowland forest, especially along rivers, but ranges up to 2200 m (7260') in Zimbabwe, where it occurs commonly in *Brachystegia* woodlands, but has adapted well throughout the range to non-native plantations like coconuts, gums, wattle and pine.

BEHAVIOUR Generally a shy, secretive forest dweller but becomes tame and approachable in suburban gardens, safari camps and cultivated areas. Usually alone or in pairs; breeding territories are defended aggressively throughout the year. Forages on the ground and has a characteristic gait of running with head held forward and long tail flat, then stopping upright and alert, searching for prey. When alarmed, flicks tail in nervous agitated manner, usually then flying into cover of bushes or low trees; flight strong, swift and direct. Feeds mainly on invertebrates and their larvae, including beetles, grasshoppers, crickets, spiders, molluscs and worms, but also small lizards and some fruit such as wild figs and berries; has been known to feed on ripening avocado pears and readily comes to bird-tables in gardens to take bread, cheese and household scraps.

BREEDING Season: has been found nesting in every month from August to March but most records are from September to January. Nest: a large, untidy, deep-cupped structure of grass, twigs and mud often including lichens, flower-heads, paper, string, cotton and pieces of rags, and lined with finer plant material and mud, usually up to 10 m (33') from the ground and secured with mud on a branch or in the fork of a tree, in a mistletoe clump or saprophytic fern occasionally in the gutter of a house; used traditionally over a number of years with new nests being built on top of the previous year's; also builds on old nests of other species such as Laughing Dove *Streptopelia senegalensis* and Fiscal Shrike *Lanius collaris*. Eggs: 2–3, exceptionally 4, pale greenish, turquoise or deep blue, spotted or speckled reddish-brown or bluish-grey (white with reddish-brown spots recorded). Incubation period 11–14 days; by female only. Fledging period 12–15 days. An occasional host to the Red-chested Cuckoo *Cuculus solitarius* (Pitman 1961). Two or three broods (Ginn *et al.* 1990).

MOULT Juveniles in Botswana moult from worn plumage to first-year plumage in early February; adults at the same time of year are either in heavily worn plumage or have completed the post-breeding moult (Traylor 1965).

MEASUREMENTS (n=43) Wing, male 110–127, female 106–119; tarsus 26–33; bill (culmen) male 16–21, female 17–24; *tropicalis* wing 101–125; *chobiensis* wing 107–114; *verreauxi* 109–117; *peripheris* 103–123. Weight (n=66) 51–82 g (Dowsett 1965, Urban *et al.* 1997).

REFERENCES Dowsett (1965), Ginn *et al.* (1990), Pitman (1961), Traylor (1965), Zimmerman *et al.* (1996).

100 OLIVACEOUS THRUSH *Turdus olivaceofuscus* Plate 31
(Gulf of Guinea Thrush)

***Turdus olivaceofuscus* Hartlaub, 1852,** *Abh. Geb. Naturw. Hamburg* **2(2): 49, pl. 3 – São Tomé.**

IDENTIFICATION 24 cm (9–9½″). Endemic to the Gulf of Guinea islands of São Tomé and Príncipe, although the race *xanthorhynchus* on Príncipe is extremely scarce (and until recent sightings in 1996 considered possibly extinct) and very rarely observed. Head and upperparts, including wings and tail, brown to olive-brown; underparts heavily barred with pale bases and dusky-brown tips. The nominate bird on São Tomé is fairly common in the moist forests; the slightly darker race on Príncipe was discovered in 1901 and since then seen on only c.4 occasions (J. Baillie pers. comm.). **Confusion species** No other thrush occurs on either island and it is unlikely to be confused with any other species.

DESCRIPTION Sexes alike. **Adult** Entire upperparts deep brown or olive-brown, forehead to crown and nape slightly darker. Tail brown tinged olive on central feathers, outers slightly paler. Median and greater coverts as on upperparts but edges to flight feathers and tertials pale olive-buff, innerwebs slightly darker brown; underwing has coverts light or pale orange to slightly deeper orange, some feathers tipped brown, secondaries pale creamy. Face to sides of nape and neck brown as upperparts. Chin and throat to upper breast pale whitish- or buffish-brown, heavily spotted or speckled brown; centre and lower breast to belly and flanks white at base and broadly tipped brown, forming bars; more closely barred on flanks; undertail-coverts whitish and barred brown (sometimes more heavily barred on breast and flanks). Bill fairly large and robust, dark brownish-horn with yellow-brown cutting edges. Legs and feet dark brown to darker grey, soles yellow. **Immature** First-year bird very similar to adult but some fine pale central shafts to upperparts and more spotted than barred on underparts, with dark spots at tips of feathers; very fine pale orange-buff tips to median and greater coverts. Throat greyish with grey-brown tips or darker spots. Bill largely horn-brown becoming yellowish towards tip.

GEOGRAPHICAL VARIATION Two races; variation not well marked. Race *xanthorhynchus* is like nominate but slightly smaller and darker above, underparts with whiter bases and broad dusky margins or tips to throat, browner on belly and vent; underwing-coverts paler orange. Bill, legs and feet yellower (legs and feet pale brown on some).

VOICE Usually silent but in flight gives a soft *zeek*, *zik* or *chik*; alarm note is a low *chup* or *chupchup*. Song is a slow, desultory piping not unlike some of the notes given by Blackbird (111): *jerooeee*, *pwee*, *teroooee*, *peewee...* or *tyoo-tooeeyoo-teeyoo-tss-tss*, varying to *twee-tooeeyoo-teewoh-tooee-too-tss-trrr-trrr-tss*, some notes more slurred

than others and repeated at intervals (Snow 1950, Urban *et al.* 1997). Song frequently uttered, especially at dawn and dusk.

STATUS AND DISTRIBUTION The nominate race is fairly common; *xanthorhynchus* is extremely rare and only recently recorded again following a gap of over 50 years (Christy & Gascoigne 1996), with population estimation at under 1,000 individuals (J. Baillie pers. comm.). Species considered Near-Threatened (Collar *et al.* 1994); race *xanthorhynchus* qualifies for inclusion in at least Vulnerable category.

T. o. olivaceofuscus São Tomé, Gulf of Guinea.
T. o. xanthorhynchus Restricted to south-west Príncipe, Gulf of Guinea.

MOVEMENTS Sedentary.

HABITAT Moist forests, forest edges and woodlands (including savanna woodlands). On São Tomé also in cocoa and coffee plantations and throughout the rainforest up to about 2000 m (6600′); the Príncipe race occurs in mid- to low-level forests of the coastal lowlands and adjacent montane slopes.

BEHAVIOUR Usually alone or in pairs; not shy (birds on Príncipe allowed observer to within 2 m/6′) but often wary or cautious; may be crepuscular or more obvious in early morning and towards dusk. Keeps low down in understorey vegetation but also up to lower mid-height in forest trees. Forages on the ground and in shrubs or tops of tall trees; on the ground hops and searches through leaf-litter in typical thrush fashion – hopping a few feet, then stopping to look and listen. In flight the wings make light rustling or vibrating noise. Food mainly large insects and their larvae, mostly beetles, but also worms and snails; also small lizards and some seasonally ripe fruit, e.g. figs.

BREEDING Little known. Season: end July to January, mostly in the latter half of the period. Nest: a bulky cup-shaped structure of dry or rotten vegetation, roots, ferns and plant fibres including palm threads, grasses and leaf-stems, usually placed up to 4 m (13–14′), exceptionally 12 m (40′), from the ground in dense vegetation, often along a horizontal branch or in bamboo clumps or cocoa tree. Eggs: 2, greenish or bluish-green, erratically spotted or speckled with reddish-brown.

MOULT No information.

MEASUREMENTS Wing, male 123–136, female 122–128; tarsus, male 39–43, female 38–41; bill (to feathers) male (n=3) 21–22, female (n=6) 19.5–23; (to skull) male 24–29, female 21–28; *xanthorhynchus* (n=1) wing 120; tarsus 38.5; bill 23. Weight (n=6) 77–92 g (Urban *et al.* 1997).

REFERENCES Christy & Gascoigne (1996), Snow (1950).

101 OLIVE THRUSH *Turdus olivaceus*

Turdus olivaceus Linnaeus, 1766, *Syst. Nat.* (ed. 12) 1: 292 – Cape of Good Hope.

IDENTIFICATION 20.5–24 cm (8–9½"). A medium-sized thrush widely distributed over much of East and southern Africa, with many races. Closely related to both the African Thrush (97) and Kurrichane Thrush (99) with which it forms a superspecies. Nominate birds (from South Africa) have the head and upperparts dark olive-brown, with wings and tail blackish-brown. Chin and throat white streaked blackish-brown, breast pale buffish, grey or light olive-brown becoming yellowish-orange on the belly and flanks, under-tail-coverts white. Some variation in the intensity of the colour of the upper- and underparts through-out the range; two races, *helleri* and *ludoviciae*, are particularly distinctive. **Confusion species** Most likely to be confused with Kurrichane and African Thrushes. From Kurrichane by lack of white (except in two races from parts of East Africa) on chin, throat and centre of breast and belly, has orange lower breast, belly and flanks, no heavy malar stripes; may also show a pale super-cilium. From African (ranges overlap in Ethiopia, northern Uganda, central Kenya, north-west Tan-zania and eastern Zaire) by much darker upper-parts lacking any grey (except in two races from central and north-east Africa) and extensive yel-lowish-orange (variable between races) on the underparts; the bill of Olive is also slightly smaller and deeper orange (not as yellow), and its eye-ring (only prominent in some races) is bright orange, duller in African (see also African Thrush for struc-tural differences). Songs of the two differ in struc-ture and phrases but those of Central African races generally little known and may show dialectal variation. Differs from Bare-eyed Thrush (98) by olive-brown (not grey or grey-brown) upperparts, yellowish orange-buff (not grey) breast and lack of a large bare eye-patch. Told from all rock-thrushes of the region (5–8) by larger size and longer shape, bright yellow-orange bill and olive upperparts lacking any grey on the head.

Taxonomic note This species and the very sim-ilar African Thrush are found throughout almost all sub-Saharan Africa and are absent only from the densest areas of equatorial rainforest and the drier areas of the south-west. Because they are so alike they continue to present a problem to tax-onomists over their exact relationship. The simi-larity in plumages – largely differing in the intensity or colour saturation of the upperparts, the amount of streaking on the throat and the presence (and intensity) or absence of orange or white on the underparts across the ranges – has given rise to considerable disagreement over the definition of specific and subspecific limits; indeed, several of the races currently recognised as belonging to African Thrush were previously ascribed to Olive. The problem is further con-founded by the presence within the range of the apparently more distinct *T (o). helleri* and *T (o). ludoviciae*.

Mackworth-Praed & Grant (1960) separated the races of both African and Olive Thrushes on similar-ity of plumages but White (1960, 1962a,b) and Rip-ley (1964) combined many of races from both species and divided them into Northern or Mountain *T. abyssinicus* and Southern *T. olivaceus* Olive Thrushes and gave both *helleri* and *ludoviciae* spe-cific status (Taita Thrush and Somali Blackbird respectively). Later editions of Mackworth-Praed & Grant (1973 onwards) also adopted this treatment. Hall & Moreau (1962) gave full species status to both *helleri* and *ludoviciae*, and later (1970) divided the races of *olivaceus* on altitude which, with some exceptions, marked a return to a treatment closer to that originally proposed by Mackworth-Praed & Grant. Keith & Urban (1992) summarised the differ-ences between African and Olive together with Kur-richane and Bare-eyed Thrushes based on plumage, voice, range and habitat occupation. Together with Dowsett & Dowsett-Lemaire (1980) they also reviewed the races of Olive and African Thrushes and established the subspecific arrangement as fol-lowed here, except that the intermediate *stormsi*, *bocagei* and *graueri*, which they placed with African, are here retained within Olive on the basis of plumage similarities (*stormsi* is extremely similar to *nyikae*) and lack of evidence from song or display that they can confidently be regarded as belonging to African Thrush. In addition both *helleri* and *ludoviciae* were considered as conspecific with Olive Thrush; *helleri*, whilst admittedly distinctive, is now considered to be within the subspecific level on the basis of *roehli* (from northern Tanzania) showing intermediate characters with those of *nyikae* (central Tanzania). Furthermore, Keith & Urban established that *nigrilorum* and *poensis*, previously considered distant and isolated races of Olive, are now more properly referable to African Thrush.

There is still division of opinion over these approaches to the species complex, which will perhaps only be resolved to some degree by DNA analysis (which could, however, just as easily complicate our understanding of the relationships still further). The treatment adopted here is closer to that originally proposed by Mackworth-Praed & Grant in 1960 with acknowledgments to the work of later authors. Although it may contain inexacti-tudes, it is based largely on similarities in plumage, voice and behaviour which, for identification pur-poses, are criteria more easily understood by field ornithologists. This treatment (somewhat reluc-tantly) retains both *helleri* and *ludoviciae* in Olive Thrush, although recent East African field guides, notably van Perlo (1995) and Zimmerman *et al.* (1996) (perhaps anticipating the results of DNA analysis), have maintained both as full species.

DESCRIPTION (*T. o. olivaceus*) Sexes alike. **Adult** Head and face to mantle, back, scapulars, rump and uppertail-coverts dark olive-brown; wings darker and tail browner or tinged warm brown but wing-coverts and base of tail as upperparts, thin pale buff-brown edges to secondaries and bases to primaries; underwing-coverts reddish-orange. Lores blackish-brown, cheeks and ear-coverts flecked slightly paler. Chin and throat white but obscured by diffuse blackish-brown streaks, upper breast pale buffish-brown or grey-brown spotted finely with darker brown (extending in some to lower breast and flanks) becoming orange washed brown on central and lower breast and deep orange, occasionally tipped paler or yellowish on flanks and belly, rear or lower flanks often tinged olive or brownish, vent and undertail-coverts white or pale orange with grey-brown tips to some longer feathers. Bill mostly bright yellow or yellowish-orange with dark culmen ridge and base to upper mandible. Legs and feet deep tan-yellow or yellowish-brown. **Immature** Juvenile has upperparts slightly paler or more olive and finely spotted, streaked or flecked with pale orange; pale orange streaks to shafts and tips of scapulars, shaft-streaks on median and greater coverts broadening to form pale orange-buff spots at tips, thus two indistinct wing-bars; chin whitish, rest of underparts pale or dull orange heavily blotched or spotted blackish-brown on breast, more finely on lower breast, flanks and belly. Bill brownish tinged yellow, sides of mandible orange or reddish-horn. First-winter bird more like adult but (depending on time of year) retains some juvenile feathers and may show pale tips to some greater coverts; edges to scapulars may also have fine pale shaft-streaks; in the hand tail feathers more tapered than rounded.

GEOGRAPHICAL VARIATION Eighteen races; except in two well-marked races (*ludoviciae* and *helleri*) variation slight, mainly concerning the depth of colour or intensity of the olive-brown upperparts and the colour of the flanks and belly.

Race *abyssinicus* (together with races *baraka*, *deckeni*, *oldeani*, *bambusicola*, *roehli*, *nyikae* and *milanjensis*) previously treated as a separate species – Northern Olive Thrush – is similar to nominate but less olive and slightly paler brown with a greyish cast or wash on nape and sides of neck to mantle, back and scapulars and wing-coverts; rump and uppertail-coverts slightly greyer. Wings and tail dark brown but flight feathers edged lighter or more buff-brown, outerwebs of outer tail feathers light olive-brown. Lores blackish-brown, cheeks and ear-coverts olive-brown; eye-ring thin, bright yellow to orange, becoming reddish-orange when breeding. Chin and throat whitish-buff, sides of throat streaked dark brown, becoming greyish-buff or greyish-olive on lower throat and breast and more orange on central and lower breast; sides of belly, flanks and thighs to underwing-coverts rich rufous-orange, flanks sometimes also tinged greyish-brown; centre of belly to undertail-coverts white, latter with greyish-brown bases and central shafts. Bill orange to reddish-orange in breeding season. Legs and feet pale yellowish-brown to orange.

Elsewhere in East and east-central Africa there are a number of races similar to *abyssinicus* with rather small or restricted distributions: *baraka* has upperparts brownish-grey and breast to belly and underwing-coverts deep tawny, lower breast and flanks more often heavily tinged chestnut; *bambusicola* like *baraka* but more olive and less grey above, whiter on chin and throat and ashy-brown on breast, paler on flanks to belly and underwing-coverts, bill deep orange; *deckeni* like previous two but darker above, duller greyish- or tawny-brown on throat with fine pale brown streaks, greyish upper breast, olive-brown on sides of belly and flanks, orange-tinged brown belly; *oldeani* like *deckeni* and *nyikae* (see below) but darker olive above and greyish below with a faint wash of brown or dull olive tinged orange on belly, flanks lack tawny and tinged grey-brown, the underwing-coverts variable from tawny to bright orange, eye-ring orange, bill deep orange, legs and feet pale orange to yellowish-brown.

Race *helleri* (known as Taita Thrush – see above) is very distinctive and, with the exception of *roehli*, unlike any of the other races – blackish-grey on forehead to crown, face, chin, throat and sides of neck to lower breast. Rest of upperparts browner or dark brown except for alula, primary coverts and innerwebs to flight and tail feathers, which are also blackish-brown. Thin yellow to yellowish-orange eye-ring. Flanks deep orange or rufous-orange but rest of underparts entirely white. Bill bright orange-yellow. Legs and feet pale orange. Juvenile similar to nominate but darker above with pale orange-buff streaks to crown and mantle and streaks and tips to scapulars and wing-coverts; breast heavily mottled or spotted blackish-brown, rest of underparts paler. Race *roehli* initially similar to *helleri* (and almost adjacent in range) but has dark olive-brown upperparts and greyer or greyish-brown on breast and dull orange flanks with white on centre of breast and belly to vent and undertail-coverts, thighs greyish or sandy-buff, underwing-coverts slightly paler.

Race *ludoviciae* (21.5–24 cm/8½–9½") (known as Somali Blackbird – see above) is also very distinctive with entire head to hindcrown and nape, ear-coverts, chin, throat and upper breast dark slate-grey or blackish, with thin pale yellow eye-ring; rest of upperparts dark lead-grey or tinged brown; edges to flight feathers olive-grey, slightly paler on edges to greater coverts and secondaries; pale greyish-buff edges to outer primaries when worn; innerwebs to wing-coverts and flight feathers blackish-brown; tertials same but broadly edged greyish-buff. Underwing-coverts plain grey, faintly tinged warm buff or pale orange on tips to greater coverts. Tail also blackish-brown, outermost feathers with white at tip. Some birds have black on lower throat and upper breast broken with blackish streaks (on grey ground colour); can also show pale grey tips to chin and throat; rest of underparts grey, slightly paler on belly and washed olive on lower flanks, with narrow white central shafts on undertail-coverts. Bill, legs and feet yellow. Female very similar but browner-black on head, restricted to lores and cheeks merging into dark grey on ear-coverts; chin and throat streaked blackish, becoming pale grey on upper breast and sides of neck. Bill dull pale or straw-yellow. Legs and feet flesh- to pale orange-yellow. Juvenile paler dull grey tinged brown on upperparts and heavily spotted and streaked on crown to nape; mantle and scapulars have prominent pale whitish-buff streaks; median and greater coverts have pale whitish-buff central shaft-streaks becoming whitish spots at tips; entire underparts dull grey-brown, mottled yellowish or whitish-buff and brown at tips, creating a heavily spotted appearance. Bill dark or horn-brown.

In Central Africa race *stormsi* has upperparts dark brownish-olive but with considerable variation (sometimes greyish-olive), chin and throat also variable from off-white, greyish, light buff to pale orange and streaked or flecked pale brown or darker; breast deep orange suffused with light brownish-olive and the orange on the upper belly and flanks is deeper or rufous-cinnamon, lower belly and undertail-coverts white or washed light orange; underwing-coverts orange. Bill dull yellow to orange-yellow. Legs and feet pale brownish-white to dull yellow or yellowish-brown. Race *williami* (which occupies the area south of *stormsi*) is slightly larger than *stormsi* and greyer or greyish-olive on crown and most upperparts, and has darker orange on flanks and underwing-coverts. Race *bocagei* has upperparts tinged grey and stripes on throat much finer than in other races, breast ashy-brown becoming tinged orange on slightly paler sides of breast and flanks; centre of lower breast and belly white. Race *graueri* is also like *stormsi* (both have been considered races of African Thrush) but brownish-olive above and pale buff-brown on breast washed orange and becoming deeper orange on lower breast and bright tawny- or pale orange on upper belly and flanks; centre of belly to undertail-coverts white or lightly washed orange; chin and throat variably streaked brownish or blackish on light buffish to tawny-white ground colour.

In southern Africa race *smithi* is similar to nominate but slightly paler grey or less olive (absent in some) above; pale yellow eye-ring; chin and throat white, streaked brown but not as heavily as on nominate; breast to flanks variable from grey or greyish-buff tinged orange; centre of lower breast to belly and vent light orange, undertail-coverts whitish tinged yellow or yellowish-orange with brown bases. Bill bright yellow or orange to reddish-orange. Eye pale brown. Legs and feet bright yellow, orange-yellow or reddish-orange, claws whitish. Juvenile as nominate but eye-ring dull whitish-yellow or yellow. Race *pondoensis* intermediate between *smithi* and nominate, more olive above than nominate with less grey on breast, which is brighter orange and extends to belly.

Race *milanjensis* has upperparts slightly darker olive-brown than nominate, chin and throat buffish-white with distinct blackish stripes, upper breast olive-buff to -brown tinged orange extending to flanks; centre of breast and upper belly rich or deep orange; undertail-coverts olive-brown with white central shafts; *nyikae* like *smithi* but with slightly heavier streaks on dull off-white to buffish chin and throat; lower throat and breast dull orange-buff variably tinged grey or dingy olive (French mustard) brown, becoming pale dull whitish to very pale orange on sides of belly and tinged rusty on flanks; centre of belly, vent and undertail-coverts white, latter with brown shaft-streaks. Underwing-coverts bright orange. Eye-ring variable from pale orange to reddish-orange. Bill orange-yellow to reddish-orange to red. Legs and feet orange-brown.

Race *swynnertoni* is dark olive above (but not as dark as *milanjensis*), lores, cheeks and ear-coverts dark brown; underparts predominantly pale orange but breast (occasionally extending to belly and flanks) suffused brown or brownish-orange, becoming light orange on belly and flanks to vent; undertail-coverts pale brown with whitish bases. Chin and throat whitish-buff heavily streaked dark brown. Bill orange or with dark brown culmen. Eye dark brown. Legs and feet dark sienna-yellow.

Two other races from South Africa, *transvaalensis* (northern Transvaal) and *culminans* (Drakensberg of Natal), have been described but are doubtfully separable from *pondoensis*.

VOICE Contact note a whistling or piping *gew, gew-gew* or *tooee tooeee*, with a thin *tseep* uttered just before taking flight; a harsher version of the latter, e.g. *tsrk-tsrk*, serves in alarm; also a soft *chuk-chuk-chuk* or *chook-chook-chook*. Song a leisurely series of varied and alternately (in East Africa) fluty, whistled, lilting and trilling phrases: *siu-joil, sii-yu-joy, chuu chou* (*baraka*), generally longer and faster in delivery than those of Kurrichane Thrush. Birds in South Africa have a more hurried delivery and generally shorter phrases, *weety-weety-weety, prrr, tweet-weet, weety*, or with a more rolling quality *wheeu-wheee-wheeu-wheee-wheeu-trrrrrrri*, or ending with a longer *reeeeeetew-eeeeee* (Maclean 1988, Zimmerman *et al.* 1996); often includes whistled imitations of other songbirds including Cape White-eye *Zosterops pallidus* and Orange-breasted Sunbird *Nectarinia violacea*. Gives a short song at dawn, a rolling *trrrip-trrree-eet* and a high-pitched *swee-turr-tee-turr* or repeated *tsurr-tchee-tsurr-tsee-tsur*. Sings at dawn and dusk from the upper branches of a tall tree, occasionally low down or on the ground; mostly in the spring and autumn, especially November and December, and silent at midsummer. Song of *helleri* most often given at dusk; that of *ludoviciae* unknown.

STATUS AND DISTRIBUTION Common or locally common except for *helleri* which is extremely scarce.

T. o. ludoviciae The mountain ranges of northern Somalia (mostly the Golis range, the Warsangli escarpment and possibly also Mt Surud) between 1300 and 2000 m (4290–6600') (Ash & Miskell 1998).

T. o. abyssinicus Extreme south of Sudan, Imatong Mountains (and possibly Dongotona and Didinga Mountains) to Eritrea and Ethiopia south into the highlands of western and most of Kenya east to the Chyulu Hills, northern and eastern Uganda and south to Loliondo in northern Tanzania.

T. o. baraka Southern Virunga and Ruwenzori range in north-east Zaire east to western and south-west Uganda.

T. o. graueri Extreme eastern Zaire, Rwanda and Burundi south to the northern shores of Lake Tanganyika including Kigoma province in north-west Tanzania (intergrades in the south with *stormsi*).

T. o. bocagei Southern Zaire in southern Kasai west to Kwango and south to northern Angola, also the Benguela highlands of west-central Angola (intergrades in the north with *stormsi*).

T. o. stormsi East-central Angola, northern and north-western Zambia (from about the Mwinilunga district) and south-east Zaire to the southern shores of Lake Tanganyika (intergrades with *graueri* and *bocagei*).

T. o. williami Mwinilunga area, north-west Zambia.

T. o. deckeni Longido to Monduli and Mt Kilimanjaro, north-east Tanzania.

T. o. oldeani Mt Meru, Mt Lolkissale, Mbulu district, Mt Hanang, Ufiome, Gerui and the crater highlands of northern Tanzania.

T. o. bambusicola Impenetrable Forest in south-west Uganda and north-east Zaire, from the highlands of the Kivu district south to Mt Kabobo and the highlands of Burundi, Rwanda and extreme north-west Tanzania.

T. o. roehli North-east Tanzania from the North Pare Mountains to the East and West Usambara Mountains.

T. o. nyikae Central, east and south-west Tanzania (Nguru Mountains, Udzungwa Mountains, Uluguru Mountains to Mt Rungwe) south to the Mafinga Mountains and the Nyika Plateau of northern Malawi and north-east Zambia.

T. o. milanjensis Southern Malawi, Dedza to Milanje and Cholo to Namuli, central Mozambique.

T. o. helleri Scarce resident (above 1500 m/4950′) of the Ngaongao, Mbololo and Chawia forests in Taita Hills of south-east Kenya (Collar & Stuart 1985). Thought to occur on Mt Kasigau but recently shown not to; a record from Mt Kilimanjaro (100 km west of Taita Hills) in February 1956 (Collar & Stuart 1985) now considered to be in error (Urban *et al.* 1997). Population of birds in Taita Hills very small in confined area; survey of Ngaongao forest in 1985 estimated a population of 90–100 birds, and the taxon is regarded as Critically Endangered (Collar *et al.* 1994). Its forest habitat has suffered extensive clearance in recent years and it now occupies an area of forest approximately 350 ha in total, although a revised estimate puts the total population at a few hundred. A DNA study has shown that there are significantly more males than females (Lens *et al.* 1998) which could have serious implications. The Kenyan Forest Department has now indicated that it will safeguard the remaining fragments of the Taita hills forest and the National Museums of Kenya are instigating a major project which will, hopefully, result in a conservation policy to protect this and other endemic species of the hills (Brooks 1997).

T. o. swynnertoni Eastern Zimbabwe, isolated areas of the Honde valley and the Lucite-Haroni rivers, also more continuously in the Inyanga Highlands south to Chirinda Forest and the borders of Mozambique north to the Pungue River watershed, also Mt Gorongosa and possibly elsewhere in southern Mozambique.

T. o. smithi Southern Namibia (except for isolated area in the Naukluft Mountains) from about Oranjemund, the lower Fish River and east along the Orange River south through Namaqualand to western Cape Province, South Africa, to about Little Karoo east to the Orange Free State, southern and western Transvaal, western Lesotho, with an isolated outpost in extreme south-east Botswana.

T. o. olivaceus South-west Cape Province to about Grahamstown and East London, South Africa.

T. o. pondoensis Eastern Cape from East London through Transkei to eastern and northern Transvaal and Natal, South Africa, to about Lake St Lucia and southern Swaziland; possibly also this race in isolated outpost at Delagoa, Mozambique.

MOVEMENTS Partial or altitude migrant but some races, e.g. *helleri* and *ludoviciae*, entirely sedentary (but one record of *ludoviciae* away from juniper forest – a single in a citrus grove at Haraf, Hargeisa, in November 1958: G. Clarke pers. comm.). Some birds disperse to lower altitudes following the breeding season. Lowland birds are completely sedentary but some higher-altitude breeders move to lower levels for the winter or non-breeding months, e.g. *swynnertoni* has been recorded down to 350 m (1150′) and *abyssinicus* to 900 m (2970′).

HABITAT Breeds in the dense undergrowth and scrub of mainly montane and (in parts of the range) lowland evergreen forests; all races breeding in East Africa – *abyssinicus, baraka, deckeni, bambusicola, oldeani, nyikae, swynnertoni, milanjensis, roehli* and *helleri* – are montane birds occurring mainly between 1500 and 3400 m (4950–11,200′), *baraka* occurring up to 3780 m (12,500′), with the exception of *roehli* and *swynnertoni* which occur down to 900 m (2950′) in the eastern highlands of Zimbabwe and the East Usambara Mountains (Tanzania). Also bamboo forests and moist lowland woodlands along river valleys, forest edges and glades, open hillsides with montane heath, moorland, brush or scrub (particularly in savanna scrub – *smithi*), plantations (in particular coffee or bananas – *abyssinicus*) and, in parts of its range, parks, gardens and orchards; *ludoviciae* is confined to forests of African cedar *Juniperus procera* and their edges.

BEHAVIOUR Primarily a retiring deep forest species which has now, in parts of its range (e.g. South Africa), adapted well to suburban areas with tall trees, large gardens and parks, where it has become tame and approachable and readily feeds in the open. Usually in pairs or small groups (up to about 12) but may form flocks to roost or when feeding at fruiting trees at certain times of year; *ludoviciae* occurs in groups of up to 30 at fruiting junipers. At lower altitudes often found near streams or lakes. Feeds mostly on the ground where it hops in typical thrush fashion but flies up into trees when alarmed; also feeds in fruit trees on ripening fruit; on the ground runs with head held low before becoming erect to search the ground for prey. Searches through leaf-litter with characteristic flicking aside of leaves. Race *roehli* said to crack snails against a stone anvil in the manner of a Song Thrush (124); *helleri* very shy and skulking, inhabiting dense thickets and forest undergrowth where it spends much time on the ground, perching only on stumps and in low trees usually less than 2 m (6½') high. Flight is fast and, when crossing open spaces, usually direct and into cover. Feeds mostly on the ground on a wide range of invertebrates including spiders, termites, ants (follows ant columns), millipedes, grasshoppers and molluscs, but also takes worms, small frogs and lizards, including chameleons, small fish and nestling birds, plus a variety of berries (*ludoviciae* feeds on the berries of African cedar) and fruit (both ripening and fallen) such as strawberry, mulberry, figs and seeds. In parts of its range very destructive to cultivated fruit. Urban-living birds in South Africa behave like urban Blackbirds in Europe and feed on a wide variety of household scraps and tit-bits. **BREEDING** Season: main period varies throughout the range, March/April to July/August in the north, with second broods in July to December or January; breeds throughout the year in Cape Province (for full range of regional laying dates see Urban *et al.* 1997). Nest: large untidy cup-shaped structure of dry leaves, bracken, bark strips, grass, twigs, rootlets and moss, variably supplemented by mud, paper and plastic and lined with mud and fine grass; in parts of its range entirely of moss with a few dry leaves as inner lining; usually placed up to 6 m (20') from the ground, though up to 21 m (70') is not uncommon, well hidden in cover in the fork of a tree, against the trunk, or along a large horizontal branch; in some suburban areas in gutters or eaves of houses; usually built entirely by female in up to 10 days. One pair (Malawi) known to

occupy same territory in 6 successive years (Dowsett 1985). Eggs: 2–3, occasionally 4, glossy, pale bluish tinged greenish or dark blue and spotted, streaked or blotched variably with brown, yellowish to reddish-brown, grey or pale mauve. Incubation period 14–15 days; mostly by the female, with occasional relief periods by male. Fledging period 16 days, but young remain with parents in natal area for up to two months. **MOULT** Little known but adults undergo complete post-breeding moult in Malawi from December to March.

MEASUREMENTS Wing, male 108–138, female 119–128 (Urban *et al.* 1997); (Zimbabwe – race unspecified) male, wing 108–120.5, female 101–115.5; (South Africa – race and sex unspecified) wing 110.5–125; tarsus, male 30–35, female 29–33 (Urban *et al.* 1997) (wing measurements by race below); (Zimbabwe – race unspecified) tarsus 26–30; *stormsi* tarsus 31–33; *swynnertoni* tarsus 28; *williami* tarsus 35; bill (culmen) (all races) 19–24.5; *stormsi* bill 24–26. Weight *abyssinicus* 54–81 g; (South Africa – race unspecified) 57.5–85 g, exceptionally 98 g (Urban 1975, Maclean 1988); *ludoviciae* 55–70 g (Ash & Miskell 1998).

Wing (listed alphabetically) *abyssinicus* 104–124; *bambusicola* 113–120; *baraka* 107–120; *bocagei* male 114–132, female 107–115; *deckeni* 109–124; *graueri* 116–125; *helleri* 113.5–122; *ludoviciae* 110–122; *milanjensis* 115–125; *nyikae* 108–123; *oldeani* 106–116; *roehli* 105–112; *stormsi* male 117–133, female 113–131; *swynnertoni* 110–118; *williami* 135–136 (White 1949, Benson 1960, 1969, Mackworth-Praed & Grant 1960, 1973, Ash & Miskell 1998).

REFERENCES Ash & Miskell (1998), Benson (1960a, 1969), Brooks (1997), Collar & Andrew (1988), Collar & Stuart (1985), Collar *et al.* (1994), Dowsett (1985), Dowsett & Dowsett-Lemaire (1993), Hall & Moreau (1962), Keith & Urban (1992), Lens *et al.* (1998), Urban (1975), White (1949, 1960, 1962a,b), Winterbottom (1996).

102 YEMEN THRUSH *Turdus menachensis* Plate 32

Turdus menachensis Ogilvie-Grant, 1913, *Bull. Brit. Orn. Club* 31: 86 – Menacha, Yemen.

INTRODUCTION 23 cm (9″). A dark brown thrush with a bright yellow bill and rusty-brown underwing-coverts, closely resembling an out-of-range female Blackbird (111). Endemic to the highlands of south-west Saudi Arabia and North Yemen. **Confusion species** Within its extremely limited range the only conceivable problem might bes with Black Bush Robin *Cercotrichas podobe*, which is smaller and blacker with a long thin tail and thin, all-dark bill.

Taxonomic note The exact status of Yemen Thrush either as a full species or as a northern outlying subspecies of Olive Thrush, as has been proposed by some authorities, remains unclear. Given

the unresolved questions arising over relationships with other congeners on the grounds of behaviour, voice and ecological niche occupation, it is (in line with current taxonomic treatments) considered here as a full species.

DESCRIPTION Sexes almost alike. **Adult male** Head and upperparts olive-brown with pale buff-brown edges to darker brown wings: tail similar or slightly browner than wings; wings often appear short or rounded. Face as upperparts but slightly darker around lores and eye; ear-coverts indistinctly streaked paler. Chin and throat to breast and sides of neck light yellowish-buff broadly streaked darker brown with smaller or less distinct streaks on sides of breast and upper flanks, plus some dark tips to upper belly (in spring when plumage more worn, spots or streaks become less prominent and throat to breast appears more uniform); lower breast, belly and vent pale grey-brown; flanks dull olive washed rufous or orange; undertail-coverts similar to belly, dull off-white but with dark grey-brown crescent- or arrow-shaped tips. In flight shows deep orange-buff to rust- or rufous-orange underwing-coverts. Bill bright yellow. Legs and feet pale greyish or tinged flesh or yellowish. In fresh plumage (autumn and winter) may show paler or fine whitish-buff edges and tips to greater coverts. **Adult female** Slightly paler or more extensively yellowish-buff on underparts; belly and flanks may also have narrow dark brown central shaft-streaks. **Immature** Juvenile unknown. First-year bird very similar to adult but with pale buff tips to some or all greater coverts and an all-dark bill.

GEOGRAPHICAL VARIATION None. Monotypic.

VOICE A variety of *chuck* notes often given quietly or repeated, some of which recall those given by Blackbird as well as the more explosive notes of both Ring Ouzel (109) and Fieldfare (122), particularly a metallic *shrrrd shrrrrd chuck*; also has a thin high-pitched *seep* or *psiii* and a harsh *shee-ak*; alarm call a chatter similar to that of Blackbird but faster and shorter. Song a short series of 3–4 soft low phrases broken by higher-pitched notes, e.g. *treep-treep* followed by a weak *tsik-tsik* or *tissik-tissik-tseechup*, a stuttering trill or a soft, frog-like croaking note; may end with shorter phrases of *ip-chu-ip* and an upslurred *chissik* or *tissik*; recalls Blackbird in tone but much less melodious and without the fluty notes (Bowden 1987, Hollom *et al.* 1988). Song period mostly prior to, or during, the breeding season but also sings at other times of year, e.g. November.

STATUS AND DISTRIBUTION Considered to be numerous in south-west Saudia Arabia (Jennings 1981) but scarce in Yemen, and thought to be under some threat from habitat destruction by the collection of firewood; regarded as Vulnerable in Collar *et al.* (1994). Highlands of the Asir region of south-west Saudi Arabia from about 21°N south to about Ibb in the highlands of western Yemen.

MOVEMENTS Partial migrant. Birds from south-west Saudi Arabia are apparently absent from September to February and are presumably present in adjacent North Yemen.

HABITAT Steep rocky hillsides, slopes and wadis with a substantial growth of remnant vegetation, including acacia or juniper scrub between 1200 and 3100 m (3960–10,200'), but mostly at 1800–2000 m (5950–6600'); also occurs in cultivated fields or terraced hillsides, notably of qat *Catha edulis* (Bowden 1987).

BEHAVIOUR A retiring and little-known species living in dense areas of natural scrub, spending long periods on the ground where it is difficult to see as it forages in decaying vegetation and often searches through leaves in the manner of a Blackbird. Feeds on a variety of small invertebrates, apparently cracking snails open on 'anvils', and fruit, particularly *Olea chrysophylla* and wild rosehips.

BREEDING Season: April to June. Nest: cup of dead grasses lined with mud and placed up to 2 m (6½') in ferns and similar shrubs or even in the fork of a small tree. Eggs: 2–3, pale blue with spots or blotches of reddish-brown.

MOULT No information.

MEASUREMENTS Wing, male 119–127, female (n=4) 111–118; tarsus (n=6) 27–32; bill (to feathers) 19–22.5; (to skull) 25.5–28. Weight 72–79 g (Ogilvie-Grant 1913, Bowden 1987).

REFERENCES Bowden (1987), Collar *et al.* (1994), Hollom *et al.* (1988), Jennings (1981).

103 COMORO THRUSH *Turdus bewsheri* Plate 31

Turdus bewsheri Newton, 1877, *Proc. Zool. Soc. London*: 299, pl. 34 – Anjouan Island.

IDENTIFICATION 24 cm (9½"). Endemic to the forests of the Comoro Islands in the Indian Ocean. A brown thrush tinged olive on the upperparts and tail, wings slightly warmer brown; some slight variation in colour tones between birds (and races) on different islands; underparts white except for brown on sides of the neck, but heavily scaled or scalloped with dark brown fringes creating a distinctive pattern; centre of belly to undertail-coverts mainly white. Shows some affinities in plumage to Olivaceous Thrush (100) of São Tomé in the Gulf of Guinea. **Confusion species** The only thrush in the Comoro Islands.

DESCRIPTION Sexes almost alike. **Adult male** Entire upperparts deep brown tinged dark olive, forehead and crown slightly darker. Wings similar but slightly warmer brown than back, edges to

outer primaries pale brown; underwing-coverts light russet to pale orange. Tail uniform with upperparts. Lores brown flecked paler, cheeks and ear-coverts brown, cheeks spotted and ear-coverts finely streaked whitish and pale buff. Chin and throat white or flecked pale brown, becoming streaked with pale buff on sides of throat; broad brown breast-band, each feather with a pale brown centre and darker brown fringe, creating indistinct scaly effect; sides of breast more evenly brown and merging with brown on sides of neck. Lower breast to sides of belly and flanks white with brown tips, creating heavier scaled pattern; centre of belly to undertail-coverts white but latter may show some olive-brown streaks. Upper mandible dark slate, lower and cutting edges to upper brown or yellowish-brown. Legs and feet ochre-brown.

Adult female As male or slightly browner with broader or more uniform tips to breast and flanks. **Immature** Juvenile similar to adult but more rufous above with fine pale buffish streaks on crown and scapulars and mottled buffish on breast.
GEOGRAPHICAL VARIATION Three races; variation slight to moderate, mainly affecting the plumage of the underparts.

Race *comorensis* similar to, but marginally smaller than, nominate and slightly darker brown above (including wings), head and face slightly darker than upperparts, cheeks and ear-coverts with fine (occasionally indistinct) pale shafts, sides of chin and throat more visibly streaked brown, especially in fresh plumage, pale or dull brown (no scales) on breast and flanks; perhaps slightly darker or tinged warmer brown on flanks; centre of lower breast and belly white and undertail-coverts warm rufous. Underwing-coverts as nominate or slightly more russet in tone.

Race *moheliensis* similar to *comorensis* except for slightly browner or more obvious spots and streaks on cheeks and ear-coverts. Chin and throat white spotted or streaked brown, extending (often indistinctly) onto warm brown breast with slightly darker tips forming scaly pattern; belly and flanks to vent greyer-brown than breast. Vent and undertail-coverts whitish, heavily obscured with pale brown centres or bases; underwing-coverts white or tinged pale russet-orange. Sexes alike but female warmer brown on breast and flanks.

VOICE A soft contact note; a sharp *twit* given repeatedly when alarmed; and a sharp *krrrk*. Song a series of beautiful, rich, mellow, typically thrush-like notes usually given as *chri-chri-chri* but with some variablity or dialect as *richi-richi-richi*, *teeu-* *teeu-teeu*, *tiree-tiree-tiree*, *kwiyi-kwiyi-kwiyi* or *kwicher-chip-chip-chip-kwich*. May also have a short subsong before the breeding season in April.
STATUS AND DISTRIBUTION Common.
T. b. bewsheri Anjouan, Comoro Islands.
T. b. comorensis Grand Comoro.
T. b. moheliensis Mohéli, Comoro Islands.
MOVEMENTS Sedentary.
HABITAT Evergreen primary forests and forest edges from sea-level to about 700 m (2300') except for nominate *bewsheri*, which occurs above this range owing to lack of any lower-level forests.
BEHAVIOUR Usually low down in trees or thick vegetation within 3 m (10') of the ground. Often occurs in mixed-species flocks. Forages low down or on the ground. Feeds mostly on invertebrates and their larvae, particularly spiders, grasshoppers, bugs, small snails and slugs; also some fruit and seeds.
BREEDING Season: mid-August to October. Nest: an open cup mostly of plant fibres and tendrils and covered in damp moss and lined with fine grasses, placed up to 3 m (10') from the ground in an epiphytic fern, on a tree-stump or along a horizontal branch of a tree. Eggs 2, pale blue with fine reddish-brown or rufous speckles overlying larger lavender-grey blotches.
MOULT No information.
MEASUREMENTS Wing, male 106–113, female 99–107; tarsus 39–41; bill (culmen) 22–24; *comorensis* wing 105–114; tarsus 36–37; bill (culmen) 23–25; *moheliensis* wing, male 109–115, female 108–109; tarsus 38–42 (Benson 1960b). Weight apparently unrecorded.
REFERENCES Benson (1960b).

104 GREY-BACKED THRUSH *Turdus hortulorum* Plate 38
Turdus hortulorum Sclater, 1863, *Ibis* 5: 196 – Camoens Garden, Macao.

IDENTIFICATION 19–23 cm (7½–9"). A distinctive medium-sized thrush of the eastern Palearctic. Adult male has ash-grey head, face and upperparts with slightly darker wings and tail and slightly paler grey chin to breast, orange or rufous breast, flanks and underwing-coverts, white centre of belly to undertail-coverts. Female is very similar but tinged more olive-brown above and lacks grey below which is replaced with white and rows of black streaks or spots on the sides of the breast. **Confusion species** Most likely to be confused with Eyebrowed Thrush (116) but lack of bold white supercilium and any brown on the upperparts, plus rich orange on the underwing-coverts, are the most obvious differences. Out-of-range male Black-breasted Thrush (106) has much darker grey head and upperparts to breast; female also extremely similar but has brown or olive-brown (not grey) upperparts, and although similarly spotted usually shows more extensive orange on the underparts; centre of breast on female Grey-backed usually whitish to pale yellow. Female Grey-backed is sim-ilar to female Japanese Thrush (107) and shares the same underwing colour, but the former has grey not grey-brown upperparts and a pale yellow (not all dark) bill, the latter a reddish wash on the flanks and spots on the breast and flanks.

Taxonomic note Previously considered by some authorities (e.g. Ripley 1964) to be a race of Black-breasted Thrush.
DESCRIPTION Sexes differ. **Adult male** Entire head to nape, mantle, scapulars, rump and tail ash-grey or tinged bluish, with slightly darker lores and perhaps slightly paler over the eyes and ear-coverts; cheeks slightly paler grey and may (in fresh plumage) be tinged warm buff; forehead and forecrown may also be tinged olive; thin pale yellow eye-ring. Wings as upperparts but centres to median and greater coverts blackish-brown; alula and primary coverts blackish-brown and flight feathers blackish, all edged slate-grey; tertials similar but more broadly edged pale grey; under-wing-coverts bright orange-rufous (as on flanks). Chin and throat variably whitish to pale or ash-

grey (deeper in some), tinged buffish-orange at sides of lower throat; centre of breast pale ash-grey (slightly paler than on head and upperparts), sides of lower breast to flanks and thighs bright orange-rufous (sides of upper flanks may be tinged grey), upper belly (in some from centre of lower breast) to vent and undertail-coverts white, latter may be washed buff or light orange. Upper mandible brownish-horn or yellowish-brown, lower yellow, or entire bill yellow darkening slightly towards tip. Legs and feet variable from yellow, pale yellowish-orange to chestnut-brown or flesh-brown. **Adult female** Upperparts olive-brown, lower back, rump and uppertail-coverts sometimes ashier-grey. May have paler crown and paler area above lores, eye and ear-coverts, often joining with moustachial stripe to form pale sur-round to cheeks and ear-coverts; narrow eye-ring pale yellow, malar blackish often extending as row of small spots or arrowheads onto whitish sides of neck. Wings browner than upperparts with paler edges to outerwebs of primaries. Chin, throat and breast white (or pale yellowish on breast) spotted faintly with brown on centre of lower throat; sides of throat to centre of breast variable from light to heavily spotted, with rows of blackish arrowhead spots continuing to upper flanks (spots sometimes much lighter or not extending to flanks); flanks, thighs, sides of lower belly to underwing-coverts rich orange; centre of belly to vent and undertail-coverts white. Bill dusky-yellow with pale brown tip to upper mandible. Legs and feet brown or yellowish at rear. **Immature** Juvenile mostly olive-brown on head and upperparts, becoming slightly greyer on edges of primaries and central tail feathers; tips of median or greater coverts warm brown or pale buffish-orange, often extending some way up central shaft. Underparts white, heavily spotted dark brown on sides of throat; may show broad pale submoustachial, long dark malar and heavy blackish (and sometimes some indistinct) spots on breast; flanks washed pale orange. Bill light brown. Legs and feet flesh-brown. First-year bird very similar to adult but female slightly duller olive-brown and male dull grey with paler fore-head to face; both show retained pale orange-buff tips to median or greater coverts (first-winter bird also shows retained pale central shafts on mantle and scapulars). Underparts as immature but with pale buffish or yellowish-buff sides of throat (below cheeks and ear-coverts), variably broad black malar extending to sides of lower throat on whitish base, and variably spotted (sparsely or heavily) with black or dusky-brown arrowheads extending to breast; sides of lower breast and flanks deep orange as adult but centre of lower breast, belly and undertail-coverts white, some-times retaining vestigial spots on belly into April. Bill mostly dark horn. Legs and feet pinkish.
GEOGRAPHICAL VARIATION None. Monotypic.
VOICE Little known. Call a soft or low chuckle, a harsh *chack-chack* and a shrill whistled *tsee* or *cheee* alarm. Song a series of variable, loud whis-tles. Reported by Dementiev & Gladkov (1954)

and La Touche (1925–1930) to have a superlative song, loud, pure and highly versatile, surpassing many of the thrushes that breed in Siberia: a series of loud fluty whistles, *tvet-tvet-tvet, qwee-qwee-qwee, tveeu-tveeu-tveeu, tveeu-tve* (pause) *tevetee-tevetee-tevetee* (with emphasis on the first syllable), followed by *k'yuu-qwo, tvee-tvee-tvee, trryuuu, tevtee-tevetee-tevetee*, some phrases sim-ilar to and recalling those of Song Thrush. Song period confined to the breeding season.
STATUS AND DISTRIBUTION Common through-out most of the breeding range. Breeds in eastern Siberia, north to about 62°N on the Aldan River and west to the Stanovoy Range, east through Ussuriland to Amurland and south to Heilungkiang (Manchuria), north-east China; has also bred (once) in Korea in 1965, where it is oth-erwise a scarce passage migrant. In winter in south and south-east China from south-east Yunnan east to Kiangsi, Chekiang, Fukien, Kwangtung and south to Hainan (where uncommon or rare) and north Vietnam (E Tonkin and North Annam).
MOVEMENTS Migratory. All breeding birds move south or slightly west of south to winter in south and south-east China. Departs from breeding grounds in September and moves through north-ern China from Inner Mongolia to Hopeh in small numbers in mid- to late September and October, although some are still on passage in southern China in early to mid-November; in Hong Kong main arrival is in November. A regular passage migrant in small numbers along the lower Yangtze River in both spring and autumn. A widespread winter visitor to Hong Kong from November to April (exceptionally September to May). Return passage begins in early April with birds in breed-ing areas of Ussuriland in late April, but many do not return to the north of the range until early or mid-May; records of birds in Kwangtung in May not exceptional.
A rare passage migrant to Taiwan (up to 4 birds in some years) and Hung-t'ou Hsu (Lanyu Island); an erratically rare or accidental visitor to Japan; an individual in Germany in October 1996 was con-sidered to be an escape.
HABITAT Breeds in dense oakwoods and thickets up to c.1100 m (3300'), often near water or rivers; found also in mixed woods of cedar and horn-beams; in Ussuriland occurs in montane valleys with dense stands of alders, elms, giant poplars and scattered groves of hazelnut and birch. On migration and in winter occurs in more open woods, bamboo clumps, scrub woodlands and groves on lower-altitude foothills and in the plains mostly along rivers.
BEHAVIOUR Usually alone or in pairs in the breeding season but occurs in loose flocks in win-ter. Most actions and behaviour similar to Song Thrush (with which it is not known to associate) but generally wary and unapproachable; spends long periods in the foliage of trees. Feeds on the ground often in thick cover, where it actively searches through decaying vegetation and noisily scatters leaves; food is mostly invertebrates and their larvae.

BREEDING Season: early May to mid-August. Nest: a cup of dry grasses, thin twigs and similar vegetation held together with mud and lined with fine grasses; usually well concealed in bushes or a small tree-fork, occasionally in a hollow up to 2 m (6½') from the ground. Eggs: 4–5, variably coloured from pale greenish to bluish and sparsely or completely covered with rusty-brown speckles, spots, streaks or lilac-pink blotches. Two broods. **MOULT** Full post-breeding moult of adults from end of July to middle or late August, completed before departure to wintering area. Juveniles undergo partial post-fledging moult from early to mid-July, complete by end of August.

MEASUREMENTS Wing, male 110–122, female 109–122; tarsus 29–31; bill (culmen) male (n=7) 14.5–18, female (n=6) 15.5–18. Weight 68 g (La Touche 1925–1930, Dementiev & Gladkov 1954).

REFERENCES La Touche (1925–1930), Ripley (1964).

105 TICKELL'S THRUSH *Turdus unicolor*   Plate 37
(Indian Grey Thrush)

Turdus unicolor Tickell, 1833, *J. Asiat. Soc. Bengal* 2: 577 – Bansigar in Borabhum.

IDENTIFICATION 21–25 cm (8¼–9¾"). A small to medium-sized thrush of the Himalayas. Males are almost entirely ash-grey or faintly tinged bluish, paler grey on the breast becoming white on the belly; females are brown or olive-brown with a whitish throat, paler buff-brown belly and whitish undertail-coverts. **Confusion species** Males are unlikely to be mistaken but females are similar to female Blackbird (111) and best separated on white throat, buff-brown breast and flanks and whitish belly to undertail-coverts; female could also be confused with female or immature Eye-browed Thrush (116) but lacks prominent supercilium and orange tones to breast and flanks.

DESCRIPTION Sexes differ. **Adult male** Entire head and face to rest of upperparts ash-grey with a light or faint tinge of bluish, slightly paler or greyer on rump and uppertail-coverts; tail slightly darker grey or grey-brown. Wings as upperparts except for darker grey or grey-brown alula and flight feathers, which have pale grey edges to primaries and, more broadly, on tertials; axillaries and underwing-coverts pale grey (variable in extent) fringed orange or pale orange-buff. Eye-ring bright yellow. Lores to eye dark grey. Chin and throat to breast pale grey becoming whitish-grey on belly and flanks and white on vent and undertail-coverts; thighs pale ash-grey. Bill bright yellow to orange-yellow in breeding season but otherwise duller or dusky-brown at base and tip. Eye brown, dark brown or reddish-brown. Legs and feet pale brown to brownish tinged yellow. **Adult female** Head and face to rest of upperparts brown to olive-brown tinged greyish on rump and uppertail-coverts; indistinct pale buff supercilium (or sides of the crown) and lores slightly paler or streaked finely with buff on ear-coverts; eye-ring buff or pale buffish to greenish-yellow. Tail dark brown. Wings as upperparts except for slightly darker brown flight feathers and olive-brown outerwebs to alula and flight feathers; underwing-coverts as male or slightly paler orange-buff. Submoustachial stripe slightly paler buff-brown than rest of head and bordered by malar stripe of blackish spots. Chin and throat white becoming buffish, tawny-brown or pale grey-brown on breast, centre of upper belly streaked or spotted darker brown, flanks slightly paler olive-brown or lighter tawny, centre of belly to vent and undertail-coverts white. Bill as male but duller brown on upper mandible. Legs and feet variably olive-brown to pale grey or yellow. **Immature** Juvenile similar to adult female but slightly darker brown with pale buff central shaft-streaks to most upperparts except rump and uppertail-coverts; pale buff-brown triangle-shaped tips to median and greater coverts forming wing-bar across tips of greaters. Wings (including under-wing-coverts) and tail as adult female. Underparts whitish tinged buffish-brown, sides of throat, breast and flanks variably pale to deep orange heavily barred or spotted darker; underwing-coverts tinged brown or buffish-brown. First-year male as adult but head and face to mantle tinged brownish, similar to adult female except for grey-ish tinge (progressively more extensive) on mantle, back, rump, uppertail-coverts and tail; eye-ring much duller than adult, retained outer greater coverts from juvenile plumage showing pale tips in early part of winter; white on chin bordered by dark malar stripe and breast washed olive- or buff-ish-brown with occasional dark streaks. First-year female as adult female or slightly browner and separated by pale tips to median and outer greater coverts; also shows more extensive amount of arrowhead spots on sides of lower throat to centre of upper breast.

GEOGRAPHICAL VARIATION None. Monotypic.

VOICE A variety of *dew-dew* or *wiw-wiw* notes, also a chuckling *chuck-chuck*, *quoit-quoit* or *juk-juk*; alarm similar to *chuck* or *juk* notes but harsher. Song a series of typical thrush-like notes, consisting of a short but rich warbling broken by short pauses and usually repeated 3–4 times followed by a series of short twittering or squeaking notes. Variable (or dialectal) from region to region, but generally monotonous in tone and inferior to other thrushes of the region; has been rendered as *chellya, chellya, chirrali – cherlya, cherlya, chellya – chellya, chellya, juliu* (Ali & Ripley 1983). Song given mostly from tops of trees, and mostly in the early morning, often

341

from before first light, but also in the afternoon and again in the evening. Song period end of March to mid-August.

STATUS AND DISTRIBUTION Locally common to common. Breeds in the Himalayas between 1200 and 2700 m (3960–8900′), exceptionally to 3000 m (10,000′), ranging discontinuously from northern Pakistan (Murree Hills, Chitral and Gilgit) through Kashmir and the mountains of northern India to Nepal, Sikkim and western Bhutan. In winter occurs at lower altitudes within the breeding range but also (generally sparsely or locally) across the adjacent plains and foothills to the south and east of the breeding range east to southern Assam – perhaps also the foothills of Arunachal Pradesh (Ali & Ripley 1983) – and south to Orissa and the Eastern Ghats in extreme north-east Andhra Pradesh, southern Bengal and the Chittagong region of Bangladesh; in the west occurs south to Quetta, northern Baluchistan and erratically to Lahore.

MOVEMENTS Partial and altitude migrant. Departs from the breeding range at the onset of the first winter snows, usually in September and October. Most movements are eastwards along the Himalayas to the main wintering range to the south and east. Occurs as a winter visitor to parts of central India from the end of October to late March, in north-east Madhya Pradesh exceptionally to early May. Return movements in spring less noticeable than those in autumn; arrives back on breeding area in late March and April to early May.

An irregular or scarce migrant to Ladakh and (possibly overlooked) south to Mt Abu, Rajasthan and Goa. A vagrant elsewhere in Bangladesh (3 records) and an extreme vagrant to Europe: an adult male on Heligoland, Germany, October 1932.

HABITAT Breeds in open broadleaved or heavy mixed forest with grassy edges or open clearings, occasionally with shrubs or similar vegetation as undergrowth, also groves of willows, orchards and scattered bushes on slopes; in parts of its range, e.g. Kashmir, penetrates the edges of villages and large gardens where it forages on lawns and in flowerbeds. In winter in similar types of habitat generally at lower altitudes.

BEHAVIOUR Actions on the ground fairly typical of many thrushes, walking or running with short steps, or hops often for a few feet at a time before pausing to survey the area before digging into the soft earth or leaf-litter to extract a worm or insect. Usually alone, in pairs or small flocks in winter, occasionally in company with Black-throated Thrushes (120), when often seen feeding on the ground in woods or clearings; shy and when disturbed flies quickly up into the canopy of a tree, but can be tame or approachable in winter when accustomed to human presence, e.g. edges of villages or cultivation; often indulges in periods of Blackbird-like clucking and scolding before going to roost. Feeds on the ground and in fruiting trees or shrubs, mostly on vegetable matter, fruit (including apples, apricots and plums) and berries, also insects and earthworms.

BREEDING Season: April to August. Nest: a fairly deep open cup of dry grasses, roots, fern stems, leaves and moss lined with fine grasses and roots, sometimes animal (e.g. horse) hair, usually placed in the fork of a tree or bush, in a hollow tree, amid the roots of a fallen tree or on a bank 2–7 m (6½–23′) from the ground. Eggs: 3–4, occasionally 5, variable in colour from pale whitish-buff to pale green, heavily spotted or blotched with reddish-brown. Incubation period 13–14 days; by female only. Both parents feed the nestlings. Possibly two broods.

MOULT Little known but probably very similar to other thrushes, with adults undergoing complete post-breeding season moult from July or early August to September. Partial post-juvenile moult of first-year birds about the same time, possibly slightly earlier.

MEASUREMENTS Wing, male 114–30, female 111–132; tarsus, male 29–32, female 28–32; bill, male 17–24, female (from skull) 16.5–24. Weight 57–75 g (Ali & Ripley 1983).

REFERENCES Ali & Ripley (1983).

106 BLACK-BREASTED THRUSH *Turdus dissimilis* Plate 39
Turdus dissimilis Blyth, 1847, *J. Asiat. Soc. Bengal* 16 144 – lower Bengal.

IDENTIFICATION 22–23.5 cm (8¾–9¼″). A small to medium-sized, brightly coloured thrush with a limited range in north-east India. Male has an all-black head, nape and upper breast, bright yellow eye-ring, grey upperparts and bright orange or rufous breast and flanks; female lacks the black head to breast and has the head and upperparts brown, chin and throat white, orange on the sides of the breast heavily streaked blackish, and central breast to undertail-coverts white. **Confusion species** Combination of all-black head, grey upperparts and bright orange underparts make confusion unlikely. Bears greatest similarity to out-of-range Grey-backed Thrush (104) from eastern Siberia to Manchuria, with which it used to be

(and sometimes still is) considered conspecific. Male Dark-throated Thrush (120) race *atrogularis* has grey to pale grey-brown top of head to nape and white on belly and flanks (male of race *ruficollis* lacks any black on head or face); female Dark-throated Thrush (especially nominate *ruficollis*) similar but lacks bright yellow eye-ring and warm orange/rufous tones on sides of breast, belly and/or flanks. Eyebrowed Thrush (116) is initially similar but lacks any black on head to breast (male) or streaks on throat and breast (female), and also has distinctive white supercilium.

DESCRIPTION Sexes differ. **Adult male** Entire head and face to nape and chin, throat and upper breast jet-black (upper chin may be white). Eye-ring bright yellow or orange-yellow. Black on nape merges into slate-grey on upper mantle; rest of upperparts to rump and uppertail-coverts also slate-grey. Wings and tail slightly darker grey but tips to greater coverts and edges of flight feathers slightly paler grey; innerwebs of both flight and tail feathers slate-brown. Centre and sides of breast to flanks, thighs and axillaries and underwing-coverts orange to orange-rufous, rest of underparts white. Bill bright yellow or orange-yellow, paler in winter. Eye brown or dark brown. Legs and feet pale tan- to orange-brown. **Adult female** Entire upperparts including head and face brown to dark olive-brown with pale or dull yellow eye-ring. Flight feathers blackish-brown edged olive-brown, wing-coverts also edged olive-brown. Long white sub-moustachial bordered by equally long black malar stripe at sides of chin; chin and throat otherwise white or faintly streaked black on lower throat, sides of neck whitish but finely streaked blackish, lower throat whitish becoming dull brownish-orange on upper and central breast, heavily marked with blackish spots often in rows. Lower breast to flanks and thighs pale orange, occasionally as strong as on male but sometimes central lower breast white extending to undertail-coverts. Bill more usually yellow than orange-yellow. **Immature** Juvenile similar to adult female but generally dusky-brown with pale central shaft-streaks to feathers on crown, becoming browner-buff streaks on mantle, back, scapulars and median coverts; tips of greater coverts also orange-rufous or pale buffish-brown. Breast brown to pale buffish-brown or tinged slightly warmer on flanks, throat and breast feathers barred darker with blackish tips; belly whitish or tinged buff. Bill yellow. Legs and feet brownish-yellow. First-year bird closely resembles adult but with pale tips to retained juvenile greater coverts.

GEOGRAPHICAL VARIATION None. Monotypic.

VOICE Call a sharp *seeee* and resounding *tock, tock, tock* or *tup-tup tup-tup-tup-tup-tup* often repeated; alarm call similar but extended into a harsher-toned rattle and ending with a slurred *took*. Song a sweet, lilting and often far-carrying *tew-tew weet, tew-tew-tiwi, pieu-pieu-pieu twi, wui-ui'ui-tri-tri*, interspersed with *wirriwi-wu iih* and often delivered for several hours.

STATUS AND DISTRIBUTION Fairly common, but habitat destruction in range presumably responsible for listing as Near-Threatened (Collar *et al.* 1994). Resident in the hills of north-east India from southern Assam, Meghalaya and Nagaland and Manipur south of the Brahmaputra (Garo, Khasi and Cachar Hills) from 1200 to about 2500 m (3950–8250'), possibly also western Arunachal Pradesh (Ali & Ripley 1983), western, northern and eastern Burma (Chin Hills and northern Shan States) and east into north-west, western and

southern Yunnan and (up to about 3000 m/c.10,000') in south-east Yunnan, southern Kweichow and western Kwangsi, also northern Vietnam; formerly considered a vagrant but regular in small numbers and widespread in northern and central Laos (Duckworth *et al.* 1999) and frequently traded in markets. In winter some birds move south to eastern and south-west Bangladesh. A rare but annual winter visitor in small numbers to north-west Thailand; vagrant to about 450 m (1485') in eastern Tonkin, Vietnam.

MOVEMENTS An altitude migrant with many birds moving to lower levels in adjacent plains where they occur in Tripura and eastern Bangladesh south to about Chittagong. Dates of movements little recorded but migrants noted in southern China in late August. A rare migrant or visitor to Kaziranga National Park, central Assam (March 1992, November 1997).

HABITAT Breeds in moist or damp evergreen woods and forests, particularly oak, rhododendron and conifer forests with a good undergrowth layer; in subtropical forests in trees overgrown with moss, orchids and ferns; in Burma occurs on Mt Victoria in light or open pine forest with very little undergrowth; in the northern Chin Hills breeds in scrub and secondary growth. In winter occurs in similar habitat at lower elevations; also in scrub jungle.

BEHAVIOUR Generally very shy in breeding area; elusive and only infrequently seen in the open, preferring the interior of woods and forests, but may become less shy in winter. Forages on the ground beneath trees and shrubs, often turning over leaves in the manner of a Blackbird (111); also feeds in trees, often at the tops of the tallest trees; several birds may gather together at fruiting trees. Feeds mainly on insects and slugs, snails and fruit, especially berries and ripe figs.

BREEDING Season: April to July. Nest: a deep well-built cup of green moss, dry grasses, roots and leaves held together with small amounts of mud and lined with fine grass and thin rootlets, usually placed in a fork of a branch in a thickly clad tree or bush, 1–6 m (3–20') from the ground or occasionally on it. Eggs: 3–4, pale buff, pale green or pale bluish with variable amounts of fine reddish or purple-brown spots or blotches.

MOULT Very little known. Adults probably undergo complete post-breeding moult in late summer or early autumn; partial post-juvenile moult of immatures at same time of year, with outer greater coverts retained into first summer.

MEASUREMENTS Wing, male (n=20) 115–125, female (n=22) 116–124; tarsus 28–34; bill (from skull) 19–25. Weight (n=1) 75 g (Ali & Ripley 1983).

REFERENCES Ali & Ripley (1983), Duckworth *et al.* (1999).

(Grey Thrush, Japanese Grey Thrush)

***Turdus cardis* Temminck, 1831, *Pl. Col.* livr. 87, pl. 518 – Japan.**

IDENTIFICATION 21–22.5 cm (8¼–8¾"). A distinctive small to medium-sized thrush from two areas of Japan and central China. Adult male is unmistakable, mostly jet-black with blackish to slate-grey upperparts, white lower breast and belly spotted with black, central flanks black but undertail-coverts white. Female is grey-brown on the face and upperparts with whitish underparts variably washed reddish-orange on the sides of the breast to the underwing-coverts, and sides of throat to belly and flanks spotted dark brown. **Confusion species** Male could possibly be confused with poorly seen Blackbird (111). Male Siberian Thrush (36) has broad white supercilium and lacks white underparts. Female and immature likely to be confused with same-age/sex Brown-headed Thrush (118) but not so extensively orange below; adult female Brown-headed is unspotted and immature shows pale orange supercilium; Grey-backed Thrush (104) has paler upperparts, pale yellow bill and generally fewer or more sparsely distributed spots below.

DESCRIPTION Sexes differ. **Adult male** Entire head and face to mantle and breast jet-black (chin in some may be paler or whitish) with yellow eye-ring; upper back and scapulars to rump and upper-tail-coverts slate-grey, darker in some individuals, or slightly tinged bluish. Tail jet-black but with thin slate-grey edges to outer feathers. Median and greater coverts black with slate-grey edges; alula and primary coverts black; flight feathers and tertials also jet-black finely edged slate-grey, more broadly on tertials; underwing-coverts slate-grey tipped with orange. Lower breast to belly and undertail-coverts white with large blackish spots, belly often unspotted, spots on flanks often merging into a slate-grey smudge. Bill in spring and summer bright yellow, becoming brown or brownish-horn in autumn and winter, especially on culmen. Eye brown. Legs and feet pale yellowish. **Adult female** Entire upperparts from forehead and crown to back and scapulars olive-brown tinged grey; rump and uppertail-coverts similar but more greyish. Tail grey-brown or greyer with pale greyish fringes to outer feathers. Thin pale yellow eye-ring; cheeks and ear-coverts warm brown finely streaked darker, often showing pale buffish area from white moustachial area to below ear-coverts; submoustachial stripe a blackish row of spots. Wings as upperparts with rust-brown fringes to median and greater coverts, alula and primary coverts; finer paler edges to flight feathers, tertials edged warm brown. Chin and throat white, but heavy black streaks on lower throat continue as blackish spots on sides and centre of breast; underparts mostly white but sides of breast orange to rusty reddish-buff extending to flanks and underwing-coverts; spots continue (occasionally as arrowheads) onto belly and lower flanks. Bill yellowish in breeding season, otherwise mostly dark horn, but some show paler or yellowish base to lower mandible. **Immature** Juvenile similar to adult female but upperparts brownish or olive-brown tinged slate-grey especially on lower back and rump of immature male (wings and tail browner in juvenile female): pale orange-buff or brownish-yellow spots to tips of feathers of nape, sides of neck and mantle, edges of tertials, secondaries and outer primaries pale buff-brown, tips (and central shaft-streaks) to median coverts orange-buff, tips to greater coverts paler buff; underwing-coverts pale orange to rusty-brown in both sexes; chin and throat pale buff or whitish with dark malar stripes, becoming more orange on sides of neck to breast and flanks, and heavily spotted brownish-black on lower throat and upper breast; belly white with brown spots. Bill dark horn or blackish. Legs and feet yellowish.

First-winter male very similar to adult male on upperparts except for being slightly paler or blackish-grey (some show slightly darker centres to feathers and edges to blackish-brown flight feathers browner, including alula and primary coverts). Wing-coverts retain pale buff-brown tips to retained juvenile feathers. Face black but smudged brown. Chin and throat whitish with varying extent of blackish streaks; throat and breast blackish on yellowish-white ground colour, or blackish with dull buffish edges or fringes; rest of underparts white with erratically spaced black to greyish spots, thighs grey. Upper mandible blackish-horn with yellowish cutting edges; entire lower mandible yellow. Legs dark reddish-brown.

GEOGRAPHICAL VARIATION Birds breeding in China have previously been separated as *T. c. lateus* but variation now considered clinal. Differs weakly from nominate by the black on the head of the male being more sharply defined from the slate-grey upperparts, and the flanks being more uniform dark grey, legs brownish (La Touche 1925–1930).

VOICE Call a thin *tsweee* or *tsuuu*. Song a series of rich, clear, musical whistles and trills, fluted as in Song Thrush (124), often repeated several times in quick succession: *see tew, see tew, see tew, titupi-tit, seea tyew, see a tyu, see a tyu, se a tyu, tilit tilit tillit, tyu tyatyew, tyatyew, tullut tullut tillit...*, etc.; also includes *tutulee tutulee tutulee* and *pee chew, pee chew, pee chew* and variations; may also include some rising or spiralling notes before repeating previous phrases; phrases and pauses both vary in length, with some rapid/short and others slower/longer. Song often delivered for long period; usually from the tops of trees; usually most song given at dawn and dusk when several males may sing in chorus.

STATUS AND DISTRIBUTION Fairly common but only local in southern Japan. Breeds in two discrete areas. Throughout Japan from Hokkaido south to Kyushu, and in central and eastern China from Kweichow, though Hunan to Hupeh, southern Henan and Anwei. In winter both populations merge and, except for a few birds which occasionally remain in southern Japan, occur in southern China from southern Yunnan east through southern Kiangsi to Kwangtung and Hainan and to northern-central Vietnam (Tonkin, North and Central Annam) and occasionally to northern and central Laos.

MOVEMENTS Migratory. All breeding birds (apart from a few in southern Japan) move south or south-west through the Nansei Shoto/Ryukyu Islands, Korea and eastern and central China to winter in southern China and northern Indochina. Departures from breeding areas in Japan in late August to mid-October, but some birds have left parts of Anwei and Hupeh by the end of September whilst others linger in central and southern Japan into late October and early November. A passage migrant and winter visitor in small numbers to Hong Kong from November to the end of April, most often between January and April. Return movements in eastern China and southern and central Japan in early April and early May but through the rest of Japan and north-central China not usually seen until late April or early May (La Touche 1925–1930).

A vagrant to Sakhalin Island and southern Laos; an annual but rare passage migrant to Taiwan (W.-H. Fang pers. comm.); has also occurred (mostly April and September) in Korea and Thailand, with 3 records in latter: Doi Inthanon (February 1993), Sakaerat, near Khao Yai National Park (December 1998) and Phu Jong Na Yoi National Park, north-east Thailand (January 1999).

HABITAT Breeds in dense, well-shaded woods or forests on hills or sides of mountains at 400–1500 m (1300–5000'), sometimes lower (e.g. in seaside woodlands in northern Japan); either in mixed or deciduous woods with brush or scrub and sparse understorey vegetation; prefers wooded valleys with streams and rivers although in Japan also occurs in open deciduous woods, gardens of shrines and large gardens in wooded hills. Occurs in similar habitat on migration and in winter but also in lowland woods, thickets and edges of cultivation.

BEHAVIOUR Shy and inconspicuous; many habits typical of *Turdus* thrushes. Usually alone or in pairs but in winter associates with flocks of Siberian Thrushes in broadleaved evergreen forests and undergrowth in Central Annam, Vietnam, and with Grey-backed Thrush in Hong Kong. Feeds on a variety of insects, earthworms and fruit, in winter also on the fruit of *Schefflera octophylla*.

BREEDING Season: April to July (China) or to August (Japan). Nest: consists of dry grasses, rootlets, twigs, mud and moss, lined with fine grasses and hair, usually placed in a fork in a tree (usually a fir but occasionally a deciduous tree) or branch or in a tangle of vines and creepers up to 10 m (33') from the ground. Eggs: usually 4 but exceptionally 2–5, variable in colour from light creamy-grey and pale greenish to reddish-cream with lilac blotches and pale or dark reddish-brown spots. Incubation period 12–13 days. Double- or triple-brooded except in the north of the range.

MOULT Adults have a complete post-breeding moult, completed before departure to winter quarters; juvenile also completes first-winter moult before autumn departure.

MEASUREMENTS Wing, male 111–121, female 109–119; tarsus, male 29–31, female 27.5–30; bill 18.5–21 (La Touche 1925–1930, Dementiev & Gladkov 1954). Weight apparently unrecorded.

REFERENCES La Touche (1925–1930).

108 WHITE-COLLARED BLACKBIRD *Turdus albocinctus* Plate 32

Turdus Albicollis Royle, 1839, *Illus. Bot. Himalayan Mountains* 2 (1835), pl. 8, fig. 3 – Himalayas [restricted to Dehra Dun by Ripley (1961) *Synopsis Birds India Pakistan*: 531].

IDENTIFICATION 27–28.5 cm (10½–11¼"). A virtually all-black or blackish-brown thrush with a distinctive bright white throat to breast and collar. Adult male is very similar to Blackbird (111) but entire white collar is diagnostic. Female a duller version of male, generally dull rufous-brown with a buffish throat, breast and collar. **Confusion species** Once seen well the presence of the broad whitish-buff throat to breast and collar separates both sexes from any other black or dark brown thrush. No white in wing makes confusion with Grey-winged Blackbird unlikely at any age.

DESCRIPTION Sexes differ. **Adult male** Head and face jet-black or glossy black on cheeks, ear-coverts, forehead and crown extending to mantle and back. Broad white collar across nape from sides of neck and upper mantle joins with white on chin and throat to centre of breast, white often spotted finely with buff or brown and chin and sides of throat often finely spotted with black. Rest of upperparts including wings and tail black with some glossy black edges to greater coverts, flight feathers and outer tail feathers; underwing-coverts also black. Rest of underparts brownish-black, undertail-coverts black with whitish shaft-streaks; may also show some greyer-black tips or fringes to upper- and undertail-coverts. Bill orange-yellow, slightly dusky along culmen or at tip. Eye brown or dark brown. Legs and feet greyish-yellow to dark brown tinged yellow. **Adult female** Black of male replaced by brown or warm gingery-brown, forehead to crown and wings and tail brown, face slightly ashy-brown, cheeks and ear-coverts often finely streaked pale buff; collar and throat to breast buffish- or pale greyish-white, often with some dark tips on sides of neck and nape. Flight feathers and tail dark brown edged lighter on innerwebs; underwing-coverts rufous-brown. Lower breast, belly and flanks more russet-brown than upperparts with fine buffish fringes; vent and undertail-coverts brown with white central shafts and tips. Much individual variation with some much darker below. May show pale brown eye-ring. **Immature** Juvenile similar to adult female but with rusty buff-brown shaft-streaks to head, nape and mantle; median and greater coverts brown with rusty-buff to buff-brown tips forming pale wing-bars; chin and throat as in adult but duller and less extensive, rest of underparts pale to orange-brown mottled with blackish-brown tips to most feathers.

GEOGRAPHICAL VARIATION None. Monotypic.

VOICE Call a characteristic thrush-like throaty or chuckling *chuck-chuck* or *tuck-tuck-tuck-tuck*; alarm note similar but with greater emphasis. Song sad or mellow in tone and recalls those of Blackbird or Song Thrush (124) but with less varied phrases and given in repeated bursts, a descending *tew-i, tew-u, tew-o* or *hoo-ee, hoo-ou, hoo-uu*, varied with *tew-eeo* and interspersed with pauses of up to 10 seconds; sings usually at dawn or in the pre-dawn hour, also at dusk, usually from atop a tall tree; song period from late March or mid-April to early August.

STATUS AND DISTRIBUTION Common or locally common. Breeds in the Himalayas between 2270 and 4250 m (7500–14,000'), from southern Kashmir and northern Himachal Pradesh east through northern India, Nepal (2700–3400 m/8900–11,220'), southern and south east Tibet (to north of Lhasa) to Bhutan, Arunachal Pradesh and Assam east to central Szechwan. Winters at lower elevations between 1500 and 3000 m (4950–10,000') but mainly above 2000 m (6600'), within the breeding range and south to northern Bengal, Meghalaya and Manipur.

MOVEMENTS An altitude migrant to lower levels within the breeding range; noted as leaving wintering areas in central Nepal in early April. Has occurred as a vagrant to north-west Burma in February, and to Bangladesh (1 record in February 1989).

HABITAT Breeds in oak, horse chestnut and rhododendron forests, open conifer forests and mixed deciduous and conifer woods with a good layer of moss or other ground cover, forest edges and margins; also found in dwarf rhododendron scrub above the treeline and may forage in open pastures and meadows at some distance from trees. In winter usually in more extensive deciduous woods or forests but also in open areas such as large gardens in the vicinity of villages.

BEHAVIOUR Generally shy and wary; quick to give alarm call in breeding season, slightly more approachable in winter; flight through trees swift and fairly direct. Often in the upper parts of tall trees. Usually alone or in pairs in the breeding season; more sociable at other times and often in small flocks or in company with other thrushes including Grey-winged Blackbird (110). Feeds in trees and bushes and on the ground, mainly on fruit and berries, particularly cotoneaster, crab-apples, hawthorn and holly, showing a preference in Nepal for *Hedera nipalensis*; also a wide variety of invertebrates.

BREEDING Season: late April (possibly late March in some areas) to mid-July. Nest: a large cup of dry grasses, moss, roots and leaves lined with dry grass and fine roots, sometimes also mud; usually on a branch or in a tree-fork, occasionally in a hole in a dead tree-trunk or on a stump, up to 3 m (10') from the ground, or on the ground concealed with moss. Eggs: 3–4, greyish-white to pale blue, similar to those of Blackbird but with larger or bolder reddish-brown blotches. Incubation by female only.

MOULT No information.

MEASUREMENTS Wing, male (n=48) 133–151, female (n=40) 131–143; tarsus 33–38; bill (from skull) 24.5–30. Weight, male 90–103, female 92–107 g (Ali & Ripley 1983).

REFERENCES Ali & Ripley (1983).

109 RING OUZEL *Turdus torquatus*   Plate 33
Turdus torquatus Linnaeus, 1758, *Syst. Nat.* (ed. 10): 170 – Europa [restricted to Sweden by Hartert (1910) *Vög. pal. Fauna* 1: 663].

IDENTIFICATION 23–24 cm (9–9½"). A sturdy thrush of open moorlands, uplands and mountainsides with sparse or stunted bushes. Male is black or blackish-grey with a distinctive white crescent across the breast, whitish edges to the wings and fine whitish fringes to some of the underparts. Female similar but duller and browner, with the crescent absent or duller and obscured with buffish-brown fringes; also usually shows more extensive whitish fringes or tips to the underparts. Both sexes give a distinctive harsh rattling call. **Confusion species** Poorly seen Blackbirds (111) may pose problems. Male distinguished by white edges to flight feathers and bright white crescent on breast.

Female and first-winter less easily told (particularly from immature Blackbirds with whitish throat and breast) owing to lack of or obscured crescent on breast; in such cases best told by extent of pale edges and tips to the underparts, particularly the lower breast, belly and flanks, and by the prominent frosted grey edges to the greater coverts, secondaries and tertials; also by call. Ring Ouzel unlikely to occur in Blackbird habitat except on passage, although the species can be be adjacent in gardens and plantations in or near moorland. Call of Fieldfare (122) is similar to that given by Ring Ouzel, especially the note given in flight, but where Fieldfare has a *chack* or a chuckling *chack-*

chack-chack Ring Ouzel gives a hard, abrupt *tak-tak-tak*.

DESCRIPTION Sexes differ. **Adult male** Entire head and face to scapulars, rump and uppertail-coverts jet- or sooty-black, at close range feathers of mantle and scapulars to rump edged blackish-brown. Tail blackish-brown, outer feathers very narrowly edged greyish-white, undertail greyish. Lesser and median coverts blackish or blackish-grey finely edged and tipped pale grey or whitish, greater coverts similar but more broadly edged pale greyish-white, alula and primary coverts as median but finely edged and tipped pale greyish; flight feathers same but secondaries and tertials broadly edged pale greyish forming a pale panel on closed wing and contrasting pattern, against the blacker coverts, in flight. Axillaries and under-wing-coverts blackish-brown narrowly fringed white. Chin and throat to upper breast black; broad white crescent or gorget across upper breast, sometimes narrowly fringed greyish-brown, lower breast blackish-brown but grading into black on centre of belly and flanks, which are fringed pale brown or greyish-brown (in fresh plumage), ven-tral area blackish; lower flanks and undertail-coverts like belly but more broadly fringed paler with whitish shafts. Bill yellow to greenish-yellow with tip and culmen ridge, occasionally also base of lower mandible, blackish or brownish-horn; yellow more extensive in summer. Eye blackish-brown. Legs dark brown to dull or dark pink. In worn plumage (spring and early summer) the grey or brown fringes on body are lost and plumage is more sooty-black, crescent on breast pure white. **Adult female** Similar to male and often inseparable in the field, but generally duller or browner (not black) on head and back. Upperparts brownish-black with broad brownish-black edges to feath-ers. Wings blackish-brown with pale buffish or buffish-white edges to median and greater coverts, tertials and flight feathers but generally duller and thinner than male. Underparts slightly variable with either blackish lower face, chin and throat to upper breast or with whitish tips to feathers. Cres-cent across upper breast generally narrower and duller white and obscured with buffish-brown tips, but in some may be pure white in summer. Lower breast, belly and flanks blackish but feathers heav-ily fringed white, whitish or pale buffish-brown, sometimes with pale shaft-streaks; vent usually blacker or with narrower fringes but undertail-coverts as belly or with pale buff-brown or whitish only on tips to feathers. Legs and feet brown to dark brown. In worn plumage slightly darker, as brown-black edges are lost. Bill brown or brown-ish-horn with dull yellow along lower mandible or restricted to base. **Juvenile** Similar to adult female but browner with fringes of upperparts deep brown; mantle, upper back and scapulars often show varying amounts of fine white edges and shaft-streaks. Wings and tail generally more visibly browner than adults with pale buffish fringes to deep brown wing-coverts, fringes broadening towards tip, flight feathers more like those of adult female but with thin whitish shaft-streaks. In the hand tail feathers more pointed than adult. Chin and throat like adult female or with pale buff base colour, but with blackish-brown streaks; generally lacks or faintly shows crescent, breast blackish-brown with warm buff-brown edges and buff tips; rest of underparts blackish-brown with pale whitish-buff edges and tips, undertail-coverts sim-ilar with broader or paler fringes or with whitish tips and shaft-streaks. **First-winter male** Very like adult (some indistinguishable) but on average duller; underparts blackish-grey with whitish tips to chin and throat; off-white breast-band; fairly broad white fringes to belly and lower flanks (occasionally to undertail-coverts); browner greater coverts (usually outers), broadly edged whitish and contrasting with newer inners, which have narrower greyish-white edges (contrast between different-aged feathers sometimes still obvious in following spring); pale buffish edges to median coverts; flight and tail feathers retained from juvenile plumage. **First-winter female** Like same-aged male but also more like adult female in winter (may be equally indistinguishable); throat pale or dull whitish and crescent usually indistinct or obscured by broad dark brown barring at tips of feathers; may retain some outer juvenile greater coverts with creamy-whitish tips (as in same-aged male, sometimes still shows these in following spring); many have broad dark tips obscuring cres-cent into first-summer plumage and are very simi-lar to adult summer female.

GEOGRAPHICAL VARIATION Three races; varia-tion largely clinal and concerns the extent of white fringes to body feathers.

Adults of race *alpestris* are similar to those of nominate but much broader, whiter edges to wing-coverts and flight feathers show as a paler, more frosted area; also broad pale fringes to underparts, particularly lower breast, belly and undertail-coverts, create pronounced scaly pattern; some paler brown edges and tips to upperparts variable in extent. Adult female as nominate but with broad white fringes to chin and throat, often merging to form a pale area finely spotted black; white on breast often shaded or spotted brown; lower breast, belly and undertail-coverts as male but with more extensive white fringes. Juvenile told by paler tips to feathers on underparts, first-winter similar but with retained inner greater coverts (some with white tips but many indistinguishable from adult).

Race *amicorum* has larger, whiter crescent and broader (than other races) white edges and tips to greater coverts and flight feathers (particularly edges of secondaries), forming a prominent panel on closed wing; underparts of male black or black-ish-brown, in female with narrow white fringes (absent in worn plumage).

VOICE Most frequent note is a dry or harsh *chak*, *tchack* or *tchuck* or even *djook*, frequently drawn out into a rattling *chack-ack-ack* given either on the ground or in flight, also heard at night from migrat-ing birds; flight calls also include a dry rolling *tcherrr* or *djuerrr* or in some a drawn-out *tschweerr*, a trilling *cherree* and a high-pitched *ssierk* or buzzing *zzierp* and a more abrupt or startled

347

tschirk. Alarm calls, frequently given in presence of man, are a rapid harsh version of the *tchack* call note, more usually run together as *tack-tac-tac* or *tac-a-tac-tac-tac* or *clack-clac-clac*, like two sharp stones hit together, often repeated at length especially if disturbance continues. Has one or two calls similar to Blackbird, a thin high-pitched *ssiii* and a more penetrating but thinner and frequently very high-pitched *zieeh* given on territory. Song a repeated series of melancholy and monotonous fluty whistled phrases interspersed with a hesitating pause given as *pi-ree pi-ree pi-ree...* or *choouee-chouee-chouee...* or even a more emphatic *ter-wee, ter-wee, ter-wee*; in some the phrase is often on one note as in *pee pee pee* or *tru-tru-tru*, whilst others can be slightly more melodious like *trruu-trruu-trruu-chee-chee-chee* or *tu-li tu-li chiv chiv* fading away at the end; also known to end with a rattling twitter or chuckling notes often given softly as a subsong, recalling subsong of Redwing (123). Appears to have dialectal variation in song pattern between parts of the breeding range e.g. song of birds in central England differs in pattern of notes from those further north (Appleyard 1994): overall structure of phrases recalls Song Thrush (124) but sad or melancholy tone more like Mistle Thrush (126). Song given from low but fairly prominent perch such as a rock, crag, wall, tall heather clump, bush or tree; mostly in the early morning and again in the evening, also occasionally at night and exceptionally in flight; has been known to sing on spring migration. Song period late March to mid- or late June, exceptionally into early July.

STATUS AND DISTRIBUTION Common throughout much of the range but often widely dispersed.

T. t. torquatus Discontinuously in western Europe from Ireland (where restricted mainly to the north-west and the south-west with several isolated outposts in the west, east and north-east) and the British Isles east more continuously through Scandinavia from southern Norway north to North Cape, Lapland and then south-east through the Kola Peninsula and eastern Finland, small outposts in northern Latvia and south-west Estonia, occasionally northern Denmark and northern France (Brittany); has also bred in Faeroes (single pairs in 1981 and 1982) and may also breed occasionally in northern Algeria (Urban *et al.* 1997). In winter to higher areas of north-central France and the Massif Central, central and south-east Spain, Middle and High Atlas ranges of central Morocco and oases of southern lowlands, High Plateau and Saharan Atlas of northern Algeria (south to about Beni Abbes and Ghardaia), north-west Tunisia (to about Gafsa and Gabes and the Tripoli area of north-west Libya – where scarce – south to Jebel Nafusa); may also occur in small numbers in Bulgaria and Greece.

T. t. alpestris Northern, central and southern Spain and the Pyrenees, also more continuously from southern Germany, southern Poland, Czech Republic and Slovakia, south to central and southern France, east through the Alps to Austria and northern Italy (south to Lombardy and Veneto –

erratically south to the northern Apennines to about Tuscany – decreasing in frequency southwards) and south through Yugoslavia to Albania and northern Greece (where generally rare or very scarce – first nests discovered in May 1979); also in extreme south-west Ukraine and Romania to Bulgaria, Thrace and western Turkey. In winter to lower elevations of similar ranges as nominate in northern Algeria, north-west Tunisia, Sardinia, Sicily, Malta and Cyprus (where scarce or irregular), central Romania, central Bulgaria, Greece, many islands in the Aegean and parts of southern Turkey. Irregular or uncommon visitor to the north coast of Egypt (west to about Bahig), the Nile delta, south to about Cairo and the Suez Canal area; scarce in winter to northern and central Israel, becoming rare in the south and in Sinai, Libya and Sudan (Khartoum and Dongola).

T. t. amicorum Isolated parts of the Taurus range, south-central Turkey (this may be an area of *alpestris–amicorum* intergradation) discontinuously east to the Caucasus (Azerbaijan and Armenia) and northern Iran, also discontinuously east through the Elburz range to the Kopet Dagh area of southern Turkmenia. In winter to lower altitudes of western and south-west Iran (Zagros range), parts of Iraq and occasionally to the Sinai in northern Egypt; rare or vagrant to south and east Israel. Has also wintered in eastern Saudi Arabia (where generally a rare or scarce migrant): a few at Dhahran (December 1970 to January 1971) and singles (January 1972), at Abu Ali (January 1977), Dammam (February 1980), Shadgum (December 1982) and Al-Sinaiyah (November 1986) (Bundy *et al.* 1989).

MOVEMENTS Migratory or partial migrant. Breeding birds in the British Isles, Scandinavia, northwest Russia and central Europe move south or south-south-west to winter in parts of France but mainly around the Mediterranean in southern Spain, Morocco, northern Algeria plus Greece and western Turkey. Birds breeding in the Pyrenees, southern France, Switzerland, Romania and Bulgaria are largely altitude migrants moving to lower levels in the winter. Autumn departures begin in September with most movement in mid-September and October when passage around or over the North Sea heaviest; arrival in Spain, North Africa and through Greece and Cyprus in mid-October and November but some juvenile birds depart later than adults with November records in Britain not unusual. Birds from southern Germany and southern Poland winter in Yugoslavia and Bulgaria; passage over the Bosphorus is from August to October but mainly from mid-September. Further east *amicorum* moves about the same time with passage through Turkey and the southern Caucasus in September and October, through Israel and into Egypt from late October to early or mid-December.

Return movements begin in early or mid-February in Middle East and March in southern Europe with some birds back on breeding territories by the end of that month. Birds in Estonia and Lithuania in February and early March were exceptionally early migrants or had wintered further north than usual. Passage through central and northern Europe and arrivals in Scandinavia mainly April and May. In Caucasus arrival on breeding areas often delayed by persistence of winter snows.

A rare or irregular migrant to inland oases of Libya (Fezzan), November to January. A rare visitor or vagrant to Iceland (24 records to end of 1995), Portugal (where probably annual), Canary Islands (Tenerife, El Hierro), Mauretania (2), Sudan (2), Syria, Jordan (2 records but up to 10 mid-March 1995), Saudi Arabia, Bahrain (1), U.A.E., Kuwait (1) and Oman (2); *alpestris* is a vagrant to Sweden (June 1998).

HABITAT Breeds in wild and rock-strewn uplands to 300–620 m (1000–2000′) in British Isles, higher elsewhere in Europe, including heather moorlands with rocky outcrops, crags, scree-slopes or boulders, mountains and hilly areas with sparse stunted trees; in Scandinavia breeds in open flat areas above the treeline but also occurs on the edge of birch or spruce plantations; in some places breeds down to sea-level. Race *alpestris* usually higher, at 1100–1300 m (3630–4300′) in Switzerland in edges of moist conifer woods or stands of pines. In Turkey *alpestris* breed from near sea-level to about 1500 m (4950′) but in the east *amicorum* breeds between 2000 and 3000+m (6600–9900′). In Russia breeds in conifer and occasionally beech forest; in the Caucasus breeds mostly in the upper levels of forest where it occurs in rhododendrons, junipers and other stunted bushes. On migration occurs regularly at lower altitudes mostly on the coast where it inhabits hedgerows, bushes and coastal scrub, also on downland habitat in southern England. In winter mainly in the same type of habitat or on dry slopes, ravines and hillsides up to 1800 m (6000′) or 2700 m (8900′) in North Africa but also at lower altitudes; in North Africa also inhabits open cedar forests, evergreen oaks and palm groves in oases.

BEHAVIOUR Usually occurs alone or in pairs, but may form large loose flocks on migration; may also mix with other thrushes, e.g. Song Thrush or Redwings, at fruiting trees. Actions on ground and in flight similar to Blackbird but usually much bolder, more alert or purposeful; raises tail on landing, then lowers it slowly. Perches on rocks, bushes, trees (more usual in the central and south of the range) and clumps of heather. Strongly territorial but neighbouring birds may feed in neutral areas between territories. Flight usually direct and often flies for some distance; generally shyer than Blackbird; when disturbed dashes swiftly low over

terrain into gullies, crevices or breaks in rocks or hills. Usually roosts in rocky or open habitat but some breeding birds roost in conifers. Feeds mostly on the ground on invertebrates, both adult and larvae, including earwigs, bugs, flies, sawflies, moths, beetles, millipedes, snails, slugs and earthworms; has also been known to eat small lizards, newts and salamanders; also takes berries and fruits of bramble, bilberry, blueberry, buckthorn, cherry, cloudberry, cranberry, crowberry, currant, elder, hawthorn, ivy, juniper, mistletoe, olive, rowan, sloe and wild strawberry.

BREEDING Season: early April to mid- to late July or early August in the north. Nest: mostly coarse grasses, heather, twigs and some earth or mud, lined with thin moor grasses; usually placed on or close to the ground in low vegetation, especially heather and bracken, also on ledge, crevice or earth bank, under rocks or (*amicorum*) rhododendrons, occasionally in mine-shaft or pot-hole (up to 5 m/16½′ below ground), rarely in trees in west of the range (more frequently by *alpestris* in central and southern Europe, where usually placed next to trunk or main branches and up to 16 m/53′ from the ground, but more usually within 3.5 m/12′); built by female. Eggs: 4–5, exceptionally 3–6, pale bluish and variably spotted, splashed or blotched with reddish or purplish-brown, occasionally unmarked or entirely spotted with reddish-brown. Incubation period 12–14 days, mostly by female but also apparently sometimes by male. Fledging period 11–15 days. Usually two broods except for the more northerly breeding birds. Breeds in first year of life.

MOULT Adults have complete post-breeding moult from late June to early September, usually completed before leaving the breeding area. Juveniles have a partial moult of the head, body, median coverts and varying numbers of the greater coverts between July and September; however, some can retain all greater coverts into late October (Svensson 1992); most *alpestris* complete their moult by mid-September, but some take longer.

MEASUREMENTS Wing (nominate and *alpestris*) male 136–149, female 133.5–144; tarsus 28–35.5; bill (from skull) 22–25; *amicorum* wing, male 134–151, female 132–139; bill (to feathers) male 16–18, female 16–19. Weight 92–138 g (Dementiev & Gladkov 1954, Cramp *et al.* 1988).

REFERENCES Appleyard (1994), Bundy *et al.* (1989), Cramp *et al.* (1988), Delgado *et al.* (1988), Dementiev & Gladkov (1954), Tucker & Heath (1994).

110 GREY-WINGED BLACKBIRD *Turdus boulboul* Plate 32

Lanius boulboul Latham, 1790, *Index Orn.* 1: 80 – India [restricted to Darjeeling by Baker (1924) *Fauna Brit. India, Birds* (ed. 2) 2: 130].

IDENTIFICATION 28–29 cm (11–11½″). A large, distinctive, almost entirely black thrush with pale grey panels in the wing obvious both in flight and at rest. Adult male is like European and most Asian races of Blackbird (111) including yellow bill and eye-ring but greater coverts, secondaries and tertials broadly pale grey, tips to median coverts also pale grey or whitish. Adult female is almost entirely olive-brown tinged with grey and replaces the pale wing-panel of the male with a broad diffuse wing-bar formed of warm or rufous-brown and pale tips to the greaters. Immature is like female but has less defined wing marking and is streaked with dull buff-brown on the crown to mantle and barred or scaled brownish on the breast and belly. **Confusion species** Within range only likely problems are White-collared Blackbird (108) and Blackbird, but obvious pale white (male) or buffish-grey (female) collar is diagnostic of former, as are the unpatterned wings of both species for both sexes.

DESCRIPTION Sexes differ. **Adult male** Almost entirely jet-black or glossy black except for narrow orange-yellow eye-ring, brownish tinge to crown and mantle and grey tinge to rump in fresh plumage; dark grey or blackish uppertail-coverts; pale grey to whitish tips to median coverts and broad silvery-grey edges and tips to outer greater coverts and lead-grey on outerwebs of inner greaters; inner secondaries edged pale grey increasing in extent inwardly, and inner secondaries and tertials broadly grey on outerwebs, forming panel on closed wing and very obvious in flight; innerwebs of secondaries and tertials glossy black, some secondaries also tipped white. Lower breast and belly to undertail-coverts as upperparts but duller or tinged browner, belly and flanks edged pale grey and creating a scaled effect. Bill orange or orange-yellow with darker tip. Eye brown or dark brown. Legs and feet brownish-yellow to yellow, soles of feet always yellow. **Adult female** Head and face dark olive-brown to dark brown with pale flecks or fine streaks on cheeks and ear-coverts. Wings and tail brown, slightly warmer than on rest of upperparts, median coverts brown to dark brown, outers finely tipped white, greater coverts warm brown finely edged and becoming greyish, greyish-whitish at tips and contrasting with blackish primary coverts; secondaries and tertials warm or rufous-brown on outerwebs and dark brown on innerwebs. Underparts olive-brown or slightly tinged grey on breast and belly and warm brown on flanks; chin and throat pale buffish faintly spotted or streaked darker. Bill as male or variably bright or dull yellow on upper and orange on lower mandible, or dark brown with yellow cutting edges and base to lower mandible. Eye-ring slightly paler or whiter than male. Legs and feet brown or yellowish-brown. **Immature** Juvenile male blackish-brown on upperparts and cheeks and ear-coverts, with pale buff shaft-streaks on crown, mantle and scapulars, also some dark tips to nape, mantle and back; median coverts have pale brown shaft-streaks and pale buff tips, greater coverts pale or greyish-buff on outers, becoming greyer-brown on inners; secondaries and tertials similar but broadly edged grey or buffish-brown, flight feathers blackish-brown. Chin and throat to breast pale creamy-buff but spotted dark brown on breast, belly similar but barred or scaled brown or dark brown. Juvenile

female like same-aged male but more olive-brown or warm olive-brown on coverts and secondaries and lacks any grey in wings as median and greater coverts are warm buff-brown.

GEOGRAPHICAL VARIATION None. Monotypic.

VOICE Call a series of fairly typical Blackbird-like chucklings including the *chuck-chuck* variations, given with some emphasis, e.g. *chook-chook*, as an alarm call; also *churi* used as a contact note, a harsh *churr* during the breeding season, and a harsh series of typical churring calls when the nest or young are approached; also has a characteristic repeated roosting call, a mournful three-note whistle, *pie oooh-tie* with the middle note slurred downward. Song far-carrying and similar to both Blackbird and Song Thrush (124) in tone but with a slightly slower delivery of rich, fluty, mellow notes; consists mainly of a soft opening note followed by four high-pitched notes descending in tone, but apparently some variation or dialectal differences, with some birds having complex series of notes including chuckles, trilling or ringing whistles and *seechoo*, *weeteeoo* and *der-did-dleoo* phrases or *tweee-toooh tweee-toooh chuiyui-twit weear-twit weear-trtrtrtt-whih-whih-which wheeeyar-wheeeyar*, but generally only very few phrases repeated. In Nepal rendered as *chir-bles-we-bullie-dee*; *we-put-kur-we-put-kur*; *who-bori-chal-et-cha-he* (Fleming *et al.* 1979). Sings during the day but mostly towards dusk from tree-tops, including isolated trees in clearings; song period mid-March to mid-August.

STATUS AND DISTRIBUTION Common or locally common; rare in southern China. Breeds in the Himalayas mostly between 1500 and 2300 m (4950–8000') from northern Pakistan (Murree Hills and Kaghan valley), but apparently absent from Kashmir, east through northern India, Nepal (regularly up to 2700 m and exceptionally to 3300 m/ 8900–10,900'), Sikkim, Bhutan, northern Bengal and Arunachal Pradesh and the hill states of northeast India east into western and southern Yunnan and south-west Szechwan with an outpost on the Yao Shan range in Kwangsi; possibly a rare resident in northern Laos (Xiangkhouang and Bokeo provinces) (Duckworth *et al.* 1999) and North Tonkin, Vietnam. In winter spreads out more widely at lower altitudes, usually between 1200 and 2100 m (3960–6950') but down to about 600 m (2000') in northern Pakistan, within and slightly south of the breeding range; also Assam and into northern and eastern Burma and south along the Arakan Yoma.

A vagrant to Bangladesh (2 records: March 1978 and March 1985) and a rare winter visitor to northwest Thailand (but probably occurs annually in small numbers).

MOVEMENTS An altitude migrant occurring at lower altitudes in winter; some birds may move some way south to the plains of north-central India (e.g. Bharatpur, Rajasthan). Most movements are undertaken at the onset of severe weather, usually in October and early November; return movements are in March and early April although bad weather may then keep some birds at low altitudes.

HABITAT Breeds in damp or moist broad-leaved forests of oak and rhododendron with a thick layer of ground vegetation, also in tall conifer forests, clearings and dry scrub on open hillsides; usually found in thicker woods and forests than the similar White-collared Blackbird. In winter found in similar habitats usually at lower levels but also in more open woods, bush scrub and large wooded gardens in the vicinity of villages.

BEHAVIOUR Generally shy and quick to take flight at the sight of an intruder; when disturbed flies to mid-levels of tree, then moves upwards staying close to the trunk; on the ground hops or bounds in typical *Turdus* thrush fashion; usually alone or in pairs in the breeding season when males become aggressive towards others; in winter occurs in small flocks and may associate with White-collared Blackbird and other thrushes. Feeds mostly on the ground or in fruiting or moss-covered trees and along branches on a variety of invertebrates and their larvae, snails, slugs and earthworms, also various seasonally available fruit and berries, particularly *Cotoneaster* and *Berberis*.

BREEDING Season: March to August (mostly May–June). Nest: a large but fairly delicate or flimsy cup of grass, leaves, moss, lichens and some roots, often with a lining of mud, fine grasses, small fern stems, lichens and hair (occasionally entirely of moss lined with fine plant material and animal hairs), usually placed close to the trunk or in the fork of a mossy tree, on a stump or between branches 2–5 m (6½–16½') from the ground or on the ground on a steep bank or among fallen tree roots. Eggs: 3–4, pale sea-green or yellowish-green and blotched, spotted or streaked with pale reddish-brown or light purple. Incubation by female but both parents build the nest and feed the nestlings. Two broods.

MOULT No information.

MEASUREMENTS Wing, male (n=66) 140–153, female (n=56) 131–155; tarsus 33–37; bill (from skull) 22.5–30. Weight, male 88–105 g, female 88–111 g (Ali & Ripley 1983).

REFERENCES Ali & Ripley (1983), Duckworth *et al.* (1999), Fleming *et al.* (1979), Roberts (1992).

111 BLACKBIRD *Turdus merula* Plates 33, 34

Turdus merula Linnaeus, 1758, *Syst. Nat.* (ed. 10): 170 – in *Europae sylvis* [restricted to Sweden by Hartert (1910) *Vög. pal. Fauna* 1: 665].

IDENTIFICATION 24–29 cm (9½–11½"). Indian subcontinent races usually 24–25 cm (9½–9¾"); three races from the Himalayas to China are the largest 28–29 cm (11–11½"). A medium to large thrush. Males are distinctive with all glossy black plumage and bright orange-yellow bill, prominent eye-ring and dark legs. Females are dull or dark brown on the head, upperparts, wings and tail and slightly paler brown below with a rufous tinge to the breast and some faint mottling or darker streaking. Juveniles are paler than the adult female and heavily spotted, mottled or flecked with orange, rufous or chestnut on the underparts; first-year birds resemble the adult female. Several races in India and Sri Lanka are more distinct in their plumage differences. **Confusion species** Most likely confusion may be between race *kinnisii* and Sri Lankan Whistling-thrush (18) – for differences see Geographical Variation below – and with male Tickell's Thrush (105). Differs from Tickell's by more uniform slate-grey plumage and lack of white on belly to undertail-coverts. Unlikely to be confused with any other species within its extensive range; there are, however, similarities to a number of other allopatric species, e.g. Yemen Thrush (102), Island Thrush (112), and several all-black thrushes of Central and South America such as Sooty Thrush (131), Black Thrush (133) and Glossy-black Thrush (134) which may need to be considered when individuals in unfamiliar locations are encountered.

DESCRIPTION Sexes differ. **Adult male** Entirely black except for the orange-yellow bill and prominent orange-yellow eye-ring. Fresh plumage (late autumn) has a glossy sheen, particularly noticeable on upperparts and wings; worn plumage (late spring to late summer) much duller and sooty- or matt black; abrasion causes flight feathers to appear browner, often visible on closed wing from midwinter. In the hand innerwebs of flight feathers are an opaque greyish-black. Eye dark brown. Legs and feet blackish-brown. **Adult female** Head and face to lower back dark brown, sometimes much darker, approaching colour of male, sometimes a faint or brownish supercilium/sides of crown, or cheeks and ear-coverts slightly paler and finely streaked darker; wings, rump and tail blackish-brown. Underparts slightly paler or browner with some birds having pale or whitish-buff on chin; throat and upper breast often mottled darker with brown spots or streaks, breast and lower belly often a warmer tinge of brown but can be variably pale or buffish and mottled with darker spots; flanks, lower belly and undertail-coverts dusky-brown with some paler edges to feathers on flanks. Warm or rufous tinge to underparts most prominent in fresh plumage (late autumn) and disappears with wear so that by spring and summer most birds dull or dark brown on breast. Bill dark or horn-brown with variable amount of pale or dull yellow either confined to base of lower mandible or extending some way towards dark tip. Eye dark brown. Legs and feet dark brown. **Leucistic birds** Individuals showing leucistic plumage aberrations are not unusual. Most are males, some showing one or two white feathers or pairs of feathers in wings and tail, sometimes white outer tail feathers, also areas of whitish-cream either as a splash or over whole areas such as the head, wings or tails; occasionally entirely white individuals occur. Females can also show similar markings but rarely as white or as extensive as in males. **Immature** Juvenile similar to adult female but heavily speckled, spotted or streaked orange-buff or pale rufous on head, mantle and scapulars; back and rump darker brown and more sparsely spotted or flecked with rufous or orange spots or streaks. Tail narrower and pointed at tip, blackish in male and browner in female. Wings also like female but median and greater-coverts dark brown with wedge-shaped rufous-buff spots at tips, greaters similar but inners also have pale orange-buff central shafts; alula, primary coverts and flight feathers dark brown. Lores to over the eye dull rufous or orange-brown; cheeks and ear-coverts buffish-brown finely flecked or streaked paler; pale or indistinct yellowish eye-ring. Chin and throat dull yellowish with dark brown streaks becoming heavier or deeper rufous-buff on lower throat and upper breast. Breast orange or deep orange-buff heavily mottled or obscured with dark brown spots; flanks and belly paler orange or rufous-brown with darker smudges not as heavily defined as on breast. Lower belly and vent often dull whitish; undertail-coverts blackish-brown with whitish central shafts and orange-buff tips. Bill dark and similar to adult female. Separation of sexes at this age not reliable but male frequently darker or blacker than female (especially on flight feathers) with heavier rufous tones. **First-winter male** In fresh plumage resembles adult female with upperparts uniform blackish-brown to dingy grey-brown. Wing-coverts (see Moult), tertials, flight and tail feathers are retained into first-summer plumage; variable numbers of the (mostly inner) greater coverts are replaced in first autumn, the outer greater coverts usually unmoulted and contrasting with darker newer inner feathers, some birds showing pale orange central shaft to unmoulted greater coverts. Chin and throat whitish streaked fairly heavily dark brown; breast and upper belly brown to blackish-brown, occasionally deep rufous-brown mottled with darker edges or tips, flanks and lower belly to undertail-coverts similar to upperparts with flanks showing some darker edges and tips to feathers. Bill dark brownish-horn (until about January). **First-winter female** Very similar to adult female but slightly paler with breast rufous, variably spotted darker and flanks, belly, vent and undertail-coverts paler grey; birds in this plumage can show paler chestnut sides of crown. As in first-winter male some juvenile feathers are retained which are paler or more olive-brown than those of adult and may show grey or buffish tips (or remains of) on retained greater coverts. Bill dark brownish-horn. **First-summer male** Similar to adult but browner-black with some crown and mantle feathers edged brown-black, feathers on underparts with paler or greyish edges; unmoulted flight feathers browner than adult and outer greater coverts also browner than new and blacker inners as they are retained

from first winter. Bill becomes progressively all yellow but sometimes can still be mostly dark on upper mandible. **First-summer female** Very similar to adult female and not always told with certainty but some have upperparts not as dark, flight feathers browner and unmoulted outer greater coverts (if present) paler. Chin and throat streaked darker or blackish and may be indistinctly spotted or blotched darker on breast. Bill assumes dull yellow base to both mandibles and dark horn tip.

GEOGRAPHICAL VARIATION Fifteen races (at least three others have been proposed); variation mainly concerns the size and colour of adults. Birds of the races *maximus* (here including *buddae*), *mandarinus* and *intermedius* are the largest (28–29 cm/11–11½"), with broad bases to wings, long primary projection, prominent head and neck in flight and heavy undulating flight silhouette; *mandarinus* has entirely black or sooty-black upperparts and brownish-black underparts, a thin or narrow pale yellow eye-ring and sometimes (probably first-summer birds) a rufous tinge to sides of throat; *maximus* less glossy black and more blackish or dark sooty-brown, lacks an eye-ring and has a dull orange bill (may become bright orange in breeding season); female similar but generally dull dark brown with dark brown bill; *intermedius* very similar to previous two and apart from a slightly larger bill (larger than *maximus*) differs principally only in measurements. All three, together with *sowerbyi* from north-east China, are probably best regarded as an incipient species, Eastern Blackbird *Turdus mandarinus*, since they are clearly separated from the Indian and Palearctic races on distribution and size and there are also differences in voice and song structure.

Female *mandarinus* similar to male, mostly sooty-black to blackish-brown but with a narrow buffish-white throat becoming tinged rust-brown on breast and flanks and generally lacking any spotting or speckling on lower throat and breast, bill dull horn to dark brown with lower mandible green to horn-green; immature dark rufous-brown heavily barred with darker tips on mantle and barred or mottled with rufous-brown on underparts. Female *intermedius* has chin and centre of throat whitish-buff streaked dark brown on throat and suffused dull brown on lower throat and breast; breast also spotted darker brown; some birds also show slightly paler or greyer fringes to belly feathers. Juvenile *maxima* very blackish-brown (male) or browner (female) with paler centres to feathers on crown, mantle, back and rump; uppertail-coverts darker than rump. Chin and throat streaked buff, breast dark brown but lower breast to flanks, vent and undertail-coverts spotted or scaled yellowish-buff or light brown on tips.

Races *mauretanicus*, *cabrerae* and *azorensis* are the smallest (only in terms of millimetres). Male *mauretanicus* slightly glossier than nominate and female, on average, slightly darker or sootier-grey, underparts also dark and breast with mottled pattern of large dark spots finely bordered paler, also a much yellower bill than in other races; *aterrimus* slightly smaller and, on average, smaller-billed than nominate and duller black or tinged brownish with female paler brown above and greyer below. Race *azorensis* has short rounded wing-tips, female blackish-brown with greyish-white throat and well-defined dark streaks and yellow bill. Considerable variation exists in populations on the Canary Islands and some birds, particularly on Hierro and Palma, are darker than those of typical *cabrerae*; female *cabrerae* also yellow-billed, blackish-brown generally without rufous or brown tones and reduced pale area on throat. Both sexes of *syriacus* also darker or greyer than *merula* with male slatier grey-black and female generally greyer and less rufous below; juvenile also distinctive with much darker brown above and finely spotted pale orange on crown and nape becoming broad streaks on mantle and scapulars; underparts more visibly barred brown and whitish with warm buff-brown tinge to breast.

Several races in the Indian subcontinent and Sri Lanka very distinctive, particularly adult *nigropileus*, which have forehead to crown, lores, cheeks and ear-coverts black or blackish-brown, noticeably paler or greyish-brown on lower nape, mantle and scapulars to uppertail-coverts; tail blackish-brown edged slate-grey on outerwebs at base; wing-coverts grey-brown, alula, primary-coverts and flight feathers blackish-brown, edges of primaries narrowly paler grey (becoming greyish-brown when worn). Underwing-coverts pale ash-grey. Chin and throat mottled or speckled whitish, breast to central upper belly light buffish-brown, possibly also tinged browner on breast, belly whitish with buffish or duller brown; flanks suffused grey-brown; thighs and undertail-coverts pale ash-grey, latter with broad whitish central shafts. Narrow orange-yellow eye-ring with similarly coloured post-ocular spot. Bill orange-yellow to reddish-orange, legs and feet pale or lemon yellow. Female similar to male but darkest on cap, on average browner and less dark than male; underparts as male with a few indistinct blackish streaks on throat; ear-coverts brown with fine pale central shafts, sometimes with paler areas on chin to throat and on belly to vent. Juvenile dusky-brown with narrow white central shafts on crown, mantle, back and edges to scapulars; tips to wing-coverts whitish or yellowish-buff; underparts light reddish-buff mottled darker with dusky-black tips.

Race *spencei* extremely similar to *nigropileus* – Ripley *et al.* (1988) found no consistent characters to separate them and combined them within *nigropileus* – but, on average, slightly darker grey-brown or brown on upperparts, and blackish-brown crown to nape less clearly distinct on very slightly paler nape. Wing and tail feathers also slightly darker brown than *nigropileus* but with same pale grey edges to primary coverts, primaries (whitish-grey) and outer secondaries. Underparts differ very little from *nigropileus* but chin and throat possibly more clearly streaked and slightly greyer on breast and upper belly (especially on females) and grey-brown on flanks; centre of belly to undertail-coverts dull whitish.

Male *simillimus* has lores, cheeks, forehead, crown and nape blackish or very heavily dark brown on rest of body and tail. Wings dark grey-brown but edges to outer greater coverts, primary coverts and outer secondaries narrowly paler (slightly more extensively grey on primary coverts, flight feathers), innerwebs to tertials, tips of flight feathers, and underwing-coverts dark brown. Cheeks, chin and throat to breast deep brown or washed chocolate-brown on cheeks, throat, breast and belly; undertail-coverts also brown with fine white central shafts. Bill yellow to reddish-orange. Legs and feet orange-yellow. Female slightly paler and not always so dark above and slightly paler below; chin and throat may be pale whitish-buff finely streaked brownish, breast to belly and vent grey-brown slightly darker on flanks to undertail-coverts. Juvenile as same-aged nominate but with paler mottling of yellowish-white bases to broad brown tips below; fine pale buff central shaft-streaks on upperparts and tips to median and greater coverts.

Male *bourdilloni* similar to *simillimus* but darker or blacker on head and wings, rest of plumage (including bases to tail feathers) slate-grey tinged bluish, edges to wing-coverts (including primary coverts) and secondaries paler bluish-slate and outer primaries broadly edged pale bluish; bill, eye-ring, legs and feet yellow to deep orange-yellow. Small post-ocular spot at rear of eye-ring may be same colour as eye-ring or bare dark skin. Female dark brown (more like nominate female) above with slight olive tinge; edges to primary coverts, primaries and outer secondaries similar to male, pale grey or grey-brown, tail brown to grey-brown; cheeks and ear-coverts finely streaked pale brown. Underparts umber-brown, slightly greyer on flanks, thighs and undertail-coverts; throat may also be pale buffish with a few dusky-brown spots or streaks. Bill yellow. Legs straw-brown.

Male *kinnisii* more like nominate but with black entirely replaced by slate-grey or tinged bluish-grey with black centres to feathers, at close range tips to crown, mantle and scapulars black forming scaly pattern, edges to flight feathers also bluish-slate, tail black washed bluish-slate. Underwing-coverts slate-grey. Female similar but browner, especially on head, with underparts suffused brownish-slate, slightly paler on belly and flanks, and undertail-coverts may show pale shafts, edges to flight feathers also grey-brown. Bill orange-yellow and eye-ring (and small post-ocular spot) orange; legs and feet of both sexes pale yellow. Immature male brownish on head and neck with darker lores, mantle and back slightly more bluish than adult male with blackish-brown wings and tail, both edged dull slate-grey; tips of greater coverts with pale buffish-brown spots; throat and breast pale brown spotted or tipped darker. Immature female like adult female but face slightly darker and forehead, throat and breast earth-brown faintly spotted or mottled paler. Bill usually black or dark horn becoming progressively yellow at base and along edges of lower mandible. Confusion possible between *kinnisii* and both

Sri Lanka Whistling Thrush (18) and (out-of-range) Tickell's Thrush (105), distinguished from former by lack of blue in plumage, particularly the pale blue on median coverts, with bright yellow (not black) bill and legs; from male Tickell's by more uniform slate-grey plumage and lack of white belly to undertail-coverts.

VOICE Extremely vocal. One of the commonest calls is a fairly strident and slightly rising *chook chook chook* or a *tuc, tuc, tuc*; other calls are variations on this with a high-pitched repeated *chick, chip* or *chup, chup, chup* when alarmed or mobbing a predator. Eastern races give a harsher *chak-chak-chak-chak* version of this note, recalling Fieldfare (122), together with a thin high-pitched *queeeiik*. Commonly utters an alarm note, especially when going to communal roost or suddenly disturbed, which is an extension of the *chook* series of call notes, usually faster, more strident and drawn out with a rattling *tchweetcheweetch-weechewee* and followed by a slower *chook chook*; eastern races, notably *mandarinus*, have a softer *sook sook* or *psook*. Contact call a thin high-pitched *sri* or *ssree* often heard at night from migrants, especially in autumn. Also in autumn and winter gives a very thin and high-pitched drawn out *tseeee...* which recalls that of Robin *Erithacus rubecula* and also very similar to but less wheezing than Penduline Tit *Remiz pendulinus*; *mandarinus* has a higher-pitched series of Fieldfare-like notes including *whiiik*. Female generally silent except for alarm call but has a rapid but soft tittering when being displayed to by male; juvenile has a persistent sharp high-pitched begging call *tsi-tsi-tsi* often followed by a *tsri-tsi* when recently out of the nest and still being fed by adults; also a *chup* note.

Song consists of clear rich fluty notes which merge into short but almost continuous warbled phrases interspersed with short pauses. Rich and mellow in tone but generally slower and more languid than Song Thrush (124) and without the repeated phrases; frequently ends with weak phrases or a series of subdued notes; mimicry of up to about 12 species noted in nominate *merula* (*nigropileus* has a wider range), also cats, human whistles and car alarms, but usually delivered quietly and not always apparent to the human ear. Also gives a quiet subsong with bill imperceptibly open, consisting of a low but sweet warble, often mellow or tinkling but also with some subdued high notes, generally more continuous than normal song but still broken into phrases; also recalls that of Robin and includes or terminates with a subdued version of the chattering call or alarm cry. Eastern races, particularly *maximus*, have a comparatively poor song with very limited repertoire, lacking the variety of musical phrases given by the western birds; gives a mournful *piew-piew* or *tieuw-quoit*, repeated monotonously at intervals of 5–6 seconds (Roberts 1992). Song of *kinnisii* is like nominate but not as loud or as rich in tone; usually sings only at dusk and dawn. Songs of the Indian subcontinent races apparently similar to nominate except where stated above; but detailed analysis of similarities and differences required.

Song usually delivered from exposed perch in tree, tall bush or building, sometimes also in flight or from the ground; singing at night not uncommon, usually stimulated by some form of light, e.g. street-lighting; subsong usually given from lower and more concealed perch, often low down in bush. Song period restricted to the breeding season, March to early August; subsong from mid-December, more frequent through the winter when weather mild.

STATUS AND DISTRIBUTION Common throughout much of the range but scarce in the northern and eastern parts.

T. m. merula Breeds commonly throughout much of Europe from Iceland, the Faeroes (50–75 pairs and increasing) and British Isles eastwards to the Urals. In Iceland up to 3 pairs bred in the Reykjavik area between 1985 and 1995 although several attempts in 1960, 1969, 1974 and 1975 may also have been successful; from 1995 to 1997 all eggs laid (probably by one female) have been infertile (G. Petursson pers. comm.). Absent from much of central Norway and largely only present in coastal areas from about 62°N and extends north to about 70°N where fairly scarce; occurs throughout much of Sweden, central and southern Finland east or south-east through Russia to the Urals. In the south from Portugal and Spain, including the Balearics, to Corsica, Sardinia, Italy, Sicily, northern Yugoslavia south-east through the Balkans where it intergrades with *aterrimus*; also small breeding population in the Nile Delta, northern Egypt appearing to hold intermediate *merula* and *syriacus* (Goodman & Meininger 1989). In recent years (since 1979) small numbers have frequently summered on Cyprus (mainly Mt Troodos).

In winter birds from Norway, northern and central Sweden, central Finland and western Russia winter in Iceland (where it is a scarce resident and winter visitor) and throughout Europe and around the Mediterranean, Cyprus and North Africa north of the Saharan Atlas (central and coastal Morocco south to about Cape Draa, northern Algeria, northern and coastal Tunisia, coast of Libya south to about Jebel Nafusa, and Cyrenaica east along the coast of Egypt to the Nile Delta, where it breeds, south to about Cairo and the Suez Canal); rare winter visitor to northern and central Israel.

Birds of this race have been released into southeast Australia, and now range from Port Lincoln (South Australia) to about Newcastle (New South Wales) and elsewhere in northern NSW and north, almost to Queensland; also occurs on Norfolk (south-west Pacific), Kangaroo and Flinders Islands and throughout Tasmania; has also been released into New Zealand where it is now widespread throughout and has colonised several outlying islands from the Kermadecs to Campbell Island.

T. m. azorensis Azores.

T. m. cabrerae Madeira and the western Canary Islands to Gran Canaria.

T. m. mauretanicus Central and northern Morocco, northern (coastal) Algeria to northern Tunisia.

T. m. aterrimus Hungary, central and southern

Balkans, southern Greece and Crete, Romania and parts of Bulgaria to southern Ukraine, with an isolated population in the Crimea, also on islands in the Ionian and Aegean Seas including Rhodes, much of northern, western and southern Turkey but largely absent or local from the central Taurus and the south-east; north through the Caucasus into northern Iran. In winter south to southern Turkey and probably also to Cyprus though no definite records, Israel (scarce or less common than *syriacus*), north coast of Egypt and the Nile Delta; in the east to Iraq, the lowlands of central and southern Iran and probably northern Saudi Arabia.

T. m. syriacus Mediterranean coast of southern Turkey (east of about Antalya and south of 38°N and west of 38°E), Lebanon and western Syria south to north-west Jordan (possibly further south), northern and central Israel and the northern Sinai, possibly also this race (or intermediates with *merula*) in the Nile Delta in Egypt, and discontinuously east into Iraq and most of Iran except the Dasht-e-Lut and Dasht-e-Kavir deserts to southern Turkmenia and south through the Zagros range to western Baluchistan. Mostly resident but part of the population moves south-west or west to winter in the Jordan Valley, Azraq and in northern Egypt in the Nile Delta south to about Cairo.

T. m. intermedius Central Russia from the Dzungarian Ala Tau and the Tien Shan ranges to western Sinkiang, south to Tadzhikistan, western and north-east Afghanistan and east through the Pamirs to the Kun Lun range on the borders of Sinkiang and Tibet east to Lop Nor and Zaidam in north-east Tsinghai. Many birds are resident but some are altitude migrants and occur in southern Afghanistan and southern Iraq in winter.

T. m. maximus The higher slopes of the Safed Koh, eastern Afghanistan/Pakistan border (Whistler 1944, Roberts 1992) and east through the Himalayas between 3200 and 4800 m (10,560–16,000′) from northern Pakistan and Baltistan, Kashmir and Gilgit to Himachal Pradesh, Sikkim, Assam and southern parts of Tibet and western Szechwan. May also breed in Nepal where it is principally an erratic spring migrant and winter visitor but some birds remain throughout the summer above the treeline. An altitude migrant and in winter occurs down to 2100 m (6930′) in south-east Tibet but not below 3000 m (9900′) in the western and central Himalayas, and many remaining at fairly high altitudes, up to 4600 m (15,200′) in Sikkim.

T. m. mandarinus Resident throughout much of south-central China, mainly south of the Yangtze from eastern Szechwan, south-east Kansu, southern Shensi to southern Honan and east to Chekiang and Fukien, south to western Yunnan, Kwangsi and Kwangtung. In 1996 one pair bred in Hong Kong (Robson 1997). In winter part of the population moves south to winter in Hong Kong, Hainan and western and eastern Tonkin, and erratically south to central and southern Laos and central Annam, Vietnam. Recently also recorded from Cambodia, May 1995 (Duckworth *et al.* 1998).

T. m. sowerbyi Central Szechwan.

T. m. nigropileus Western Ghats (up to about 1820 m/c.6000′) of western India from southern Rajasthan (north to about Mt Abu), eastern Gujarat and much of Madhya Pradesh south to the northern and central parts of the Western Ghats.

T. m. spencei Eastern India in the Eastern Ghats from northern Orissa west to about Hyderabad south to the hills of Nellore, Andhra Pradesh.

T. m. simillimus A common resident of the hills in Kerala and Tamil Nadu, south-west India, from the Brahmagiris and the Biligirirangans south to the Nelliampathis and Palnis (where it intergrades with *bourdilloni*).

T. m. bourdilloni A common resident of the hills above 900 m (3000′) of southern Kerala and Tamil Nadu, south-west India, generally south of *simillimus* in the Nelliampathi and Palni Hills south to the Ashambu Hills, but exact limits of range unclear and intergrades occur where the ranges overlap. Generally resident but Abdulali & Unnithan (1996) recorded a specimen collected in Goa, December 1979.

T. m. kinnisii A local resident in the hills of Sri Lanka above 900 m (3000′).

MOVEMENTS Resident and migratory. Nominate birds breeding in the northern and eastern parts of the range move south or west to winter within the breeding range, and others breeding in Scandinavia and central and eastern Europe move south or south-west to winter in southern Europe, some of the Mediterranean islands, e.g. Malta, Cyprus, and along the coasts of North Africa from Morocco to Egypt. Birds from Scotland and northern England move south-west to winter in Ireland whilst those from southern England move west to Ireland or south to France; birds from Norway, Sweden, Finland, north-west Russia, Baltic states, Low Countries and Germany move south-west and west to winter around the coast of Iceland (where common but variable in numbers annually) and throughout the British Isles between mid- to late October and mid- or late April. Race *mauretanicus* mostly sedentary but some southward movement evident from records in southern Morocco, central Algeria and southern Tunisia from early November to early April.

Birds of both *aterrimus* and *syriacus* winter south into northern Egypt, mainly in the Nile Delta south to about Cairo, with *aterrimus* present along the Mediterranean coast from October to mid-April and *syriacus* mainly in parts of Jordan (principally the Jordan valley), western Sinai and Nile Delta (where it may be resident) from November to March. There are also unspecified records from the western desert of Egypt. A few individuals, probably *aterrimus* (mostly first-year males or occasionally females), occur in eastern Saudi Arabia (Dammam to Abqaiq area).

Breeding birds from western and south-west Russia leave the breeding areas from mid-September, although some migrants are recorded in August, with large-scale movements noted in mid-October; most birds have left by early November, but some remain in the northern Caucasus throughout the winter. Occurs as a regular passage migrant through Turkey and Jordan and is a scarce winter visitor (late October to March) to U.A.E. and Kuwait.

Race *nigropileus* is a partial migrant with many birds from Madhya Pradesh leaving the breeding area; occurs south in winter from the Gil Forest, Farahabad and throughout the Western Ghats, to Kerala and western Tamil Nadu (apparently absent from Nilgiri Hills). Race *mandarinus* occurs in larger numbers than in summer in southern Yunnan from October to May and is a regular winter visitor to Hong Kong and Hainan from November to March, some remaining in the Hong Kong area into April; winter visitor to central and southern Laos mostly in December to April with latest on 12 May (Duckworth *et al.* 1998); also noted on passage through Zhoushan Dao (Shaweishan Island) off coast of Chekiang, eastern China, in April. First recorded on Taiwan in January 1981 and now more than 100 records to 1999 (also on Hung-t'ou Hsu/Lanyu Island) and best regarded as a rare passage migrant (W.-H. Fang pers. comm).

Return movements (for all races) to the breeding areas take place from early March and April with arrivals at the northern boundaries of the range in early May. Mostly a nocturnal migrant but some movements by day, also some arrivals noted in the daytime from long crossings, e.g. over the North Sea; usually moves singly but many individuals may move at the same time, giving the impression of loose association. Hard-weather movements occur at the onset of severe winters and these may be either by day or night.

A rare winter visitor to inland Libya (2 records at Serir oasis), Bahrain (1 record), Saudi Arabia (at least 5 records in the eastern province) and Sudan (1 record). Further east the races are mostly sedentary although *intermedius* has occurred in late winter in Quetta and Peshawar and may be commoner in north-west Pakistan and eastern Afghanistan than records suggest. There are also records of vagrants from Bangladesh (January 1982), Thailand (3 records), Cambodia (single, May 1995), Ryukyu Islands (March 1982), Japan (April–May 1985); Greenland (12+), Spitsbergen, Jan Mayen and Bear Islands. In North America a male found dead on 16 November 1994 at Bonavista, Newfoundland, is regarded as the first natural vagrant (Mactavish 1995); other birds in U.S.A. and Canada (California in 1891, Montreal, Quebec, in November 1970 and Ericau, Ontario, in April 1981) are regarded as escapes; 16 pairs are reported to have been released in Portland, Oregon, in May 1989.

HABITAT Principally deciduous forests and woodlands, usually those with dense undergrowth, but also glades and forest edges, copses, edges of cultivation and farmland with hedges, heaths and moorland edges, parks, orchards, plantations, bushes, scrub, gardens and town and city squares; birds of the race *mandarinus* are principally birds of lowland China but *maximus* inhabits trees and forests, grass and scrub-covered slopes or rocky screes along the treeline, and in summer occurs in high-altitude dwarf juniper scrub; *kinnisii* occurs in forests and copses and on hillside tea-estates, thick undergrowth, elephant grass scrub and, in some areas, large gardens. Occurs up to 1000 m (3300′) in Europe, to 4500 m (14,850′) in the Tien Shan and the Himalayas, and to 4575 m (15,100′) in western China; in North Africa occurs to about 2300 m (7590′), exceptionally to 2700 m (8900′).

BEHAVIOUR Generally active, sociable and conspicuous, with up to 60 or more in a loose association, but some populations (notably in Asia, e.g. *kinnisii*) shyer, more secretive and usually alone or in pairs. Race *kinnisii* usually only active at dawn and dusk, spending long periods of the day hidden in undergrowth. All other races usually occur in open areas including woods; on the ground runs, hops and walks; usual gait when feeding is to hop a few yards and then pause to survey the ground; rapidly dives into shelter in undergrowth or ivy-covered trees when alarmed. Flight is fast or dashing but fairly low, slightly undulating and usually over short distances. On migration flight tends to be more direct and broken with short glides. On landing the tail is habitually raised and slowly lowered, wings often drooped when on the ground or at rest. When excited or alarmed rapidly shakes or jerks wings and flicks, flirts or cocks tail. Roosts loosely communally, especially in winter with up to 200 together, exceptionally up to 2,000, frequently with other thrushes, each bird regularly spaced apart from the next; indulges in noisy aggressive pre-roosting display with others. Feeds both on the ground and in trees and bushes; when on the ground feeds by pulling worms from the surface or in woods or hedges scratches at piles of fallen leaves with feet, then turns over leaves with bill; feeds in trees on berries and fruit in late summer to early winter. Food is mostly insects and their larvae, also some spiders, millipedes, small snails and earthworms; fruit includes apple, pear, cherry, strawberry, raspberry, currant, gooseberry, etc. and berries of *Cotoneaster*, rowan, hawthorn, rose, holly, ivy, juniper, yew, mistletoe, lantana, blackberry, bilberry, barberry, buckthorn, honeysuckle, privet, sandalwood, elderberry, guelder-rose, etc.; eastern birds also take banyan berries and mulberries, whilst southern Indian birds (*nigropileus* and *bourdilloni*) take large numbers of berries of *Maesa perrottetiana*, *Trema orientalis* and flower nectar of *Erythrina lithosperma*. Also takes household scraps and boiled rice and has been recorded catching small fish, frogs, tadpoles, newts and small lizards; and known to feed on dead mice and human excreta.

BREEDING Season: early March to early September; eastern races April–July; *simillimus* March–August, *bourdilloni* and *kinnisii* April–June, *nigropileus* June–September; New Zealand birds from late August to mid-November. Nest: a cup (eastern race nests have been described as bulky) of dry grass, straw or fine twigs or similar material, usually including some moss, lined with mud and dry grasses or pine needles; built by female and placed on a fork of (or along) a branch of a small tree, in a hedge or bush (deciduous and evergreen), also in ivy or other creeper on sides of trees and buildings, also on stump of dead tree, in piles of dead wood, holes in walls, in sheds or occasionally (more often in montane races) on the ground or on a bank. Eggs: usually 3–5 (exceptionally 2–6), pale blue tinged greenish, but can be buffish or rarely white and variably mottled, spotted or splashed with pale reddish-brown (can also be unmarked); eggs of southern Indian races may more closely resemble those of Song Thrush with those in the north more similar to the nominate (Baker 1924). Incubation period: 12–13 days, exceptionally 10–19; by the female but male (which lacks brood-patch) has been known to sit on the eggs. Fledging period: 13–14 days, but as short as 10 or up to 19 days. Young often fed by both adults for up to 21 days after leaving the nest. Breeds in first year of life; usually two broods but three (in the south of the range) not unknown.

MOULT Adults have complete moult following the breeding season from August to early November, but some may begin wing moult as early as late May and not be complete in some until December; birds in the southern parts of the range moult earlier than those in the north. May also replace some body feathers in March. Juveniles moult the head, body and lesser and median coverts, some of the (usually inner) greater coverts and also some of the tertials and tail feathers about 6 weeks after fledging, usually July to late August; complete by October. In the British Isles and much of Europe, and occasionally parts of Scandinavia, all the greater coverts are regularly moulted (Svensson 1992).

MEASUREMENTS Wing, male 117–140, female 112–132; tarsus, male 28–36, female 24–34; bill (from skull) male 23–27, female 19–21; *aterrimus* wing, male 120–138, female 118–129; *syriacus* wing, male 123–136, female 120–131; *cabrerae* wing, male 121–130, female 115–124; *azorensis* wing, male 117–129, female 112–123; tarsus 32–36; bill 16–19; *mauretanicus* wing, male 122–135; *mandarinus* wing, male 152–164, female 144–153; bill 23–27; tarsus 35–37; *intermedius* wing, male 130–143, female 127–139; bill 27–32; *maximus* wing, male 144–167, female 144–161; tarsus 32–38; bill 25–29; *nigropileus* wing, male 126–132, female 121–130; bill 20.5–28; tarsus 30–35; *spencei* wing, male 119–132, female 116.5–127; tarsus 26.5–33; bill 21–28; *simillimus* wing, male 119–134, female 118–130; tarsus 29.5–35; bill 20.5–28; *bourdilloni* wing, male 117–124, female 110–124; tarsus 26.5–34; bill 20.5–24.5; *kinnisii* wing, male 104–119, female 105–116; tarsus 27.5–33; bill 20–26. Weight *merula* male 60–149 g, female 60–140 g; *aterrimus* male 69–98 g, male 88–102 g; *intermedius* male 84–121 g, female 85–106 g (Whistler & Kinnear 1932, Ali & Ripley 1983, Cramp *et al.* 1988, Micali *et al.* 1981, Svensson 1992).

REFERENCES Abdulali & Unnithan (1991), Ali & Ripley (1983), Brazil & Suzuki (1988), Cramp *et al.* (1988), Duckworth *et al.* (1998), Mactavish (1995), Micali *et al.* 1981, Ripley *et al.* (1988), Robson (1997), Svensson (1992), Tucker & Heath (1994), Whistler (1944), Whistler & Kinnear (1932).

112 ISLAND THRUSH *Turdus poliocephalus* Plates 44, 45, 46, 47
(Mountain Blackbird)
T*urdus poliocephalus* Latham, 1801, *Index Orn.* suppl.: 44 – Norfolk Island.

IDENTIFICATION (nominate race) 20.5–25 cm (8–9¾"), size varying considerably throughout the range; see Geographic Variation. An enigmatic species widely scattered across a large number of islands in the south-west Pacific, Wallacea and Malaysia from northern Sumatra east to Fiji and north to Taiwan and formerly south to Lord Howe Island. Occurs entirely on islands and usually a montane species but some occur at sea-level; virtually all races are island endemics and as such have suffered from the introduction of rats or cats and at least four (including the nominate) are known or thought to have become extinct within recent times, while several others have low or unknown populations which may be at risk, e.g. *pritzbueri*. Several races have only recently been described (e.g. *tolokiwae* in the late 1980s) and several more probably remain undetected. Nominate birds had the head and face buff or brownish-buff, in some restricted to the crown forming a cap; rest of the upperparts including wings and tail black, flight and tail feathers slightly browner than upperparts. Sides of the neck, throat to upper breast pale yellowish-buff to buff-brown; rest of the underparts sooty or brownish-black with white

central shaft-streaks to undertail-coverts. Bill, legs and feet yellow to dark yellow or orange. Plumage varies considerably throughout the range and some races may show 'leap-frog' similarities to others which are separated by one or more completely different races (see note at introduction to Geographic Variation). The species as a whole remains poorly known and requires considerable investigation to determine its exact affinities and ancestral origins; under modern-day species concepts it would be easy to consider all races as full species (a treatment already afforded by some authorities to some races occurring in several well-known areas and comparatively better studied).

Confusion species Unlikely to be confused with any other species within its native range, but several races are easily confusable with each other but are unlikely, in life, to come into contact. In parts of Indonesia and Wallacea occurs on islands with equally rare or little known deep-forest *Zoothera* thrushes, e.g. Moluccan Thrush (27), but unlikely to be confused with any of these on plumage or call.

DESCRIPTION (Nominate race) Not seen since 1969 when the population was less than 50

357

individuals (King 1981) and now considered extinct. Sexes differ. **Adult male** Entire head and face pale grey or light buffish-brown; lower nape, sides of neck, throat to upper breast pale yellowish-buff to buff-brown, centre and sides of breast duller than throat; some have entire head and face buffier or more brownish-buff than others or colour is restricted to crown, forming cap. Rest of upperparts including wings and tail black, flight and tail feathers slightly browner than upperparts; in fresh plumage outer edges to flight feathers slightly paler or buff-brown. Rest of underparts and underwing-coverts sooty- or brownish-black with white central shaft-streaks to undertail-coverts. Bill yellow, dark yellow or orange. Eye dark brown. Legs and feet yellow to dark yellow or orange. **Adult female** Almost identical to adult male but forehead to hindcrown browner forming a dark cap, breast darker grey-brown or grey-buff; belly and flanks more heavily tinged or edged warm brown or chestnut. Bill yellow to blackish-yellow. Legs and feet brownish or blackish-yellow. **Juvenile** Similar to adult but generally browner on body with pale central shaft-streaks to crown, mantle and scapulars, and pale buffish tips to median and greater coverts; heavily mottled with dark brown and pale buff tips on throat and upper belly; dark brown head, face and breast gradually becomes progressively paler towards first summer; also has rufous-brown tinge to lower breast, belly and flanks.

GEOGRAPHICAL VARIATION Fifty-two races; considerable variation between them with a range of plumages and with a curious and marked lack of consistency throughout the range, so that races from distant parts of the range frequently show greater similarity to each other than those which are nearer e.g. *loeseri* from northern Sumatra is extremely similar to *samoensis* from the eastern end of the range and to *bougainvillei* from the centre than to *indrapurae*, its nearest neighbour; in other instances races which show close similarities and geographical distribution are broken or interrupted by dissimilar birds on adjacent islands, e.g. in Fiji the all-black *hades* on Gau Island and the similar but greyer *vitiensis* on Vanua Levu are separated by *ruficeps* with a bright golden or golden-buff head and breast. The following division groups those races with greatest similarities of plumage and is intended for ease of reference; identification of race by location is given under Distribution. It should also be noted that within the divisions some birds (particularly females) show sufficient variation they could equally be classed in other divisions.

1. Head pale, body black or brown (including nominate)

Race *niveiceps* (23 cm/8½–9″) male has pure white head to nape, sides of neck and upper breast or with some darker tips to feathers, and may show dark spot behind eye; rest of upperparts including wings and tail black with some glossy edges; axillaries and underwing-coverts black. Centre of breast black becoming dark olive-cinnamon on lower breast and orange to chestnut on flanks and

belly to vent; undertail-coverts black but with broad whitish central shaft-streaks, thighs grey or grey-brown. Female has forehead and (very conspicuously in some) sides of crown white (forming supercilium and extending to nape in some), crown to hindneck also white but heavily streaked or entirely obscured with brown or may show narrow white collar; rest of upperparts olive-brown, darker on wings and tail, or greyish-olive on lower back, rump and uppertail-coverts. Face to chin and throat white but flecked or streaked brown, submoustachial usually whiter with broken malar of brown spots, rest of underparts as male but generally paler or tinged brown on flanks; undertail-coverts white with fine brown edges; underwing-coverts dusky-brown. Bill yellow to yellowish-orange. Legs and feet yellowish or bright orange-brown. Juvenile similar to female but has head brown and more uniform with rest of upperparts; sides of crown white, top of crown, ear-coverts and throat (all often spotted brown) to nape and mantle streaked with pale buff central shafts, becoming spots at tips of median and greater coverts; narrow dark malar of brown spots. Rest of underparts dull orange-buff mottled with blackish tips. Bill olive-brown. Legs and feet brownish-yellow.

Male *tempesti* (19–20.5 cm/7½–8″) very similar to nominate with most upperparts, including forehead to nape, brown or brownish-black; chin, throat, sides of neck to face and centre of breast grey or greyish-buff tinged light-brown, slightly darker or browner on female; lores blackish and rest of underparts black or blackish-brown except for brown thighs; female has warm brown tips to some underparts. Bill, legs and feet bright yellow or yellow-orange. Female similar but slightly duller or browner and face to breast, sides of neck and nape dark brown (duller or less contrasting), tips of lower breast, belly and flanks broadly and variably black or blackish-brown or with warm brown edges and tips. Juvenile generally dark brown, paler on underparts with darker spotting or mottling, pale buff central shaft-streaks to crown and nape to mantle, pale tips to greater coverts and also sometimes pale rufous tips to belly and flanks.

Adult *deningeri* (23 cm/9″) has entire head, nape, sides of neck and chin to breast creamy-white or tinged buff (in some only crown white, and some moulting or worn plumage birds show darker or browner bases to crown, nape, lower throat and breast); rest of upperparts, including wings and tail, dull brown or brownish-black with some whitish-brown tips to upper mantle; underwing-coverts brown. Underparts dull brown slightly paler than above, thighs pale buffish-brown. Eye-ring yellow. Bill, legs and feet yellow. Female identical but head and neck to breast may be duller or more infused with brown; brown on breast may merge with darker belly. Juvenile has head, face and upperparts dingy brown with fine pale shaft-streaks on mantle and scapulars; chin and throat whitish and breast mottled or flecked whitish or pale buff, bases of belly feathers pale or orange-buff.

Male *albifrons* (19.5–20.5 cm/7¼–8") has entire head to nape, sides of neck, chin and throat to breast white or creamy-white; rest of plumage black or blackish-brown but some birds show brown tinge or edges to feathers on belly and flanks, or whitish tips to lower belly and vent. Female has entire head to breast much duller or light greyish-buff; rest of body slightly browner with rufous on centre of lower breast to belly becoming darker on flanks; undertail-coverts brownish, broadly streaked and tipped white. Underwing-coverts dark brown edged rufous. Juvenile generally drab-brown above with pale orange-buff tips to median and greater coverts, face and nape heavily flecked pale yellowish-buff with fine pale streaks on crown, mantle and scapulars; underparts yellowish-buff on chin and throat bordered by dark brown malar; rest of underparts dull rufous-brown heavily spotted and barred darker brown.

Probably extinct *pritzbueri* (19–20.5 cm/7½–8") male similar to *tempesti* and *canescens* with entire head to nape and sides of neck, chin and throat to breast creamy- or greyish-white; rest of body, including wings and tail, sooty-black or blackish-brown, thighs tinged browner. Eye-ring orange. Female has head and face to breast much duller, greyish-buff to grey-brown on crown and nape, and browner-black with dusky or warm rufous fringes to feathers on lower breast, belly and flanks. Juvenile entirely rich or rufous-brown with paler central shaft-streaks and mottled or spotted paler on underparts; lower belly and vent whitish.

Male *canescens* (19–20.5 cm/7½–8") like *pritzbueri* and *tempesti* but forehead to nape, face, sides of neck, chin, throat and breast dull grey washed (quite heavily in parts) with brown, darkest on crown and nape; rest of body, wings and tail black. Female slightly darker grey or greyish-brown on face, crown, sides of neck and breast; lower breast and belly tinged rufous.

Race *ruficeps* (19–20.5 cm/7½–8") has the entire head to nape and face, chin, throat and breast light golden-brown or rufous-buff; rest of plumage, including wings (but axillaries and underwing-coverts brown) and tail black, slightly glossy black above, some females having lower breast and/or upper belly duller or browner. Bill, legs and feet yellow. Juvenile male similar to adult but has dark feather edges to crown and pale orange central shaft-streaks on mantle and scapulars; tips to median and greater coverts pale orange; underparts pale orange becoming rufous orange-buff finely spotted dark brown. Juvenile female has entire head, face and upperparts brown to olive-brown with darker tips to crown, mantle and back; orange or orange-buff underparts heavily mottled or spotted dark brown.

2. Entirely dark brown or jet-black

Race *xanthopus* (21.5 cm/8½") almost entirely plain sooty- or dark brown but mantle, back, scapulars, rump and uppertail-coverts warmer or deep ruddy-brown as are edges to flight feathers and tail feathers; face to sides of neck, chin and throat duller, slightly paler or greyer-brown,

becoming vinous- or deep cinnamon-brown on sides and lower breast, belly and flanks; vent to undertail-coverts brown. Bill yellow or yellowish-brown to orange. Eye brown. Legs and feet straw-yellow to orange. Female like male but head slightly darker, underparts slightly duller.

Now probably extinct (not seen since 1920s) *vinitinctus* (20.5–21.5 cm/8–8½") has head and face brown to greyish-brown; mantle and scapulars to uppertail-coverts, edges to wing-coverts, flight feathers and tertials warm russet-brown with olive tinge to back; innerwebs to flight feathers and all tail feathers brown. Chin and throat to sides of neck light brown becoming vinous- or cinnamon-brown on breast, belly and flanks; undertail-coverts brown. Underwing-coverts pale brown. Eye-ring yellow. Bill yellow. Legs and feet light yellow. Female slightly paler and more olive-brown above and paler below. Immature light brown on head and face becoming olive-brown on upperparts with fine pale buff central shaft-streaks and sooty- or dusky-brown spots on throat and breast; belly warm buffish-brown.

Now probably extinct *mareensis* male black above, underparts blackish-brown (not jet-black), undertail-coverts black with white central shafts and tips, underwing-coverts blackish-brown; flanks, belly and vent have faint white tips. Eye-ring and bill yellow or orange-yellow. Legs and feet bright yellow. Female similar but more uniform brownish-black or very dark brown on head and upperparts, warmer or rufous to chestnut-brown below, some birds showing grey on belly; undertail-coverts as male. Juvenile drab-brown with pale orange-buff central shaft-streaks to mantle, scapulars, crown and ear-coverts, tips to greater coverts pale orange; face streaked and finely spotted pale buff; chin and throat pale or whitish-buff and spotted brown, breast orange-brown to buffish-orange spotted pale and yellowish-buff, flanks and belly yellowish- to orange-buff spotted or blotched dark brown, vent and undertail-coverts whitish.

Male *samoensis* (19.5–20.5 cm/7¼–8") entirely sooty-black or has blackish-brown head, face and throat; in worn plumage innerwebs of secondaries and tertials slightly brown-black and edges of primaries brownish. Bill orange-yellow. Legs and feet yellow. Female similar but tinged brown below. Legs brownish-orange. Juvenile has head black but body and wings blackish-brown and underparts warm dark brown.

Adults of race *hades* (19–20.5 cm/7½–8") similar to *samoensis* but entirely glossy black except for bright yellow eye-ring, bill, legs and feet. Immature resembles adult but with broad rufous brown edges to underparts.

Race *loeseri* entirely blackish or blackish-brown, female very slightly paler and forehead to crown, nape, face, chin, throat and upper breast slightly paler or infused buff, wings (including underwing-coverts) marginally browner than rest of plumage; feathers on centre of belly edged warmer brown. Bill orange-yellow. Legs and feet brownish-yellow.

Male *carbonarius* (23–24 cm/9–9½") almost entirely blackish with bright yellow eye-ring, except for slightly browner-black flight feathers and underparts (some birds have head to breast browner and may also show white tips to area around vent and lower flanks and thighs greyer-black). Bill orange or yellow with dark tip. Legs and feet orange or yellowish-orange. Eye brown to dark brown. Female almost identical but browner with slightly paler underparts, belly feathers edged pale or warm buffish-brown; vent grey-brown and undertail-coverts brown with creamy-buff streaks and tips. Bill as male or with dark upper mandible. Legs and feet dull orange.

Race *whitneyi* (17.5–18 cm/6¾–7") entirely sooty-black, slightly paler brown on face and sides of neck to chin, throat and breast. Bill, legs and feet yellow. Female very similar but with brownish tinge to upperparts and reddish or chestnut edges to feathers of belly and flanks, occasionally extending to lower breast, undertail-coverts with whitish-buff central shaft-streaks. Juvenile as adult but face finely mottled pale buff; centre of chin and throat light orange-buff, rest of underparts same but heavily spotted or mottled blackish-brown except on centre of belly to vent where spots smaller. First-year and subadult birds similar to adult female with broad rufous edges to belly and flanks; undertail-coverts have broad white central shaft-streaks.

Race *rennellianus* (19–20.5 cm/7½–8") entirely sooty-black above and blackish-brown below with rufous or cinnamon-brown, occasionally whitish, edges to feathers on belly and flanks, thighs rust-brown and undertail-coverts blackish-brown with rust or cinnamon tips. Female slightly browner on head and rufous on belly and flanks extending in some to undertail-coverts, lower belly and vent with whitish tips. Bill, legs and feet yellow. Immature similar to female but variably browner or paler below with pale lores to chin.

Male *bougainvillei* (19–20.5 cm/7½–8") entirely blackish-brown with throat to upper breast marginally paler; female similar but with olive-grey tinge to mantle, back and rump and some paler or browner fringes to feathers of belly and flanks. Bill, legs and feet yellow. Juvenile as adult with slightly more extensive pale fringes to underparts.

Race *heinrothi* almost entirely blackish-brown but head and most upperparts browner. Bill yellow. Legs and feet yellowish-brown.

Male *becki* (19–20.5 cm/7½–8") generally dark brown or brownish-black on upper- and under-parts, some birds showing olive-brown edges on mantle and back at close range; face, sides of neck, chin and throat to breast pale grey, sides of belly and flanks dark grey but some with flanks tipped or edged paler grey; centre of belly whitish; undertail-coverts dark brown with whitish central shaft-streaks and tips. Bill, legs and feet yellow. Female as male or slightly paler overall and often with rufous edges to flanks. Juvenile similar but generally paler or tinged olive above and has pale tips to edges of scapulars and tips to median and greater coverts; underparts paler with pale or yellowish-buff on sides of breast and whitish edges to

centre of belly and vent, all spotted darker brown. First-year and subadult birds as adults but with belly and flanks infused orange or orange-buff, fairly strongly or prominently in some.

Race *kulambangrae* (19 cm/7½") entirely blackish-brown; female and first-year have some feathers fringed rusty-orange on lower throat, breast, belly and flanks. Bill, legs and feet yellow.

Race *sladeni* (20.5 cm/8") similar to *kulambangrae* but slightly larger with longer tail, entirely dull blackish-brown, including underwing-coverts but undersurfaces of flight feathers contrastingly paler brown; edges to upperwing-coverts and flight feathers slightly warmer brown and edges to feathers of underparts tinged bright or warm brown. Eye-ring yellow. Bill orange-yellow. Legs and feet dull yellow.

Male *tolokiwae* darker than either *bougainvillei* or *heinrothi* but slightly paler than *kulambangrae* and *rennellianus* (and probably also *sladeni*); upperparts dull dark grey-brown and underparts slightly paler with indistinctly pale edges to belly and undertail-coverts. Female slightly paler, feathers of belly and undertail-coverts with broad rufous edges. Juvenile similar to female with rich brown or rufous tips to sides of crown, ear-coverts and nape and tips to median and greater coverts, underparts with pale or buffish central shaft-streaks. Eye-ring, bill, legs and feet yellowish-orange.

Race *efatensis* (19–19.5 cm/7½–7¾") shorter-tailed than most races, mostly dull or sooty-blackish, slightly browner or dark olive-brown in female, but nape, chin, throat, sides of neck to breast (especially on female) browner with paler brown fringes, whitish on vent, thighs brownish flecked white, undertail-coverts with whitish edges and central shaft-streaks and white tips to longest feathers. Bill, legs and feet yellow. Juvenile like female but with pale flecks to head, mantle and scapulars; tips to greater coverts finely tipped light orange-buff; face also flecked yellowish-buff. Chin and throat yellowish-buff with brown malar stripe; rest of underparts dull buffish-brown spotted darker brown. First-year similar to adult but slightly paler above with rufous-brown on lower breast, belly and flanks.

Race *vanikorensis* (18–19 cm/7–7½") has upperparts sooty blackish-brown with slightly blacker forehead and crown; female tends to have browner edges to flight feathers; whitish or buffish-white tips to undertail-coverts. Underparts slightly paler or greyer black (especially female); underwing-coverts brown or dark grey-brown. Bill, legs and feet yellow. Juvenile browner, heavily mottled below with orange-buff and dark brown spots and bars. First-year and subadult are as adults but with light orange-buff edges to lower breast, belly and flanks.

Male *thomassoni* (23–24 cm/9–9½") glossy black except for dark brown forehead to crown and upper nape; nape and sides of neck paler or brown (or tinged with grey), face and sides of throat and neck grey or blackish-brown; undertail-coverts with fine white central shafts. Some birds, probably immature, both with and without paler heads and throats, show bright rufous edges to belly and flanks. Female similar to male but head, face and breast sometimes uniform with rest of plumage; centre of belly to flanks and vent fringed rufous-brown, undertail-coverts with pale creamy-buff tips. Legs and feet yellow to straw-yellow.

Male *malekulae* (19 cm/7½") has forehead and crown to nape and rest of upperparts blackish-brown and tinged olive on mantle, back and scapulars to rump, tail dark brown, wings slightly darker brown, underwing-coverts brown; face and sides of neck grey-brown, slightly paler or greyer-brown on chin, throat, sides of neck and breast; belly and flanks orange or rufous-buff, overlying brown or blackish bases, vent whitish, thighs grey-brown and undertail-coverts blackish with white central shaft-streaks and tips. Bill yellow. Legs and feet bright yellow. Female similar to male but has head and upperparts tinged olive, breast pale buff-brown and belly and flanks orange or rufous overlying grey-brown bases. Juvenile similar to adult but paler or more olive above with pale central shaft-streaks on face, nape, mantle and scapulars; underparts whitish- or light orange-buff across breast and flanks, heavily spotted blackish-brown. First-year or subadult blackish above and dark grey below with whitish undertail-coverts.

Adult *versteegi* (23–24.5 cm/9–9½") almost entirely blackish-brown with nape, sides of neck and chin to breast very slightly paler or lighter brown; some birds may show orange or rufous-orange feathers or tips on belly and flanks. Female virtually identical but has less contrast between top of head and underparts, also shows pale orange or cinnamon on edges to feathers of belly and flanks, and white on central shafts and tips of longest undertail-coverts. Juvenile browner above with extensive pale orange-buff spots and central shaft-streaks to entire upperparts and prominently on forehead, nape, scapulars and back; tips to median and greater coverts pale yellowish-buff, tips to tertials more finely yellowish-buff. Cheeks and ear-coverts brown, finely streaked pale buff; chin and throat pale or whitish-buff with well-defined brownish malar stripes; breast, belly and flanks dull rusty-orange heavily spotted with brown or dark brown on breast.

Smallest race *placens* (16.5–18 cm/6½–7") has upperparts, including wings and tail, dull brown with slightly darker forehead and crown; face, sides of neck to chin, throat and breast slightly paler or greyer; belly also tinged rufous-buff, especially in female which is warmer brown or lighter chestnut below. Bill, legs and feet yellow. Juvenile male has pale orange tips to greater coverts and outer median coverts, and fine pale orange tips to tertials. First-year and subadult birds similar to female but have fairly broad whitish central shaft-streaks on undertail-coverts.

Male *layardi* (19.5–21 cm/7¾–8¼") has dark olive-brown lores and face to forehead and rest of upperparts, including wings and tail, except edges to flight feathers and tertials which are warmer or sepia-brown; underwing-coverts dark grey washed

rufous. Chin and centre of throat pale ash-grey or greyish-buff becoming deep tawny-brown on breast (darker on sides of breast) and rust- or rufous-orange on lower breast, sides of belly and flanks; vent white or suffused white, thighs buffish-grey; undertail-coverts dull brown with broad, light orange or rufous central shaft-streaks. Bill, legs and feet bright orange or orange-yellow. Female same but slightly duller, sides of neck pale grey to grey-brown, tinged paler grey-brown on throat to centre of breast, and belly to flanks dull orange or chestnut. Juvenile paler and more uniform brown with pale buff central shaft-streaks to head, mantle and scapulars, and tips to median and greater coverts; underparts are spotted or mottled dark brown or black.

Race *papuensis* (22–23 cm/8¼–9") almost entirely uniform except for blackish-brown wings and tail and slightly paler or lighter brown on sides of head and face; chin and throat to centre of upper breast tinged paler buffish-brown. Female has rufous or rufous-brown edges to belly and flanks. Eye brown-black. Bill, legs and feet yellow. Juvenile like adult but central shaft-streaks on crown and nape buffish-orange extending onto mantle and scapulars; tips of greater coverts also finely buffish-orange; heavily streaked below with pale buff or buffish-orange on tips of breast; flanks, belly and undertail-coverts all heavily spotted or mottled rufous and dark brown.

Race *nigrorum* (21.5–23 cm/8½–9") has head and upperparts, including wings and tail, dull or dark grey-brown, lores and face to forehead and crown slightly darker and paler on nape. Chin and throat to central breast and sides of neck pale grey-ish-buff or buff-brown, paler on belly and flanks and whitish around vent, becoming darker on undertail-coverts, which are narrowly edged white. Eye-ring bright yellow. Juvenile as adult but slightly warmer brown with darker tips to crown, nape, mantle, back and upper rump, giving faint barred appearance; yellowish-buff on chin and throat, spotted browner on breast and orange-buff on lower breast, belly and flanks; belly indistinctly spotted brown, thighs and undertail-coverts brown, latter streaked pale buff. Bill bright yellow. Legs and feet straw-yellow.

Race *javanicus* (21.5–23 cm/8½–9") has upperparts dull dark brown, slightly paler on head, face and nape; flight feathers and tertials also dark brown. Face, chin and throat to sides of neck light buff-brown, duller or grey-brown on rest of underparts and underwing-coverts, darkest on lower flanks and undertail-coverts (tinged white) with white central shaft-streaks; centre of belly to vent orange but sometimes interspersed among the grey-brown feathers. Bill, legs and feet yellow.

Race *stresemanni* differs from *javanicus* in being slightly larger, with more reddish-brown wings, breast somewhat browner and rather darker reddish on the belly.

Race *keysseri* (23–24.5 cm/9–9½") also entirely dark brown, including wings, tail and underwing-coverts, but eye-ring yellow, face, chin, throat, sides of neck and breast tinged slightly paler, and edges to belly feathers rusty-orange. Bill, legs and feet yellow. Female marginally paler or browner with pale yellow eye-ring and slightly more extensive orange or rufous-orange on belly, flanks and undertail-coverts, latter also having fine whitish central shaft-streaks. Bill, legs and feet medium yellow.

3. All dark with brown head/face, rufous/chestnut belly/flanks

Male *celebensis* (21.5–23 cm/8½–9″) has entire head and face to nape and centre of breast dusky- or olive-brown, sometimes slightly paler grey- or buffish-brown on chin, throat and breast; rest of upperparts including wing-coverts and edges to inner secondaries and tertials dull or dark greyish olive-brown (sometimes with warm brown edges to greater coverts); rest of flight feathers and tail brown, underwing-coverts also brown. Flanks to sides of belly rufous to deep orange-chestnut, centre of belly to vent and undertail-coverts white, latter flecked or streaked brown. Legs and feet yellowish-brown. Female similar to male but has slightly paler olive-brown upperparts, brown on lower breast often tipped orange, and orange on belly and flanks also paler; undertail-coverts as male. Bill brownish-orange, paler on lower mandible.

Race *hygroscopus* (23–25.5 cm/9–10″) very similar to *celebensis* (and often treated as synonymous) but larger and deeper-toned; face and crown pale brown, with slightly paler buff-brown nape, sides of neck, chin and throat; slightly browner on breast. Rest of upperpart as *celebensis* but slightly darker or olive-grey, including flight and tail feathers. Belly, flanks and vent rich rufous-orange; vent and undertail-coverts brown or brownish-olive with pale buff central shaft-streaks and pale orange-buff tips. Bill yellow. Legs and feet yellowish-brown.

Race *seebohmi* (24–25.5 cm/9½–10″) has entire head, face to chin, breast and upperparts, including wings and tail, uniform sooty blackish-brown; underwing-coverts also blackish-brown. Eye-ring broad, bright yellow. Sides of lower breast to belly and flanks rufous- or rusty-orange; centre of belly with white tips and lower belly to vent white, thighs and undertail-coverts blackish-brown, latter streaked broadly with pale orange and white tips. Bill, legs and feet bright yellow. Female slightly sootier-brown above and duller below. Juvenile duller black than adult with fine buff central shafts on nape, mantle, scapulars and tips to wing-coverts; cheeks and ear-coverts mottled with rufous; broad blackish malar stripe; throat orange- or rufous-buff, heavily spotted or mottled black.

Race *mayonensis* has forehead to crown black, hindcrown and nape to sides of neck, chin, throat and breast brown or blackish-brown, sometimes with black chin; rest of plumage glossy black except for white central shafts and tips of longest undertail-coverts. Bill and legs yellow.

Race *katanglad* (21.5 cm/8½″) has entire head and upperparts brown. Chin and throat to face, sides of neck (sometimes to nape) and breast pale buffish-brown, slightly darker or browner on lower breast. Upper flanks and belly rufous, lower flanks

to undertail-coverts dark brown, latter broadly streaked and tipped white; thighs and undertail-coverts brown. Juvenile like adult but with pale orange-buff flecks on crown and nape (including sides of nape), edges of scapulars and tips of greater coverts. Chin and throat off-white or dull yellowish, sides of chin and throat to sides of neck brown as upperparts, breast also brown but becoming broken or finely mottled yellowish-buff with pale buff central shaft-streaks, lower breast pale buff becoming dull orange or orange-buff and diffusely tipped or spotted brown, belly orange-buff diffusely barred or tipped darker brown, flanks dull buffish-brown tinged warm brown and barred with dark or brown tips. Bill yellow but upper mandible can be mostly brown. Legs and feet pale yellow to orange-yellow.

Race *schlegelii* (21.5–23 cm/8½–9″) very similar to *fumidus* and *sterlingi* and has entire head and face to nape, sides of neck, chin, throat and breast (to centre of upper belly in some) greyish-buff to buffish-brown (sometimes paler on face and darker on crown), eye-ring bright yellow; mantle, back, scapulars and rump grey-brown tinged olive but edges to lower scapulars, greater coverts, inner secondaries and tertials olive-grey, rest of wings and tail brown. Underwing-coverts brown or grey-brown. Belly and vent rich red- or rust-orange, undertail-coverts greyish buff-brown. Bill, legs and feet yellow. Adult female as male but breast less well defined as reddish/rufous-orange merges into buffish-brown of breast and some show brownish tips to belly and flanks. Juvenile as adult but with extensive yellowish-buff on sides of neck, pale buff streaks to crown and nape and pale orange central shaft-streaks to mantle, back and, prominently, scapulars, also on tips to median and greater coverts. Chin and throat whitish- or creamy-buff with brownish edges to throat; rest of underparts orange or orange-buff with broad brown bars or spots at tips of breast and upper flanks.

Race *sterlingi* (23.5–24.5 cm/9¼–9½″) virtually identical to *schlegelii* but has face and throat to upper breast darker or sooty-brown, belly deeper chestnut-brown and possibly slightly darker on undertail-coverts.

Race *fumidus* (21.5–24 cm/8½–9½″) has head and upperparts brown faintly tinged olive on mantle and back to uppertail-coverts, forehead to nape slightly paler brown, eye-ring yellow. Chin and throat to face pale brown, slightly paler on sides of neck and breast; belly and flanks rufous-orange; lower belly white, vent and undertail-coverts brown with broad white central shaft-streaks. Bill, legs and feet yellow. Juvenile similar to adult but finely streaked on crown, mantle and scapulars. Face and most of underparts heavily mottled yellowish-buff and brown, becoming orange on belly and flanks with some brown spotting.

Race *whiteheadi* (21.5–24 cm/8½–9½″) very similar to *fumidus* but has head and face to centre of breast slaty- or dark grey-brown, slightly darker on lower throat and breast, also slightly darker or more rusty-rufous on belly and flanks; latter, thighs and undertail-coverts sometimes dark slate-brown with narrow central shafts (broader in female);

underwing-coverts and axillaries dark brown or tinged grey-brown. Eye-ring deep yellow. Bill, legs and feet yellow.

Race *biesenbachi* is like previous two but with breast grey as in *javanicus*; throat and sides of head are greyer than in *whiteheadi* and paler than in *fumidus*.

Race *indrapurae* (22–24 cm/8¾–9½") has forehead to crown and nape creamy-buff but in worn plumage partially or entirely flecked or mottled darker or browner (some birds in intermediate plumage have face to breast pale buffish and forehead to crown dark brown); rest of upperparts, including wings and tail, dark brown; underwing-coverts dark brown. Face, chin and throat pale or buffish-brown, browner on sides of neck to breast; belly and flanks rufous orange, lower flanks to undertail-coverts dark brown, latter finely streaked paler centrally. Eye-ring pale yellow. Bill yellow. Legs and feet yellowish-flesh. Juvenile has mantle and edges to scapulars with narrow buff central shafts and throat to upper belly mottled buffish-chestnut and blackish, undertail-coverts broadly whitish-buff on central shafts.

Race *mindorensis* (23 cm/9") has forehead to crown and upper nape greyish-brown, rest of upperparts, including wings and tail, sooty-black, underwing-coverts dark grey-brown; lores dark brown, cheeks and ear-coverts slightly paler or greyer than crown. Chin whitish and throat to breast, sides of neck and nape pale or ashy greyish-buff, sides of lower breast brown or blackish-brown becoming rufous on belly and flanks; lower flanks dark brown, centre of lower breast to belly and vent white, undertail-coverts black heavily streaked white, but upper feathers white with fine black fringes; thighs dark slate-grey. Eye-ring greenish-yellow. Bill, legs and feet yellow. Female as male but head more uniform with upperparts, and chestnut or rufous underparts, belly white slightly tinged rufous. Immature similar to female but with narrow rufous-buff shafts on mantle, back and wing-coverts; throat, breast and flanks rust-coloured and spotted black, crown to nape dark brown.

4. Dark upperparts, paler underparts (notably chin to breast)

Race *malindangensis* (23.5–24 cm/9¼–9½") has upperparts, including head, wings and tail, entirely dark grey-brown, slightly paler on nape (in fresh plumage edges of flight feathers and tertials slightly paler brown); chin and throat to sides of neck and breast pale greyish-buff, browner on belly, vent and underwing-coverts; undertail-coverts also brown but broadly streaked and tipped white. Bill pale yellow. Legs and feet straw-yellow.

Male *kelleri* (20.5–21.5 cm/8–8½") has upperparts including wings and tail deep dark brown, lores to cheeks, forehead and forecrown darker brown. Chin and throat to ear-coverts and sides of neck and nape pale brown or buffish-brown, rest of underparts dull dark brown. Eye-ring and bill yellow. Legs and feet straw-yellow. Female more uniform brown but can have buff-brown on nape, sides of neck, chin and throat to upper breast. Bill, legs and feet yellow.

Race *vitiensis* (19–21.5 cm/7½–8½") predominantly deep grey-brown from head to uppertail-coverts including wings (but primaries finely edged paler) and tail; lores to cheeks and ear-coverts, sides of neck (and nape) to chin, throat and breast greyish-buff, darker grey on belly and flanks; lower breast and belly only lightly tinged rufous, vent white, undertail-coverts dark brown. Bill yellow to light orange. Legs and feet bright yellow. Eye dark brown. Female has face to breast pale greyish-buff becoming warmer or tinged orange or rufous on lower breast, belly and flanks, lower flanks and undertail-coverts warm brown to dark brown. Bill light orange. Legs and feet yellow. First-year bird, including subadult male, similar to adult female with chestnut or light chestnut on belly and flanks.

Race *erythropleurus* (20.5 cm/8") has upperparts olive-brown tinged ashy (slightly duller or darker on forehead to nape), extending to wing-coverts, edges to flight feathers and tertials, most heavily tinged olive-brown on rump and uppertail-coverts; alula, tips of primary coverts and innerwebs to flight feathers brown. Tail also brown but all feathers edged olive-brown. Eye-ring bright or golden-yellow. Chin and throat white streaked brown at sides of throat, becoming light buff or tawny tinged greyish on sides of neck and breast; belly and flanks orange or deep orange, centre of belly to vent white extending to undertail-coverts, which are also pale orange. Underwing-coverts pale buff or light beige with light orange edges to underwing-coverts. Bill, legs and feet golden-yellow.

Male *beehleri* similar to *heinrothi* (in section 2 above) with blackish forehead to nape and olive wash to blackish upperparts, but has face to lower throat deep greyish-brown. Female similar but dark brown with dark cap and paler brown face to chin and lower throat, brown on belly edged paler brown.

VOICE A variety of throaty Blackbird-like chuckles or clucking notes; has a short *tchook* or *tchooo* or *tchack* contact note, often given as a double *chook chook* which becomes a brisk, clear, rapid or higher-pitched chattering *tchick-tchick-tchick*, *tchink-chink-chink* or *tchook-tchook-toaweet-oweet-toaweetoweet* when excited or alarmed; also a short but repeated *chep* and a thin weak downslurred hissing *sss...* Displaying birds or parents with young often give a persistent *ptink*, and has a drawn-out descending *chweee*.

Song a rather subdued melody of flute-like whistles and musical phrases similar to Blackbird in tone and to Song Thrush in structure and pace but with less tendency to repetition; songs of individual races and variation between them not well known but some, e.g. on Java, have a short stuttering song of relatively unmelodious notes. Usually given in early morning but sometimes also during the day and at dusk, mostly from a prominent perch atop a bush or tree although forest birds may sing from within the canopy. Nominate *erythropleurus* has a subdued version of the main song given as a sub-song from a low perch (Pearson 1966).

STATUS AND DISTRIBUTION Variably rare or scarce to fairly common but four races, including nominate *poliocephalus*, are now believed to be extinct.

Taiwan

T. p. niveiceps Uncommon or rare resident in the mountains of Taiwan between 1400 and 2500 m (3950–9200') and formerly (at least 20 years ago) on Hung-t'ou Hsu (Lanyu Island).

Philippines

T. p. thomassoni Mountains of northern Luzon, Philippines.

T. p. mayonensis Mountains of southern Luzon, perhaps including the southern peninsula (Sorsogon and Camarines Sur), Philippines.

T. p. mindorensis Mountain forests between 1210 and 2420 m (4000–8000') of Mindoro, Philippines.

T. p. nigrorum 1515–1800 m (5000–6000') on mountains of Negros, Philippines.

T. p. malindangensis 1360–1880 m (4500–6200') on Mt Malindang, north-west Mindanao, Philippines.

T. p. katanglad Above 1450 m (4785') on Mt Katanglad, central Mindanao, Philippines.

T. p. kelleri Mt Hilong Hilong, Mt Apo and Mt Matutum, north-east and southern Mindanao, Philippines.

Malaysia

T. p. seebohmi Above 2420 m (8000') on Mt Kinabalu and above 2120 m (7000') on Mt Trus Madi, Sabah, northern Borneo.

Indonesia

T. p. loeseri Mt Leuser and several other peaks south to Mt Kerinci, Sumatra.

T. p. indrapurae Mountains of south-west central Sumatra.

T. p. biesenbachi Mt Papandajan, West Java.

T. p. fumidus Above 2420 m (8000') on Mt Gede-Pangrango, West Java.

T. p. stresemanni Mt Lawu, Central Java.

T. p. javanicus Mountains over 2000 m (6600') of Central Java.

T. p. whiteheadi Mountains of East Java.

T. p. celebensis Above 1810 m (6000') on Bonthain Peak and Wawa Kareng, Lompobattang mountains, south-western Sulawesi. Coates & Bishop (1997) record further, as yet undescribed birds near Lake Matano, south-east Central Sulawesi and in East Sulawesi.

T. p. hygroscopus 2500–3500 m (8250–11,550') in Latimodjong Mountains southern-central Sulawesi (see previous entry).

T. p. schlegelii 1600–2000 m (5280–6600') on Mt Mutis, West Timor.

T. p. sterlingi 2300–2600 m (7600–8580') on Mt Ramelan, East Timor.

T. p. deningeri Above 1800 m (5950') on Mt Pinaia, Seram.

Indian Ocean

T. p. erythropleurus Christmas Island (to Australia), where it remains common and widespread; introduced to Cocos-Keeling Island between 1885 and 1900 but not seen there since the 1980s.

New Guinea

T. p. versteegi Oranje and Snow Mountains, western New Guinea, extending marginally into the western Star Mountains, Papua New Guinea.

T. p. carbonarius Tari and Porgera areas east to Mt Wilhelm, Mt Giluwe and Mt Hagen (possibly elsewhere in the Wahgi Valley area), Bismarck Mountains, central New Guinea.

T. p. keysseri Saruwaged Mountains, Huon Peninsula and between 1160 and 1520 m (3830–5010') on Karkar Island, north-central New Guinea.

T. p. papuensis Wharton and Owen Stanley ranges, south-east New Guinea.

T. p. tolokiwae Above 750 m (2475') on Tolokiwa Island, Vitiaz and Dampier Straits.

T. p. beehleri Above 1500 m (4950') in Hans Meyer range, southern New Ireland.

T. p. canescens Above 1600 m (5280') on Goodenough Island, D'Entrecasteaux Archipelago, New Guinea.

T. p. heinrothi Mussau Island, St Matthias group, Bismarck Archipelago, New Guinea (common in forest at all levels but scarce in secondary growth).

Also one other, as yet unnamed subspecies: 1380–1650 m (4550–5440') in Nakanai Mountains, central New Britain (Coates 1990).

South-west Pacific

T. p. bougainvillei Above 1200 m (3960') in Crown Prince Range, Bougainville, Solomon Islands.

T. p. kulumbangrae Above 1040 m (3430') in montane moss forests on Kolombangara, Solomon Islands.

T. p. sladeni Over 1200 m (3960') on mountains of Guadalcanal, Solomon Islands.

T. p. rennellianus Rennell Island, Solomon Islands.

Vanuatu (formerly New Hebrides)

T. p. vanikorensis Vanikoro and Utupua Islands, Santa Cruz Islands and Espiritu Santo and Malo, Vanuatu.

T. p. placens Ureparapara (Bligh) and Vanua Lava Islands, Banks Islands.

T. p. whitneyi Gaua (Santa Maria Island), Banks Islands.

T. p. malekulae Pentecost, Malekula and Ambrim Islands, Vanuatu.

T. p. becki Paama, Lopevi, Epi and Emae Islands, Vanuatu.

T. p. efatensis Efate and Nguna islands, Vanuatu.

T. p. albifrons Eromanga Island, Vanuatu.

T. p. pritzbueri Tanna Island, New Hebrides, and formerly Lifu Island, Loyalty Islands (where now probably extinct).

New Caledonia

T. p. mareensis Formerly occurred down to sea-level on Mare Island, Loyalty Islands, but regarded as near extinction in 1939 and although little fieldwork has since been carried out on Mare, now considered extinct.

T. p. xanthopus New Caledonia, where very rare, last mainland record in 1968, but still present in small numbers on Grande Terre and Yande (where population estimated at 100 birds in 1982).

Tasman Sea
T. p. poliocephalus Norfolk Island; probably extinct.
T. p. vinitinctus Lord Howe Island; extinct.
Fiji
T. p. layardi Viti Levu, Koro, Ovalau and Yasawa Islands, Fiji.
T. p. ruficeps Kadavu Island, Fiji.
T. p. vitiensis Vanua Levu Island, Fiji.
T. p. hades Gau island, Fiji.
T. p. tempesti Taveuni Island, Fiji.
Samoa
T. p. samoensis Savai'i and Upolu Islands, Samoa.

MOVEMENTS Sedentary.

HABITAT Most races occur at a variable range of high altitudes (above 2750 m/9075' on New Guinea; above 1175 m/3880' on Karkar Island; 1500 m/4950' on New Ireland; 1200 m/3960' on Bougainville and Guadalacanal; 1040 m/3430' on Kolombangara, and above 750 m/2475' on Tolokiwa) in montane temperate cloud-forest and mossy thicket and pine forest, or above the timberline in sparse or dense scrub, tree heather, tree ferns, alpine grasslands and boulderfields, also in underbrush in ravines or on steep slopes and dwarf forest edges; a few, particularly those in Melanesia, Polynesia, Mussau and Rennell Island and some of the Vanuatu islands, occur in thick humid lowland rainforest or well-wooded areas down to sea-level (e.g. *erythropleurus, vanikorensis*); in areas where it is common, may also visit areas of secondary growth or overgrown gardens.

BEHAVIOUR In forest fairly shy and difficult to see or approach; usually alone or in pairs, occurring mostly low down or on the ground where it forages in typical fashion on the ground amongst the leaf-litter, usually running or hopping but quick to take alarm, and has swift escape flight with sharp alarm call or chatter; forest-dwelling birds also take seasonal fruits from the canopy of fruiting trees. Montane scrub birds feed in shrubs and low-growing vegetation as well as on the ground, and are usually more approachable, especially where accustomed to human presence, e.g. Mt Kinabalu; usually singly or in pairs, but occasionally several may gather at food source, such as a fruiting tree. Flight usually swift and straight, even through fairly thick growth; on landing the tail is nervously raised and lowered, often accompanied by flicking the wings. Food invertebrates and their larvae, including centipedes, millipedes, small crickets, beetles, spiders, worms, small molluscs (including small snails) and (*albifrons*) small scorpions; also small lizards; plus berries (e.g. wild raspberries), seeds and fruits, particularly guava.

BREEDING Season: April–May and September–December (nominate and *malindangensis*), February–September (*fumidus*), August–November (*mareensis*), September–January (*efatensis, xanthopus*); October–March (*erythropleurus*), July–September (*rennellianus*), November–December (*vinitinctus*); January and March (*seebohmi*), possibly later elsewhere. Nest: a bulky cup of small roots,

bark, grasses, vine stems, palms or plant fibres and leaves, covered with green moss or lichens and lined with finer grasses and other soft vegetation; usually placed low down in forest undergrowth or up to 5 m (16.5') from the ground in a shrub or tree-fork, on a branch or close to the trunk, sometimes in tangled vegetation, tree-hole or crown of pandanus palm or tree-fern. Eggs: 1–2, occasionally 3–4, pale green or greenish-blue or bluish or olive-green, some (e.g. *poliocephalus, fumidus*) blotched lilac and all flecked or finely spotted tawny- or reddish-brown, usually at the larger end. Incubation period 18 days; by female alone (*erythropleurus*). Fledging period 17–19 days.

MOULT No information.

MEASUREMENTS (arranged alphabetically) Wing *albifrons* (n=18) male 103–109, female 97–98; *becki* (n=26) male 95.5–110, female 92–103; *beehleri* (n=4) male 97–105.5, female 97–99; *bougainvillei* (n=15) male 105–115, female 103.5–116.5; *celebensis* (n=17) male 118–125, female 113–123; *deningeri* (n=6) male 112–122, female 107–117; *efatensis* (n=15) 92–114; *erebus* (n=11) male 124.5–132, female 120–126; *erythropleurus* (n=28) male 100–116, female 100–111; *fumidus* (n=17) 118–126; *hades* (n=6) male 105–111, female 101; *heinrothi* (n=2) 110–112; *hygroscopus* (n=11) male 131–135, female 120–130.5; *indrapurae* (n=8) 118–122; *javanicus* (n=15) male 116–130, female 116–119; *katanglad* (n=6) 112–116; *kelleri* (n=12) male 112–118, female 109–116; *keysseri* (n=5) male 113–124, female 117–120; *kulambangrae* (n=3) 103–114; *layardi* (n=18) male 102–116, female 102–114; *loeseri* (n=3) 130–135; *malekulae* (n=17) male 99–109, female 94–107; *malindangensis* (n=20) male 119–131, female 118.5–123.5; *mareensis* (n=14) male 104–109, female 100–102.5; *mayonensis* (n=4) 120–132; *mindorensis* (n=6) male 100–112, female 100–103; *nigrorum* (n=15) male 114–120, female 111–119; *niveiceps* (n=11) male 114.5–121, female 116–118; *papuensis* (n=9) male 127–135, female 120–129; *placens* (n=8) 97–109.5; *poliocephalus* (n=56) male 104–116, female 101–112; *pritzbueri* (n=10) male 100.5–113, female 97–107; *rennellianus* (n=28) male 96–107, female 96–104; *ruficeps* (n=27) male 104–113, female 100.5–105; *samoensis* (n=27) male 98–107.5, female 97–105; *schlegelii* (n=14) male 115–122, female 112–118; *seebohmi* (n=12) male 129–130, female 120–124; *sladeni* (n=5) male 107–112; *sterlingi* (n=5) male 116–125, female 117; *tempesti* (n=18) male 102–117, female 105–116; *thomassoni* (n=27) male 116–123, female 109–115; *vanikorensis* (n=13) male 99–107, female 95.5–98; *versteegi* (n=7) male 128–135.5, female 128.5–133; *vinitinctus* (n=23) male 98–109, female 96–106; *vitiensis* (n=14) male 103.5–112, female 105–109; *whiteheadi* (n=3) 121–124; *whitneyi* (n=6) male 94–102, female 91–96; *xanthopus* (n=5) male 120–124.5, female 110.5–118.

Bill (culmen) (arranged alphabetically, specimen sample sizes as above) *beehleri* 19–22; *bougainvillei* 17.5–20; *celebensis* 16–18; *efatensis* 18–23; *erebus* 17.5–20; *erythropleurus* 17–19.5;

fumidus 16–19; hades 17–21; heinrothi 24–25; indrapurae 15.5–18; javanicus 16.5–19; kelleri 16.5–19; kulambangrae 18–23; layardi 17.5–20; malekulae 17.5–22; mareensis 16–21; mindorensis 15.5–18; nigrorum 18–20; niveiceps 15.5–19; papuensis 19–23; placens 16.5–22; poliocephalus 15–20; pritzbueri 16.5–21; rennellianus 17.5–19; ruficeps 22–24; samoensis 16.5–22; seebohmi 17–19.5; sladeni 20.5–24; tempesti 17.5–21; thomassoni 16–18; vanikorensis 16.6–18; vinitinctus 17–20; vitiensis 20.5–24; whiteheadi 17.5–20; whitneyi 17.5–23; xanthopus 18–23.

Tarsus deningeri, heinrothi, layardi, pritzbueri 34; becki, hades, ruficeps, tempesti, vitiensis, whitneyi, xanthopus 31–33; bougainvillei, indra-

purae, kulambangrae, malekulae, pritzbueri, samoensis, sladeni 30–31; rennellianus 31–32; placens, sladeni 32; beehleri 33–36; keysseri 36; erebus 36.5–37.5; papuensis 33.5–40; versteegi 39.5–42.

Weight beehleri 48–52.5 g; erythropleurus 56–61 g; keysseri 69–78 g; layardi 55–61 g; malindangensis male 75 g, female 84–86 g; papuensis 74–80 g; rennellianus 52–67 g; sladeni 57–67.5 g; tolokiwae 52–67 g.

REFERENCES Beehler (1978), Bregulla (1992), Cain & Galbraith (1955), Coates (1990), Diamond (1989), King (1981), Mayr (1941, 1945), Mayr & Gilliard (1951), Pearson (1966), Rand & Rabor (1960), Ripley (1977), Rowland (1995).

113 CHESTNUT THRUSH Turdus rubrocanus   Plate 35
(Grey-headed Thrush, Gould's Thrush)
Turdus rubrocanus 'Hodgs.' 1846, in Gray, Cat. Mamm. Birds Nepal Thibet 34: 52.

IDENTIFICATION 24–28 cm (9½–11″). A large, brightly coloured thrush of the Himalayas and mountains of south-west China; occurs in two distinct races – western (nominate) with pale buffish-grey on the head and face becoming whiter on the neck, and eastern with the corresponding area blackish-grey; rest of upper- and underparts chestnut, wings and tail black, centre of belly whitish becoming barred black with white tips on the undertail-coverts. Female like male but paler or duller chestnut with extensive areas of pale buff on the belly. **Confusion species** Eastern race initially similar to Kessler's Thrush (114), which has all-black head (male) or brown head with pale buff supercilium, spotted chin and throat (female), with broad pale whitish-buff on mantle and lower breast/upper belly.

DESCRIPTION Sexes differ. **Adult male** Head and face to sides of neck pale ash-grey or tinged grey-brown, becoming paler or whiter on chin and throat and on nape and sides of breast, eye-ring yellow. Mantle to scapulars, rump and uppertail-coverts chestnut. Wings, including coverts and tail, black with edges to coverts, scapulars and outer tail feathers glossy black; underwing-coverts dusky-brown to blackish and greater coverts edged rufous or chestnut. Sides of lower breast, upper belly and flanks chestnut, centre of belly whitish, occasionally with dusky or blackish spots or tips, becoming more heavily barred blackish with white tips and shaft-streaks; undertail-coverts black with broad white centres. Bill yellow, duller in non-breeding season. Legs and feet dull brownish-yellow. **Adult female** Similar to male but duller or browner; head, face and nape duller ash-grey and tinged buffish-brown, often with some dull greyish-brown spotting or streaks on sides of lower throat and a dark brown submoustachial. Wings and tail brown. Chestnut on body duller or browner and shows extensive pale or greyish-buff tips to breast, belly and flanks; undertail-coverts as those of male. **Juvenile** Head, face and neck pale brown with some pale centres to feathers;

upperparts dark brown or chestnut on lower back and rump and mottled with darker tips except for pale buff shaft-streaks on mantle and browner tips to median and greater coverts; flight feathers blackish in immature male and brown in same-age female. Chin and throat cream or buffish-cream, becoming brownish at sides of breast, rest of underparts brown with warm brown centres and blackish tips more visible or marked in male than female.

GEOGRAPHICAL VARIATION Two races; differences well marked in males. Eastern gouldii has head, face and neck dark slate-brown or blackish grey when worn, chestnut on body (to underwing-coverts) brighter or more rust-brown and lacks white on belly, but may show some on vent; undertail-coverts black, broadly white on centres. Female very similar to male but head and face grey, chestnut on body duller or browner and wings and tail more visibly tinged browner.

VOICE Contact note similar to the chuck-chuck notes of Blackbird (111) but the alarm is a rapid, repeated kwik-kwik kwik-kwik. Song recalls Song Thrush (124) in tone and quality but less sustained and with longer pauses: short warbled phrases repeated several (up to 7–8) times before changing to another yee-bre, yee-bre, yee-bre – diddiyit, diddiyit diddiyit – yip-bru, yip-bru... usually given from the tops of conifers in the morning and again towards dusk; song period from early April to July (perhaps only very infrequently towards late June or early July).

STATUS AND DISTRIBUTION Locally common or scarce.

T. r. rubrocanus Breeds eastwards from the Safed Koh on the eastern Afghanistan/Pakistan border discontinuously through northern Pakistan (south through Indus Kohistan to about Murree Hills) to Kashmir, Ladakh and the Himalayas of northern India, Nepal (but breeding not proven) to Sikkim. In winter to lower altitudes within and immediately south of the breeding range in northern Pakistan and northern India.

T. r. gouldii Eastern Arunachal Pradesh (generally scarce) and south-east Tibet, Szechwan, north-west Yunnan, eastern Tsinghai north to Kansu, Ningsia and southern Shensi and east to south-east Hupeh. In winter to lower altitudes within the breeding range, also in small numbers to the north-east Indian hill states (Khasi and Cachar Hills), northern Burma and north-west Thailand (mainly in irruptive years to Doi Inthanon and Doi Pui).

MOVEMENTS An altitude migrant. Moves to lower altitudes at the onset of severe winter weather usually in late September and early October but some still at fairly high levels in early November. In years of poor food supply occurs erratically or in irruptive flocks south of the usual wintering range. Return movements in March and April.

Birds of the eastern race *gouldii* have occurred east to Shantung province, west to Sikkim and once to Nepal; also birds, presumably this race, occurred in Luang Namtha province, northern Laos, in mid-March 1997 and Khammouane province, central Laos, in February 1998. Also a vagrant (one record) to East Tonkin, Vietnam, 27 March 1989 (C. R. Robson *in litt.*).

HABITAT Breeds in both conifer and mixed forests (mainly fir and birch or horse chestnut), usually with a good ground layer of vegetation between 2300 and 3300 m (7500–11,000′), occasionally higher; also deciduous wooded hills and open wooded country; in winter to similar habitats at lower altitude (to about 1500 m/4950′), including orchards and fruiting trees.

BEHAVIOUR Generally shy and unobtrusive, perching mainly in the tops of trees; usually singly or in pairs in the breeding season; in winter often in small flocks and occasionally in company with White-collared Blackbirds (108), Grey-winged Blackbirds (110) and Dark-throated Thrushes (120). Feeds on the ground, also in bushes and trees, but usually deep in the forest and rarely in the open, mainly on invertebrates (ants, beetles, millipedes, grasshoppers, caterpillars, pupae, slugs and small snails), seeds and berries; also known to take fruit, especially wild pears, and visits rhododendron blossoms for nectar.

BREEDING Season: April to the end of July. Nest: a cup of grass, moss, plant stems, twigs, roots and dead leaves lined with mud, fine grasses and pine needles; usually in a tree or sapling and placed against a trunk or thick branch, in a thick tangle of branches up to 3.5 m (11½′) from the ground, or else on the ground, on a bank, amongst the roots of a fallen tree, on a ledge or in a tree-hole. Eggs: 2–4, exceptionally 5, light green, greenish-blue or -grey covered with reddish-brown or light purple spots or blotches. Incubation and nest building by female.

MOULT Adults undergo a complete post-breeding moult from the end of July.

MEASUREMENTS Wing, male 135–144, female 132–135; tarsus 27.5–33; bill 21–30; *gouldii* wing 137–148. Weight 84–100 g (Ali & Ripley 1983).

REFERENCES Ali & Ripley (1983), Roberts (1992).

114 KESSLER'S THRUSH *Turdus kessleri*　　　　Plate 36
(White-backed Thrush)
Merula Kessleri **Przewalski, 1876,** *Mongol. i Strana Tangut.* **2: 62, pl. 10 – Kansu.**

IDENTIFICATION 28 cm (11″). A large distinctive thrush with a restricted range in east-central Asia. Adult male has all-black head to upper mantle and breast, black wings and tail, pale buff mantle to sides of upper breast and upper belly, and warm brown or light chestnut scapulars to rump and lower belly. Adult female similar but generally paler, with a dull brown head to breast and a pale buffish supercilium, chin and throat. **Confusion species** Chestnut Thrush (113) has a pale buffish or buffish-grey head, face and neck (slightly duller or dingier in female) and lacks the pale buffish areas on the upper- and underparts, with black undertail-coverts streaked white. Female Chestnut lacks the dull brown head and face and pale buffish supercilium of Kessler's.

DESCRIPTION Sexes differ. **Adult male** Entire head, face, neck, to breast and upper mantle jet-black and slightly glossy; bright yellow eye-ring. Mantle and edges of upper scapulars pale buff or buffish-white (sharply delineated against black hood), grading to chestnut on back and lower scapulars; rump and uppertail-coverts slightly paler than back, with pale buffish tips and blackish centres to uppertail-coverts. Wings (including all coverts) and tail jet-black, edges of coverts, scapulars and outer tail feathers slightly glossy black with fine rufous edges and tips; underwing-coverts dull rufous or darker at bases of feathers. Sides of upper breast to lower breast and upper belly dull whitish-buff, rest of belly, flanks and thighs chestnut, undertail-coverts black. Bill yellow; may be dusky at tip. Legs and feet brown, soles paler or yellower. **Adult female** General pattern like male but much duller without heavy contrast. Head to nape and upper mantle dull grey-brown extending to sides of neck and breast; pale yellow eye-ring; cheeks and ear-coverts dull brown with fine pale whitish-buff shaft-streaks; pale buff or light greyish-buff on mantle and back, paler than on male and often with dark central shaft-streaks, in fresh plumage becoming orange-rufous or chestnut on lower back, rump and uppertail-coverts, or when worn paler greyish-buff faintly tinged light orange. Wings and tail dark brown but wings edged paler or ashy-brown, broadly on inner secondaries and tertials. Chin and throat pale or dull buffish, streaked or spotted with dark brown tips and broad dark brown malar at sides. Lower breast/upper belly pale greyish-cream or dull buff, rest of underparts dull grey-brown tinged grey-brown on breast and chestnut, tawny-brown or tawny-rufous on belly to vent; undertail-coverts like male, dusky-brown with rufous fringes. Bill dull yellowish-brown, becoming yellower at tip and base of lower mandible. **Juvenile** Forehead and crown to mantle and upper back brown to dark brown, flecked with pale buffish shaft-streaks; scapulars, back and rump barred pale buff or whitish-buff and dark brown. Tail dark brown. Wing-coverts as scapulars but lesser and median coverts have broad pale buff shaft-streaks and median and greater coverts have whitish tips. Chin and throat to breast pale whitish or greyish-buff, heavily spotted or mottled with dark brown tips, belly and flanks barred with dark brown, undertail-coverts dark brown with fine pale buff edges.

GEOGRAPHICAL VARIATION None. Monotypic.

VOICE Call a soft *squack* becoming harsher *squawk* when alarmed; also a soft *dug-dug* and a series of *chock-chock-chock* usually given when disturbed, and a loud harsh piping *swi-swi-swi-swi* alarm similar to that of Blackbird (111) and a chuckling note similar to the dry rattling call of White-collared Blackbird (108). Song rarely heard: a series of short melancholy phrases similar to that of Mistle Thrush (126).

STATUS AND DISTRIBUTION Scarce, rare or locally common. Breeds in western China from eastern Tsinghai and Kansu south to north-west Yunnan, western Szechwan, eastern and north-east Tibet. In winter to south-east Tibet (one specimen collected in November close to the Sikkim border), east-central Nepal (mainly Khumbu) where very scarce (though up to 100 recorded in winter 1999–2000 and previously regarded as a vagrant (not recorded prior to 1986), and infrequently in northern Arunachal Pradesh (where possibly overlooked) and probably southern Tsinghai.

MOVEMENTS Migratory. All breeding birds move south or south-west to winter in extreme south-west China and south-east Tibet. Very little information on dates of movements but migrants recorded in southern and south-east Tibet in March and April, exceptionally in May and early June, and in autumn from August to October.

A vagrant to Bhutan (1 record) and possibly Sikkim (Meinertzhagen recorded of a party of 4 at 3700 m at Changu, Sikkim, in December).

HABITAT Breeds in the upper or montane zones of dwarf juniper and conifer forests, low rhododendron and willow scrub above the timberline between 3600 and 4500 m (11,900–14,850'), and in open rocky country with stunted scrub. In winter to lower elevations (but mostly above 1500 m/5000') where it occurs in similar habitat but also in edges of cultivation, especially orchards and potato fields.

BEHAVIOUR Gregarious and often in flocks even in the breeding season; in winter often in company with Dark-throated (120) and Dusky Thrushes (121). On the ground a large or robust-looking thrush with a long tail and wings frequently drooped at side of the body. In flight recalls Mistle and other large thrushes with a series of about 10–15 wing-strokes followed by a short glide. Feeds on the ground and in vegetation; food little known but probably little different in composition from other large thrushes, i.e. mostly invertebrates such as earthworms, plus berries (known to take juniper berries in winter) and fruit.

BREEDING Season: May to July or early August. Nest: a cup-shaped structure of grass roots, animal hair and feathers, often in a hollow in a rock or bank along a stream. Eggs: little known but according to Baker (1924) like those of Fieldfare (122).

MOULT No information.

MEASUREMENTS Wing, male (n=21) 152–163, female (n=8) 143–157; tarsus 34–38; bill (from skull) 25–27 (Ali & Ripley 1983). Weight apparently unrecorded.

REFERENCES Ali & Ripley (1983), Baker (1924).

115 GREY-SIDED THRUSH *Turdus feae* Plate 38
(Fea's Thrush)

Merula Feae Salvadori, 1887, *Ann. Mus. Civ. Genova* 5: 514 – Mulayit Mountain, Tenasserim.

IDENTIFICATION 22–23.5 cm (8¾–9¼"). A medium-sized, plain-looking thrush with a limited but imprecisely known range in north-east China. Adults are bright olive-brown above, and the only real field characters are a prominent white supercilium reaching over the ear-coverts, a white crescent below the eye, and a dull whitish or whitish-buff chin to breast, becoming grey or greyish-buff on the remaining underparts (in some more heavily grey on the flanks). **Confusion species** Once the long white supercilium seen, only problem may be with Eyebrowed Thrush (116), which has a similar supercilium but greyer-brown upperparts, deep orange wash on the breast (always present although often pale in first-year birds) and flanks (where no grey) and white belly to undertail-coverts. First-winter birds are extremely similar to same-age female Eyebrowed and require good views of the flank colour to separate them: always grey in Grey-sided and pale orange to whitish-orange in Eyebrowed. Female Tickell's Thrush (105) is similar but duller brown and lacks a supercilium.

DESCRIPTION Sexes almost alike. **Adult male** Entire upperparts including wings and tail warm olive-brown, slightly paler or tinged russet on forehead to crown and nape; wing-coverts, tertials and edges of flight feathers slightly paler brown. Lores blackish-brown, long white supercilium from base of bill over eye and fading at rear of ear-coverts, short dark eye-stripe, cheeks and ear-coverts warm russet-brown with small white crescent below eye. Chin and throat whitish-buff, becoming variably washed rusty-buff or greyish on breast and sides of neck, lower breast buffish to grey washed brownish, becoming whitish-grey on belly and flanks, sometimes with flanks heavily washed grey; lower belly, vent and undertail-coverts white with grey-brown fringes. Underwing-coverts ash-grey. Bill brownish-horn, becoming yellowish-horn on lower mandible and yellowish at base. Eye dark brown. Legs and feet pale brown to brownish-yellow. **Adult female** Like male except for dark brown (not black) lores, cheeks and ear-coverts finely streaked or flecked white, faint spotting on sides of chin and dark brown streaks on throat or at sides of throat, and grey on underparts visibly tinged brownish-grey, but breast and flanks also sometimes warm or russet-brown and lower flanks to undertail-coverts white. **Immature** First-winter bird similar to adult female with warm or russet-brown head and nape to mantle; white tips to greater coverts, fine whitish flecks or streaks on cheeks and ear-coverts, and white on chin and throat with thin brown streaks on sides of throat; breast may be as brown as upperparts, ending abruptly as a breast-band.

GEOGRAPHICAL VARIATION None. Monotypic.

VOICE Range of notes very poorly known. Call similar to that of Eyebrowed Thrush but a thinner *zeeee* or *sieee*. Song a rather jerky repeated series of short double- or treble-note phrases, mostly consisting of *sit tewuu* or *sit-tewoo*, *wet-too*, *chit-to-loo* or varied with *pwt-too-too* and broken by long pauses. Sings from an exposed perch at the tops of tall trees.

STATUS AND DISTRIBUTION Scarce or uncommon but poorly known. The population is considered to be small and threatened by habitat loss, and listed as Vulnerable (Collar *et al.* 1994). Breeds in north-eastern China in the hills and mountains of Hebei province, including the Eastern Tombs area near Peking, and at Old Peak near Beidahe; possibly also in Luliang Shan, west-central Shanxi province, northern China, where recorded in May (King 1987).

Winters locally, mainly above 1200 m (4000') in extreme north-east India (but may be very rare or erratic here, given lack of recent published reports; but see Movements) from Nagaland and Meghalaya, North Cachar Hills to Manipur; possibly regular in small numbers to western and eastern Burma discontinuously south to Tenasserim and east to north-west Thailand; 2 birds recently (February 1995) recorded at c.1700 m (5600') on the Nakai Plateau (Nakai-Nam Theun), central Laos (Duckworth *et al.* 1998).

MOVEMENTS Migratory. Breeding birds move south to south-west to winter from north-east India to north-west Thailand and central Laos, south to Tenasserim, Burma. Arrive in northern India from mid- to late October onwards and leave for the breeding area from early to late April. Scarce or irregular on spring migration on western shore of Gulf of Bohai. Single recently recorded in May 1999 as a vagrant to Lava, north Bengal (A. Prasad pers. comm.).

HABITAT Dense and often damp broadleaf forests on hills, and montane woods usually well above 1500 m (5000') in summer, slightly lower to about 1000–1100 m (3300–3630') in winter. On migration occurs in a variety of wooded habitats including plantations. Winter habitat similar to that of summer and often found near rhododendrons.

BEHAVIOUR A fairly shy and retiring species, often in flocks and in company or loose association with Eyebrowed Thrush. Has a rapid flight, usually into thick cover, appearing very similar in shape to other medium-sized thrushes. Forages in trees and on the ground amongst moss-covered rocks and in low vegetation or beneath rhododendrons, taking invertebrates, mainly spiders, plus wild strawberries and berries; also recorded taking nectar from a flowering tree.

BREEDING Unknown; Baker (1924) was under the impression that the bird was 'probably resident' in the hills of north-east India, south of the Brahmaputra, and went on to describe a nest and eggs which are now considered in error.

MOULT No information.

MEASUREMENTS Wing, male (n=5) 124–131; female (n=4) 119–121; tarsus 30–33; bill 24–25 (Ali & Ripley 1983). Weight apparently unrecorded.

REFERENCES Ali & Ripley (1983), Baker (1924), Collar *et al.* (1994), Duckworth *et al.* (1998), King (1987).

116 EYEBROWED THRUSH *Turdus obscurus*   Plate 38
(Dark Thrush, Grey-headed Thrush [Japan])

Turdus obscurus Gmelin, 1789, *Syst. Nat.* 1(2): 816 – 'Sibiriae silvis, ultra lacum Baical.'

IDENTIFICATION 20.5–24.5 cm (8–9½"). A medium-sized thrush from central and eastern Siberia, best recognised by grey or greyish-brown head and face and long, fairly broad white supercilium from the lores to over the eye and ear-coverts, sometimes with a white crescent on the cheeks. Upperparts mostly deep brown, breast and flanks variably pale to warm or rufous-orange, belly to undertail white. Juveniles browner on the crown and nape and have the grey of the face broken by fine whitish streaks; upperparts generally paler brown than adult and show a row of fine white tips to the greater coverts; chin and throat whitish but underparts variably pale, warm or dingy orange. **Confusion species** Likely to be confused with Grey-sided (115) and Pale Thrushes (117) (formerly considered a race of Pale Thrush) and Redwing (123). Best told from Grey-sided by colour of underparts (see also that species). From Pale Thrush by long white supercilium, paler brown upperparts, paler or brighter orange underparts and no obvious white tips to outer tail feathers; female Pale Thrush may show similarly marked underparts but is usually also blotched grey on sides of breast, has darker upperparts and lacks well-defined supercilium. Initially like Redwing, which has slightly darker upperparts and well-defined streaks below, with red confined to the flanks and underwing-coverts. Immature possibly confused with same-age Brown-headed Thrush (118), which has darker upperparts, darker spots on the breast and pale tail-tips. Grey-backed Thrush (104) has browner upperparts, long white supercilium and orange (or pale orange) not pale grey on the breast. In eastern Siberia the songs of Eyebrowed, Pale and Grey-backed Thrushes are extremely similar and probably not separable by ear alone.

DESCRIPTION Sexes similar but usually separable. **Adult male** Forehead to crown and nape blackish-grey with an olive-brown tinge, lores and slightly behind eye black; supercilium from upper lores to over eye (or above ear-coverts in some) white (broadest over or behind eye); pale yellowish-grey eye-ring; small crescent of white below eye on upper cheeks (not always present), white submoustachial with blackish malar; rest of face, chin, throat and sides of neck charcoal-grey or faintly washed brown. Mantle, back and scapulars brown to olive-brown, lower back, rump and uppertail-coverts similar but with warmer or rufous-brown wash. Tail dark brown with no obvious white tips but may show narrow whitish tip to innerweb of outermost feather and fine whitish fringe to tip of next innermost at close range or in the hand. Wings-coverts as scapulars; alula and primary coverts brown or darker brown but edged pale buff, flight feathers and tertials dark brown with outer edges of secondaries and tertials paler brown; underwing-coverts similar to upperparts, pale greyish-brown tinged olive. Chin as rest of face or white with black malar stripe, breast and flanks variable from warm buff-brown to orange or orange-rufous, centre of lower breast, belly, vent and undertail-coverts white, latter sometimes showing brownish edges and olive-grey tips to some feathers. In worn plumage (April to July) head and face browner and rest of body also paler brown. Upper mandible and tip to lower blackish-horn, base of lower and cutting edges to upper yellow in breeding season; at other times bill generally darker with less yellow. Eye dark brown. Legs and feet variable from light or yellowish-brown to dark pinkish- or flesh-brown. **Adult female** Similar to male but can also be much paler with forehead to nape pale olive-brown extending to face; ear-coverts dark slate-grey finely streaked pale brown and whitish; chin and throat

generally more whitish or with dark malar streaks and whitish submoustachial becoming greyer on lower throat and upper breast; breast and flanks generally paler, varying from pale tawny to light orange or even pale grey on centre of upper breast; in worn plumage tone of upper- and underparts paler and breast to flanks more faded. Bill as male or greenish-horn with pale yellow base to lower mandible. Legs and feet yellowish-green. **Immature** Juvenile has crown, mantle and scapulars dark or olive-brown with pale central streaks to feathers, creating heavily spotted effect; back unspotted, rump and uppertail-coverts similar to mantle but with pale spots on tips of feathers. Tail as adult but feathers narrower and pointed at tip, uniformly dark. Face pale buffish-brown or lightly streaked grey and slightly mottled darker on cheeks and ear-coverts; whitish submoustachial and sooty-grey malar stripes. Wings pale olive-brown with pale buffish-brown tips to lesser and median coverts and whitish tips to greaters; tertials similarly have pale buff tip on outerweb. Chin and throat whitish or streaked grey at sides; breast and flanks pale buff to buffish-orange, centre of lower breast and belly whitish with dark spots to tips of breast feathers, becoming paler or browner on lower breast and flanks. **First-winter and -summer male** Similar to but paler than adult male with dark olive-brown crown to nape, thin pale buff to whitish supercilium over black lores broadening behind eye, lower lores to eye whitish, sometimes with whitish area below eye as a separated small whitish crescent, cheeks and ear-coverts greyish or grey-brown streaked paler, whitish submoustachial and dark grey sides to whitish chin and throat, sides to lower throat and upper breast pale brown to greyish-brown. Rest of upperparts as adult or slightly paler olive-brown, but has fine whitish-buff fringes or spots at tips of (mostly inner) greater coverts, occasionally pale tips to tertials, and edges to flight feathers pale buffish. Breast and flanks pale orange or tawny-orange fading to whitish central lower breast and belly to vent and undertail-coverts, some birds showing very little or very pale wash, or may be confined to flanks. **First-winter and -summer female** As same-age male or adult female (not always distinguishable) but head and face lack any grey, breast duller or very faded, occasionally greyish-brown in spring. Bill as non-breeding adult but yellow at base duller or less extensive. Underparts as first-winter bird.

GEOGRAPHICAL VARIATION None. Monotypic.

VOICE Contact-call in flight a Blackbird-like *zieeh* or harsher *seee* or *tseee* recalling a Redwing, and a thin *sip-sip*, *zip-zip* or *che-e* given by wintering birds; other contact notes heard from flocks feeding on the ground include a chuckling *dack-dack* or *tuck-tuck* and a *tchup* or *tchuck* given from cover. Song a series of 2–3 clear melodic but mournful phrases and whistles, usually delivered at medium-slow pace, some recalling the delivery of a Song Thrush (124) or Redwing: *teveteu trrrutetyute... trrryutetyutyu*, followed by a pause, then a lower-pitched twittering, disordered warbling and subdued chattering interspersed with short pauses;

may include some poor imitations of neighbouring species e.g. the fluty yodelling *dweep* or *elooeet* of Greenshank *Tringa nebularia* together with calls of Willow Tit *Parus montanus*, Coal Tit *P. ater*, Nuthatch *Sitta europea* or Two-barred Crossbill *Loxia leucoptera*. In parts of the range, e.g. Amurland and Ussuriland, the songs of Eyebrowed, Pale and Grey-backed Thrushes are extremely similar and probably not always separable with certainty by ear alone, at least without local experience of all three. Song period begins with first arrivals back on breeding territory from end of May to mid-July.

STATUS AND DISTRIBUTION Locally scarce to common or abundant in parts of the breeding range. Breeds in central and eastern Siberia from about 78°E along the River Pur and the middle reaches of the Ob north to about 63°N along the Pur and 69°N along the Yenisey east (generally south of 65°N) to about 144°E in Yakutia. In the south to the north-east Altai, western Sayan range, Khamar Daban (south of Lake Baikal) and possibly the Hentiy (Hentiyn Nuruu) range in northern Mongolia, also the middle reaches of the Amur and the northern Sikhote-Alin in extreme eastern Russia; separate populations in southern and eastern Kamchatka and may possibly breed in the northern Kuriles.

In winter to southern China from southern Yunnan through Kwangsi and Kwangtung to Taiwan, in the south from north-east India in much of Arunachal Pradesh and the north-east hill states (vagrant to peninsular India with c.5 records) and throughout South-East Asia (except south-west Burma, central, eastern and south-east Thailand and northern Annam) including Peninsular Malaysia, islands in the Gulf of Thailand, Singapore (where uncommon), northern Borneo (including Sarawak), Brunei, Sumatra, also Java, Bali (where less common) and the Philippines (Apo Reef, Calayan, Guimaras, Luzon, Siquijor, Mindanao, Negros, Caluya, Busuanga, Palawan and Cebu) including the Sulu Archipelago (Tawitawi); a few also winter in southern Japan.

Has been reported in summer from Mt Fuji, Mt Daisetsu and on Tsushima, Japan, but breeding has yet to be proved.

MOVEMENTS Migratory; entirely deserts breeding area in the winter. Post-breeding dispersal of both adults and immatures in central Siberia from mid-July. More purposeful migration begins with movements south or south-east through Mongolia, central and eastern China and Japan to winter throughout much of South-East Asia from north-east India to the Greater Sundas and southern China. Most birds begin southward movement from central and northern Siberia in mid-August and most have departed from the breeding areas by early September; passage in eastern part of the range in middle to late September. Passage through Japan begins in September but most birds pass through early October to early November. Arrives in north-east India late October or early November about the same time or slightly ahead of birds wintering to the east; birds wintering in southern Malaysia and northern Borneo arrive (exceptionally in early October) from mid-November to mid-December; most migrants at Fraser's Hill, Malaysia, late November onwards. Uncommon or moderately common on passage in Thailand (where only numerous from early December) and Korea (mostly May and November); common passage migrant and scarce winter visitor to Hong Kong (flocks of over 100 regular in November) from November to May, but most in March and April and uncommon on passage and rare winter visitor to Taiwan; also rare winter visitor to the Philippines from the end of November to April or exceptionally to early May.

Most move in small to medium-sized flocks but may congregate in larger numbers at peak times. Return movements in spring appear to be reverse of direction taken in autumn. Birds begin moving in the southern part of the wintering range in late March but most passage through north-east India, Thailand (when much more numerous than in autumn) and across central China is in April, when birds also noted in southern and central Japan; passage through Mongolia early to mid-May. Common spring migrant through Sakhalin from mid-May to first 10 days of June; arrives back on breeding territory in eastern Siberia from mid-May, and late May or early June on Kamchatka.

An accidental or scarce (but annual) vagrant to much of Europe with records from British Isles (16 records to 1999, last in 1995), Norway (3), Finland (2), France (10), Belgium (8), Netherlands (4), Germany (18), Poland (8), Czech Republic (at least 20), Malta (2), Portugal (1); elsewhere there are records from Israel (1), Oman (1), U.A.E. (1), Nepal (6), northern India (West Bengal and northern Assam), southern India (Karnataka and Tamil Nadu – 2), and Andaman Islands (3), Maldives (1), Sri Lanka (1), Bangladesh (4); has occurred as an annual vagrant to north-east Sulawesi (including a flock of 15 in April 1978), twice on Flores (in April 1976, and flock of c.30 in April 1988). Over 40 records in Alaska (north to Barrow), including the Aleutians (where considered almost annual in spring on western islands east to Amchitka) and Pribilof Islands; in May 1998 a total of 180 were conservatively estimated to have passed through the Aleutians (mostly Attu) and the Pribilofs, with up to 13 a day on St Paul Island at the height of this movement. Also a rare winter visitor to Palau (Caroline Islands).

HABITAT Breeds in dense forests of spruce and fir, usually in extensive taiga, the greatest densities in valleys and slopes of mid-age *Pinus sibirica* forests with dense canopy cover; may also breed in mixed forests and broadleaved woods up to 1500 m (4950') or occasionally to 2400 m (7920') in places; often nests in damp depressions, near streams or water. In Sakhalin and the north of the range breeds in lowland and montane larch–birch forests with dwarf cedar pine *Pinus pumila* bushes; also montane stone-birch *Betula ermani* groves with similar undergrowth layer. On Kamchatka breeds mainly in birch forests with a good undergrowth. Also occurs (in winter or on migration) on the edge of agricultural land, in orchards, parks and large gardens in towns and cities. On passage and in winter occurs in open forest but, in some parts of the range, in open country, including mangroves, casuarina groves, open beaches with vegetation and gardens. In southern Malaysia occurs from sea-level to at least 2000 m (6600′) and up to 2420 m (8000′) on Mt Kinabalu, northern Borneo. **BEHAVIOUR** Occurs alone, in pairs or more usually on passage and in winter in small flocks. Fairly shy and unapproachable on breeding territory but may be more confiding outside this period. On the ground has gait and actions of other *Turdus* thrushes of same size, e.g. Redwing or Song Thrush, with upright stance and tail held straight out or at a slightly depressed angle, hopping or running with frequent pauses to check and search for food; flight fast and direct; when disturbed usually flies into tops of tree or bushes; most active in the early morning and evening, spending the day in the shade of trees. Often in flocks and frequently associates with Dark-throated (120) and Dusky Thrushes (121), especially in winter. Vagrants to Europe have often occurred with the first-arriving Redwings. Feeds mostly on the ground on a wide variety of invertebrates and in the canopy of trees on berries and fruit.

BREEDING Season: late May to late July. Nest: a large untidy cup-shaped structure mainly of grasses including some sedges, leaves, small spruce twigs, moss, roots, bark and larch needles, lined with mud and fine grasses, usually in a fork or close to a tree-trunk (usually fir) or in a bush up to 9 m (c.30′) from the ground. Eggs: 4–6, exceptionally 3–7, pale or dull blue with rusty-red or reddish-brown mottling, speckles or blotches. Nestlings fed by both parents. Fledging period 10+ days. Two broods in the south and centre of the range.

MOULT Adults undergo full post-breeding moult from late July or early August; complete before autumn departure from breeding area. Juveniles undergo partial post-breeding moult of the head, body, lesser, median and some inner greater coverts before leaving the breeding area; usually completed by mid-August.

MEASUREMENTS Wing, male (n=73) 117–136, female (n=57) 115–127; tarsus 27.5–33; bill 17–23. Weight, male 61–117, female 50–110 g (Ali & Ripley 1983).

REFERENCES Ali & Ripley (1983), Dickinson *et al.* (1991).

117 PALE THRUSH *Turdus pallidus* Plate 36
Turdus pallidus Gmelin, 1789, Syst. Nat. 1(2): 815 – 'Sibiria, ultra lacum Baikal.'

IDENTIFICATION 22–23 cm (8¾–9″). A rather dark thrush with pale brown olive-tinged upperparts, dark grey head, wings and tail, and white-tipped outertail; underparts variable from whitish to pale brown. Female similar or paler brown with the head and face paler grey tinged olive, and a white chin and central throat. Both sexes can show a whitish spot/submoustachial at the base of the bill. Breeds in far eastern Siberia, wintering in Japan and southern China. **Confusion species** Could be mistaken for Brown-headed Thrush (118) but lacks the bright orange underparts and male has a grey not brown head and face; both sexes also told from this and similar Eyebrowed (116) by much paler and olive underparts, white spots on outer tail tips and no supercilium. Female told from adult and immature Dark-throated Thrush (120) by paler face, lack of black on throat or breast, and pale yellowish eye-ring; white outertail tips in both sexes is always a good feature in flight. **Taxonomic note** Occasionally treated as conspecific with Eyebrowed, Brown-headed and also Izu Islands Thrush (Dementiev & Gladkov 1954, Cheng 1987).

DESCRIPTION Sexes differ. In worn plumage both sexes become duller olive or tinged greyish-olive. **Adult male** Forehead to upper nape, face and sides of throat grey or deep greyish, forehead often tinged pale olive or grey-brown, and lores to eye blackish; thin yellow eye-ring. Lower nape to mantle, scapulars, rump and uppertail-coverts pale brown or light chestnut-brown (may appear olive-brown or tinged greyish in some lights); in fresh plumage male is more heavily tinged warm chestnut. Tail dark grey with olive on central feathers and white tips to outer two (most extensive on outermost) and small whitish spot at tip of third inner feather. Median coverts as scapulars or on outer-webs, tips to greaters grey or blackish; alula and primary coverts brown but finely edged warm brown; flight feathers grey-brown but also finely edged pale brown; inner secondaries and tertials more broadly edged warm brown; underwing-coverts pale grey or edged whitish. Chin variably white, whitish or grey and usually shows small white spot at base of bill which, in some, becomes indistinct whitish submoustachial. Lower chin and throat either entirely grey or greyish-olive. Breast light orange to warm brown or with brown spots in centre, belly variably whitish, greyish-olive or darker olive; flanks similar or slightly browner-olive becoming olive-brown on lower flanks; centre of belly to vent white, undertail-coverts pale buff or whitish with brownish spots at tips; thighs grey-brown. Bill brown or greyish-horn with yellowish-orange base to lower mandible. Eye dark brown. Legs and feet yellowish to pale fleshy-brown. **Adult female** Generally similar to male but upperparts (including edges to wings and tail) slightly more olive-brown and head and face paler grey (or entirely greyish-olive); forehead to crown and most of face may also be tinged olive, except for some fine whitish flecks or narrow streaks on cheeks and ear-coverts and a pale olive-buff upper edge to dark grey lores to eye; has a small pale base or submoustachial from sides of bill. Wings as male but generally warmer brown edges to primary coverts, inner primaries and secondaries, outer 3–4 primaries narrowly edged whitish on outerweb. Chin and throat whitish finely streaked dark brown, sometimes with short dark grey malar; rest of underparts pale or gingery-brown with greyish-olive smudges on sides of breast and flanks, sometimes also mottled duller across breast; rest of underparts whitish. Bill may have slightly more yellow at base of lower mandible. Legs and feet straw-yellow to brown. **Immature** Juvenile brown or dull olive-brown above, heavily flecked with pale buff or buffish-orange spots on crown and nape and longer, finer streaks on mantle, back and scapulars; tips to greater coverts pale or whitish-buff. Underparts whitish or tinged yellowish-buff in places and mottled or spotted dark brown. First-year bird similar to adult female but generally duller olive, especially head and face which are olive-grey; cheeks and ear-coverts heavily flecked pale or whitish-buff; prominent whitish submoustachial and long dark greyish malar, sides of chin and throat mottled and streaked olive with broad whitish central shafts. Has (some) retained juvenile wing-coverts and may (notably in autumn and early winter) show white tips to greater coverts (in some retained into first summer but usually absent by January).

GEOGRAPHICAL VARIATION None. Monotypic.

VOICE Call a dry sharp *chook*, *tuck-tuck* or *chuck-chuck*, very similar to that of Brown-headed Thrush, often given very softly; also a thin harsh *tsee* or *tsee-ip* and some softer chuckling notes; alarm note a long sibilant *seee* followed by a series of loud sharp *quack quack* or *tchink tchink* notes, very like those given by Blackbird (111). Song similar to that of Brown-headed Thrush and Mistle Thrush (126) but with emphasis on different notes: a simple series of far-carrying, repeated double or treble whistles, phrases varying from *tuvee-tulee tulee-tuvee* or *tve-tveeu-weet-weet-tveeu-trrrsss* to *tveng-tvee-tyu-tryuu*, *tvee-tvee-tyu-trengg* or *tfeeu-fyu-tryu-fyu...*; may end with a slurred *tsss-ss-ss*. Usually sings from atop a tall tree, mostly at dusk and around sunrise, sometimes in chorus with others.

STATUS AND DISTRIBUTION Locally common or scarce. Far eastern Siberia in Amurland and Ussuriland north to about Khungari and the Gorin river, in the south from Heilungkiang in northern Manchuria and the Khabarovsk region south to southern and eastern Liaoning; also in the mountains of Korea (where generally uncommon but locally numerous). Bred in summer 1991 on Mt Garyu, Honshu, Japan, following several summering records (Totune & Yamamoto 1993); also reported to breed on Tsushima (in Korea Strait) but requires confirmation. In winter to central and southern Japan (from Honshu southwards) through the Ryukyu/Nansei Shoto Islands to Taiwan; also in southern Korea and mainland China south of the Yangtze west to Kweichow and south to Kwangsi and occasionally to south-east Yunnan.

MOVEMENTS Migratory. Entirely deserts the breeding area in winter. Moves south through Korea, northern China and Japan to winter in southern Japan, Taiwan and southern China. Departs from breeding areas in Amurland and Ussuriland in mid- to late September, with passage through northern Japan and north-east China in late September and early October. Passage through east coast of China in September with arrival in Taiwan and southern China from early October, but first visitors to Hong Kong not usually before late November or early December. Return movements begin in the south in late March and early April; arrives in Korea in mid-April where passage and breeding birds present together; passage then more visible and often in larger numbers in eastern China and throughout Japan than in autumn. Deserts wintering areas in Japan from mid-April to early May, although June/July records on northern Honshu and Hokkaido not unknown. Arrives in Amurland and Ussuriland in late April and early May.

A rare winter visitor (3 records) to the Philippines (Calayan, Luzon and Batan).

HABITAT Breeds in dense mixed montane and sub-montane forests, mostly spruces or cedar woods but also bamboo thickets and plantations of cedars and deciduous trees. On migration it occurs in more open habitats in woodlands, hillside woods, copses and scrub, particularly in berry-bearing bushes. In winter in similar habitat at lower levels plus wooded groves, orchards, suburban areas, parks, gardens, edges of cultivation, and open fields.

BEHAVIOUR Generally shy or wary during the breeding season, when usually alone or in pairs; on migration and in winter occurs in small to large flocks which feed together in open fields and in woodland areas, often alongside Eyebrowed Thrushes. On the ground stands upright and forages in typical thrush manner in leaf-litter and open grassy areas. Feeds also in low vegetation and bushes, mostly taking a variety of berries, e.g. whortleberry, plus seeds and invertebrates such as beetles and worms.

BREEDING Season: mid-May to mid- or late August. Nest: a bulky cup of mud, dry grasses, sedges or roots lined with fine grasses, moss, dry leaves or cedar needles and some mud; usually placed in a tree-fork at least 1.5 m (5') from the ground. Eggs: 4–5, like Fieldfare (122) pale greenish-blue with sparse covering of reddish-brown spots or fine streaks. Incubation period 13–14 days; by female. Fledging period 13–15 days; nestlings fed by both parents. Probably two broods.

MOULT Adults undergo full post-breeding moult following the breeding season, completed before departure on autumn migration. Partial post-breeding moult of juveniles begins soon after becoming independent but usually affects the head, body, lesser and median and some (inner) greater coverts, completed before mid- to late August or early September.

MEASUREMENTS Wing, male (n=50) 123–134, female (n=45) 117–130.5; tarsus 30–32; bill (to feathers) male 17–20.5, female 16–19.5 (to skull) 21–24.5. Weight 79 g (La Touche 1925–1930, Dementiev & Gladkov 1954).

REFERENCES Dementiev & Gladkov (1954), La Touche (1925–1930), Totune & Yamamoto (1993).

(Brown Thrush, Red-bellied Thrush, Japanese Brown Thrush)
Turdus chrysolaus Temminck, 1831, *Pl. Col.* livr. 87, pl. 537 – Japan.

IDENTIFICATION 23–24 cm (9–9½″). A medium-sized thrush of the Far East, similar to several other thrushes each of which are distinctively marked. Adults dark brown above and bright rufous below except for contrasting pale underwing-coverts in flight and white from the belly to undertail-coverts. Adult male has a blacker face than female, which shows white streaks on the chin and throat and a thin whitish supercilium. Juvenile similar to female but has paler orange underparts, orange supercilium, heavily white-spotted upperparts and blackish-spotted lower breast. **Confusion species** Pale Thrush (117) (sometimes considered conspecific with Brown-headed) has much paler underparts, dark grey head and pale warm brown or light chestnut-brown on rest of upperparts, and white tips to tail. Eyebrowed Thrush (116) is similar but has generally paler orange underparts, broad white supercilium, pale crescents below eye and pale sides to neck. Izu Islands Thrush (119) is also similar but has very limited range, black head to breast and generally much deeper rufous underparts; females are generally browner with white-streaked throat.

DESCRIPTION Sexes differ. **Adult male** Forehead pale brown, crown and nape to scapulars, rump and uppertail-coverts deep olive-brown tinged russet. Lores to cheeks slightly blacker, becoming browner on ear-coverts and sides of nape; thin bright yellow eye-ring. Tail blackish-brown, broadly edged pale grey-brown on all outer feathers. Median and greater coverts blackish-brown edged slightly paler or warm russet-brown, flight feathers blackish-brown fairly broadly edged pale or buffish-grey on primaries, alula and primary coverts blackish, tertials like coverts; underwing-coverts pale or whitish-grey with greyish-white fringes at bases. Chin and throat variable from blackish-brown to pale brown merging into deep orange or orange-rufous on breast to flanks and sides of belly to sides of rump; rear of flanks brownish; central lower breast, central belly to vent and undertail-coverts white, latter with brown or rusty-brown spots at tips. Bill dark brown or blackish except for bright yellowish or yellowish-orange lower mandible which has dark tip. Legs and feet pale brown to yellowish or orange-brown. **Adult female** Similar but slightly paler or more gingery-brown on head and face, also on rest of upperparts; wings and tail as male, but tertials often warmer or buffish-brown. Face much browner than male and shows indistinct pale or ill-defined buffish supercilium over or more usually behind eye and over ear-coverts, thin pale yellow eye-ring. Chin and throat white finely streaked dark brown, sometimes with thin whitish moustachial and broad brown or dark brown malar; centre of lower throat sometimes unstreaked. Underparts slightly paler than male and streaked dusky-brown, area of white more extensive on belly, undertail-coverts often spotted or edged dark brown. Bill as male but in breeding season lower mandible orange-yellow. **Immature** Juvenile similar to adult female but heavily speckled or spotted white or yellowish on sides of head and neck to nape and upper mantle, feathers on crown and mantle streaked white or yellowish on central shafts; longest uppertail-coverts have pale buffish or yellowish-buff tips. Wings dark brown with central shaft-streaks to tips of median and greater coverts; tips of outerwebs of median coverts whitish, tips of greater coverts pale whitish-buff, flight feathers and centres of tertials blackish with broad whitish tips. Pale supercilium finely flecked white, whitish to pale orange submoustachial bordered below by dark brown malar; chin and throat whitish, upper breast to centre of breast smudged with brownish spots, lower breast to upper belly pale yellowish or orange occasionally spotted blackish, flanks to vent orange with a few blackish spots, vent to undertail-coverts white. Bill like adult but with duller yellow base. First-winter bird closely resembles adult female but can usually be separated by vestigial pale tips to greater coverts. Legs pale flesh-pink.

GEOGRAPHICAL VARIATION None. Birds from northern and central Kuriles were previously separated as *orii* but are now considered to be within the range of *chrysolaus* (Vaurie 1955b).

VOICE Common call a series of *chuck-chuck* notes; a thin high-pitched Blackbird-like *tsi* or *tsiii*; alarm is a series of *tsssup ssup sup sup* notes. Song similar to that of Pale Thrush but with accent more on first syllable: a persistent series of trisyllabic rich upslurred whistled phrases *tseefee-tseetee-tseetsssyu, tsvee-tsvevee-tsyutsitsrrr* or *tsvyu-tsvyu, tsvee-tsvee-tsyurrr* or *tseefeetsee-tsyuu, tlee-too-yooo* or *tvyu-tvee-phyu-veee*; may end with a *tringtststsss* or a rising and querulous *wewwi-kwer—sli*, and occasionally a drier *z'korrn-korrn-tsui*. Song period May to late July, but some birds sing in wintering areas in March and April; sings throughout the day from the tops of trees.

STATUS AND DISTRIBUTION Common to locally abundant on Sakhalin and in Japan. Breeds throughout the Kuriles (north to Shumshu Island), central and southern Sakhalin and northern Japan south to central Honshu. In winter occurs from central and southern Japan and in small numbers throughout the Nansei Shoto/Ryukyu Islands, also in southern China from southern Yunnan, Kwangsi and Kwangtung to Taiwan, possibly also north to Chekiang and south to Hainan; rare winter visitor to Hong Kong and uncommon in the Philippines (Calayan, Luzon, Batan, Fuga and Palaui).

MOVEMENTS Migratory. Breeding birds move south and south-west to wintering areas. Passage migrant through eastern China (Hopeh and Shantung to Fukien and Kwangtung) and Korea. Autumn departures from Sakhalin begin in late

September and continue through October, with some birds still on passage through northern Japan in November. A rare but regular (not annual) winter visitor to Hong Kong from November to April. Uncommon in winter on the Philippines from November (exceptionally mid-September) to the end of February (exceptionally to end of March). In spring begins northward movement in late March; in Taiwan gathers in large flocks prior to departure from February to April; passage in central Japan mid- to late April when it also appears on Sakhalin but many northern breeding birds arrive on territory only in early May. Recorded as an overshooting migrant in western Kamchatka in May 1997 (K. Mikhailov pers. comm) and a scarce migrant or vagrant to the lower Amur River (Sharpe 1902).

HABITAT Breeds in dense forest and scrub, most usually in mixed deciduous woods and groves of conifer and birch in valleys and plains, also in birch–spruce forests along river valleys, the edges of lakes and by inlets of the sea. In Japan breeds in dry deciduous and mixed woods with a good scrub layer, or in open conifer woods from sea-level up to 2400 m (7920') in subalpine woods and scrub; on Sakhalin in spruce–birch zone or birch–larch forests, but may also utilise secondary forests and alder–willow forests. In winter occurs in cultivated areas in the lowlands, edges of fields and scattered woodlands, also orchards, parks and suburban gardens; often in undergrowth and shaded areas.

BEHAVIOUR Sociable and often in large flocks in winter; on migration often occurs with flocks of Eye-browed or Pale Thrushes. Feeds low down in vegetation, in shaded or secluded places or on the ground, usually under the cover of bushes or shrubs but also in the open but with cover nearby. Feeds mostly on invertebrates and seasonal fruits; during the breeding season takes adult and larval ants, bees, beetles, butterflies, cicadas, moths, slugs, small snails and weevils; in autumn and early spring takes a variety of fruit or seeds of bilberry, cranberry, currant, honeysuckle, juniper, rowan and whortleberry.

BREEDING Season: May to August. Nest: a cup of thin twigs and dry grasses, pine needles, moss and earth, lined with small dry leaves; usually placed in bushes, saplings and young evergreen trees up to c.5 m (16') from the ground. Eggs: 3–4, rarely 2–5, variably bluish-green to pale greyish-green to grey-brown, and blotched with light purplish-grey and densely flecked or spotted rust-brown. Incubation period 13–14 days.

MOULT Imperfectly known but adult birds on Sakhalin undergo a complete post-breeding moult in August to mid-September.

MEASUREMENTS Wing, male (n=43) 118–132; female (n=38) 114–125; tarsus 29–32; bill (to feathers) 16.5–20. Weight, male 64–74 g, female 64–69 g (La Touche 1925–1930, Dementiev & Gladkov 1954).

REFERENCES Dementiev & Gladkov (1954), La Touche (1925–1930), Vaurie (1955b).

119 IZU ISLANDS THRUSH *Turdus celaenops* Plate 39
(Izu Thrush, Seven Islands Thrush)

Turdus celaenops Stejneger, 1887, *Science* 10: 108; also 1887, *Proc. U.S. Natn. Mus.* 10: 484 – Miyakeshima, Idzu, Japan.

IDENTIFICATION 23 cm (9"). A medium-sized thrush with a limited range; endemic to the Izu Islands of south-central Japan and one or two others further south. Similar to Brown-headed Thrush (118) but generally darker. Male has a black head, face and breast, brown upperparts and bright rufous or deep orange-red underparts except for a thin strip of white on the belly to vent and under-tail-coverts. Female similar but without the black on the head to breast; has warmer brown head and upperparts, white streaks on throat and more white on the belly. **Confusion species** Brown-headed Thrush lacks the all-black to breast of the male and has paler orange underparts; female and immature Izu Islands Thrush are very similar to same-age and -sex Brown-headed but have warmer brown on the face and upperparts, lack any white over the eye and usually have bolder or more obvious streaks on the chin and throat. Bill of both sexes more extensively yellow than in Brown-headed. Eyebrowed (116) is also similar but generally greyer on the head and upperparts, much paler below, with bold white supercilium and cheek-patch.

DESCRIPTION Sexes differ. **Adult male** Entire head to nape, chin, throat and upper breast jet-black; bright yellow eye-ring. Mantle to rump, uppertail-coverts and scapulars deep olive-brown or tinged russet, some feathers on upper mantle sometimes tipped blackish; rump and uppertail-coverts tinged slightly warmer or rufous-brown than back. Tail glossy black. Median coverts blackish broadly edged (may obscure black centres) warm brown, greater coverts blackish-brown edged greyish with blackish central shafts; alula, primary coverts and flight feathers black with greyish edges and tips to primary coverts and flight feathers; tertials similar to scapulars but broadly edged brown or olive-brown on outerwebs; under-wing-coverts slate-grey with paler grey tips. Rest of underparts from sides of upper breast bright rufous or deep orange-red except a thin strip of white from centre of lower breast across belly to under-tail-coverts; thighs greyish and sides of undertail-coverts fringed rufous-brown. Bill mostly bright yellow, dusky-horn along culmen and at tip. Legs and feet brown, dark brown, pinkish or fleshy-brown, soles paler. **Adult female** Forehead to

375

crown and nape dark olive-brown, sometimes with the head and face much darker or greyer and looking more like male but not extending so far onto breast. Mantle to back and scapulars warm or olive-brown tinged russet; rump and uppertail-coverts deep olive-brown. Tail blackish or black-ish-grey but edged brown on outer feathers, more broadly at base. Lores (occasionally extending across base of forehead) dark brown or blackish; sides of neck warm brown with fine pale shaft-streaks on ear-coverts; pale yellow eye-ring slightly duller than in male. Lesser coverts similar to mantle and scapulars or can be duller with blackish centres, median coverts dark grey edged paler; greater coverts similar or slightly greyer edged paler, alula and primary coverts dark grey edged paler brown, flight feathers dark grey or blackish edged warm or russet-brown on secondaries and outerwebs of tertials (innerwebs as flight feathers); underwing-coverts grey or fringed paler. Chin and throat to upper breast whitish but streaked dark brown; broad dark grey or brown malar. Upper breast tinged brownish, becoming rich or deep orange-rufous on sides of neck to flanks, similar to that on male but slightly paler in some; may also show paler or whitish tips to some flank feathers; centre of upper belly to vent and undertail-coverts more extensively white than on male. Bill dark greyish-brown with yellowish base. Legs as male. **Immature** Juvenile almost entirely russet-olive above, darker or greyer on face with long pale buffish or yellowish-buff central shaft-streaks on sides of crown, mantle, back and scapulars; wing-coverts slightly darker brown but with broad central shaft-streaks becoming spots at tips of medians and pale buffish spots at tips of greaters; rest of wings dark brown but broadly edged deep russet-olive on outerwebs, tail similar. Face finely flecked with fine pale buffish shaft-streaks, poorly defined pale submoustachial obscured by small brownish spots but prominent pale yellowish sides of throat below cheeks and ear-coverts. Underparts heavily mottled with rich brown and orange spots on breast, becoming more predominantly orange-brown on lower breast and belly with smaller brown tips. Bill dark horn. **First-year bird** Similar to respective adult but has chin and throat white streaked black, may extend to breast and may show irregular dark tips to upperparts and paler fringes or tips to underparts. Head and face similar to adult female but may show fine pale flecks on cheeks and ear-coverts.

GEOGRAPHICAL VARIATION None, but birds from Yakushima have previously been separated as *yakushimensis*.

VOICE Calls similar to Brown-headed Thrush but more grating in tone; alarm appears to be a series of dry grating notes. Song a distinctive series of short notes or a long phrase followed by a shorter one and running into a second or third. Most frequent song is a repeated harsh rattling *tche-e-e-e-e*, *tche-e-e-er* or *tch-ee-ee-ew*, which may be given on a level pitch or slightly wavering with a fading finish; and a rising or more bubbling *cheeer-tew-tew-tchew-tew*; also a dry rattling phrase.

STATUS AND DISTRIBUTION Common to abundant. Resident on the Izu Islands south of Tokyo, from Toshima to Aogashima with the exception of Oshima; possibly also resident on Yakushima in the Tokara Islands prior to 1905 and has recently (1988) been found breeding in small numbers on Nakanoshima (Kawaji *et al.* 1989) in the Tokara Islands. Has declined rapidly in numbers on Miyake-jima following the introduction of weasels *Mustela sibirica* in the late 1970s to control rats; the weasels are now preying on other species (Collar *et al.* 1994). Volcanic eruptions in the early 1980s have also reduced the amount of available habitat. Occurs on Oshima in winter and is a vagrant to southern Honshu; also several recent records from islands south of Kyushu, e.g. Yakushima (but none since 1960), Danjo Islands and Tairajima.

MOVEMENTS Mostly sedentary although some birds move in winter to Oshima and some of the islands south of Kyushu; also occasionally between December and February to southern Honshu.

HABITAT Breeds in deciduous and mixed woods from dense fir or laurel forests to open second-growth woods, orchards and large gardens; birds on Yakushima are reported to have inhabited the juniper and rhododendron zone in the upper levels of mixed forests. On Nakanoshima birds occur in deciduous trees, mainly *Persea thunbergii*, *Castanopsis sieboldii*, *Pleioblastus linearis* and *Mallotus japonicus*, with a ground layer of bamboo.

BEHAVIOUR Usually in pairs or small flocks; often breeds semi-colonially with several pairs in close proximity. Forages in trees from the canopy to low down in the forest undergrowth and on the ground, where it feeds on insects and their larvae, also on some seasonally available fruit.

BREEDING Season: March to June, occasionally to August. Nest: a deep cup-shaped structure of dried pine needles, moss and twigs, usually placed 1.5–6 m (5–20′) in a tree-fork. Eggs: 3–4, rarely 2–5, pale blue-grey with fine or small reddish-brown spots.

MOULT No information.

MEASUREMENTS Wing (n=11) 112–124; tarsus 28.5–32.5; bill 17–19.5. Weight apparently unrecorded.

REFERENCES Brazil (1991), Collar *et al.* (1994), Kawaji *et al.* (1989).

120 DARK-THROATED THRUSH *Turdus ruficollis*   Plates 40, 42
(Black-throated Thrush)

Turdus ruficollis Pallas, 1776, *Reise Versch. Prov. Russ. Reichs* 3: 694 – Dauria [Transbaicalia].

IDENTIFICATION 24–27 cm (9½–10½"). A very distinctive thrush divided into two well-marked races, one ('Black-throated') in western Siberia, the other ('Red-throated') in south-central Siberia) but with considerable areas of overlap where intermediates occur. Nominate male has brick-red chin to breast and in tail, female less well defined but generally showing rufous streaks on breast. Western race male has black chin to breast, greyish-black in tail. Upperparts grey to grey-brown in both races and rest of underparts whitish, except for the underwing-coverts which are rufous in Red-throated and more orange-red in Black-throated. Immatures are like the respective adult females. Intermediate birds (of any age) are predominantly like same-age Black-throated but with varying amounts of red to reddish-black on the chin to breast and in the tail. **Confusion species** Most likely to be confused with slightly larger and more robust (in shape and stance) adult Dusky Thrush (121) of the nominate race *naumanni*, which is extensively rufous on the flanks extending in some to the undertail-coverts; the upperparts are much browner in Dusky and adult males are visibly flecked with orange or orange-buff on the scapulars, rump and uppertail-coverts; the supercilium is paler and often shorter in adult Dusky but some first-winter Red-throateds have very pale orange supercilia. Adult female Red-throated is similar to some adult female *naumanni* but differs chiefly on colour of underparts which in Red-throated are off-white and streaked greyish mainly on the sides of the breast, sometimes tinged dull orange and with white or buffish-white undertail coverts (apart from the dark brown and greyish spots on the breast of both), while *naumanni* has a more definite rufous tinge or streaks or blotches on the breast and flanks with a paler rufous wash on the whitish-tipped undertail-coverts. Eyebrowed Thrush (116) has more extensive orange on the underparts and usually a darker head with a white supercilium and cheek-patch. Adult male Black-throated (race *atrogularis*) is unlikely to be confused with any other species by the amount of black on the face or chin to breast; male (including first-winter birds) *eunomus* race of Dusky Thrush is similar but has a large white supercilium, variable amounts of white on the chin and throat, and darker (or blackish in adults) upperparts or centres to the mantle and scapulars, and warm brown to rich coppery-brown coverts and edges of flight feathers; females and immature Black-throated are more confusable with other thrushes with streaked underparts, notably Redwing (123) which is slightly smaller and has a pronounced white supercilium and submoustachial, heavily streaked underparts and bright red flanks (occasionally obscured on birds in the field) to underwing-coverts.

Taxonomic note Stepanyan (1978, 1990) considered *ruficollis* and *atrogularis* to be distinct species but we follow Portenko (1981) in regarding them as conspecific, as there is a wide area of overlap between the two where the ranges meet. Portenko also considered that the two races of Dusky Thrush were closely related to *ruficollis* on the basis of a small number of hybrids between *atrogularis* and *naumanni* and a much smaller area of overlap. However, the ranges of the latter two taxa are largely allopatric with little or no real evidence of frequent or widespread hybridisation between them. Until the relationships of these thrushes are resolved through DNA profiling we feel that the treatment by Vaurie (1959) remains valid. The contact zones, breeding ranges and the problems of intergradation within *T. ruficollis* and between *T. ruficollis* and *T. naumanni* were discussed by Clement (1999b).

DESCRIPTION 'Red-throated Thrush' (*T. r. ruficollis*). Sexes differ (but not always separable with certainty). **Adult male** Upperparts from forehead and crown to rump uniform grey-brown or slightly paler or greyer-olive on nape and hindneck, uppertail-coverts with slightly browner centres and warmer brown at tips. Tail has central feathers mostly dark brown or blackish with all outers mostly deep or reddish-rufous with variable dark or reddish-brown. Lesser coverts as scapulars, median coverts dark grey tipped pale grey or greyish-buff, greater coverts blackish edged and tipped pale or whitish-grey (in late winter and spring up to 7 unmoulted greater coverts have paler off-white edges than newer, moulted feathers); flight feathers dark grey or blackish, finely edged pale grey or pale greyish-brown on primaries and primary coverts; alula black, tertials grey-brown broadly fringed pale grey; underwing-coverts deep red or rufous. Lores blackish; cheeks and sides of throat reddish or deep reddish-brown, thin red or reddish-brown supercilium to rear of ear-coverts, ear-coverts and sides of neck grey or tinged brown. Chin and throat to breast rich brick-red or brown-tinged deep rufous (in fresh plumage red is partially obscured by pale or whitish-buff tips or fringes), occasionally extending to sides of upper breast, and may have small dark brown or blackish spots; rest of underparts whitish, flanks tinged greyish and tips of undertail-coverts sometimes orange to pale rufous. Bill blackish-horn with pale or bright yellow base to lower mandible and cutting edges to upper mandible. Eye dark brown or blackish. Legs and feet deep brown tinged pinkish. **Adult female** Similar to adult male but tinged slightly more olive on crown and rest of upperparts; brick-red on face and chin to breast can be as complete as male (so attribution of sex to such individuals not advisable of this single character), but tends to be more

broken up as pale orange and reddish-brown mottling on cheeks and sides of chin and throat, sometimes streaked darker in a prominent dark malar stripe, and with centre of chin and upper throat whitish to pale grey or pale orange; red on breast darker and more streaked, spotted or blotchy but still forming a pectoral band. Lores blackish-brown and supercilium often paler (occasionally whitish) or much less distinct than in male. Rest of underparts as male but may also show greyish spots and smudges on flanks; undertail-coverts white or buffish-white. **Immature** Juvenile has the upperparts and wings mostly dark grey becoming paler grey on rump and uppertail-coverts; crown, mantle, back, scapulars and rump have pale or whitish-buff central shaft-streaks and tips to median coverts have narrow whitish-buff spots forming broken wing-bar; greaters more indistinctly edged and tipped paler. Some individuals – probably males – have light or pale orange to orange-brown innerwebs to (some or all) outer tail feathers. Face generally blackish-brown with pale or buffy-orange supercilium and creamy submoustachial and broad dark malar stripe; lower throat, breast and upper flanks deep cream to orange-buff, heavily mottled or spotted with brown. **First-winter male** Initially similar to adult female but shows fine dark centres to crown, mantle and back, broad pale buff or greyish edges to greater coverts, scapulars and tertials, the retained juvenile outer (occasionally all) greater coverts having whitish tips. Face and throat to sides of neck generally off-whitish or pale orange, spotted or streaked darker reddish (with or without darker spotting in malar area) and becoming deeper orange on tips of breast to form an incomplete or slightly mottled pectoral band (first-year male has more extensive area of rufous than same-age female), belly and flanks greyish or washed buff and spotted with slightly darker smudges or streaks. Tail as adult but tends to show more extensive darker outerwebs to outer feathers except for outermost pair. Throat and breast colour of adult is acquired during late winter/early spring of first-summer plumage. **First-winter female** Similar to adult female but can also lack any red or orange on throat and breast, thus similar to same-age 'black-throated', and has pale buffish supercilium, off-white to pale buffish chin and throat, and black streaks on sides of chin and malar stripe, upper breast spotted blackish to warm brown on greyish ground colour, with spots on centre and lower breast becoming warmer or even rufous-brown. Wings and tail as first-winter male.
GEOGRAPHICAL VARIATION Two races; variation well marked. Portenko (1981) separated birds from the western slopes of the central and northern Urals as *vogulorum* on the basis of the upperparts being more heavily olive-brown, but was unable to determine an eastern border for the race or where *vogulorum* met *atrogularis*. On the basis of such slim differences, which at best appear to be no more than clinal, *vogulorum* is not considered to be a valid race.
'Black-throated Thrush' (*T. r. atrogularis*). Sexes differ. **Adult male** Upperparts pale grey or brown-

tinged grey; at close range can show olive-brown centres to some feathers of crown to upper mantle; uppertail-coverts similar to back or slightly paler tinged brown. Tail blackish-brown finely edged pale grey or grey-brown at base of outer feathers. Wings as nominate above but underwing has pale orange or orange-buff coverts, paler on flight feathers. Lores to cheeks dark grey or blackish, ear-coverts pale grey or mottled olive-brown. Chin and throat to breast jet-black or, in fresh plumage (autumn/winter) variably tipped whitish-grey (abrasion of paler tips reveals uniform black on chin to breast). Rest of underparts white, mottled or smudged with dark grey spots on sides of belly and streaks on flanks; bases of undertail-coverts often show as dark brown. Bill dark brown with yellow base to lower mandible. Legs and feet yellowish-brown to dark brown tinged greyish. In late autumn and winter (fresh plumage) shows variable amounts of pale or whitish tips to black on chin, throat and upper breast, face and forehead also finely streaked black, and edges to median and greater coverts, flight feathers and tertials broadly pale buff. **Adult female** Similar to adult male but more heavily tinged olive-brown and often shows slightly darker streaks on crown and mantle; tail as male but innerwebs of all outer feathers may be tinged brown. Wings as male but edges to lower scapulars greyish-white with greater coverts and secondaries edged brownish-buff, becoming paler when worn. Lores dark brown or blackish with pale indistinct supercilium from base of bill over eye and fading over ear-coverts, thin whitish eye-ring often incomplete or obscured; cheeks and ear-coverts as upperparts or mottled slightly darker, sometimes with whitish submoustachial and bordered by row of blackish spots forming malar on sides of whitish chin and throat (centre of throat may form whitish patch), becoming streaked with blackish-brown; streaks become broader on breast over pale grey-buff ground colour, but variation considerable, some birds with streaks very broad and thus resembling males, some with pale to brown edges so broad that dark centres almost obscured and only visible at close range. Sides of lower breast, upper belly and flanks pale grey with finer streaks on centres of feathers, fringes more buffish-brown, centre of belly to vent white tinged grey-brown, undertail-coverts whiter. In worn plumage (summer) abrasion makes darker centres to throat and breast more prominent. **Immature** Juvenile similar to adult female but crown, mantle, scapulars and lesser coverts have pale buff shaft-streaks (broadest or most prominent on edge of mantle and scapulars) and blackish tips; back to rump and uppertail-coverts as adult but with fine pale greyish-white shaft-streaks and tips. Tail as adult or with browner outerwebs to outer feathers. Wings as adult except for pale yellowish or greyish-white tips to median and edges to greater coverts, those on medians and inner greaters appearing more wedge-shaped on birds in hand, tertials similar but with poorly defined whitish-grey spots at tips; inner secondaries and tertials broadly edged brownish. Supercilium whitish but poorly defined and pale grey or buff, fading over eye; cheeks and ear-coverts brown, finely flecked, spotted or streaked whitish. Chin and throat as adult female, upper breast dull off-white or buffish-white heavily mottled or spotted with dark brown; spots become smaller on lower breast (those of immature male are, on average, slightly larger than on same-age female), flanks similar or greyish with dark brown tips, centre of belly to vent and undertail-coverts white. Juveniles of both nominate and *atrogularis* are very similar and (depending on age) may be indistinguishable in the field. **First-winter bird** Shows intermediate characters of both adults. First-winter male shows variable upperparts from that of the adult male or is more olive-brown as adult female; wings and tail as adults but inner (or sometimes all) greater coverts retained from juvenile plumage and show pale greyish-white tips. Dark feathers of lores to cheeks, ear-coverts and breast have fine pale grey fringes; chin and throat similar but more often streaked whitish. First-winter female very similar but breast usually greyer and shows fewer (or narrower) dark brown or black streaks, and streaks continue on lower breast and flanks; retained greater coverts from juvenile plumage have prominent pale grey tips.

Intermediates Intermediates or hybrids most usually resemble 'Black-throated Thrush' but in adults the black on chin to breast usually more purple-black or black suffused with red either in streaks (females) or more solidly as a band (males); in some males the face may be black whilst the chin to breast is purple-black (see plates). Both sexes have some rust-brown or reddish in the tail (usually on the innerwebs), but this can vary in extent from very little (and possibly not visible in the field) in the outer feathers to as much as on nominate *ruficollis*. Exceptionally some individuals (of any age or sex) may show extensive amounts of rufous edges in the tail and some reddish or purple on the chin to breast. First-winter birds are similar to the female and have variable amounts of reddish-black spotting or streaks on the chin to breast and show a similar variation in the amount of red or reddish-orange in the tail.

Hybrids between Black-throated (both *atrogularis* and *ruficollis*) and Naumann's Thrush are also known from the area of overlap between the two. According to Portenko (1981) these hybrids resemble *T. naumanni eunomus* but have rust-coloured tail feathers and underparts, although in some individuals the rust on the underparts is reduced in extent, to tips of some feathers or a light wash on the breast; hybrids between *atrogularis* and *eunomus* have grey upperparts with diffuse blackish spots and black on the throat and spots on the underparts.

VOICE Most frequent call is a soft *jak* or *tack-tack* similar to but not as throaty as that of Fieldfare (122); also a chattering *chuck, chack, tchak* or *tjuk* or a slightly shorter abrupt *chk, chik, chap, chit* or *qui-kwea* contact call and a single *seee, ziet* or *ziep*, and a trisyllabic *puk peer-up* from birds in Nepal (Fleming *et al.* 1979); occasionally repeated

or run together as a short phrase, *tack-tack-tack* or *tsak-tsak-tsak*, recalling similar note of Ring Ouzel (109) and Fieldfare, as does the harsh *schrieh* noted in Mongolia (Mauersberger *et al.* 1982); other contact notes between members of a flock noted as a rapid *hetetetet* and a hoarser *retet riep*, with a rapid *wiwiwi* on take-off. Gives a variety of single harsh notes such as *squeeetch*, etc.; alarm note varies from single *kack* or *char* when disturbed near nest to a shriller *chit cheet, quich-quich-quoit-oit-toit* or *pee-wit chip-chi-chip* in winter in Nepal; other alarm notes are similar to Blackbird (111) although *ruficollis* also has a softer chuckling *which-which-which*.

Songs of the two races apparently differ quite markedly. Song of nominate *ruficollis* simple and generally less melodious than Song Thrush (124), with whistling phrases replaced by rambling and cackling *chve-che-chve-che... chvya-chya-chvya-chvya...* or *chooee whee-oo-ee oo* or *hoo-eee whee-oo-ee oo* (Cramp *et al.* 1988). Song of *atrogularis* a variety of hoarse raucous whistled notes, *t'eee... t'yuyuu... teeu-'eet*, broken by pauses of equal length; the initial phrases are loud, drawn-out and descending, the last two ascending, short and sharp; may give several other phrases, e.g. *hweet* or *hweet-a* in a ponderous manner (Rogacheva 1992, K. Mikhailov pers. comm.) before repeating the song several times in slow succession, or may include more drawn-out phrases such as a ringing *hweeeeee*. Sings usually from a high vantage point at the top of a tree; song period appears to be confined to just before and towards the end of the breeding season; very little song recorded in Siberia after the end of June; occasionally sings in late winter in March and early April before departing from wintering areas. **STATUS AND DISTRIBUTION** Nominate *ruficollis* locally common throughout but in Sayan range locally abundant; *atrogularis* locally common to abundant, e.g. middle reach of the Yenisei, East Sayan Mountains.

T. r. ruficollis South-central Siberia (south and east of *atrogularis* with which it interbreeds in overlap areas; see below) in the central and eastern Russian Altai Range from about Teletskoye Lake north and east through the Sayan ranges and Tuva north to about 60°N on the upper Lena, about 58°N on the upper Nizhnyaya Tunguska, the upper reaches of the Podkamennaya Tunguska and east along the Lena to about Zhigalov on the River Tutura and the River Vitim south to the Yablonovy range (Vitimskoye plateau and the Kalar valley) and along the River Kharige into northern Mongolia east to the Hentiyn Nuruu (Khentei) range. Southern limits of the range extend to Khangay range and the upper reaches of the River Khoit-Tomrin-Gul, the River Shurugin-Gul/Dzavhan Gol (south of Uliastay) and north-west to the Karga River and the Tannu-Ola range.

In winter to the Himalayas, possibly into eastern Afghanistan and southern Turkmenistan, east through northern India and Nepal (mostly the north where also scarce) to northern Bengal and Arunachal Pradesh and the north-east India hill states (south to Nagaland and Manipur and the hills of Khasi and Cachar); a few may winter in central China especially around Beijing, more regularly southern or south-east Tibet and northern and western Yunnan (in some years may be more extensive than shown on map) south to the plains of Sind, Madhya Pradesh, north-east Burma (where it is commoner than *atrogularis*) and northern and central Bangladesh (mostly along the Brahmaputra and the Garo hills).

T. r. atrogularis Extreme eastern Europe and western Siberia from the upper reaches of the Kama River (in European Russia – west of the Urals), the middle and northern Urals east across the lower Ob River (north to about Nadym) and thence east mostly along the treeline between 64°N and 67°N to the taiga of the lower Yenisei, then south (from about Turukhansk) along the valley of the Yenisei and east along the Angara and Chadobets rivers; from about Krasnoyarsk the range extends erratically south into the Sayan ranges, western Tuva and the north-east Altai (common throughout the Altai extending to the foothills) into northern, western (possibly also central) Sinkiang, north-west Mongolia and south into the Tarbagatay. In north-west Mongolia it breeds near Dzshuk-kul and the upper flows of the Karga River. From the western Altai the range extends south to the Tarbagatay (eastern Kazakhstan) and north-west through Barnaul oblast (region) and through the southern parts of the forest zone of south-west Siberia north of the Barabinskaya steppe, Tara–Irtysh confluence and Tobol'sk to about 59°N in the middle Urals.

Small numbers regularly winter in the valleys of eastern Kazakhstan (and possibly elsewhere in central Siberia) and in some years considerable numbers may winter in Central Asia. The majority winter from southern Iraq eastward through most of Iran (except the north-west but common around Tehran) including Gulf coast and coastal Baluchistan, Afghanistan north to southern Turkmenistan and southern Tadzhikistan to the Himalayas (including the northern Himalayas in southern Tibet, southern Sinkiang and east to northern Yunnan), also throughout most of Pakistan (generally less common across the southern half of the Indus plain and rare in Karachi) and the plains and foothills of northern India and Nepal east to Assam, Bhutan, Arunachal Pradesh, Nagaland, Manipur, Bangladesh and northern, central and eastern Burma. Occurrence in the plains of northern India largely governed by severity of weather in northern foothills; has occurred south to southern Rajasthan and northern Gujarat and once (March 1985) in Andhra Pradesh. Small numbers winter in Hebei province and around Beijing but elsewhere in north-east China generally scarce. A scarce or irregular winter visitor (November to early March) to eastern Saudi Arabia (and rare in Central Province), Bahrain (common in some winters, e.g. 1990/1991), U.A.E. and Oman.

Intermediate zone In the south-east and east of the range *atrogularis* interbreeds with nominate *ruficollis*, from the upper Lena and the upper Nizhnyaya Tunguska (possibly as far east as northern Lake Baikal and the upper Olekma), through the Russian Altai and the Sayan ranges. Within this area there are both hybrid and pure pairs and areas of higher density of hybrids than pure pairs. There are very few published examples of the extent of hybridisation in this area, and various authors have described areas of both pure and hybrid pairs. Sushkin (1929, 1938) reported that of 22 birds collected near Podvolochnaya (near the source of the Nizhnyaya Tunguska) 18 were hybrids, and in a second area near Werchne-Kalininsk he found that all 9 birds collected were hybrids. Detailed information on the extent and degree of hybridisation within this area of overlap is patchy and requires much more intensive studies to map more accurately the extent of the area from which intermediates originate.

MOVEMENTS Migratory, with virtually all birds leaving the breeding areas except for a few *atrogularis* which remain in the valleys of eastern Kazakhstan and possibly elsewhere in central Siberia; also winter records from southern Lake Baikal and Kashgar (Sinkiang).

Nominate *ruficollis* departs from breeding areas in late September and early October and migrates through Mongolia and much of northern, central and western China to Sinkiang and Tibet west to the borders of Turkmenia; in the east occurs as a migrant through Shensi and is regular in autumn around Beijing. Post-breeding dispersal movements of *atrogularis* begin as early as mid-July from the breeding areas but true southward movements occur from early September to mid-November; in the southern Caucasus of Armenia, Azerbaijan, Tadzhikistan and Afghanistan the first migrants usually appear in mid-September but in some years as early as late August; further south and east (e.g. northern Tibet) large-scale movements not usual until late September. Most have left Siberia by the end of September; arrives in the Himalayas of northern India and Nepal in October, although occasionally in mid-September; in northern Iran most numerous in winter from mid-December to early March. Return movements of *ruficollis* noted on passage in Mongolia and around Lake Baikal in mid- to late April (but early birds often forced to return south in years of late snowfall) with passage continuing into mid- and late May; *atrogularis* occurs in Afghanistan as a spring migrant through Nuristan from late February to April; along the middle reaches of the Yenisei passage begins in early May (average 10 May) and becomes widespread across the taiga in the following weeks, with most birds on territory in southern and central Siberia by first week of June. Departs from wintering areas in March and early April, exceptionally early May in northern India or mid-May in northern Pakistan; northward passage through Tadzhikistan continues into early May, arrives in central Siberia from mid-April to early May.

A diurnal and nocturnal migrant; in Siberia frequently seen in flocks of up to 40 moving north over large areas of taiga, often in company with Dusky Thrushes; in exceptional weather conditions flocks of over a hundred occur, usually as part of a large movement of birds lasting several hours.

Rare or accidental to Japan (9 records – 3 *ruficollis* and 6 *atrogularis* – Hokkaido to southern Ryukyu/Nansei Shoto Islands) and north-west Thailand (both races); nominate *ruficollis* is a vagrant to northern Pakistan (2 records) and *atrogularis* has occurred (November 1997) in Taiwan; both races have also occurred as vagrants to most of the western Palearctic (mostly *atrogularis* except where stated) with records in British Isles (43 including 1 *ruficollis*), Norway, Sweden, Finland, Denmark (6), Estonia, Spain, France (11), Belgium, Netherlands (4), Germany, Poland, Czech Republic, Austria, Italy, Romania, Bulgaria (1 record, January 1964), Greece (1 record, March 1956). In the Middle East has occurred in Israel (11 records 1978–1988, November–February), Egypt (Sinai, January 1982) and Yemen. Most records have been in the autumn and early winter period, with occasional birds remaining throughout the winter.

HABITAT Race *atrogularis* breeds along the edges of or clearings in coniferous and mixed deciduous forests, often in the undergrowth of dense taiga forest of *Pinus sibirica* or spruce–fir mixed forest where it occurs in swamp forest or alder thickets near streams or rivers, along the Yenisei in maximum densities of up to 46 pairs per km² in middle-aged (20–70 years) stands of previously burned regenerating forest sites (K. Mikhailov pers. comm.); also in more montane woods up to 2200 m (6600′), e.g. larch clumps and sparse dry woods of birch, willow and poplar with scrub or buckthorn. Nominate *ruficollis* breeds in sparse or open forests at high altitudes (in overlap zones usually breeds at higher levels) and the upper limits of cedar forests and mossy scrub-tundra, also in scrub and dwarf forest along the treeline and above. Only around Baikal, in north-west Mongolia and along the Lena and Tunguska rivers does it breed in taiga forest at relatively low levels. In winter found more commonly in open habitat, e.g. fields, edges of cultivation and grassy areas as well as forest edges, rhododendron thickets and groves; nominate *ruficollis* generally winters (alone or in small flocks) at higher altitudes than *atrogularis*, between 2400 m and 3900 m in Nepal where the latter winters occurs on the edges of the plains and lowland hills.

BEHAVIOUR Actions on the ground similar to those of Fieldfare; characteristic gait is a series of long hops often with head held erect. Often raises tail in manner of Blackbird when landing and occasionally flicks wings. Generally shy and quickly takes cover in nearby trees or bushes when disturbed. May breed in single pairs or loose aggregations; in winter often found in flocks of several hundred and (particularly *atrogularis*) in company with other thrushes, e.g. Tickell's (105), Eyebrowed (116) and Mistle (126) and on passage with Dusky (121); roosts in flocks in firs or other densely packed trees. Feeds on the ground and in trees, mainly on invertebrates, including grasshoppers, beetles, caterpillars, grubs, flies, ants, spiders, earthworms and small snails; also berries including those of *Magnolia*, blueberry, cherry, rosehips and haws, plus seeds of spruce, juniper and docks; also known to take nectar from flowers.

BREEDING Season: late May (in the south) or early June to mid- or late July. Nest: mostly of grasses or thin twigs and other similar material, often bound together with earth and lined with fine grasses and some moss and lichens; cup of nest apparently quite deep, usually placed low down (within 1.5–2 m/4½–6½′ of ground) along branches or in the crown of shrubs, in or on a tree stump or fork in branches of larches, poplars or other deciduous trees, in the roots of fallen or windblown trees and occasionally on the ground. Eggs: 4–5, occasionally 6 or 7, similar to those of Mistle Thrush, pale greenish, greenish-blue or slightly deeper blue and marked with numerous brown or deep brown spots or blotches. Incubation period 10–12 days; by female alone. Nestling period 11–13 days.

MOULT Adults have complete post-breeding moult from late July to late August extending in some to early September. Partial moult of juveniles involves the head and body, lesser and median coverts and some of the greater coverts, from late June or early July, usually completed by mid-August or exceptionally to early September; some birds may replace all greater coverts in autumn.

MEASUREMENTS Wing, male 127–145, female 127–141; bill 15–22; *atrogularis* wing, male 128–143, female 125–138; tarsus, male 26–35, female 25.5–34; bill 17–25. Weight *ruficollis* male 76–94 g, female 63–103 g; *atrogularis* male 59–110 g, female 68–105 g (Dementiev & Gladkov 1954, Ali & Ripley 1983, Cramp *et al* 1988).

REFERENCES Ali & Ripley (1983), Clement (1999b), Fleming *et al.* (1979), Mauersberger *et al.* (1982), Piechocki *et al.* (1982), Portenko (1981), Roberts (1992), Rogacheva (1992), Stepanyan (1978, 1990), Sushkin (1929, 1938).

121 DUSKY THRUSH *Turdus naumanni*   Plates 41, 42
(Naumann's Thrush, Rufous-tailed Thrush)

***Turdus naumanni* Temminck, 1820, *Man. Orn.* (ed. 2) 1: 170 – Silesia and Austria... Hungary.**

IDENTIFICATION 23–25 cm (9–9¾″). A medium-sized robust-looking thrush with a stout bill and upright carriage from central and eastern Siberia.

Very brightly coloured and divided into two races, although intermediate forms are not uncommon. Nominate birds are brown to warm brown above with slightly brighter rufous on rump and tail, a whitish-orange supercilium, pale chin and throat with dark malars and bright reddish underparts often with paler or whitish 'scales'; race *eunomus* is equally distinctive with black on crown and sides of face and long white supercilium (often quite broad) and most of the upperparts also blackish with varying amounts of rich brown fringes with bright coppery-red edges to wing-coverts and bases of flight feathers; underparts white with varying amounts of black to blackish-brown spots. Underwing-coverts (on both) are bright chestnut to deep orange or reddish-buff. Juveniles are like the adults but upperparts broadly streaked with pale buffish-orange central shafts and underparts pale orange mottled with black spots. Intermediate birds can resemble either but with blackish areas variable, from reddish-brown through purple-brown to brown; sometimes similar above to one race and below to the other. **Confusion species** Generally unmistakable once seen well but at distance nominate males (and some females) could be confused with nominate race of Dark-throated Thrush (120); but red on underparts of nominate Dusky is generally more extensive (underparts on nominate *ruficollis* have red confined to the chin to breast, with whitish or greyish-white on belly and flanks), while the upperparts are usually pale uniform grey on Dark-throated and brown or black on Dusky; supercilium usually better defined on Dusky (especially *eunomus*) than on either race of Dark-throated. Adult female nominate *naumanni* could be confused with initially similar adult female nominate *ruficollis* but best separated by presence on Dusky of rufous on the breast and flanks (as a tinge, blotches or streaks) and dull rufous or rufous-

orange with whitish tips to the undertail-coverts; female nominate *ruficollis* has the red or rufous on the underparts often more broken (with whitish fringes) or streaked or spotted with blackish spots. Redwing (123) is smaller with better defined, whiter supercilium (and sides of neck-patch) than nominate *naumanni*, lacking either the black or reddish or rufous tones to the upperparts and/or tail, and the red on the underparts is restricted to sides of the breast and flanks; otherwise has rather bold blackish streaks on underparts. Eyebrowed Thrush (116) also initially similar but much paler and generally more uniform grey-brown, males with grey head and both sexes with pale (or paler) orange on breast and flanks.

Taxonomic note Portenko (1981) considered both races of *naumanni* to be subspecies of Dark-throated Thrush *T. atrogularis* (see comments under Dark-throated Thrush).

DESCRIPTION 'Naumann's Thrush' (*T. n. naumanni*). Sexes similar. **Adult male** Forehead and crown to mantle, lower back and scapulars greyish to warm-brown with pale cinnamon-orange or chestnut edges to some scapulars; rump and uppertail-coverts as mantle and back. In fresh plumage forehead to crown may be (finely) and rump and uppertail-coverts (broadly) streaked or mottled rufous or rufous-orange, tips of longest uppertail-coverts more usually orange or russet-brown. Tail has central feathers brown to greyish-brown as are outerwebs of outer feathers (except outermost); innerwebs broadly orange increasing in extent outwardly to pale orange outer feathers, which are edged and tipped brown except for a pale or whitish-buff spot at extreme tip (in fresh plumage tips to all tail feathers finely edged

Dusky Thrush showing typical relaxed pose with wings held down from sides of body.

whitish-buff). Wing-coverts as scapulars with slightly darker centres, edges and tips to greater coverts pale or orange-rufous (becoming paler grey-brown when worn), flight feathers and tertials dark brown finely edged greyish-brown to pale rufous or reddish, broader on edges to tertials. Lores dark brown or blackish, ear-coverts as upperparts or slightly paler brown; supercilium pale or whitish-orange, fairly broad and extending to rear of ear-coverts; cheeks whitish, pale orange submoustachial bordered by darker brown malars, sides of neck pale yellowish to orange or finely spotted reddish-buff. Chin and throat whitish or pale cream to orange-buff or reddish finely edged buff, breast usually more heavily orange, rust-red, rufous or finely fringed (broadly in fresh plumage, frequently obscuring rufous centres to feathers) pale buff or spotted brown (sometimes paler or whiter on belly and vent to undertail-coverts, but latter often tipped with orange). Thighs whitish-orange. In flight shows all-brown wings with slightly paler area on secondaries, underwing-coverts and bases to flight feathers variably red-dish-orange or pale orange. Bill entirely dark horn with a pale yellowish base to lower mandible, becoming more extensive along cutting edge of upper mandible in summer. Legs and feet pale brown or tinged yellowish. **Adult female** Very similar to adult male but duller and shows less rufous tones to upperparts and in edges of tail feathers. Underparts may also be somewhat duller (but not always) or more broadly edged with white, chin and throat more heavily spotted or lightly streaked and shows broader or more distinct malar stripe with blackish-brown, paler brown and less extensive brown or chestnut-brown edges to scapulars and wing-coverts. **Immature** Juvenile has forehead to crown brown, finely streaked with fine whitish-buff central shafts, nape similar but with pale buff tips; mantle, back and scapulars also brown to grey-brown with light-orange or rufous-buff central shaft-streaks (broadest on sides of mantle and scapulars), rump and uppertail-coverts rufous-brown with paler central shaft-streaks and darker tips to longer uppertail-coverts. Tail warm or rufous-brown at base, becoming brown towards tip; feathers narrower and more pointed in shape than on adult. Median and greater coverts brown edged warm or chestnut-brown, inner greaters with pale or chestnut-brown central shafts, medians narrowly tipped pale buff; underwing-coverts as adult but paler. Supercilium as adult but paler and poorly defined, especially in front of eye, becoming paler or whitish over ear-coverts; cheeks to sides of neck and throat creamy-white finely spotted or streaked black, breast pale orange or orange-buff and heavily spotted brownish-black, flanks similar but with smaller blackish centres to feathers. **First-winter bird** Very similar to adult female but slightly darker or duller and with finely mottled upperparts with fine dark centres and paler grey-brown tips to crown to mantle; scapulars and coverts often show very fine pale central shaft-streaks, but edges of scapulars orange to deep reddish-buff; centres to back, rump and

uppertail-coverts orange to deep reddish-buff with brown fringes (which may sometimes obscure centres), longest uppertail-coverts pale orange. Tail brown to blackish-brown broadly edged (in some entirely covering brown at base of tail) orange to reddish-brown at bases to outers, inner-webs as adults, tips of feathers more pointed than adults (only visible in hand or on good or close view of spread tail in field). Edges and tips to median coverts pale buff, greaters (most, if not all, retained from juvenile plumage) similar but tips variable from whitish-buff (outer, unmoulted feathers) and pale orange to rich brown with dark brown inners (fresh feathers); alula and primary coverts dark brown finely edged pale buff or orange-buff, flight feathers dark brown finely edged whitish-buff on primaries and more broadly edged brown, variably pale buffish-brown to warm brown, on secondaries and tertials; tips to tertials more broadly pale buff. Face like adult but often shows paler, greyish-flecked supercilium, lores blackish but cheeks and ear-coverts paler than adult with rear ear-coverts grey-brown or flecked white; lower ear-coverts and sides of neck also whitish-buff. Poorly defined whitish or dull creamy-buff submoustachial and row of blackish spots forming malar. Chin and throat whitish, becoming mottled (variable in extent) with red-dish-orange to dark or reddish-brown on centres and tips to feathers of breast and flanks and can be either uniformly or broadly edged white, whitish-grey or grey-brown; centre of belly to vent and undertail-coverts whitish. Very difficult to sex but brightly coloured birds probably male and those with dull tones and heavy spotting on breast and flanks probably female. Bill mostly dark horn or with dull yellow at base of lower mandible and cutting edges to upper. **First-summer bird** Very similar to adult but some males in breeding season retain broad pale submoustachial and dark malar, and are very similar to same-age or adult females. **GEOGRAPHICAL VARIATION** Two races; variation well marked.

'Dusky Thrush' (*T. n. eunomus*). Sexes differ. **Adult male** Forehead and crown to nape blackish or blackish-grey; mantle, back and scapulars the same but variably black in worn plumage (summer) or finely edged pale buff or pale rufous to chestnut or rust-brown in fresh plumage (autumn and early winter); lower back, rump and uppertail-coverts blackish-grey with broad warmer russet-brown fringes, some centres of rump and uppertail-coverts also dark brown. Tail blackish-brown with bases of feathers edged rich chestnut-brown. Median coverts vary from blackish centres with rich or russet-brown tips to entirely rich russet or chestnut-brown with fine pale buff tips; greater coverts mostly rich chestnut or deep russet-brown or with darker brown central shafts and tip of innerweb, edge of outerweb whitish; alula blackish-brown or with a paler brown outer edge; primary coverts blackish-brown broadly edged rich or russet-brown, tips dark brown; flight feathers and tertials blackish-brown broadly edged at bases of outerwebs rich chestnut or deep russet-brown, (together with that on coverts) forming a bright panel on closed wing (sometimes with thin pale edges to outer primaries and tertials with dark brown innerwebs); underwing-coverts orange to reddish-buff finely edged whitish. Broad pale cream or whitish supercilium from upper lores over eye and ear-coverts, fading on sides of nape. Lores black and ear-coverts similar, dark brownish or washed grey, cheeks creamy-white mottled with fine black spots. Chin and throat to upper breast and sides of neck white or creamy-white, irregularly flecked or spotted with dark brownish tips forming narrow submoustachial, breast black but feathers with variable amounts of white on fringes, creating either a uniform/broken breast-band pattern or a large area of white within black (becomes blacker as fringes wear down), whilst others (probably first-winter birds) have throat and breast white heavily streaked black; flanks and sides of belly similar to breast or tinged rusty-brown and often with more white showing, belly to vent and undertail-coverts white or finely tipped dark brown, deep rust-brown or blackish. Bill dark brownish-horn but base of lower mandible bright yellow to orange-yellow, usually more extensive in breeding season. Legs and feet brown to dark brown. **Adult female** Very similar to male but duller, crown to mantle browner, not as black and wing-coverts and flight feathers less broadly edged chestnut on outerwebs, blacker brown on innerwebs; pattern of longest primary coverts often distinctive in separation from immature male – mostly brown or brownish and diffusely paler on innerweb. As in female *naumanni* throat more heavily spotted or streaked blackish and shows a more pronounced malar stripe. Breast usually browner and flanks tend to be more rusty than black. **Immature** Juvenile has forehead to crown brownish-black but finely streaked with narrow whitish-buff central shaft-streaks, nape similar but with pale buff tips, mantle, back and scapulars brownish-black but with reddish or rufous-buff central shaft-streaks (broadest on sides of mantle and scapulars), rump and uppertail-coverts brown with paler central shaft-streaks and dark tips or greyish tips to longer uppertail-coverts. Tail has slightly narrower, more pointed feathers. Median and greater coverts blackish-brown edged chestnut-brown, inner greaters have pale or chestnut-brown central shafts, medians tipped pale buff; underwing-coverts as adult but paler. Supercilium as adult but finely spotted black, cheeks to sides of neck and throat creamy-white finely spotted black, breast whitish thickly spotted brownish-black on centres of feathers, flanks similar but dark centres smaller. **First-winter bird** As adult female (not always distinguishable in field with certainty from adult) but shows blackish centres to much of upperparts, intensity of brown to coppery-brown on upperparts variable but first-year female browner than same-age male or adult female; in hand differs from adult by tail feathers as for *naumanni*. First-year female tends to have paler chestnut or buffish-brown edges to mantle, upper back and scapulars. Some (if not all) outer greater coverts retained from juvenile plumage and have pale central spot at tip, whereas fresh feathers have rufous edges, median coverts

usually showing pale brown or chestnut shaft-streaks, longest primary coverts with blackish edges and tips, and rufous on innerwebs (Svensson 1992); tips of inner secondaries whitish, usually more so in male than female.

Intermediates Dusky Thrushes show a high degree of variation as a result of intergradation between nominate and *eunomus* in the overlap areas of the range. Thus for example birds with extensive areas of russet in the plumage of the upperparts regularly occur along the Anadyr River in eastern Siberia, almost at the extreme northern edge of *eunomus*. One of the commonest (*naumanni*) variations has the head and upperparts of Naumann's except for more extensive areas of orange on the edges to the secondaries and tertials; the feathers on the breast are usually black centred with whitish fringes, becoming dark orange to chestnut on the lower breast, belly and flanks – on some merging gradually whilst on others the black/orange border is sharp. Most, however, have orange to extensive bright orange-chestnut on the rump, uppertail-coverts and edges to the base of the tail – some males have extensively reddish-chestnut on the edges to the mantle, back and more obviously on the rump and uppertail-coverts. Others are much darker and resemble *eunomus* except that the mantle, back and scapulars are heavily washed with deep copper-brown (especially on the edges of the scapulars), the median coverts are golden-brown with darker or browner innerwebs, greaters bright golden with brown innerwebs, flight feathers dark brown broadly edged pale golden-brown at base. A distinct *eunomus* variation shows areas of coppery-brown restricted to the edges of the mantle, back and scapulars or only on the wing-coverts and edges to the secondaries and tertials; the face is whiter with a broad white supercilium over dark grey-brown lores, cheeks and ear-coverts, a whitish moustachial bordered by a blackish submoustachial, dark streaks at the sides of the throat becoming heavier and more continuous across the breast to the sides of the belly and flanks on orange-tinged brown ground colour, rump and uppertail-coverts tinged with warm or orange-brown, and base of the tail rusty-brown.

VOICE Most frequent call is a loud shrill *cheeh-cheeh*, often repeated several times, also a series of rather harsh *ket-ket-ket*, *cha-cha-cha* or *kra-kra-kra* and a chuckling *chak-chak* recalling Fieldfare (122), or shortened to *chk* or a harsher *tacktack-tack*, occasionally a *tsepit-tack-tack* given when in a flock or when going to roost, and a chattering *quaawag* or *kvaevaeg* from *eunomus*; some calls given with musical or squeaky tone, on take-off gives a *kwet-kwet* and a starling-like *spirr*, *shurr* or *swic*; alarm call a hard *tock-tock* or a harsher and more drawn-out version of the *cha-cha* call note, given as *chak-cha-cha-cha*; in flight a thin *geeeh*, *shrree* or *kweee* often repeated and a thin high-pitched *huuit* similar to that of Fieldfare.

Song contains phrases similar to those of Redwing and the Fieldfare-like call, but less varied and more fluting and melodious, frequently ending in a faint trill or twitter, a rather flat and unhurried *tvee-tryuuu-tee... tvee-tryuuuu-tvee* with the middle phrase longest and accentuated, ending with a rising three-note Fieldfare-like *tsee-tsee-tee*. Song of *eunomus* similar but with the emphasis falling on the first phrase, *tryuuuu-tvee-tryu... tyuu-trrryuuute, tryuute, tryuute frrrrr*; may be interspersed with harsher chirping notes or short trills suggestive of excitement or alarm notes such as *ki-chur chi-kiyur* or terminating with a *chi-yo* or series of dry *ket-ket-ket* notes. In Ussuriland (where present as a migrant from April to early June) and Japan considered a poor singer giving a subdued Fieldfare-like song comprising chuckling phrases, squeaks and other quiet sounds (K. Mikhailov pers. comm.). In the Lena valley of north-east Russia song given as *veet tyulir-tyulir fru-fru fir-fee veetveet tyulir-tyulir che-che-che-che veet-veet-veet fru-fru pryupee-pryupee* (Cramp *et al.* 1988).

May also have regional or dialectal song, or true song only given on breeding grounds; Yakhontov (1976 in Cramp *et al.* 1988) described the song of *eunomus* (no location given) as loud and powerful with beautiful whistles and fluting notes of rich quality recalling Nightingale *Luscinia megarhynchos*, Blackbird (111) and Song Thrush (124). Song period undetermined but presumably much as in other *Turdus* thrushes through the spring and summer months; has been recorded singing in northern parts of breeding range in mid-August. Song usually given from a tree, typically in mornings and evenings but also at night and throughout the day in dull or wet weather.

STATUS AND DISTRIBUTION Common to abundant in breeding range except for Kamchatka and the extreme east of the range where generally sporadic or rare; common in parts of southern China in winter.

T. n. naumanni Breeds in central and eastern Siberia from about 63°N 85°E along the Yenisey east along the middle Nizhnyaya Tunguska (from about the Turku River area), Podkamennaya Tunguska (from about the Gaingda and Birobchana rivers) and Chunya rivers east to the middle and upper Lena River and east to the Aldan and probably also parts of the Maya rivers and south to the Stanovoi Ranges; also in small and apparently isolated areas of the lower reaches of the Lena (i.e. within the range of *eunomus*). The southern boundary is poorly known and may only be discontinuous east of Lake Baikal through Transbaikalia to the Stanovoi Range; in the west of the range the southern boundary includes the tributaries of the Angara River and the southern parts of Lake Baikal. Broadly (though not commonly) overlaps with *eunomus* in the north and west of the range. Possibly on the basis of small areas of breeding *naumanni* in the area of the mouth of the Lena, Stepanyan (1990) gave the eastern part of the range as the Sea of Okhotsk south to the Uda River (see note below).

In winter small numbers remain in extreme eastern Russia (around Vladivostok and possibly elsewhere along the coasts of the Sea of Japan), then sporadically through north-east China from southern Manchuria southward; very common around Beijing, with most occurring north of the Yangtze but also in the south to south-east Tibet, Yunnan, Kwangsi, Kwangtung and Fukien, also to Korea and Taiwan and less commonly in Japan and the Ryukyu/Nansei Shoto Islands.

T. n. eunomus Breeds mainly north of the range of *naumanni* (but see below); east from about 78°E on the Pur and Taz rivers and from about 85°E on the lower Yelogui rivers north to the treeline and tundra at the mouth of the lower Yenisei and the south-west Taymyr to the confluence of the Novaya and Khatanga rivers and eastwards through the extensive taiga forest to the mouth of the Lena and Kolyma rivers (north to about 71°N in the region of the Kolyma delta and about 72°N on the Indigirka) east to about Anadyr (on the Bering Sea) and south through Kamchatka to the Karaginski Islands (where irregular or scarce). In the south the breeding range extends east from about 57°N 93°E on the Yenisei–Angara confluence, the watershed of the Podkamennaya Tunguska and the Lena rivers east (mostly north of 59–60°N) through the lower Olekma and middle reaches of the Aldan to Okhotsk and Magadan to about 62°N. Stepanyan (1990) also included the Shantarskiye Islands (55°N 138°E) within the range (see note below).

In winter has been (exceptionally) recorded along the Yenisei in early February and there are specimens collected from Ussuriland in December and January (Vorobiev 1954); otherwise most move to Japan and south through the Ryukyus/Nansei Shoto Islands to Taiwan, and in mainland China from Hopeh, but most winter in south and south-east China, south of the Yangtze (may also winter in small numbers in Korea) to Assam, north-east Indian hill states and north, central and south Burma (where scarce or irregular) and east Tonkin, Vietnam.

Intergrade zone Overlaps with *naumanni* in the area of the middle Angara River and tributaries and along the middle and upper Podkamennaya Tunguska, the upper Lena and possibly south to Lake Baikal; eastwards the overlap range includes the upper Vitim and possibly also the lower reaches of the Olekma and middle Aldan rivers and the northern parts of the Stanovoi Range, but much of this vast area remains ornithologically unexplored.

In addition to these overlap areas, there is new evidence to show that in areas near the delta of the Lena and Olenek rivers (at about 73°N) small groups of *naumanni* are breeding (and doubtless elsewhere within the extensive areas of Yakutia, e.g. the upper reaches of the Kotuy River) (K. Mikhailov pers. comm.). This apparent range extension takes *naumanni* north of the more northerly breeding *eunomus*, which is apparently absent from these areas. In addition the definition of a regular breeding area for these birds, in areas so poorly known ornithologically, becomes further confused in that both *naumanni* and *eunomus* (together with other species, e.g. Brambling *Fringilla montifringilla*) breed erratically south of their 'normal' ranges in eastern Siberia and south-east Russia. In particular in years when poor weather delays northward migration Dusky Thrushes are known to wander in groups throughout May and early June in the Sikhote–Alin and Bikin areas of southern Amurland (where there are good areas of suitable breeding habitat) and occasionally or regularly breed up to 500 km south of the Stanovoi Range. In successive years a small and isolated population becomes temporarily established only for the area to be abandoned in years when there is no barrier to the entire population migrating further north to breed.

MOVEMENTS Migratory. Both races leave the breeding areas. Nominate birds move south through Mongolia and much of north-central China, Ussuriland, Amurland (rare migrant through Sakhalin) and Korea to winter in Japan, the Ryukyu/Nansei Shoto Islands, and China from Manchuria south to Yunnan and east to Fukien and Taiwan, also to north-east India and northern Burma. Depart from breeding areas in far eastern Russia in mid-September to mid-October but some still on passage in early November and arrivals in north-east India not usually before mid-November. Race *eunomus* departs from northern parts of breeding range in Kamchatka in early September and most have gone by the end of the month, although late passage continues through Ussuriland and Sakhalin (where common to abundant) to mid-October, exceptionally early November. Arrives in northern Japan in late September to November with most arriving in central Japan and Taiwan from mid- to late October. Both races occur in winter in Hong Kong from November to April but *eunomus* erratically common (good influxes in 1983/1984 and 1994/1995 winters, including flocks of over 100) in some years, virtually absent in others. Return movements begin in mid-March in Japan or slightly later in southern China; first back in Ussuriland and Sakhalin late March, *naumanni* usually ahead of *eunomus* by about two weeks, and continuing through April with early arrivals on breeding territory in late April and May; passage through Sayans and the upper Yenisei in early May, both races more numerous from mid-April to early May in Korea than in autumn; in central E Siberia (Yakutia) and the north of the range *eunomus* (or intermediates) do not arrive until second half of May and many not on territory until last week of May or first week of June. May regularly overshoot into the tundra of the Taymyr Peninsula in the summer months (Rogacheva 1992).

A scarce or probably annual visitor to central or eastern Nepal, rare or irregular winter visitor to north-west Thailand (*eunomus*) mostly in irruption years and occasionally in flocks including over 100 together January 1982. Rare winter visitor or vagrant to much of Europe from the Faeroes (1; December 1947), British Isles (10 records including 2 *naumanni*), Norway, Sweden (sole record *naumanni*), Finland, Denmark (2, both *eunomus*), Germany, Poland, Czech Republic (3, all *naumanni*), France (9), Belgium, Netherlands (2 *eunomus*), Switzerland, Austria, Italy, Yugoslavia, Hungary, Cyprus, also Israel (November 1982), Kuwait (January 1987), northern Pakistan and Bangladesh (March 1989). Most of the above records have been in the period September to March but one bird in Finland was a singing male on 17 May 1983. *Eunomus* has also occurred as a vagrant to Alaska (mostly the western Aleutian Islands, and St Lawrence Island and north to Barrow and on the mainland at Petersburg, south-east Alaska) and the Mariana Islands (single records on Uracas and Maug) in the western Pacific.

HABITAT Breeds in open forests and woods, both races showing similar habitat preferences but *eunomus* also extending into more montane areas than *naumanni*; stunted larches and dwarf willow thickets in the shrub–tundra zone and on the edges of larch woodlands and forests, also poplar, birch, alder and stone pine *Pinus sibirica* woods or thickets; riverside scrub with tall trees. On passage and in winter occurs in similar but more open habitat such as edges of woods or forests, hillside scrub, edges of cultivated areas, pastures and fields especially of winter stubbles, riverbanks and suburban parks and gardens.

BEHAVIOUR Usually alone or in small loose flocks on passage or in winter; in China on migration occurs in large flocks of up to several hundred. Many actions recall those of Fieldfare; on the ground hops and walks for short distances before pausing; often holds bill tilted slightly upwards and wings held below level of body. In flight looks fairly dumpy, again recalling Fieldfare. Frequently occurs in flocks especially on passage and in winter, when many congregate at roost or common food source, often with Dark-throated Thrush. Variably tame and approachable or shy and cautious; when disturbed flies off some distance and hesitant to return. Feeds on invertebrates and their larvae, especially mosquitoes in the breeding season, also large numbers of worms; seeds and berries, including Amur cork *Phellodendron amurense*, berries and rowan, bilberries, grapes and buckthorn.

BREEDING Season: mid- or late May to early August. Nest: rough and untidy, mainly of grass or thin twigs, moss and lined with mud and fine grasses, usually placed low in tree or bush 3–5 m (10–17') from the ground. Eggs: 3–5, occasionally 6, and similar to those of Blackbird or Mistle Thrush (126).

MOULT Similar to other *Turdus* thrushes. Post-breeding adults have complete moult from July to early September, and birds in moult reported in breeding area in mid- to late August. Juveniles undergo partial moult of head, body, lesser and median coverts and some inner greater coverts between August and October.

MEASUREMENTS Wing 122–137, exceptionally 142; bill 14–17; *eunomus* wing, male (n=65) 124–139, female (n=60) 121–133; tarsus 29–34; bill (culmen) 14–17.5 (from skull) 20.5–24. Weight 62–88 g, exceptionally 57–106 g (44 g in exhausted vagrant, Netherlands) (Dementiev & Gladkov 1954, Cramp *et al.* 1988, Svensson 1992).

REFERENCES Cramp *et al.* (1988), Dementiev & Gladkov (1954), Svensson (1992), Vorobiev (1954).

Turdus pilaris Linnaeus, 1758, *Syst. Nat.* (ed. 10): 168 – Europa [restricted to Sweden by Hartert (1910) *Vög. pal. Fauna* 1: 646].

IDENTIFICATION 25–26.5 cm (10–10½"). A distinctively marked thrush from central Europe, northern Russia to eastern Siberia. Adults have grey head, face, rump and uppertail-coverts separated by rich chestnut-brown mantle, back and scapulars, blackish wings and black tail. In flight shows prominent broad silvery-white underwing-coverts. Juveniles closely resemble the adults but are duller. Very vocal and frequently in small flocks or loose aggregations even in the breeding season. **Confusion species** None.

DESCRIPTION Sexes almost alike. **Adult male** Forehead to nape uniform bluish-grey streaked very finely with black, lower forehead/base of bill to lores and upper cheeks black, thin pale yellow eye-ring, fairly narrow white supercilium fading over ear-coverts; ear-coverts perhaps slightly darker than crown along lower and rear edge. Mantle, back and scapulars deep chestnut with paler buffish edges to some feathers. Rump and uppertail-coverts grey with slightly paler tips to uppertail-coverts. Tail black or brownish-black. Median and greater coverts as scapulars but with pale buffish fringes; may retain one or two juvenile greater coverts into late winter, and in early spring may show contrast between old, shorter, dull brown feathers with whitish tips and new rufous-brown feathers. Often shows patch of white at bend of wing (made up of protruding underwing-coverts); alula and primary coverts black, flight feathers and tertials also black but partially obscured with greyish edges to primaries and warm brown or chestnut edges and buffish-grey tips to secondaries and tertials; underwing-coverts silvery-white. Chin and throat pale yellow broadly streaked black especially on lower and sides of throat, breast similar or rusty buff-brown at sides of breast, also heavily streaked black. Belly and flanks whitish-buff heavily streaked with blackish or dark brown centres, lower belly to vent and undertail-coverts white or faintly marked with pale brown chevrons. Bill in breeding season yellow except for blackish tip (in some perhaps entirely yellow), becoming more extensively dark brown from tip of upper mandible in non-breeding season but some males may retain extensively yellow upper mandible. Legs and feet blackish-brown. In worn plumage black streaks on crown more visible, mantle and back paler and underparts paler buff with more obvious black spots or chevrons.

Adult female As adult male and many probably inseparable in field but usually with less streaking on crown; mantle to scapulars in some birds less rufous or duller earth-brown; in hand bases or centres to feathers dark grey or blackish-brown (black in male), tail feathers also dark brownish-olive and not black as in male. Underparts have slightly paler ground colour and chevrons on flanks brown and less distinct. Bill generally duller yellow. **Juve-**nile Extremely similar to adult but grey on head and rump tinged buffish-brown; mantle to scapulars paler with pale buff central shaft-streak; median and greater coverts and tertials as adult but with pale buff or whitish central shafts and fringes. Underparts also as adult but breast and flanks heavily spotted (not streaked or in chevrons) black. **First-year bird** Virtually identical to adults (especially in first-winter) but slightly duller and may show buffish-brown tinge to grey on head and rump. Retained outer greater coverts (from juvenile plumage) very slightly shorter and duller brown with whitish tips (and possibly edges), and contrast with newer brown feathers. In the hand, tail feathers more clearly pointed than the blunt, more rounded tips of adults, this being the best method for ageing first-winter and first-summer birds (Svensson 1992).

GEOGRAPHICAL VARIATION Monotypic but birds from central Europe and central-western Russia have been separated as *subpilaris* on the basis of very slight differences in size, colour of mantle and back deeper reddish-brown and spots on underparts rusty-brown (not black); birds from east of the Yenisei have been proposed as *tertius* on the basis of longer wings on average, slightly paler grey head and rump, paler rufous mantle and back, and paler buff on breast. However, these races are poorly substantiated as Fieldfares show a considerable degree of individual variation in plumage tones and measurements.

VOICE Extremely vocal. Most frequent call *chuck* or *chack* or a chuckling *chack-chack* repeated either as a contact call or more frequently in flight between members of flocks, occasionally varied into a *cha-cha-chack* or dry *cher-chack-chack*; a thin nasal *tseee* or *tsree*, occasionally rendered as *huit* or *huuie huit* in flight; alarm call a sharp agitated *chetchetchetje,* and a high-pitched rattling *trt-trt-trrrrt-trrt* rather like that of Mistle Thrush (126), often increasing in intensity and usually directed at intruder. Song a series of harsh chattering, twittering or warbling notes interspersed with thin wheezing or squeaky notes and chuckles rather like a poor Blackbird (111) but lacking any clear or fluty tones; often begins with *chack* call notes before developing into twittering notes or a slow *took-took-tcheree-cherri-weeoo,* interspersed with *chack* notes. Has a low subsong, consisting of a subdued twittering warble broken by long pauses.

Song given from tree but also in flight; subsong often given by roosting birds in chorus with others, especially in late winter and spring. Flight song usually given as part of courtship display. Full song given usually only in the morning and evening during the breeding season; subsong more frequent at other times.

STATUS/DISTRIBUTION Common to locally abundant throughout much of the breeding range but scarce or local at edges of the range especially in the extreme north and west.

Discontinuous and sparsely distributed from the isolated outpost in Julianehaab District, southern Greenland (small population established in 1937 but very scarce since the severe winter of 1966/1967; may still survive in small numbers – most recently seen in 1990), Iceland where it has bred about 14 times since 1950 (with 1–2 pairs in seven years between 1967 and 1996), to central and northern England and north-central Scotland (where very scarce and local with never more than 25 pairs in any one year and widely dispersed). Much more numerous throughout Scandinavia to the southern Kola Peninsula and northern Russia (south of 68°N) to about 73°N (possibly further north in some years on the Taymyr Peninsula) and 135°E in eastern Siberia, east of the Aldan River. In the south discontinuously in eastern France, Belgium, the Netherlands and northern Denmark and continuously east through Switzerland, Germany, northern Italy, northern Yugoslavia and probably south-west Slovakia (Stollmann 1996) to central Romania, southern Ukraine, southern Kazakhstan and east to the western Sayan range and Lake Baikal. May have bred Faeroes 1982 but first confirmed breeding 1997 and may also breed in Bulgaria; has also bred in northern and central Greece on three occasions (1981, 1986 and 1992), the most southerly breeding Fieldfares in the world (Handrinos & Akriotis 1997).

In winter in Iceland (usually fewer than 50 individuals), southern Sweden, southern Finland, Estonia, Latvia and Lithuania and south-west Russia south of about 60°N in the north, throughout Europe (including coastal areas of Iceland and the Faeroes), but largely absent from western and central Portugal, Corsica, Sardinia, parts of Sicily and southern Italy, central Bulgaria and southern Greece south to Crete; present (in varying numbers) from about 45°N in France east to central and southern Turkey, Cyprus, Lebanon, northern and western Syria and in variable numbers (from common to occasionally none) in Israel, highlands of north-west Jordan and the eastern desert, northern coasts of Egypt including much of the Nile Delta, east to Alexandria and south along the Nile Valley to about Luxor; also winters throughout the Caucasus and north-west Iran to south and southeast of the Caspian also (perhaps not annually) at isolated outposts in Syria, Iraq, north-west Saudi Arabia and southern Kazakhstan.

MOVEMENTS Migrant. Birds breeding in Scandinavia and Russia north of about 60°N move west-south-west to south to winter within the breeding range in Europe west to Ireland and northern Spain and south to the northern shores of the Mediterranean, east to the Middle East and south to northern Egypt. Breeding birds from this area also move between west and south but are shorter-distance migrants; most occurrences in the extreme south of the range usually only in severe winters. Most departures follow post-breeding flocking or local movements in late July to early September but birds from northern parts of the range in Russia

begin moving in mid-August. Elsewhere most departures from late September to November (or onward movements even later, especially in the south of the range), also in December and January if food scarce or weather severe. Arrivals or passage through Iceland mostly in November with most having moved on by early December. Wintering flocks mostly nomadic and wander widely in search of feeding areas, moving on when source exhausted. Birds from Finland and southern Sweden move west into Norway before moving on a broad front between south-west and south; birds from the east of the range winter from the Black Sea to the Caspian. In years when southern limits of the wintering range in north-west Africa are occupied, arrives from mid-October to late December and usually leaves by mid- to late February, although not unknown to mid-April in Algeria; in Sinai and the Nile valley of Egypt most records mid-November to mid-February.

Return movements begin early depending on severity of weather; some birds move in early February (or late January in extreme south or southeast of the wintering range) but most departures are in March to mid-April with late migrants still on the move in late April and early May. Arrives back in breeding areas from mid- to late March but Siberian breeding birds rarely encountered before early May.

A nocturnal migrant, although many movements and arrivals undertaken by day, the latter mostly onward or local nomadic movements or dawn arrivals of large numbers of birds, e.g. across North Sea in autumn. In some years migrants drift far off intended course and are probably the causes of original appearances in Iceland and Faeroes; some also recorded far out into Atlantic. Most migration is at a fairly low level, hence it is one of the most frequently seen migrants at the start and end of winter in parts of Europe; some movements, particularly those of longer distance and duration, are at higher levels and flocks have been tracked by radar at 3270 m (10,800').

An uncommon or irregular visitor to Morocco, Algeria, Tunisia, (but has occurred in good numbers in severe winters in northern and central Europe, e.g. 1965/1966) and Libya (where has occurred south to Wadi Kamm, Wadi Turghat and the Jefren Escarpment); accidental or rare visitor to Greenland (away from Julianehaab area 8+ records, including several hundred in October 1976), Spitsbergen, Bear Island, Jan Mayen, Madeira, Iraq, Gulf coast of Saudi Arabia (6+ records November–March), Bahrain (8 records), UAE (c.6 records), Kuwait; single record in Uttar Pradesh, India, Mongolia, China (Kansu), Japan (3 records). Canada: Baffin Island and Foxe basin, Keewatin and Point Pelee, Ontario, Quebec (including one long-staying individual from early January to mid-March 1976), Newfoundland (including 4 together winter 1985/1986) and Nova Scotia, all mostly January to mid-May or October. U.S.A. 29 records: Alaska (3 records of 4 birds, the first at Point Barrow, June 1968, all in the period 2–20 June) and north-east U.S. (Connecticut, New York and New Jersey west to Minnesota);

Connecticut individual listed as an escape by Bull (1964).

HABITAT Breeds in woods and edges of forest of birch, pine, spruce, alder and mixed species, often in moist areas or near meadows and along river valleys and edges of bogs; occasionally in parks, orchards, edges of cultivation and gardens, in montane areas breeding in dwarf birch forest up to (or occasionally beyond) the treeline; in the north to edge of open tundra of *Salix* and *Betula* shrubs. On migration and in winter frequents more open habitat of open fields (including playing fields), open pastures, cultivated and arable fields, also woodlands and scrub with berry bushes. On migration occurs in a wide variety of habitats especially along river valleys and coasts.

BEHAVIOUR Bold and fairly vocal in breeding season, aggressive in defence of territory; in winter warier. Extremely sociable and (except for vagrants) rarely seen alone; may nest in single pairs or small scattered colonies, in core of breeding range occurs at densities of up to 120 pairs per km², exceptionally to over 500 pairs per km² in southern Finland (Cramp *et al.* 1988). In winter flocks may number several hundreds or thousands, especially on passage, but individual feeding flocks usually much smaller. Roosts communally, up to several hundred or thousands (exceptionally to about 15,000) together, occasionally with Redwings (123), Blackbirds or other species, e.g. Yellowhammer *Emberiza citrinella*, usually in trees, particularly evergreens, also plantations, hedgerows, reedbeds; possibly occasionally in winter stubble and on the ground in long grass and in furrows on ploughed fields (Witherby *et al.* 1938). Forages mostly in large areas of open ground in small to large flocks where gait and actions recall those of Mistle Thrush (126), with head and neck held high and tail horizontal and (unlike Mistle Thrush) wings often drooped at sides of rump; has rapid hopping or bounding gait; flight also like Mistle Thrush but less laboured and gliding. When disturbed flock takes rapidly to tops of nearby bushes or trees; perches in the open on prominent branches of trees or bushes. Feeds mainly in the open by searching the ground and locating prey visually in typical thrush-like manner, probing soft earth and digging into rotting fruit and vegetation; takes flying ants in the air and has been known to take leeches and small fish from water. Food is mainly insects and seasonally available fruit; invertebrate prey includes ants, beetles, bugs, crickets, earthworms, flies, harvestmen, millipedes, moth larvae, sawflies, snails and spiders; also fruit and seeds of alder, apple (mostly when on ground), barberry, bilberry, bramble, buckthorn, cherry, crowberry, currant, elder, grasses, hawthorn, holly, juniper, mistletoe, pear, rose, rowan, sedges, wild strawberry and yew; also grain.

BREEDING Season: early April to late August. Nest: bulky cup-like structure of grass, twigs, leaves and roots, lined with mud, fine grasses, horse hair or similar materials, built mostly by female. Usually markedly or loosely colonial, with up to c.50 nesting together, in trees (up to 20 m from the ground though most within 10 m) and placed against a trunk or in tree-fork, mostly in or on the edges of woods, occasionally in gardens, exceptionally in rocks or on the ground. Eggs: 5–6, exceptionally 3–7, pale blue finely speckled or spotted or in some more heavily blotched with reddish-brown. Incubation period 10–14 days; by female. Fledging period 12–15 days; independent of adults at 30 days. Two broods.

MOULT Adults undergo complete post-breeding moult between July and September. Following breeding season juveniles undergo moult of head, body, median coverts and some inner greater coverts from July to early October (mainly August and September); completed before autumn migration.

MEASUREMENTS Wing, male 137–159, female 133–153; 'tertius' male 146–153; tarsus 29–36; bill (from skull) 23–24.5. Weight 80–128 g; in winter male 105–132 g, female 101–141 g (Dementiev & Gladkov 1954, Cramp *et al.* 1988, Norman 1994).

REFERENCES Bull (1964), Green (1998), Handrinos & Akriotis (1997), Norman (1994), Stollmann (1996), Witherby *et al.* (1938–1941).

123 REDWING *Turdus iliacus* Plate 43

***Turdus iliacus* Linnaeus, 1766, *Syst. Nat.* (ed. 12): 292 – Europe (Sweden).**

IDENTIFICATION 21–24 cm (8¼–9½"). A distinctive small to medium-sized thrush of the northern Palearctic, similar to Song Thrush (124) in size and plumage. In winter occurs throughout most of Europe to the Middle East. Has a characteristic thin high-pitched call, given frequently, especially in flight. **Confusion species** From Song Thrush by slightly smaller size with distinctive white supercilium, streaked (not spotted) underparts and rust- or rufous-red flanks and underwing; also a much higher-pitched *tseee* call. The only other thrush (in range) with orange flanks is Eyebrowed (116), which is slightly larger and has a grey head and face and lacks any spots or streaks on the underparts.

DESCRIPTION Sexes alike. **Adult** Forehead, crown and nape grey-brown, extending to mantle, back and scapulars which are perhaps slightly paler; rump and uppertail-coverts tinged olive-brown. Tail brown or medium-brown but with fine buffish edges to outer feathers. Medium-brown wing-coverts, centres to median coverts slightly darker and edges to greater-coverts finely pale buff or more broadly pale greyish-buff on edges of inner feathers, tertials same; alula and primary coverts blackish finely edged pale buff-brown, flight feathers dark brown or blackish finely edged pale greyish-buff, more broadly on secondaries. Underwing-coverts rich or rusty-rufous. Lores blackish, upper lores and supercilium pale yellowish or creamy-white (becomes whiter in spring and summer), supercilium broadens behind eye and extends to rear of ear-coverts or sides of nape. Thin white line from lower lores to below eye, cheeks and ear-coverts dark brown streaked whitish or buffish-white, broad whitish submoustachial broadening and extending to sides of neck (below ear-coverts) and edged finely with row of fine dark streaks. Chin and throat white or creamy either unstreaked or with fine malar stripe, becoming heavier on sides of lower throat, sides of neck pale or whitish-buff heavily streaked black; breast pale buffish-white heavily streaked blackish, belly white also heavily streaked; flanks rich rufous- or rusty-red (but not always visible on perched birds) with short brown streaks, vent and centre of undertail-coverts white, sides of lower flanks tinged pale orange becoming pale brown chevrons at sides of undertail-coverts. Bill blackish-brown with yellow base to lower mandible and cutting edges to upper. Legs and feet pale yellowish- or tawny-brown. In worn plumage (summer) upperparts become paler or grey-brown and streaks on underparts more clearly defined. **Immature** Juvenile has forehead and crown to entire upperparts brown or warm brown but with centres of crown to mantle and back blackish; mantle, back and scapulars have pale buff shaft-streaks and broad wedge-shaped tips, tail dark brown, wing-coverts similar or darker with individual broad pale buff wedge-shaped tips to outer median coverts, greaters similar but with pale or whitish tips and edges, tertials also similar but with pale buff or whitish spot at tips, flight feathers black but edges to secondaries pale brown and tips to primaries finely buffish. Face like adult but supercilium, sides of nape and submoustachial yellowish-buff, cheeks and ear-coverts mottled blackish with white streaks. Chin and throat whitish, lower throat and breast pale yellowish-buff heavily spotted (with inverted heart-shaped spots) black, becoming shorter bars on lower breast, flanks pale to rufous-orange with fine black tips, belly whitish with sparse covering of blackish spots. Bill blackish or dark horn or brownish base to lower mandible. Legs and feet pinkish-brown. **First-winter and first-summer bird** Resembles adult but outer greater coverts, tertials, flight feathers and tail retained from juvenile plumage; tertials and outer greater coverts have pale buff spots at tips (often retained into following spring). Tail feathers slightly narrower and more clearly pointed at tip, compared to rounded tips of adults.

GEOGRAPHICAL VARIATION Two races; variation largely clinal and not well marked. Race *coburni* similar to but very slightly larger than nominate, the upperparts slightly darker or deeper warm brown, black streaks on breast heavier and, together with sides of belly, flanks and undertail-coverts, washed olive-brown. Legs dark brown with paler or yellowish rear.

VOICE Calls very distinctive and characteristic. Commonest call is a thin high-pitched and far-carrying *seeeh, seeih, tseeeep* or *tsiiieh* note, given frequently in flight as a contact call, including by

nocturnal migrants and on the ground; also a harsh scolding *zieh* and a rather short or abrupt *chup* or *chep* or even *chittick*, given as a contact note in flocks mostly in winter or when going to roost. Alarm call a series of sharp rattling *trrrt trrrt trrt* notes repeated and faintly recalling Wren *Troglodytes troglodytes* in tone and delivery; also a shorter but still sharp *jipp jipp*; in extreme alarm or disturbance gives a series of squealing notes similar to that of the panic note of Song Thrush interspersed with the rattling notes.

Full song divided into two (or more) parts: at first a few short, rather melancholy flute-like notes, rendered as a descending or downslurred *truui truui truui* or *tiruppi tiruppi tiruppi* or *teecheu teecheu* or variations thereon, including *chirree cherree churree*, followed by a faster or levelled-out twittering, also variable in pitch and length; a low chuckling warble and a quieter chattering sequence which includes some harsh scratchy notes, often increasing in pace towards the end. Subsong consists of the fast twittering warble interspersed with a low churring or rattling *trrrt trrrt trrrrt* similar but less emphatic than the alarm note and often given softly but rising to a crescendo at end.

Song period spring to early autumn in Scandinavia, given mostly from some way up in a tree or tall bush, often by several males in concert. Subsong often given on warm fine days in mid- to late winter within wintering area and at other times, e.g. before roosting in the summer months; also sings at night, particularly in the north of the range.

STATUS AND DISTRIBUTION Common to abundant.

T. i. iliacus Discontinuously (and variable in numbers) in central and northern Scotland (mostly north of the Great Glen) through Scandinavia and northern Russia mostly between 50°N and about 73°N, north to the tundra line and several of the inshore islands, e.g. Vaigach, east to Siberia, east of the River Lena and possibly to about 160°E on the lower Kolyma (where generally scarce). In the south from isolated outposts in Poland and southern Ukraine, continuously from north-east Poland through the Baltic states east to the Sayan range (where generally scarce or rare) and the southern shore of Lake Baikal and north-east to about Yakutsk. Occasionally breeds further south and west to Denmark (last bred 1983, 1–2 pairs) and northern France.

Winters throughout most of Europe from the British Isles south to the Iberian Peninsula and north-west Africa east to coastal areas of Poland and north through the Baltic states to the Gulf of Finland, south through eastern Austria, Yugoslavia, Albania, northern and central Greece, Cyprus (where annually variable in numbers); also the southern Ukraine (including the Crimea) and much of the Black Sea coastlands from southern Romania, Bulgaria and all coastlands of Turkey (where scarce or rare but may be commoner some years in the north) south to northern Syria, most of Israel (except the Negev) and northern Sinai (varies annually in numbers but generally very rare). Further east it winters (in variable numbers) through the Caucasus into north-west Iran and the south-east Caspian; possibly also in isolated areas of southern Kazakhstan. In North Africa winters from central and northern Morocco (mainly west and north of the High Atlas) east through the coastal plain of northern Algeria to the coasts of northern Tunisia and extreme north-west Libya (where generally scarce or uncommon).

T. i. coburni Iceland; Faeroes (5–15 pairs); a pair considered to be this race bred on Fair Isle, Shetland, in 1935. In winter several hundred birds remain in Iceland and on the Faeroes but rest move to British Isles (mainly Scotland and Ireland), south-west England, western France and Spain; also recorded in the Netherlands and recently (October 1995) Denmark. Bred in southern Greenland in 1948 and 1967, and in 1990/1991 a small population became established in the Julianehaab area of southern Greenland.

MOVEMENTS Migratory. Almost entire population deserts the breeding range in winter, except for birds in Iceland, Faeroes, Britain and northern Poland and the Baltic states (where, in the latter case, breeding birds are probably replaced by others from further north or east), and moves between west and south to most of Europe south to central Morocco, northern Algeria, northern Tunisia and the Middle East; in the east of the wintering range occurs around the Black Sea and through the Caucasus to north-west Iran and the Caspian. In the extreme south of the wintering range numbers fluctuate annually; in some years virtually absent from some traditional sites.

Post-breeding dispersal takes place from mid-July to the end of August but autumn departures from Scandinavia begin in mid- to late September and occur through to mid-November; departures from further east in central Siberia begin in late August, with most birds gone by late October; passage through areas to the south of the breeding range and arrivals in Britain and northern France from late September (although individuals in midsummer and arrivals in July and early August are not unknown), and may reach central Europe shortly after, or as late as November but, depending on food abundance, in some years not until January. In the south of the range birds arrive in northern Greece and Cyprus from late October to mid-November and winter in Morocco and Israel from November to mid- to late February and early March.

Individuals show little sign of winter site-fidelity, with birds recovered in subsequent winters in widely different areas, e.g. from Britain to France, Italy and Greece; also some long-distance recoveries of birds ringed in the autumn and recovered the following winter, e.g. Scotland to Germany and Greece, the Netherlands to Turkey. Longest-distance migrants are those from the eastern borders of the range with a minimum distance of 6500 km west-south-west to the wintering area; thus most records in the southern Caspian are from January to early March. Migrant *coburni* depart from Iceland as nominate birds leave Scandinavia or slightly later, to Scotland (most records Shetland, Hebrides) and northern Ireland, with notable passage along west coast of England; probably also make direct crossing to northern Spain.

Return passage is reverse of autumn routes, beginning in mid- to late February to early March (although many from southern areas of the wintering range have begun moving north earlier in February), depending of severity of weather, and continues through to mid-April, but arrivals in far north and east of the range in early to mid-May. Late-returning birds in early or mid-June in British Isles and elsewhere in northern Europe, more rarely later in summer (away from breeding areas), e.g. up to 15 records late June to mid-August on Fair Isle.

A nocturnal migrant usually in flocks of up to a hundred but also in pairs and smaller flocks which are frequently detectable at night by the almost constant series of contact calls; moves on both clear and starry nights but seemingly able to move in thick cloud or foggy conditions; also makes diurnal movements ahead of, or during, severe winter weather when flocks seen on the move across large stretches of water, along coasts, lines of hills or rivers or arriving from over the sea.

An irregular or scarce winter visitor to southern Morocco (possibly even further south) and the eastern Canary Islands, in north-west Egypt erratic, very rare (Sinai) or uncommon in winter to the Nile Delta, Wadi el Natrun, west along the coast to about Burg el Arab and south to about Cairo. Rare vagrant to Spitsbergen, Bear Island, Jan Mayen, Novaya Zemlya, the Azores, Madeira and Jordan (3 records), north-west and eastern Saudi Arabia (9+ records late November–February), Bahrain and Kuwait, also Iraq (3 records) and Japan (3 records). A casual visitor (including nominate *iliacus*) to Greenland where frequently recorded October to May (Salomonsen & Gitz-Johansen 1950, Boertmann 1994). There are two records from North America: Jamaica Bay Refuge, Long Island, New York, February 1959 (often considered to refer to an escape from captivity, e.g. Bull 1964), and St Anthony, Newfoundland, June–July 1980. Two undated records of *iliacus* in Iceland (G. Petursson pers. comm.). The 19th-century records from northern Pakistan (Kohat and Drosh) are now considered to be unsubstantiated (Roberts 1992).

HABITAT Breeds mostly in birch or mixed conifer woodland but also low thickets of dwarf birch, willow, larch and juniper in lowlands, along river valleys, floodplains, edges of fjords or edges of wet- or moist-ground areas. In Iceland breeds in birch scrub and on the ground in rocky or boulder-strewn country; also breeds beyond the treeline in the northern tundra. In Iceland and Scandinavia nests locally in town parks and large gardens, also hedgerows, small alder carr woods, damp or swampy woodlands, and willow scrub along the edges of lochs in Scotland. On migration can occur almost anywhere along coasts or on hilltops. In winter in woods, copses, hedgerows and more open habitat, fields, pastureland, parks, gardens and orchards; in North Africa in olive groves and cedar forests. In severe weather tame and approachable, frequently entering gardens in towns and cities.

BEHAVIOUR Very similar to Song Thrush when on the ground, but much more likely to be in flocks (up to several hundred), especially in winter when often in company (both feeding and roosting) with Fieldfares (122), Song and Mistle Thrushes (126) or, in North Africa, with Ring Ouzels (109); when disturbed from open ground quickly flies to nearest trees and returns when threat has passed; at a distance in flight the slightly smaller size and shorter tail recalls Starling *Sturnus vulgaris*, but flight, especially on migration, more thrush-like, undulating and with brief glides. Call frequently given in flight, especially by low-flying migrants at night. Roosts communally in winter with hundreds gathering in (especially conifer) woods, copses, thickets, plantations and old hedgerows; usually shares roost with other thrushes, particularly Fieldfare, also Starlings. Feeds on ground and in trees or bushes; on ground has manner similar to Song Thrush but more likely to take food from surface and less occasionally digs for earthworms; snail shells are broken by striking the smaller end with the bill, but uses rocks, stones or other 'anvils' on which to break open shells; also searches leaf-litter and cattle dung. Takes a wide variety of invertebrates, particularly ants, beetles, crickets, earthworms, grasshoppers, mayflies, millipedes, moths, sandhoppers, snails, slugs,and spiders. Has been known to take small crabs and marine worms from along the tideline. Fruits include berries and/or seeds of apple (particularly when on the ground), bramble, buckthorn, cherry, currant, elder, hawthorn, holly, ivy, juniper, madder, pear, pine, rose, rowan, olive, wild strawberry and yew, plus a variety of root crops; in Spain (and probably elsewhere around the Mediterranean) takes fallen olives and a number of crop-damaging pests.

BREEDING Season: mid-April to late July, rarely early August. Nest: small neat cup-shape of grass, twigs, moss or lichen, lined with mud and fine grass or leaves, usually placed on ground under bushes, on banks or in fairly dense vegetation in trees, tree-stumps, willow thickets or bushes, occasionally in old buildings, e.g. sheds and outhouses. Semi-colonial and nests in loose association with others or Fieldfares, but single pairs frequently in isolated territory. Eggs: 4–6, exceptionally 3–7, pale blue to greenish-blue, finely speckled or lined with reddish-brown, occasionally unmarked; smaller than most similar-sized thrushes. Incubation period 12–14 days; usually by female only. Fledging period 9–13 days; young become independent 14 days after fledging. Two broods throughout most of the range except northern areas and alpine areas of Scandinavia.

MOULT Full post-breeding moult of adults from late June to late September, completed before autumn departure to wintering area. Juvenile post-breeding moult confined to head, body, lesser and median coverts, some inner greater coverts, and occasionally a few tertial or tail feathers, during July to September.

MEASUREMENTS Wing, male (n=142) 111–129, female (n=78) 110–127; tarsus, male 22–30, female 23–28; bill (to feathers) male 13–19, female 13–16.5; *coburni* Wing (n=45) 116–128; tarsus 26–34; bill, male 12.5–17.5, female 13–16.5. Weight, male 47–65 g, female 58.5–77 g (Dementiev & Gladkov 1954, Micali *et al.* 1981, Cramp *et al.* 1988); 2 male, 2 female migrant *coburni*, Outer Hebrides (March 1935), 82–97 g.

REFERENCES Boertmann (1994), Bull (1964), Micali *et al.* 1981, Salomonsen (1950).

124 SONG THRUSH *Turdus philomelos*   Plate 43
(Common Song Thrush, European Song Thrush)

Turdus philomelos **Brehm, 1831, Hb. *Naturgesch. Vög. Deutschl.*: 382 – central Germany.**

IDENTIFICATION 20–23.5 cm (8–9¼"). A small to medium-sized thrush of the western Palearctic. Distinguished by variably warm brown or colder and greyer-brown upperparts, spotted underparts often forming lines on flanks, no supercilium or white in the tail and warm yellowish or orange-buff underwing. Legs and feet distinctly pale flesh-pink. Has distinctive calls and very musical song. **Confusion species** Most commonly confused with the Redwing (123) and the much larger Mistle Thrush (126). Easily told from Redwing by lack of red on the underwing and flanks, lack of bold white supercilium, more rounded crown (flatter on Redwing) and different call notes. Mistle Thrush is larger, longer-tailed and generally paler and more plump-bellied, with a different pattern of spots on the underparts and a semi-gorget pattern of merging spots and streaks on the breast; tail is long with white tips to outer feathers (uniform in Song Thrush, which lacks the pale grey edges to the flight feathers except for pale yellowish-buff, not white tips to the median coverts); colours of underwing-coverts also differ. Mistle Thrush has a heavier, more bouncing gait, often with head held high. Out-of-range Chinese Song Thrush (125) is very similar but with distinctive blackish facial mark and prominent broad white tips to wing-coverts. **DESCRIPTION** Sexes alike. **Adult** (Western end of range of nominate; see Geographical Variation) Forehead to crown and nape brown or washed grey-brown; mantle, back and scapulars warm or light brown washed light grey and tinged olive-grey on rump and uppertail-coverts; tail warm brown or umber-brown. Lores a thin dark line, upper lores a thin pale cream or yellowish line from base of bill to eye, some showing an indistinct or vestigial pale

line over eye and ear-coverts, pale creamy eye-ring (not always visible), cheeks and ear-coverts brown or olive-brown finely spotted or flecked yellowish and edged brown or blackish on rear edge, pale cream or whitish submoustachial stripe and black spotted malar stripe. Coverts as rest of upperparts with indistinct yellowish-buff or pale orange-buff tips to median coverts (usually only visible on outer feathers) and smaller or finer pale buff tips to greater coverts; primary coverts brown or dark brown edged paler, edges to flight feathers paler or warm brown on basal half of feathers; tertials warm brown becoming edged paler or greyer-brown; underwing-coverts and axillaries yellowish-buff. Chin and upper throat whitish becoming finely streaked with black on sides of lower throat towards blackish malar; breast and sides of neck heavily spotted, often forming incomplete lines on a cream or yellowish-buff ground colour extending to flanks; belly whiter and more individually spotted, vent to undertail-coverts white, sometimes with (indistinct) spots at sides of undertail-coverts. Bill dark horn with pale yellowish or flesh-yellow base to lower or cutting edges to upper mandible. Legs and feet pale flesh-pink. In summer worn plumage slightly paler or duller, tips of median coverts paler and underparts whiter (less buffish). **Immature** Juvenile like adult but distinguished by dark tips to most upperparts; crown to nape with pale buff tips or streaks; mantle, back and scapulars with larger pale yellowish-buff central shaft-streaks and tips; rump and uppertail-coverts paler, tawnier-brown; tail with dark brown shafts. Inner median and greater coverts have short, broad yellowish-buff shaft-streaks and tips to both medians and inner greaters. Underparts show smaller or more widely spaced spots; breast and upper belly washed buff and mottled with large blackish spots, undertail-coverts pale buff. Bill and legs as adult. **First-year bird** Closely resembles adult from August/September onwards and only told with certainty in field by retained inner juvenile greater coverts showing pale yellowish-buff shaft-streaks, unmoulted browner outer coverts (but in *clarkei* contrast is reduced or absent and a small number of birds retain all greater coverts into their first summer), yellowish-buff to pale brown outer edges to primary coverts and yellowish-buff cheeks and ear-coverts. Face paler or more yellowish than adult. In the hand differs from adult by narrower, more pointed tail feathers.
GEOGRAPHICAL VARIATION Three races; variation clinal and not well marked. Birds in west of range of nominate as described but progressively colder brown or washed more heavily above with grey from Sweden eastwards to Siberia. Nominate slightly paler or greyer above and whiter in ground colour below than races (*clarkei* and *hebridensis*) breeding in the British Isles. Upperparts of *clarkei* are warmer or more rufous-brown with an olive tinge to rump and uppertail-coverts and not grey-ish-tinged as in *hebridensis* and nominate *philomelos*; underparts heavily spotted on deep yellowish-buff ground colour on breast and flanks;

axillaries and underwing-coverts deeper yellowish or light orange-buff. Race *hebridensis* darkest, with darker earth-brown on upperparts than *clarkei*, with greyish tinge to rump and uppertail-coverts; underparts have paler buff ground colour on breast and edges to lower flanks, with greyish-brown on rest of flanks, and larger, blacker, denser spotting; underwing-coverts slightly more heavily tinged orange than in other races. Birds of the doubtful race *nataliae* are very slightly larger (in mm) but otherwise extremely similar to nominate, with greyish-brown upperparts without any olive on rump.
VOICE Most frequent note is a short sharp *tsip*, *sipp* or *zip* usually uttered on taking flight, especially when disturbed, and often given as a contact-note in flight, especially at night, and occasionally as a warning or threat note. In Iran migrants give a call rarely heard elsewhere, a disyllabic *zili* or *zilip*, slightly metallic in tone. Migrant *philomelos* give a thin and high-pitched *seep* or *seeh* very similar to that given by Redwing but differing in tone and not as drawn-out. Alarm note is a *kup-kup* or *chook-chook* given softly at first but increasing with continued alarm; develops into a more frantic strident repeated series of *tuk-chick-chick* notes. When caught by predator (including man) utters a panic-stricken and increasingly shrieking series of *ksick-ksick*, *shree* or *tchri* notes.
Song a loud clear series of ringing musical phrases rhythmically repeated after a brief pause; musical or fluty phrases interspersed with harsher or grating notes, each phrase repeated 2–4 times, and rendered as *filip filip filip codidio codidio quitquitquit tittitt tittitt tereret tereret tereret kviet kviet kviet...* or interspersed with phrases like *wit-weeooo-too, ti-ti-huwee ti-ti-huwee, wit-wit-wit, teeeooo-teeeooo-teeeooo* or *cheri-too cheri-too* (Cramp *et al.* 1988). May also include imitations of a wide range of other species, mostly waders but also mechanical noises such as ringing telephones. Subsong rather subdued and infrequently heard, consisting of a series of low warbling, jumbled or interspersed with twittering notes, usually given with some emphasis by displaying males disputing a territory, mostly in early spring but also in autumn.
Nominate birds and *clarkei* sing throughout the year but most frequently and with increased intensity from mid-November to early July; *hebridensis* song period February to end of June; usually sings from well up in a tree, hedgerow bush, or top of a building; occasionally in flight or on the ground; most often in the early morning and evening, sometimes as many as 10 singing within earshot of each other; occasionally at night.
STATUS AND DISTRIBUTION Common in the British Isles (except Shetland) and across most of Europe, but less numerous in the north and in the extreme south of the range.
T. p. philomelos Isolated outposts in west-central and eastern Spain, more continuously from northern Spain and extreme north-east Portugal east through southern France, Switzerland and south

through the central Apennines to southern Italy and east through Yugoslavia, Albania and northern Greece to Bulgaria and the Black Sea coast of Turkey to the eastern Pontic Mountains and Western Anatolia in western Turkey. In northern Europe the range extends from eastern Netherlands, central Germany and southern Czech Republic and Slovakia north to about 70°N in Norway and east to about 65°N through Archangel to the Urals. North of the Black Sea the range extends north-east through the Ukraine, with an isolated outpost in the Crimea, to western and central Siberia, north to about 65°N but generally scarce or rare north of about 60°N along the Yenisei; in the east to the western shore of Lake Baikal and the eastern Sayan range; also south-east through the Caucasus and into north-west Iran to the northern slopes of the Elburz range south of the Caspian Sea.

In winter most of the breeding birds in Russia, Scandinavia and eastern Europe winter in western and central Europe south to the Mediterranean and east through the southern Balkans, Greece, islands in the Ionian and Aegean Seas, Crete, western and southern Turkey to the Middle East and northern Sinai; also small numbers to northern, central and eastern Saudi Arabia to northern Oman; Mediterranean islands and North Africa from central and southern Morocco (north and west of the High Atlas) east through northern Algeria (occasionally to some central oases) to central and northern Tunisia (north of about Gafsa), northern Libya (Tripoli and coast of Cyrenaica), north coast of Egypt and south through the Nile Delta, Suez Canal and (becoming less frequent or numerous) down the Nile to Aswan and occasionally south to Khartoum in Sudan (where there are also single records from western desert oases), also at one or two oases in the eastern desert (of Egypt) and along the Red Sea coast to Eritrea; an uncommon visitor to northern Sudan; also variable in numbers annually to northern and central Israel, northern highlands of Jordan (where common most winters) and smaller numbers south to the Jordan valley, eastern Saudi Arabia, U.A.E. (frequent November–March, exceptionally late October–mid-April), Bahrain (occasionally common November–March), Kuwait, Oman (small numbers November–March) and in the extreme south to Yemen, north-east Ethiopia and Djibouti. In the east the winter range extends south-east from southern Turkey down the valleys of the Euphrates and Tigris in Iraq (usually in small numbers) to north-central Iran (around the southern Caspian) and western Baluchistan and the coasts of the Arabian Sea.

T. p. hebridensis Outer Hebrides and Skye; interbreeds with *clarkei* in Inner Hebrides, coastal areas of western Scotland, Arran and County Kerry in western Ireland; mostly sedentary but a few move south-south-west to winter in Ireland; has also been recorded in northern England, where it may be more regular than the few records suggest (Hazelwood & Gorton 1954).

T. p. clarkei Ireland, British Isles (except for areas occupied by *hebridensis*) to west and north-west France, Belgium and western and central

Netherlands. Birds in Denmark, central France, central Germany and central Italy possibly also to northern Spain, northern Greece, Bulgaria and Romania are intermediate with nominate *philomelos*. Some move south in winter to France, Corsica, northern Spain, Portugal and the Balearics.

A further race 'nataliae' has been proposed from Krasnoyarsk, central Siberia, but is little known and not currently recognised by Russian authorities. Vaurie (1959) examined several individuals in southern Iran (Luristan and Fars) and considered them to correspond with this race, concluding that they were either of local origin or from an unknown area further north in Siberia (possibly towards the eastern end of the range).

Nominate race has been introduced into Australia, Lord Howe Island and New Zealand and now occurs on most of the surrounding islands north to Kermadec Islands and south to Campbell Island. In Australia it is now mostly confined to the suburbs of Melbourne, north to about Mt Macedon and south to the Geelong district and the Mornington Peninsula; in New Zealand it has become widely established and fairly common up to 1300 m (4300′).

MOVEMENTS A partial migrant with populations in Scandinavia, Russia and eastern Europe moving west, south-west or south to winter in Europe, around the Mediterranean and parts of North Africa, the Middle East and east to the Persian Gulf. Departures from northern and eastern parts of the range begin in late August but main passage from the central parts of the range from September to early November or mid-December, mid-winter movements and influxes not uncommon in southern Europe or the Middle East; severe weather can induce southward movements at any time and some birds are still on the move (e.g. into Ireland) in February.

A nocturnal migrant but dawn and daytime arrivals in coastal areas not unusual; moves in loose flocks, sometimes alone, often on a broad front with large-scale departures from the northern areas taking place simultaneously. Birds from northernmost parts of the range, northern Scandinavia and northern Russia, are the longest-distance migrants and winter furthest south in the Canary Islands, northern Morocco to northern Tunisia, Cyprus, Israel and Cyrenaica (Libya). Birds from Scandinavia, Russia, eastern and central Europe move between west and south to winter in southern England, France (mainly the south-west), Spain and Portugal and to Greece and the Aegean islands. Breeding birds in Britain, Denmark, Netherlands, Belgium and north-east France are mostly resident or short-distance migrants and considerable numbers from the Netherlands winter in Britain and Ireland whilst British breeding birds also winter in Ireland, north-west France, northern Spain and Portugal, occasionally south to the Balearics. Birds from Switzerland and southern Europe are the shortest-distance migrants and the last to move, with many remaining until November before moving to winter in northern Italy and adjacent areas of the Mediterranean, Corsica and

Cyrenaica (Libya). Ringing recoveries show that birds wintering in Greece originate in Scandinavia, western Russia and also Italy and Malta.

Return movements begin in North Africa and across the Mediterranean from mid- to late February (Israel, Cyprus, Greece and northern Morocco) to mid-April, when passage also noted through the Caucasus and southern Ukraine. Arrivals in northern Europe and southern Scandinavia from March to mid-April, although some birds noted on south coast of England late February; arrivals in northern Sweden east to central Siberia in early May, and in northern Russia in late April and early May; passage of northern breeding birds occurs at time when local (resident) birds are on eggs.

Occurs regularly as a vagrant or scarce migrant to Iceland (where it is possibly annual, with up to 30 birds in one year; recorded every year, except one, 1979–1995) and the Faeroes and elsewhere as an extremely scarce overshooting migrant or vagrant to Greenland, the Azores, Madeira, Mauretania (mostly along the coast but also in the Sahara: November, January and February), Senegal (1, November), Mali (1, December), Chad (1, March), Central African Republic (1), the most southerly record; outside Africa vagrant to Pakistan and India (2). A single bird on Vanuatu in the 1930s is considered a vagrant from New Zealand.

HABITAT Forests, woods and copses (both deciduous and coniferous) with a good undergrowth layer, also thickets, hedgerows, plantations, roadside embankments or open scrub and virtually anywhere with trees or bushes close to open ground; in the west of its range occurs as an urban bird in gardens and town and city parks; *hebridensis* inhabits more open country including heather moors with bracken, gorse and willow saplings, also frequently on the seashore especially in winter. Has a preference for shaded moist woods with adjacent bushy or areas, avoiding dry and persistently cold, frosty or frequently snowy areas. In the east and south of its range more restricted to woods and edges of conifer forests, up to the treeline (c.2200 m/7250') in Switzerland, in subalpine birchwoods in the Urals and in tundra birch-scrub on the Kola Peninsula. On migration can occur almost anywhere in coastal scrub or bushes.

BEHAVIOUR On the ground has rather upright stance but runs with head held lower; typical gait similar to that of Blackbird (111), consisting of a series of short runs or hops followed by a pause with head tilted to one side and then repeated. Flight fairly fast – faster than Mistle Thrush – and direct or slightly undulating, usually with typical short call note. Mostly alone or in pairs, but roosts with other thrushes in groups up to 10; also feeds in loose association with others and Blackbirds, Fieldfares (122) and Redwings in open fields or scrub. In central Siberia often in company with migrating flocks of Dark-throated Thrushes (120). Feeds actively in the open and under bushes; breaks open snails on 'anvils' of stones, rocks, paths or walls; searches for food in leaf-litter by clearing leaves with a sideways sweeping action of head and bill. Feeds largely on invertebrates, notably earthworms, slugs and snails, but also ants, spiders, centipedes and millipedes; takes ripe soft fruits including cherry, currant, grape, olive, raspberry and strawberry, fallen apples and plums; also berries such as barberry, bilberry, blackberry, elder, hawthorn, holly, juniper, mistletoe, rowan, sea-buckthorn and yew; in gardens takes kitchen scraps and bread. Nestlings are fed mostly on worms, slugs, snails and insect larvae.

BREEDING Season: early nests in early March with some young still fledging early August; in New Zealand from end June to mid-December. Nest: a neat cup of thin twigs, grasses and moss, lined with mud and dry grass, usually in trees or bushes, also in ivy or similar creepers on walls or on a ledge, up to 2.5 m (8') but occasionally (e.g. *hebridensis*) on the ground in long heather or bracken or among rocks; built entirely by female. Eggs: 3–5, exceptionally 2–6, but 2 more usual in north of range; pale blue, occasionally pale whitish-blue or even white, sparingly spotted or blotched dark purplish- or blackish-brown. Incubation period 10–17 days; entirely by female. Fledging period 11–17 days. Usually two or three broods (often from the same nest) but in the north of the range only one. Breeds in first year of life.

MOULT Adults have full post-breeding moult beginning as early as mid-June and completed from August to late September or mid-October. Young birds have post-juvenile moult shortly after fledging and completed between July and October: the head, body, wing-coverts (but usually only 3–5 inner greater coverts, and in a few birds all greater coverts are retained into the first summer), tertials and some tail feathers are replaced.

MEASUREMENTS Wing, male (n=140) 111–126, female (n=90) 107–123; tarsus 27–35; bill (from skull) 20–24; *clarkei* wing, male (n=23) 111–121, female (n=10) 111–119; '*nataliae*' wing 112–128. Weight 50–107 g (Dementiev & Gladkov 1954, Micali *et al.* 1981, Cramp *et al.* 1988).

REFERENCES Cramp *et al.* (1992), Dementiev & Gladkov (1954), Hazelwood & Gorton (1954), Micali *et al.* 1981, Tucker & Heath (1994).

125 CHINESE SONG THRUSH *Turdus mupinensis*   Plate 43
(Chinese Thrush, Mongolian Song Thrush, Eastern Song Thrush,
Verreaux's Song Thrush)

Turdus auritus **Verreaux, 1871,** *Nouv. Arch. Mus. Hist. Nat.* **[Paris], 6 (1870): 34 –
mountains of Chinese Tibet [= Muping (now Paohing, western Szechwan)** *fide* **Verreaux (1872); name amended to** *Turdus mupinensis* **Laubmann (1920)** *Orn.
Monatsber.* **28: 17, as** *T. auritus* **preoccupied].**

IDENTIFICATION 23 cm (9″). A medium-sized
thrush, very similar in general appearance to Song
Thrush (124), its better-known western counterpart,
but slightly larger, the face markings heavier or
more defined, and with large bold spots on the
underparts. Pale grey-brown upperparts, warm
brown edges to wings with creamy or whitish tips
to median and greater coverts forming prominent
double wing-bar, cinnamon-brown underwing-
coverts and heavily spotted underparts. Generally
little known and details habitat preferences, voice
and breeding remain sketchy. **Confusion species**
No serious problems within range; plain upperparts
and spotted underparts instantly separate it from
vaguely similar, slightly larger White's Thrush (50);
out-of-range Song Thrush is slightly (but usually
appreciably) smaller, browner above, much duller-
or browner-faced, and lacks the distinctive face
markings, prominent wing-bars, heavy spots below
and stronger-looking bill.
DESCRIPTION Sexes alike. **Adult** Entire upperparts from forehead and crown to rump and uppertail-coverts pale greyish-brown, slightly darker on
crown and nape, paler or greyer on mantle, back
and scapulars and warmer or more gingery-brown
on rump and uppertail-coverts. Tail brown or dark
brown on innerwebs broadly edged paler or greyish-brown on outers. Median and greater coverts
dark brown or dark greyish-brown with broad
creamy or white tips forming two wing-bars; alula
dark brown, primary coverts blackish-brown
edged warm brown, flight feathers similar but
broadly edged warm brown on primaries and
(slightly duller) secondaries, tertials dull brown but
edged warm brown on outerweb; underwing-
coverts cinnamon. Lores dusky with upper lores
whitish, broad white eye-ring usually broadest
above and behind eye; cheeks and ear-coverts
pale greyish (or finely spotted black) and may
show whitish crescent in front of eye; broad black
line extends down from eye, and broad black line
at rear of ear-coverts; often bordered with whitish-
buff on sides of nape; occasionally shows dark but
ill-defined moustachial and equally ill-defined
whitish submoustachial spotted black, but always
has broad blackish malar from base of bill to sides
of neck. Chin and throat white or spotted finely
with black at sides; rest of underparts whitish,
heavily marked with large black spots which often
merge to become two or three together in a randomly spaced pattern; centre of belly to vent and
undertail-coverts usually unspotted white. Thighs
pale or greyish-brown. Bill robust, dark horn, with
base of lower mandible pale yellow. Eye dark

brown or blackish. Legs pale pinkish-brown. In
worn plumage or moulting birds, wing-bars can be
absent or greatly reduced. **Immature** First-winter
bird similar to adult but possibly slightly more
olive-brown on head and upperparts; mantle, back
and scapulars have fine or ill-defined darker
fringes and pale buff central shafts, broadest on
mantle and upper back. Wing-coverts black
basally with whitish-buff spots at tips. Underparts
as adult but more heavily mottled with larger or
darker spots.
GEOGRAPHICAL VARIATION None. Monotypic.
VOICE Very poorly known and possibly mostly
silent. Song similar to Song Thrush, with clear but
slower delivery of whistled or fluted phrases rising
slightly in tone, some phrases repeated and others
slightly slurred, followed by pauses of several seconds: *drrip-dee-du dudu-du-twi dju-wu-wi chu-
wii-wr'wup chu-wi'i-wu-wrrh dju-dju-weee'u
dju-dju-weee'u* or *chee-dlee-wee, tlee dup, tlee
dewee, see tewee, tluu tluu towit,* and interspersed
with several shorter twittering and *wit-wit-wit, wit-
weet-too* and *se-wee* phrases (from recordings by
C. Robson and P. Doherty).
STATUS AND DISTRIBUTION Uncommon to
locally common; considered Near-Threatened
(Collar *et al.* 1994). Resident in central and central-southern China from central Hopeh (north of
Peking) south through southern Shansi and southern Shensi to southern Kansu, Szechwan and most
of Yunnan (where it occurs up to 3050 m/10,000′,
in the Likiang range) to western Kweichow.
MOVEMENTS Although largely sedentary, occurs
as a scarce or rare spring and autumn migrant on
the coast of Hopeh at Beidaihe and possibly elsewhere; has also occurred in Shantung province.
Birds in the north of the range are thus most probably migrants to the extreme south in winter. A
vagrant to East Tonkin (Vietnam): Cuu Long, Red
River delta, 27 March 1989 (C. Robson *in litt.*).
HABITAT Breeds in both montane broadleaved
and mixed forests, plantations and woodlands
with an abundance or undergrowth.
BEHAVIOUR On the ground has a rather sturdy
upright gait emphasised by the long legs and bill
held slightly uptilted; walks or runs in the usual
manner although often recalls the characteristics
of a larger thrush, e.g. Fieldfare (122) in flight.
Food very probably similar to other thrushes, consisting largely of invertebrates, especially slugs,
snails and ants, together with a variety of berries
and other fruit.
BREEDING Poorly known. Season: May–June.
Nest: usually placed up to 2.5 m (7′) from the

ground on a branch or broken tree-stump. Eggs: 2–4, whitish-grey to dull reddish-white with violet-grey blotches and irregular brown or pale reddish-brown spots.
MOULT No information.

MEASUREMENTS (n=7) Wing, male 16–120, female 114–118; tarsus 32–36; bill (from feathers) 16–19. Weight apparently unrecorded.
REFERENCES Cheng (1987), Meyer de Schauensee (1984).

126 MISTLE THRUSH *Turdus viscivorus*   Plate 43
(Mistletoe Thrush, Stormcock)
***Turdus viscivorus* Linnaeus, 1758, *Syst. Nat.* (ed. 10): 168 – Europa [restricted to Essex by BOU List Committee (1948) *Ibis* 90: 320].**

IDENTIFICATION 27–28 cm (10½–11″). A large, stocky thrush of Europe, western Asia and much of Asia Minor with small outposts in central Asia and the western Himalayas. Large size and long-tailed shape an obvious feature, and on the ground tends to be more upright than other thrushes. Pale grey-brown above; heavy spotting below often forms a gorget pattern across the breast; the long tail has distinctive white tips to the outer feathers, and the wings have silvery-white underwing-coverts. The flight is distinctively undulating or bounding and interspersed with glides recalling that of a pigeon.
Confusion species Much paler, larger and longer-tailed than Song Thrush (124) with which it is often found (see that species for further differences). Birds in the western Himalayas are very similar to both Plain-backed Thrush (48) and Long-tailed Thrush (49), the former being slightly more rufous above, generally lacking any visible wing-bars in the field, with a pronounced eye-ring and closely spaced blackish bars, not spots, on the lower breast, belly and flanks. Long-tailed Thrush is slightly more olive above, shows two buffish wing-bars and lacks the breast-band effect; the spots on the breast and upper belly form short broad bars. White's Thrush (50) is also initially similar but has a heavily spotted appearance of golden-yellow and black crescent on the upperparts and by dark brown or blackish crescents below. Juveniles could be mistaken for White's but lack the golden-yellow tones and distinctive underwing pattern, have a less robust shape and show pale buffish spots to the mantle, back and scapulars with darker tips to feathers, and spots (not scallops) on the underparts.
DESCRIPTION Sexes alike. **Adult** Forehead to crown and nape pale brown tinged grey; sides of neck to mantle, back and scapulars pale grey-brown, scapulars frequently slightly browner; rump paler and more washed with yellowish-buff, uppertail-coverts similar but finely tipped greyish-white. Tail grey-brown with white tips to outer three feathers varying in extent but usually decreasing inwardly and forming wedge. Lores pale yellow or creamy-yellow becoming greyish-white on cheeks; pale buffish-white eye-ring most visible behind eye; ear-coverts slightly darker than cheeks and finely mottled darker, some showing more heavily pronounced tear-drop line below eye; blackish border to rear of ear-coverts extend-

ing along lower edge; has short line of fine blackish spots forming vestigial moustachial stripe bordering whitish submoustachial and blackish malar stripe. Median coverts have black centres broadly tipped white, greater coverts grey-brown tipped finely with pale buff or buffish-white and edged pale buff; alula and primary coverts darker brown, finely edged olive; flight feathers and tertials brown to dark brown tinged olive and broadly edged pale greyish-buff on secondaries. Chin and throat whitish with lines of fine blackish spots at sides of throat becoming heavier on sides of neck; breast yellowish-buff strongly marked with black wedge-shaped spots which merge across lower breast to form a gorget or breast-band effect; sides of lower breast olive, flanks pale yellowish-buff; belly to vent white heavily spotted black, under-tail-coverts white tinged buff with a few grey-brown arrowhead marks at sides. In flight axillaries and underwing-coverts silvery-white. Bill blackish or dark horn-brown except for yellowish base to lower mandible and cutting edge of upper. Eye dark brown. Legs and feet pale yellowish-brown. In worn plumage upperparts become paler and buff tones on underparts less visible; also pale edges to flight feathers and tertials become whiter or are completely abraded. **Immature** Juvenile similar to adult but upperparts variably paler buffish or greyish-brown and many feathers have pale creamy-buff centres and blackish tip, especially those on mantle, scapulars and rump; uppertail-coverts have less visible pale centres but dark tips and edges; median and greater coverts also as adult but finely edged whitish or whitish-buff, greaters broadly tipped buff, flight feathers broadly edged and finely tipped pale greyish-buff, tertials broadly edged yellowish-buff. Underparts as adult but spots generally smaller; some birds lack spots on chin and throat. **First-winter bird** Very similar to adult but may retain some pale shaft-streaks on scapulars, rump and wing-coverts; underparts usually more heavily buffish. Retains juvenile flight and tail feathers and 3–4 outer greater coverts and primary coverts into first summer; unmoulted/retained greater coverts edged off-white and contrast against pale olive-buff edges of newer feathers, a contrast which remains into following spring (in exceptional cases all greater coverts are moulted in first autumn, then only separable from adult on tail feather shape: Svensson 1992). In the hand tail feathers are narrow and more pointed than in adult.

GEOGRAPHICAL VARIATION Three races now considered valid; variation clinal. A considerable number of other races (at least eight) have been proposed, mainly from areas along the cline of increasingly paler birds from western Europe east to Siberia (Vaurie 1955b). Nominate birds indeed reduce their colour saturation and the amount of black spotting on the underparts from north-west Scotland east to the palest birds in Siberia and south-east Europe and Turkey. Eastern race *bonapartei* is slightly larger (c.30 cm/11¾") than nominate, with longer wings and paler (pale grey) upperparts, paler or whiter underparts with the spots correspondingly less black. Race *deichleri* is similar in coloration to *bonapartei* but similar in size to nominate, with a slenderer bill.

VOICE Call a series of harsh chattering or rattling notes, usually louder when excited or alarmed; also a dry or slightly muted *krr*, *trrr* or *rrr* given either when perched or in flight, especially when disturbed, this note often developed into a higher-pitched *terterter* alarm note varied by a rapid dry *tuc-tuc-tuc* in the breeding season. Song a loud, far-carrying and rather mellow or melancholy melodious whistling, comprising 3–6 short phrases of fluted swirling whistles recalling those of Blackbird (111) but lacking the quick changes in pitch, e.g. *chuwee-trewuu... trureetruruu... truwutru... truwuwutru*, interspersed with short phrases of a second or two and repeated again with similar tone and pitch; some regional or seasonal variations, with addition of *quick-quick-quick* or *weepeeep eepwee*. Overall effect is of a fairly limited repertoire and a rather slow, drawn-out delivery. May give a descending *diuiuiju* at start or towards end of normal song; also a subdued but rather rapid warbling containing 1–2 chattering notes, similar to that of Fieldfare (122).

Song usually delivered from well up in a tree or from roof-top, occasionally in flight or even from the ground; usually early on sunny mornings but also in short periods throughout the day, especially after, or even during, wet or stormy weather (hence the old English name 'Stormcock'). Song period mostly from mid-November to early June, but also exceptionally in late August, early September and October.

STATUS AND DISTRIBUTION Common throughout much of the range but in northern and eastern districts of Russia, the Balkans and parts of eastern Germany scarce or infrequent.

T. v. viscivorus Most of Europe, from the British Isles (with the exception of the Western Isles, Orkney and Shetland Islands) to south-east Norway, Sweden (except the west and north-west), Finland (except northern Lapland), the southern part of the Kola Peninsula and much of western Russia south of 65°N east to about 63°N in the Urals and the western bank of the Ob River; in the south the range extends eastwards from Spain and Portugal, the central Apennines to southern Italy and northern Sicily (but avoids much of northern Italy) south-east through much of the Balkans,

where the range is fragmentary and mostly restricted to the high ground of central and southern Greece (present but generally scarce or rare on the Aegean and Ionian Islands; has bred Lesbos, Kefallinia, Ikaria and Samos), discontinuously in Bulgaria and Hungary, but continuously through central Romania to the Ukraine and east to about 52°N in the southern Urals; the isolated population in Crimea was formerly separated as *tauricus*, but also occurs through the Caucasus east to Azerbaijan. Occurs throughout much of southern and western Turkey (but largely absent from west-central inland areas, southern coastal lowlands and the central Taurus range) and northern and eastern Turkey (up to about 2600 m/8580') east to extreme northern Iraq (in the Ser Amadiya) and in north-west Iran in parts of the Elburz range and elsewhere south of the Caspian, possibly also in the southern Zagros Mountains.

In winter breeding birds from Scandinavia, northern Denmark, the Baltic states, Poland, western Russia, Slovakia, Hungary and western Romania move between west and south to winter within Europe, North Africa, northern Morocco, northern Algeria, northern Tunisia (south to about Gabes) and irregularly or exceptionally to coastal north-west Libya (to Wadi Rami, Wadi Turghat and the Jefren Escarpment), Balearic Islands, Crete, Cyprus, north and east Romania, south-east Turkey, Syria, northern Iraq, Lebanon and northern and central Israel. Occasional individuals winter further north, in central Norway and Sweden, and further east, in western Russia.

T. v. deichleri Resident in northern Morocco from Tangier south to the Middle Atlas, central plateau and High Atlas; more numerous inland and up to about 1800 m (6000') in the Middle Atlas; discontinuously east through northern Algeria south to the Saharan Atlas (usually in cork oak forests) and north-west Tunisia; also Corsica and Sardinia.

T. v. bonapartei Siberia from the eastern bank of the Ob River (birds on the west banks of the Ob and Irtysh are intermediate with nominate) east to about 60°N along the Yenisei, the Podkamennaya Tunguska River basin and south-west Baikal, south through the Sayan range to the Altai and Tien Shan ranges and east into northern and south-west Sinkiang, also south through Ferghana, Tadzhikistan to northern Afghanistan (Herat and Nuristan at 1600–3100 m/5280–10,230') and the Safed Koh, eastern Afghanistan; also Chitral, Kashmir and Gilgit south to north-central Baluchistan, Pakistan and east through the western Himalayas (to west-central Nepal) where it breeds between 1800 and 3900 m (5950–12,850'). Several small isolated populations in northern and north-east Iran such as those in the Kopet Dagh (Turkmenistan). In winter moves to lower altitudes in Ferghana and the western Himalayas (1200 m/3950') in northern India (south to about Dehra Dun) and Pakistan, but only down to between 2135 and 3050 m (7050–10,050') in Nepal, occasionally more widely in northern Pakistan to Lahore and Quetta; also occurs widely in southern Kazakhstan, southern

Turkmenistan, southern Tadzhikistan and much of northern Iran.

MOVEMENTS Partial and altitude migrant. Autumn departures of birds in Scandinavia and western Russia occur between mid- or late September and November with birds moving in gradual stages between south-south-west and south-south-east to winter mostly within Europe, western Turkey, Cyprus and the Middle East, in the south some birds still on passage at beginning or mid-December. In western Russia southward movement conspicuous from late September to mid-October; passage across Strait of Gibraltar usually mid- to late October and eastward passage through Cyprus from mid-October to mid-November. Very little migration across the North Sea, with very few noted at northern observatories; single recovery in south-east England of a bird ringed in Estonia. Breeding birds in British Isles and probably much of north-west Europe sedentary or make only short-distance movements with very few recoveries beyond 50 km. Movements noted in Britain from August to November but forms post-breeding family parties or flocks in late July. Birds from Britain recovered mostly in Ireland and France. Breeding birds in the Himalayas are altitude migrants, moving down to the foothills and valleys surrounding the breeding areas.

Return movements begin in the Middle East in mid-February but elsewhere in southern and central Europe from late March, and continue through April with birds reaching the northern limits of the breeding range in late April and early May, depending on the weather; in some years not back in the Archangel region until 20 May; in central and eastern Europe birds arrive on breeding territory from late February and in central Sweden in late March.

Whilst some birds are nocturnal migrants a considerable number move by day, either alone or in small groups. Large numbers moving or flocking together are rare but 280 flying west in southern England in September and 1500 in Mordovia, Russia, also in September are extremes.

Occurs as a scarce or irregular winter visitor to Tripoli area of north-west Libya and in harsh or severe winters in Europe to northern Egypt (mostly along the coast to about Matruh, Nile Delta, south to about Cairo and the Suez Canal) where recorded from mid-October to early March. In Israel it is variably an absent, rare, scarce or common spring and autumn passage migrant or winter visitor in the northern half of the country; usually single birds but with records of flocks (50+) in November and December; it is also a very rare winter visitor to Sinai (mostly November and March) and extremely scarce in Jordan November–mid-March, mostly in northern highlands to the Azraq area, once south to Aqaba. A rare passage migrant to Iceland (37 records to end 1995, including a nest with 5 eggs in spring 1988 but probably only a single female involved), and winter vagrant (fewer than 12 records) to Crete, U.A.E. and most of the Gulf States (single records in Bahrain and Qatar) to northern and eastern Saudi Arabia; also Faeroes (7 records), Azores, Sikkim

(flock of 8, October 1998), China (1 record in Sinkiang) and Japan (1 record).

HABITAT Woods, plantations, edges of forests, open forest, copses, hedgerows, open fields, orchards, parks and town and city squares; in some parts of the range occurs in almost treeless areas. In the south and east of the range it occurs in upland and montane woodlands of conifers, including cedar and juniper forests or mixed with oak and birch; also dwarf juniper above the tree-line; in North Africa above 600 m (1980') and occasionally to c.1700 m (5600'). In winter to more open areas of farmland or rough pasture, moorland, hillsides and grassy areas.

BEHAVIOUR Occurs alone and in pairs but frequently gathers in family parties or small loose flocks in late summer, with groups of up to 50 not uncommon but above 150 exceptional. Roosts singly or in pairs in trees, tall bushes and hedgerows; family parties in autumn more sociable and roost together. In Europe in winter often associates or shares feeding areas with Redwings (123) and Fieldfares (122). Spends time in the open on the ground where typical gait is erect or upright with head held up and tail down, actions similar to Song Thrush although hops are longer and more pronounced; when excited or alarmed flicks wings and tail. In flight regularly closes wings for a second or two; thus while short flights are fairly direct, longer ones are more undulating. Pairs are often quarrelsome; males are intolerant of intruders into territory and bold in its defence; fearlessly attack birds or prey and crows, etc., especially near the nest. Forages mostly within habitat but more in open fields and rarely in undergrowth or hedgerow bottoms. Food mostly invertebrates, fruit and berries. Invertebrates include earthworms, snails, slugs, beetles, ants, millipedes, earwigs, grasshoppers and spiders; vegetable matter includes fruits and seeds of alder, barberry, bilberry, blackberry, buckthorn, cherry, currant, elder, grape, hawthorn, holly, juniper, mistletoe, olive, rose, rowan, snowberry, strawberry and yew, flowers and shoots of grasses, sycamore, etc.; will take fallen apples and plums, Has been known to attack and kill young Song Thrush, Blackbird and Hedge Sparrow *Prunella modularis* and slow worm.

BREEDING Season: mid-March (late February in Britain) to mid- or late July. Nest: a large cup of fine sticks, dry grasses, roots and moss, occasionally lichens, bracken fronds, bits of wool, cloth or feathers lined with mud, fine grasses and leaves; usually up to 20 m (66') from the ground (but many within 2–9 m/ 6.5–30') along a branch or in a fork, against the trunk of a tree, in a hedgerow bush or tree, on a ledge in a building, bank, cliff-face or amongst rocks. Nest built by female but assistance from male not unknown. Eggs 3–5, exceptionally 2–6, pale or greenish-blue, also pale creamy-buff or buffish-brown spotted, dappled or blotched with reddish, purple or blackish-brown; can also be unmarked. Incubation period 12–15 days; usually by female. Fledging period 14–16 days; young fed by both adults. Two broods throughout most of the range (except in Siberia);

adult male feeds young of first brood when adult female on eggs of second.

MOULT Adults have full post-breeding moult beginning in late May to late June, occasionally whilst birds are still breeding; completed between mid-August and early October. Juveniles have partial moult of head, body, lesser, median and some inner greater coverts, depending on hatching but begins May to August and completed by early to mid-October. No spring or summer moult but may renew some body feathers January to March.

MEASUREMENTS Wing, male (n=90) 143–170, female (n=69) 142–168; tarsus 28.5–35; bill (from skull) 22–25; *bonapartei* wing, male (n=45) 156–176, female (n=15) 155–171; *deichleri* wing, male (n=23) 147–160; female (8)145–153. Weight 100–167 g; *bonapartei* male 100–150 g, female 93–140 g (Dementiev & Gladkov 1954, Vaurie 1959, Cramp *et al.* 1988).

REFERENCES Cramp *et al.* (1988), Ctyroky (1987), Dementiev & Gladkov (1954), Tucker & Heath (1994), Vaurie (1955b, 1959).

127 WHITE-CHINNED THRUSH *Turdus aurantius*　　　　**Plate 55**
(Turdus) aurantius Gmelin, 1789, *Syst. Nat.* 1(2): 832 – Jamaica.

IDENTIFICATION 24–26.5 cm (9½–10½"). Endemic to Jamaica, like White-eyed Thrush (155). Has dark grey upperparts except for slightly darker or browner head and paler grey underparts, with distinctive white patch in the wing (formed by two white webs to the inner greater coverts), small area of white on the chin, and bright orange-red bill, legs and feet. **Confusion species** None likely; apart from wintering American Robin (161), White-eyed Thrush is the only other thrush on Jamaica but lacks the white patch in the wing and the bright red bill and legs and has a pale eye and brown-streaked white chin and throat.

DESCRIPTION Sexes alike. **Adult** Forehead to crown, nape and face sooty-black, face streaked or flecked paler in some birds but in others as dark as crown. Mantle, back, scapulars, rump and upper-tail-coverts dark grey tinged brown or sooty-brown. Wings and tail darker uniform brown but not as dark as crown, with two broad white edges to innermost greater coverts forming small white patch; edges to outerwebs of flight feathers dark greyish-slate; underwing-coverts slate greyish-black with whitish edges. Chin, whitish; throat grey-brown or paler in some, rest of underparts greyish-buff except for whitish-buff belly (sometimes from lower breast) to vent; breast can also show whitish tips; undertail-coverts grey-brown or with white tips. Bill bright yellow-orange to deep orange with blackish tip. Eye brown or orange-brown. Legs and feet yellow or yellowish-orange. **Immature** First-year bird similar to adult including white edges to inner wing-coverts; chin and throat sooty or blackish-brown as rest of head except for centre of chin, which is dull whitish. Underparts duller than adult with darker brown-grey on breast, with dull rufous-brown tips or spots and dull whitish bases to feathers on lower breast and belly; flanks dull brown, undertail-coverts grey with some white streaks or tips. Bill dark with yellow or orange tip. Legs and feet dull yellow or yellowish-orange.

GEOGRAPHICAL VARIATION None. Monotypic.

VOICE Variable from a lilting melodious song in breeding season, often including shrill whistles (or given on their own) *p'lice, p'lice* or a *piuu* and a repeated *wichu wichu wichu...* and a deep cluck-

ing *kek* scolding note often repeated monotonously; alarm a rapid high-pitched series of notes very similar to those given by Blackbird (111). Song slow and lilting, containing shrill drawn-out notes usually in pairs on a rising scale, such as a continually repeated *ture-tee-too-too-tee-tee*, but richer and recalling both American Robin and Blackbird in tone; also has a softer, more subdued subsong. Sings mostly in the early dawn; song period from late February to August.

STATUS AND DISTRIBUTION Very common resident. Endemic to Jamaica.

MOVEMENTS Largely sedentary but some, possibly first-year birds, disperse to lower levels in winter.

HABITAT Mostly in hills and mountains, where it is chiefly a woodland bird, but also enters citrus and banana plantations, pastures and gardens; on the north and south-west coasts occurs down to sea-level.

BEHAVIOUR Generally alone or in pairs but may roost semi-colonially. Most habits like other *Turdus* thrushes, habitually spending long periods on the ground; when in trees or on the ground the tail is often held high or semi-erect over the back; tail also flicked rapidly when alarmed or nervous, and wings drooped at sides of the body. An active and easily seen bird (but can also be elusive, and more often heard than seen) with quick movements; usually flies low and fast, especially when in escape flight, when gives high-pitched alarm call. Forages on the forest floor in typical thrush fashion; frequently seen along roadsides and especially active following rain. Takes small lizards, frogs, small mice, worms, slugs, beetles, moths, fruit and berries.

BREEDING Season: May to August. Nest: a bulky, untidy cup mostly of leaves, plant fibres (especially of pimento) and twigs usually placed in a shrub, bromeliad, base of a palm frond, stump, fork or span of a branch. Eggs: 2–4, dull whitish or pale green, finely spotted darker or with reddish-brown. Two broods.

MOULT No information.

MEASUREMENTS Wing, male (n=22) 116–127, female (n=14) 112–123; tarsus 32–40.5; bill (to feathers) 21–25.5. Weight apparently unrecorded.

REFERENCES Levy & Downer (1992).

128 GRAND CAYMAN THRUSH *Turdus ravidus* Plate 53

Mimocichla ravida Cory, 1886, *Auk* 3: 499 – Grand Cayman, West Indies.

IDENTIFICATION 27–28 cm (10½–11″). A large, rather long-tailed thrush endemic to the Cayman Islands; not seen since 1938 and now regarded as extinct. Almost entirely ash-grey except for darker lores, white vent to undertail-coverts, white spots at tips of outer tail feathers and coral-red bill and legs. **Confusion species** None. Combination of long tail, almost uniform plumage and red bill and legs made it unmistakable.

DESCRIPTION Sexes almost alike. **Adult male** Entire upperparts uniform deep ash- or slate-grey with slightly darker or blacker lores and base of upper mandible. Tail blackish-grey, slightly darker on outer edges with black central shafts, inner-webs of outer four feathers with large white spots at tip. Coverts uniform with scapulars, except for slightly darker or blackish-grey shafts to greaters; alula and primary coverts slate-grey, flight feathers blackish-grey with thin pale or whitish-grey edges to primaries and broadly edged darker or slate-grey on secondaries, outerwebs of tertials entirely slate-grey; underwing-coverts dark grey. Face to sides of nape, chin, throat and most of underparts pale grey or tinged buff on breast; vent and under-tail-coverts white; small area of bare skin around eye. Bill, eye-ring, legs and feet coral-red. **Adult female** Identical to male except for slightly less grey on wings, and innerwebs to tertials brown or dark brown. **Immature** Juvenile similar to adult but with pale buffish-brown central shaft-streaks on crown and nape; chin and throat to breast pale tawny-brown becoming white and indistinctly mottled or smudged grey-brown or buffish-brown; undertail-coverts white. Wings and tail as adult.

GEOGRAPHICAL VARIATION None. Monotypic.

VOICE Unknown except for a prolonged series of quiet or subdued warbled notes.

STATUS AND DISTRIBUTION Extinct; last seen in 1938. When first described in 1886 it was regarded as common but by the early 1900s it had become rare and local; 13 specimens were col-lected in 1916. The reasons for its demise are not clear and the rapid rate of its disappearance remains a mystery, but the destruction of its forest habitat possibly contributed to its extinction (Raf-faele 1998). Formerly north and east Grand Cay-man Island.

MOVEMENTS Sedentary.

HABITAT Previously inhabited dense lowland forests.

MOULT No information.

MEASUREMENTS Wing, male (n=3) 125.5–133, female (n=2) 124.5–127; tarsus 36.5–40.5; bill (culmen) 21–22 (to skull) 26.5–28. Weight appar-ently unrecorded.

REFERENCES Raffaele *et al.* (1998).

129 RED-LEGGED THRUSH *Turdus plumbeus* Plate 53

Turdus plumbeus Linnaeus, 1758, *Syst. Nat.* (ed. 10): 169 – America [later cor-rected to Islands of Andros and Eleuthera, Bahamas, based on Catesby (1731) *Nat. Hist. Carolina, Florida, Bahama Islands* 1: 30, pl. 30].

IDENTIFICATION 26–27 cm (10¼–10½″). The res-ident and widespread thrush of most of the West Indies from Cuba to Dominica and the Bahamas, but absent from Jamaica. A large, well-marked thrush; nominate birds are slate- or deep grey with a white chin, red base of the bill, bright red eye-ring, pale greyish edges to the wing feathers, and white spots to the tips of the outer tail feathers. Variation between island races is well marked. **Confusion species** None likely.

DESCRIPTION Sexes almost alike. **Adult male** Face and forehead to most upperparts dark slate-grey, slightly lighter on rump and uppertail-coverts; base of forehead can also be paler than rest; lores black or blackish-grey. Tail black on central pair, outers blackish-brown edged greyish with large white tips to outermost two or three, spots decreas-ing in size inwardly. Median coverts black broadly tipped grey, greater coverts also black but largely obscured by broad pearl-grey edges to outerwebs and slightly darker grey tips; alula brownish-black, primary coverts black broadly edged pale grey on outerweb, flight feathers black or blackish-grey finely edged and tipped pale grey, becoming broadly edged grey on secondaries and tertials (outerwebs of tertials mostly grey); underwing-coverts grey, darker on axillaries. Base of bill whitish, becoming short whitish-grey submous-tachial; chin white (may extend slightly onto upper malar area), throat to centre of upper breast black, rest of underparts slate-grey, slightly paler than on upperparts, with tinge or band of tawny-buff on centre of belly and sometimes paler tips around vent. Bill black to dusky or reddish-dusky. Eye light hazel. Eye-ring, legs and feet bright vermilion or coral-red. **Adult female** Usually indistinguishable from male but may show duller slate-grey upper-parts and less extensive white tips to tail. **Immature** Juvenile similar to adult but duller or tinged buffish-brown and with paler bases and darker grey or grey-brown tips to forehead and crown to mantle and scapulars, latter with fine pale buff or dull

whitish central shafts; wing-coverts dark grey (paler grey on outer greater coverts) and pale orange-buff tips to both medians and greaters. Broad whitish submoustachial flecked sooty-black, chin and throat to breast heavily spotted or mottled sooty-blackish, spots on breast more widely spaced, becoming dull brown bars on belly and flanks. Bill pale horn-brown with yellow base to lower mandible. **First-year bird** Very similar to adult but has retained primary coverts, and varying number of retained flight feathers which contrast with new ones and with new greater coverts; retained juvenile primary coverts brownish-black with dull grey edges and generally faded appearance; retained flight feathers also blackish-brown with less distinct and brownish wash to outerwebs; but note that birds with extensive replacement of primary coverts and flight feathers may not always be reliably aged (G. Wallace pers. comm.).
GEOGRAPHICAL VARIATION Six races; variation clinal and well marked. Races *ardosiaceus* and *albiventris* are regarded by some as representing a distinct species – Eastern Red-legged Thrush – and further research is considered likely to support this division.

Race *schistacea* similar to nominate but slightly darker slate-grey above with larger area of white on chin and submoustachial, black on lores extending to cheeks; ear-coverts dark grey; black on lower throat extends further onto centre of upper breast and is often in broad streaks; grey breast is, on average, darker than on nominate, lower flanks and vent pale buffish-white and usually tinged light orange; undertail-coverts variably bluish-grey (as on breast) to white with black bases. Bill sealing-wax red, darker or reddish-horn at tip. Eye-ring, legs and feet bright coral-red.

Race *rubripes* has white on chin extending to upper malar area and upper throat, and black on throat to centre of upper breast often in broad streaks broken by thin or fine white streaks (western birds of this race are more extensively black on throat: G. Wallace pers. comm.); centre of lower breast, belly to vent, thighs and sides of flanks rich orange-buff or light orange-rufous, underwing-coverts edged pale orange, undertail-coverts whitish. Bill deep red, darkening towards tip. Eye-ring orange or orange-red to vermilion. Legs and feet bright orange-red.

Race *coryi* similar to (but slightly smaller than) *rubripes* with marginally paler upperparts; has similar amount of white on chin and black on throat and centre of upper breast, but may show slightly more white flecks on lower throat; white malar stripe. Forehead to crown and hindcrown may be more heavily streaked blackish. Rust-orange on underparts restricted to centre of lower belly and vent, with paler orange (over grey bases) on sides of belly, extending to flanks and thighs. Bill as *rubripes*. Eye-ring bright coral-red. Legs and feet bright red.

Race *ardosiaceus* also paler grey on upper- and underparts than nominate; forehead and crown have distinct blackish centres, tail black and all feathers (except central pair) broadly tipped with white, broadest on outermost. Most of breast pearl-grey becoming whiter on lower flanks, belly and undertail-coverts; chin, throat and centre of upper breast white, boldly streaked black, heaviest at sides of throat; thin white submoustachial and black on lores to cheeks becoming dark grey on ear-coverts (some birds may show several thin black streaks to centre of upper breast). Bill, eye-ring, legs and feet bright coral-red.

Race *albiventris* similar to *ardosiaceus* but has shorter, more rounded wings and (on average) longer tarsi, also more white on belly (extending to lower breast in some), white tips to tail as in *ardosiaceus*; female like male but belly tipped yellowish-buff. Bill, legs and feet yellow.

VOICE Call a series of creaking notes or whistles, usually uttered in pairs and broken by a short pause *chirruit chirruit* or *pert squeeer* or *pert seeer*, also a thin, weak and sibilant *sleee*, *pzeet* or *weecha* and a soft *wuk wuk*, *chuk chuk* or *weet weet* when alarmed or disturbed; the typical alarm or distress call is a loud repeated *week week*, usually rising to a crescendo, often given in territorial or pairing disputes in the early breeding season. Song a slow, hesitant or melancholy series of 2–3 phrases similar to that of Pearly-eyed Thrasher *Margarops fuscatus*, repeated in varying order and broken or interrupted by pauses of varying length: *chirri chirri eeyu chirr biyuyu... tewi... shooh... tewii*, often incorporating the calls of other species, e.g. Black-necked Stilt *Himantopus himantopus*, Red-tailed Hawk *Buteo jamaicensis*, Northern Flicker *Colaptes auratus*, Yellow-throated Vireo *Vireo flavifrons*, Oriente Warbler *Teretistris fornsi*, Cuban Bullfinch *Melopyrrha nigra* and Red-legged Honeycreeper *Cyanerpes cyaneus*. Race *coryi* on breeding territory gives repeated, insect-like *tzzz-tu-it* which may be followed by a bell-like trill; also a less strident subsong given in winter and early spring. Race *ardosiaceus* (and possibly others) has a distinctive sharp *wit* or *pit* note given at regular intervals during the song, providing a distinctive difference from the very similar song of La Selle Thrush (160). Usually sings from a high exposed perch such as the top of a dead tree. Song period from the last few days of April but peak period from mid-May to the end of July, although some birds sing infrequently to mid-August.
STATUS AND DISTRIBUTION Common or fairly common resident (may become seasonally conspicuous when breeding).

T. p. plumbeus Grand Bahama, the Abacos, Andros, New Providence, Eleuthera and Cat Island.

T. p. schistaceus Eastern Cuba (provinces of Holguín, Santiago de Cuba and Guantánamo).

T. p. rubripes Central and western Cuba (east to western Holguín where it intergrades with *schistaceus*), Isle of Pines and possibly formerly on the Swan Islands.

T. p. coryi Cayman Brac.

T. p. ardosiaceus Hispaniola, Gonave, Tortue and Puerto Rico.

T. p. albiventris Dominica.

MOVEMENTS None, but may have occurred formerly more widely in, or have been a non-breeding visitor to, southern Bahamas. Records from Grand Cayman are considered to refer to escaped cage-birds.

HABITAT Woodlands, including edge of coastal woodland, mangrove and scrub, also edges of rainforest, pinewoods, coppices and coffee plantations, cactus and dry thorn-scrub and thick undergrowth in deciduous woods and tangled areas or thickets in large gardens.

BEHAVIOUR Usually alone or in pairs and generally shy in forests but may become fairly approachable in gardens. Spends long periods early in the morning foraging low in vegetation or on the forest floor searching the leaf-litter for invertebrates; runs or walks with tail held semi-erect. May remain motionless for long periods but otherwise forages actively, noisily turning over fallen leaves and other decaying vegetation. When disturbed hops quietly away from view or flies rapidly short distance to low branch. Becomes noisy and actively indulges in pair and territorial fights at the onset of the breeding season; also noisy at and before going to roost, which outside the breeding season can be communal. Food in the breeding season mostly insects and some fruit, most commonly that of the royal palm *Roystonea regia*; in non-breeding season largely a fruit-eater (making local movements in response to fruiting trees) and berries; also known to take frogs and small lizards.

BREEDING Season: March–November; *coryi* March–September; *ardosiaceus* December–January. Nest: a bulky, untidy cup-shaped structure of grasses, cactus needles, bits of paper, wool, plant down or fibres, feathers and dry leaves, lined with horsehair and fine grass; usually placed in tree-fork or crown of a palm up to 9–10 m (30') from the ground, occasionally lower on a tree-stump or even on the ground; in Cayman Islands has nested in drainpipes on a house roof (Bradley 1995). Eggs: 3–5, pale greenish-blue or bluish-white (*ardosiaceus*), blotched light violet-grey and heavily spotted or speckled reddish-brown.

MOULT No information.

MEASUREMENTS Wing, male (n=17) 116–128, female (n=12) 113–123; tarsus 34.5–40.5; bill (culmen) 21.5–29; *ardosiaceus* wing, male (n=11) 119–138.5, female (n=9) 114.5–136.5; *albiventris* wing 120; *rubripes* wing, male (n=15) 100–129, female (n=8) 100–127.5; tarsus 29–38; *coryi* (n=3) wing 116.5–130; *schistaceus* (n=7) wing, male 120.5–137, female 111–127. Weight (*rubripes*) 50–82 g (G. Wallace pers. comm.).

REFERENCES Bradley (1995), Brudenell-Bruce (1975).

130 CHIGUANCO THRUSH *Turdus chiguanco* Plate 58

Turdus chiguanco Lafresnaye & d'Orbigny, 1837, Synop. Av. 1 in Mag. Zool. 7, cl. 2: 16 – Tacua, Peru.

IDENTIFICATION 26–28 cm (10¼–11"); 27–30 cm (10½–11¾") in Argentina. A large, robust thrush of Ecuador to Argentina; in the north of its range a montane species of open country, but in the south more associated with arboreal habitats and occurs almost down to sea-level. Nominate birds are olive-grey above and slightly paler or greyer below with no eye-ring; southern race *anthracinus* is much blacker and males have a prominent yellow eye-ring. **Confusion species** Great Thrush (132) very similar but larger, longer-tailed and (in Ecuador and northern to central Peru) with an eye-ring. Nominate birds are paler than Great with paler chin and throat and generally narrower or poorly defined streaks; in south-east Peru race *ockendeni* of Great Thrush is darker than Chiguanco but in Bolivia (to northern Chile and Argentina) race *anthracinus* of Chiguanco is darker than co-existing race of Great. **DESCRIPTION** Sexes almost alike. **Adult** Entire upperparts olive-grey or tinged pale brown except forehead which is flecked paler or whitish; crown to hindcrown sometimes slightly darker and flight and tail feathers browner; underwing has coverts pale orange, flight feathers pale or silvery-grey. Lores to cheeks and ear-coverts paler brown or latter flecked pale buff-brown. Chin, whitish or whitish-buff, extending to throat in some; throat pale greyish-olive and indistinctly streaked darker with triangular-shaped spots; sides of neck, breast, belly and flanks greyer-buff than upperparts, becoming paler or greyer on centre of belly to undertail-coverts, although latter can also be grey and tipped or edged white; thighs pale or whitish-grey. Bill bright yellow, sometimes with a dark horn base to upper mandible. Eyes chestnut to red or reddish-hazel. Legs and feet yellow. Some females slightly paler buff or buffish-brown with chin and throat whitish and broadly streaked dark brown on sides of lower throat. **Immature** Juvenile dull greyish-olive tinged brown above with pale buff central shaft-streaks to mantle; wings and tail browner than adult, with pale grey or buffish-grey edges to primaries; median and greater coverts tipped with small pale or whitish-buff spots. forehead to over eyes also with small whitish spots. Chin and throat pale buff mottled with brown spots or bars at tips; breast more boldly marked with pale buff centres and broad pale brown tips, forming a spotted pattern and becoming more barred with broad dark brown tips on lower breast, belly and flanks. Undertail-coverts buff-brown with broad pale buff central shaft-streaks. Bill, legs and feet dull yellow. **First-year bird** More like adult above and juvenile below, with retained pale buff tips to median and greater coverts and mottled darker or dark brown on face (to over eye) and most underparts. Mottling of underparts replaced by adult-type plumage before end of non-breeding period.

GEOGRAPHICAL VARIATION Three races; variation clinal and not well marked.

Race *anthracinus* much sootier-black with bright yellow eye-ring, blackish-brown flight feathers, dull dark brown underwing-coverts. In fresh plumage underparts sooty-brown tinged grey and edged buff. Bill, legs and feet orange-yellow. Female paler or browner with pale chin and throat streaked dusky-brown, but not always easily separable from nominate female. Bill like male but duller and duskier-brown at base especially of upper mandible. Note that birds from Mendoza, Argentina, have long bills whilst those from central Bolivia are much shorter. Juvenile has pale buffish-orange spots to tips of greater coverts, and underparts heavily spotted or mottled with pale yellowish-buff and blackish-brown spots, heaviest on breast.

Race *conradi* larger and paler than nominate; however, not considered valid by several authorities (e.g. Ridgely & Tudor 1989), since it is extremely similar to and doubtfully distinguishable in the field from the nominate.

VOICE Most usual note is a repeated *check-check-check* or *tuck-tuck*; has a thin, high-pitched wheezing alarm note and, when disturbed, a loud sharp *tsi tsi tsi* in flight. Juveniles have a short wren-like churring trill as a contact note for parents. Song a series of pleasant, melodious, piping whistled phrases, *wee-see-seeu*, containing up to 6 notes and interspersed with short whistled trills, repeated several times but rather weak in tone; only given when breeding and mainly at dusk and dawn, usually from a prominent perch such as a branch or roadside wire. In areas of overlap with Great Thrush caution needed in identification on voice alone as songs similar.

STATUS AND DISTRIBUTION Common or fairly common.

T. c. conradi Andes of Chimborazo (to about Riobamba and possibly further north – in 1989–1991 there were records from Volcán Iliniza, western Cotopaxi, and further north from Tumbaco, near Quito), central Ecuador to central Peru.

T. c. chiguanco Coastal Peru to La Paz, northwest Bolivia, and south to Tarapaca, northern Chile.

T. c. anthracinus Bolivia, from central La Paz, Cochabamba and Santa Cruz south to Mendoza in the Andes and in the sierras of Córdoba and San Luis in west-central Argentina and to Antofagasta and Atacama, northern Chile, occasionally or erratically south to the foothills of Santiago, Talca and Bio Bio, central Chile.

MOVEMENTS Generally sedentary but movements little known; may be a seasonal or non-breeding visitor to parts of the range, occurring around Lima only between June and October; some birds may make short-distance movements to areas with fruiting trees.

HABITAT A bird of dry, open country, usually found in short-grass areas with scattered or stunted bushes or cacti of the temperate zone, between 2000 and 4300 m (6600–14,200') in Ecuador, Bolivia and central Peru but lower, almost to sea-level, in southern Peru; also along streams and edges of cultivation, occasionally in bushy areas such as hedgerows, ravines and (particularly in the south) edges of deciduous woodlands; in montane areas in *Polylepis* woodland and small shrubs; in places found in town parks, orchards and gardens where it often becomes tame, and in the Andes of Peru considered a garden bird.

BEHAVIOUR Usually alone or in pairs; may form loose family flocks (often of several families) at the end of the breeding season. In forests generally a shy bird, quickly taking flight at first sign of intrusion, but in other parts of the range has acclimatised well to human presence. Exhibits typical *Turdus* thrush habits of hopping or running rapidly along the ground and regularly flicks wings, especially when alarmed or on landing. Frequently adopts deep- or full-breasted appearance when on the ground, with wings lowered, rump and upper-tail-coverts exposed, and tail slightly raised. Spends much time foraging in the open on short grass. Food mainly a variety of insects and their larvae and worms, also some fruit, especially olives, and has been seen feeding at an animal carcass (M. Pearman pers. comm.).

BREEDING Season: November to June or July. Nest: a large mossy cup usually placed up to 4 m (c.13') from the ground in a small tree, e.g. *Salix*. Eggs: January in Argentina. Fledglings March to July.

MOULT No information.

MEASUREMENTS Wing, male 126–133, female 128–130; *conradi* male 131–145, female 130–138; *anthracinus* bill central Bolivia 24–27, Tucumán (Argentina) 25–29, Mendoza 30–32 (Hellmayr 1934). Weight apparently unrecorded.

REFERENCES Fjeldså & Krabbe (1990), Krabbe (1992), Ridgely & Tudor (1989).

131 SOOTY THRUSH *Turdus nigrescens*   Plate 57
(Sooty Robin)

***Turdus nigrescens* Cabanis, 1860, *J. Orn.* 8: 324 – Volcán de Irazu, Costa Rica.**

IDENTIFICATION 24–25.5 cm (9½–10"). A large dark thrush (the only one of the region) with a noticeably pale eye and bright orange bill and legs. Female is similar but paler or browner. Inhabits mountains and volcanic lavafields with low scrubby vegetation, also bushy scrub on páramo and clearings in oak forests. A poor singer with a monotonous series of short chirping vireo-like notes. **Confusion species** Mountain Thrush (145) is initially similar but told from both sexes by uniform dull brown plumage, all-dark bill, dark eye and legs. Pale-vented Thrush (148) is similar to adult female but slightly smaller, has dark eye and white lower belly to undertail-coverts. Clay-coloured Thrush (151) is also very similar to both sexes but much paler coffee-brown with a greenish-yellow bill, dark or reddish-brown eye and grey-brown legs. Male also confusable with much smaller Slaty-backed Nightingale-thrush (83) but lacks pale chin and throat and white or yellowish-white belly; bill of Sooty Thrush also larger and less orange. Black-faced Solitaire (74) is initially similar but much greyer with a black face, white wing-bar and more erect stance.

DESCRIPTION Sexes differ slightly. **Adult male** Head and upperparts to scapulars sooty-black; lores and base of bill to eye, cheeks and sometimes front of ear-coverts black. Lesser, median and greater coverts darker brown than scapulars and mantle; alula, primary coverts, flight feathers and tertials blackish-brown, tertials diffusely edged warmer brown; underwing-coverts dark-brown. Uppertail-coverts and tail blackish-brown with central tail feathers slightly browner. Underparts almost entirely sooty-brown, slightly darker on flanks and belly, and undertail-coverts black edged brown. Bill yellowish-orange. Eye white with pale orange eye-ring. Legs and feet orange or deep orange. **Adult female** Similar to male but generally deep chocolate-brown on upperparts, wings and tail, sometimes paler yellowish-buff below, streaked brown on chin and throat and with pale yellowish-buff edges to some breast and belly feathers; undertail-coverts darker brown than belly. Eye as male. Bill and legs as male but slightly darker or duller orange. **Immature** Juvenile sooty-brown with darker wings and tail, but crown, mantle and scapulars to rump have pale yellowish-buff central shaft-streaks, becoming slightly orange at tips; median and greater coverts have short shaft-streaks becoming yellowish-orange spots at tips; tips to lower tertials also have yellowish-orange tips. Ear-coverts finely streaked or flecked yellowish-buff, sides of neck also have yellowish-buff tips, chin and throat yellowish-white or -buff becoming heavily spotted with blackish-brown over yellowish on breast; sides of breast to flanks with more widely spaced brown spots and more diffusely spotted on belly, vent and undertail-coverts; thighs grey. **First-year bird** Similar to adult, i.e. immature male darker than same-age female with slightly paler upperparts, pale tips to median and greater coverts retained into first winter, underwing-coverts generally more buffish-brown. Bill, legs and feet brownish-yellow. Eye-ring also paler or more yellowish.

GEOGRAPHICAL VARIATION None. Monotypic.

VOICE Call a low grating *grrrrk, grrek* or *trrrr*, a soft *chirp*, a slightly harsher, wren-like, repeated *tchweerp, tchweerp* or *chrr-chrr-chrr-chrr*, a thin and rolling *prrreee* and a typical robin-like *ssss* note. Song only given during the breeding season: a series of short, simple and rather unmusical, vireo-like, throaty, buzzing or squeaky phrases, each given up to 6 times and broken by a pause of several seconds *chuweek chuweek chuweek chuweek... seechrrrzit seechrrzit seechrrzit... tseeur tseeur tseeur tseeur* (Ridgely 1976, Stiles & Skutch 1989).

STATUS AND DISTRIBUTION Common to abundant in Costa Rica, local or uncommon in western Panama. Breeds above 2500 m (8250') in Cordillera Central and Cordillera de Talamanca, Costa Rica, and above 2270 m (7000'), exceptionally down to 1850 m (6100'), on Volcán de Chiriquí, western Chiriquí, Panama.

MOVEMENTS Mostly resident but some birds occur down to 2270 m (7000') in Costa Rica after the breeding season.

HABITAT Open areas at high altitudes, including volcanic lavafields, páramo, bushy areas of scrub, bogs, pastures above the treeline, oak and secondary forest edges and clearings.

BEHAVIOUR Usually in pairs or small loose groups foraging on the ground and in low branches of trees and in tall scrubby bushes. Fairly tame and approachable; on the ground behaves very like American Robin (161) but also adopts a very erect stance, hops and makes short runs; the flight is swift, low and direct. Actively forages by turning over leaves and investigating grass tussocks and cushions of ground-covering herbaceous plants. Feeds on invertebrates, berries, particularly *Solanum*, melostomes, blackberries, and arillate seeds (Stiles & Skutch 1989).

BREEDING Season: March to May. Nest: a bulky cup-shaped structure of twigs, rootlets, lichens, grasses and mosses with a tightly woven inner lining of fine grasses, usually placed 2–8 m (7–26') from the ground in a tall shrub or tree. Eggs: 2, greenish-blue and unspotted.

MOULT No information.

MEASUREMENTS Wing, male 136–147.5, female 132.5–140; bill (culmen) 20–23; tarsus 33.5–39. Weight 96 g (Stiles & Skutch 1989).

REFERENCES Stiles & Skutch (1989).

132 GREAT THRUSH *Turdus fuscater*　　　　　Plate 58

Turdus Fuscater Lafresnay & d'Orbigny, 1837, *Synop. Av.* 1 in *Mag. Zool.* 7, cl. 2: 16 – Andibus (Bolivia) [= La Paz, Hellmayr (1934) *Field Mus. Nat. Hist. Publ. Zool. Ser.* 13(7): 415].

IDENTIFICATION 28–33 cm (11–13″). The largest (by far) of the South American thrushes, and size alone makes it very distinctive even in silhouette (which in flight recalls small *accipiter* and has been misidentified as such). Generally dark olive-brown all over with yellow eye-ring (in male); variation in intensity of plumage between races but usually has distinctive long tail uptilted when on the ground. **Confusion species** Most likely to be confused with the smaller and generally shorter-tailed Chiguanco Thrush (130) but, where the two species overlap in Ecuador to north-west Bolivia, Great is distinguished by habitat preference (humid cloud-forest and open country) and presence of an eye-ring (absent in the two northern races of Chiguanco). Particular care is needed in distinguishing the races of the two in south-east Peru where Great race *ockendeni* is darker than nominate race of Chiguanco, while in Bolivia Great nominate is paler than race *anthracinus* of Chiguanco. Songs of the two species are also very similar and care is needed in separating them on voice alone. See Glossy-black Thrush (134) for differences from the blackish races of Great (*quindio, gigantodes* and *ockendeni*).
DESCRIPTION Sexes alike, except that female usually lacks eye-ring. **Adult** Head and face very blackish-brown, lores to eye and cheeks black, with narrow bright yellow to orange eye-ring (possibly paler in older birds). Nape to mantle and uppertail-coverts dark brown tinged olive or greyish-olive, wings (including coverts) and tail deeper or blackish-brown; outer greater coverts, alula and primary coverts black; underwing-coverts uniform with flanks but may be edged and tipped with pale or dull orange. Chin whitish (may form small spot) becoming pale greyish-brown on throat, indistinctly streaked darker or blackish; rest of underparts paler or greyish-brown, especially centre of belly. Bill orange to reddish-orange. Legs and feet yellowish-orange to brownish-yellow. **Immature** Juvenile paler greyish-olive with pale buff or light orange-buff central shaft-streaks on crown, nape and mantle to scapulars and median and greater coverts; tips of median and greater coverts spotted with pale buff; underparts mottled buff and dark or with blackish-brown spots or bars at tips. **First-year bird** Slightly paler than adult with extensive streaks on throat, upper breast to centre of upper belly. Lacks eye-ring in all but adult plumages. Bill yellow or brownish at base and along culmen. Legs and feet brownish-yellow, becoming yellow in male and brownish in female.
GEOGRAPHICAL VARIATION Seven races; variation well marked in depth or intensity of overall plumage between races.
Race *ockendeni* darkest; sooty-black or deep blackish-brown on entire upperparts, tail blackish;

underparts uniform dark brown and tinged olive except for slightly paler lower breast and belly; underwing-coverts blackish-brown; legs and feet orange. Female brownish-olive on underparts and bill orange.
Races *quindio* and *gigantodes* very similar to each other (*quindio* is, on average, more deeply coloured than *gigantodes*) and slightly paler than *ockendeni* (but still darker than nominate): sooty- or dark grey brownish-black above and sooty-brown below including underwing-coverts or occasionally tipped buffish, streaks on throat indistinct but probably stronger in females. Juveniles as nominate but have orange tips to greater underwing-coverts and paler buffish-white underparts on *gigantodes* and buffish-white chin and throat becoming grey-brown on breast, belly and flanks on *quindio*.
Race *gigas* largest; uniform dark olive-brown, appearing to lack darker streaks on throat but may show slightly paler chin; immature as nominate but has pale buff-brown greater underwing-coverts. Race *clarus* similar to *gigas* but generally lighter olive-brown. Race *cacozelus* palest, with lighter olive-brown upperparts and olive-brown on wings; buffish-olive breast and flanks becoming whitish on lower breast and belly; underwing-coverts buffish-brown becoming light orange to cinnamon on tips of greater underwing-coverts.
VOICE Call a loud liquid *sleeu*; also a sharp ringing *keeyert* or *see-ert* and a repeated Blackbird-like (but sharper) *kert!-kert!-kert!-kert!* especially in flight or when alarmed; a loud throaty *chee-yop* also given in flight, along with a thin wavering *eeeee...*; other alarm notes are a repeated *kee* and low *chuck* or *tjuck* notes when disturbed. Song more rarely heard: a fairly limited series of weak lilting whistled musical phrases, often including *ooweetyu* phrases, delivered at medium-slow pace similar to that of American Robin (161), and repeated several times or broken by clear whistles, similar to (and mistakable for) song of Chiguanco Thrush (130) in areas of sympatry; usually from mid- to upper levels of a tree, only at (or just before) dawn and dusk at the start of or during the early part of the breeding season. Quality of song or preferred phrases varies greatly throughout the range (Ridgely & Tudor 1989, Fjeldså & Krabbe 1990).
STATUS AND DISTRIBUTION Common or very common.
T. f. cacozelus Sierra Nevada de Santa Marta, northern Colombia.
T. f. clarus Cerros Tetari and Pie Cerro, Perijá Mountains, west of Lake Maracaibo, Colombia–Venezuela border.
T. f. quindio Central and western Andes, Colombia, south to south-east Nariño to about the latitude of Baños, northern Ecuador.

T. f. gigas Eastern Andes of Colombia from Norte de Santander south to about Cundinamarca and western Venezuela in Lara, Trujillo and Mérida to south-west Táchira.

T. f. gigantodes Southern Ecuador (Huigra) south in the western Andes to northern Lima, Peru, and through the temperate zone of the central Andes to about Junín; birds further south in Huancavelica and Apurimac, south-central Peru, are possibly also this race.

T. f. ockendeni South-east Peru (Cuzco and Puno).

T. f. fuscater Andes of Central and north-west Bolivia (La Paz and Cochabamba).

MOVEMENTS Sedentary.

HABITAT A wide choice of forest or woodland habitats between 1400 and 4250 m (4620–14,000') but more usually above 2000 m (6600'); in humid cloud-forest edges and clearings (generally absent from heavily forested areas) to scattered or secondary woods, hedges and isolated patches of scrub or *Polylepis* woodland high above the treeline to open country where it inhabits páramo grassland, especially areas with scattered small bushes. In recent years has become common around farmland and cultivation and in gardens (even in cities such as Quito and La Paz), and appears to have increased in areas of widespread deforestation.

BEHAVIOUR Usually alone or in pairs during the breeding season, when extremely territorial; at other times may occur in small flocks, occasionally up to 40 together; possibly roosts communally in trees during the non-breeding period. Most active at dawn and dusk; spends long periods on the ground where it hops or runs; flicks tail frequently and raises tail on landing. Frequents short grassy areas or well-grazed pastures, gardens and occasionally roadsides; also forages in fruiting trees. Feeds mainly on fruit and berries (including strawberries), also insects and worms.

BREEDING Season: probably throughout the year. Nest: a huge cup-shaped structure of a variety of plant material, usually without a mud lining and placed low in a bush or spreading tree. Eggs: 2, pale greenish-blue with darker or reddish-brown spots.

MOULT No information.

MEASUREMENTS *fuscater* wing, male 149–154, female 140–145; bill (culmen) male (n=11) 20–24.5, female (n=11) 21–24, (to skull) 25–27; *cacozelas* wing, male 145–153, female 140–153 (exceptionally to 160); bill (to feathers) both sexes (n=3) 24–26, (to skull) 28–30.5; *ockendeni* wing, male 149–150, female 146; bill (to feathers) both sexes (n=2) 25, (to skull) 28–29 (Hellmayr 1934). Weight apparently unrecorded.

REFERENCES Fjeldså & Krabbe (1990), Hellmayr (1934), Ridgely & Tudor (1989).

133 BLACK THRUSH *Turdus infuscatus*   Plate 57
(Black Robin)
Merula infuscata Lafresnaye, 1844, *Rev. Zool.* [Paris] 7: 41 – Mexico.

IDENTIFICATION 21.5–24 cm (8½–9"). Male is a very distinctive all-black thrush with bright yellow bill and legs; female is brown with warmer brown underparts and streaked throat. Occurs in cloud-forests in limited range in Central America. **Confusion species** Male is very similar to (and previously considered conspecific with) Glossy-black Thrush (134) of South America, also Blackbird (111) of the Palearctic, but within native range unlikely to be confused with any other thrush. Female extremely similar to both sexes of Mountain Thrush (145) but has pale yellowish or dull orange, not dark, legs; Mountain is also grey-brown and lacks darker-streaked pale chin and throat and has pale under-tail-coverts edged pale buff. Clay-coloured (151) is also similar but favours more open areas, is somewhat warmer in tone and has paler or yellowish bill and dull flesh-coloured legs. Immature Rufous-collared Thrush (162) from same-age Black by bulkier size, lack of yellow eye-ring and (depending on age) no black patches in plumage.

DESCRIPTION Sexes differ. **Adult male** Dull sooty-black except for bright yellow eye-ring; overall like slightly smaller version of European Blackbird; very slightly glossy black on head, nape, mantle, back, chin, throat and breast; flight feathers browner-black than rest of upperparts. Bill, legs and feet bright yellow or orange-yellow. **Adult female** Head and upperparts olive tinged russet-brown including wings, edges to median, greater and primary coverts; flight feathers and tail browner. Lores dark brown with short buffish line to eye, rest of face dark olive or tinged brown and fine pale shaft-streaks on cheeks and ear-coverts. Chin and throat pale buff or buffish-white flecked or streaked slightly darker on chin and sides of throat and neck. Breast and belly light olive tinged grey, becoming darker or tinged warm brown or ginger on flanks; undertail-coverts pale sandy-brown with whitish central shafts. Underwing-coverts pale orange, slightly duller or more olive on innerwebs of coverts. Bill black or blackish-brown. Legs and feet pale yellowish or dull orange. **Immature** Juvenile very similar to adult female with fine pale orange-buff central shaft-streaks on grey-brown crown to mantle and more prominent edges to scapulars and pale orange tips (wedge-shaped on median and greaters) to all (except primary) wing-coverts. Underparts dull orange or orange-buff spotted brown on sides of chin and throat; upper breast more closely spotted dark brown or blackish; rest of underparts more sparsely spotted. In older birds underparts mottled whitish-buff and barred browner on throat to belly and flanks. Bill as female but darker on juvenile female. First-summer male has yellow eye-ring, bill, legs and feet, grey-brown head and upperparts with some black feathers on mantle and back; throat heavily streaked black, rest of underparts greyish with some black feathers on belly. Can breed at this age in this plumage. Attains adult plumage by or just before second winter, after prebasic moult.

GEOGRAPHICAL VARIATION None. Monotypic.

VOICE Call a dry, clucking or scolding *chuh-chuh-chuh-chuh-chuh* and a harsher *chehk-chehk...*, also a thin *ssii* usually given in flight. Song a variable series of fairly typical thrush-like rich warbling whistles or musical phrases broken or interrupted with frequent pauses and followed by 2–3 repetitions of the same phrase (Howell & Webb 1995); may be interspersed with short, subdued or fading trills and frequently mimics the notes of other nearby species, particularly Eastern Bluebird *Sialia sialis*, Steller's Jay *Cyanocitta stelleri*, Whip-poor-will *Caprimulgus vociferus* and Grey Silky-Flycatcher *Ptilogonys cinereus*, with notes recalling Brown-backed Solitaire (71) and Yellow-backed Oriole *Icterus chrysater*; overall tone and quality recalls Northern Mockingbird *Mimus polyglottos*; given from top or high in tall forest tree. Song period March to at least May.

STATUS AND DISTRIBUTION Common or fairly common. Resident. Eastern Mexico from southern Tamaulipas south-east through San Luis Potosi to Puebla and northern Oaxaca; western Mexico in southern and Guerrero and southern Oaxaca; eastern Mexico from interior Chiapas to Guatemala, central Honduras and western El Salvador.

MOVEMENTS Largely resident but moves to lower altitudes in winter; has occurred down to 300 m (990') in Guatemala. Vagrant to Morelos, central Mexico, in March 1982.

HABITAT Humid evergreen and pine–oak cloud-forests and forest edges of the subtropical and temperate zones, usually between 1200 and 3500 m (3960–11,550'), possibly lower in Mexico.

BEHAVIOUR Usually alone or in pairs for most of the breeding season, but in winter often in small flocks or loose associations of up to 20, especially at fruiting trees. Usually at middle to upper levels of trees and thick bushes, but often also on the ground in clearings and on trails. Forages both in trees and on the ground, mainly taking insects and fruit, especially berries.

BREEDING Season: April to June. Eggs: blue and usually unspotted.

MOULT No information.

MEASUREMENTS Wing, male 121–133, female 122.5–125; tarsus 27.5–32.5; bill (culmen) 18.5–21 (Hellmayr 1934, Dickey & van Rossem 1938). Weight apparently unrecorded.

REFERENCES Dickey & van Rossem (1938).

134 GLOSSY-BLACK THRUSH *Turdus serranus* Plate 59

Turdus serranus Tschudi, 1844, *Arch. Naturg.* 10(1): 280 – Peru.

IDENTIFICATION 23–25.5 cm (9¼–10"). An aptly named bird, the male being entirely lustrous or glossy black with a thin orange eye-ring and bright orange-yellow bill and legs. Female is duller, deep rufous-brown, slightly paler or greyish-olive on the underparts, and has a narrow orange-yellow eye-ring. Both sexes are very similar to but smaller (and the male is much glossier) than the respective sexes of Blackbird (111) of the Palearctic. **Confusion species** Most likely problem is Great Thrush (132), especially the races *quindio*, *gigantodes* and *ockendeni*, which are very dark; but it is much larger and the black is less intense and duller, the male with a bright yellow eye-ring; female is very slightly browner than male Great with a pale or whitish throat in some races and, in race *gigantodes*, with throat streaked dark brown. Moreover, Glossy-black is almost entirely a forest bird whilst Great occurs along forest and woodland edges and is more likely to be seen on the ground in open clearings, pastures, roadsides and high grasslands. The race *anthracinus* of Chiguanco Thrush (130) is very similar and best told by duller brownish-black plumage with much larger orange-yellow bill; it is also unlikely to occur within same habitat, preferring more open areas, edges of cultivation and light woodlands. Male Pale-eyed Thrush (95) has a yellower bill, pale whitish-blue eye and no eye-ring, the female with a dark eye and darker-streaked yellowish-buff chin and throat, off-whitish belly to vent. Female Glossy-black also likely to be mistaken for female Yellow-legged (94) and Black-hooded (138) Thrushes in northern Colombia, but all-dark chin and throat and generally much darker rufous-brown underparts separate it from Yellow-legged, which has buffish-white lower centre of belly to vent and undertail-coverts, and from Black-hooded, which has a paler or buffish-brown belly and flanks below an ill-defined browner 'breast-band'. Pale-vented (148) is also initially similar but is a lower-altitude bird and does not occur within the range of Glossy-black. In Ecuador and extreme north-west Peru confusion likely with female Ecuadorian Thrush (153) but Glossy-black generally occurs higher (i.e. above 1500 m), has a darker brown head and upper breast, and lacks Ecuadorian's prominent streaks on the chin and throat.

DESCRIPTION Sexes differ. **Adult male** Entirely glossy black except for bright orange-yellow eye-ring; wings and tail slightly sooty-black. Bill orange or orange-yellow. Legs and feet bright yellow. **Adult female** Most of head and upperparts dull olive-brown tinged orange or rust-orange on underparts (recalling female Blackbird) with forehead to nape and rump and uppertail-coverts slightly richer brown; thin orange-yellow eye-ring; wings and tail also slightly richer olive-brown. Underwing has coverts dark rufous-brown with pale orange edges to greater coverts. Underparts slightly paler, greyish-olive and washed brownish-olive on lower throat, breast, belly and flanks, sometimes with faint streaks on throat; undertail-coverts slightly darker chocolate or dark rufous-brown. Bill dull or dirty yellow. Legs and feet as male. Some birds (possibly not fully adult) paler or brighter brown on head, face and nape; chin and throat deep buffish-brown, becoming warmer or more rufous-brown on wing-coverts, breast and belly to undertail-coverts. **Immature** Juvenile dull or dark olive-brown with fine pale buff central shaft-streaks to forehead (where most heavily streaked), crown, nape, mantle and edges to scapulars; also shows paler bases to mantle, back and rump; fine pale buff tips to median and greater coverts. Tail dull or dusky-brown. Underparts mottled with pale buff-brown centres, whiter central shaft-streaks and dark brown tips to chin, throat, breast and upper flanks. In first winter becomes more uniformly dark but female especially rufous-brown on forehead to crown and wings and retains thin, pale orange-buff shaft-streaks on chin to upper belly and flanks.

GEOGRAPHICAL VARIATION Four races; variation clinal and not well marked.

Race *fuscobrunneus* extremely similar to nominate but in the hand has slightly smaller bill and female darker or duller olive-brown above, underwing-coverts dull cinnamon; wings and tail shorter than nominate. Underparts deep umber- or cinnamon-brown except for throat which is pale or greyish-olive, sometimes with faint streaks. Bill dark or horn-brown with yellowish base. Legs and feet straw-yellow.

Female of race *atrosericeus* generally light olive-brown above with edges to wings richer russet-brown, tail dark olive-brown with rich russet edges, underwing-coverts olive or tinged brownish-olive with broad pale orange fringes; underparts paler or greyish-brown, dull brown or washed olive on throat, breast and flanks, and slightly paler on belly; undertail-coverts paler than on nominate with whitish central shafts. Bill slightly longer and more often brighter or yellower. First-year female much more rufous on upperparts (particularly on forehead and edges to wings), underparts also similarly tinged rufous except for greyer belly.

Male *cumanensis* dark chocolate-brown on both upper- and underparts with rufous-brown edges to wings and blackish-brown tail; underwing-coverts also blackish-brown. Female like that of *atrosericeus* but less olive above and deep sooty-grey tinged brown below; underwing-coverts have fine orange-buff fringes. Bill entirely yellow.

VOICE Call a fairly typical clucking *chick-chip-chip-chip-chip-chip* or *tjick-tjick-tchi-tchi-tchi* and a sharp or rasping *rrrrrt-rrrrrt*. Song a rather untypical (for a thrush) weak, short but rapid series of squeaky, high-pitched or shrill notes, *tee-do-dede-do-deet* or *ee-te-jeete-o-et* with an upward inflection, sometimes including a short trill or slurred notes; repeated monotonously at short intervals (Hilty & Brown 1986). Usually sings at dawn and dusk, from a high perch, e.g. a bromeliad high in a tree, often in the open. In western Andes sings from February to late July.

STATUS AND DISTRIBUTION Fairly common. Resident.

T. s. cumanensis Mountains of north-east Venezuela in Anzoategui, Sucre and Monagas.

T. s. atrosericeus Coastal mountains of northern Venezuela (east to Sucre) and the Andes of Mérida and Táchira and the Perijá mountains of north-east Colombia.

T. s. fuscobrunneus Colombia, Páramo de Tamá and all three ranges of the Andes and the eastern and western slopes of Ecuador.

T. s. serranus Northern Peru, the western slope of the Andes south to Cajamarca to western Bolivia (La Paz and Cochabamba) and north-west Argentina (Salta and Jujuy).

MOVEMENTS Largely sedentary, but has occurred in suitable habitat down to about 320 m (1050').

HABITAT Humid, montane cloud-forests and secondary forests and woods of the subtropical zone between 1500 and 2800 m (4950–9240'), rarely to 3000–3500 m (9900–11,550'), also forest edges and clearings, in places also venturing into large gardens with suitable habitat; in south-east Ecuador and north-west Peru it also occurs, perhaps seasonally, in dry deciduous forest. In Ecuador the race *fuscobrunneus* is rare above 2800 m (9240') but several birds were recorded singing at 3750 m (12,375') in mid-March 1996 on Volcán Pichincha (Krabbe *et al.* 1997).

BEHAVIOUR Generally shy and inconspicuous, and quick to take flight at the approach of an intruder; usually alone or in pairs from mid-stages to the upper canopy, occasionally low down or on the ground. Forages in canopy, also along branches in creepers and epiphytes and on the ground. Food mostly berries and small fruits together with some insects and their larvae.

BREEDING Season: February to November. Nest: a small cup of moss or lichens usually low down in tangled creeper or vines. Eggs: 2, pale blue spotted with purple and light brown. Fledglings from June onwards.

MOULT No information.

MEASUREMENTS Wing, male 125–135, female 124–128; bill 21–25.5; tarsus 32.5–35; *fuscobrunneus* wing, male 120–125, female 117–122; bill 20–24; *atrosericeus* wing, male 119–127, female 114–121; bill 24–27.5; *cumanensis* wing, male 117–123, female 116–117; bill 23–24 (Hellmayr 1934). Weight apparently unrecorded.

REFERENCES Hellmayr (1934), Hilty & Brown (1986), Krabbe *et al.* (1997).

Turdus nigriceps 'Jelski' = Cabanis, 1874, *J. Orn.* 22: 97 – Peru.

IDENTIFICATION 19–23 cm (7½–9″). Male is the only entirely grey thrush of the Andes from Ecuador to north-west Argentina; female is browner or more olive-brown on the upperparts, brown on the breast and greyish on the belly and flanks; chin and throat as male but some birds show an unstreaked crescent-like area of white on the lower throat. **Confusion species** Males are virtually unmistakable; Plumbeous-backed Thrush (137) is initially similar but is paler above and below with a distinctive whitish eye and a creamy-buff tinge to lower flanks. Female is more likely to be confused with female Pale-eyed Thrush (95), which is mostly brown above and below and has poorly defined streaks on chin and throat and dull greyish-white on centre of belly to vent. Female Glossy-black Thrush (134) is more uniform dark brown with no pale areas on the chin and throat, and has a dusky-yellow bill. White-necked Thrush (157) is also very similar but is much greyer below with a a broad orange-yellow eye-ring and prominent white crescent on the lower throat.

DESCRIPTION Sexes differ. **Adult male** Forehead to hindcrown blackish, merging into deep bluish-tinged slate-grey, with black centres to nape and upper mantle. Mantle to uppertail-coverts, scapulars and lesser coverts deep slate- or bluish-grey, slightly paler grey on lower back, rump and uppertail-coverts. Tail dark brown, appearing black at distance. Median and greater coverts dark brown tinged bluish-grey, alula blackish-brown, primary coverts dark brown but broadly edged bluish-grey, flight feathers dark brown finely edged paler, tertials similar indistinctly edged bluish-grey on outerwebs; underwing-coverts pale ash-grey. Lores to eye blackish; thin pale yellow or yellowish-green eye-ring; cheeks, ear-coverts and sides of nape as forehead and crown or slightly paler. Chin and throat white, heavily streaked black. Breast to flanks uniform pale ash-grey, becoming white on centre of belly to vent, undertail-coverts similar but with grey edges and tips. Bill yellow to yellow-orange, slightly paler towards tip. Legs and feet dull yellow. **Adult female** Forehead to nape and sides of neck brown or warm brown, becoming darker or tinged with greyish-olive on mantle to uppertail-coverts and scapulars. Tail olive-brown. Median and greater coverts warm or gingery-brown, alula and primary coverts dark brown, flight feathers dark brown edged paler or warmer brown; tertials as flight feathers but edged olive-brown; underwing-coverts pale orange to ruddy-brown. Lores to cheeks and ear-coverts brown as crown but finely spotted or flecked paler buff-brown; thin or inconspicuous yellowish-buff or pale yellow eye-ring. Chin and throat whitish-buff with short dark brown streaks; edge of chin and throat darker brown forming broad malar, some birds with lower throat unstreaked and thus appearing as whitish crescent; breast to flanks

variable from warm cinnamon or gingery-brown to darker brown; centre of belly off-white or pale grey, thighs dull grey and undertail-coverts whitish flecked darker or with grey-brown. Bill dark horn or blackish-brown tinged yellow at base of lower mandible. Legs and feet buffish-yellow to brownish-horn. **Immature** Juvenile as adult female but slightly darker olive-brown on head and upperparts; crown and nape heavily tipped pale orange-buff, becoming longer streaks on shafts of upper mantle; small orange-buff spots at tips of median and greater coverts; underwing-coverts cinnamon. Face heavily spotted orange-buff on cheeks with fine streaks or flecks on ear-coverts. Chin and throat pale buff; breast feathers pale whitish-buff or warm buffish-orange with broad brown tips and fringes creating a scaly pattern extending to flanks. Centre of belly white with thinner blackish-brown fringes and tips; undertail-coverts whitish with or yellowish-buff edges and brown tips. Bill dusky or dark brown. Legs and feet dark brown.

GEOGRAPHICAL VARIATION None. Monotypic.

VOICE Call a dry *tsok* and a frequent harsh *kraa* contact note. Song a series of typical thrush-like phrases, with rather drawn-out, musical, high-pitched whistles combined with a variable series of jumbled metallic notes, often including or initiated by *tooee, too-oo...* (the first phrase rising, the second falling) and followed by several notes of similar quality before repeating some whistled phrases; broken by long pauses; very ventriloquial, the bird usually extremely difficult to see in dense vegetation.

STATUS AND DISTRIBUTION Locally common to scarce. Isolated outpost (small numbers) on western slope of Andes in Piura and Cajamarca, north-west Peru, and Loja, southern Ecuador; ranges continuously (but see Movements) from the east Andean slope in Peru from Piura, Lambayeque and Amazonas to central Bolivia and south into north-west Argentina south to La Rioja and Córdoba.

MOVEMENTS Partial migrant; mostly resident but recent evidence suggests that birds north of about Cochabamba, central Bolivia, are (with the possible exception of birds in north-west Peru and southern Ecuador) austral migrants from at least July, returning to breeding areas between October and April. Birds in eastern Peru may also be non-breeding austral migrants, being recorded only from the end of May to early September (Schulenberg 1987).

HABITAT Humid montane forest usually between 500 and 2000 m (1650–6600′), exceptionally to 2550 m (8400′) in Cochabamba, Bolivia, and to 2300 m (7590′) in La Rioja, Argentina (where common: M. Pearman pers. comm.), also in dense shrubbery, especially alders, wooded ravines, particularly on edges and along clearings of forests or near streams.

BEHAVIOUR Usually alone or in pairs. Very shy or unobtrusive, often staying within dense foliage and extremely hard to observe, even whilst singing, except when up to 4 m (c.13') in fruiting bushes and trees.

BREEDING Very poorly known. Season: November to March or April; November–December (Argentina). Juveniles noted in January–April. Nest: usually placed up to 4 m (13') in well shaded or dense vegetation. Eggs: 3.

MOULT No information.

MEASUREMENTS Wing (n=10) male 105–118, female 101–109; tarsus 24.5–28.5; bill (culmen) 15.5–18.5. Weight 47–57 g.

REFERENCES Fjeldså & Krabbe (1990), Rasmussen *et al.* (1996), Schulenberg (1987).

136 EASTERN SLATY-THRUSH *Turdus subalaris* Plate 56

Merula subalaris 'Leverkuhn' = Seebohm, 1887, *Proc. Zool. Soc. London*: 557 – Jutuba, [presumably in the valley of the Rio Grande], São Paulo, Brazil.

IDENTIFICATION 20–21.5 cm (8–8½"). The distant eastern counterpart of Andean Slaty-Thrush (135), which it closely resembles but has paler and more uniform upperparts. Confusion species The grey plumage of the male makes it distinctive within the range and should cause no confusion with any other thrush of the region. Females, however, are extremely similar to a number of other thrushes, particularly White-necked Thrush (157), which is generally darker brown above and not tinged grey, the throat streaking is better defined and less closely streaked, and the flanks are washed orange. Creamy-bellied Thrush (144) is also similar but has a prominent yellow bill, black lores, very bold streaks on the chin and throat, no white crescent on the lower throat, generally paler underparts and a different habitat. The allopatric race *debilis* of Black-billed Thrush (146) is also extremely similar but more generally olive-brown above, brownish below with well defined areas of white on the belly to undertail-coverts and a much darker bill.

DESCRIPTION Sexes differ. Adult male As Andean Slaty-Thrush but upperparts slightly paler, more uniform with forehead and crown less black (may only show slightly darker centres to feathers) and whole upperparts bluish or light bluish-grey washed faintly with olive; wings and tail dusky-grey with pale grey edges to flight feathers; underwing-coverts white or occasionally pale grey. Lores dark grey, cheeks and ear-coverts deep ash-grey; thin yellow or orange-yellow eye-ring. Chin and throat white, becoming heavily streaked black on centre and sides of throat, and with prominent crescent of white on lower throat; breast to flanks uniform ash-grey, lower breast and centre of belly to vent and undertail-coverts pure white; thighs grey. Bill orange-yellow or with a blackish tip. Legs and feet yellow to pale orange. Adult female Similar to male but greyish-brown on head and upperparts, wings and tail duskier greyish-brown. Chin and throat white but brown streaks on centre reduced in extent and lower throat and upper breast has pale or whitish crescent, breast to flanks pale grey-brown becoming white on lower belly, vent and undertail-coverts. Bill yellowish-brown. Legs and feet yellow. Immature Juvenile very like same-age Andean Slaty-Thrush. Head and most upperparts dark olive-brown finely streaked pale buff or light orange-buff on central shafts, mantle and back similar but pale shaft-streaks larger or more visibly spaced; tips to median and greater coverts with pale buff spots. Underparts mottled white or buffish-white, and breast, belly and flanks barred with blackish-brown tips. Bill dark or dusky-horn. Legs and feet brown.

GEOGRAPHICAL VARIATION None. Monotypic.

VOICE Call a soft *tsuk*, given more sharply in alarm. Song a series of weak, hesitant, high-pitched, squeaky but musical notes with a bell-like tone (differs considerably from the jumbled ventriloquial phrases of Andean Slaty) beginning with a sharp thin whistle *tsree* followed shortly by *tsree tsing, tsing chewluh chewluh chuh, tsree ting, ting, ting sing, sing, sing kile, kile, kile, kile, kle, kli, kli, sree...* (Sick 1993), some notes given with more emphasis than others and the introductory *tsree* or concluding *sree* often repeated on its own between long pauses. Typical song perches are secluded branches high in the tree canopy; often sings in groups.

STATUS AND DISTRIBUTION Locally common; very common in the north but uncommon in the extreme south. South-east Brazil from north-central Mato Grosso, Goiás and western (and probably eastern) Minas Gerais to eastern and central Paraguay (south to about Depto. Paraguari, where extremely scarce to rare) and north-east Argentina (Misiones). In Brazil has extended its breeding range southward during the 20th century into Rio Grande do Sul.

MOVEMENTS Not fully understood, possibly an austral migrant; the northern limit of the breeding range is uncertain. It occurs in Minas Gerais in the breeding season and elsewhere in Mato Grosso and Goiás (where it is not reported breeding) during the austral winter, some birds lingering and even singing into October; returns to the breeding areas in late September and October.

HABITAT Mostly humid and dense riverine forest and woodland canopy up to about 1000 m (3300') but in parts of the range also in plantations (including eucalyptus), parks and villages or gardens with large trees. In parts of the range found in the same forested habitat as Yellow-legged (94), Rufous-bellied (141) and White-necked (157) Thrushes.

BEHAVIOUR Poorly known but not regarded as being as shy or wary as its western counterpart.

411

Usually alone or in pairs; sometimes associates with Rufous-bellied Thrush.

BREEDING Very poorly known or documented; probably very similar to that of Andean Slaty-Thrush.

MOULT No information.

MEASUREMENTS Wing (n=3) 108–115; tarsus 24–26.5; bill (culmen) 14–15, (to skull) 17–19. Weight apparently unrecorded.

REFERENCES Ridgely & Tudor (1989), Sick (1993).

137 PLUMBEOUS-BACKED THRUSH *Turdus reevei*　　　Plate 56

Turdus reevei Lawrence, 1870, *Ann. Lyc. Nat. Hist. New York* 9: 234 – Puna Island, Gulf of Guayaquil, Ecuador.

IDENTIFICATION 23–24 cm (9–9½″). A little known thrush of fairly restricted range from Ecuador to north-west Peru; distinctive blue-grey upperparts with slightly darker head and face, underparts creamy with a greyish breast. In good view best field character is the pale bluish-white eye and indistinct narrow eye-ring. **Confusion species** None likely; Andean Slaty-Thrush (135) primarily occurs in the Andes and has a dark eye, slightly darker grey upperparts and paler grey underparts.

DESCRIPTION Sexes almost alike. **Adult male** Entire upperparts slate bluish-grey, palest on forehead and sides of crown and darkest on centre of crown and nape; tail blackish but central pair and outerwebs to all outer feathers deep grey, edges of outermost only thinly edged. Median coverts deep grey slightly paler than rest of upperparts, greater coverts same with black central shafts; alula black very finely edged grey, primary coverts black broadly edged deep grey; flight feathers black or blackish-brown finely edged dark grey on primaries, becoming broadly edged deep blackish-grey on secondaries and tertials; underwing-coverts whitish with warm peachy-buff tips to greater underwing-coverts. Lores dark brown, cheeks and ear-coverts to sides of neck slate grey-brown with fine dark tips; indistinct thin white eye-ring. Chin and throat creamy- to buffish-white, heavily streaked greyish-brown on sides of throat; breast creamy-white or tinged greyish-buff, belly and flanks whitish with warm peachy-buff tinge on flanks; thighs off-white; vent to undertail-coverts white. Bill yellow. Eye light blue or pale bluish-white. Legs and feet pale yellow. **Adult female** Almost identical to male except for browner tinge to head and face. **Immature** Juvenile similar to adult except for darker olive-brown upperparts with extensive pale buff central shaft-streaks on forehead, crown and nape, mantle and back, becoming prominent on scapulars. Wings blackish-brown with fan-shaped buff spots at tips of median coverts, greater coverts pale with fine spots at tips of primary coverts and tertials. Face also dark olive-brown with fine pale buffish shaft-streaks on cheeks and ear-coverts. Underparts creamy-white

to -buff mottled with brown tips forming an unevenly scaled pattern. In first winter pale shaft-streaks on edges of scapulars and some pale tips to greater coverts retained and broad grey-brown bars on tips of breast feathers. Bill brown. Legs and feet light brown.

GEOGRAPHICAL VARIATION None. Monotypic.

VOICE Poorly known. Song a series of rapid musical, whistling notes given in a jumbled or rambling manner, often interspersed with a series of single descending whistled notes; several birds may sing in concert.

STATUS AND DISTRIBUTION Rare to seasonally locally common; in north-west Peru abundant in its limited range. Breeds in western Ecuador from Manabí and Pichincha (including Puna Island) north to the Río Palenque and south to Lambayeque, north-west Peru.

MOVEMENTS Not fully understood but becomes seasonally common in drier areas in the rains in the early months of the year.

HABITAT Tropical-zone forests and secondary woodlands, both humid and deciduous, up to about 1800 m (5940′), exceptionally to 2500 m (7590′), e.g. in Loja; also forest edges, clearings, quebradas and adjacent scrub areas. Most numerous in the Chongon Hills, Chimborazo, and further south in El Oro, Ecuador; common in Tumbes National Forest, northern Peru, and less common (but not uncommon) in Lambayeque.

BEHAVIOUR Little known but an arboreal species of middle stages to canopy level in forests, often forming sizeable concentrations of up to c.30 in fruiting trees, sometimes with Ecuadorian Thrush (153). Otherwise usually singly or in small groups, frequently feeding unobtrusively in trees and shady areas on the ground.

BREEDING Nest only recently discovered (Best *et al.* 1995). Season: January to at least March. Nest: a cup-shaped structure of dried grasses, fine twigs and dried leaves placed up to 2 m (6–7′) in a small tree.

MOULT No information.

MEASUREMENTS (n=6) Wing 112–126.5; tarsus 29.5–30.5; bill (culmen) 17.5, (to skull) 23–25. Weight 63–66 g (R. G. Pople pers. comm.).

REFERENCES Best *et al.* (1995).

138 BLACK-HOODED THRUSH *Turdus olivater*   **Plate 60**

Merula olivatra Lafresnaye, 1848, *Rev. Zool.* [Paris] 11: 2 – Caracas, Venezuela.

IDENTIFICATION 23–24 cm (9–9½"). Male very distinctive with bright yellow bill, eye-ring and legs, all-black head to nape and breast, olive-brown upperparts, and dull to bright buffish or rufous-buff underparts. Female similar but head and upper breast dark brown contrasting variably (depending on the intensity of brown) with the light olive-brown upperparts and warm buff-brown underparts. **Confusion species** Male is unlikely to be confused with any other species but female similar to females of both Yellow-legged (94) and Pale-eyed (95) Thrushes; separable on the uniform underparts, lacking any white or greyish-brown on the belly; also female Pale-eyed Thrush lacks an eye-ring. Female Glossy-black Thrush (134) is extremely similar but is darker brown above and lacks the faint contrast between the head to breast and rest of body. Clay-coloured Thrush (151) is more uniformly paler, dull sandy-brown with slightly duller breast and flanks, and has a dull greenish or olive-yellow bill, with no dark head or eye-ring.

DESCRIPTION Sexes differ. **Adult male** Forehead to hindcrown, cheeks, ear-coverts, chin, throat and upper breast black, thin yellow eye-ring; nape and sides of neck to rest of upperparts including wing-coverts and edges of flight feathers and tertials deep olive-brown; alula, primary coverts and innerwebs of flight feathers dark brown; underwing has coverts as breast and flanks, tips of greater coverts lighter orange. Tail blackish-brown narrowly washed olive at edges of outers. Rest of underparts from centre and sides of lower breast variable from sandy to ochre or buffish-brown washed olive extending to undertail-coverts, which have fine whitish central shafts and light olive tips. Bill yellow. Eye dark. Legs and feet dull or brownish-yellow. **Adult female** Similar to male but lacks well-defined black head, has paler head and only faint indication of hooded effect, thin pale yellow eye-ring; rest of upperparts slightly paler olive-brown; wings and tail not as dark as male. Chin and throat to sides of neck dull buff streaked brown and becoming washed dull yellowish-orange or orange-buff and extending to rest of underparts except for flanks and underwing-coverts, which are slightly darker orange. Bill dusky or dull yellow. Legs and feet yellowish-brown. **Immature** Juvenile as adult but with pale buff streaks on blackish crown and nape and dark brown cheeks and ear-coverts; narrow buffish streaks to mantle and scapulars and orange to orange-buff tips to wing-coverts. Chin and throat spotted blackish-brown on orange-buff ground colour becoming heavily blackish-brown bars and tips to breast and centre of belly.

GEOGRAPHICAL VARIATION Seven races; variation slight.

Race *roraimae* has black on head less extensive and merging with upperparts across hindneck and sides of neck, upperparts (extending to wing-coverts and edges of flight feathers and tertials) darker olive-brown than nominate, tail black or blackish. Chin and throat broadly streaked black and merging into dull olive-brown on lower throat, upper breast and sides of neck; breast to flanks and belly light orange washed dull olive, slightly paler on lower belly and undertail-coverts, latter also showing pale orange tips; sides of belly and flanks washed dull or dusky-olive extending to undertail-coverts with paler fringes. Underwing-coverts dull olive-brown edged pale orange. Female has chin and throat more clearly streaked and black extends from lores to ear-coverts and sides of nape; chin and throat dull olive-brown becoming dull olive on lower throat, streaked blackish (occasionally forming blackish malars); generally duller on underparts but some can be orange on belly and upper flanks.

Races *duidae*, *paraquensis* and *kemptoni* from the tepuis of southern Venezuela have black on chin and throat broken into streaks and underparts bright rufous-buff. *T. o. duidae* resembles *roraimae* but has a darker bill, larger tail and, on average, longer wings and bill. Race *kemptoni* differs from the other two by its darker, more greyish-brown abdomen; *paraquensis* from *duidae* by its darker upperparts and paler underparts (more obvious in the male).

Race *caucae* has head and face black and throat dingy whitish streaked black; breast and upper flanks greyish-olive becoming pale sandy-buff on belly to undertail-coverts; female like male but with dull brown hood; race *sanctaemartae* more like nominate but has breast pale brown and lower breast with olive-brown edges, rest of underparts pale brownish-olive.

VOICE Song a typical thrush-like series of very slow, hesitant musical phrases usually given loudly or deliberately, in pairs broken by short pause *too-doo*, *too-dee* or *chur-dee* and *chu-chee*, often separated by ringing *clee* or thinner *ee-ee* notes (Hilty & Brown 1986); also gives a softer, more melodious song containing similar notes but more usually a single repeated syllable. Sings mostly in the early morning and evening.

STATUS AND DISTRIBUTION Resident. Common or locally common, except race *caucae* (no recent reports and may now be extinct).

T. o. olivater Norte de Santander, northern Colombia and the adjacent coastal cordillera east to northern Guarico and Miranda, Venezuela; also central Venezuela from the Sierra de Perijá, Zulia, south-west Táchira, north-west Barinas, southern Lara to Falcón and Yaracuy.

T. o. sanctaemartae Santa Marta Mountains, Colombia.

T. o. paraquensis Cerro Paraque, Amazonas, Venezuela.

T. o. kemptoni Cerro de la Neblina, Amazonas, Venezuela.

T. o. duidae Cerros Yavi, Paru, Huachmacare

413

and Mount Duida, Amazonas, plus Cerro Tabaro, Bolívar, Venezuela.

T. o. roraimae Sierra de Lema, and the Gran Sabana of Bolívar and Amazonas, southern Venezuela, to Cerro Twek-quay, Guyana, and extreme Pico de Neblina, Roraima, northern Brazil.

T. o. caucae Central Andes from Patia valley (La Sierra) to Urubamba south of Popayán, Colombia. There are no recent reports of this race, which has been extremely threatened by extensive deforestation of the upper Cauca valley.

Taxonomic note As *T. o. caucae* is (or was) so distinct and so distantly remote from the nominate and other races, Ridgely & Tudor (1989) questioned whether it merited full species status, but concluded that as it is so poorly known it should for the present remain as a race of *T. olivater*.

MOVEMENTS Mostly resident but recently reported from Surinam (Donahue & Pierson 1982), possibly indicating a small population on the western border.

HABITAT Mostly in humid or cloud-forest of the tropical and subtropical zones, forest edges, clearings and more open woodland between 800 and 2300 m (2640–7600′), also coffee plantations with tall trees, open country with scattered trees and bushes.

BEHAVIOUR Very similar in most respects to many other forest thrushes but generally more approachable; frequently occurs on the forest floor but also in lower levels of trees up to the canopy. Food is mostly insects, berries and fruit.

BREEDING Season: January to July. Nest: a fairly large cup-shaped structure of plant material, lined with mud and moss. Eggs: 2–3; similar to those of White-necked Thrush (157) but slightly larger and more heavily marked.

MOULT No information.

MEASUREMENTS *olivater* wing, male 113–120, female 110–115; bill 21–23; *roraimae* wing, male 118–125; bill 24–25; *duidae* male 125–133; bill 25–26; *sanctaemartae* wing, male 119–121, female 112–122; bill 23–25; *caucae* wing, male 123, female 119; bill 24–25 (Hellmayr 1934). Weight apparently unrecorded.

REFERENCES Donahue & Pierson (1982), Hellmayr (1934), Hilty & Brown (1986), Ridgely & Tudor (1989).

139 MARAÑÓN THRUSH *Turdus maranonicus*　　Plate 56

Turdus maranonicus Taczanowski [ex Stolzman MS], 1880, *Proc. Zool. Soc. London*: 189, pl. 20 – Callacate, northern Peru.

IDENTIFICATION 21.5–23 cm (8½–9″). A poorly known but distinctive thrush with a restricted range from southern Ecuador and northern Peru. Head and upperparts brown with a faintly scaly pattern, underparts white but barred or scaled darker with arrow-marked spots on the breast becoming darker brown bars on the lower breast to flanks. **Confusion species** None likely except perhaps poorly seen juveniles, which may be confused with same-age Plumbeous-backed Thrush (137) but have paler buff flecks to the head and upperparts; all other juvenile sympatric thrushes have much heavier spotted plumage on upperparts.

DESCRIPTION Sexes alike. **Adult** Entire upperparts from lores and forehead to tail earth-brown to dark olive-brown, forehead to crown slightly darker and feathers of crown to back and scapulars edged darker, creating slightly scaly pattern; innerwebs of greater coverts, alula, primary coverts and flight feathers dark brown contrasting against paler brown outerwebs; axillaries and underwing has coverts whitish-buff, flight feathers creamy-white. Thin bluish-grey eye-ring, cheeks and ear-coverts brown flecked paler buff. Entire underparts white but chin and throat streaked brown becoming spotted with dark brown arrowhead streaks on sides of chin and throat and extending to breast, becoming dark brown bars at tips of feathers, forming crescents or spots on lower breast, belly and flanks; centre of belly to vent and undertail-coverts unbarred white. Bill quite large and deep at base, greyish-horn to olive-brown. Legs and feet bluish-grey. **Immature** Juvenile similar to adult but brown upperparts have broad pale buff central shaft-streaks to forehead, crown and nape, more widely spaced on mantle, back and scapulars; median and greater coverts also have pale orange-buff central shaft-streaks and broad pale orange tips. Ear-coverts brown with fine pale central shafts. Underparts as adult or slightly more heavily mottled or spotted with broad dark tips to feathers.

GEOGRAPHICAL VARIATION None. Monotypic.

VOICE Poorly known. The contact note is a frequent *bip* with a resounding nasal quality (M. Pearman pers. comm.); also a series of *chup chup* notes, and an alarm call similar to that of other thrushes. Song (unrecorded) consists of fairly typical *Turdus* thrush notes, quite melodious with a series of flute-like phrases but less musical than other thrushes of the region. Sings from high but often concealed perches in tree-tops.

STATUS AND DISTRIBUTION Common or locally common. Southern Ecuador, Zumba–Chito trail and Palanda, Zamora-Chinchipe province and the upper Marañón Valley and tributaries, north-west Peru, from Cajamarca, La Libertab and Piura.

MOVEMENTS Largely sedentary but reported to be a dry-season visitor to Tombillo, June–August (Seebohm 1902).

HABITAT Dry deciduous woodlands of the subtropical zone, also forest edge, mimosa and dry scrub, irrigated agricultural areas and mango groves, usually between 200 and 2000 m (660–6600′).

BEHAVIOUR Usually alone or in pairs but up to 6 may feed together in favoured spots. Mostly arboreal during the day and spends long periods in shaded parts of the forest; at dusk calls frequently and feeds in well-watered or moist areas apparently in search of worms. On alighting shivers tail nervously; when disturbed flies to low branch up to 3 m (10') from the ground and remains motionless except for shivering tail; frequently raises the crown feathers slightly.

BREEDING Unrecorded.

MOULT No information.

MEASUREMENTS (n=3) Wing 114.5–117; tarsus 29–31; bill 19.5–21.5. Weight apparently unrecorded.

REFERENCES M. Pearman in Best *et al.* (1997), Ridgely & Tudor (1989), Williams & Tobias (1994).

140 CHESTNUT-BELLIED THRUSH *Turdus fulviventris* Plate 49

Turdus fulviventris Sclater [ex Verreaux MS], 1857, *Proc. Zool. Soc. London*: 273 – Nova Grenada [= Bogotá].

IDENTIFICATION 23–25 cm (9–10"). A very brightly coloured South American thrush with a blackish head, grey upperparts and breast and rufous-orange belly, flanks and underwing-coverts. The only thrush of the northern Andes with an orange belly. **Confusion species** Bears greatest similarity to out-of-range Rufous-bellied Thrush (141), which has a browner head concolorous with the upperparts, heavily streaked chin and throat and brown, not grey, breast. Also rather like American Robin (161), which even in the northern winter occurs much further north and is more extensively red below, darker above, with white eye-crescents. **DESCRIPTION** Sexes similar but separable. **Adult male** Entire head to chin and throat, sides of neck and nape sooty brownish-black, slightly blacker on forehead to nape, some showing grey streaks on throat. Black on head sharply divided from slate grey-brown on lower nape to rump, uppertail-coverts, scapulars, inner wing-coverts and edges to tertials; dark brown outer greater coverts, alula and primary coverts; flight feathers also dark brown except for broad slate grey-brown edges to secondaries; in hand has long first primary (about half length of second). Tail dark blackish-brown, outer feathers paler. Sides of neck to breast grey or olive-grey tinged buff-brown; lower breast, flanks and belly bright orange or rufous becoming whitish on vent and grey or olive-grey on undertail-coverts. Underwing has coverts bright or warm orange, flight feathers silvery-whitish. Bill yellow to yellowish-orange. Eye dark with thin orange eye-ring. Legs and feet dull or yellowish-brown. **Adult female** Very similar to adult male but slightly duller or browner above; head browner-black and less sharply distinct from rest of upperparts, heavily streaked blackish on grey throat, cheeks and ear-coverts flecked grey. Legs and feet fleshy-brown. **Immature** Nestlings and juveniles very poorly known. First-year bird similar to adult above but crown and nape may be slightly darker with varying amounts of pale or orange-buff central shafts to upper mantle and scapulars. Median coverts have dull orange central shafts broadening slightly at tips, greaters have narrow orange-buff tips. Chin and throat to sides of neck and breast narrowly barred with pale orange and dark brown tips, becoming more prominent across upper breast; rest of underparts dull orange to orange-chestnut with browner tips forming bars on lower breast and flanks.

GEOGRAPHICAL VARIATION None. Monotypic.

VOICE Call a dull *peent*. Song a slow series of thrush-like phrases, given in a hesitant, deliberate manner recalling Black-hooded Thrush (138) but more musical in quality, with some sharper, higher-pitched single notes and others more extended into short trills: *che'e e-chert chee-rtee e'r'r, chu-wurt, titi, t't't', ett... peert... peet-peet... wit-wit... toooo-oo-oo...* May also contain other trills and buzzes (Hilty & Brown 1986) and mimic other species, e.g. Black-mandibled Toucan *Ramphastos ambiguus* (Hardy & Parker 1992). Sings from tops of trees usually within the canopy.

STATUS AND DISTRIBUTION Locally common to uncommon. North-west and western Venezuela south through the Andes from Trujillo to eastern Colombia in the East Andes in Norte de Santander north to the Perijá Mountains (east to north-west Zulia, Venezuela); head of the Magdalena Valley in Huila to the eastern slope of the East Andes in western Putumayo and eastern Nariño, Colombia, south through central and south-east Ecuador to northern and north-east Cajamarca (where fairly common), extreme northern Peru.

MOVEMENTS Sedentary.

HABITAT Resident between 1300 and 2700 m (4290–8900') of the subtropical zone in mossy cloud-forests particularly on steep hillsides, also forest edges including roadsides and clearings, secondary woodlands and in some shrubby areas; in northern Peru favours páramo with low bushes.

BEHAVIOUR Very similar to that of American Robin; usually alone or in pairs; often hops on ground and at all levels in bushes and trees where it forages for berries and fruit.

BREEDING Very poorly known. Season: January to June with fledglings and juveniles in February to July.

MOULT No information.

MEASUREMENTS (n=5) Wing 119–126.5; tarsus 30–33; bill (culmen) 20–20.5. Weight, male 71 g, female 69 g (Rahbek *et al.* 1993).

REFERENCES Hardy & Parker (1992), Rahbek *et al.* (1993).

141 RUFOUS-BELLIED THRUSH *Turdus rufiventris*   Plate 49

Turdus rufiventris Vieillot, 1818, *Nouv. Dict. Hist. Nat.* (nouv. ed.) 20: 226 – Brazil.

IDENTIFICATION 23–25.5 cm (9–10"). A thrush with very brightly coloured underparts from eastern and southern Brazil south to northern Argentina. Head, face and upperparts uniform olive-brown tinged greyish, chin and throat white, prominently streaked brown, becoming buffish or pale buffish-brown on the breast and bright orange or orange-rufous on rest of underparts. **Confusion species** The only other South American thrush with a bright orange belly – Chestnut-bellied Thrush (140) – occurs in the north-west, from Venezuela to Peru. Austral Thrush (142) from further south has a darker head to nape, much paler buffish or warm buffish-brown underparts and a bright yellow bill and legs.

DESCRIPTION Sexes alike but female (on average) slightly paler below. **Adult** Forehead to crown and nape olive or greyish-olive (sometimes extending onto face) becoming more heavily tinged olive-brown on mantle to scapulars, median coverts, inner greater coverts and edges to secondaries and tertials; outer greaters, alula, primary coverts and flight feathers dark brown finely edged paler or olive-grey on outerwebs of primaries; secondaries sometimes edged olive-brown. Rump and upper-tail-coverts mostly greyish-olive; tail greyish olive-brown or brown tinged with grey except for outers which are paler brown. Face grey-brown tinged olive, ear-coverts with fine pale or whitish central shafts. Chin and throat to sides of neck white spotted (particularly on adult female) or diffusely or prominently streaked brown, extending in some onto upper breast; upper breast tawny-buff, becoming yellowish- or greyish-buff and rich orange on upper belly, rufous-orange on lower belly, flanks and vent, axillaries and underwing-coverts; under surfaces to flight feathers pale silvery-yellow; undertail-coverts as belly or duller orange, thighs ashy or greyish. Upper mandible olive-yellow to yellowish-green, lower slightly paler. Eye sooty-brown or black. Eye-ring thin and yellowish to pale orange. Legs and feet variably grey to light pinkish- or purplish-horn. **Immature** First-winter bird resembles adult (may show retained juvenile feathers with pale orange-buff central shaft-streaks to outer scapulars) but median and greater coverts have dull orange spots at tips of coverts; tips to tertials also pale orange-buff. Chin and throat dull buffish-white, faintly spotted brown; breast dull yellowish, heavily but diffusely spotted brownish; belly pale orange, sometimes also spotted with brown tips (forming bars) extending onto flanks.

GEOGRAPHICAL VARIATION Two races; variation not well marked. Race *juensis* is, on average, paler above and on wings; breast creamy-buff, sometimes tinged grey, upper belly pale orange becoming orange on belly to flanks, underwing and undertail-coverts.

VOICE Call *djok*, *pup-pup*, *cluck cluck* or a rising but somewhat slurred *dru-uip* or *dru-wip*, recall-

ing similar notes of Pale-eyed (95), Ecuadorian (153) and Clay-coloured (151) Thrushes; alarm is a sharp *tsri*; also gives a range of chuckling or laughing notes at dusk. Song typically slow and thrush-like; in breeding season gives a loud melodious lilting series of varied phrases rich in tone, *koro koro – cheeere cheeeerie – tooodle*, less broken by pauses; also has a simple monotonous dialect song, *dewee-dewo dewee-dewo, fewri-tewri*, etc. (Sick 1993). In non-breeding season gives a different, more resonant song *juh-JOEit, drew-wip, drew-wip, drew-wip...* Sings mostly in the early morning and again at dusk, from a prominent or hidden perch in the tops of medium to tall trees (Ridgely & Tudor 1989, Fjeldså & Krabbe 1990).

STATUS AND DISTRIBUTION Common or locally common (possibly less numerous in north-east Brazil).

T. r. rufiventris Southern Brazil from southern Bahia west to central Mato Grosso, Paraguay (uncommon or rare in the north-east and west) and eastern Bolivia (south-east Santa Cruz), and south to Rio Grande do Sul, Uruguay and northern Argentina south to Córdoba and Buenos Aires.

T. r. juensis north-east Brazil from Maranhão, Piauí and Ceará to Paraíba and Pernambuco, also northern and western Bahia.

MOVEMENTS Sedentary.

HABITAT Lowland humid woodlands, groves, plantations, forest clearings and edges or patches of bushes and scrub, from sea-level to 2600 m (8580') in Bolivia; in the south occurs in gardens (including centres of cities like Rio de Janeiro and Buenos Aires), parks and edges of cultivation; in drier parts of the range is virtually restricted to areas near water (Ridgely & Tudor 1989). In southern Brazil it shares the same area of forest with White-necked Thrush (157), Cocoa Thrush (149) and Eastern Slaty-Thrush (136).

BEHAVIOUR In the west and south of its range a conspicuous and approachable bird but elsewhere considered shy and retiring, spending long periods hiding in dense foliage but occasionally seen hopping or running about on the ground near cover or venturing into the open on paths, forest trails and riverbanks. Feeds on the ground mostly beneath vegetation. Becomes active and vocal in the late afternoon before going to roost. Food is mostly invertebrates, especially earthworms, and fruit (mostly berries); also known to take very small fish and freshwater shrimps.

BREEDING Season: late August or early September to late December but eggs in Argentina October to January and dependent young in May. Nest: a large cup-shaped structure of roots and plant fibres with a lining of mud, dried grasses and small twigs usually up to 3 m (10') – exceptionally 12 m (c.40') – from the ground in the fork of a branch in a shrub or tree. Eggs 3–4, exceptionally 6, pale yellowish-green to greenish-blue and heavily spotted or blotched deep red or chestnut. Incubation period 13 days. Fledgling period 13–14 days. Probably two broods. Shiny Cowbird *Molothrus bonariensis* brood-parasitises nests but apparently without effect on the overall population (Lichtenstein 1998).

MOULT No information.
MEASUREMENTS (n=42) Wing, male 113–124.5, female 115–124; tarsus 29.5–35; bill (culmen) 17–20.5. Weight 78 g.
REFERENCES Lichtenstein (1998), Madroño *et al.* (1997).

142 AUSTRAL THRUSH *Turdus falcklandii*   Plate 60

Turdus falcklandii Quoy & Gaimard, 1824, in Freycinet, *Voy. Uranie Physicienne, Zool.* livr. 3: 104 – Falkland Islands.

IDENTIFICATION 23–26.5 cm (9–10½"). A long-legged, fairly plump thrush with dark head, olive-brown upperparts and slightly browner wings and tail; underparts rich buff-brown or tinged orange. Juveniles distinctively spotted with pale buff or sandy-buff below with heavy blackish tips. Widely distributed over much of southern South America and the only thrush on the Falklands. **Confusion species** Creamy-bellied Thrush (144), the only other thrush in the range of Austral, is initially similar but has a uniform brown head and upperparts and much paler underparts with a pale creamy-white belly to undertail-coverts and pinkish legs. **DESCRIPTION** Sexes almost alike. In worn plumage both adults become much paler. **Adult male** Forehead to crown, nape, lores, cheeks and ear-coverts blackish, slightly infused with paler brown centres to forehead and crown; pale yellowish-orange eye-ring. Lower nape to lower back, including greater coverts and edges to secondaries and tertials, warm brownish-olive; outer greaters, alula, primary coverts, flight feathers and innerwebs of tertials blackish-brown. Tail blackish-brown with olive-brown bases to central feathers. Chin and throat whitish-buff becoming yellowish on throat (and sides of throat), heavily spotted or streaked blackish-brown; lower throat and upper breast rich buff-brown becoming ochre-brown on sides of neck and more variably paler orange to darker on breast, belly and flanks to undertail-coverts; underwing-coverts as breast and flanks. Bill yellow to pale orange. Eye coffee or dark brown. Legs and feet long, yellow to bright yellow or orange-yellow. **Adult female** Very like adult male (often indistinguishable) but head often less deeply black and tinged warm buff-brown; upperparts sometimes paler or tinged olive-yellow. **Immature** Upperparts brown with prominent pale buff central shaft-streaks to head, nape, mantle, back and scapulars, slightly heavier on mantle and back with dark tips to feathers; median and greater coverts have pale buff to orange-buff spots at tips. Underparts yellowish to yellowish-orange on breast and belly, heavily spotted with heavy blackish-brown at tips of breast, belly and flanks and streaks on sides of chin and throat. Bill brown or brownish-horn. Legs and feet dull yellowish-brown.
GEOGRAPHICAL VARIATION Three races (others proposed but no longer accepted); differences not well marked and mostly clinal. Race *magellanicus*

(includes birds once separated as '*pembertoni*') has more greyish-olive upperparts, greyer on rump and uppertail-coverts, tail blackish with greyish outerwebs. Blackish forehead and crown often obscured by olive-brown fringes; chin and throat also paler but more heavily or extensively streaked blackish on sides of throat and upper breast, rest of underparts whitish, buffish-grey or light peachy-orange edged olive; in fresh plumage belly and undertail-coverts may be pinkish-buff. Female usually has black head and face less well defined and lower face as upperparts. Race *mochae* paler with, on average, a longer bill.
VOICE Commonest calls a low-pitched *huit*, a harsher rattling *wreet* or *sreep*, a sharp *trrrt trrrt* and a strong deep *choyz-choyz-choyz* in alarm; gives a *skwuk* or *squack* note at intruders in breeding territories (Woods 1988).
Song rather weak and unobtrusive, hesitant, broken and descending, *chew – chew – char – chear* (with slightly longer stress on last note), individual notes separated by short pause, but with some rich musical whistling or piping notes and some soft whistles and wheezes, e.g. *cheee – tsss-sss-sss*, and may include a series of half-hearted *chwee, dizee* or *dizwee* notes; some of the thin repeated piping notes form slow, sad, broken phrases; also imitates calls and songs of other birds in the vicinity; frequently repeats several phrases for many minutes. Sings mostly at dawn and dusk but may give shorter burst over the day in the early breeding season; song period late August to late December. In Falklands sings from any available high perch including tussock-grass clumps, exposed rocks, shrubs and trees, roofs of buildings, but also from the ground; in South America mostly from tree-tops or high in the canopy, sometimes from lower branches.
STATUS AND DISTRIBUTION Common resident.
T. f. falcklandii Falkland Islands.
T. f. magellanicus Central and southern Chile (south of Atacama) and the Juan Fernandez archipelago south to Tierra del Fuego, Staten Island and islands in the Beagle Channel, and in southern Argentina intermittently south from (but mainly in west of) Neuquén and Río Negro south to Santa Cruz.
T. f. mochae Mocha Island (Araucania), Chile.
MOVEMENTS Mostly sedentary but has been recorded (once) in austral winter north into Mendoza, Argentina. Of 200 ringed in Falklands

in seven years (1957–1963) longest-distance recovery was 3.6 km (R. Woods pers. comm.).

HABITAT In Falklands found mainly in areas of dense mature tussock-grass usually up to 3 m (11') high near boulder beaches with accumulated heaps of rotting kelp, also on upper slopes with rocky outcrops and tall fern *Blechnum magellanicum*, diddle-dee heathland, valleys with fachine *Chiliotrichum diffusum*, gardens with introduced trees, gorse patches and other shrubs. In South America occurs in a wide variety of forests or woodlands (notably southern beech in Argentina) up to c.2150 m (7100'), from open understorey to light woodland, secondary woods and edges of thick forest, plantations, parks, gardens and brush.

BEHAVIOUR Usually alone or in pairs and often inquisitive and tame. Spends much time on the ground where it hops and runs in search of prey, particularly on bare soil or in rotting kelp (in which it digs substantial holes, presumably for larvae and small crustaceans). Diet consists of worms, snails and a range of arthropods and their larvae; also berries and some fruit, particularly strawberries; in parts of the range readily comes to bird feeders and takes household scraps.

BREEDING Season: late August to December (Falklands), elsewhere September to February. Nest: a large deep cup-shaped structure of dry grasses, stems and roots, often including scraps of wool or pieces of string, lined with mud, cattle droppings or horsehair; up to 6 m (20') but mostly within 2 m (6.6') of the ground, in crevices between rocks or on the ground but secluded by grass or ferns, also in tussocks, cypress trees or bushes and frequently in sheds or outhouses. Eggs: 2–3, blue-green closely spotted brown or purple. Incubation period 14–16 days. Fledging period 16–18 days. Two or possibly three broods reared in a year (Woods 1988). Breeding information in South America less well known.

MOULT Juveniles begin losing their blackish ventral spots from about January onwards but some first-winter birds (probably late brood) may show irregular black spots or even a gorget in mid-April. First-year birds have usually replaced wing-coverts by mid-March but some may retain them to the end of September.

MEASUREMENTS Wing, male 134.5–142.5, female 128.5–136.5; bill (culmen), 24–26; tarsus 36–40. Weight 100–111 g (R. Woods pers. comm.).

REFERENCES Woods (1988).

143 PALE-BREASTED THRUSH *Turdus leucomelas*   Plate 51

Turdus leucomelas Vieillot, 1818, *Nouv. Dict. Hist. Nat.* (nouv. ed.) 20: 238 – Paraguay.

IDENTIFICATION 23–27 cm (9–10½"). A grey-headed thrush with warm brown upperparts, brown-streaked whitish throat, greyish-buff breast and flanks, and white central belly to undertail-coverts. Fairly common and widely distributed over much of northern South America. **Confusion species** Combination of grey head and face (although restricted on some to the nape) and warm brown upperparts distinctive. White-necked Thrush (157) has an all-brown head and upperparts, white unstreaked lower throat and grey breast and flanks. Creamy-bellied Thrush (144) has a bright yellow bill, brown head, heavily streaked throat and very pale creamy-buff breast and flanks. Black-billed Thrush (146) has an all-black bill, much darker brown head and upperparts and pale grey-brown breast. Cocoa Thrush (149) is much warmer or rufous-brown on head and upperparts, cinnamon or rufous-brown below.

DESCRIPTION Sexes almost alike. **Adult male** Forehead to nape, including sides of nape and around eye, grey to greyish-olive merging across nape to rust-brown tinged olive on mantle and upperparts, including edges to outer primaries, secondaries and innerwebs to greater and primary coverts; tertials darker brown. Underwing has coverts pale buff to bright orange, bases to flight feathers pale orange. Tail dark brown washed grey. Lores blackish; ear-coverts finely streaked with white central shafts. Chin and throat white, heavily streaked brown or blackish-brown; breast grey or greyish-buff (browner in fresh plumage) becoming tinged warmer on upper flanks; centre of belly to undertail-coverts white but latter diffusely marked with brown towards tips. Bill dull horn-brown with yellowish-brown or olive-yellow on lower mandible, more extensively darker in non-breeding season. Eye reddish or light brown. Legs and feet pale or horn-brown. In worn or summer breeding plumage upperparts duller or greyer. **Adult female** Identical to male but can have grey on head restricted to nape with rest of head brown or olive-brown; in hand can show warmer or light orange tinge to breast. **Immature** Juvenile similar to adult but has buff flecks or light streaks to centres of feathers of pale grey-brown forehead and crown, nape greyer with fine streaks extending to mantle and scapulars; median and greater coverts have broad pale orange spots at tips, edges to greater coverts, secondaries and tertials light orange-brown. Sides to chin and throat cinnamon-brown diffusely spotted brown, breast grey diffusely spotted darker brown.

GEOGRAPHICAL VARIATION Three races; differences not very well defined and largely clinal. Races *albiventer* and *cautor* are ash-grey on head, face and nape and on rump and uppertail-coverts, but some *albiventer* show brown to rust-brown on forehead; *albiventer* very similar to nominate but can, especially in fresh plumage, have russet-brown edges to flight feathers and tertials, and some show a light gingery-brown wash to mantle and back. Female *albiventer* slightly smaller and less heavily grey than male and some have head and face uniform with rest of upperparts. Birds from eastern Colombia west to French Guiana and northern Brazil, previously proposed as *ephippialis* on paler grey upperparts and grey, not brown, breast, are here treated as synonymous with *albiventer* as the differences are not constant and only evident in fresh-plumage birds.

VOICE Call a distinctive single or repeated and rather harsh or grating *wert, wert-wert-wert* or *shreh, shreh, shreh*, also *quwaak*; alarm note *cha cha, zit* or *zeezit* also given repeatedly. Prior to roosting gives a variable series of notes including *pseep, shuh-DEE-dididi... shrewee...* Song recalls several other thrushes in quality, particularly American Robin (161): a series of musical mellow (and typically thrush-like) phrases including *hereit, hereit, tuweeee* or *chreIT, chrewIT glewo CHEWluh, CHEWluh TIrewd TIrewd...* with the individual phrases repeated several times; may also give some (or subdued version of) harsh scratchy call notes at the start of, or following, the song. Song usually delivered at dawn and dusk from a secluded position in low to middle canopy. Birds in Argentina begin singing in September.

STATUS AND DISTRIBUTION Common or locally common.

T. l. leucomelas Southern Brazil from Rio de Janeiro west to southern Goiás and Mato Grosso south to east-central Paraguay (rare or uncommon south to Depto. Paraguari, also north-east and west), northern and eastern Bolivia (Santa Cruz and La Paz), eastern Peru (around Moyobamba in San Martín) and south-eastern Peru (Pampas del Heath, Madre de Dios) and extreme north-east Argentina (Misiones and Corrientes).

T. l. cautor Guajira Peninsula, Colombia.

T. l. albiventer Northern Colombia (Santa Marta to the upper Magdalena Valley, Tolima, and in the eastern lowlands south to Meta and Vichada), through Venezuela (except southern Amazonas), Guyana, Surinam, Guiana and most of northern Brazil (western and central Amazonas to the Tapajos–Amazon confluence but absent from eastern

Santa Catarina and Rio Grande do Sul) south to about Bahia, probably intergrading with nominate in central Brazil.

MOVEMENTS Sedentary.

HABITAT Edges of humid forests and clearings to dry or subhumid deciduous woodlands of the tropical and lower subtropical zones, also gallery forest, forest islands in open grasslands, dense thickets, pine plantations, often near water, from sea-level to about 1900 m (6270'), exceptionally to 2000 m (6600'); in some areas frequents pastures, edges of cultivation, parklands and gardens (including the suburbs of Caracas).

BEHAVIOUR Usually in pairs or small loose flocks, can be retiring but in some areas frequently feeds in the open on the ground (and may become tame); also feeds in low to mid-height trees. Runs rapidly on the ground; flight usually low and fast through the trees. In Santarem, Brazil, has been seen foraging at night under electric lights (Sick 1993). Often becomes active or vocal prior to roosting. Food is mostly insects and their larvae and fruit.

BREEDING Season: January to August or throughout the year, e.g. eggs in October in north-east Argentina. Nest: a cup-shaped structure mainly of moss, roots, small vines and similar fibrous plant material bound together with mud, dry grass and small roots; usually in a shrub, creeper or tree-stump or on a building up to 3 m (10') from the ground, occasionally on the ground on a bank; built by female only. Eggs: 2–3, pale bluish-green to pale bluish-white, spotted with reddish-brown. Fledged young in May. Incubation period 12 days. Often brood-parasitised by Shiny Cowbird *Molothrus bonariensis*.

MOULT No information.

MEASUREMENTS Wing (n=10) male 113–121, female 113.5; tarsus 27.5–32; bill (to feathers) 16–17.5 (to skull) 23; *albiventer* (n=27) wing, male 116.5–125, female 113–121. Weight, male 55–67 g, female 47–76 g.

REFERENCES Sick (1993).

144 CREAMY-BELLIED THRUSH *Turdus amaurochalinus*   Plate 52

Turdus amaurochalinus Cabanis, 1851, *Mus. Hein.* 1: 5 – Brazil [restricted to Rio Grande do Sul by Pinto (1944) *Cat. Aves Brasil* (Publ. Dept. Zool., Sao Paulo) pt. 2: 370].

IDENTIFICATION 22–25 cm (8¾-10"). An olive-brown thrush with pale underparts ranging from southern lowland Brazil to central Argentina. Best distinguished by its very erect stance when on the ground, bright yellow bill (when breeding), blackish lores, heavily streaked throat and creamy-white belly to undertail-coverts. **Confusion species** Most like Pale-breasted Thrush (143), which has a grey head, pale lores, richer rufous mantle, back and wings, less heavy streaks on throat and paler bill; also more extensively buffish-brown below. Black-billed Thrush (146) race *debilis* overlaps the wintering range and possibly

confusable with female or immature Creamy-bellied by the white belly to undertail-coverts; readily separated by the all-black bill, much browner plumage and lack of well-defined streaks on the throat. White-necked Thrush (157) is darker above with an orange-yellow eye-ring and heavily streaked throat above a brighter white crescent across the upper breast.

DESCRIPTION Sexes alike except bills. **Adult** Forehead to crown and nape olive-brown with slightly darker centres; rest of upperparts slightly paler olive-brown or tinged grey, especially on rump and uppertail-coverts. Tail olive-brown on central pair and edges to all outers, rest brown. Wing-coverts as upperparts; alula, innerwebs to primary coverts and flight feathers brown to dark brown, outer edges to primary coverts and flight feathers pale olive-brown; tertials olive-brown. Underwing has coverts pale yellowish-orange to orange-buff, secondaries light orange at base. Lores to eye black or blackish-brown, eye-ring dark brown, cheeks and ear-coverts olive-brown, slightly darker than that on upperparts. Chin and throat pale whitish-buff, heavily streaked blackish-brown on lower throat; centre of lower throat often unstreaked white. Breast and flanks buff or buffish-brown, becoming slightly browner on lower flanks; belly to vent and undertail-coverts creamy-white; thighs grey or greyish-olive. Sometimes breast pale grey or greyish-olive, centre of lower breast white and belly buffish. Bill bright yellow in male, horn or dull yellow at base and duskier towards tip in female; outside of breeding season bill of male blackish and more like female's. Legs and feet light brown to blackish. **Immature** Juvenile slightly duller or browner than adult with pale buff central shaft-streaks to crown, nape, mantle and back, those on mantle and back much larger. Median and greater coverts also have pale buff central shaft-streaks becoming pale orange-buff spots at tips to broken or disjointed wing-bar. Fine or small pale orange-buff tips to tertials. Face heavily mottled or flecked pale yellowish-buff with dark brown bars. Chin and throat whitish-buff, spotted or mottled with dark brown streaks. Breast and flanks yellowish or buff heavily barred brown on flanks; belly whitish and faintly barred brown at tips. Undertail-coverts dull yellowish-buff mottled brown. Bill dull or dusky-brown.

GEOGRAPHICAL VARIATION None. Monotypic.
VOICE Call a sharp mewing note and a soft or low *pok*, *bock* or *back*; in flight, or about to fly, gives a thin *pseep* or *psib*; alarm or distress call is a sharp *chup* or *pup*, also a cat-like *pshewo* or *pchuo*. Song a series of typical thrush phrases but jumbled, rambling, repetitive, monotonous and seemingly half-hearted, with by long pauses between phrases: *yo Plant AY, nAAo nasSAYoo, aprodraySAYoo, FREEo, FREEo* (Sick 1993); usually from a high open perch at the tops of trees.
STATUS AND DISTRIBUTION Common or locally common. Breeds in southern Brazil (southern Mato Grosso, Minas Gerais and Rio de Janeiro; exact northern limits of breeding range uncertain)

west to western Bolivia (to La Paz) and south through Paraguay and Uruguay to northern and central Argentina (south to Neuquén and Río Negro). In austral winter occurs north into southeast Peru (Puno, Madre de Dios and south-east Ucayali) and central and northern Brazil (to south and east Pará and northern Maranhão).
MOVEMENTS Partial or erratic migrant. Occurs north of the breeding range during the austral winter from the end of April or early May to October, but considerable numbers remain within the breeding range, south to northern Argentina. Northbound migrants have been noted in Rio de Janeiro from 20 April to early May and return south from about July. Recorded once in Atacama, Chile.
HABITAT Mainly a lowland species of the tropical and subtropical zones, but occurs up to 2100 m (6930') (in Cochabamba and Chuquisaca, Bolivia) in semi-open habitats from humid, subhumid and dry areas mainly along forest edges, clearings, small woods and thickets, and in southern parts of the range in edges of cultivation, parks and large gardens including around large cities. In parts of southern Brazil often found in the same area of forest as Black-billed Thrush. Austral migrants in south-east Peru occur in large gardens and on small farms.
BEHAVIOUR Usually alone or in pairs and generally very retiring; occasionally, in non-breeding season and on migration, in small flocks. Found in trees or bushes; generally less often on the ground than other thrushes of the region, but has an upright stance and runs erratically with wings drooped and, with tail, jerked or flicked upwards; shakes or quivers tail vertically on landing. Feeds mostly on fruit.
BREEDING Little known. Season: October to December; fledglings noted in February and March in Bolivia and northern Argentina (de la Peña 1995, M. Pearman pers. comm.). Nest: a deep cup-shaped structure of plant fibres mixed with mud and occasionally with fragments of nylon and thread, lined with rootlets, usually 1–8 m (26') from the ground in bushes or trees. Eggs 3, rarely 4; green spotted with grey, chestnut or brown. Brood-parasitised by Shiny Cowbird *Molothrus bonariensis*.
MOULT No information.
MEASUREMENTS Wing (n=48) male 113–125, female 118–122; tarsus 28–32; bill (culmen) 15–20. Weight, male 52–67, female 50–63 g.
REFERENCES Hartert & Venturi (1909), de la Peña (1995), Sick (1993).

145 MOUNTAIN THRUSH *Turdus plebejus*   Plate 57
(Mountain Robin, American Mountain Thrush)
Turdus plebejus Cabanis, 1861, *J. Orn.* 8 (1860): 323 – Costa Rica.

IDENTIFICATION 23–26 cm (9–10¼"). A dull olive-brown thrush of Central America (sometimes considered conspecific with Black-billed Thrush [146] of South America), almost entirely uniform but slightly paler on the central belly to

the undertail-coverts with some faint streaks on the chin and throat; the all-dark bill is also a useful feature. **Confusion species** Similar to Clay-coloured Thrush (151) but much greyer-olive and with an all-dark bill. Pale-vented Thrush (148) also has a blackish bill but Mountain usually occurs higher, is more uniformly darker and has pale greyish-olive spots, not white, on the lower belly to undertail-coverts. Black Thrush (133) male is black with yellow bill and eye-ring (present also in immature males); female has all-dark bill but yellow legs and feet, lacks the paler throat and has buffier-brown undertail-coverts. Immature Rufous-collared Robin (162) is almost entirely darker grey with a yellow bill.

DESCRIPTION Sexes alike. **Adult** Entire upperparts olive-brown but lores to eye, forehead to nape, and tail slightly warmer brown; mantle, back, rump, uppertail-coverts, wings, edges of scapulars and tertials more heavily tinged olive; outer greater coverts, alula and primary coverts brown, but latter also edged olive-brown. Underwing-coverts pale buffish-brown edged light orange. Chin and throat dull whitish-buff or greyish on throat and diffusely streaked darker, rest of underparts dull greyish-brown on sides of breast, belly and flanks; centre of lower belly whiter extending to undertail-coverts, which are diffusely spotted brown. Bill black or blackish horn-brown. Eye hazel-brown. Legs and feet horn- or dark brown. **Immature** Juvenile like adult but darker olive, with pale buff to light cinnamon shaft-streaks to most upperparts and pale orange-buff tips to median and greater coverts (some of which are retained into first-winter plumage). Juvenile also mottled buff below, paler on throat and spotted with darker brown tips to buff bases on breast, belly and flanks; belly more plainly pale or greyish-buff. First-year bird closely resembles adult but has retained wing and tail feathers and greater coverts may show pale buff tips into first spring.

GEOGRAPHICAL VARIATION Three races; differences not well marked and some authorities (e.g. Hellmayr 1934, Monroe 1968) merge *rafaelensis* with *differens*. Race *differens* slightly more olive or tinged olive-brown on upperparts, particularly crown and nape and wings and tail; underparts lack grey tones and more heavily tinged olive or light olive-brown on breast and flanks (some birds, possibly female, show grey-brown on breast and upper belly), streaks on chin and throat fainter and virtually invisible in the field, undertail-coverts dull whitish edged pale olive. Race *rafaelensis* intermediate between nominate and *differens* and slightly darker brown above, with indistinct streaks on throat and buffier-brown undertail-coverts; also differs slightly in measurements.

VOICE Calls include a variety of frequently given (including in flight) *whip whip* or *pip pip*, occasionally *kwek-kwek* or *chowk-chowk* notes; a low *toc* similar to the deeper, more aggressive *tock tock tock* alarm usually given on territory, but also gives the typical throaty chuckle or cackle when disturbed or alarmed; in flight has a high-pitched, thin, nasal *seee* or *peeent*. Song a

distinctive sustained machine-like series of erratic unmusical sharp piping notes varying little in pitch: *chir chip chip cher chip chip cher cher tsup chip...* occasionally broken by a harsher *chirk cheep churry chirk chirk chip cher...* (Skutch 1960, 1967). Song usually given from a high concealed perch at dawn, through the morning and early afternoon; frequently sings in rainy weather. Song period early April to about the first week of June.

STATUS AND DISTRIBUTION Common or locally common.

T. p. differens Pacific slope of south-east Oaxaca and Chiapas, Mexico, to interior and Caribbean slope in Guatemala.

T. p. rafaelensis Highlands of Honduras to Los Esesmiles, El Salvador, and north-western Nicaragua.

T. p. plebejus Mountains of Costa Rica to Chiriquí and Bocas del Toro, western Panama.

MOVEMENTS Partial or altitude migrant, moving to lower levels, down to c.900 m (2970') during the wet season, and returning to higher ground in January and February.

HABITAT Tall evergreen cloud-forests, open woodlands and forest edges of the subtropical and lower temperate zones above 1800 m (5950') to the treeline (about 2725 m/9000' in El Salvador), particularly oaks and those with an abundant growth of epiphytes, mosses, liverworts and ferns; also edges and clearings, pastures and grassy areas with scattered moss-covered trees; outside the breeding season frequents secondary growth and small stands of fruiting trees away from the mountain forests (Skutch 1967).

BEHAVIOUR Usually alone or in pairs in the breeding season, at other times forms small to medium-sized flocks. An active bird but not always easy to see as it can be wary of intruders but also occasionally perches at the tops of tall trees. Actions as many other thrushes; hops when on the ground. Forages on the ground but mainly in trees at medium to high levels, also in epiphyte-covered branches. Food mainly arillate seeds, a wide variety of berries, and invertebrates.

BREEDING Season: March–June. Nest: a spacious cup of green moss and leaves such as bamboo, lined with black roots and fine grasses, placed in an epiphyte, moss-covered branch, vine or fork 3–12 m (10–40') up in a tree, including isolated trees outside the forest. Eggs: 2–3, bluish-green unmarked.

MOULT No information.

MEASUREMENTS Wing, male 128–143, female 129.5–138; *differens* wing 130–141.5; *rafaelensis* wing 127–134.5; bill (culmen) 20–24; tarsus 30–35 (Hellmayr 1934, Dickey & van Rossem 1938). Weight apparently unrecorded.

REFERENCES Dickey & van Rossem (1938), Hellmayr (1934), Monroe (1968), Stiles & Skutch (1989).

Turdus ignobilis **Sclater, 1857,** *Proc. Zool. Soc. London*: **273 – Nova Grenada [= Bogotá].**

IDENTIFICATION 21.5–24 cm (8½–9½"). A rather dingy thrush of large areas of northern South America. Generally dull or deep olive-brown with slightly paler underparts, brown-streaked whitish chin and throat (race *debilis* has a white crescent across the lower throat) and white on the central belly to undertail-coverts. **Confusion species** Very like several other thrushes of the region. Pale-vented Thrush (148) is slightly warmer brown without the olive tinge to the upperparts, has brighter or cinnamon-brown underwing-coverts usually visible in flight, a warmer brown lower breast, upper belly and flanks, and more finely streaked chin and throat on a duller yellowish-brown ground colour. Hauxwell's Thrush (150) is less olive and warmer earth-brown above, warmer buff-brown below, bill dark grey or dark brown but not black; it is more likely to occur in forest than Black-billed. Lawrence's Thrush (147) has a yellow bill and eye-ring. Female Yellow-legged Thrush (94) is similar to Pale-vented but has more prominent streaks on the chin and throat and a narrow yellow eye-ring, pale or dull yellowish legs and feet and dull whitish (buff-tinged) centre of belly to undertail-coverts. Female Pale-eyed Thrush (95) has yellow legs and feet, indistinct chin and throat streaks and much less extensive pale centre of belly to undertail-coverts. Creamy-bellied Thrush (144) is more extensively white or pale creamy-white below and has a bright yellow bill. White-necked Thrush (157) is very similar to race *debilis* but has much paler, greyer underparts and darker olive-brown head and upperparts; grey, not pale buff underwing-coverts, narrow yellow eye-ring, much heavier streaks on the flanks, larger white patch on the lower throat and upper breast, and paler bill. White-throated Thrush (156) is like White-necked but with dull brown breast and flanks and a yellowish bill.

DESCRIPTION Sexes alike. **Adult** Entire head and face to upperparts including edges of scapulars, median and inner greater coverts, tertials and uppertail-coverts, dull olive-brown; outer greater coverts, alula, primary coverts and innerwebs to flight feathers dark brown, edges to secondaries and tertials grey or greyish olive-brown. Tail brown with paler brown outer feathers and olive-brown central feathers. Lores to eye, cheeks and ear-coverts dark brown. Chin and throat whitish, diffusely streaked or spotted pale brown extending to lower throat; sides of throat to breast and sides of breast dull grey-brown tinged olive, extending as greyish buff-brown wash to flanks; centre of belly to vent and undertail-coverts white or creamy-whitish. Underwing-coverts dull buff to off-white but edges of greater underwing-coverts finely light-orange buff. Bill dark brown or black. Eye light brown. Legs and feet dark brown. **Immature** Juvenile similar to adult but has crown and nape to

back, mantle and scapulars flecked or streaked pale orange-buff; median and greater-coverts have pale orange-buff central shaft-streaks and small spots at tips. Underparts light or creamy-buff spotted diffusely with brown on chin and throat, more heavily spotted or streaked on breast to flanks; centre of belly to undertail-coverts white diffusely barred or spotted with brown.

GEOGRAPHICAL VARIATION Five races; most differences clinal and not particularly well marked; mostly concerns intensity of colour of head and upperparts.

Race *goodfellowi* slightly warmer or darker olive-brown on head and upperparts; chin and throat whitish prominently but diffusely streaked with fine brown, sides of chin and throat to breast much deeper brown-buff, becoming paler on sides of lower breast and flanks to underwing-coverts, or slightly darker on lower flanks; underwing-coverts lightly tipped orange-buff; centre of belly to vent and undertail-coverts white.

Race *arthuri* much darker greyish or grey-brown on face, sides of neck and upperparts, slightly heavier or sooty-grey on sides of head; wings similar but tinged olive or olive-brown; underparts predominantly pale greyish tinged buffish-olive on breast and flanks and underwing-coverts pale orange-buff.

Race *debilis* birds similar to nominate or very slightly darker but has slightly smaller bill, chin and throat more extensively white, streaked pale brown; breast paler grey or greyish-buff extending to lower sides of breast and upper flanks; centre of belly to undertail-coverts pure creamy-white. Underwing-coverts pale buff becoming light orange-buff on tips of greater underwing-coverts.

Race *murinus* darker in tone than nominate with olive-brown on head and upperparts, including wings and tail, underparts similarly darker with chin and throat white, spotted or becoming streaked with brown on throat and sides of throat; sides of neck and breast brown washed with grey, rest of underparts pale whitish-grey washed with light brown on lower flanks; undertail-coverts white.

VOICE Gives a soft *bok* contact note and a sharper, higher-pitched *sree* alarm. Song fairly typical of several South American thrushes, especially Creamy-bellied Thrush, also (the more distant) American Robin (161); generally a rapid continuous series of fairly soft, pleasant, musical or fluting phrases which may begin with a *wert* note and includes several *your-your-we*, *tu-lee* or *su-wee* phrases (second or concluding phrase usually upwardly inflected) often repeated in pairs, some ending in a slurred manner. Sings infrequently from an exposed perch, e.g. tree-top, mostly around dawn, much less after midday.

STATUS AND DISTRIBUTION Common.

T. i. ignobilis Western slopes of the Central

Andes, Antioquia and Caldas and the Magdalena Valley from Santander south to Huila, eastern Colombia.

T. i. goodfellowi Cauca Valley from Quindío south to Cauca, and the Pacific slope from northern Antioquia south to Cauca, Colombia.

T. i. debilis Eastern slope of the East Andes in Norte de Santander and Boyacá and sporadically east to southern Amazonas, Colombia; Táchira, Mérida and western Apuré and Barinas, Venezuela; eastern Ecuador east to central Amazonas, Brazil east to lower Rio Negro and upper Rio Tapajos, central Peru and northern Bolivia (south to Cochabamba and western Santa Cruz).

T. i. murinus Southern Venezuela from Cerros Yavi, Guanay and Camani and subtropical zone of Mts Duida and Paru, Amazonas, and in Bolívar on the upper Río Caura and the cerros of the Gran Sabana to the foothills of Roraima and Merumé Mountains, Guyana.

T. i. arthuri Lowlands and lower slopes of Mts Yapacana and Duida, Amazonas, southern Venezuela, east to Guyana and Surinam.

MOVEMENTS Sedentary.

HABITAT Subtropical and tropical zones; edges of low forests to the tops of some tepuis, mainly in clearings or lightly wooded areas, often near water; also grassy plains with tall gallery woods to parks, pastures, gardens and suburban areas mainly between 900 and 2100 m (2970–6950')

but recorded up to 2800 m (9240') in the eastern Andes of Colombia; in Ecuador mainly up to about 1300 m (4290') in eastern foothills. In parts of the range (western Colombia) frequents gardens and lawns. In Brazil often occurs in the same area of forest as Creamy-bellied Thrush.

BEHAVIOUR Usually alone or in pairs; a conspicuous bird, often seen hopping or walking on the ground (but less terrestrial in eastern parts of the range); also forages in bushes and trees. Food mostly worms and insects, plus some fruit and berries.

BREEDING Not well known. Season: all year. Nest: a large, coarsely built cup-shaped structure of local plant material and some mud, usually placed low in a bush or tree, occasionally on a tree-stump. Eggs: 2, pale blue, heavily spotted with brown.

MOULT No information.

MEASUREMENTS Wing (n=10) 114.5–120; tarsus 29–31; bill (culmen) 16.5–18.5; *goodfellowi* (n=6) wing, male 112–118, female 110–115; tarsus 27.5–30.5; bill 15–16; *debilis* (n=11) wing, male 108–115, female 104–110; bill (culmen) 16.5–17.5, (to skull) 17–19; *murinus* (n=13) wing, male 118–123, female 116–119; bill (culmen) 16–18.5, (to skull) 19–21; *arthuri* (n=2) wing 104–105; tarsus 28; bill 16.6–18.5. Weight apparently unrecorded.

REFERENCES Hilty & Brown (1986), Meyer de Schauensee & Phelps (1978).

147 LAWRENCE'S THRUSH *Turdus lawrencii*   Plate 52

Turdus lawrencii Coues 1880, *Bull. U.S. Geol. Geog. Surveys Terr.* 5, no. 4: 570 – upper Amazons.

IDENTIFICATION 21.5–23 cm (8½–9"). An almost uniform olive-brown thrush with slightly paler breast and flanks and white belly to undertail-coverts; has a prominent bright yellow eye-ring and a yellow (male) to dusky (female) bill. Extremely shy, very hard to locate even when singing, and only rarely seen in the open; most notable for its extensive vocal powers, being one of the best mimics in the world, sustaining perfect imitations of other birds (up to 50 species per session) for several hours. **Confusion species** Visible confusion possible with any of the following, but singing birds unmistakable. Cocoa Thrush (149) is much warmer or cinnamon-brown above and below, lacks an eye-ring and usually shows an all-dark bill. Hauxwell's Thrush (150), with which Lawrence's frequently occurs, lacks bright yellow eye-ring, is generally paler or more rufous-brown above and has much stronger dark streaks on the throat and a dark grey or brown bill. In the hand it has a longer second primary than Hauxwell's which falls between 5th and 7th – Hauxwell's falls between 7th and 9th. Pale-vented Thrush (148) has a pale grey head, brighter brown upperparts, dusky (not brown) and paler buff underparts. Yellow-eyed Thrush (152) is duller brown above and

below with a pale yellow bill and a large bright yellow area around the eye. Female from similar Black-billed Thrush (146) by thin yellow eye-ring, dull but not black bill and lack of white on the lower throat. For differences from extremely similar, but out-of-range, Unicoloured Thrush (154) see that species.

DESCRIPTION Sexes almost alike. **Adult male** Entire upperparts deep olive-brown, slightly darker on crown and paler olive-brown on face and sides of neck; prominent bright yellow eye-ring; wings all dark, dusky-brown with medium and greater-coverts and edges to flight feathers olive-brown as on upperparts. Tail more dusky-brown than upperparts with olive tinge to outer feathers. Lores sooty-black. Chin and throat whitish, heavily streaked brown or blackish-brown; sides of throat light brown tinged olive, paler olive-brown on sides of lower breast and flanks; lower flanks heavier brown, centre of belly to vent whitish, undertail-coverts dark brown, tipped pale grey-brown. Underwing-coverts pale cinnamon to pale orange. Bill in breeding season bright yellow with dark tip, dark horn-brown in non-breeding season. **Adult female** From male by slightly narrower eye-ring, duller yellow bill and slightly paler underparts.

423

Immature Juvenile similar to adult on upperparts except for pale orange-buff streaks to crown, nape, mantle and scapulars, and pale orange-buff spots to tips of median and greater coverts (retained into first-winter plumage). Underparts paler than adult, generally pale buffish or olive heavily spotted or blotched blackish-brown. Bill dark or dusky.

GEOGRAPHICAL VARIATION None. Monotypic.

VOICE Mostly silent but makes distinctive soft *kuk* and a sharp or piercing *peer*, possibly uttered together as *kuk-cheer* in alarm; variations include *perwheee* or *weecheee* or a repeated *pedep peep peep*; often responds to playback of calls (but not song).

An extremely accomplished mimic when singing, considered by some to be the best bird mimic in the world; only rarely is the song not interspersed with imitated notes of other species. A loud, unhurried but continuous series of virtually perfectly imitated songs, phrases or calls of other species within the general area of the bird, including tinamous, cuckoos, antbirds, parrots and grosbeaks; also includes calls of frogs and insects. The delivery is halting, as if the singer is choosing the next species to imitate; one individual was noted mimicking up to 50 other species (Hardy & Parker 1992), whilst studies of 30 birds produced a total of 173 bird species imitated (full list in Hardy & Parker 1997). Birds that do few or poor imitations (i.e. unrecognisable species) are thought to be young, whilst the more accomplished mimics are several years old. The song is given throughout much of the day, including the hottest parts, sometimes for several hours almost without a break or with only short breaks of up to 15 minutes, during which the bird is presumably feeding or drinking. It is usually delivered from a regular, secluded perch in the topmost canopy where the singer is frustratingly hard to see and its presence is only betrayed by the song; singer does not respond to playback tapes and hence considered solely to be advertising to a female. Within-year pattern variable: in southern Peru recorded April–October but in northern Peru most vocal January–February, silent May–September (Hardy & Parker 1997).

STATUS AND DISTRIBUTION Uncommon or local; possibly overlooked. Upper Amazonia in Amazonas and Bolívar, Venezuela, to western Brazil (east to the Negro and Tapajos rivers) south to northern Mato Grosso, south-eastern Colombia (to western Putumayo and Vaupés), eastern Ecuador, north-eastern Peru (Pebas and Chamicuros) and north-western Bolivia (Pando and La Paz).

MOVEMENTS Sedentary.

HABITAT Wooded swamps, along streams and up to 500 m (1650') in areas of seasonally flooded low-lying humid dense rainforest in the transitional zone between *terra firme* and *várzea*; often absent from apparently suitable habitat (Hardy & Parker 1997).

BEHAVIOUR Generally shy and unobtrusive, probably overlooked in many parts of the range; most likely to be detected only when singing. Spends much time high in trees where it remains hidden from view except when making short flights through the canopy; occasionally in mixed-species flocks. Forages especially at mid-level in fruiting trees and on the ground where it searches through the leaf-litter in damp areas. Food unknown but probably worms, insects and fruit.

BREEDING Very poorly known. Season: probably November to March, but possibly all year. Nest: typically cup-shaped, mostly of grass and mud and placed on branches or between bromeliads and the trunks of trees, usually over water in flooded forest.

MOULT No information.

MEASUREMENTS Wing, male 112–120, female 109–113; tarsus 24–25; bill 15.5–19.5 (Hellmayr 1934). Weight apparently unrecorded.

REFERENCES Davis *et al.* (1994), Hardy & Parker (1992, 1997).

148 PALE-VENTED THRUSH *Turdus obsoletus*   Plate 52

***Turdus obsoletus* Lawrence, 1862, *Ann. Lyc. Nat. Hist. New York* 7: 470 – Panama Rail Road, Atlantic side of the Isthmus of Panama.**

IDENTIFICATION 21.5–23 cm (8½–9"). A dark brown thrush of southern Central America and western Colombia with rufous-tinged upperparts, bright orange underwing-coverts, and white lower belly to undertail. **Confusion species** Very like several other dark thrushes of the region but allopatric from much warmer, more rufous Hauxwell's (150) and Cocoa (149) Thrushes. In Central America Clay-coloured Thrush (151) is much lighter brown with a pale greenish bill and no white belly to undertail. Mountain Thrush (145) is similar in overall plumage tones but lacks white belly to undertail. In Colombia, Black-billed Thrush (146) is darker, less rufescent and without the bright orange underwing-coverts; race *debilis* of the eastern Andes to southern Amazonas has a more extensive area of white on chin and throat.

Taxonomic note This species and the following two (Cocoa and Hauxwell's Thrushes) are closely allied but the exact nature of the relationships is unclear and this has led to a range of treatments over the last 50 years (at least one subspecies has been assigned to two species as here constituted: see Geographical Variation under Cocoa Thrush). Hartert (1920) and Hellmayr (1934) classified all three as races of Cocoa but Gyldenstolpe (1945) found evidence that Hauxwell's and Cocoa are sympatric in several areas of Brazil. Hauxwell's and Cocoa are perhaps more closely related than either is to Pale-vented, as the latter is more montane. However, Ripley (1964) classed both Cocoa and Hauxwell's as separate species and Pale-vented as a race of Cocoa. Meyer de Schauensee (1966, 1970) also separated Cocoa and Hauxwell's but considered Pale-vented a race of Hauxwell's. Snow (1985) looked at the species complex in great depth from museum skins and found considerable variation in the contact zone between *fumigatus* and *hauxwelli* although individuals of both types were more associated with their own type. He concluded however, that all populations should be treated as conspecific pending further investigation. However, Ridgely & Tudor (1989) separated all three as allospecies (parts of a superspecies) based on habitat and altitudinal preferences together with morphological characters. Further investigation into behavioural and breeding aspects of the birds together with DNA analysis will reveal a better understanding of their relationships, and until such time we follow the arrangement in Ridgely & Tudor (1989).

DESCRIPTION Sexes almost alike. **Adult male** Entire upperparts rich brown with warm rufous tinge to mantle, back, scapulars, rump and upper-tail-coverts. Tail brown but central pair rich brown. Wing-coverts as scapulars with some pale orange-buff tips to greater coverts, flight feathers brown but edged warm cinnamon-brown; underwing has coverts pale orange but carpal area brownish-olive. Face brown but streaked grey-brown with pale buff-brown shaft-streaks. Chin and throat pale whitish-buff flecked or finely spotted darker or buff-brown with indistinct streaks on sides of throat. Breast dingy brownish-buff or tinged olive, becoming slightly darker on flanks; centre of belly and vent either as breast and flanks or white to under-tail-coverts. Bill dark horn to blackish-brown. Eye chocolate-brown. Legs and feet brown, olive- or grey-brown. **Adult female** Probably indistinguishable when seen alone but in pairs are slightly paler or duller. **Immature** Juvenile slightly duller than adult with deep brown on forehead to nape and mantle, back and scapulars, most of which have pale central shaft-streaks and (usually) largest or most prominent on edges to scapulars. Lesser coverts have orange-buff central shaft-streaks and pale orange tips, median and greater coverts dull orange triangular spots at tips and fine pale orange-buff tips to tertials and edges of longest uppertail-coverts. Chin and throat mottled from off-white tinged brown to pale orange-buff and brown spots becoming browner on breast with paler yellowish centres and dark brown bars at tips; belly and flanks paler off-white or light yellowish-buff with small or indistinct brown bars; lower flanks duller or washed olive-brown. Centre of lower belly to undertail-coverts off-white. Some birds, presumably later in first year, like adult but with fine pale central shafts to crown and upper mantle and dull orange tips to median and greater coverts.

GEOGRAPHICAL VARIATION Three races; variation clinal and not well marked. Most variation concerns overall brown tones of head and upperparts; nominate intergrades through *colombianus* to *parambanus*. Race *colombianus* very similar to nominate but on average paler or more fulvous-brown above and on edges to wing-coverts and flight feathers; breast and flanks are tinged olive. Race *parambanus* slightly darker brown above and central tail feathers uniform with rest of tail; lacks any rich brown tones; centre and lower belly white.

VOICE A thin dry twittering *bzeeek* and throaty *wuk, wak* or rising *weep*, often repeated several times; alarm note is a series of successively rising querulous whistles, often given in an agitated manner at dusk by birds going to roost. Immature birds make weak parrot-like squawks and trills. Song typically thrush-like in quality; similar to the long musical caroling phrases of Clay-coloured but richer, less varied, frequently interspersed with *tewee* or *weeooweet* phrases and more rapidly delivered. Usually sings from hidden perch high in canopy.

STATUS AND DISTRIBUTION Common resident in Costa Rica, becoming uncommon or local in Panama and Colombia.

T. o. obsoletus Caribbean slope of Costa Rica north to Cerro Santa María and south through Panama where it also occurs on the Pacific slope in Veraguas on Cerro Campana and Cerro Azul, the Caribbean slope in San Blas and in eastern Darién to the borders of extreme north-west Colombia (western shore of Gulf of Urabá).

T. o. parambanus Pacific slope of West Andes of Colombia from Valle south to Ecuador (Esmeraldas and Pichincha).

T. o. colombianus Eastern slope of West Andes of Colombia from middle Cauca Valley (Valle) to upper Patia valley (Cauca).

May be more widespread in Colombia than previously thought: a male collected in the Magdalena Valley in September 1997 represents the most easterly record of the species but subspecific status was not determined (Stiles *et al.* 1999).

MOVEMENTS Largely sedentary but in Costa Rica descends to lower elevations (regularly to 100 m/330', occasionally to sea-level) after breeding. Single instance of vagrancy or possible range extension further south in Ecuador: one recent record in El Oro (Ridgely & Tudor 1989).

HABITAT Breeds from 500 to 1500 m (1650–4950'), exceptionally to 200 m (660') in Pichincha, Ecuador; in the upper tropical zone through the subtropical and into the lower montane zones in humid and wet forests, also gallery forests. Occurs mainly in deep forest but sometimes forest edges and tall secondary growth, usually in the foothills of the Central American cordilleras and lower slopes of the Andes.

BEHAVIOUR Generally shy and alone or in pairs, but in Costa Rica in the non-breeding season it is found in loose, roving flocks of up to 30. Essentially a tree-loving bird usually at mid- to upper canopy levels where it is very inconspicuous; also forages amidst leaf-litter but nowhere near as terrestrial as Hauxwell's and Cocoa Thrushes. Unlike most *Turdus* thrushes appears not to flick its tail. Feeds on small fruits, seeds, berries and insects.

BREEDING Season: April–May. Nest: a large untidy bulk of leaves, fibres and mud with moss on the outside, lined with fine, usually dark roots and fibres; usually placed up to 18 m (60') on a branch covered in, or even inside, epiphytes or occasionally in crown of tree-fern. Eggs: 2–3, pale bluish-green, finely spotted or blotched with pale or dull reddish-brown at the larger end.

MOULT No information.

MEASUREMENTS Wing, male (n=7) 117–129.5, female (n=6) 110–122; tarsus 29–31.5; bill (cul-men) 17–19 (to skull) 20–23; *colombianus* wing, male (1) 110; *parambanus* wing, male (2) 115–120, female (4) 110–116. Weight apparently unrecorded.

REFERENCES Gyldenstolpe (1945), Hellmayr (1934), Ridgely & Tudor (1989), Snow (1985), Stiles *et al.* (1999).

149 COCOA THRUSH *Turdus fumigatus*   Plates 52, 53

Turdus fumigatus Lichtenstein, 1823, *Verz. Doubl.*: 38 – Brazil [restricted to Rio Espirito Santo, by Hellmayr (1934) *Field Mus. Nat. Hist. Publ.* Zool. Ser. 13(7): 385].

IDENTIFICATION 21.5–24 cm (8½–9½"). An almost uniformly warm rufous or cinnamon-brown thrush of the south Caribbean and South America, lacking any olive tinge to the plumage but with varying amounts of white on the belly; throat whitish, streaked brown. **Confusion species** Only problems may be Lawrence's (147), Pale-vented (148) and Hauxwell's (150) Thrushes (see taxonomic note under Pale-vented and comment at start of Geographical Variation below), but neither is as rufous or cinnamon and Cocoa usually (not always) has a buffier belly and a paler yellow bill. Lawrence's is darker brown and has yellow eye-ring and bill. Hauxwell's is also darker above and tinged olive below, vent to undertail usually much whiter. Allopatric Pale-vented is also darker but tinged russet-brown above, only lightly streaked on the throat and usually has whiter vent to undertail and an all-dark bill.

DESCRIPTION Sexes alike. **Adult** Entire upperparts brown, varying in intensity from plain brown on head and neck to rufous or warm cinnamon-brown on lower mantle, back and rump, brightest or deepest on uppertail-coverts; same colour on edges to scapulars and wing-coverts, deeper cinnamon-brown on edges to secondaries and tertials; inner-webs to coverts and flight feathers deep brown. Underwing has coverts pale orange and deeper orange on tips to greater coverts, secondaries pale orange. Tail dark cinnamon on central feathers and edges to all outers, rest of tail dark brown. Ear-coverts have pale shafts or tips. Chin and throat dull white or yellowish-white streaked brown or pale brown; breast, flanks and belly uniformly dull cinnamon or orange-brown; centre of lower belly and vent white, undertail-coverts whitish with orange-brown edges and tips; thighs pale buffish-brown. Some birds, particularly females, duller below, with no orange or cinnamon, and much duller buff-brown or brown. Bill mostly brownish-horn or dingy yellow. Eye dark reddish-brown. Legs and feet light horn-brown. **Immature** Juvenile generally deep ruddy-brown with fine pale or orange-buff flecks to crown and spots on nape, and variably broad or narrow central shaft-streaks to mantle, back and scapulars; tips of longest upper-tail-coverts may also be slightly paler; more heavily orange-brown on lesser coverts, and orange-buff shaft-streaks becoming spots at tips of

median and greater coverts; edges to median and greater coverts rich russet-brown extending to edges of secondaries and tertials, and more narrowly on primaries, rest of innerwebs of flight feathers and tail dark brown. Chin and throat off-white to dull yellowish, mottled or indistinctly spotted browner, breast with yellowish to light orange-buff centres and dull brown tips forming bars; belly and flanks same but paler or yellowish with finer dull brown tips; lower belly and vent (possibly to undertail-coverts) may be whitish.

GEOGRAPHICAL VARIATION Five races; differences largely clinal and not well marked. The racial affinity of some of these forms requires further scrutiny; *orinocensis* is here considered a race of Cocoa Thrush (following the treatment by Ridgely & Tudor (1989) but has previously (Meyer de Schauensee & Phelps 1978, Hardy & Parker 1992) been assigned to Pale-vented Thrush. Moreover, some authorities (Howard & Moore 1980) consider *bondi* and *personus* as a full species, Lesser Antillean Thrush *Turdus personus*.

Race *personus*, on average, slightly darker above than nominate except for dark rufous tones to wings, rump, uppertail-coverts and base of tail; underwing-coverts orange-buff, more heavily buff in some birds; underparts dull buffish-brown faintly tinged orange on breast and belly; under-tail-coverts white, streaked browner on central shafts and edged paler brown.

Race *bondi* slightly smaller and very similar to *aquilonalis* but duller and more uniform olive-brown, less rufous on mantle and back, and with warm brown or dark rufous-brown edges of wing-coverts, flight feathers, rump and uppertail-coverts. Chin and throat white heavily streaked brown, rest of underparts washed grey buff-brown or isabelline, slightly warmer on flanks, centre of belly to undertail-coverts white, latter streaked brown.

Race *aquilonalis* similar to nominate but paler brown above and has chin and throat whitish variably streaked finely or heavily pale brown; rest of underparts much paler with uniform light orange-brown on breast and flanks and lighter on central belly; undertail-coverts whitish or washed orange-buff. Bill dark or grey-brown. Legs and feet pale grey-brown to slate-brown.

Race *orinocensis* doubtfully (in the field) separable from nominate but upperparts, on average, slightly darker or browner and less rufous (but more rufous than *aquilonalis*), underparts paler or more olive; white on belly less extensive and undertail-coverts buffish-white.

VOICE A harsh *bak* contact note, a *chuck* or *cluck* flight note, and a harsh scraping rapid *chat-shat-shat* or *kik-ik-ik-ik* alarm call. Song a series of musical phrases, mostly consisting of short, largely warbled phrases, *teew-too*, repeated with some variation, *john pierre oh – john pierre oh – mi yes, mi yes, mi yes* occasionally ending in an *sree*; also a burst of rapid *deww-eh deww-eh deww-eh..., wee-a-wee-a-wee-a...* or *fee-ow fee-ow* repeated and descending in pitch, incorporated into the main phrases of the song. Usually only given in breeding season, when several males can be heard singing together in an evening chorus.

STATUS AND DISTRIBUTION Common (Trinidad), locally common to uncommon (South America).

T. f. bondi St Vincent, Lesser Antilles.

T. f. personus Grenada, Lesser Antilles.

T. f. aquilonalis Trinidad and northern Venezuela from Sucre west along the coastal cordilleras to Yaracuy and eastern Lara, also north-west Zulia to southern end of Lake Maracaibo and northern Táchira; north-east Colombia at Palogordo and Petrolea, Norte de Santander.

T. f. orinocensis Venezuela, in two (possibly three) widely separated areas, (a) east of the Andes in southern Táchira to northern Barinas, (b) along the upper Orinoco in Amazonas from Nericagua to Cano Casiquiare. Snow (1985) considered there to be an isolated small population in central Colombia but range now considered to be contiguous.

T. f. fumigatus Venezuela from Delta Amacuro and eastern Bolívar through Guyana and Surinam east to northern Brazil (northern Maranhão to eastern Pará) west and south to lower Rio Negro and Rio Madeira to central Mato Grosso and Goiás. Also Atlantic coastal forests from Pernambuco to about Rio de Janeiro.

MOVEMENTS Sedentary.

HABITAT Mostly lowland forests (below 1000 m/ 3300') but also in montane forests of the tropical and subtropical zones to about 1800 m (5940') in Venezuela north of the Orinoco, including dense tropical forest and lighter deciduous secondary growth woodlands, gallery forests, forest edges and clearings, open woodlands and plantations (mostly cocoa), usually near water, especially streams or swamps; in parts of the range enters gardens. In southern Brazil often found in the same area of forest as Rufous-bellied (141) and White-necked (157) Thrushes.

BEHAVIOUR Generally shy, retreating into cover when disturbed but in places appears to be more frequently encountered, e.g. in roadside ditches in northern Trinidad. Usually alone or in pairs in lower vegetation and understorey of forests or on the ground. Forages low down or on forest floor but also climbs higher in fruiting trees and the upper canopy. Feeds on invertebrates, especially ants and their larvae, also fruit and berries.

BREEDING Season: all months of the year except September but mostly February to July (Trinidad). Nest: bulky structure of plant and vegetable material, reinforced with mud, covered with moss and lined with finer roots; usually placed up to 5 m (16½') from the ground in holes in trees or on stumps or crowns of tree-ferns, occasionally on the ground in a sloping bank. Eggs: 2–3, exceptionally 4, pale greenish-blue mottled or blotched with light reddish-brown. Incubation period 12.5–13.5 days; solely by female. Fledging period 13–15 days.

MOULT No information.

MEASUREMENTS Wing (n=35) male 111–118, female 106–111; tarsus 33–36; bill (culmen) 15.5–20; *bondi* (n=16) male 113–120, female 110–118.5; *aquilonalis* (n=17) wing, male 109–118, female 104–119; *orinocensis* male 106–112, female 102–113; bill (culmen) 23–25, female 22–24. Weight, male 55.5–75 g, female 66.5–83 g.

REFERENCES ffrench (1973), Hardy & Parker (1992), Meyer de Schauensee & Phelps (1978), Ridgely & Tudor (1989), Snow (1985), Zimmer & Phelps (1955).

150 HAUXWELL'S THRUSH *Turdus hauxwelli*   Plate 52
Turdus hauxwelli Lawrence, 1869, *Ann. Lyc. Nat. Hist. New York* 9: 265 – Pebas, Peru.

IDENTIFICATION 23 cm (9"). Sometimes considered a race of Pale-vented (148) and Cocoa (149) Thrushes (see taxonomic note under Pale-vented Thrush). A uniformly brown thrush of lowland forests of much of western Brazil to eastern Ecuador and south-east Colombia. Generally shy and easily overlooked in low level dense vegetation in the depths of humid forest. Almost featureless, it differs from several other similar thrushes within the range in finer plumage details. **Confusion species** Closely resembles Cocoa, Black-billed (146) Lawrence's (147) and Unicoloured (154) Thrushes. Cocoa occurs mainly north and east of the range but may overlap in places, and is brighter or more rufous-brown notably on breast and upper belly, generally becoming buffish on belly to undertail (but some can be whitish-bellied while some Hauxwell's can have buff-tinged belly and undertail). Black-billed is duller brown and tinged olive above, with less distinct throat streaking and, in race *debilis* which occurs throughout much of Amazonia, more extensively whitish on chin and throat; it is less a forest species than Hauxwell's and more likely to occur in cleared areas. Lawrence's occurs in similar forest habitat to

427

Hauxwell's but is darker brown above (including head) and dingier olive-brown below, with a bright yellow bill and (in male) yellow eye-ring; in the hand Hauxwell's has a shorter second primary (between the 7th and 9th primary) than Lawrence's (between 5th and 7th on Lawrence's). From Unicoloured by darker brown (rufous-tinged) upperparts, including wings and tail, paler underparts with white on the central belly and undertail-coverts (latter may be washed buff) and buffish-white underwing-coverts (pale brown in Unicoloured, which has whitish chin and throat indistinctly streaked sandy-brown, rest of underparts dull sandy-buff or buffish-brown and narrow orange eye-ring).

DESCRIPTION Sexes alike. **Adult** Entire head and upperparts dark brown with rufous or cinnamon-olive tinge to mantle, back and rump, becoming richer on uppertail-coverts and darker rufous-brown on central tail feathers and edges to all outers; rest of tail dark brown; wings dark brown with warm brown or chestnut on outerwebs of flight feathers; underwing-coverts orange or deep orange. Cheeks and ear-coverts finely streaked or flecked pale buff, sometimes with thin olive eye-ring. Chin and throat white heavily streaked dark brown; breast, sides of belly and flanks warm earth-brown or tinged buff; centre of belly (from centre of lower breast) to undertail-coverts white, latter with pale brownish tips. Bill dark grey or dark brown, sometimes showing yellowish tip. Legs and feet grey. **Immature** Juvenile similar to adult but slightly richer brown above and with fine central shaft-streaks on crown and nape and slightly heavier on mantle and scapulars, those on scapulars becoming orange or orange-buff at edges; tips to median and greater coverts pale orange or orange-buff. Face finely streaked pale; underparts dull orange-buff, spotted or mottled darker with brown or dark brown edges and tips, heaviest or most densely spotted on breast.

GEOGRAPHICAL VARIATION None. Monotypic.

VOICE Song a distinctively slow, rambling series of fluty whistled phrases, rising and falling in pitch, containing *see-you*, *lee-du* and *plee-uuu* phrases,

also a more structured *see-it-ooo, wit-tuu, woo-it* and interspersed with softer, almost subdued churrs or trills and longer querulous whistled phrases. Also an accomplished mimic (includes Pied Lapwing *Vanellus cayanus* and Ringed Antpipit *Corythopsis torquata* in its repertoire) and known to give perfect imitations of other species within the area.

STATUS AND DISTRIBUTION Scarce or uncommon; common around Amazonia Lodge, Madre de Dios, Peru. Southern and south-east Colombia (Putumayo, Amazonas and Vaupés), eastern Ecuador and eastern Peru, west across western and central Amazonas, Brazil, to the Rio Madeira and north probably to the lower Rio Negro, in the south to northern Bolivia (La Paz and north-west Santa Cruz). Snow (1985) considered (from examination of skins) that populations along the middle Amazon, lower Madeira and lower Purus rivers were intermediate with Cocoa Thrush.

MOVEMENTS Sedentary.

HABITAT Found mostly in dense humid lowland forests (both *terra firme* and *várzea*), secondary forest and re-grown areas, usually near water and including forested islands in rivers up to about 800 m (2640') but very rare above 400 m (1320') in Ecuador.

BEHAVIOUR A shy, elusive and retiring thrush of dense undergrowth and lower to mid-canopy levels of humid forests where it is easily overlooked; most frequently seen foraging on the ground in clearings, forest edges or along riverbanks. Spends most time, alone or in pairs, low down in vegetation or on the ground foraging for invertebrates such as worms; also in fruiting trees.

BREEDING Unknown but probably not greatly dissimilar to that of the closely related Cocoa Thrush.

MOULT No information.

MEASUREMENTS Wing, male 112–120, female 107–120; tarsus 25.5–28; bill (culmen) 17–17.5. Weight 49–73 g (Hellmayr 1934).

REFERENCES Gyldenstolpe (1945), Hartert (1920), Hellmayr (1934), Meyer de Schauensee (1966, 1970), Ridgely & Tudor (1989), Snow (1985).

151 CLAY-COLOURED THRUSH *Turdus grayi* Plate 54
(Gray's Thrush)

Turdus Grayi Bonaparte, 1838, *Proc. Zool. Soc. London* (1837): 118 – Guatemala [restricted to Alta Vera Paz. Guatemala, by Griscom (1930)].

IDENTIFICATION 23–26.5 cm (9–10½"). The common or familiar thrush replacing American Robin (161) over much of its range from southern Mexico and Central America (apart from the high mountains) to north-west South America. An almost uniform dull or clay-brown thrush with slightly darker or more olive-brown upperparts, a whitish throat diffusely streaked, and a dull greenish-yellow bill and similarly (but somewhat variably) coloured legs. **Confusion species** In Central America similar

to both Mountain (145) and Pale-vented (148) Thrushes, both of which have black bills; moreover, Mountain Thrush is much darker brown and lacks the pale buff-brown underparts; Pale-vented has a white lower belly to undertail-coverts. Both Yellow-eyed (152) and Ecuadorian (153) Thrushes are allopatric, the former (with which Clay-coloured is sometimes considered conspecific) having a large yellowish-flesh eye-ring and white central belly to undertail-coverts, while Ecuadorian has a thin yellowish-orange eye-ring and more usually occurs in forests. Pale-breasted Thrush (143) occurs in range of Clay-coloured but has a grey head and nape and greyish-white to white on the central belly; the upperparts are slightly warmer and the edges of the flight feathers more rufous-brown. Female Black-hooded Thrush (138) overlaps in north-east Colombia but Black-hooded usually above 800 m (2640') with a usually yellow (can also be dusky) bill, thin yellowish eye-ring and generally darker brown underparts, particularly on the chin to breast, which is an indistinct version of the black head and breast of the male.

DESCRIPTION Sexes alike. **Adult** Entire upperparts uniform dull clay- or cold coffee-brown, including median and inner greater coverts and central tail feathers; outer greater coverts, alula, primary coverts and flight feathers darker brown on inner-webs, tertials also darker brown but outers to secondaries and tertials thinly edged with colour of upperparts; forehead and crown occasionally show some darker centres. Outer tail feathers darker coffee-brown than rest of upperparts. Face and sides of neck slightly darker brown than upperparts. Chin and throat pale buff, diffusely streaked darker brown becoming light orange-buff or tinged brown on lower throat; streaks on some extend to lower throat and upper breast, sides of neck and upper breast; slightly paler orange-buff or sandy on rest of underparts. Underwing has coverts slightly heavier orange, flight feathers pale orange. Bill greenish-horn to olive-yellow, paler or more yellow on lower mandible; brighter in breeding season. Eye dark brown or reddish-brown. Legs and feet variable from dull pinkish to pale slate-grey or greenish-brown. Some individuals, particularly females, are often paler below and tinged grey or greyish-buff on breast and pale or whitish-buff on breast to belly and vent. **Immature** Juvenile similar to adult but has dark brown upperparts with blackish tips to mantle and back, fine pale buff streaks to crown, nape, mantle, scapulars and median coverts, latter with fine, pale buff tips (and probably greater coverts). Chin and throat dull buff becoming yellowish on throat; lower throat and upper breast heavily spotted or blotched dull brown, breast and belly yellowish-orange obscured by diffuse dull brown bars at tips of feathers. Bill dusky- or horn-brown. Legs and feet horn-brown. **First-year bird** Closely resembles adult but juvenile median and some greater wing-coverts and some flight feathers retained into first summer.

GEOGRAPHICAL VARIATION Six races; variation clinal and not well marked. Race *umbrinus* much richer brown above and brighter on breast, belly and undertail-coverts, lighter brown on flanks; becomes paler overall when worn and confusable with birds of following race. Race *tamaulipensis* very similar to nominate but slightly paler or greyer above and noticeably paler or creamy-buff on breast, belly and flanks; some are pinkish-buff on lower belly and undertail-coverts in fresh plumage. Race *microrhynchus* poorly separated from *tamaulipensis* but has, on average, slightly shorter tarsus and bill. Race *casius* also very like

nominate but browner-olive above with underparts deep (clay-coloured) buff-brown on breast, flanks and underwing-coverts, and paler buffish tinged light orange on belly to undertail-coverts. Race *incomptus* similar to *casius* but slightly duller or washed pale buff on breast to central belly, flanks brownish or coffee-brown washed grey, vent to undertail-coverts pale off-white lightly washed yellowish-orange; underwing-coverts also paler buffish-brown.

VOICE Call a slurred or querulous and cat-like rising *quirre, jerereeee, hoouree, clee-ee-eu, sreer, keyaah* or *keyoooo*, especially used in contacting young and when going to roost; and a drawn-out, nasal *wee-ee-gwa* and nuthatch-like *ung-ung-ung* as well as some typical thrush-like chuckling notes including *tock tock*, sometimes varied with *kluh-kluh* or *pup pup pup pup*, etc.; also a high thin *siii* or *sip* note in flight. Song a very rich, musical, mellow series of clear, caroling, rhythmic, typical thrush notes including trills, warbles, whistles and some high-pitched piercing notes recalling American Robin, but considerable variation between males across range. Sings at various times of the day but particularly in the early dawn and at dusk. Song period usually only before and during breeding period, January to August in the north, and March to October in Costa Rica and further south; may give brief fragments of subsong usually in the early morning.

STATUS AND DISTRIBUTION Common to locally abundant in Central America, less common or locally common in south of range.

T. g. grayi Eastern and southern Mexico (except the area occupied by *tamaulipensis*), the Sierra Madre range in eastern San Luis Potosi, Veracruz, Puebla, Hidalgo, Oaxaca (including around Oaxaca City where probably derived from cage-birds of uncertain race), Tabasco and Chiapas (except the extreme south) to eastern Guatemala, Belize, El Salvador, Honduras and Nicaragua.

T. g. tamaulipensis South-east Texas (where a scarce resident in Rio Grande valley; see Movements), U.S.A., eastern Mexico from southern Tamaulipas to central and southern Nuevo León, the lowlands of south-east San Luis Potosi, Veracruz, northern Tabasco, northern Chiapas, Campeche, Yucatán, Quintana Roo and the islands of Meco, Mugeres and Cozumel to Lake Petén in northern Guatemala.

T. g. microrhynchus Interior of south-central San Luis Potosi to Querétaro, Mexico.

T. g. umbrinus Extreme southern Chiapas, Mexico, and the Pacific coast lowlands of Guatemala.

T.G. casius Costa Rica, Panama on both Caribbean and Pacific slopes (except for Darién) and northern Coloumbia (northern Chocó east to Guarjira Peninsula and south to southern Bolívar).

T. g. incomptus Northern Colombia (Barranquilla to Santa Marta Peninsula).

MOVEMENTS Resident in southern Texas, where it has bred, with peak occurrence December–March (mostly Rio Grande Valley State Park, Brownsville, as far north as San Ygnacio and inland as far north as Huntsville); *umbrinus* may also be a sporadic winter visitor to El Salvador.

HABITAT Principally a bird of moist, damp or wet open lowland woods and edges of cultivation (e.g. coffee and banana plantations) in the tropical and lower subtropical zones, up to about 300 m (990'), but reaches the timberline at about 2450 m (8000') in Central America; forest edges and clearings but outside the breeding season occurs deeper in broadleaved forests and dense secondary growth or scrub, also scattered trees, orchards, clearings and gardens, even in the suburbs of large cities, including San José, Costa Rica, where it favours open lawns, usually in dry areas.

BEHAVIOUR Mostly alone or in pairs but small flocks gather to roost (often with other species) and at common source of food. Behaviour similar to many other (especially northern hemisphere) thrushes; in parts of the range a familiar bird in suburban areas – taking the place of the northern American Robin – but further south not always conspicuous and much warier; dowdy plumage assists in avoiding detection; but aggressive in defence of nest. Many habits recall other thrushes, particularly American Robin; habitually flicks wings open briefly on landing, whilst also raising and gently lowering closed tail. Outside the breeding season occasionally forms roosts in groves of trees. Forages in bushes, low vegetation and the canopy of fruiting trees, also on the ground where it works through fallen leaf-litter. Feeds mainly on worms, slugs, insects (frequent at ant trails) and their larvae, occasionally small lizards, plus seeds and fruit, notably figs, frequently occurring in numbers at fruiting trees; in parts of the range often attracted to garden feeders.

BREEDING Season: March to July (Costa Rica), March to May (Colombia), December to late April (Panama). Nest: a large, sturdy but fairly shallow cup-shaped structure of loose (often living) vegetation, grasses and plant stems held together with mud and lined with coarse fibres, roots or leaves, often covered with moss; placed low down or up to 10 m (30'), exceptionally to 30 m (100'), from the ground in a fork in a bush or low tree or on a well-covered tree-stump, often well hidden in foliage; occasionally in bananas or coconut palms, and in the highlands frequently utilises crowns of epiphytes. Eggs: 2–3, exceptionally 4, pale green or blue or pale greyish-blue and variably marked with heavy rufous- or rusty-brownish spots or lilac blotches. Incubation period 12 days; by the female. Fledging period 15–16 days; nestlings fed by both adults. Occasionally second brood.

MOULT First-year birds complete their moult by the end of August; adults commence in mid-August and complete by mid-September.

MEASUREMENTS Wing (n=55) male 116–132.5, female 110–130.5; tarsus 28–34; bill (culmen) 17–23; *tamaulipensis* (n=27) wing, male 116–128, female 116.5–128; *casius* (n=23) wing, male 110–129, female 110–128; *umbrinus* (n=3) 109–122; *incomptus* wing 105–112; *microrhynchus* tarsus (n=2) 33–35. Weight 76 g.

REFERENCES Dickey & van Rossem (1938), Howell & Webb (1995), Skutch (1960), Stiles & Skutch (1989).

152 YELLOW-EYED THRUSH *Turdus nudigenis*   Plate 51
(Bare-eyed Thrush, Bare-eyed Robin)
Turdus nudigenis **Lafresnaye, 1848, *Rev. Zool.* [Paris] 11: 4 – Caracas.**

IDENTIFICATION 23–24 cm (9–9½"). A generally plain or dull olive- brown thrush with whitish-buff underparts and whiter lower belly to undertail-coverts; most distinctive feature is the broad area of bright yellow around the eye. **Confusion species** Similar in general plumage to a number of other thrushes of the region, particularly female Glossy-black (134), Black-hooded (138) and Lawrence's (147), but easily separated by presence of fairly large, conspicuous bright yellow area around the eye; Lawrence's is much darker olive-brown above and paler on the breast and flanks, with a thin bright yellow eye-ring and (male) bright yellow bill. Ecuadorian Thrush (153) – sometimes considered a race of Yellow-eyed – is virtually identical except for the slightly paler underparts and only narrow yellow eye-ring.

DESCRIPTION Sexes alike but adult female slightly paler below than male. **Adult** Entire upperparts, including lores, olive-brown tinged grey (paler grey when worn), more heavily grey on rump and uppertail-coverts with slightly darker centres to crown and hindcrown. Darker grey centres to median and greater coverts, alula and innerwebs of flight feathers and tertials; outerwebs of secondaries, tertials and edges of primary coverts slightly more heavily tinged olive. Tail brown to dark brown washed olive on central pair, outer two feathers paler brown. Cheeks and ear-coverts olive-brown with large bright yellow to yellowish-orange patch around eye but usually larger behind eye and more developed when breeding. Chin and throat off-white streaked brown extending to sides of throat; lower throat and upper breast to sides of neck whitish or greyish-buff, more heavily buff-brown on sides of breast, flanks similar but darker coffee-brown; centre of belly to undertail-coverts white, some feathers tipped dark brown. Underwing has coverts as flanks but tips to greater coverts vary from pale whitish to bright or warm orange, secondaries pale creamy-whitish. Bill yellow to olive-yellow. Eye brown to blackish-brown. Legs and feet olive-brown or slightly paler brown. **Immature** Juvenile similar to adult but has pale buffy-white streaks or flecks to forehead and crown, finer streaks on nape and hindcrown, and more boldly light orange-buff streaks on mantle, scapulars, median and greater coverts, with small triangular tips to median and greater coverts. Has broad pale buffish-white submoustachial with small dark spots bordered by dark malar stripe; chin and throat dull white or buffish, broadly spotted or barred brown on breast to flanks; centre of belly to lower flanks and undertail-coverts dull buffish. Spots and streaks disappear with age towards first-winter plumage.

GEOGRAPHICAL VARIATION Two races; poorly differentiated and not well marked. Race *extimus* darker or browner, upperparts deep buffish-olive and underparts darker umber-brown or tawny-olive, and area of white on vent generally smaller.

VOICE Call a querulous, cat-like or rising *keer-leee, queeeow, pee-ou-wa* or *shuh-ey, uhEEuh* and a more musical *chareera* and a harsh *tak-tak-tak*, also a monosyllabic frog-like note which may be used as a contact note (M. Pearman pers. comm.). Song a series of sweet rich musical fluted phrases similar to that of Cocoa Thrush (149) but slower, lower-pitched, more hesitant, including *ture-too-too* and *cheerily cheer-up cheerio*, plus ringing trills, but generally with little repetition of phrases and broken with frequent pauses. Sings from a high position, usually throughout the year but more regularly from April to August.

STATUS AND DISTRIBUTION Common, locally common to uncommon.

T. n. nudigenis Lesser Antilles from Martinique south (excluding Barbados where it was introduced but failed to become established) to Margarita and Patos Islands, Trinidad and Tobago, extreme eastern Colombia, eastern Andes in eastern Norte de Santander, Boyacá, Cundinamarca and Meta (Macarena Mountains) and the lowlands from Arauca to Meta and the Orinoco; widespread in most of Venezuela except the extreme northwest (Zulia, Falcón, Trujillo, Lara and parts of Amazonas), Guyana, Surinam and French Guiana,

also north-east Brazil north of the Amazon and west to the Rio Negro.

T. n. extimus Northern Brazil, to the south bank of the lower Amazon.

MOVEMENTS Sedentary.

HABITAT Deciduous gallery and rainforest edges and clearings, bamboo clumps, lightly wooded areas of open forest, savannas with scattered groves of trees, secondary forests and dry scrub to edges of cultivation (particularly fruit and cocoa), open fields and gardens (including Port of Spain and the outskirts of Caracas) in the tropical and lower subtropical zones up to 600 m (2000') in Trinidad but occurs to 1600 m (5280') in South America, but most often below 1000 m (3300').

BEHAVIOUR Alone or in pairs but may gather in some numbers at abundance of fruit; mostly in lower levels of trees but also walks, hops and runs on the ground where it frequently forages for food; fairly shy but in parts of the range (Trinidad) recorded at feeding-tables. Occasionally aggressive in defence of food or territory, a behaviour thought to have contributed to the decline of Forest Thrush (64) on St Lucia (Raffaele *et al.* 1998). Feeds mostly on berries and fruit, particularly pawpaw, guava and avocado, also earthworms and insects and their larvae.

BREEDING Season: April–September but mostly May–August. Nest: a large cup-shaped construction of plant material, twigs, mixed with mud and lined with fine roots, placed 2–7.5 m (6–25') from the ground in the fork of a branch or in a shrub. Eggs: 2–3, occasionally 4, deep blue to greenish-blue with deep reddish-brown spots mostly at the broader end. Incubation solely by female but both adults feed nestlings. Usually has two broods.

MOULT No information.

MEASUREMENTS (n=30) Wing, male 104–122, female 107–115; tarsus 28–31.5; bill (culmen) 17–20.5. Weight, male 55–74.5 g, female 56.5–74 g.

REFERENCES Bond (1979), Hilty & Brown (1986), Meyer de Schauensee & Phelps (1978), Raffaele *et al.* (1998).

153 ECUADORIAN THRUSH *Turdus maculirostris*   Plate 51

Turdus ignobilis maculirostris **Berlepsch and Taczanowski, 1883,** *Proc. Zool. Soc. London***: 538 – Chimbo, western Ecuador.**

IDENTIFICATION 21.5–23 cm (8½–9"). Previously considered a race of Yellow-eyed Thrush (152) but lacks a wide bare area of skin around the eye, occupies a more heavily forested habitat and is widely separated from Yellow-eyed in northern South America. **Confusion species** Closely resembles allopatric Yellow-eyed and Clay-coloured (151) Thrushes; females of both Pale-eyed (95) and Glossy-black (134) Thrushes are similar but generally occur at higher elevations and are somewhat more uniformly darker brown or sandy buff-brown respectively, the latter having a darker brown head and upper breast.

DESCRIPTION Sexes alike. **Adult** Very similar to Yellow-eyed Thrush but lacks broad bright yellow area around eye; has narrow yellow or yellowish-orange eye-ring; face and upperparts entirely brownish-olive extending to edges to greater coverts, primary coverts, inner secondaries and tertials, rest of flight and tail feathers brown but edges to tail olive-brown; underwing-coverts pale buff becoming orange-buff towards tips of greaters. Chin and throat whitish or whitish-buff finely streaked brown; breast, upper belly and flanks ash- or buffish-brown variably tinged olive;

lower belly and vent to undertail-coverts white, spotted or streaked olive-brown. Bill dark olive-yellow or slightly paler or greenish-yellow at tip; may become wholly dark (or darker) when not breeding. Legs and feet grey-brown. **Immature** Juvenile similar to adult and same-age Yellow-eyed Thrush. Forehead and crown to nape finely spotted or flecked pale buff; mantle, scapulars and back also flecked with long pale buff streaks; tips to median and greater coverts have pale orange-buff spots and paler central shaft-streaks. Streaks on throat pale or ill-defined, breast, belly and flanks dull whitish or buffish and faintly spotted with brownish tips.

GEOGRAPHICAL VARIATION None. Monotypic.

VOICE Call a thin whining querulous note, similar to both Yellow-eyed and Clay-coloured Thrushes. Song apparently unknown.

STATUS AND DISTRIBUTION Local to uncommon; fairly common in El Oro, Ecuador, and Tumbes National Forest, north-west Peru. Western Ecuador north to coastal Esmeraldas and Imbabura, south through central Andes to Tumbes, extreme north-west Peru.

MOVEMENTS Sedentary.

HABITAT Forests including secondary forest edges, particularly damp areas in deciduous and semi-deciduous forests and clearings, also open areas with grass, scattered trees or hedges up to about 1800 m (5950') but to over 2000 m (6600') near Ibarra, Ecuador.

BEHAVIOUR Shy and generally hard to see, usually occurring singly or in pairs; similar to many other thrushes of the region but little known and apparently more closely tied to forests than nearest relatives. May be crepuscular since it is known to be most active, or visible, at dawn. Feeds in trees and may congregate in fruiting trees with Plumbeous-backed Thrush (137).

BREEDING Nest only recently discovered (Best et al. 1995). Season: January to April. Nest: a thick cup-shaped structure of dried grass, fine twigs and dried leaves, placed 1.5 m (c.5') from the ground in low vegetation or tree-stump. Eggs 3.

MOULT No information.

MEASUREMENTS (n=8) Wing 105–120; tarsus 28–33; bill (culmen) 16.5–18, (to skull) 21.5–26. Weight 62–76 g (R. G. Pople pers. comm.).

REFERENCES Best et al. (1995).

154 UNICOLOURED THRUSH *Turdus haplochrous*   Plate 51

Turdus haplochrous Todd, 1931, *Proc. Biol. Soc. Washington* 44: 54 – Palmarito, Río San Julián, Chiquitos, Bolivia.

IDENTIFICATION 24 cm (9½"). An extremely rare and little known species of the lowland forests of east-central Bolivia. Discovered in 1931 and seen only a few times by ornithologists, taped only once, and about nine specimens exist in museum collections. Head and upperparts olive-brown, paler or sandier-brown below with indistinct streaks on the throat; belly, flanks and undertail-coverts are brownish. **Confusion species** Most likely to be confused with extremely similar Hauxwell's Thrush (150), which occurs in the same habitat and region, and Lawrence's Thrush (147); great care needed in confirming identity of Unicoloured. Hauxwell's has darker brown upperparts, including wings and tail, with rufous-russet tinge, paler underparts with white on central belly to undertail-coverts (the latter may be washed buff) and buffish-white underwing-coverts (pale brown in Unicoloured, which has whitish chin and throat indistinctly streaked sandy-brown and rest of underparts dull sandy-buff or buffish-brown, with narrow orange eye-ring). Lawrence's is not known to be sympatric with Unicoloured; best told by broad orange-yellow eye-ring, bright orange-yellow bill (in breeding season; dark horn when not breeding), dusky-brown upperparts and whitish belly to undertail-coverts. Out-of-range Cocoa Thrush (149) is also warmer rufous-brown above and below with buffish belly and undertail-coverts; very similar to Clay-coloured Thrush (151) of central and northern South America.

DESCRIPTION Sexes alike except possibly for bill. **Adult** Entire upperparts and face buffish-olive or light olive-brown; wings slightly darker brown but edges of secondaries and tertials darker brownish-olive; underwing-coverts light warm brown with edges and tips to greater underwing-coverts paler or orange-buff. Tail dark brown. Eye-ring narrow and dull orange. Chin and throat whitish, becoming buffish and indistinctly streaked deep sandy- or dusky-brown, rest of underparts pale sandy- or dull buffish-brown or light brownish-olive on flanks and undertail-coverts. Bill (brownish-black in original description) olive or greenish-yellow; base of lower mandible dark brown in male and pale grey in female (this requires confirmation). Legs and feet dark brown. **Immature** Unknown.

GEOGRAPHICAL VARIATION None. Monotypic.

VOICE Call a repeated squawking or rattling note similar to the extreme anxiety notes of other thrushes notably, in Europe, Fieldfare (122) and Song Thrush (124), probably used in alarm. Song a series of typically thrush-like whistling phrases, *tioooo-it toodle-it, teww-it, woo-woo-wooo-wit, tew-wooo*, similar in tone to Hauxwell's Thrush but given at slightly faster pace (Whyte et al. 1995, Brace et al. 1997).

STATUS AND DISTRIBUTION Extremely rare; considered Near-Threatened (Collar et al. 1994). Beni and Santa Cruz departments, northern Bolivia. Two were collected in 1918 from Palmarito, Río

San Julián, Chiquitos province, Santa Cruz, two more in 1944 from the banks of the Río Mamoré, Marbán province, Beni, and a further two 7 km south-east of Trinidad (Beni) in 1984. Seen and recorded by Ted Parker in September 1989 near La Junta (between Santa Rosa de la Roca and Florida) near Noel Kampff Mercado National Park (Santa Cruz). Further sightings (and a specimen collected) were made in September 1992 in a small area of forest within Beni Biological Station, along the south bank of the Río Manique approximately 70 km north-east of San Borja (White *et al.* 1995); in 1993 two specimens were collected in Isiboro Secure National Park in southern Beni (Brace *et al.* 1997).

MOVEMENTS Sedentary.

HABITAT Largely unknown but specimens were taken from semi-open lowland woodland and seasonally flooded riverine (*várzea*) forest with well developed undergrowth.

BEHAVIOUR Only known records refers to single birds or pairs; occurs in the same habitat and associates with both Hauxwell's and Creamy bellied (144) Thrushes. No known threats and occurs in extensive amounts of apparently suitable habitat. Requires further and extensive survey and research into habitat requirements and overall ecology. Food unknown.

BREEDING Unknown.

MOULT No information.

MEASUREMENTS (n=2) Wing, male 114, female 115; bill 17–20; tarsus 32. Weight 84 g.

REFERENCES Brace *et al.* (1997), Collar *et al.* (1992, 1994), Hellmayr (1934), White *et al.* (1995).

155 WHITE-EYED THRUSH *Turdus jamaicensis*   Plate 55
(Turdus) jamaicensis Gmelin, 1789, *Syst. Nat.* 1(2): 809 – Jamaica.

IDENTIFICATION 23–24 cm (9–9½"). A Jamaican endemic with a rich brown head with pale bluish eyes, deep grey upperparts, grey or greyish-brown underparts, whitish chin and throat heavily streaked brown except for white crescent on centre of lower throat, which often appears as a 'bow-tie' pattern. **Confusion species** No other thrush within the range has a pale eye; White-chinned Thrush (127), the other endemic thrush of Jamaica, has only a small area of white on the chin, 1–2 white edges to inner greater coverts, white spots on dark brown undertail-coverts and bright reddish-orange bill and legs.

DESCRIPTION Sexes alike. **Adult** Lores to eye blackish, forehead to nape and face including cheeks, ear-coverts and sides of nape deep rich or rufous-brown, on some face and nape slightly paler or warm gingery-brown. Sides of neck, mantle, back, scapulars, rump and uppertail-coverts deep or lead-grey, base of longest uppertail-coverts brown. Tail black or blackish-brown. Median coverts brown edged slightly paler, greater coverts similar but edged grey or grey-brown on outerwebs; alula, primary coverts, tertials and flight feathers deep brown, edges to tertials and inner secondaries grey-brown, edges to primaries pale buff-brown. Underwing-coverts pale slate-grey. Centre of chin and throat white streaked warm brown, lower throat and upper breast with band or crescent of white, breast grey or grey-brown becoming slightly paler grey on belly and flanks; central belly to vent white, undertail-coverts white with blackish or grey-brown bases, thighs greyish-white. Bill black, base of lower mandible occasionally yellow. Eye pale bluish- to greyish-white (known locally as 'glass-eye'). Legs brown or dark brown, soles of feet yellow. **Juvenile** Similar to adult but no streaks on throat, heavy streaks on breast.

GEOGRAPHICAL VARIATION None. Monotypic.

VOICE Call a shrill harsh *dzee* or *dzaw* note, often used in alarm. An exemplary singer likened to Northern Mockingbird *Mimus polyglottos*, with a varied musical song, with each phrase repeated 2–3 times. Usually begins with a high-pitched but descending *seeooo… seeooo… seeooo* and *weeesp* or *wee-issp*, plus trilling whistles, chimes and harsher notes together with a frequently repeated ringing *hee-haw* bell-like whistle.

STATUS AND DISTRIBUTION Fairly common. Endemic to Jamaica.

MOVEMENTS Moves to lower levels in cooler, non-breeding months but rare in lowlands and valleys.

HABITAT Damp mountain forests and wooded hills, gullies and ravines from about 100 m (330') to the highest peaks, sometimes in coffee plantations and other mid-elevation woodlands.

BEHAVIOUR Shy and secretive and rarely seen away from dark areas of forest. Forages at all levels in trees and occasionally in ground-level shrubs or, more rarely, on the ground in the open. Flight through trees is low, swift and dashing. Feeds mainly on fruit, especially berries and small figs, also insects.

BREEDING Season: April to June. Nest: large, cup-shaped and placed in a small tree. Eggs 2–3, pale bluish-green, heavily speckled darker.

MOULT No information.

MEASUREMENTS Wing, male 115–121, female 112–121.5; tarsus 34–36; bill (culmen) 17–20 (Ridgway 1907). Weight apparently unrecorded.

REFERENCES Bond (1979), Ridgway (1907).

IDENTIFICATION 22–26.5 cm (8¾–10½"). A variably brown to grey-brown or slate-grey thrush of Mexico to northern South America; differs in tone of grey or brown on underparts, but heavy streaks on white throat and white crescent on lower throat and centre of upper breast constant. Similar in size, shape and song to American Robin (161). **Confusion species** Extremely similar to White-necked Thrush (157) which occurs in north-east Colombia and east of the Andes, but no overlap between the two; White-necked has grey breast to flanks whilst the South American race *daguae* of White-throated is pale or dull brown. White-necked is generally hard to see and prefers thick low forest vegetation. Presence of white crescent across lower throat prevents confusion with other species. Clay-coloured Thrush (151) has some faint streaks on throat but is otherwise almost uniform tawny-brown. Black Thrush (133) male is uniformly black; female has all-dark bill and is entirely brown, including the undertail-coverts.

Taxonomic note This and the following species have sometimes been regarded as conspecific (e.g. Ripley 1964) but we follow Miller & Griscom (1925), Hellmayr (1934) and AOU (1983) in treating them as distinct species. Although extremely similar in plumage there are clear differences in range, habitat, song and behaviour. Some authorities have also proposed *daguae* as a separate species.

DESCRIPTION Sexes alike. **Adult** Entire upperparts dark brown tinged olive, slightly darker brown on head and face and paler olive on rump and uppertail-coverts. Eye-ring bright yellow. Wings and tail brown but edges to wing-coverts, flight feathers and tertials lighter or olive-brown; in worn plumage median coverts and flight feathers slightly paler brown; underwing-coverts pale orange. Chin and throat to centre of upper breast whitish, broadly streaked dark brown; lower throat and centre of upper breast has unstreaked white crescent. Breast and upper belly to flanks pale buffish to olive-grey, slightly warmer or washed warmer buffish-brown on lower breast and flanks, sometimes with a slightly heavier tinge on lower flanks; thighs as rest of underparts or buffish-grey; centre of belly to undertail-coverts white. Bill yellowish or dull yellow with darker base and culmen. Legs and feet dull yellow or yellow tinged olive-brown. In worn plumage (breeding season) body, wings and tail much greyer, breast and flanks ashy-brown and bill darker. **Immature** Juvenile has entire head and upperparts brown or brownish-olive, slightly darker on wings and tail, eye-ring brownish or greenish-yellow becoming orange-yellow; forehead to crown and nape finely streaked light orange-buff, becoming larger streaks of orange or cinnamon-brown on mantle, back and edges of scapulars; tips to median and greater coverts also spotted with deep orange-buff (retained into first year). Face as upperparts with

fine pale buff spots or streaks on cheeks and ear-coverts. Chin and throat whitish finely spotted darker, breast to belly and flanks mottled with warmer buff centres to feathers and darker brown tips, paler or less spotted or barred on belly. Bill greyish. Legs and feet dull greenish-olive or grey.

GEOGRAPHICAL VARIATION Ten races; considerable variation in tones of upperparts and bill and leg colour; *daguae* a candidate for species status.

Race *lygrus* (including *renominatus*) very like nominate and probably inseparable with certainty in worn plumage, best told in fresh autumn/winter plumage; head and upperparts slightly paler brown and rump more clearly olive, with dark or greyish eye-ring; breast, upper belly and flanks paler greyish-brown or approaching buff-brown tinged grey. Bill dusky-brown or blackish on upper mandible and pale grey on lower. Legs and feet dull or pale grey.

Race *calliphthongus* very similar to (and weakly separated from) *lygrus* but less rufous-brown above and paler or duller below; race *rubicundus* somewhat variable, from olive to deeper or more heavily tinged rufous-brown above (including wing-coverts, outerwebs of flight feathers and tertials); rest of flight and tail feathers slightly browner; breast dull olive or olive-grey, flanks similar or faintly tinged orange-buff, becoming deep olive on lower flanks, centre of belly paler. Race *cnephosus* very similar to *assimilis* but more heavily tinged olive-brown above and browner or warmer brown on breast to flanks. Bill yellowish or greenish-olive but tip of culmen usually dark brown.

The races *lecauchen*, *atrotinctus* and *oblitus* much greyer or darker on head and upperparts than other races. Male *lecauchen* quite distinct from nominate and has head and upperparts olive- or dark grey tinged light brown, bright yellow bill, eye-ring, legs and feet (legs and feet sometimes greyish-yellow); streaks on throat blackish-brown contrasting more strongly against background white; breast, upper belly and flanks grey or olive-greyish-brown tinged with golden or peachy-buff extending to axillaries and underwing-coverts. Female similar but more olive-grey on head and upperparts, bill yellow to greenish or orange-yellow, and legs and feet straw-yellow to yellowish-brown. Race *atrotinctus* like *lecauchen* but head and upperparts slaty-black with wings and tail slightly duller or sooty-black; female paler or greyer, less blackish, with breast, upper belly and flanks grey or tinged olive. Race *oblitus* also like *lecauchen* but more heavily tinged olive-brown on head and upperparts, and breast, upper belly and flanks browner or buffish-brown.

Race *daguae* smallest with a shorter bill, has head and face brown and rest of upperparts including tail, wing-coverts and edges to flight feathers and tertials deep brownish-olive heavily tinged rusty-brown and similar to rufous individuals of race *rubicundus*; innerwebs to flight and tail feathers much darker; underwing-coverts brown with thin whitish edges and tips to greater underwing-coverts; breast to belly and flanks sepia-brown or dull olive-brown, slightly paler or greyish on flanks in some; vent and undertail-coverts white. Eye-ring variable from dull lemon-yellow to greenish-yellow. Bill black, base of lower mandible greyer or pale olive-green. Legs and feet grey or brownish-grey. Race *coibensis* slightly smaller than nominate and similar to or marginally darker than *rubicundus*, crown uniform with rest of upperparts; female slightly paler above and browner on flanks. Bill blackish at base, greenish-yellow or yellow at tip. Legs and feet light brown.

VOICE Has several short but characteristic guttural contact notes, *ep, ek, kek, ok, unk, enk*, etc., plus a harsh buzzing and somewhat frog-like *krrt, unk* or *urrrk*; also a gruff nasal *rreuh*, sometimes slightly more drawn-out and repeated, a clucking *kyow, keyooo* or *ch-uhk*, which may also be given as part of a more prolonged yodelling *wheeljeeujeeujeeu*, and a harsher, more screeching *dzeeyoo* and whistled *peeyuu* often given as an alarm note or when going to roost. In flight gives a typical thin *ssii* or *ssee*. Race *coibensis* has a characteristic *chur-r-r* or *pru-r-r* (Wetmore *et al.* 1984). Not all races give all calls given here; some populations may only utter certain calls, e.g. Mexican birds are not known to have the harsh buzzing or frog-like call of individuals in Nicaragua and elsewhere (Hardy & Parker 1992).

Appears to have two distinct songs. The more frequent is an unmistakable thrush song, very similar to that of American Robin: lively with a loud, full repertory of rich warbling and fluty caroling phrases, frequently but unpredictably repeated in mockingbird-like fashion and interspersed with spiralling whistles, chatters and trilling notes; usually given from a tall, often conspicuous perch in the canopy. The less frequent song is series of rich melodic notes repeated for several minutes, recalling similar songs of mockingbirds Mimidae or wrens Troglodytidae. Sings early morning and afternoon, most races from mid- to late March (exceptionally early February) to late July or early August, but breeding birds rarely sing once young have hatched; *coibensis* sings from mid-January.

STATUS AND DISTRIBUTION Common or fairly common, more numerous in Mexico and Central America. Resident or partial migrant.

T. a. calliphthongus Mexico from south-east Sonora to north-east Sinaloa and Chihuahua.

T. a. lygrus Mexico from central and southern Sinaloa south through western Mexico (east to Morelos) to Oaxaca and south-west Chiapas.

T. a. assimilis Mexico from southern Tamaulipas south through eastern Mexico to northern Veracruz, Hidalgo, eastern Mexico and northern Oaxaca.

T. a. lecauchen South-east Veracruz, north-east Oaxaca and Chiapas, Mexico, to northern and central Guatemala, Belize and north-west Honduras.

T. a. rubicundus Pacific slope of southern Guatemala to western Honduras (south of

lecauchen) and El Salvador (Volcán de San Miguel, Volcán de San Salvador and Volcán Santa Ana).

T. a. atrotinctus Caribbean slope of Nicaraguan highlands; probably also in extreme eastern Honduras (Arenal).

T. a. oblitus Costa Rica in the Pacific slope foothills and lower mountains.

T. a. cnephosus South-west Costa Rica (Terraba valley) to Cerro Campana, western Panama (Chiriquí, Veraguas and Cocle).

T. a. coibensis Coiba Island (possibly also Isla Rancheria and Isla Brincanco), Veraguas, Panama; possibly a winter visitor to Cebaco (see below).

T. a. daguae Eastern Panama (Pacific slope, Darién), western Colombia (west of the Andes) from lower Atrato valley east to Mutata, Antioquia, south to Esmeraldas and Pichinchas, north-west Ecuador; recently recorded in moist forest at 500 m (1650′) in Guayas, southern Ecuador (Pople *et al.* 1997).

MOVEMENTS Partial migrant; apparently largely sedentary but birds in Costa Rica and Panama (and possibly elsewhere in the range) move or wander to lower elevations when not breeding; found down to about sea-level in the south-west around Golfo Dulce and recorded several times on Barro Colorado Island, along the Panama Canal. A vagrant to Chiriquí Grande, Bocas del Toro province, northern Panama (Olson 1993), also Nuevo León and Campeche, Mexico; has been recorded (presumably *daguae*) in Rio Palenque, Pichincha and Quevedo, Los Ríos, Ecuador. The type specimen of *coibensis* was collected on Cebaco Island, Veraguas, in February where considered to be a possibly regular winter visitor. A vagrant to southern Texas with up to 4 birds present at 2 localities in March–April 1998.

HABITAT Wet or moist lowland and foothill evergreen subtropical forests, and lower elevation cloud-forests, to c.900 m (2970′) in South America, but only to c.250 m (825′) in Ecuador; 1360–1970 m (4500–6500′) in El Salvador; 1850 m (6100′) in Costa Rica, 2000 m (6600′) in southern Mexico and 3000 m (9900′) further north; *coibensis* breeds at sea-level in drier forests and edges of mangrove swamps. Seen mostly in forest edges and clearings but also occurs in forest interior, adjacent bush and tangled scrubby areas such as stands of wild cane, secondary growth, plantations, hedgerows and (usually outside the breeding season) savannas.

BEHAVIOUR Fairly sociable, but usually alone or in pairs in the breeding season; forms loose groups (e.g. in fruiting trees) when not breeding and mixes with other species. Mostly a shy, unobtrusive bird of mid-levels to canopy in forests, more rarely on the ground. Forages in vegetation along branches and on or near the ground where it follows army ants and flicks aside leaf-litter with its bill. Feeds mainly on variety of seasonal fruit, especially berries; also insects and earthworms.

BREEDING Season: March to early July. Nest: a large bulky cup of vegetable matter and plant fibres with a middle layer of mud, outer covering of green moss and inner lining of finer grasses, stems or other

suitable material; usually placed up to 8 m (26′) in a tree, creeper, bamboo or vine. Eggs: 2–3, variably dull white or greenish-white to pale blue and heavily mottled with fine reddish-brown and grey spots.
MOULT No information.
MEASUREMENTS Wing (24) male 121–133.5, female 107–123; tarsus 28–32; bill (to feathers) 16.5–23; *daguae* (n=13) wing, male 102.5–112, female 97–110; bill (to feathers) 14.5–19.5; tarsus 25–30; *coibensis* wing, male 109.5–117.5, female 108–113.5; tarsus 27.5–31.5; *lygrus* wing, male 121–124, female 116.5–124; *atrotinctus* (n=11)

wing 114–123; *cnephosus* (n=12) wing, male 113–125.5, female 114–124.5; bill (to feathers) 15.5–18; *lecauchen* (n=32) wing 114–127; *oblitus* (n=13) wing 115–125.5; *rubicundus* (n=36) wing, male 120.5–132, female 115–124; tarsus 26–31. Weight *rubicundus* female 62 g; *cnephosus* (male and female) 66–72 g; *lecauchen* male 74 g (Dickey & van Rossem 1938, Ridgway 1907, Skutch 1960, 1967).
REFERENCES Dickey & van Rossem (1938), Eisenmann (1950), Hardy & Parker (1992), Miller & Griscom (1925), Olson (1993), Pople *et al.* (1997).

157 WHITE-NECKED THRUSH *Turdus albicollis*   Plate 50
Turdus albicollis Vieillot, 1818, *Nouv. Dict. Hist. Nat.* (nouv. ed.) 20: 227 – Brazil [= Rio de Janeiro, *vide* Hellmayr (1934) *Field Mus. Nat. Hist. Publ.* Zool. Ser. 13(7): 336].

IDENTIFICATION 20.5–24 cm (8–9½″). The counterpart of White-throated Thrush (156) east of the Andes and in large parts of the Amazon rainforest (see taxonomic note under that species). Best identified by its overall dark brown upperparts, heavily brown-streaked white throat (can appear all dark when seen from the side) above a white crescent on the lower throat, and grey underparts. **Confusion species** Almost identical to White-throated but there is no overlap in range (although the distance between the two in southern Colombia can only be a few hundred kilometres) and White-throated differs in song and habitat preference while its southern race *daguae* has a brown or buffish-brown breast, belly and flanks. Black-billed Thrush (146), particularly race *debilis*, is very similar but has less definite streaks on throat, no eye-ring, black bill, smaller area of white on lower throat and brown (not grey) breast, upper belly and flanks. Pale-breasted Thrush (143) has streaks on throat but lacks white crescent on lower throat/upper breast, has grey on head, paler brown upperparts and pale brown breast and flanks. Lawrence's (147), Cocoa (149), Pale-vented (148) and Yellow-eyed (151), together with female Yellow-legged (94), Pale-eyed (95) and Glossy-black (134), are initially similar but generally more uniform brown, show reduced (if any) amount of streaking on the throat, and lack the broad white crescent across the lower throat and upper breast.
DESCRIPTION Sexes alike. **Adult** Entire head and face dusky-brown extending to nape in some or becoming olive-brown on nape and deeper brownish-olive on mantle, back, scapulars and rump; uppertail-coverts greyish-brown. Tail dark brown. Median and greater coverts and outerwebs of tertials olive-brown as scapulars; innerwebs dark brown; alula, primary coverts and flight feathers medium brown with fine russet-olive edges to outer primaries and secondaries; underwing-coverts pale orange or buffish-orange. Lores to eye blackish or very dark brown; promi-

nent yellow or yellowish-orange eye-ring. Chin and throat white but broadly streaked dark brown; lower throat and centre of upper breast has white crescent. Centre of breast grey, tinged olive-brown at sides and merging into brown on sides of neck; centre of lower breast paler grey, becoming white on belly to vent and undertail-coverts; thighs greyish; sides of lower breast and flanks bright orange-rufous becoming tinged olive or olive-brown on lower flanks. Bill yellow with blackish culmen. Legs and feet brown to dark horn-brown. **Immature** Juvenile has head and upperparts rich brown, slightly darker on wings and tail; fine pale orange-buff central shaft-streaks to face, crown, nape and sides of neck, becoming larger streaks on mantle to back and rump and more broadly on edges to scapulars. Tips to median and greater coverts have pale orange spots; greaters also have pale buff central shaft-streaks; underwing has coverts brown with pale orange tips to greater coverts. Chin and throat whitish, lightly spotted or flecked brown; breast mottled orange-brown with dark brown tips, belly and flanks similar but more broken with white bases, tips to flanks finer and not as broad, vent and undertail-coverts pale or whitish-buff.
GEOGRAPHICAL VARIATION Seven races; differences clinal but well marked in birds from southern parts of the range. Nominate *albicollis*, *paraguayensis* and probably *crotopezus* differ significantly from other races in range and presence of warm buff to rufous on the flanks, and may in due course be separated at the species level. At least two further subspecies have been proposed but we regard '*minusculus*' and '*berlepschi*' as synonyms of *phaeopygoides* and *spodiolaemus* respectively.
Race *phaeopygus* has upperparts, including forehead to crown, darker or greyish-olive (may be tinged brown but variable between individuals) and innerwebs to flight and tail feathers also darker brown, axillaries grey and underwing-coverts grey-brown with thin white edges and tips;

rump and uppertail-coverts also darker or greyer-brown and more uniform with tail. Chin and throat off-white and streaked grey or olive-brown; breast to flanks and sides of belly buffish-grey or pale grey, centre of belly, vent and undertail-coverts white. Race *phaeopygoides* very like *phaeopygus* but has longer wing, reddish eye-ring, upperparts less brown and more heavily tinged olive.

Race *spodiolaemus* tinged more rufous-olive above and black streaks on throat heavier; upper breast grey but can be tinged brown, and underwing has coverts pale grey with brown centres to greater coverts and buffish edges and tips to axillaries; lower mandible partly or entirely yellow. Race *crotopezus* (intermediate in intensity of plumage coloration, especially on flanks) similar to *spodiolaemus* and tinged darker or slightly rufous on mantle to rump and scapulars (including wing-coverts and edges to flight feathers) than nominate but has longest uppertail-coverts grey-brown (as in *phaeopygus*) and breast to upper belly dingy grey or tinged buffish, flanks tawny or tinged olive and underwing-coverts pale buff or tinged orange; bill in this and following race mostly blackish with lower mandible yellowish. Race *contemptus* similar to *crotopezus* but has brighter or more olive-tinged upperparts and flanks heavier brown; underwing-coverts light buff-brown edged pale orange. Race *paraguayensis* similar to nominate (both larger than other races with upperparts, including wing-coverts and edges to flight feathers, pale olive-brown) but streaks on throat and grey on breast slightly heavier, flanks orange-brown and underwing-coverts brownish-buff.

VOICE Call a low cluck *chack*; also *jup*, often repeated or run into *jup, few-up*, and occasionally used more sharply as *youp* or *yoow-up* in alarm (sounding like a human yell); also a repeated *jjig-wig* or *jjig-wig-wig* and a thin high-pitched *tsri*. Song considered tuneful and pleasant, with a slow, typical thrush-like structure of paired rich fluty phrases *two-e-o, two-ee*, including rising ringing phrases repeated loudly but in a lazy, slurred or tired and melancholy fashion, usually without pause and varying little in tone. Far-carrying but given from deep cover and not easy to trace to source. Often one of earliest dawn songs and continues throughout the day.

STATUS AND DISTRIBUTION Fairly common or locally common.

T. a. phaeopygoides North-east Colombia in the Santa Marta and Perijá Mountains and on the western slope of the East Andes in Norte de Santander and on the eastern slope from Norte de Santander and Vichada south to Vaupés and south-east Nariño. In Venezuela from north-west Zulia south to Táchira, western Barinas and western Apuré and north-east from Mérida to Carabobo and Distrito Federal, also Sucre and Anzoategui; Trinidad and Tobago.

T. a. phaeopygus Venezuela in Bolívar and Amazonas east to Surinam, French Guiana and northern Brazil, east to about Belem and northern Maranhão and south along the Rio Tapajos to north-west Mato Grosso.

T. a. spodiolaemus Eastern Ecuador, north-east and eastern Peru east to Amazonas, western Brazil south of the Rio Solimões in the Rio Purus area and south to Beni, northern Bolivia.

T. a. contemptus Bolivia in La Paz, Santa Cruz and Tarija to Salta and Jujuy, north-west Argentina.

T. a. crotopezus Eastern Brazil in Bahia, Espírito Santo and Alagoas.

T. a. albicollis South-eastern Brazil from Rio de Janeiro to Rio Grande do Sul.

T. a. paraguayensis South-west Brazil from Mato Grosso through eastern Paraguay (where uncommon to scarce) to north-east Argentina in Misiones and Corrientes.

MOVEMENTS Sedentary.

HABITAT Tropical and lower subtropical zones in dense tangled undergrowth, clearings and edges of humid, mostly lowland *terra firme* rainforest and mature secondary growth, reaching montane forest in places; to 1900 m (6270′) north of the Orinoco and about 1500 m (4950′) south of it, but to about 2400 m (7900′) in the Yungas of La Paz, Bolivia. In southern Brazil often found in the same area of forest as Eastern Slaty (136), Rufous-bellied (141) and Cocoa (149) Thrushes; in northern Argentina (Misiones) often found in company with Rufous-bellied Thrush.

BEHAVIOUR Generally inconspicuous and very retiring, more often heard or glimpsed than seen well, but in places (Trinidad and northern Venezuela in Henri Pittier National Park) emerges to feed on the ground at roadside edges, forest clearings, pastures and picnic areas; in the south of its range more easily observed in non-breeding season. Mostly alone or in pairs but also occurs in small groups of up to 6; in austral winter in larger numbers and mixed-species flocks at fruiting bushes and trees. Favours low branches and dense undergrowth at or just above ground-level, but occasionally feeds in mid-storey. Mostly takes invertebrates (regularly follows army ant swarms); also fruits, berries, seeds.

BREEDING Season: November–August (Trinidad) but mostly (including Colombia) March–June. Nest: a small, generally shallow cup of plant and rough vegetable material covered with an outer layer of moss and lined with fine roots; usually low down in vegetation or thick bush but often in open or exposed. Eggs: 2–3, exceptionally 4, pale greenish-blue, spotted or blotched with lavender overlain with brown or rich reddish-brown. Incubation period 12.5–13 days; both parents feed the young. Probably three broods.

MOULT May and June but may have a partial moult in September and October.

MEASUREMENTS Wing (n=12) 110–120; tarsus 27.5–32; bill (culmen) 16.5–20.5; *phaeopygus* (n=20) wing, male 103.5–112.5, female 101–110; *paraguayensis* (n=6) wing 99.5–110; *phaeopygoides* (n=12) wing, male 103–115, female 107–114; *crotopezus* (n=22) wing 105–118; tarsus 24–30; *contemptus* (n=6) wing 113–121; *spodiolaemus* (n=15) wing, male 103–115, female 95–111. Weight 43–67.5 g.

REFERENCES ffrench (1973).

158 RUFOUS-BACKED THRUSH *Turdus rufopalliatus*   Plate 54

Turdus rufo-palliatus Lafresnaye, 1840, *Rev. Zool.* [Paris] 3: 259 – Monterey, California [corrected to Acapulco, Mexico, by Bangs & Penard (1919) *Bull. Mus. Comp. Zool.* 63: 37].

IDENTIFICATION 21.5–24 cm (8½–9½"). A large attractive-looking thrush from western Mexico. Mainly cinnamon or deep rufous but with a grey head and blackish wings and tail, chin and throat have heavy black streaks. Found mostly in lowland woodlands and frequently at fruiting trees. **Confusion species** Recently separated Grayson's Thrush (159) is paler grey on head and face, duller or colder olive-brown above, duller or greyer-brown below, and chiefly confined to the Tres Marias Islands (but may overlap occasionally in Nayarit: see Movements). American Robin (161) – a winter visitor to higher areas of central Mexico – has much darker head and upperparts, white patches around the eye and more reddish-orange underparts. Clay-coloured Thrush (151) occurs in similar parts of the range but is more uniformly duller brown above and paler below, and lacks the warm tones of Rufous-backed.

DESCRIPTION Sexes almost alike. **Adult male** Forehead to crown and nape pale grey with slightly darker centres and forehead to nape washed olive-brown. Mantle, back and scapulars rich cinnamon becoming slate-grey washed cinnamon on rump and uppertail-coverts, longest uppertail-coverts grey. Tail black or blackish-brown on central shafts edged pale grey on central pair, outer feathers browner. Median and greater coverts bright rufous as edges of scapulars; alula black broadly edged pale grey, primary coverts grey, outerwebs black; flight feathers black or blackish-brown broadly edged pale grey, especially on secondaries; tertials slate-grey but broadly overlain with rich brown on outerwebs. Lores to eye black, eye-ring yellow; cheeks and ear-coverts grey with fine whitish shaft-streaks. Chin and throat (including malar region) to centre of upper breast white boldly streaked blackish, rest of breast (may be tinged with grey) to flanks and underwing-coverts rich cinnamon or rufous-orange and brightest on flanks, slightly paler orange on underwing-coverts. Centre of belly to undertail-coverts white. Bill yellow or with dusky-brown tip. Legs and feet flesh-pink. **Adult female** Extremely similar but much duller or browner, generally lacking rufous and tinged olive on mantle, back and most scapulars, but edges of scapulars and wing-coverts rufous brown; breast, flanks and underwing-coverts duller orange. **Immature** Juvenile like adult but head and most upperparts duller with pale, whitish or buff flecks and central shaft-streaks on crown and nape; mantle to scapulars paler brown with variably fine or broad buffish central shafts and dark fringes; rump and uppertail-coverts brown but heavily streaked paler on central shafts. Tail as adult but lacks black on central feathers. Median coverts light olive-brown with

broad orange central shafts broadening across outerwebs at tips; alula and primary coverts dark grey as in adult, greater coverts browner or light olive-brown with broad pale orange tips and slightly darker edges at tips; innerwebs to flight feathers grey or grey-brown and inner secondaries and tertials edged olive. Face to sides of neck grey or pale grey. Chin and throat white finely spotted with olive to olive-brown at sides; upper breast pale orange-buff with brown tips forming bars, sides of belly and flanks also pale orange finely barred darker with olive-brown tips; centre of lower belly, vent and undertail-coverts white.

GEOGRAPHICAL VARIATION None. Monotypic.

VOICE Call a plaintive, mellow, drawn-out whistling *peeeooooo* or *cheeoo* or *teeeuu*, often given with partner or members of small group; a fairly hard throaty clucking *chuck chuck chuck...* or *chok chok chok...*, and a thin, high-pitched *ssiii* or *ssip* given mostly in flight. Song a slow leisurely series of rich clear or warbled liquid thrush notes, recalling American Robin (161), including *weedleeoo* trills, chuckling notes and repeated phrases.

STATUS AND DISTRIBUTION Common or fairly common. Resident along the Pacific slope of western Mexico from southern Sonora (Río Yaquí) and extreme south-west Chihuahua south to Jalisco, Michoacán, Guerrero and southern Oaxaca (to about the Isthmus of Tehuantepec), interior to Morelos and western Puebla; recently established populations in Distrito Federal and Oaxaca City are probably of captive origin.

MOVEMENTS Mostly sedentary but regularly occurs north of the breeding range in non-breeding season (mid-October to mid-April) but also in June and July, to northern Sonora, south-west Texas (6 records), Arizona (38+ records 1978–1994) and southern New Mexico (4 records); also a vagrant west to California (8 records to 1998, all between 5 November and 13 April, including four that appeared to overwinter, and most in the south-east desert) but some may be escaped cage-birds. In the south of the range a scarce or rare winter visitor to eastern Oaxaca and Chiapas.

HABITAT Deciduous and mixed forests, woodland edge, dense shrubbery and scrub, plantations and large gardens usually in the lowlands of the tropical and subtropical zones; occurs up to 1500 m (4950') in foothills and the higher valleys.

BEHAVIOUR Usually alone or in pairs in the breeding season but occurs in loose flocks in winter, especially at fruiting trees; forages low in vegetation, on the ground and high in trees and bushes. Food is mostly insects, fruit and berries.

BREEDING Very poorly known. Eggs: whitish, heavily marked or spotted with reddish-brown.

MOULT No information.
MEASUREMENTS (n=31) Wing, male 117.5–133.5, female 115.5–128.5; bill (culmen) 19–22.5; tarsus 29.5–34 (Phillips 1981). Weight apparently unrecorded.
REFERENCES Phillips (1981).

159 GRAYSON'S THRUSH *Turdus graysoni* Plate 54

Merula flavirostris graysoni Ridgway, 1882, *Proc. U.S. Natn. Mus.* 5: 12 – Tres Marias.

IDENTIFICATION 24–25.5 cm (9½-10"). An endemic to the Tres Marías Islands of western Mexico. Extremely similar to but paler (or more washed-out) than the closely related Rufous-backed Thrush (158) from which it has only recently been separated. Head and face greyish tinged with olive becoming more orange to pale cinnamon tinged olive on the mantle and back, but scapulars and rump grey or grey-brown. Breast greyish-buff becoming warmer or cinnamon on the flanks and off-white on the central belly to undertail-coverts. Remains little known despite its apparent abundance. Confusion species Rufous-backed Thrush has darker grey head and face and more obvious eye-ring, richer or warmer brown upperparts and deeper brown underparts. Clay-coloured Thrush (151) is almost uniform dull olive-brown but sootier-brown above with a dull-coloured bill, indistinct throat streaks and paler central belly to undertail-coverts. White-throated Thrush (156) has the head uniform with the grey-brown olive-tinged upperparts, lacks an eye-ring and rufous/orange tinges to the body, and has chin and throat white boldly spotted black.
DESCRIPTION Sexes alike (female slightly smaller and duller than male). Adult Forehead to crown and nape pale grey lightly tinged brown or brownish-olive; mantle and back grey or greyish-orange tinged warm olive-brown on centre of back; scapulars grey; rump and uppertail coverts grey-brown becoming grey on longest tail-coverts; Tail blackish-grey with grey edges to bases of most outer feathers. Median and inner greater coverts grey-brown with coppery-brown tips, outer greater coverts pale grey, alula blackish, flight feathers blackish or blackish-brown finely edged pale grey; edges to inner secondaries and tertials olive-grey.

Underwing-coverts pale orange. Lores to eye dusky-brown, cheeks and ear-coverts grey or finely flecked paler on ear-coverts; thin pale yellow eye-ring. Chin and throat white boldly streaked blackish-brown, or spotted on lower throat. Breast greyish buff-brown tinged lightly with cinnamon, becoming warmer brown or cinnamon on flanks; upper belly as breast or slightly paler, centre of belly to undertail-coverts dull off-white. Bill yellow with dusky tip. Legs and feet pinkish-flesh. Immature Juvenile undescribed but probably similar to that of Rufous-backed Thrush.
GEOGRAPHICAL VARIATION None. Monotypic.
VOICE Unrecorded.
STATUS AND DISTRIBUTION Resident. Common. Tres Marías Islands, western Mexico. Restricted range causes it to be considered Near-Threatened (Collar *et al.* 1994).
MOVEMENTS An uncommon to rare visitor, from December to June (mainly December–April), to adjacent mainland of Nayarit, mostly around San Blas and south to about Las Varas, western Mexico.
HABITAT Dry or semi-arid forests, including edges and clearings plus plantations, from sea-level to about 600 m (1980').
BEHAVIOUR As in Rufous-backed Thrush, with which it may occur as a scarce visitor to mainland Nayarit. Food as for Rufous-backed Thrush, often occurring in small numbers in fruiting trees.
BREEDING Undescribed.
MOULT No information.
MEASUREMENTS (n=7) Wing, male 121.5–132.5, female 119–127.5; bill (culmen) male 22–23, female 20.5–25.5; tarsus, male 33–36, female 32–38 (Phillips 1981). Weight apparently unrecorded.
REFERENCES Phillips (1981).

160 LA SELLE THRUSH *Turdus swalesi* Plate 55

Haplocichla swalesi Wetmore, 1927, *Proc. Biol. Soc.* Washington 40: 55 – Massif de la Selle, Haiti.

IDENTIFICATION 26–27 cm (10–10½"). A shy endemic of the upper rainforest and cloud-forest of Hispaniola. Very distinctive with blackish head and upperparts to centre of breast; lower breast and flanks deep rufous or chestnut and white on centre of the belly. Uncommon or scarce (still fairly easily seen at a few sites). Confusion species Similar to American Robin (161) in overall size

and shape, long legs and relatively long tail.
DESCRIPTION Sexes alike. Adult Forehead to crown, nape and sides of neck black extending across rest of upperparts; wings and tail glossy or bronzed black but flight feathers and outer tail feathers browner. Face also black but cheeks and ear-coverts flecked greyer; bright yellow-orange eye-ring. Chin and throat black, heavily flecked or

streaked whitish on centre of throat. Breast blackish-brown tinged brown at sides. Belly and flanks to vent deep rufous or chestnut, centre of belly white; lower flanks and thighs grey, undertail-coverts white but centres of feathers grey or dark grey. Bill orange. Legs and feet brown or blackish-brown, soles of feet paler brown. **Immature** Juvenile undescribed but first-year bird probably very similar to adult.

GEOGRAPHICAL VARIATION Two races; variation clinal but fairly well marked. Race *dodae* has nape, mantle, back and scapulars olive-brown.

VOICE Virtually silent except when singing but gives fairly typical short soft *sip* or *wip* contact notes often as a double note in flight or when about to fly. Song a series of individual whistles, chuckles and chirps strung together with long pauses, very similar in tempo and phrasing to that of Red-legged Thrush (129) without the distinctive sharp *wit* or *pit* note; also a drawn-out low soft whistle which may be extended into *ture-too* or *tu-re-oo* and *cho-ho-cho* and a louder, more strident *poo-ip, poo-ip* or *whewry-whewry-wheury* and some low chuckling or gurgling notes (Bond 1979). Given from exposed perches at dawn but becomes progressively more hidden during the rest of the day and by evening delivered from perches within the upper canopy.

STATUS AND DISTRIBUTION Locally common to uncommon or scarce; endemic to Hispaniola. Described as common at the time of discovery but never widespread, and in recent years the range has decreased rapidly with the destruction of its forest habitat. Now classed as Vulnerable by Collar *et al.* (1994); may no longer occur in Haiti as recent reports suggest that all remaining rainforest has been destroyed (A. Sander pers. comm.). Habitat destruction in the Dominican Republic (including within the 'protected' national parks) puts this species at increasing risk of extinction within a matter of decades. Thus within its remaining range it is in need of enforced protection measures.

T. s. swalesi Restricted to the Massif de la Selle ridge, Haiti, east to the Sierra de Bahoruco (mostly the area between Lomo de Toro, Zapoten and Pueblo Viejo), Dominican Republic. Reported to be 'very common' in Parc National La Visite, Haiti (Woods & Ottenwalder 1986) but with continuing habitat loss (see above) this assessment may now need revising.

T. s. dodae Sierra de Neiba and the vicinity of Alto Banderas, Cordillera Central, Dominican Republic, where locally common within the restricted amount of remaining habitat (Graves & Olson 1986, Keith *et al.* in prep.).

MOVEMENTS Sedentary.

HABITAT Dense understorey shrubbery and vegetation of subtropical rain- and cloud-forests and pine forests above 1360 m (4500') on the high ridges of central Hispaniola; may also sometimes wander to edges of cultivation and gardens (Collar *et al.* 1992). Habitat destruction in recent years has now brought it into contact with Red-legged Thrush which may compete with it for food.

BEHAVIOUR Shy and generally timid, usually seen taking cover along forest paths or in flight through the mid- to lower canopy. Conversely, territorial birds are also fairly inquisitive and respond to 'pishing' provided the observer remains hidden and completely still. Spends long periods inactive; forages low down in trees, moist understorey vegetation and on the ground and variably reported as difficult or easy to observe. Has been recorded as feeding in the open on edges of paths or trails especially in the early dawn; also reported to forage in the open in cultivated gardens (Stockton de Dod 1978) and may inhabit thickets near villages. Forages in typical thrush manner on the ground where it hops or runs rapidly with head held low, stops abruptly and raises its head erect, taking worms and arthropods; also takes fruit in trees (notably *Persea anomala*).

BREEDING Very poorly known. Season: May–July. Nest: a bulky cup, mostly of moss and placed in a shrub, low tree or bush at low or moderate heights from the ground (Bond 1979). Eggs: 2–3, greenish-blue and finely spotted.

MOULT No information.

MEASUREMENTS Wing, unsexed (n=7) 119.5–135 (C. Rimmer pers. comm.); male (n=4) 127–131.5, female (n=3) 121–128; tarsus 42–47; bill, male 23–25, female 21.5–22 (culmen) 15.5–17; *dodae* wing, male (n=1) 129, female (n=1) 125. Weight (n=9) 88–106 g.

REFERENCES Collar *et al.* (1992, 1994), Graves & Olson (1986), Keith *et al.* (in prep.), Stockton de Dod (1978), Wetmore & Swales (1931).

161 AMERICAN ROBIN *Turdus migratorius*   Plate 48

Turdus migratorius Linnaeus, 1766, *Syst. Nat.* (ed. 12) 1: 292 – in America *septentrionali.*

IDENTIFICATION 25–28 cm (10–11″). The common large thrush of North America, widely distributed through most of Canada, the U.S.A. and Mexico; northern birds move south in winter. A large distinctive thrush often seen in suburban gardens and town parks as well as more rural and deep-forest habitats. Male has blackish head and face (except chin and throat) with broad but broken white eye-ring, grey upperparts and wings, blackish-brown tail

with small whitish tips to outer feathers, blackish-streaked white chin and throat, deep reddish-chestnut breast to vent, and white undertail-coverts. Female similar but generally paler, with duller, more orange underparts. Juveniles like female but paler, mottled or flecked with paler tips or shafts above and spotted black below. Birds in northern Mexico are much paler. **Confusion species** Rufous-backed Thrush (158) lacks any eye-ring on a dark grey head, and has very strong rufous- or reddish-brown on the mantle and scapulars and a white central lower breast to undertail. Varied Thrush (37) is slimmer, with darker grey upperparts, orange supercilium and a broad black breast-band. In western U.S.A. American Robins can be paler grey above and below and may show pale supercilium, recalling Eyebrowed Thrush (116).

DESCRIPTION Sexes differ. **Adult male** Forehead to nape and face to sides of neck black or blackish-grey with broken white eye-ring usually extending as short white stripe above lores (may also be broken or separated from it over eye), white on lower half forming crescent on upper cheeks; mantle to back and scapulars dark grey or dusky greyish-brown, often with blackish centres; rump and uppertail-coverts slightly paler grey than rest of upperparts; tail black but tips of outermost feathers have large white spots on innerweb, tips of next inner one or two feathers white. Median coverts as scapulars or slightly darker, may be edged or tipped warm brown or orange-brown in fresh plumage; greater coverts similar or darker in centre and edged grey or brown; alula black, primary coverts dark grey or black finely edged pale grey; flight feathers black finely edged pale or whitish-grey on outerwebs, tertials edged slightly browner. Underwing has coverts as belly and flanks but base of flight feathers light or silvery-brown. Chin and throat white with thin black streaks at sides; breast to belly and flanks deep orange-rufous to chestnut with fine white fringes which disappear with wear; lower belly, vent and undertail-coverts white; thighs brown flecked white. Bill yellow or orange-yellow darker, blackish at tip in breeding season becoming darker horn-brown or blackish on culmen with yellow to orange-yellow base to lower mandible. Eye dark brown. Legs and feet brown, dark brown or tinged yellowish-brown. In worn plumage head becomes darker and rest of upperparts greyer, edges to wing-coverts, secondaries and tertials paler or whitish, and underparts duller and without white tips. **Adult female** As male (sometimes not reliably sexed by plumage alone) but generally duller with browner-black on head and upperparts slightly browner, buffish-white broken eye-ring, paler or brownish fringes to wing-coverts, blackish-brown streaks on sides of chin and throat, and slightly duller orange on breast to belly and flanks; may also show darker orange bases to feathers on breast and frequently shows more white on fringes to lower breast, flanks and sides of belly; thighs and undertail-coverts dull or off-white. **Leucistic birds** Total albino and leucistic individuals occur frequently throughout the range; there are also rare occurrences of melanistic individuals. **Immature** Juvenile heavily mottled with paler tips, broadly pale buff along central shafts of mantle to rump and scapulars, and pale buff central shafts and rusty-buff tips to median and tips to greater coverts; tertials also show small whitish spot at tips; more pale or whitish areas on face and base of bill, with short pale sub-moustachial and dark brown malar stripe; sides of throat have small dark spots becoming large dark brown spots on pale tawny-buff or dull orange breast and flanks, belly to undertail-coverts whitish spotted

or smudged blackish-brown. Bill as adult but duller or paler. **First-winter bird** Similar to adult but paler or duller brown with sooty-brown on head and face and paler or buffish eye-ring; tail and wing-coverts (retained from juvenile plumage) with greyish-white tips to median and greater coverts, amount of white at tip of outer tail feathers usually less than in adult; underparts as female but with fine yellowish or whitish fringes to lower breast, belly and flanks, sometimes also retaining a few black tips on breast into following spring. First-summer bird difficult to age with certainty.

GEOGRAPHICAL VARIATION Seven races; clinal and moderately to weakly defined; only one, con-finis, is distinctive in the field, and often classed as a separate species, the San Lucas Robin.

Race achrusterus smaller than nominate and has black on forehead to crown finely (or more broadly in female) tipped pale grey (quite broadly in female) or orange-brown; upperparts slightly browner or dusky-brown; white tips to tail moderately distinct to indistinct; breast to belly and flanks paler, on average, and more tawny-rufous (paler or sandier-brown in female) than deep orange; juvenile similar to that of nominate but has whiter underparts, less heavily (or even un-) spotted.

Race caurinus very slightly smaller than nominate and very dark grey to black on head, extending in some onto upper mantle or back; rest of upperparts variable from brownish-grey to dusky-brown; underparts may, on average, be slightly deeper rust-orange, white on tips of innerwebs of outer two tail feathers more restricted and not always visible in field.

Race nigrideus also uniformly darker or blackish on head; mantle, back and scapulars grey to dark grey with blackish centres showing, but some females can be darker above (as dark as in males of other subspecies); tail like nominate; underparts, on average, slightly deeper rufous or more chestnut than nominate, chin and throat more heavily streaked and often merging on throat; undertail-coverts greyer than in other races; juvenile has larger black spots, often merging across breast.

Western birds, race propinquus, are same size or slightly larger and paler than nominate and tinged more heavily brownish-grey in fresh plumage (some males can be as pale as females of other subspecies); virtually lacking any white or has only a very narrow white tips to outermost tail feather. Some birds (probably females from more northern parts of breeding range) so pale as to lack almost any red below or show only slight wash on breast, males usually darker or more rufous; may also show pale or whitish sides of head or as supercilium (D. Roberson pers. comm.).

Race phillipsi from Mexico is similar to propinquus but on average slightly smaller but with a larger bill; male also less brick-red and tinged more rust- or rich brown below.

Race confinis slightly smaller generally, and palest, with uniform pale grey-brown on head, face and upperparts or slightly paler grey on rump and uppertail-coverts; also generally lacks any white spots to tips of outer tail feathers but has white edge to extreme tip of outermost feather. Has short thin whitish supercilium; dark lores may be indistinct or obscured in some; cheeks and ear-coverts dark grey to blackish and may have fine whitish shaft-streaks; broad white crescent on lower half of eye. Chin and throat white and may show indistinct dusky malar; throat to upper breast also whitish and streaked dusky; rest of underparts lack any orange or rufous and are instead pale buffish or pale yellow (especially in female) or creamy-buff (often heaviest on flanks and extending to underwing-coverts) except for mostly white undertail-coverts; flanks on female washed pale brownish-grey. Bill mostly yellow with dusky tip more extensively brownish in winter. Legs and feet brown.

VOICE Most frequent call is a series of *tut-tut-tut* notes, often preceded by an explosive or exclamatory *seeech* or *seech-ook* or a high-pitched *pleent*; a thin *sss sss tut-tut-tut* or *skeet skeet*; a high-pitched screaming alarm *seech each-each-each*; a rapid chuckling and musical *he-he-he-he-he* running up and down the scale; and a tinkling *chill-ill-ill-ill* with the first note most striking and the following notes dropping gradually in pitch. Song a loud, rich, pleasant *cheerily-cheery-cheerily-cheery* interspersed with short pauses and changes in tone; may also include some other thrush-like phrases, e.g. *teedle-teedle*; also a whispered *hisselly-hisselly* song usually given as part of the courtship display. Sings usually from a high perch, e.g. top of a tall tree, mostly in early morning from before dawn and in the evening until well after dark; several birds often sing in close proximity. Song period from early March (California) to late July or early August; some birds, particularly in the east, sing infrequently into late August and September and sporadically throughout the winter. The song of *confinis* is like the nominate but with a weaker delivery and lacking any clear notes.

STATUS AND DISTRIBUTION Common or fairly common; may be erratically common or scarce in winter. Birds in central California (*propinquus*) and probably elsewhere in the U.S.A. are considered to be still increasing (Roberson & Tenney 1993).

T. m. migratorius Breeds in the U.S.A. and Canada to the edge of the trees and along the edge of the tundra from northern and western Alaska, northern Yukon, northern Mackenzie east to about the Thelon River, southern Keewatin, northern and central British Columbia, central Alberta, northern Manitoba and east to eastern and south-central Quebec and Nova Scotia south into western North Dakota to Kansas, Oklahoma, Missouri, Indiana east to the New England states and south to Maryland and in the Appalachians to North Carolina and north-west Virginia. In winter to southern coastal Alaska (where local) and southern Canada from southern British Columbia to southern Ontario, south-west Quebec (more rarely or locally in southern Alberta, southern Saskatchewan and southern Manitoba), New Brunswick, Prince Edward Island, southern Newfoundland and Nova Scotia to most of the U.S.A., south to southern Florida, Bermuda, northern Bahamas and western Cuba (where rare in winter), also eastern Mexico from eastern Durango south to southern Veracruz (but generally rare or scarce in lowlands of eastern Mexico).

T. m. nigrideus Breeds coastal northern Quebec (west to James Bay) to Labrador, Newfoundland, St Pierre and Miquelon islands. In winter from southern Newfoundland south through most of the eastern states to southern Louisiana, southern Mississippi, central South Carolina and northern Georgia (possibly also to north-west Florida).

T. m. achrusterus Breeds from southern Oklahoma east through southern Missouri to Maryland and western Virginia south to northern Florida and the Gulf states to central Texas. In winter throughout much of the southern part of the breeding range south to southern Florida, southern Texas, occasionally or exceptionally to Cuba (singles collected in December 1963 and January).

T. m. caurinus Breeds in south-east Alaska from about Glacier Bay south through coastal British Columbia to Washington and north-west Oregon, mostly in the coastal belt where the annual rainfall exceeds 75". In winter from south-west British Columbia south to central and southern California and east to northern Idaho, exceptionally some birds remaining in south-east Alaska during winter; also recorded as a casual migrant to south-east California and central Arizona (Phillips 1986).

T. m. propinquus Breeds from south-east British Columbia, southern Alberta, south-west Saskatchewan south to Montana and south-east Oregon, western South Dakota, western Nebraska to southern California (but absent from desert areas) and more recently the Sierra Juarez in northern Baja California (Howell & Webb 1992); also central, southern and north-east Arizona and Mexico south to western Zacatecas (possibly also south-west Nuevo León) and Guanajuato (where it intergrades with *phillipsi*). In winter throughout much of the southern part of the breeding range and south to Baja California, Oaxaca. Possibly also winters into the highlands of central and south-central Guatemala (Land 1970) but this considered doubtful (Phillips 1986) and in need of verification (Howell & Webb 1995).

T. m. confinis Breeds between 1000 and 2000 m (3300–6600') in the Todos Santos range and Las Lagunas, Cape San Lucas, southern Baja California.

T. m. phillipsi Resident in Mexico from southern Nuevo León and south-west Tamaulipas west to Jalisco and south to Guerrero and central-southern Oaxaca.

MOVEMENTS Migrant or partial migrant. Breeding birds in Alaska and virtually all Canada (except the southernmost areas) move south to winter in the U.S.A., Bahamas, most of Mexico and the highlands of southern Guatemala. Most birds leave the breeding area in September and October but those from Alaska and much of northern Canada depart in mid- to late August and September. Arrives in wintering areas from October onwards, some birds still arriving in the south of the range in late December. Present on Bermuda (where regular but uncommon) from mid-September to mid-April, most in December and January, and in Bahamas from late October to early March. Rare winter visitor (*migratorius*) to Cuba from between late September and March to mid-April.

Return movements from the southern and central U.S.A. begin early, usually in mid- to late February and early March, progressively later for birds in northern U.S.A.; arrival in central Alaska and the Seward Peninsula from first week of May; late migrants pass through Florida in mid- to late April. Ringing recoveries show that migrants move along river valleys and along southern and eastern coasts. Race *confinis* is a vertical migrant, occurring at lower elevations in the non-breeding months.

Nominate birds have occurred (as overshoots) west to the Pribilof Islands, north to Point Barrow and Prudhoe Bay, Herschel Island, Yukon and at Frobisher Bay, Baffin Island. In the south birds (race uncertain, possibly *achrusterus*) are uncommon to scarce visitors to the Yucatán Peninsula and Cozumel Island, south-east Mexico; vagrant (January 1981) to Belize. Irregular or rare vagrant to Greenland (3 *migratorius* and 3 *nigrideus*), Jamaica, Hispaniola, Puerto Rico and most of Europe from Iceland (2 records), Norway, British Isles (31 to 1996), France, Belgium, Germany, Czech Republic and Austria.

HABITAT Mainly an inhabitant of forests, woods in high-rainfall areas, occurring from wooded tundra, swamps and bottomlands to the timberline at c.3700 m (12,200'), and in meadows or glades in conifer tracts, alder thickets, farms with wooded edges. Throughout most of the 'lower 48' states it is widespread in farmland with woods, hedges and adjacent open areas such as edges of cultivation, fields, lawns, gardens, golf courses, parks, orchards and shrubberies in urban and suburban areas (including the centre of most towns and cities, e.g. New York). In winter in similar habitat but usually in more open or grassy areas.

BEHAVIOUR Outside the northern, north-western and extreme southern parts of its range it is a tame species, often feeding and nesting in suburban gardens; *caurinus* inhabits dense conifer and spruce forests and only rarely comes into suburban areas. General actions and gait similar to those of the Blackbird (111) in Europe but more robust or bolder with a nervous, alert stance, head often held high, wings slightly drooped and tail flicked occasionally; on the ground walks, hops or runs. In flight the shape is easily recognisable by the straight upperparts and a relatively rounded belly; as in other large thrushes, deep wing-beats and brief swift glides create undulating flight. Roosts communally even in the breeding season; some roosts in late July and August can number several thousand birds at their peak. Feeds mostly on the ground but also in trees and bushes, mainly on a range of wild and cultivated fruits, berries and invertebrates including fruits of red cedar, juniper, bayberry, mulberry, pokeweed, juneberry, spiceberry, blackberry, raspberry, rowan, chinaberry, hawthorn, cherry, woodbine, grape, flowering dogwood and blueberry; also grass-seed; invertebrates mostly beetles and caterpillars, but also ants, bugs, flies, grasshoppers, spiders, snails, millipedes and earthworms. Nestlings are fed mostly on small worms and other soft invertebrate prey.

In places (particularly *caurinus*) feeds on open beaches along the tideline, taking a variety of small insects and molluscs; in others it is fond of crab-apples and has been known to take dead mice and small snakes, and to become intoxicated by the effects of large quantities of ripe chinaberries (Bent 1949).

BREEDING Season: April to late August. Nest: a large untidy construction of grasses, twigs, weed stalks, string and cloth, with a smooth lining of mud often forming a rim, the mud itself lined with fine grasses and soft plant material; usually placed 1.5–5 m (5–15') from the ground in a tree-fork, along a branch, on/in buildings with suitable ledges, top of post, gutter, fire-escape, etc.; will nest anywhere remotely suitable, including clumps of phragmites, occasionally on the ground and also in old nests of other birds; has even been known to share a nest and feeding of the young with a Mourning Dove *Zenaida macroura*. Eggs: 3–4, rarely 5–6, variable in shape from oval to round, pale blue or more rarely white, usually unmarked or with tiny dots or spots of dark brown. Incubation 11–14 days; almost entirely by the female. Fledging period 15–16 days. Two broods.

MOULT Full post-breeding moult of adults from late summer, completed in August or early September. Post-juvenile partial moult of the body feathers, wing-coverts (except some inner greater coverts) and tertials occurs from August to October; remaining greater coverts, flight feathers and tail retained into first-winter plumage.

MEASUREMENTS Wing, male (n=100) 120–140, female (n=100) 118–132.5; bill (culmen) 18.5–22 (to 24 in *confinis*); tarsus 29.5–35.5; *nigrideus* wing, male (n=10) 128–136, female (n=10) 123–131; *achrusterus* wing, male (n=50) 119–133, female (n=54) 116–129; *caurinus* wing, male (n=37) 120–137, female (n=39) 115–132; *propinquus* wing, male (n=100) 128–145, female (n=100) 124–142; *phillipsi* wing 129–139; *confinis* wing, male 133–140.5, female 124–136.5 (Pyle *et al.* 1997). Weight, male 59–91 g, female 72–94 g.

REFERENCES Bent (1949), Boertmann (1994), Howell & Webb (1992).

162 RUFOUS-COLLARED ROBIN *Turdus rufitorques* Plate 49

Turdus (Merula) rufitorques Hartlaub, 1844, *Rev. Zool.* [Paris] 7: 214. – Guatemala.

IDENTIFICATION 23–25.5 cm (9–10"). An attractive and distinctive thrush of the mountains of southern Mexico to El Salvador. Adult male is black on the head and face with a broad rufous or reddish-orange collar on the lower nape to upper belly, the rest of plumage being sooty-black with some gloss on the wings and tail. The adult female is similar but dark or grey-brown and the collar to belly is duller or less complete. **Confusion species** Male offers no problems if seen well: the rufous collar is diagnostic. Female initially similar to female Black Thrush (133) and Mountain Thrush (145) but both lack any collar and the latter has an all-dark bill and whitish belly to vent; Clay-coloured Thrush (151) is paler with tawny-buff underparts and no collar.

DESCRIPTION Sexes differ. **Adult male** Forehead to upper nape, lores, cheeks and ear-coverts black; thin whitish or pale yellow eye-ring. Lower nape to sides of neck and breast and upper belly rufous-orange or deep chestnut, narrowest on nape and broadest on breast (some birds, perhaps not full adults, have forehead and crown finely edged orange and belly and flanks also orange with blackish edges). In fresh plumage (October) shows fairly broad pale or grey edges to dark-centred feathers on mantle and scapulars to uppertail-coverts. Rest of plumage above and below deep sooty-black with some glossy edges on upperparts, wings, underwing-coverts and tail. Chin pale or whitish-buff becoming dark brown or tawny-orange on throat and streaked black, or can be entirely blackish-brown with rufous edges to feathers; breast and upper belly also variable from deep reddish-orange and bright rufous to brick-red; belly to vent and undertail-coverts black with a few whitish central shafts but variable as some birds show reddish or reddish-brown tinge on belly. Bill bright yellow or yellowish-orange except tor blackish tip. Legs and feet bright yellow. In fresh plumage head, upperparts, breast and belly have greyish-brown edges and tips. **Adult female** Similar to male but black replaced with brown, blackish- or greyish-brown, forehead to nape perhaps slightly darker brown; collar (usually fairly indistinct on nape) often begins on sides of nape, paler or light orange-buff to orange-brown or brownish-rufous, continuing to breast and upper belly. Face as crown; chin and throat pale tawny-buff streaked more finely with dusky or black; breast, belly and flanks grey-brown or washed buff, vent to undertail-coverts grey-brown or tinged olive, latter with broad white central shafts. Bill, legs and feet light orange-brown, upper mandible often dusky-brown. In worn plumage (breeding season) rufous collar abraded or almost absent and becomes pale grey-brown. **Immature** Juvenile very similar to same-age American Robin (161); head and face dark brown with pale yellowish-buff centres and dark brown fringes; nape has pale yellowish-buff centres and, in some, may merge to form pale collar; upperparts dark brown but upper mantle and scapulars have pale yellow or light orange-buff central shafts and dark brown tips, becoming broader shaft-streaks on lower mantle and edges of scapulars. Juvenile male has larger spots/shaft-streaks than same-age female; rump and upper-tail-coverts have smaller or duller central shaft-streaks. Median and greater coverts have pale yellowish or orange-buff tips; tertials have pale orange-buff tips; underwing-coverts pale or yellowish-orange; underparts whitish-buff on chin and throat, becoming mottled with yellow or yellowish-orange subterminally and dark brown bars or tips on rest of underparts except for dark olive on lower flanks and whitish undertail-coverts with olive-brown edges. Bill mostly brown with paler base to lower mandible. First-year male similar to adult female but slightly darker and usually with brighter collar. First-year female very dull or drab brown with darker edges and tips to nape; also usually red on breast greatly reduced or entirely lacking so that upperparts appear almost uniform. Males appear to breed in subadult plumage which is much less rufous or chestnut and hence appear more like females than do older males, which, in certain areas, are relatively rare. Thus it seems likely that males take two years to reach full adult plumage.

GEOGRAPHICAL VARIATION None. Monotypic.

VOICE A sharp *whip whip whip* and a single sharp *chick* or *chuck*, recalling American Robin; also a thin weak lisping note recalling Cedar Waxwing *Bombycilla cedorum* given in flight or when about to fly. Song similar to song of American Robin but despite some rich fluty phrases lacks the latter's variety of phrase and is often given with little emphasis or apparent enthusiasm, trailing off into a weak chattering at the end; sings late into the evening and again at the first signs of dawn (Skutch 1960). Song period late January to late May.

STATUS AND DISTRIBUTION Common to abundant. Resident between 1500 and 3630 m (5000–12,000') in the mountains of Chiapas, southern Mexico, to central and southern Guatemala (possibly also western Honduras) and Volcán de Santa Ana, western El Salvador.

MOVEMENTS Little known but some may move to lower altitudes in severe weather. Has occurred infrequently (vagrant?) in Honduras.

HABITAT Occurs in cloud-forest and conifer or pine-oak woods and forest, also in woodland with brush or scrub, pastures and edges of cultivation of the subtropical and lower temperate zones, occasionally at the edges of villages; also found above the treeline (including the main cones of extinct volcanoes) in undulating prairie with isolated cypresses, pines and agaves.

BEHAVIOUR Shy and unobtrusive, usually alone or in pairs but very sociable at roosts, when it often forms sizeable flocks in cypress trees or pinewoods; also forms loose gatherings in the non-breeding season; appears to be tolerant of extremely cold weather at high altitudes. On the ground hops in typical thrush manner and flies short distances when disturbed. Forages on the ground in open pastures.

BREEDING Season: April and May, possibly to late July. Nest: very similar to that of American Robin, a large open nest of grey lichens, small twigs and flower stems, together with some moss and mud or cow dung and lined with fine grasses and plant fibres, usually placed up to 4.5 m (15') from the ground in tree- and branch-forks and in clumps of creepers or parasitic tree-ferns. Eggs

2–3, pale blue, unmarked and identical to those of American Robin. Low-altitude birds are double-brooded.

MOULT No information.

MEASUREMENTS Wing, male (n=32) 127–139, exceptionally 142, female (n=15) 121.5–134.5; tarsus 30.5–33.5; bill (culmen) 19–21 (Dickey & van Rossem 1938). Weight apparently unrecorded.

REFERENCES Dickey & van Rossem (1938), Skutch (1960).

REFERENCES

Abdulali, H. & Unnithan, S. 1991. A catalogue of the birds in the collection of Bombay Natural History Society 34: Muscicapidae (Turdinae). *J. Bombay Nat. Hist. Soc.* 88: 73–80.

Ali, S. & Ripley, S. D. 1983. *Compact handbook of the birds of India and Pakistan.* Bombay: Oxford University Press.

Allport, G., Ausden, M., Hayman, P. V., Robertson, P. & Wood, P. 1989. The conservation of birds of Gola Forest, Sierra Leone. *ICBP Study Report* 38.

American Ornithologists' Union 1983. *Check-list of North American birds: the species of birds of North America from the Arctic through Panama, including the West Indies and Hawaiian Islands.* Sixth edition. American Ornithologists' Union.

American Ornithologists' Union 1998. *Check-list of North American birds: the species of birds of North America from the Arctic through Panama, including the West Indies and Hawaiian Islands.* Seventh edition. American Ornithologists' Union.

Ames, P. L. 1975. The application of syringeal morphology to the classification of the Old World insect eaters (Muscicapidae). *Bonn. Zool. Beitr.* 26: 107–134.

Andersson, S. 1996. Bright ultraviolet coloration in the Asian whistling-thrushes (*Myiophonus* spp.). *Proc. R. Soc. Lond.* B. 263: 843–848.

Andersson, S. 1999. Morphology of UV reflectance in a whistling-thrush: implications for the study of structural colour signalling in birds. *J. Avian Biol.* 30: 193–204.

Andrews, I. J., Khoury, F. & Shirihai, H. 1999. Jordan Bird Report 1995–97. *Sandgrouse* 21: 10–35.

Appleyard, I. 1994. *Ring Ouzels of the Yorkshire Dales.* Leeds: W. S. Maney & Sons.

Ash, J. S. & Miskell, J. E. 1983. Birds of Somalia: their habitat, status and distribution. *Scopus* special supplement No.1.

Ash, J. S. & Miskell, J. E. 1998. *Birds of Somalia.* Robertsbridge, East Sussex: Pica Press.

Atwood, J. L., Rimmer, C. C., McFarland, K. P., Tsai, S. H. & Nagy, L. R. 1996. Distribution of Bicknell's Thrush in New England and New York. *Wilson Bull.* 108: 650–661.

Avise, J. C., Patton, J. C. & Aquadro, C. F. 1980. Evolutionary genetics of birds 1. Relationships among North American thrushes and allies. *Auk* 97: 135–147.

Baker, E. C. S. 1924. *The fauna of British India.* Vol. II. London: Taylor & Francis.

Baker, E. C. S. 1932. *The nidification of birds of the Indian Empire.* 4 Vols. London: Taylor & Francis.

Baker N. E. & Baker, E. M. 1992. Four Afrotropical migrants on the East African coast: evidence for a common origin. *Scopus* 15: 122–124.

Bannerman, D. A. 1936. *The birds of Tropical West and Equatorial Africa.* Vol. 2. London: Crown Agents for the Colonies.

Bannerman, D. A. 1953. *The birds of West and Equatorial Africa.* London: Oliver & Boyd.

Batten, L. A. 1977. Studies on the population dynamics and energetics of Blackbirds *Turdus merula*, Linnaeus. PhD thesis, University of London (unpublished).

Beaman, M. 1994. *Palearctic birds: a checklist of the birds of Europe, North Africa and Asia.* Stonyhurst, Lancashire: Harrier Publications.

Beehler, B. 1978. Notes on the mountain birds of New Ireland. *Emu* 78: 65–70.

Behrstock, R. A. & Eubanks, T. L. 1997. Additions to the avifauna of Nuevo León, Mexico, with notes on new breeding records and infrequently seen species. *Cotinga* 7: 27–30.

Beltrán, W. 1992. First description of the nest and eggs of the Black Solitaire. *Wilson Bull.* 104: 551–552.

Bennun, L. A. 1987. Ringing and recapture of Spotted Ground Thrushes *Turdus fischeri fischeri* at Gede, Kenya Coast: indications of site fidelity and population size. *Scopus* 11: 1–5.

Benson, C. W. 1946. Notes on the birds of southern Abyssinia. *Ibis* 88: 180–205.

Benson, C. W. 1960a. Recent records from north-western Northern Rhodesia. *Bull. Brit. Orn. Club* 80: 106–112.

Benson, C. W. 1960b. Birds of the Comoro Islands: results of the BOU Centenary Expedition 1958. *Ibis* 103b: 5–106.

Benson, C. W. 1969. The relationship of *Turdus pelios bocagei* (Cabanis) and *Turdus pelios stormsi* Hartlaub. *Bull. Brit. Orn. Club* 89: 133–134.

Bent, A. C. 1949. Life histories of North American thrushes, kinglets and their allies. *U. S. Natn. Mus. Bull.* 196.

Berger, A. J. 1972. *Hawaiian birdlife.* Honolulu: University of Hawaii.

Best, B. J., Checker, M., Thewlis, R. M., Best, A. L. & Duckworth, W. 1995. Bird breeding data from southwestern Ecuador. *Ornitologia Neotropical* 6.

Best, B. J., Heijnen, T. and Williams, R. S. R. eds. 1997. *A guide to bird-watching in Ecuador and the Galápagos Islands.* Leeds: Biosphere Publications.

Betts, F. N. 1966. Notes on some resident breeding birds of southwest Kenya. *Ibis* 108: 513–530.

BirdLife International in prep. *Threatened birds of the world.* Cambridge: BirdLife International.

Bishop, K. D. & Brickle, N. W. 1998. An annotated checklist of the birds of the Tanimbar Islands. *Kukila* 10: 115–150.

Biswas, B. 1961. The birds of Nepal, part 5. *J. Bombay Nat. Hist. Soc.* 58: 653–677.

Boertmann, D. 1994. An annotated checklist to the birds of Greenland. *Bioscience* 38: 1–63.

Boesman, P. 1997. Some new information on the distribution of Venezuelan birds. *Cotinga* 9: 27–39.

Bond, J. 1979. *Birds of the West Indies*. London: Collins.

Bowden, C. G. R. 1987, The Yemen Thrush in North Yemen. *Sandgrouse* 9: 87–89.

Bowen, R. V. 1997. Townsend's Solitaire (*Myadestes townsendi*). In *The birds of North America*, No. 269 (A. Poole & F. Gill, eds.). Philadelphia: Academy of Natural Sciences, & Washington, D.C.: American Ornithologists' Union.

Bowler, J. & Taylor, J. 1989. An annotated checklist of the birds of Manusela National Park, Seram. *Kukila* 4: 3–29.

Bowler, J. & Taylor, J. 1993. Birdwatching areas: Manusela National Park, Seram, Maluku, Indonesia. *Oriental Bird Club Bull.* 18: 21–25.

Brace, R. C., Hornbuckle, J. & Pearce-Higgins, J. W. 1997. The avifauna of the Beni Biological Station, Bolivia. *Bird Conserv. Internatn.* 7: 117 159.

Bradley, P. 1995. *Birds of the Cayman Islands*. Second edition. Italy: Caerulea Press.

Brazil, M. A. 1991. *The birds of Japan*. London: Christopher Helm.

Brazil, M. A. & Suzuki, T. 1988. Blackbird *Turdus merula* new to Ishikawa Prefecture. *Japanese J. Orn.* 37: 33–34.

Bregulla, H. L. 1992. *Birds of Vanuatu*. Oswestry: Anthony Nelson.

Britton, P. L. (ed.). 1980. *Birds of East Africa*. Nairobi: East African Natural History Society.

Brooks, D. J., Evans, M. I., Martins, R. P. & Porter, R. F. 1987. The status of birds in North Yemen and the records of the OSME Expedition in autumn 1985. *Sandgrouse* 9: 4–66.

Brooks, T. 1997. Threatened birds of Kenya 9: Taita Thrush. *Kenya Birds* 5: 102–104.

Brosset, A. & Erard, C. 1986. *Les oiseaux des regions forestières du nord-est du Gabon*. Vol.1. Paris: Société Nationale de Protection de la Nature.

Brown, L. H. 1970. Recent new breeding records for Kenya. *Bull. Brit. Orn. Club* 90: 2–6.

Brudenell-Bruce, P. G. C. 1975. *The Birds of New Providence and the Bahama Islands*. London: Collins.

Buckingham, D. L., Dutson, G. C. L. & Newman, J. L. 1995. Birds of Manus, Kolombangara and Makira (San Cristobal) with notes on mammals and records from other Solomon Islands. Report of the Cambridge Solomons Rainforest Project 1990. Unpublished.

Bull, J. 1964. *Birds of the New York area*. New York: Harper & Row.

Bundy, G., Connor, R. J. & Harrison, C. J. O. 1989. *Birds of the Eastern Province of Saudi Arabia*. London: Witherby.

Butchart, S. H. M., Brooks, T. M., Davies, C. W. N., Dharmaputra, G., Dutson, G. C. L., Lowen, J. C. & Sahu, A. 1994. Preliminary Report of the Cambridge Flores / Sumbawa Conservation Project 1993. Unpublished.

Cain, A. J. & Galbraith, I. C. J. 1955. Five new subspecies from the mountains of Guadalcanal (British Solomon Islands). *Bull. Brit. Orn. Club* 75: 90–93.

Carroll, R. W. 1988. Birds of the Central African Republic. *Malimbus* 10: 177–200.

Chapin, J. P. 1953–1954. The Birds of the Belgian Congo. Pts III & IV. *Bull. Amer. Mus. Nat. Hist.* 75A & B.

Chapman, F. M. 1924. Descriptions of New Birds from Ecuador, Colombia, Peru and Bolivia. *Amer. Mus. Novit.* 138.

Chasen, F. N. 1935. A handlist of Malaysian birds. *Bull. Raffles Mus.* 11: 1–389.

Chasen, F. N. 1940. A new race of Rock Thrush from the Malay States. *Bull. Brit. Orn. Club* 60: 97–98.

Cheng, Tso-hsin, 1987. *A synopsis of the avifauna of China*. Beijing: Science Press.

Cherry, J. D. 1985. Early autumn movements and prebasic moult of Swainson's Thrush. *Wilson Bull.* 97: 368–370.

Chong, M. H. N. in prep. Breeding record of Chestnut-capped Thrush (*Zoothera interpres*) in Peninsular Malaysia.

Christy, P. & Gascoigne, A. 1996. Principe Thrush rediscovered after more than 50 years. *Gulf of Guinea Conservation Newsletter* 4: 2.

Clancey, P. A. 1955. Geographical variation in the Orange Thrush *Turdus gurneyi* Hartlaub of eastern and south eastern Africa. *Bull. Brit. Orn. Club* 75: 70–78.

Clancey, P. A. 1968. The status of *Monticola pretoriae* Gunning and Roberts 1911. *Bull. Brit. Orn. Club* 88: 126–128.

Clancey, P. A. 1971. *A handlist of the birds of southern Mozambique*. Lourenco Marques: Instituto de Investigação Cientifica de Moçambique.

Clancey, P. A. 1993. The Ground Thrush *Zoothera guttata* (Vigors 1831) in the southern Afrotropics. *Gerfaut* 82–83: 45–50.

Clement, P. 1999a. The African *Zoothera* thrushes: identification, distribution and some problems with classification. *Bull. African Bird Club* 6: 17–24.

Clement, P. 1999b. Kennzeichen und Taxonomie von Bechsteindrossel *Turdus ruficollis* und Naumanndrossel *T. naumanni*. *Limicola* 13: 217–250.

Coates, B. J. & Bishop, K. D. 1997. *A guide to the birds of Wallacea*. Alderley, Queensland: Dove Publications.

Coates, B. J. 1990. *The birds of Papua New Guinea*. Vol. 2. Alderley, Australia: Dove Publications.

Cochran, W. W. 1972. Long-distance tracking of birds. Pp.39–59 in S. R. Galler, K. Schmidt-Koenig, G. J. Jacobs & R. E. Belleville, eds. *Animal orientation and navigation.* Washington D. C.: National Aeronautics and Space Administration SP262.

Cochran, W. W., Montgomery, G. G. & Graber, R. R. 1967. Migratory flights of *Hylocichla* thrushes in spring: a radiotelemetry study. *Living Bird* 6: 213–224.

Collar, N. J. 1999. The type locality and conservation status of *Monticola bensoni. Ostrich* 70: 151.

Collar, N. J. & Andrew, P. 1988. *Birds to watch: the ICBP world checklist of threatened birds.* Cambridge: International Council for Bird Preservation.

Collar, N. J. & Stuart, S. N. 1985. *Threatened birds of Africa and related islands: the ICBP/IUCN Red Data Book.* Cambridge: International Council for Bird Preservation.

Collar, N. J. & Tattersall, I. 1987. J. T. Last and the type-locality of Benson's Rockthrush *Monticola bensoni. Bull. Brit. Orn. Club* 107: 55–59.

Collar, N. J., Crosby, M. J. & Stattersfield, A. J. 1994. *Birds to watch 2: the world list of threatened birds.* Cambridge: BirdLife International.

Collar, N. J. Gonzaga, L. P., Krabbe, N., Madroño Nieto, A., Naranjo, L. G., Parker, T. A. & Wege, D. C. 1992. *Threatened birds of the Americas: the ICBP/IUCN Red Data Book.* Cambridge: International Council for Bird Preservation.

Collar, N. J., Mallari, N. A. D. & Tabaranza, B. R. 1999. *Threatened birds of the Philippines.* Manila: Bookmark, Inc.

Cramp, S., ed. 1988. *The birds of the Western Palearctic.* Vol. 5. Oxford: Oxford University Press.

Ctyroky, P. 1987. Ornithological observations in Iraq. *Beitr. Vogelkund.* 33: 141–204.

Davidson, P. & Stones, T. 1993. Birding in the Sula Islands. *Oriental Bird Club Bull.* 18: 59–63.

Davidson, P., Stones, T. & Lucking, R. 1995. The conservation and status of key bird species on Taliabu and the Sula Islands, Indonesia. *Bird Conserv. Internatn.* 5: 1–20.

Davis, P. 1959. A second Gray-cheeked Thrush at Fair Isle. *Brit. Birds* 52: 316.

Davis, S. E., Rocha O., O., Sarmiento, J. & Hanagarth, W. 1994. New departmental records and notes for some Bolivian birds. *Bull. Brit. Orn. Club* 114: 73–85.

Dee, T. J. 1986. *The endemic birds of Madagascar.* Cambridge: International Council for Bird Preservation.

Deignan, H. G. 1965. Notes on the nomenclature of the whistling-thrushes. *Bull. Brit. Orn. Club* 85: 3–4.

Delacour, J. 1942. The whistling thrushes (genus *Myiophoneus*). *Auk* 59: 246–264.

Delacour, J. 1947. *The birds of Malaysia.* New York: Macmillan.

Delgado, G., Nogales, M. & Naeslund, C. 1988. *Turdus torquatus* on El Hierro (Canary Islands). *Malimbus* 10: 221.

Dementiev, G. P. & Gladkov, N. A. (eds.) 1954. *Birds of the USSR.* Vol. 5. (English translation 1966) Jerusalem: Israel Program for Scientific Translations.

Demey, R (comp.) 1999. Recent reports. *Bull. African Bird Club* 6: 76.

Diamond, A. W. 1973. Ecology of St Lucia forest birds. *Ibis* 115: 313–329.

Diamond, J. M. 1989. A new subspecies of the Island Thrush *Turdus poliocephalus* from Tolokiwa Island in the Bismarck Archipelago. *Emu* 89: 58–60.

Dickey, D. R. & van Rossem, A. J. 1938 *The birds of El Salvador.* Chicago: Field Museum of Natural History.

Dickinson, E. C., Kennedy, R. S. & Parkes, K. C. 1991. *The birds of the Philippines.* Tring, Hertfordshire: British Ornithologists' Union (Check-list No.12).

Donahue, P. K. & Pierson, J. E. 1982. *Birds of Suriname: an annotated checklist.* South Harpswell, Maine.

Dowsett, R. J. 1965. Weights of some Zambian birds. *Bull. Brit. Orn. Club* 85: 150–152.

Dowsett, R. J. 1985. Site-fidelity and survival rates of some montane forest birds in Malawi, south-central Africa. *Biotropica* 17: 145–154.

Dowsett-Lemaire, F. 1990. Eco-ethology, distribution and status of Nyungwe Forest birds (Rwanda). *Tauraco Res. Rep.* 3: 87–109.

Dowsett, R. J. & Dowsett-Lemaire, F. 1993. A contribution to the distribution and taxonomy of Afrotropical and Malagasy birds. *Tauraco Res. Rep.* 5.

Dranzoa, C. 1995. Lyre-tailed Honeyguide *Melichneutes robustus* and Grey Ground Thrush *Zoothera princei batesi:* new records for Uganda. *Scopus* 18: 128–130.

Duckworth, J. W., Tizard, R. J., Timmins, R. J., Thewlis R. M., Robichaud, W. G. & Evans T. D. 1998. Bird records from Laos, October 1994–August 1995. *Forktail* 13: 33–68.

Duckworth, J. W., Salter, R. E. & Khounboline, K. (compilers) 1999. *Wildlife in Lao PDR: 1999 Status Report.* Vientiane: IUCN-The World Conservation Union/Wildlife Conservation Society/Centre for Protected Areas and Watershed Management.

Earlé, R. A. & Oatley, T. B. 1983. Populations, ecology and breeding of the Orange Ground Thrush at two sites in eastern South Africa. *Ostrich* 54: 205–212.

Eck, S. 1974. Katalog der ornithologischen Sammlung des Staatlichen Museums fur Tierkunde, Dresden. 5. Gattung *Myiophonus* Temminck (Turdidae). *Zool. Abhand. Staatl. Mus. Tierh. Dresden* 33: 95–102.

Eck, S. 1976. Die Vögel der Banggai-Inseln insbesondere Pelengs. *Zool. Abhand. Staatl. Mus. Tierh. Dresden* 34: 53–100.

Eisenmann, E. 1950. Some notes on Panama birds collected by J. H. Batty. *Auk* 67: 364–367.

Elgood, J. H., Heigham, J. B., Moore, A. M., Nason, A. M., Sharland, R. E. & Skinner, N. J. 1994. *The birds of Nigeria.* Tring, Hertfordshire: British Ornithologists' Union (Check-list No.4) (second edition).

Elliott, H. F. I. 1957. A contribution to the ornithology of the Tristan da Cunha Group. *Ibis* 99: 545–586.

Evans, P. G. H. 1993. *Birds of the eastern Caribbean.* Oxford: Macmillan.

Evans, W. R. 1994. Nocturnal flight call of Bicknell's Thrush. *Wilson Bull.* 106: 55–61.

Fancy, S. G., Jacobi, J. D., Pratt, T. K. & Ralph, C. J. 1994. Determining age and sex of Omao (*Myadestes obscurus*). *Elepaio* 54: 25–27.

Farkas, T. 1962. Zur Biologie und Ethologie der südafrikanischen Arten der Gattung *Monticola* (Boie). *Vogelwelt* 83: 11–22.

Farkas, T. 1966. Zur systematischen Stellung des Pretoria-Steinrotels *Monticola pretoriae* Gunning and Roberts. *Vogelwelt* 87: 33–48.

Farkas, T. 1971. *Monticola bensoni,* a new species from south-western Madagascar. *Ostrich* suppl. 9: 83–90.

Farkas, T. 1973. The biology and a new subspecies of *Monticola sharpei. Bull. Brit. Orn. Club* 93: 145–155.

Farkas, T. 1974. On the biology of *Monticola imerinus* (Hartlaub). *Bull. Brit. Orn. Club* 94: 165–170.

Farkas, T. 1979. A further note on the status of *Monticola pretoriae* Gunning and Roberts. *Bull. Brit. Orn. Club* 99: 20–21.

ffrench, R. P. 1973. *A guide to the birds of Trinidad and Tobago.* Wynnewood, Pennsylvania: Livingston Publishing Co.

Fjeldså, J. & Krabbe, N. 1990. *Birds of the high Andes.* Copenhagen: Zoological Museum, University of Copenhagen.

Fleischer, R. C., & McIntosh, C. E. in prep. Molecular systematics, geographical origins and estimated lineage ages of the Hawaiian avifauna. *Studies in Avian Biology.*

Fleming, R. L., Fleming, R. L. & Bangdel, L. S. 1979. *Birds of Nepal with reference to Kashmir and Sikkim.* (Second edition). Kathmandhu, Nepal: Avalok.

Ford, J. 1983. Speciation in the Ground-Thrush complex *Zoothera dauma* in Australia. *Emu* 83: 141–151.

Fraser, M. W., Ryan, P. G., Dean, W. R. J., Briggs, D. J. & Moloney, C. L. 1994. Biology of the Tristan Thrush *Nesocichla eremita. Ostrich* 65: 14–25.

Friedmann, H. & Williams, J. G. 1968. Notable records of rare or little known birds from western Uganda. *Rev. Zool. Bot. Afr.* 77: 11–36.

Friedmann, H., Kiff, L. F. & Rothstein, S. J. 1977. A further contribution to knowledge of the host relations of parasitic cowbirds. *Smithson. Contrib. Zool.* 235: 1–75.

Galbraith, I. C. J. & Galbraith, E. H. 1962. Land birds of Guadalcanal and the San Cristoval group, eastern Solomon Islands. *Bull. Brit. Mus. Nat. Hist. (Zool.)* 9: 1–86.

Garrido, O. & Kirkconnell, A. (in prep.) *Birds of Cuba.*

Gaston, K. J. 1994. *Rarity.* London: Chapman and Hall.

Gatter, W. 1997. *Birds of Liberia.* Robertsbridge, East Sussex: Pica Press.

Gibbs, D. 1996. Notes on Solomon Island birds. *Bull. Brit. Orn. Club* 116: 18–25.

Ginn, P. J., McIlleron, W. G. & Milstein, P. le S. 1989. *The complete book of South African birds.* Cape Town: Struik.

Glenister, A. G. 1971. *The birds of the Malay Peninsula.* Singapore & Penang: Oxford University Press.

Godfrey, W. E. 1979. *The birds of Canada.* Ottawa: National Museums of Canada.

Gómez de Silva, H. 1999. Distributional and temporal records of some Mexican birds. *Cotinga* 9: 16–20.

Goodwin, D. 1957. Remarks on some genera of Turninae. *Bull. Brit. Orn. Club* 77: 110–113.

Graves, G. R. & Olson, S. L. 1986. A new subspecies of *Turdus swalesi* (Aves: Passeriformes: Muscicapidae) from the Dominican Republic. *Proc. Biol. Soc. Washington* 99: 580–583.

Green, P. 1998. Possible anywhere: Fieldfare. *Birding* 30: 212–219.

Gregory, P., Burrow, I. & Burrows, R. & Burrows, G. 1996. Blue Rock Thrush at Manokwari, a new record for Irian Jaya. *Kukila* 8: 154.

de Greling, C. 1992. New records from northern Cameroun. *Bull. Brit. Orn. Club* 92: 24–27.

Grimmett, R., Inskipp, C. & Inskipp, T. 1998. *Birds of the Indian subcontinent.* London: A. & C. Black/Christopher Helm.

Griscom, L. 1930. Studies from the Dwight Collection of Guatemala Birds. *Amer. Mus. Nov.* 438.

Gundlach, J. 1893. *Ornitología cubana, o católogo descriptivo de todas las especies de aves tanto indigenas como de paso annual o accidental observadas en 53 años.* Habana: Arquivos de la Policlínica.

Gyldenstolpe, N. 1945. The bird fauna of Rio Jurua in western Brazil. *Kungl. Svenska Vetenskap. Handl.* 22.

Hachisuka, M. & Udagawa, T. 1950–1951. Contributions to the ornithology of Formosa. *Q. J. Taiwan Mus.* 3: 187–279, 4: 1–180.

Hadden, D. 1981. *Birds of the North Solomons.* Wau, Papua New Guinea: Wau Ecology Handbook No.8.

Hall, B. P. 1966. A new name for *Geocichla princei graueri* Sassi. *Bull. Brit. Orn. Club* 36: 123–124.

Hall, B. P. & Moreau, R. E. 1962. A study of the rare birds of Africa. *Bull. Mus (Nat. Hist.) Zool.* 8: 313–378.

Hall, B. P. & Moreau, R. E. 1970. *An atlas of speciation in African passerine birds.* London: British Museum (Natural History).

Handrinos, G. & Akriotis, T. 1997. *The birds of Greece.* London: Christopher Helm.

Hardy, J. W. & Parker III, T. A. 1992. *Voices of the New World thrushes.* Ara Records (tape).

Hardy, J. W. & Parker III, T. A. 1997. The nature and probable function of vocal copying in Lawrence's Thrush, *Turdus lawrencii. Ornithological Monographs* 48: 307–320.

Harebottle, D. M., Taylor, P. J. & Berruti, A. 1997. The subspecies status of the spotted ground thrush *Zoothera guttata guttata* (Aves: Turdidae) in South Africa: a multivariate analysis. *Durban Mus. Novit.* 22: 32–36.

Harrison, J. A., Allan, D. G., Underhill, L. G., Herremans, M., Tree, A. J., Parker, V. & Brown, C. J. 1998. *The atlas of southern African birds.* Vol. 2: Passerines. Johannesburg: BirdLife South Africa.

Harrison, J. M. 1954. Notes on the song of the Blue Rock Thrush, *Monticola solitarius* (Linnaeus). *Bull. Brit. Orn. Club* 74: 96.

Hartert, E. 1910. *Die Vögel der paläarktischen Fauna.* Berlin: R. Friedlander.

Hartert, E. 1920. Types of birds in the Tring Museum. *Novit. Zool.* 27: 425–505.

Hartert, E. 1924. Notes on some birds from Buru. *Novit. Zool.* 31: 104–111.

Hartert, E. & Venturi, S. 1909. Notes sur les oiseaux de la République Argentine. *Novit. Zool.* 16: 159–267.

Hayes, F. E., Scharf, P. A. & Ridgely, R. S. 1994. Austral bird migrants in Paraguay. *Condor* 96: 83–97.

Hazelwood, A. & Gorton, E. 1954. A Hebridean Song Thrush *Turdus ericetorum hebridensis* Clarke in England. *Bull. Brit. Orn. Club* 74: 10.

Hellebrekers, W. P. J. & Hoogerwerf, A. 1967. A further contribution to our oological knowledge of the island of Java (Indonesia). *Zool. Verhand.* 88.

Hellmayr, C. 1934. Catalogue of birds of the Americas and the adjacent islands. Part VII. *Field Mus. Nat. Hist., Zool. Ser.* 13.

Henry, G. M. 1971. *A guide to the birds of Ceylon.* Delhi: Oxford University Press.

Hicks, R. & Finch, B. W. 1987. Blue Rock Thrush on Paga Hill, Port Moresby. First record for the Australian Region, east of the Moluccas. *Muruk* 2(2): 66–67.

Hilty, S. L. & Brown, W. L. 1986. *A guide to the birds of Colombia.* Princeton: Princeton University Press.

Hoffmann, T. W. 1984. *National red data list of endangered and rare birds of Sri Lanka.* Colombo: Ceylon Bird Club.

Hoffmann, T. W. 1998. *Threatened birds of Sri Lanka: National Red List.* Colombo: Ceylon Bird Club.

Hollom, P. A. D., Porter, R. F., Christensen, S. & Willis, L. 1988. *Birds of the Middle East and North Africa.* Calton, UK: Poyser.

Holmes, D. & Phillipps, K. 1996. *The birds of Sulawesi.* Kuala Lumpur: Oxford University Press.

Holmes, G. 1984. Ecological evidence for distinguishing two species of ground-thrushes in central eastern Australia. *Australian Bird Watcher* 10: 164–166.

Holsten, B., Bräunlich, A. & Huxham, W. 1991. Rondo Forest Reserve, Tanzania: an ornithological note including new records of the East Coast Akalat *Sheppardia gunningi*, the Spotted Ground Thrush *Turdus fischeri*, and the Rondo Green Barbet *Stactolaema olivacea woodwardi. Scopus* 14: 125–128.

Hoover, J. P. & Brittingham, M. C. 1993. Regional variation in cowbird parasitism of Wood Thrushes. *Wilson Bull.* 105: 228–238.

Howell, S. N. G., Dowell, B. A., James, D. A., Behrstock, R. A & Robbins, C. S. 1992. New and noteworthy bird records from Belize. *Bull. Brit. Orn. Club* 112: 235–242.

Howell, S. N. G. & Webb, S. 1992. Noteworthy bird observations from Baja California, Mexico. *Western Birds* 23: 153–163.

Howell, S. N. G. & Webb, S. 1995. *A guide to the birds of Mexico and northern Central America.* Oxford: Oxford University Press.

Humphrey, P. S. & Parkes, K. C. 1959. An approach to the study of molts and plumages. *Auk* 76: 1–31.

Humphrey, P. S. & Parkes, K. C. 1963. Comments on the study of plumage succession. *Auk* 80: 496–503.

Inskipp, C. & Inskipp, T. P. 1991. *A guide to the birds of Nepal.* Second edition. London: Christopher Helm (A. & C. Black).

Irwin, M. P. S. 1984. The genera of African thrushes and the systematic position of the Groundscraper Thrush. *Honeyguide* 30: 13–20.

Irwin, M. P. S. & Benson, C. W. 1966. Notes on the birds of Zambia, part 1. *Arnoldia* (Rhodesia) 2(32): 1–19.

Isherwood, I. S., Willis, J. D. A., Edwards, T. R. K., Ekstrom, J. M. M., Kuriake, S., Lubis, I. R., Notanubun, H., Putnarubun, J., Robinson-Dean, J. C. & Tobias, J. A. 1997. *Biological surveys and conservation priorities in northeast Seram, Maluku, Indonesia.* Cambridge: CSB Conservation Publications.

Ishihara, T. 1986. The Amami Thrush distinct from the White's Ground Thrush. *Strix* 5: 60–61.

Jennings, M. C. 1981. *The birds of Saudi Arabia: a check-list.* Cambridge: M. C. Jennings.

Jensen, F. P. 1989. A review of some genera of African chats (Aves, Muscicapidae, Erithacini). *Steenstrupia* 15: 161–175.

Jones, J. P. G., Ferry, C. D., Isherwood, C. E., Knight, C. G., Kumara, C. L. & Weerakoon, K. 1998. *A conservation review of three wet zone forests in south-west Sri Lanka: final report of Project Sinharaja '97.* Cambridge: CSB Conservation Publications.

Junge, G. C. A. 1938. On a collection of birds from Enggano. *Treubia* 16: 339–356.

Karthikeyan, S. 1994. Some notes on Pied Ground Thrush *Zoothera wardii* (Blyth). *J. Bombay Nat. Hist. Soc.* 91: 145–146.

Kawaji, N., Higuchi, H. & Hori, H. 1989. A new breeding record or the Izu Island Thrush *Turdus celaenops* from the Tokara Islands, southwest Japan. *Bull. Brit. Orn. Club* 109: 93–95.

Keith, A. R., Wiley, J. W., Ottenwalder, J. A. & Latta, S. C. in prep. *Check-list of the birds of Hispaniola.* London: British Ornithologists' Union.

Keith, S. 1968. Notes on birds of East Africa, including additions to the avifauna. *Amer. Mus. Novit.* 2321.

Keith, S. & Garrett, K. L. 1994. Oberlaenders Ground Thrush *Zoothera oberlaenderi* in the Impenetrable Forest, Uganda. *Scopus* 17: 141–142.

Keith, S. & Twomey, A. 1968. New distributional records of some East African birds. *Ibis* 110: 537–548.

Keith, S. & Urban, E. K. 1992. A summary of the present knowledge of the status of thrushes in the *Turdus olivaceus* species group. *Proc. VII Pan-Afr. Orn. Congress* 249–260.

Keith, S., Urban, E. K. & Fry, C. H. 1992. *The birds of Africa* Vol. 4. London: Academic Press.

Kepler, C. B. & Kepler, A. K. 1983. A first record of the nest and chicks of the Small Kauai Thrush. *Condor* 85: 497–499.

Khan, A. A. & Takashi, M. in prep. Intra-specific divergence of Oriental *Zoothera dauma* with notes on Island Endemic Amami Thrush, *Z. d. amami* (Hartert), Amami Oshima, Ryukyu Islands, Japan.

King, B. 1987. Some bird observations at Pangquangua Reserve in west central Shanxi Province in NE China. *Hong Kong Bird Report* 1984–1985: 112–114.

King, B. F., Woodcock, M. & Dickinson, E. C. 1975. *A field guide to the birds of South-East Asia.* London: Collins.

King, W. B. 1981. *Endangered birds of the world: the ICBP Bird Red Data Book.* Washington, D. C.: Smithsonian Institution Press.

Krabbe, N. 1992. Notes on distribution and natural history of some poorly known Ecuadorean birds. *Bull. Brit. Orn. Club* 112: 169–174.

Krabbe, N., Poulsen, B. O., Frolander, A. & Barahona, O. R. 1997. Range extensions of cloud forest birds from the high Andes of Ecuador: new sites for rare or little-recorded species. *Bull. Brit. Orn. Club* 117: 248–256.

Lack, D. 1971. *Ecological isolation in birds.* Oxford: Blackwell Scientific Publications.

Lane, D. & Jaramillo, A. 2000. Identification of *Hylocichla/Catharus* thrushes, part I: molt and aging of spotted thrushes and field ID of Wood Thrush and Hermit Thrush. *Birding* 32: 120–135.

Langrand, O. 1990. *Guide to the birds of Madagascar.* New Haven, Connecticut: Yale University Press.

Langrand, O. & Goodman, S. M. 1996. Current distribution and status of Benson's Rockthrush *Pseudocossyphus bensoni*, a Madagascar endemic. *Ostrich* 67: 49–54.

La Touche, J. D. D. 1925–1930. *A handbook of the birds of eastern China.* Vol. 1. London: Taylor & Francis.

Levy, C. & Downer, A. 1992. Life history of the White-chinned Thrush *Turdus aurantius. Gosse Bird Club Broadsheet* 58: 11–13.

Lewis, A. 1993. Birding in Tanimbar and Kai. *Oriental Bird Club Bull.* 18: 52–54.

Lichtenstein, G. 1998. Parasitism by Shiny Cowbirds of Rufous-bellied Thrushes. *Condor* 100: 680–687.

Macdonald, J. D. 1948. A new race of Orange Thrush from Uganda. *Bull. Brit. Orn. Club* 69: 16.

MacKinnon, J. & Phillipps, K. 1993. *A field guide to the birds of Borneo, Sumatra, Java and Bali.* Oxford: Oxford University Press.

Mackworth-Praed, C. W. & Grant, C. H. B. 1960. *Birds of eastern and north eastern Africa.* Vol. 2. London: Longmans.

Mackworth-Praed, C. W. & Grant, C. H. B. 1973. *Birds of west central and western Africa.* Vol. 2. London: Longmans.

Maclean, G. L. 1988. *Roberts birds of southern Africa.* Cape Town: Trustees of the John Voelker Bird Book Fund.

Maclean, G. L. 1993. *Roberts birds of southern Africa.* Sixth edition. Cape Town: Trustees of the John Voelker Bird Book Fund.

Mactavish, B. 1995. Eurasian Blackbird specimen for Newfoundland. *Birders J.* 4: 82–83.

Madroño N., A., Clay, R. P., Robbins, M. B., Rice, N. H., Faucett, R. C. & Lowen, J. C. 1997. An avifaunal forest survey of the vanishing interior Atlantic forest of San Rafael National Park, Departments Itapua/Caazapa, Paraguay. *Cotinga* 7: 45–53.

van Marle, J. G. & Voous, K. H. 1988. *The birds of Sumatra.* London: British Ornithologists' Union (Checklist No.10).

Martens, J. & Eck, S. 1995. Towards an ornithology of the Himalayas: systematics, ecology and vocalizations of Nepal birds. *Bonn. Zool. Monographien* 38.

Martínez del Río, C. 1992. Ecological and evolutionary implications of digestive processes: bird preferences and the sugar constituents of floral nectar and fruit pulp. *Experientia* 48: 544–551.

Mauersberger, G., Wagner, S., Wallschlager, D. & Warthold, R. 1982. *Mitt. Zool. Mus. Berlin* 58: 11–74.

Mayr, E. 1935. Birds collected during the Whitney South Sea Expedition. *Amer. Mus. Novit.* 820.

Mayr, E. 1936. Birds collected during the Whitney South Sea Expedition: description of 25 species and subspecies. *Amer. Mus. Novit.* 828.

Mayr, E. 1941. Birds collected during the Whitney South Sea Expedition. 37. On some undescribed races of *Turdus poliocephalus. Amer. Mus. Novit.* 1152.

Mayr, E. 1945. *Birds of the Southwest Pacific.* New York: Macmillan.

Mayr, E. & Gilliard, E. T. 1951. New species and subspecies of birds from the highlands of New Guinea. *Amer. Mus. Novit.* 1524.

McLaren, I. A. 1995. Field identification and taxonomy of Bicknell's Thrush. *Birding* 5: 358–366.

Mearns, B. & Mearns, R. 1988. *Biographies for birdwatchers. The lives of those commemorated in western Palearctic bird names.* London: Academic Press.

Medway, Lord & Wells, D. R. 1976. *Birds of the Malay Peninsula.* Vol. 5. London & Kuala Lumpur: Witherby & Penerbit Universiti Malaya.

Mees, G. F. 1977. Additional records of birds from Formosa (Taiwan). *Zool. Meded.* 51: 243–264.

Mees, G. F. 1996. Geographic variation in the birds of Java. *Publ. Nutall Orn. Club.* No. 26.

Meyer de Schauensee, R. 1966. *The species of birds of South America with their distribution.* Narberth, Pa.: Livingston Publishing Co.

Meyer de Schauensee, R. 1970. *A guide to the birds of South America.* Narberth, Pa: Livingston Publishing Co.

Meyer de Schauensee, R. 1984. *The birds of China.* Oxford: Oxford University Press.

Meyer de Schauensee, R. & Phelps, W. H. 1978. *A guide to the birds of Venezuela.* Princeton: Princeton University Press.

Micali, G., Vigorita, V. & Massa, R. 1981. Body measurements of some passerine migrants caught in the autumn in Lombard Pre Alps. *Atti I Convegno Italiano di Aulla Ornitologica –1981.*

Miller, W. & Griscom, L. 1925. Notes on Central American birds with descriptions of new forms. *Amer. Mus. Novit.* 183.

Milstein, P. le S. 1968. Affinity of *Turdus litsitsirupa. Bull. Brit. Orn. Club* 88: 1.

Monroe, B. L. 1968. A distributional survey of the birds of Honduras. *Ornithological Monographs* No.7.

Moreau, R. E. 1966. *The bird faunas of Africa and its islands.* New York: Academic Press.

Morris, A. K. & Burton A. 1993. NSW Annual Bird Report. *Australian Birdwatcher* 27: 97–139.

Morris, P. & Hawkins, F. 1998. *Birds of Madagascar: a photographic guide.* Robertsbridge, East Sussex: Pica Press.

Moskoff, W. 1995. Veery (*Catharus fuscescens*) in A. Poole & F. B. Gill, eds. *The Birds of North America,* No. 142. Philadelphia and Washington, D.C.: Academy of Natural Sciences and American Ornithologists' Union.

Munro, G. C. 1960. *Birds of Hawaii.* Rutland, Vermont: C. E. Tuttle.

Newman, K. 1983. *Birds of southern Africa.* Johannesburg: Macmillan.

Newton, I. 1998. *Population limitation in birds.* London: Academic Press.

Nikolaus, G. 1982. A new race of the Spotted Ground Thrush (*Turdus fischeri*) from South Sudan. *Bull. Brit. Orn. Club* 102: 45–47.

Norman, D. 1994. *The Fieldfare.* London: Hamlyn.

Noske, R. A. 1995. At the crossroads of two avifaunas: Timor. *Oriental Bird Club Bull.* 21: 34–38.

Odum, E. P., Connell, C. E. & Stoddard, H. L. 1961. Flight energy and estimated flight ranges of some migratory birds. *Auk* 78: 515–527.

Olson, S. L. 1987. The relationships of the New Guinean ground-robins *Amalocichla. Emu* 87: 247–248.

Olson, S. L. 1989. Preliminary systematic notes on some Old World passerines. *Riv. Ital. Orn.* 59: 183–195.

Olson, S. L. 1993. Contributions to avian biogeography from the archipelago and lowlands of Bocas del Toro, Panama. *Auk* 110: 100–108.

Olson, S. L. 1996. The contribution of the voyage of H. M. S. Blonde (1825) to Hawaiian ornithology. *Arch. Nat. Hist.* 23: 1–8.

Ornat, A. L., Lynch, J. F. & de Montes, B. M. 1989. New and noteworthy records of birds from the eastern Yucatan Peninsula. *Wilson Bull.* 101: 390–409.

Ouellet, H. 1993. Bicknell's Thrush: taxonomic status and distribution. *Wilson Bull.* 105: 545–572.

Palmer, R. S. 1972. Patterns of molting. In D. S. Farner & J. R. King (eds.) *Avian Biology* 2: 65–102.

Papish, R., May, J. L. & Brewer, D. 1997. Orange-billed Nightingale-Thrush: first record for Texas and the U.S. *Birding* 29: 128–130.

Pasquet, E., Cibois, A., Baillon, F. & Erard, C. in prep. Relationships between the ant-thrushes *Neocossyphus* and the flycatcher-thrushes *Stizorhina,* and their position relative to *Myadestes, Entomodestes* and some other Turdidae (Passeriformes). *J. Zool. Syst. Evol. Res.*

Payne, R. B. 1972. Mechanisms and control of molt. In D. S. Farner & J. R. King (eds.) *Avian Biology* 2: 103–155.

Payne, R. B. 1980. A new ground-thrush from Africa. *J. Field Orn.* 51: 199.

Pearson, A. J. 1966. The birds of Christmas Island (Indian Ocean). *Bull. Brit. Orn. Club* 86: 66–70.

de la Peña, M. R. 1995. *Ciclo reproductivo de las aves argentinas.* Santa Fe: Universidad Nacional del Litoral.

Perkins, R. C. L. 1903. Vertebrata. Pp.365–466 in D. Sharp, ed. *Fauna Hawaiiensis.* Vol. 1, Part IV. Cambridge: The University Press.

Peters, J. L. 1926. The present distribution and status of the Lesser Antillean solitaires. *Auk* 43: 430–433.

Phillips, A. R. 1969. An ornithological comedy of errors: *Catharus occidentalis* and *C. frantzii. Auk* 86: 605–623.

Phillips, A. R. 1986. *The known birds of North and Middle America.* Part 1. Denver, Colorado: A. R. Phillips.

Phillips, A. R. 1991. *The Known Birds of North and Middle America.* Part 2. Denver, Colorado: A. R. Phillips.

Phillips, A. R., Marshall, J. T. & Monson, G. 1964. *The birds of Arizona.* Tucson: University of Arizona Press.

Phillips, A. R. & Rook, W. 1965. A new race of the Spotted Nightingale-Thrush from Oaxaca, Mexico. *Condor* 67: 1–5.

452

Phillips, A. R. 1981. Subspecies vs forgotten species: the case of Grayson's Robin (*Turdus graysoni*). *Wilson Bull.* 93: 301–309.

Pitman, C. R. S. 1961. The Kurrichane Thrush *Turdus libonyanus tropicalis* (Peters) a host of the Red-chested Cuckoo *Cuculus solitarius* (Stephens) in Southern Rhodesia. *Bull. Brit. Orn. Club* 81: 48–49.

Pople, R. G., Burfield, I. J., Clay, R. P., Cope, D. R., Kennedy, C. P., Lopez L., B., Reyes, J., Warren, B. & Yagual, E. 1997. *Bird surveys and conservation status of three sites in western Ecuador. Final report of Project Ortalis '96.* Cambridge: CSB Conservation Publications.

Portenko, L. A. 1981. Geographical variation in Dark-throated Thrushes (*Turdus ruficollis* Pallas) and its taxonomical value. *Proc. Zool. Inst. Acad. Sci. USSR* 102: 72–109. (In Russian.)

Portenko, L. A. 1989. *Birds of the Chukchi Peninsula and Wrangel Island.* Vol. 2. Washington, D.C.: Smithsonian Institution Libraries.

Pratt, H. D. 1982. Relationships and speciation of the Hawaiian thrushes. *Living Bird* 19: 73–90.

Pratt, H. D., Bruner, P. L. & Berrett, D. G. 1987. *A field guide to the birds of Hawaii and the tropical Pacific.* Princeton: Princeton University Press.

Prigogine, A. 1965. Notes sur quelques *Geokichla* de la République du Congo. *Rev. Zool. Bot. Afr.* 71: 230–244.

Prigogine, A. 1977. The Orange Ground-Thrush *Turdus tanganjicae* (Sassi) a valid species. *Bull. Brit. Orn. Club* 97: 10–15.

Prigogine, A. 1978. A new ground-thrush from Africa. *Gerfaut* 68: 482–492.

Prigogine, A. 1985. Revision des espèces africaines appartenant au genre *Zoothera*. *Gerfaut* 75: 285–319.

Prigogine, A. & Louette, M. 1984. A new race of the Spotted Ground-thrush, *Zoothera guttata* from Upemba, Zaire. *Gerfaut* 74: 185–186.

Pyle, P., Howell, S. N. G., DeSante, D. F., Yunick, R. P. & Gustafson, M. 1997. *Identification guide to North American birds.* Part I. Bolinas, California: Slate Creek Press.

Quantrill, R. 1995. Red-tailed Ant-Thrush *Neocossyphus rufus* in Central African Republic. *Malimbus* 17: 103–104.

Raffaele, H., Wiley, J., Garrido, O., Keith, A. & Raffaele, J. 1998. *A guide to the birds of the West Indies.* Princeton, New Jersey: Princeton University Press.

Rahbek, C., Bloch, H., Poulsen, M. K. & Rasmussen, J. F. 1993. Avian body weights from southern Ecuador. *Bull. Brit. Orn. Club* 113: 103–108.

Ralph, C. J. 1981. Age ratios and their possible use in determining autumn routes of passerine migrants. *Wilson Bull.* 93: 164–188.

Ralph, C. J. & Fancy, S. G. 1994. Demography and movements of the Omao (*Myadestes obscurus*). *Condor* 96: 503–511.

Rand, A. L. 1936. Distribution and habits of Madagascar birds. *Bull. Amer. Mus. Nat. Hist.* 72: 436–437.

Rand, A. L. 1995. The origin of the land birds of Tristan de Cunha. *Fieldiana Zool.* 37: 139–166.

Rand, A. L. & Rabor, D. S. 1960. Birds of the Philippine Islands: Siquijor, Malindang, Bohol and Samar. *Fieldiana: Zoology* 35(7).

Rappole, J. H., Ramos, M. A. & Winker, K. 1989. Wintering Wood Thrush movements and mortality in southern Veracruz. *Auk* 106: 402–410.

Rasmussen, J. F., Rahbek, C., Poulsen, B. O., Poulsen, M. K. & Bloch, H. 1996. Distributional records and natural history notes on threatened and little known birds of southern Ecuador. *Bull. Brit. Orn. Club* 116: 26–46.

Reynolds, M. & Snetsinger, T. 2000. The Hawaii Rare Bird Search 1994–1996. In J. M. Scott, S. Conant & C.van Riper (eds.) Ecology Conservation and Management of Endemic Hawaiian Birds: a vanishing Avifauna. *Studies in Avian Biology* 21.

Ridgely, R. S. & Tudor, G. 1989. *The birds of South America.* Vol.1. Austin: University of Texas Press.

Ridgway R. 1907. The birds of North and Middle America. Part IV. *U.S. Natn. Mus. Bull.* 50.

Rimmer, C. C. 1996. A closer look: Bicknell's Thrush. *Birding* 28: 118–123.

Rimmer, C. C., Atwood, J. L., McFarland, K. P. & Nagy, L. R. 1996. Population density, vocal behaviour and recommended survey methods for Bicknell's Thrush. *Wilson Bull.* 108: 639–649.

Rimmer, C. C., McFarland, K. P. & Goetz, J. E. 1999. Demographics and ecology of Bicknell's Thrush and other montane forest birds in the Dominican Republic. Report to American Bird Conservancy. Unpublished.

van Riper III, C. & Scott, J. M. 1979. Observations on distribution, diet and breeding of the Hawaiian Thrush. *Condor* 81: 65–71.

van Riper III, C., van Riper, S. G., Goff, M. L. & Laird, M. 1986. The epizootiology and ecological significance of malaria in Hawaiian landbirds. *Ecol. Monogr.* 56: 327–344.

Ripley, S. D. 1952. The Thrushes. A Taxonomic Study. *Postilla* 13.

Ripley, S. D. 1964. Family Muscicapidae, subfamily Turdinae. Pp.13–227 in E. Mayr & R. A. Paynter, eds. *Check-list of birds of the world: a continuation of the work of James L. Peters.* Vol. 10. Massachusetts: Museum of Comparative Zoology.

Ripley, S. D. 1977. A new subspecies of Island Thrush, *Turdus poliocephalus*, from New Ireland. *Auk* 94: 772–773.

Ripley, S. D., Beehler, B. M. & Krishna Raju, K. S. R. 1988. Birds of the Visakhapatnam Ghats, Andhra Pradesh, 2. *J. Bombay Nat. Hist. Soc.* 85: 90–107.

Ripley, S. D. & Hadden, D. 1982. A new subspecies of *Zoothera* (Aves: Muscicapidae: Turdinae) from the northern Solomon Islands. *J. Yamashina Inst. Orn.* 14: 103–107.

Roberson, D. 1980. *Rare birds of the West Coast of North America*. Pacific Grove, California: Woodcock.

Roberson, D. & Tenney, C. 1993. *Atlas of the breeding birds of Monterey County, California*. Carmel, Ca.: Monterey Peninsula Audubon Society.

Roberts, T. J. 1992. *The Birds of Pakistan*. Vol.2. Karachi: Oxford University Press.

Robinson, H. C. and Kloss, C. B. (1918) Results of an expedition to Korinchi Peak, Sumatra 2, birds. *J. Fed. Malay States Mus.* 8: 81–284.

Robson, C. 1997. From the field. *Oriental Bird Club Bull.* 25: 63.

Robson, C. 1999. From the field. *Oriental Bird Club Bull.* 29: 53.

Robson, C. R., Buck, H., Farrow, D. S., Fisher, T. & King, B. F. 1998. A birdwatching visit to the Chin Hills, West Burma (Myanmar), with notes from nearby areas. *Forktail* 13: 109–120.

Rogacheva, H. 1992. *The birds of Central Siberia*. Husum, Germany: Husum-Druck und Verlagsgesellschaft.

Roth, R. R., Johnson, M. S. & Underwood, T. J. 1996. Wood Thrush (*Hylocichla mustelina*) in A. Poole & F. B. Gill, eds. *Birds of North America*, No. 246. Philadelphia and Washington, D.C.: Academy of Natural Sciences and American Ornithologists' Union.

Rouchouse, C. 1985. Sedentarisation de *Monticola solitarius* au Cap de Naze, Sénégal. *Malimbus* 7: 91–94.

Round, P. D. 1983. Some recent bird records from northern Thailand. *Nat. Hist. Bull. Siam Soc.* 31: 123–138.

Round, P. D. & Treesucon, U. 1997. Nesting records of Chestnut-capped Thrush (*Zoothera interpres*) from peninsular Thailand. *Nat. Hist. Bull. Siam Soc.* 45: 225–230.

Rowland, P. 1995. Island Thrush (*Turdus poliocephalus*) in Western Province, Papua New Guinea. *Muruk* 7: 41–43.

Rowley, J. S. & Orr, R. T. 1964. The status of Frantzius' Nightingale Thrush. *Auk* 81: 308–314.

Ryan, P. G. & Moloney, C. L. 1991. Tristan Thrushes kill adult White-bellied Storm-Petrels. *Wilson Bull.* 103: 130–132.

Salempo, E. 1994. Birds recorded from the Loliondo area of northern Tanzania. *Scopus* 17: 124–127.

Salomonsen, F. 1950. *The birds of Greenland*. Copenhagen: Ejnar Munksgaard.

Schodde, R. & Mason I. J. 1999. *Directory of Australian birds (Passerines)*. Collingwood, Victoria, Australia: CSIRO Publishing.

Schulenberg, T. S. 1987. New records of birds from western Peru. *Bull. Brit. Orn. Club* 107: 184–189.

Scott, J. M., Mountainspring, S., Ramsey, F. L. & Kepler, C. B. 1986. *Forest bird communities of the Hawaiian Islands: their dynamics, ecology and conservation*. Cooper Ornithological Society (Studies in Avian Biology 9).

Seebohm, H. 1881. *Catalogue of the birds of the British Museum*. Vol. 5. London: Trustees of the British Museum.

Seebohm, H. & Sharpe, R. B. 1898–1902. *A monograph of the Turdidae*. 2 vols. London.

Serle, W. 1950. A contribution to the ornithology of the British Cameroons. *Ibis* 92: 602–638.

Serle, W. 1954. A second contribution to the ornithology of the British Cameroons. *Ibis* 96: 47–80.

Serle, W. 1957. A contribution to the ornithology of the eastern region of Nigeria. *Ibis* 99: 628–685.

Serle, W. 1962. Remarks on the taxonomy of *Turdus nigrilorum* Reichenow and *Turdus saturatus* (Cabanis) in southern British Cameroons. *Bull. Brit. Orn. Club* 82: 124–126.

Sheldon, F. H. & Gill, F. B. 1996. A reconsideration of songbird phylogeny with emphasis on the evolution of titmice and their sylvioid relatives. *Systematic Biology* 45: 473–495.

Sibley, C. G. & Ahlquist, J. E. 1990. *Phylogeny and classification of birds: a study in molecular evolution*. New Haven: Yale University Press.

Sibley, C. G. & Monroe, B. L. 1990. *Distribution and taxonomy of birds of the world*. New Haven: Yale University Press.

Sick, H. 1993. *Birds in Brazil*. Princeton: Princeton University Press.

Simms, E. 1978. *British thrushes*. London: Collins.

Simms, E. 1990. *Woodland birds*. London: Collins.

Sinclair, I. & Langrand, O. 1998. *Birds of the Indian Ocean islands*. Cape Town: Struik.

Skutch, A. F. 1960. *Life histories of Central American birds* Vol. 2. Berkeley, California: Cooper Ornithological Society (Pacific Coast Avifauna no.34).

Skutch, A. F. 1967. *Life histories of Central American highland birds*. Cambridge, Mass.: Publications of the Nuttall Ornithological Club No.7.

Slud, P. 1964. The birds of Costa Rica: distribution and ecology. *Bull. Amer. Mus. Nat. Hist.* 128.

Smith, K. D. 1957. An annotated list of the birds of Eritrea. *Ibis* 99: 307–337.

Smythies, B. E. 1981. *The birds of Borneo*. Third edition. Kota Kinabalu: The Sabah Society; and Kuala Lumpur: Malayan Nature Society.

Smythies, B. E. 1986. *The birds of Burma*. Liss, Hampshire: Nimrod Press.

Snetsinger, T. J., Wakelee, K. M. & Fancy, S. G. 1999. Puaiohi (*Myadestes palmeri*) in A. Poole & F. B. Gill, eds. *The Birds of North America*, No. 461. Philadelphia and Washington, D.C.: Academy of Natural Sciences and American Ornithologists' Union.

Snow, D. W. 1950. The birds of São Tomé and Príncipe in the Gulf of Guinea. *Ibis* 92: 579–595.

Snow, D. W. 1958. *A study of blackbirds.* London: George Allen & Unwin.

Snow, D. W. 1985. Systematics of the *Turdus fumigatus/hauxwelli* group of thrushes. *Bull. Brit. Orn. Club* 105: 30–37.

Snow, D. W. 1997. Should the biological be superseded by the phylogenetic species concept? *Bull. Brit. Orn. Club* 117: 110–121.

Speirs, J. M. 1985. *Birds of Ontario.* Toronto: Natural Heritage/Natural History Inc.

Stejneger, L. H. 1887. Birds of Kauai Island, Hawaiian Archipelago, collected by Mr. Valdemar Knudsen. *Proc. U.S. Natn. Hist. Mus.* 10: 75–102.

Stepanyan, L. S. 1964. Geographical variation of the Rock Thrush *Monticola saxatilis* L. *Sb. Trudy Zool. Mus. MGU* 9: 228–231.

Stepanyan, L. S. 1978. [*The composition and distribution of the bird fauna of the USSR.*] Moscow: Nauka (in Russian).

Stepanyan, L. S. 1990. [*Conspectus of the ornithological fauna of the USSR.*] Moscow: Nauka (in Russian).

Stiles, F. G. & Skutch, A. F. 1989. *A guide to the birds of Costa Rica.* London: Christopher Helm.

Stiles, F. G., Rosselli, L. & Bohórquez, C. I. 1999. New and noteworthy records of birds from the middle Magdalena valley of Colombia. *Bull. Brit. Orn. Club* 119: 113–127.

Stockton de Dod, A. 1978. *Aves de la Republica Dominicana.* Santo Domingo: Museo Nacional de Historia Natural.

Stollmann, A. 1996. Fieldfare (*Turdus pilaris*) observations in the Danube Area during nidification. *Tichodroma* 9: 213–214.

Stones, A. J., Lucking, R. S., Davidson, P. J. & Raharjaningtrak, W. 1997. Checklist of the birds of the Sula Islands (1991) with particular reference to Taliabu Island. *Kukila* 9: 37–55.

Stotz, D. F., Bierregaard, R. O., Cohn-Haft, M., Petermann, P., Smith, J., Whittaker, A. & Wilson, S. V. 1992. The status of North American migrants in central Amazonian Brazil. *Condor* 94: 608–621.

Stresemann, E. 1931a. Vorläufiges über die ornithologischen Ergebnisse der Expedition Heinrich 1930–1931. *Orn. Monatsber.* 39: 7–14.

Stresemann, E. 1931b. Vorläufiges über die ornithologischen Ergebnisse der Expedition Heinrich 1930–31. *Orn. Monatsber.* 39: 77–85.

Sushkin, P. P. 1929. On two groups of hybrids in shrikes and thrushes. *Verh. VI Int. Ornithol. Kongr. Kopenhagen* 1926: 379–381.

Sushkin, P. P. 1938. *Birds of the Soviet Altai and adjacent parts of north-western Mongolia.* 2 vols. (in Russian). Moscow: Academy of Sciences of USSR Press.

Suthers, H. B. 1993. Effect of age class separation on sex determination by wing and tail in Veery and Wood Thrush. *North American Bird-Bander* 18: 142–147.

Svensson, L. 1992. *Identification guide to European passerines.* Fourth edition. Stockholm: L. Svensson.

Totune, T. & Yamamoto, H. 1993. First breeding record of the Pale Ouzel *Turdus pallidus* from Honshu. *Strix* 41: 17–19.

Traylor, M. A. 1965. A collection of birds from Barotseland and Bechuanaland. *Ibis* 107: 137–172.

Tucker, G. M. & Heath, M. F. 1994. *Birds in Europe: their conservation status.* Cambridge, UK: BirdLife International.

Tyabji, H. N. 1994. The birds of Bandhavgarh National Park, M. P. *J. Bombay Nat. Hist. Soc.* 91: 51–74.

Unitt, P. & Estrella, R. R. 1996. Winter distribution of Hermit Thrush subspecies in the Sierra de la Laguna, Baja California Sur. *Western Birds* 27: 65–69.

Urban, E. K. 1975. Weights and longevity of some birds from Addis Ababa, Ethiopia. *Bull. Brit. Orn. Club* 95: 96–98.

Urban, E. K. & Brown, L. H. 1971. *A checklist of the birds of Ethiopia.* Addis Ababa: Haile Selassie I University Press.

Urban, E. K., Fry, C. H. & Keith, S. 1997. *The birds of Africa.* Vol. 5. London: Academic Press.

Vaurie, C. 1955. Notes on Palearctic birds, No. 14. *Amer. Mus. Novit.* 1731.

Vaurie, C. 1955a. Systematic notes on Palearctic birds. No.13: *Zoothera mollissima* and *Zoothera dixoni*. *Amer. Mus. Novit.* 1706.

Vaurie, C. 1955b. Systematic notes on Palearctic birds. No.15 Turdinae: the genera *Turdus, Grandala* and *Enicurus*. *Amer. Mus. Novit.* 1733.

Vaurie, C. 1959. *Birds of the Palearctic fauna: passeriformes.* London: Witherby.

Verhoeye, J. & Holmes, D. A. 1998. The birds of the islands of Flores – a review. *Kukila* 10: 3–59.

Vorobiev, K. A. 1954. *Birds of the Ussuri area.* Moscow: Academy of Science of the USSR (in Russian).

Wakelee, K. M. 1996. Life history of the Omao (*Myadestes obscurus*). Master's thesis, University of Hawaii, Honolulu.

Wakelee, K. M. & Fancy, S. G. 1999. Omao (*Myadestes obscurus*), Kamao (*Myadestes myadestinus*), Olomao (*Myadestes lanaiensis*), and Amaui (*Myadestes oahensis*) in A. Poole & F. B. Gill, eds. *The Birds of North America*, No. 460. Philadelphia and Washington, D.C.: Academy of Natural Sciences and American Ornithologists' Union.

Wallace, G. J. 1939. Bicknell's Thrush, its taxonomy, distribution and life history. *Proc. Boston Soc. Nat. Hist.* 41: 211–402.

Walsh J. F. & Walsh, B. 1983. Possible thrush 'anvils' in Upper Volta. *Malimbus* 5: 54–55.

Warakagoda, D. 1997. Some observations on the Sri Lanka Whistling Thrush. *Oriental Bird Club Bull.* 26: 32–34.

Wells, D. 1992. Night migration at Fraser's Hill, Peninsular Malaysia. *Oriental Bird Club Bull.* 16: 21–24.

Wetmore, A. & Swales, B. H. 1931. Birds of Haita and the Dominican Republic. *Bull. U.S. Natn. Mus.* 155: 338–339.

Wetmore, A., Pasquier, R. & Olson, S. L. 1984. *Birds of the Republic of Panama.* Part 4. Washington, D.C.: Smithsonian Institution Press.

Whistler, H. 1944. Materials for the ornithology of Afghanistan, part II. *J. Bombay Nat. Hist. Soc.* 45: 61–72.

Whistler, H. & Kinnear, N. B. 1932. The Vernay Scientific Survey of the Eastern Ghats (Ornithology Section), part III. *J. Bombay Nat. Hist. Soc.* 15: 67–93.

White, A. G., Brace, R. C. & Payne, A. J. 1995. Additional records of and notes on the Unicoloured Thrush *Turdus haplochrous*, a little known Bolivian endemic. *Bull. Brit. Orn. Club* 115: 29–33.

White, C. M. N. 1949. A new race of thrush from Northern Rhodesia. *Bull. Brit. Orn. Club* 69: 57–58.

White, C. M. N. 1960. A check list of the Ethiopian Muscicapidae (Sylviinae). Part I. *Occas. Pap. Natn. Mus. S. Rhodesia.* 24B: 399–430.

White, C. M. N. 1962a. A check list of the Ethiopian Muscicapidae (Sylviinae). Part 2. *Occas. Pap. Natn. Mus. S. Rhodesia* 26B: 653–738.

White, C. M. N. 1962b. *A revised check list of African shrikes, orioles, drongoes, starlings, crows, waxwings, cuckoo-shrikes, bulbuls, accentors, thrushes and babblers.* Lusaka: Government Printer.

White, C. M. N. 1967. Taxonomic notes on African Turdinae. *Bull. Brit. Orn. Club* 87: 150–152.

White, C. M. N. & Bruce, M. D. 1986. *The birds of Wallacea: an annotated check-list.* London: British Ornithologists' Union (Check-list No. 7).

Whitney, C. L. 1989. Geographical variation in Wood Thrush song: a comparison of samples recorded in New York and South Carolina. *Behaviour* 111(1–4): 49–60.

Williams, R. S. R. & Tobias, J. A. 1994. The conservation of Ecuador's threatened avifauna: final report of the Amazulu 1990–1991 projects. *Birdlife Study report* 60.

Williamson, K. 1954. Gray-cheeked Thrush at Fair Isle: a new British bird. *Brit. Birds* 47: 266–267.

Winker, K., Oehlenschlager, R. J., Ramos, M. A., Zink, R. M., Rappole, J. H. & Warner, D. W. 1992. Avian distribution and abundance records for the Sierra de los Tuxtlas, Veracruz, Mexico. *Wilson Bull.* 104: 699–718.

Winker, K., Warner, D. W. & Weisbrod, A. R. 1992. Migration of woodland birds at a fragmented inland stopover site. *Wilson Bull.* 104: 580–598.

Winker, K. & Rappole, J. H. 1988. The relationship between *Hylocichla* and *Catharus* (Turdinae). *Auk* 105: 392–394.

Winterbottom, M. G. 1996. A study of the Cape Thrush *Turdus olivaceus* L. *Ostrich* 37: 17–22.

Witherby, H. F., Jourdain, F. C. R., Ticehurst, N. F. & Tucker, B. W. 1938–1941. *The handbook of British birds.* 5 Vols. London: Witherby.

Woods, R. W. 1988. *Guide to birds of the Falkland Islands.* Oswestry: Anthony Nelson.

Zimmer, J. T. & Phelps, W. H. 1955. Three new subspecies of birds from Venezuela. *Amer. Mus. Novit.* 1709.

Zimmerman, D. A. 1991. The Aztec Thrush in the United States. *Birding* 23: 318–329.

Zimmerman, D. A., Turner, D. A. & Pearson, D. J. 1996. *Birds of Kenya and northern Tanzania.* London: Christopher Helm.

Zink, R. M. & Dittmann, D. L. 1992. Review of 'The Known Birds of North and Middle America, Part II' by Allan R. Phillips. *Wilson Bull.* 104: 764–767

INDEX OF SPECIES

Figures in bold are plate numbers